TUTORIAL
LOCAL NETWORK TECHNOLOGY

Second Edition

William Stallings

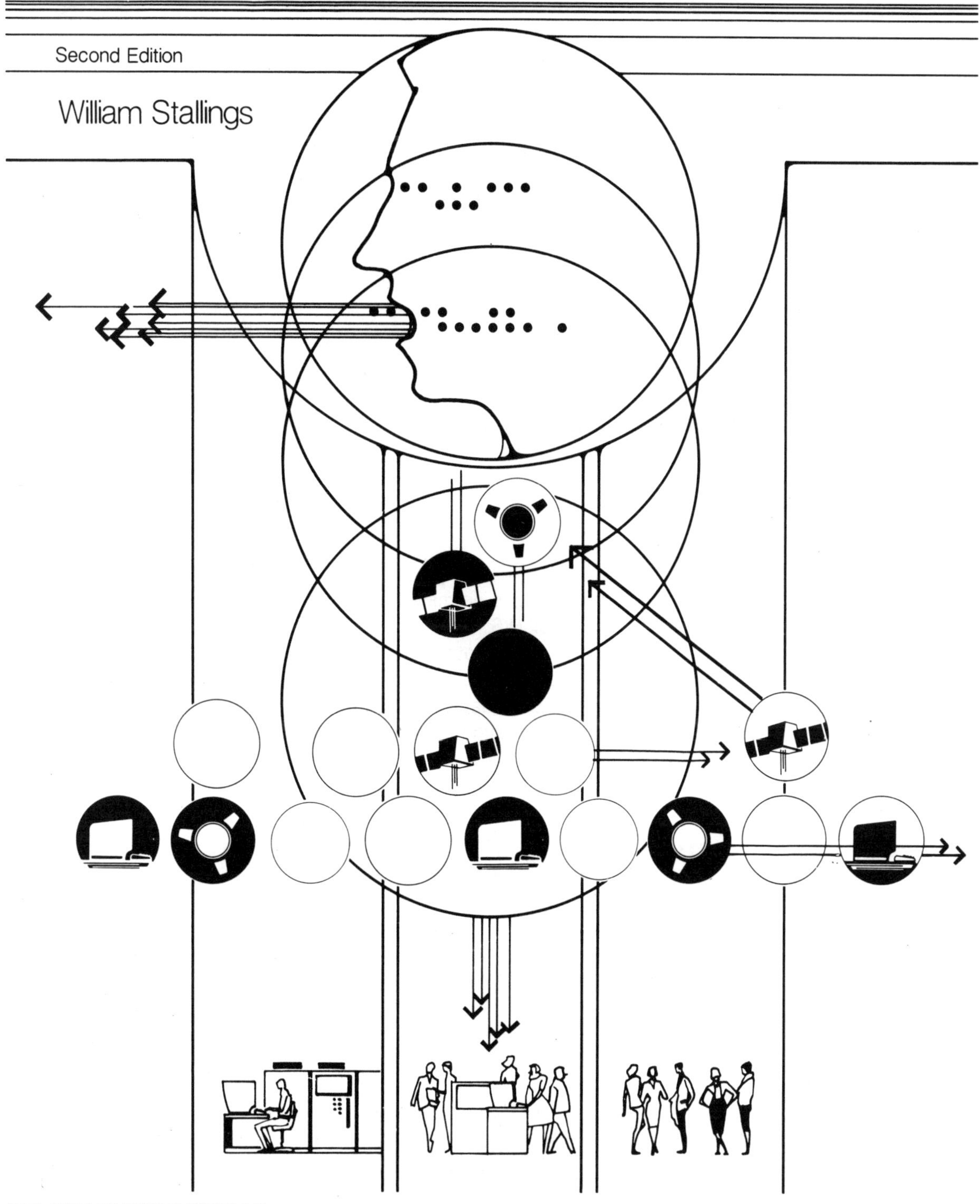

IEEE CATALOG NUMBER EHO234-5
LIBRARY OF CONGRESS NUMBER 85-80332
IEEE COMPUTER SOCIETY ORDER NUMBER 657
ISBN 0-8186-0657-6

THE INSTITUTE OF ELECTRICAL AND ELECTRONICS ENGINEERS, INC.

Published by IEEE Computer Society Press
1730 Massachusetts Avenue, N.W.
Washington, D.C. 20036-1903

COVER DESIGNED BY JACK I. BALLESTERO

IEEE Catalog Number EHO234-5
Library of Congress Number 85-80332
IEEE Computer Society Order Number 657
ISBN 0-8186-0657-6 (Paper)
ISBN 0-8186-4657-8 (Microfiche)

Order from: IEEE Computer Society
Post Office Box 80452
Worldway Postal Center
Los Angeles, CA 90080

IEEE Service Center
445 Hoes Lane
Piscataway, NJ 08854

THE INSTITUTE OF ELECTRICAL AND ELECTRONICS ENGINEERS, INC.

PREFACE

Perhaps no other major innovation in data processing or data communications has been so widely discussed or so eagerly anticipated before its maturity as that of local networks. Local networks are attractive for such features as high availability and the ability to support multiple vendor equipment. Although the technology is still evolving, the principal architectural forms and design approaches have emerged.

P.1 Tutorial Focus

This tutorial focuses on the broad and rapidly evolving field of local networks. Consequently, the aims of the text, constrained by space, are dictated by concerns of breadth rather than depth. The articles and original material have been selected on the bases of topics and style to support these aims.

In terms of topics, the tutorial explores the key issues in the field in the following general categories:

- *Technology and architecture*: There is a small collection of ingredients that serves to characterize and differentiate local networks, including transmission medium, network topology, communication protocols, switching technique, and hardware/software interface.
- *Network type*: It is convenient to classify local networks into three types, based partly on technology and partly on application. These are local area network (LAN), high-speed local network (HSLN), and digital switch/digital private branch exchange (PBX).
- *Design approaches*: While not attempting to be exhaustive, the tutorial exposes and discusses important issues related to local network design.

Conspicuously missing from this list is a category with a title such as "Typical Systems." This tutorial is focused on the common principles underlying the design and implementation of all local networks and should, therefore, give the reader sufficient background to judge and compare local network products. A description of even a small sample of such systems is beyond the scope of this book. Articles about specific systems are included herein only when they are the best vehicle for communicating the concepts and principles under discussion.

In terms of style, the tutorial is primarily:

- *Descriptive*: Terms are defined, and the key concepts and technologies are discussed in some detail.
- *Comparative*: Wherever possible, alternative or competing approaches are compared, and their relative merits, based on suitable criteria, are discussed.

On the other hand, analytic and research-oriented styles are present to a much lesser degree. Virtually all of the mathematical content is confined to the section on performance, and, even there, the emphasis is on results rather than derivations.

Also, much of the material presents concepts and approaches that have moved beyond research and are commercial realities today. Both the Bibliography (Section 10) and the references contained in each article suggest additional sources for the interested reader.

P.2 Intended Audience

This tutorial is intended for a broad range of readers interested in local networks.

- *Students and professionals in data processing and data communications*: The tutorial is a convenient means of reviewing some of the important papers in the field. Its organization and the original material aid the reader in focusing on this exciting aspect of data communications and data processing.
- *Local network designers and implementors*: The tutorial discusses the critical design issues and illustrates alternative approaches to meeting user requirements.

- *Local network customers and system managers*: This text alerts the reader to some of the key issues and tradeoffs, as well as what to look for in the way of network services and performance.

Most of the material can be comfortably read with no background in data communications. The glossary and original material provide supporting information for the reprinted articles.

P.3 Organization of Material

This tutorial is a combination of original material and reprinted articles. Its organization is intended to clarify both the unifying and the differentiating concepts underlying the field of local networks. The organization of the sections is as follows:

1. *Introduction*: This section discusses local network technology, focusing on the key characteristics of transmission medium and topology. The classification of types of local networks used in this book is presented and discussed.
2. *Local Area Networks*: The term LAN is often mistakenly identified with the entire field of local networks. LANs have a general-purpose application, and most of the better-known local networks fall into this class. The major types of LANs (baseband bus, broadband bus/tree, and ring) are described and compared. The important issue of medium access control protocols is explored. The standards currently being developed for LANs are also described.
3. *High-Speed Local Networks*: This section focuses on a special-purpose high-speed type of local network and examines current technology and standards as well as possible future directions.
4. *Digital Switches and Digital Private Branch Exchanges*: Networks in this category constitute the major alternative to LANs for meeting general local interconnection needs. This section explores the technology and architecture of these devices and examines their pros and cons relative to LANs.
5. *The Network Interface*: The nature of the interface between an attached device and a LAN or an HSLN is an important design issue. This section explores some alternatives.
6. *Performance*: The purpose of this section is to give some insight into the performance problems and the differences in performance of various local networks.
7. *Internetworking*: In the majority of cases, local networks will be connected in some fashion to other networks. Some alternatives are explored.
8. *Design Issues*: The purpose of this section is to give the reader some feel for the breadth of design issues that must be addressed in implementing and operating local networks.
9. *Glossary*: Includes definitions for most of the key terms appearing in this text.
10. *Bibliography*: Provides a guide to further reading.

P.4 Related Materials

Local Networks: An Introduction (Macmillan, 1984) by William Stallings is a companion to this tutorial text, and follows the same topical organization. It is intended as a textbook as well as a reference book for professionals (available from Macmillan Publishing, 866 Third Avenue, New York, NY 10022; 800-223-3215). The author has also prepared a videotape course on communication networks. About half the course is devoted to local networks and the digital PBX; the remainder covers packet-switched, packet-radio, and satellite networks (available from the Association for Media-Based Continuing Education for Engineers, 225 North Avenue NW, Atlanta, GA 30332; 404-894-3362).

P.5 The Second Edition

In the two years since *Local Network Technology* was published, the field has continued to evolve and expand, necessitating an early second edition. This is reflected in the makeup of this edition, which includes a total of 19 new articles and a net gain of seven articles over the first edition. Among the noteworthy additions are several papers on fiber optic local networks, reflecting the fact that this most promising of transmission media is at last arriving on the local network scene. Also included are a more comprehensive survey article, articles on new technical approaches for LANs, and more. The revision of this text has been an interesting and rewarding experience and I hope that its readers find it a useful guide to this fascinating field.

Table of Contents

Section 1: Introduction

1.1 Overview

This section provides an overview of the major types of local networks and their key architectural features. As background we begin with a brief discussion of the applications of local networks. The range of applications is wide so, to give some flavor for the potential uses of local networks, we discuss four distinct types of application.

Personal Computer Networks

We start at one extreme, a system designed to support microcomputers, such as personal computers. With the relatively low cost of such systems, individual managers within organizations are independently procuring personal computers for standalone applications, such as spreadsheet programs or project management tools. Today's personal computers put processor, file storage, high-level languages, and problem-solving tools in an inexpensive, "user-friendly" package. The reasons for acquiring such a system are compelling.

However, a collection of standalone processors will not meet all of an organization's needs; central processing facilities are still required. Some programs, such as econometric forecasting models, are too big to run on a small computer. Corporate-wide data files, such as accounting and payroll, require a centralized facility but should be accessible to a number of users. Plus, there are other kinds of files that, though specialized, must be shared by a number of users. Further, there are sound reasons for connecting individual intelligent work stations not only to a central facility but also to each other. Members of a project or organization team need to share work and information. By far, the most efficient way to do so is electronically.

The capabilities of each work station can be matched to the tasks of the particular work station user. Each type of user is provided with electronic mail and word processing to improve the efficiency of creating and distributing messages, memos, and reports. Managers are also given a set of program and budget management tools. With the amount of automation that personal computers supply, the role of a secretary becomes less that of a typist and more that of an administrative assistant. Tools such as an electronic calendar and graphics support become valuable for these workers. Similarly, engineers and technical writers can be supplied with tailored systems.

Certain expensive resources, such as a disk and printer, can be shared by all users of the departmental local network. In addition, the network can tie into larger corporate network facilities. For example, the corporation may have a buildingwide local network and a long-haul corporate-wide network. A communications server can provide controlled access to these resources.

A key requirement for the success of such a network is low cost. The cost of attachment to the network for each device should be on the order of one to a few hundred dollars; otherwise, the attachment cost will approach the cost of the attached device. However, the capacity and data rate need not be high, so this is a realizable goal.

Computer Room Networks

At the other extreme from a personal computer local network is one designed for use in a computer room containing large, expensive mainframe computers. This is an example of what we refer to as a high-speed local network (HSLN). The HSLN is likely to find application at very large data processing sites. Typically, these sites will be large companies or research installations with large data processing budgets. Because of the size involved, a small difference in productivity can mean millions of dollars saved.

Consider a site that uses a dedicated mainframe computer. This implies a fairly large application or set of applications. As the load at the site grows, the existing model may be replaced by a more powerful one, perhaps by a multiprocessor system. At some sites, a single-system replacement will not be able to keep up. The facility will eventually require multiple independent computers. Again, there are compelling reasons for interconnecting these systems. The cost of system interrupt is high, so it should be possible to shift applications easily and quickly to backup systems. It must be possible to test new procedures and applications without degrading the production system. Large bulk storage files must be accessible from more than one computer. Load leveling should be possible to maximize utilization.

It can be seen that some key requirements for HSLNs are the opposite of those for personal computer networks. High data rates are required to keep up with the work, which typically involves the transfer of large blocks of data. The electronics for achieving high speeds are expensive, on the order of tens of thousands of dollars per attachment. Fortunately, given the much higher cost of attached devices, such costs are reasonable.

Office Automation

Most local network applications will fall between the two extremes of personal computer networks and computer room networks. Moderate data rates and moderate attachment costs are requirements. In some cases, the local network will support one or a few types of devices and rather homogeneous traffic. In others, it will support a wide variety of devices and traffic types.

A good generic example of the latter case is an office automation system, which can be defined as the incorporation of appropriate technology to help people manage information more effectively.

The key motivation for the move to office automation is productivity. As the percentage of white-collar workers has increased, the volume of information and paperwork has grown. In most installations, secretarial and other support functions are heavily labor intensive. Increased labor costs combined with low productivity and increasing workload have caused employers to seek effective ways of increasing the level of automation of this type of work.

At the same time, principals (managers and skilled "information workers") are faced with their own productivity bind. Work must be done faster with less wait time and waste time between segments of a job. This requires better access to information and better communication and coordination with others.

An office automation system, then, should include not only intelligent work stations but also a variety of other devices, such as minicomputers with text and data files, facsimile machines, intelligent copiers, and so forth. For this system to work and be truly effective, a local network is needed that can support the various devices and transmit the various types of information.

Integrated Voice and Data Local Networks

In virtually all offices today, the telephone system is separate from any local network that might be used to interconnect data processing devices. With the advent of digital voice technology, the capability now exists to integrate the telephone switching system of a building with the data processing equipment, providing a single local network for both.

Such integrated voice/data networks might simplify network management and control. They will also provide the required networking for the kinds of integrated voice and data devices to be expected in the future. An example is an executive voice/data work station that provides verbal message storage, voice annotation of text, and automated dialing.

1.2 Article Summary

The lone article in this section, "Local Networks," serves as an overview to the entire tutorial. It lists and briefly describes the various transmission media and topologies for local networks and then defines and compares the three types of local networks as they are classified in this tutorial. They are: local area network (LAN), high-speed local network (HSLN), and digital private branch exchange (PBX). The article then expands on the technology and standards for LANs and HSLNs. The topics introduced in this article are the subject of more detailed description in the remainder of this tutorial text.

Local Networks

WILLIAM STALLINGS

Honeywell Information Systems, Inc., McLean, Virginia 22102

The rapidly evolving field of local network technology has produced a steady stream of local network products in recent years. The IEEE 802 standards that are now taking shape, because of their complexity, do little to narrow the range of alternative technical approaches and at the same time encourage more vendors into the field. The purpose of this paper is to present a systematic, organized overview of the alternative architectures for and design approaches to local networks.

The key elements that determine the cost and performance of a local network are its topology, transmission medium, and medium access control protocol. Transmission media include twisted pair, baseband and broadband coaxial cable, and optical fiber. Topologies include bus, tree, and ring. Medium access control protocols include CSMA/CD, token bus, token ring, register insertion, and slotted ring. Each of these areas is examined in detail, comparisons are drawn between competing technologies, and the current status of standards is reported.

Categories and Subject Descriptors: B.4.1 [**Input/Output and Data Communications**]: Data Communications Devices—*receivers*; *transmitters*; B.4.3 [**Input/Output and Data Communications**]: Interconnections (subsystems); C.2.5 [**Computer-Communication Networks**]: Local Networks

General Terms: Design, Performance, Standardization

INTRODUCTION

Local networks have moved rapidly from the experimental stage to commercial availability. The reasons behind this rapid development can be found in some fundamental trends in the data processing industry. Most important is the continuing decrease in cost, accompanied by an increase in capability, of computer hardware. Today's microprocessors have speeds, instruction sets, and memory capacities comparable to medium-scale minicomputers. This trend has spawned a number of changes in the way information is collected, processed, and used in organizations. There is an increasing use of small, single-function systems, such as word processors and small business computers, and of general-purpose microcomputers, such as personal computers and intelligent terminals. These small, dispersed systems are more accessible to the user, more responsive, and easier to use than large central time-sharing systems.

As the number of systems at a single site—office building, factory, operations center, etc.—increases, there is likely to be a desire to interconnect these systems for a variety of reasons, including

- sharing expensive resources, and
- exchanging data between systems.

Sharing expensive resources, such as bulk storage and line printers, is an important measure for cost containment. Although the cost of data processing hardware has dropped, the cost of such essential

CONTENTS

electromechanical equipment remains high. Even in the case of data that can be uniquely associated with a small system, economies of scale require that most of that data be stored on a larger central facility: The cost per bit for storage on a microcomputer's floppy disk is orders of magnitude higher than that for a large disk or tape.

The ability to exchange data is an equally compelling reason for interconnection. Individual users of computer systems do not work in isolation and will want to retain some of the benefits provided by a central system, including the ability to exchange messages with other users, and the ability to access data and programs from several sources in the preparation of a document or the analysis of data.

A Definition

This requirement for communication, both among multiple computer systems within an organization and between those systems and shared resources, is met by the local network, which is defined as follows:

A local network is a communications network that provides interconnection of a variety of data communicating devices within a small area.

There are three significant elements in this definition. First, a local network is a communications network, not a computer network. In this paper, we deal only with issues relating to the communications network; the software and protocols required for attached computers to function as a network are beyond the scope of the paper.

Second, we broadly interpret the phrase "data communicating devices" to include any device that communicates over a transmission medium, including

- computers,
- terminals,
- peripheral devices,
- sensors (temperature, humidity, security alarm sensors),
- telephones,
- television transmitters and receivers,
- facsimile.

Of course, not all types of local networks are capable of handling all of these devices.

Third, the geographic scope of a local network is small, most commonly confined to a single building. Networks that span several buildings, such as those on a college campus or military base, are also common. A network with a radius of a few tens of kilometers is a borderline case. With the use of appropriate technology, such a system can behave like a local network.

Another element that could included in the definition is that a local network is generally a privately owned rather than a public or commercially available utility. Usually a single organization owns both the network and the attached devices.

Some of the key characteristics of local networks are

- high data rates (0.1–100 megabits per second, Mbps),

- short distances (0.1–50 kilometers),
- low error rate (10^{-8}–10^{-11}).

The first two parameters differentiate local networks from two cousins: long-haul networks and multiprocessor systems.

These distinctions between the local network and its two cousins have an impact on design and operation. Local networks generally experience much fewer data transmission errors and lower communications costs than long-haul networks, and cost–performance trade-offs therefore differ significantly. Also, it is possible to achieve greater integration between the local network and the attached devices, as they are generally owned by the same organization.

A major distinction between local networks and multiprocessors systems is the degree of coupling: Multiprocessor systems are tightly coupled, have shared memory, usually have some central control, and completely integrate the communications function, whereas local networks tend to have the opposite characteristics.

Benefits and Pitfalls

We already have mentioned resource sharing as an important benefit of local networks. This includes not only expensive peripheral devices, but also data.

A local network is also more reliable, available to the user, and able to survive failures. The loss of any one system should have minimal impact, and key systems can be made redundant so that other systems can quickly take up the load after a failure.

One of the most important potential benefits of a local network relates to system evolution. In a nonnetworked installation such as a time-sharing center, all data processing power is in one or a few systems. In order to upgrade hardware, existing applications software must be either converted to new hardware or reprogrammed, with the risk of error in either case. Even adding new applications on the same hardware, or enhancing those that exist, involves the risk of introducing errors and reducing the performance of the entire system. With a local network it is possible to gradually replace applications or systems, avoiding the "all-or-nothing" approach. Another facet of this capability is that old equipment can be left in the system to run a single application if the cost of moving that application to a new machine is not justified.

Finally, a local network provides the potential to connect devices from multiple vendors, which would give the customer greater flexibility and bargaining power.

These represent the most significant benefits of a local network. Alas, there are potential pitfalls as well.

There is a certain amount of loss of control in distributed systems; it is difficult to manage this resource, to enforce standards for software and data, and to control the information available through a network. The prime benefit of networking—distributed systems—also incorporates its prime pitfall.

It is likely that data will be distributed in a local network, or at least that access to data will be possible from multiple sources. This raises the problems of integrity of data (e.g., two users trying to update a database at the same time), security of data, and privacy.

Another pitfall might be referred to as "creeping escalation." With the dispersal of systems and ease of adding computer equipment, it becomes easier for managers of suborganizations to justify equipment procurement for their department. Although each procurement may be individually justifiable, the total may well exceed an organization's requirements.

Finally, as we mentioned, one of the significant benefits of a local network is the potential to connect devices from multiple vendors. However, the local network does not guarantee interoperability, that is, that these devices can be used cooperatively. Two word processors from different vendors can be attached to a local network, but will most likely use different file formats and control characters. Some form of format-conversion software will be required to take a file from one device and edit it on the other.

A further discussion of the applications, benefits, and pitfalls of local networks is contained in Derfler and Stallings [1983].

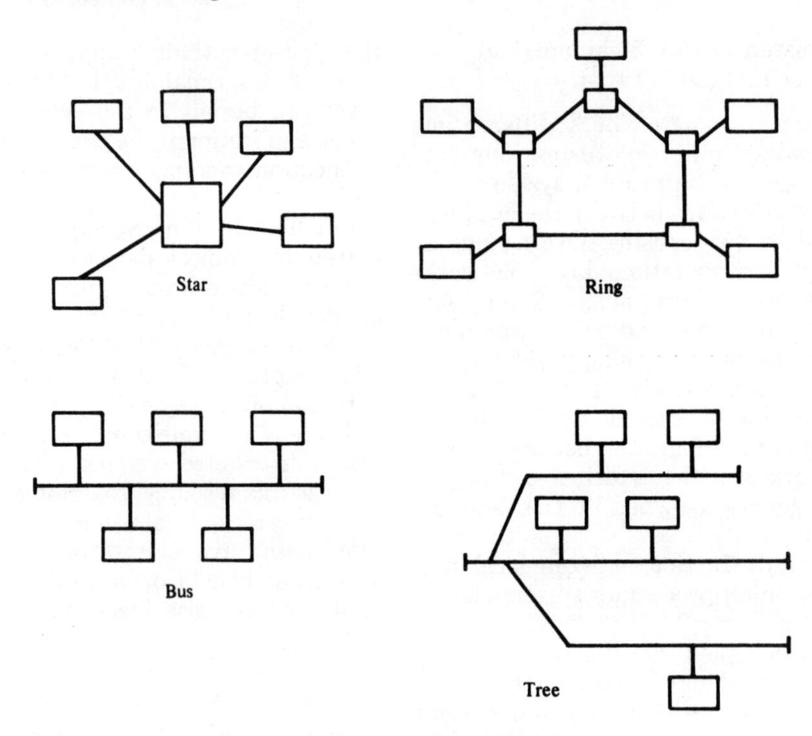

Figure 1. Local network topologies.

1. LOCAL NETWORK TECHNOLOGY

The principle technological alternatives that determine the nature of a local network are its topology and transmission medium [Rosenthal 1982], which determine the type of data that may be transmitted, the speed and efficiency of communications, and even the kinds of applications that a network may support.

In this section we survey the topologies and transmission media that are currently appropriate for local networks, and define three types of local networks based on these technologies.

1.1 Topologies

Local networks are often characterized in terms of their topology, three of which are common (Figure 1): star, ring, and bus or tree (the bus is a special case of the tree with only one trunk and no branches; we shall use the term bus/tree when the distinction is unimportant).

In the star topology, a central switching element is used to connect all the nodes in the network. A station wishing to transmit data sends a request to the central switch for a connection to some destination station, and the central element uses circuit switching to establish a dedicated path between the two stations. Once the circuit is set up, data are exchanged between the two stations as if they were connected by a dedicated point-to-point link.

The ring topology consists of a closed loop, with each node attached to a repeating element. Data circulate around the ring on a series of point-to-point data links between repeaters. A station wishing to transmit waits for its next turn and then sends the data out onto the ring in the form of a packet, which contains both the source and destination address fields as well as data. As the packet circulates, the destination node copies the data into a local buffer. The packet continues to circulate until it returns to the source node, providing a form of acknowledgment.

The bus/tree topology is characterized by the use of a multiple-access, broadcast medium. Because all devices share a common communications medium, only one device can transmit at a time, and as with the

Table 1. Typical Characteristics of Transmission Media for Local Networks

	Signaling technique	Maximum data rate (Mbps)	Maximum range at maximum data rate (kilometers)	Practical number of devices
Twisted pair wire	Digital	1–2	Few	10's
Coaxial cable (50 ohm)	Digital	10	Few	100's
Coaxial cable (75 ohm)	Digital	50	1	10's
	Analog with FDM	20	10's	1000's
	Single-channel analog	50	1	10's
Optical fiber	Analog	10	1	10's

ring, transmission employs a packet containing source and destination address fields and data. Each station monitors the medium and copies packets addressed to itself.

1.2 Transmission Media

Table 1 is a list of characteristics of the transmission media most appropriate for local networks: twisted pair wire, coaxial cable, and optical fiber. The characteristics listed in the table serve to distinguish the performance and applicability of each type of transmission medium.

Twisted pair wiring is one of the most common communications transmission media, and one that is certainly applicable to local networks. Although typically used for low-speed transmission, data rates of up to a few megabits per second can be achieved. One weakness of twisted pair wire is its susceptibility to interference and noise, including cross talk from adjacent wires. These effects can be minimized with proper shielding. Twisted pair wire is relatively low in cost and is usually preinstalled in office buildings. It is the most cost-effective choice for single-building, low-traffic requirements.

Higher performance requirements can best be met by coaxial cable, which provides higher throughput, can support a larger number of devices, and can span greater distances than twisted pair wire. Two transmission methods, baseband and broadband, can be employed on a coaxial cable; these are explained in detail in Sections 2.2 and 2.3, respectively. The key difference is that baseband supports a single data channel, whereas broadband can support multiple simultaneous data channels.

Optical fiber is a promising candidate for future local network installations. It has a higher potential capacity than coaxial cable, and a number of advantages over both coaxial cable and twisted pair wire, including light weight, small diameter, low noise susceptibility, and practically no emissions. However, it has not been widely used thus far due to cost and technical limitations [Allan 1983]. From a technical point of view, point-to-point fiber-optic topologies like the ring will become feasible as the cost of optical fiber drops. Multipoint topologies like the bus/tree are difficult to implement with optical fiber because each tap imposes large power losses and causes optical reflections. One approach to this problem is the passive star coupler (Figure 2) [Freedman 1983; Rawson and Metcalfe 1978]. The passive star coupler consists of a number of optical fibers fused together: Light entering from one fiber on the input side is equally divided among and output through all fibers on the other side of the coupler.

1.3 Relationship between Medium and Topology

The choices of transmission medium and topology cannot be made independently. Table 2 illustrates desirable combinations.

The bus topology can be implemented with either twisted pair wire or coaxial cable.

The tree topology can be employed with broadband coaxial cable. As we shall see, the unidirectional nature of broadband signaling allows the construction of a tree architecture. The bidirectional nature of baseband signaling on either twisted pair wire or coaxial cable would not be suited to the tree topology.

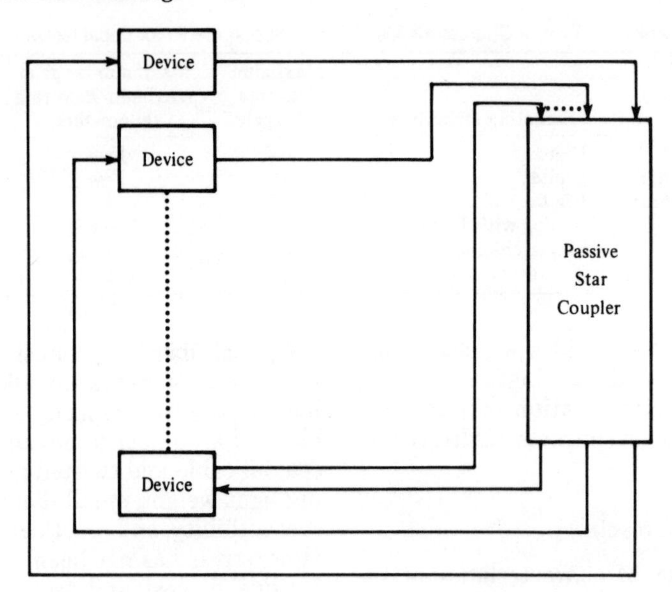

Figure 2. Optical fiber passive star configuration.

Table 2. Relationship between Transmission Medium and Topology

Medium	Topology: Bus	Tree	Ring	Star
Twisted pair	×		×	×
Baseband coaxial	×		×	
Broadband coaxial	×	×		
Optical fiber			×	

The ring topology requires point-to-point links between repeaters. Twisted pair wire, baseband coaxial cable, and fiber all can be used to provide these links. Broadband coaxial cable would not work well in this topology, as each repeater would have to be capable, asynchronously, of receiving and retransmitting data on multiple channels. It is doubtful that the expense of such devices could be justified.

The star topology requires a single point-to-point link between each device and the central switch. Twisted pair wire is admirably suited to the task. The higher data rates of coaxial cable or fiber would overwhelm the switches available with today's technology.

1.4 Types of Local Networks

Three categories of local networks can be distinguished: local area network (LAN), high-speed local network (HSLN), and computerized branch exchange (CBX). These categories reflect differences in types of applications, possible choices of topologies and media, and, especially in the case of the CBX, differences in technology. Table 3 is a summary of representative characteristics of each category. Although we have included the CBX as a category of local network because it is an alternative means of locally interconnecting digital devices, its technology and architecture are so different from that of the LAN and HSLN that it is often not considered a local network. We mention its characteristics briefly, but in the remainder of this paper we shall concentrate on the LAN and HSLN.

1.4.1 Local Area Network

The term "local area network" (LAN) refers to a general-purpose local network that can serve a wide variety of devices. LANs support minicomputers, mainframes, terminals, and other peripheral devices. In many cases, these networks can carry not only data, but voice, video, and graphics.

The most common type of LAN is a bus or tree using coaxial cable; rings using twisted pair wire, coaxial cable, or optical

Table 3. Classes of Local Networks

Characteristics	Local area network	High-speed local network	Computerized branch exchange
Transmission medium	Twisted pair, coaxial (both), fiber	CATV coaxial	Twisted pair
Topology	Bus, tree, ring	Bus	Star
Transmission speed (Mbps)	1–20	50	0.0096–0.064
Maximum distance (kilometers)	~25	1	1
Switching technique	Packet	Packet	Circuit
Number of devices supported	100's–1000's	10's	100's–1000's
Attachment cost ($)	500–5000	40,000–50,000	250–1000

fiber are an alternative. The data transfer rates on LANs (1–10 Mbps) are high enough to satisfy most requirements and provide sufficient capacity to allow a large numbers of devices to share the network.

The LAN is probably the best choice when a variety of devices and a mix of traffic types are involved. The LAN, alone or as part of a hybrid local network with one of the other types, will become a common feature of many office buildings and other installations.

1.4.2 High-Speed Local Network

The high-speed local network (HSLN) is designed to provide high end-to-end throughput between expensive high-speed devices, such as mainframes and mass storage devices.

Although other media and topologies are possible, the bus topology using coaxial cable is the most common. Very high data rates are achievable—50 Mbps is standard—but both the distance and the number of devices are more limited in the HSLN than in the LAN.

The HSLN is typically found in a computer room setting. Its main function is to provide I/O channel connections among a number of devices. Typical uses include file and bulk data transfer, automatic backup, and load leveling. Because of the current high prices for HSLN attachment, they are generally not practical for microcomputers and less expensive peripheral devices, and are only rarely used for minicomputers.

1.4.3 Computerized Branch Exchange

The computerized branch exchange (CBX) is a digital on-premise private branch exchange designed to handle both voice and data connections, usually implemented with a star topology using twisted pair wire to connect end points to the switch.

In contrast to the LAN and HSLN, which use packet switching, the CBX uses circuit switching. Data rates to individual end points are typically low, but bandwidth is guaranteed and there is essentially no network delay once a connection has been made. The CBX is well suited to voice traffic, and to both terminal-to-terminal and terminal-to-host data traffic.

2. THE BUS/TREE TOPOLOGY

The bus and tree topologies have been most popular to date in implementing both LANs and HSLNs. Well-known bus or bus/tree architectures include Ethernet [Metcalfe and Boggs 1976], one of the earliest local networks; HYPERchannel [Christensen 1979], the oldest and most popular HSLN; and MITRENET [Hopkins 1979], the basis of much United States government-sponsored research. Most of the low-cost, twisted pair LANs for microcomputers use a bus topology. In this section we describe key characteristics of bus and tree configurations, and present a detailed description of the two transmission techniques used in these configurations: baseband and broadband.

2.1 Characteristics of Bus/Tree LANs and HSLNs

The bus/tree topology is a multipoint configuration; that is, it allows more than two devices at a time to be connected to and capable of transmitting on the medium.

This is opposed to the other topologies that we have discussed, which are point-to-point configurations; that is, each physical transmission link connects only two devices. Because multiple devices share a single data path, only one device may transmit data at a time, usually in the form of a packet containing the address of the destination. The packet propagates throughout the medium and is received by all other stations, but is copied only by the addressed station.

Two transmission techniques are in use for bus/tree LANs and HSLNs: baseband and broadband. Baseband uses digital signaling and can be employed on twisted pair wire or coaxial cable. Broadband uses analog signaling in the radio frequency (RF) range and is employed only on coaxial cable. Some of the differences between baseband and broadband are highlighted in Table 4, and in the following two sections we explore these techniques in some detail. There is also a variant known as "single-channel broadband," which has the signaling characteristics of broadband but some of the restrictions of baseband; this technique is also covered below.

The multipoint nature of the bus/tree topology gives rise to several problems common to both baseband and broadband systems. First, there is the problem of determining which station on the medium may transmit at any point in time. Historically, the most common access scheme has been centralized polling. One station has the role of a central controller. This station may send data to any other station or may request that another station send data to the controller. This method, however, negates some of the advantages of a distributed system and also is awkward for communication between two noncontroller stations. A variety of distributed strategies, referred to as "medium access control protocols," have now been developed for bus and tree topologies. These are discussed in Section 4.

A second problem with the multipoint configuration has to do with signal balancing. When two devices exchange data over a link, the signal strength of the transmitter must be adjusted to be within certain limits.

Table 4. Bus/Tree Transmission Techniques

Baseband	Broadband
Digital signaling	Analog signaling (requires RF modem)
Entire bandwidth consumed by signal—no FDM	FDM possible—multiple data channels, video, audio
Bidirectional	Unidirectional
Bus topology	Bus or tree topology
Distance, up to a few kilometers	Distance: up to tens of kilometers

The signal must be strong enough so that, after attenuation across the medium, it meets the receiver's minimum signal strength requirements, and is strong enough to maintain an adequate signal-to-noise ratio. On the other hand, if it is too strong, the signal will overload the circuitry of the transmitter, which creates harmonics and other spurious signals. Although it is easily done for a point-to-point link, signal balancing for a multipoint configuration is complex. If any device can transmit to any other device, then the signal balancing must be performed for all permutations of stations taken two at a time. For n stations that works out to $nx(n-1)$ permutations. For example, for a 200-station network (not a particularly large system), 39,800 signal strength constraints must be staisfied simultaneously. With interdevice distances ranging from tens to possibly thousands of meters, this can become an impossible task. In systems that use RF signals, the problem is compounded, owing to the possibility of RF signal interference across frequencies. The solution to these difficulties is to divide the medium into segments within which pairwise balancing is possible (i.e., signals between pairs of devices can be balanced within each segment). Amplifiers or repeaters are used between segments to maintain signal strength.

2.2 Baseband Systems

A baseband LAN or HSLN is by definition one that uses digital signaling. The entire frequency spectrum of the medium is used to form the digital signal, which is inserted on the line as constant-voltage pulses. Baseband systems can extend only about a

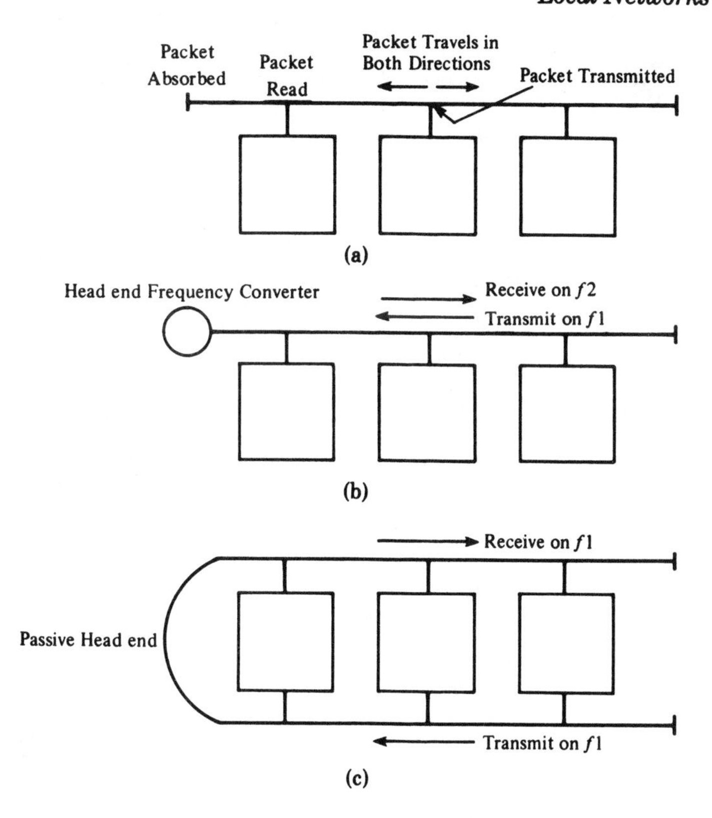

Figure 3. Baseband and broadband transmission: (a) bidirectional (baseband, single-channel broadband); (b) mid-split broadband; (c) dual cable broadband. [From W. Stallings, *Local Networks: An Introduction*, Macmillan, New York, 1984. Copyright Macmillan 1984.]

kilometer at most because the attenuation of the signal, especially at higher frequencies, causes a blurring of the pulses and a weakening of the signal to the extent that communication over longer distances is impractical. Baseband transmission is bidirectional; that is, a signal inserted at any point on the medium propagates in both directions to the ends, where it is absorbed (Figure 3a). In addition, baseband systems require a bus topology. Unlike analog signals, digital signals cannot easily be propagated through the splitters and joiners of a tree topology.

2.2.1 Baseband Coaxial

The most well-known form of baseband bus LAN uses coaxial cable. Unless otherwise indicated, this discussion is based on the Ethernet system [DEC 1983; Metcalfe and Boggs 1976; Metcalfe et al. 1977; Shoch et al. 1983] and the almost-identical IEEE standard [IEEE 1983].

Most baseband coaxial systems use a special 50-ohm cable rather than the more common 75-ohm cable used for cable television and broadband LANs. For digital signals, the 50-ohm cable suffers less intense reflections from the insertion capacitance of the taps, and provides better protection against low-frequency electromagnetic noise.

The simplest baseband coaxial LAN consists of an unbranched length of coaxial cable with a terminator at each end to prevent reflections. A maximum length of 500 meters is recommended. Stations attach to the cable by means of a tap. Attached to each tap is a transceiver, which contains the electronics for transmitting and receiving. The distance between any two taps should be a multiple of 2.5 meters

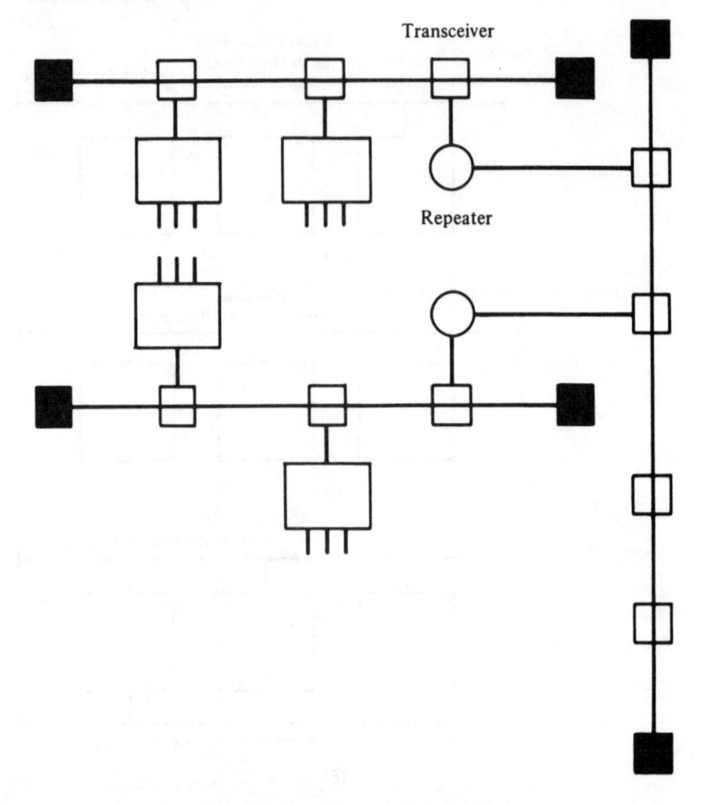

Figure 4. Baseband system.

to ensure that reflections from adjacent taps do not add in phase [Yen and Crawford 1983], and a maximum of 100 taps is recommended.

The above specifications are for a 10-Mbps data rate. They are based on engineering trade-offs involving data rate, cable length, number of taps, and the electrical characteristics of the transmit and receiver components. For example, at lower data rates the cable could be longer.

To extend the length of the network, a repeater may be used. A repeater consists, in essence, of two transceivers joined together and connected to two different segments of coaxial cable. The repeater passes digital signals in both directions between the two segments, amplifying and regenerating the signals as they pass through. A repeater is transparent to the rest of the system; since it does no buffering, it in no sense isolates one segment from another. So, for example, if two stations on different segments attempt to transmit at the same time, their packets will interfere with each other (collide). To avoid multipath interference, only one path of segments and repeaters is allowed between any two stations. Figure 4 is an example of a baseband system with three segments and two repeaters.

2.2.2 Twisted Pair Baseband

A twisted pair baseband LAN is intended for low-cost, low-performance requirements. Although this type of system supports fewer stations at lower speeds than a coaxial baseband LAN, its cost is also far lower.

The components of the system are few and simple:

- twisted pair bus,
- terminators,
- controller interface.

The latter can simply be a standard two-wire I/O or communications interface.

Typically, the electrical signaling technique on the cable conforms to RS-422-A. This is a standard inexpensive interface.

With this kind of network, the following parameters are reasonable:

- length, up to 1 kilometer,
- data rate, up to 1 Mbps,
- number of devices, 10's.

For these requirements, twisted pair wire is a good medium for several reasons: It is lower in cost than coaxial cable and provides equal noise immunity, and virtually anyone can install the network. The task of installation consists of laying the cable and connecting the controllers. This requires only a screwdriver and a pair of pliers, and is similar to hooking up hi-fi speakers.

Examples of these systems can be found in Malone [1981], Bosen [1981], and Hahn and Belanger [1981].

2.3 Broadband Systems

Within the context of local networks, a broadband system is by definition one that uses analog signaling. Unlike digital signaling, in which the entire frequency spectrum of the medium is used to produce the signal, analog signaling allows frequency-division multiplexing (FDM). With FDM, the frequency spectrum on the cable is divided into channels or sections of bandwidth; separate channels can support data traffic, TV, and radio signals.

A special case of a broadband system is a low-cost system using only a single channel. To distinguish between the two cases, we will refer to "FDM broadband" and "single-channel broadband" in this section. In Section 2.3.1, we examine FDM broadband, describing two different physical configurations, dual cable and split cable, and three different data transfer techniques, dedicated, switched, and multiple access. In Section 2.3.2, we describe single-channel broadband.

2.3.1 FDM Broadband

Broadband systems use standard, off-the-shelf community antenna television (CATV) components, including 75-ohm coaxial cable. All end points are terminated with a 75-ohm terminator to absorb signals. Broadband components allow splitting and joining operations; hence both bus and tree topologies are possible. Broadband is suitable for a range of tens of kilometers and hundreds or even thousands of devices. For all but very short distances, amplifiers are required.

A typical broadband system is shown in Figure 5. As with baseband, stations attach to the cable by means of a tap. Unlike baseband, however, broadband is a unidirectional medium; signals inserted onto the medium can only propagate in one direction. The primary reason for this is that it is not feasible to build amplifiers that will pass signals of one frequency in both directions. This unidirectional property means that only those stations "downstream" from a transmitting station can receive its signals. How, then, can one achieve full connectivity?

Clearly, two data paths are needed. These paths are joined at a point on the network known as the head end. For the bus topology, the head end is simply one end of the bus; for the tree topology, the head end is the root of the branching tree. All stations transmit on one path toward the head end (inbound). Signals received at the head end then are propagated along a second data path away from the head end (outbound). All stations receive on the outbound path.

Physically, two different configurations are used to implement the inbound and outbound paths (see Figure 3). On a dual cable configuration, the inbound and outbound paths are separate cables, the head end being simply a passive connector between the two. Stations send and receive on the same frequency.

In contrast, in the split configuration, the inbound and outbound paths are different frequencies on the same cable. Bidirectional amplifiers pass lower frequencies inbound and higher frequencies outbound. The head end contains a device, known as a frequency converter, for translating inbound frequencies to outbound frequencies.

The frequency converter at the head end can be either an analog or a digital device. An analog device simply translates signals

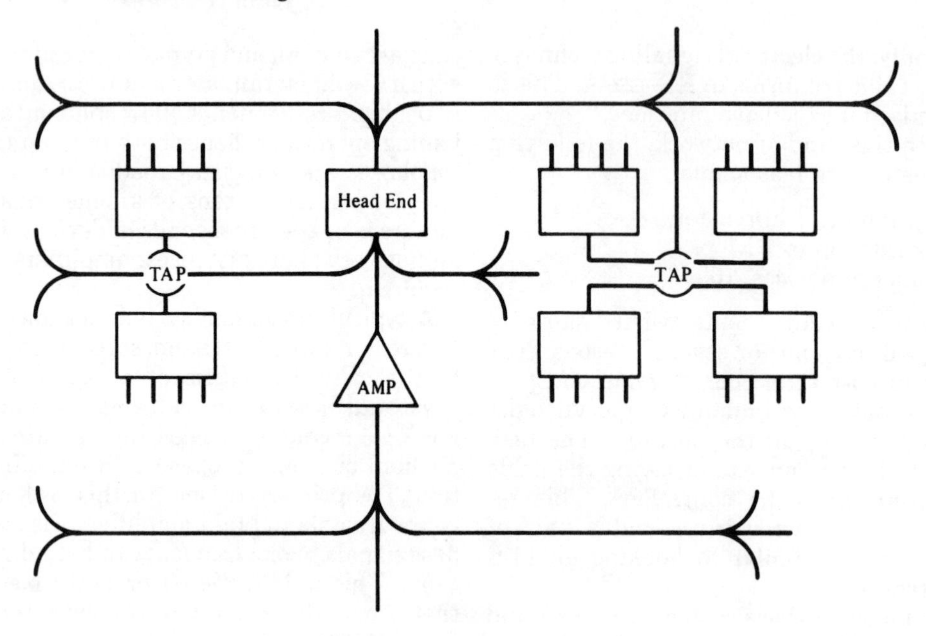

Figure 5. Broadband system.

to a new frequency and retransmits them. A digital device recovers the digital data from the head end and then retransmits the cleaned-up data on the new frequency.

Split systems are categorized by the frequency allocation to the two paths. Subsplit, commonly used by the CATV industry, provides 5–30 megahertz (MHz) inbound and 40–300 MHz outbound. This system was designed for metropolitan area TV distribution, with limited subscriber-to-central office communication. Mid-split, more suitable for LANs, provides an inbound range of 5–116 MHz and an outbound range of 168–300 MHz. This provides a more equitable distribution of bandwidth. Midsplit was developed at a time when the practical spectrum of a CATV cable was 300 MHz. Spectrums surpassing 400 MHz are now available, and either "supersplit" or "equal-split" is sometimes used to achieve even better balance by splitting the bandwidth roughly in half.

The differences between split and dual are minor. The split system is useful when a single-cable plant is already installed in a building, and the installed system is about 10–15 percent cheaper than a dual cable system [Hopkins 1979]. On the other hand, a dual cable has over twice the capacity of mid-split, and does not require the frequency translator at the head end. A further comparison can be found in Cooper and Edholm [1983].

The broadband LAN can be used to carry multiple channels, some used for analog signals, such as video and voice, and some for data. For example, a video channel requires a 6-MHz bandwidth. Digital channels can generally carry a data rate of somewhere between 0.25 and 1 bit per second per hertz. A possible allocation of a 350-MHz cable is shown in Figure 6.

One of the advantages of the use of multiple channels is that different channels can be used to satisfy different requirements. Figure 7 depicts three kinds of data transfer techniques that can be used: dedicated, switched, and multiple access.

For dedicated service, a small portion of the cable's bandwidth is reserved for exclusive use by two devices. No special protocol is needed. Each of the two devices attaches to the cable through a modem; both modems are tuned to the same frequency. This technique is analogous to securing a dedicated leased line from the telephone company. Transfer rates of up to 20 Mbps are achievable. The dedicated service could be used to connect two devices when a heavy

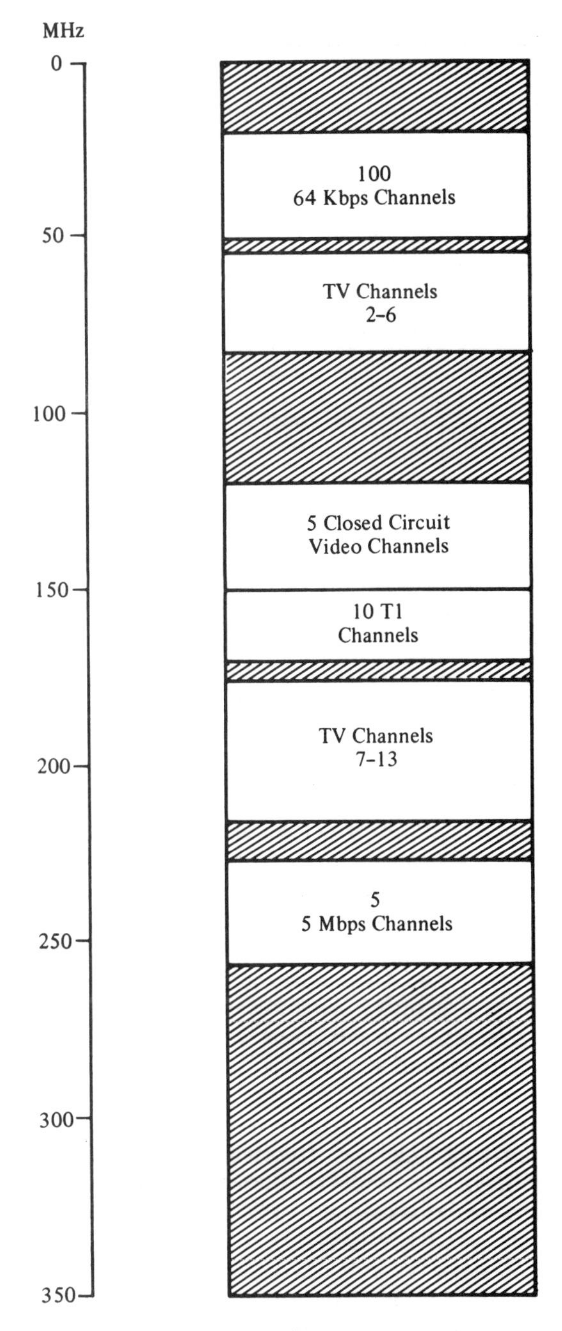

Figure 6. Broadband spectrum allocation.

traffic pattern is expected; for example, one computer may act as a standby for another, and need to get frequent updates of state information and file and database changes.

The switched transfer technique requires the use of a number of frequency bands. Devices are attached through "frequency-agile" modems, capable of changing their frequency by electronic command. All attached devices, together with a controller, are initially tuned to the same frequency. A station wishing to establish a connection sends a request to the controller, which assigns an available frequency to the two devices and signals their modems to tune to that frequency. This technique is analogous to a dial-up line. Because the cost of frequency-agile modems rises dramatically with data rate, rates of 56 Kbps or less are typical. The switched technique is used in Wang's local network for terminal-to-host connections [Stahlman 1982], and could also be used for voice service.

Finally, the multiple-access service, by far the most common, allows a number of attached devices to be supported at the same frequency. As with baseband, some form of medium access control protocol is needed to control transmission. It provides for distributed, peer communications among many devices, which is the primary motivation for a local network.

Further discussions of FDM broadband LANs can be found in Cooper [1982, 1983], Dineson and Picazo [1980], and Forbes [1981].

2.3.2 Single-Channel Broadband

An abridged form of broadband is possible, in which the entire spectrum of the cable is devoted to a single transmission path for analog signals. In general, a single-channel broadband LAN uses bidirectional transmission and a bus topology. Hence there can be no amplifiers, and there is no need for a head end. Transmission is generally at a low frequency (a few megahertz). This is an advantage since attenuation is less at lower frequencies.

Because the cable is dedicated to a single task, it is not necessary to ensure that the modem output is confined to a narrow bandwidth; energy can spread over the cable's spectrum. As a result, the electronics are simple and inexpensive. This scheme would appear to give comparable performance, at a comparable price, to baseband.

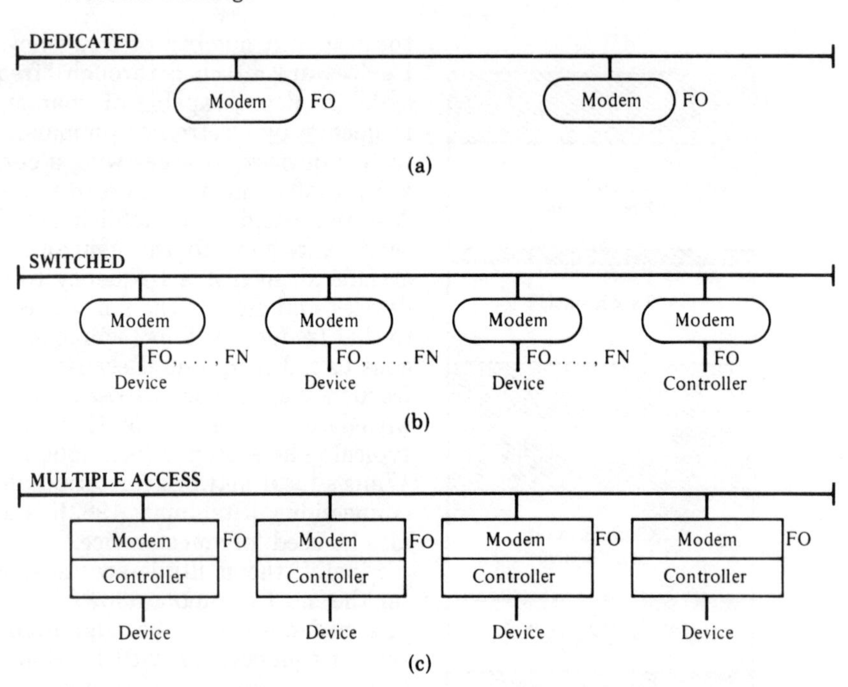

Figure 7. Broadband data transfer services: (a) dedicated; (b) switched; (c) multiple access.

The principle reason for choosing this scheme over baseband appears to be that single-channel broadband uses 75-ohm cable. Thus a user with modest initial requirements could install the 75-ohm cable and use inexpensive single-channel components. Later, if the needs expand, the user could switch to full broadband by replacing modems, but would avoid the expense of rewiring the building with new cable.

2.4 Baseband versus Broadband

One of the least productive aspects of the extensive coverage afforded local networks in the trade and professional literature is the baseband versus broadband debate. The potential customer will be faced with many other decisions more complex than this one. The fact is that there is room for both technologies in the local network field. For the interested reader, thoughtful discussions may be found in Hopkins and Meisner [1982] and Krutsch [1981].

To briefly summarize the two technologies, baseband has the advantages of simplicity, and, in principle, low cost. The layout of a baseband cable plant is simple: A relatively inexperienced local network engineer should be able to cope with it. Baseband's potential disadvantages include limitations in capacity and distance—but these are only disadvantages if one's requirements exceed those limitations.

Broadband's strength is its tremendous capacity. Broadband can carry a wide variety of traffic on a number of channels, and with the use of active amplifiers can achieve very wide area coverage. Also, the system is based on a mature CATV technology, with reliable and readily available components. A disadvantage of broadband systems is that they are more complex than baseband to install and maintain, requiring experienced RF engineers. Also, the average propagation delay between stations for broadband is twice that for a comparable baseband system. This reduces the efficiency and performance of the system, as discussed in Section 5.

As with all other network design choices, the selection of baseband or broadband must be based on the relative cost and benefits. Neither is likely to win the LAN war.

2.5 Bus HSLNs

HSLNs using a bus topology share a number of characteristics with bus-based LANs. In particular, data are transmitted in packets, and because the configuration is multipoint, a medium access control protocol is needed. From the user's point of view, the key difference between a LAN and an HSLN is the higher data rate of the latter. Commercial HSLN products and the proposed American National Standards Institute (ANSI) standard both specify 50 Mbps, whereas 10 Mbps or less is typical for LANs. The higher data rate of the HSLN imposes cost and technical constraints, and the HSLN is limited to just a few devices (10–20) over a relatively small distance (less than 1 kilometer).

Two techniques have been used for bus HSLNs: baseband and single-channel broadband. In both cases a 75-ohm coaxial cable is used. Baseband is used for the most widely available HSLN product, HYPERchannel [Christensen 1979; Thornton 1980]. Single-channel broadband is used on CDC's product [Hohn 1980] and is the approach taken in the proposed ANSI standard [Burr 1983].

It is difficult to assess the relative advantages of these two schemes. In general, the two approaches should give comparable performance at comparable cost.

3. THE RING TOPOLOGY

The major alternative to the bus/tree topology LAN is the ring. The ring topology has been popular in Europe but is only slowly gaining ground in the United States, where Ethernet and MITRENET were largely responsible for shaping the early direction of activity. Several factors suggest that the ring may become more of a competitor in the United States: IBM has conducted research on ring LANs and is expected to announce a product, and the IEEE 802 ring LAN standard is moving toward completion.

3.1 Characteristics of Ring LANs

A ring LAN consists of a number of repeaters, each connected to two others by unidirectional transmission links to form a single closed path. Data are transferred sequentially, bit by bit, around the ring from one repeater to the next. Each repeater regenerates and retransmits each bit.

For a ring to operate as a communications network, three functions are required: data insertion, data reception, and data removal. These functions are provided by the repeaters. Each repeater, in addition to serving as an active element on the ring, serves as an attachment point for a station. Data are transmitted in packets, each of which contains a destination address field. As a packet circulates past a repeater, the address field is copied. If the attached station recognizes the address, then the remainder of the packet is copied. A variety of strategies can be used for determining how and when packets are added to and removed from the ring. These strategies are medium access control protocols, which are discussed in Section 4.

Repeaters perform the data insertion and reception functions in a similar manner to taps, which serve as station attachment points on a bus or tree. Data removal, however, is more difficult on a ring. For a bus or tree, signals inserted onto the line propagate to the end points and are absorbed by terminators, which clear the bus or tree of data. However, because the ring is a closed loop, data will circulate indefinitely unless removed. There are two solutions to this problem: A packet may be removed by the addressed repeater when it is received, or each packet could be removed by the transmitting repeater after it has made one trip around the ring. The latter approach is more desirable because: (1) it permits automatic acknowledgment, and (2) it permits multicast addressing, that is, one packet sent simultaneously to multiple stations.

The repeater then can be seen to have two main purposes: (1) to contribute to the proper functioning of the ring by passing on all the data that comes its way, and (2) to provide an access point for attached stations to send and receive data. Corresponding to these two purposes are two states (Figure 8): listen and transmit.

In the listen state, each bit that is received by the repeater is retransmitted, with a small delay to allow the repeater to perform required functions. Ideally, this delay should be on the order of one bit time (the time it takes for a repeater to transmit one complete bit onto the outgoing line). The required functions are

(1) Scan the passing bit stream for pertinent patterns, chiefly the address or addresses of attached stations. Another pattern, used in the token control strategy, is discussed in Section 4. Note that to perform the scanning function, the repeater must have some knowledge of packet format.
(2) Copy each incoming bit and send it to the attached station, while continuing to retransmit each bit. This will be done for each bit of each packet that is addressed to this station.
(3) Modify a bit as it passes by. In certain control strategies, bits may be modified, for example, to indicate that the packet has been copied. This would serve as an acknowledgment.

When a repeater's station has data to send and the repeater has permission to transmit (based on the medium access control strategy), the repeater enters the transmit state. In this state, the repeater receives bits from the station and retransmits them on its outgoing link. During the period of transmission, bits may appear on the incoming ring link. There are two possibilities, and they are treated differently:

(1) The bits could be from the same packet that the repeater is still sending. This will occur if the "bit length" of the ring is shorter than the packet. In this case, the repeater passes the bits back to the station, which can check them as a form of acknowledgment.
(2) For some control strategies, more than one packet could be on the ring at the same time. If the repeater, while transmitting, receives bits from a packet that it did not originate, it must buffer them to be transmitted later.

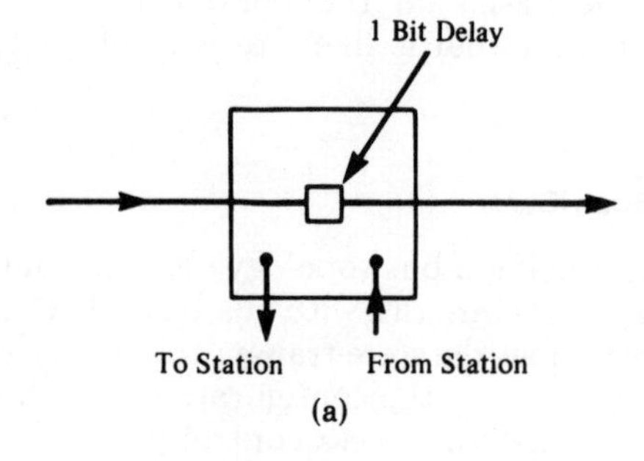

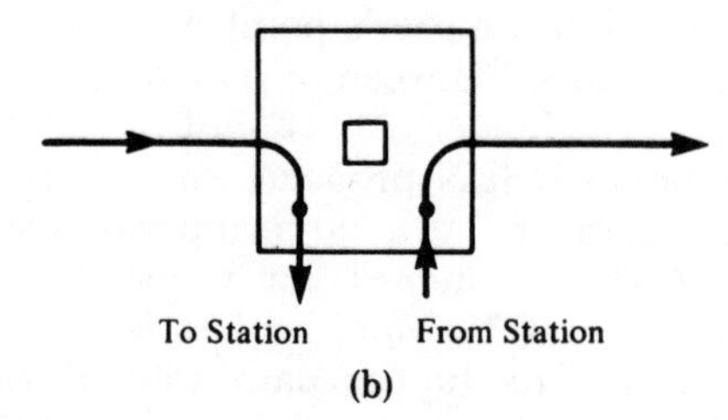

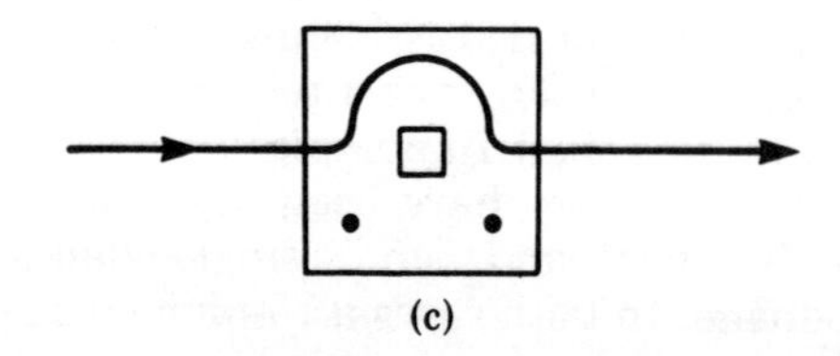

Figure 8. Ring repeater states: (a) listen state; (b) transmit state; (c) bypass state.

These two states, listen and transmit, are sufficient for proper ring operation. A third state, the bypass state, is also useful. In this state, a bypass relay can be activated, so that signals propagate past the repeater with no delay other than medium propagation. The bypass relay affords two benefits: (1) it provides a partial solution to the reliability problem, discussed later, and (2) it improves performance by eliminating repeater delay for those stations that are not active on the network.

Twisted pair wire, baseband coaxial cable, and fiber optic cable all can be used to provide the repeater-to-repeater links. Broadband coaxial cable could not be used easily, as each repeater would have to be capable of receiving and transmitting data on multiple channels asynchronously.

3.2 Potential Ring Problems

One of the principal reasons for the slow acceptance of the ring LAN in the United

States is that there are a number of potential problems with this topology [Saltzer and Pogran 1979]:

Cable Vulnerability. A break on any of the links between repeaters disables the entire network until the problem can be isolated and a new cable installed.

Repeater Failure. A failure of a single repeater also disables the entire network. In many networks, some of the stations may not be in operation at any given time; yet all repeaters must always operate properly.

Perambulation. When either a repeater or a link fails, locating the failure requires perambulation of the ring, and thus access to all rooms containing repeaters and cable. This is known as the "pocket full of keys" problem.

Installation Headaches. Installation of a new repeater to support new devices requires the identification of two topologically adjacent repeaters near the new installation. It must be verified that they are in fact adjacent (documentation could be faulty or out of date), and cable must be run from the new repeater to each of the old repeaters. There are several possible consequences: The length of cable driven by the source repeater may change, possibly requiring returning; old cable will accumulate if not removed; and the geometry of the ring may become highly irregular, exacerbating the perambulation problem.

Size Limitations. There is a practical limit to the number of stations on a ring. This limit is suggested by the reliability and maintenance problems cited earlier and by the accumulating delay of large numbers of repeaters. A limit of a few hundred stations seems reasonable.

Initialization and Recovery. To avoid designating one ring node as a controller (negating the benefit of distributed control), a strategy is required to ensure that all stations can cooperate smoothly when initialization and recovery are required. This cooperation is needed, for example, when a packet is garbled by a transient line error; in that case, no repeater may wish to assume the responsibility of removing the circulating packet.

The last problem is a protocol issue, which we discuss later. The remaining problems can be handled by a refinement of the ring topology, discussed next.

3.3 An Enhanced Architecture

The potential ring problems cited above have led to the development of an enhanced ring architecture that overcomes these problems of the ring and allows the construction of large local networks. This architecture is the basis of IBM's anticipated local network product [Rauch-Hindin 1982] and grows out of research done at IBM [Bux et al. 1982] and Massachusetts Institute of Technology [Saltzer and Clark 1981]. The result is a ring-based local network with two additions: ring wiring concentrators and bridges.

The ring wiring concentrator is simply a centralized location through which inter-repeater links are threaded. The link between any two stations runs from one station into the concentrator and back out to the second station. This technique has a number of advantages. Because there is central access to the signal on every link, it is a simple matter to isolate a fault. A message can be launched into the ring and tracked to see how far it gets without mishap. A faulty segment can be disconnected and repaired at a later time. New repeaters can easily be added to the ring: Simply run two cables from the new repeater to the site of ring wiring concentration and splice into the ring.

The bypass relay associated with each repeater can be moved into the ring wiring concentrator. The relay can automatically bypass its repeater and two links for any malfunction. A nice effect of this feature is that the transmission path from one working repeater to the next is approximately constant; thus the range of signal levels to which the transmission system must automatically adapt is much smaller.

The ring wiring concentrator permits rapid recovery from a cable or repeater failure. Nevertheless, a single failure could temporarily disable the entire network. Furthermore, throughput considerations

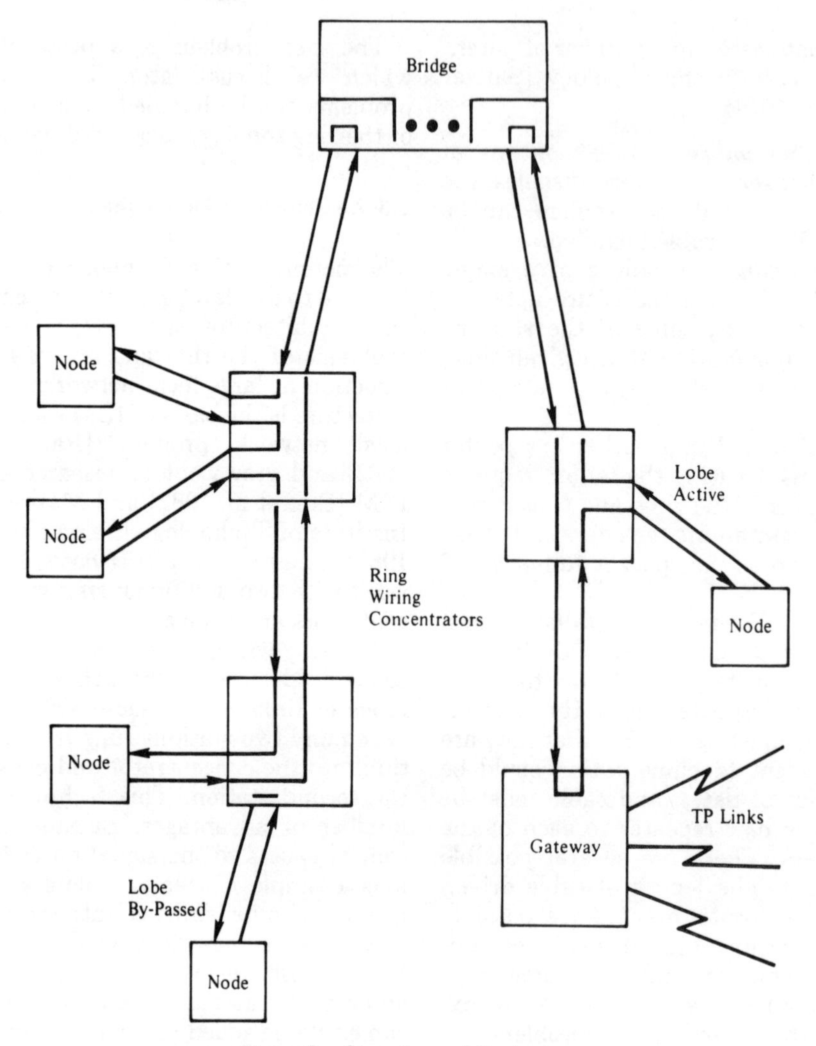

Figure 9. Star–ring architecture.

place a practical upper limit on the number of stations in a ring, since each repeater adds an increment of delay. Finally, in a spread-out network, a single wire concentration site dictates a lot of cable.

To attack these remaining problems, consider a local network consisting of multiple rings (Figure 9). Each ring consists of a connected sequence of wiring concentrators; the set of rings is connected by a bridge. The bridge routes data packets from one ring subnetwork to another on the basis of addressing information in the packet so routed. From a physical point of view, each ring operates independently of the other rings attached to the bridge. From a logical point of view, the bridge provides transparent routing between the two rings.

The bridge must perform five functions:

Input Filtering. For each ring, the bridge monitors the traffic on the ring and copies all packets addressed to other rings on the bridge. This function can be performed by a repeater programmed to recognize a family of addresses rather than a single address.

Input Buffering. Received packets may need to be buffered, either because the interring traffic is peaking, or because the output buffer at the destination ring is temporarily full.

Switching. Each packet must be routed through the bridge to its appropriate destination ring.

Output Buffering. A packet may need to be buffered at the threshold of the destination ring, waiting for an opportunity to be inserted.

Output Transmission. This function can be performed by an ordinary repeater.

Two principal advantages accrue from the use of a bridge. First, the failure of a ring, for whatever reason, will disable only a portion of the network; failure of the bridge does not prevent intraring traffic. Second, multiple rings may be employed to obtain a satisfactory level of performance when the throughput capability of a single ring is exceeded.

There are several disadvantages to be noted. First, the automatic acknowledgment feature of the ring is lost; higher level protocols must provide acknowledgment. Second, performance may not significantly improve if there is a high percentage of interring traffic. If it is possible to do so, network devices should be judiciously allocated to rings to minimize interring traffic.

3.4 Bus versus Ring

For the user with a large number of devices and high capacity requirements, the bus or tree broadband LAN seems the best suited to the requirements. For more moderate requirements, the choice between a baseband bus LAN and a ring LAN is not at all clear-cut.

The baseband bus is the simpler system. Passive taps rather than active repeaters are used. Thus medium failure is less likely, and there is no need for the complexity of bridges and ring wiring concentrators.

The most important benefit of the ring is that, unlike the bus/tree, it uses point-to-point communication links, which has a number of implications. First, since the transmitted signal is regenerated at each node, transmission errors are minimized and greater distances can be covered. Second, the ring can accommodate optical fiber links, which provide very high data rates and excellent electromagnetic interference (EMI) characteristics. Third, the electronics and maintenance of point-to-point lines are simpler than those for multipoint lines. Another benefit of the ring is, assuming that the enhanced ring architecture is used, that fault isolation and recovery is simpler than for bus/tree.

Further discussion of ring versus bus is contained in Salwen [1983].

4. MEDIUM ACCESS CONTROL PROTOCOLS

All local networks (LAN, HSLN, CBX) consist of a collection of devices that must share the network's transmission capacity. Some means of controlling access to the transmission medium is needed so that any two particular devices can exchange data when required.

The key parameters in controlling access to the medium are "where" and "how." The question of where access is controlled generally refers to whether the system is centralized or distributed. A centralized scheme has the advantages of

- possibly affording greater control over access by providing such things as priorities, overrides, and guaranteed bandwidth,
- allowing the logic at each station to be as simple as possible, and
- avoiding problems of coordination,

and the disadvantages of

- a single point of failure, and
- possibly acting as a bottleneck, reducing efficiency.

The pros and cons for distributed control are mirror images of the above points.

How access is controlled is constrained by the topology and is a trade-off among competing factors: cost, performance, and complexity.

The most common medium access control protocols for local networks are categorized in Figure 10. In all cases, multiple data transfers share a single transmission medium. This always implies some sort of multiplexing, either in the time or frequency domain. In the frequency domain, any technique on a multiple-channel broadband system is by definition based on frequency-division multiplexing (FDM).

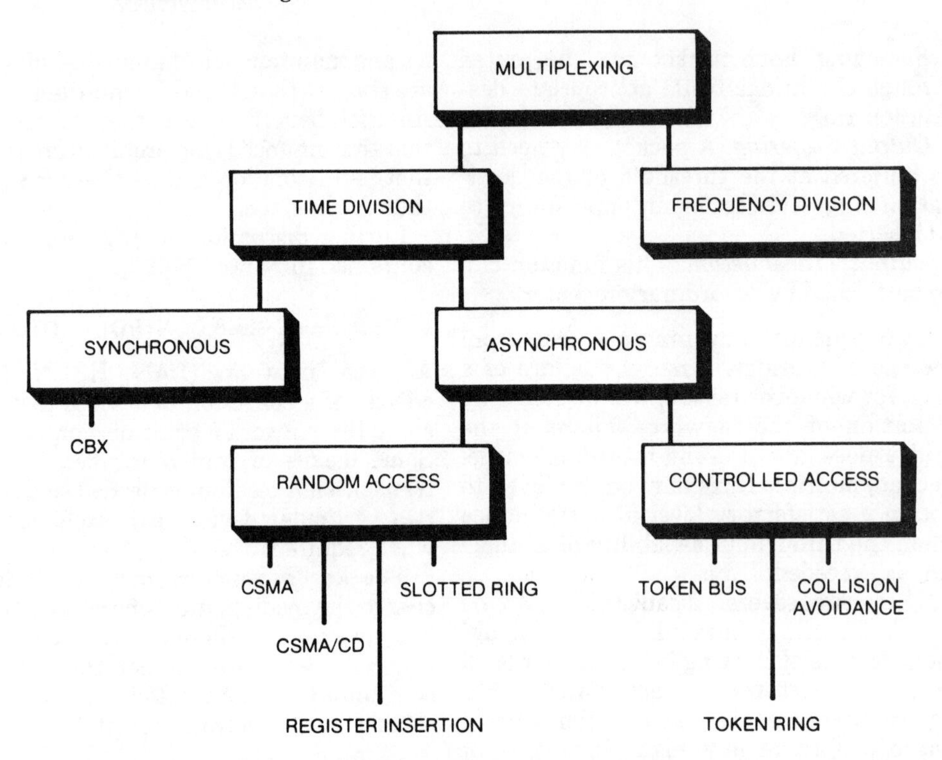

Figure 10. Local network access control techniques.

Within a single channel, however, some form of time-division multiplexing is required.

Time-division access control techniques are either synchronous or asynchronous. With synchronous techniques, a specific capacity is dedicated to a connection, as, for example, in the CBX. This is not optimal in bus/tree and ring networks: The needs of the stations are unpredictable, and the transmission capacity should be allocated in an asynchronous (dynamic) fashion in response to these needs.

Access to the medium using asynchronous time-division multiplexing (TDM) may be random (stations attempt to access the medium at will and at random times) or regulated (an algorithm is used to regulate the sequence and time of station access). The random access category includes two common bus techniques, carrier sense multiple access (CSMA) and carrier sense multiple access with collision detection (CSMA/CD), and two common ring techniques, register insertion and slotted ring. The regulated access category includes both token bus and token ring for LANs and collision avoidance, the most common HSLN technique. All of the asynchronous techniques have found widespread application in LANs or HSLNs, and are discussed in this section.

4.1 Bus/Tree LANs

Of all the local network topologies, the bus/tree topologies present the most challenges, and the most options, for medium access control. In this section we do not survey the many techniques that have been proposed; good discussions can be found in Luczak [1978] and Franta and Chlamtec [1981]. Rather, emphasis will be on the two techniques for which standards have been developed by the IEEE 802 Committee and that seem likely to dominate the marketplace: CSMA/CD and token bus. Table 5 is a comparison of these two techniques on a number of characteristics.

Table 5. Bus/Tree Access Methods

Characteristic	CSMA/CD	Token bus
Access determination	Contention	Token
Packet length restriction	Greater than 2× propagation delay	None
Principal advantage	Simplicity	Regulated/fair access
Principal disadvantage	Performance under heavy load	Complexity

4.1.1 CSMA/CD

The most commonly used medium access control protocol for bus/tree topologies is CSMA/CD. The original baseband version is seen in Ethernet, and the original broadband version is part of MITRENET [Hopkins 1979; Roman 1977].

We begin the discussion by looking at a simpler version of this technique known as CSMA or listen before talk (LBT). A station wishing to transmit listens to the medium to determine whether another transmission is in progress. If the medium is idle, the station may transmit. Otherwise, the station backs off for some period of time and tries again, using one of the algorithms explained below. After transmitting, a station waits for a reasonable amount of time for an acknowledgment, taking into account the maximum round-trip propagation delay and the fact that the acknowledging station must also contend for the channel in order to respond.

This strategy is effective for systems in which the packet transmission time is much longer than the propagation time. Collisions only occur when more than one user begins transmitting within the period of propagation delay. If there are no collisions during the time that it takes for the leading edge of the packet to propagate to the farthest station, then the transmitting station has seized the channel and the packet is transmitted without collision.

With CSMA, an algorithm is needed to specify what a station should do if the medium is found to be busy. Three approaches or "persistence algorithms," are possible:

(1) *Nonpersistent.* The station backs off a random amount of time and then senses the medium again.

(2) *1-Persistent.* The station continues to sense the medium until it is idle, then transmits.

(3) *p-Persistent.* The station continues to sense the medium until it is idle, then transmits with some preassigned probability p. Otherwise, it backs off a fixed amount of time, then transmits with probability p or continues to back off with probability $(1 - p)$.

The nonpersistent algorithm is effective in avoiding collisions; two stations wishing to transmit when the medium is busy are likely to back off for different amounts of time. The drawback is that there is likely to be wasted idle time following each transmission. In contrast, the 1-persistent algorithm attempts to reduce idle time by allowing a single waiting station to transmit immediately after another transmission. Unfortunately, if more than one station is waiting, a collision is guaranteed! The p-persistent algorithm is a compromise that attempts to minimize both collisions and idle time.

CSMA/CD, also referred to as listen while talk (LWT), attempts to overcome one glaring inefficiency of CSMA: When two packets collide, the medium remains unusable for the duration of transmission of both damaged packets. For packets that are long in comparison to their propagation time, the amount of wasted bandwidth can be considerable. This waste is reduced with the CSMA/CD protocol: A station continues to listen to the medium while it is transmitting. Hence the following rules are added to the CSMA protocol:

(1) If a collision is detected during transmission, immediately cease transmitting the packet and transmit a brief jamming signal to ensure that all stations know there has been a collision.

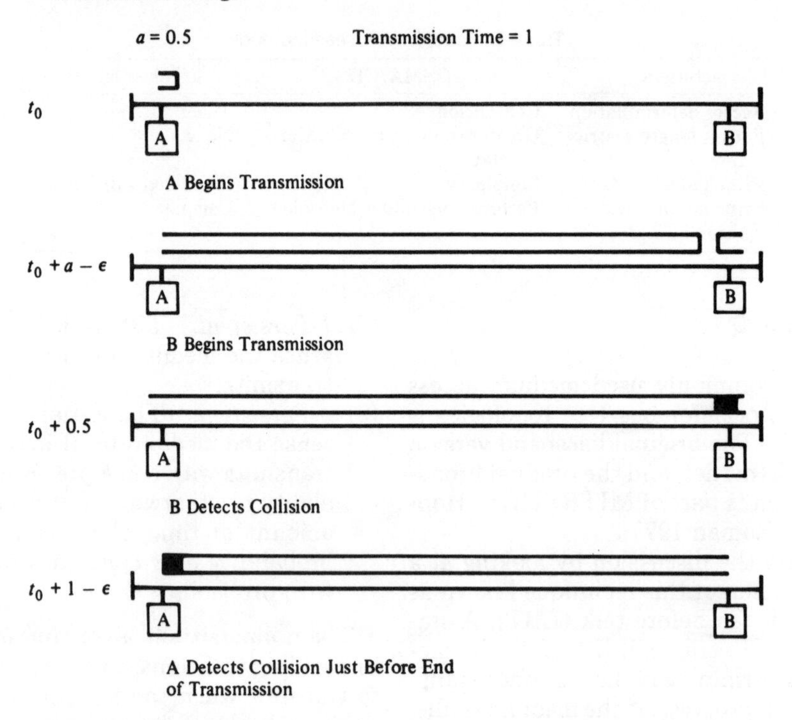

Figure 11. Baseband collision detection timing (transmission time is normalized to 1; a = propagation time). [From W. Stallings, *Local Networks: An Introduction*, Macmillan, New York, 1984. Copyright Macmillan 1984.]

(2) After transmitting the jamming signal, wait a random amount of time, then attempt to transmit again, using CSMA.

When these rules are followed, the amount of wasted bandwidth is reduced to the time that it takes to detect a collision. For proper operation of the algorithm, the minimum packet size should be sufficient to permit collision detection in the worst case. For a baseband system, with two stations that are as far apart as possible (worst case), the time that it takes to detect a collision is twice the propagation delay (Figure 11). For a broadband system, in which the worst case is two stations close together and as far as possible from the head end, the wait is four times the propagation delay from the station to the head end (Figure 12).

As with CSMA, CSMA/CD employs one of the three persistence algorithms. Unexpectedly, the most common choice is 1-persistent; it is used by both Ethernet and MITRENET, and used in the IEEE 802 standard. As was mentioned, the problem with the nonpersistent scheme is the wasted idle time. Although it is more efficient, p-persistent still may result in considerable waste. With the 1-persistent scheme, that waste is eliminated at the cost of wasted collision time.

What saves the day is that the time wasted due to collisions is mercifully short if the packets are long relative to propagation delay. With random back off, two stations involved in a collision are unlikely to collide on their next tries. To ensure stability of this back off, a technique known as binary exponential back off is used. A station attempts to transmit repeatedly in the face of repeated collisions, but the mean value of the random delay is doubled after each collision. After a number of unsuccessful attempts, the station gives up and reports an error.

Although the implementation of CSMA/CD is substantially the same for baseband and broadband, there are a few differences. One difference is the means for performing carrier sense. For baseband systems, the carrier sense operation consists of detecting

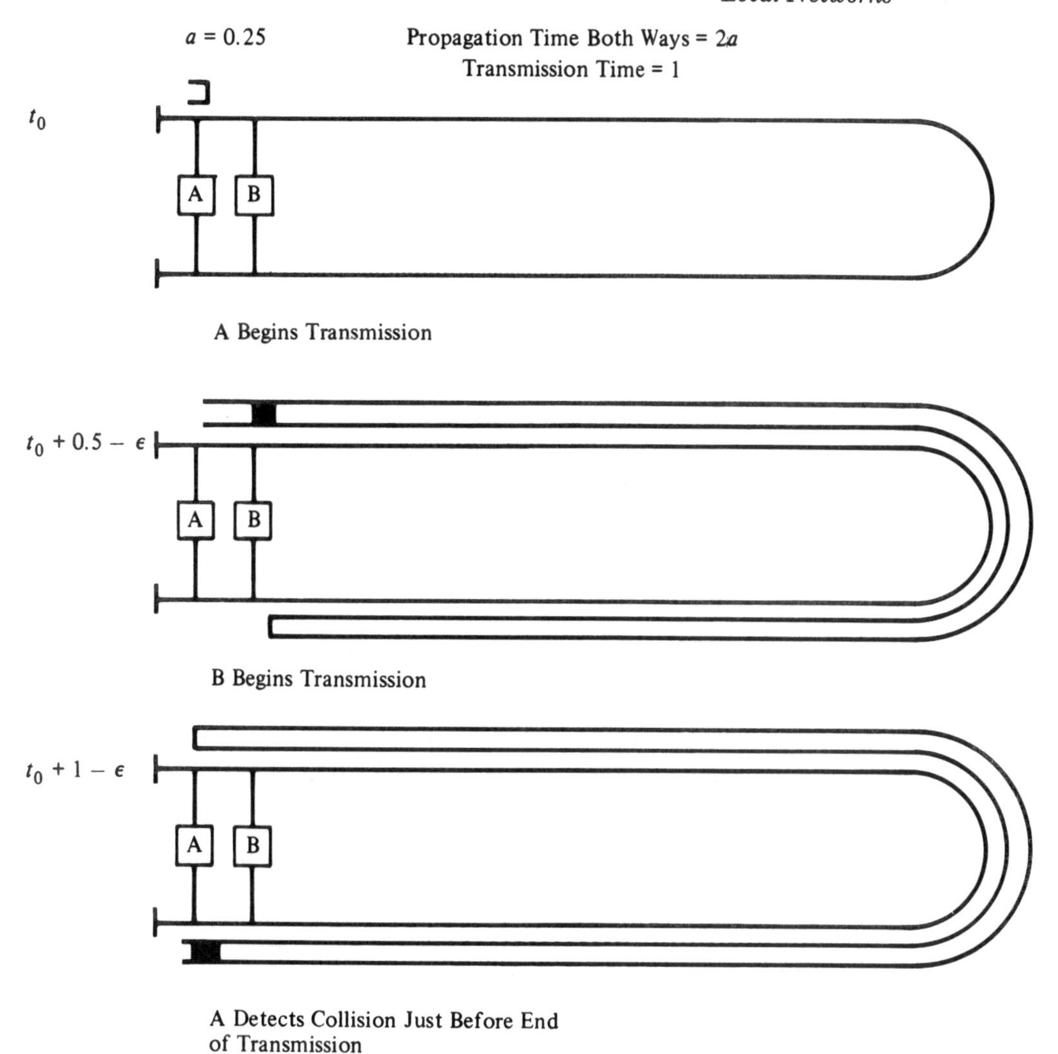

Figure 12. Broadband collision detection timing (transmission time is normalized to 1; a = propagation time one way). [From W. Stallings, *Local Networks: An Introduction*, Macmillan, New York, 1984. Copyright Macmillan 1984.]

a stream of voltage pulses; for broadband, the RF carrier is detected.

Another difference is in collision detection (CD). In a baseband system, a collision produces higher voltage swings than those produced by a single transmitter. A transmitting transceiver detects a collision if the signal on the cable exceeds the maximum that could be produced by the transceiver alone. Attenuation presents a potential problem: If two stations that are far apart are transmitting, each station will receive a greatly attenuated signal from the other. The signal strength could be so small that when added to the transmitted signal at the transceiver, the combined signal does not exceed the CD threshold. This is one reason that Ethernet retricts the maximum length of cable to 500 meters. Because frames may cross repeater boundaries, collisions must cross as well. Hence, if a repeater detects a collision on either cable, it must transmit a jamming signal on the other side.

There are several approaches to collision detection in broadband systems. The most common of these is to perform a bit-by-bit comparison between transmitted and received data. When a station transmits on

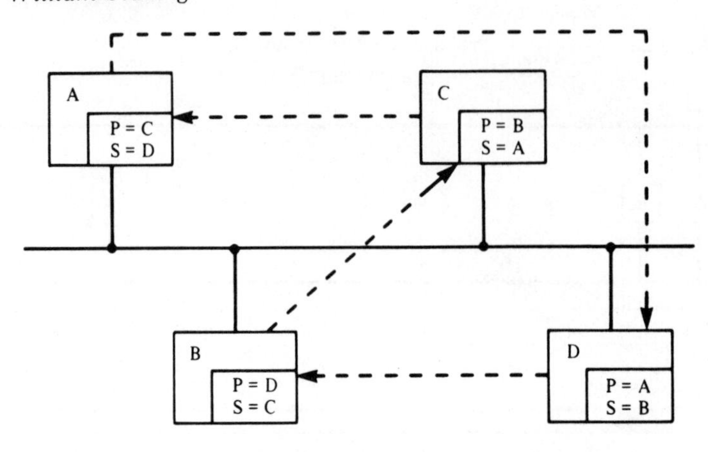

Figure 13. Token bus.

the inbound channel, it begins to hear its own transmission on the outbound channel after a propagation delay to the head end and back. In the MITRE system, the first 16 bits of the transmitted and received signals are compared and a collision is assumed if they differ. There are several problems with this approach. The most serious is the danger that differences in signal level between colliding signals will cause the receiver to treat the weaker signal as noise, and fail to detect the collision. The cable system, with its taps, splitters, and amplifiers, must be carefully tuned so that attenuation effects and differences in transmitter signal strength do not cause this problem. Another problem for dual cable systems is that a station must simultaneously transmit and receive on the same frequency. Its two RF modems must be carefully shielded to prevent cross talk.

An alternative approach for broadband is to perform the CD function at the head end. This is most appropriate for the midsplit system, which has an active component at the head end anyway. This reduces the problem of tuning, ensuring that all stations produce approximately the same signal level at the head end, which then can detect collisions by looking for garbled data or higher-than-expected signal strength.

4.1.2 Token Bus

Token bus is a technique in which the stations on the bus or tree form a logical ring; that is, the stations are assigned positions in an ordered sequence, with the last member of the sequence followed by the first. Each station knows the identity of the stations preceding and following it (Figure 13).

A control packet known as the token regulates the right of access: When a station receives the token, it is granted control of the medium for a specified time, during which it may transmit one or more packets and may poll stations and receive responses. When the station is done, or time has expired, it passes the token on to the next station in logical sequence. Hence steady-state operation consists of alternating data transfer and token transfer phases.

Non-token-using stations are allowed on the bus, but these stations can only respond to polls or requests for acknowledgment. It should also be pointed out that the physical ordering of the stations on the bus is irrelevant and independent of the logical ordering.

This scheme requires considerable maintenance. The following functions, at a minimum, must be performed by one or more stations on the bus:

Addition to Ring. Nonparticipating stations must periodically be granted the opportunity to insert themselves in the ring.

Deletion from Ring. A station can voluntarily remove itself from the ring by splicing together its predecessor and successor.

Fault Management. A number of errors can occur. These include duplicate address (two stations think that it is their turn) and broken ring (no station thinks that it is its turn).

Ring Initialization. When the network is started up, or after the logical ring has broken down, it must be reinitialized. Some cooperative, decentralized algorithm is needed to sort out who goes first, who goes second, etc.

In the remainder of this section we briefly describe the approach taken for these functions in the IEEE 802 standard.

To accomplish *addition to ring*, each node in the ring is responsible for periodically granting an opportunity for new nodes to enter the ring. While holding the token, the node issues a *solicit-successor* packet, inviting nodes with an address between itself and the next node in logical sequence to request entrance. The transmitting node then waits for a period of time equal to one response window or slot time (twice the end-to-end propagation delay of the medium). If there is no request, the node passes the token to its successor as usual. If there is one request, the token holder sets its successor node to be the requesting node and transmits the token to it; the requestor sets its linkages accordingly and proceeds. If more than one node requests to enter the ring, the token holder will detect a garbled transmission. The conflict is resolved by an address-based contention scheme: The token holder transmits a *resolve-contention* packet and waits four response windows. Each requestor can respond in one of these windows, based on the first two bits of its address. If a requestor hears anything before its window comes up, it refrains from requesting entrance. If the token holder receives a valid response, it is in business; otherwise it tries again, and only those nodes that requested the first time are allowed to request this time, based on the second pair of bits in their address. This process continues until a valid request is received, no request is received, or a maximum retry count is reached. In the latter two cases, the token holder gives up and passes the token to its logical successor in the ring.

Deletion from ring is much simpler. If a node wishes to drop out, it waits until it receives the token, then sends a *set-successor* packet to its predecessor, instructing it to splice to its successor.

Fault management by the token holder covers a number of contingencies. First, while holding the token, a node may hear a packet, indicating that another node has the token. In this case, it immediately drops the token by reverting to listener mode, and the number of token holders drops immediately to 1 or 0. Upon completion of its turn, the token holder will issue a token packet to its successor. The successor should immediately issue a data or token packet. Therefore, after sending a token, the token issuer will listen for one slot time to make sure that its successor is active. This precipitates a sequence of events:

(1) If the successor node is active, the token issuer will hear a valid packet and revert to listener mode.
(2) If the issuer does not hear a valid packet, it reissues the token to the same successor one more time.
(3) After two failures, the issuer assumes that its successor has failed and issues a *who-follows* packet, asking for the identity of the node that follows the failed node. The issuer should get back a set-successor packet from the second node down the line. If so, the issuer adjusts its linkage and issues a token (back to Step 1).
(4) If the issuing node gets no response to its who-follows packets, it tries again.
(5) If the who-follows tactic fails, the node issues a solicit-successor packet with the full address range (i.e., every node is invited to respond). If this process works, a two-node ring is established and the procedure continues.
(6) If two attempts of Step 5 fail, the node assumes that a catastrophe has occurred; perhaps the node's receiver has failed. In any case, the node ceases activity and listens to the bus.

Logical *ring initialization* occurs when one or more stations detect a lack of bus activity lasting longer than a time-out value: The token has been lost. This can

Table 6. Ring Access Methods

Characteristic	Register insertion	Slotted ring	Token ring
Transmit opportunity	Idle state plus empty buffer	Empty slot	Delimiter with free indicator
Frame purge responsibility	Receiver or transmitter	Transmitter node	Transmitter node
Principal advantage	Maximum ring utilization	Simplicity	Regulated but fair access
Principal disadvantage	Purge mechanism	Bandwidth waste	Token monitor required

result from a number of causes, for example, the network has just been powered up, or a token-holding station fails. Once its time-out expires, a node will issue a *claim-token* packet. Contending claimants are resolved in a manner similar to the response-window process.

4.1.3 CSMA/CD versus Token Bus

At present, CSMA/CD and token bus are the two principal contenders for medium access control technique on bus/tree topologies. In this section we examine their comparative disadvantages and advantages.

It should be obvious that the principal disadvantage of token bus is its complexity; the logic at each station far exceeds that required for CSMA/CD. A second disadvantage is the overhead involved; under lightly loaded conditions, a station may have to wait through many fruitless token passes for a turn.

Indeed, in considering these disadvantages, it would seem difficult to make a case for token bus. Such a case can be made, however [Miller and Thompson 1982; Stieglitz 1981], and includes the following elements. First, it is easy to regulate the traffic in a token bus system; different stations can be allowed to hold the token for differing amounts of time. Second, unlike CSMA/CD, there is no minimum packet length requirement with token bus. Third, the requirement for listening while talking imposes physical and electrical constraints on the CSMA/CD system that do not apply to token systems. Finally, token bus is significantly superior to CSMA/CD under heavy loads, as discussed below.

Another advertised advantage of token bus is that it is "deterministic"; that is, there is a known upper bound to the amount of time that any station must wait before transmitting. This upper bound is known because each station in the logical ring only can hold the token for a specified time. In contrast, the delay time with CSMA/CD can only be expressed statistically, and since every attempt to transmit under CSMA/CD can, in principle, produce a collision, there is a possibility that a station could be shut out indefinitely. For process control and other real-time applications, this "nondeterministic" behavior is undesirable. Unfortunately, in actual application there is always a finite possibility of transmission error, which can cause a lost token. This adds a statistical component to the behavior of a token bus system.

4.2 Ring LANs

Over the years, a number of different algorithms have been proposed for controlling access to the ring (surveys are presented by Penny and Baghdadi [1979] and Liu [1978]). The three most common ring access techniques are discussed in this section: token ring, register insertion, and slotted ring. In Table 6 these three methods are compared on a number of characteristics:

Transmit Opportunity. When may a repeater insert a packet onto the ring?

Packet Purge Responsibility. Who removes a packet from a ring to avoid its circulating indefinitely?

Number of Packets on Ring. This depends not only on the "bit length" of the ring relative to the packet length, but on the access method.

Principal Advantage.

Principal Disadvantage.

The significance of the table entries will become clear as the discussion proceeds.

4.2.1 Token Ring

The token ring is probably the oldest ring control technique, originally proposed in 1969 [Farmer and Newhall 1969] and referred to as the Newhall ring. This has become the most popular ring access technique in the United States. Prime Computer [Gordon et al. 1980] and Apollo both market token ring products, and IBM seems committed to such a product [Rauch-Hinden 1982]. This technique is the ring access method selected for standardization by the IEEE 802 Local Network Standards Committee [Andrews and Shultz 1982; Dixon 1982; Markov and Strole 1982].

The token ring technique is based on the use of a small token packet that circulates around the ring: When all stations are idle, the token packet is labeled as a "free" token. A station wishing to transmit waits until it detects the token passing by, alters the bit pattern of the token from "free token" to "busy token," and transmits a packet immediately following the busy token (Figure 14).

There is now no free token on the ring, and so other stations wishing to transmit must wait. The packet on the ring will make a round trip and be purged by the transmitting station. The transmitting station will insert a new free token on the ring when both of the following conditions have been met:

- the station has completed transmission of its packet, and
- the busy token has returned to the station.

If the bit length of the ring is less than the packet length, then the first condition implies the second. If not, then a station could release a free token after it has finished transmitting but before it receives its own busy token. However, this might complicate error recovery, since several packets will be on the ring at the same time. In any case, the use of a token guarantees that only one station at a time may transmit.

When a transmitting station releases a new free token, the next station downstream with data to send will be able to seize the token and transmit.

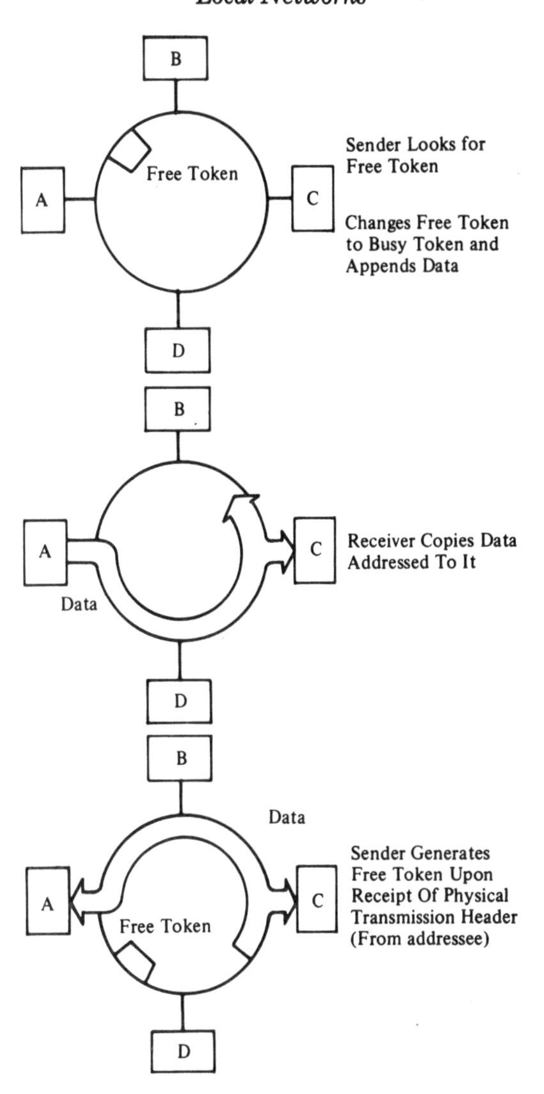

Figure 14. Token ring.

One nice feature of token ring, and all ring protocols, is this: If the source station has responsibility for removing the circulating packet, then the destination station can set bits in the packet as it goes by to inform the sender of the result of the transmission. For example, the IEEE 802 standard includes three such control bits in the packet format: address recognized (A), packet copied (C), and error (E). The A and C bits allow the source station to differentiate three conditions:

- station nonexistent/nonactive,
- station exists but packet not copied,
- packet received.

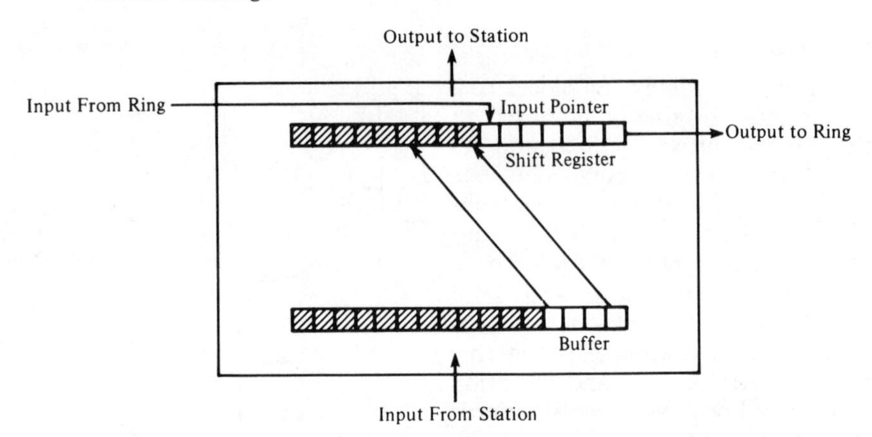

Figure 15. Register insertion technique.

The E bit can be set by any station if an error is detected.

There are two error conditions that could cause the token ring system to break down. One is the loss of the token so that no token is circulating; the other is a persistent busy token that circulates endlessly. To overcome these problems the IEEE 802 standard specifies that one station be designated as "active monitor." The monitor detects the lost token condition using a time-out, and recovers by issuing a new free token. To detect a circulating busy token, the monitor sets a "monitor bit" to one on any passing busy token. If it sees a busy token with the bit already set, it knows that the transmitting station has failed to absorb its packet and recovers by changing the busy token to a free token.

Other stations on the ring have the role of passive monitor. Their primary job is to detect failure of the active monitor and assume that role. A contention-resolution algorithm is used to determine which station takes over.

The token ring technique shares many of the advantages of token bus. Perhaps its principal advantage is that traffic can be regulated, either by allowing stations to transmit differing numbers of data when they receive the token, or by setting priorities so that higher priority stations have first claim on a circulating token.

The principal disadvantage of token ring is the requirement for token maintenance. The active/passive monitor system described above must be employed for error recovery.

4.2.2 Register Insertion

The register insertion strategy was originally developed by researchers at Ohio State University [Hafner et al. 1974], and is the technique used in the IBM Series 1 product [IBM 1982] and a Swiss product called SILK [Huber et al. 1983]. It derives its name from the shift register associated with each station on the ring, which is equal in size to the maximum packet length, and used for temporarily holding packets that circulate past the station. In addition, the station has a buffer for storing locally produced packets.

The register insertion ring can be explained with reference to Figure 15, which shows the shift register and buffer at one station. First, consider the case in which the station has no data to send, but is merely handling packets of data that circulate by its position. When the ring is idle, the input pointer points to the rightmost position of the shift register, indicating that it is empty. When a packet arrives along the ring, it is inserted bit by bit in the shift register, with the input pointer shifting left for each bit. The packet begins with an address field. As soon as the entire address field is in the buffer, the station can determine if it is the addressee. If not, then the packet is forwarded by shifting one bit out on the right as each new bit arrives from the left, with the input pointer stationary. After the last bit of the packet has arrived, the station continues to shift bits out to the right until the packet is gone. If no additional packets arrive during this time, the input pointer will return to its initial position. Otherwise, a second packet will begin to accumulate in the register as the first is shifted out.

If the arriving packet is addressed to the node in question, it can either erase the address bits from the shift register and divert the remainder of the packet to itself, thus purging the packet from the ring, or retransmit the data as before, while copying it to the local station.

Now consider the case in which the station has data to transmit. A packet to be transmitted is placed in the output buffer. If the line is idle and the shift register is empty, the packet can be transferred immediately to the shift register. If the packet consists of some length n bits, less than the maximum frame size, and if at least n bits are empty in the shift register, the n bits are parallel transferred to the empty portion of the shift register immediately adjacent to the full portion; the input pointer is adjusted accordingly.

The principal advantage of the register insertion technique is that it achieves the maximum ring utilization of any of the methods. A station may transmit whenever the ring is idle at its location, and multiple packets may be on the ring at any one time.

The principal disadvantage is the purge mechanism. Allowing multiple packets on the ring requires the recognition of an address prior to removal of a packet. If a packet's address field is damaged, it could circulate indefinitely. One possible solution is the use of an error-detecting code on the address field.

4.2.3 Slotted Ring

The slotted ring technique was first developed by Pierce [1972], and is sometimes referred to as the Pierce loop. Most of the development work on this technique was done at the University of Cambridge in England [Hopper 1977; Wilkes and Wheeler 1979], and a number of British firms market commercial versions of the Cambridge ring [Heywood 1981].

In the slotted ring, a number of fixed-length slots circulate continuously on the ring. Each slot contains a leading bit to designate the slot as empty or full. All slots are initially marked empty. A station wishing to transmit waits until an empty slot arrives, marks the slot full, and inserts a packet of data as the slot goes by. The station cannot transmit another packet until this slot returns. The slot may also contain response bits, which can be set on the fly by the addressed station to indicate accepted, busy, or rejected. The full slot makes a complete round trip, to be marked empty again by the source. Each station knows the total number of slots on the ring and can thus clear the full/empty bit that it had set as it goes by. Once the now empty slot goes by, the station is free to transmit again.

In the Cambridge ring, each slot contains room for one source and one destination address byte, two data bytes, and five control bits for a total length of 37 bits.

The Cambridge ring contains several interesting features. A station may decide that it wishes to receive data only from one other station. To accomplish this each station includes a source select register. When this register contains all ones, the station will receive a packet addressed to it from any source; when it contains all zeros, the station will not accept packets from any source. Otherwise the station is open to receive packets only from the source whose address is specified by the register.

In addition, the Cambridge ring specifies two response bits in each packet to differentiate four conditions:

- destination nonexistent/nonactive,
- packet accepted,
- destination exists but packet not accepted,
- destination busy.

Finally, the Cambridge ring includes a monitor, whose task it is to empty a slot that is persistently full.

The principal disadvantage of the slotted ring is that it is wasteful of bandwidth.

First, a slot typically contains more overhead bits than data bits. Second, a station may send only one packet per round-trip ring time. If only one or a few stations have packets to transmit, many of the slots will circulate empty.

The principal advantage of the slotted ring appears to be its simplicity. The interaction with the ring at each node is minimized, improving reliability.

4.3 HSLNs

In this section, we review the only technique that thus far has gained favor for HSLNs, known as prioritized CSMA. It is also referred to as CSMA with collision avoidance. The technique will be described in terms of the ANSI draft standard [Burr 1983]; the algorithm for HYPERchannel is very similar.

The protocol is based on CSMA; that is, a station wishing to transmit listens to the medium and defers if a transmission is in progress. In addition, an algorithm is used that specifically seeks to avoid collisions when the medium is found idle by multiple stations.

For this scheme, the stations or ports form an ordered logical sequence (PORT(1), PORT(2), ..., PORT(N)), which need not correspond to physical position of the bus.

The scheme is initialized after each transmission by any port. Following initialization, each station, in turn, may transmit if none of the stations in sequence before it have done so. So PORT($I + 1$) waits until after PORT(I) has had a chance to transmit. The waiting time consists of

(1) the earliest time at which PORT(I) could begin transmitting (which depends on the transmission opportunity for PORT($I - 1$)), plus
(2) a port delay time during which PORT(I) has the opportunity to transmit, plus
(3) the propagation delay between the two ports.

As we shall see, this rather simple concept becomes more complex as we consider its refinements.

The basic rule can be described as follows. After any transmission, PORT(1) has the right to transmit. If it fails to do so in a reasonable time, then PORT(2) has the chance, and so on. If any port transmits, the system reinitializes.

The first refinement is to permit multiframe dialogues. To accommodate this, an additional rule is added: After any transmission, the port receiving that transmission has the first right to transmit. If that port fails to transmit, then it is the turn of PORT(1), and so on. This will permit two ports to seize the medium, with one port sending data frames and the other sending acknowledgment frames.

The second refinement is to accommodate the case in which nobody has a frame to transmit. HYPERchannel solves this by entering a free-for-all period, in which collisions are allowed. ANSI has a more elegant solution: If none of the stations transmit when they have an opportunity, then the highest priority station times out and transmits a dummy frame. This serves to reinitialize the network and start over.

With these two refinements, we can depict the MAC protocol as a simple sequence of events:

1. Medium is active
2. Medium Goes Idle
   If Receiver Transmits,
   Then Go To 1
   Else Go To 3
3. If PORT(1) Transmits,
   Then Go To 1
   Else Go To 4

⋮

$N + 3$. If No Port Transmits, Then Go To 1.

The third refinement has to do with balancing this scheme, which at this point is biased to the lower number ports [PORT(1) *always* gets a shot, for example]. To make the scheme fair, a port that has just transmitted should not try again until everyone else has had a chance.

To concisely describe the algorithm with these three refinements, we need to define some quantities:

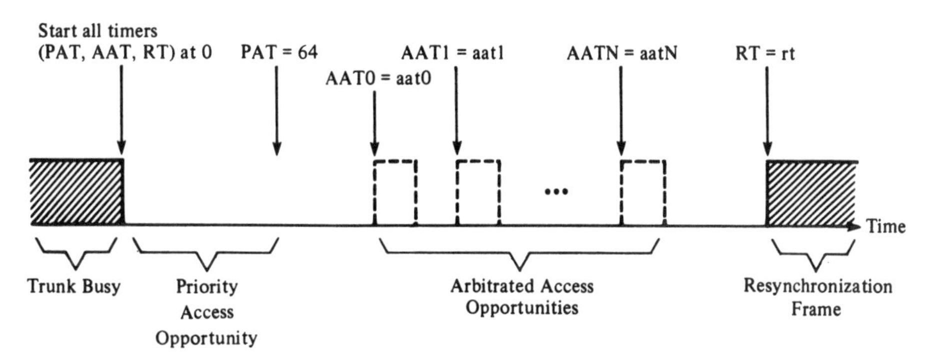

Figure 16. Operation of the ANSI medium access control protocol.

Priority Access Opportunity. A period of time granted to a port after it receives a frame. May be used to acknowledge frame and/or continue a multiframe dialogue.

Priority Access Timer (PAT). Used to time priority access opportunities: 64-bit times.

Arbitrated Access Opportunity. A period of time granted to each port in sequence, during which it may initate a transmission: 16-bit times. Assigned to individual ports to avoid collisions.

Arbitrated Access Timer (AAT). Used to provide each port with a unique, nonoverlapping, arbitrated access opportunity.

Resynchronization Timer (RT). Time by which the latest possible arbitrated transmission should have been received. Used to reset all timers.

Arbiter Wait Flag (WF). Used to enforce fairness. When a port transmits, its WF is set so that it will not attempt another arbitrated transmission until all other ports have an opportunity.

Figure 16 depicts the process of this refined algorithm. For the timers listed, we use the convention that uppercase letters refer to the variable name and lowercase letters to a specific value. A timer that reaches a specified maximum value is said to have expired.

This technique seems well suited to HSLN requirements. The provision for multiframe dialogue permits rapid transfer of large files. A typical HSLN consists of only a small number of stations; under these circumstances, the round-robin access technique will not result in undue delays.

5. COMPARATIVE PERFORMANCE OF LAN PROTOCOLS

Although there have been a number of performance studies focusing on a single protocol, there have been few systematic attempts to analyze the relative performance of the various local network protocols. In what follows, we look at the results of several carefully done studies that have produced comparative results. A lengthy survey of performance studies is found in Tropper [1981].

5.1 CSMA/CD, Token Bus, and Token Ring

One important study was done by a group at Bell Laboratories, under the sponsorship of the IEEE 802 Local Network Standards Committee [Arthurs and Stuck 1981; Stuck 1983a, 1983b]. Naturally enough, the study analyzed the three protocols being standardized by IEEE 802: CSMA/CD, token bus, and token ring. Two cases of message arrival statistics are employed. In the first case, only one out of one hundred stations has data to transmit, and is always ready to transmit. In such a case, one would hope that the network would not be the bottleneck, but could easily keep up with one station. In the second case, all one hundred stations always have data to transmit. This represents an extreme of congestion, and one would expect that the network may be a bottleneck. In both cases, the one station or one hundred stations provide enough

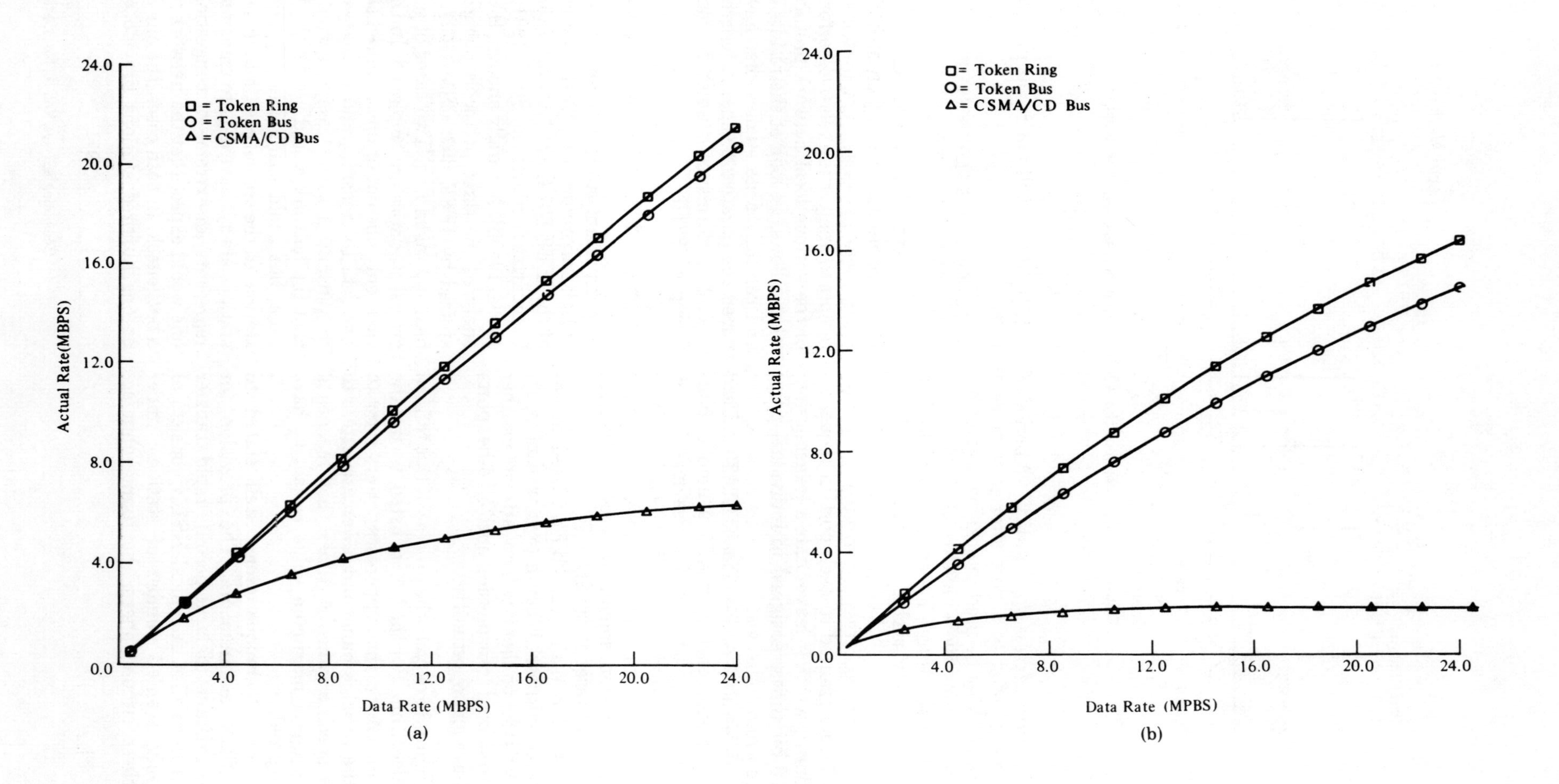
□ = Token Ring
○ = Token Bus
Δ = CSMA/CD Bus
Actual Rate(MBPS)
24.0
20.0
16.0
12.0
8.0
4.0
0.0
4.0
8.0
12.0
16.0
20.0
24.0
Data Rate (MBPS)
(a)
□= Token Ring
○= Token Bus
Δ = CSMA/CD Bus
Actual Rate (MBPS)
24.0
20.0
16.0
12.0
8.0
4.0
0.0
4.0
8.0
12.0
16.0
20.0
24.0
Data Rate (MPBS)
(b)

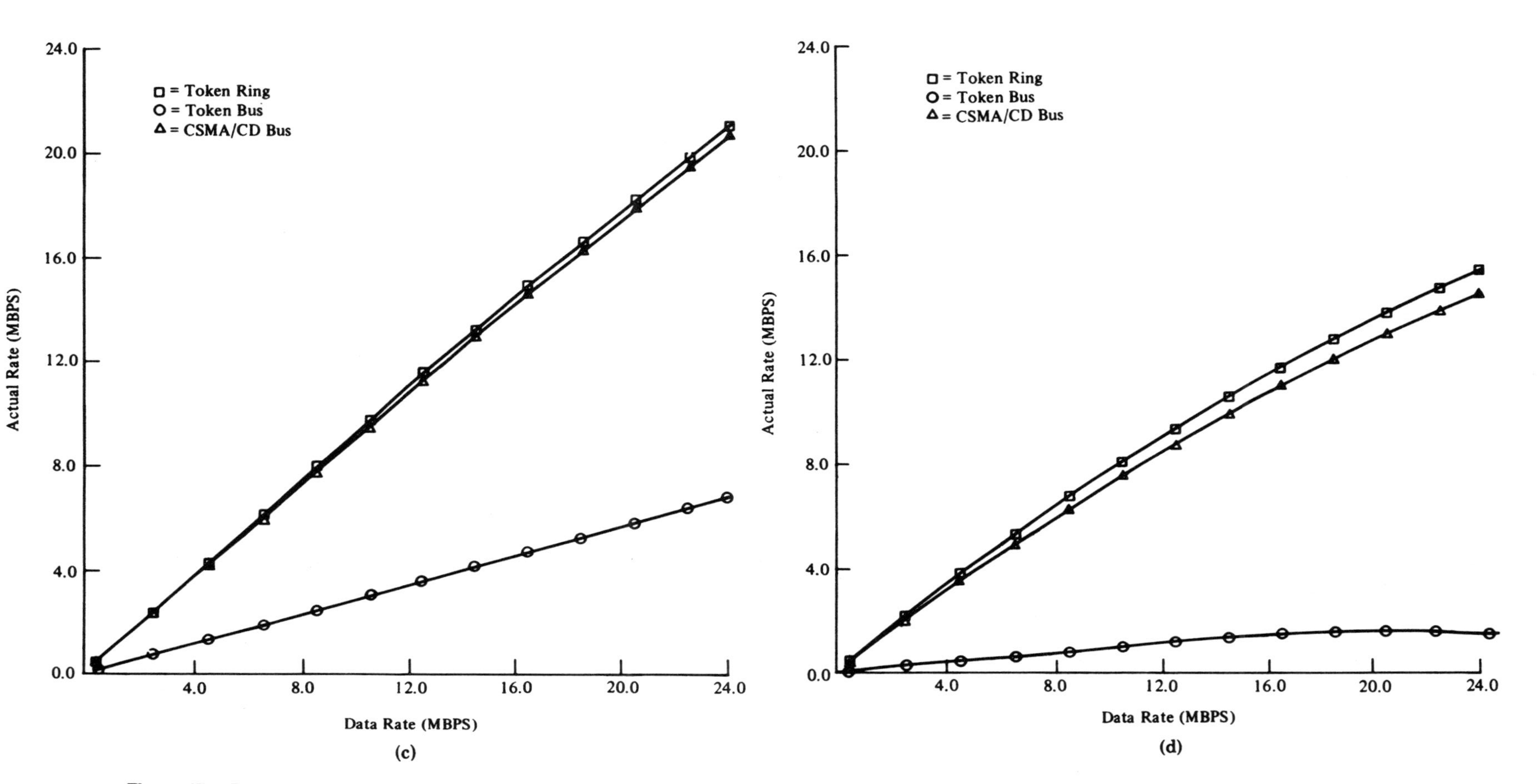

Figure 17. Potential throughput of IEEE 802 protocols: (a) 2000 bits per packet, 100 stations active out of 100 stations total; (b) 500 bits per packet, 100 stations active out of 100 stations total; (c) 2000 bits per packet, 1 station active out of 100 stations total; (d) 500 bits per packet, 1 station active out of 100 stations total.

input to fully utilize the network. Hence the results are a measure of maximum potential utilization. In addition, results were obtained by using two different packet sizes to determine the relative effect of this parameter on the three protocols. Thus a total of four different cases was analyzed.

The results are given in Figure 17, which shows the actual data transmission rate versus the transmission speed of the medium for the four cases. The length of the medium (bus or ring) is assumed to be 2 kilometers. Note that the abscissa in the plots is not offered load but the actual capacity of the medium. Three systems are examined: token ring with a 1-bit latency per station, token bus, and CSMA/CD. The analysis yields the following conclusions:

(1) For the given parameters, the smaller the mean packet length, the greater is the difference in maximum mean throughput rate between token passing and CSMA/CD. This reflects the fact that, for a given amount of data, smaller packets mean more packets and hence more collisions under CSMA/CD.
(2) Token ring is the least sensitive to workload.
(3) CSMA/CD offers the shortest delay under light load, whereas it is most sensitive under heavy load to the workload.

Note also that in the case of a single station transmitting, token bus is significantly less efficient than the other two protocols. This is so because the assumption is made that the delay in token processing is greater for token bus than that for token ring.

Another interesting phenomenon is seen most clearly in Figure 17b. For a CSMA/CD system under these conditions, the maximum effective throughput at 5 Mbps is only about 1.25 Mbps. If expected load is, say, 0.75 Mbps, this configuration may be perfectly adequate. If however, the load is expected to grow to 2 Mbps, raising the network data rate to 10 Mbps or even 20 Mbps will not accommodate the increase!

The reason for this disparity between CSMA/CD and token passing (bus or ring) under heavy load has to do with the instability of CSMA/CD. As offered load increases, so does throughput, until, beyond some maximum value, throughput actually declines as offered load increases. This results from the fact that there is an increased frequency of collisions: More packets are offered, but fewer successfully escape collision. Worse, those packets that do collide must be retransmitted, further increasing the load.

5.2 CSMA/CD and Ring Protocols

It is far more difficult to do a comparative performance of the three major ring protocols than to do a comparison of bus and token ring protocols, as the results depend on a number of parameters unique to each protocol, for example,

- *Token Ring.* Size of token, token processing time.
- *Slotted Ring.* Slot size, overhead bits per slot.
- *Register Insertion.* Register size.

Although there have been a number of studies on each one of the techniques, few have attempted pairwise comparisons, much less a three-way analysis. The most systematic work in this area has been done by Liu and his associates [Liu et al. 1982]. Liu made comparisons based on analytic models developed by others for token ring, slotted ring, and CSMA/CD, plus his own formulations for register insertion. He then obtained very good corroboration from simulation studies.

Figure 18 is a summary of the results, on the basis of the assumption that relatively large packets are used and that register insertion ring packets are removed by the destination station, whereas slotted ring and token ring packets are removed by the source station. This is clearly an unfair comparison since register insertion under this scheme does not include acknowledgments, whereas token ring and slotted ring do. The figure does show that slotted ring is the poorest performer, and that register insertion can carry a load greater than 1.0, since the protocol permits multiple packets to circulate.

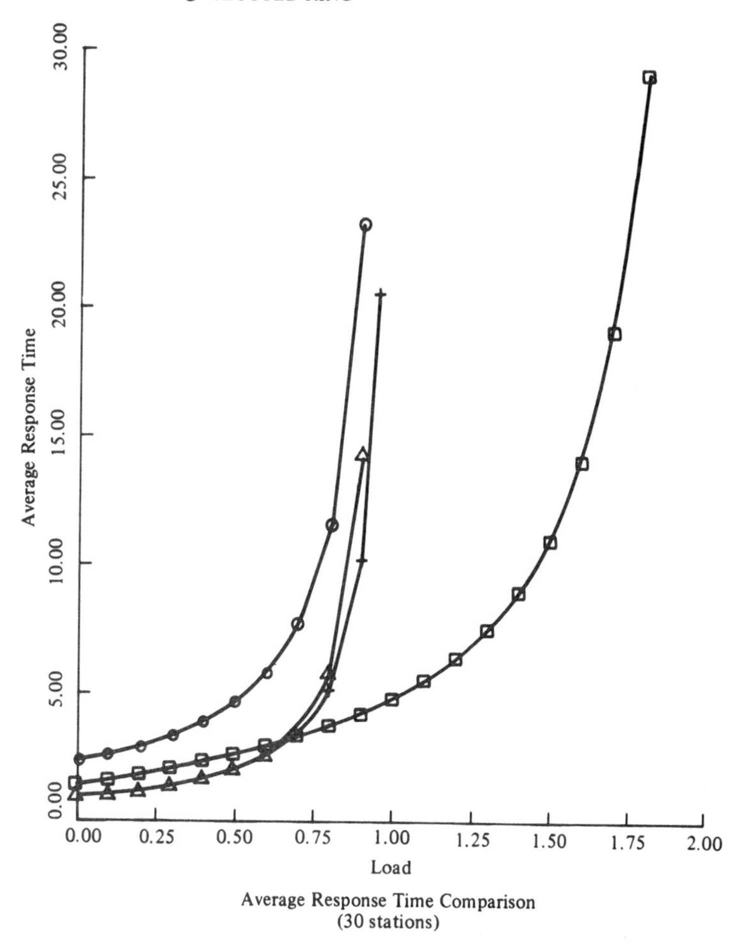

Figure 18. Delay for various protocols.

Bux performed an analysis comparing token ring, slotted ring, and CSMA/CD, yielding results similar to those of Liu [Bux 1981]. He confirmed several important conclusions: that token ring suffers greater delay than CSMA/CD at light load but less delay and more stable throughput at heavy loads, and further, that token ring has superior delay characteristics to slotted ring.

It is difficult to draw conclusions from the efforts made thus far. The slotted ring seems to be the least desirable over a broad range of parameter values, owing to the considerable overhead associated with each small packet. As between token ring and register insertion, the evidence suggests that at least for some sets of parameter values, register insertion gives superior throughput and delay performance.

6. STANDARDS

6.1 Local Area Networks

The key to the development of the LAN market is the availability of a low-cost interface; the cost to connect equipment to a LAN must be much less than the cost of the actual equipment. This requirement, as

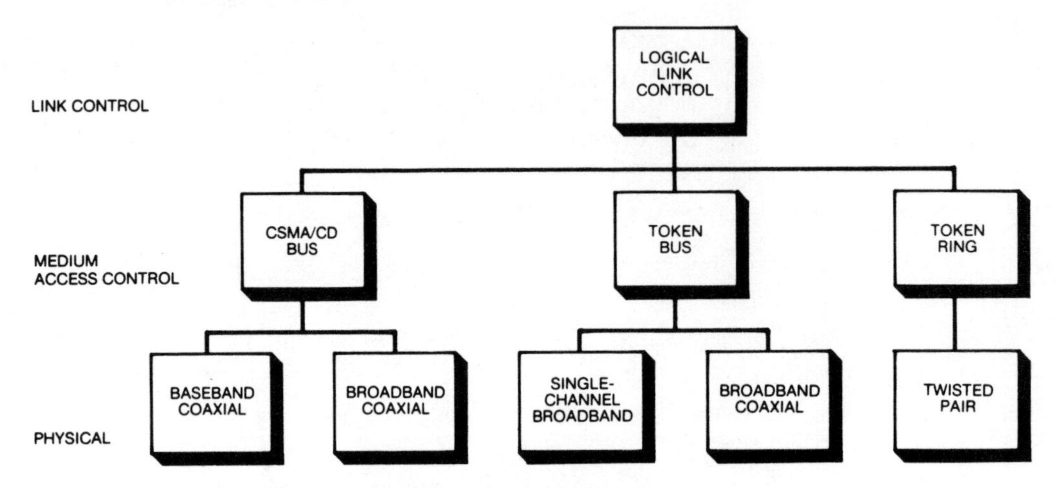

Figure 19. The IEEE 802 standard.

well as the complexity of the LAN protocols, dictates a very large scale integration (VLSI) solution. However, chip manufacturers are reluctant to commit the necessary resources unless there is a high-volume market. A LAN standard would ensure that volume and also enable equipment of a variety of manufacturers to intercommunicate.

This is the rationale of the IEEE 802 committee [Clancy et al. 1982], which has developed a set of standards for LANs [IEEE 1983]. The standards are in the form of a three-layer communications architecture with a treelike expansion of options from top to bottom (Figure 19). The three layers, known as logical link control, medium access control, and physical, encompass the functionality of the lowest two layers (data link and physical) of the International Organization for Standardization (ISO) reference model.

The logical link control (LLC) layer provides for the exchange of data between service access points (SAPs), which are multiplexed over a single physical connection to the LAN. The LLC provides for both a connectionless, datagramlike service, and a connection-oriented, virtual-circuit-like service. Both the protocol and the frame format resemble HDLC.

At the medium access control layer, there are three standards: CSMA/CD has converged with the Ethernet specification, which is well suited to typical office applications, and two forms of token access have been standardized, for time-critical applications, such as process control, as well as for office applications.

For CSMA/CD, a 10-Mbps baseband physical layer has been approved. Several broadband options are still under consideration, ranging in data rate per channel from 1 to 5 Mbps.

For token bus, three physical layers are provided as options. The simplest and least expensive is a single-channel broadband system using frequency shift keying (FSK) at 1 Mbps. A more expensive version of this system runs at 5 or 10 Mbps and is intended to be easily upgradable to the final option, which is multichannel broadband. The latter provides data rates of 1, 5, or 10 Mbps.

For token ring, twisted pair has been defined, which will provide data rates of 1 and 4 Mbps.

The range of options offered may be disheartening to the reader. However, the IEEE 802 Committee has at least narrowed the alternatives, and it is to be expected that the bulk of future LAN development work will be within the scope laid down by IEEE 802.

More detailed discussions of the standard may be found in Nelson [1983], Graube [1982], Allan [1982], and Myers [1982].

6.2 High-Speed Local Networks

For HSLNs, the necessity for standards seems less compelling. Because of the high data rate requirement, the HSLN vendor must provide a high-throughput interface to the attached device. Such an interface has a cost in the tens of thousands of dollars range, and a VLSI protocol implementation will not significantly affect the price.

The X.3T9.5 Committee sponsored by ANSI has prepared a draft HSLN standard [ANSI 1982; Burr 1983; Parker 1983] using a two-layer model, corresponding to the data link and physical layers of the ISO model. The data link layer specifies a simple connectionless service. The physical layer specification includes the collision-avoidance protocol discussed earlier, and it specifies a data rate of 50 Mbps.

7. SUMMARY

Local networks can be characterized, in large measure, by the transmission medium and topology employed. Common combinations are

Twisted Pair Bus or Ring. An inexpensive, easily installed network for a small number of low-cost, low-throughput devices.

Baseband Coaxial Cable Bus or Ring. A general-purpose network; supports moderate numbers of devices over moderate distances; suitable for many office applications.

High-Speed Baseband Coaxial Cable Bus. Supports a small number of high-throughput devices; suitable for computer-room requirements.

Broadband Coaxial Cable Bus. The most flexible and general-purpose network; supports a large number of devices over a wide area, and can handle a variety of traffic requirements using FDM.

Twisted Pair Star. The architecture of the CBX. Suitable for supporting at moderate cost a large number of limited throughput devices.

For descriptive clarity, and to reflect differences in standards and technology, three categories of local networks can be defined. The category local area network (LAN) covers a variety of local networks using a bus, tree, or ring topology and that support a variety of applications and loads. The high-speed local network (HSLN) is specifically designed to support high-speed data transfer among a limited number of devices. The third category, the computerized branch exchange (CBX), is a digital private branch exchange designed to handle both voice and data connections.

An important design issue for LANs and HSLNs is the choice of medium access control protocol. The most important ones for the bus/tree topology are CSMA/CD, token bus, and collision avoidance, and, for the ring topology, token ring, register insertion, and slotted ring.

The literature on local networks is growing as rapidly as the field itself. Annotated bibliographies may be found in Shoch [1980] and Stallings [1983]. Stallings [1984] is a textbook on the subject.

REFERENCES

ALLAN, R. 1982. Local-area networks spur moves to standardize data communications among computers and peripherals. *Electron. Des.* Dec. 23, 107–112.

ALLAN, R. 1983. Local networks: Fiber optics gains momentum. *Electron. Des.* June 23.

ANDREWS, D. W., AND SCHULTZ, G. D. 1982. A token-ring architecture for local area networks: An update. In *Proceedings of COMPCON Fall 82* (Washington, D.C., Sept. 20–23). IEEE Computer Society, Los Angeles, pp. 615–624.

ANSI 1982. *Draft Proposed American National Standard Local Distributed Data Interface.* American National Standards Institute, New York.

ARTHURS, E., AND STUCK, B. W. 1981. A theoretical performance analysis of polling and carrier sense collision detection communication systems. In *Proceedings of the 7th Symposium on Data Communications* (Mexico City, Oct. 27–29). *Comput. Commun. Rev. 11,* 4, 156–163.

BOSEN, R. 1981. A low-speed local net for under $100 per station. *Data Commun. 10,* 2 (Dec.), 81–83.

BURR, W. 1983. An overview of the proposed american national standard for local distributed data interfaces. *Commun. ACM, 26,* 10 (Oct.), 554–561.

BUX, W. 1981. Local-area subnetworks: A performance comparison. *IEEE Trans. Commun. COM-29,* 10 (Oct.).

BUX, W., CLOSS, F., JANSON, P. A., KUMMERLE, K., MILLER, H. R., AND ROTHAUSER, H. 1982. A local-area communication network based on a reliable token ring system. In *Proceedings of the International Symposium on Local Computer Networks.*

CHRISTENSEN, G. S. 1979. Links between computer-room networks. *Telecommunications 13*, 2 (Feb.), 47–50.

CLANCY, G. J., et al. 1982. The IEEE 802 Committee states its case concerning its local network standards efforts. *Data Commun. 11*, 4 (Apr.), 13, 238.

COOPER, E. 1982. 13 often-asked questions about broadband. *Data Commun. 11*, 4 (Apr.), 137–142.

COOPER, E. 1983. Broadband network design: Issues and answers. *Comput. Des. 22*, 3 (Mar.), 209–216.

COOPER, E., AND EDHOLM, P. 1983. Design issues in broadband local networks. *Data Commun. 12*, 2 (Feb.), 109–122.

DEC 1980. *The Ethernet: A Local Area Network Data Link Layer and Physical Layer Specifications*, Sept. 30. Digital Equipment Corp., Intil Corp., and Xerox Corp., Digital Equipment Corp., Maynard, Mass.

DERFLER, F., AND STALLINGS, W. 1983. *A Manager's Guide to Local Networks.* Prentice-Hall, New York.

DINESON, M. A., AND PICAZO, J. J. 1980. Broadband technology magnifies local network capability. *Data Commun. 9*, 2 (Feb.), 61–79.

DIXON, R. C. 1982. Ring network topology for local data communications. In *Proceedings of COMPCON, Fall 82* (Washington, D.C., Sept. 20–23). IEEE Computer Society, Los Angeles, pp. 591–605.

FARMER, W. D., AND NEWHALL, E. E. 1969. An experimental distributed switching system to handle bursty computer traffic. In *Proceedings of the ACM Symposium on Problems in the Optimization of Data Communications.* ACM, New York.

FORBES, J. 1981. RF prescribed for many local links. *Data Commun. 10*, 9 (Sept.).

FRANTA, W. R., AND CHLAMTEC, I. 1981. *Local Networks.* Lexington Books, Lexington, Mass.

FREEDMAN, D. 1983. Fiber optics shine in local area networks. *Mini-Micro Syst. 16*, 10 (Sept.), 225–230.

GORDON, R. L., FARR, W. W., AND LEVINE, P. 1980. Ringnet: A packet switched local network with decentralized control. *Comput. Networks 3*, 373–379.

GRAUBE, M. 1982. Local area nets: A pair of standards. *IEEE Spectrum* (June), 60–64.

HAFNER, E. R., NENADAL, Z., AND TSCHANZ, M. 1974. A digital loop communications system. *IEEE Trans. Commun. COM-22*, 6 (June), 877–881.

HAHN, M., AND BELANGER, P. 1981. Network minimizes overhead of small computers. *Electronics*, Aug. 25.

HEYWOOD, P. 1981. The Cambridge ring is still making the rounds. *Data Commun. 10*, 7 (July), 32–36.

HOHN, W. C. 1980. The Control Data loosely coupled network lower level protocols. In *Proceedings of the National Computer Conference* (Anaheim, Calif., May 19–22), vol. 49. AFIPS Press, Reston, Va., 129–134.

HOPKINS, G. T. 1979. Multimode communications on the MITRENET. *Proceedings of the Local Area Communications Network Symposium* (Boston, May). Mitre Corp., McLean, Va., pp. 169–178.

HOPKINS, G. T., AND MEISNER, N. B. 1982. Choosing between broadband and baseband local networks. *Mini-Micro Syst. 16*, 7 (June).

HOPPER, A. 1977. Data ring at Computer Laboratory, University of Cambridge. In *Local Area Networking.* NBS Publ. National Bureau of Standards, Washington, D.C., pp. 500–531, 11–16.

HUBER, D., STEINLIN, W., AND WILD, P. 1983. SILK: An implementation of a buffer insertion ring. *IEEE J. Selected Areas Commun. SAC-1*, 5 (Nov.), 766–774.

IBM CORP. 1982. *IBM Series/1 Local Communications Controller Feature Description.* GA34-0142-2. IBM Corporation.

IEEE 1983. *IEEE Project 802, Local Network Standards.* Institute of Electrical and Electronic Engineers, New York.

KRUTSCH, T. E. 1981. A user speaks out: Broadband or baseband for local nets? *Data Commun. 10*, 12 (Dec.), 105–112.

LIU, M. T. 1978. Distributed loop computer networks. In *Advances in Computers*, vol. 17. Academic Press, New York, pp. 163–221.

LIU, M. T., HILAL, W., AND GROOMES, B. H. 1982. Performance evaluation of channel access protocols for local computer networks. In *Proceedings of COMPCON FALL 82* (Washington, D.C., Sept. 20–23). IEEE Computer Society, Los Angeles, pp. 417–426.

LUCZAK, E. C. 1978. Global bus computer communication techniques. In *Proceedings of the Symposium on Computer Networks* (Gaithersburg, Md., Dec.). IEEE Computer Society, Los Angeles, pp. 58–67.

MALONE, J. 1981. The microcomputer connection to local networks. *Data Commun. 10*, 12 (Dec.), 101–104.

MARKOV, J. D., AND STROLE, N. C. 1982. Token-ring local area networks: A perspective. In *Proceedings of COMPCON FALL 82* (Washington, D.C., Sept. 20–23). IEEE Computer Society, Los Angeles, pp. 606–614.

METCALFE, R. M., AND BOGGS, D. R. 1976. Ethernet: Distributed packet switching for local computer networks. *Commun. ACM 19*, 7 (July), 395–404.

METCALFE, R. M., BOGGS, D. R., THACKER, C. P., AND LAMPSON, B. W. 1977. Multipoint data communication system with collision detection. U.S. Patent 4,063,220.

MILLER, C. K., AND THOMPSON, D. M. 1982. Making a case for token passing in local networks. *Data Commun. 11*, 3 (Mar.), 79–88.

MYERS, W. 1982. Towards a local network standard. *IEEE Micro 2*, 3 (Aug.), 28–45.

NELSON, J. 1983. 802: A progress report. *Datamation* (Sept.), 136–152.

PARKER, R. 1983. Committees push to standardize disk I/O. *Comput. Des. 22*, 3 (Mar.), 30–34.

PENNY, B. K., AND BAGHDADI, A. A. 1979. Survey of computer communications loop networks. *Comput. Commun. 2*, 4 (Aug.), 165–180; *2*, 4 (Oct.), 224–241.

PIERCE, J. R. 1972. Network for block switches of data. *Bell Syst. Tech. J. 51*, 6 (July–Aug.).

RAUCH-HINDIN, W. 1982. IBM's local network scheme. *Data Commun. 11*, 5 (May), 65–70.

RAWSON, E., AND METCALFE, R. 1978. Fibernet: Multimode optical fibers for local computer networks. *IEEE Trans. Commun. COM-26*, 7 (July), 983–990.

ROMAN, G. S. 1977. *The design of broadband coaxial cable networks for multimode communications.* MITRE Tech. Rep. MTR-3527. Mitre Corp., McLean, Va.

ROSENTHAL, R., Ed. 1982. The selection of local area computer networks. NBS Special Publ. 500-96, National Bureau of Standards, Washington, D.C., Nov.

SALTZER, J. H., AND CLARK, D. D. 1981. Why a ring? In *Proceedings of the 7th Symposium on Data Communications* (Mexico City, Oct. 27–29). *Comput. Commun. Rev. 11*, 4, 211–217.

SALTZER, J. H., AND POGRAN, K. T. 1979. A star-shaped ring network with high maintainability. In *Proceedings of the Symposium on Local Area Communications Network* (Boston, May). Mitre Corp., McLean, Va., pp. 179–190.

SALWEN, H. 1983. In praise of ring architecture for local area networks. *Comput. Des. 22*, 3 (Mar.), 183–192.

SHOCH, J. F. 1980. *An Annotated Bibliography on Local Computer Networks.* Xerox Palo Alto Research Center, Palo Alto, Calif., Apr.

SHOCH, J. F., DALA, Y. K., AND REDELL, D. D. 1982. Evolution of the Ethernet local computer network. *Computer 15*, 8 (Aug.), pp. 1–27.

STAHLMAN, M. 1982. Inside Wang's local net architecture. *Data Commun. 11*, 1 (Jan.), 85–90.

STALLINGS, W. 1983. *Tutorial: Local Network Technology.* IEEE Computer Society Press, Silver Spring, Md.

STALLINGS, W. 1984. *Local Networks: An Introduction.* Macmillan, New York.

STIEGLITZ, M. 1981. Local network access tradeoffs. *Comput. Des. 20*, 12 (Oct.), 163–168.

STUCK, B. 1983a. Which local net bus access is most sensitive to congestion? *Data Commun. 12*, 1 (Jan.), 107–120.

STUCK, B. 1983b. Calculating the maximum mean data rate in local area networks. *Computer 16*, 5 (May), 72–76.

THORNTON, J. E. 1980. Back-end network approaches. *Computer 13*, 2 (Feb.), 10–17.

TROPPER, C. 1981. *Local Computer Network Technologies.* Academic Press, New York.

WILKES, M. V., AND WHEELER, D. J. 1979. The Cambridge digital communication ring. In *Proceedings of the Symposium on Local Area Communications Network* (Boston, May). Mitre Corp., McLean, Va., pp. 47–62.

YEN, C., AND CRAWFORD, R. 1983. Distribution and equalization of signal on coaxial cables used in 10 Mbits baseband local area networks. *IEEE Trans. Commun. COM-31*, 10 (Oct.), 1181–1186.

Received January 1983; final revision accepted March 1984

Section 2: Local Area Networks

2.1 Overview

The term local area network (LAN) is generally used to refer to a general-purpose local network that can serve a wide variety of devices over a large area. LANs support mini computers, mainframes, terminals, and other peripherals. In many cases, these networks can carry not only data but also voice, video, and graphics transmissions.

A LAN (rather than a high speed local network (HSLN) or a digital PBX) is probably the best choice when a variety of devices and a mix of traffic types are involved. The LAN, alone or as part of a hybrid local network with one of the other types, will become a common feature of many office buildings and other installations.

This section looks at the major alternative architectural approaches to LANs and focuses on some key design issues. As was described in Section 1, the key technology aspects of a LAN are transmission medium, topology, and medium access control technique. The current status of standards for LANs is also described.

2.2 LAN Transmission Media

To date, the transmission media most commonly used for LANs have been twisted pair and coaxial cable. Baseband transmission is used on twisted pair; baseband or broadband transmission is used on coaxial cable. Baseband and broadband technologies were introduced in Section 1 and are examined in greater detail in the articles of this section.

In recent years, there has been increasing interest in the use of optical fiber as a LAN transmission medium. In the remainder of this subsection, we first describe the medium and then discuss its use to construct a LAN.

Physical Description

An optical fiber is a thin (50-100 μm), flexible medium capable of conducting an optical ray. Various glasses and plastics can be used to make optical fibers. The lowest losses have been obtained by using fibers of ultrapure fused silica. Ultrapure fiber is difficult to manufacture; higher-loss multicomponent glass fibers are more economical and still provide good performance. Plastic fiber is even less costly and can be used for short-haul links, for which moderately high losses are acceptable.

For a single optical fiber, the glass or plastic fiber, having a high index of refraction, is surrounded by a cladding layer of a material with slightly lower index. The cladding layer isolates the fiber and prevents crosstalk with adjacent fibers. Fiber optic cable consists of a bundle of fibers, sometimes with a steel core for stability. Stacked ribbon cable is an alternative method of bundling; the cable consists of a stack of flat ribbons, each with a single row of fibers.

Benefits

One of the most significant technological breakthroughs in data transmission has been the development of practical fiberoptic communications systems. Optical fiber already enjoys considerable use in long-distance telecommunications, and its use in military applications is growing. The continuing improvements in performance and decline in prices, together with the inherent advantages of optical fiber, will result in new areas of application, such as local networks and short-haul video distribution. The following characteristics distinguish optical fiber from twisted pair and coaxial cable.

- *Greater bandwidth*: The potential bandwidth and, hence, data rate of a medium increases with frequency. At the immense frequencies of optical fiber, data rates of 2 Gbps over tens of kilometers have been demonstrated. Compare this to the practical maximum of hundreds of Mbps over about 1 km for coaxial cable and just a few Mbps over 1 km for twisted pair.
- *Smaller size and lighter weight*: Optical fibers are considerably smaller than coaxial cable or bundled twisted pair cable, at least an order of magnitude smaller in diameter for comparable data transmission capacity. For cramped conduits in buildings and underground along public right-of-way, the advantage of small size is considerable. The corresponding reduction in weight reduces structural support requirements.
- *Lower attenuation*: Attenuation is significantly lower for optical fiber than for coaxial cable or for twisted pair and is constant over a wide range.
- *Electromagnetic isolation*: Optical fiber systems are not affected by external electromagnetic fields. Thus, the system is not vulnerable to interference, impulse noise, or crosstalk. By the same token, fibers do not radiate energy, causing little interference with other equipment and providing a high degree of security from eavesdropping; in addition, fiber is inherently difficult to tap.
- *Greater repeater spacing*: Fewer repeaters mean lower cost and fewer sources of error. Bell Labs has successfully tested a 119-km repeaterless link at 420 Mbps

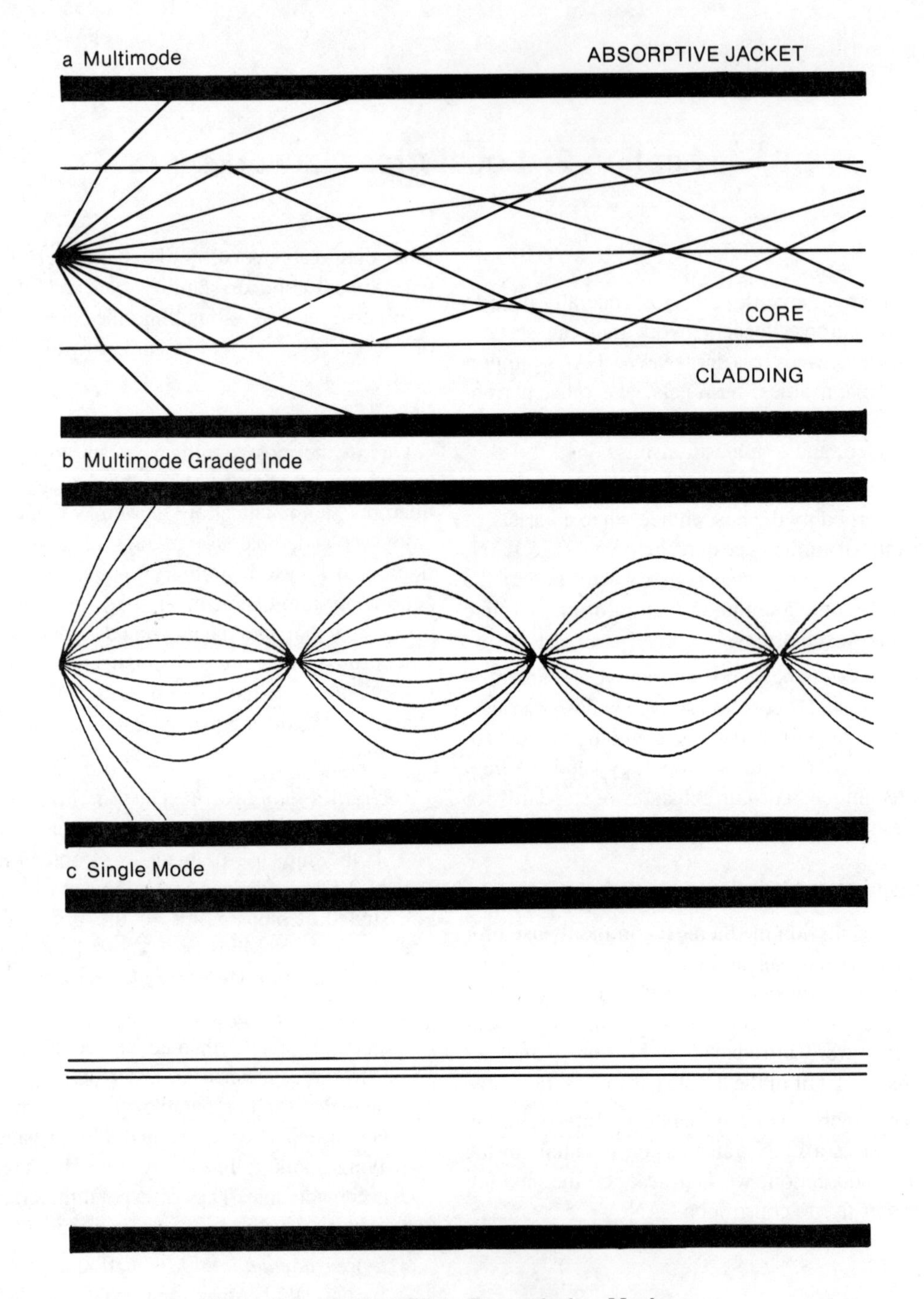

Figure 2.1 Optical Fiber Transmission Modes

with a bit error rate of 10^{-9}. Coaxial and twisted-pair systems generally have repeaters every few kilometers.

Transmission Characteristics

Optical fiber transmits a signal-encoded beam of light by means of total internal reflection. Total internal reflection can occur in any transparent medium that has a higher index of refraction than the surrounding medium. In effect, the optical fiber acts as a waveguide for frequencies in the range 10^{14}-10^{15} Hz, which covers the visible spectrum and part of the infrared spectrum.

Figure 2.1 shows the principle of optical fiber transmission. Light from a source enters the cylindrical glass or plastic core. Rays at shallow angles are reflected and propagated along the fiber; other rays are absorbed by the surrounding material. This form of propagation is called multimode, referring to the variety of angles that will reflect. When a fiber core radius is reduced, fewer angles will reflect. By reducing the radius of the core to the order of a wavelength, only a single angle or mode can pass: the axial ray. Table 2.1 compares these two modes. The reason for

Table 2.1 Comparison of Single-Mode and Multimode Optical Fiber

SINGLE-MODE	MULTIMODE
Used for long distances and high data rates	Used for short distances and low data rates
Expensive	Inexpensive
Narrow core: requires laser light source	Wide core: gathers light well
Difficult to terminate	Easy to terminate
Minimum dispersion; very efficient	Large dispersion; inefficient

Table 2.2: Medium Access Control Techniques

	CENTRALIZED	DISTRIBUTED
ROUND-ROBIN	Polling	Token Bus Token Ring Collision Avoidance
RESERVATION	Centralized Reservation	Distributed Reservation
CONTENTION		CSMA/CD Slotted Ring Register Insertion

the superior performance of single-mode is this. With multimode transmission, multiple propagation paths exist, each with a different path length and hence time to traverse the fiber. This causes signal elements to spread out in time and limits the rate at which data can be accurately received. Since there is a single transmission path with single-mode transmission, such distortion cannot occur. Finally, by varying the index of refraction of the core, a third type of transmission, known as multimode graded index, is possible. This type is intermediate between the other two in characteristics. The variable refraction has the effect of focusing the rays more efficiently than ordinary multimode.

Two different types of light source are used in fiber optic systems: the light-emitting diode (LED) and the injection laser diode (ILD). The LED is a solid-state device that emits light when a current is applied. The ILD is a solid-state device that works on the laser principle in which quantum electronic effects are stimulated to produce a superradiant beam of narrow bandwidth. The LED is less costly, operates over a greater temperature range, and has a longer operational life than the ILD. The ILD is more efficient and can sustain greater data rates.

The detector used at the receiving end to convert the light into electrical energy is a photodiode. Two solid-state devices have been used: the PIN detector and the APD detector. The PIN photodiode has a segment of intrinsic (I) silicon between the P and N layers of a diode. The APD, avalanche photodiode, is similar in appearance but uses a stronger electric field. Both devices are basically photon counters. The PIN is less expensive and less sensitive than the APD.

Of course, only analog signaling is possible in optical fiber, since only light waves may be transmitted. With appropriate modulation, either digital or analog data may be carried.

LAN Applications

The application of fiber to LANs has lagged its use in other areas because of cost and technical concerns, which include difficulties in tapping a signal from the fiber, connecting fibers to other LAN components, and splicing. The article by Finley accurately captures the current status and most promising technical approaches for fiber LANs.

2.3 LAN Topologies

The topologies that have been most commonly used for LANs are bus/tree and ring. Again, these were introduced in Section 1 and are examined in greater detail in this section. To date, efforts at standardization have focused on these two topologies.

A more recent topology, which might be termed the star-LAN or centralized bus, has been introduced by AT&T and is under consideration by the IEEE 802 standards committee (see Section 2.5). This architecture is similar to the more traditional LAN bus. The difference is that in this case the bus is very short and, consequently, the connecting cable to the attached device may be very long. The short bus allows for a simplified access control protocol and for efficient centralized control. This architecture is explored in the paper by Acampora and Hluchyz.

2.4 Medium Access Control

With all types of local networks, a key technical issue is that of access control. An access control technique is required to regulate the use of the shared medium. The key parameters in any medium access control technique are where and how. "Where" refers to whether control is exercised in a centralized or distributed fashion. In a centralized scheme, a controller is designated that has the authority to grant access to the network. A station wishing to transmit must wait until it receives permission from the controller. In a decentralized network, the stations collectively perform a medium access control function to dynamically determine the order in which stations transmit.

IEEE 802 REFERENCE MODEL RELATIONSHIP TO OSI MODEL

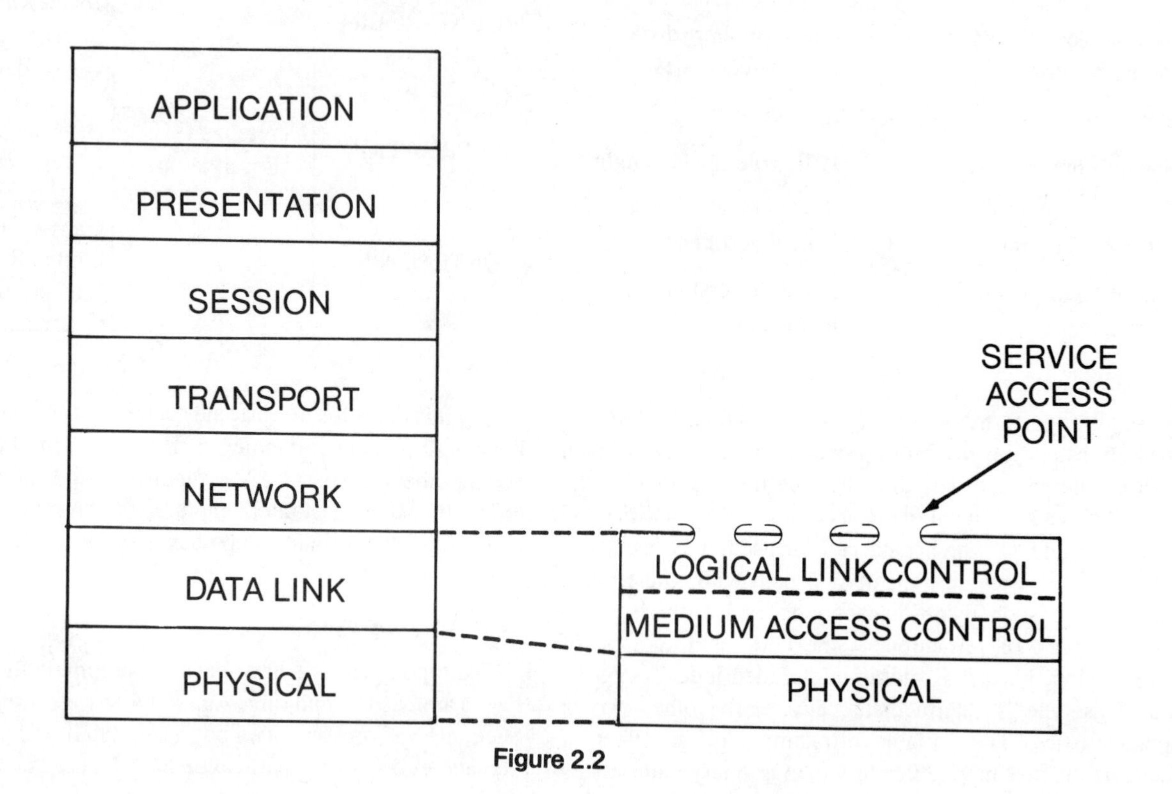

Figure 2.2

A centralized scheme has certain advantages, such as, (1) It may afford greater control over access for providing such things as priorities, overrides, and guaranteed bandwidth, (2) It allows the logic at each station to be as simple as possible, and (3) It avoids problems of coordination. Its principal disadvantages are that (1) It results in a single point of failure; (2) It may act as a bottleneck, reducing efficiency; and (3) If propagation delay is high, the overhead may be unacceptable. The pros and cons for distributed control are mirror images of the points made above.

The second parameter, "how," is constrained by the topology and is a tradeoff among competing factors: cost, performance, and complexity. In general, we can categorize access control techniques as being either synchronous or asynchronous. With synchronous techniques, a specific capacity is dedicated to a connection. We see this in the digital PBX. Such techniques are not optimal in broadcast networks because the needs of the stations are generally unpredictable. It is preferable to be able to allocate capacity in an asynchronous (dynamic) fashion, more or less in response to immediate needs. The asynchronous approach can be further subdivided into three categories: Round robin, Reservation, and Contention.

Round Robin

Round robin techniques are conceptually simple, being based on the philosophy of "give everybody a turn." Each station in turn is given an opportunity to transmit. During that opportunity the station may decline to transmit or may transmit subject to a certain upper bound, usually expressed as a maximum amount of data or time for this opportunity. In any case, the station, when it is finished, must relinquish its turn, and the right to transmit passes to the next station in logical sequence. Control of turns may be centralized or distributed. Polling on a multidrop line is an example of a centralized technique.

When many stations have data to transmit over an extended period of time, round robin techniques can be very efficient. If only a few stations have data to transmit at any give time, other techniques may be preferable, largely depending on whether the data traffic is "stream" or "bursty." Stream traffic is characterized by lengthy and fairly continuous transmissions. Examples are voice communication, telemetry, and bulk file transfer. Bursty traffic is characterized by short, sporadic transmissions. Interactive terminal-host traffic fits this description.

Reservation

For stream traffic, reservation techniques are well suited. In general for these techniques, time on the medium is divided into slots, much as with synchronous TDM. A station wishing to transmit reserves future slots for an extended or indefinite period. Again, reservations may be made in either a centralized or distributed fashion.

Contention

For bursty traffic, contention techniques are usually appropriate. With these techniques, no control is exercised to determine whose turn it is; all stations contend for time in a way that can be, as we shall see, rather rough and tumble. These techniques are of necessity distributed in nature. Their principal advantage is that they are simple to implement and, under light to moderate load, efficient. For some of these techniques, however, performance tends to collapse under heavy load.

Although both centralized and distributed reservation techniques have been implemented in some LAN products, round robin and contention techniques are the most common. Specific examples are shown in Table 2.2.

2.5 Standards

Standards for LANs have been developed by a committee set up by The Institute of Electrical and Electronics Engineers, Inc., known as the IEEE 802 committee. The task of the IEEE 802 was to specify the means by which devices could communicate over a local area network. The committee characterized its work in this way:

> A Local Network is a data communications system which allows a number of independent devices to communicate with each other. This Standard defines a set of interfaces and protocols for the Local Network.
>
> A Local Network is distinguished from other types of data networks in that the communication is usually confined to a moderate size geographic area such as a single office building, a warehouse or a campus. The network can generally depend on a communications channel of moderate to high data rate which has a consistently low error rate. The network is generally owned and used by a single organization. This is in contrast to long distance networks which interconnect facilities in different parts of the country or are used as a public utility. The Local Network is also different from networks which interconnect devices on a desktop or components within a single piece of equipment.
>
> The objective of the Local Network Standard is to ensure compatibility between equipment made by different manufacturers such that data communications can take place between the devices with a minimum effort on the part of the equipment users or the builders of a system containing the equipment. To accomplish this, the Standard will provide specifications which establish common interfaces and protocols for local area data communications networks.

Two conclusions were quickly reached. First, the task of communication across the local network is sufficiently complex that it needs to be broken up into more manageable subtasks. Second, no single technical approach will satisfy all requirements.

The first conclusion is reflected in a "local network reference model," compared in Figure 2.2 to the better-known open systems interconnection (OSI) model. The model has three layers:

- *Physical*: The layer is concerned with the nature of the transmission medium, and the details of device attachment and electrical signaling.
- *Medium access control*: A local network is characterized by a collection of devices all needing to share a single transmission medium. A means to control access is needed so that only one device attempts to transmit at a time.
- *Logical link control*: This layer is concerned with establishing, maintaining, and terminating a logical link between devices.

The second conclusion was reluctantly reached when it became apparent that no single standard would satisfy all committee participants. There was support for both ring and bus topologies. Within the bus topology, there was support for two access methods (CSMA/CD and token bus) and two media (baseband and broadband). The response of the committee was to standardize all serious proposals rather than to attempt to settle on just one.

The work of the IEEE 802 committee is currently organized into the following subcommittees: (1) IEEE 802.1 Higher Layer Interface Standard (HILI), (2) IEEE 802.2 Logical Link Control Standard (LLC), (3) IEEE 802.3 CSMA/CD, (4) IEEE 802.4 Token Bus, (5) IEEE 802.5 Token Ring, and (6) IEEE 802.6 Metropolitan Area Network (MAN).

The HILI subcommittee is not developing standards, but rather is working on a variety of related issues such as higher layer interfaces, internetworking, addressing, and network management.

Work has been completed on LLC, CSMA/CD, token bus, and token ring for an initial standard, and approved IEEE standards have been adopted for each. Work on new options and features continues in each subcommittee.

The work on metropolitan area networks is just beginning to make progress. The subcommittee is attempting to develop a small number of reasonable alternatives for further study.

The acceptance of the IEEE 802 standards has been remarkably widespread. The National Bureau of Standards, which issues Federal Information Processing Standards (FIPS) for U.S. government procurements, has issued FIPS for CSMA/CD and LLC. The others will probably follow. The International Organization for Standardization (ISO) has decided to adopt the IEEE 802 documents in toto as a Draft Proposal. This is the first step in the development of international standards. The influential European Computer Manufacturers Association (ECMA), which had been actively drafting its own LAN standards, has now officially deferred to IEEE 802.

2.6 Article Summary

The first two articles describe a specific baseband and broadband LAN, respectively. They are chosen because of the breadth of description of the two approaches that they provide. The article by Shoch et al. describes one of the earliest baseband LANs, Ethernet. Developed jointly by Xerox, DEC, and Intel, Ethernet is a widely used baseband system. The second article discusses the Sytek broadband local network, which is representative of the approach.

The next article, "A User Speaks Out: Broadband or Baseband for Local Nets?" is a revealing discussion of the relative merits of the two approaches. As might be expected, the author concludes that neither approach dominates; each has a place, depending on the requirements. A final article on bus/tree LANs is by Flatman. This article looks at a system called "Cheapernet," which is a proposed standard for a low-cost LAN.

The next two articles deal with the ring. Strole describes in considerable detail IBM's approach to the ring, which heavily influenced the IEEE 802 ring standard. The article deals with the architectural approach and the token ring protocol and the measures employed to enhance system availability. "Why a Ring?" compares the ring and bus/tree architectures.

The next article deals with the IEEE 802 standard. "Toward a Local Network Standard" is a concise but remarkably complete description of the standard.

Until recently, virtually all LAN products on the market were either bus/tree or ring products. A quite different approach has been taken by AT&T using a centralized bus architecture, and this is described in the next article.

Finally, "Optical Fibers in Local Area Networks" provides a status reported on the long-anticipated emergence of optical fiber in the LAN marketplace.

Evolution of the Ethernet Local Computer Network

John F. Shoch, Yogen K. Dalal, David D. Redell, and Ronald C. Crane

Evolution of the Ethernet Local Computer Network

As it evolved from a research prototype to the specification of a multi-company standard, Ethernet compelled designers to consider numerous trade-offs among alternative implementations and design strategies.

John F. Shoch, Yogen K. Dalal, and David D. Redell, Xerox
Ronald C. Crane, 3Com

With the continuing decline in the cost of computing, we have witnessed a dramatic increase in the number of independent computer systems used for scientific computing, business, process control, word processing, and personal computing. These machines do not compute in isolation, and with their proliferation comes a need for suitable communication networks—particularly local computer networks that can interconnect locally distributed computing systems. While there is no single definition of a local computer network, there is a broad set of requirements:

- relatively high data rates (typically 1 to 10M bits per second);
- geographic distance spanning about one kilometer (typically within a building or a small set of buildings);
- ability to support several hundred independent devices;
- simplicity, or the ability "to provide the simplest possible mechanisms that have the required functionality and performance";[1]
- good error characteristics, good reliability, and minimal dependence upon any centralized components or control;
- efficient use of shared resources, particularly the communications network itself;
- stability under high load;
- fair access to the system by all devices;
- easy installation of a small system, with graceful growth as the system evolves;
- ease of reconfiguration and maintenance; and
- low cost.

One of the more successful designs for a system of this kind is the Ethernet local computer network.[2,3] Ethernet installations have been in use for many years. They support hundreds of stations and meet the requirements listed above.

In general terms, Ethernet is a multi-access, packet-switched communications system for carrying digital data among locally distributed computing systems. The shared communications channel in an Ethernet is a passive broadcast medium with no central control; packet address recognition in each station is used to take packets from the channel. Access to the channel by stations wishing to transmit is coordinated in a distributed fashion by the stations themselves, using a statistical arbitration scheme.

The Ethernet strategy can be used on many different broadcast media, but our major focus has been on the use of coaxial cable as the shared transmission medium. The Experimental Ethernet system was developed at the Xerox Palo Alto Research Center starting in 1972. Since then, numerous other organizations have developed and built "Ethernet-like" local networks.[4] More recently, a cooperative effort involving Digital Equipment Corporation, Intel, and Xerox has produced an updated version of the Ethernet design, generally known as the Ethernet Specification.[5]

One of the primary goals of the Ethernet Specification is compatibility—providing enough information for different manufacturers to build widely differing machines in such a way that they can directly communicate with one another. It might be tempting to view the Specification as simply a design handbook that will allow designers to develop their own Ethernet-like network, perhaps cus-

EHO234-5/85/0000/0050$01.00 © 1982 IEEE

tomized for some specific requirements or local constraints. But this would miss the major point: Successful interconnection of heterogeneous machines requires equipment that precisely matches a single specification.

Meeting the Specification is only one of the necessary conditions for intermachine communication at all levels of the network architecture. There are many levels of protocol, such as transport, name binding, and file transfer, that must also be agreed upon and implemented in order to provide useful services.[6-8] This is analogous to the telephone system: The common low-level specifications for telephony make it possible to dial from the US to France, but this is not of much use if the caller speaks only English while the person who answers the phone speaks only French. Specification of these additional protocols is an important area for further work.

The design of any local network must be considered in the context of a distributed system architecture. Although the Ethernet Specification does not directly address issues of high-level network architecture, we view the local network as one component in an *internetwork* system, providing communication services to many diverse devices connected to different networks.[6,9] The services provided by the Ethernet are influenced by these broader architectural considerations.

As we highlight important design considerations and trace the evolution of the Ethernet from research prototype to multicompany standard, we use the term Experimental Ethernet for the former and Ethernet or Ethernet Specification for the latter. The term Ethernet is also used to describe design principles common to both systems.

General description of Ethernet-class systems

Theory of operation. The general Ethernet approach uses a shared communications channel managed with a distributed control policy known as *carrier sense multiple access with collision detection*, or CSMA/CD. With this approach, there is no central controller managing access to the channel, and there is no preallocation of time slots or frequency bands. A station wishing to transmit is said to "contend" for use of the common shared communications channel (sometimes called the Ether) until it "acquires" the channel; once the channel is acquired the station uses it to transmit a packet.

To acquire the channel, stations check whether the network is busy (that is, use *carrier sense*) and defer transmission of their packet until the Ether is quiet (no other transmissions occurring). When quiet is detected, the deferring station immediately begins to transmit. During transmission, the transmitting station listens for a collision (other transmitters attempting to use the channel simultaneously). In a correctly functioning system, collisions occur only within a short time interval following the start of transmission, since after this interval all stations will detect carrier and defer transmission. This time interval is called the *collision window* or the *collision interval* and is a function of the end-to-end propagation delay. If no collisions occur during this time, a transmitter has acquired the Ether and continues transmission of the packet. If a station detects collision, the transmission of the rest of the packet is immediately aborted. To ensure that all parties to the collision have properly detected it, any station that detects a collision invokes a *collision consensus enforcement procedure* that briefly jams the channel. Each transmitter involved in the collision then schedules its packet for retransmission at some later time.

To minimize repeated collisions, each station involved in a collision tries to retransmit at a different time by scheduling the retransmission to take place after a random delay period. In order to achieve channel stability under overload conditions, a controlled retransmission strategy is used whereby the mean of the random retransmission delay is increased as a function of the channel load. An estimate of the channel load can be derived by monitoring the number of collisions experienced by any one packet. This has been shown to be the optimal strategy among the options available for decentralized decision and control problems of this class.[10]

Stations accept packets addressed to them and discard any that are found to be in error. Deference reduces the probability of collision, and collision detection allows the timely retransmission of a packet. It is impossible, however, to guarantee that all packets transmitted will be delivered successfully. For example, if a receiver is not enabled, an error-free packet addressed to it will not be delivered; higher levels of protocol must detect these situations and retransmit.

Under very high load, short periods of time on the channel may be lost due to collisions, but the collision resolution procedure operates quickly.[2,11-13] Channel utilization under these conditions will remain high, particularly if packets are large with respect to the collision interval. One of the fundamental parameters of any Ethernet implementation is the length of this collision interval, which is based on the round-trip propagation time between the farthest two points in the system.

Basic components. The CSMA/CD access procedure can use any broadcast multi-access channel, including radio, twisted pair, coaxial cable, diffuse infrared, and fiber optics.[14] Figure 1 illustrates a typical Ethernet system using coaxial cable. There are four components.

Station. A station makes use of the communication system and is the basic addressable device connected to an Ethernet; in general, it is a computer. We do not expect that "simple" terminals will be connected directly to an Ethernet. Terminals can be connected to some form of terminal controller, however, which provides access to the network. In the future, as the level of sophistication in terminals increases, many terminals will support direct connection to the network. Furthermore, specialized I/O devices, such as magnetic tapes or disk drives, may incorporate sufficient computing resources to function as stations on the network.

Within the station there is some interface between the operating system environment and the Ethernet controller. The nature of this interface (often in software) depends upon the particular implementation of the controller functions in the station.

Controller. A controller for a station is really the set of functions and algorithms needed to manage access to the channel. These include signaling conventions, encoding and decoding, serial-to-parallel conversion, address recognition, error detection, buffering, the basic CSMA/CD channel management, and packetization. These functions can be grouped into two logically independent sections of each controller: the transmitter and the receiver.

The controller functions are generally implemented using a combination of hardware, microcode, and software, depending on the nature of the station. It would be possible, for example, for a very capable station to have a minimal hardware connection to the transmission system and perform most of these functions in software. Alternatively, a station might implement all the controller functions in hardware, or perhaps in a controller-specific microprocessor. Most controller implementations fall somewhere in between. With the continuing advances in LSI development, many of these functions will be packaged in a single chip, and several semiconductor manufacturers have already announced plans to build Ethernet controllers. The precise boundary between functions performed on the chip and those in the station is implementation-dependent, but the nature of that interface is of great importance. As many of the functions as possible should be moved into the chip, provided that this preserves all of the flexibility needed in the construction and use of system interfaces and higher level software.

The description of the controller in this article is functional in nature and indicates how the controller must behave independent of particular implementations. There is some flexibility in implementing a correct controller, and we will make several recommendations concerning efficient operation of the system.

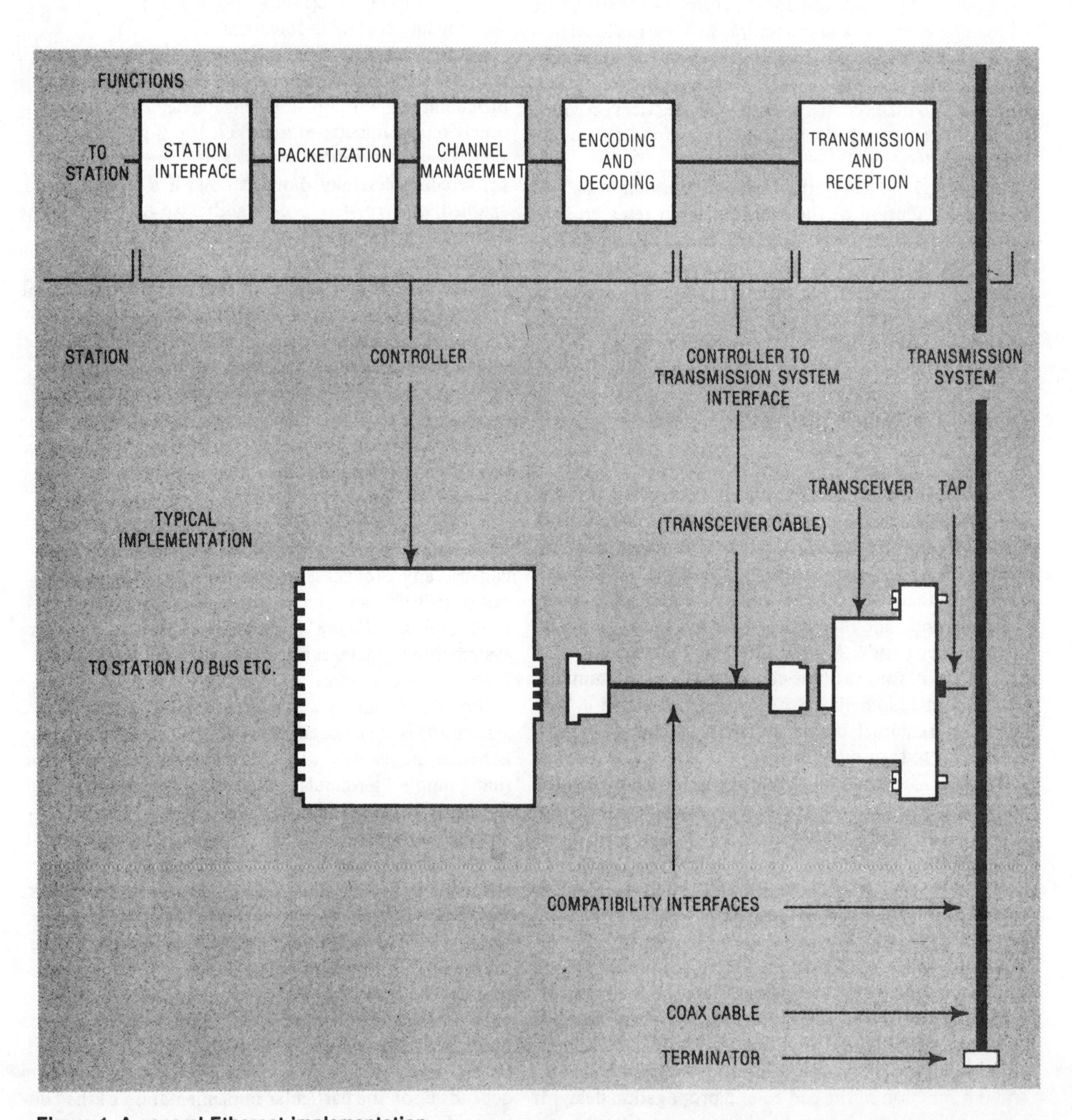

Figure 1. A general Ethernet implementation.

Transmission system. The transmission system includes all the components used to establish a communications path among the controllers. In general, this includes a suitable broadcast transmission medium, the appropriate transmitting and receiving devices—transceivers—and, optionally, repeaters to extend the range of the medium. The protocol for managing access to the transmission system is implemented in the controller; the transmission system does not attempt to interpret any of the bits transmitted on the channel.

The broadcast transmission medium contains those components that provide a physical communication path. In the case of coaxial cable, this includes the cable plus any essential hardware—connectors, terminators, and taps.

Transceivers contain the necessary electronics to transmit and receive signals on the channel and recognize the presence of a signal when another station transmits. They also recognize a collision that takes place when two or more stations transmit simultaneously.

Repeaters are used to extend the length of the transmission system beyond the physical limits imposed by the transmission medium. A repeater uses two transceivers to connect to two different Ethernet segments and combines them into one logical channel, amplifying and regenerating signals as they pass through in either direction.[15] Repeaters are transparent to the rest of the system, and stations on different segments can still collide. Thus, the repeater must propagate a collision detected on one segment through to the other segment, and it must do so without becoming unstable. A repeater makes an Ethernet channel longer and as a result increases the maximum propagation delay of the system, meaning delay through the repeater and propagation delay through the additional segments. To avoid multipath interference in an Ethernet installation, there must be only one path between any two stations through the network. (The higher level internetwork architecture can support alternate paths between stations through different communications channels.)

Controller-to-transmission-system interface. One of the major interfaces in an Ethernet system is the point at which the controller in a station connects to the transmission system. The controller does much of the work in managing the communications process, so this is a fairly simple interface. It includes paths for data going to and from the transmission system. The data received can be used by the controller to sense carrier, but the transmission system normally includes a medium-specific mechanism for detecting collisions on the channel; this must also be communicated through the interface to the controller. It is possible to power a transceiver from a separate power source, but power is usually taken from the controller interface. In most transmission systems, the connection from the controller is made to a transceiver, and this interface is called the transceiver cable interface.

Two generations of Ethernet designs. The Experimental Ethernet circa 1972 confirmed the feasibility of the design, and dozens of installations have been in regular use since then. A typical installation supports hundreds of stations and a wide-ranging set of applications: file transfer, mail distribution, document printing, terminal access to timesharing systems, data-base access, copying disks, multimachine programs, and more. Stations include the Alto workstation,[16] the Dorado (an internal research machine),[17] the Digital Equipment PDP-11, and the Data General Nova. The system has been the subject of extensive performance measurements confirming its predicted behavior.[12,13]

Based upon that experience, a second-generation system was designed at Xerox in the late 1970's. That effort subsequently led to the joint development of the Ethernet Specification. Stations built by Xerox for this network include the Xerox 860, the Xerox 8000 Network System Processor, and the Xerox 1100 Scientific Information Processor (the "Dolphin").

The two systems are very similar: they both use coaxial cable, Manchester signal encoding, and CSMA/CD with dynamic control. Some changes were made based on experience with the experimental system or in an effort to enhance the characteristics of the network. Some of the differences between the systems are summarized in Table 1.

An "Ethernet Technical Summary," which brings together the important features of Version 1 of the joint specification on two pages, is included for reference (pp. 14-15). (In building a compatible device or component, the full Ethernet Specification[5] remains the controlling document. In describing the Ethernet Specification, this article corresponds to Version 1.0; Version 2.0, including extensions and some minor revisions, will be completed later this year.)

Figure 2 is a photograph of some typical components from the Experimental Ethernet, including a transceiver and tap, transceiver cable, and an Alto controller board. Figure 3 is a photograph of similar components based on the Ethernet Specification. Note that both controller boards have been implemented with standard MSI circuits.

Transmission system design

A number of design issues and trade-offs emerged in the development of the Ethernet transmission system, and several lessons were learned from that experience.

Coaxial cable subsystem. In addition to having favorable signaling characteristics and the ability to handle multimegabit transmission rates, a single coaxial

Table 1.
Comparison of Ethernet systems.

	Experimental Ethernet	Ethernet Specification
Data rate	2.94M bps	10M bps
Maximum end-to-end length	1 km	2.5 km
Maximum segment length	1 km	500 m
Encoding	Manchester	Manchester
Coax cable impedance	75 ohms	50 ohms
Coax cable signal levels	0 to +3V	0 to −2V
Transceiver cable connectors	25- and 15-pin D series	15-pin D series
Length of preamble	1 bit	64 bits
Length of CRC	16 bits	32 bits
Length of address fields	8 bits	48 bits

Ethernet 1.0 Technical Summary

Packet Format

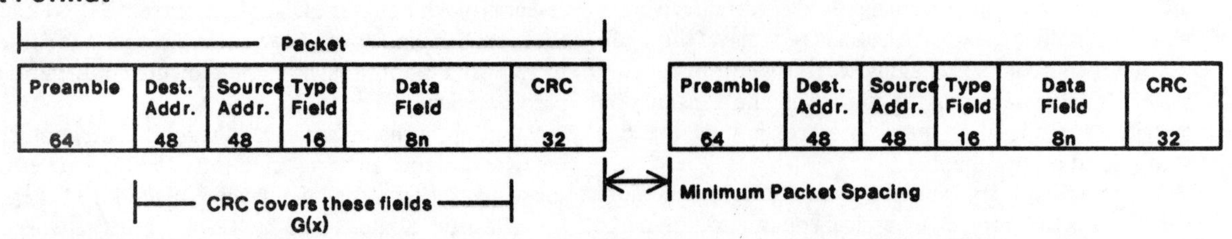

Stations must be able to transmit and receive packets on the common coaxial cable with the indicated packet format and spacing. Each packet should be viewed as a sequence of 8-bit bytes; the least significant bit of each byte (starting with the preamble) is transmitted first.

Maximum Packet Size: 1526 bytes (8 byte preamble + 14 byte header + 1500 data bytes + 4 byte CRC)

Minimum Packet Size: 72 bytes (8 byte preamble + 14 byte header + 46 data bytes + 4 byte CRC)

Preamble: This 64-bit synchronization pattern contains alternating 1's and 0's, ending with two consecutive 1's.
The preamble is: 10101010 10101010 10101010 10101010 10101010 10101010 10101010 10101011.

Destination Address: This 48-bit field specifies the station(s) to which the packet is being transmitted. Each station examines this field to determine whether it should accept the packet. The first bit transmitted indicates the type of address. If it is a 0, the field contains the unique address of the one destination station. If it is a 1, the field specifies a logical group of recipients; a special case is the broadcast (all stations) address, which is all 1's.

Source Address: This 48-bit field contains the unique address of the station that is transmitting the packet.

Type Field: This 16-bit field is used to identify the higher-level protocol type associated with the packet. It determines how the data field is interpreted.

Data Field: This field contains an integral number of bytes ranging from 46 to 1500. (The minimum ensures that valid packets will be distinguishable from collision fragments.)

Packet Check Sequence: This 32-bit field contains a redundancy check (CRC) code, defined by the generating polynomial:

$$G(x) = x^{32} + x^{26} + x^{23} + x^{22} + x^{16} + x^{12} + x^{11} + x^{10} + x^{8} + x^{7} + x^{5} + x^{4} + x^{2} + x + 1$$

The CRC covers the address (destination/source), type, and data fields. The first transmitted bit of the destination field is the high-order term of the message polynomial to be divided by G(x) producing remainder R(x). The high-order term of R(x) is the first transmitted bit of the Packet Check Sequence field. The algorithm uses a linear feedback register which is initially preset to all 1's. After the last data bit is transmitted, the contents of this register (the remainder) are inverted and transmitted as the CRC field. After receiving a good packet, the receiver's shift register contains 11000111 00000100 11011101 01111011 ($x^{31}, \ldots, x^{0}$).

Minimum Packet Spacing: This spacing is 9.6 usec, the minimum time that must elapse after one transmission before another transmission may begin.

Round-trip Delay: The maximum end-to-end, round-trip delay for a bit is 51.2 usec.

Collision Filtering: Any received bit sequence smaller than the minimum valid packet (with minimum data field) is discarded as a collision fragment.

Control Procedure

The control procedure defines how and when a station may transmit packets into the common cable. The key purpose is fair resolution of occasional contention among transmitting stations.

Defer: A station must not transmit into the coaxial cable when carrier is present or within the minimum packet spacing time after carrier has ended.

Transmit: A station may transmit if it is not deferring. It may continue to transmit until either the end of the packet is reached or a collision is detected.

Abort: If a collision is detected, transmission of the packet must terminate, and a *jam* (4-6 bytes of arbitrary data) is transmitted to ensure that all other participants in the collision also recognize its occurrence.

Retransmit: After a station has detected a collision and aborted, it must wait for a random *retransmission delay*, defer as usual, and then attempt to retransmit the packet. The random time interval is computed using the backoff algorithm (below). After 16 transmission attempts, a higher level (e.g. software) decision is made to determine whether to continue or abandon the effort.

Backoff: Retransmission delays are computed using the *Truncated Binary Exponential Backoff* algorithm, with the aim of fairly resolving contention among up to 1024 stations. The delay (the number of time units) before the nth attempt is a uniformly distributed random number from $[0 \text{ to } 2^{n}-1]$ for $0 < n \leq 10$ ($n = 0$ is the original attempt). For attempts 11-15, the interval is *truncated* and remains at [0 to 1023]. The unit of time for the retransmission delay is 512 bit times (51.2 usec).

Channel Encoding

Manchester encoding is used on the coaxial cable. It has a 50% duty cycle, and insures a transition in the middle of every bit cell ("data transition"). The first half of the bit cell contains the complement of the bit value, and the second half contains the true value of the bit.

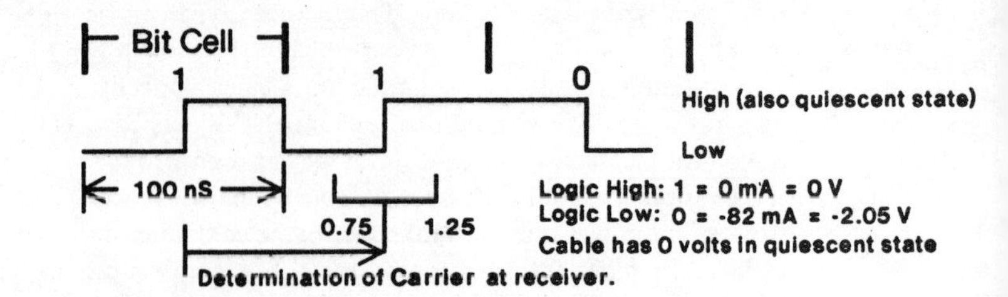

Data Rate

Data rate is 10 M bits/sec = 100 nsec bit cell ± 0.01%.

Carrier

The presence of data transitions indicates that carrier is present. If a transition is not seen between 0.75 and 1.25 bit times since the center of the last bit cell, then carrier has been lost, indicating the end of a packet. For purposes of deferring, carrier means any activity on the cable, independent of being properly formed. Specifically, it is any activity on either receive or collision detect signals in the last 160 nsec.

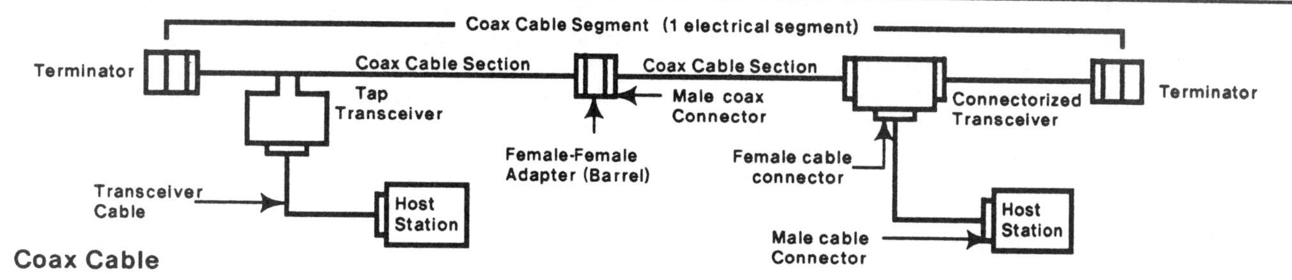

Coax Cable

Impedance: 50 ohms ± 2 ohms (Mil Std. C17-E). This impedance variation includes batch-to-batch variations. Periodic variations in impedance of up to ± 3 ohms are permitted along a single piece of cable.

Cable Loss: The maximum loss from one end of a cable segment to the other end is 8.5 db at 10 MHz (equivalent to ~500 meters of low loss cable).

Shielding: The physical channel hardware must operate in an ambient field of 2 volts per meter from 10 KHz to 30 MHz and 5 V/meter from 30 MHz to 1 GHz. The shield has a transfer impedance of less than 1 milliohm per meter over the frequency range of 0.1 MHz to 20 MHz (exact value is a function of frequency).

Ground Connections: The coax cable shield shall not be connected to any building or AC ground along its length. If for safety reasons a ground connection of the shield is necessary, it must be in only one place.

Physical Dimensions: This specifies the dimensions of a cable which can be used with the *standard tap*. Other cables may also be used, if they are not to be used with a tap-type transceiver (such as use with connectorized transceivers, or as a section between sections to which standard taps are connected).

Center Conductor:	0.0855" diameter solid tinned copper
Core Material:	Foam polyethylene or foam teflon FEP
Core O.D.:	0.242 " minimum
Shield:	0.326" maximum shield O.D. (>90% coverage for outer braid shield)
Jacket:	PVC or teflon FEP
Jacket O.D.:	0.405"

Coax Connectors and Terminators

Coax cables must be terminated with male N-series connectors, and cable sections will be joined with female-female adapters. Connector shells shall be insulated such that the coax shield is protected from contact to building grounds. A sleeve or boot is acceptable. Cable segments should be terminated with a female N-series connector (can be made up of a barrel connector and a male terminator) having an impedance of 50 ohms ± 1%, and able to dissipate 1 watt. The outside surface of the terminator should also be insulated.

Transceiver

CONNECTION RULES

Up to 100 transceivers may be placed on a cable segment no closer together than 2.5 meters. Following this placement rule reduces to a very low (but not zero) probability the chance that objectionable standing waves will result.

COAX CABLE INTERFACE

Input Impedance: The resistive component of the impedance must be greater then 50 Kohms. The total capacitance must be less than 4 picofarads.

Nominal Transmit Level: The important parameter is average DC level with 50% duty cycle waveform input. It must be -1.025 V (41 mA) nominal with a range of -0.9 V to -1.2 V (36 to 48 mA). The peak-to-peak AC waveform must be centered on the average DC level and its value can range from 1.4 V P-P to twice the average DC level. The voltage must never go positive on the coax. The quiescent state of the coax is logic high (0 V). Voltage measurements are made on the coax near the transceiver with the shield as reference. Positive current is current flowing out of the center conductor of the coax.

Rise and Fall Time: 25 nSec ± 5 nSec with a maximum of 1 nSec difference between rise time and fall time in a given unit. The intent is that dV/dt should not significantly exceed that present in a 10 MHz sine wave of same peak-to-peak amplitude.

Signal Symmetry: Asymmetry on output should not exceed 2 nSec for a 50-50 square wave input to either transmit or receive section of transceiver.

TRANSCEIVER CABLE INTERFACE

Signal Pairs: Both transceiver and station shall drive and present at the receiving end a 78 ohm balanced load. The differential signal voltage shall be 0.7 volts nominal peak with a common mode voltage between 0 and +5 volts using power return as reference. (This amounts to shifted ECL levels operating between Gnd and +5 volts. A 10116 with suitable pulldown resistor may be used). The quiescent state of a line corresponds to logic high, which occurs when the + line is more positive than the - line of a pair.

Collision Signal: The active state of this line is a 10 MHz waveform and its quiescent state is logic high. It is active if the transceiver is transmitting and another transmission is detected, or if two or more other stations are transmitting, independent of the state of the local transmit signal.

Power: +11.4 volts to +16 volts DC at controller. Maximum current available to transceiver is 0.5 ampere. Actual voltage at transceiver is determined by the interface cable resistance (max 4 ohms loop resistance) and current drain.

ISOLATION

The impedance between the coax connection and the transceiver cable connection must exceed 250 Kohms at 60 Hz and withstand 250 VRMS at 60 Hz.

Transceiver Cable and Connectors

Maximum signal loss = 3 db @ 10 MHz. (equivalent to ~50 meters of either 20 or 22 AWG twisted pair).

Transceiver Cable Connector Pin Assignment

1.	Shield*		
2.	Collision +	9.	Collision -
3.	Transmit +	10.	Transmit -
4.	Reserved	11.	Reserved
5.	Receive +	12.	Receive -
6.	Power Return	13.	+ Power
7.	Reserved	14.	Reserved
8.	Reserved	15.	Reserved

*Shield must be terminated to connector shell.

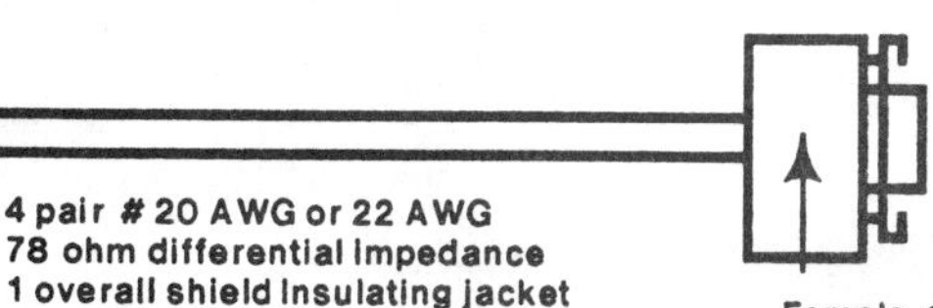

Male 15 pin D-Series connector with lock posts.

Female 15 pin D-Series connector with slide lock assembly.

cable can support communication among many different stations. The mechanical aspects of coaxial cable make it feasible to tap in at any point without severing the cable or producing excessive RF leakage; such considerations relating to installation, maintenance, and reconfigurability are important aspects in any local network design.

There are reflections and attenuation in a cable, however, and these combine to impose some limits on the system design. Engineering the shared channel entails trade-offs involving the data rate on the cable, the length of the cable, electrical characteristics of the transceiver, and the number of stations. For example, it is possible to operate at very high data rates over short distances, but the rate must be reduced to support a greater maximum length. Also, if each transceiver introduces significant reflections, it may be necessary to limit the placement and possibly the number of transceivers.

The characteristics of the coaxial cable fix the maximum data rate, but the actual clock is generated in the controller. Thus, the station interface and controller must be designed to match the data rates used over the cable. Selection of coaxial cable as the transmission medium has no other direct impact on either the station or the controller.

Cable. The Experimental Ethernet used 75-ohm, RG-11-type foam cable. The Ethernet Specification uses a 50-ohm, solid-center-conductor, double-shield, foam dielectric cable in order to provide some reduction in the magnitude of reflections from insertion capacitance (introduced by tapping into the cable) and to provide better immunity against environmental electromagnetic noise. Belden Number 9880 Ethernet Coax meets the Ethernet Specification.

Terminators and connectors. A small terminator is attached to the cable at each end to provide a termination impedance for the cable equal to its characteristic impedance, thereby eliminating reflection from the ends of the cable. For convenience, the cable can be divided into a number of sections using simple connectors between sections to produce one electrically continuous segment.

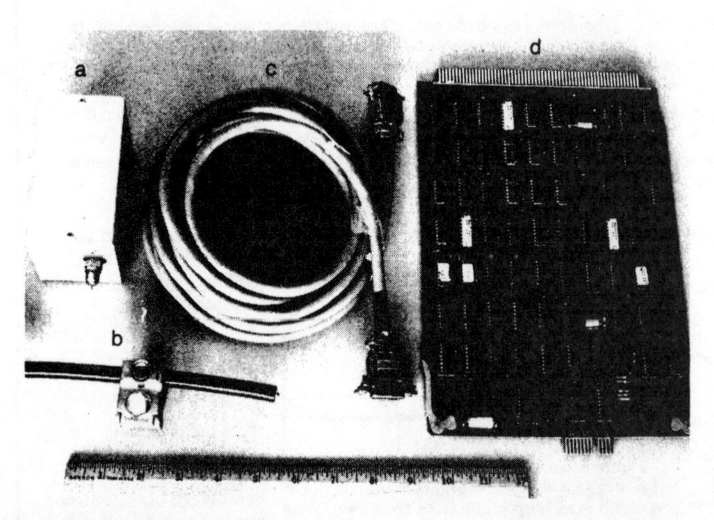

Figure 2. Experimental Ethernet components: (a) transceiver and tap, (b) tap-block, (c) transceiver cable, and (d) Alto controller board.

Segment length and the use of repeaters. The Experimental Ethernet was designed to accommodate a maximum end-to-end length of 1 km, implemented as a single electrically continuous segment. Active repeaters could be used with that system to create complex topologies that would cover a wider area in a building (or complex of buildings) within the end-to-end length limit. With the use of those repeaters, however, the maximum end-to-end length between any two stations was still meant to be approximately 1 km. Thus, the segment length and the maximum end-to-end length were the same, and repeaters were used to provide additional flexibility.

In developing the Ethernet Specification, the strong desire to support a 10M-bps data rate—with reasonable transceiver cost—led to a maximum segment length of 500 meters. We expect that this length will be sufficient to support many installations and applications with a single Ethernet segment. In some cases, however, we recognized a requirement for greater maximum end-to-end length in one network. In these cases, repeaters may now be used not just for additional flexibility but also to extend the overall length of an Ethernet. The Ethernet Specification permits the concatenation of up to three segments; the maximum end-to-end delay between two stations measured as a distance is 2.5 km, including the delay through repeaters containing a point-to-point link.[5]

Taps. Transceivers can connect to a coax cable with the use of a *pressure tap,* borrowed from CATV technology. Such a tap allows connection to the cable without cutting it to insert a connector and avoids the need to interrupt network service while installing a new station. One design uses a tap-block that is clamped on the cable and uses a special tool to penetrate the outer jacket and shield. The tool is removed and the separate tap is screwed into the block. Another design has the tap and tap-block integrated into one unit, with the tap puncturing the cable to make contact with the center conductor as the tap-block is being clamped on.

Alternatively, the cable can be cut and connectors fastened to each piece of cable. This unfortunately disrupts the network during the installation process. After the connectors are installed at the break in the cable, a T-connector can be inserted in between and then connected to a transceiver. Another option, a connectorized transceiver, has two connectors built into it for direct attachment to the cable ends without a T-connector.

Experimental Ethernet installations have used pressure taps where the tap and tap-block are separate, as illustrated in Figure 2. Installations conforming to the Ethernet Specification have used all the options. Figure 3 illustrates a connectorized transceiver and a pressure tap with separate tap and tap-block.

Transceiver. The transceiver couples the station to the cable and is the most important part of the transmission system.

The controller-to-transmission-system interface is very simple, and functionally it has not changed between the two Ethernet designs. It performs four functions: (1) transferring transmit data from the controller to the transmission system, (2) transferring receive data from the transmission system to the controller, (3) indicating to the controller that a collision is taking place, and (4) providing power to the transmission system.

It is important that the two ground references in the system—the common coaxial cable shield and the local ground associated with each station—not be tied together, since one local ground typically may differ from another local ground by several volts. Connection of several local grounds to the common cable could cause a large current to flow through the cable's shield, introducing noise and creating a potential safety hazard. For this reason, the cable shield should be grounded in only one place.

It is the transceiver that provides this ground isolation between signals from the controller and signals on the cable. Several isolation techniques are possible: transformer isolation, optical isolation, and capacitive isolation. Transformer isolation provides both power and signal isolation; it has low differential impedance for signals and power, and a high common-mode impedance for isolation. It is also relatively inexpensive to implement. Optical isolators that preserve tight signal symmetry at a competitive price are not readily available. Capacitive coupling is inexpensive and preserves signal symmetry but has poor common-mode rejection. For these reasons transformer isolation is used in Ethernet Specification transceivers. In addition, the mechanical design and installation of the transceiver must preserve this isolation. For example, cable shield connections should not come in contact with a building ground (e.g., a cable tray, conduit, or ceiling hanger).

The transceiver provides a high-impedance connection to the cable in both the power-on and power-off states. In addition, it should protect the network from possible internal circuit failures that could cause it to disrupt the network as a whole. It is also important for the transceiver to withstand transient voltages on the coax between the center conductor and shield. While such voltages should not occur if the coax shield is grounded in only one place, such isolation may not exist during installation.[1]

Negative transmit levels were selected for the Ethernet Specification to permit use of fast and more easily integrated NPN transistors for the output current source. A current source output was chosen over the voltage source used in the Experimental Ethernet to facilitate collision detection.

The key factor affecting the maximum number of transceivers on a segment in the Ethernet Specification is the input bias current for the transceivers. With easily achievable bias currents and collision threshold tolerances, the maximum number was conservatively set at 100 per segment. If the only factors taken into consideration were signal attenuation and reflections, then the number would have been larger.

Controller design

The transmitter and receiver sections of the controller perform signal conversion, encoding and decoding, serial-to-parallel conversion, address recognition, error detection, CSMA/CD channel management, buffering, and packetization. Postponing for now a discussion of buffering and packetization, we will first deal with the various functions that the controller needs to perform and then show how they are coordinated into an effective CSMA/CD channel management policy.

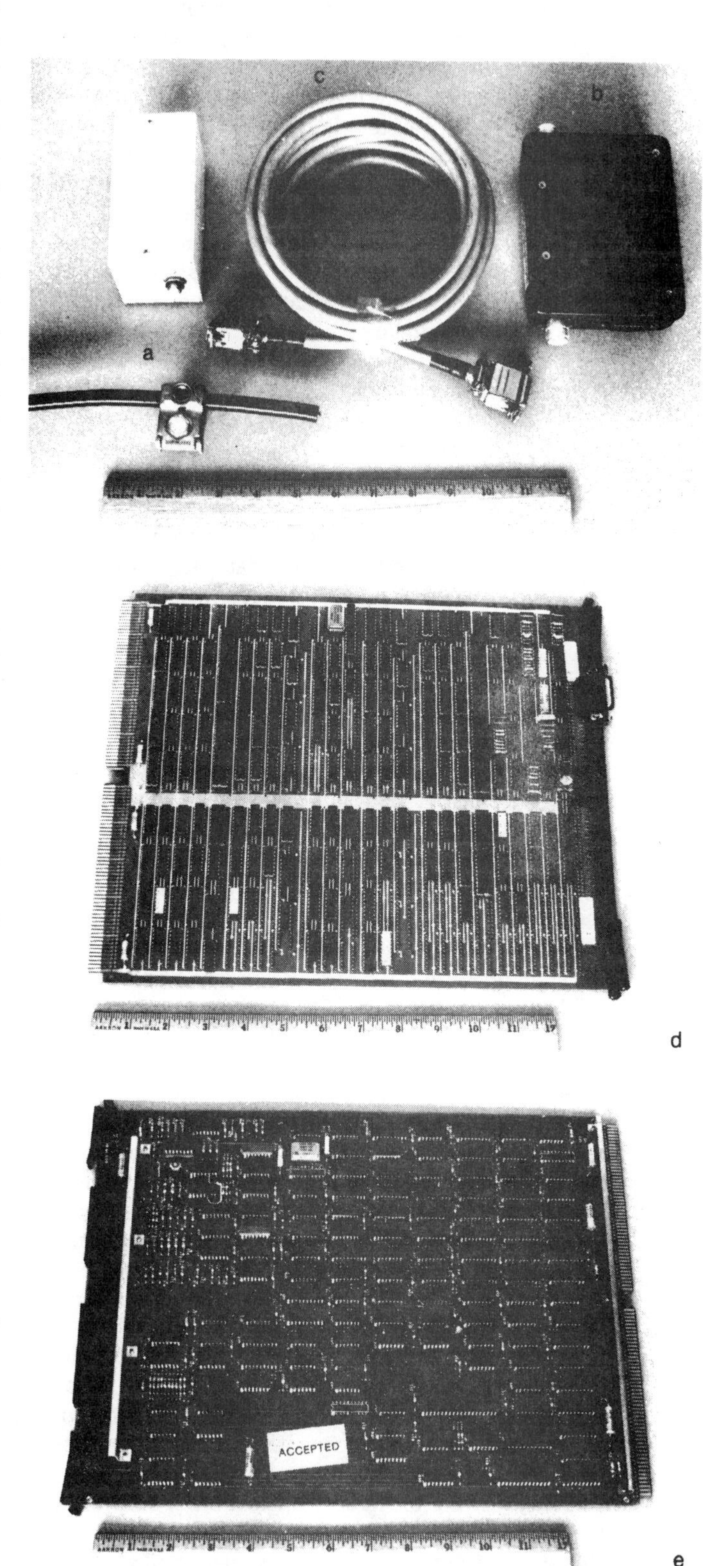

Figure 3. Ethernet Specification components: (a) transceiver, tap, and tap-block, (b) connectorized transceiver, (c) transceiver cable, (d) Dolphin controller board, and (e) Xerox 8000 controller board.

Signaling, data rate, and framing. The transmitter generates the serial bit stream inserted into the transmission system. Clock and data are combined into one signal using a suitable encoding scheme. Because of its simplicity, Manchester encoding was used in the Experimental Ethernet. In Manchester encoding, each bit cell has two parts: the first half of the cell is the complement of the bit value and the second half *is* the bit value. Thus, there is always a transition in the middle of every bit cell, and this is used by the receiver to extract the data.

For the Ethernet Specification, MFM encoding (used in double-density disk recording) was considered, but it was rejected because decoding was more sensitive to phase distortions from the transmission system and required more components to implement. Compensation is not as easy as in the disk situation because a station must receive signals from both nearby and distant stations. Thus, Manchester encoding is retained in the Ethernet Specification.

In the Experimental Ethernet, any data rate in the range of 1M to 5M bps might have been chosen. The particular rate of 2.94M bps was convenient for working with the first Altos. For the Ethernet Specification, we wanted a data rate as high as possible; very high data rates, however, limit the effective length of the system and require more precise electronics. The data rate of 10M bps represents a trade-off among these considerations.

Packet framing on the Ethernet is simple. The presence of a packet is indicated by the presence of carrier, or transitions. In addition, all packets begin with a known pattern of bits called the *preamble*. This is used by the receiver to establish bit synchronization and then to locate the first bit of the packet. The preamble is inserted by the controller at the sending station and stripped off by the controller at the receiving station. Packets may be of variable length, and absence of carrier marks the end of a packet. Hence, there is no need to have framing flags and "bit stuffing" in the packet as in other data-link protocols such as SDLC or HDLC.

The Experimental Ethernet used a one-bit preamble. While this worked very well, we have, on rare occasions, seen some receivers that could not synchronize with this very short preamble.[18] The Ethernet Specification uses a 64-bit preamble to ensure synchronization of phase-lock loop receivers often used at the higher data rate. It is necessary to specify 64 bits to allow for (1) worst-case tolerances on phase-lock loop components, (2) maximum times to reach steady-state conditions through transceivers, and (3) loss of preamble bits owing to squelch on input and output within the transceivers. Note that the presence of repeaters can add up to four extra transceivers between a source and destination.

Additional conventions can be imposed upon the frame structure. Requiring that all packets be a multiple of some particular byte or word size simplifies controller design and provides an additional consistency check. All packets on the Experimental Ethernet are viewed as a sequence of 16-bit words with the most significant bit of each word transmitted first. The Ethernet Specification requires all packets to be an integral number of eight-bit bytes (exclusive of the preamble, of course) with the least significant bit of each byte transmitted first. The order in which the bytes of an Ethernet packet are stored in the memory of a particular station is part of the controller-to-station interface.

Encoding and decoding. The transmitter is responsible for taking a serial bit stream from the station and encoding it into the Manchester format. The receiver is responsible for decoding an incoming signal and converting it into a serial bit stream for the station. The process of encoding is fairly straightforward, but decoding is more difficult and is realized in a *phase decoder.* The known preamble pattern can be used to help initialize the phase decoder, which can employ any of several techniques including an analog timing circuit, a phase-locked loop, or a digital phase decoder (which rapidly samples the input and performs a pattern match). The particular decoding technique selected can be a function of the data rate, since some decoder designs may not run as fast as others. Some phase decoding techniques—particularly the digital one—have the added advantage of being able to recognize certain phase violations as collisions on the transmission medium. This is one way to implement collision detection, although it does not work with all transmission systems.

During transmission a controller must recognize that another station is also transmitting.

The phase decoders used by stations on the Experimental Ethernet included an analog timing circuit in the form of a delay line on the PDP-11, an analog timing circuit in the form of a simple one-shot-based timer on the Alto, and a digital decoder on the Dorado. All stations built by Xerox for the Ethernet Specification use phase-locked loops.

Carrier sense. Recognizing packets passing by is one of the important requirements of the Ethernet access procedure. Although transmission is baseband, we have borrowed the term "sensing carrier" from radio terminology to describe the detection of signals on the channel. Carrier sense is used for two purposes: (1) in the receiver to delimit the beginning and end of the packet, and (2) in the transmitter to tell when it is permissible to send. With the use of Manchester phase encoding, carrier is conveniently indicated by the presence of transitions on the channel. Thus, the basic phase decoding mechanism can produce a signal indicating the presence of carrier independent of the data being extracted. The Ethernet Specification requires a slightly subtle carrier sense technique owing to the possibility of a saturated collision.

Collision detection. The ability to detect collisions and shut down the transmitter promptly is an important feature in minimizing the channel time lost to collisions. The general requirement is that during transmission a controller must recognize that another station is also transmitting. There are two approaches:

(1) *Collision detection in the transmission system.* It is usually possible for the transmission system itself to recognize a collision. This allows any medium-dependent technique to be used and is usually implemented by comparing the injected signal with the received signal. Comparing the transmitted and received signals is best done in the transceiver where there is a known relationship between the two signals. It is the controller, however, which needs to know that a collision is taking place.

(2) *Collision detection in the controller.* Alternatively, the controller itself can recognize a collision by comparing the transmitted signal with the received signal, or the receiver section can attempt to unilaterally recognize collisions, since they often appear as phase violations.

Both generations of Ethernet detect collisions within the transceiver and generate the collision signal in the controller-to-transmission-system interface. Where feasible, this can be supplemented with a collision detection facility in the controller. Collision detection may not be absolutely foolproof. Some transmission schemes can recognize all collisions, but other combinations of transmission scheme and collision detection may not provide 100-percent recognition. For example, the Experimental Ethernet system functions, in principle, as a wired OR. It is remotely possible for one station to transmit while another station sends a packet whose waveform, at the first station, exactly matches the signal sent by the first station; thus, no collision is recognized there. Unfortunately, the intended recipient might be located between the two stations, and the two signals would indeed interfere.

There is another possible scenario in which collision detection breaks down. One station begins transmitting and its signal propagates down the channel. Another station still senses the channel idle, begins to transmit, gets out a bit or two, and then detects a collision. If the colliding station shuts down immediately, it leaves a very small collision moving through the channel. In some approaches (e.g., DC threshold collision detection) this may be attenuated and simply not make it back to the transmitting station to trigger its collision detection circuitry.

The probability of such occurrences is small. Actual measurements in the Experimental Ethernet system indicate that the collision detection mechanism works very well. Yet it is important to remember that an Ethernet system delivers packets only with high probability—not certainty.

To help ensure proper detection of collisions, each transmitter adopts a *collision consensus enforcement* procedure. This makes sure that all other parties to the collision will recognize that a collision has taken place. In spite of its lengthy name, this is a simple procedure. After detecting a collision, a controller transmits a *jam* that every operating transmitter should detect as a collision. In the Experimental Ethernet the jam is a phase violation, while in the Ethernet Specification it is the transmission of four to six bytes of random data.

Another possible collision scenario arises in the context of the Ethernet Specification. It is possible for a collision to involve so many participants that a transceiver is incapable of injecting any more current into the cable. During such a collision, one cannot guarantee that the waveform on the cable will exhibit any transitions. (In the extreme case, it simply sits at a constant DC level equal to the saturation voltage.) This is called a *saturated collision.* In this situation, the simple notion of sensing carrier by detecting transitions would not work anymore. In particular, a station that deferred only when seeing transitions would think the Ether was idle and jump right in, becoming another participant in the collision. Of course, it would immediately detect the collision and back off, but in the extreme case (everyone wanting to transmit), such jumping-in could theoretically cause the saturated collision to snowball and go on for a very long time. While we recognized that this form of instability was highly unlikely to occur in practice, we included a simple enhancement to the carrier sense mechanism in the Ethernet Specification to prevent the problem.

We have focused on collision detection by the transmitter of a packet and have seen that the transmitter may depend on a collision detect signal generated unilaterally by its receiving phase decoder. Can this receiver-based collision detection be used just by a receiver (that is, a station that is not trying to transmit)? A receiver with this capability could immediately abort an input operation and could even generate a jam signal to help ensure that the collision came to a prompt termination. With a reasonable transmitter-based collision detection scheme, however, the collision is recognized by the transmitters and the damaged packet would come to an end very shortly. Receiver-based collision detection could provide an early warning of a collision for use by the receiver, but this is not a necessary function and we have not used it in either generation of Ethernet design.

CRC generation and checking. The transmitter generates a cyclic redundancy check, or CRC, of each transmitted packet and appends it to a packet before transmission. The receiver checks the CRC on packets it receives and strips it off before giving the packet to the station. If the CRC is incorrect, there are two options: either discard the packet or deliver the damaged packet with an appropriate status indicating a CRC error.

While most CRC algorithms are quite good, they are not infallible. There is a small probability that undetected errors may slip through. More importantly, the CRC only protects a packet from the point at which the CRC is generated to the point at which it is checked. Thus, the CRC cannot protect a packet from damage that occurs in parts of the controller, as, for example, in a FIFO in the parallel path to the memory of a station (the DMA), or in the memory itself. If error detection at a higher level is required, then an end-to-end software checksum can be added to the protocol architecture.

In measuring the Experimental Ethernet system, we have seen packets whose CRC was reported as correct but whose software checksum was incorrect.[18] These did not necessarily represent an undetected Ethernet error; they usually resulted from an external malfunction such as a broken interface, a bad CRC checker, or even an incorrect software checksum algorithm.

Selection of the CRC algorithm is guided by several concerns. It should have sufficient strength to properly detect virtually all packet errors. Unfortunately, only a limited set of CRC algorithms are currently implemented in LSI chips. The Experimental Ethernet used a 16-bit CRC, taking advantage of a single-chip CRC generator/checker. The Ethernet Specification provides better error detection by using a 32-bit CRC.[19,20] This function will be easily implemented in an Ethernet chip.

Addressing. The packet format includes both a source and destination address. A local network design can adopt either of two basic addressing structures: *network-specific* station addresses or *unique* station addresses.[21] In the first case, stations are assigned network addresses that must be unique on *their* network but may be the same as the address held by a station on another network. Such addresses are sometimes called *network relative* addresses, since they depend upon the particular network to which the station is attached. In the second case, each station is assigned an address that is unique over all space and time. Such addresses are also known as absolute or universal addresses, drawn from a flat address space.

To permit internetwork communication, the network-specific address of a station must usually be combined with a unique network number in order to produce an unambiguous address at the next level of protocol. On the other hand, there is no need to combine an absolute station address with a unique network number to produce an unambiguous address. However, it is possible that internetwork systems based on flat (internetwork and local network) absolute addresses will include a unique network number at the internetwork layer as a "very strong hint" for the routing machinery.

If network-specific addressing is adopted, Ethernet address fields need only be large enough to accommodate the maximum number of stations that will be connected to one local network. In addition, there must be a suitable administrative procedure for assigning addresses to stations. Some installations will have more than one Ethernet, and if a station is moved from one network to another it may be necessary to change its network-specific address, since its former address may be in use on the new network. This was the approach used on the Experimental Ethernet, with an eight-bit field for the source and the destination addresses.

We anticipate that there will be a large number of stations and many local networks in an internetwork. Thus, the management of network-specific station addresses can represent a severe problem. The use of a flat address space provides for reliable and manageable operation as a system grows, as machines move, and as the overall topology changes. A flat internet address space requires that the address space be large enough to ensure uniqueness while providing adequate room for growth. It is most convenient if the local network can directly support these fairly large address fields.

For these reasons the Ethernet Specification uses 48-bit addresses.[22] Note that these are station addresses and are not associated with a particular network interface or controller. In particular, we believe that higher level routing and addressing procedures are simplified if a station connected to multiple networks has only one identity which is unique over all networks. The address should not be hard-wired into a particular interface or controller but should be able to be set from the station. It may be very useful, however, to allow a station to read a unique station identifier from the controller. The station can then choose whether to return this identifier to the controller as its address.

In addition to single-station addressing, several enhanced addressing modes are also desirable. *Multicast* addressing is a mechanism by which packets may be targeted to more than one destination. This kind of service is particularly valuable in certain kinds of distributed applications, for instance the access and update of distributed data bases, teleconferencing, and the distributed algorithms that are used to manage the network and the internetwork. We believe that multicast should be supported by allowing the destination address to specify either a physical or logical address. A logical address is known as a *multicast ID. Broadcast* is a special case of multicast in which a packet is intended for all active stations. Both generations of Ethernet support broadcast, while only the Ethernet Specification directly supports multicast.

Stations supporting multicast must recognize multicast IDs of interest. Because of the anticipated growth in the use of multicast service, serious consideration should be given to aspects of the station and controller design that reduce the system load required to filter unwanted multicast packets. Broadcast should be used with discretion, since all nodes incur the overhead of processing every broadcast packet.

Controllers capable of accepting packets regardless of destination address provide *promiscuous* address recognition. On such stations one can develop software to observe all of the channel's traffic, construct traffic matrices, perform load analysis, (potentially) perform fault isolation, and debug protocol implementations. While such a station is able to read packets not addressed to it, we expect that sensitive data will be encrypted by higher levels of software.

CSMA/CD channel management

A major portion of the controller is devoted to Ethernet channel management. These conventions specify procedures by which packets are transmitted and received on the multi-access channel.

Transmitter. The transmitter is invoked when the station has a packet to send. If a collision occurs, the controller enforces the collision with a suitable jam, shuts down the transmitter, and schedules a retransmission.

Retransmission policies have two conflicting goals: (1) scheduling a retransmission quickly to get the packet out and maintain use of the channel, and (2) voluntarily backing off to reduce the station's load on a busy channel. Both generations of Ethernet use the *binary exponential back-off algorithm* described below. After some maximum number of collisions the transmitter gives up and reports a suitable error back to the station; both generations of Ethernet give up after 15 collisions.

The binary exponential back-off algorithm is used to calculate the delay before retransmission. After a collision takes place the objective is to obtain delay periods that will reschedule each station at times quantized in steps at least as large as a collision interval. This time quantization is called the *retransmission slot time.* To guarantee quick use of the channel, this slot time should be short; yet to avoid collisions it should be larger than a collision interval. Therefore, the slot time is usually set to be a little longer than the round-trip time of the channel. The real-time delay is the product of some retransmission delay (a positive integer) and the retransmission slot time.

Collisions on the channel can produce collision fragments, which can be eliminated with a fragment filter in the controller.

To minimize the probability of repeated collisions, each retransmission delay is selected as a random number from a particular retransmission interval between zero and some upper limit. In order to control the channel and keep it stable under high load, the interval is doubled with each successive collision, thus extending the range of possible retransmission delays. This algorithm has very short retransmission delays at the beginning but will back off quickly, preventing the channel from becoming overloaded. After some number of back-offs, the retransmission interval becomes large. To avoid undue delays and slow response to improved channel characteristics, the doubling can be stopped at some point, with additional retransmissions still being drawn from this interval, before the transmission is finally aborted. This is referred to as *truncated binary exponential back-off.*

The truncated binary exponential back-off algorithm approximates the ideal algorithm where the probability of transmission of a packet is 1/Q, with Q representing the number of stations attempting to transmit.[23] The retransmission interval is truncated when Q becomes equal to the maximum number of stations.

In the Experimental Ethernet, the very first transmission attempt proceeds with no delay (i.e., the retransmission interval is [0-0]). The retransmission interval is doubled after each of the first eight transmission attempts. Thus, the retransmission delays should be uniformly distributed between 0 and $2^{\min(\text{retransmission attempt},\ 8)} - 1$. After the first transmission attempt, the next eight intervals will be [0-1], [0-3], [0-7], [0-15], [0-31], [0-63], [0-127], and [0-255]. The retransmission interval remains at [0-255] on any subsequent attempt, as the maximum number of stations is 256. The Ethernet Specification has the same algorithm with ten intervals, since the network permits up to 1024 stations; the maximum interval is therefore [0-1023]. The back-off algorithm restarts with a zero retransmission interval for the transmission of every new packet.

This particular algorithm was chosen because it has the proper basic behavior and because it allows a very simple implementation. The algorithm is now supported by empirical data verifying the stability of the system under heavy load.[12,13] Additional attempts to explore more sophisticated algorithms resulted in negligible performance improvement.

Receiver. The receiver section of the controller is activated when the carrier appears on the channel. The receiver processes the incoming bit stream in the following manner:

The remaining preamble is first removed. If the bit stream ends before the preamble completes, it is assumed to be the result of a short collision, and the receiver is restarted.

The receiver next determines whether the packet is addressed to it. The controller will accept a packet in any of the following circumstances:

(1) The destination address matches the specific address of the station.
(2) The destination address has the distinguished broadcast destination.
(3) The destination address is a multicast group of which the station is a member.
(4) The station has set the controller in promiscuous mode and receives all packets.

Some controller designs might choose to receive the entire packet before invoking the address recognition procedure. This is feasible but consumes both memory and processing resources in the controller. More typically, address recognition takes place at a fairly low level in the controller, and if the packet is not to be accepted the controller can ignore the rest of it.

Assuming that the address is recognized, the receiver now accepts the entire packet. Before the packet is actually delivered to the station, the CRC is verified and other consistency checks are performed. For example, the packet should end on an appropriate byte or word boundary and be of appropriate minimum length; a minimum packet would have to include at least a destination and source address, a packet type, and a CRC. Collisions on the channel, however, can produce short, damaged packets called collision fragments. It is generally unnecessary to report these errors to the station, since they can be eliminated with a fragment filter in the controller. It is important, however, for the receiver to be restarted promptly after a collision fragment is received, since the sender of the packet may be about to retransmit.

Packet length. One important goal of the Ethernet is data transparency. In principle, this means that the data field of a packet can contain any bit pattern and be of any length, from zero to arbitrarily large. In practice, while it is easy to allow any bit pattern to appear in the data field, there are some practical considerations that suggest imposing upper and lower bounds on its length.

At one extreme, an empty packet (one with a zero-length data field) would consist of just a preamble, source and destination addresses, a type field, and a CRC. The Experimental Ethernet permitted empty packets. However, in some situations it is desirable to enforce a minimum overall packet size by mandating a minimum-length data field, as in the Ethernet Specification. Higher level protocols wishing to transmit shorter packets must then pad out the data field to reach the minimum.

At the other extreme, one could imagine sending many thousands or even millions of bytes in a single packet. There are, however, several factors that tend to limit packet size, including (1) the desire to limit the size of the buffers in the station for sending and receiving packets, (2) similar considerations concerning the packet buffers that are sometimes built into the Ethernet controller itself, and (3) the need to avoid tying up the channel and increasing average channel latency for other stations. Buffer management tends to be the dominant consideration. The maximum requirement for buffers in the station is usually a parameter of higher level software determined by the overall network architecture; it is typically on the order of 500 to 2000 bytes. The size of any packet buffers in the controller, on the other hand, is usually a design parameter of the controller hardware and thus represents a more rigid limitation. To insure compatibility among buffered controllers, the Ethernet Specification mandates a maximum packet length of 1526 bytes (1500 data bytes plus overhead).

Note that the upper and lower bounds on packet length are of more than passing interest, since observed distributions are typically quite bimodal. Packets tend to be either very short (control packets or packets carrying a small amount of data) or maximum length (usually some form of bulk data transfer).[12,13]

The efficiency of an Ethernet system is largely dependent on the size of the packets being sent and can be very high when large packets are used. Measurements have shown total utilization as high as 98 percent. A small quantum of channel capacity is lost whenever there is a collision, but the carrier sense and collision detection mechanisms combine to minimize this loss. Carrier sense reduces the likelihood of a collision, since the acquisition effect renders a given transmission immune to collisions once it has continued for longer than a collision interval. Collision detection limits the duration of a collision to a single collision interval. If packets are long compared with the collision interval, then the network is vulnerable to collisions only a small fraction of the time and total utilization will remain high. If the average packet size is reduced, however, both carrier sense and collision detection become less effective. Ultimately, as the packet size approaches the collision interval, system performance degrades to that of a straight CSMA channel without collision detection. This condition only occurs under a heavy load consisting predominantly of very small packets; with a typical mix of applications this is not a practical problem.

If the packet size is reduced still further until it is less than the collision interval, some new problems appear. Of course, if an empty packet is already longer than the collision interval, as in the Experimental Ethernet, this case cannot arise. As the channel length and/or the data rate are increased, however, the length (in bits) of the collision interval also increases. When it becomes larger than an empty packet, one must decide whether stations are allowed to send tiny packets that are smaller than the collision interval. If so, two more problems arise, one affecting the transmitter and one the receiver.

The transmitter's problem is that it can complete the entire transmission of a tiny packet before network acquisition has occurred. If the packet subsequently experiences a collision farther down the channel, it is too late for the transmitter to detect the collision and promptly schedule a retransmission. In this situation, the probability of a collision has not increased, nor has any additional channel capacity been sacrificed; the problem is simply that the transmitter will occasionally fail to recognize and handle a collision. To deal with such failures, the sender of tiny packets must rely on retransmissions invoked by a higher level protocol and thus suffer reduced throughput and increased delay. This occasional performance reduction is generally not a serious problem, however. Note that only the sender of tiny packets encounters this behavior; there is no unusual impact on other stations sending larger packets.

While occasional collisions should be viewed as a normal part of the CSMA/CD access procedure, line errors should not. One would therefore like to accumulate information about the two classes of events separately.

The receiver's problem with tiny packets concerns its ability to recognize collision fragments by their small size and discard them. If the receiver can assume that packets smaller than the collision interval are collision fragments, it can use this to implement a simple and inexpensive fragment filter. It is important for the receiver to discard collision fragments, both to reduce the processing load at the station and to ensure that it is ready to receive the impending retransmission from the transmitter involved in the collision. The fragment filter approach is automatically valid in a network in which there are no tiny packets, such as the Experimental Ethernet. If tiny packets can occur, however, the receiver cannot reliably distinguish them from collision fragments purely on the basis of size. This means that at least the longer collision fragments must be rejected on the basis of some other error detection mechanism such as the CRC check or a byte or word alignment check. One disadvantage of this approach is that it increases the load on the CRC mechanism, which, while strong, is not infallible. Another problem is that the CRC error condition will now be indicating two kinds of faults: long collisions and genuine line errors. While occasional collisions should be viewed as a normal part of the CSMA/CD access procedure, line errors should not. One would therefore like to accumulate information about the two classes of events separately.

The problems caused by tiny packets are not insurmountable, but they do increase the attractiveness of simply legislating the problem out of existence by forbidding the sending of packets smaller than the collision interval. Thus, in a network whose collision interval is longer than an empty packet, the alternatives are

(1) *Allow tiny packets.* In this case, the transmitter will sometimes fail to detect collisions, requiring retransmis-

sion at a higher level and impacting performance. The receiver can use a partial fragment filter to discard collision fragments shorter than an empty packet, but longer collision fragments will make it through this filter and must be rejected on the basis of other error checks, such as the CRC check, with the resultant jumbling of the error statistics.

(2) *Forbid tiny packets.* In this case, the transmitter can always detect a collision and perform prompt retransmission. The receiver can use a fragment filter to automatically discard all packets shorter than the collision interval. The disadvantage is the imposition of a minimum packet size.

Unlike the Experimental Ethernet, the Ethernet Specification defines a collision interval longer than an empty packet and must therefore choose between these alternatives. The choice is to forbid tiny packets by requiring a minimum data field size of 46 bytes. Since we expect that Ethernet packets will typically contain internetwork packet headers and other overhead, this is not viewed as a significant disadvantage.

Controller-to-station interface design

The properties of the controller-to-station interface can dramatically affect the reliability and efficiency of systems based on Ethernet.

Turning the controller on and off. A well-designed controller must be able to (1) keep the receiver on in order to catch back-to-back packets (those separated by some minimum packet spacing), and (2) receive packets a station transmits to itself. We will now look in detail at these requirements and the techniques for satisfying them.

Keeping the receiver on. The most frequent cause of a lost packet has nothing to do with collision or bad CRCs. Packets are usually missed simply because the receiver was not listening. The Ethernet is an asynchronous device that can present a packet at any time, and it is important that higher level software keep the receiver enabled.

The problem is even more subtle, however, for even when operating normally there can be periods during which the receiver is not listening. There may, for instance, be turnaround times between certain operations when the receiver is left turned off. For example, a receive-to-receive turnaround takes place after one packet is received and before the receiver is again enabled. If the design of the interface, controller, or station software keeps the receiver off for too long, arriving packets can be lost during this turnaround. This occurs most frequently in servers on a network, which may be receiving packets from several sources in rapid succession. If back-to-back packets come down the wire, the second one will be lost in the receive-to-receive turnaround time. The same problem can occur within a normal workstation, for example, if a desired packet immediately follows a broadcast packet; the workstation gets the broadcast but misses the packet specifically addressed to it. Higher level protocol software will presumably recover from these situations, but the performance penalty may be severe.

Similarly, there may be a transmit-to-receive turnaround time when the receiver is deaf. This is determined by how long it takes to enable the receiver after sending a packet. If, for example, a workstation with a slow transmit-to-receive turnaround sends a packet to a well-tuned server, the answer may come back before the receiver is enabled again. No amount of retransmission by higher levels will ever solve this problem!

It is important to minimize the length of any turnaround times when the receiver might be off. There can also be receive-to-transmit and transmit-to-transmit turnaround times, but their impact on performance is not as critical.

Sending to itself. A good diagnostic tool for a network interface is the ability of a station to send packets to itself. While an internal loop-back in the controller provides a partial test, actual transmission and simultaneous reception provide more complete verification.

The Ethernet channel is, in some sense, half duplex: there is normally only one station transmitting at a time. There is a temptation, therefore, to also make the controller half duplex—that is, unable to send and receive at the same time. If possible, however, the design of the interface, controller, and station software should allow a station to send packets to itself.

Recommendations. The Ethernet Specification includes one specific requirement that helps to solve the first of these problems: There must be a minimal interpacket spacing on the cable of 9.6 microseconds. This requirement applies to a transmitter getting ready to send a packet and does not necessarily mean that all receivers conforming to the Specification must receive two adjacent packets. This requirement at least makes it possible to build a controller that can receive adjacent packets on the cable.

Satisfying the two requirements described earlier involves the use of two related features in the design of a controller: full-duplex interfaces and back-to-back receivers. A full-duplex interface allows the receiver and the transmitter to be started independently. A back-to-back receiver has facilities to automatically restart the receiver upon completion of a reception. Limited back-to-back reception can be done with two buffers; the first catches a packet and then the second catches the next without requiring the receiver to wait. Generalized back-to-back reception can be accomplished by using chained I/O commands; the receiver is driven by a list of free input buffers, taking one when needed. These two notions can be combined to build any of the following four interfaces: (1) half-duplex interface, (2) full-duplex interface, (3) half-duplex interface with back-to-back receive, and (4) full-duplex interface with back-to-back receive.

The Experimental Ethernet controller for the Alto is half duplex, runs only in a transmit or receive mode, and must be explicitly started in each mode. The need to explicitly start the receiver (there is no automatic hardware turnaround) means that there may be lengthy turnaround times in which packets may be missed. This approach allows sharing certain components, like the CRC function and the FIFO.

Experimental Ethernet controllers built for the PDP-11 and the Nova are full-duplex interfaces. The transmit-to-receive turnaround has been minimized, but there is no provision for back-to-back packets.

The Ethernet controller for the Xerox 8000 processor is a half-duplex interface with back-to-back receive. Although it cannot send to itself, the transmit-to-receive turnaround delay has been avoided by having the hardware automatically revert to the receive state when a transmission is completed.

The Experimental Ethernet and Ethernet Specification controllers for the Dolphin are full-duplex interfaces with back-to-back receivers. They are the ultimate in interface organization.

Our experience shows that any one of the four alternatives will work. However, we strongly recommend that all interface and controller designs support full-duplex operation and provide for reception of back-to-back packets (chained I/O).

The controller-to-station interface defines the manner in which data received from the cable is stored in memory and, conversely, how data stored in memory is transmitted on the cable.

Buffering. Depending upon the particular data rate of the channel and the characteristics of the station, the controller may have to provide suitable buffering of packets. If the station can keep up with the data rate of the channel, only a small FIFO may be needed to deal with station latency. If the station cannot sustain the channel data rate, it may be necessary to include a full-packet buffer as part of the controller. For this reason, full compatibility across different stations necessitates the specification of a maximum packet length.

If a single-packet buffer is provided in the controller (a buffer that has no marker mechanism to distinguish boundaries between packets), it will generally be impossible to catch back-to-back packets, and in such cases it is preferable to have at least two input buffers.

Packets in memory. The controller-to-station interface defines the manner in which data received from the cable is stored in memory and, conversely, how data stored in memory is transmitted on the cable. There are many ways in which this parallel-to-serial transformation can be defined.[24] The Ethernet Specification defines a packet on the cable to be a sequence of eight-bit bytes, with the least significant bit of each byte transmitted first. Higher level protocols will in most cases, however, define data types that are multiples of eight bits. The parallel-to-serial transformations will be influenced by the programming conventions of the station and by the higher level protocols. Stations with different parallel-to-serial transformations that use the same higher level protocol must make sure that all data types are viewed consistently.

Type field. An Ethernet packet can encapsulate many kinds of client-defined packets. Thus, the packet format includes only a data field, two addresses, and a type field. The type field identifies the special client-level protocol that will interpret the data encapsulated within the packet. The type field is never processed by the Ethernet system itself but can be thought of as an escape, providing a consistent way to specify the interpretation of the rest of the packet.

Low-level system services such as diagnostics, bootstrap, loading, or specialized network management functions can take advantage of the identification provided by this field. In fact, it is possible to use the type field to identify all the different packets in a protocol architecture. In general, however, we recommend that the Ethernet packet encapsulate higher level internetwork packets. Internetwork router stations might concurrently support a number of different internetwork protocols, and the use of the type field allows the internetwork router to encapsulate different kinds of internetwork packets for a local network transmission.[25] The use of a type field in the Ethernet packet is an instance of a principle we apply to all layers in a protocol architecture. A type field is used at each level of the hierarchy to identify the protocol used at the next higher level; it is the bridge between adjacent levels. This results in an architecture that defines a layered tree of protocols.

The Experimental Ethernet design uses a 16-bit type field. This has proved to be a very useful feature and has been carried over into the Ethernet Specification.

Summary and conclusions

We have highlighted a number of important considerations that affect the design of an Ethernet local computer network and have traced the evolution of the system from a research prototype to a multicompany standard by discussing strategies and trade-offs between alternative implementations.

The Ethernet is intended primarily for use in such areas as office automation, distributed data processing, terminal access, and other situations requiring economical connection to a local communication medium carrying bursts of traffic at high peak data rates. Experience with the Experimental Ethernet in building distributed systems that support electronic mail, distributed filing, calendar systems, and other applications has confirmed many of our design goals and decisions.[26-29]

Questions sometimes arise concerning the ways in which the Ethernet design addresses (or chooses not to address) the following considerations: reliability, addressing, priority, encryption, and compatibility. It is important to note that some functions are better left out of the Ethernet itself for implementation at higher levels in the architecture.

All systems should be reliable, and network-based systems are no exception. We believe that reliability must be addessed at each level in the protocol hierarchy; each level should provide only what it can guarantee at a reasonable price. Our model for internetworking is one in which reliability and sequencing are performed using end-to-end transport protocols. Thus, the Ethernet provides a "best effort" datagram service. The Ethernet has been designed to have very good error characteristics, and, without promising to deliver all packets, it will deliver a very large percentage of offered packets without error. It includes error detection procedures but provides no error correction.

We expect internetworks to be very large. Many of the problems in managing them can be simplified by using absolute station addresses that are directly supported within the local network. Thus, address fields in the Ethernet Specification seem to be very generous—well beyond the number of stations that might connect to one local network but meant to efficiently support large internetwork systems.

Our experience indicates that for practically all applications falling into the category "loosely coupled distributed system," the average utilization of the communications network is low. The Ethernet has been designed to have excess bandwidth, not all of which must be utilized. Systems should be engineered to run with a sustained load of no more than 50 percent. As a consequence, the network will generally provide high throughput of data with low delay, and there are no priority levels associated with particular packets. Designers of individual devices, network servers, and higher level protocols are free to develop priority schemes for accessing particular resources.

Protection, security, and access control are all system-wide functions that require a comprehensive strategy. The Ethernet system itself is not designed to provide encryption or other mechanisms for security, since these techniques by themselves do not provide the kind of protection most users require. Security in the form of encryption, where required, is the responsibility of the end-user processes.

Higher level protocols raise their own issues of compatibility over and above those addressed by the Ethernet and other link-level facilities. While the compatibility provided by the Ethernet does not guarantee solutions to higher level compatibility problems, it does provide a context within which such problems can be addressed by avoiding low-level incompatibilities that would make direct communication impossible. We expect to see standards for higher level protocols emerge during the next few years.

Within an overall distributed systems architecture, the two generations of Ethernet systems have proven to be very effective local computer networks.■

Acknowledgments

Many people have contributed to the success and evolution of the Ethernet local computer network. Bob Metcalfe and David Boggs built the Experimental Ethernet at the Xerox Palo Alto Research Center, and Tat Lam built and supplied the many transceivers. Since then, Ed Taft, Hal Murray, Will Crowther, Roy Ogus, Bob Garner, Ed Markowski, Bob Printis, Bob Belleville, Bill Gunning, and Juan Bulnes have contributed to the design and implementation of the Ethernet. Cooperation among Digital Equipment Corporation, Intel, and Xerox also produced many important contributions to the Ethernet Specification.

References

1. R. C. Crane and E. A. Taft, "Practical Considerations in Ethernet Local Network Design," *Proc. 13th Hawaii Int'l Conf. Systems Sciences,* Jan. 1980, pp. 166-174.
2. R. M. Metcalfe and D. R. Boggs, "Ethernet: Distributed Packet Switching for Local Computer Networks," *Comm. ACM,* 19:7, July 1976, pp. 395-404.
3. R. M. Metcalfe, D. R. Boggs, C. P. Thacker, and B. W. Lampson, "Multipoint Data Communication System with Collision Detection," US Patent No. 4,063,220, Dec. 13, 1977.
4. J. F. Shoch, *"An Annotated Bibliography on Local Computer Networks"* (3rd ed.), Xerox Parc Technical Report SSL-80-2, and IFIP Working Group 6.4 Working Paper 80-12, Apr. 1980.
5. *The Ethernet, A Local Area Network: Data Link Layer and Physical Layer Specifications,* Version 1.0, Digital Equipment Corporation, Intel, Xerox, Sept. 30, 1980.
6. D. R. Boggs, J. F. Shoch, E. A. Taft, and R. M. Metcalfe, "PUP: An Internetwork Architecture," *IEEE Trans. Comm.,* Apr. 1980, pp. 612-624.
7. H. Zimmermann, "OSI Reference Model—The ISO Model of Architecture for Open Systems Interconnection," *IEEE Trans. Comm.,* Apr. 1980, pp. 425-432.
8. Y. K. Dalal, "The Information Outlet: A New Tool for Office Organization," *Proc. On-line Conf. Local Networks and Distributed Office Systems,* London, May 1981, pp. 11-19.
9. V. G. Cerf and P. K. Kirstein, "Issues in Packet-Network Interconnection," *Proc. IEEE,* Vol. 66, No. 11, Nov. 1978, pp. 1386-1408.
10. F. C. Shoute, "Decentralized Control in Computer Communication," Technical Report No. 667, Division of Engineering and Applied Physics, Harvard University, Apr. 1977.
11. R. M. Metcalfe, "Packet Communication," Thesis Harvard University, Project MAC Report MAC TR-114, Massachusetts Institute of Technology, Dec. 1973.
12. J. F. Shoch and J. A. Hupp, "Performance of an Ethernet Local Network—A Preliminary Report," *Local Area Comm. Network Symp.,* Boston, May 1979, pp. 113-125. Revised version *Proc. Compcon Spring 80,* San Francisco, pp. 318-322.
13. J. F. Shoch and J. A. Hupp, "Measured Performance of an Ethernet Local Network," *Comm. ACM,* Vol. 23, No. 12, Dec. 1980, pp. 711-721.
14. E. G. Rawson and R. M. Metcalfe, "Fibernet: Multimode Optical Fibers for Local Computer Networks," *IEEE Trans. Comm.,* July 1978, pp. 983-990.
15. D. R. Boggs and R. M. Metcalfe, Communications network repeater, US Patent No. 4,099,024, July 4, 1978.
16. C. P. Thacker et al., "Alto: A Personal Computer," Xerox Palo Alto Research Center Technical Report CSL-79-11, Aug. 1979.
17. "The Dorado: A High-Performance Personal Computer," Three Reports, Xerox Palo Alto Research Center, CSL-81-1, Jan. 1981.

18. J. F. Shoch, *Local Computer Networks,* McGraw-Hill, in press.

19. J. L. Hammond, J. E. Brown, and S. S. Liu, "Development of a Transmission Error Model and an Error Control Model," Technical Report RADC-TR-75-138, Rome Air Development Center, 1975.

20. R. Bittel, "On Frame Check Sequence (FCS) Generation and Checking," ANSI working paper X3-S34-77-43, 1977.

21. J. F. Shoch, "Internetwork Naming, Addressing, and Routing," *Proc. Compcon Fall 78,* pp. 430-437.

22. Y. K. Dalal and R. S. Printis, "48-bit Internet and Ethernet Host Numbers," *Proc. Seventh Data Comm. Symp.,* Oct. 1981.

23. R. M. Metcalfe, "Steady-State Analysis of a Slotted and Controlled Aloha System with Blocking," *Proc. Sixth Hawaii Conf. System Sciences,* Jan. 1973. Reprinted in *Sigcom Review,* Jan. 1975.

24. D. Cohen, "On Holy Wars and a Plea for Peace," *Computer,* Vol. 14, No. 10, Oct. 1981, pp. 48-54.

25. J. F. Shoch, D. Cohen, and E. A. Taft, "Mutual Encapsulation of Internetwork Protocols," *Computer Networks,* Vol. 5, No. 4, July 1981, pp. 287-301.

26. A. D. Birrell et al., "Grapevine: An Exercise in Distributed Computing," *Comm. ACM,* Vol. 25, No. 4, Apr. 1982, pp. 260-274.

27. H. Sturgis, J. Mitchell, and J. Israel, "Issues in the Design and Use of a Distributed File System," *ACM Operating Systems Rev.,* Vol. 14, No. 3, July 1980, pp. 55-69.

28. D. K. Gifford, "Violet, an Experimental Decentralized System," Xerox Palo Alto Research Center, CSL-79-12, Sept. 1979.

29. J. F. Shoch and J. A. Hupp, "Notes on the 'Worm' Programs—Some Early Experiences with a Distributed Computation," *Comm. ACM,* Vol. 25, No. 3, Mar. 1982, pp. 172-180.

Yogen K. Dalal is manager of services and architecture for office systems in the Office Products Division of Xerox Corporation. He has been with the company in Palo Alto since 1977. His research interests include local computer networks, internetwork protocols, distributed systems architecture, broadcast protocols, and operating systems. He is a member of the ACM and the IEEE. He received the B. Tech. degree in electrical engineering from the Indian Institute of Technology, Bombay, in 1972, and the MS and PhD degrees in electrical engineering and computer science from Stanford University in 1973 and 1977, respectively.

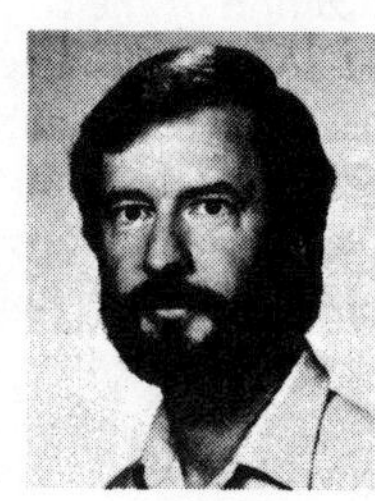

David D. Redell is a staff scientist in the Office Products Division of Xerox Corporation. He was previously on the faculty of the Massachusetts Institute of Technology. His research interests include computer networks, distributed systems, information security, and computer architecture. He received his BA, MS, and PhD degrees in computer science from the University of California at Berkeley.

John F. Shoch is deputy general manager for office systems in the Office Products Division of Xerox Corporation. From 1980 to 1982, he served as assistant to the president of Xerox and director of the corporate policy committee. He joined the research staff at the Xerox Palo Alto Research Center in 1971. His research interests have included local computer networks (such as the Ethernet), internetwork protocols, packet radio, and other aspects of distributed systems. In addition, he has taught at Stanford University, is a member of the ACM and the IEEE, and serves as vice-chairman (US) of IFIP Working Group 6.4 on local computer networks. Shoch received the BA degree in political science and the MS and PhD degrees in computer science from Stanford University.

Ronald C. Crane, a founder of 3Com Corporation in Mountain View, California, now heads advanced engineering for the firm. From 1977 to 1980 he served as a technical staff member and subsequently a consultant to Xerox's Office Products Division in Palo Alto where he was a principal designer of the Digital, Intel, Xerox Ethernet system. His research interests have included adaptive topology packet networks, digital broadcasting systems (Digicast), and baseband transmission systems. He is a member of the ACM and IEEE. He received the BS degree in electrical engineering from the Massachusetts Institute of Technology in 1972 and the MS degree in electrical engineering from Stanford University in 1974.

Mark A. Dineson and J. J. Picazo,
Network Resources Corporation, San Jose, Calif.

Broadband technology magnifies local networking capability

Conventional coaxial cable is yielding to broadband—a medium that offers almost fifty times more capacity and bandwidth

Although baseband coaxial cable has long been used for data transmission, especially in local area networks, broadband cable may well supplant it in large networks of the 1980s. Broadband—historically relegated to television, security video, and audio applications—has advantages in capability, configuration, and compatibility that can no longer be ignored by network planners. It has been a sleeping giant of the data communications world, but it is about to awake.

There is not much physical difference between baseband coaxial cable and broadband (or CATV) cable. The former is a carrier wire surrounded by a woven mesh of copper, while the latter has a sleeve of extruded aluminum instead. The baseband, typically 3/8 inch in diameter, presently sells for about 21 cents per foot. Broadband, only slightly wider, costs about 33 cents. In terms of transmission capacity, however, the differences are significant.

Broadband coaxial local area networks use radio frequency (RF) transmission, and, in contrast with baseband coaxial networks, a single broadband cable can support a transmission rate of almost 150 Mbit/s. One very attractive feature is that this increased capacity (almost 50 times that of conventional baseband coax) can be wholly or partly dedicated to data communications and implemented at a cost comparable to that of baseband coaxial networks.

Why has this technology only recently emerged in the data communications industry? The answer, quite simply, is that the computer world and the cable television industry have evolved in two completely different dimensions, with little or no cross-fertilization, until recently. Spurred by the phenomenal growth of data communications and local area networking in recent years, broadband coaxial local networks have made impressive advances. In response to growing demands for high-capacity, multichannel and megabit-range communications, this technology has been recently rediscovered, and has already been implemented in business, industry, research, and education. Specific applications include automotive plants, steel mills, hospitals, banks, universities, research centers, military bases, government buildings, chemical plants, and oil refineries, to name a few.

In addition to providing a flexible and expandable high-capacity data network, this technology allows for ancillary services such as video and audio telephone. Because of the exceptionally wide bandwidth, the "snake farm" of coax that exists in many local networks today can usually be replaced with a single cable. Modems which provide high-capacity, multilevel communications for all these applications are now commercially available. For data transmission, RF modems can support point-to-point and multipoint links, and also perform as time-division multiplexers, packet network interfaces, and/or intelligent controllers.

Broadband cable has a capacity that is midrange between fiber optics and conventional media. For each coaxial node (or trunk) cable, an ultimate of approximately 150 Mbit/s of transmission path, full-duplex, is available. All channel assignments are done by frequency-division multiplexing, similar to the stacking of channel services on satellite or microwave links. The network manager, or planner, may freely assign these channels at 9.6-kbit/s, 56-kbit/s, 230.4-kbit/s, 1-Mbit/s, or 3-Mbit/s slots, for example, up to the capacity of each cable in the network.

Table 1 shows the maximum number of links which

Table 1 Ultimate capacities of single coaxial cable in broadband network*

DATA RATE	LINKS†	AVAILABLE BANDWIDTH	REQUIRED BANDWIDTH PER LINK	NUMBER‡ OF LINKS
9.6 KBIT/S	FDX, S, A	105 MHz	10 KHz	10,500
19.2 KBIT/S	FDX, S, A	105 MHz	20 KHz	5,250
56 KBIT/S	FDX, S	105 MHz	60 KHz	1,750
230.4 KBIT/S	FDX, S	105 MHz	240.4 KHz	437
512 KBIT/S	FDX, S	105 MHz	520 KHz	200
1.544 MBIT/S	SX, S	105 MHz	1,600 KHz	65
3.088 MBIT/S	SX, S	105 MHz	3,200 KHz	32

*ASSUMES HIGH-QUALITY, BUT PRESENTLY AVAILABLE, MODEM EQUIPMENT.

†LINK TYPES: SX = SIMPLEX, FDX = FULL-DUPLEX, S = SYNCHRONOUS, A = ASYNCHRONOUS

‡DIVIDE BY 2 FOR FULL-DUPLEX, AS EACH CHANNEL UTILIZES SEPARATE FACILITIES FOR TRANSMISSION.

can be carried over a single broadband carrier. Performance such as that shown in the table, while achievable, requires relatively expensive modems. Most networks today, however, employ something less than state-of-the-art technology. Of course, as cost of the modem decreases, so does its efficiency.

Effectiveness versus cost is one major consideration in deciding whether or not to install a broadband network. The efficiency of the broadband network is its capability of carrying a multiplicity of signals with little or no distortion of their character. The RF technology offers an unusually high signal-to-noise ratio, and this equates to bit error rates of less than 1 in 10^8 for large geographic networks using low-cost modems. With better-quality modems and smaller geographic settings, bit error rates of 1 in 10^{11} are possible.

Broadband networks are extremely flexible. The basic topology may first be a tree, a star, or a hybrid (Fig. 1). Network growth can be simply an addition of new or planned extensions. This network concept is hard to compare to conventional hard-wired systems. Broadband networks provide the capability for instantly reconfiguring the interconnection of the cabling to provide a data path for a user moving to any location served by the network. This strengthens the case for broadband for those who spend endless days studying cable charts, terminal diagrams, and cable catalogs, on their way to fighting snarls of complex cable interconnections. And this doesn't include the difficulty experienced in adding "just one more line" to that conduit already filled to capacity.

With broadband technology, the user expands the network simply by procuring appropriate hardware, securing a short piece of coaxial cable (if necessary), adding the station to the network control database, and installing the modems. When a new building or floor of a building is added, a simple cable extension is normally all that is required. When the traffic load approaches cable capacity, the network is reconfigured to a hierarchy, with subnetworks.

A broadband network does not require a switch to unusual protocols and interfaces; it is simply the media, which is protocol-transparent. Interfaces for RF modems may be procured in all normal conventions: RS-232,-422,-423, V.24, V.35, DS-1, teletype, even parallel. It is even possible to mate the network to phone lines, microwave, and satellite for outside connections. Fiber-optic sublinks, which have been designed to provide isolation and security for network nodes, are also compatible with broadband networks. Assume that a user is to be restricted to an assigned line and denied access to anything else on the lines. This is accomplished by simply locking up the modems at the building node or high-rise closet area and providing hardwire or fiber to the fellow. He is then hardware-constrained to his operating channel.

A broadband network may also be added to an existing system (if there is room left). Instead of pulling in the next set of conventional cables, the user simply pulls in appropriate broadband cable and, if necessary, repeaters. The broadband network may easily extend existing services without necessarily removing or modifying currently operating network facilities.

Broadband networks are relatively low priced—as low as $1.50 per foot installed. The data communications network planner or manager must analyze his environment to determine the applicability of this technology to his needs and the overall cost effectiveness of a broadband network. The primary criteria for analysis are (1) mix of service, (2) number of devices, and (3) plant size.

Multiple services

If the plant, building, or complex needs multimode service (differing types of services), broadband may provide tremendous reductions in cable counts. This multimode characteristic may be exemplified as a mixture of low-speed asynchronous data channels (to 9.6 kbit/s), synchronous point-to-point or multipoint data channels, high-speed data channels (up to 3 Mbit/s, synchronous), surveillance video, graphics video, audio, telephone, and television. When the requirements include some or all of the above functions, the conventional approach would normally be a layered topology using various available media: twisted pairs, video coaxial cable, pulse coaxial cable, and specialized cables. Multimode requirements are key in determining applicability.

Network density should be analyzed to determine the suitability of broadband based on sheer volume of data. A single-cable network with suitable terminal equipment can support several thousand users. Since devices may be randomly located throughout the network, physical implementation becomes much less complex than its conventionally wired alternative. There are, however, broadband networks installed with less than 40 devices interconnected on the lines. Such networks are poised for growth, and the growth capability is substantial. In general, if the terminal devices number 100 or more and are spread out geographically to some extent, the reduced system complexity is an advantage of broadband-type networks.

Physical layout

Broadband is a "not-so-local" network medium. Coverage may be as high as 300 square miles of surface, with several thousand user points. For a large installation where many users access many computers, broadband is particularly applicable. In evaluating the physical plant, the manager or planner should examine the costs and capacities of underground ducting, tunnels, conduit, and poles, and compare the lengths and amounts of standard cabling required to the one or two coaxial cable lines normally required in a broadband network.

Anticipated growth is another significant factor. Historically, it has been difficult to sell management on growth orientation, or future services. However, in many plant sites data communications growth has been awesome. There are current installations in which the ceilings sag under the weight of cables falling from overloaded cable trays. Underground ducts are filled to the point that streets are being excavated for new, larger, and incredibly expensive duct networks. In some cases, high-speed fiber-optics links are being installed on a point-to-point basis to ease congestion. Broadband coaxial technology can prevent this.

One major responsibility of the active planner/manager is to analyze trends in his own network. The need to install underground services may delay the implementation of a newly delivered system by several months. The broadband cabling which is necessary for a large data system is condensed dramatically and at the same time allows for expansion. For example, it is easily possible to set up a network between several buildings supporting 400 separate users and 10 independent computers, and still have room to grow and expand—all with one coaxial cable looping between buildings.

In considering broadband, the network planner should examine the physical conduit plan generally required for installation. For large plants, a star/tree

1. Single-cable networking. *Broadband networks support any traditional network topology, typically with less cabling than used in conventional coaxial networks.*

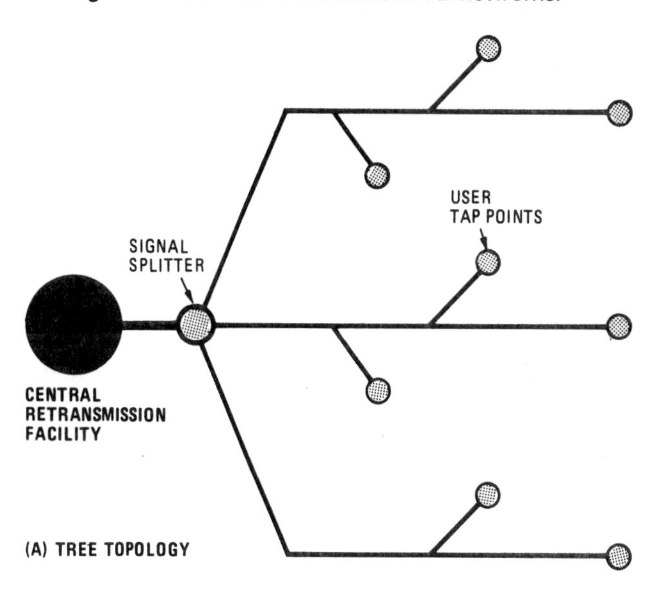

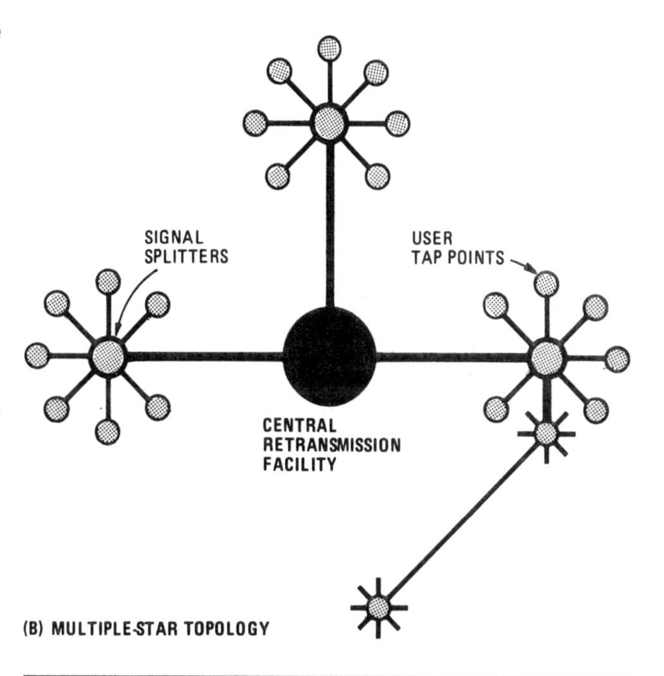

2. Retransmission. *A key component of the broadband network is the central retransmission facility (CRF), a "translator" that filters and regenerates signals.*

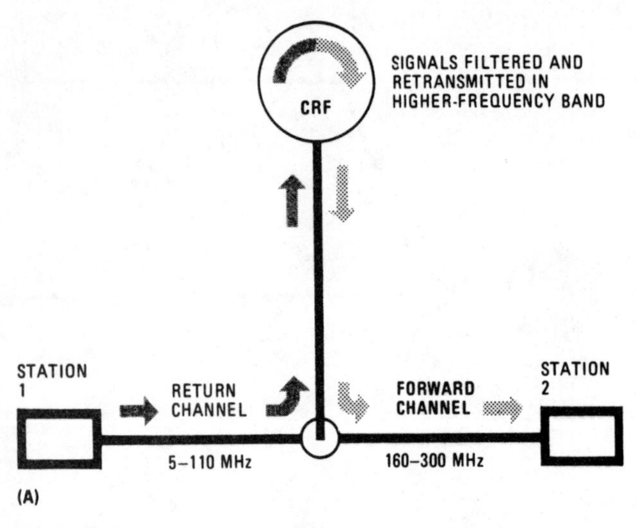

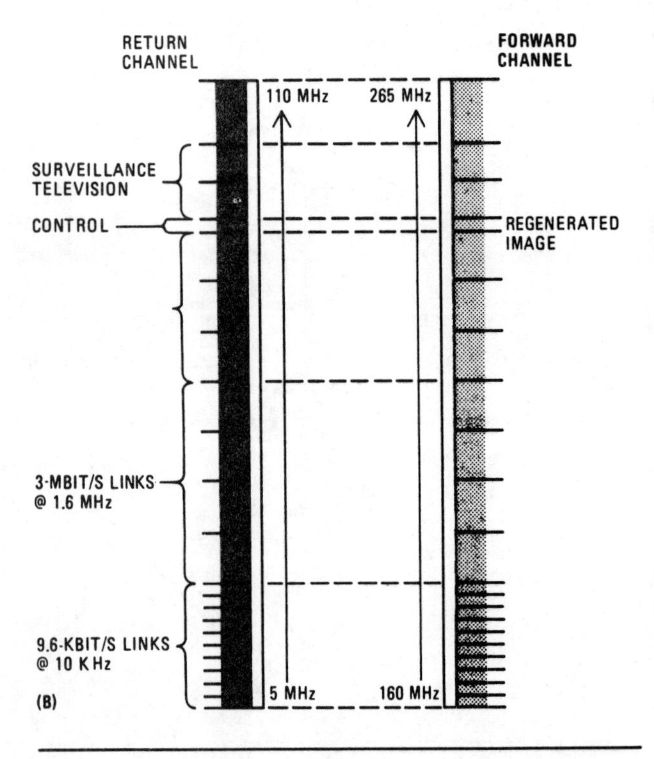

hybrid configuration is normally used, and if density is increased, a multiple-star/tree hybrid may be needed. In general topological layouts for broadband, the cabling connectivity is basically independent of the physical layout. With broadband, all links are available at all points, so a simple topology can provide service to multiple buildings with multiple users. As discussed later, there are several considerations and constraints in developing a detailed topographic model.

In its most simple form (a single coaxial cable), the broadband network may be characterized as a two-way radio frequency medium with a forward bandwidth (Fig. 2) of 140 MHz and a return bandwidth of 105 MHz. For operation, signals are transmitted on a return spectrum channel and retransmitted at a higher frequency on a mathematically related, forward bandwidth channel. All points attached to the broadband coaxial cable can receive the retransmitted signal (analogous to our satellite comparison). To establish a full-duplex link, each location to be connected is assigned a frequency that will allow direct communication with the other locations.

In multipoint broadband networks, this retransmission is performed by the central retransmission facility (CRF). The basic functions of the CRF are to accept signals from the cable(s) of the coaxial distribution system, amplify them, convert them to mirror images for retransmission in a higher frequency band, and provide ancillary functions (such as tech control) required by the system.

For purposes of this article, all user access point appliances are referred to as modems, by virtue of their function: translating digital information into radio frequency signals for the broadband medium. The channel assignments are characterized by their positions within the spectrum available (frequency) and the space they require (bandwidth).

Network topology

As a first step in developing a realistic topographical model, the network designer must review the physical layout of the plant and consider any near-future network expansion. In a high-rise building, for example, the user cable may appear at floors not active in the network, since that would be the simplest routing. In the case of a large site, it would be advantageous to avoid areas with little or no potential for network connection because of the cost of extra cabling. As shown in Figure 3, the cabling complexity in the interconnection of buildings is minimal.

In establishing the topographical shape of a broadband network, there are several considerations. A network center point must be identified, and a topography selected to meet overall network needs. For relatively small physical plants, a simple tree configuration could be used. Examples are a high-rise building in which the central retransmission facility (CRF) is placed at the top or bottom of the building, or a large single building, such as an automotive assembly plant, in which the central retransmission facility is in the computer center, with the "tree" branching from this point.

For multibuilding facilities, analysis is more complex. The designer should place the CRF in a central location, if possible, because of line-length constraints placed on the system for best signal-to-noise ratio. In this case, the topology will appear to be more of a star. or "hub." The hub and tree topologies are both capable of phenomenal growth, as will be later discussed. When using the star/hub topology, the designer has some freedom in placing the CRF, as the network requires only its general centrality.

The star topology has some interesting advantages. Since the broadband network is active, an outage caused by a repeater (amplifier) failure is not as critical

3. Network layout. *The broadband network uses a hierarchical cable layout. The trunk cable carries all traffic to the central retransmission facility, where it is retransmitted, in a higher bandwidth range, back into the network. Feeder cables interface the trunk with directional splitters. Users access the feeders over individual tap lines.*

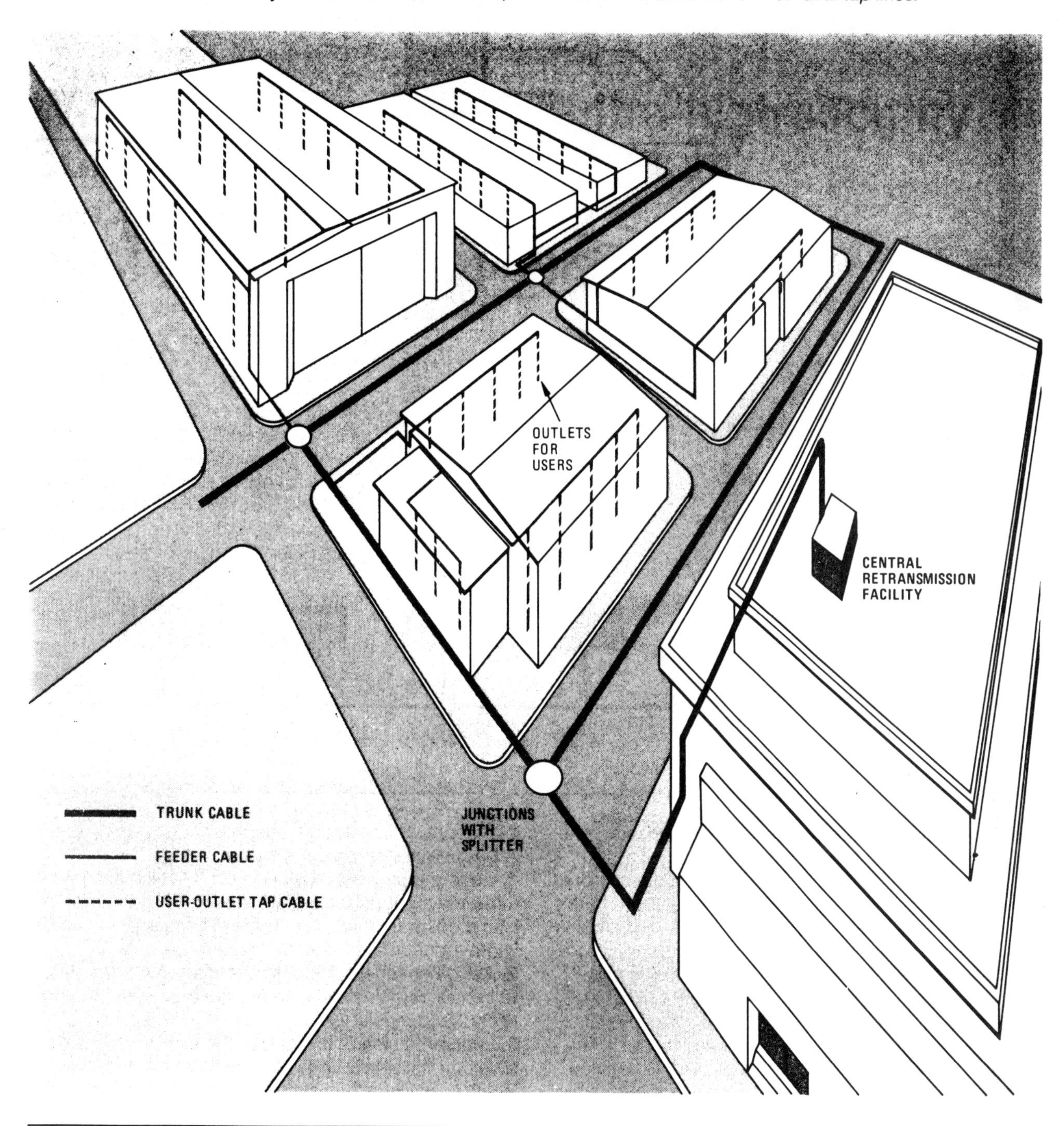

in a network of several radial lines. Also, each radial arm may have differing services provided, as controlled by the CRF. This is an additional capability of broadband as a network medium.

After the cable layout is determined, values indicating user loads and data rates must be assigned to each user area. This procedure helps the designer evaluate cables, internal distribution, and hardware selection. If an area has nodes remote to most users (for instance, a site several miles from the central core of data communications activities), the planner might consider, based on the site's capacity requirements, whether microwave or existing conventional cable would be the most cost-effective.

When the initial layout has been made, it is necessary to characterize the planned services and categorize their rates, types, and number. As mentioned before, broadband uses a random-interconnect scheme, and as such, may comprise layers of connected networks and subsystems. The "layers," or channels, can

__4. User interface.__ Each user access, or tap point, to the broadband network requires a radio frequency (RF) modem. A single modem may service a standalone intelligent terminal, a terminal-cluster controller, a minicomputer, a mainframe, or nondata voice/video equipment. Directional-coupler taps interface the cables.

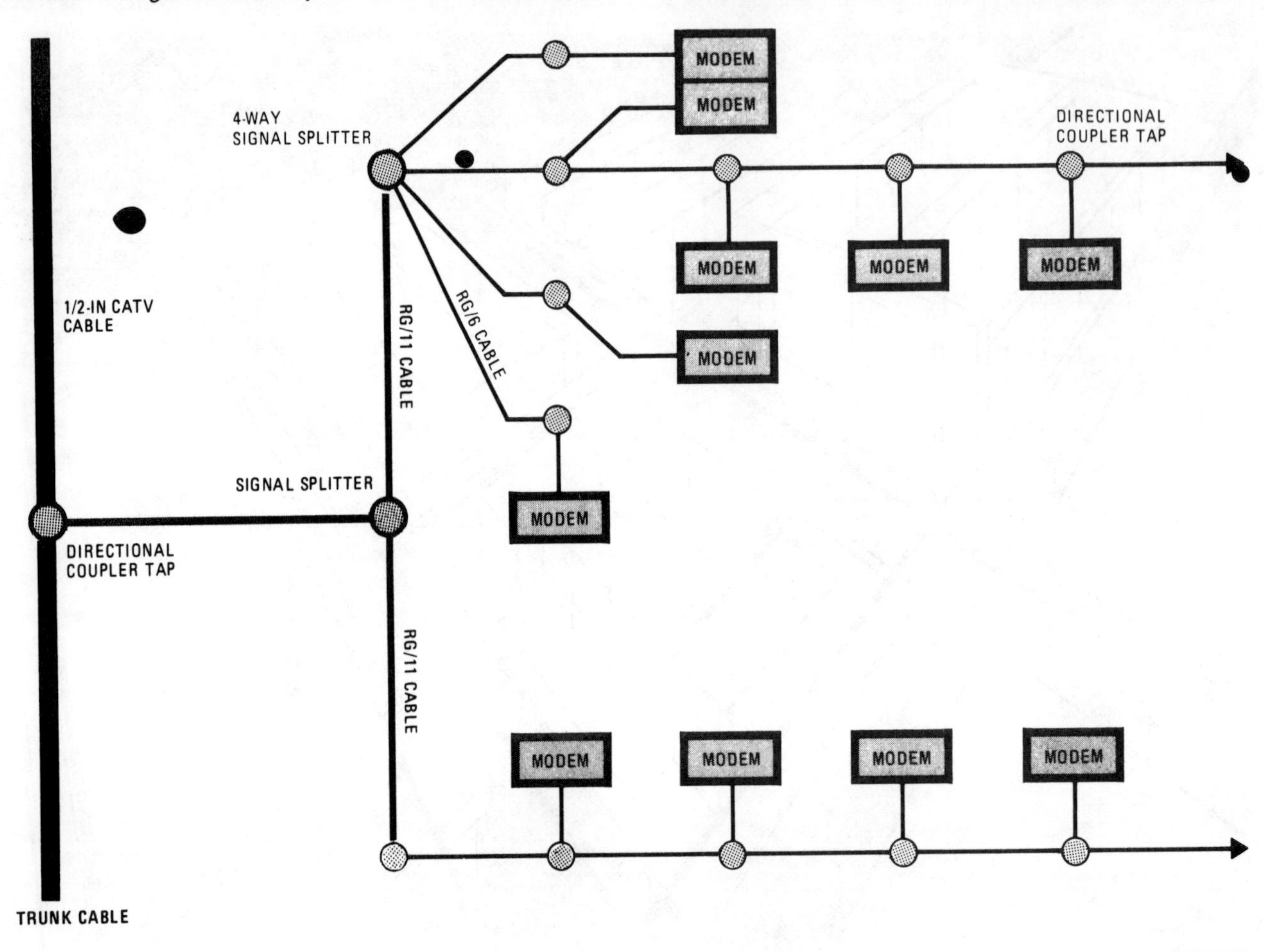

aid in analyzing the planned services and the percentage of loading they will lend the system.

The first layer will include data relating to common-system/common-rate links. For instance, if one network requirement is a multipoint link (such as an IBM 3705 port and modem to 20 polled devices and modems), this becomes a basic common-system/common-rate layer in the stack of channels (Fig. 2B). An asynchronous point-to-point link belongs in the same layer, even though fewer devices are connected. The similarity is that each line, or link function, is detailed to the same extent as the link that uses conventional wiring. In this regard, we are analyzing only line layer assignment—without the addition of multiplexers and/or packet networks.

Once the designer has detailed the data requirements and isolated each function in terms of commonality and rate, he can analyze the channel allocations and cable capacities in order to complete the broadband network topography.

Configuring the media

To determine the number of coaxial cable lines (one or more) required to serve the network functions, the planner must construct a channel and capacity model. A basic four-step process is used:

1. Generate channels. Using Table 2, which describes available modems, select a corresponding characteristic modem for each link. This will generate the bandwidth requirement for stacking channels.

2. Assign channels. Allocate channels that carry data to center frequencies in the available bandwidth of the broadband medium.

3. Look at the loading. Analyze the total loading to ensure that the total bandwidth does not exceed that which is available. If a simple cable scheme is used, and additional services will be added later, more efficient modems may be called into play, increasing the service density within the available bandwidth.

4. Establish the location. Physically locate the terminals and provide for their connection to the network. At this point, hardware will have been selected by function, and detailed design of the network may begin.

For more-complex networks, these same considerations apply for each coaxial cable, but much more planning is required for channel assignment, modem selection, and intersystem patches and subnetworks.

The distribution of terminal point "outlets" within

the plant deserves special attention and care. When the access node has been brought to the floor or building of interest, the user must decide how to properly distribute its resources. Access points, or outlets, can literally be placed anywhere. There are several approaches to providing service to the desired area:

■ Total access. This provides "user utopia," or an outlet in each room or area in the facility. As users demand services, appropriate hardware is procured, assignments are established, and the service is added up to the capacity of the system.

■ Access by application. This allots access points or "outlets" in only the required areas. Although much less expensive than the "user utopia" approach, as new needs arise this method requires continually accomodating branch wiring.

Distribution of "outlets," or network access ports, is accomplished using "feeder" cables from the major node (trunk cable). This is analogous to a river system fed by tributaries: each feeder, or tributary, is in turn

Table 2 Broadband network devices

DESCRIPTION	CLASS*	RATE	EFFICIENCY	BANDWIDTH	MODE	APPROXIMATE PURCHASE PRICE	VENDORS
RF MODEMS							
MODEM, DATA	1	TO 9.6 KBIT/S	10 Hz/BIT	100 KHz	ASYNC	$ 800–1,200	AMER. MODEM, INTERACTIVE SYSTEMS
MODEM, DATA	1	TO 19.2 KBIT/S	5 Hz/BIT	100 KHz	SYNC	2,000	AMER. MODEM, E-COM
MODEM, DATA	1	TO 512 KBIT/S	1 Hz/BIT	1 Hz/BIT	SYNC	3,000–6,000	AMER. MODEM, E-COM, COMTECH
MODEM, DATA	1	TO 3 MBIT/S	0.55 Hz/BIT	0.55 Hz/BIT	SYNC	4,000–6,000	AMER. MODEM, E-COM, COMTECH
MODEM, DATA	1	TO 6 MBIT/S	0.55 Hz/BIT	0.55 Hz/BIT	SYNC	7,400	AMER. MODEM
MODEM, DATA	2	TO 56 KBIT/S	10 Hz/BIT	100 KHz	SYNC/ ASYNC	1,000	NETWORK RESOURCES
MODEM, AUDIO	3	VOICE GRADE	7 Hz/Hz	25 KHz	AUDIO	700	AMER. MODEM
MODEM, AUDIO	3	15-50 KHz	12 Hz/Hz	200 KHz	AUDIO	1,000	CATEL DIV. (UNITED SCIENTIFIC)
MODULATOR, VIDEO	4	4.2 MHz	1.5 Hz/Hz	6 MHz	VIDEO	2,000	JERROLD ELEC.
MODULATOR, VIDEO	4	4.2 MHz	2.4 Hz/Hz	10 MHz	VIDEO	1,600	CATEL DIV.
MODULATOR, VIDEO	4	8 MHz	1.5 Hz/Hz	12 MHz	VIDEO	900	BLONDER-TONGUE LABS
MODULATOR, VIDEO	4	10 MHz	2.4 Hz/Hz	24 MHz	VIDEO	2,400	CATEL DIV.
DEMODULATOR, VIDEO	5	4.2 MHz	1.5 Hz/Hz	6 MHz	VIDEO	1,000	JERROLD ELEC.
DEMODULATOR, VIDEO	5	4.2 MHz	2.4 Hz/Hz	10 MHz	VIDEO	1,600	CATEL DIV.
DEMODULATOR, VIDEO	5	8 MHz	1.5 Hz/Hz	12 MHz	VIDEO	1,000	BLONDER-TONGUE LABS
DEMODULATOR, VIDEO	5	10 MHz	2.4 Hz/Hz	24 MHz	VIDEO	$1,600	CATEL DIV.
OTHER EQUIPMENT							
TRANSLATORS (CRF)				18 MHz	RETRANS	$2,500	AMER. MODEM, NETWORK RESOURCES
REPEATERS (TRUNK AMPLIFIERS)						800–2,000	JERROLD, C-COR
SPLITTERS, TAPS, OUTLETS, ACCESSORIES						VARIES	JERROLD, MAGNAVOX, RCA, GILBERT, BLONDER-TONGUE, GTE SYLVANIA, ETC.
TECH. MONITOR AND NETWORK CONTROL (MANUAL & AUTOMATIC)						$11,000–300,000	NETWORK RESOURCES

*CLASSES: 1, 3, 4, 5 ARE FIXED-FREQUENCY DEVICES, CRYSTAL-CONTROLLED.
CLASS 2 ACCOMMODATES MULTIPLE FREQUENCIES.

Broadband 'carrier' offers T1 links

Manhattan Cable, the broadband-based subsidiary of Time Inc., reportedly now offers 1.544-Mbit/s data channels on its downtown local cable network. The company, which began as a cable television firm about 10 years ago, started to provide commercial data transmission services in 1975. This year's revenues from local data transmission are expected to exceed $1 million, according to a company spokesman.

At present, about a half dozen New York banks are using Manhattan Cable's facilities to move data between their locations. The "facilities" are actually a dedicated CATV cable that runs about 5 miles along Broadway, from Columbus Circle south to the Battery. Another cable spanning about the same distance is now being installed to provide complete backup redundancy.

The single-cable network utilizes 30 repeaters, or amplifiers, along its course and presently supports about 130 data communications links. Data rates average about 4.8 kbit/s, but range from 1.2 kbit/s to 56 kbit/s. Most of the traffic being carried is RJE/batch, and most of the links are point-to-point. The company indicated, however, that about 5 percent of the terminal devices connected to the cable are polled.

Manhattan Cable reported that its revenue from data services has doubled every year since 1975 and that use of its dedicated data cable has not yet begun to approach capacity. The single cable can support up to 470 low-speed channel links (of 56 kbit/s and below) and still handle up to 70 T1-capacity channels (of 1.544 Mbit/s each).

Manhattan Cable attributes its success to both good service and cost-effectiveness. It claims to offer complete interface-to-interface service, including installation of the RF modems, plus cheaper prices than those for the phone company's leased lines, DDS, or other services. The company guarantees network availability of 99.98 percent and a bit error rate no worse than 1 in 10^7.

---

fed by tap lines, which correspond to the springs or run-off streams of the river system. In Figure 4, the device used to split from the node (or trunk) cable to the feeder is known as a splitter. From the feeder to the tap line, the device is a directional coupler; and from the tap line to the outlets, a directional coupler tap. These devices allow distribution to a large number of user service outlets.

Physical routing of feeder and tap lines is accomplished in a manner similar to that of TV distribution. The cables may be run in conduit or floor duct, above ceilings, or in walls. The network topology and all its branches are essentially completed once the location of the outlets and their wiring has been diagrammed.

The next consideration is the placement and values of repeater units, splitters, taps, couplers, and outlets. Design values vary with the installation, length of cables, and number of outlets. Signals from the CRF must appear at each outlet at the same level, and signals from the outlet to CRF must also follow this rule.

Signal specifications

There are many suppliers for all cable components used in implementing a broadband network, as most of it is CATV-type hardware. The network requires the following signal characteristics (decibel, or dB, is the unit of measurement for signal strength):

- Each broadband outlet must provide a +6-dB return signal (referenced to 1,000 microvolts/75 ohms ±3 dB) for an input injected into the same outlet of +56 dB.
- Each outlet must allow frequencies in the range of 5 to 110 MHz to be passed to the CRF.
- Each outlet must allow frequencies in the range of 160 to 300 MHz to be delivered from the CRF.
- For the above requirements, the level characteristics must be flat with frequency of transmission, ±0.5 dB.

Some of these requirements seem stringent, but they are achievable with today's "off-the-shelf" hardware. Reports available from most of the equipment suppliers and consultants, including Network Resources Corporation, describe the engineering, equipment, and coaxial requirements of a broadband network.

Equipment and modems

Broadband equipment is available commerically in many different configuration and performance levels. Table 2 presents characteristics of several classes of data modems, including devices providing closed circuit video and audio functions.

Modems for broadband, or RF transmission, are direct descendants of the satellite and microwave industry. The size and structure of the broadband network influences to some extent the performance of these devices, but bit error rates of less than 1 in 10^8 may be expected, and where the network is contained within a small area, rates of 1 in 10^{11} or less are known.

A significant factor of the broadband network is that the low-speed and high-speed links can coexist on the same medium without interfering with each other. Broadband allows tech monitoring of the medium in many locations on the network. Wraparound and loopback tests are more easily done on this common medium, as the wiring of the tech control is simpler than that of conventional scanning approaches.

A typical monitor system collects and evaluates the condition of the medium in real time, provides detailed fault analysis, recommends repair procedures, and provides a database containing information for network management. It may be expanded to provide the standard patching and allocation facilities necessary to support a large-scale system.

The central retransmission facility (CRF) equipment consists of translation and control components assembled to the specific requirements of the network. It requires careful engineering in its selection and placement. If the CRF is also the location of the technical monitor facility, an extremely powerful central control point can be established, which may be expanded as

5. Extensions. *The broadband network may be extended locally through repeaters (amplifiers) or, when links to remote networks/devices are required, through modems to fiber-optic, microwave, or satellite facilities. Broadband can typically accommodate such links without requiring additional cabling or special interface equipment.*

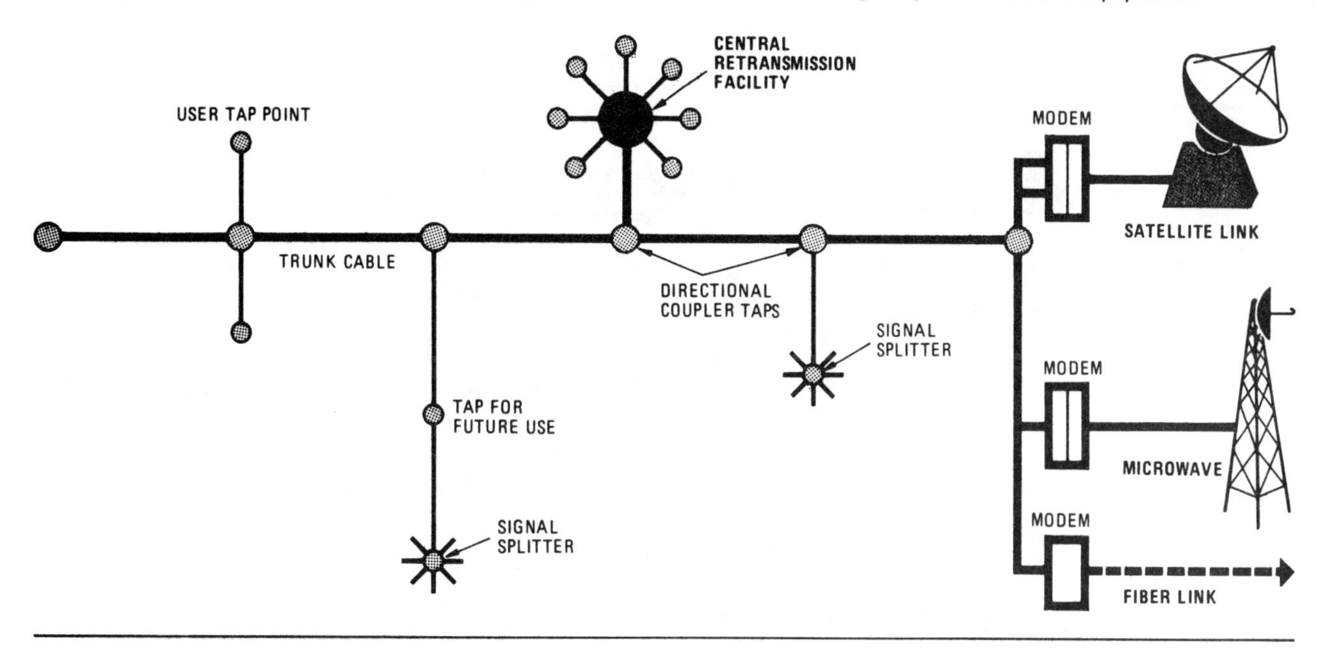

system use and scope increases. In the CRF, the data signals are not normally decoded from the cable signals. The radio frequency composite spectrum arriving from the coaxial network is processed by filters and converted up, to be sent right back down the same coaxial network.

The broadband concept lends itself to hierarchies within the network, where local subnetworks within buildings can use a broadband-type facility themselves. At this point, the major topological nodes (or trunks) become essentially file carriers or high-speed buses. The advantages of this type of hybrid topology are:

■ A relatively basic service network may be modularly expanded to the limits of its capabilities, or beyond, with no major cable changes.

■ As limits are approached, the planner may choose to use an auxiliary cable (installed earlier), form subnetworks generated from existing cabling by the addition of distributed processing equipment, or provide multiplexers to condense the user data stream.

Broadband advantages

Up to this point, we have addressed a very basic broadband system that is nevertheless capable of supporting several thousand individual links, comprised of varying services. With terminal-cluster multiplexers, operating in a basic time-division multiplexing (TDM) mode, the number of usable lines in terminal-oriented applications can be increased by factors of 8 to 20 or more. More exotic TDM techniques will improve line use by perhaps 50 times.

The broadband network does not restrict the planner to single-supplier equipment, and it may be integrated with wired plant subnets and fiber optics. Connections between broadband locations remote to each other can be made over fiber optics, T-1 carriers, microwave, or satellite, as shown in Figure 5.

When evaluating the capabilities of broadband, the planner can determine cost based on the size of the physical plant and the density of needed services.

Applications

Many colleges, universities, and schools may have campus configurations ideal for broadband networks. If properly designed cabling is already in place for distributing educational television, it is not hard to include service links for data.

On the "Wall Street" of any major city there are banks, brokerages, and transaction facilities with hundreds of people using terminal devices, which are invariably connected in some type of network. Many of these networks are enormous. The cabling required from floor to floor and building to building often makes a good case for these firms' investments in wire and cable companies.

Where system density is high and multiple floors or buildings must be interconnected, broadband technology should be considered. Although on a single floor of a building the technology may not be cost-feasible, for multifloor interconnection or multiple services, a broadband network may be the most appropriate.

The broadband network replaces many conventional cables and allows flexibility in change. When sites require frequent additions, deletions, and upgrading of services, broadband may be the easiest route.

Research and government facilities are generally large enough to justify the presence of broadband, based on distances, buildings, and required services. The numbers of distributed terminals, computers, and subsystems found in these installations are generally such that high-density communications is not a consideration for the future—it was needed 10 years ago. ■

A user speaks out: Broadband or baseband for local nets?

Thomas E. Krutsch, Security Pacific National Bank, Glendale, Calif.

Which coaxial-cable approach is most convenient and reliable? The author examines the strengths and weaknesses of the two technologies.

Networking trends foretell that the coaxial-cable bus topology will be the widespread choice for general-purpose local information networks. And although many users agree that coaxial cable is the best medium, it remains to be seen whether baseband or broadband emerges as the predominant technology.

The bus design has several advantages over a centralized configuration of conventional communications networks. A new or relocated device may be connected to any conveniently located network-access point without necessitating physical changes to the network. Also, portions of the bus may be extended with relative ease to serve devices not originally included in the network; expanding centralized setups requires multiple cable runs back to the switching equipment. A bus-based design makes it possible for numerous relatively "bursty" devices to share, as needed, a common, high-capacity transmission link economically. In addition, it enables the distribution of the necessary intelligence for control of the network among many intelligent bus-interface units. This can decrease or eliminate the number of network components, possibly increasing the fault tolerance of the total network.

A local network contains several characteristic elements, not the least of which is the transmission medium. The transmission medium must be rugged, able to endure a lifetime of manhandling by construction and maintenance personnel and by users who pull it through conduits and step on it—all this, while remaining highly reliable. The medium must be immune to noise and maintain low loss, enabling it to be used for reasonable distances at adequate data rates, with a minimum number of amplifiers and repeaters. According to many users, coaxial cable best satisfies these needs (see "Which transmission medium?").

Since numerous devices can share a common cable bus, it is necessary to multiplex the data passing over it. One technique used is time-division multiplexing (TDM). The form of TDM generally used in baseband local networks allows multiple access, with the bandwidth of the transmission medium being shared as needed. Examples of networks using TDM techniques are Net/One, (Ungermann-Bass), Ethernet (Xerox Corporation), and Hyperbus and Hyperchannel (Network Systems Corporation.

Frequency-division multiplexing (FDM) is used in broadband local networks and is much like the multiplexing technique used for years in conventional analog microwave networks and in CATV. An FDM local network can be almost identical to a CATV distribution scheme (see "Local networks' consensus: High speed," DATA COMMUNICATIONS, December 1980, p. 56). .

One advantage of a broadband network is that, unlike TDM-based networks, it can carry analog as well as digital information. For example, numerous channels of full-bandwidth video (used in teleconferencing and building-security applications) could be distributed, along with data. Another advantage is its ability to accommodate multiple, special-purpose applications on a noninterfering basis, even to the extent of containing subnetworks operating on TDM principles.

A disadvantage is the need for radio-frequency (RF)

Which transmission medium?

Twisted pair. Twisted pair has the advantage of relative low cost but has several serious disadvantages. Single twisted pair lacks the physical ruggedness required by a local network. It tends to both emit and pick up electrical noise and possesses relatively unpredictable impedance characteristics under conditions of practical use, resulting in relatively low data rates.

Optical fiber. Near the opposite end of the bandwidth spectrum lies optical fiber. The fiber itself offers digital bandwidths up to many hundreds of megabits per second. Practical lightwave transmitter/receivers already yield 100-Mbit/s performance in point-to-point applications, and higher speeds are expected in the future. A major difficulty in using optical fiber to form a practical bus configuration is that a great number of bus taps and couplers are necessary. Unfortunately, the science of fiber optics and the communications marketplace have not yet come together to make available couplers and taps with adequate low loss, high reliability, and low cost.

Coaxial cable. Coaxial cable has been in use for many years, in numerous applications which impose requirements similar to local networks'. Its advantage is that many types of coaxial cable, connectors, splitters, and taps are available, and installation and maintenance personnel are familiar with its use. Coaxial cable is the medium generally used in modern local networks.

modems, which are often more expensive than the relatively simple transceivers used in baseband schemes. Moreover, since these modems often have components that do not readily lend themselves to LSI (large-scale integration) or VSLI (very-large-scale integration), their cost may remain high relative to that of their baseband counterparts. Another disadvantage is that the propagation delay through a broadband network is likely to be much greater than that in a baseband network.

Subnetworks on a cable

FDM/TDM networks are a subdivision of the FDM classification and use a combination of the two techniques. Into this category fall LocalNet (Network Resources Corporation), Cablenet (Amdax Corporation), and Mitrenet (Mitre Corporation). Although designed basically like a broadband (FDM) network, FDM/TDM networks contain, in effect, one or more subnetworks, each of which operates internally according to TDM principles.

The communicating devices belonging to each subnetwork are equipped with bus-interface units much like those used with baseband (TDM) networks, except that they incorporate RF modems whose outputs are compatible with the frequency plan of the broadband network. These bus-interface units buffer data from their respective devices just as in a pure TDM network and enact access protocols similarly.

An important difference is that in a TDM network, the interface units occupy the entire cable bandwidth during transmission. In an FDM/TDM network, they occupy only that portion of the bandwidth allotted to them by the network designer, leaving the remainder for other uses. Just as in a TDM network, the interface units may be used to communicate between otherwise incompatible devices. In such a network, the cable bandwidth might be divided into a number of different user groups, with several independent subnetworks provided for the various groups. These could coexist in real time with numerous virtual point-to-point and multipoint circuits, depending on network requirements. Since such a network is basically an FDM design, numerous bands could be reserved for video or additional analog services.

In a typical baseband network, there is essentially a single communications channel, which all using devices can access. Network control is generally distributed among the many interface units that share the network. Consequently, it is the network-access protocol that stands between efficient network operation and chaos.

One access scheme, token passing, ensures relatively tight control over the network. It achieves "fairness"; that is, there is little possibility that any one device or interface unit will hog more than its share of bus capacity. It also eliminates the inefficiency caused by collisions between contending bus-interface units. A priority-access arrangement can be used, with designated interface units being sent the token more often than others.

But there are also disadvantages to token passing. Bandwidth is not entirely available on demand, and there is overhead associated with passing the token. That is, if the control token is passed to each interface unit in turn, including those that have nothing to send, then those that do have traffic to send will have somewhat less network capacity at their disposal. Token passing also requires error recovery mechanisms that enable the network to recognize and recover from the effects of garbled or lost tokens and from the failure of an interface unit to forward the token.

Most baseband local networks, including Net/One, Ethernet, Hyperbus, and Hyperchannel, use contention-type control. The bandwidth of the bus is available on demand, so that contention is well suited to environments in which each device using the network possesses bursty (low-duty-cycle) traffic characteristics.

A basic contention-based access protocol is carrier-sense multiple access with collision detection (CSMA/CD). Under this protocol, the interface unit through which each communicating device is connected to the network first "listens" to the bus (senses carrier) to see if it is free before transmitting its own accumulated frame. A contention-based access protocol for control of either a baseband or a broadband network involves trade-offs between speed, frame size, maximum allowable round-trip propagation delay throughout the network, and efficiency.

A priority-access scheme can refine contention: Each interface unit is pre-assigned a fixed value that must effectively be added to the random-retry interval that it computes on detecting a collision. The interface unit with the lowest pre-assigned fixed value will have the shortest retry interval, giving it the highest priority in beginning the retransmission of its packet. To maintain efficiency during peak traffic periods, the interface units can adjust the length of their retry intervals upward as the frequency of collisions increases. This operation is known as back-off.

Independent paths

Unlike baseband networks, broadband networks may possess a physical focal point (the head-end facility) at which amplification and frequency translation take place. However, this does not necessarily mean that control of the network is centralized.

With broadband networks, a great many simultaneous, independent communications paths are possible in real time, and it is not necessary to depend on an access protocol to mediate between numerous interface units vying for time on the bus. An FDM network, like conventional communications media, simply supplies a transparent communications medium. Any conventional circuit configuration (that is, point-to-point or multipoint) may be implemented using broadband cable by substituting RF modems for the conventional modems or line drivers. Then control may be imposed through conventional communications link protocols [such as binary synchronous communications (BSC) and synchronous data link control (SDLC)] enacted by the communicating devices themselves.

A network-control technique unique to broadband networks uses frequency separation between channels. However, rather than using a static, semipermanent frequency assignment, the channels are allocated dynamically, through the use of frequency-agile RF modems. Such a network may use a contention channel for requests for channel allocation and demand-allocated dedicated channels for the actual traffic.

Figure 1 compares typical baseband and broadband networks configured to supply communications services under the same physical circumstances. In the baseband network shown in Figure 1B each cable segment follows the bus layout, with the main cable itself connected to each transceiver serving a network-access point. Active repeaters are required to regenerate the signal when the desired cable length is greater than the maximum allowed (typically 500 to 1,200 meters) or when the maximum number of transceivers per cable segment (typically from 100 to 250) would otherwise be exceeded.

Repeaters can lend flexibility to baseband-network design. Although passive bus splitters cannot be used in baseband networks, active repeaters can connect several cable segments to form a tree or star configuration. However, only a small number of repeaters may be allowed between any two communicating stations. Regardless of the physical layout eventually reached with baseband and broadband, the logical design is still considered to be that of a bus.

Since there are propagation time limits beyond which the access protocol loses efficiency, the number of cable segments that can be connected by simple repeaters is restricted. To extend the network beyond these limits, the network must be divided in two, with the portions separated by a buffered repeater, or filter repeater. Unlike the simple repeater, it ignores (filters) all frames that do not bear the address of a device on the other portion of the network. When a frame bearing an appropriate address is detected, it is momentarily stored while the buffered repeater acquires control of the adjacent portion of the network for which the frame is intended. It is then sent, just as if the buffered repeater were a bus-interface unit originating a frame. (While buffered repeaters are supported as a concept by most local-network vendors, there are no known buffered repeaters available for purchase at this time.)

Besides enlarging the allowable physical extent of a baseband network, buffered repeaters can be useful in alleviating network congestion when much of the traffic is between stations on the same subnetwork. A buffered repeater could place this subnetwork into semi-isolation, freeing the remainder of the network from the higher-density traffic.

The broadband layout in Figure 1A shows the same topology as the baseband layout (Fig. 1B). One obvious difference is the broadband's retransmission facility. In single-cable broadband local networks, the retransmission facility receives information from communicating devices on the low-frequency end of the spectrum and retransmits it to all devices on the spectrum's high end. A second difference is that there are no repeaters used on the cable; CATV amplifiers can be employed if necessary (see "Broadband technology magnifies local network capability," DATA COMMUNICATIONS, February 1980, p. 61).

Guidelines for bus selection

In choosing the type of coaxial cable suitable for a network, the user must evaluate design trade-offs, including size, ruggedness, electrical loss, ease of handling, and cost. In commercial CATV distribution systems, which cover long distances, requirements generally dictate that different types of cable be used for various parts of the "tree" layout. The trunk would be composed of cable with very good electrical characteristics, including very low loss, to minimize the number of amplifiers required. Such cable is generally from 0.7 to 1 inch in diameter, with a shield of solid aluminum. More loss can be tolerated in the cables extending from the trunk, known as feeder cables, so that less-expensive cable with a smaller diameter and a braid/foil shield might be used. Still more loss is acceptable in the drop cables extending to each network-access point. In broadband communications networks with shorter distances, three types of cable may not be necessary.

It is easier to start up a small-scale network using baseband than using broadband. The minimum baseband configuration is no more than two baseband transceivers, two bus interface units (which might already exist within certain office equipment), and a length of terminated coaxial cable.

A broadband network, on the other hand, typically requires a greater initial commitment, particularly if it

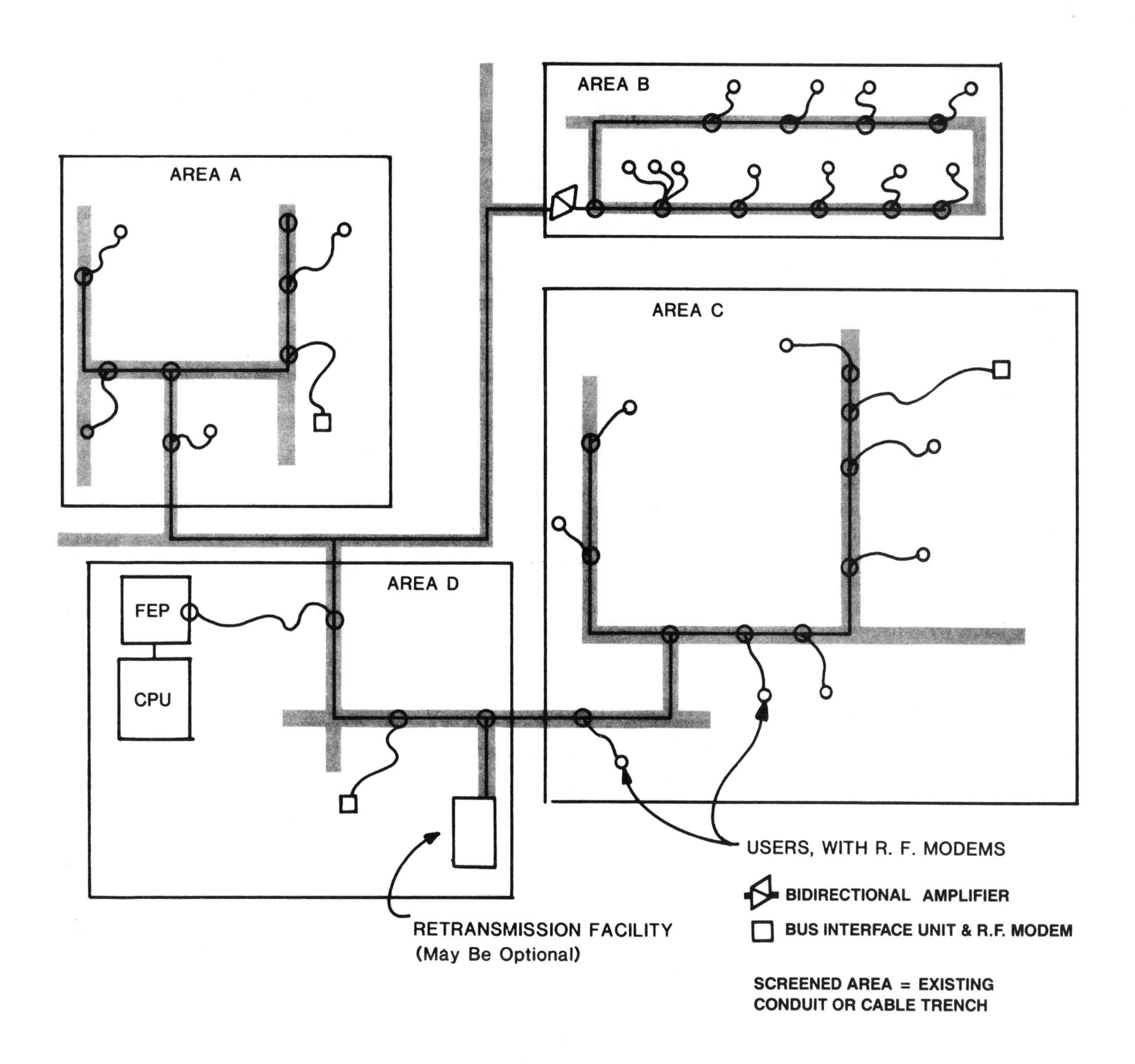

Figure 1a. Here we see how a broadband network might be used to allow communication between users in various locations. The figure illustrates the fact that practical network design is often constrained by the necessity of using existing cable trenches, conduit, and entry points between locations. Areas A through D could be separate buildings, floors in a single building, or areas on a single floor. The drop cables are considered to extend from the cable trench or conduit to the network users via raised floor, false ceiling, etc. Any necessary active equipment is considered to be located at the retransmission facility, with the exception of the use of an amplifier to boost signal levels in area B.

will handle analog video and if it is to offer maximum future adaptability. The network should be designed by competent personnel, with attention paid to RF power levels at various points and the likely location and ultimate number of access points. The location of the retransmission facility (if used) must be planned, and its equipment purchased and installed. Once in place, the network must be aligned, with frequency and amplitude equalized and standing wave ratios taken, among other things.

Baseband capacity and performance

Baseband/TDM and broadband/FDM have different strengths and limitations in their capacity and performance. General-purpose baseband networks accept data at rates ranging from approximately 4 to 10 Mbit/s. The effective network throughput must always be less, for several reasons.

One reason is the way user devices share the bus. Under the CSMA/CD access protocol, frame collisions will inevitably occur, requiring back-off and retransmis-

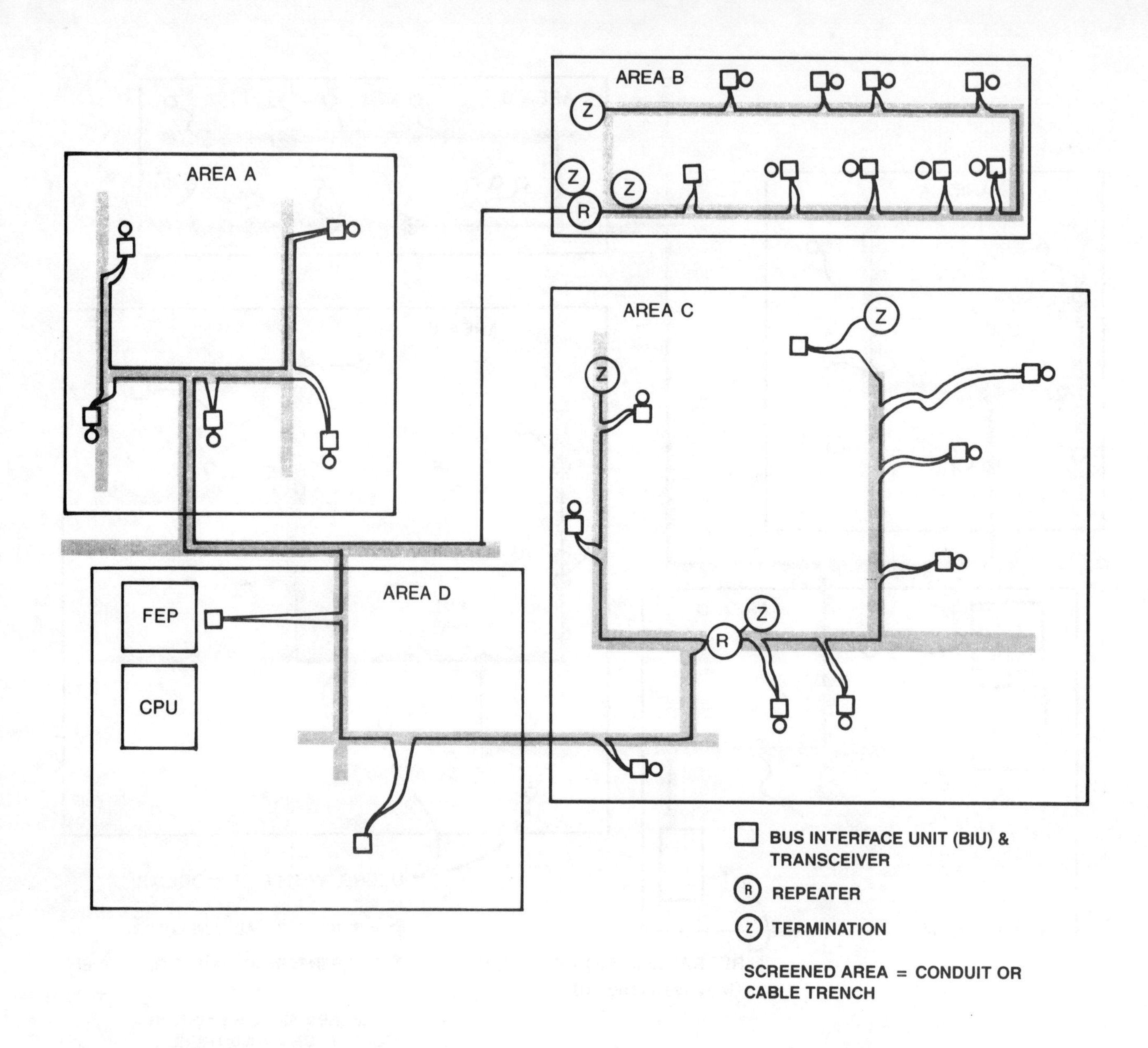

Figure 1b. This is an illustration of how a baseband network might be used in the same situation as the broadband network of Figure 1a. In area B, the baseband cable is accommodated in an existing trench or conduit, so as to be easily looped about the area. In area A, however, we see that if for some reason, we cannot make an easy loop around the entire area (for instance, if the cable must enter and leave the area at a single point), it may be necessary to double the cable back on itself, thus making for a longer cable segment than would otherwise be necessary. In area C, we see a repeater used in order to allow the bus to branch, in order to avoid the doubling back that we see in area A. Limitations on the number of repeaters allowed between any two transceivers may limit the use of this technique. In area B, we see a repeater used in order to extend the permissible length of the cable. Note that a baseband network would have served any one of the four areas very easily, and without the need for a retransmission facility.

sion. The collision rate—and its consequences—depend on several factors, including the degree of network loading, the frame length, the time required for a frame to be propagated throughout the network, and the possible existence of a priority-access scheme. Studies of one local network using CSMA/CD indicate that when the total traffic load that devices are trying to send rises above 100 percent of the bus transfer rate, actual bus use remains above 95 percent.

All the bits counted toward bus use do not represent user data, however. A more serious factor lowering effective network throughput is overhead from various sources. On one local network, which did not require an acknowledgment for each frame successfully received, approximately 21 percent of all bits transiting the bus during actual use represented overhead traceable to the network and internetwork environment itself. (This figure is influenced by a great many variables and should be taken only as a very rough indicator of the network's expected performance.)

Effective bus throughput is only one aspect of baseband network capacity. Another, and one that more directly concerns each network user, is the maximum data rate that the network can accept from and deliver to an individual device. The interface unit often imposes limitations that may be more severe than expected from looking at network specifications.

Still another performance issue is delay. The length of this period depends on a number of factors. When a contention access protocol is used, this delay may vary with network conditions and may also be imposed "unfairly"; that is, last-in/first-out contention may occur during high-traffic periods. When a token-passing access protocol is used, the delay tends to be more constant and predictable.

A local network's capacity and performance can be greatly influenced by the characteristics of the traffic applied to it. For instance, the efficiency of a network using contention can be greatly reduced if it is used to serve devices generating short frames at a high duty cycle, in contrast to "bursty," low-duty-cycle traffic.

Broadband capacity

The first step in evaluating the capacity of a broadband network is to consider its total bandwidth: the complete range of frequencies usable for information transmission. The greater the bandwidth of the network or of one channel, the greater the potential information-carrying capacity. Typical single-cable broadband networks have bandwidths of approximately 250 MHz.

The second step is evaluating the modems' use of the bandwidth. RF modems accept the data from the communicating device and convert it into RF signals, whose frequencies lie within a pre-assigned portion of the bus's total bandwidth. The range of the frequencies used by the modem constitute its bandwidth. As a general rule, the higher a modem's transmission speed, the larger the amount of bandwidth it will occupy.

RF modems presently provide speeds from a few bits per second to several megabits per second. (A few bits per second is unusual, but there are RF modems in building-monitoring setups that operate at 1 bit every several seconds.) The amount of bandwidth required by each modem depends not only on its speed but on its bandwidth efficiency. For instance, two modems from different manufacturers, each capable of a data rate of 1.5 Mbit/s, may occupy bandwidths from 1.5 Mhz to 6 MHz. Of course, the more efficient the modem, the greater its cost—in this case, by a factor of about 3. RF modems of lower maximum speeds tend to be relatively less bandwidth-efficient. For instance, modems capable of 19.2 kbit/s may require bandwidths in the neighborhood of 100 kHz.

The ultimate digital capacity of a broadband network, then, depends on the available network bandwidth and the efficiency of the modems. For example, with multiple 1.5-Mbit/s modems, a single-cable broadband network of 250-MHz bandwidth would have a maximum digital capacity approaching 250 Mbit/s, if the relatively efficient modems were used, or about 63 Mbit/s, with the inefficient (but less-expensive) ones. If a double-cable design were used, the above figures would be more than doubled.

Evaluating capacity becomes more complicated when a broadband network serves video and facsimile applications, as well as digital data. Full-bandwidth video is the service most demanding of bandwidth, with each video channel occupying 6 Mhz. For two-way video as used in teleconferencing, 12 MHz is required.

Vulnerability to failure

Every communications network has areas of vulnerability to accidental or deliberately caused failure. Most conventional networks, for instance, have multiple parallel communications links converging on a central point at which switching equipment is located. This type of network is relatively immune to serious consequences resulting from the failure of a single link, since such a failure would tend to impact only a single user of a single service. On the other hand, such a conventional network is vulnerable to problems affecting the centralized switching equipment, particularly since such equipment is complex enough to be difficult to troubleshoot, and its expense generally prevents it from being provided in fully redundant form.

The vulnerabilities of a bus-based distributed intelligence network are reversed. There is no centralized switching equipment serving the entire network. In the case of broadband networks, the relatively low expenses of the head-end equipment permits redundancy, and its simplicity promotes high reliability and rapid fault isolation. Instead, a bus-based network is vulnerable to problems affecting the bus.

The cable generally used in baseband networks has 50-ohm impedance, comprises a combination braided-foil shield, and is in the neighborhood of 0.4 inch in diameter. Since the tree topology is not possible on a single cable segment within a baseband network, there are no couplers, splitters, or drop cables. Instead, the main cable itself is connected to each baseband transceiver. The connection to the bus is generally made with a pressure-type of tap. To make the connection, the bus cable is pierced and "cored" with a special tool, and the tap is clamped onto the cable while a sharp point makes contact with the center conductor.

The baseband transceiver must generally be attached directly to the tap to minimize the length of the "stub." There are several advantages to these arrangements. The cable is fairly flexible and easily handled (although the minimum bend radius can be a problem), making for convenient installation. A tap may be installed at nearly any point along the cable (subject to spacing limitations), lending adaptability, since the location of possible future taps along the cable need not be anticipated.

However, if a vital main cable is stepped on, pinched, twisted, or kinked, its electrical characteristics may be altered at the damaged point, causing an impedance mismatch. When a frame, beginning to be propagated along the cable, encounters an impedance mismatch, several abnormalities occur. A portion of its transmission power (how much depends on the degree of mismatch) is reflected from the mismatch, back toward the bus-interface unit that transmitted the frame. The nonreflected portion of the signal continues past the damaged point with reduced power. If of sufficient magnitude, these reflections can result in each bus-interface unit detecting an apparent collision (with itself) each time it attempts to transmit.

The impedance mismatch resulting from the disconnection of a section of cable or loss of a segment termination has a similar effect. Since this problem disrupts all communication on that portion of the network not isolated by a buffered repeater, it appears that there is no rapid and effective way of isolating the problem, short of time-domain reflectometry, possibly after turning off each affected interface unit to prevent interference from the attempted frame transmission. Using a time-domain reflectometer, a technician sends an electrical pulse along the cable. The pulse detects any fault it encounters. A portion of the pulse is reflected back to the reflectometer, hence its name. The amount of time from the pulse emission to its arrival back at the reflectometer is measured to gauge the distance to the fault, whereon the technician can plan remedial action. In actual practice, sections of cable will probably have to be systematically disconnected and terminated, until the interface units on remaining cable sections cease detecting constant spurious collisions and begin to function normally. The precise location of the damaged point along the affected section would then have to be determined, and the damage repaired, or the entire cable section replaced.

A large baseband network, consisting of multiple subnetworks connected by buffered repeaters, would not be totally disabled by such a failure, since the problem would not extend beyond the buffered repeaters into adjoining subnetworks. Portions of the network on either side of the affected subnetwork would be totally isolated, however. The susceptibility of baseband networks to problems of this kind in actual large-scale use remains to be seen.

Broadband cable has 75-ohm impedance. The trunk cable may be semi-rigid with a shield of solid aluminum and may range in diameter from approximately 0.4 inch to 1.1 inches. It is less apt to be damaged than the baseband bus cable because of its ruggedness and its distance from the connections to each network-access point. In other words, less trunk cable is used, and it can be better protected.

In a mid-split broadband network equipped with bus-interface units employing a CSMA/CD access protocol, the modem of each interface unit uses one frequency in transmitting and "listens" for a different frequency in receiving. This means that in case of an impedance mismatch, the reflection of a transmitted signal back to its source would not be "heard" by the modem and would not be interpreted as a collision by the interface unit. To affect the network, a cable would have to be damaged badly enough to reduce the signal level passing through the damaged point so that other modems could not satisfactorily receive it after it had been frequency-shifted and retransmitted. If this occurred, only that portion of the network on the "downstream" (from the retransmission facility) side of the damaged point would be adversely affected. The rest of the network would continue to operate.

Ways around problems

With both baseband and broadband networks, there are procedures to reduce cable damage and similar failures and to minimize their consequences. One is simply to place the cable in conduit when it passes through areas particularly vulnerable to damage. Another is to plan for "inevitable" failures by building in serviceability during network design. This includes devising means to rapidly detect and bypass a damaged section of cable or other fault.

In baseband networks, a physical layout that segments the cable permits rapid fault isolation. Multiple cable segments radiating from a single point allow users to systematically disconnect cable segments so as to identify the segment with the failure. Once the affected segment has been bypassed, the remainder of the network can resume normal operation while the fault on the disconnected segment is pinpointed. Each cable segment should be broken into sections, by placing the appropriate connectors at intervals on the cable, to facilitate this process.

Also, users might limit the number of transceivers placed on each segment to some figure below the allowed maximum to minimize the impact of disconnecting a segment and to ease the task of locating the source of the failure. In this case, the decrease in reliability due to the use of greater numbers of repeaters would have to be weighed against the expected benefits resulting from a reduction of the MTTR (mean time to repair). Also, the use of time-domain reflectometry (TDR) would indicate to maintenance personnel both the magnitude of any cable discontinuity and its distance along the cable from the test equipment. If TDR were used, accurate cable routing and transceiver-placement records would have to be maintained to relate the output of the test equipment to the physical location of the fault.

The best insurance against serious consequences resulting from damage to the bus might be a redundant cable. This redundancy can be provided in broadband in several ways, one of which is illustrated in Figure 2.

In the baseband realm, only one special purpose network (Hyperchannel) currently provides the capability of making use of more than one cable bus without the necessity of manually changing from one to another. In general purpose baseband networks, even if a manual change were considered acceptable, the transceivers used are generally required to be securely attached directly to the bus cable. They are often deliberately placed in somewhat inaccessible locations (such as above a false ceiling) to discourage accidental or deliberate tampering or damage. This means that manually

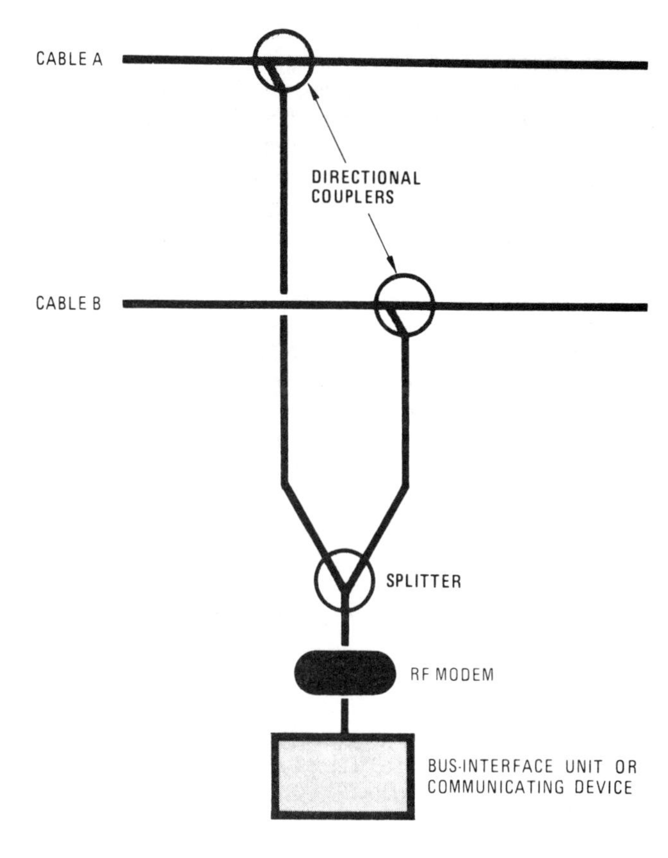

Figure 2. Redundancy. A bus-interface unit (BIU) or communicating device is connected to only one cable at a time. If one cable fails, its output is switched to the second cable.

making the change from one bus to the other might be difficult unless redundant transceivers were also provided, with one permanently attached to each bus. Users would then manually change their bus-interface units from one transceiver to the other in the event of a failure. If redundant cables are used, it is wise to consider the principle of diverse routing, which provides enough physical separation of cables so that an accident or other occurrence causing damage to one would not be likely to affect the other.

Network control

The equipment common to both baseband networks and broadband networks includes active devices such as amplifiers, power supplies, modulators, and repeaters—the failure of which would affect all or large portions of the network. In a broadband network, the common equipment is generally located at the cable head-end, at the retransmission facility. This location also serves as a convenient central point for network technical control. Standard CATV components are generally used, taking advantage of the maturity of the technology and reliability of the equipment. Statistics gathered by one CATV operator indicated a mean time between failures for amplifiers of over 48,000 hours and for power supplies of over 100,000 hours, although typical figures are somewhat lower.

In spite of this reliability, it is wise to provide a full complement of backup equipment, along with adequate patching facilities, test equipment, and training. During network design, when possible, an attempt should be made to place all active equipment within the head-end and technical-control facility, to facilitate fault isolation. However, if the number of network-access points or the distances involved are great enough, it may be necessary to locate amplifiers remote from the head-end facility.

Such amplifiers can be powered from the cable itself, by power supplies located at the retransmission facility, so that it is not necessary to obtain power externally in areas where commercial power backup may not be readily available. If such an amplifier fails, only the portion of the network "downstream" from the cable head-end would likely be affected, with the remainder of the network operating normally. Depending on the reliability requirements of the network, parallel redundant amplifiers could be used, as illustrated in Figure 3.

Other problems

Dedicated equipment is that which is devoted to the use of relatively few communicating devices, and whose failure would generally not seriously disrupt large portions of the network. The bus-interface unit used in both baseband pure TDM and FDM/TDM networks typically supplies bus access to form one to four communicating devices. Although reliability figures on interface units are not readily available, the fact that they use the same technology as typical microcomputers, and are of approximately the same complexity, may be a rough indicator as to their reliability. The baseband transceiver is a piece of dedicated equipment unique to baseband networks. Again, reliability figures are not readily available, but their simplicity is a point in their favor in this regard.

Since in baseband networks each interface unit or transceiver occupies the entire bus bandwidth when transmitting, and since baseband transceivers are generally connected directly to the bus without isolation, baseband networks are potentially vulnerable to two types of dedicated equipment failure which could occasionally impact the entire network: streaming and impedance changes.

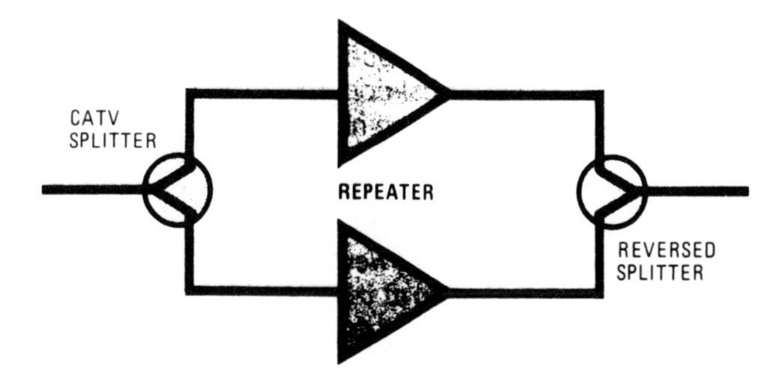

Figure 3. Amplified reliability. Duplicate broadband amplifiers are used for continuous operation. If one amplifier fails, however, the collective output level will drop.

A streaming-terminal condition occurs when a terminal on a multidrop line does not wait to be polled, insteand transmitting in a continuous stream. When this occurs, data from all other terminals on the line becomes unintelligible and useless. On a baseband network, a streaming bus-interface unit that ignored the normal access protocol would disable the network, but transceivers are equipped to prevent this.

Of course, the bus-interface units used in an FDM/TDM network could fail in a similar way. Even though the consequences would not be as serious, since only the bandwidth accessible to the RF modem is affected, an independent fail-safe timing circuit is desirable.

The second potentially serious problem concerns the baseband transceiver, which normally presents a high impedance to the bus. Since it is generally connected directly to the bus cable, any individual transceiver failure (such as a shorted transistor or faulty drive circuitry) that resulted in anything other than the normal high impedance could cause reflections that would disable the entire network, just as in the case of a damaged bus cable. Here also, locating a faulty transceiver could be difficult.

RF modems, because of features such as loopback switches, can assist in problem diagnosis. They are connected to the bus through CATV taps. Since each RF modem has access to only a specific frequency band, a modem failure which resulted in, say, constant carrier being transmitted (rather than controlled carrier) would affect only a particular frequency band, rather than the entire network. ■

Low-cost local network for small systems grows from IEEE-802.3 standard

Differing microcomputer systems can communicate easily thanks to Cheapernet, an extension of a new local-area network standard.

Existing standards for local-area networks define a utility that can serve the communications requirements of an entire building or plant site a lengthy period of time. But the meteoric success of the personal computer and workstation is creating a need for still simpler systems.

Indeed several such networks already exist, giving rise to numerous and confusing permutations of access method, cable type, data rate, and so on. But thus far, no single dominant candidate has emerged to set a de facto standard. Accordingly, the IEEE 802 Local Area Network Standards Committee has undertaken to provide one that conforms to the Open Systems Interconnection reference model formulated and adopted by the International Standards Organization and approved by the IEEE and the European Computer Manufacturers Association. This new open system network has been dubbed Cheapernet.

Alan V. Flatman
International Computers Ltd.
Besides serving as manager of local network applications for ICL in Kidsgrove, Staffs., U.K., Alan V. Flatman is chairman of the Cheapernet Task Group of the IEEE's 802 Local Area Network Standards Committee. He has also worked in the areas of displays and fiber optics. A member of IEE, he holds a BS in electronics engineering and a PhD in thermionic storage and speech synthesis from Staffordshire Polytechnic.

By accommodating common communications protocols, Cheapernet will enable different manufacturers' equipment to be interconnected. It draws heavily on the technology and protocols for the IEEE-802.3 standard (see the table, p. 186), which is based on the access method known as carrier-sense multiple access with collision detection (CSMA/CD) and is derived from the earlier Ethernet specification.

Essentially a smaller version of the 802.3 network, Cheapernet trades off cable span and the number of stations to obtain lower cost and easier installation. Yet because it is spawned from the earlier standard, it will be

able to use the same highly integrated chips that are just becoming available for 802.3-based networks. The result will be additional savings as the cost of the three chips involved—a transceiver, serial encoder-decoder, and network controller—drops further to reflect the economy of large volume production of both types of local networks. (See pp. 193 and 203 for a description of three such chips.)

Data rate is OK

Interestingly, Cheapernet's definers decided not to reduce the data rate from the original standard's 10 Mbits/s, even though such a move would have further reduced the cost. Only marginal savings would have been produced by cutting the data rate to 4 Mbits/s; slowing the rate still further would have congested the channel and required extensive data-packet buffering for certain applications. Worse, lowering the data rate would have rendered Cheapernet incompatible with the original 802.3 standard, which it is intended to complement.

However, one effective cost-cutting method that was adopted was reducing the range, or overall cable span, of the system. A single Cheapernet segment is limited to 600 ft, compared with about 1600 ft permitted by the earlier standard. This allows the use of RG-58, a cable that is thinner and more flexible and therefore costs much less than the one specified in 802.3.

For further economy, Cheapernet terminals connect directly to the network's primary cable. The tradeoff here is that the new net accepts only 30 nodes, whereas the standard 802.3 system accepts up to 100.

That direct connection, a result of placing the network's transceiver inside the user's data terminal equipment (DTE), is physically the most substantial departure from the original 802.3 specification (Fig. 1). The latter calls for external (and therefore more expensive)

IEEE-802.3 and Cheapernet local-area networks compared

Parameter	IEEE-802.3	Cheapernet
Data rate	10 Mbits/s	10 Mbits/s
Segment length	1600 ft	600 ft
Network span	8000 ft	3000 ft
Nodes per segment	100	30
Nodes per network	1024	1024
Node spacing	2.5 m (at cable marker bands)	0.5 m min.
Segment cabling system	0.4-in. diameter, 50-Ω coaxial cable with N-series connectors	0.25-in. diameter, 50-Ω coaxial cable with BNC connectors
Transceiver interface	0.38-in.-diameter multiway cable with 15-pin D connectors (length up to 165 ft)	Not applicable
Installation	Installer required	Simple, mainly by user

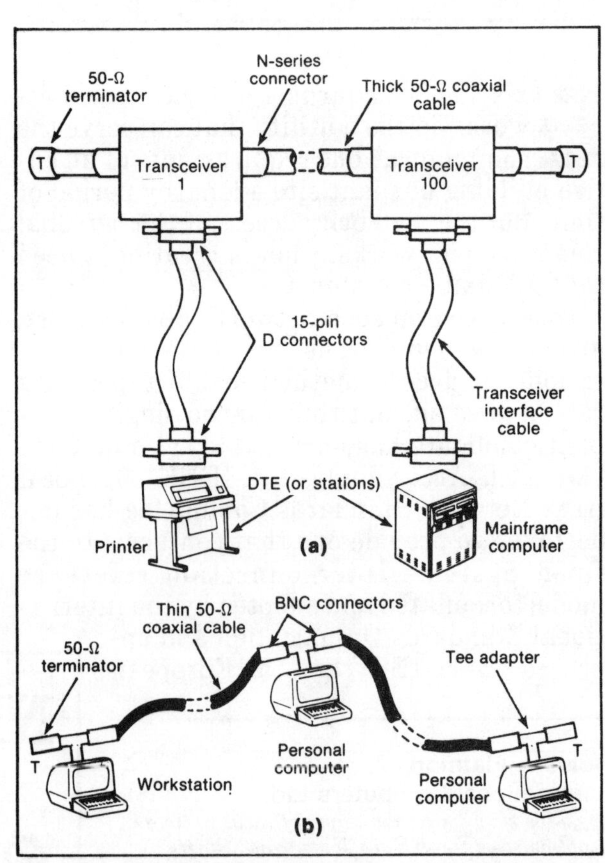

1. The acceptance of the Ethernet-like IEEE-802.3 local-area network standard (a) has created interest in a related but less expensive version suitable for small microcomputer systems. To reduce the cost, the newly proposed Cheapernet standard (b) shortens the cable length to make less expensive cables and connectors practical. The data terminal equipment (DTE) incorporates a transceiver IC and so connects directly to the primary cable.

transceivers at the primary cable and connecting cables extending to the DTE.

With Cheapernet, in contrast, each user will likely connect to the primary cable using ready-made cables prefitted with connectors. Alternatively, users can construct their own connector and cable assemblies if they know how, but ready-mades with molded strain reliefs are expected to be more reliable and less expensive. In either case, each user station attaches to a tee adapter in the primary cable. In addition, each tee must be separated from its nearest neighbor by at least 0.5 meter. No other restrictions apply, however, unlike 802.3, where connections are made only at specified cable markers.

Although Cheapernet is intended for very local use, several 600-ft segments can be joined together with the help of signal repeaters. Alternatively, several segments can be similarly attached to a standard 802.3 network, which would thus be made to form the overall network's "backbone" (Fig. 2). The compatibility between the two networks' transmission levels, data rates, and protocols means that the same basic repeater (except for having different coaxial connectors) could be used throughout.

Best of both worlds

Of the two extended configurations, the two-system collaboration is particularly appealing. Such a hybrid unites the attributes of both types of nets: Local users are free to configure their own equipment while enjoying the resilience and reliability of the backbone's data communications infrastructure. Moreover, connections between the systems need no complex and expensive bridges or any additional designing.

The length of such a network is limited by the 25-μs maximum end-to-end delay time that can be tolerated by each network's CSMA/CD protocol. Translated into cable length, this means that the maximum length of a standard local network alone is 8000 ft and that of the Cheapernet is 3000 ft. For a hybrid setup, the maximum length depends on the number of repeaters, the individual lengths of each segment, and other factors. The rules for configuring hybrid systems will be laid out in the Cheapernet specification.

Despite the low cost and simplicity of connecting to a node in the Cheapernet standard, the basic cable components—the RG-58 coaxial cable and BNC connectors—are well proven and reliable. Tests have shown the cable and the BNC connector to meet the need at hand. In fact, both pass the FCC rf emission requirements for Class A and Class B tests. The cable's susceptibility to electromagnetic noise is also acceptably low.

As for the BNC connector, its military rating ensures a low contact resistance even after hundreds of remating cycles. In addition, it resists environmental contamination and the

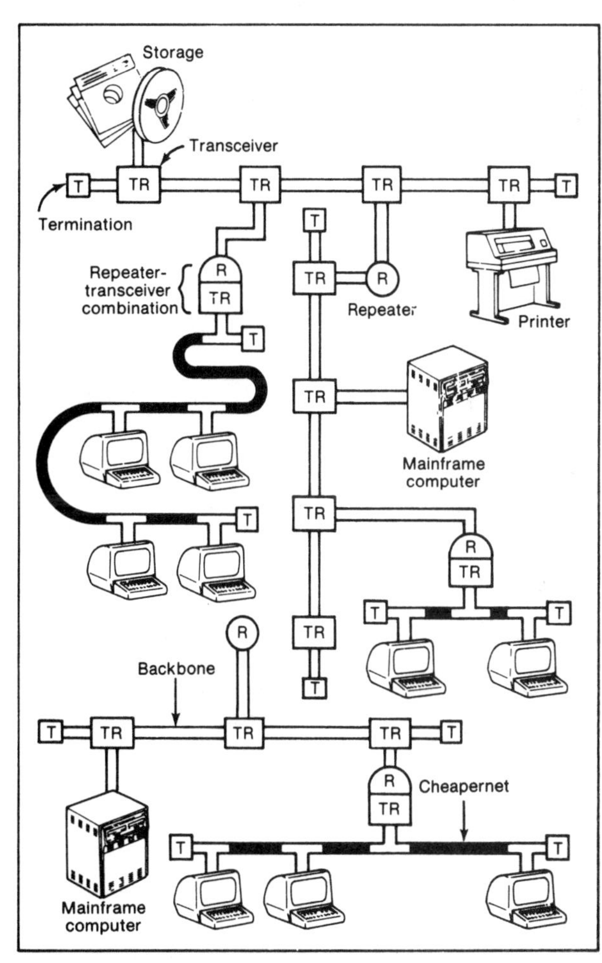

2. To overcome its limited range (600 ft per segment), several Cheapernet lengths can be joined by a repeater or tied into a larger local network "backbone." In the latter configuration, a system can offer the best of both worlds: a low-cost and easy-to-use Cheapernet backed up by a flexible and powerful Ethernet-like network.

Networking: Low-cost local network

degrading effects of long storage periods. Despite these strengths, the wide application of the BNC connector keeps its cost low.

In connecting individual lengths of cable to the system, the designer must take care to cover any exposed metal, be it at a connector, tee adapter, or line terminator, in order to prevent accidental multiple ground connections and their resulting current loops. Such loops would reduce the signal integrity of transmission line. Cheapernet accordingly specifies that plastic moldings be snapped over the exposed metal at each junction, both to prevent ground loops and to help secure the connection they protect. Deliberate grounding should be limited to a single point along the coaxial cable, but even this is optional, since each station will contain a high-value resistor to discharge any static electricity that builds up on the line.

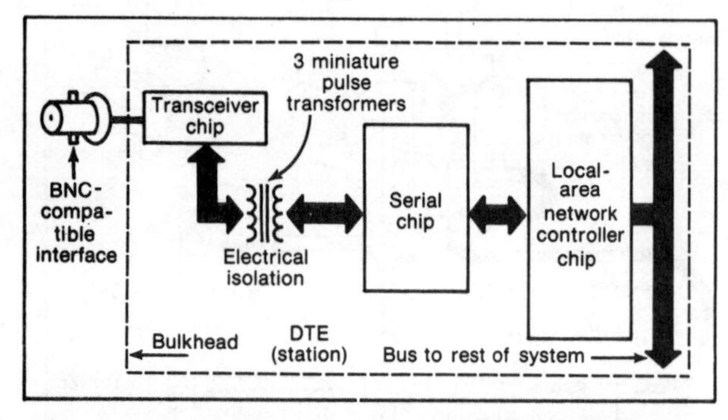

3. Cheapernet chips are well on their way to the user because of the low-cost network's compatibility with the already accepted IEEE-802.3 Ethernet derivative. The same trio of IC components—a transceiver, a serial encoder and decoder, and a controller—will work with both systems. In Cheapernet, however, the pulse transformers that isolate the terminal from the network's primary cable are located within the DTE, not outside it.

Despite Cheapernet's newness, some semiconductor companies are well on their way toward integrating the three active elements of the system. These elements are the transceiver, the serial encoder and decoder, and the controller (Fig. 3). As noted, integrated versions of these parts, which have begun to appear this year, are being developed for the network defined by the 802.3 standard and will automatically apply to Cheapernet as well.

Of the three chips, it is the transceiver that transmits and receives data and senses a collision on the line. As mentioned, this device will be located within the DTE, close to the BNC connector and the primary line itself. Placing the transceiver close to the primary line helps maintain the network's low shunt capacitance (8 pF).

What's more, pulse transformers between the transceiver and serial encoder and decoder chips electrically isolate each DTE from the others in a segment—a separation that is called for in the Cheapernet specification. The DTE is isolated between the transceiver and serial chips and not at the interface to the primary line, because there it would obstruct the sophisticated collision-sensing system, a mechanism that relies on monitoring the line's dc level.

The second chip of the system, the serial encoder and decoder, translates data into the Manchester biphase format for transmission on the system and into the NRZ (non-return-to-zero) coding needed by the controller chip. The Manchester code, having abundant clock pulses, eases the task of decoding data.

Finally, all transmission protocol functions, serial-to-parallel conversion, and communication with the host are the job of the last of the three chips, the controller. This IC could ultimately be combined with the serial encoder and decoder and so cut the system's cost even further.□

Norman C. Strole

A Local Communications Network Based on Interconnected Token-Access Rings: A Tutorial

Local area networks are expected to provide the communications base for interconnecting computer equipment and terminals over the next decade. The primary objective of a local area network (LAN) is to provide high-speed data transfer among a group of nodes consisting of data-processing terminals, controllers, or computers within the confines of a building or campus environment. The network should be easily accessible, extremely reliable, and extendible in both function and physical size. The rapid advances in computing and communications technology over the last two decades have led to several different transmission schemes and media types that could be used in these networks. The star/ring wiring topology with token-access control has emerged as a technology that can meet all of these objectives. The requirements of small networks with just a few nodes, as well as those of very large networks with thousands of nodes, can be achieved through this one architecture. This paper is a tutorial of the fundamental aspects of the architecture, physical components, and operation of a token-ring LAN. Particular emphasis is placed on the fault detection and isolation capabilities that are possible, as well as the aspects that allow for network expansion and growth. The role of the LAN relative to IBM's Systems Network Architecture (SNA) is also discussed.

Introduction

A local area network (LAN) can be defined as an information transport system for high-speed data transfer among a group of nodes consisting of office or industrial system terminals and peripherals, cluster controllers, or computers, via a common interconnecting medium within the bounds of a single office building, building complex, or campus [1]. The geographical constraints together with advanced transmission technologies enable data transfer rates of many millions of bits per second within the local network. These transmission rates, coupled with a reliable access control scheme, permit a large number of devices to share a common physical interconnection link with minimum interference to one another, while allowing large blocks of data to be transferred with simple error-recovery procedures and data management protocols.

This paper is a tutorial of a LAN communication system based on a ring topology with token-access control. The concepts presented here have been the subjects of research investigations on token-ring local area networks conducted at the IBM Research Laboratory in Zurich, Switzerland [2–4] and at IBM's Research Triangle Park laboratory in North Carolina [5–9]. A brief historical perspective on the evolution of teleprocessing and a description of some basic LAN topologies, control schemes, and transmission techniques are presented. A discussion of the criteria that should be considered in designing a LAN is followed by a functional description of several of the key physical components that comprise a token-ring network. The token-access control protocol for regulating data flow on the ring is explained, including the data frame format and addressing structure, and mechanisms for ensuring token integrity and uniform token access to all attached nodes. The implementation of a LAN in the context of IBM's Systems Network Architecture (SNA) [10] is also discussed. Finally, some of the fault detection and isolation capabilities that enhance the overall reliability of the token-access ring LAN are presented.

Historical perspective

The factors influencing the present surge in office automation and the use of computer terminal equipment in industry have arisen as a natural outgrowth of the revolution in technology that has occurred during the last twenty-five years in both computing and communications. Through the

1960s, large host computers were used primarily in batch processing modes, with punched cards or magnetic tape as the primary input medium. In 1964, one of the first commercial interactive systems, known as the Semi-Automatic Business-Related Environment (SABRE), became fully operational for handling airline passenger information and reservations. This project introduced a new era in telecommunications and contained many significant innovations in the areas of line control, multiplexors, and real-time operating systems [11]. In 1968, one of the earliest and largest nationwide nonmilitary computer networks was established for air-route traffic control using the IBM 9020 system [12]. Data concerning each flight are established at the point of takeoff and are passed from one control sector to the next in the path as the flight progresses. This system introduced new concepts in hardware and software reliability, having such features as a distributed data base, a failsafe system design with gradual degradation, and highly interactive application programs.

The 1970s brought new technologies to both computing and communications that enabled more and more users to have direct access to a computing facility. Advances in microelectronics led to the development of minicomputers which offered good performance capabilities at substantially lower cost. Also, interactive processing came into general use with the advent of the keyboard/printer and keyboard/display terminals as costs decreased and as operating systems shifted to allow both batch mode and interactive processing. The introduction of commercial distributed processing permitted multiple users to share access to common data bases and remote input/output equipment. Distributed processing has now expanded to a global level with the advent of satellite communications and packet-switching. The ARPANET is one of the better-known examples of a nationwide computer communications network [13]. Structured communications functions, such as those implemented in SNA [10, 14], provide well-defined protocols for the reliable exchange of information between network nodes. At the local level, the increased installation of terminals and workstations has resulted in a steady growth in the volume of information that must be transferred over the communications network. High-speed local networks are emerging to meet this growing demand as it becomes economically feasible to implement networking within an establishment. New technologies, such as very-large-scale integrated (VLSI) circuits, have greatly reduced the cost of implementing high-speed transmission and sophisticated communication functions that are necessary to interface a large number of devices to the local area networks.

Current LAN concepts

• *LAN configurations and control schemes*

A fundamental understanding of the basic LAN configurations and control schemes that are prevalent today will enable the reader to comprehend the more detailed discussions in subsequent sections of this paper. There are basically three network configurations that are particularly suited to LANs, namely the *ring*, the *bus*, and the *star* [15]. There are also a number of control schemes that can be implemented with each of these network configurations for regulating access among the network nodes.

Ring A ring network configuration consists of a series of nodes that are connected by unidirectional transmission links to form a closed path. Information signals on the ring pass from node to node and are regenerated as they pass through each node. The application of ring communication systems as local networks has been the object of significant research investigations including such projects as the Distributed Computing System (DCS) [16], the Pierce ring [17], the MIT ring [18], the Cambridge ring [19], and the experimental ring network at the IBM Research Laboratory in Zurich, Switzerland [3].

The Pierce ring and the Cambridge ring utilize a slotted-ring control scheme in which several fixed-length data "slots" flow continuously around the ring. Any node can place a data packet in one of the empty slots, along with the appropriate address information. Each node on the ring examines the address information in each packet and copies those frames that are directed to that node. A "message received bit" can be set by the receiving node to indicate to the originator that the message was received. The originating node must remove the packet from the ring when it returns, thus freeing that slot on the ring.

A second control scheme applicable to ring systems is known as *register insertion*. Each node must load the frame it wishes to transmit into a shift register and insert the entire contents of the register into the ring whenever the ring becomes idle. The shift register, in effect, becomes a part of the ring. The frame is shifted out onto the ring and any incoming frame is shifted into the register temporarily until it too is shifted onto the ring. A frame may be purged (removed from the ring) by either the sending or the receiving node. The sending node can only remove its register from the ring whenever the register contains only idle characters (i.e., no frame data) or the returned original frame itself. A new message cannot be loaded into the shift register until it has been removed from the ring. The IBM local communications controller for Series/1 uses a control scheme based on the register insertion concept [20].

A third control scheme, known as *token-access* control, has been implemented in the DCS, the MIT ring, and the Zurich ring. A unique bit sequence, called a *token*, is passed from one node to another. If a node has no data to transmit, the token is simply passed on to the next node. The receipt of a token gives permission to the receiving node to initiate a transmission. Upon completion of the transmission, the token is passed implicitly (without addressing information) to the next node on the ring.

In all three of the above ring control schemes, the sending node can determine on its own when it may begin transmitting based on the status of the ring at the time. This is contrasted with other ring (or loop) control schemes in which a single master node is responsible for initiating all data transfers. An example of this is the IBM 8100 communication loop. Here, the master node polls the nodes around the loop, allowing each of them in turn to send data if they have any waiting when they are polled.

Bus The *bus* provides a bidirectional transmission facility to which all nodes are attached [15]. Information signals propagate away from the originating node in both directions to the terminated ends of the bus. Each node is tapped into the bus and copies the message as it passes that point in the cable. One bus control scheme that is particularly suited for LAN systems is carrier sense, multiple access, with collision detection (CSMA/CD) [21]. With this scheme, any node can begin transmitting data whenever it detects that the bus is idle. The node continues to monitor the bus for interference from another node that may have begun transmitting at about the same time. Any "collisions" will be detected by all transmitting nodes, causing those nodes to halt transmission for a short random time period before attempting to transmit again.

The token control scheme can also be employed on a bus system. The operation is similar to that for a ring except that an explicit token (containing a specific node address) is employed for a bus, resulting in a logical ordering of the nodes that resembles a ring [5]. Polling can also be used in multidrop-bus configurations where a master controller polls each node to initiate data transfers.

Star The *star* topology, which derives its name from the radial or star-like connection of the various nodes to a centralized controller or computer, is implemented in point-to-point communication schemes that enable each node to exchange data with the central node. This topology is also used in private branch exchanges (PBXs) or computerized branch exchanges (CBXs) where the central node acts as a high-speed switch to establish direct connections between pairs of attached nodes. CBX systems are well suited for voice communications, and they can also accommodate the transfer of data between two nodes. Transmission speeds are presently in the 56-kb/s or 64-kb/s range, which is much less than the multiple-megabit-per-second rates achievable with ring and bus LAN systems.

The bus and ring network topologies are examples of what are called "shared-access links." That is, all nodes share access to a common communications facility, and any signal that is generated at a node propagates to all other active nodes. However, for a meaningful and reliable exchange of data to take place, two nodes must establish a logical, point-to-point link with one another [1]. The physical network thus provides a mechanism for moving the information between nodes that have established logical connections.

- *Transmission techniques*

The various transmission techniques that are implemented within LANs can be generally categorized by the signaling scheme used to transfer the electrical energy onto the medium. The digital information to be transmitted over the medium must first be electrically encoded such that the bits (*1*s and *0*s) are distinguishable at the receiving node(s). The rate at which the encoded bit information is applied to the medium by a sending node is referred to as the transmission speed, expressed in bits per second. The encoded information is applied to the medium in one of two basic methods, commonly referred to as *baseband* and *broadband* signaling.

Baseband In *baseband* signaling, the simpler of the two methods, the encoded signal [22] is applied directly to the medium as a continuous stream of voltage transitions on a copper medium or as a stream of light pulses on an optical fiber medium. One node at a time may apply signals to the medium, resulting in a single channel over which signals from multiple nodes must be time-multiplexed to separate the energy. Baseband data rates exceeding 100 million bits per second (Mb/s) are possible. However, practical limitations, such as the rates at which the attached nodes can continuously send or receive information and the maximum signal drive distance for a given data rate and medium, result in typical LAN data rates of up to 16 Mb/s. Baseband signals must be periodically repeated over a long distance to avoid data loss or interference due to signal degradation. The maximum distance between repeaters is a function of the properties of the transmission medium, use of intermediate connectors, and the data rate. In general, a decrease in the distance between repeaters is needed as the data rate is increased [7].

Broadband *Broadband* transmission schemes, unlike baseband, employ analog signals and multiplexing techniques on the LAN medium to permit more than one node to transmit at a time. Multiple channels or frequency bands can be created by a technique known as frequency division multiplexing (FDM). A typical broadband system has a bandwidth of 300 megahertz (MHz) which can be divided into multiple 6-MHz channels (as used in cable television signal distribution) with pairs of channels designated for bidirectional communications over a single cable. A standard 6-MHz channel can readily accommodate data rates up to 5 Mb/s. Two adjacent 6-MHz channels can be used to provide a single 12-MHz channel for data rates up to 10 Mb/s [23]. Access to a channel that is shared by a large number of nodes must be regulated by some type of control scheme, such as token passing or CSMA/CD. Broadband operation requires that a modulate/demodulate function be performed by radio-frequency modulator/demodulators (rf modems) at the sender and receiver, respectively, resulting in a higher cost per attachment than with baseband schemes. However, this enables broadband signals to be transmitted for longer distances between repeaters over a specially designed broadband cable.

• *Data frames or packets*
The control scheme that is selected for a particular topology governs the access of the various nodes to the network. In all of the transmission control schemes, the data being transferred from one node to another must be transmitted in a particular format that is recognizable by the receiving node. The actual format of a packet or frame varies depending upon the specific communication requirements. In addition to the data (information) field, the frame contains some type of delimiter field that is distinguishable from all other fields to mark the beginning and end of the frame. There may also be some control fields that contain status information, specific commands, format qualifiers, or the frame length. Most of the schemes require that the frame contain address information to identify the sender (source) and intended receiver (destination). Finally, one or more check bits are normally included to enable the receiver to detect possible errors that may have occurred after the sender transmitted the frame. A more complete description of a frame format is given later.

Selection criteria for a LAN

There are a number of factors that must be considered when selecting or designing a LAN. Each of the LAN configurations and control schemes described earlier has both strong and weak points, requiring the designer or user to make trade-offs in selecting the appropriate system design. One criterion that may be used is a comparison of the information transfer characteristics of the various schemes. The performance characteristics of several LAN transmission schemes, including token-access rings, slotted rings, and CSMA/CD buses, were evaluated by Bux [24]. He compared their data-throughput characteristics as affected by system parameters such as transmission rate, cable length, packet lengths, and control overhead. He concluded that the token ring performs well at high throughputs and transmission speeds of 5 and 10 Mb/s. The CSMA/CD bus also performed well at these speeds as long as the ratio of propagation delay to mean packet transmission time was on the order of 2 to 5%. The requirement to minimize propagation delay on a bus restricts the length of the bus in a LAN system, a factor that is not as critical in a token ring system. Another performance study by Stuck [25] showed the token ring to be the least sensitive to workload, offering short delays under light load and controlled delays under heavy load. The token bus was shown to be not as efficient as the token ring under heavy load and to have greater delay under light load. Stuck also found the CSMA/CD bus to have the shortest delay under light load, but to be quite sensitive to heavy workload, and to be sensitive to the bus length and message length, performing better with a shorter bus and longer messages.

A primary criterion in selecting a LAN is to minimize the cost of installing, operating, and maintaining the system without sacrificing network performance and reliability. In general, a baseband token-access communication scheme can be implemented with low-cost interface adapters and does not require the more sensitive rf modems associated with broadband systems. Also, the token-access ring wiring medium can be installed within a building using a radial (star) wiring scheme. Star wiring implies that the transmission cable is installed from concentration points within a building to the various user work areas, such as offices or laboratories. Wall outlets in each of these areas can provide physical interfaces to the network to permit fast, reliable attachment or relocation of the nodes.

Another design criterion is that any network faults or disruptions should be quickly detected and isolated to restore normal operation. The wiring concentration points provide centralized access to some of the primary network components to enhance the maintenance and reliability aspects of the overall system [18]. In addition, the flow of data and control signals around a closed ring provides an inherent capability for monitoring normal token operation from a single point on the ring and enables ring faults (such as a break in a segment of the ring) to be quickly detected. A more comprehensive discussion of the fault detection and isolation capabilities within a token-ring LAN is presented later in this paper.

The above LAN design criteria and others are incorporated into the token-ring architecture described here. This description is intended to give the casual reader an understanding of the fundamental aspects of a token-ring system while providing enough detail to permit further comparison with other LAN architectures.

Token-ring topology and network components

A star/ring wiring scheme combines the basic star wiring topology with the unidirectional, point-to-point signal propagation of the ring configuration. A major benefit of radial wiring is the capability of isolating those links that have failed, or are not in use, from the network [18]. Also, additional links may be added at any time. Major components of a two-ring system are represented in Fig. 1 and described next.

• *Ring interface adapter*
The term *node* encompasses a wide variety of machine types that can attach to and communicate over the local network. The primary functions associated with token recognition and data transmission are distributed to each node within the network. Advances in VLSI technology make it possible to delegate a large portion of this communication function to a ring interface adapter within each node, thus freeing the node from this processing. The adapter handles the basic transmission functions that are described later, including frame recognition, token generation, address decoding, error checking, buffering of frames, and link fault detection.

There may be instances where a device with an incompatible communication interface is to be attached to the local network. In this case a separate interface converter may be attached between the device and the token ring to perform the protocol and timing conversions that are required to send and receive data over the local network.

• *Wiring concentrators*
Wiring concentrators which contain a series of electronic relays are the central elements for structuring the star/ring wiring layout. Wiring lobes, consisting of two pairs of conductors for separate send and receive paths, emanate from the wiring concentrators to the various network interface points (e.g., wall outlets) at each of the node locations throughout a building. The lobes are physically connected within the concentrators to form a serial link, with the wiring concentrators then being interconnected in a serial fashion to complete the ring (Fig. 1). A lobe is only included in the ring path when the node is active; otherwise, an electronic relay within the wiring concentrator causes that lobe to be bypassed [4, 26]. Nodes may easily be moved from one location to another without requiring the installation of a new cable. The wiring is segmented at the wiring concentrators rather than being a continuous cable, thus permitting the intermixing of transmission media. For example, shielded twisted-pair wire can be used to interconnect the wiring concentrators to nodes, while optical fibers can be used for transmission links between wiring concentrators.

The wiring concentrators provide points within the star/ring network that facilitate reconfiguration and maintenance, thus enhancing network reliability. As described earlier, electronic relays within the wiring concentrators are activated whenever a node is powered on to bring that node and the associated wiring lobe into the active ring. Should the attached adapter detect a fault within either its own components or the wiring lobe between itself and the wiring concentrator, it can deactivate the relay and remove itself

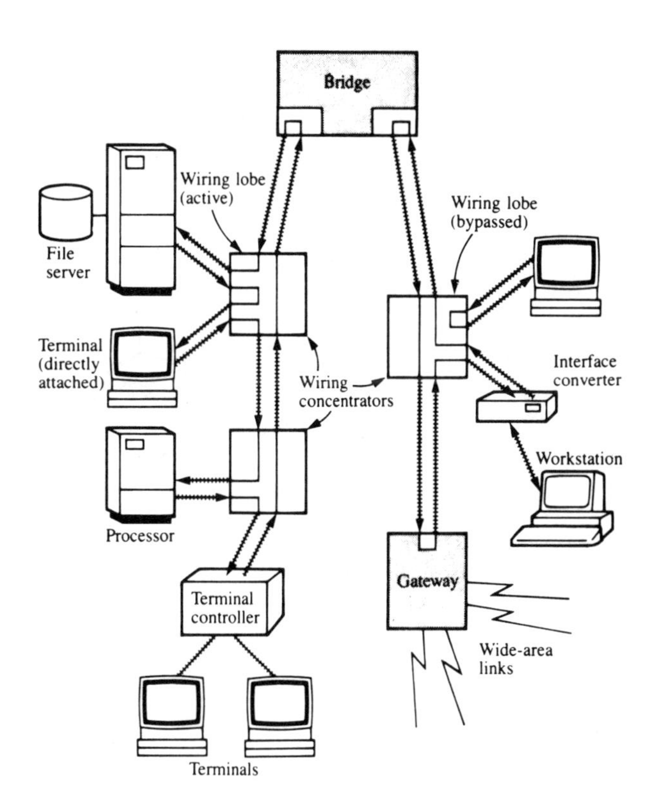

Figure 1 Wiring topology and components of a two-ring network. *Wiring concentrators* are the central elements for structuring a star/ring wiring layout. *Bridges* provide high-speed links between multiple rings. *Gateways* are used to access wide-area networks for long-distance communications.

from the ring. This lobe-bypass function may also be accomplished by manually deactivating the faulty node in case a faulty adapter is unable to remove itself from the ring. Passive concentrators contain electronic relays but no active elements, such as processing logic or power supplies, and require only enough power from an attached node to activate the relays to insert a node into the ring [18, 26]. Active wiring concentrators, on the other hand, contain processing logic and their own power supplies, and thus have the ability to detect and bypass faults that occur in the ring segments between concentrators. Active concentrators may also be remotely activated through the receipt of appropriate network management commands to bypass faults.

• *Bridge function*
Multiple rings may be required in a LAN when the data transfer requirements exceed the capacity of a single ring or when the attached nodes are widely dispersed, as in a multifloor building or campus environment. Therefore, large networks may typically have several rings with 100 to 200 nodes per ring. Two rings can be linked together by a high-speed switching device known as a *bridge* (Fig. 1). A

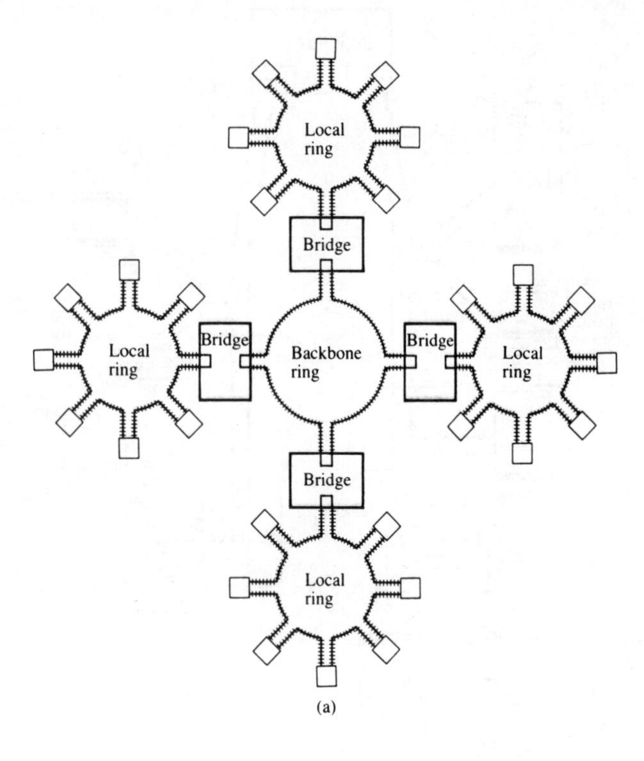

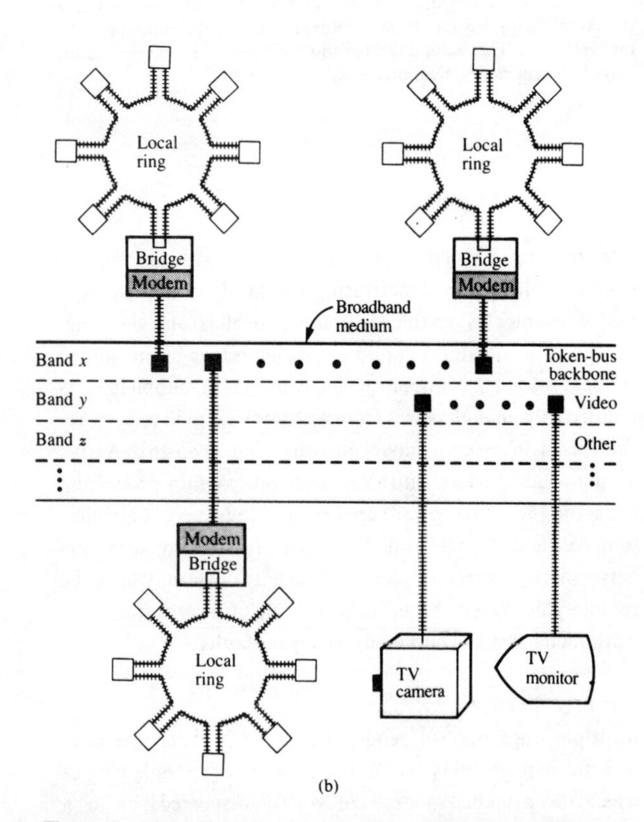

Figure 2 Multiple-bridge local area network: (a) A token-ring backbone wherein the bridges provide a logical routing of frames among rings and perform a speed conversion between the local rings and the backbone ring; (b) A broadband-bus backbone in which the bridges switch the ring data onto a channel of the broadband medium.

bridge is capable of providing a logical routing of frames between the rings based on the destination address information contained in the headers of the frames. An additional capability of the bridge is to perform transmission speed changes from one ring to another. Each ring retains its individual identity and token mechanism, and can therefore stand alone in the event the bridge or another ring is disrupted. The bridge's interface to a ring is the same as any other node's, except that it must recognize and copy frames with a destination address for one of the other rings within the network. Also, several frames may be temporarily buffered in the bridge while awaiting transfer to the next ring.

The local network can be further expanded to meet larger data capacity requirements by interconnecting multiple bridges. This results in a hierarchical network in which multiple rings are interconnected via bridges to a separate high-speed link known as a *backbone*. The backbone itself may be a high-speed token ring, Fig. 2(a), or it may be a token-access bus link, such as a channel within a broadband CATV system, Fig. 2(b). The address field format described later is structured to designate the specific ring to which a node is attached, thereby facilitating the routing of packets through bridges [17].

- *Gateway function*

In today's networking environment, a growing number of users require access to nationwide communication links as well as to the local network. For example, the primary host processing system may be located in another city or state, requiring that access be provided over a geographically dispersed area. A *gateway* node provides an interface between a LAN and a wide-area network for establishing long-distance communications between nodes within the LAN and nodes that are within other LANs or that are accessible directly on the wide-area network. Wide-area networks include private and commercial satellite links, packet-switching networks, leased lines, or other terrestrial links. They generally operate at lower transmission rates than most LANs, usually in the kb/s transmission range. A gateway can perform the necessary address translations as well as provide the speed and protocol conversions that are required to interface the LAN to these various transmission facilities. There may also be applications where a gateway could be used as an intermediate node between a token-ring LAN and a node in either a CSMA/CD- or PBX-based LAN.

- *Transmission media in a ring network*

The most prevalent LAN wiring media today are twisted-pair copper wire and coaxial cable. However, the use of optical fiber media in LAN systems will certainly increase in the coming years. Unshielded twisted-pair copper medium is used extensively for normal voice communications. However, voice transmission frequencies are much lower than those of local networks, and the impact of environmental noise is not as detrimental to analog voice signals as it could be to digital LAN traffic. Thus, "voice-grade" twisted-pair media cannot satisfy all of the requirements of a high-speed LAN. A high-quality "data-grade" twisted-pair medium has a higher characteristic impedance and is shielded to reduce the external electromagnetic interference (EMI), as well as the outward electromagnetic radiation from the cable itself. Also, the data-grade pair is a balanced medium (i.e., both wires have the same impedance to ground) which, in combination with the shielding, reduces the crosstalk interference from other twisted pairs within the same cable. (See Park and Love [27].) Thus, a well-designed twisted-pair cable can provide a reliable transmission medium for a local network system operating at baseband data rates of 1 to 10 Mb/s [7].

Optical fibers offer several advantages over copper media for use in LANs, including low susceptibility to electromagnetic interference and low signal attenuation over long distances at speeds greater than 100 Mb/s [7]. As this technology matures, lower-cost splicing techniques, as well as lower production costs, will make the use of optical fibers more economical than it is today. As noted earlier, the token-ring control scheme and the radial wiring topology enable optical fibers to be used within the LAN. For example, optical fibers could be used between buildings where lightning poses a hazard that requires additional protection with metallic media but not with optical fiber. Fibers could also be used in industrial environments where higher levels of EMI are found.

Broadband coaxial cable systems can be incorporated within a LAN for transmitting both analog video and digital data signals. While television systems do not play a major role in the office today, they may do so in the future. As noted earlier, standard CATV channels could be used for data transmission between rings by means of broadband bridges or for the interconnection of LANs via appropriate gateways.

- *Differential Manchester encoding scheme*

The binary data that originate within a node must be encoded for effective transmission over the ring. Many different encoding schemes are possible, including 8B/10B encoding [28] and differential Manchester encoding [22]. The differential Manchester code is being considered by the IEEE Project 802 Local Area Network Committee as the standard scheme for baseband ring transmission [29]. This code allows for simpler receive/transmit and timing recovery circuitry and offers a smaller delay per station than do block codes. Also, the differential Manchester code allows for the interchanging of the two wires of a twisted pair without introducing data errors [4]. A series of contiguous *1*s and *0*s

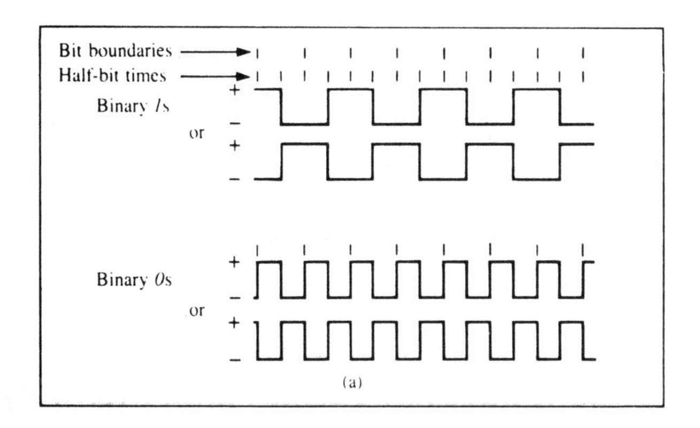

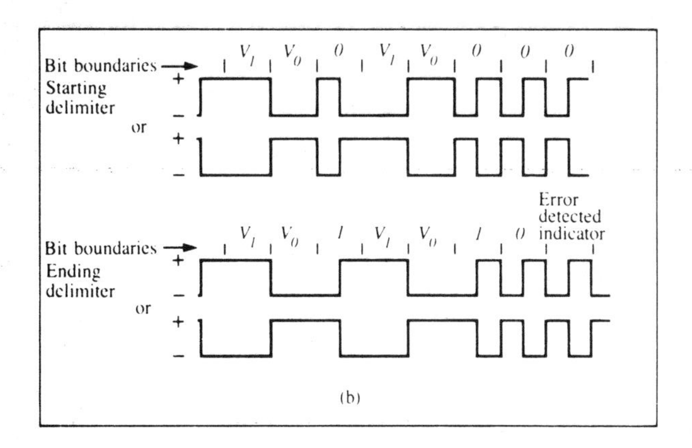

Figure 3 Differential Manchester encoding: (a) A *1* is distinguished from a *0* by the presence or absence of a polarity change at the bit boundary followed by a polarity change at the half-bit time of the synchronous signal on the medium; (b) Starting and ending delimiters contain code violations to distinguish them from data for delineating a frame.

(bits) would appear as shown in Fig. 3 when encoded. Each bit is encoded as a two-segment signal, with a signal transition (polarity change) at the middle or half-bit time. This transition at the half-bit time effectively cancels the dc component of the signal and provides a signal transition for clock synchronization at each adapter. The *1*s are differentiated from the *0*s at the leading bit boundary; a value of *1* has no signal transition at the bit boundary, while a value of *0* does. In decoding the signal, only the presence or absence of the signal transition, and not the actual polarity (positive or negative), is detected.

A code violation results if no signal transition occurs at the half-bit time. Code violations can be intentionally created to form a unique signal pattern that can be distinguished from normal data (*1*s and *0*s) by the receiving adapter(s). Such unique signal patterns can be inserted to mark the start and end of a valid data frame. Four code violations are used in pairs to maintain the dc balance, as well as to prevent spurious signals from being recognized as valid delimiters.

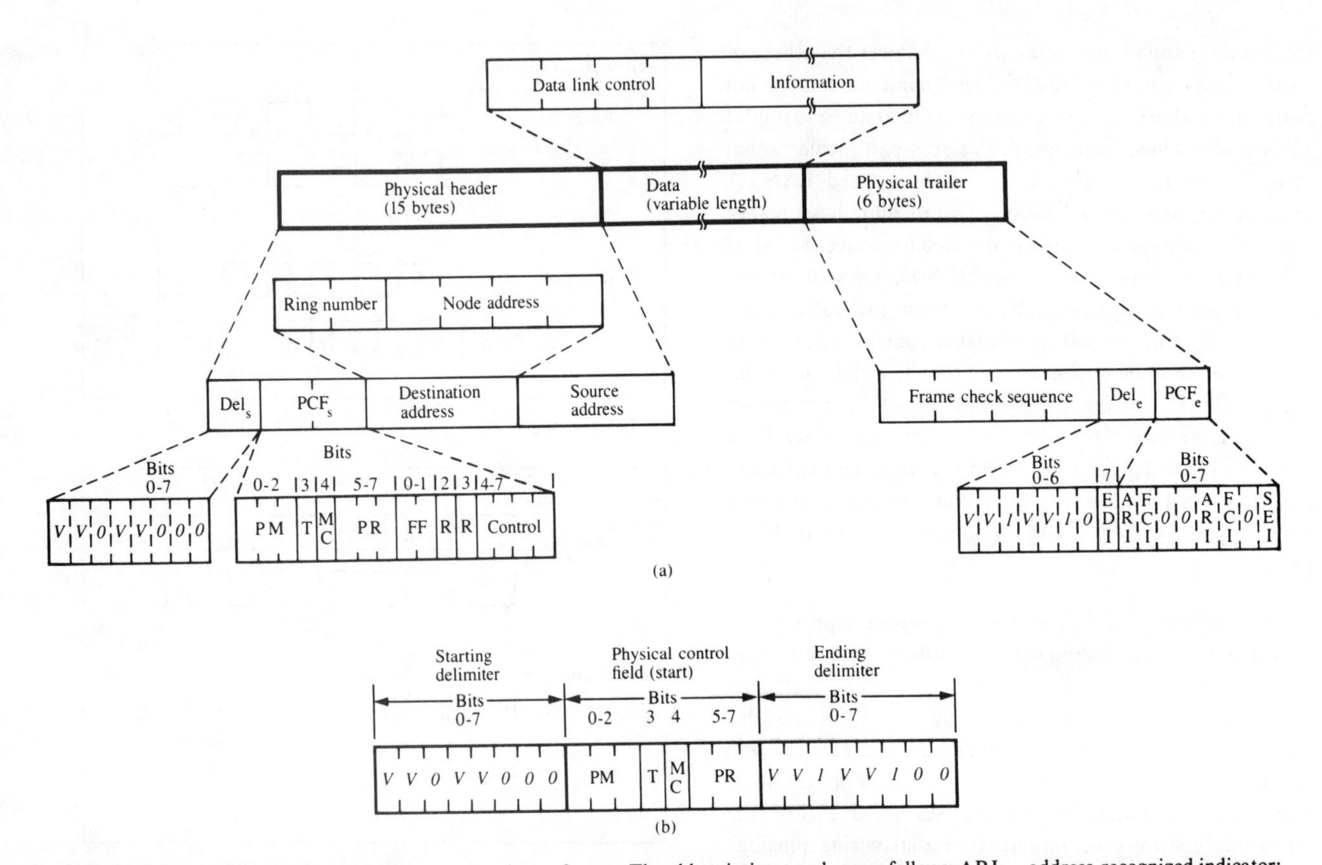

Figure 4 (a) Overall frame format. (b) Free token frame format. The abbreviations used are as follows: ARI = address-recognized indicator; Del_e = ending delimiter; Del_s = starting delimiter; EDI = error-detected indicator; FCI = frame-copied indicator; FF = frame format; MC = monitor count; PCF_e = ending physical control field; PCF_s = starting physical control field; PM = priority mode; PR = priority reservation; R = reserved; SEI = soft error indicator; T = token: *1* means busy, *0* means free; V = code violation.

Also, within each violation pair, the first is a violation of the normal *1* bit, V_1 (i.e., no signal transition at the leading bit boundary), while the second is a violation of the normal *0* bit, V_0 (i.e., signal transition occurs at the leading bit boundary). Thus the bit pattern $V_1V_0 0 V_1V_0 0$ is used to denote the starting delimiter, while the pattern $V_1V_0 1 V_1V_0 1$ is used to denote the ending delimiter (Fig. 3). These code patterns comprise the first six bit-times of either delimiter, leaving two bit-times within the byte (eight bit-times) for other uses. Any other code violations that occur are assumed to be transmission errors.

Token-ring architecture

• *Data frame format*

The general format for transmitting information on the ring, called a frame, is shown in Fig. 4(a). The "data" portion of the frame is variable in length (up to a fixed maximum) and contains the information that the sender is transferring to the receiver. The data field is preceded by a physical header, which contains three subfields. The first is a starting delimiter (Del_s) that identifies the start of the frame. The starting delimiter is a unique signal pattern that includes pairs of code violations of the differential Manchester encoding scheme as described earlier. Next, a starting physical control field (PCF_s) is defined for controlling the access to the transmission facility and for passing encoded information to the adapters. This two-byte field includes a one-bit token indicator that indicates whether the token is free (*0*) or busy (*1*). The frame format shown in Fig. 4(a) would contain a busy token indication. A free token, on the other hand, contains only the first byte of the PCF_s and the starting and ending delimiters [Fig. 4(b)]. A token priority mode, in conjunction with the priority reservation indicators within the first byte of the PCF_s, provides different priority levels of access to the ring. The monitor count bit is used in conjunction with a token monitor function to maintain the validity of the token. Both the priority access scheme and the token monitor function are described subsequently. The second byte of the PCF_s contains a two-bit frame format (FF), two reserved bits, and a four-bit control indicator. The FF bits enable the receiving node to determine whether the information within the data field of the frame contains medium-access control (MAC) information (FF = *00*) or user data (FF = *01*). MAC frames may optionally include frame status information or other urgent ring management information within the control indicator subfield. Finally, the header includes a field containing the address of the node that originated the information and the address of the node (or nodes) destined to receive the information. Both address fields contain six bytes, with the first two bytes indicating the specific ring number (in multiple ring networks) and the last four bytes indicating the unique node address.

The data field itself may be subdivided to include a data link control subfield as well as the user information field. Data link control information is necessary for the higher-level protocols that are normally used within data communication networks [14].

The dàta field is followed by a physical trailer which is also composed of three subfields. The first portion of the trailer contains a four-byte frame check sequence (FCS) that is calculated by the source node and used for detecting errors that occur during transmission within the second byte of the physical control field, the address fields, or the data field itself. The FCS is a 32-bit cyclic redundancy check (CRC) that is calculated using a standard generator polynomial [29]. Next, an ending delimiter (Del_e) is provided to identify the end of the frame. This delimiter also contains pairs of code violations such as were found in the starting delimiter, but with *1*s following the violations to distinguish the Del_e from the Del_s. The last bit of the Del_e is designated as the error-detected indicator (EDI). This indicator is always *0* during error-free ring operation, but is set to *1* by any intermediate ring adapter that detects an error with the FCS of a frame. The Del_e is followed by an ending physical control field (PCF_e), which is also employed for certain physical control functions. The PCF_e contains bits that can be modified while the frame is traversing the ring and is therefore not included in the calculation of the FCS character. For this reason the frame-copied indicator (FCI) and the address-recognized indicator (ARI) bits are duplicated to provide a redundancy check to detect erroneous settings. The uses of the FCI, the ARI, and the soft error indicator (SEI) within the PCF_e are discussed later.

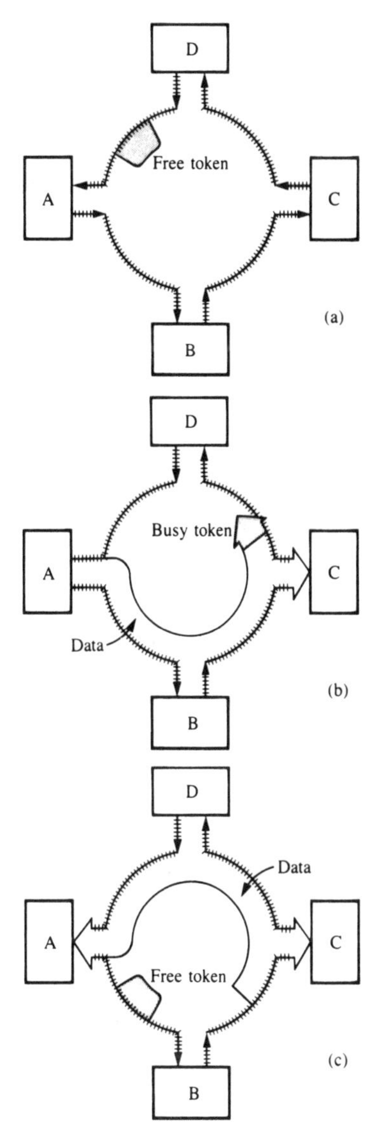

Figure 5 Token-ring access control protocol. (a) Sender (node A) looks for a *free* token, then changes *free* token to *busy* and appends data. (b) Receiver (node C) copies data addressed to it; token and data continue around the ring. (c) Sender (node A) generates free token upon receipt of physical header and completion of transmission, and continues to remove data until receipt of the physical trailer.

- *Token-access control protocol*

The token-access control mechanism for regulating data flow in a ring topology is based on the principle that permission to use the communications link, in the form of a "free" token, is passed sequentially from node to node around the ring. The "free" token, as described earlier, contains a one-bit indication that the token is "free" (T = *0*). With the token-access control scheme, a single free token circulates on the ring (Fig. 5), giving each node in turn an opportunity to transmit data when it receives the token. Each node introduces into the ring approximately a one-bit delay as the time to examine, copy, or change a bit as necessary. A node having data to transmit can change the token indicator from free (*0*) to busy (*1*) and begin data transmission by appending the remainder of the physical header field (second byte of PCF_s and destination/source address fields), the data field, and the physical trailer. The node that initiates a frame transfer must remove that frame from the ring and issue a free token upon receipt of the physical header, allowing other nodes an opportunity to transmit. If a node finishes transmitting the entire frame prior to receiving its own physical header, it continues to transmit idle characters (contiguous *0*s) until the header is recognized. This ensures that only one token (free or busy) is on the ring at any given time. The single-token protocol is thus distinguished from a multiple-token protocol in which a new free token is released immediately

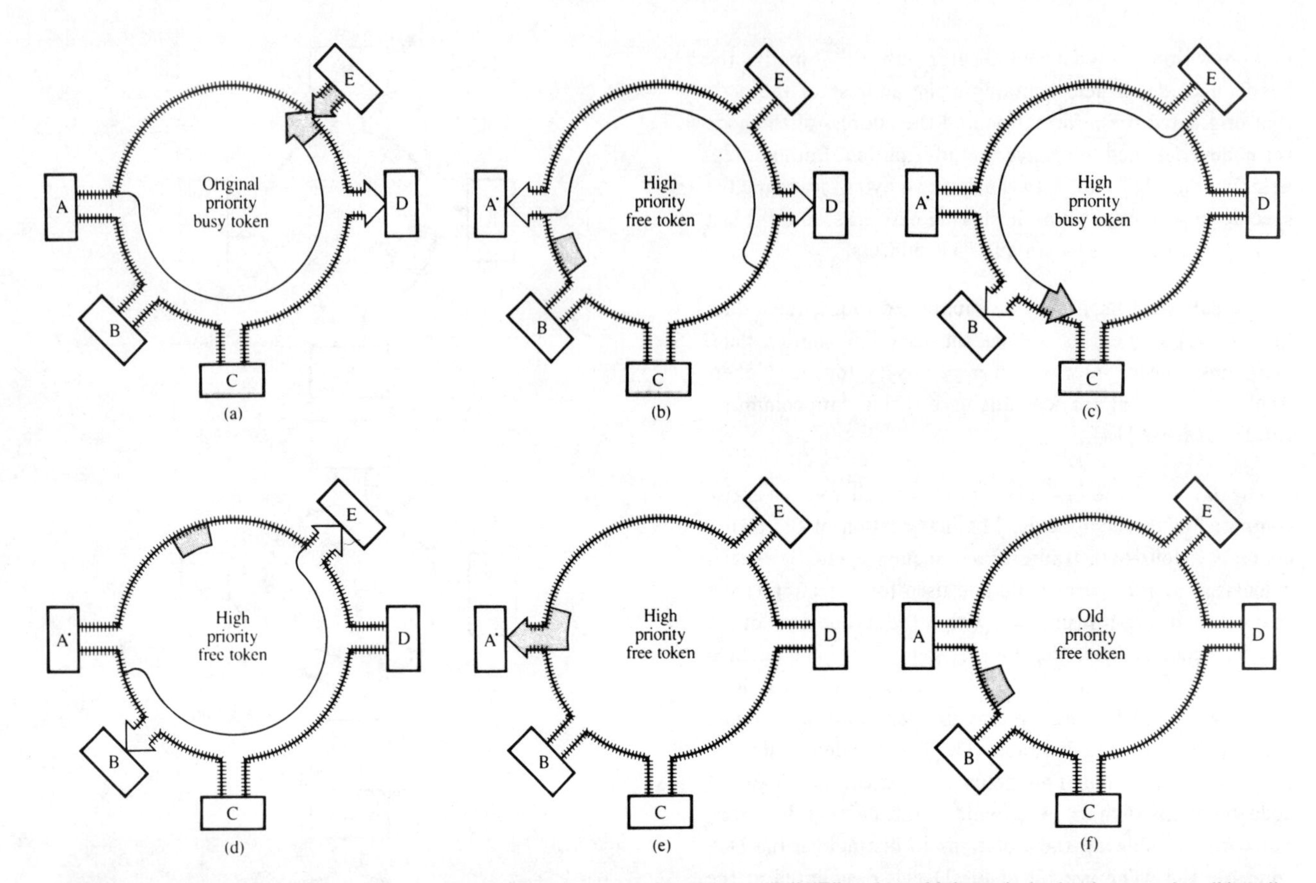

Figure 6 Priority with "uniform access." (a) "A" is in the process of sending to "D." "E" makes a higher priority level reservation. (b) "A" generates a higher priority level free token and saves the original priority level. Since "B" is at a lower priority level, it cannot use the higher level token. (c) "E" uses the free token to send data to "B." (d) "E" generates a free token at the current (higher) priority level. (e) "A" sees the higher priority level free token and generates a free token at the saved preempted priority level. (f) Now "B" is given the chance it missed earlier to use the free token.

following the last byte of the trailer. Only one free token is permitted in either case, with multiple busy tokens (frames) possible in the latter case if the length of a data frame is short compared to the time that it takes the leading busy token to travel completely around the ring. However, multiple-token error recovery is much more complex, while performance improvements of a multiple-token protocol over a single-token protocol are marginal when adapter delays are small [24].

Note that the ARI bits in the physical trailer of a frame are set by a node whenever it recognizes its own address within the destination field of that frame. The FCI bits are set by a node whenever it copies a frame from the ring. If a node cannot copy a frame from the ring, only the ARI bits are set, indicating to the sending node that the destination node is active but did not copy the frame. The ARI and FCI bits are used only for passing status information on a ring and do not provide an end-to-end acknowledgment of frame transfer in a multiple ring network.

The token-access control protocol provides uniform access to the ring for all nodes. A node must release a free token after each transmission and is not allowed to transmit continuously (beyond a maximum frame size or preset time limit) on a single token. All other nodes on the ring will have a chance to capture a free token before that node can capture the token again. In some system configurations, it may be necessary for selected nodes, such as bridges or synchronous devices, to have priority access to the free tokens. The priority mode and reservation indicators in the PCF_s are used in regulating this access mechanism. Various nodes may be assigned priority levels for gaining access to the ring, with the lowest priority being *000*. This means that a selected node can capture any free token that has a priority mode setting equal to or less than its assigned priority. The requesting node can set its priority request in the reservation field of a frame if the priority of that node is higher than any current reservation request (Fig. 6). The current transmitting node must examine the reservation field and release the next free token with the new priority mode indication, but retain the interrupted priority level for later release. A requesting node uses the priority token and releases a new token at the same priority so that any other nodes assigned that priority can also have an opportunity to transmit. When the node that originally released the priority free token recognizes a free token at that priority, it then releases a new free token at the level that was interrupted by the original request. Thus, the lower-priority token resumes circulation at the point of interruption.

Network addressing and frame routing The local network environment is expected to be changing frequently as nodes are added to a ring, moved from one ring to another, or removed completely [6]. The addressing and routing schemes for transferring frames from the source node to the destination node must be efficient and reliable in this changing environment. There are three types of addresses that could be used to identify a particular node. One type of identification is an identifier address that could be preset by hardware components within a node and remain unique no matter where the node is located within the network. Another type of address could be assigned to the specific wall outlet or wiring concentrator lobe to which the node is attached, denoting the physical location of the node within the network. A third logical address could be assigned to a node by a separate address server whenever the node becomes active in the network. The important point is that an address exists that distinguishes one particular node from all the others. This address is appended to the ring number to form the complete source or destination address that is included in each frame [Fig. 4(a)].

Certain addresses can be defined to be "all-stations" or "all rings" addresses that can be used when a frame is to be sent to all nodes in the network or on a particular ring. Otherwise the sender must determine at least the unique portion of the intended receiver's address before the first message can be sent. This information could be obtained from a central address management function or from a published source (similar to a telephone book). The sender then transmits a special MAC frame, known as an *address resolution request* frame, containing the unique portion of the destination address and an "all-rings" address, since the sender does not yet know which ring the destination node is attached to, or even if that node is currently active. If the target node is active, it will receive the address resolution request and respond to the requesting source node with another MAC frame containing its full address information (including ring number). Both nodes then know the complete address of the other and can continue communicating. Saltzer describes how a similar scheme could be used to determine the exact route through the network that the resolution request frame traversed in reaching the destination node [30].

The ring number portion of the destination address within frames is examined by a bridge and those frames that are directed to another ring are transferred within the bridge to the appropriate destination ring (if multiple rings are attached to a single bridge) or to the backbone. A frame is removed from the backbone by a bridge only if the destination ring number can be reached directly through that bridge or if the frame contains a general "all-rings" broadcast address.

A communication path between a node, A, within the local network and another node, B, in a separate network is established through an intermediate gateway node. Node A can communicate directly with the gateway node using the addressing scheme described above. However, the address information that identifies node B must be contained within the information portion of the frames which the gateway node examines to route the frames. Thus, routing through a gateway node can be associated with those functions performed at the path control layer of an SNA node or the network control layer of the ISO model [10].

Token monitor function Normal token operation is monitored by a special function, known as the token monitor, that is always active in a single node on each ring. This function can be performed by any node on the ring and is necessary to initiate the proper error recovery procedure if normal token operation is disrupted. This includes the loss of a free token or the continuous circulation of a busy token, both of which prevent further access to the ring [3]. It is important to note that this monitor function exists only for token recovery and does not play an active role in the normal exchange of data frames.

The monitor count flag in the physical control field of a frame is employed by the active token monitor to detect the continuous circulation of a busy token. When a busy token is first observed by the active monitor, the monitor count flag is set to *1* as the frame passes by. The failure of the transmitting node to remove the frame causes it to pass the token monitor a second time. The token monitor, observing the monitor count flag set, removes the frame from the ring and issues a free token. The active monitor also maintains a timer which is reset upon the passage of either a busy token or a free token. Loss of the token due to interference or noise causes the timer to expire, prompting the token monitor to reinitialize the ring with a free token.

The capability to be an active monitor exists in all active nodes attached to a ring. These other nodes maintain a standby monitor status and are prepared to become the new active monitor should a failure in the current active monitor occur. The standby monitors are essentially monitoring the ring to detect abnormal ring operation that could occur whenever the active monitor has failed. The detection of an error condition by any standby monitor initiates a recovery procedure that allows it or one of the other nodes to become the new monitor [3].

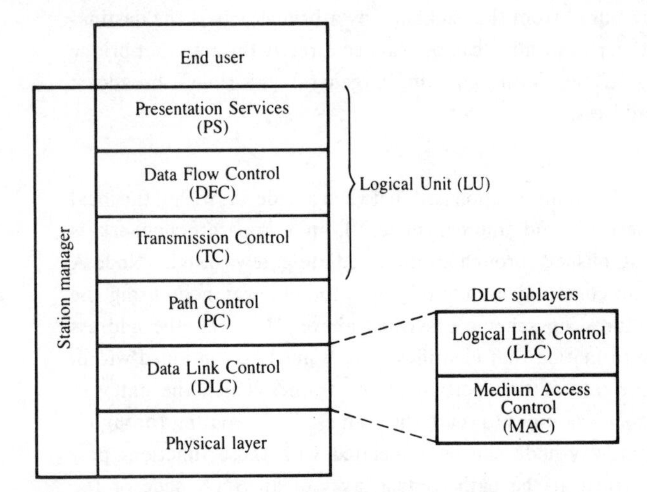

Figure 7 Systems Network Architecture (SNA) layers. Local network protocols and transmissions are performed at the data link control (DLC) and physical layer functional layers of SNA. DLC functions can be further subdivided into logical link control and medium access control sublayers.

Extension of token-access protocol for synchronous applications The token-access control protocol, in conjunction with the priority reservation scheme described earlier, provides a basis for incorporating synchronous data transfer over a token ring [1, 3, 6]. Synchronous operations require that data packets be transmitted and/or received at periodic intervals rather than asynchronously. However, the token-access mechanism is basically an asynchronous control scheme. Synchronous operations, such as real-time digitized voice transfer, can be accomplished by periodically making the ring available only for synchronous data transfer. A special function node, known as a synchronous bandwidth manager, can maintain an internal clock to provide the correct time interval. At the end of each time interval, the synchronous bandwidth manager raises the priority of the circulating free token via the reservation scheme described earlier. This unique priority frame is available only to those nodes requiring synchronous data transfer. The token remains at this priority until all synchronous nodes have had an opportunity to transmit one data frame. The synchronous bandwidth manager then releases a free token at the original priority. The synchronous bandwidth manager must be involved in the establishment of any synchronous communication connections to regulate the synchronous load added to the network so as to avoid excessive delays in the asynchronous traffic.

Token-ring architecture relative to SNA

• *Overview*

A LAN provides a basic transport mechanism for data transfer among nodes within the network. However, the LAN by itself does not provide all of the functions that are necessary for two nodes to manage and conduct a meaningful two-way exchange of information. The same higher-level communication protocols that are implemented to control data transfer across public data networks [31] are also applicable to data transfer across a LAN. IBM's Systems Network Architecture (SNA) and the International Organization for Standardization (ISO) reference model separate network functions into layers to facilitate the description of the protocols as well as their implementation [10, 32, 33]. SNA protocols can be implemented for managing the flow of information within a local network as in any other SNA environment [8]. The basic SNA layers are depicted in Fig. 7. The functions of the lowest layer, known as the *physical layer*, are unique to the particular transport mechanism that is implemented, whether it be a communications loop, a multidrop bus, or a token ring. The next higher layer, *data link control* (DLC), is traditionally independent of the actual physical transport mechanism and performs the functions that are necessary to ensure the integrity of the data that reach the layers above DLC. A modification of this concept that would allow the DLC layer to share physical access functions with the physical layer is presented later. Network flow control and message unit routing functions are provided at the next higher layer, known as *path control* (PC). The composite of the functions at the DLC and PC layers of all of the nodes within an SNA network comprises the path control subnetwork, the fundamental transport mechanism for transferring data from a source SNA node to a destination SNA node.

An end user within an SNA environment may be a person engaged in interactive work at a display terminal or an application software function that is active within a host. The end user in an SNA node is represented to the network by a *logical unit* (LU). A logical unit comprises the functions of the upper three layers of SNA, transmission control (TC), data flow control (DFC), and presentation services (PS). Two end users communicate within an SNA network by establishing a logical path, called a session, between their respective LUs. The LU-LU session provides a temporary connection for moving the data between the end users, utilizing the services of the PC subnetwork. A more detailed discussion of the logical unit functions relative to local area networks can be found in [8]. The functions of the physical layer and the data link control layer are discussed in more detail next.

• *Physical layer*

The physical layer of the model encompasses the basic functions associated with placing the electrical signals onto the transmission medium. This includes such fundamental operations as signal generation, phase timing along the ring, and the encoding of the signal information using the differential Manchester scheme. These operations are performed within the ring interface adapter at each active node in the network.

• *Data link control*

Data link control (DLC) is the next layer above the physical layer in SNA. The IEEE Project 802 Committee on Local Area Networks and the European Computer Manufacturers Association (ECMA) have proposed that for local networks, the data link layer of the ISO model, which corresponds to the DLC layer of SNA, be further subdivided into two functional sublayers: logical link control (LLC) and medium-access control (MAC), as depicted in Fig. 7 [29, 34]. This functional decomposition essentially separates those DLC functions that are hardware dependent from those that are hardware independent, thereby possibly reducing the cost of developing data equipment to interconnect to different types of physical transmission interfaces [35].

Medium-access control sublayer The medium-access control (MAC) sublayer of DLC includes those functions associated with frame and token transmission which can be, but are not necessarily, performed by the interface adapter in each node. The actual functions performed at this sublevel depend upon the LAN architecture that is being implemented. The functions for a token-ring LAN include the following:

- Token protocols—basic token access and generation, including token priority reservation scheme.
- Address recognition—copying of frames from ring based on destination address in physical header.
- Frame delimiters—identifying beginning and ending of frames (transmit and receive) via unique delimiters.
- Frame check sequence (FCS)—calculation and verification of cyclic redundancy check (CRC) for each frame.
- Token monitor—performance of all functions associated with active or standby token monitors.

Logical link control sublayer The second sublayer, logical link control (LLC), includes those functions unique to the particular link control procedures that are associated with the attached node and not the medium access. This permits various logical link protocols to coexist on a common network without interfering with one another. Logical links are established primarily to ensure data integrity to the higher layers. For example, HDLC employs a frame-sequencing protocol for verifying that frames have successfully reached their destination, with the appropriate retransmission of lost frames [14].

Multiple appearances of LLC may exist within each node. In these instances, a link multiplex function within the LLC layer directs incoming frames to the appropriate LLC task and also provides the correct address information for outgoing frames. Each LLC appearance is logically associated with one other LLC appearance in another node. Models of four nodes are shown in Fig. 8, with examples of some of the logical links that may exist. Each link within the figure is identified by the pair of addresses of the nodes at the ends of the logical link. Thus, the point-to-point connectivity discussed earlier is provided by the LLC sublayer of the DLC layer of the architecture.

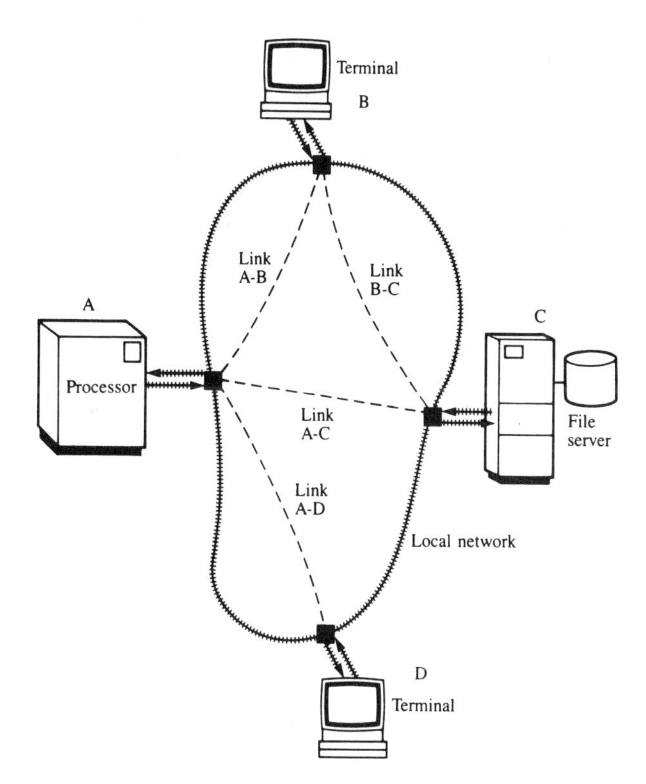

Figure 8 Logical link connectivity. The local network provides the physical transport mechanism for the transfer of data between nodes that have established a logical link connection.

• *Station manager*

The station manager function interfaces to both sublayers of the DLC layer, as well as to the higher layers of SNA. The overall function of the station manager can be partitioned according to the various levels of the architecture, such as PC manager or MAC manager functions. The MAC manager performs operations relative to fault diagnosis and statistics collection within the LAN that are described next.

Ring fault detection and isolation

The topological structure of a star/ring configuration, in conjunction with the token-access control protocol, provides an extremely reliable communication link [5]. The unidirectional propagation of information (electrical signals and data frames) from node to node provides a basis for detecting certain types of network faults which can be categorized into two types: hard faults and soft faults.

A *hard* fault is defined as a complete disruption of the electrical signal path at some point on the ring. This disruption may be caused by a break in the wiring, either in the wiring lobe between a node and the wiring concentrator or in the wiring segment interconnecting two wiring concentrators. The failure of the receiver and/or transmitter of an active node can also cause a total disruption of the signal path. A hard fault is detected immediately by the next active node downstream from the fault as a loss of signal transitions at its receiver. The node that detects the presence of a fault then begins transmitting a unique MAC frame known as a *beacon*. Contained within the beacon frame is the address of the beaconing node as well as the last received address of the active node immediately upstream. (A special function for determining the address of the upstream node is discussed later.) Even though the ring is disrupted at one point, all of the active nodes, except the beaconing node, can receive and transmit normally. Thus, the beacon frame is received by all active nodes and may even be received by the node immediately adjacent to and upstream from the break. Recovery actions at the wiring concentrator might include removing from the ring the beaconing node or the node upstream from the beaconing node, or else switching to an alternate ring, as discussed later.

A *soft* fault is characterized by intermittent errors, usually caused by a degradation in the electrical signal or environmental electromagnetic interference. The frame check sequence (FCS) of all frames is calculated and verified by all intermediate nodes as the frames are repeated. The first node on the ring that detects an FCS error can set the error-detected indicator (EDI) bit in the physical trailer of the frame as an indication to all other nodes that the error has been detected. That node also logs the occurrence of the error by maintaining a count of the errors it has detected. If a predetermined threshold of FCS errors is reached over a given time interval at any one node, an indication of the condition can be reported to a special ring network management (RNM) function. The error report message that is sent to the ring network manager contains information that can be used in locating the source of the soft errors. The node detecting the FCS errors can also send a frame with the SEI bit set to *1* to all other nodes on the ring to inform them that a soft error condition exists on the ring.

The RNM node is a special function node within the local network that is capable of monitoring the network operation and configuration. For example, the RNM node could compile error statistics on the occurrence of FCS errors throughout the network or notify an operator of an excessive number of soft errors at a particular node [6]. With this information, the operator or a software application within the RNM node could initiate an appropriate ring reconfiguration action via a command to an active wiring concentrator to bypass a faulty ring segment or node. The RNM node can also maintain an up-to-date list of what nodes are active on any given ring within the network. Network management functions may be distributed over several RNM nodes in large networks if required.

As described earlier, the ARI bits are set by a node whenever it recognizes its own address within the destination field of that frame. If two nodes on a ring were inadvertently assigned the same address, one of the nodes would detect that the ARI bits had been set by the other node. This condition is reported as an error to the RNM node for action.

The isolation of a fault is enhanced if the node detecting and reporting it can also identify the address of the next active upstream node from the fault. This address information can be considered in conjunction with the address of the reporting node to expedite the isolation of a fault, such as was described in the beaconing and soft error procedures earlier. Thus, periodically, the active monitor issues a broadcast frame called a roll-call-poll MAC frame [1]. The first active node downstream from the monitor node sets the ARI bits and copies the source address. Other nodes on the ring do not copy the address information in this particular broadcast frame when the ARI bits are set. The node that received the roll-call-poll frame then issues a roll-call-repeat MAC frame containing its own source address whenever a free token is observed. This frame is recognized and copied by the next downstream active node. This process continues around the ring until the active monitor receives the roll-call-repeat MAC frame without the ARI bits set. At that time, each node has copied and saved the specific address of the adjacent node immediately upstream. This information is transmitted with all beacon frames and soft error report frames, thereby allowing the RNM node to log the general location of the fault.

Once the general location of a fault (hard or soft) has been determined, some action is necessary to eliminate the faulty segment(s) from the ring so that normal operation can resume. The wiring concentrators provide concentration points for bypassing such faults, as was discussed earlier with lobe bypass. A separate technique is necessary if reconfiguration is required as a result of faults occurring within the ring segments interconnecting wiring concentrators. Alternate backup links can be installed between the wiring concentrators in parallel with the principal links (Fig. 9). If a fault occurs in the ring segment between two wiring concentrators, wrapping of the principal ring to the alternate ring within the two wiring concentrators restores the physical path of the ring. This wrapping function, like the lobe bypass function, may be activated manually or via automatic switching logic, or may be command initiated from an RNM node. The figure shows four wiring concentrators as they would be configured to bypass such a fault with both a principal and an alternate ring. The signals on the alternate ring are propagated in the direction opposite to those on the principal ring, thus maintaining the logical order of the nodes on the ring. In other words, node N remains immediately downstream from node M. Consequently, configuration tables associated with the network management functions do not have to be altered [1]. In addition to the procedure for bypassing faults, each node can perform self-diagnostic tests of its own circuitry and wiring lobe to ensure that it does not disrupt the signal path when it is inserted into the ring. If these tests indicate a potential problem, the node is not inserted into the ring until after the situation is remedied [6].

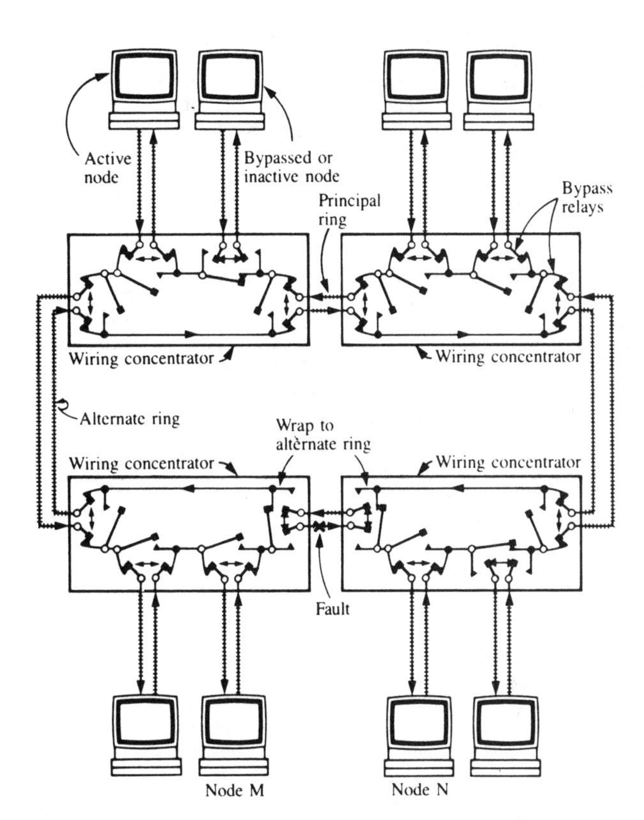

Figure 9 Ring reconfiguration with alternate ring. A fault on the ring between two wiring concentrators can be bypassed by wrapping the connections within the wiring concentrators, thereby using the alternate path and maintaining the same node ordering that existed before the fault occurred.

Summary

This tutorial has highlighted many of the key aspects of a token-ring local area network. The star/ring topology with token-access control offers a network architecture that can satisfy today's requirements while allowing for future growth and expansion. Wiring concentrators provide points throughout a building for a radial wiring scheme in which any node can be isolated from the network in case of failure. This concept forms the basis for a network management scheme that should provide quick isolation and recovery from both hard faults and soft faults. Token-ring networks are extendible in that additional token-controlled rings may be added to the network through the use of bridges. Furthermore, a hierarchical network structure can be implemented in a large building or a campus environment by interconnecting multiple bridges via a high-speed backbone. The backbone link may utilize the token-access control scheme on either another baseband ring or a channel within a broadband communication system (e.g., CATV). A token-ring LAN provides the basic transport mechanism for the transfer of data among nodes within the LAN. Higher-level communication protocols, such as those within SNA, must be implemented to ensure meaningful and reliable information exchange across the network.

Acknowledgments

The author wishes to acknowledge Roy C. Dixon, Don W. Andrews, and James D. Markov for their contributions and suggestions in preparing this tutorial, and Frank P. Corr and Edward H. Sussenguth for their technical review and comments. Several IBM researchers have contributed to the overall token-ring concepts presented here. The basic research within IBM that led to the development of this token-ring LAN architecture was conducted at the IBM Research Laboratory in Zurich, Switzerland.

References

1. R. C. Dixon, N. C. Strole, and J. D. Markov, "A Token-Ring Network for Local Data Communications," *IBM Syst. J.* **22**, 47–62 (1983).
2. W. Bux, F. Closs, P. A. Janson, K. Kümmerle, and H. R. Müller, "A Reliable Token Ring System for Local-Area Communication," *Proceedings of the National Telecommunications Conference*, November 1981, pp. A.2.2.1–A.2.2.6.
3. W. Bux, F. Closs, P. A. Janson, K. Kümmerle, H. R. Müller, and E. H. Rothauser, "A Local-Area Communication Network Based on a Reliable Token Ring System," *Proceedings of the International Symposium on Local Computer Networks*, Florence, Italy, April 1982, pp. 69–82.
4. H. R. Müller, H. Keller, and H. Meyer, "Transmission in a Synchronous Token Ring," *Proceedings of the International Symposium on Local Computer Networks*, Florence, Italy, April 1982, pp. 125–147.
5. R. C. Dixon, "Ring Network Topology for Local Data Communications," *Proc. COMPCON Fall '82*, Washington, DC, IEEE Catalog No. 82CH1796-2, pp. 591–605, available through the IEEE, 445 Hoes Lane, Piscataway, NJ 08854.
6. D. W. Andrews and G. D. Schultz, "A Token-Ring Architecture for Local-Area Networks—An Update," *Proc. COMPCON Fall '82*, Washington, DC, IEEE Catalog No. 82CH1796-2, pp. 615–624, available through the IEEE, 445 Hoes Lane, Piscataway, NJ 08854.
7. P. Abramson and F. E. Noel, "Matching the Media to Local Network Requirements," *Data Communications* **12**, No. 7, pp. 115–123 (July 1983).

8. J. G. Rusnak, "Local-Area Networking and Higher-Level Protocols: An SNA Example," *Contribution of Working Papers to IEEE Project 802 on Local Area Networks*, IBM CPD Publication, March 8, 1982; available through IBM branch offices.
9. J. D. Markov and N. C. Strole, "Token Ring Local Area Networks—A Perspective," *Proc. COMPCON Fall '82*, Washington, DC, IEEE Catalog No. 82CH1796-2, pp. 606–614, available through the IEEE, 445 Hoes Lane, Piscataway, NJ 08854.
10. *Systems Network Architecture: Concepts and Products*, Order No. GC30-3072, available through IBM branch offices.
11. David R. Jarema and Edward H. Sussenguth, "IBM Data Communications: A Quarter Century of Evolution and Progress," *IBM J. Res. Develop.* **25,** 391–404 (1981).
12. J. F. Keeley et al., "An Application-Oriented Multiprocessing System," *IBM Syst. J.* **6,** 78–133 (1967).
13. P. M. Karp, "Origin, Development and Current Status of the ARPA Network," *Proceedings of the Seventh Annual IEEE Computer Society International Conference*, San Francisco, 1973, pp. 49–52.
14. *Data Communication—High-Level Data Link Control Procedures—Frame Structure*, ISO Draft Proposal ISO/DP 3309 (Revision of ISO Standard ISO/3309-1976), October 1981; available through the American National Standards Institute, 1430 Broadway, New York, NY 10018.
15. D. D. Clark, K. T. Pogran, and D. P. Reed, "An Introduction to Local Area Networks," *Proc. IEEE* **66,** 1497–1517 (1978).
16. David J. Farber, Julian Feldman, Frank R. Heinrich, Marsha D. Hopwood, Kenneth C. Larson, Donald C. Loomis, and Lawrence A. Rowe, "The Distributed Computing System," *Proceedings of the Seventh Annual IEEE Computer Society International Conference*, San Francisco, 1973, pp. 31–34.
17. J. R. Pierce, "Network for Block Switching of Data," *Bell Syst. Tech. J.* **51,** 1133–1145 (1972).
18. J. H. Saltzer and K. T. Pogran, "A Star-Shaped Ring Network with High Maintainability," *Proceedings of the Local Area Communications Network Symposium*, Boston, May 1979, pp. 179–189.
19. M. V. Wilkes and R. M. Needham, "The Cambridge Model Distributed System," *ACM Oper. Syst. Rev.* **14,** 21–29 (1980).
20. *IBM Series/1 Local Communications Control, General Information*, Order No. GA27-3093, available through IBM branch offices.
21. R. M. Metcalfe and D. R. Boggs, "Ethernet: Distributed Packet Switching for Local Computer Networks," *Commun. ACM* **19,** 395–404 (1976).
22. "A Survey of Digital Baseband Signaling Techniques," *NASA Technical Memorandum X-64615*, University of Tennessee, June 1971.
23. "Token-Passing Bus Access Method and Physical Layer Specifications," *IEEE Standard 802.4*, Draft D, Sections 14–15, December 1982; available from the Director of Standards, IEEE, 345 East 47th St., New York, NY 10017.
24. W. Bux, "Local-Area Subnetworks: A Performance Comparison," *IEEE Trans. Commun.* **29,** 1465–1473 (1981).
25. B. W. Stuck, "Calculating the Maximum Mean Data Rate in Local Area Networks," *Computer* **16,** No. 5, 72–76 (1983).
26. K. Kümmerle and M. Reiser, "Local-Area Communication Networks—An Overview," *J. Telecommun. Networks* **1,** 349–370 (1982).
27. D. I.-H. Park and R. D. Love, "An Analysis of the Tolerance to Crosstalk Noise of a Pulse Width Modulation System," *IBM J. Res. Develop.* **27,** 432–439 (1983, this issue).
28. A. X. Widmer and P. A. Franaszek, "A DC-Balanced, Partitioned-Block, 8B/10B Transmission Code," *IBM J. Res. Develop.* **27,** 440–451 (1983, this issue).
29. *IEEE Project 802, Local Network Standard, Draft C*, May 1982; available from the Director of Standards, IEEE, 345 East 47th St., New York, NY 10017.
30. J. H. Saltzer, D. P. Reed, and D. D. Clark, "Source Routing for Campus-Wide Internet Transport," *Local Networks for Computer Communications*, North-Holland Publishing Co., New York, 1981, pp. 1–23.
31. F. P. Corr and D. H. Neal, "SNA and Emerging International Standards," *IBM Syst. J.* **18,** 244–262 (1979).
32. *ISO Reference Model of Open-Systems Interconnection* ISO/TC97/SC16, DP 7498; available from the American National Standards Institute, 1430 Broadway, New York, NY 10018 (Rev., January 1983).
33. P. François and A. Potocki, "Some Methods for Providing OSI Transport in SNA," *IBM J. Res. Develop.* **27,** 452–463 (1983, this issue).
34. Standard ECMA-80-81-82, Local Area Networks: Coaxial Cable System—Physical Layer—Link Layer, September 1982.
35. K. N. Larson and W. R. Chestnut, "Adding Another Layer to the ISO Net Architecture Reduces Costs," *Data Communications*, 215–222 (1983).

Received March 29, 1983; revised June 28, 1983

Norman C. Strole *IBM Communication Products Division, P.O. Box 12195, Research Triangle Park, North Carolina 27709.* Dr. Strole is a staff engineer at the Research Triangle Park laboratory, where he is currently involved in the performance evaluation and analysis of local area network systems. He joined IBM in 1973 and prior to his current assignment worked in the development and performance evaluation of the IBM supermarket/retail store systems. His research activities have included the development of a simulation methodology for the performance evaluation of shared-resource computer architectures. Dr. Strole received a B.S. in electrical engineering from North Carolina State University, Raleigh, in 1973. He received the M.S. and Ph.D. in electrical engineering from Duke University in 1975 and 1980, respectively. He currently holds an adjunct appointment in the School of Electrical Engineering at Duke University and is a member of Eta Kappa Nu, the Institute of Electrical and Electronics Engineers, and Tau Beta Pi.

WHY A RING?*

Jerome H. Saltzer and David D. Clark

Massachusetts Institute of Technology
Laboratory for Computer Science
Cambridge, Massachusetts

Kenneth T. Pogran

Bolt Beranek and Newman Inc.
Cambridge, Massachusetts

Abstract

In a world increasingly populated with Ethernets and Ethernet-like nets a few sites continue to experiment with rings of active repeaters for local data communication. This paper explores some of the engineering problems involved in designing a ring that has no central control, and then compared the M.I.T.-designed ring with the Ethernet on a variety of operational and subtle technical grounds, on each of which the ring may possess important or interesting advantages.

Introduction

The M.I.T. Laboratory for Computer Science has, for more than two years, been operating a prototype one Mbit/sec. distributed control ring network of eight nodes. The laboratory is engaged in checkout of an improved, simpler, ten Mbit/sec. ring design, intended to link groups of up to 250 desktop computers. Since there are already several competing local network designs that use contention-controlled broadcast on passive coaxial cable rather than a repeater ring, we are often asked why one should bother to develop an alternative approach--the contention-controlled broadcast technology is field proven, its properties are well understood and adequate for the application. In addition, there are at least three difficult engineering problems involved in the design of a distributed control ring network: reliability of the repeater string, distributed initialization and recovery, and closed-loop clock coordination. Of course the ring approach has also been field-proven[1,2,3], but in no case in a form that settles all the questions. Upon analysis, it appears that an apparent preference for contention-controlled broadcast networks in the United States but for ring networks in Europe has been more determined by accidental historical precedents than by persuasive technical arguments.

This paper examines briefly nine technical differences between the contention-controlled broadcast approach and the ring, and argues that it seems interesting to pursue the ring technology. It assumes that the reader is familiar with the basic concepts involved in local networks and in ring networks as described in published papers[4,5]. There are a wide variety of possible designs both for rings and for passive proadcast networks, and these design choices have both gross and subtle differences that affect comparisons. To be specific, the kind of ring network assumed in this discussion is a token-controlled system in which the originator removes his own message and in which there is no central control or monitor station. Both the one and ten Mbit/sec. rings at M.I.T. mentioned earlier are of this design. For contrast, the Ethernet local communication network developed by the Xerox Palo Alto Research Center will be used, with the understanding that it is typical of a contention-controlled passive coaxial cable broadcast design[6,7,8]. The Mitre Corporation MITREBUS[9], another contention-controlled broadcast design, is mentioned for comparison also.

These specific designs are chosen because they reflect two distinct and important design choices:

- access control by contention (Ethernet) versus token (ring), and

- communication by broadcast (Ethernet) versus point-to-point (ring).

As shall be seen, the nine technical differences discussed all flow directly from these two choices. This point should be kept in mind when applying the observations to other local network designs that use a different combination of design choices, for example, a token-controlled broadcast net or a contention-controlled ring.

*Authors' addresses: J.H. Saltzer and D.D. Clark, M.I.T. Laboratory for Computer Science, 545 Technology Square, Cambridge, Mass. 02139. K.T. Pogran, Bolt Beranek and Newman Inc., 50 Moulton Street, Cambridge, Mass. 02138. Please address correspondence to J. H. Saltzer, telephone (617) 253-6016.

This research was supported by the Advanced Research Projects Agency of the Department of Defense and was monitored by the Office of Naval Research under contract number N00014-75-C-0661.

Reprinted from *The Proceedings of the Seventh Data Communications Symposium*, 1981, pages 211-217.

Ring design problems

The three difficult ring engineering problems referred to above appear to have elegant and straightforward solutions, and one of the reasons for trying out ring technology in the field is to verify that these solutions work well in practice. Other papers[5,10,11,12] explore these three engineering problems and considerations in their solution in some depth, so they are only summarized here:

1. Reliability of the repeater string. The basic problem here is that a failure in any one repeater can disrupt the entire local network and, if one strings together one hundred or more active repeaters, one would expect to end up with a very fragile system. Further, locating the troublesome repeater could require perambulation of the entire network. Very reliable repeaters and careful system engineering seem to be needed at first glance. However, a simpler solution to these problems is to arrange the transmission links between successive nodes so that each internode link loops through a central point, a wire center. At the wire center, bypass relays that are energized remotely by the network stations can do a majority of the reconfiguration operations automatically. The resulting configuration, a star-shaped ring, creates a centralized location for maintenance and reconfiguration and at the same time provides reliability, without compromising the distributed nature of the ring control. Further, clusters of nodes can be connected by nearby wire centers that are in turn connected hierarchically through more distant wire centers. This approach reduces the wiring cost that one might anticipate in a star topology.

2. Distributed initialization and recovery. To avoid designating some one ring node as special (and thereby making ring operation depend on that node's continued good health) some algorithm is required whereby all active repeaters can quickly and simply agree upon the need for initialization and recovery, and not fall all over one another trying to accomplish it. A suitable strategy can be devised using two ideas developed for passive broadcast networks. First, when any node detects ring trouble, it jams (as in Ethernet) the ring net with a characteristic signal that insures agreement among all participants. Second, after jamming, a virtual token, whose time of arrival is based on the station's address (as in the Chaosnet[13],) determines which single station actually performs network reinitialization.

3. Closed-loop clock coordination. A subtle problem of distributed agreement on data transmission rate arises in a ring. The issue is that not only must the collection of repeaters agree on a common clock rate, but that clock rate must result in an integral number of bit times of delay when traversing the closed ring. Fortunately, there appear to be at least three different, workable ways of achieving this agreement. The simplest of these ways is to open the ring when originating a message, and thereby allow all non-originating repeaters simply to track the originator. An intermediate approach based on inserting time wedges in the clock at repeaters that fall behind the fastest repeater was used in the prototype ring[5]. The most sophisticated approach is to have a phase-locked-loop in each repeater tracking its preceding neighbor, and design loop filters so that the resulting ring of PLL's is stable[12].

These three problems are, of course, problems only until they are solved. Since good solutions appear to be in hand, the following discussion assumes that the ring design being compared with the Ethernet includes the star topology, automatic decentralized reinitialization, and any one of the clock coordination techniques.

Nine points of comparison of rings with Ethernets

1. The contention-controlled broadcast net has a significant analog engineering component, while the ring net is almost entirely a digital design. This difference looks very interesting to explore, because of its possible ramifications in ability to exploit rapidly advancing progress in digital technology and VLSI. To understand this difference, consider that a broadcast net transmitter's signal must be receivable by all receivers on the cable. These receivers are at varying distances from the transmitter and therefore will experience different attenuations and echoes. Similarly each receiver must be able to hear every transmitter. In all, there are , N(N-1) such combinations that must work in an N-node network, and the transceiver system must be designed conservatively enough that the worst possible receiver-transmitter placement combination (in terms of echo buildup and attenuation) must deliver acceptable performance. The analog noise level contributed by idle transmitters grows with the number of nodes, though probably less than linearly. Finally, in order for a "listen-while-transmit" collision detection feature of an Ethernet to work, an active transceiver must be able to notice that it is not the only active one. Thus the receiver part must be capable of detecting the weakest other transmitter during its own transmissions and distinguishing that other transmitter from its own transmitter's echoes. This set of requirements is not impossible to meet, but very careful analog transmission system engineering is needed, and the resulting design has many analog components. In contrast, the analog part of a ring network repeater is more tractable. Any given transmitter sends a signal down a private line to only one receiver. The receiver has one echo environment and one received signal level to cope with. Thus, a relatively simple line driver/line receiver combination can suffice. For this reason, the passive broadcast technology is straining to reach a 10 Mbit/sec. signalling rate with a 200 node net, while the ring can operate at

that speed and scale with a fairly elementary analog system.

While engineering in the analog domain is substantially easier in the ring, in the digital domain the situation reverses. Note that two of the three difficult ring engineering problems discussed earlier (initialization and clock coordination) can be handled by techniques that are mostly digital. This difference in the character of the hard engineering problems of the two technologies offers an exploitation opportunity that may favor the ring network. The recent and projected waves of technology improvement have benefited the digital domain more than the analog, mostly because it is easy to see how to solve problems systematically by increasing digital component count; it often seems to be harder to take systematic advantage of increased numbers of components in the analog domain. A less compelling, but still interesting, argument is that because of the simple analog transmission system required by the ring, even the line drivers and receivers might be integrable into a future VLSI implementation; it is probably harder to do this integration for the more complex analog transceiver technology of the passive broadcast net.

2. A problem with the Ethernet that is closely related to its analog domain engineering emphasis lies in ground reference and power supply. It is important that a local network not impose a uniform ground reference on all attached hosts. If it did, the network risks carrying large ground currents or creating ground loops. In order to obtain maximum transceiver performance, all present Ethernet designs seem to require direct coupling of an active component (e.g., the base of a transistor) to the cable, with consequent need for a power supply whose ground reference is the cable shield. To avoid adding a central, shared component, a per-node, isolated power supply for the active part of the transceiver electronics seems to be a requirement of an Ethernet. The ring, on the other hand, can be designed to deliver enough energy that ground isolation can be achieved in the signal path ahead of the first active component of the receiver. (The prototype M.I.T. ring used optical isolators for this purpose; the ten Mbit/sec. ring uses pulse transformers.) Finally, because sensitive, active electronic components are directly attached to the Ethernet coaxial cable conductors, transient suppression (e.g., from lightning) requires that the coaxial cable ground shield system be grounded at no more than one point. To enforce this requirement and maintain the ability to divide a long cable into sections for trouble shooting, the Ethernet specification[8] requires that there be no ground for the cable. Such a floating conductive system becomes a severe personnel hazard in the case in which it accidentally becomes shorted to an electric power conductor.

3. Electromagnetic compatibility between the net and other physically adjacent electrical equipment is generally easier to engineer with a balanced transmission medium than with an unbalanced one. One of the attractions of the Ethernet is the ease of attaching to it at any point, which ease relies on the use of clamp-on connectors with coaxial cable, an unbalanced medium. If one tried to use a balanced transmission medium for the Ethernet, it would probably become necessary to install ordinary connectors every time a new node is added, and the easy attachment virtue would be compromised. In addition, the Ethernet strategy of listening for collisions depends on the transmitter being off half the time. Collision detection with balanced lines would probably become more complex, since in the most obvious balanced waveform modulation schemes the transmitter runs continuously rather than for half of each bit time. In contrast, the ring network can use shielded twisted pair and balanced waveform modulation, thereby reducing both radiation to other equipment and susceptibility of the network to noise spikes and electrical interference originating elsewhere. At the same time, the passive star arrangement for a ring captures much of the easy attachment property.

4. An attraction of the passive broadcast net is the intrinsic high reliability that comes from having a minimum number of active components whose failure can disrupt the net. The most important shared component--the coaxial cable--is completely passive. In contrast, the primary objection to a ring network is the operational fragility of a series string of 100 or more repeaters. However, this fragility appears to be easy to overcome by the passive star arrangement of the ring network.

5. Another attraction of the passive broadcast net is that it is exceptionally easy to install--a single cable is routed through the building, near every office or other location in which a network node might be needed. Actual attachment of nodes can be deferred until the node is required, at which time attachment can be accomplished by clamp-on connectors; attachment does not disrupt network operation. However, hand-in-hand with this convenience goes an associated inconvenience, namely that trouble isolation and first-aid repair cannot easily be centralized. Some kinds of failures will require foot-by-foot inspection of the network and each node attachment, involving access to offices and other spaces throughout the building. The passive star configuration of the ring network appears to completely overcome this potential problem. With a passive star, addition of a new station involves running a cable from the office to a nearby wire center, so one might consider wiring a building in advance by running one such cable per office. Then, installation of a station is done by attaching a connector and plugging it in. No extra disruption is associated with this kind of installation. Further, many buildings are already designed with cable trays and wire ducts in place that emanate from a wire center, because both telephone and electric power wiring practice also call for wire centers. Field experience with both kinds of networks is really required to determine which is more effective on day-to-day operational issues such as this and the previous two. Such experience is being reported for the Ethernet[7,14]; corresponding experience with a ring is not yet so extensive.

6. There is an intrinsic limitation in the contention-controlled broadcast net approach in its ability to make effective use of higher speed transmission media, such as optical fibers. In a contention network, at the beginning of each packet transmission there is a period when there is a risk of collision: this period is proportional to the length of the transmission medium, since the packet is exposed to collision until its first bit propagates to the farthest transceiver. The duration of this exposure is thus fixed by the physical configuration. As the transmission speed increases, the time required to transmit an average size packet decreases, until the packet transmission time becomes as short as the cable propagation time. At that point, most of the advantage of carrier sense is lost and the system becomes an ordinary Aloha channel, with an intrinsic data capacity limit of about 18% of the channel capacity[6,15]. For a 1 Km. coaxial cable, the end-to-end propagation time is typically 4500 nsec. This is comparable to the time required to transmit a 60-octet packet at 100 Mbit/sec. Thus an attempt to build a 100 Mbit/sec. passive broadcast net might result in an effective performance limit near 20 Mbit/sec. The ring, because it does not use a contention access scheme, does not have any corresponding limiting effect, and thus can be scaled up directly to a 100 Mbit/sec. configuration. (The importance of this limitation in contention-controlled nets depends critically on the distribution of packet sizes. If most packets are 6000, rather than 60, octets in length the limitation would be inconsequential at a 100 Mbit/sec. rate. One can make a good argument that any application that requires a 100 Mbit/sec. transmission rate for 100 nodes will not typically generate small packets because of per-packet software overhead, so there should be an opportunity to avoid the Aloha phenomenon. Until some more experience is gained with applications that really require this bandwidth, the questions will remain unanswered. Experience with the Hyperchannel[16] network, which is a contention-controlled net that runs at 50 Mbit/sec., may be useful in this regard.

7. A second limitation of the passive broadcast net approach that appears to require some considerable ingenuity to overcome is to take advantage of fiber optic technology. This technology offers the attraction of very high speed, excellent electromagnetic compatibility, avoidance of lightning and ground reference problems, and (predicted) low cost. However, the problems of turning optical fiber into a broadcast medium are formidable. One must invent a satisfactory technique for tapping an optical fiber and detecting a signal without diverting too much optical energy or else the system will not scale up very well in number of nodes. Yet the same tap must allow introducing a new signal without loss. (Some recent experiments with many-tailed star couplers are promising, but that approach gives up the single cable routed by every office that is one of the chief attractions of the Ethernet[17].) In contrast, since a ring network uses one-way, point-to-point transmission, replacing the wire links in a ring network with fiber optic links is quite straightforward. The Cambridge ring has operated for some time with one fiber optic link[1].

8. Because it uses repeaters, a ring network can with ease span much greater physical distances than can the passive broadcast net. The passive broadcast net can also be augmented with repeaters, as in the new Ethernet standard and the Mitrebus. However, use of contention control, which makes the propagation time between the two most widely separated stations a critical, performance-limiting parameter, limits the distance that one can extend a broadcast net even with repeaters. Since in order to arrange a ring to span a longer distance at least parts of it must be "stretched out" rather than fully looped back in a passive star, one trades away some maintenance ease to gain a greater geographical span. Thus the contention-controlled broadcast net trades both performance and maintenance ease with increased geographical coverage, while the ring trades only maintenance ease. The distance spanning effect is quite substantial, for two reasons. First, when using comparably expensive driver, receiver, and cable technology, a single ring link, being point-to-point rather than broadcast, can be slightly longer than a single broadcast cable segment. Second, when successive ring links are placed in tandem the maximum geographical span is multiplied by half the number of stations--perhaps a factor of 100. Thus for an area such as a campus of a hundred buildings and building wings, a ring may have a considerable advantage over a passive broadcast network.

9. A final, practical question to consider is whether or not there might be anything about a ring network that intrinsically requires either more or less complex logic than a contention-controlled broadcast network. Only examination of in-field designs can answer this question, but such examination is trickier than one might expect, because every local net designer seems to have chosen a different function packaging approach. Thus one design includes packet buffers, another doesn't but includes a direct memory access channel for some popular computer bus, the next assumes that part of the network control will be handled by software rather than hardware. To compare more carefully, implementations for the experimental Ethernet, the M.I.T. Artificial Intelligence Laboratory Chaosnet, and the ten Mbit/sec. ring network were compared by measuring the board area required to hold the implementation of the network control logic up to but not including speed-matching buffers. All three were found to require something less than 50 square inches of densely packed wire-wrap card. Casual observation of the implementation of a Mitrebus interface and a Prime Computer ring net controller suggested that these two network designs were similar in complexity to the others.

The conclusion is that there is no significant intrinsic difference in the complexity of implementation of the two approaches, and a straightforward TTL implementation of a ring network should require about the same amount of hardware as an equivalent function contention-controlled broadcast net operating at the same speed. (This comparison of hardware complexity is distinct from that of point one, earlier, which raised some questions about the ease of VLSI implementation of the analog components of the broadcast network.)

Non-determinism

A sometimes-mentioned point of difference between token control as used in the ring and contention control as used in the Ethernet is the ability to predict the maximum time one must wait to obtain access. Superficially, it appears that a carefully-designed token control net could have an advantage here. If one limits the maximum message length, and insists that the token must be passed along after sending one message, then every network user has a guarantee that the token makes steady progress, and one can calculate with confidence the maximum length of time one might have to wait for access. In contrast, in the case of the Ethernet, since every attempt to transmit could in principle produce a collision, there is a worrisome possibility that one could go on engaging in collisions indefinitely. Such a possibility would be of concern, for example, in a distributed real-time process control application in which a deadline might be missed. This property is sometimes summarized by saying that the Ethernet is "non-deterministic".

That analysis is, however, superficial, because it omits a real-world consideration that intervenes to make the contention network and the token network much more similar than one might expect. In any network, no matter how access is controlled, there is a finite probability of transmission error. In a token-controlled ring, an error may destroy the token at the worst possible time, or when a station nearing a deadline finally receives the token the message it sends may be damaged by an error, and retransmission may be needed. Thus the prospective recipient of the message can find that the deadline has been missed; the token ring is non-deterministic, too. One must accept the fact that the real-world provides no guarantees, only a probability of success. Once that principle is clear, one can specify a required success probability and choose system parameters accordingly. However, this approach applies equally well to the token and contention networks. Given a required probability of successfully meeting a deadline, one can calculate immediately a loading level for an Ethernet that meets the deadline with more than the required probability in the face of contention. The rest of the system must, of course, be designed to insure that the intended Ethernet load is not exceeded, either absolutely or else with a probability consistent with the system success goal.

The numbers that result can be quite practical. For example, in a 50-node ring, one must plan to wait for as many as 50 maximum length messages to be sent until the token arrives. The probability that an Ethernet is busy for n or more successive message intervals when it is loaded to a fraction of its capacity r ($r<1$, exponential message arrivals, fixed message length) is approximately r^n. For $r = 0.5$ (a 50% loaded network) the probability that a wait of more the 50 message intervals occurs is thus less than about 10^{-16}, probably 5 orders of magnitude smaller than the probability of a transmission error that calls for retry or reinitialization.

In practice there is one more level of subtlety to this line of argument. Suppose we have designed both an Ethernet and a ringnet for a time-critical application, and have determined the error rates on both nets and the maximum allowed load on the Ethernet so that the chance of missing the deadline is acceptably small. In the case of a token-controlled ring, if any host attempts to present an abnormal traffic load to the network, the token-control mechanism effectively throttles the runaway host, and other network participants still have their usual chance of meeting their deadlines. In the contention-controlled Ethernet, an abnormally active host can increase the probability of contention and perhaps thereby lower the chance of meeting deadlines. This difference represents a genuine advantage of the token ring. But if the system is correctly designed, this effect must be second order, when one considers that any single host is normally throttled internally by software overhead anyway. Although one might hypothesize a conspiracy of several runaway nodes, such a hypothesis takes us into the realm of predictably low-probability events. (One can also argue about whether incorrectly designed Ethernets fail more spectacularly than incorrectly designed token rings, but that somehow seems to be an uninteresting discussion.)

Thus it appears to us that the non-determinism of the contention system is an unimportant difference with the token approach.

Broadband

A related idea is that of using radio frequency broadcast signalling on coaxial cable ("Broadband") as, for example, the Mitre Corporation has done[9]. In these systems, both broadcast and contention control of access are used, so this scheme boils down to translating an Ethernet from baseband to some carrier frequency. It thus has most of the same attractions and disadvantages of the Ethernet, but with three extra appeals:

a) The same coaxial cable can also carry other radio frequency signals with different purposes, for example cable television. Thus bringing the data network into an office would automatically bring the CATV system there, too.

b) The coaxial cable is used in a frequency range where there is less dispersion (change of propagation velocity with frequency) so a greater bandwidth can be obtained.

c) The cable television industry has developed a useful collection of modestly priced components, including cable attachment hardware and radio frequency linear integrated circuits that one could exploit. In particular, high bandwidth, low delay analog repeaters are available at a modest price; this availability leads to more uniform, higher signal levels. Higher signal levels in turn allow simpler analog design and ground isolation techniques to be used.

The radio frequency signalling approach, however, ends up with the same kind of large analog engineering component as does the Ethernet-type broadcast net, this time in the form of wide-band linear amplifiers, voltage controlled oscillators, filters, modems, and phase-locked loops. Although there are available integrated circuits that help perform those functions, in real applications those circuits must be surrounded by additional analog components--capacitors, resistors, transformers, etc. In exploiting cable television industry developments, one misses the opportunity to exploit what may be even more potent (by reason of volume and potential total integration) economic forces in the digital logic area. Finally, if one tries to make use of the potential for higher bandwidth it turns out that one cannot so easily take advantage of the television industry chips. But if one uses discrete components, the cost climbs substantially.

Apart from these considerations, the broadband network is an example of a contention-controlled broadcast system, so the earlier technical comparisons with the token-controlled ring seem to apply to it also.

Conclusions

Considering these various technical arguments, it appears that one cannot make a clear case for either the contention-controlled broadcast net or the ring technologies. Both approaches have good arguments in their favor, and it is likely that operational issues such as ease of installation, maintenance, and administration will dominate the detailed technical issues. Thus practical experience with 100-node ring networks is really required to establish concrete comparisons of reliability and ease of maintenance and reconfiguration in the field. The answer to the question asked in the opening paragraph is that there seems to be substantial technical interest in continuing to develop ring technology.

A second conclusion concerns the interpretation of standards for local networks, such as the recently announced Ethernet standard of Xerox, Intel, and Digital Equipment Corporation[8]. With the current state of understanding and with substantial technical issues still to be resolved, such standards today can only provide guidance on how to implement a particular technology, not on choice of technology itself. A second standard may be required for ring technology, just as separate standards apply to phonograph records and magnetic tapes. It is possible that one could define a local network interconnection interface standard that is technology-independent although one may anticipate substantial technical arguments about what functions are desirable or feasible in a compatibility interface. (The IEEE Data Link Media Access Committee seems to have started some of these arguments rolling[18].)

Acknowledgements

This paper is a collection of conclusions and thoughts developed in conversations over several years with ring and Ethernet advocates too numerous to identify. Comments on drafts of this paper by Butler Lampson and David Reed sharpened up several of the observations.

References

1. Wilkes, M.V., and Wheeler, D.J., "The Cambridge Digital Communication Ring," Proc. Local Area Comm. Network Symposium, May, 1979, pp. 47-61.

2. Gordon, R.L., et al., "Ringnet: A packet switched local network with decentralized control," 4th Conf. on Local Networks, Minneapolis, October, 1979, pp. 13-19.

3. Okuda, N., Kunikyo, T., and Kaji, T., "Ring Century Bus-an Experimental High Speed Channel for Computer Communications," Proc. Fourth Int. Conf. on Computer Communications, September, 1978, pp. 161-166.

Clark, D.D., Pogran, K.T., and Reed, D.P., "An Introduction to Local Area Networks," Proc. IEEE 66, 11 (November, 1978), pp. 1497-1517.

5. Mockapetris, P.V., et al., "On the Design of Local Network Interfaces," 1977 IFIP Congress Proceedings, pp. 427-430.

6. Metcalfe, R.M., and Boggs, D.R., "Ethernet: Distributed Packet Switching for Local Computer Networks," CACM 19, 7 (July, 1976) pp. 395-404.

7. Crane, R.C., and Taft, E.A., "Practical Considerations in Ethernet Local Network Design," Hawaii Int. Conf. on System Sciences. January, 1980.

8. "The Ethernet," Version 1.0, Digital Equipment Corp., Intel Corp., and Xerox Corp., September, 1980.

9. Meisner, N.B., et al., "Time Division Digital Bus Techniques Implemented on Coaxial Cable," Proc. Comp. Network Symposium, National Bureau of Standards, Gaithersburg, Md., December 15, 1977, pp. 112-117.

10. Saltzer, J.H., and Pogran, K., "A Star-Shaped Ring Network with High Maintainability," Proc. Local Area Communications Network Symposium, Mitre Corp., May, 1979, pp. 179-190.

11. Saltzer, J.H., "Communication ring initialization without central control," M.I.T. Laboratory for Computer Science

Technical Memorandum TM-202, July, 1981.

12. Leslie, I.M., "Frequency Stability in a Unidirectional Ring of Phase Locked Loops," unpublished working paper of University of Cambridge Computer Laboratory, ca. 1979.

13. Moon, D.A., "Chaosnet," Massachusetts Institute of Technology Artificial Intelligence Laboratory Memorandum 628, (June, 1981).

14. Shoch, J.E., and Hupp, J.A., "Performance of an Ethernet Local Network: A Preliminary Report," Proc. of Local Area Comm. Network Symposium, May, 1980, pp. 113-125.

15. Abramson, N., "Packet switching with satellites," AFIPS Conf. Proc. (NCC 1973), New York, June 1973, pp. 695-702.

16. Thornton, J.E., "Overview of Hyperchannel," COMPCON Spring 1676, San Francisco, CA., February 1979, pp. 262-265.

17. Rawson, E.G., "Application of Fiber Optics to Local Networks," Proc. Local Area Networks Symposium, Mitre Corp., May, 1979, pp. 155-167.

18. IEEE Data Link Media Access Committee draft standard, in preparation.

A standard with choices? Though some object to the notion, the proposed IEEE standard for local networking reflects reality. Two general approaches are being standardized, each appropriate to certain applications.

Toward a Local Network Standard

Reprinted from *IEEE Micro*, August 1982, pages 28-45.

Ware Myers

Contributing Editor

Local computer networks have captured the interest and inspired the imagination of a host of people not only in the United States but across the world. A standard network could be the sinew that binds the various components of automation systems in factory and office. In October 1979 Kenneth J. Thurber and Harvey A. Freeman identified 44 major local computer network system concepts and classified them into seven categories.[1] Some had been developed in universities, and others in industry. The number of different developments made it clear that if people were going to communicate beyond a narrow circle, and if manufacturers were going to mass-produce the requisite equipment, there had to be some standardization.

For this purpose IEEE Standards Project 802 was established by the IEEE Computer Society in February 1980, with Maris Graube of Tektronix as chairman. By the end of that year the 802 committee had decided that a single method for accessing the network medium would not satisfy the diverse applications it foresaw. At its December 1980 meeting it tentatively accepted two general approaches encompassing three specific methods, leading some observers to express disappointment at the idea of a standard with choices.

By May 1981 the committee had pulled together a package of documents, which it called Draft A, describing the technical state of the art. This draft was admittedly far from a standard, but it did begin to get the subject matter in writing. At its July meeting in Seattle the committee authorized the preparation of Draft B. This draft was reviewed in September in Toronto and approved for release. In October it was mailed to the members of the committee. Subsequently it was distributed by the IEEE Computer Society.[2]

Hundreds of comments were returned by the committee members and were entered into word processing systems by the drafting subcommittees. For example, the comments on the baseband section of the proposed standard came to about 1000 lines of text; those on one of the medium access methods, to more than 1200 lines.

The intent in seeking these comments was not to approve or disapprove a standard; that would have been premature. Rather the purpose was to ask, Does the technical approach make sense? Is the set of chapters consistent one with another? Are there technical errors? Will the material be understandable to prospective users (expected to be manufacturers, system specifiers, and protocol programmers, but not workstation operators)? Is the material organized to best meet these different needs? The many comments received in response to Draft B helped answer these questions. The comments were reviewed at the committee's December 1981 meeting in San Diego and helped guide the decisions from which the committee could proceed with Draft C.

During the first quarter of 1982 the subcommittees and working groups reworked the document in terms of a new outline which the committee had agreed in December would make the standard more understandable. In early March the entire committee met in Phoenix. Further rewriting was completed in April and in May Draft C was mailed to the qualified voters.[3] Ballots and comments were returned in early July. Another committee meeting was scheduled for early August to consider further changes. When the committee decides that all significant differences have been resolved, the standard will be submitted to the IEEE Standards Board for formal approval.[4] The committee's reporting relationships are charted in Figure 1.

The 802 committee has about 120 qualified voters, that is, people who have been attending the meetings, participating in the discussions, and acquiring the knowledge needed to cast an informed vote. Over 100 attend each quarterly meeting. Those not qualified to vote are free to read the drafts and submit comments, but these reactions are given less weight, particularly if a commenter seems to be unfamiliar with the arguments already considered in committee. Interest in the proposed standard is global, with about 90 of the 900 people on the mailing list outside the United States. Representatives from Great Britain, Scandinavia, Germany, France, and Japan, as well as from other countries, have attended the meetings.

Some 250 to 300 companies are represented, including mainframe and minicomputer manufacturers, semiconductor companies, telephone companies, and office equipment manufacturers. In terms of technical expertise there are committee members who are at the state of the art in each access method considered for the standard. Others have been involved in the development of the International Standards Organization's reference model, the Open Systems Interconnection, within whose scope the local network standard is to fit. Still others have experience in standards writing.

Looked at from the applications side, committee members range over a broad spectrum. Some are concerned with a network connecting a few bays of equipment within a single room; others are interested in covering a campus-sized area. Some are involved in connecting units in office environments; some in tying together test equipment, computers, and workstations in light industry environments; and others in linking automated processes in heavy industries such as petrochemical plants and pulp and paper mills. In an automated pulp and paper mill, if a critical message misses its time window, tons of paper slurry may spill out. Naturally those involved with such real-time applications place great importance on reliability, integrity, and deterministic timing. And finally, there are those interested in communicating over more than local distances, such as from one plant to another, leading the committee to include internetwork connections on its agenda.

With this wide range of interests and expertise, the committee has had some difficulty in focusing on a manageable set of objectives. A simple set of requirements might have led to a simple standard. With a broad spectrum of requirements, however, it is perhaps not surprising that multiple access mechanisms and multiple media have found their way into Draft C.

Goals of the 802 committee

The purpose of the local network committee is to standardize the means of connecting digital equipment within a local area, as opposed to the longer distances served by telecommunications common carriers. The standardization process has to take place within the constraints imposed by technology, both current and prospective. It has to consider existing products and services and the economics associated with them. It has to serve the range of applications found in local network environments.

In today's local network environment, there are scores of implementations and innumerable conflicting interests.

If the standardization process could arrive at one best way to accomplish these purposes, the resulting standard would permit manufacturers to supply just one type of equipment, systems designers to specify this one type, and users to benefit from the resulting simplicity and low cost. In the present instance, however, there are several application areas, scores of implementations, and innumerable conflicting interests.

One approach—and that chosen by the committee—is to standardize several methods. This approach has the merit of meeting the needs of different applications and satisfying the desires of differing interest groups. It has the drawbacks of limiting the size of production runs—thus increasing the cost of equipment, and adding to the length and complexity of the standard—perhaps confusing manufacturers, system specifiers, and protocol programmers.

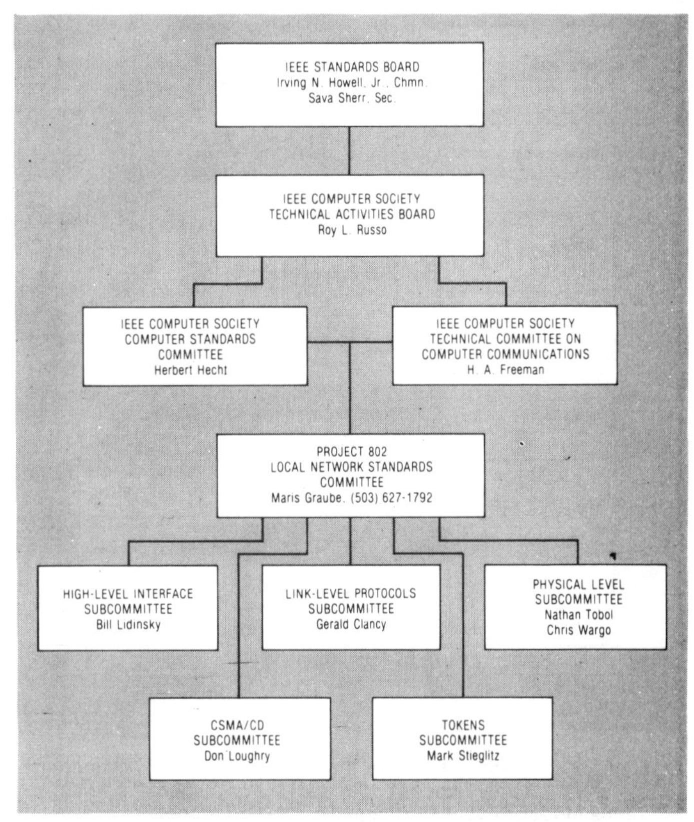

Figure 1. Organizational chart showing the reporting path and structure of the IEEE P802 committee.

The committee has accepted the latter drawback as a challenge. If it can properly structure the standard, readers can find what they need and bypass sections irrelevant to them. If it can present the options in a logical order, system specifiers can more easily assemble systems.

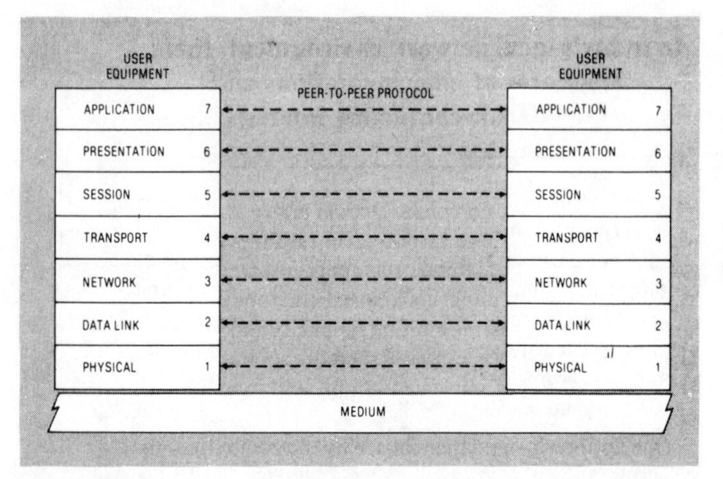

Figure 2. The International Standards Organization's Open Systems Interconnection reference model consists of seven layers which are relatively independent of each other. A message originating in an upper layer of a sending station passes down through the layers and over the medium to the receiving station, where it passes up to the layer corresponding to its originating layer. From a protocol standpoint, the message may be thought of as passing directly from one layer to a corresponding layer (dotted lines).

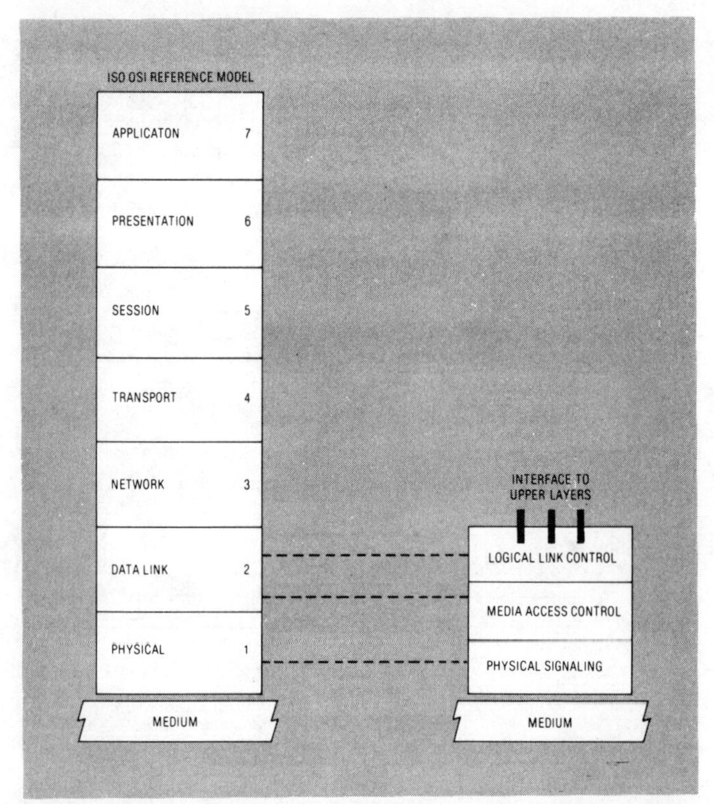

Figure 3. The two lower layers of the ISO Open Systems Interconnection reference model map onto three layers of the local area network reference model. Levels 3 through 7 of the OSI model are outside the scope of the local network model except to the degree that the logical link control layer has to interface to the network layer (symbolized by the vertical bars at top right).

Applications supported. The committee intends that networks conforming to its standard will support application processes and services such as

- file transfer and access protocols,
- access to remote data bases,
- graphics, word processing, and electronic mail,
- process control, and
- digitized voice transmission.

The last application might include, in addition to person-to-person communication, digital code originating in a speech synthesizer. It might service intercom, public address, and limited teleconferencing facilities.

The network is also intended to support data devices such as

- computers and terminals,
- mass storage devices,
- printers and plotters,
- copiers and telecopiers,
- monitoring and control equipment, and
- bridges and gateways to other networks.

These devices involve three types of services: short-burst data transfers; substantial transfers, as to mass storage; and frequent transfers, as in monitoring and control.

Functional requirements. The committee approached these many circumstances by first formulating functional requirements. The list of requirements went through many drafts in the early days. Appendix A of Draft B set forth the characteristics a local network should possess at the current state of the art. For example, it should support at least 200 data devices distributed along a communications medium of at least two kilometers in length. Its data rate should fall within the range of one megabit per second to 20 megabits per second. It should allow easy addition or deletion of devices, and a transient fault caused by such addition or deletion should last less than one second.

The undetected bit-error rate at the interface to the device being supported should be less than one part in 10^{14}. A more recent formulation of this goal is a mean time between undetected errors of one year. Failure of any data device should not cause failure of the network as a whole. If a device failure causes a transient, the rest of the network should be able to recover from it.

It should be possible to address one station, to simultaneously address two or more stations, or to simultaneously address all stations connected to the network.

The committee discovered, however, that the functional requirements stated in Draft B had led to many misunderstandings. It decided to delete them and did so in Draft C. Nevertheless, they give an indication of the committee's informal goals.

Reference models. One of the first requirements to be set was the decision to work in terms of the International Standards Organization's Open Systems Interconnection layered architecture.[5] This concept was developed by

Subcommittee 16 of ISO Technical Committee 97, beginning in March 1978. After 18 months of work its draft was adopted by the parent committee on data processing as the basis for the development of standards at each layer.[6]

The OSI reference model consists of seven layers, shown in Figure 2. Layering divides a very complex task into smaller pieces, each of which is relatively independent of the others. The first two layers are tailored to the network technology being used in some category of operations. The physical layer establishes, maintains, and releases the physical connection between two pieces of equipment; that is, it transmits the 1's and 0's. The next layer, called the data link, contains the techniques used to send packets between devices. If the error rate at the physical level is unacceptable, the data-link level may include a means of error detection.

The three levels at the top—session, presentation, and application—engage in end-to-end data transfer. These levels and the two intermediate levels—network and transport—are outside the scope of the local network standard. The 802 standard will be a particular implementation of levels 1 and 2, as diagrammed in Figure 3. The local area network reference model sets up three layers to provide the functions of the two lower layers of the OSI model.

The local network model is detailed further in Figure 4. It is not only a model, but also serves as a guide to the committee's terminology and to the organization of the standard document. Figure 5 shows the correspondence between the reference model and the chapters of Draft C. The key terms used in Figures 4 and 5 are defined in the box on the next page.

There are two types of specifications in the standard: service specifications and layer specifications. The first specifies the services provided by a layer to the next-higher layer. For example, at the top of Figure 5 a service specification describes the relationship between the logical link control layer and the network layer of the OSI model.

A layer specification describes a way of implementing a particular layer. At the logical link control layer just one approach is needed, but at the other layers two general approaches, encompassing three methods, are provided. These approaches are CSMA/CD (carrier-sense multiple-access with collision detect) and token passing, the latter including token bus and token ring techniques. At the media access unit level, access may be provided to three media: twisted pair, coaxial cable, and optical fiber. The coaxial cable may be operated in baseband or broadband.

Media access methods

When the 802 project was getting under way during 1980, Xerox's Ethernet was the most talked-about local network.[7] It is an instance of what the committee later termed the CSMA/CD access method. Xerox had been operating prototype three-megabit-per-second networks in some of its plants since 1976 and was getting ready to make the concept more widely available. The committee accepted much of the Ethernet work as at least part of the basis for a standard. However, because other approaches were also under development, the committee looked at token-passing access methods as well.

An IEEE standards committee is not a dictatorial body that can arbitrarily impose a standard on the world.

An IEEE standards committee is not a dictatorial body that can arbitrarily impose a standard on the world. It is a representative body that talks out disagreements at

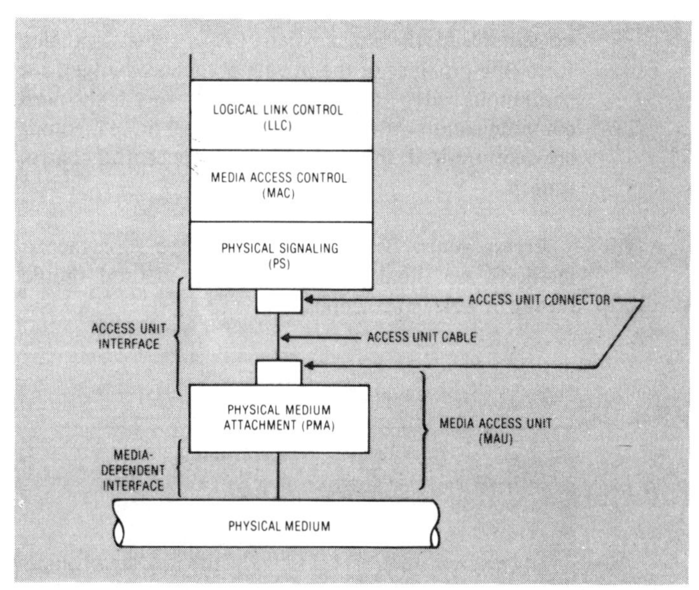

Figure 4. This version of the local area network reference model, called the implementation reference model, illustrates the terminology adopted by the committee.

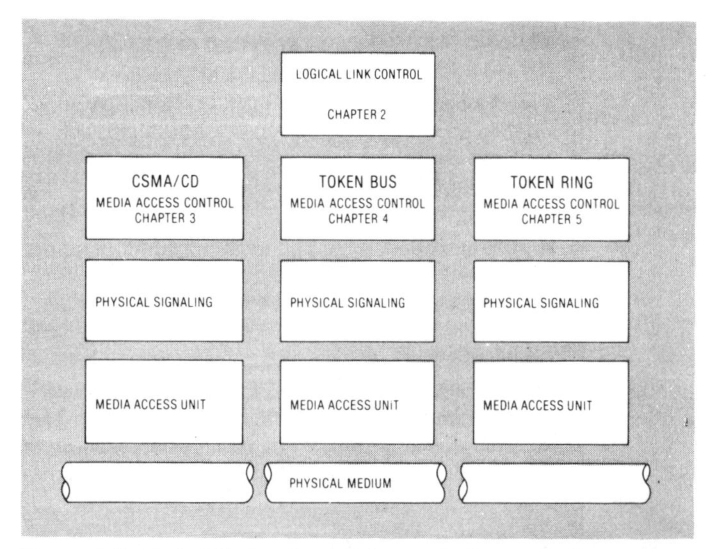

Figure 5. Draft C of the local network standard proposes two types of medium access: CSMA/CD (carrier-sense multiple-access with collision detect) and token passing. The latter is further divided into token bus and token ring methods. The logical link control layer is the same for all three, but then the standard splits into three long chapters, each covering one of the three methods.

length—that is one reason standard-making takes time—and attempts to reach a consensus. It does not make decisions simply by majority vote.

In the 802 committee there were groups favoring each access method, a division undoubtedly reflecting the real world. A British business magazine, *The Economist*, termed the situation "a technological jungle in which experts violently disagree and potential buyers stand aghast."[8]

In December 1980 the committee agreed to include both CSMA/CD and token passing in its deliberations. Furthermore, it decided to implement token passing in both a broadcast topology—the token bus—and a sequential topology—the token ring.

All three of these media access methods are directed at transmitting digital data over a local network. They are not suitable for the transmission of voice signals in analog form (the province of the private branch exchange), for continuous video transmission, or for very-high-speed communication between mainframes. All three methods are decentralized; there is usually no one central control station.

Access goals. Before we examine the three access methods, we should consider what a method should ideally be able to accomplish:

- *Initialization.* The method should enable network stations, upon power-up, to enter the state required for operation.
- *Fairness.* The method should treat each station fairly in terms of the time it is made to wait until it gains entry to the network (access time) and the time it is allowed to spend on the network (communications time).
- *Priority.* In managing access and communications time, the method should be able to give priority to some stations over other stations.
- *Limitation to one station.* The method should limit transmission to one station at a time.
- *Receipt.* The method should ensure that message packets are actually received (no lost packets), are delivered only once (no duplicate packets), and are received in the proper order.
- *Error limitation.* The method should be capable of encompassing an appropriate error-detection scheme.
- *Recovery.* If two packets collide (are present on the network at the same time), or if notice imitative of a collision appears, the method should be able to recover, i.e., be able to halt all transmissions and select one station to retransmit.
- *Reconfigurability.* The method should enable a network to accommodate the addition or deletion of a

Key terms—local area network implementation reference model

(adapted from Draft C[3])

Logical link control. That part of the link layer which supports media-independent data link functions and uses the services of the media access control sublayer to provide services to the network layer. Specifically, logical link control initiates control signal interchange, organizes data flow, interprets commands and generates responses, and carries out error control and recovery functions for the layer.

Type 1 operation. A type of local network operation wherein data units may be exchanged without establishment of a link connection. These link data units are not acknowledged, nor is there any flow control or error recovery.

Type 2 operation. A type of local network operation wherein a link connection must be established prior to data unit exchange. All link data units are acknowledged, and flow control and error recovery functions are provided.

Media access control. That part of the link layer which supports media-dependent functions and uses the services of the physical layer to provide services to logical link control. Three methods are included in the proposed standard:

1. **CSMA/CD** (carrier-sense multiple-access with collision detect). The generic term for a class of medium access procedures which (a) allows multiple stations to access the medium at will without explicit prior coordination; (b) avoids contention by means of carrier sense and deference; (c) resolves contention by means of collision detection and retransmission. (These concepts are discussed in more detail in a later section.)
2. **Token bus.** A token access procedure used with a broadcast topology.
3. **Token ring.** A token access procedure used with a sequential (ring) topology.

Token access procedure. A means of managing the mutually exclusive use of a shared medium, based on possession of a token.

Token. A symbol of authority which is passed between stations that use a token access procedure. Possession of the token indicates which station is in control of the medium.

Physical signaling. Performs data encapsulation/decapsulation and data transmit/receive management functions.

Access unit interface. Carries control and data signals.

Physical medium attachment. Encodes signals for transmission on the medium and decodes signals received from the medium.

Physical medium. A twisted pair of wires, coaxial cable (baseband or broadband), or optical fiber used to transmit bits.

station with no more than a noise transient from which the network's stations can recover.

- *Compatibility*. The method should accommodate equipment from all vendors who build to its specification.
- *Reliability*. The method should enable a network to continue operating in spite of the failure of one or several stations.

Carrier-sense multiple-access method

The CSMA/CD access method is related to the model of Figure 5 as shown in Figure 6. The principal function of the transmit data encapsulation sublayer is to construct a frame by supplying a preamble, a start-frame delimiter (00010011), a destination address, a source address, a length count, a medium-access-control information field, the message itself, a pad (to achieve minimum frame size), and a frame-check sequence. The message is obtained from the logical link control sublayer. Transmit link management ascertains whether the medium is free and initiates transmission. The transmit data encoding sublayer takes the bit-serial stream from link management and generates the electrical signal placed on the medium—in this case using Manchester phase encoding.

Similarly, the receive data decoding sublayer converts the data on the medium into a bit stream and passes it on to receive link management. This sublayer's function is to establish, in accordance with certain rules, that the frame received is valid. The receive data decapsulation sublayer recognizes the frame's destination address, determines if it matches its own, disassembles the frame, and passes the message part along to the logical link control sublayer.

Operation. All CSMA stations have independent access to the medium—there is no central controller. Thus, at any moment the transmit data encapsulation sublayer may generate a frame and present it to transmit link management, ready for transmission. Meanwhile, the physical signaling sublayer has been listening to the medium and providing a carrier-sense signal to the link management sublayer.

If no station's carrier is sensed, link management is free to initiate transmission. If a carrier is sensed, link management defers to it. If a carrier is sensed but then ends, link management waits for 9.6 microseconds or more and then initiates transmission. This delay is called the interframe delay and lasts long enough to allow the network to clear.

Once a transmission begins, it has to propagate over the entire network so that all the other stations can sense its carrier and defer their own transmissions. The time this propagation takes is called the slot time. Once past the slot time, the transmission continues to completion, since the other stations have good manners—deference—built in. On the other hand, if another transmission begins during the slot time—its physical signaling sublayer not yet having sensed the first transmission's carrier—the two transmissions are said to collide.

While transmitting, a station's physical signaling sublayer listens for a collision. If one is detected, transmit link management initiates a jam signal to ensure that all stations know a collision has occurred. All transmitting stations cease transmitting and each waits for a random period of time determined by its own internal logic. The station whose random backoff period happens to be the shortest then begins its transmission again. The other station, or stations, continue to wait, since their backoff periods are still running. As their backoff periods expire, they sense the transmitting station's carrier and defer their own transmissions until that station finishes.

The randomization process used to determine the backoff periods is called "truncated binary exponential backoff." The minimum backoff period must be at least one slot time long. Other backoff periods are integral multiples of the slot time. The backoff algorithm may be thought of in terms of a counter, implemented in either hardware or software. After one collision, either a 0 or a 1, randomly selected, is tranferred to the lowest bit position of the counter. Countdown then takes one or two clock intervals, providing a backoff period of one or two slot times.

One station may draw a one-count backoff, another a two-count backoff. The first will count once and initiate retransmission. The second will count twice, sense the carrier of the first, and defer. If both stations happen to draw one-count (or two-count) backoffs, their transmissions will again collide.

Each station maintains a record, perhaps in a counter, of collision frequency. If this frequency is high, indicating that the network is busy, the station increases the average length of its backoff interval. After two collisions, for example, a station transfers two bits to the low-order positions of its countdown counter. Since the two bits are selected randomly, the count entered may be 0, 1, 2, or 3. The retransmission attempts are now spread out over four

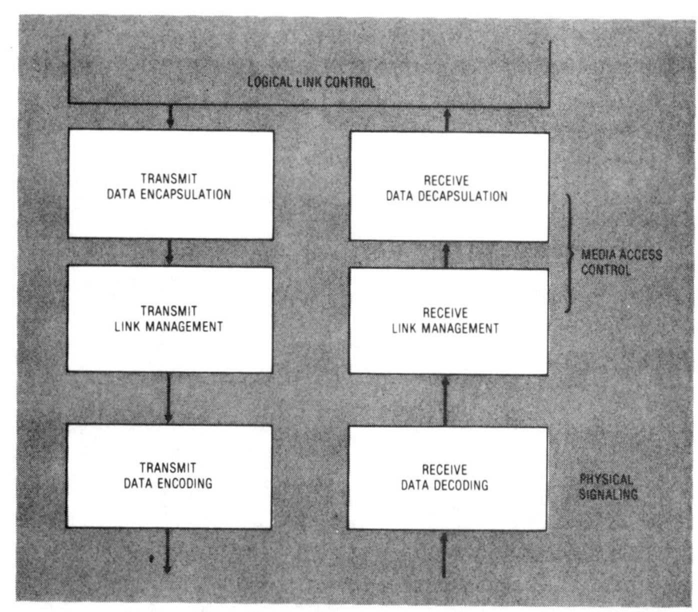

Figure 6. The architectural model of the CSMA/CD access method consists of six functions below the logical link control sublayer. Three functions transmit data to the physical medium and three receive data from the physical medium.

slot times, reducing the probability of another collision. However, the average backoff period has been doubled, slightly reducing the efficiency of the network. Under this scheme, a network which had counted eight collisions would stretch out its retransmission attempts over 2^8, or 256, slot times.

Assuming the countdown counter is of finite size, the backoff algorithm will reach the counter's limit. If collisions still occur, something else is probably wrong, and the circumstance is reported as an error.

Complexity. The CSMA/CD method's complexity is suggested by the 11 states of the transmit access logic shown in Figure 7. Table 1 summarizes the activities in each state. In addition, there are three states of receiver logic (not illustrated). The CSMA/CD method has been precisely defined in the form of a Pascal program, and the size of this program—approximately 500 lines—also indicates the method's complexity.

Disadvantages. In a network connecting office machines, which is the application Xerox presumably had in mind when it developed Ethernet, the uncertainty of access to the medium, resulting from the random factor in the backoff algorithm, is not a matter of consequence. One can imagine a particularly unlucky station that competes in a series of backoff sequences and always loses the countdown race to another station. Thus, the maximum delay that any one message may encounter is not deterministic.

Some members of the 802 committee felt that such an open-ended access delay might present a problem to applications such as process control, in which hazardous conditions must be controlled within a specified reaction period. This concern led to consideration of the token passing method, since it ensures that each station gets access to the medium within some specified time.

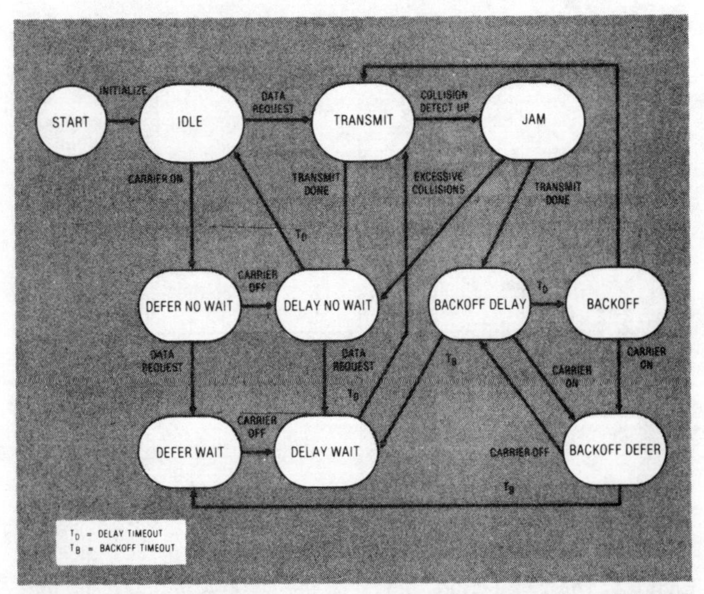

Figure 7. The state diagram of the transmit portion of the CSMA/CD method suggests the degree of complexity encountered in implementing the method. For complete information refer to Draft C.[3]

Ethernet performance. In considering the matter of deterministic or nondeterministic access time, it is pertinent to examine the performance of an actual Ethernet installation. The network studied, said to be one of the oldest in existence, runs at 2.94 megabits per second, spans 550 meters, and connects over 120 machines. Applications include sending files to printers, transferring files to a storage system, accessing shared data bases, downloading programs, accessing timesharing computers, and performing remote diagnosis.[9]

Actual traffic on this network is almost 300 million bytes per 24-hour day, mostly in the daytime. This volume represents a great deal of activity—it is about half that carried by the Arpanet. Yet average utilization of the medium is less than one percent, although it rises to 37 percent over the busiest one second of the day. Under these circumstances, 99.18 percent of the packets access the medium with zero waiting time. Only 0.79 percent have to defer because of carrier-sense, and less than 0.03 percent collide.

Still, in a critical application an occasional message could be delayed for an indeterminable time. In other words, the network might treat a particular station unfairly, purely as a matter of chance.

To test fairness, John F. Shoch and Jon A. Hupp operated the network (at night when other users were not around) at an offered load of 100 percent, made up of 10 stations each generating a load at a 10-percent rate[9]—i.e., each station was given a queue of messages sufficient, if all the messages in the queue were transmitted, to occupy 10 percent of the theoretical bandwidth of the system. Because of factors such as deference, collision, and backoff, however, the medium cannot accommodate ten 10-percent loads. But Shoch and Hupp found that 9.3 to 9.6 percent of each offered 10-percent load was transmitted, for a total network utilization of 94 percent. Absolute fairness among the stations would have resulted in 9.4 percent each. Thus, even under an extreme load condition, the network transmitted fairly equal portions of each offered load.

On the other hand, the CSMA/CD access method does not give one station priority over the others. All stations have an equal probability of accessing the medium. Draft C calls this "the most aggressive behavior that a station may exhibit in attempting to retransmit after a collision." The draft also states that "in the course of implementing the retransmission scheduling procedure . . . [a station may] . . . introduce extra delays which will degrade its own throughput, but in no case may a station's retransmission scheduling result in a lower average delay between retransmission attempts than the procedure defined above." This language seems to imply that some stations might be adjusted for lower priority, leaving the "aggressive" station in possession of the normal retransmission schedule.

Token-bus method

The token-bus method may be characterized as a logical ring on a physical bus, as shown in Figure 8. In normal operation, a node passes a token when it completes its transmission. In a logical sense, it passes the token to the next node address in descending order. In a physical sense, it broadcasts a token frame with a destination address over the bus to all nodes; the destination node recognizes its address and accepts the frame and with it, the token.

The token authorizes that node (and only that node) to put a message frame on the bus. Thus, there is no possibility of collision, as in the CSMA/CD method. Since collision is impossible, a token-bus frame need be no longer than the information it is to convey. A CSMA/CD frame, on the other hand, must be filled out to a length that will permit a collision to be detected by the most distant station. Thus, token-bus frames used for control purposes can be very short, and the transmission capacity of the network will be somewhat increased.

If the node with the token has a message to send, it sends it and then passes the token to the next node. If the node has no message to send, it passes the token immediately. Each node receives the token in sequence; thus, the scheme provides fair access to the transmission medium. Moreover, the length of time that a node has to wait for access is deterministic, since a message frame is not allowed to exceed a specified maximum length. If all the nodes have messages to send, the worst-case wait for access is the sum of all the token-passing times and message times. On the other hand, if only one node has a message to send, the worst-case access time is the sum of the token-passing times only. In the latter case, the *average* access time can be as short as half that of the worst case, since at times the token will be only one station away, at other times the maximum number of stations

Table 1.
State transitions for the transmit portion of the CSMA/CD method (see Figure 7).

CURRENT STATE	EVENT	ACTION	NEXT STATE
0. START	INITIALIZE	-PERFORM INITIALIZATION	IDLE
1. IDLE	DATA REQUEST	-CONSTRUCT FRAME -START FRAME TRANSMISSION	TRANSMIT
	CARRIER ON	-NO ACTION	DEFER NO WAIT
2. TRANSMIT	COLLISION DETECT UP	-START JAM TRANSMISSION -INCREMENT ATTEMPT COUNT	JAM
	TRANSMIT DONE	-START DELAY TIMER -RESET ATTEMPT COUNT -INDICATE SUCCESSFUL TRANSMISSION	DELAY NO WAIT
3. JAM	TRANSMIT DONE	-START DELAY TIMER -START BACKOFF TIMER	BACKOFF DELAY
	EXCESSIVE COLLISIONS	-START DELAY TIMER -INDICATE TRANSMIT EXCESSIVE COLLISIONS	DELAY NO WAIT
4. BACKOFF	CARRIER ON	-NO ACTION	BACKOFF DEFER
	BACKOFF TIMEOUT	-START FRAME TRANSMISSION	TRANSMIT
5. BACKOFF DEFER	CARRIER OFF	-START DELAY TIMER	BACKOFF DELAY
	BACKOFF TIMEOUT	-NO ACTION	DEFER WAIT
6. BACKOFF DELAY	CARRIER ON	-STOP DELAY TIMER	BACKOFF DEFER
	DELAY TIMEOUT	-NO ACTION	BACKOFF
	BACKOFF TIMEOUT	-NO ACTION	DELAY WAIT
7. DEFER NO WAIT	DATA REQUEST	-CONSTRUCT FRAME	DEFER WAIT
	CARRIER OFF	-START DELAY TIMER	DELAY NO WAIT
8. DELAY NO WAIT	DATA REQUEST	-CONSTRUCT FRAME	DELAY WAIT
	DELAY TIMEOUT	-NO ACTION	IDLE
9. DEFER WAIT	CARRIER OFF	-START DELAY TIMER	DELAY WAIT
10. DELAY WAIT	DELAY TIME OUT	-START FRAME TRANSMISSION	TRANSMIT

Note: This table is intended to be illustrative; those seriously concerned with applying CSMA/CD should refer to Draft C.[3]

away, and at yet other times somewhere in between. For time-critical applications such as process control, the number of nodes and the maximum length of messages can be selected so as to provide access within some fixed period of time.

Priority can be achieved in several ways. A node performing less critical functions than other stations can be permitted to place a message on the medium only every second time—or every *n*th time—it receives the token. High-priority stations can be set up to send every time. High-priority stations can also be authorized to send longer frames than less important stations.

Token-passing characteristics. Certain features distinguish token passing from other access methods:*

- Coordination of the nodes requires only a small percentage of the medium's capacity when the offered load is high. Under overload conditions each node's expected access delay grows no faster than the total offered load. Thus, the method is said to be efficient.
- The method works at the data rates and distances originally considered by the committee. (These rates and distances have the potential for growth, however.)
- Although each node receives an equal share of the medium's capacity, no node is *required* to take its full share.
- The method permits multiple classes of service—i.e., priorities.
- By coordinating the nodes' authority to transmit (by means of the token), the method prevents the nodes from interfering with each other's transmissions.
- The method imposes no requirements on the medium beyond those necessary for transmission and reception of multibit, multiframe sequences at the specified mean bit-error rate.
- In the absence of system noise, the method provides computable, deterministic, worst-case bounds on access delay for any given network and loading configuration.
- Since periods of controlled interference can be distinguished from noise, system noise measurements can be made.
- The method permits the presence of low-cost, reduced-function nodes together with one or more full-function nodes. At least one full-function node is needed to make the system operational—for example, to initialize it. An example of a reduced function node is one that can "receive only" and therefore does not contain access control logic.
- The method places few constraints on how the node which momentarily controls the medium uses its time. In particular, it does not prohibit a node from using other specialized access methods during its access period.

*This summarization is adapted from Draft C; see reference 3.

Complexity. Normal operation of a token-bus network is quite straightforward. However, a network must be able to initialize itself, that is, it must be able to create an ordered sequence of access; it must be able to recover from faults, principally those caused by a lost token or by the presence of multiple tokens; and it must be able to admit an inactive node to its ordered sequence and to allow an active node to transfer to inactive status. These additional functions increase complexity.

The degree of complexity is suggested by the 11 states of the token-bus access logic, shown in Figure 9. Table 2 summarizes the nature of the activities in each state. Draft C provides, as an example, an implementation of this logic written in the Ada language—it occupies approximately 2350 lines. Such complexity has always implied correspondingly high costs.

However, as the logic of each access method is reduced to a single chip, the cost differences among the methods

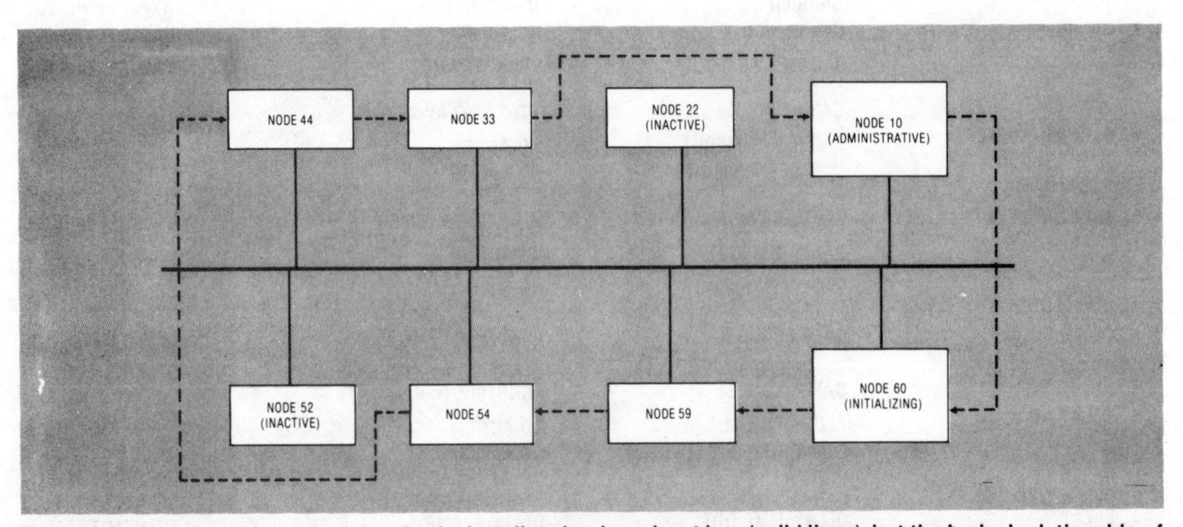

Figure 8. In the token-bus method the physical medium is a broadcast bus (solid lines), but the logical relationship of the nodes is a ring (dotted lines). Some nodes are administrative or initializing and may perform functions that occur infrequently, such as recovery, while other less expensive nodes perform only the minimum functions, such as accepting the token and sending or receiving messages. A node may withdraw from the logical ring and become inactive.

may no longer be significant. Western Digital, for example, is working on a token controller chip.[10] It is also possible to reduce cost by having several classes of nodes. An administrative node can be employed, for example, to watch for and resolve unusual network conditions, permitting the other nodes to have limited capability and lower cost.

Token-ring method

The token-ring method is based on a physical ring and operates on the same ring, as illustrated in Figure 10. In many respects it operates in much the same way as the token-bus. The principal difference is that a frame, instead of propagating in a broadcast fashion, passes directly from one node to the next over a point-to-point link. At a node, the frame is always passed on, or repeated, to the following node. In addition, the frame's address is examined. If it is the same as the node's address, the frame is also relayed to the logical link control sublayer.

Operation. Figure 11 diagrams the passing of a token to a node A, the transmission of data over the ring, the removal of the transmitted data, and the passing of the token to a node G. A node accepts the token only when it has data to send; otherwise, it repeats the field which contains the token (called the access control field) without modification. When a node has data to send, a token field appears, and the node modifies the field as it passes by and inserts its data after the token field.

On the ring configuration a frame could repeat from node to node indefinitely. Therefore, positive action has to be taken to remove the frame from the ring. This responsibility is assigned to the originating node. When the circulating frame reaches that node, it is deleted. At that point the originating node puts another token field onto the ring.

A node can drop out of the ring by closing its bypass "relay," which in actuality may be an electronic circuit. One potential deficiency of the physical ring approach is that a malfunction in the path through a node could break the ring medium; breaking it renders the entire network inoperative. To avoid such a breakdown, a node design goal is to devise circuits that, upon detecting a break, will close the bypass relay. The defective node is cut out of the ring, but the rest of the network continues to operate.

Priority. The token-ring method can be operated on a nonpriority basis or on a multiple-priority basis. The start-delimiter field of the frame format assigns three bits

Table 2.
Token-bus logic involves transitions among 11 states.

STATE	DESCRIPTION
0	UNPOWERED: Virtual state prior to power-up.
1	IDLE: Node is listening to medium and is not transmitting.
2	DEMAND IN: Node is observing medium for evidence of other contending nodes before bidding to succeed the token-holding node.
3	DEMAND DELAY: Having sent a request to enter the ring to the station holding the token, the node waits, listening for a response.
4	CLAIM TOKEN: Node is attempting to initialize or reinitialize the logical ring by sending claim-token frames.
5	ACCEPT TOKEN: Having just received or claimed a token, node is considering removing itself from the logical ring before using the token.
6	USE TOKEN: Node is sending data for its logical link layer.
7	CHECK SERVICE CLASS: Node is controlling the transmission of frames for different service classes or priorities.
8	PASS TOKEN: Node is attempting to pass the token to its successor and/or to solicit a successor.
9	CHECK TOKEN PASS: Node is waiting for a reaction from the node to which it has just passed the token.
10	AWAIT RESPONSE: Node is attempting to sequence candidate successors—by means of a distributed contention resolution algorithm—until it receives a next-node frame from one of them or determines that no successor is going to appear.

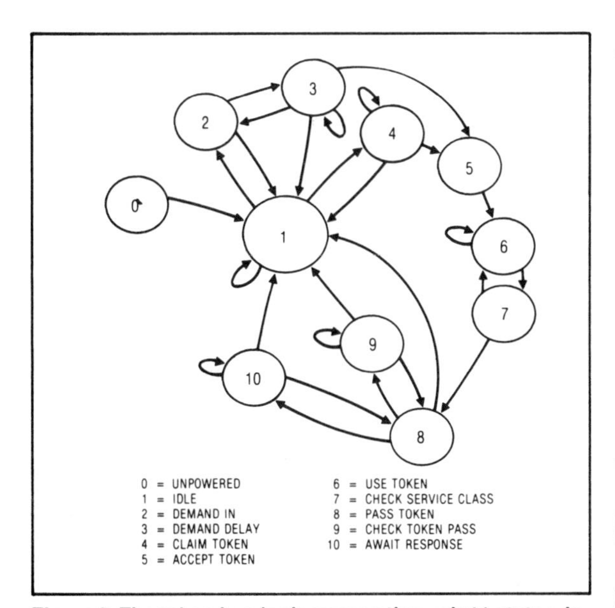

Figure 9. The token-bus logic passes through 11 states, involving a number of state transitions (taken from Draft C^3).

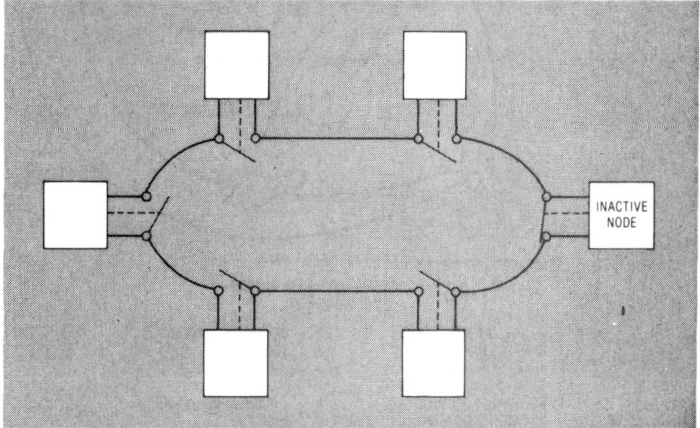

Figure 10. In the token-ring method the nodes are located around a physical ring. The order in which the token is passed is the same as the physical order, except that a node can opt out of the ring by closing its bypass relay.

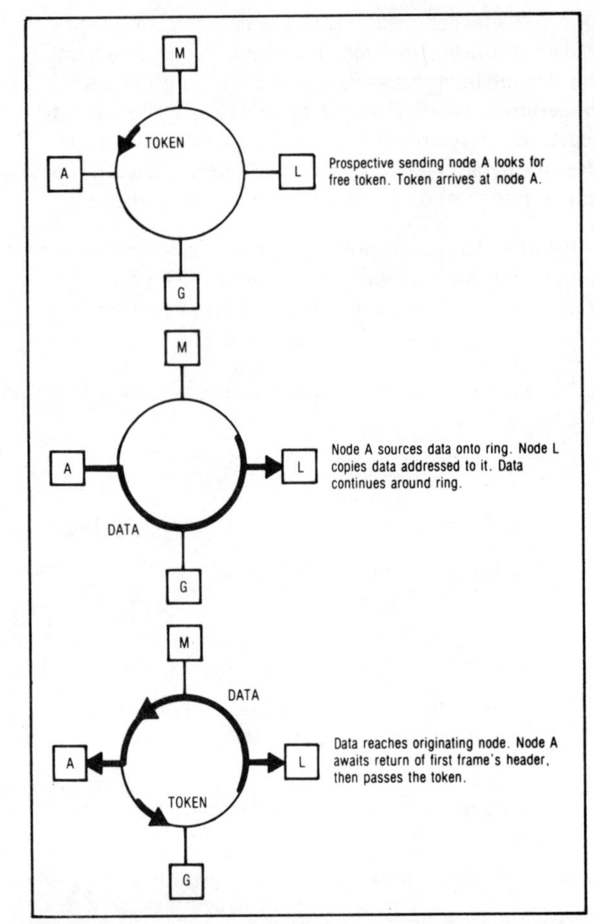

Figure 11. The successive stages in transferring a token, then data, and then the token again, in a sequential medium.

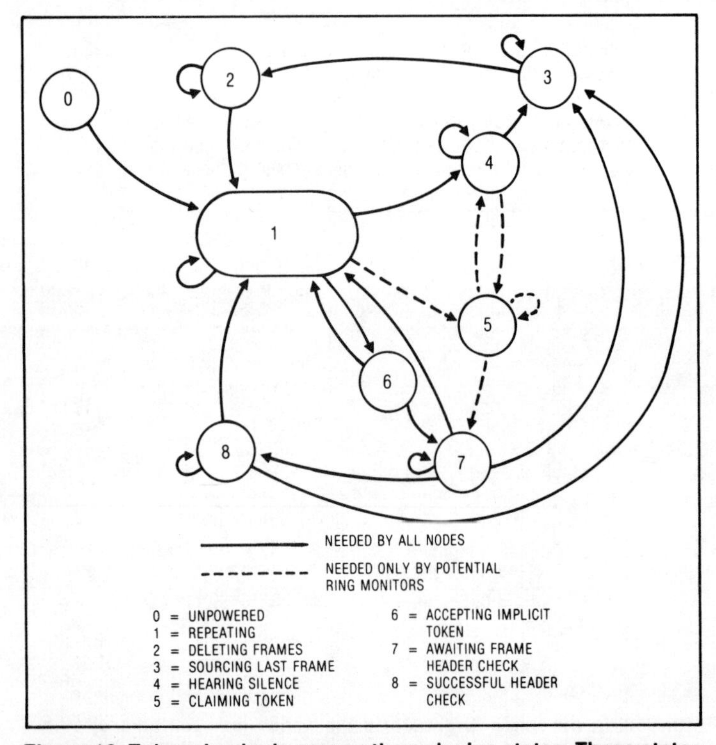

Figure 12. Token-ring logic passes through nine states. These states are similar to, and approximately the same number as, those in token-bus logic. (This diagram is based on Draft B.[2])

to designate priority. (In a nonpriority system, these bits are assigned zeros.) When a node receives a token frame, it compares the priority bits of the start-delimiter field with the priority bits of the message to be transmitted. If the comparison is favorable, the node transmits the message. If the comparison shows that the message's priority is lower than that set in the token frame, the message is held and the node immediately forwards the token to the next node.

The start-delimiter field also has three priority-reservation bits. A node with a high-priority message to send may transmit a brief message with the priority-reservations bits set to those of its message, asking that the next token be issued at this priority. Thus, it acquires precedence for its message over any lower-priority message waiting at a node.

Complexity. As in the token-bus method, there is much more to the token-ring method than the bare outline above gives. Its complexity is suggested by Figure 12, in which the relationships between nine states are shown. These states may be grouped into three modes, as listed in Table 3. The degree of complexity is suggested by the 300 Ada instructions needed to formally set forth the logic of operation.

IBM contribution. At the March 1982 meeting of the 802 committee, the IBM Communication Products Division, Research Triangle Park, North Carolina, submitted four technical papers to contribute to "the further development of the IEEE LAN Standards, particularly in the area of token rings." The first paper describes various techniques for providing local-area data communications and focuses on two shared-access topologies, the ring and the bus.[11] After discussing techniques for controlling access contention, it explores the rings in greater depth.

The second paper, dealing with system-level considerations, considers configuration, cabling, expandability, and the migration of existing products.[12] The third proposes a specific architecture and presents formats and protocols.[13] It includes priority schemes that could be used to accommodate both synchronous and asynchronous data on the same token-ring system. The fourth paper argues the importance of higher-level protocols in local-area networking.[14]

These papers are working documents for use by the committee and hence are not currently available. However, they are scheduled to be delivered at the IEEE Computer Society's Compcon Fall '82 conference, to be held September 20-24 in Washington, DC. They will be included in the conference's digest of papers. IBM warns that "submission of this information to the IEEE is not an IBM product offering nor an implied commitment to any future product offerings."

Several advantages of the token-ring method, in addition to those mentioned above, are described in these papers. One is the relative ease of isolating a fault in the ring configuration. For example, Dixon suggests the addition of an alternate ring to convey a signal around the fault when one is found.[11] The insertion of this path can be accomplished with manual switches, with automatic switching logic, or with a command initiated from a remote command facility. Moreover, because signals are regenerated at each node, a ring network can encompass a considerable area.

If a single span is held to a short distance—less than a kilometer, for example—a four-megabit-per-second data rate can be achieved with data-grade, twisted-pair cable.[12] This rate will be able to be greatly increased when fiber-optic cables become generally available. An optical-fiber medium can be easily integrated into a ring, Dixon says.

The priority interrupt mechanism, previously described, can be used by network management functions to rapidly access the network for monitoring, error recovery, congestion control, reconfiguration, orders, and other activities.[11]

Markov and Strole conclude that "the delay-throughput characteristics of the token-access ring are superior to those of the random-access bus when the ratio of propagation delay to packet transmission time is high."[12]

Nondeterminism. Unlike the CSMA/CD access method, both the token-bus and the token-ring methods are logically deterministic. Maximum access time in a token network is the sum of the token-passing and message-transmitting times for all nodes, when each has a message waiting. In a contention network this time is nondeterministic because of the random backoff algorithm which delays access in the event of a collision.

At the electrical level, however, all networks become nondeterministic because of the finite probability of the occurrence of a transmission error. In a token-controlled network, for example, noise might damage the token just as a key node was finally about to obtain the otherwise deterministic access, or the critical message itself, when finally sent, might encounter noise.

Error or noise is, of course, nondeterministic, but a probability value for its occurrence can be calculated. Similarly, the probability of access to a CSMA/CD network under given circumstances may be calculated. Thus, design of both types of networks involves various nondeterministic factors. In both cases a designer can only reduce the probability of not obtaining access within some maximum time period to some low value appropriate to the particular application. That probability can never quite reach zero.

Addressing

The operation of the international telephone network appears to be based on a few simple principles. Its users' names are related to their telephones by a number, and the relationship between the names and numbers is documented in directories on the basis of locality. The telephone number serves two purposes. It is a guide to the address of the telephone in a hierarchical numbering system. At the same time it serves to route a call through a series of switches from the originating telephone to the receiving telephone.

As the number of displays, workstations, terminals, personal computers, or host computers connected to networks increases, some similar set of concepts will have to be applied to interconnected local networks. Just as the telephone numbering system requires a hierarchy of levels—country code, area code, and so on—computer networks appear to need a hierarchy of at least three addressing levels:

(1) network identification,
(2) node identification, and
(3) software process identification.

Only the second of these, the node address, is considered to be a responsibility of the data link layer, which is included within the scope of the 802 committee. The data link header, therefore, need contain at a minimum only an address recognizable on a particular local network. In early networks, such as the Experimental Ethernet at the Xerox Palo Alto Research Center, the address was contained in eight bits. At that time 256 hosts on a single local network seemed to be an ample number.

As local networks were interconnected, however, additional addressing mechanisms became necessary. Within Xerox, for example, the internetwork system in use in

Table 3.
Token-ring logic involves transitions among nine states grouped into three modes.

STATE	DESCRIPTION
0	UNPOWERED: Virtual state prior to power-up.
A	MODE: WATCHING THE MEDIUM
1	REPEATING: Node is repeating each bit it receives and is also examining each group of bits for its address; if address is found, node passes addressed frame to its logical link control sublayer.
2	DELETING FRAMES: Node is deleting a frame it has transmitted, has completed transmission, and is waiting for an appropriate point, e.g., between frames, at which to switch to the repeating state.
3	SOURCING LAST FRAME: Node is finishing the transmission of the last frame prior to entering the deleting-frames state.
B	MODE: RECOVER
4	HEARING SILENCE: Not hearing any transmissions, node is either sourcing idle or sending report-silence frames.
5	CLAIMING TOKEN: Node is attempting to initialize or reinitialize the logical ring by sending claim-token frames.
C	MODE: HOLDING THE TOKEN
6	ACCEPTING IMPLICIT TOKEN: Having accepted an implicitly addressed (one octet) token, node is awaiting the entire token frame and ending delimiter.
7	AWAITING FRAME HEADER CHECK: Having accepted a token, node is waiting to check the access-control and source-address fields of a frame.
8	SUCCESSFUL HEADER CHECK: Having passed the header check, the node is using the token.

1981 as a research network included 35 Experimental Ethernets, 30 internet routers, and over 1200 hosts.[15] The network identification and process identification procedures, however, were assigned to protocol levels above the data link layer.[16]

Address space. The number of hosts that can be connected to any one local network is limited. The Ethernet specification, for example, sets an upper limit of 1024.[17] If hosts are numbered relative to the network to which they are attached, two bytes (65,536 addresses) will provide ample space. However, there are arguments for giving every host in the world a unique and permanent address. Under this scheme a host could be moved from one network to another without ever losing its identification number. How large an address space might this approach take?

There are arguments for giving every host in the world a unique and permanent address. Under such a scheme a host could be moved from one network to another without ever losing its identification number.

After surveying market projections of the number of host computers to be built in the 1980's, Dalal and Printis concluded that the number will be very large—in the tens of millions.[15] If embedded microcomputers are added, the number becomes much larger. While such microcomputers may not require constant access to a network, they may well be accessed periodically for program updating or operation diagnosis.

Dalal and Printis decided that 32 bits (4.3 billion addresses) would probably be enough, but after further considering the problem of allocation, they recommended 48-bits (281×10^{12} addresses). This number was subsequently embodied in the Ethernet specification. However, one problem was that the assigning of this space in blocks to manufacturers and users would result in many unused numbers. Also, in addition to what they called physical host numbers, which are individual addresses, Dalal and Printis wanted to allow space for "multicast" addresses—ones that provide the ability to target packets to a group of hosts.

Thus, 281,474,977,000,000 numbers permit every computer and microprocessor on earth to have a unique address and a group address for a long time to come. Unfortunately, 48-bit source and destination addresses in each packet add to the communications overhead, both by reducing transmission efficiency and by increasing the logic that hosts have to devote to address processing. The 802 committee found that those who just wanted to install a little network for isolated use were not happy with addresses this long.

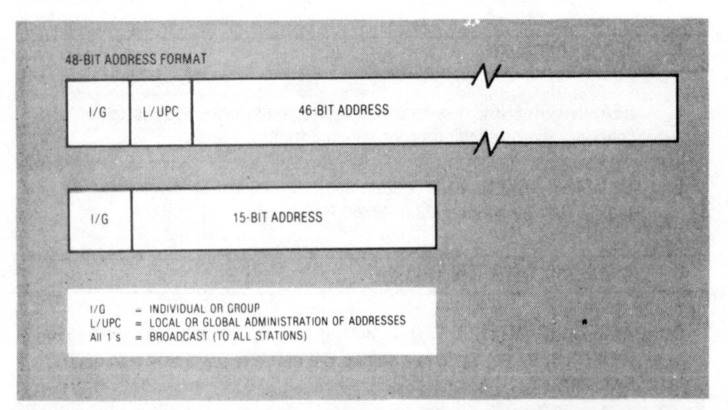

Figure 13. Draft C recommends a 16-bit or 48-bit destination and source-address format. The first bit in both formats divides the address space into single or multicast address assignments. The second bit in the 48-bit format divides the space into local or global administration of the addresses. Xerox is administering the Ethernet space, but an assignment scheme for global address administration has not yet been established. This task is considered to be outside the scope of the 802 committee's responsibility.

Committee approaches. The first attempt to effect a compromise between the two points of view, contained in Draft B, resulted in an extendable address format. The first bit of each byte was to indicate whether that byte was the final one of the address or whether it extended to the following byte. Under this plan a small network could use a one-byte address, the first bit signifying nonextension, the second bit indicating an individual or group address, and the remaining six bits providing 64 addresses. The maximum address was to be seven bytes—56 bits. Since seven bits were devoted to extension decisions and one bit to the individual/group address decision, the remaining 48 bits provided approximately the same address space as the Ethernet specification. Draft B permitted a manufacturer to support any address length, from one to seven bytes, "as an implementation decision."

This solution had the drawback, however, of using additional logic to sort the extension bits from the address bits and, in the maximum implementation, of employing one more byte than Ethernet. The second solution, embodied in Draft C, repeals the extendable address format and offers users the choice of 16-bit addresses for isolated networks (these are called network-specific host addresses) or 48-bit addresses for worldwide unique addresses. Figure 13 illustrates these choices. The *unique* addresses have also been termed *absolute* or *universal* addresses and are said to be drawn from a *flat* address space in contrast to a "nonflat" hierarchical structure. Under Draft C the Ethernet space, already being allocated by Xerox to manufacturers and users licensing the network, will become a part of the space specified by the 802 standard.

Addressing modes. Individual and group addresses have already been mentioned. There are two other addressing modes. One is *broadcast*—a single host sending the same message at the same time to all other nodes on the network. The second is *promiscuous*—a single host receives all packets no matter to whom they are addressed. A promiscuous host can "observe all of the channel's traffic and construct traffic matrices, perform load analysis, potentially perform fault isolation, and debug protocol implementations."[18]

Media

The 802 committee intends to standardize, for all three network access methods, media access units (see again Figure 3) for suitable media. The possible media include twisted-pair cable, coaxial cable, and fiber-optic cable. The coaxial-cable medium is further divided into baseband and broadband. The higher levels of the standard do not change when the medium used for transmission changes. Thus, the same medium-access-controller chip can be used with different medium access units.

There has been much argument about the merits of each medium. The reasons for disagreement appear to lie in the application characteristics that affect a choice. Different spokesmen, like the three blind men trying to describe an elephant by touch, are obviously apprehending different parts of the network beast. These differences leave to the potential user the task of harnessing his own beast. The first thing to do when shopping for a local-area network, according to Kenneth J. Thurber of Architecture Technology Corporation, is to assess requirements.[19]

The second thing, perhaps, is to consider the goals. The physical transmission medium, says one survey article, should be "reliable, simple, inexpensive, high-speed, noise-free, and physically robust."[20] Furthermore, it should be "easy to install, maintain, and configure." We might add the obvious—it should have the capacity to accommodate not only current traffic, but also more growth than is usually anticipated.

Capacity. The media are located over a considerable capacity range—from up to one megabit per second for twisted pair to 150 megabits per second for coaxial cable and optical fiber. Twisted pair is on the low end of the 1-to 20-megabit-per-second capacity range the committee is considering. The committee will probably specify several data rates within this range. Ethernet, for example, which uses baseband coax, is specified at 10 megabits per second.

The coaxial cable used in broadband transmission is frequency-division multiplexed into a number of channels, some of which can be designed to 802 values. Sytek's LocalNet System 40, for example, is based on five 2.5-megabit-per-second channels multiplexed on a 300-MHz broadband CATV cable.[21]

The capacity of a medium does not exist in isolation. The capacity needed depends on the communication requirements that the user wants to place on the medium. There are three principal services: voice, data, and video.

Voice. The telephone network has provided this service for 100 years, and most organizations have private branch exchanges on their premises. A PBX system is implemented by twisted pairs in a star configuration; older systems make connections by circuit switching, that is, by establishing a continuous line from one telephone to another by closing switches within the PBX. In such a system only a small part of the potential capacity of a twisted pair is required to transmit voice, so the balance can be used to transmit data. The latest PBXs are more sophisticated than the traditional series of switches. What they actually do is convert a voice input into a pulse-code-modulated, or PCM, digital signal and multiplex it, along with other voice inputs, onto a single line. This line can transmit PCM signals at rates of up to 56 kilobits per second. To transmit data through such a system, it is necessary merely to provide the appropriate interface units to convert the data device's digital signal into a PCM signal. Several vendors have PBXs of this type on the market and others are readying offerings.[22,23]

What's the best network medium? There has been much argument over this. The advocates of the various media are like the three blind men trying to describe an elephant by touch—each is apprehending a different part of the network beast.

The principal advantage of the PBX approach is that the wiring is already installed in existing buildings. The disadvantage is that the data rate is low—in fact, outside the 802 committee's scope. Consequently, the type or number of devices that can be attached to a PBX-based network is limited to those with low data-rate requirements.

Data. Having enough transmission capacity to handle high-data-rate devices requires coaxial cable or optical fiber. A baseband coaxial cable system is one in which information is directly encoded and impressed upon the medium. Signals can travel in both directions on this medium, suiting it to a bus topology (although it can also be employed in a ring topology). In a bus topology there can be only one signal at a time at any one point; more than one signal results in a collision. The network must be designed to recover from it.

Data rates in the 1-to-20-megabit-per-second range are feasible. A system must be able to drive a section of 500 meters without a repeater. Baseband coax is relatively inexpensive and is easily installed. An additional station can be tapped into an active cable with no more than a momentary interrruption of service (which baseband systems are designed to accommodate).

Although baseband systems were originally designed to handle data only, it was to be expected that someone would complain that they do not accommodate voice. A baseband network is based on packets and obviously cannot accommodate a continuous analog signal as such. However, analog voice signals can be converted into digital form, transmitted in packets, and buffered before being transformed back into analog.

Whether a particular digital packet network can handle a certain number of digitized voice and data signals is a matter of the relative bandwidth of the network and of the signals under consideration. A 10-megabit-per-second network can accommodate a number of channels of digitized voice along with other digital data. However, the number of simultaneous calls that a baseband system can handle is relatively small, compared to PBX or broadband. For example, Melvin estimates that a 35-percent-data/65-percent-voice Ethernet operating at 10 megabits per second could accommodate from 40 to 80 simultaneous calls, depending on the length of the round-trip delay.[24] If only one-third of an office's phones were engaged at any one time, a system of 120 to 240 phones could be accommodated. Such numbers might be sufficient for a small local network.

At the practical level the integration of voice and data involves a number of factors of which the two most important, according to Melvin, are delay and echo. He concludes that "voice on an Ethernet local-area network is implementable today in standalone voice/data systems and in PABX-enhancing applications." Furthermore, he believes that this conclusion applies to "any other integrated voice/data local-area network distribution scheme which uses packet transmission techniques such as tokens, slotted loops, etc., having performance which is load-dependent." Connection of Ethernet voice terminals to the public switched-telephone network can also be achieved, he believes, but may require "additional research, experimentation, field trial, and performance standardization before becoming widely used."

An optical-fiber medium operates in the visible part of the spectrum. Hence, transmission over it is unaffected by electrical interference.

Video. In addition to voice and data, an ultimate local network should also be able to transmit video signals, permitting it to handle teleconferencing, security observation, training films, and other high-bandwidth applications. These functions are already being provided by broadband CATV coaxial cable systems. All three services—voice, data, and video—can be impressed on a broadband coaxial cable system.

Broadband is a transmission technique in which a number of different signals can be present on a medium at the same time without disrupting one another. Using coaxial cable as the medium, the technique utilizes standard CATV taps, connectors, amplifiers, and power supplies. Both single-trunk and dual-cable systems are possible. In a single-trunk system two-way transmission is accomplished by transmitting data on the lower range of the available spectrum in the upstream direction with one amplifier, and data on the upper range downstream with a second amplifier. The head end of the system has a device called a remodulator, which shifts the data on the low band up to the high band and reflects them back downstream.

Optical fiber. This medium, relatively new and hence unfamiliar to some designers, provides a high bandwidth over a considerable distance. In addition, transmission, being in the visible part of the spectrum, is not affected by electrical interference.

According to Rawson and Metcalfe, however, an optical-fiber medium presents two problems to the CSMA/CD network designer.[25] In this access method, it will be recalled, stations are attached to the medium by a T-connection and transmission is bidirectional. To use optical fiber in this configuration would require an optical T-connection producing a very low insertion loss. Secondly, reflections would have to be low enough not to interfere with collision detection.

However, for their experimental Fibernet, the two researchers devised a star topology that could be operated in a passive and unpowered mode using the Ethernet access method. The key component, which they called the transmissive star coupler, enabled optical transmission to be unidirectional. In one 22-minute test sequence, 150-megabit-per-second pseudorandom data was transmitted without error over a distance of more than 500 meters. Writing in 1978, the experimenters felt that their work had demonstrated "the practicality of a 100-megabit-per-second local computer network using today's technology."

In April 1982 a prototype version, called Fibernet II, was reported.[26] Based on an interactive star architecture, the 10-megabit-per-second system handles up to 25 transceivers through dual fibers.

Neff and Senzig rejected a ring topology for an optical-fiber network on the ground of poor reliability—if a single node fails, the entire network goes down.[27] They were also concerned about the "fragility" of Rawson and Metcalfe's star coupler. They turned instead to a new interconnection technique, Anarchy, in which "nodes are connected with bidirectional point-to-point links forming an arbitrary topology." The originating node broadcasts its messages over all the links to which it is connected. Intermediate nodes rebroadcast the message. The receiving node recognizes its address, accepts the message, and returns an acknowledgment along the sending path. The transmissions on off-path links, in effect, die out.

Standardization of an optical-fiber medium in the 802 context appears to be several years off. One reason is that basic optical-fiber parameters are still being standardized by a committee of the Electronic Industries Association.

Media status. The 802 committee has begun to standardize access to several media. The CSMA/CD subcommittee has added sections on both baseband and broadband in Draft C. The token-bus subcommittee has provided sections on several varieties of baseband and broadband transmission, while the token-ring subcommittee has included material on baseband, shielded, twisted-pair, and baseband-coaxial cable.

The local networking era

The advent of local networks is bringing changes of order-of-magnitude scope. When station interfaces to networks are reduced to VLSI chips, costs could drop tenfold—from thousands of dollars to hundreds of dollars.[28] Data transmission rates are going up about three orders of magnitude—from 9600 bits per second over modems to 10 megabits per second over local networks. Transmission distances are increasing from room-length buses linking a few computers to several-kilometers-long buses joining hundreds of hosts.

These changes are coming even if three access methods, instead of one, are standardized by the 802 committee. The cost of each method should be low, since VLSI implementation will damp out the differences in the complexity among the three, and the volume of applications for each method should be high enough to obtain economies of scale. If it were ever to become possible to standardize on just one method, the cost of development, manufacture, installation, and maintenance would fall still further.

Order-of-magnitude changes in the ability to do something have led in the past to more doing of it, and to doing it differently. In this case the growth in local networking capability promises to lead to distributed computing, resource sharing, and common data bases. For the individual it will mean access to more computing power, more peripherals, and more information; it will enable him to communicate more widely; it will enhance his ability to work. Local networks will provide a new generation of applications, some of them perhaps now unsuspected.

If experience with the CSMA/CD, token-bus, and token-ring access methods reveals real differences in performance and cost, the lowest-cost, highest-performance method will become dominant in the next five to ten years. It could then be chosen as the sole standard.

On the other hand, if performance and cost differences turn out to be small and difficult to quantify, or if each access method is found to be best for a particular group of applications, then we may expect all three methods to endure.

Yet a third scenario is possible. Researchers are still developing new access methods. Conceivably one of them could become the eventual winner in the local network sweepstakes. Or one or more new methods could take a place alongside some of the methods now being standardized. That outcome might raise network costs, but presumably—under the laws of competition—the better fit of a new method to an application would offset the extra cost.

To the potential local network user who would like to put his saddle on the ultimate winner this year, the prospect of having to ride just one of the horses in a lengthy race is a bit disheartening. All he can do at present is study the horses (methods) and the condition of the track (applications) and make his judgment. ■

Acknowledgments

Robert Stewart, former chairman of the IEEE Computer Society's Standards Committee, recognized the need for an article of this type and referred me to Maris Graube, chairman of the 802 committee. He, in turn, referred me to subcommittee chairmen Donald C. Loughry, Mark Stieglitz, and Nathan Tobol. I express my appreciation to them for explaining the situation orally and supplementing their comments with many documents. Harvey Freeman, chairman of the Technical Committee on Computer Communications, offered comments on the first draft.

References

1. Kenneth J. Thurber and Harvey A. Freeman, "Architectural Considerations for Local Computer Networks," *Proc. First Int'l Conf. Distributed Computing Systems,* Oct. 1979, pp. 131-142 (reprinted in Thurber, *Tutorial: Office Automation Systems,* 1980, pp. 165-176; available from IEEE Computer Society, 10662 Los Vaqueros Cir., Los Alamitos, CA 90720).
2. *A Status Report—Local Network Standards Committee, IEEE Project 802, Draft B,* Oct. 19, 1981, 408 pp.
3. *IEEE Project 802: Local Network Standards, Draft C,* May 17, 1982, 698 pp.
4. J. R. Fragola, "The IEEE Standards Generation Process," *Proc. Compsac 78,* IEEE Computer Society, Los Alamitos, CA, pp. 545-550.
5. "Reference Model of Open Systems Interconnection," International Standards Organization documents ISO/TC97/SC16/N227 and ISO/TC97/SC16/N309.
6. Hubert Zimmermann, "OSI Reference Model—The ISO Model of Architecture for Open Systems Interconnection," *IEEE Trans. Communications,* Vol. COM-28, No. 4, Apr. 1980, pp. 425-432 (reprinted in Thurber, *Tutorial: Office Automation Systems,* pp. 104-111).
7. Robert M. Metcalfe and David R. Boggs, "Ethernet: Distributed Packet Switching for Local Computer Networks," *Comm. ACM,* Vol. 19, No. 7, July 1976, pp. 395-404 (reprinted in Thurber and Freeman, *Tutorial: Local Computer Networks,* 2nd ed., 1981, pp. 262-271; available from IEEE Computer Society, 10662 Los Vaqueros Cir., Los Alamitos, CA 90720)..
8. "Local Networks—A Matter of Choice," *The Economist,* Dec. 12, 1981, pp. 99-100.
9. John F. Shoch and Jon A. Hupp, "Peformance of an Ethernet Local Network—A Preliminary Report," *Digest of Papers—Compcon Spring 80,* IEEE Computer Society, Los Alamitos, CA, pp. 318-322.
10. Mark Stieglitz, "An LSI Token Controller," *Digest of Papers—Compcon Spring 82,* IEEE Computer Society, Los Alamitos, CA, pp. 115-120.
11. R. C. Dixon, "Ring Network Topology for Local Data Communications," working paper, IBM Communication Products Division, Research Triangle Park, NC, Mar. 8, 1982, 31 pp. (To appear in *Digest of Papers—Compcon Fall 82,* IEEE Computer Society, Los Alamitos, CA, 1982.)
12. J. D. Markov and N. C. Strole, "Token-Ring Local Area Networks: A Perspective," working paper, IBM Communication Products Division, Research Triangle Park, NC, Mar. 8, 1982, 18 pp. (To appear in *Digest of Papers—Compcon Fall 82,* IEEE Computer Society, Los Alamitos, CA, 1982.)
13. D. W. Andrews and G. D. Schultz, "A Token-Ring Architecture for Local-Area Networks," working paper,

IBM Communication Products Division, Research Triangle Park, NC, Mar. 8, 1982, 27 pp. (To appear in *Digest of Papers—Compcon Fall 82,* IEEE Computer Society, Los Alamitos, CA, 1982.)

14. J. G. Rusnak, "Local-Area Networking and Higher-Level Protocols: An SNA Example," working paper, IBM Communication Products Division, Research Triangle Park, NC, Mar. 8, 1982, 13 pp. (To appear in *Digest of Papers—Compcon Fall 82,* IEEE Computer Society, Los Alamitos, CA, 1982.

15. Yogen K. Dalal and Robert S. Printis, "48-bit Absolute Internet and Ethernet Host Numbers," *Proc. 7th Data Communications Symp.,* IEEE Computer Society, Los Alamitos, CA, 1981, pp. 240-245.

16. David R. Boggs, John F. Shoch, Edward A. Taft, and Robert M. Metcalfe, "Pup: An Internetwork Architecture," *IEEE Trans. Communications,* Vol. COM-28, No. 4, Apr. 1980, pp. 612-624 (reprinted in Thurber, *Tutorial: Office Automation Systems,* pp. 131-143).

17. *The Ethernet: A Local Area Network; Data Link Layer and Physical Layer Specifications,* version 1.0, technical manual, DEC-Intel-Xerox, Sept. 30, 1980, p. 26.

18. John F. Shoch, Yogen K. Dalal, David D. Redell, and Ronald C. Crane, "Evolution of the Ethernet Local Computer Network," *Computer,* Vol. 15, No. 8, Aug. 1982, pp. 10-27.

19. Bruce Howard, "Local Nets, PBXs To Coexist in Future," *Computerworld,* Mar. 1, 1982, p. 67.

20. David D. Clark, Kenneth T. Pogran, and David P. Reed, "An Introduction to Local Area Networks," *Proc. IEEE,* Vol. 66, No. 11, Nov. 1978, pp. 1497-1517 (reprinted in Thurber and Freeman, *Tutorial: Local Computer Networks,* pp. 16-36).

21. K. J. Biba, "LocalNet: A Digital Communications Network for Broadband Coaxial Cable," *Digest of Papers—Compcon Spring 81,* IEEE Computer Society, Los Alamitos, CA, pp. 59-63.

22. Harvey J. Hindin, "Controlling the Electronic Office: PBXs Make Their Move," *Electronics,* Apr. 7, 1981, pp. 139-148.

23. James P. McNaul, "Applications Utilizing Integrated Voice/Data PABXs," *Digest of Papers—Compcon Spring 82,* IEEE Computer Society, Los Alamitos, CA, pp. 308-311.

24. Donald K. Melvin, "Voice on Ethernet—Now!," Intel paper presented at Nat'l Telecommunications Conf., Nov. 30, 1981, 22 pp.

25. Eric G. Rawson and Robert M. Metcalfe, "Fibernet: Multimode Optical Fibers for Local Computer Networks," *IEEE Trans. Communications,* Vol. 26, No. 7, July 1978, pp. 983-990 (reprinted in Thurber and Freeman, *Tutorial: Local Computer Networks,* pp. 61-68).

26. "Xerox Develops Optical Ethernet," *Electronics,* Apr. 21, 1982, p. 34.

27. Randall Neff and Don Senzig, "A Local Network Design Using Fiber Optics," *Digest of Papers—Compcon Spring 81,* IEEE Computer Society, Los Alamitos, CA, pp. 64-69.

28. Philip L. Arst and David Yeh, "The Changing Economics for Computer and Terminal Interconnection—An Overview," technical report, Intel Corp., Santa Clara, CA, Feb. 24, 1982, 20 pp.

Ware Myers is a freelance writer specializing in computer subject matter and a contributing editor for *IEEE Micro.* From 1965 until Xerox withdrew from the mainframe business in 1975, he was a member of the Systems Development Group, Computer Systems Division, in El Segundo, California, where he worked on the development of analog instruments, color display stations, a microprogrammed controller, and several MOS memories. His principal contribution to these developments was the preparation of design specifications, technical descriptions, operating instructions, and reference manuals. From 1956 to 1965 he was with Consolidated Electrodynamics Corporation and its subsidiary, Consolidated Systems Corporation. He has also worked as an instructor and lecturer in engineering at the University of California, Los Angeles.

Myers received his BS from the Case Institute of Technology and his MS from the University of Southern California. He is a member of Tau Beta Pi and the IEEE Computer Society.

Myers' address is c/o *IEEE Micro*, 10662 Los Vaqueros Circle, Los Alamitos, CA 90720.

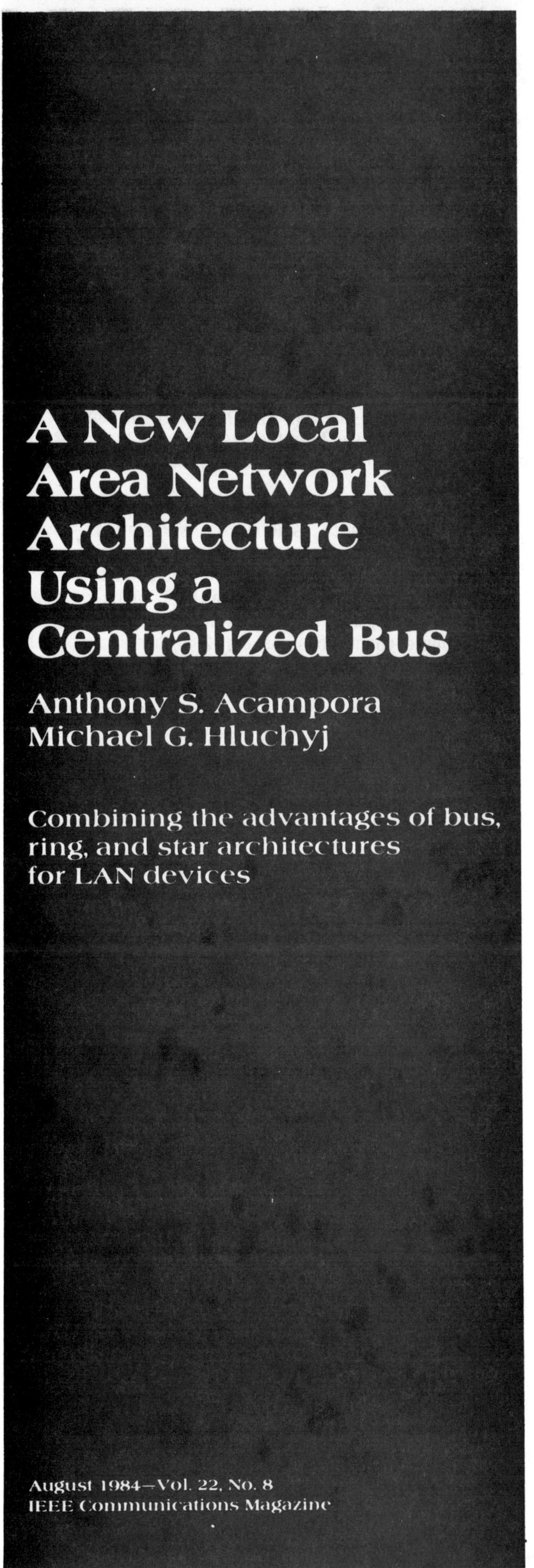

LOCAL AREA NETWORKS are currently enjoying tremendous popularity as a means for providing wideband interconnection and communications among data terminals, host computers, and other types of digital equipment located throughout a single building or a campus of buildings. Such networks are typically based on bus, ring, or star architectures, each of which manifests its own set of advantages and disadvantages. In this paper, an architectural approach is described that draws upon and integrates the advantages found separately in these three different architectures, while avoiding the major disadvantages found in any one. This new architecture employs a centrally located short bus that provides an extremely efficient packet-switching service to the devices attached to the network. Bandwidth on the short bus is dynamically allocated in response to instantaneous demands by means of a highly efficient but flexible priority-based bus contention scheme. The approach permits multiple priority classes with fair allocation of bandwidth within each class, along with a capability for integrated circuit and packet switching. The architecture can also make use of existing twisted-pair building wiring, and at the same time take advantage of emerging optical-fiber technology. In addition, the architecture provides a means to expand the network beyond a local area, resulting in a wide-area network capability.

Introduction

In recent years, many different architectures have emerged for Local Area Networks (LAN's) based on star, bus, and ring topologies [1]. Arguments abound concerning the superiority of one LAN architecture over another, but in fact, on close examination, each has its own set of advantages and disadvantages.

Star topologies, as applied to LAN's, are typically implemented around a digital PBX core. A digital PBX enjoys the advantage of superior network management features, where centralization eases fault detection and isolation and permits careful system configuration and performance tracking by an administrator. Also, centralization makes for a more secure system, and although it can be cumbersome at the switch itself, the twisted-pair building wiring is uniform and backed by years of installation and maintenance experience.

On the negative side, the circuit-switched architecture of traditional digital PBX's does not permit high-speed statistical multiplexing of data; the end devices are often limited to a single 64-kb/s digital pipe through the switch. Not only is this circuit-switched connection poorly matched to the demands of bursty data traffic, with switch ports unnecessarily tied up for long periods with little or no interactive traffic, but the limited data rate is not conducive to high-speed host-to-host communications. Furthermore, the lack of statistical multiplexing hinders the trend toward multiple virtual connections between devices, and does not make efficient use of generally expensive leased trunking facilities between locations.

Distributed-bus and ring LAN architectures avoid the major pitfalls of a traditional circuit-switched PBX by providing shared, packet-switched access to a single high-speed data channel. The distributed nature of these architectures also allows for simple modular growth. In addition, some contend that distributed architectures are inherently more reliable.

Reprinted from *IEEE Communications Magazine*, August 1984, pages 12-21.

EHO234-5/85/0000/0129$01.00 © 1984 IEEE

This, however, is arguable since even with these architectures there exist failure modes capable of bringing down the entire network; these are often more difficult and time consuming to isolate than with a centralized architecture.

In the literature, most LAN comparisons are made between distributed-bus and ring architectures and their respective media-access techniques [2,3]. Beyond questionable security, arguments against distributed-bus architectures center on the CSMA/CD media-access scheme and its limitations: cable length, bus transmission rate, packet size vs. efficiency trade-off (see the section entitled "Bus Contention"), instability at high utilizations, and nondeterministic delays. Furthermore, it has been argued that a distributed bus cannot make use of current optical-fiber technology. Arguments against token-passing rings center on the protocol complexity to protect against lost tokens, and hardware complexity to protect against broken rings and failed ring interface units. It is also argued that, when devices are added to or removed from a distributed bus, no disruption in service is experienced, in contrast to rings. Finally, with both architectures, the associated protocols are geared for one network located on one premises; interconnection of networks for either on-premises growth or interpremises communications requires gateways.

In what follows, we describe a new LAN architecture—based on a centrally located short bus—that combines the advantages of the digital PBX, distributed-bus, and ring architectures while avoiding their disadvantages. Like the digital PBX, the centralized nature of this new LAN architecture allows for secure communications with a rich set of network management features for fault detection and isolation, and system configuration and performance tracking. However, as with distributed-bus and ring architectures, it avoids the major drawbacks of a circuit-switched PBX by providing shared, packet-switched access to a single high-speed data channel—the short bus.

Unlike distributed-bus and ring architectures, the media-access scheme, which takes advantage of the small propagation delay on the bus, is both simple and efficient. It achieves a perfect scheduling of packet transmissions wherein there are neither destructive collisions nor periods when the bus is idle with packets awaiting transmission. Moreover, this desirable characteristic is robust with respect to the geographical separation among the attached devices, the bus transmission rate, and the selected packet size. In particular, a small packet size, say under 200 bits, can be selected to provide a high degree of pipelining through the system. In addition, the scheduling of packet transmission is flexible, permitting multiple priority classes, round-robin-like scheduling within a priority class, and even integrated circuit and packet switching. With these features, efficient integration and servicing of disparate traffic types are readily achieved.

Two other areas in which the centralized-bus architecture has important advantages over other LAN architectures are building distribution and networking. The building distribution allows for the use of twisted-pair wiring from an office to a satellite closet, while avoiding wire congestion at the central location through the use of a fiber-optic backbone. Besides its small size and light weight, fiber also enjoys the advantages of high bandwidth, high noise immunity, and security from tapping. Finally, as we describe in the next section, the basic building block in the centralized-bus architecture is a node containing a fast hardware packet switch designed specifically for use with virtual circuits. As such, nodes can be interconnected via simple interfaces, to both permit on-premises growth and provide metropolitan and nationwide networking without the need for complex gateways.

Basic Network Architecture

The shared transmission medium in the centralized-bus architecture is a short bus, consisting of backplane wiring in a cabinet, with the bus interface units (referred to as interface modules) residing in the cabinet on separate circuit cards (as shown in Fig. 1). The short-bus backplane and interface modules form the basic building blocks of the LAN, from which concentrators and network nodes are constructed.

As illustrated in Fig. 2, the concentrators, nodes, and attached devices (such as terminals, workstations, hosts, and printers) are interconnected using point-to-point transmission media. The nodes may be interconnected in a flexible mesh topology, using optical fiber for on-premises connections and leased or private transmission facilities for interpremises connections. As Fig. 2 further shows, each node taken alone is the root of a tree—the attached devices form the leaves and the concentrators form the branch points. Fiber again would be used for connecting the concentrators to the node and also for attaching devices, such as host computers, that require a high-speed multiplexed data link to the network. Terminal and workstation connections to a node or concentrator may be made with twisted-pair wiring.

The architecture of the node has its origins in the DATAKIT[1] Packet Switch invented by A. G. Fraser [4]. All data enters and exits a node via the interface modules which all have a common interface to the backplane. Each interface module contains bus contention logic and packet buffers, along with any functionality associated with the particular interface (for example, an asynchronous terminal interface module would have a packet assembly and disassembly function). As Fig. 3 shows, a node also contains a clock module, a switch module, and a common control processor, along with the three data busses that reside on the backplane—the transmit, broadcast, and contention busses.

[1]DATAKIT is a trademark of AT&T.

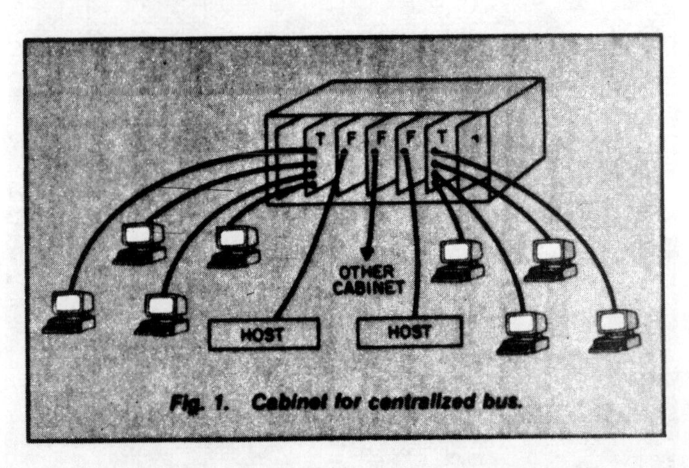

Fig. 1. Cabinet for centralized bus.

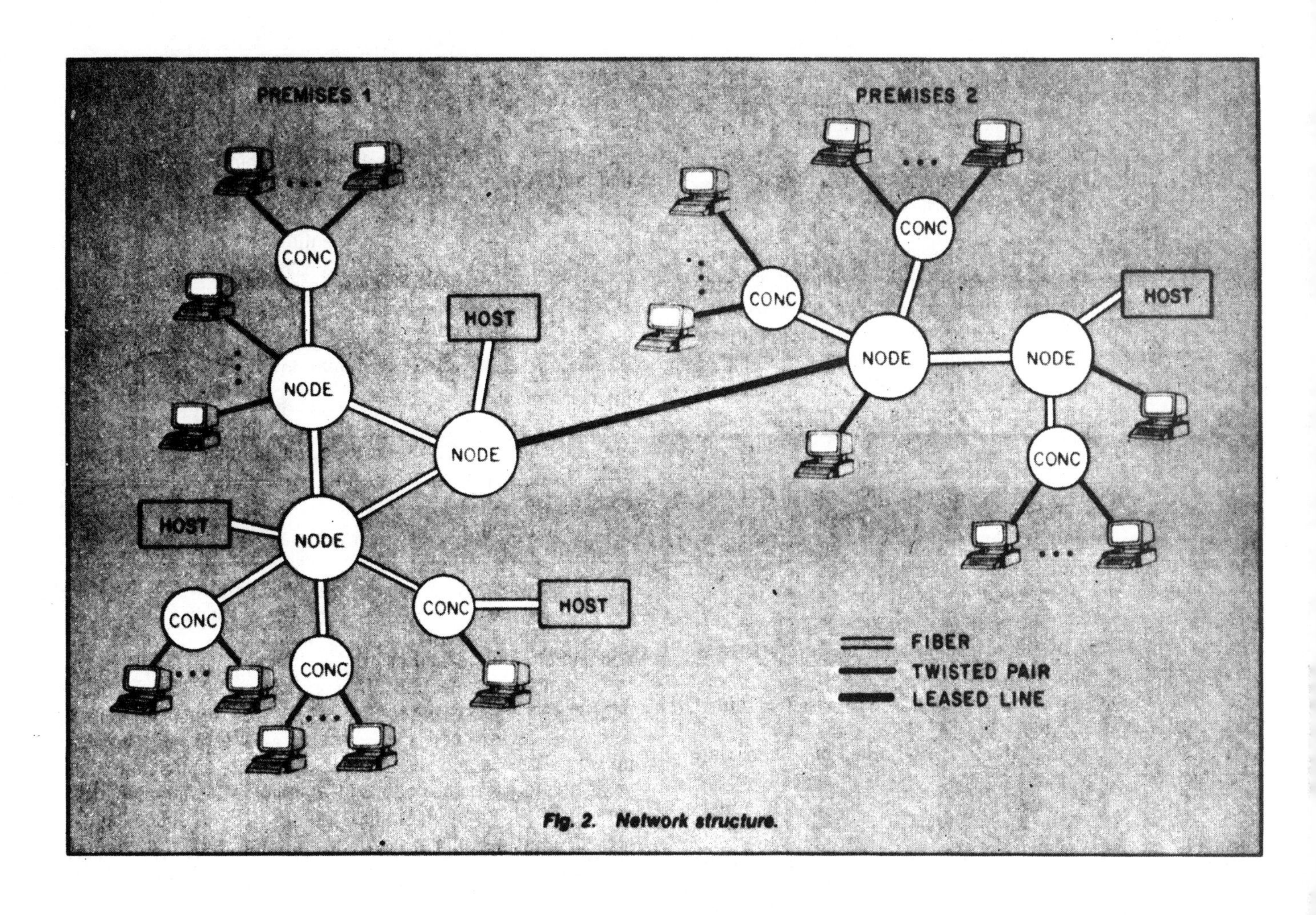

Fig. 2. Network structure.

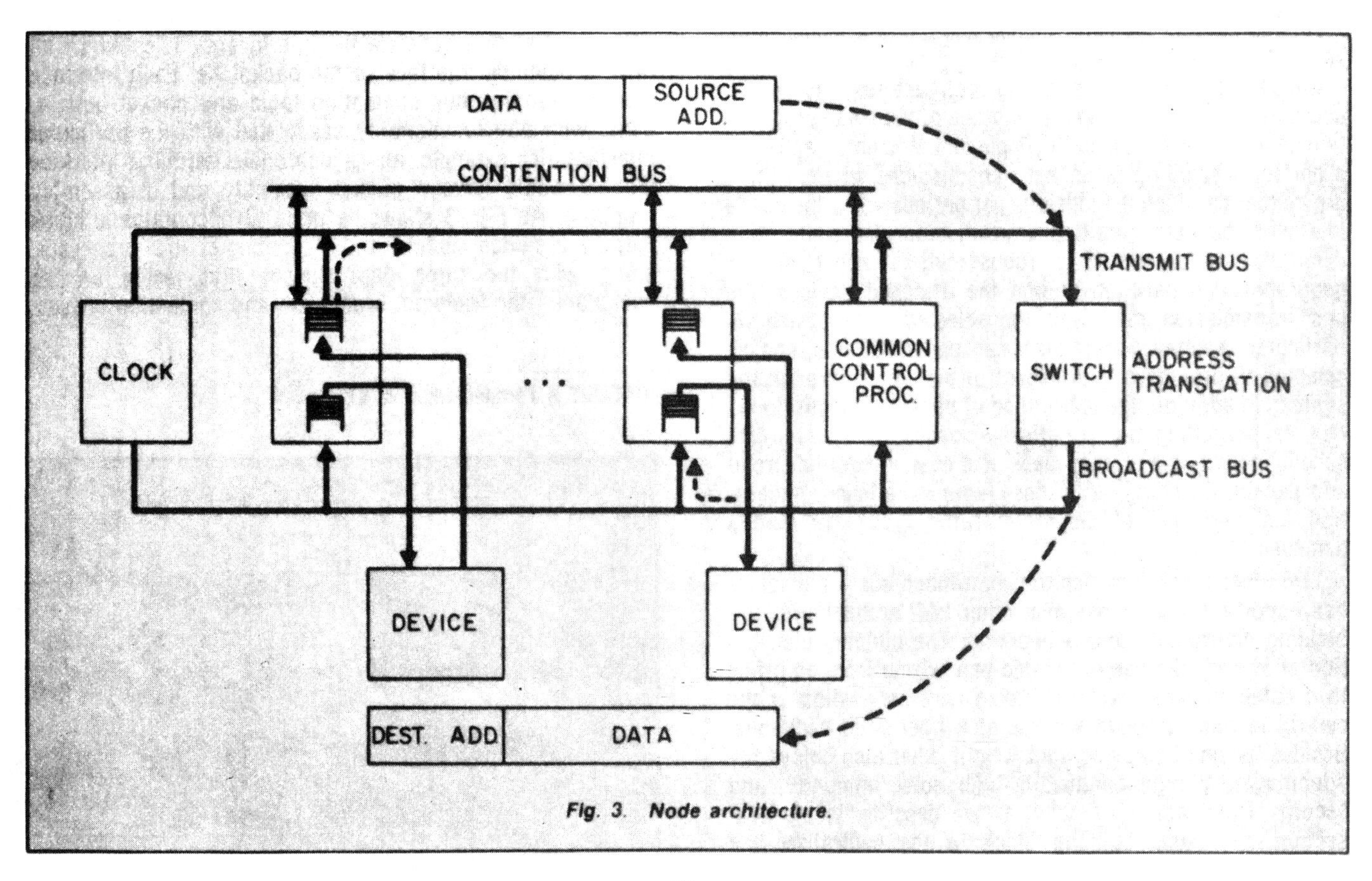

Fig. 3. Node architecture.

As we describe later, the contention bus is used by the interface modules to gain access to the time-slotted transmit bus. The transmit bus and broadcast bus are used for sending and receiving packets, respectively. The header of each packet placed on the transmit bus by an interface module contains a source address consisting of a module number followed by a channel number. The module number uniquely identifies the transmitting interface module, and the channel number is used to distinguish among the different conversations passing through that module. As Fig. 3 shows, each packet placed on the transmit bus is removed by the switch module, which translates the source module and channel numbers to the destination module and channel numbers. The specific translation is established by a prior call-set-up procedure. The packet is then retransmitted on the broadcast bus where it is received by the specified destination module. In this way, a virtual circuit transport mechanism is implemented, wherein the common control processor at the node handles call step-up and take-down along with necessary maintenance and administration functions.

A packet passing through two or more nodes first has its source module and channel numbers translated, by the switch module at the first node, to those of a trunk interface module, also located at the first node. After receiving the packet, this trunk module strips the module number and, retaining the channel number information, transports the packet over the trunk to a trunk interface module located at the second node. Here, the packet contends for access to the transmit bus of the second node, and is transmitted with the new trunk module number and the same channel number used over the trunk. The switch module at the second node translates this address to the destination address at the second node, which may be that of the end device or, if the packet is destined for another node, that of another internode trunk module. The proper address translation at each node along the path is established during the call-set-up procedure. Note that, although we are discussing the centralized-bus architecture in the context of LAN's, the nodes and trunk interface modules can be used to construct wide-area networks with an arbitrary mesh topology.

The last major component of the centralized-bus architecture is the concentrator. Although a concentrator cabinet may be smaller than that of a node, both may share a common backplane design, thus permitting the same interface modules to be used in either the concentrator or node. Unlike the node, however, the concentrator would not contain a switch module or a common control processor (CCP). All packets placed on the concentrator transmit bus are forwarded, via optical fiber, to a fiber interface module at the node. (Contention for the concentrator's transmit bus is resolved via the same mechanism applied at the node.) Likewise, all packets coming from the node are placed on the concentrator broadcast bus to be received by the destination interface module. In this way, neither switching nor call control processing is done at the concentrator, which functions only as a statistical multiplexor.

Having described the basic components of the centralized-bus architecture, the remainder of the paper will focus on four important aspects: bus contention, networking, building distribution, and network management. The centralized-bus architecture finds its major strengths in these four areas.

Bus Contention

Often emphasized when comparing packet-switching LAN architectures are the performance and complexity of the associated media access schemes. The simplicity, efficiency, and flexibility of the bus contention scheme emerge as clear advantages of the centralized-bus architecture. In this section we describe the contention scheme, compare its performance with other access schemes, and describe its inherent flexibility.

Short-Bus Contention Scheme

Access to the transmit bus in both the node and concentrator is governed by a bus contention scheme operating on a separate serial contention bus. As shown in Fig. 4, both the transmit bus and contention bus use the same slot timing (generated by the clock module) and operate in parallel; contention for a given time slot on the transmit bus occurs in the previous time slot on the contention bus. A contention code is transmitted in each access time slot on the contention bus; this consists of a priority code followed by the module number for the "winning" module. This module has won the sole right to transmit one fixed-length packet onto the transmit bus in the next time slot. Messages arriving to a module of length greater than this fixed-length packet are decomposed into a sequence of fixed-length packets; all such packets independently contend, in sequence, for access to the transmit bus. The contention process, which occurs at the beginning of each time slot, is such that the module having the highest contention code wins contention and transmits its packet in the next time on the transmit bus. Although the module number is fixed and unique to each interface module on the backplane, the priority code can change with time, allowing a flexible distributed scheduling of packet transmissions.

The contention mechanism itself relies on two properties of the contention bus. First, the bus is short in the sense that the end-to-end propagation delay is less than the time to transmit one bit. Second, each module can simultaneously transmit and receive with the (open collector) contention bus

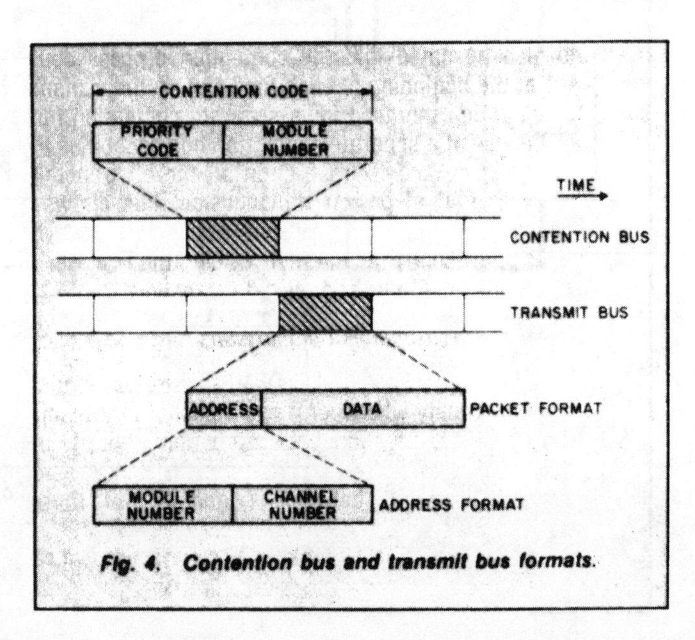

Fig. 4. Contention bus and transmit bus formats.

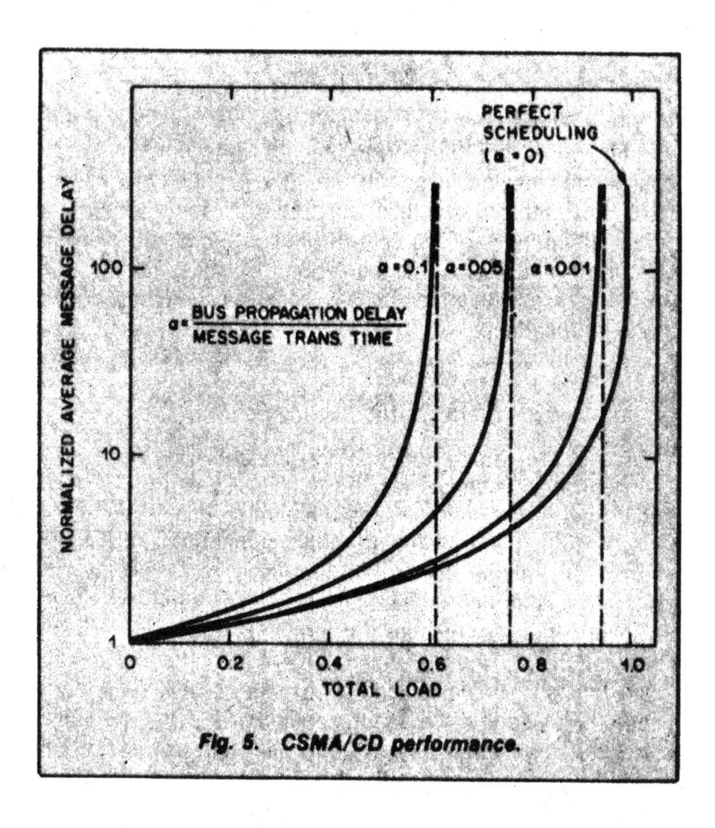

Fig. 5. CSMA/CD performance.

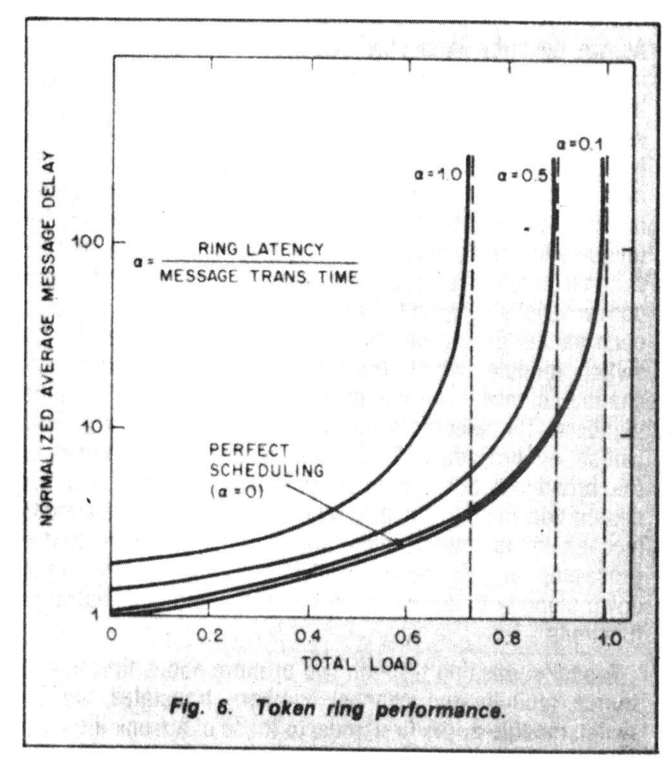

Fig. 6. Token ring performance.

functioning as a logical OR. Hence, before the end of a bit transmission on the contention bus, each module observes the state of the bus to be the logical OR of all transmitted bits. This leads to the following simple scheme for resolving contention. At the start of each time slot, each contending module begins transmitting its contention code on the contention bus. If what a module transmits differs from what is read off the bus after each bit, it stops contending. That is, if a module transmits a 0 and reads a 1, it drops out of contention and waits for the next time slot before contending again. Hence, by the end of the time slot, the contending module with the highest contention code wins contention and then transmits, without interference, its packet in the next time slot on the transmit bus.

One may view the contention process as a simple binary tree search, similar to one proposed by Hayes [5]. Mark [6] proposed a similar contention scheme for a distributed bus. It should also be noted that the contention process could take place at the beginning of each time slot on the transmit bus [7], eliminating the need for a separate contention bus. However, the use of a separate contention bus decouples the contention process, and its restriction on the bit transmission time, with that of packet transmission; this allows a higher packet transmission rate than would otherwise be possible. In particular, a parallel rather than a serial transmission bus could be used for data transport.

Performance Comparisons

With the short-bus contention scheme, an interface module contends continuously whenever it has a packet to transmit; modules that lose contention back off without interfering with the transmission of the eventual winner. Hence, aside from a small delay of between 1 and 2 slot times[2] (corresponding to the time waiting for the start of the next time slot and contention for access to the transmit bus), packet transmissions are perfectly scheduled, avoiding both collisions and bus idle periods when there are packets awaiting transmission. This is to be contrasted with popular media-access schemes, such as CSMA/CD and token passing for distributed-bus and ring architectures, respectively [1]. Figures 5 and 6 show what have now become well-known delay vs. load performance results for CSMA/CD and token passing (single-token system). Here, the average delay is normalized with respect to the mean message-transmission time, and the total load is the fraction of bus capacity utilized in the successful transmission of messages. The CSMA/CD performance curves in Fig. 5 were obtained from results derived in [8] under the assumptions of Poisson message arrivals and exponentially distributed message lengths. The token passing performance curves in Fig. 6 were obtained under the same assumptions from results derived in [9].

For CSMA/CD, the parameter α in Fig. 5 corresponds to the ratio of the bus end-to-end propagation delay and the mean time to transmit a message. Note from Fig. 5 that the delay vs. load performance for CSMA/CD degrades from that of perfect scheduling as α increases from zero. An increase in α results from an increase in the bus length or transmission rate, or a decrease in the mean message size. For a system with a 2-km cable length and a mean message length of 1000 bits, the three values of α—0.01, 0.05, and 0.1—in Fig. 5 correspond respectively to a bus transmission rate of 1, 5, and 10 Mb/s. Note that as α increases, the fraction of usable bandwidth provided by the bus diminishes, that is, the delay experienced approaches infinity at smaller normalized offered loads. This trade-off between bus length, transmission rate, and message length is a fundamental limitation of CSMA/CD systems arising from finite speed-of-light considerations.

[2]Note that at 10 Mb/s, a 200-bit packet size corresponds to a slot time of only 20 μs.

With token-ring architectures, the media-access efficiency decreases as the ring latency increases. The ring latency is the delay in transmitting a bit completely around the ring, which includes both the ring propagation delay and the processing delay at each ring interface unit. Figure 6 shows the degradation in performance for a single token system as α (now the ratio of the ring latency and the mean message transmission time) increases. Note that α increases with an increase in the ring length, transmission rate, number of interface units, or processing delay per interface unit; or with a decrease in the mean message size. For a system with 50 interface units, a 2-km cable length, and a mean message length of 1000 bits, the three values of α—0.1, 0.5, and 1.0—in Fig. 6 correspond respectively to a transmission rate and per-interface-unit processing delay of 5 Mb/s and 1 bit, 10 Mb/s and 8 bits, and 20 Mb/s and 16 bits. Again, we note that the usable bandwidth decreases as α increases.

From these comparison results, we conclude that the perfect scheduling performance for the short-bus contention scheme is superior to that of CSMA/CD and token passing. In particular, its performance is robust with respect to the bus transmission rate, geographical separation and number of attached devices, and selected packet size. The ability to use small packets, in fact, becomes important when considering the pipelining performance of a system.

Pipelining Considerations

The performance results shown thus far have ignored the effects of the access line speed. Implicit in the results is an assumption that each message generated by a device arrives instantly to its respective network interface unit. For LAN's, the speed of the shared transmission media (bus or ring) is typically much greater than the access line speed, particularly when considering that most terminals connected to LAN's today operate at less than 20 kb/s. Figure 7 illustrates the reduction in transport delay, under these conditions, that is possible by dividing messages into small packets and pipelining them on a high-speed bus. It is assumed that the line speeds for both transmitting and receiving devices are equal but less than the bus transmission rate, and that there is no other traffic on the bus (that is, the bus contention delay is zero). The "excess delay" indicated in each case is that delay in excess of the situation where the two devices are directly connected. The excess delay for the pipelined case is simply the time to receive one packet of data over the access line plus the time to transmit the packet on the bus. For the nonpipelined case, the excess delay consists of the entire line delay for the message plus the time to transmit the message on the bus. Hence, the excess delay for the pipelined case is proportional to the packet size, while the excess delay for the nonpipelined case is proportional to the message size.

There is, of course, a limit on how small a packet size one can select. With a fixed overhead per packet, as one reduces the packet size there results an increase in the percentage of overhead. However, the use of virtual circuits reduces the address overhead for each packet, so that even a small packet, containing say 16 data bytes, can maintain a per-packet addressing overhead of under 10%.

The advantage of the centralized-bus architecture and its ability to pipeline traffic becomes clear by considering a specific example. Suppose that a large number of sources are attached, by means of 64-kb/s access lines, to an LAN bus operating at 10 Mb/s. Furthermore, assume that each source generates exponentially distributed messages of mean length $\overline{M}$ according to a Poisson process; the LAN traffic load is increased by increasing the message arrival rate. Two cases are compared with the results shown in Fig.

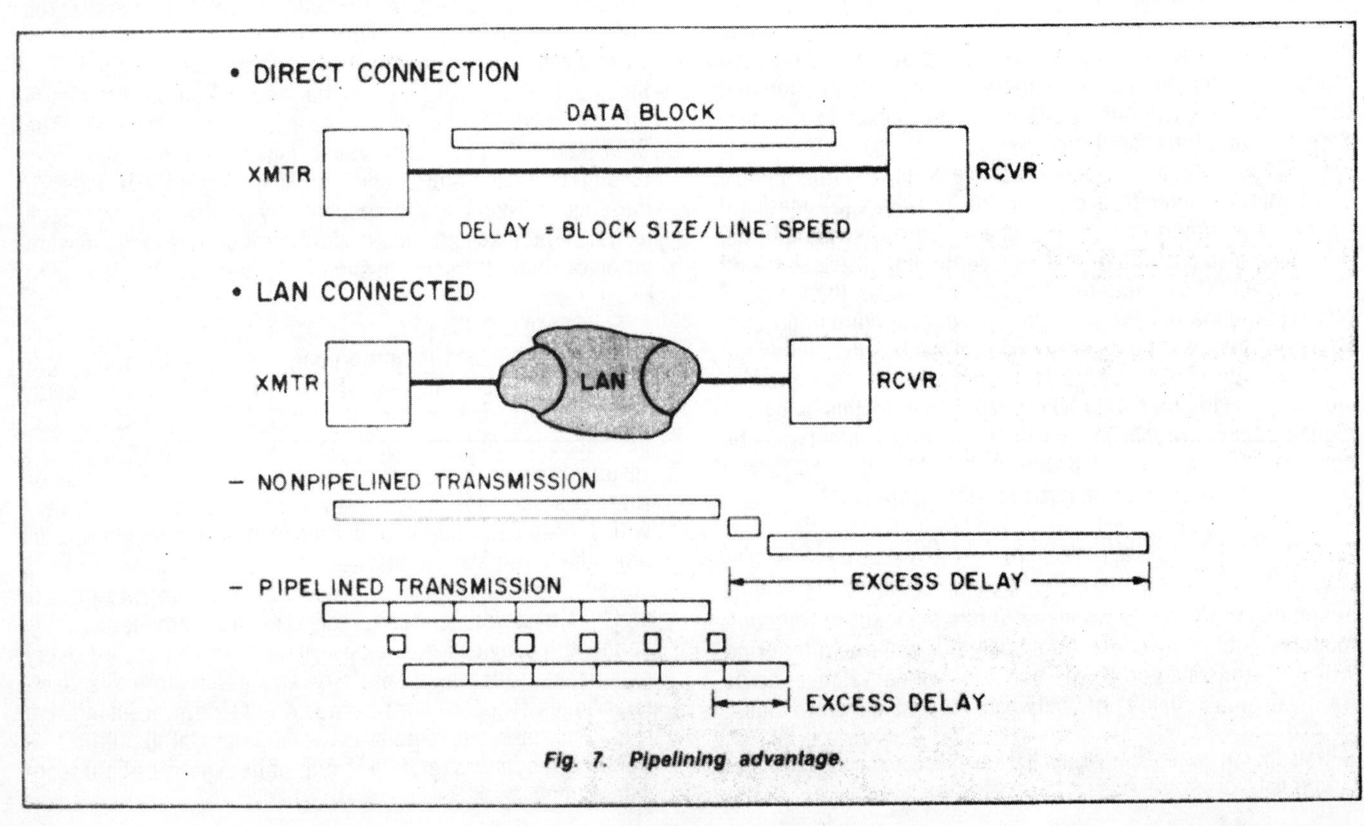

Fig. 7. Pipelining advantage.

8. For the first case, the mean message length M is 1000 bytes, and the LAN is a short bus with a packet size of 16 bytes. For the second case, the LAN is a 2-km distributed bus using the CSMA/CD contention protocol and, to bring out all relevant points, mean message lengths of 16 bytes and 100 bytes are considered, along with the 1000-byte mean message length assumed for the short-bus LAN. The short-bus performance curve in Fig. 8 was obtained through an approximate analysis based on the $M/M/m$ queuing model (where the number of servers $m = 10 \cdot 10^6/64 \cdot 10^3 \simeq 156$) [10]. The CSMA/CD curves were obtained by adding a message line delay to the results derived in [8]. In both cases, any per-message or per-packet overhead was ignored.

We note from Fig. 8 that, as a result of pipelining, the average excess delay for the short bus is about 2 ms (this is the time it takes for 16 bytes to arrive over the 64-kb/s access line) for traffic loads as high as 80%. In this regime, the bus-contention delay is negligible in comparison to the 2-ms packetization delay. Above 80% load, however, the contention delay overshadows the packetization delay and so the average excess delay grows rapidly with increasing load. Note that one can view the 10-Mb/s bus as providing 156 time slots every 2 ms; each time slot contains 16 bytes, and access to one time slot every 2 ms provides a 64-kb/s channel. Hence, up to 156 simultaneous messages can be pipelined through the short bus with the bus contention delay upper bounded by 2 ms. Only when the number of simultaneous messages arriving at the bus exceeds 156 can transmission delays grow beyond 2 ms.

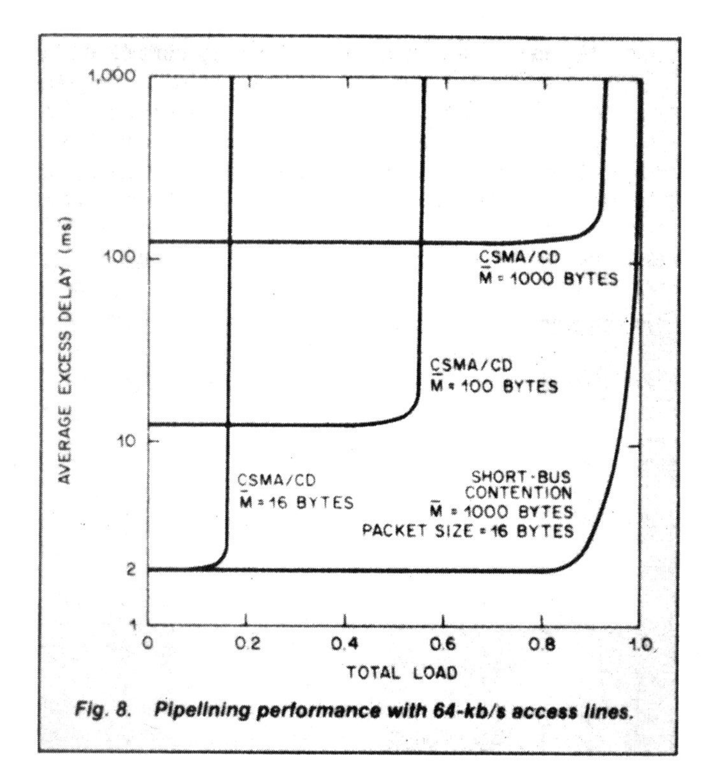

Fig. 8. **Pipelining performance with 64-kb/s access lines.**

For the 2-km distributed bus, several effects are noted. First, for a mean message length of 1000 bytes, good bus utilization efficiency is achieved since α (the ratio of the bus end-to-end propagation delay and the mean message transmission time on the bus) is small. However, the average excess delay for light loads is about 125 ms. To reduce this excess delay, suppose that sources are restricted to transmit messages with mean lengths of 100 bytes rather than 1000 bytes. Then the delay at light loading falls to about 12.5 ms, but the distributed-bus LAN becomes unstable at traffic loads greater than 55%. Similarly, if the mean message length is limited to 16 bytes to provide an excess delay of 2 ms at light loading (comparable to the short bus), then the distributed-bus LAN becomes unstable for offered loads greater than 17%. Thus, we see that a distributed bus with CSMA/CD cannot simultaneously provide low-excess delay and high-bandwidth utilization efficiency. By contrast, the short-bus contention scheme provides a lower bound on excess delay as compared to any distributed-bus parameter set.

The pipelining advantage becomes even more dramatic when one considers networking among LAN nodes by means of off-premises transmission facilities. Here, because bandwidth is generally much more expensive, the transmission rates of off-premises communications links might be 2 or 3 orders of magnitude lower than typical LAN rates. Under these conditions, the pipelining advantage is enjoyed along each link on a path from source to destination. Specifically, suppose that a particular network connection involves K nodes, as shown in Fig. 9. For simplicity, suppose that the access lines connecting the end devices, as well as all internode trunks, operate at a data rate of R b/s. Without pipelining, the entire message is assembled at each node input port before placing the message on the corresponding high-speed bus, and at each output port before the message is sent over a trunk or device access line. Following the single-node discussion, and ignoring any message overhead, it follows that, without pipelining, the excess delay incurred at light loading is

$$D_{\text{excess}} = K[M/R + M/S]$$

where S is the data rate on the high-speed bus and M is the length of the message. With pipelining, it is only necessary that single packets from a long message be assembled before placing the packet onto the high-speed bus or the lower-speed internode trunks and access lines. Hence, the excess

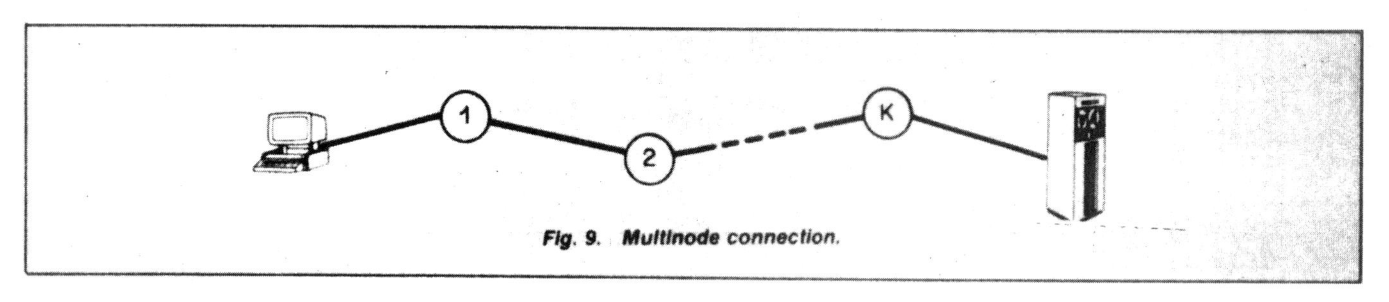

Fig. 9. **Multinode connection.**

delay with pipelining is independent of the message length and is given by

$$D_{excess} = K[P/R + P/S]$$

where P is the packet size and, again, any packet overhead is ignored.

A simple numerical example is instructive. Suppose that a particular path in the network passes through three nodes, and R = 64 kb/s. Let the bus speed S be 10 Mb/s and the message length M be 1000 bytes; and, for pipelining, let the packet size be 16 bytes. Then, at light loading, the excess delay without pipelining is 377 ms; with pipelining, the excess delay is only 6 ms. Improvement of almost two orders of magnitude is noted with pipelining.

The concept of dividing messages into small units before transmission in a data-communications network is not new. The advantages of such an approach have long been recognized and, in fact, have resulted in the acceptance of packet-switching over message-switching techniques. The point to be made here, however, is that the media-access efficiency of the short-bus contention scheme is, unlike that in CSMA/CD and token passing, insensitive to the selected packet size. Hence, one has the flexibility to select a small packet size without incurring a loss of media-access efficiency, and thereby enjoy a small end-to-end delay by virtue of message pipelining.

Flexible Distributed Scheduling

Along with perfect scheduling of packet transmissions and its associated performance advantages, the bus contention mechanism also provides considerable flexibility in the way packets are scheduled. As described earlier, the contention code used by an interface module is composed of two parts: a priority code followed by the module number. The module number ensures that no two interface modules ever contend using the same contention code. Basing contention on the module number only, however, would result in an unfair allocation of the bus. Under heavy loading, packets from lower-numbered modules would incur a larger delay than those from higher-numbered modules. This could be avoided by having the module number itself change with time [11], but this requires a certain amount of coordination among the interface modules to ensure that no two ever use the same number. Preceding the fixed module number with a priority code, which can change with time, avoids this problem and in fact permits much flexibility in scheduling packet transmissions on the bus.

One may, for example, make use of the priority code to assign different types of traffic to different priority classes. Network control messages could use a higher priority code than interactive data messages, which in turn could use a higher priority code than long file transfers. In addition, by using two consecutive priority codes (say differing in the least-significant bit) for each priority class, one can achieve a fair round-robin-like scheduling within the priority class. This technique, which is based on an algorithm that has been around for some time [12], has modules switching from the lower priority code to the higher to ensure a fair sharing within the priority class. Specifically, a module first contends using the lower of the two priority codes. If the module loses contention because either: 1) a module in a higher priority class won, or 2) a module in its own priority class won using the higher priority code, it continues to contend using the lower priority code. If the module loses contention and the winner was in its priority class using the lower priority code, the module contends in the next time slot and all subsequent time slots, until it wins, using the higher priority code. Whenever a module wins contention, it begins its next contention using the lower priority code.

For each priority class using this scheme, variable-length cycles appear on the contention bus for which all time slots won by the priority class (except the first in the cycle) have the priority code set at the higher value. In effect, each module in the priority class is given the opportunity to transmit one packet in each cycle, with the proviso that a packet newly arriving to an interface module must wait until the next cycle before it can be transmitted.

Another use of the priority code, described in [7] and illustrated in Fig. 10, guarantees a module access to a time slot on a periodic basis, much like circuit-switched TDMA. With this technique, a module first contends with a low-priority code and then, after winning a time slot, contends periodically using a higher priority code. A variation on this technique allows a module holding such a synchronous circuit to relinquish unused slots to asynchronous traffic.

Hence, we see that the perfect scheduling performance of the short-bus contention scheme is further enhanced by its great scheduling flexibility. This flexible scheduling is made possible by the inherent priority structure in the contention mechanism.

Networking

An important feature of the centralized-bus architecture is its ability to conveniently support internode networking to accommodate both on-premises growth and interpremises

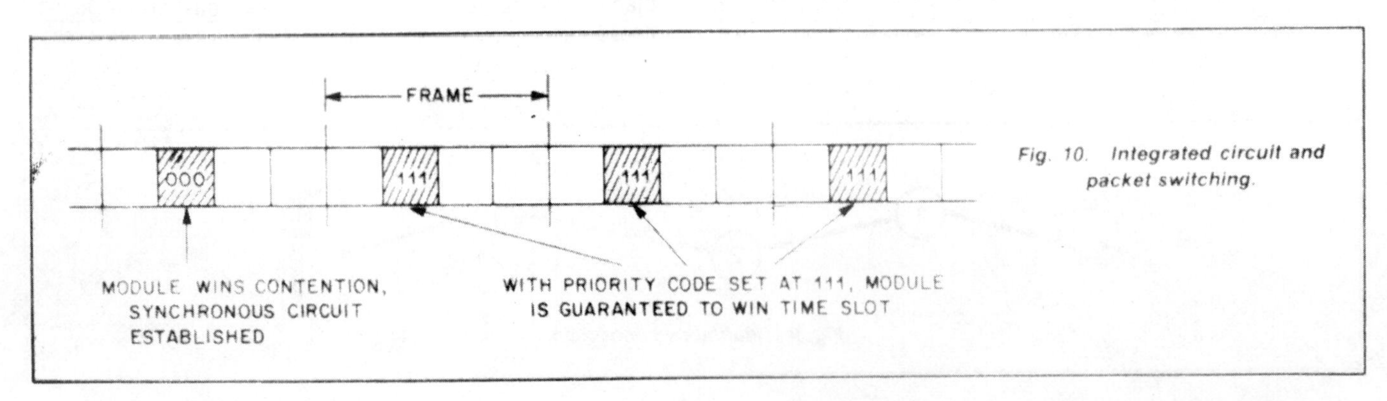

Fig. 10. Integrated circuit and packet switching.

communications. As Fig. 2 shows, nodes can be interconnected in an arbitrary mesh topology using bidirectional, point-to-point transmission facilities carrying statistically multiplexed traffic between nodes. For on-premises growth, optical fiber can be used for node interconnection; for interpremises communications, use may be made of leased (for example, DDS or T1) or private (for example, microwave) transmission facilities. In both cases, two nodes are interconnected simply by inserting, into the backplane of each, a trunk module that interfaces to one end of the communications link. The trunk modules themselves need not contain much intelligence since their main functions involve bus contention, packet buffering, and interfacing to the internode transmission facility. The real intelligence for internode networking resides in the CCP located at each node.

The CCP's communicate with each other over the internode trunks to establish end-to-end virtual circuits through the network. A device (such as a terminal) originating a call to another device (such as a host computer) first communicates its request to the CCP located at its node. The CCP determines whether the called device resides at its node; if it does not, it proceeds to select, according to a routing algorithm, an outgoing trunk to another node to communicate the request. This next CCP in turn determines whether the called device resides at its node and, if not, selects an outgoing trunk to another node to communicate the request. This process repeats until arriving at the node at which the called device resides. Then, assuming the destination device accepts the call, the process works its way backwards to the originating device, across the established path, with the appropriate address translations written into the switch module memory at each node. Once established, this path through the network remains fixed for the duration of the call, thus maintaining the proper sequence of packets delivered to the destination.

The virtual circuit service provided for both single and multinode configurations in the centralized-bus architecture makes for a highly effective data-transport capability. By using the same basic building blocks to construct both local-area and wide-area networks, one eliminates the need for complex gateways required in other architectures for network growth. Also, since full source-destination addressing is not required in each packet, addressing overhead can be kept to a minimum. Coupled with the bus contention efficiency, this permits the use of short packets to achieve a high degree of message pipelining, as discussed in the previous section. Finally, if desired, a permanent virtual circuit connection can be established between devices to remove the need for call set-up, while still using bandwidth only when there is data to transmit.

Building Distribution and Network Management

Important components of any LAN are its building distribution system and its network management features and services. Coaxial cable (both broadband and baseband), optical fiber, and twisted-pair wiring are all prominent candidates for an LAN transmission medium. The centralized-bus architecture conveniently exploits the latter two in a manner consistent with conventional building wiring for voice transmission. Referring to Fig. 11, we note that conventional voice wiring consists of two types of cabling: riser cables (between floors) and lateral cables (horizontal at each floor). The lateral cables terminate in remote apparatus and satellite equipment closets, from which emanate the individual twisted-pair cables running to each telephone.

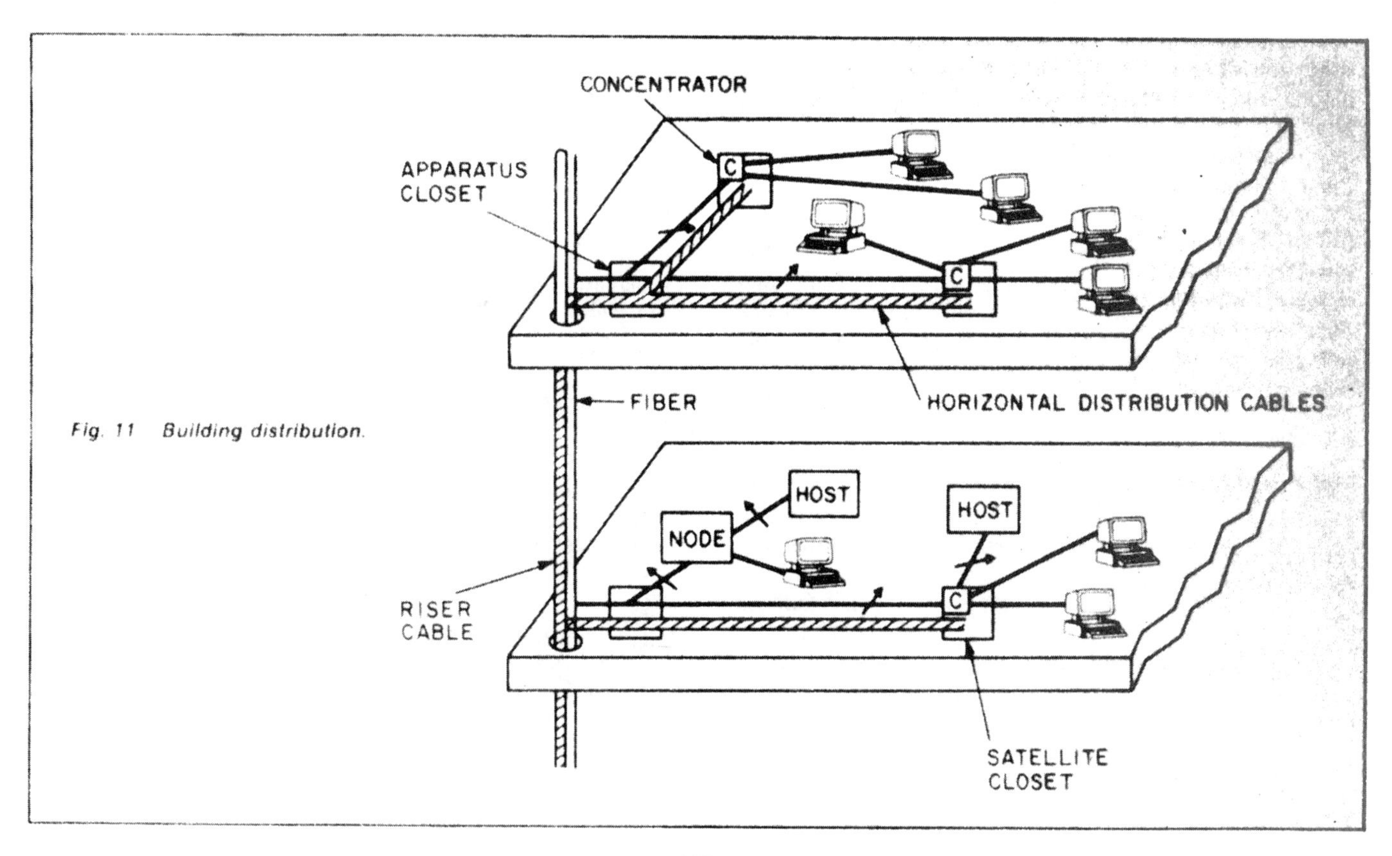

Fig. 11 Building distribution.

Appropriate cross-connect panels are housed in the apparatus and satellite closets.

The centralized-bus architecture permits the superposition of LAN transmission media onto such a topology. Using relatively short-length (new or existing) twisted-pair wiring, devices can be attached via cross-connect panels to concentrators located in satellite closets. Each concentrator is then connected to a node via a dedicated optical-fiber pair that shares wiring ducts and risers with existing cabling. The small-diameter, high-bandwidth, and light-weight advantages of fiber are exploited to reduce or eliminate the physical congestion problems prevalent in the wiring conduits of many existing buildings. In addition, the fiber links do not interfere with voiceband signals, and are themselves immune to electrical interference. Wideband devices (host computers, for example) requiring bandwidth in excess of that allowable on twisted-pair wiring would be allocated dedicated fibers to a concentrator or back to the node.

With the interface modules and common equipment residing in a relatively small number of locations on a premises, network management in the centralized-bus architecture is made easier. Nodes and concentrators located in computer rooms and satellite closets permit ease of monitoring and servicing of the various network components, and yet can be made secure from access by unauthorized personnel. The CCP could, in addition, play an important role in network management by periodically polling the interface modules for status. The status responses from the modules can be used to monitor the health, performance, and configuration of the network. The CCP might even have an attached, dedicated console for maintenance and administration functions. Finally, the interface modules can be designed so that the removal or, in many cases, malfunctioning of one does not interfere with the operation of the network.

Conclusions

We have described a new LAN architecture that has applications for both on-premises and interpremises data communications. This architecture combines the advantages of digital PBX, distributed-bus, and ring architectures to provide a low-delay, end-to-end virtual circuit connection service to the attached devices. The basic building blocks of the architecture, contained in both the concentrators and packet-switching nodes, are a short-bus backplane, and interface modules for attaching user devices to the network and interconnecting network components. The associated bus contention scheme, taking advantage of the short propagation delay on the bus, eliminates performance problems associated with other LAN architectures and at the same time provides considerable flexibility for scheduling packet transmissions; multiple priority groups, round-robin-like scheduling within a priority group, and even integrated circuit and packet switching are permitted. The architecture can also make use of a twisted-pair/optical-fiber building distribution system that both complements and enhances existing building wiring. In addition, its overall architecture is conducive to maintenance and administration services commonly found onlv in centralized networks.

References

[1] C. David Tsao, "A local area network architecture overview," *IEEE Communications Magazine*, vol. 22, no. 8, p. 7, Aug. 1984.

[2] J. H. Saltzer, K. T. Pogran, and D. D. Clark, "Why a ring?," *Comput. Networks*, vol. 7, pp. 223-231, 1983.

[3] W. Bux, "Local-area subnetworks: a performance comparison," *IEEE Trans. Commun.*, COM-29, pp. 1465-1473, Oct. 1981.

[4] A. G. Fraser, "Datakit—a modular network for synchronous and asynchronous traffic," *Proc. ICC*, pp. 20.1.1-20.1.3, June 1979.

[5] J. F. Hayes, "An adaptive technique for local distribution," *IEEE Trans. Commun.*, COM-26, pp. 1178-1186, Aug. 1978.

[6] J. W. Mark, "Distributed scheduling conflict-free multiple access for local area communication networks," *IEEE Trans. Commun.*, COM-28, pp. 1968-1976, Dec. 1980.

[7] A. S. Acampora, M. G. Hluchyj, and C. David Tsao, "A centralized-bus architecture for local area networks," *Proc. ICC*, pp. 932-938, June 1983.

[8] S. S. Lam, "A carrier sense multiple access protocol for local networks," *Comput. Networks*, vol. 4, pp. 21-32, 1980.

[9] O. Hashida, "Analysis of multiqueue," *Review of the Elect. Comm. Lab.*, Nippon Telegraph and Telephone Public Corp., vol. 20, 1972.

[10] L. Kleinrock, *Queueing Systems, Vol. 1: Theory*, New York, NY: John Wiley & Sons, 1975.

[11] A. K. Mok and S. A. Ward, "Distributed broadcast channel access," *Comput. Networks*, vol. 3, pp. 327-335, 1979.

[12] R. C. Chen, "Bus Communication Systems," Ph.D. Thesis, Computer Science Dept., Carnegie-Mellon University, Pittsburgh, PA, Jan. 1974.

Anthony S. Acampora was born in Brooklyn, NY on December 20, 1946. He received the B.S.E.E., M.S.E.E., and Ph.D. degrees from the Polytechnic Institute of Brooklyn in 1968, 1970, and 1973, respectively. From 1968 through 1981 he was a member of the technical staff at Bell Laboratories, initially working in the fields of high-power microwave transmitters and radar system studies, and signal processing. From 1974 to 1981 he was involved in high-capacity digital satellite systems research, including modulation and coding theory, time division multiple access methods, and efficient frequency reuse techniques.

In 1981, he became supervisor of the Data Theory Group at Bell Laboratories, working in the field of computer communications and LAN's. In January 1983 he transferred with his group to AT&T Information Systems to continue work on LAN's. In November 1983 he was appointed head of the Radio Communications Research Department at AT&T Bell Laboratories, where his current responsibilities include management of research in the areas of antennas, microwave and millimeter wavelength propagation, terrestrial radio and satellite communication systems, and multiuser radio communications.

Dr. Acampora is a member of Eta Kappa Nu, Sigma Xi, and of the IEEE, and serves as editor for Satellite and Space Communications of the *IEEE Transactions on Communications*.

Michael G. Hluchyj was born in Erie, PA on October 23, 1954. He received the B.S.E.E. degree in 1976 from the University of Massachusetts at Amherst; and the S.M., E.E., and Ph.D. degrees in Electrical Engineering from the Massachusetts Institute of Technology in 1978, 1978, and 1981, respectively. In 1981 he joined the technical staff at Bell Laboratories and in 1983 transferred to AT&T Information Systems. Dr. Hluchyj's work at Bell Laboratories and AT&T Information Systems has centered around the architectural design and performance analysis of LAN's. ■

Optical Fibers in Local Area Networks

Marion R. Finley, Jr.

The burgeoning potentials of optical-fiber transmission technology in LAN's

August 1984—Vol. 22, No. 8
IEEE Communications Magazine

IN THE following paragraphs, we will examine the application of optical transmission technology to the local interconnection structures that we call local area networks (LAN's). These networks are a singular technological development with an application scope which may eventually overlap that of older conventional network structures, such as the local subscriber loop in telephone systems.

By the term LAN we understand a data communications system that allows a number of independent, nonhomogeneous devices to communicate with each other [1]. LAN's are usually distinguished from other types of data networks in that communication is confined to a modestly sized geographic area such as a single office building or a complex of buildings and laboratories such as a university campus. LAN application environments include the commercial, the industrial, and the institutional. Perhaps the major thrust of LAN's will be in office applications. LAN's must, therefore, support services such as file transfer, graphics applications, word processing, electronic mail, distributed data bases, interconnection to other LAN's, digital telephony, and, eventually, some kind of video service. Moreover, LAN's must support a wide variety of data devices: computers of all vintages (micro, mini, and maxi), video terminals, mass storage devices, printers, plotters, facsimile printers, and gateways to other networks.

Some of the distinguishing features of LAN's are:

- Distances between network interfaces are typically less than 1 km; a network interface is a concentrator/deconcentrator interface which usually includes packetization/depacketization facilities as well, to which the various network devices may be connected.
- Aggregate bandwidth is modest, ranging from 1-20 Mb/s, although newer systems are now emerging in the range of 32-several hundreds of Mb/s, with one recent prototype potentially capable of achieving 1 Gb/s.
- Uniformly low bit error rates are assumed, usually less than 10^{-9}.
- Network architecture is such that total connectivity is achieved and complex routing algorithms are not needed.
- The Open Systems Interconnection Reference Model (OSI/RM), proposed by the International Standards Organization (ISO) [2], is susceptible to simplifications as a consequence of the preceeding point. The IEEE Computer Society Project 802 has developed standards for three classes of LAN's, namely contention networks using CSMA-type protocols, token buses, and token rings [3]. It remains to be seen whether these will become industry standards, but they have at least forced designers to consider the issue.
- A high degree of connectability/reconnectability is required.

As a transmission medium, optical fibers have proven to be extremely effective in CATV and telephone trunking applications [4]. However, when one restricts attention to LAN's, optical fibers have yet to be exploited to the limits of their enormous information-carrying capacity. Such things as optical tap losses, optical transmitter-receiver pair behavior, and complexity of the medium-access mechanisms needed limit their applicability at the present stage of technology.

EHO234-5/85/0000/0139$01.00 © 1984 IEEE

Optical-Fiber Communications Systems

Optical fibers enjoy a number of charming properties that make them natural candidates for high-capacity transmission systems. The most important of these are:

- Large bandwidth × distance products supporting data attaining transmission at rates up to, say, 100 Gb/s over 100 km [5]. Today's fibers typically offer bit rates of several hundred Mb/s [6].
- Since glass is a dielectric medium, immune to electromagnetic interference and free from sparking, optical fibers are useful in EMI-rich and other hostile environments.
- Extremely small physical dimensions—the diameter of an uncabled optical fiber may vary from as little as 5–10 μm for the high-performance single-mode fibers to between 50 to several hundred μm for multimode fibers (see below for the definitions of these terms).
- Low attenuation, typically several decibels per kilometer, although values as low as 0.2 dB/km have been obtained [5].

The basic components of an optical fiber communications system are [7]: optical transmitters, optical receivers, optical fibers connecting transmitter-receiver pairs, connectors and splices, and couplers. For further details regarding the nature of these components in an optical-fiber communications system, the interested reader might consult [7a]. We deal primarily with systems using multimode fibers in this paper, that is, fibers that permit transmission of several modes of light injected from noncoherent sources, as opposed to systems using single-mode fibers which allow only one mode of the injected light to propagate through the fiber. Single-mode fibers offer very-high bandwidth and low loss, and their application to LAN's is the subject of current research and development [7c].

Let us now examine a simple link consisting of a transmitter-receiver pair interconnected by a single optical fiber (see Fig. 1): The optical transmitter consists of electronic circuitry that drives an optical source such as a light-emitting diode or a laser diode. The source output, a light beam in effect, is modulated according to the electrical input signals and launched into the fiber. At the opposite end of the fiber, light impinges on the surface of an optical detector such as a p-i-n or avalanche photodiode. The light energy is reconverted into an electrical signal and the electronic detecting circuitry of the optical receiver reconstructs the signal originally presented to the transmitter. Connectors serve to connect the fiber to the output fiber of the transmitter or the input fiber of the receiver, and to connect any two segments of fiber that must be joined. Connection may also be made by splicing, a procedure involving fusing together the ends of two fiber segments.

Several crucial system parameters determine whether the link just described works:

- the optical power of the signal received at the detector,
- the distortion of the signal transmitted through the fiber, and
- the system rise time.

Since the optical power of the received signal must exceed a certain threshold value, which is a function of the optical receiver, the optical power loss should satisfy a power

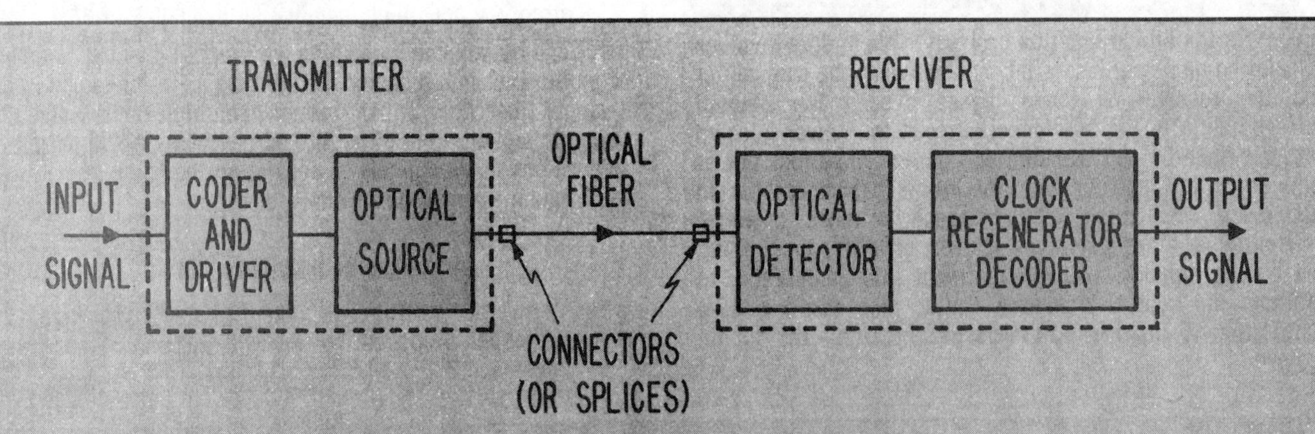

Fig. 1. A simple optical fiber communications link.

Optical Sources—*LED's or laser diodes, transmission wavelengths in the 800–1300 (1550 on occasion) nm range.*

Optical Detectors—*p-i-n or APD photodiodes, similar wavelength windows as for source.*

Optical Fiber—*Glass fiber, perhaps plastic coated; pure plastic fibers for some applications. Wavelength windows as for sources.*

Optical Connectors—*Fiber-to-fiber interface, several types available. While great improvements have been made in these devices, the author finds them still a bit delicate for LAN applications in which frequent reconnections are made.*

Optical Splices—*Fiber-to-fiber permanent join, achieved through electric arc fusion or by other techniques. Perhaps better than connectors if no or very few disconnects/reconnects are foreseen.*

The coding and driver circuits prepare the electrical signal modulated in the appropriate format, and present it to the LED or laser diode source. The modulated light beam emitted by the source is coupled into a fiber "pigtail" which terminates in a connector. By the latter, the transmission fiber is connected to the source "pigtail." The beam thus traverses the connector and the fiber to the "pigtail" that enters the receiver unit. This "pigtail" is then coupled to the detector, the light converted to electricity, and amplified. Clock recovery and decoding take place next, and the original input signal is reconstructed.

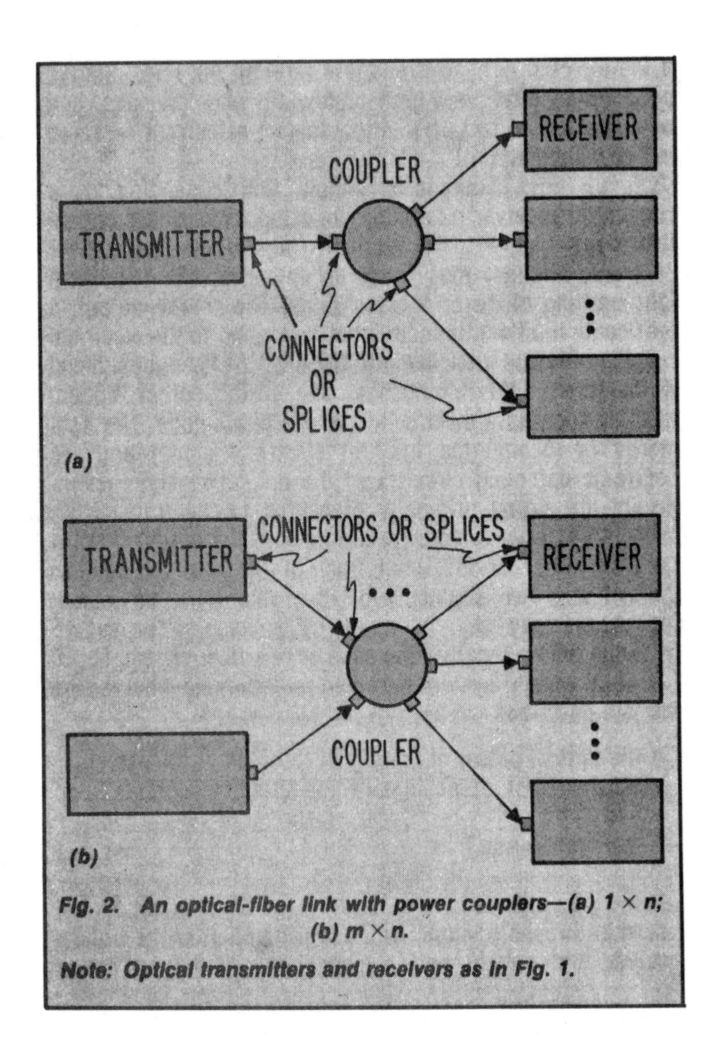

Fig. 2. An optical-fiber link with power couplers—(a) 1 × n; (b) m × n.

Note: Optical transmitters and receivers as in Fig. 1.

budget for the link to function properly. This budget involves calculating all power losses incurred between the transmitter and the receiver. If these losses exceed the amount corresponding to the difference between the power injected into the fiber by the transmitter and the minimum power required by the receiver, then the link is not acceptable. In this event, one must either choose a more powerful transmitter, a more sensitive receiver, or a less-lossy fiber. The coding scheme used also affects this calculation. In addition, the system rise time should also conform to a budget that is imposed by the desired bit rate. This budget involves two crucial fiber parameters—the material and the modal dispersions—both of which can cause pulse spreading, and hence intersymbol noise, as the light traverses the fiber. Material dispersion refers to the light impulse broadening due to the differential delay of the various wavelengths present in the beam, whereas modal dispersion refers to spreading caused by differential optical path lengths present in a multimodal fiber. For those interested in more details on these two budget calculations and the relevant parameters, [7a] and [7b] may be helpful.

Optical losses may occur at the transmitter-to-fiber coupling points, at all connectors and splices, and at the fiber-to-receiver coupling and throughout the fiber itself. Moreover, fiber cabling and environmental conditions may introduce additional optical losses and should be included in the power budget calculations.

A $1 \times n$ power coupler splits the light beam into n outgoing ports (Fig. 2(a)). The amount of optical power coupled into each leg is a function of the coupler's construction and is determined by system requirements. In general, one has $m \times n$ couplers in which there are m input ports and n output ports (Fig. 2(b)). Assuming equal distribution of power over each of the output ports of a $1 \times n$ coupler, power is reduced by at least a factor of $1/n$ while traversing the coupler, in logarithmic terms, decreased by $-10 \log n$ dB. Additional losses occur due to the coupler itself, and it is difficult to make the power division uniformly equal. It is clear that even when a transmitter-receiver pair conforms to power budget requirements, the careless use of power couplers may introduce extra optical power losses, resulting in link failure.

Another source of power loss is optical multiplexing and coupling, namely the multiplexing of several optical signals at different wavelengths onto the same fiber. This technique is called wavelength division or color multiplexing (WDM), where light signals from n sources, each one at different wavelengths, are combined by a wavelength division coupler or multiplexer into a composite light signal and injected into a single fiber (Fig. 3). An optical demultiplexer is used to separate signals from different sources. Thus, WDM permits several physical channels to coexist on the same fiber, and these channels may go in either direction.

Architecture for Fiber-Optic LAN's

The term "architecture" is taken to mean the layered network model proposed by the International Standards

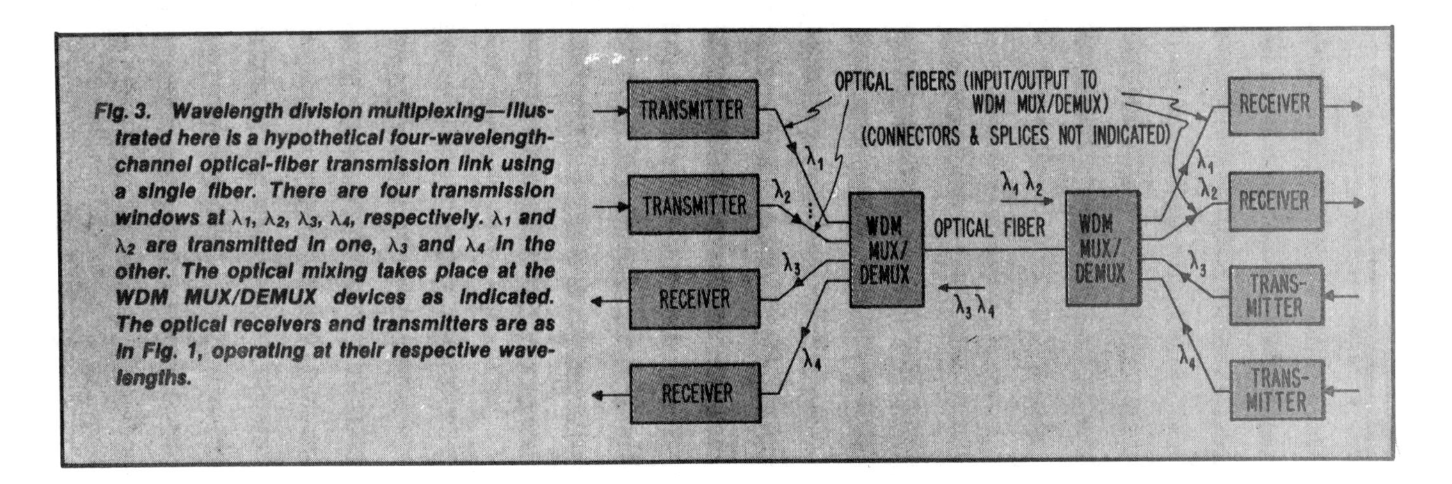

Fig. 3. Wavelength division multiplexing—Illustrated here is a hypothetical four-wavelength-channel optical-fiber transmission link using a single fiber. There are four transmission windows at λ_1, λ_2, λ_3, λ_4, respectively. λ_1 and λ_2 are transmitted in one, λ_3 and λ_4 in the other. The optical mixing takes place at the WDM MUX/DEMUX devices as indicated. The optical receivers and transmitters are as in Fig. 1, operating at their respective wavelengths.

Organization, the OSI/RM mentioned [2] earlier, or the variant proposed by the IEEE Computer Society for LAN's, the LAN/RM [3]. These two models are summarized in Figs. 4 and 5, and the relationship between the two models is indicated in Fig. 6. The OSI/RM applies to computer networks in general, whereas the LAN/RM was conceived as an attempt to provide a standard for LAN's and for enforcing some degree of compatibility between products of different manufacturers.

The thrust of this article is primarily at the first two layers of these models, that is the physical and the data-link-control layers of the OSI/RM or the physical and the medium-access-control (MAC) layers of the LAN/RM. Given a network topology, one must propose a medium-access method by which transmitting and receiving nodes access the transmission medium. Such methods are known by the generic term medium access (or multi-access) protocols [8]. The primary issue to be discussed in this article is that of implementing the physical layer using optical fibers. This means, above all, determining the network topologies that are most suitable for this technology.

The following network topologies appear most promising for optical-fiber-based LAN's [8] (see Fig. 7).

1) The bus, in which network interfaces are interconnected linearly; the connectivity requirement imposes bidirectionality.
2) The ring or loop, in which network interfaces are interconnected linearly, but with the last one connected back to the first one, thus forming a closed loop; unidirectional transmission is sufficient to guarantee total connectivity.
3) The star, in which every node is connected bidirectionally to a single central node, the "hub" of the star; connectivity is clearly obtained.
4) Hybrids of the above, for example, star-ring topologies in which a number of rings are interconnected through a centralized hub.

These topologies are listed without any consideration of the manner in which the network interfaces are coupled to the transmission medium, a crucial point for optical-fiber applications to LAN's. In the case of buses and rings, the network interfaces are coupled to the medium through a passive or active device. In the first case, the network interface receives a portion of the optical energy from the medium and it injects optical energy directly into the medium. The medium is not broken, so to speak. In the second case, all the optical signal energy enters the interface, an optoelectrical conversion and regeneration take place, the converted signal is presented to the node and perhaps modified by the latter, and then reconverted to optical energy and launched onto the outgoing fiber. An active network interface will have the general structure indicated in Fig. 8(a), whereas a passive network interface will follow that of Fig. 8(b).

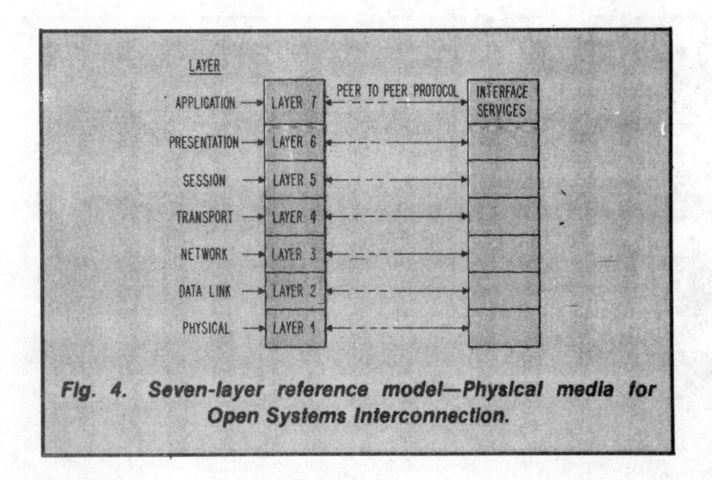

Fig. 4. Seven-layer reference model—Physical media for Open Systems Interconnection.

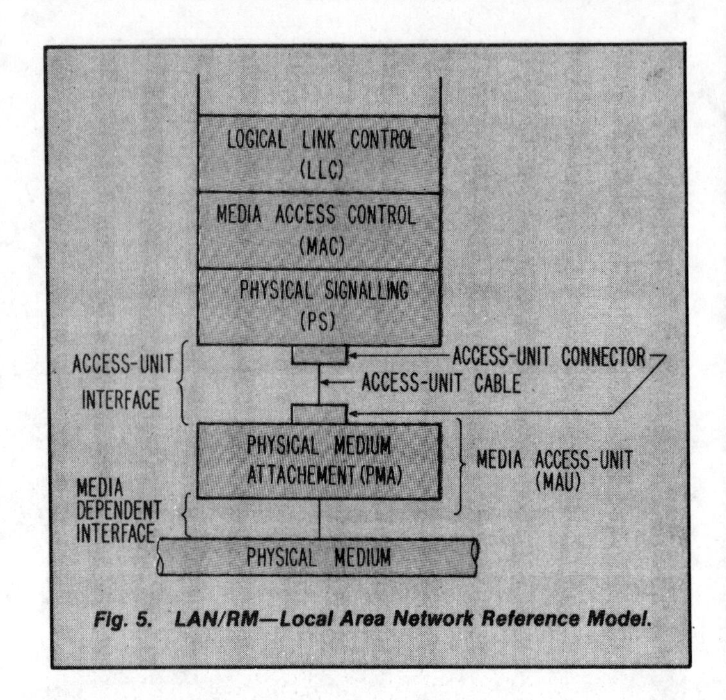

Fig. 5. LAN/RM—Local Area Network Reference Model.

Two remarks must be made at this point. First of all, optical repeaters, at the current state of the art, involve optoelectrical conversion, electrical regeneration, and electrooptical conversion, which is the case for active interfaces. True optical-to-optical repeaters not involving optoelectrical and electrooptical conversions are not yet available. Secondly, passive interfaces imply optical-to-optical coupling, hence careful considerations for distortions and power losses have to be made to satisfy the system power budgets.

Finally, in Fig. 8(c), a hybrid network interface structure is indicated that combines the advantages of the active and passive structures of Figs. 8(a) and 8(b). This gives a "fail-safe" node—if the active regenerating portion goes down, the passive part remains intact.

Let us now examine the optical fiber versions of the three principal topologies listed above.

Buses

Active and passive configurations are shown in Figs. 9(a) and 9(b). Active buses entail the active couplers described above at each network interface, one for each direction, whereas passive buses have a complex passive coupler configuration. In the former case, the interface cost and electronic complexity are drawbacks for the implementation of active buses. In the second case, the lossy nature of couplers and transmitter-receiver pairs limits the number of network interfaces one may cascade in sequence to about 13 [9]. The optical equivalent of the high-impedance electrical tap is not yet perfect.

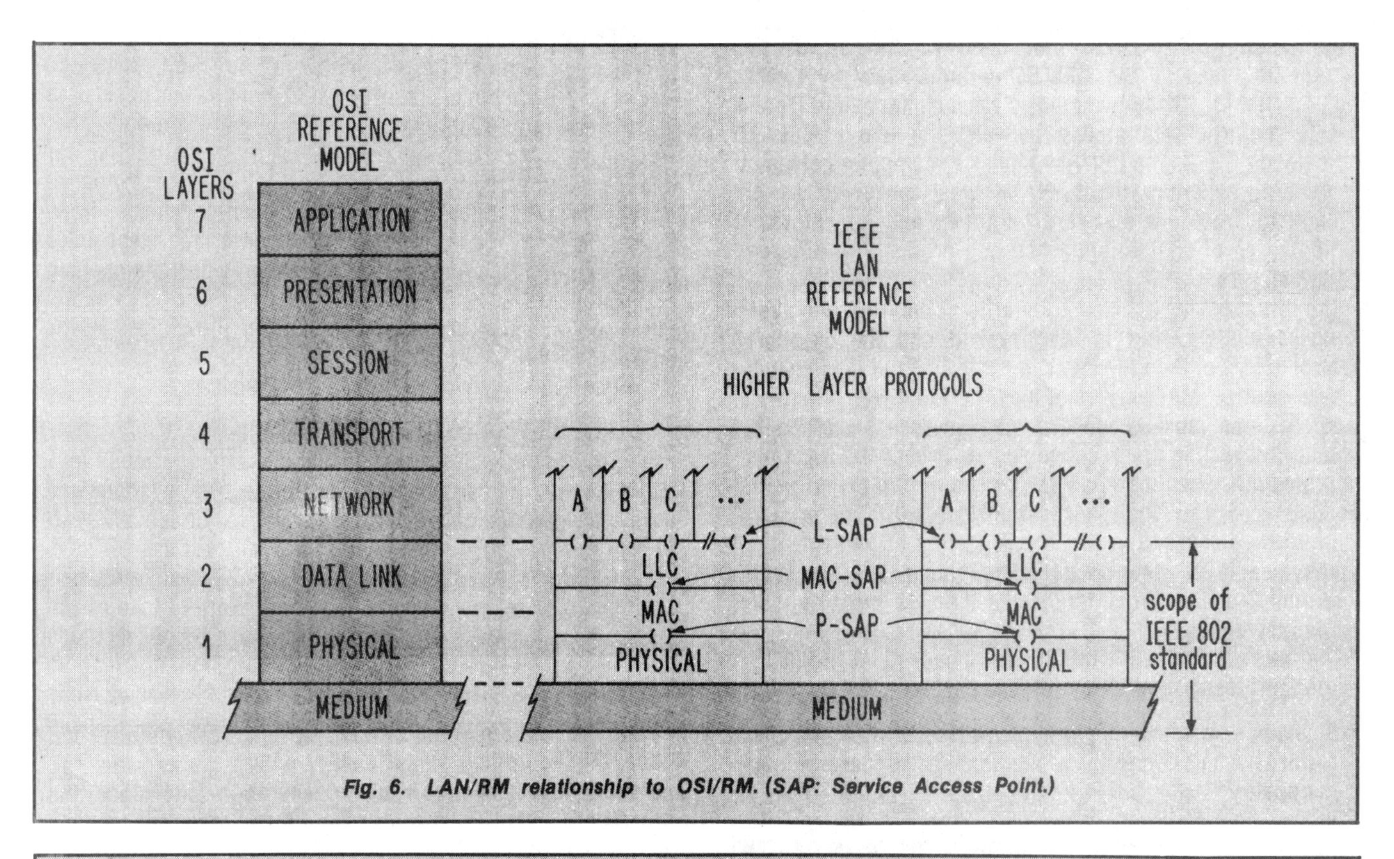

Fig. 6. LAN/RM relationship to OSI/RM. (SAP: Service Access Point.)

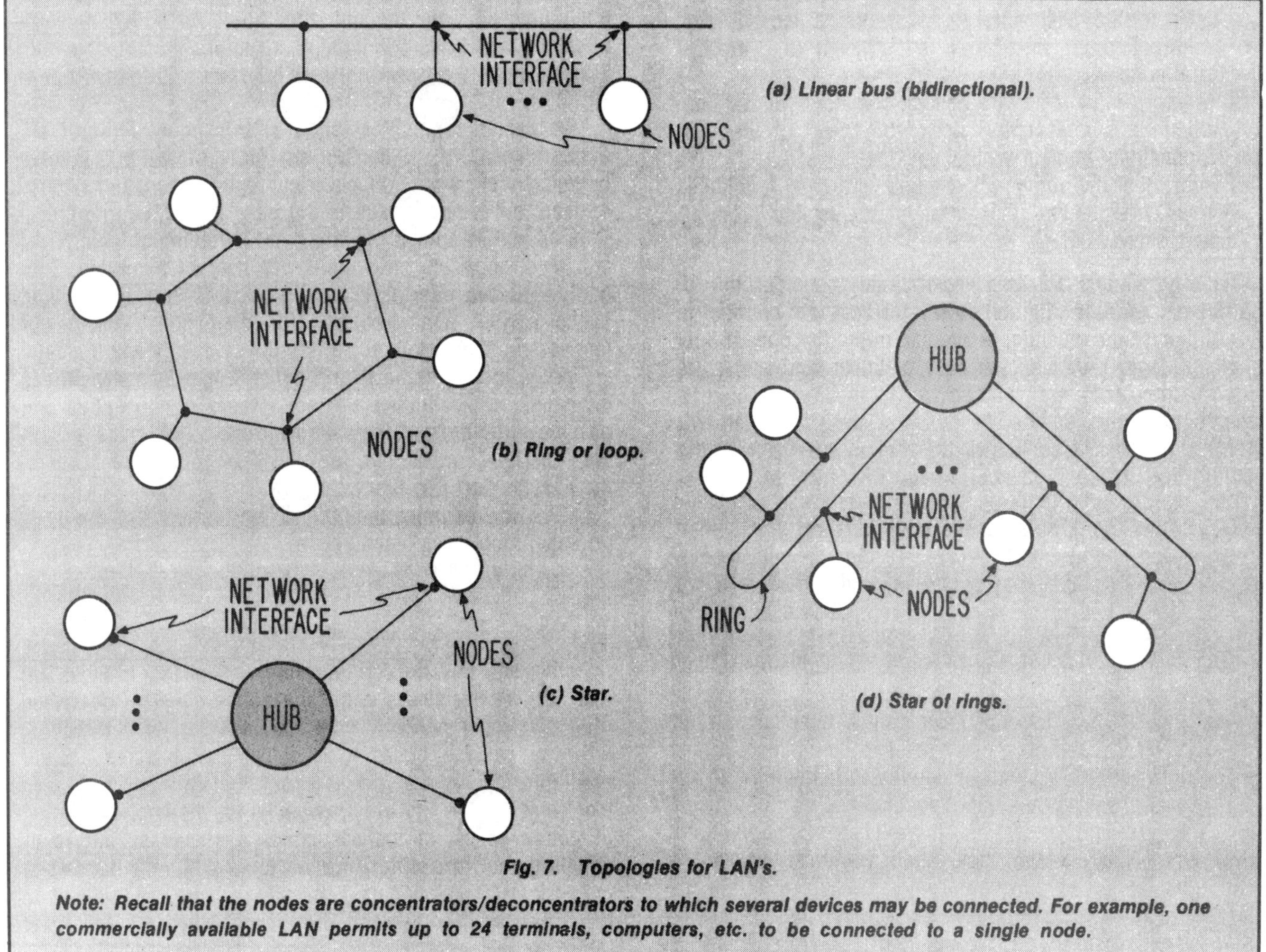

Fig. 7. Topologies for LAN's.

Note: Recall that the nodes are concentrators/deconcentrators to which several devices may be connected. For example, one commercially available LAN permits up to 24 terminals, computers, etc. to be connected to a single node.

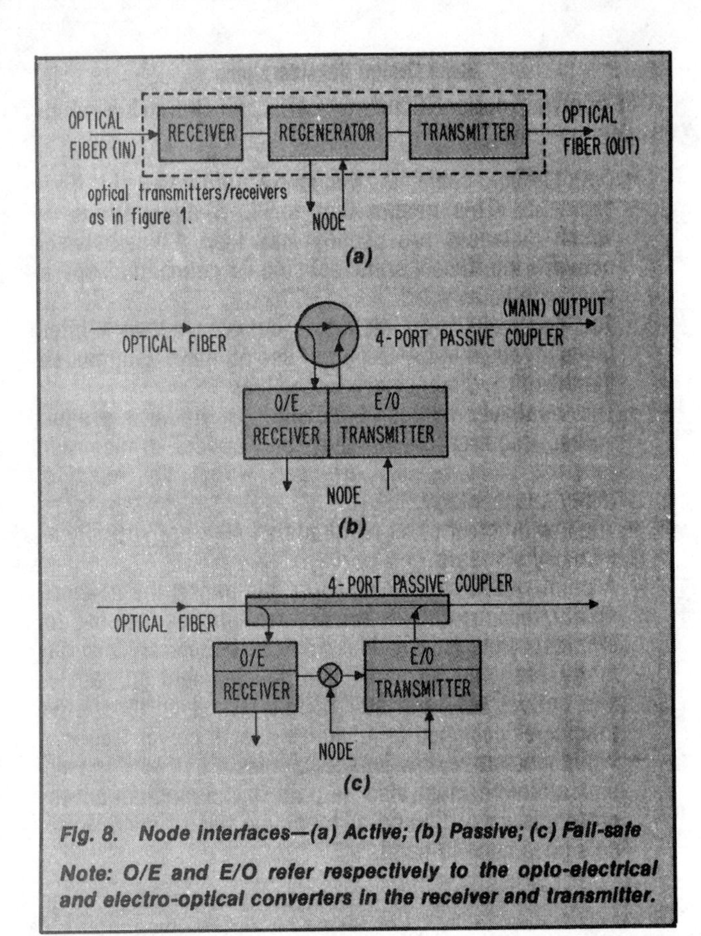

Fig. 8. Node interfaces—(a) Active; (b) Passive; (c) Fail-safe

Note: O/E and E/O refer respectively to the opto-electrical and electro-optical converters in the receiver and transmitter.

An intriguing variant of the passive bus is the unidirectional bus, shown in Fig. 9(c), in which one end of the bus is closed, giving a "U" configuration. This configuration, proposed by the author and one of his assistants in 1977 [10] and considered recently by other researchers [9], offers the advantages of a linear bus coupled with the simplicity of ring topologies, especially when medium-access protocols are concerned. Once again, however, the number of network interfaces that one can introduce is limited by coupler losses, just as is the case for passive linear buses.

Rings

Ring topologies, similarly to linear bus topologies, allow two types of configurations, active or passive, as shown in Figs. 10(a) and 10(b), with fail-safe variants as suggested in Figs. 10(c) and 10(b). For an active ring, either node failure or a fiber break will cause a fatal crash; certain nodes will remain incommunicado. In the case of a passive ring, node failure need not bring down the whole network, but a fiber break certainly will.

One should note that the signal, once injected into the fiber, will circulate until it is completely attenuated. This may give rise to echoes, as there is no way to remove the signal from the ring, unless the fiber is physically discontinuous at, say, a master control station—in which case one does not have a true passive ring. The author has not yet seen an elegant solution to this problem, although the fail-safe version of such rings proposed by Albanese [11] has been reported to function properly (Fig. 10(b)).

Fail-safe variants for active rings include that of adding another loop going in the opposite direction, with the necessary switchover electronics to handle the case of a fiber break and an optical bypass switch, at each node, that is tripped if the node fails. Active rings are attractive for their structural simplicity and for the high-performance medium-access algorithms that have been developed. However, the cost and complexity of the interface electronics needed to implement these algorithms have been dampening factors in their realization. Since this cost is steadily decreasing, active rings are now being introduced in the marketplace.

Stars

Centralized switched star network configurations have existed now for over a century in our telephone systems and represent perhaps the best-understood class of networks—at least, the one with which most people seem at ease. This is true for active stars in which the centralized hub exercises switching or medium-access functions. The PBX approach, collision detection for CSMA, "hub" accessing methods [8, 12], fast circuit switching, and other approaches may be used. Optical-fiber technology may be used in these cases in its simplest and best-understood form, namely point-to-point (Fig. 11(a)).

What is surprising is that via an $n \times n$ passive star coupler, one can create an optical bus with properties similar

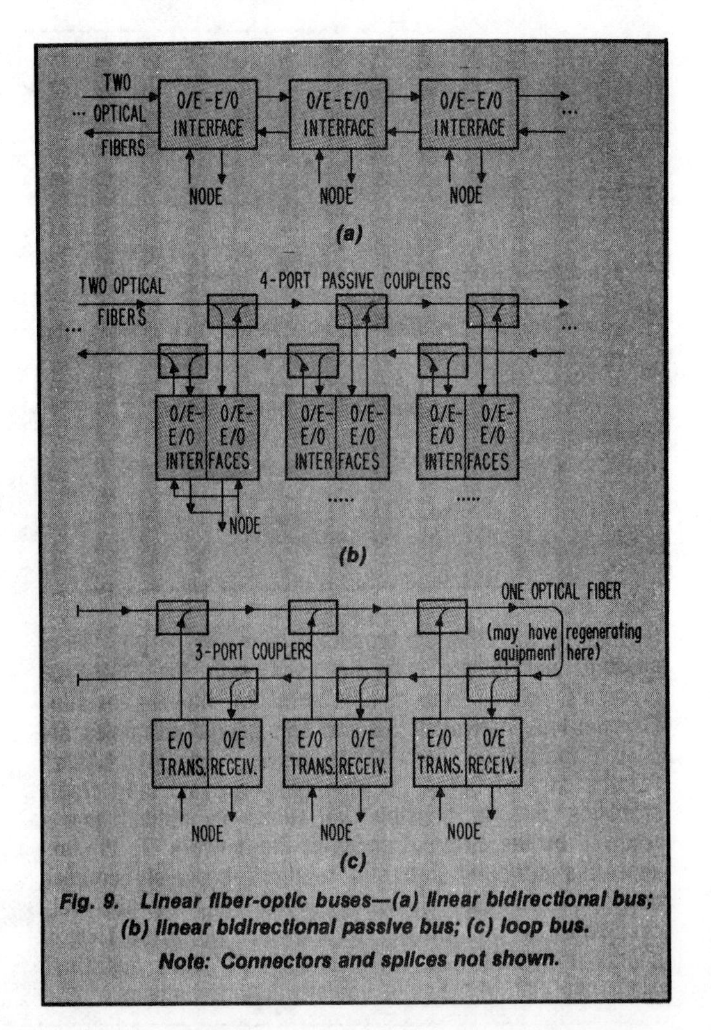

Fig. 9. Linear fiber-optic buses—(a) linear bidirectional bus; (b) linear bidirectional passive bus; (c) loop bus.

Note: Connectors and splices not shown.

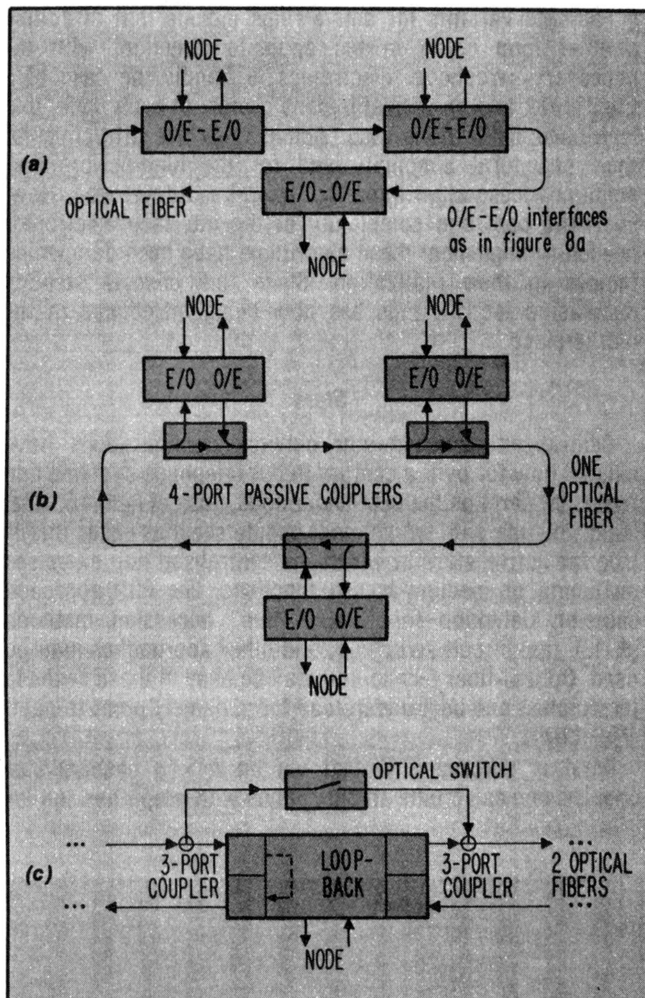

Fig. 10. Fiber-optic ring topologies—(a) Active ring: In this topology, regeneration takes place at every node. (b) Passive ring: This configuration introduces the problem of signal echo. Note: Passive ring with fail-safe mechanism: The topology is exactly the same as in (b), but the E/O-O/E mechanism is that of Fig. 8(c). If the active part of this mechanism fails, the ring may still continue to function [11]. (c) Active ring with fail-safe features (just one node interface is shown): If the interface fails, the optical switch is automatically tripped and the signals simply bypass it (note the need for couplers), and appropriate messages are sent to the maintenance modules of the network. If the principal fiber breaks, this is detected by software and the loopback mechanism of the appropriate node is evoked. Again, maintenance procedures are set in motion.

to that of an Ethernet broadcast bus (Fig. 11(b)). Thus, passive star buses may be used with the CSMA/CD protocols, giving one simple way to fiberize existing Ethernet-type networks. Several commercial examples are cited in the section "Some Contemporary Fiber-Optic LAN's." For the case of CSMA/CD, the collision event may create problems due to possible variations in optical power received by the different nodes of the network. To circumvent this difficulty and still retain a passively coupled network, a collision-detecting device may be passively coupled at the star coupler, as shown in Fig. 11(c). This, of course, influences the power budget, but does guarantee proper working of the collision-detection mechanism.

Some Design Considerations

In applying optical fibers to LAN's, the following points should be noted:

- Optical-fiber cable is frequently fabricated in 1-km segments. This means that for LAN applications, in which distances are usually less than 1 km between network interfaces, some splicing or connecting operations will be avoided.
- The relatively short distances between network interfaces involved in LAN's permit use of fibers with modest bandwidth × distance product values.
- The relatively modest bandwidth × distance product values required mean that the optical transmitter-receiver pairs needed are well within the reach of today's technology.
- The low bit error rates required by LAN's are virtually an industry standard.
- A point raised several times in this paper: the connectability/reconnectability requirement implies the need for efficient, that is, low-loss, power couplers. This has motivated much research and development on passive and active "tee" and star couplers, and on innovative topologies designed to minimize optical power losses.
- While innovative, low-loss topologies are needed, particular attention must also be paid to the medium-access protocols used. Choice of topology and of such protocols goes hand-in-hand.

There are clearly trade-offs to be made in the design process. For example, by choosing an active ring configuration, the problem of coupler or tap losses essentially disappears; one has the point-to-point link described earlier. However, one also has the problem of complexity with the medium-access method and the critical question of providing fault-tolerance mechanisms such as loop-back and bypass switching. Thus, one advantage may be outweighed by other considerations.

At this point, one may decide to throw out the active ring idea and try a passive star-coupled configuration instead. This approach is certainly interesting as it gives an optical equivalent of the Ethernet coaxial-cable bus. However, the efficiency of the CSMA/CD medium-access protocol hinges on the proper detection of the collision event. To guarantee this, it may be necessary to add special equipment at the star hub, as was mentioned in the previous section. Once again, an advantage may be countered by an inconvenience.

We do not yet have a definitive way of determining the optimal design for fiber-optic LAN's (or for any type of LAN for that matter). Moreover, the number of parameters needed for the complete description is quite large, as is the range of choices possible. In an attempt to systematize fiber-optic LAN design, the author has developed an overall heuristic procedure, part of which has been programmed. Out of this procedure, a list of the principal parameters has been derived. While neither the procedure nor the parameter list are definitive, they at least give us a way to compare different LAN configurations. The procedure is summarized below.

Outline of a Design Procedure

The procedure consists of six main steps, each one containing a large number of substeps, not given in detail here:

Step 1-Determine networks' requirements such as:

- network services to be offered and relevant constraints imposed by these services (such as priorities and delays),
- the approximate geometrical distribution of network devices and of the network interfaces to which they are to be connected,
- average and maximum traffic generated per network interface and the traffic mix expected,
- maximum number of network interfaces,
- the expected bit error rate,
- level of fault-tolerance desired,
- level of reconnectability desired,
- the cost budget,
- provisions for future expansion,
- constraints related to any compatibility needed with existing equipment—for example, fibers already in place,
- environmental constraints.

Step 2—As a function of these requirements, propose a plausible topology/medium-access protocol combination: We have seen that there are many medium-access protocols and topologies. Roughly speaking, for modest bit rates (say 1-32 Mb/s), CSMA/CD Ethernet-like passive star coupled networks are perhaps the most promising, especially if one must have compatibility with existing Ethernet equipment. Token protocol-ring combinations are now appearing in this same range and for higher bit rates. For very-high bit rates, the "locomotive" access scheme used in D-Net for example [13], on loop-bus or hybrid topologies, is very promising (see the next section).

Step 3—For the topology/medium-access protocol combination determined by the preceeding step, select feasible optical components to satisfy the constraints given in Step 1: This step includes finding transmitter-receiver pairs together with the fiber and couplers needed to respect the system constraints, such as the power budget safety margin and the rise time (for networks with bit rates higher than approximately 45 MHz). The optical components are selected from component matrices that give their most important characteristics. Unfortunately, there is no standard way of presenting these characteristics; therefore one must understand exactly what the manufacturers intend in their product announcements. (Magazines such as *LASER FOCUS* and *International Fiber Optics and Communications* publish component matrices for most known manufacturers once a year.) Notice that there are a number of hidden matching procedures in this step: wavelength of the source and of the detector with a fiber wavelength transmission window, and core diameter of the fibers leading out of or into transmitters and receivers, respectively, with that of the fiber cable used. Similarly, for the matching of coupler arms with efferent or afferent fibers.

Step 4—Specify the network interface hardware. This gets into the electronic heart of the interface and is not described here.

Step 5—Verify that all requirements have been met. If not, loop back to the appropriate step.

Step 6—Display and store the proposed configuration.

In this procedure, we assume that if—within the execution of any of the above steps—no feasible solution is found, the procedure automatically backs up to the preceding one, requesting another input from that step. For example, if, in Step 3 no feasible optical component selection is found for a given topology/medium-access protocol combination, then control is returned to Step 2, requesting a new such combination. In the final procedure, the human user will be able to interact with the search process of a solution, in the direction his intuition and experience indicate as being the most promising.

A list of the principal design parameters for fiber-optic LAN's is given in Table I. The comparison table of the next section is based upon this one. Notice that even with great simplification, there are over 20 main parameters to be dealt with. Table II shows an example for an interesting bus network constructed by the MITRE Corporation for the NASA Goddard Space Flight Center.

Some Contemporary Fiber-Optic LAN's

In this section, a number of contemporary fiber-optic LAN activities are summarized. In some cases, the networks exist as finished products available in the marketplace. In others, the networks are in varying stages of development, ranging from theoretical studies, sometimes accompanied by experimental backup, to laboratory prototypes. The examples presented, sometimes incomplete due to lack of information, were selected in order to give readers an idea of what are, in the author's opinion, the major trends in this field.

The networks presented in this section permit the following general observations:

1) the multiaccess protocols are of critical importance to the designer in determining high throughput, low delay;

TABLE I

Key Parameters for Fiber-Optic LAN's

1) Manufacturer
2) Network name
3) Operational status (experimental prototype, commercially available)
4) Date placed in service (if available)
5) Services offered
6) Span
7) Bit rate
8) Topology
9) Organization (centralized, partially distributed, distributed)
10) Multi-access methods
11) BER
12) Number of nodes
13) Number of terminals
14) Fault tolerance
15) Coding scheme (NRZ, RZ, Manchester)
16) Fiber type
17) Fiber core diameter
18) Fiber outer diameter
19) Fiber windows
20) Source type (LED, LD)
    Source power
21) Source wavelength
22) Detector type
    Detector sensitivity
23) Detector wavelength
24) Coupler characteristics
25) Switches (optical)

TABLE II
VALUES OF KEY PARAMETERS FOR A SAMPLE CONFIGURATION

To illustrate the use of the parameters of Table I, the NASA Goddard Space Flight Center network, developed by the MITRE Corporation, is examined (CRES'82) [28].

1) NASA/MITRE
2) NASA GSFC Fiber-Optic Local Area Network
3) Experimental, under development
4) Partially operational in 1982
5) Services: digital rates, 10 b/s–10 Mb/s per user,
   frames of 4800 bits
6) Span: 1.6 km (length of legs of bus)
7) Bit rate: aggregate bit rate estimated to be greater than 70 Mb/s,
   100 Mb/s for finished version, 50 Mb/s for prototype
8) Topology: rooted tree using tee couplers in one version,
   star couplers in another version
9) Organization: centralized
10) Multi-Access: slotted TDMA
11) BER: less than 10^{-9}
12) Number of nodes: in prototype 3, in finished version 100 (?)
13) Number of devices per node: 2-8
14) Fault tolerance: not specified
15) Coding scheme: NRZ (shown to be problematical with AC-coupled
    receiver; Manchester probably preferable)
16) Fiber type: GI (graded index, glass-on-glass)
17) Core diameter: 50 μm
18) Outer diameter (O.D.): 125 μm
19) Fiber window: not specified, 850 nm
20) Source type: Exxon OTX5100, LED @ 780-850 nm
    275 Mb/s
    power greater than 1000 μW
    rise time less than 1.5 ns
    price: $1100
21) Detector type: Exxon ORX5100, PIN, 850 nm
    0.1–150 Mb/s
    BER: 10^{-9}
    minimal detectable power: 5 μW @ 830 nm
24) Couplers: Version 1: biconically fused tapered 40/40, 60/20, 75/5
    insertion loss 20%
    Version 2: 6-legged transmissive star, −7.78 down per
    leg, −2 dB excess loss

Allowable optical power budget: 35 dB

2) CSMA/CD-type protocols are used up to 32 Mb/s, and ring token protocols may be used for higher bit rates;
3) token rings dominate now for the high-speed commercially available networks (50–100 Mb/s);
4) a variant of the token protocol method apparently works at 1 Gb/s on a loop-bus architecture in a laboratory prototype.

CSMA/CD Networks (Ethernet Compatible)

Certainly one of the first LAN's to attract a great deal of attention is the Ethernet developed by the Xerox Corporation. This network has stimulated the creation of a number of look-alikes, as well as versions to be implemented on standard broadband coaxial-cable systems [1]. Therefore, it is natural that fiber-optic versions are developed. Two such versions are presented below, each one using slightly different approaches. The first is the Xerox Corporation's active-star-based Fibernet II; the second is Codenet, a passive-star-based system developed by the Codenoll Corporation. The Ungermann-Bass Corporation, together with the Siecor Corporation, has recently built a similar passive-star-coupled configuration for their Ethernet-compatible Net/One. This version uses a centralized collision-detection mechanism that is passively coupled to the incoming fibers of the star coupler, as suggested in the previous section.

Besides the two efforts mentioned above, there are, of course, others. Apparently, Nippon Electric Corporation and Toshiba have developed Ethernet-compatible 10-Mb/s CSMA/CD networks. The NEC network uses a tree architecture, whereas the Toshiba network (in prototype form) uses a passive-star-coupled bus [14]. These networks are summarized in Table III.

Fibernet II [15]—Fibernet II uses an active star repeater to create the equivalent of the baseband coaxial-cable "Ether" channel (Fig. 12). Collision detection is implemented electrically in the 25-port star repeater on a backplane which behaves like a small Ethernet and which is electrically compatible with the standard 10-Mb/s Ethernet coaxial cable. The span of the network is about 2.5 km. Using 8-channel multiplexers, the network could handle up to 200 stations, whereas by cascading the repeaters on their backplane Ethernets, over 1000 stations might be accomo-

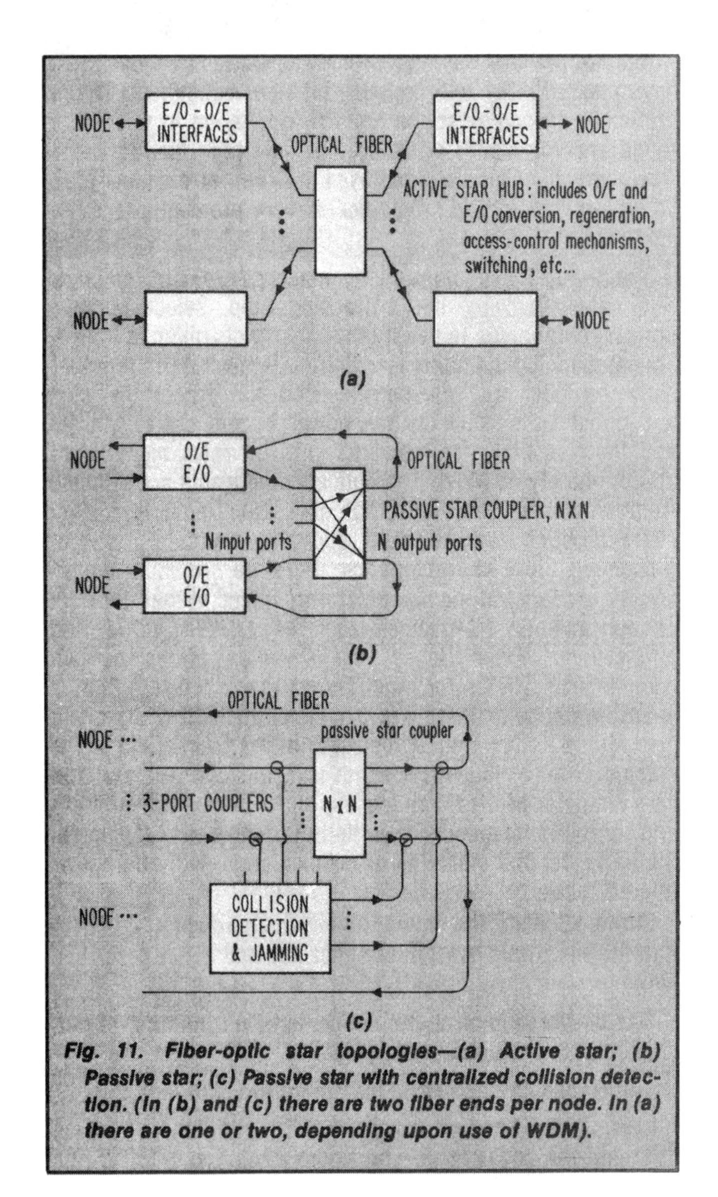

Fig. 11.* *Fiber-optic star topologies—(a) Active star; (b) Passive star; (c) Passive star with centralized collision detection. (In (b) and (c) there are two fiber ends per node. In (a) there are one or two, depending upon use of WDM).

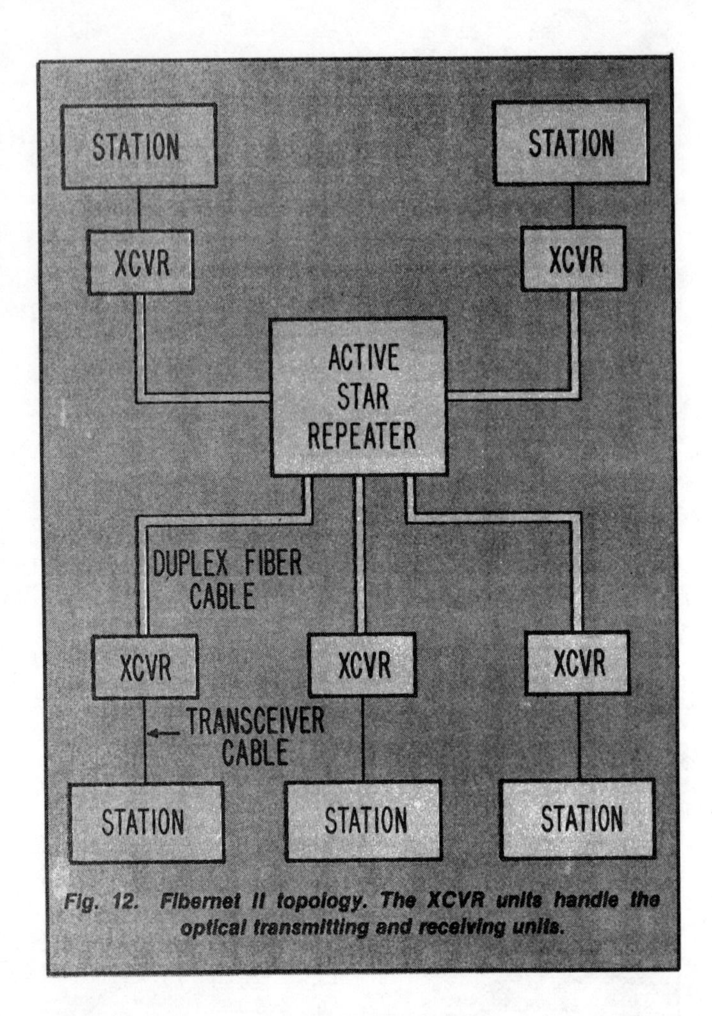

Fig. 12. Fibernet II topology. The XCVR units handle the optical transmitting and receiving units.

dated. Finally, the fiber star network might be used as a backbone to interconnect Ethernet segments.

Passive Star Configurations—Another Ethernet-compatible effort uses an 8-port passive star coupler to implement the "Ether" channel. The collision-detection mechanism is distributed, as opposed to the centralized version of Fibernet II, and is implemented in the station nodes. The latter are capable of supporting up to 24 serial RS-232 ports each, or various other combinations of serial and parallel ports. Thus, a 16-node configuration would support several hundred terminal devices. Extensions of the network might be achieved through making the star active, as in Fibernet II, or by the use of repeaters. As mentioned above, the Codenoll Corporation and Ungermann-Bass, jointly with Siecor, have produced such networks [16].

Nippon Telegraph and Telephone's Call for Bids—An interesting development is the call for bids put out by the Japanese Nippon Telegraph and Telephone Public Corporation (NTT) to United States firms, to develop medium-scale, passive-star-coupled CSMA/CD networks at 32 Mb/s. The star is to be 32 or 100 ports, depending on the system specified. This reflects Japan's current interest in pushing office and factory automation [17].

Hub Type Networks—A class of networks has recently evolved in an attempt to overcome some of the deficiencies of the Ethernet CSMA/CD type networks. This class uses an ingenious centralized selection-broadcast mechanism, hence the term "hub."

Hubnet [12]—Hubnet is being developed by the University of Toronto's Computer Systems Research Group in collaboration with the CANSTAR Corporation. A prototype has been built and tested. Hubnet's designers set about to determine a network architecture that would overcome the following shortcomings of Ethernet: poor performance under heavy traffic conditions, low efficiency at high bandwidths, and (in the optical domain) coupler (tap) losses in linear bus configurations. As a consequence, an innovative architecture was derived in which these shortcomings would appear to have been eliminated. The key idea is to shrink the "Ether" channel to a point (the hub) at which an incoming signal is selected and broadcast to all outgoing lines (Fig. 13). While one incoming signal is being handled, signals arriving on other input lines are blocked, causing their transmitting units to time out and try again. There are, therefore, no collisions in the Ethernet sense. In the case of several signals arriving simultaneously when the hub is quiescent, one is chosen arbitrarily.

Hubnet may be expanded by the cascading of subhubs. A comparison of Hubnet's performance with that of Ethernet is given in Fig. 14.

Non-CSMA/CD Buses—A number of uni- and bidirectional buses have been developed recently. One example, using a passive star-coupled topology as illustrated above but operating at much higher bit rates, was developed by ITT Electro-Optical Products Division as part of a NASA data base management system for archiving and retrieving satellite data [18]. This network uses a 16 × 16 fused biconical taper star coupler

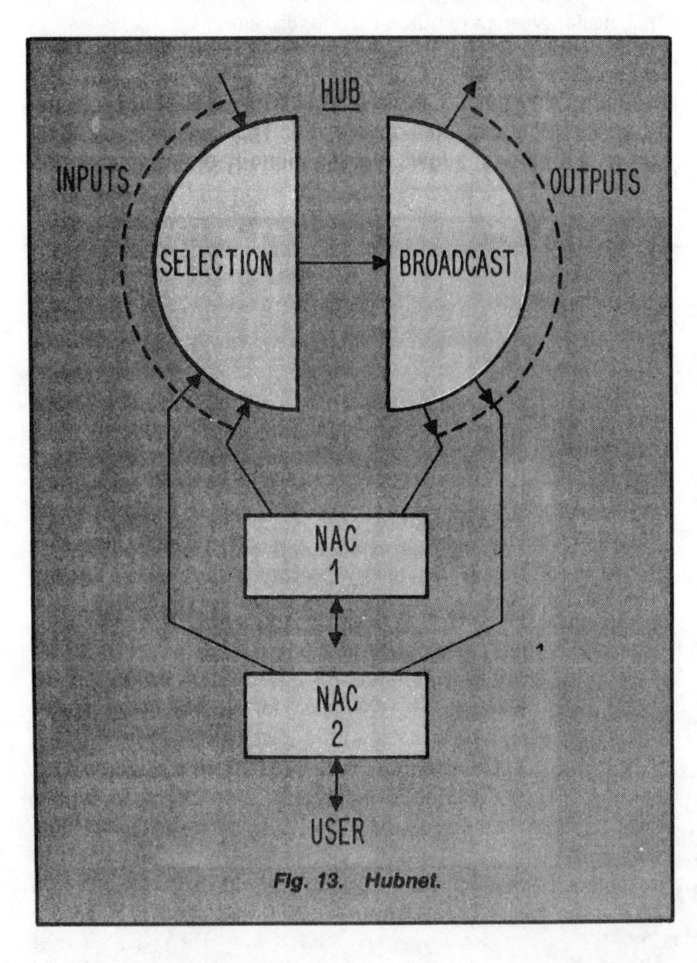

Fig. 13. Hubnet.

TABLE III—COMPARISON OF VARIOUS FIBER-OPTIC LAN'S

	Fibernet II	Codenet	Hubnet	Two-Way Bus	D-Net	Loop 6770 (NEC)	NASA/ITT	Hara's PBX
Topology	active star	passive star	star hub	loop-bus	several	active ring	passive star	active switched star
Organization	centralized	distributed	distributed	distributed	distributed	distributed	centralized	centralized
Access	CSMA/CD	CSMA/CD	hub access	centralized polled TDMA	"locomotive"	token	TDMA	circuit-switched TDMA
Bit Rate	10 Mb/s	3.4 Mb/s	50 Mb/s	100 Mb/s	100 Mb/s	32 Mb/s	100 Mb/s	55.5 MHz, 10 Mb/s sampling
Span	2.5 km	0.9–2.8 km	open	—	—	2.0 km	2.0 km	—
(max loop length)	—	—	—	—	—	—	—	—
Max. # Nodes	200–1000	200–1000	65 536	13	—	126	16	—
Fault Tolerance	—	—	—	—	—	dual fiber, switchover, loop-back	—	—
Fiber Core	100 μm	100 μm	100 or 50 μm	—	—	50 μm	50 μm	—
Fiber O.D.	140 μm	140 μm	140 μm	—	—	125 μm	125 μm	—
Fiber Type	step-index	G.I.	G.I.	—	—	G.I.	G.I.	—
Fiber Window	—	850, 1300 nm	—	—	—	—	—	—
Source	LED	LED	LED	LED/LD	—	LED/850 nm	LD/820 nm	—
Detector	PIN	PIN	PIN	PIN/APD	—	PIN	APD	—
Coding	Manchester	Manchester	—	—	—	RZ	Manchester	—

Error Rate: Presumably less than 10^{-9} in all cases.

and operates at 100 Mb/s (thus, far beyond the range of efficiency of CSMA/CD protocols). The maximum network span without repeaters is 2 km; the bit error rate is less than 10^{-10}.

Another approach to bidirectional buses is that adopted by Albanese [9], illustrated in Fig. 15. This network, using a loop-bus topology, allows two functionally distinct networks to coexist on the same fiber. This is done by using 4-port couplers and transmission at different wavelengths for the two directions. Due to limitations of current coupler technology, the number of nodes is limited *in the best case* to about 13 for a 100-Mb/s system. Polling and TDMA are used for access. A unidirectional variant called XBN (for Experimental Broadband Network) has been implemented by Hubbard and Albanese [19]. It uses dynamically assignable TDMA plus contention access methods simultaneously at a bit rate of 16.384 Mb/s.

PARAMETER	HUBNET	ETHERNET
data rate	50 Mbps	10 Mbps
span	open	2.5 km
max. # of stations	65,536	1024
medium	optical fibers	coaxial cable
topology	rooted tree, star	bus
message protocol	variable frame message size full acknowledgement delivery	variable frame message size best effort delivery
link control	multiple access echo detect of retry	CSMA/CD

Fig. 14. Comparison of Hubnet with Ethernet.

In Canada, work is underway on a joint project between the Communications Research Center of the Department of Communications, CANSTAR, and Sperry-Univac to develop a shipboard data bus with half-duplex connections at 10 Mb/s [20]. Several topologies, including a hybrid linear and a hybrid star configuration, are being examined. A critical element of these configurations are the hybrid star couplers and the asymmetric 4-port fused biconical tapered couplers.

Finally, an architecture has been proposed recently by Tseng and Chen at TRW [13], namely D-Net. D-Net may be realized using several topologies as illustrated in Fig. 16. In this network, a specialized node called the "locomotive generator" generates trains that define the access windows for the network interfaces. The result of this is an efficiency near one and, therefore, unlike Ethernet or Fibernet II, high bit rates, in the hundreds of Mb/s, may be used. Network delay is tightly bounded so that packetized voice is feasible.

According to a recent paper [13], an experimental prototype of D-Net has been built with a transmission rate of 1 Gb/s including 6 packet-switched television channels at 82 Mb/s each. A variant of this type of network has been reported by Gerla, Yeh, and Rodriguez [21] at the UCLA School of Engineering.

Table III continued

FACOM 2881 (Fujitsu)	FACOM 2883 (Fujitsu)	H-8644 (Hitachi)	Loop Network (Hitachi)	Loop 6530 (NEC)	Loop 6830 (NEC)	BRANCH 4800 (NEC)	(Prototype) (Toshiba)	SIGMA (Hitachi)	BILNET (Mitsubishi)
active ring	active ring	active ring	active ring	active ring	active ring	tree	passive star	active ring	passive ring
—	—	—	—	—	—	—	distributed	—	—
TDMA	TDMA	token passing	TDMA	hybrid	hybrid	CSMA/CD	CSMA/CD	TDMA	TDMA
4 Mb/s	33 Mb/s	32 Mb/s	32 Mb/s	32 Mb/s	32 Mb/s	10 Mb/s	10 Mb/s	32 Mb/s	50 Mb/s
3 km	9 km	2 km	2 km	7 km	12 km	1 km	1.5 km	2 km	—
96 km	576 km	100 km	—	—	—	—	—	—	—
32 (?)	54 (?)	50 (?)	—	—	—	—	—	64	around 13
(other details lacking at this writing)				(other details not available at this writing)				dual fibers, switchover, loop-back	—
								50 μm	—
								125 μm	—
								—	—
								830 nm	—
								LED/@ 830 nm	—
								PIN	—

Error Rate: Presumably less than 10 ^{9} in all cases.

TDMA and Token Passing Rings—Several examples of token ring networks are cited in Table III. For now, consider a typical example, the C&C-Net Loop 6770 built by the Nippon Electric Corporation, Ltd. [22]. This network operates at 32 Mb/s and includes fault-tolerance mechanisms for ring interface bypassing in case of a ring interface failure, alternate path selection if a fiber is broken, and battery power back-up. The ring consists of two optical-fiber loops transmitting in opposite directions. Under normal circumstances, one loop is idle and on standby, whereas the other is active. Since the ring interfaces are active, bypassing is achieved by electronic, as opposed to optomechanical, switching.

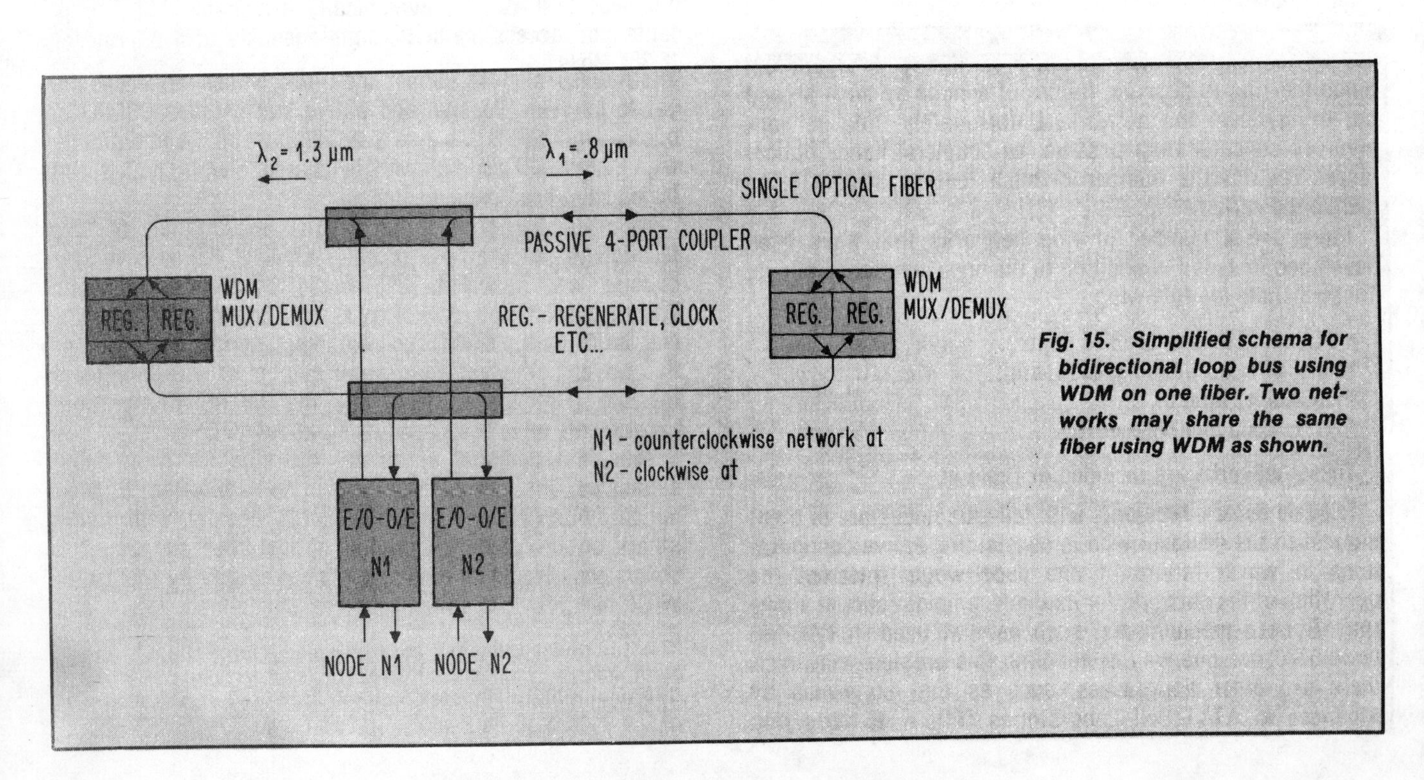

Fig. 15. Simplified schema for bidirectional loop bus using WDM on one fiber. Two networks may share the same fiber using WDM as shown.

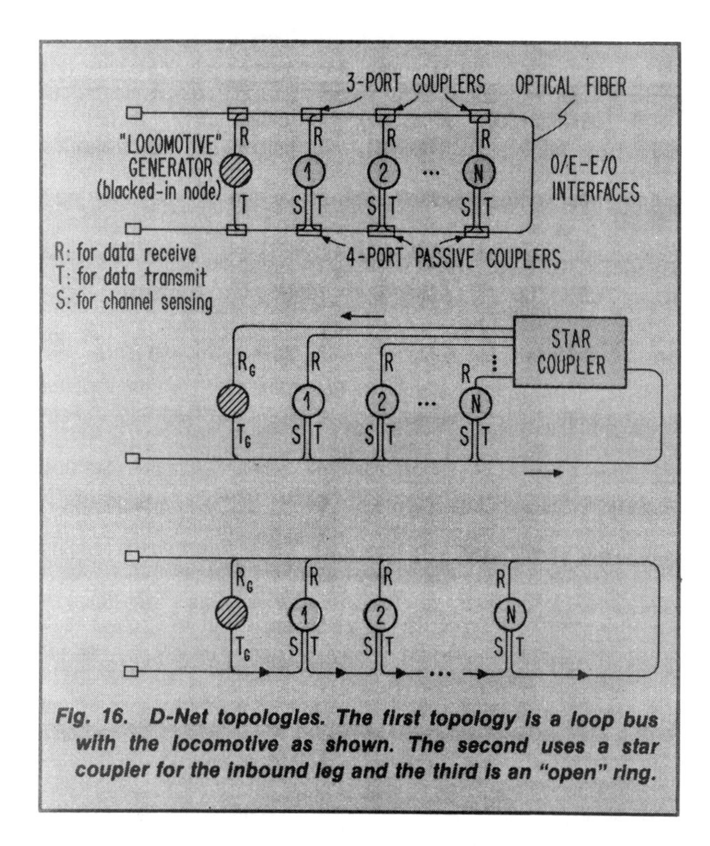

Fig. 16. D-Net topologies. The first topology is a loop bus with the locomotive as shown. The second uses a star coupler for the inbound leg and the third is an "open" ring.

An interesting approach to passive ring configurations is that of the Communication Laboratory of the Mitsubishi Electric Company in Japan with their 50-Mb/s BILNET (for BIdirectional passive Loop-structured NETwork [23]). This network transmits bidirectionally on the same fiber using WDM, one wavelength for one direction, the other for the opposite direction (840 and 900 nm, respectively). Normally the ring is "open," that is, the loop is broken at one point via an optical switch. This prevents signals from circulating more than once around the loop and thus creating echo interference. However, if the fiber cable is broken elsewhere, the switch closes, thus insuring continuity of operation. Since the ring is passive, failure of a node as such should not bring down the network. Unfortunately, this network involves concatenating passive tee couplers, hence optical losses restrict the number of such tees to about 13, as mentioned earlier.

There are a number of ring networks that have been developed in Japan in addition to the ones mentioned above. These include the following:

- Facom 2881 and 2883 of Fujitsu;
- H-8644 Loop Network of Hitachi;
- SIGMA of Hitachi;
- Loop 6530 and 6830 of NEC.

These networks are included in Table III.

Fail-Safe Nodes—Networks with fail-safe nodes are of great interest to the designer who is considering active configurations in which failure of one node would interrupt the operation of the network, for example, a unidirectional active ring. Bypass mechanisms, such as that used in C&C-Net Loop 6770, are one way of handling this problem. However, there are other approaches, such as that suggested by Albanese at AT&T Bell Laboratories [11]. A 16-Mb/s ring network was proposed whose nodes, based upon efficient 4-port couplers, allow automatic (that is, non-switched) bypass if the active portion of the node goes down. If there is no problem with echo interference, then fail-safe nodes would permit implementation of large-scale ring networks using optical fibers similar to the C&C-Net Loop 6770 mentioned above.

PBX-Like Networks—Use of a centralized switch for LAN's offers the simplicity of the circuit-switched telephone network, completely bypassing the multi-access problems associated with rings and passive stars. The penalties to be paid are the need for expensive intelligence and duplication at the switch site and access mechanisms to the nodes. For now, the price seems still too high to pay, but with the effects of economies-of-scale, this might not remain a serious barrier. A major problem is that of constructing a broadband switch that is capable of switching very-high-bit-rate channels.

The recent development of a broadband optoelectronic switch by E. Hara [24] would permit 64 kb/s and a video channel to be multiplexed on one fiber, allowing voice, video, and data on the same system. Hara's switch has been tested experimentally and is now under construction by Foundation Instruments in Ottawa. This switch uses optical fiber methods internally to deliver signals to its crosspoints with acceptable crosstalk losses. Hara proposes this switch as the basis of a network for office communications systems and for high-rise building complexes.

The major characteristics of the configurations presented in the preceding sections are summarized in Table III.

Conclusions

Optical-fiber technology for LAN applications is maturing rapidly and there are now a number of commercial fiber-optic LAN's available. Active-ring topologies using token-passing access methods and having a very high degree of fault tolerance are in the forefront, with several intriguing alternatives, such as Hubnet and D-Net, whose influences are yet to be seen. Passive and active star-coupled CSMA/CD bus configurations are also available, useful if compatibility with Ethernet-like components is desired. Several high-speed buses have been implemented.

There is the promise of greater exploitation of this technology: for example, recently a 100 × 100 passive star coupler was reported [25], made by a new process. Wavelength-division technology is maturing as well. Commercial WDM multiplexers/demultiplexers permit only four or five wavelengths, yet a far larger number of wavelengths is feasible [26]: for example, at the MITRE Corporation, experiments have been done using about 15 [27].

Thus, the potential of optical fibers is far from being exhausted. The intriguing point to note here is that a given optical-fiber network structure could coexist with many others on the same underlying optical-fiber support. The coexistence would be made possible precisely by the use of WDM, new low-loss power couplers, single-mode fibers, and the like.

Optical fibers thus hold out the promise of realizing powerful integrated-services local networks as key elements of the society of the twenty-first century.

Acknowledgments

The author would like to acknowledge the numerous contributions made by his colleagues in gathering data on fiber-optic LAN's. Special thanks are due to Dr. Paul Polishuk, President, Information Gatekeepers, Inc. of Boston, MA; to Dr. Masahiro Kawahata, Managing Director, Visual Information System Development Association (MITI), Tokyo, Japan; to A.T. Szanto, President, Foundation Instruments, Ltd., Ottawa, Canada; to Roy Pepper, President, Ungermann-Bass Canada Ltd.; and to his colleague at Laval University, Dr. Thien Vo-Dai, for his help in better understanding the role of medium-access protocols. The author also wishes to acknowledge the financial support received for his research in this area from the National Science and Engineering Research Council of Canada and the Department of Communications, Government of Canada. Finally, he wishes to thank the reviewers for their constructive remarks.

References

[1] K. J. Thurber, Ed., *The LOCALNetter Designer's Handbook*, Minneapolis, MN: Architecture Technology Corporation, 1982.

[2] H. Zimmermann, "OSI Reference Model—The ISO Model of Architecture for Open Systems Interconnection," *IEEE Trans. Commun.*, COM-28, no. 4, pp. 425–432, April 1980.

[3] IEEE Computer Society Project 802, *Local Area Network Standards*, IEEE, 1981.

[4] See, for example, the sections on telephone and CATV trunking applications in the special issue on Fiber Optic Systems of the *IEEE J. Select. Areas Commun.*, SAC-1, no. 3, pp. 381–444, April 1983.

[5] T. Li, "Advances in optical fiber communications: an historical perspective," *IEEE J. Select. Areas Commun.*, SAC-1, no. 3, pp. 356–372, April 1983.

[6] For detailed tables of currently available optical fibers and cables, please see annual publications such as the *International Fiber Optics and Communications 1983–84 Handbook & Buyers Guide, Volume V*, published by Information Gatekeepers, Inc.; or the similar volume published by *LASER FOCUS*.

[7a] S. D. Personick, "Review of fundamentals of optical fiber systems," *J. Select. Areas Commun.*, SAC-1, no. 3, pp. 373–380, April 1983.

[7b] W. Chou, *Computer Communications, Volume 1, Principles*, Prentice-Hall, pp. 299–300, 1983.

[7c] M. Marhic, "Single-mode fiber optics for local area networks," *LAN-84 Seminar, Information Gatekeepers, Inc.*, Arlington, VA, March 29–30, 1984.

[8] C. D. Tsao, "A local area network architecture overview," *IEEE Communications Magazine*, vol. 22, no. 8, pp. 7–11, Aug. 1984.

[9] A. Albanese, "Bidirectional light-wave bus," *Proc. FOC/LAN 83*, pp. 214–215, Oct. 1983.

[10] M. R. Finley and P. Chartier, "Microprocessor optic fiber network-based information systems for the small enterprise," *Proc. Canadian Inform. Process. Soc., CIPS'78*, pp. 201–208, May 1978.

[11] A. Albanese, "Fail-safe nodes for lightguide digital networks," *Bell Syst. Tech. J.*, vol. 16, no. 2, pp. 247–256, Feb. 1982.

[12] P. I. P. Boulton and E. S. Lee, "Hubnet: a 50-Mb/s glass fiber local area network," *Proc. LAN'82*, pp. 15–17, Sept. 1982.

[13] C. W. Tseng and B.-U. Chen, "D-Net, a new scheme for high data rate optical local area networks," *IEEE J. Select. Areas Commun.*, SAC-1, no. 3, pp. 493–499, April 1983.

[14] "Toshiba unveils fibre LAN," *Asian Computer Monthly*, p. 83, Feb. 1983; and "Local Area Network (LAN)," *EDP Japan Report*, pp. 57–58, Nov. 29, 1982.

[15] E. G. Rawson and R. V. Schmidt, "Fibernet II: An Ethernet-compatible fiber optic local area network," *Proc. LAN'82*, pp. 15–17, Sept. 1982.

[16] J. R. Jones, J. S. Kennedy, and F. W. Scholl, "A prototype CSMA/CD local network using fiber optics," *Proc. LAN'82*, pp. 86–90, Sept. 1982.

[17] Nippon Telegraph and Telephone Public Corporation: *Procurement Documentation—Medium Scale Local Area Optical Fiber System Equip.*, Engineering Bureau, Tokyo, 1983.

[18] D. R. Porter, P. R. Couch, and J. W. Schelin, "A high-speed fiber optic data bus for local data communications," *IEEE J. Select. Areas Commun.*, SAC-1, no. 3, pp. 479–488, April 1983.

[19] W. M. Hubbard and A. Albanese, "The experimental broadband network," *GLOBECOM'82*, Nov. 29–Dec. 2, 1982.

[20] D. C. Johnson, P. W. Rivett, and W. W. Davis, "Designing a shipboard data bus with biconical taper couplers," *Proc. Sixth Int. Fiber Optics and Commun. Expos., FOC'82*, pp. 139–144, Sept. 15–17, 1982.

[21] M. Gerla, C. Yeh, and P. Rodriguez, "Token protocol for high-speed fiber optic local networks," *Tech. Digest: Sixth Topical Meet. Optical Fiber Commun., OFC-83*, p. 88, Feb. 28–March 2, 1983.

[22] M. Kiyono, M. Tada, K. Yasue, K. Takumi, and Y. Narita, "C&C net loop 6770—a reliable communication medium for distributed processing systems," *Proc. LAN'82*, pp. 47–50, Sept. 1982.

[23] K. Ito et al., "Bidirectional fiber optic loop-structured network," *Electron. Lett.*, vol. 17, no. 2, pp. 84–86, Jan. 22, 1982.

[24] E. S. Hara, "A fiber optic LAN/OCS using a broadband switch," *GLOBECOM'82*, pp. E 1.4.1–1.4.5, Nov. 29–Dec. 2, 1982.

[25] Y. Fujii et al., "A 100 input/output-port star coupler composed of low-loss slab waveguide," *Proc. Fourth Int. Conf. Integrated Optics and Optical Fiber Commun., IOOC'83*, pp. 292–293, June 27–30, 1983.

[26] Paul Polishuk, personal communication, Fall 1983.

[27] Charles Husbands, personal communication, Spring 1983.

[28] R. Creswell and M. D. Drake, "Fiber-optic component test in high-speed data bus applications," *SPIE '82*, Washington, DC, April 1982.

Marion R. Finley, Jr., received his B.A. and M.A. in Mathematics from the Rice Institute in Houston, TX and his Ph.D. in Communications Sciences from the University of Michigan in Ann Arbor, MI. He participated in the creation of the Computer and Information Sciences Department at the Ohio State University in Columbus, OH. In Canada since 1969, he is currently professor in the Department d'Informatique (Computer Science Department) at Laval University in Quebec City. During the academic year 1978–1979, he spent part of his sabbatical at the pioneering Hi-OVIS project in Japan, the world's first wired city project to use optical fibers as transmission medium.

His research areas include telecommunications systems (in particular, broadband local area networks), new services, and new media. He has received a number of contracts and grants for work in these areas. He has lectured extensively on the subject of LAN's in the United States, Canada, the People's Republic of China, and Japan. Recently, he has been examining fifth generation implications for LAN's. Dr. Finley is a member of the IEEE and the ACM. ■

Section 3: High-Speed Local Networks

3.1 Characteristics

The subject of this section is the high-speed local network (HSLN). Recall that HSLNs are intended to satisfy user requirements for high-speed data transfer among hosts and mass storage devices.

Briefly, the key characteristics of an HSLN are as follows:

- *High data rate*: Both extant products and a draft standard have data rates of 50 Mbps or more, higher than that found with LANs.
- *High-speed interface*: HSLNs are intended to provide high throughput among computer room equipment (e.g., mainframes and high-speed peripherals). Thus, the physical link between station and network must be high-speed.
- *Distributed access*: As with LANs, it is desirable for reasons of reliability and efficiency to have distributed access control.
- *Limited distance*: Generally, an HSLN will be used in a computer room or in a small number of rooms; hence, great distances are not required.

3.2 Coaxial-Cable HSLNs

At present, HSLN technology is dominated by the coaxial cable bus architecture. Consequently, these HSLNs share a number of characteristics with bus-based LANs. In particular, a packetswitching technique is used and, because the medium is a multi-access one, a medium access control technique is needed to determine who goes next. The key difference between a bus LAN and a bus HSLN is the higher data rate of the latter.

Two signaling approaches have been used: single-channel broadband and baseband. The single-channel broadband is the basis for a pending American National Standards Institute (ANSI) standard being drafted by the X3T9.5 committee; it is also the technique used in Control Data's Loosely Coupled Network product. The baseband technique is used in the oldest and most widely used HSLN, Network Systems Corporation's HYPERchannel.

The approaches have much in common. Among the common characteristics are:

- *Data rate of 50 Mbps*: At this speed, the cost of the HSLN attachment is significantly greater than that of a LAN.
- *Maximum length of about 1 km*: This limit is dictated by the data rate, but it should be adequate for many HSLN requirements.
- *Maximum number of stations in the tens*: Again, this is dictated by the data rate. Since HSLNs are primarily intended for expensive high-speed devices, this restriction is usually not burdensome.
- *Provisions for multiple (up to four) cables*: This increases throughput and reliability.

3.3 Fiber HSLNs

Because of the potentially high data rate of optical fiber, this medium is attractive for implementing an HSLN. As with fiber LANs, fiber HSLNs have been slow in developing. The same ANSI committee that has been developing the coaxial-cable HSLN standard is also working on a fiber HSLN standard. The committee felt that the ring topology offered fewer technical problems than the bus and have concentrated their efforts there. The last article in this section deals with this standard.

3.4 HSLN Versus LAN

We have seen that there are differences in the objectives of the HSLN and the LAN. The HSLN is a special-purpose network, designed for high-speed host-to-host and host-to-storage applications. The LAN is a general-purpose network, designed to support a variety of devices generating a mix of traffic types.

Consider a site that has both a substantial computer room installation plus building-wide office automation requirements. Are two separate local networks necessary? Are they desirable?

The case for two separate networks is clear. The HSLN is tailored to the computer room requirement; the LAN, to the office automation requirement. However, it is worth considering whether a single broadband LAN, with one or more channels devoted to HSLN-style traffic, might not provide a better solution. With current technology, the broadband LAN can provide a single-channel data rate of up to 15-20 Mbps. This is certainly less than 50 Mbps; but, in general, the medium is not the bottleneck in high-speed transfer. An efficient LAN protocol at 20 Mbps could provide throughput of the same order of magnitude as does the HSLN. This approach permits the integration of a variety of network requirements on a single network. Which approach is better depends on the tradeoffs of the particular situation.

3.5 Article Summary

The article by Thornton looks at HSLNs from the point of view of a back-end network, explores related issues in some detail, and describes HYPERchannel, a commercially available HSLN.

The article by Burr looks at a proposed ANSI standard for HSLNs. This standard makes use of a CSMA-based protocol that avoids collisions and a 50-Mbps single-channel broadband bus physical layer. The article describes the standard and provides a useful discussion of the application of an HSLN for mainframe-to-disk communication.

The next article reviews the LAN architecture that is part of DEC's Vaxcluster product. The technology used is a 70-Mbps passive star coupler. With a passive star, a transmission into the central node is retransmitted out along all attached links via transformer coupling. A transmission from one station is received by all other stations, and only one station at a time can successfully transmit. Thus, the configuration is physically a star but logically a bus. This configuration is planned to be an alternative physical layer for the ANSI HSLN standard, in addition to the 50-Mbps bus described in the preceding article.

The same ANSI committee is developing an optical-fiber HSLN standard, and this is described in the last article. This is the first high-speed fiber HSLN standard, and reflects the fact that fiber optic technology is reaching maturity for local network applications. The standard specifies a token-passing ring similar to the IEEE 802.5 standard.

Reprinted from *Computer*, February 1980, pages 10-17. Copyright © 1980
by The Institute of Electrical and Electronics Engineers, Inc.

This review of existing back-end networks emphasizes the relationship of their storage aspects to the more general concept of local computer networks.

Back-End Network Approaches

James E. Thornton
Network Systems Corporation

A particularly interesting evolutionary phase of computer science and technology lies behind the term "back-end storage networks." Even if one discounts the changes arising from advances in communications technology, the computer room has steadily evolved from its early monolithic form. But when one also considers the effects of telephone terminal networks, the change is truly all-encompassing. These pressures are leading us to a new computer-room architecture, one with back-end storage systems.

Back end vs. front end

The term "back end" comes directly from the front-end communications processors now in general use, but back-end systems differ from front-end systems in both performance, such as speed of data transfer, and functional emphasis (see Figure 1). Front-end machines evolved from early hard-wired multiplexers which connected remote terminals to host computers by means of telephone lines. These multiplexers provided primitive connectability only, leaving most of the communications processing to the host computer. More modern front-end processors have progressively off-loaded the communications function from the host, contributing to the development of large-scale, geographically distributed networks.

These large-scale networks are derived largely from communications technology, which in turn was built on transmission of the human voice by analog transceivers. Digitized voice technology appeared only recently, substantially after the establishment of large-scale terminal networks. Thus, the connection of a remote terminal to a computer has had to utilize the frequency and response characteristics of long-distance voice circuits.

The functional behavior of the front-end processor has been influenced by the speed of transmission and by the early characteristics of remote terminals. Most terminals utilize a maximum transmission speed of 9600 bits per second, but most communications networks do not support even that rate. While the rate is sufficient for traffic consisting of card images and character-at-a-time or line-at-a-time text, it is unsatisfactory for transmitting a reel of tape.

The back-end system, on the other hand, addresses functions associated with file transfer and high-speed commnication between host computers. Unlike the front end, the back-end network was derived from computer technology—an exclusively digital environment that operates at speeds three or four orders of magnitude higher than telephone lines and is highly concentrated, permitting short distances for interconnection.

The reasons for a back-end network are many, but the principal one is the growth of sites with multiple hosts. At some stage in the past ten years or so, reliability and availability issues forced duplication of the computer room's critical components, including the host computer. The availability issue, in particular, is driven by the need to provide high-quality remote terminal service during prime time. Simply stated, the operator of the computer center could not tolerate having major portions of the system down for any extended period. Once embarked on a course of duplication, the process of incremental growth became an alternative to full-scale replacement. Adding host computers still required duplication of peripheral equipment, particularly

EHO234-5/85/0000/0155$01.00 © 1980 IEEE

disk storage and magnetic tape transports. Thus the back-end storage idea is bound up with pooling and sharing storage units.

One difficulty exists in classifying the back end in the more general context of local computer networks. It is fairly straight-forward to define a back-end processor in which storage management functions are off-loaded from the host computers. Not so straightforward is classifying the network scheme that permits this back end. However, for the purposes of this article, back-end storage networks are meant to include the back-end processor, the shared storage devices, and the method of interconnection with the host computers.[1]

Pioneering back-end networks

Two well-documented efforts representing significant early work on back-end networks will be discussed here. In the earlier work, begun in 1964 at Lawrence Livermore Laboratory,[2] the back end was a subnetwork of LLL's high-performance local computer network, Octopus. The second system, built by NASA for the Mission Control Center in Houston, Texas, was intended to support Skylab and the many experiments that required ground processing.

Octopus. The Octopus network supports several thousand users engaged in scientific, engineering, and support tasks in many fields of research and development. Designed to provide an interactive computing environment for both large and small problems, the network has grown to include four CDC 7600 and two CDC Star computers, as well as the DEC dual processor PDP-10 operating as a back-end processor.

Octopus was originally conceived as a star topology with a central switching node and a set of links to interconnect resources. In this early stage, the central node not only performed a packet switching function, it also handled terminal control and shared-device control. This wide range of demands on CPU bandwidth, memory bandwidth, and buffer capacity—coupled with interconnection limits—placed a major operating burden on the central node.

Consequently, the Octopus designers chose to move in the direction of functional partitioning. Figure 2 shows the various functional subnetworks shared by the worker computers. Each subnetwork consists of a connection to each worker computer, buffer memory, subnetwork control computer, and interfaces to attached resources that in turn have associated control computers. In the case of the file transport subnetwork, the subnetwork control computer is the PDP-10 and the photostore control computer is the IBM 1800. An additional subnetwork encompasses the CDC-38500 mass storage subsystem.

Interconnections from the functional subnetworks to the worker computers are bit parallel and point to point. The back-end networks (the file transport and MASS subnetworks) interface at 10 megabits per second and 40 Mbps respectively. Generally, the Octopus network has depended on excess average bandwidth capacity to reduce bottlenecks in the network communications units.

The laboratory's functional separation of shared resources and associated control computers has been very successful, but as is normal in state-of-the-art efforts, successful progress has exposed further needs and desirable extensions. One important problem area is the matter of interconnecting the subnetworks. Because the subnetworks are quite different in interface bandwidth and communications protocols, the task of providing paths from one to another falls to the worker computers. This is an undesirable use of the worker computers' memory space and CPU cycles. Routing all high-speed subnetwork data intercommunication through the workers dilutes their primary function—that of computation.

In Octopus, the back-end processor associated with the file transport subnetwork is not user programmable but performs the special-purpose function of managing the photostore. Here, the back-end

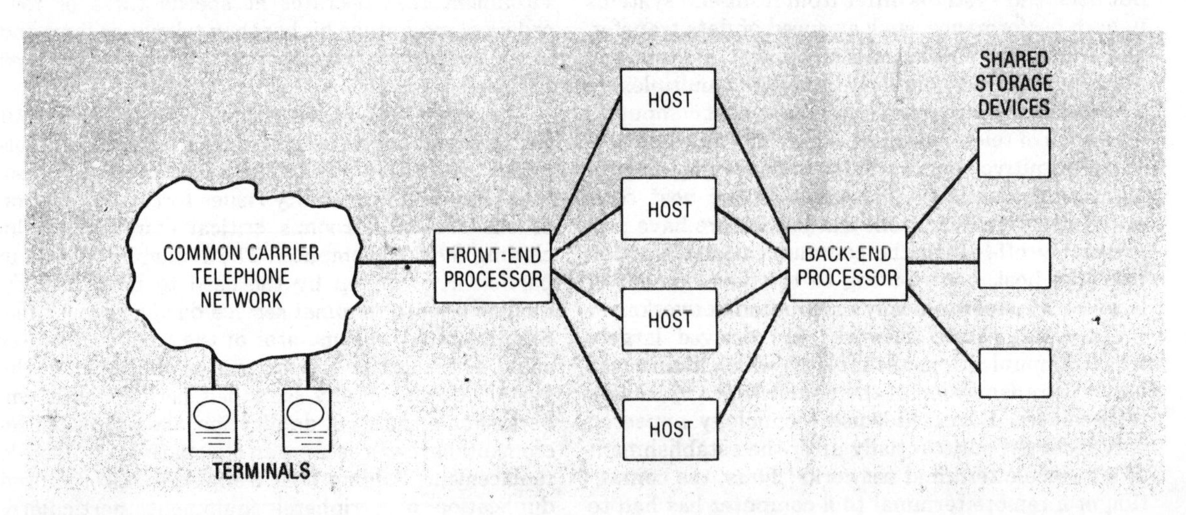

Figure 1. A back-end network.

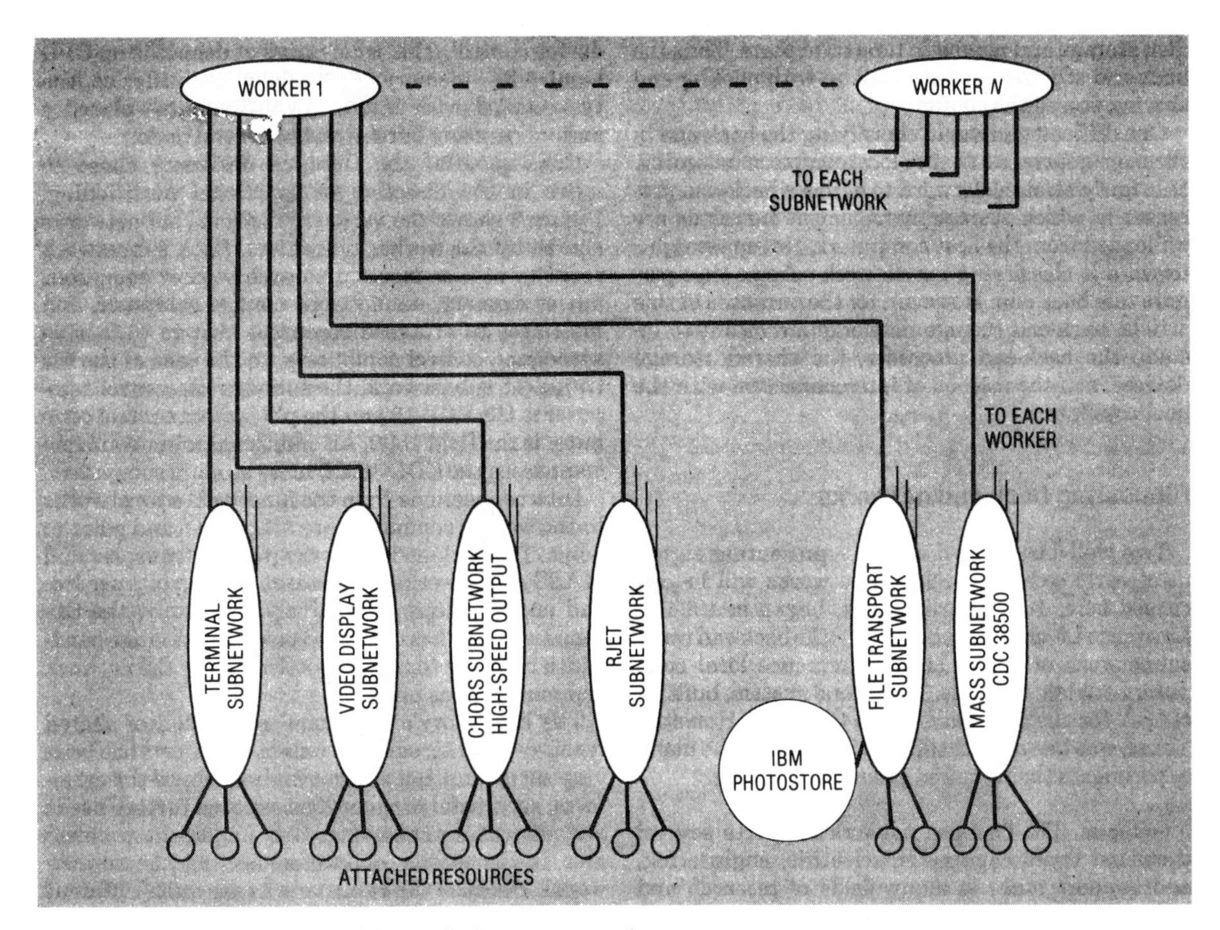

Figure 2. Lawrence Livermore Laboratory's Octopus network.

approach has much to recommend it, especially when contrasted with alternatives. It would be unreasonable to duplicate such a massive storage unit as the photostore for each worker computer. It can also be claimed that tailoring the back-end processor for the intended special-purpose function produces a more efficient unit, since overheads associated with general-purpose user programmability are at least partly eliminated.

The file transport subnetwork su' orts generation of some 3 x 10[1?] bits per year and quests to about 10^6 files per day. The compute environment at Lawrence Livermore Laboratory is very advanced, but it does indicate the direction of the back end. The generation of data to be stored and shared will soon be a major concern for all computer centers.

Skylab. Another early back-end storage network was built by NASA to support Skylab and its associated ground processing. With the Skylab terminal system, engineers and scientists could view telemetry data, received through ground stations, after the data had been processed.

Spacecraft data transmitted from the orbiting laboratory were received at remote tracking sites and then relayed to Mission Control Center. At the Houston center, a Univac 494 front-end processor received and routed the data to one or more of five IBM System/360 Model 75 computers.[3] Data to be stored were transmitted to the CDC Cyber 73 operating as a back-end processor. Three main software systems operated in the System/360s: the terminal support system, the data storage subsystem, and the data retrieval subsystem.

The design of this system addressed the time constraints associated with (1) proper receipt of the telemetry data and (2) responsiveness to terminal requests. Initially, only limited terminal capabilities for quick looks at incoming scientific data were envisioned. However, terminal requirements grew substantially during the course of the project, and their support became a major problem.

The Skylab project considered two configurations to meet the terminal system's data-base system requirement and began extensive simulation and performance evaluation activities to qualify the advantages and disadvantages of each alternative. The first option assumed the addition of disks, as needed, to the System/360 Model 75's selector channels; two channel switches and other manual switches would permit attachment of disks to any of the host computers. The second configuration option specified a separate data-base computer that would be linked to the System/360 Model 75 through a selector channel.

The comprehensive evaluation demonstrated the superiority of the configuration utilizing a back-end processor. This configuration was more responsive to data-base requests and permitted a greater data-base request rate than the first option. The simulation also provided valuable insight into the organization of the data base and of the host software versus the back-end software. Using separate functional modules for the data storage subsystem and the data retrieval subsystem provided more flexibility and effectively separated the incoming telemetry processing from the data retrieval processing. These subsystems could also be run in separate host computers for possible load sharing or multijobbing with other applications.

Substantial effort went into the design and fine tuning of this system, particularly in the relationship between batch processing requests and quick-look interactive requests. In spite of severe constraints, the system performed to expectations.

Some important comments can be made about these two pioneering efforts:

(1) The validity of a back-end storage system lies both in the sharing of a massive storage unit for economy of scale and in supporting high terminal request service for data retrieval with good response.
(2) Functional partitioning is valuable for designing efficient special-purpose modules.
(3) Partitioning into subnetworks introduces protocol issues between low-speed and high-speed subnetworks and emphasizes the need for compatible and symmetrical protocols.
(4) Point-to-point connections by standard I/O channels limit speed, distance, and total connectivity.

Current local network technology and issues

The back-end storage network is considered to be a subnetwork of a local computer network. In recent years new technologies and system architectures have become available for local computer networks. The two general approaches that have been explored—the ring network and the bus network—are differentiated only by the method of interconnection (see Figure 3). In the ring network, each node actively repeats the messages being transmitted around the ring.[4] The node may also receive or transmit data on behalf of the host computer or device to which it is interfaced. In contrast, the bus network utilizes a continuous coaxial bus which makes a passive connection at each drop or adapter.[5] Each adapter may receive or transmit data on behalf of the host computer or device to which it is interfaced.

While the ring and bus structures are different, the differences need not materially alter the points discussed in this paper. Therefore, the following description of new system's architecture concentrates on the bus structure and references HYPERchannel, a bus network developed by Network Systems Corporation.[6] (Thurber and Freeman[1] survey other bus networks.)

The major objectives of a bus network should include

(1) *Extension of interconnect distance to a 1000-foot minimum.* This will facilitate floor-space relief for the expanding computer room.
(2) *Interface to any standard channel.* To accomplish this, the network must be data format independent except at its interfaces.
(3) *Elimination of single points of failure.* For high reliability and availability, all units connected to the local network should be allowed equal access without master/slave relationship and without dependence on each other.
(4) *Network operation at computer channel speeds.* This objective is aimed at the file transfer function or computer to computer traffic.
(5) *Data rate decoupling by use of buffer memory.* Judicious use of buffer memories within the network could allow units with different data rates to communicate, each at its own rate.
(6) *Ready attachment of new technology.* New memory technologies may be more effective by network connection than by direct computer channel connection.
(7) *Unpredictable and uncoordinated access.* Units interfaced to the local high-speed communications network are assumed to require unplanned use of the network.

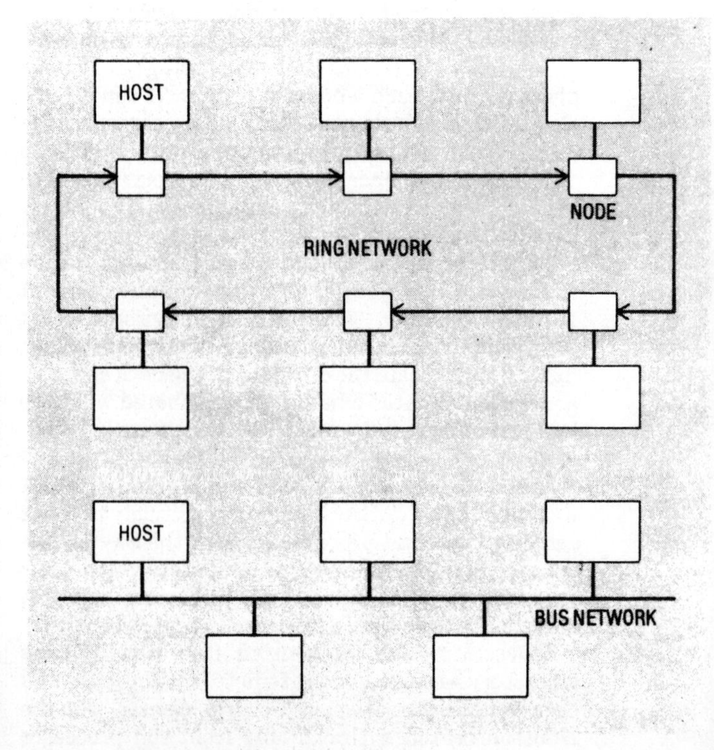

Figure 3. Ring and bus local networks.

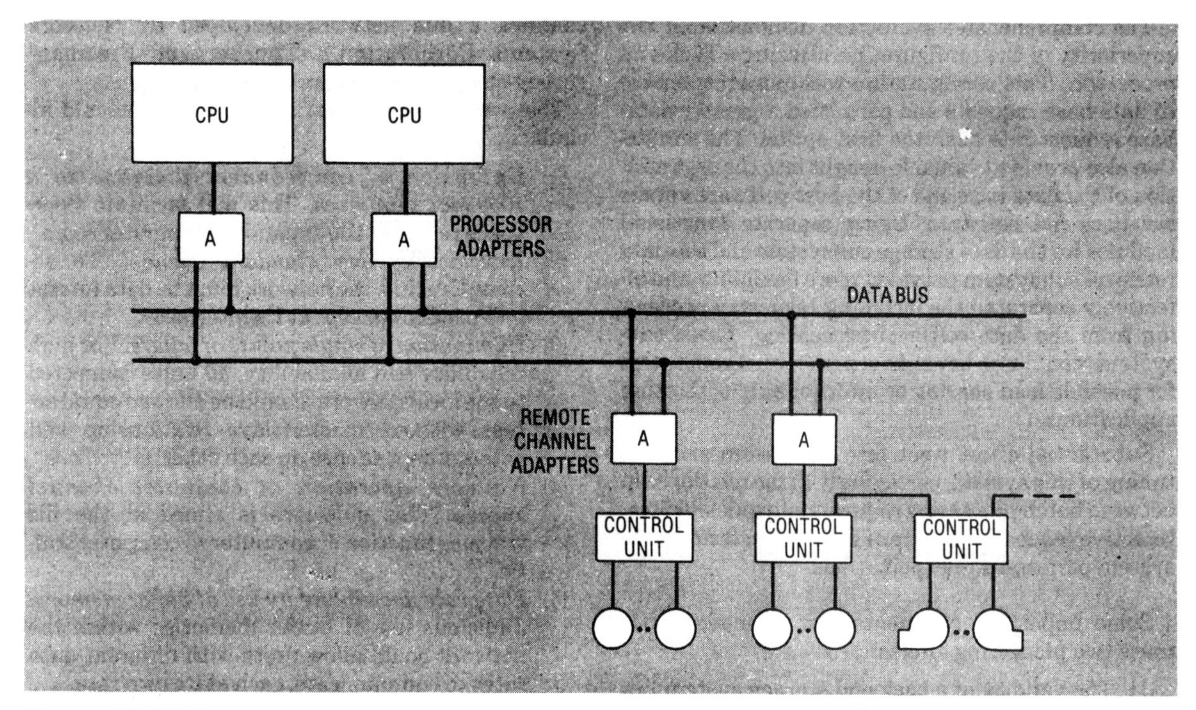

Figure 4. HYPERchannel network.

(8) *Maximum practical utilization of network capacity.* The protocols used in the network should be adaptable enough to supply high bandwidth and fast response.

Site data channel. The local network characterized above is best described as a site data channel to differentiate it from a computer data channel and from a digital phone network. As one example of a bus network, let us consider some key ingredients of HYPERchannel. As shown in Figure 4, this network is a multidrop single coax with a fixed transfer rate of 50 megabits per second. A second data bus is optional.

The connection to the bus is made passively by means of an adapter, which in turn interfaces to the standard channel of a host computer or peripheral controller. Each adapter contains hardware and firmware which implement a unique contention algorithm.[7]

Adapter models differ only at the interface to the host computer or peripheral controller. It should be obvious that the serial (single coax) stream of data on the bus can be assembled into literally any parallel interface without regard to word size or format. Thus the concept of a site data channel encompasses the interconnection of incompatible processors or peripherals, a property it shares with the telephone networks. This does not remove the incompatibility, it merely allows incompatible units to share a fully general-purpose local network.

Host-to-host messages. One class of back-end storage network can be called the "host-to-host" environment. In this structure, messages are prepared in one host such that the receiving host can interpret and act upon the message. This message preparation may be within an application program or within a service program called by the application program.

In the file transport system at Lawrence Livermore Laboratory, as shown in Figure 2, the files are transferred from the PDP-10 to a worker computer. In this type of back-end storage system, the network supports a host-to-host environment. The bus network can be readily used for this environment because of several very important presumptions:

(1) The worker computer application programs call for a file transfer service which results in a message communication to the PDP-10 server computer.
(2) The server computer is capable of fielding messages from more than one worker computer.
(3) The incompatibility between worker computers and server is resolved by predefined message formats.
(4) The bus network utilizes a message technique for communication.

HYPERchannel also transfers information by means of messages. After preparation, the message is output to the adapter and stored in a buffer within the adapter. In Figure 5 a typical message is broken down into the message proper and its associated data. In preparing this message, the host provides the source and destination addresses, alternative routing instructions, and an access code (similar to an authorization key) as a header. In the message prop-

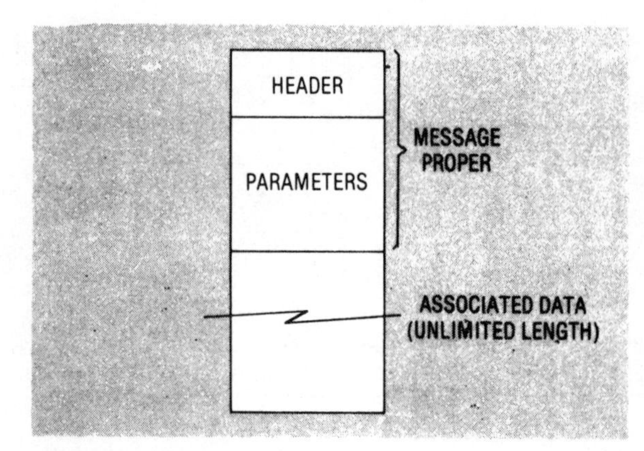

Figure 5. A standard message.

er, additional space is provided for information interpreted only by the receiving host. The associated data of unlimited length is also buffered in the adapter and transmitted. The adapter only interprets the header data in order to execute the full transfer of the message. The entire message, header and all, is transmitted to the receiving adapter and then to the receiving host.

This message is similar to a datagram as far as the network is concerned. Once delivered, the network retains nothing about it except some statistics of network activity. It is therefore assumed that in due course a return message will be transmitted from the receiving host back to the originator.

The messages are delivered on the bus in bursts at the fixed maximum rate of 50 megabits per second. The bus can be shared by a number of transmitters and receivers independently transferring messages. Time on the bus is allocated by a contention algorithm which allows equal immediate access under light loading and gradually converts to fixed priority assignment as the load approaches maximum. Each burst, or frame, is separately checked for error, and retransmissions are made where necessary. The host program which handles messages also checks for successful transfers by the use of positive acknowledgment messages.

The use of host-to-host messages to support a back-end storage system is under development at several sites. In one such system, shown in Figure 6, worker computers of two different manufacturers (IBM and Sperry Univac) will utilize a pair of IBM 3031s managing a very large mass-storage facility. In this system an initial stage does not require a common data format. Each worker machine is merely provided mass storage space without regard to sharing data. In a following stage, a common data base for each class of worker computer can be developed. A long-term process of developing a common data base for all machines may not be realistic. However, this is an example of the immediate potential of sharing the storage devices, if not the data.

Remote channels. While the host-to-host message scheme is a direct application of a back-end network, the pooling of peripherals is another application. Certain models of adapters can interface to standard peripheral controllers and, in effect, function as a remote channel. An example is a remote block-multiplexer channel which emulates the IBM standard channel. The standard IBM block-multiplexer channel executes channel programs which are prepared by host software and placed in a memory available to the channel. The channel then executes the program by reading channel command words

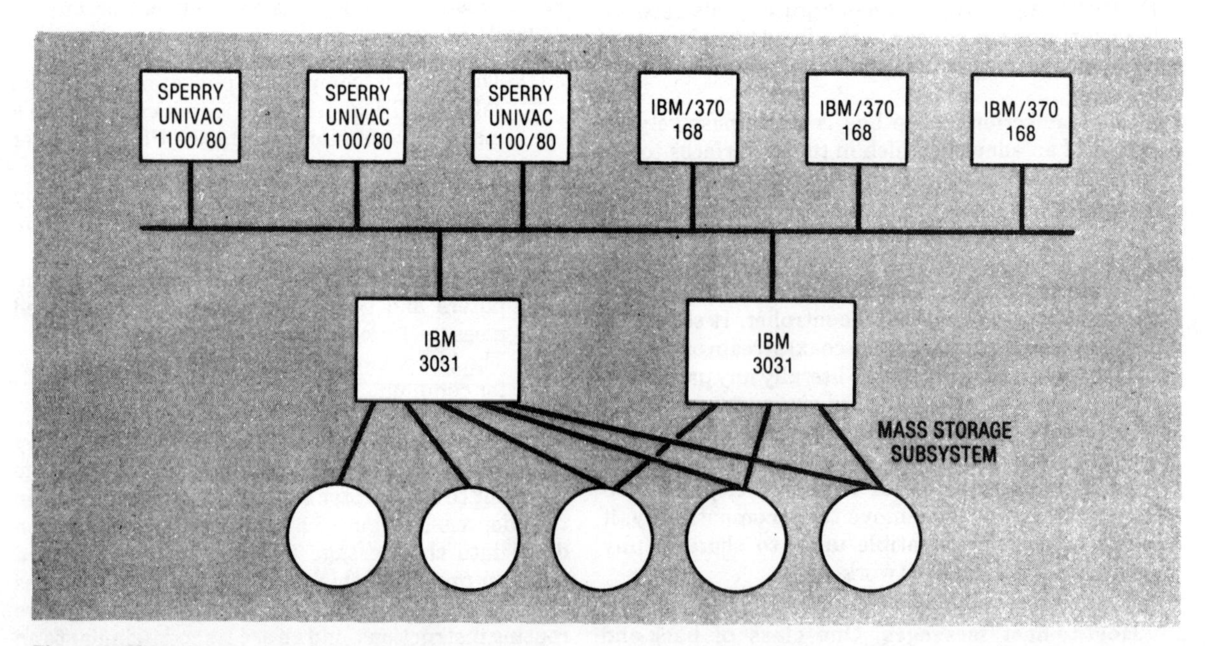

Figure 6. Shared mass storage back-end network.

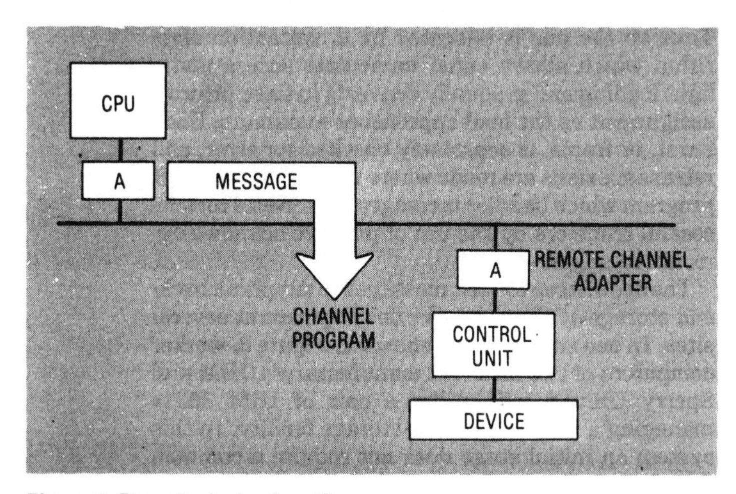

Figure 7. Remote device handling.

from the memory and delivering the appropriate channel commands to the peripheral controller.

The remote channel version in the bus network effectively stores the channel program in the remote adapter (see Figure 7). The adapter then emulates the block multiplexer channel using the adapter memory as the source of the channel program. This requires that the channel program be delivered intact and complete to the remote channel adapter, but except for this, the peripheral controller does not "know" that it is connected remotely. Delivery of the original channel program entails use of a host service program which uses a message similar to the host-to-host message. In this case, the channel program is the data portion of the message. The host service program provides header information and, where necessary, interprets the channel program to account for the fact that a network has been inserted between the host computer and the peripheral controller.

A block multiplexer channel has the ability to service more than one peripheral controller by disconnecting during periods when a controller is executing a long operation. The channel then goes on to the next channel program in its queue. The remote channel version is also capable of this kind of multiplexing.

Distribution vs. bottleneck. The principal objective of a back-end network is to provide relatively unlimited access between equipment at channel speed. The particular benefit accruing to a back-end storage system is that is allows all worker computers to off-load the storage management function to a separate back-end processor. This shared management function could become the key bottleneck for the computer center; therefore, it is well to examine the means available to at least duplicate the function. In both of the pioneering efforts described, the back-end processor was not duplicated, although the PDP-10 was a dual processor on common memory. These were vulnerable to down time and possible bottleneck under heavy loads.

Referring back to Figure 6, note that the system is configured with two server computers managing the mass storage. As advances are made in memory technology and data-base processors, the prospect of distributing the storage management function even further calls for greater network activity. It seems clear that back-end storage and back-end networks are deeply linked.

The choice of duplicating for reliability is the principal reason for the incremental, add-on growth of the computer center. Indiscriminate duplication without regard to positive objectives is not desirable. The back-end storage network, with the emphasis on network, may provide the means for both objective distribution and maximum sharing of resources.

Long-distance back end. In the first section of this article, we compared the front end to the back end and concluded that the two are quite different, principally because the front end was derived from telephone technology. But long-distance digital technology, utilizing microwave radio links and satellite links, is now on the horizon.[8] These very-high-bandwidth links have opened up the possibility of directly connected back-end networks. The HYPERchannel approach to these long-distance links is through the use of a link adapter (Figure 8).

Messages from site A are transmitted on the long-distance link, point-to-point from one link adapter to the next. The receiving link adapter then forwards

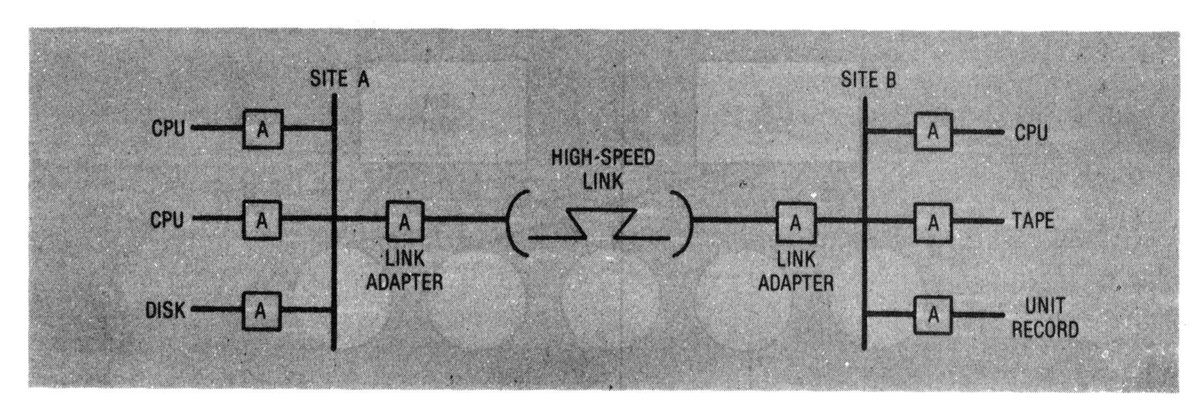

Figure 8. Interconnecting two sites by microwave link.

the message to its destination, site B, as if A were local to B. This is done by assigning a block of adapter addresses to the link adapter in each site. The destination and source addresses are carried in the message header such that the link adapter is transparent to the sender and receiver.

Although the bandwidth is high in this type of link, the effective data rate is also a function of the total distance and data block size. For file transfer purposes, block size should be relatively large to make good use of the link. In contrast, terminal traffic could be handled better by breaking the bandwidth down to voice-grade links entering the computer center by means of the front end. Hybrid use will provide some interesting properties. As a practical matter, it may be wise to ignore bandwidth considerations for anything but file transfer to retain a single-message approach, whether for local back ends or long-distance back ends.

Monitoring and maintenance. Total distribution to prevent single points of failure is a valid objective, but the other side of the coin is the matter of network control. One possible approach is monitoring in a manner that permits network operation whether or not the monitor is "alive and well." The adapters execute retry and error-handling functions, including capturing statistical information on traffic, error conditions, retransmissions, etc. This statistical data can then be called periodically from either a server computer or a worker computer which has been assigned the network monitor function. In fact, since the whole idea of a local computer network is that it run essentially unattended, one common monitor, such as a "war room" minicomputer, would be ideal.

In this regard, the network could be the vehicle for total on-line maintenance of all equipment, ranging from host computers to peripherals. This presumes that peripherals directly connected to a central processor unit in a conventional manner will use diagnostics and maintenance procedures provided for that CPU. It would be useful to initiate and monitor such diagnostics from the war room. Also, diagnostic programs delivered in the form of channel programs to the remote channel adapters would be a useful maintenance vehicle for network-connected peripherals. Depending on how the back-end processor is configured, its special maintenance requirements may also respond to a network monitor.

Compatibility. A final issue in back-end networks is the matter of compatibility. A number of HYPERchannel users have connected CPUs and peripherals from different manufacturers, proving that concepts like the back-end storage system have just as much of a place in a mixed environment as in a compatible one. Looking beyond program and software compatibility, we find a largely incompatible data environment in which conversion between character codes, while useful, barely scratches the surface.

Therefore, one of the long-term requirements for reaching the ultimate promise of the back-end storage network is the slow conversion to common data standards. Early usage of the network will provide physical accessibility, sharing, and distribution of the storage media. Where data compatibility exists, a portion of the back-end storage system can also be devoted to a shared, common data base.

In summary, the back-end processor has come to be recognized for its value in the context of local computer networks, a context providing fertile ground not only for the continuing evolution of back-end processors but also for the introduction of new technologies. ■

References

1. K. J. Thurber and H. A. Freeman, "Local Computer Network Architecture," *Digest of Papers, COMPCON 79 Spring,* San Francisco, Feb. 26-Mar. 1, 1979, pp. 258-261.
2. R. W. Watson, "The LLL Octopus Network," *3rd USA-JAPAN Computer Conference,* San Francisco, Oct. 1978, pp. 12-21.
3. R. J. Mancini, "Performance Analysis for the Skylab Terminal System," *IBM Systems J.,* No. 2, Feb. 1974, pp. 94-114.
4. D. J. Farber, "A Ring Network," *Datamation,* Vol. 21, No. 2, Feb. 1975, pp. 44-46.
5. R. M. Metcalfe and D. R. Boggs, "Ethernet: Distributed Packet Switching for Local Computer Networks," *Comm. ACM,* Vol. 19, No. 7, July 1976, pp. 395-404.
6. J. E. Thornton, "Overview of HYPERchannel," *Digest of Papers, COMPCON 79 Spring,* San Francisco, Feb. 26-Mar. 1, 1979, pp. 262-265.
7. G. S. Christensen and W. R. Franta, "Design and Analysis of the Access Protocol for HYPERchannel Networks," *3rd USA-JAPAN Computer Conference,* San Francisco, Oct. 1978, pp. 86-93.
8. G. S. Christensen, "Links Between Computer Room Networks," *Telecommunications,* Vol. 13, No. 2, Feb. 1979, pp. 47-50.

James E. Thornton is the president of Network Systems Corporation, which manufactures and markets short-haul data communications units that interconnect large-scale computers and minicomputers. While serving as vice president of Control Data Corporation's Computing Development Laboratories, he designed and co-designed the CDC 1604, 6400, and 6600 and headed laboratories which developed the CDC Star-100 and other products. Prior to joining Control Data, he was with Engineering Research Associates and Univac. Thornton, who received his BSEE degree from the University of Minnesota, is a former member of the advisory committee of the National Academy of Sciences and National Science Foundation.

An Overview of the Proposed American National Standard for Local Distributed Data Interfaces

WILLIAM E. BURR *National Bureau of Standards*

ABSTRACT: The Local Distributed Data Interface (LDDI) Project of X3 Technical Committee X3T9 has resulted in three draft proposed American National Standards for a high performance local area network. The proposed standards are organized in accordance with the ISO Reference Model for Open Systems Interconnection and encompass the lowest two protocol layers (data link and physical) of the model, plus a serial broadband coaxial bus interface. The intended application of the LDDI is as a backend network for the interconnection of high performance CPUs and block transfer peripherals such as magnetic disk and tapes. A carrier-sense multiple access with collision prevention (CSMA-CP) distributed bus arbitration protocol is employed. The cable interface supports the attachment of up to 28 ports over a cable distance of 0.5 km (8 ports may be attached to a 1 km cable) at a transfer rate of 50 Mbit/s.

William E. Burr is an electronic engineer at the National Bureau of Standards where he works on the development of computer I/O interface standards. He chairs the American National Standard Committee X3T9.2, which is developing an intelligent, parallel bus interface standard for small computers and peripherals. His research interests include formal specification, verification, and measurement of I/O interfaces and instruction set architectures as well as the use of broadcast networks as magnetic disk interfaces.

Author's Present Address: William E. Burr Institute for Computer Sciences and Technology, National Bureau of Standards, Building 225, Room A216, Washington, DC 20234.

BACKGROUND

In February 1979, X3T9, a technical committee of American National Standard Committee X3, Information Processing, formed an *ad hoc* working group to study its future interface standards projects. A principal motivation was the inadequacy of the existing disk interfaces for projected magnetic disk device transfer rates. In 1972 state-of-the-art disks recorded at about 6.4 Mbit/s per recording head, while in 1983 state of the art disks record at about 24 Mbit/s. Fundamental limits have not been approached and further increases are expected. The appetites of large mainframe computers for high bandwidth peripherals are keeping pace with the rapid progress in magnetic peripherals. Space and security considerations frequently result in a need to connect several large computers and their peripherals together over a high bandwidth, long distance (η 1 km) link.

Parallel bus interfaces can accommodate very high transfer rates, but are not satisfactory for distances which exceed 200m or so because of differences in signal propagation rates and distances. A then-new approach, serial, distributed local broadcast networks, appeared to offer many advantages. Ethernet[1] had spawned a number of experimental networks which resulted in an explosion of papers appearing in the technical literature [7], while Hyperchannel[2] demonstrated the practicality of a 1 km, 50 Mbit/s serial bus [8].

X3T9 chose to develop an interface standard for a serial 50 Mbit/s interface, able to connect a modest number of devices through up to 1 km of cable. X3T9 agreed to follow the ISO Reference Model for Open Systems Interconnection (OSI) [3] and to generate standards for layers 1 and 2 of that model, the physical and data link layers. Task group X3T9.5 was organized and began its work in August 1979, selecting the name Local Distributed Data Interface (LDDI).

[1] Trademark of the Xerox Corporation. Certain commercial computer networks are identified in this paper because of their historical importance in the development of local network technology and the LDDI proposals. Such identification does not imply any recommendation or edorsement by the National Bureau of Standards.
[2] Trademark Network Systems Corporation.

"An Overview of the Proposed American National Standard for Local Distributed Data Interfaces" by W.E. Burr from *Communications of the ACM*, Volume 26, Number , August 1983, pages 554-561. Copyright 1983, Association for Computing Machinery, Inc., reprinted by permission.

THE OSI MODEL

The OSI Model provides a layered structure for computer interconnection standards. Seven "layers" are defined Figure 1) with an application layer at the top and a physical layer at the bottom. Layer "protocols" communicate only with their "peer" protocols at distant ports. They do this by means of an "interface" to the immediately lower layer, which provides communication "services" to the higher layer. In turn, each layer except the applications layer provides communications services to the layer which is immediately higher through an interface.

Until recently, X3T9.5 has confined itself to the lowest two layers. The LDDI is consistent with the OSI Model, although its assignment of functions to layers differs from long distance communications protocols such as ADCCP [1]. Standards for at least two more layers are needed for the LDDI to fulfill its promise. A Network Layer Protocol is needed. High performance bus networks usually provide for parallel trunks as a matter of reliability and performance expansion. This implies a routing function which is the principal business of the network layer and which may well also provide service enhancements, such as automatic acknowledgments, to data link layer services. X3T9.5 has just begun work on a data link dependent Network Layer Protocol for the LDDI.

The remaining needed standard would define an application protocol for a magnetic tape and disk server (also possibly a host-to-host application protocol). This "application" process corresponds roughly to magnetic disk driver software in current operating systems and, despite the OSI designation of "application layer," would normally be an operating system rather than a user function. Other intermediate protocols would be null, since, despite the adherence of the LDDI protocols to the OSI Model, the connection of a magnetic disk to its host computer is not viewed by X3T9.5 as an "open" process in the sense of the Model. Other standards bodies are generating general purpose protocols for the internet sublayer and transport and session layers which should be useful with the LDDI protocols when open traffic passes over the LDDI.

GENERAL STRUCTURE OF THE LDDI PROPOSED STANDARDS

Figure 2 is a block diagram of the LDDI protocols and cable interface. Since it is a distributed masterless protocol, one illustration suffices for all ports. Starting at the bottom is the electrical cable interface [5]. This is separately specified because the interface could be used with other protocols, while the protocols could be used with other interfaces. The proposed interface standard [5] has three parts: a modulator, demodulator, and a cable. The modulator accepts serial digital information from the physical protocol, modulates an RF carrier, and transmits that signal on the cable. The demodulator converts the analog signal from the cable to digital bits and passes them to the Physical Layer Protocol.

The Physical Layer Protocol [6] contains three functions: (1) a transmitter which appends a preamble to a bit stream supplied by the data link layer, (2) a receiver which strips the preamble off the message before passing the received data to the data link layer, and (3) an arbiter which determines when a port may transmit without danger of collisions with messages from other ports.

The Data Link Layer Protocol [4] contains two functions: (1) a transmitter, which inserts a source address, and a 32-bit

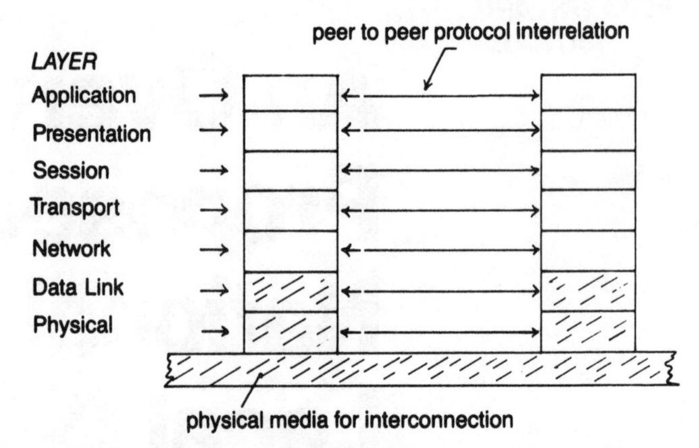

FIGURE 1. Open Systems Reference Model. (//// indicates areas covered by proposed LDDI standards.)

frame check sequence (FCS); (2) a receiver, which checks the destination address and FCS and uses a length field to determine the end of the message.

THE LDDI PHYSICAL (ELECTRICAL) INTERFACE

The proposed LDDI physical interface employs 75 Ω coaxial cable. Since the cable parts are used in CATV applications, they are readily available. The topology is a linear bus with a number of drops through passive T tap port couplers (Figure 3). The broadband interfaces uses the spectrum from 35 MHz to 200 MHz and is identical to that employed in the Loosely Coupled Network (LCN), a commercially available 50 Mbit/s local network from Control Data Corp. Bit error

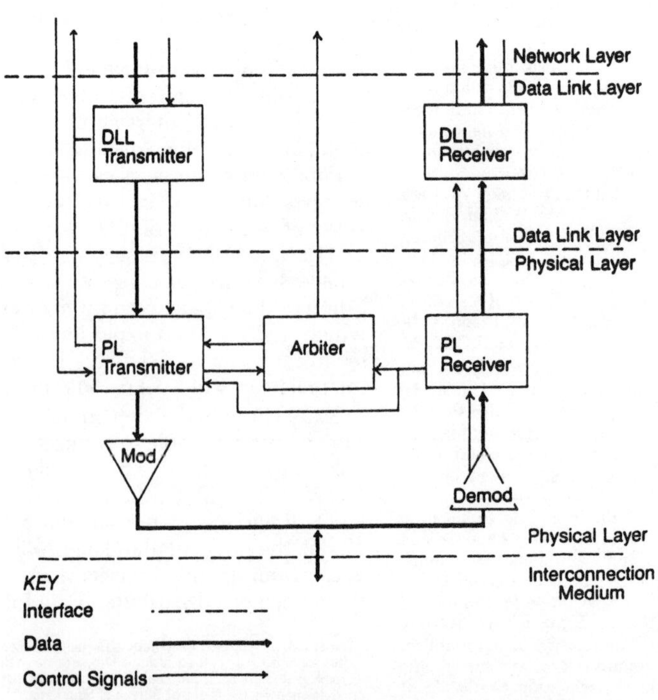

FIGURE 2. LDDI Protocol Functions. Interface: - — - —; ⟶; Control Signals: ⟶.

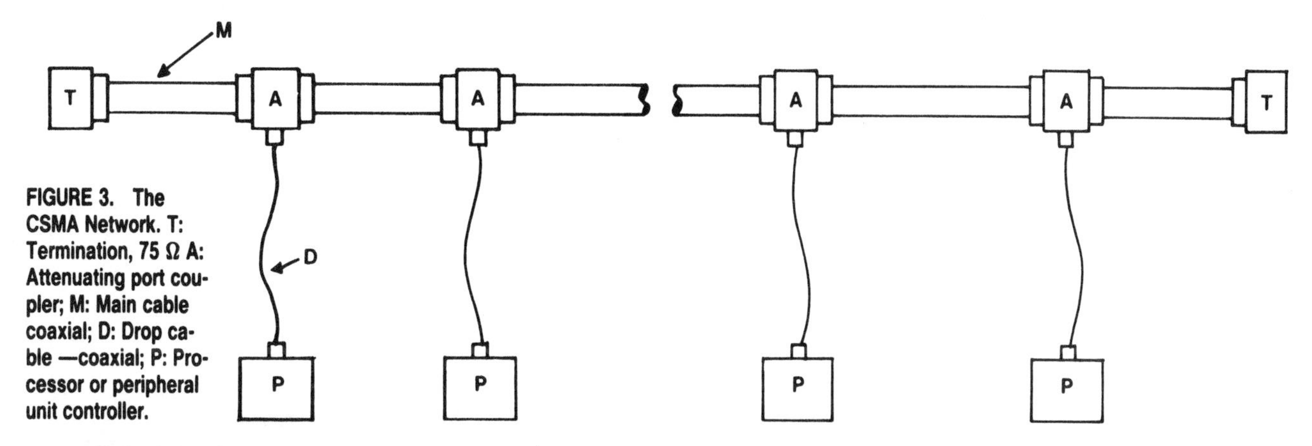

FIGURE 3. The CSMA Network. T: Termination, 75 Ω A: Attenuating port coupler; M: Main cable coaxial; D: Drop cable —coaxial; P: Processor or peripheral unit controller.

rates of less than 1 bit in error in 10^{10} transmitted bits have been achieved by Control Data Corp.

Two separate signals are employed: a 150 MHz carrier and a 50 MHz bit-clock signal. Data modulates the carrier by differential change-on-zeros 180° phase modulation. Power is 1 to 2 mW, and the dynamic range of the receivers is 60 dB. The entire receiver and transmitter can be built from inexpensive commercially available parts.

Connection to the main cable is made by passive T tap couplers which cause about 1 dB of attenuation for signals passing through the tap along the main cable, but provide about 11 dB of attenuation when passing signals from the main cable to the drop cable. With high quality foam dielectric metal sheath trunk cable and flexible 50 ft drop cables, the 60 dB dynamic range of receivers allows up to 8 taps with 1 km of cable. With shorter cables more taps can be supported (28 at 500 m). If a drop cable is improperly terminated, the reflected signal is attenuated by 22 dB, and no problem generally results on the main cable.

PHYSICAL LAYER PROTOCOL

The interface proposal described in the preceding section is one way to demodulate analog signals into the digital bits; however, the LDDI Physical Layer Protocol could be used with many other interfaces and all broadcast network topologies. The physical layer receiver expects to see a preamble of binary ones followed by a "start flag" octet before the bit stream. The receiver passes everything following the start flag to the data link layer. Whenever the received signal from the interconnection medium exceeds a power threshold specified in the interface proposal, a medium active signal is turned on.

The transmitter sends a 64 bit synchronizing preamble of ones, followed by a start flag, then it sends the bit stream supplied by the data link layer, and finally, it appends a trailing field of 16 binary ones.

The arbiter uses the on-to-off transition of the medium active signal to determine when the port may safely transmit. The arbitration algorithm is similar to the Hyperchannel algorithm and its operation is illustrated in Figures 4 and 5. When the medium active signal changes from on to off, three timers are started. The first of these, the Priority Access Timer (PAT), counts 64 bit times. While it is running, a port is permitted to initiate a priority transmission. Typical uses for this Priority Access Opportunity include immediate acknowledgments and protocols where a dialogue between two ports must hold the interconnection medium (i.e., for "streaming" of many successive blocks of data between a disk and CPU without "slipping" disk revolutions between successive blocks).

The second time, the Arbitrated Access Timer (AAT), is individually determined for each port. When it expires, a port may immediately begin a new, arbitrated transmission without danger of collision. The basic method for determining the AAT values is as follows:

(1) The highest priority port may transmit after the cable has been idle long enough for the port to have received a priority transmission from the most distant port, if one had occurred.

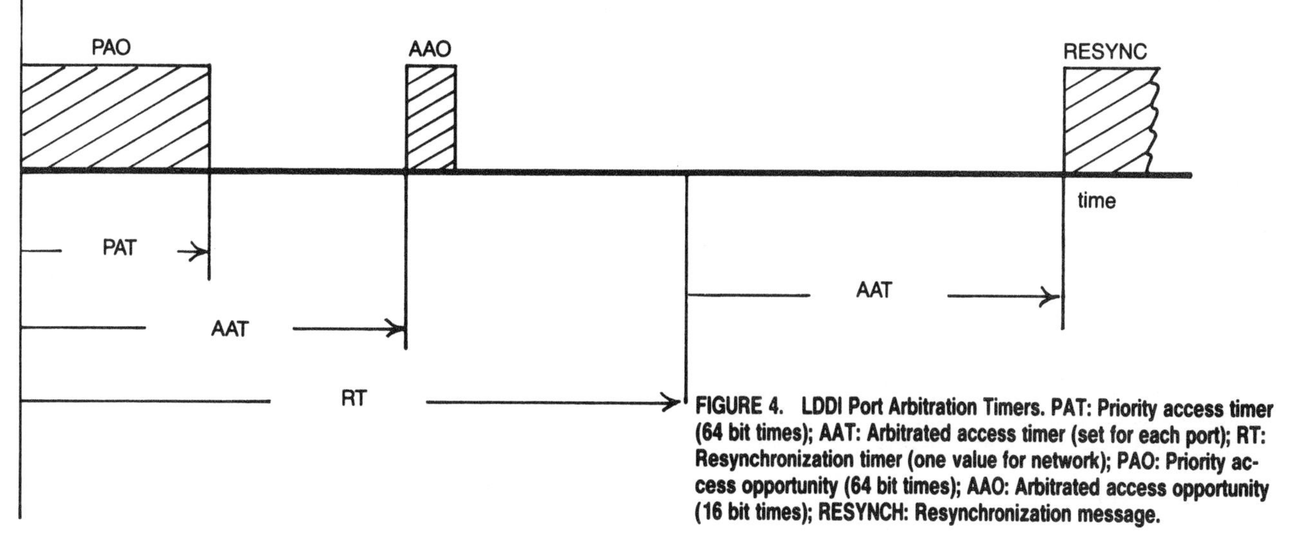

FIGURE 4. LDDI Port Arbitration Timers. PAT: Priority access timer (64 bit times); AAT: Arbitrated access timer (set for each port); RT: Resynchronization timer (one value for network); PAO: Priority access opportunity (64 bit times); AAO: Arbitrated access opportunity (16 bit times); RESYNCH: Resynchronization message.

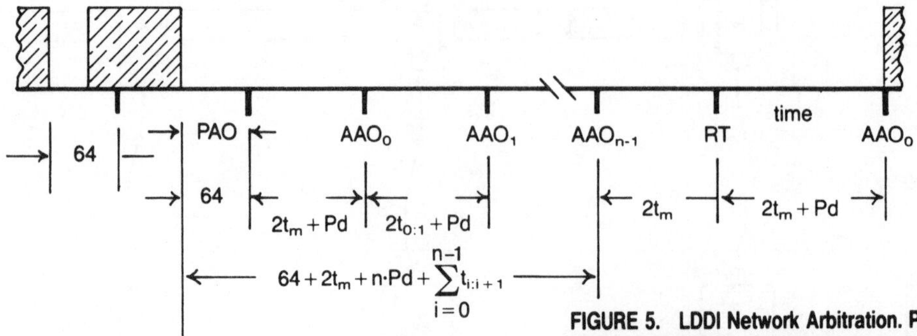

FIGURE 5. LDDI Network Arbitration. PAO: Priority access opportunity (64 bit times); AAT_x: Arbitrated access opportunity for port x; RT: Resynchronization time expires; t_m: Maximum end-to-end propagation delay; $t_{x,y}$: propagation delay from port x to port y; Pd: Port delay (includes 16 bit time arbitrated access opportunity plus turn on and recognition delays).

(2) Each successively lower priority port must delay while the cable is idle until it has had time to receive an arbitrated transmission from the immediately higher priority port, if it transmits.

The third timer, the Resynchronizing Timer (RT), may be set alike at all ports to the time by which every port would have received a transmission from the lowest priority port, if it transmits. When the RT expires, the AAT is restarted and a "wait flag" is reset. If the AAT expires again the port transmits a special resynchronizing message (or a "real" message, if one is now available) to resynchronize the timers at all ports. Thus, when traffic is light, the highest priority port periodically transmits resynch messages, preserving medium arbitration clock synchronism.

A wait flag feature is optionally observed at some or all ports. When this feature is used, the wait flag is set whenever the port transmits during an Arbitrated Access Opportunity. While set, the wait flag inhibits Arbitrated Transmissions. The wait flag is reset whenever the RT expires, after every port has had an Arbitrated Access Opportunity. The effect is round robin scheduling among all ports observing the wait flag protocol.

The LDDI arbitration algorithm is appropriate for broadcast radio nets, one- and two-channel star networks, and two-channel head-end buses and single-channel buses. A simple algorithm for assigning AAT timer values is to separate them by one round trip propagation delay plus one port delay. This results in simpler calculation but slower arbitration than by individually calculating delays between ports of successive priority. On a linear bus, best performance is obtained if the ports are arranged in priority sequence from one end to the other; then the AAT for the lowest priority port may be set to 64 bit times, plus four end-to-end propagation delays, plus the sum of the port delays of all higher priority ports.

LDDI arbitration *prevents* collisions rather than detecting them on the fly and retransmitting them, as does Ethernet. If appropriate higher layer protocols are used, the LDDI arbitration can support a "deterministic" network (worst case service times are bounded in the absence of noise). Collisions do not occur and will not degrade channel capacity or service times. The algorithm is stable at any load and passive failures at one port do not affect the arbitration of other ports. It may be used with almost any broadcast medium. Its salient disadvantage is the need to individually compute timer settings for each port for highest performance.

DATA LINK LAYER

The LDDI data link layer frame is illustrated in Figure 6. As

D	S	L	I(VARIABLE)	FCS

FIGURE 6. Data Link Frame Format. D: Destination address; S: Source address; L: Length field; I: Information (variable length); FCS: Frame check sequence.

a security measure, the LDDI Data Link Transmitter function inserts the source address in the message header. Higher layers supply the destination address, a 16 bit value for the information field length and the variable length information field. When the information field has been transmitted, a 32-bit frame check sequence, protecting both the header and the information field, is appended by the Transmitter.

The Data Link Layer Receiver first examines the destination address of incoming frames. If it matches the address of that port, the header and information field are passed up to higher layers; otherwise the frame is ignored. The length field is used to locate the end of the information field and the beginning of the FCS. If the FCS is correct, a signal is sent to the network layer saying that the frame is valid; if the FCS is not correct, an error signal is sent to the network layer.

The OSI Model states, "The objective of this layer is to detect *and possibly correct* errors which may occur in the physical layer" (emphasis added). The data link layer detects transmission errors, but does not correct them. No aspect of the LDDI caused as much discussion in X3T9.5 as error detection and correction. The committee was aware of the properties of forward error-correcting codes which are widely used to protect data stored on magnetic disks. Forward error correction is necessary for disks, because data is written today but read months or years later; it is not possible to recover from the error by going back to the original data. With a local network, it is easy to retain a copy of the transmitted frame at a source port until the destination port acknowledges the receipt of an error-free frame and to retransmit if the frame is damaged. If transmission error rates are low, the straightforward error recovery procedure for local networks is retransmission.

The LDDI data link layer protocol does not, however, acknowledge the receipt of valid frames and cannot therefore retransmit erroneous frames. The rationale is (1) that such a service is unnecessary for performance reasons, since a high quality medium can (and must) be guaranteed, and that transmission errors will be infrequent; (2) provision is made with the Arbitrated Access Opportunity for "immediate" acknowledgments by higher layers; and (3) application layer to application layer acknowledgment and recovery may still be needed. Even if correct data link layer entity to data link layer entity delivery were guaranteed, the source application would have no assurance that higher layers were operating properly. Consider writing to a disk. The source application entity needs an acknowledgment indicating that the data was correctly received, written to disk, and then read back; nothing less ensures that the data is properly recorded.

The LDDI philosophy is very similar to that of conventional parallel I/O channels, where infrequent parity errors cause host interrupts, and recovery is the responsibility of host software and also similar to that of Ethernet, another local area network. These are very different from telecommunications data link protocols, such as ADCCP [1] which does error detection, retransmission, and lost and duplicate message detection. ADCCP must deal with noisy, switched public lines, and a performance penalty would result if recovery from frequent transmission errors had to be "bounced upstairs" to higher layers. It is unnecessary for local networks to recover from transmission errors at the data link layer, since they can provide comparable reliability by virtue of a more reliable interconnection medium.

STATUS AND PROSPECTS

Three LDDI standards proposals have been completed by the task group, X3T9.5, which developed them, approved by its parent committee X3T9, and forwarded to American National Standards Committee X3, Computers and Information Processing, where they have been reviewed and ballotted. The response was 34 yes votes and 4 substantive no votes to which the technical committee must respond. X3T9 is now preparing its response, which could include changes in the proposed standard. As was mentioned earlier, X3T9 has begun work on a companion data link dependent Network Layer Protocol in addition to the three LDDI standards proposals.

The development of the LDDI proposals from their inception to complete draft proposed American National Standards has taken somewhat over three years. A roughly comparable period will probably be required for the X3 and American National Standards Institute approval process. This reflects the inherent time constants of an open, voluntary standards process; a six- or seven-year period from inception to publication of a standard is quite usual.

The protocols are being simulated in a joint National Bureau of Standards—Lawrence Livermore Laboratory effort and compared with simulations and measurements of traffic on Lawrence Livermore Laboratory's Hyperchannel network. At the National Bureau of Standards, a reduced data rate protocol testbed for the physical and data link layer protocols has been implemented. There are a few minor (for the purpose of protocol validation and performance measurement) differences. The National Bureau of Standards experimental network uses the LDDI arbitration algorithm, but uses 8 bit rather than 16 bit addresses and a 16 bit rather than a 32 bit frame check sequence. The National Bureau of Standards experimental network is a 10 Mbit/s, two-channel broadcast star, rather than the 50 Mbit/s, one-channel bus of the LDDI proposal. Adapters for four 16-bit microcomputers and a network monitor have been built, and testing and design of experimental network and higher layer protocols is underway.

The focus of the National Bureau of Standards effort is to validate and measure the efficiency of the LDDI arbitration protocol and provide a testbed for a higher layer protocols. Connecting 16 bit microcomputers with a 10 Mbit/s link scales fairly well to a 50 Mbit/s connection between mainframes. A 0.5 km optical cable segment simulates the greater propagation delay (in bit times) experienced at 50 Mbit/s.

Introdution of products based upon the LDDI is probably several years away. Three companies now make 50–70 Mbit/s networks which are similar but not compatible. Attachments to these networks are expensive today (on the order of $20K–$40K per port) which limits the market. It is unlikely that current products will be adapted to the LDDI protocols. The situation will change, however, with the introduction of large scale integration (LSI) chips for implementing such networks. One semiconductor vendor has announced a chip set, to be available in 1984, which can be used to implement the LDDI protocols at 50 Mbits/s [2]. This will change costs considerably and commercial availability of LDDI compatible products probably will follow the introduction of these chips.

If adopted, the protocol standards, which can be implemented as needed in faster new circuitry, should have a long useful life. The life expectancy of the cable interface may be shorter; within a decade, 50 Mbit/s will probably be too slow for the highest performance storage devices. In a few years, the cable interface may need to be revised to permit higher transfer rates or supplanted by a fundamentally different interface, such as an optical fiber star, which would work with the LDDI protocols.

CONCLUSIONS

The proposed LDDI American National Standards include data link and physical layer protocols as well as a serial coaxial bus physical interface. All are suitable for block transfers between a reasonable number of high data rate (50 Mbits/s) devices. Neither the protocols nor the bus interface are major departures from already proven designs. The cable and its interface can be implemented with inexpensive readily available components. The two protocols may be implemented at high rates entirely in straightforward combinational and sequential logic; no programmable engine is needed. The protocols are able to support almost any local broadcast interconnection medium and to support a wide range of network or higher layer protocols. Facilities are provided for higher layers to implement datagrams, immediate acknowledgment messages, or extended exclusive dialogues between two cooperating ports. A reliable data link layer service is provided to higher layers by virtue of a reliable cable interface and a 32-bit FCS, which will detect transmission errors. Both fair (round robin) and priority access to the broadcast medium are supported, as well as combinations of the two. Despite their derivation from proven networks, the proposed standards look to the future, are not a formalization of old "de facto" technology or any previously existing network, and, in consequence, do not favor one present vendor of high performance networks over another. They should have a long and useful life.

Tutorial follows

WHAT DOES "LOCAL" MEAN?

There are many definitions of "local" network, most of which involve some distance limit, and frequently, single ownership of the network and everything connected to it. In the author's view, the "localness" of a network is primarily a function of the number of "bits on the fly" through the network. The author offers the following definition:

A local network is a network where the end-to-end signal propagation delay is large compared with a single bit transmission duration and small compared with the typical message transmission duration.

As a consequence of this definition, the higher the transfer rate, the less local the network, and a 50 km, 1 Mbit/s network is equivalent to a 1 km, 50 Mbit/s network in locality. A satellite network is then the antithesis of a local network, even if the endpoints are just across the street. Still, most local network protocols can be used if the data transfer rate is slow enough so that packet durations are long compared with the half-second propagation delays of geosynchronous satellites. A 50 Mbit/s LDDI network with 1 km of cable (the longest supported) will have about 200 bits on the fly from one end to the other, and typical message lengths will probably be on the order of 10^3 to 10^4 bits.

An incidental property of most local networks is very low channel error rates compared with typical long distance or common carrier networks, eliminating the performance need for very quick low level error recovery; hardware error detection with relatively slow software error correction procedures will usually suffice for local networks.

LOCAL NETWORK TOPOLOGIES

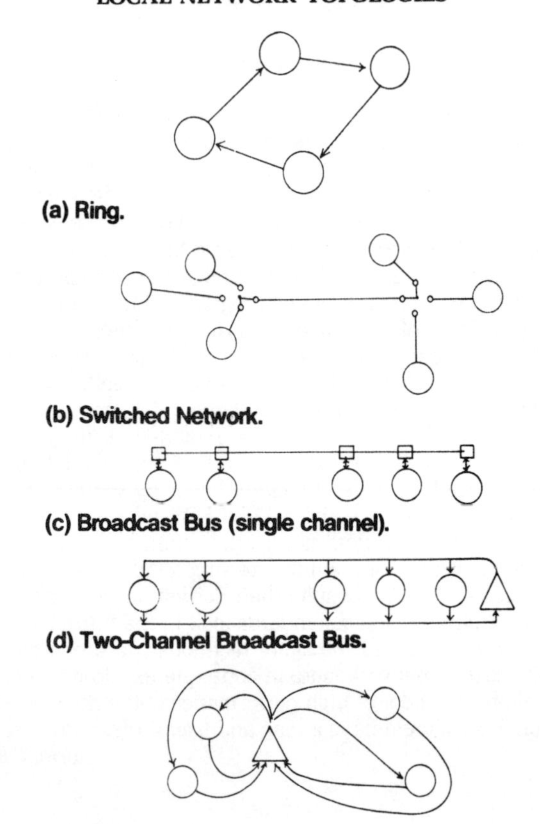

(a) Ring.

(b) Switched Network.

(c) Broadcast Bus (single channel).

(d) Two-Channel Broadcast Bus.

(e) Two-Channel Star.

Local networks can be broken into rings, broadcast, and switched networks. In ring networks, data is passed from one port to the next and regenerated at each port in a closed loop. Either the sending or the receiving port removes the message from the ring. In a broadcast network, every message transmitted by any one port is received by every other port without intervening storage or switching. A switched network, of course, involves some kind of switch and may involve storing and later forwarding messages.

Rings, of course, have a closed-loop topology. Switched networks may be a simple star, with the switch at the center, or many switches may be connected together to form a more general network, with alternative routes between ports.

The LDDI is a broadcast network. The most fundamental distinction in broadcast topologies is between those which use a single channel to both send and receive, and those which use separate send and receive channels (with two cables or by multiplexing in one cable), connected by some central amplifier, coupler, or repeater. Two channel networks may be either stars, trees, or linear buses.

Collision detection in two-channel networks is possible using bit-by-bit comparison of received data to transmitted data, or by logic at the amplifier; this makes such networks suitable for broadband signaling with a CSMA-CD protocol. In single-channel networks, broadband CSMA-CD is generally impractical, but baseband CSMA-CD can use analog means or code violations to detect collisions. The LDDI physical layer protocol prevents rather than detects collisions. It is suitable for any broadcast topology, and either baseband or broadband signaling. The present LDDI Cable Interface Proposal, however, is a single-channel, broadband linear bus. With a single-channel bus topology, the physical layer protocol can arbitrate any number of ports in four end-to-end bus propagation delays plus the sum of the individual port logic delays.

BROADCAST NETWORK ARBITRATION

Aloha. With this simple strategy, each port simply transmits as soon as it has a message to send. Two ports may transmit simultaneously causing a "collision." An error-detecting code is used by the receiver to detect collisions and a "backoff" algorithm may then be used to retransmit unacknowledged messages. Aloha works well when traffic is light, but channel throughput falls to zero with even modest offered loads. For this reason, Aloha is obviously unsuitable for a CPU-to-disk connection. Aloha, or a variation called "Slotted Aloha," is useful for long distance broadcast networks, since none of the CSMA schemes work well when propagation delays exceed typical packet transmission times.

Carrier Sense Multiple Access (CSMA). This is a listen-before-talk protocal where a port with a message to send checks for an active channel; if the channel is idle, the message is transmitted, while if it is active, the port defers to the current transmitter. When the channel becomes idle, some backoff procedure may be employed to reduce the probability that two ports will transmit simultaneously. This procedure may guarantee that collisions will not occur, or it may simply reduce the probability of collision. The LDDI uses a collision-free CSMA arbitration protocol with resynchronizing messages to maintain clock synchronism after long idle periods. Hyperchannel is similar, but enters a free-for-all mode when the channel is idle for long periods, and collisions are possible, but infrequent.

Token Bus. Just as with physical rings, broadcast media may be arbitrated by token passing. The port which receives the token may transmit one or more messages and then pass the token to the next port in the logical ring. Steady-state operation is quite simple, and token arbitration is efficient for modest numbers of ports in the arbitration ring. Lost token and duplicate token recovery are complex, however, and token bus systems frequently include some provisions for ports to dynamically enter or leave the logical arbitration ring, which is also complex. The complexity of these protocols and the "thinking time" required for token processing militate against token passing in a high bandwidth network such as the LDDI. ARCNET[1] is a widely used, commercially available broadcast token network, and IEEE Committee P802 has developed a proposed token bus standard.

BASEBAND VERSUS BROADBAND

Despite their wide use, the author is not aware of a truly satisfying definition of the terms "baseband" and "broadband" as applied to local networks. In general communications usage, baseband refers to a signal before it modulates a carrier and broadband to the signal after the carrier has been modulated. Some local network transmission schemes which are generally classified as baseband can, however, be viewed as the modulation of a carrier by the transmitted data. Nonetheless, much passion is expended in arguments about whether baseband or broadband is better for a network application.

In general, baseband schemes use the cable spectrum from dc to several times the bit rate (counting harmonics needed to get sufficiently fast signal rise times), while broadband systems use the spectrum immediately around some higher frequency carrier. If frequency division multiplexing is used, then it is a broadband system.

Frequency division multiplexing is a primary reason for using broadband transmission schemes. In principle, one can operate a large number of separate networks on a single cable by frequency division multiplexing. The goal of some broadband systems is to use a single cable to carry several networks, telephone traffic, and a number of television channels.

Because they do not require a modulator/demodulator (modem), baseband systems are generally less expensive but do not allow frequency multiplexing. Since signal attenuation (in dB) for coaxial cable varies as the square root of frequency, baseband cables of the same length have less attenuation and a smaller dynamic signal range, which may allow collision detection on single-channel systems. On the other hand, at high bandwidth, baseband cables are more affected by phase dispersion, a phenomenon resulting from differing propagation velocities at differing frequencies.

Both baseband and broadband techniques have been demonstrated to work at 50 Mbits/s. The LDDI broadband system is comparatively inexpensive to implement, partly because it uses some mass produced cable TV components, and partly because it sacrifices the usual goal of broadband systems: frequency multiplexing.

The LDDI broadband interface uses the cable spectrum from about 35 MHz to 225 MHz, which more than encompasses the broadcast spectrum of the 12 VHF TV channels, commercial FM radio, and aeronautical radio. Moreover, to allow for inexpensive transmitter implementations, suppression of out-of-band harmonics is not required, preventing the use of the remaining spectrum for other services. The LDDI, then, uses a broadband interface, which has most of the properties usually associated with baseband interfaces: it is inexpensive but does not permit frequency division multiplexing.

HOW MAGNETIC DISKS AFFECT THE LDDI

The main use for the LDDI is connecting large computers to high performance magnetic disks, as well as to each other. Magnetic disks are the primary file, swapping and paging store in most computer systems. Any interface which appreciably reduces perceived magnetic disk performance will have a marked adverse effect on overall computer system performance. Two performance parameters characterize magnetic disks fairly well: latency (which has both a head movement and rotational component), and transfer rate. State-of-the-art magnetic disks store on the order of 10^{10} bits of data on one spindle, with a 24 Mbit/s transfer rate (from one head; a few specialized disks run several heads in parallel to achieve transfer rates from 40 to 100 Mbits/s) and have latencies on the order of a few tens of milliseconds. Performance of swapping computer systems and sequential file accesses are limited primarily by the transfer rate, while paging systems and direct file accesses "see" mostly latency effects.

Disk traffic is usually inherently bursty, that is, the disk spends most of the time spinning, and transfers only occasional bursts of data at high rates. Thus, several disks may share the same cable, with only occasional interference with one another. Swapping does, however, generate long transfers which must be done quickly. The Priority Access Opportunity of the LDDI is intended to facilitate holding the network so that large amounts of data can be streamed between the disk and a host, without slipping disk revolutions between successive blocks. This may cause other network users to wait, but little is more important to a swapping system than swapping.

Paging systems and direct file accesses are, in contrast, primarily sensitive to latency. Network arbitration latencies should be on the order of 1 ms or less so that they are small compared to typical magnetic disk latencies; this is not difficult for the LDDI to achieve with a 1 km cable since 1 ms is about 200 end-to-end propagation delays.

Computer systems depend heavily on the correct operation of the disk and its communication paths. While software checksums may be selectively applied to key application data, there is no hope of general software checks of the correctness of all data read from disks; there is much too much such data and to do so would make a mainframe perform like a microprocessor. Data passed over parallel buses between computers and controllers are typically protected by careful electrical design and bus parity checks. Data passed over controller to drive ("device level") interfaces are usually protected across the interface and on the recording surfaces by forward error-correcting codes. Data are frequently protected inside the computer by parity checks on buses, and parity or Hamming codes in main store; microcomputer systems frequently dispense entirely with parity checks, relying only on electrical design.

Even before error detection and correction are applied, raw disk and network error rates must be very low, or the effects on system performance will be intolerable while undetected errors have catastrophic effects on system integrity. The LDDI prevents collisions, which reduces one source of error (collision detection has a similar effect on the unde-

[1] ARCNET is a trademark of Datapoint Corporation.

tected error rate) and uses a strong 32-bit FCS to ensure error detection.

Disk interfaces must be highly reliable and introduce little latency of their own. Networks with many successive hop-by-hop connections dynamic routing, storage at intermediate nodes, and the like, while common in communications applications, cause too much latency and are generally too complex and insufficiently reliable to be put between a disk and a CPU. Data link (that is hardware) level error recovery is not generally needed for magnetic disk interfaces because of their reliability and, as with present operating systems disk and interfaces, infrequent LDDI errors will be handled by specialized driver programs, which, since error recovery may involve using alternate cables (routing), is probably best thought of as a network layer process.

A network layer, devoted to managing the LDDI network and recovering from network errors, will be needed. This layer will apply both to communications with peripherals as well as to local host-to-host and "open" communications with other networks through standard internet and transport layer protocols, presenting a uniform and highly reliable service to all. This is similar to drivers for current parallel interfaces; that is, there is frequently a very low level operating system driver layer which handles the scheduling of I/O, the fielding of interrupts, and, sometimes, recovery from bus errors, before passing off to a device specific driver.

What would be intolerable for magnetic disks is many repetitive levels of protocol, in both the network adapter and the host CPU, which repetitively check for or correct similar errors. Telecommunications applications, with their comparatively low data rates, and more complex protocols and failure modes, may operate this way, but it is no way to run a disk. Computer system vendors cannot be expected to turn their operating systems inside out to suit an arbitrary seven-layer model of telecommunications networks in a matter so central to the local system and its performance as how disks are handled.

Consider a **read** operation. It is conventional with present parallel interfaces to receive an immediate acknowledgment from the disk controller which indicates that a **read** command has been received, parses properly, and that the disk is able to execute the command (i.e., is not offline or locked by another host). We can expect LDDI higher level disk protocols to be similar. If a data block then read from a disk is damaged by the network, if a **read** command packet is damaged in any of the buses or buffers between the network and the host's main store, or if the disk is simply momentarily busy, the recovery is the same: repeat the **Read** operation.

Consider next a write to disk. In addition to acknowledgments that the command has been accepted and that blocks have been properly received by the disk, a final acknowledgment is often needed indicating that the disk has read the data after recording it and found it to be correctly recorded. Here there is a difference between the response to a block damaged by the network and one that fails a read-back check. If the block is damaged by the network, the write operation is repeated. If there is a bad spot on the disk, however, then some sort of alternative block assignment is first needed on the disk. This may involve a complex sequence of operations to find a suitable alternative and to flag the original block with a suitable pointer. Then the bad block may be rewritten.

Intelligent disks, that is, disks with significant processing power in their controllers, may off-load most normal disk error-recovery functions, Still, it is likely that host CPUs will retain some final error recovery functions, and intelligent disks will introduce complications of their own. They may, particularly in multiprocesser systems, schedule their activity on a shortest latency first basis rather than on a first-in, first-out basis. The effect to hosts will be similar to out-of-order packets; the host will not be able to assume that **reads** are serviced on a first-in, first-out basis. The logic for coping with this in the host can probably also cope with out-of-order packets from the network (if the network can generate them).

In most systems, the volume of traffic between disks and host CPUs would dwarf all other traffic in terms of the amount of data moved over the network. In most cases, adding open message traffic on the LDDI would have a negligible effect. However, the cost of a short frame, in channel time, is nearly as great as a fairly long frame, because of network protocol overhead. It is the length of the cable, and propagation delay, rather than transfer rate, which determine the number of short packets which a broadcast network can accommodate. A 1 Mit/s or a 10 Mbit/s network can handle nearly as many short messages as a 50 Mbit/s network. The LDDI may prove to be a somewhat clumsy choice for terminal traffic. Moreover, general purpose communications protocols may generate many short control messages. Such traffic might, perhaps, significantly load a LDDI network and interfere with disk traffic, even though comparatively little actual data passed over the network. If so, another network would be needed for the open traffic.

Acknowledgments. The author wishes to thank Mr. Robert J. Carpenter of the National Bureau of Standards for his many helpful suggestions in the preparation of this paper.

REFERENCES

1. American National Standard for Advanced Data Communication Control Procedures (ADCCP). ANSI Std. X3.66-1979, American National Standards Institute, New York, 1979.
2. Coleman, V. Siliconizing the local area network. *Comput. Networks 6*, 4 (Sept. 1982), 245–254.
3. Data-Processing-Open Systems Interconnection—Basic Reference Model. ISO Draft Proposal 7498, International Standards Organization, Geneva, Switzerland, Dec. 3, 1980.
4. Draft Proposed American National Standard Data Link Layer Protocol for Local Distributed Data Interfaces. ANSI Std. X3T9.5/031, rev. 11, American National Standards Institute, New York, Aug. 24, 1982.
5. Draft Proposed American National Standard Physical Layer Interface for Local Distributed Interfaces to a Nonbranching Coaxial Cable Bus. ANSI Std. X3T9.5/088, rev. 3, American National Standards Institute, New York, May 10, 1982.
6. Draft Proposed American National Standard Physical Layer Protocol for Local Distributed Data Interfaces. ANSI Std. X3T9.5/036, rev. 8, American National Standards Institute, New York, Aug. 27, 1982.
7. Metcalfe, R.M., and Boggs, D.R. Ethernet: Distributed packet switching for local computer networks. *Comm. ACM 19*, 7 (July 1976), 395–404.
8. Thornton, J.E., Christensen, G.S., and Jones, P.D. A new approach to network storage management. *Comput. Des. 14*, 11 (1975), 81–85.

CR Categories and Subject Descriptors: B.4.2 [**Input/Output and Data Communications**]: Input/Output Devices—*channels and controllers;* C.2.2 [**Computer-Communication Networks**]: Network Protocols—*protocol architecture;* C.2.5 [**Computer-Communication Networks**]: Local Networks—*access schemes, buses*

Received 11/82; revised 3/83

Reprinted with permission from *The Proceedings of the Eighth International Fiber Optics Communications and Local Area Networks Exposition*, 1984, pages 246-250.

CI: A High Speed Interconnect for Computers and Mass Storage Controllers

W. D. Strecker
32-Bit Systems Architecture
and Advanced Development
Digital Equipment Corporation
295 Foster Street
Littleton, Ma. 01460
1-July-1984

1 INTRODUCTION

Typically, multicomputer systems fall into one of two classes: tightly coupled and loosely coupled. Tightly coupled systems are characterized by close physical proximity of the processors, high bandwidth interprocessor communication through shared primary memory, and a single copy of the operating system. In contrast, loosely coupled systems are characterized by physical separation of the processors, lower bandwidth message oriented interprocessor communication, and independent operating systems.

Recent hardware and software engineering work at DEC has focused on building multicomputer systems whose goals are (1) high availability and (2) easy extensibility to a large number of processors and mass storage controllers. To support these goals, a loosely coupled rather than a tightly coupled system was selected.

From a software perspective, the independent operating systems of the loosely coupled system increase the availability of the overall system in the presence of individual operating system failures.

From a hardware perspective, it is difficult to design the

EHO234-5/85/0000/0171$01.00 © 1984 IEEE

physical packaging and memory system of a shared primary memory multiprocessor which is both adequately low in cost for small numbers of processors and mass storage controllers and adequately high in performance for large numbers of processors and mass storage controllers. In contrast, a group of standard single processor computers linked by an external message oriented interconnect facilitates building cost effective systems over a wide range of cost and performance.

A key issue with the loosely coupled approach is system performance. The performance is gated by (1) the bandwidth of the computer interconnect and (2) the software overhead of the associated communications architecture. To address this issue, three steps were taken:

1. The development of a very high speed message oriented interconnect termed the CI (for Computer Interconnect).

2. The development of a simple, low overhead communications architecture whose functions are tailored to the needs of highly available, extensible systems. This architecture is termed SCA (for System Communication Architecture).

3. The development of an intelligent hardware interface to the CI which implements much of SCA. This interface is termed the CI Port.

The loosely coupled system concept has been applied to the DEC VAX-11 computer family and the DEC VAX/VMS operating system. The resulting structure has been given the name VAXcluster. In order to encourage the development of loosely coupled systems by multiple vendors, DEC is proposing the CI as an LDDI (Local Distributed Data

Interface) being standardized by the American National Standards Committee X3T9.5. The remainder of this paper discusses the CI, the CI port, and SCA. To set some context for this discussion, the paper also describes briefly the VAXcluster hardware structure and the central VAXcluster software concept -- the distributed file system. It is anticipated that other vendor's systems based on the LDDI would embody concepts similar to those found in the VAXcluster.

2 VAXCLUSTER HARDWARE STRUCTURE

Fig. 1 shows the hardware structure of a VAXcluster. There are four major elements: the CI, the CI Port, the host computer, and the mass storage controller.

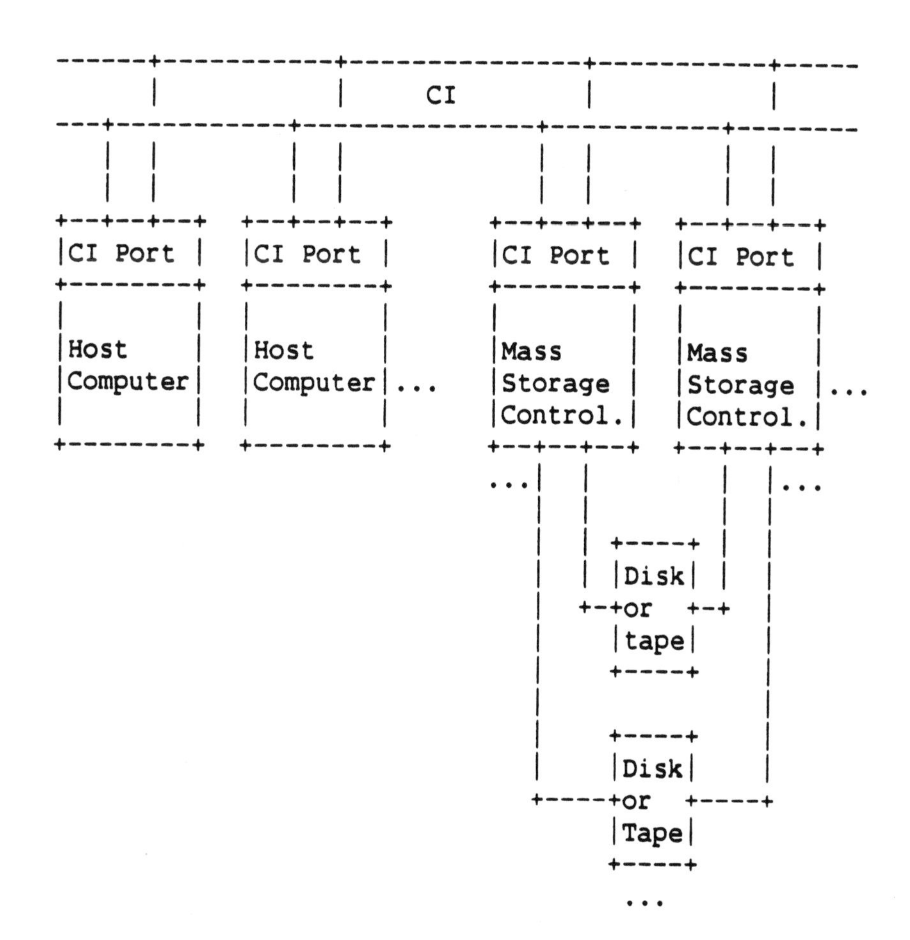

Fig. 1. VAXcluster Hardware Structure

In order to provide redundancy such that there is no single point of failure, there is a minimum of two host computers and two mass storage controllers. All of the mass storage devices are dual ported and attached to two separate mass storage controllers.

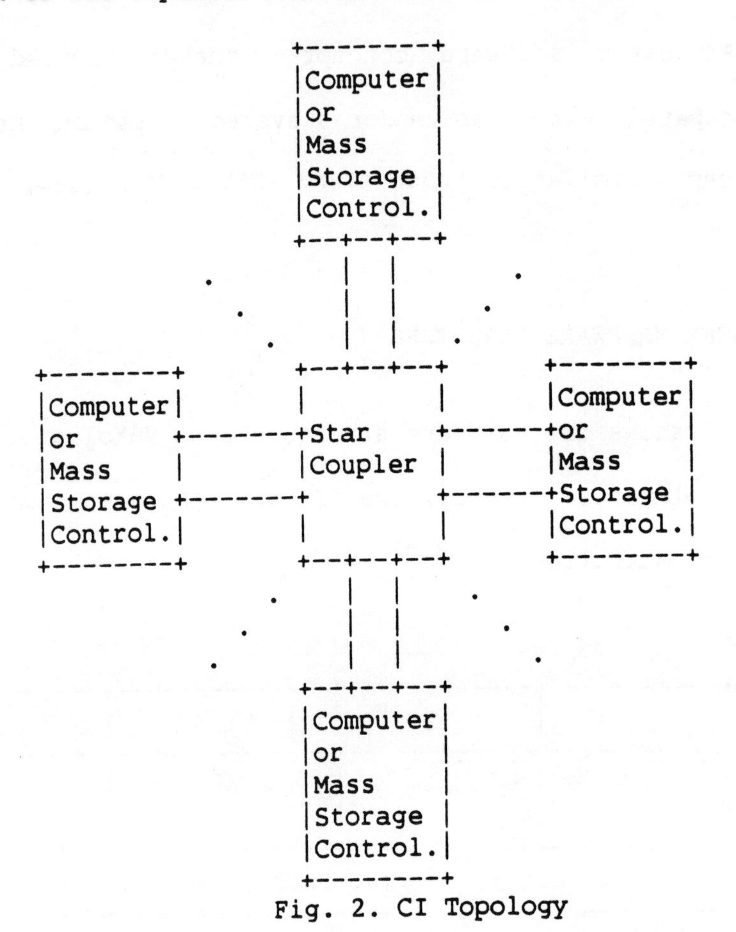

Fig. 2. CI Topology

The CI is dual path serial interconnect with each path supporting a 70 megabit/sec transfer rate. The primary purpose of the dual paths is to provide redundancy in case of path failure; but when both paths are available, they are independently useable. Each path is implemented in two coaxial cables: one for transmitted and one for received signals. Baseband signalling is employed together with Manchester encoding. The physical topology of the CI is that of a star: a central hub termed a Star Coupler with radial paths of up to 45 meters extending to each of the CI nodes. See Fig. 2. The Star Coupler is a passive device supporting up to 16 nodes each of which may be either a host computer or mass storage controller. Interfaces to the CI are transformer coupled providing electrical isolation between the nodes.

A star topology was selected over a linear topology for three reasons:

1. The efficiency of arbitration of a serial bus is related to the transit time between the most widely separated nodes. The star topology permits the nodes to be located anywhere within a 45 meter radius circle (about 6400 square meters) with a maximum node separation of 90 meters. In general, a linear bus threaded through 16 nodes in the same area would greatly exceed 90 meters in length.

2. The central Star Coupler permits the addition and removal of nodes with a minimum risk of electrical or mechanical disruption of the CI.

3. The star topology facilitates two possible future extensions to the CI: first, an active Star Coupler permitting many more than 16 nodes and, second, replacement of the coaxial cables with fiber optic cables.

Data is transferred on the CI in variable length packets (or frames) whose format is given in Fig. 3.

The source and destination address fields of the packet are 1 byte permitting architecturally up to 256 nodes in a VAXcluster. The destination address is specified in true and complement form to minimize the chance that a failure in address generation or recognition logic would cause an otherwise good packet to be received by the wrong node. The packet is protected by a 32-bit cyclic redundancy check.

Bit Sync	5 bytes
Character Sync	1 byte
Type/Length	1 or 2 bytes
Destination	1 byte
Complement of Destination	1 byte
Source	1 byte
Body (data)	up to 4K bytes
CRC	4 bytes
Trailer	6 bytes

Fig. 3. CI Packet Format

The CI is arbitrated using a carrier sense, multiple access, collision avoidance (CSMA/CA) method. Arbitration is performed independently for each path. Arbitration details are given in Fig. 4.

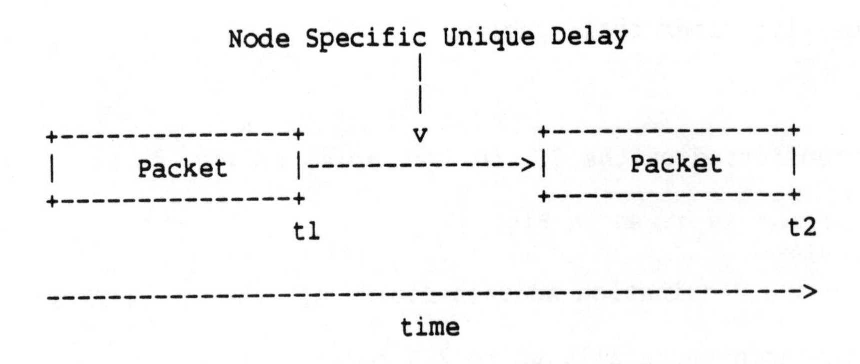

Fig. 4. CI Arbitration

A node N wishing to use the CI waits until the CI becomes quiet (no carrier sensed). Let this be t1 in Fig. 4. At this point node N waits a unique, node specific delay time. If the CI is still quiet, then node N wins the arbitration and sends its packet. If the CI is not quiet, some other node has won the arbitration and is currently using the CI. Node N waits again until the CI is quiet (t2 in Fig. 4.) and repeats the process.

Under heavy loading, this arbitration method is essentially collision free because all the nodes are effectively synchronized in their determination of when the CI becomes idle. Under light to moderate loading collisions do occur, but the colliding nodes then become synchronized and further collisions are avoided.

Nodes having shorter delay times have priority over those with longer delay times. Since for many applications this is undesireable, nodes are assigned a pair of delay times -- one relatively short and one relatively long. Under heavy loading, nodes alternate between use of the short and long delay times insuring that all nodes have equal access to the CI.

4 CI PORT

The CI Port is the interface between the CI and a host computer or mass storage controller. The CI Port offloads much of the work in communicating among host computers and mass storage controllers.

At the lowest level, the CI Port performs the CI arbitration described earlier. After winning the arbitration, the sending Port -- Port 1 in Fig. 5 -- sends a data packet and waits for receipt of an acknowledgement packet. If the data packet is correctly received, the receiving Port -- Port 2 in Fig. 5 -- immediately returns an acknowledgement packet. The amount of time required for the CI port to generate an acknowledgement packet is less than the smallest node specific delay. Hence the acknowledgement packet can be sent without re-arbitrating the CI. The acknowledgement packet effectively reuses the arbitration for the data packet. If a positive acknowledgement is not received, the sending CI Port retries the operation up to a specified retry limit.

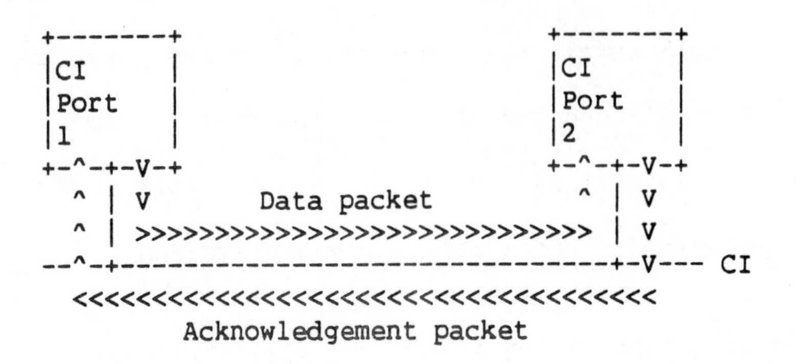

Fig. 5. Data and Acknowledgement Packets

When both CI paths are available, the CI Port statistically arbitrates and distributes transmissions across both paths. This insures path load balancing and continual verification that both paths are operational. The notion of path availability is maintained on a per node basis in each CI Port in a data structure termed the path status table. Fig. 6 shows a hypothetical path status table for node 1. Note that it is possible that path 1 might be bad to one node and good to another node.

Access to Node	Using Path 1	Using Path 2
0	bad	good
1	good	good
2	good	good
=		=
15	good	bad

Fig. 6. Hypothetical Path Status Table for Node 1

The CI Port will only attempt to use good paths as indicated in the path status table. If the CI Port is unsuccessful in sending data on a path marked good when the retry limit is exhausted, it will change the path to bad in the path status table. If the other path is good, the CI Port will automatically try up to the retry limit on the other path. Only if both paths are bad will a CI Port operation fail.

A key contributor to the performance is the capability of the CI Ports to directly transfer data between memory buffers in different nodes. By issuing a single command to its local CI port, a local node can read the contents of an arbitrarily sized buffer in remote node into a local buffer or write the contents of an arbitrarily sized local buffer to a buffer in a remote node. See Fig. 7.

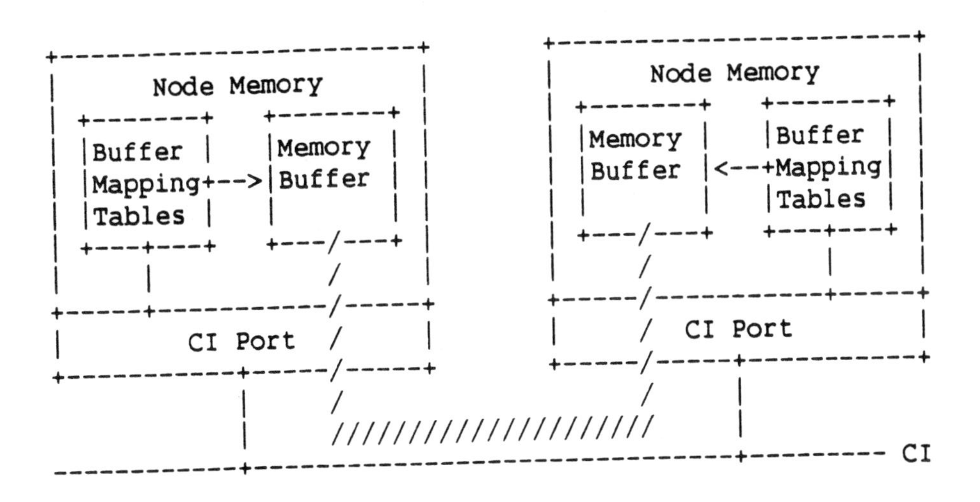

Fig. 7. Buffer to Buffer Transfers

The local and remote CI Ports cooperate in a read or write operation by:

1. Breaking the transfer up into maximum sized CI data packets.

2. Insuring that all packets of the transfer are correctly sent and received.

3. Referencing the memory buffers specified in the transfer through buffer mapping tables. In the case of a host computer, the CI port uses the host computer page tables to map the memory buffers.

5 SCA

SCA provides the mechanism by which the software components of the VAXcluster communicate. An implementation of SCA provides four basic communication services:

1. Connection management - a connection is a logical communication path between two software processes. The connection management service establishes these connections. Once a connection is established, the following three SCA services can be used.

2. Datagram transfer - a datagram is a small information unit (typically tens to hundreds of bytes) which is sent over a connection. Delivery of a datagram is not guaranteed. Datagrams, for example, are used for certain types of status information which are periodically generated and whose loss is not critical. Datagrams are also used by software components which have their own protocols for insuring reliable communication: the DECnet network manager is an example of this.

3. Message transfer - like a datagram, a message is a small unit of information sent over a connection. Delivery of a message is guaranteed and requires a more elaborate protocol than for datagram transfer to insure the delivery. Messages, for example, are used to send disk read and write requests from a host computer to a mass storage controller.

4. Block data transfer - block data is arbitrarily sized data moved between memory buffers. Delivery of block data is also guaranteed. The block data service, for example, is used by the mass storage controller to move the data associated with disk read or write requests to or from the host computer.

6 VAXCLUSTER SOFTWARE

The VAXcluster software structure is a set of independent VAX/VMS operating systems which communicate using SCA services.

The most important software concept of the VAXcluster is the distributed file system in which all files appear local to each of the operating systems in the VAXcluster. The distributed file system supports the goals of availability and extensibility as follows:

1. As new disks are added, the associated files are immediately available to all host computers. Similarly, as new host computers are added, all file storage is immediately available to the new host computers.

2. When a host computer implementing an application fails, the application can be moved to another host computer. The new host computer has exactly the same access capabilities to the application's files as did the failed host computer.

To understand the evolution of the VAX/VMS operating system from a single computer operating system to the VAXcluster operating system, a simple example of file processing is considered for both the single computer and the VAXcluster environments. Fig. 8 shows file processing in a single computer.

File requests are passed to the file manager which manages the file system. The file manager maps the file operation into reads or

Fig. 8. File Processing in a Single Computer

writes of specific disk blocks and calls the disk manager. The disk manager performs the physical reading or writing of the disk by issuing commands to the disk controller.

Fig. 9. shows the same type of file processing in a VAXcluster. In Fig. 9 the CI, CI Port, and SCA are represented abstractly. There are three nodes on the CI. Nodes 1 and 2 are host computers. Node 3 is a mass storage controller. The host computers have file managers and disk managers structured as before. In Fig. 9 there are three SCA connections: disk manager 1 to disk controller 3; disk manager 2 to disk controller 3; and file manager 1 to file manager 2. The disk manager/disk controller connection allows each disk manager to directly issue commands to the disk controller. The connection between the file managers is used to pass information to synchronize

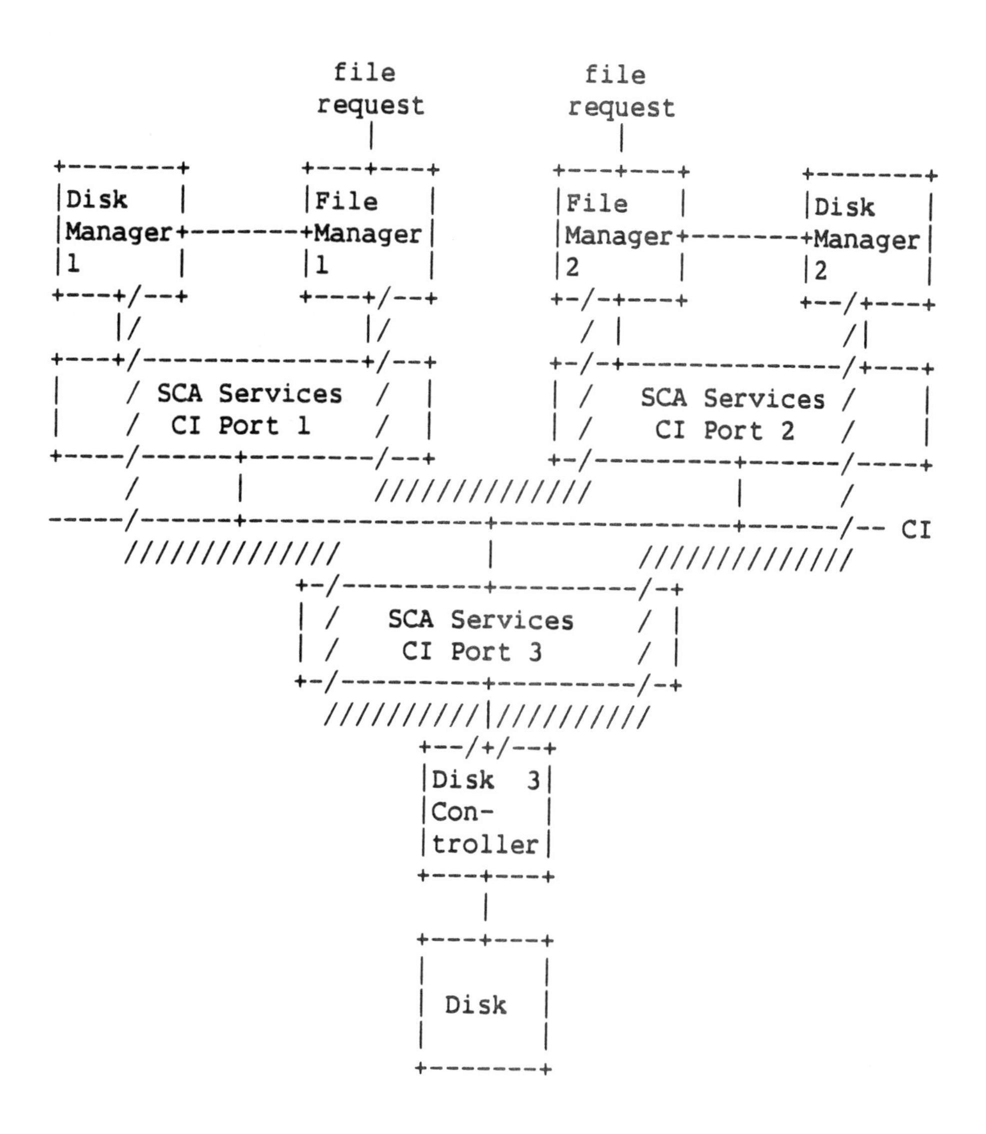

Fig. 9. File Processing in a VAXcluster

state changes in the file system to insure that each file manager has a consistent definition of the file system.

7 SUMMARY

The CI is a high speed message oriented serial interconnect for host computers and mass storage controllers. Implementing the performance critical functions of a communications architecture in the hardware interface to the CI provides the basis for a high performance loosely coupled system. Hardware redundancy and a distributed file system enable the loosely coupled system to achieve its goals of high availability and easy extensibility.

Sunil Joshi and Venkatraman Iyer, Advanced Micro Devices, Sunnyvale, Calif.

New standards for local networks push upper limits for lightwave data

Recent activities in ANSI committees foretell a different yardstick for high-speed local fiber networks.

While other standards bodies now specify top-end data rates of 10 Mbit/s for local networks, the American National Standards Institute (ANSI) is developing network standards for data rates an order of magnitude higher—around 100 Mbit/s. These are not futuristic speeds. Most companies involved in developing these standards plan to introduce products supporting such data rates during 1985 and are pushing to finalize the standard by mid-1984. Called the Fiber Distributed Data Interface (FDDI), this proposed new ANSI standard (currently in committee X3T9.5) specifies a token-passing ring architecture for local networks using optical fiber cable.

There are two reasons for the need for high data rate networks: a dramatic increase in computer processing power over the last few years and an enormous increase in the volume of stored or processed data. As a result, it is the lower-speed local networks that quickly become the weak link between devices needing to transfer huge amounts of data as quickly as possible.

Clearly, data rate requirements depend on the services supplied and the network's application. For example, back-end networks, which connect computers to other storage devices and peripherals, require high-speed data transfer. These networks have a fairly small number of nodes (frequently fewer than 50), and span relatively small distances—usually within a computer room. In general, a backbone network has to be at least as fast as the devices on it in order to minimize buffering constraints. As the speeds of hard disks and optical disks increase beyond 40 or 50 Mbit/s, back-end networks need to be even faster. In addition, protocols for such networks must provide for "streaming" operations, in which several data packets are sent end-to-end in a single network access. This is essential for disk transfers because, with streaming, disks can send entire tracks of data in one access, eliminating the wait for a complete disk revolution between network access opportunities.

Backbone

An organization wishing to connect its token bus, token ring and Ethernet networks would use a special bridge or gateway network to do so. Known as a backbone network, these interconnecting links can span distances of up to several kilometers, often connecting many floors of a building or even several buildings together. Since internetwork traffic is funneled through the backbone, it has to be able to accept fairly high data rates. Also, devices requiring high throughput can be connected directly to the backbone. Large mainframes in different buildings, for example, may have direct connections to the backbone. Or, a distributed PBX architecture can be implemented by connecting the local PBXs in each building via the backbone network, which likewise should be fast enough to carry real-time voice information.

Unlike back-ends, front-end networks typically connect computers to devices that are more user-interactive, such as terminals, word processors, workstations, and printers. Front-end networks can have hundreds of nodes spanning a few kilometers. The IEEE 802.3, 802.4, and 802.5 standards (see "Local network standards") are essentially designed for front-end applications.

Until now users have been satisfied with data rates of 10 Mbit/s or so for front-end networks. But if it were available—and affordable—most network users would welcome higher data rates and their services.

For example, a 10-Mbit/s data rate is not sufficient to support many real-time voice conversations, much

Reprinted with permission from *Data Communications*, July 1984, pages 127-138.

Local network standards

Numerous standards committees in the United States are standardizing various layers of the International Organization for Standardization (ISO) seven-layer Open System Interconnect (OSI) model. The most notable are the IEEE and ANSI committees, the primary focus of which has been ISO's physical and data link layers (table).

The IEEE is comprised of professional engineers, whereas ANSI membership is comprised of companies. ANSI is also the official body representing the United States in ISO. Hence, ANSI's organization closely parallels ISO's in terms of technical committees and subcommittees. Indeed, ANSI standards could eventually become ISO standards.

The IEEE defines standards for data rates of approximately 40 Mbit/s and below. ANSI focuses on data rates greater than 40 Mbit/s. Both committees have liaison members who represent them at the other committees' meetings—mainly to share expertise and to avoid duplication of effort.

The IEEE 802 committee is specifying a series of local network standards that define four access technologies for a variety of physical media. The four standards are described briefly as follows:

- IEEE Standard 802.3. This is essentially the same as the Ethernet standard, which uses carrier sense multiple access with collision detect (CSMA/CD) as the access method. The standard is defined at a 10-Mbit/s data rate on a coaxial cable in a bus.
- IEEE Standard 802.4. This bus standard uses a token-passing mechanism to determine network access. The primary application of this scheme is in factory automation where the advantages of bus topology are combined with the priority potential and deterministic properties of token access.
- IEEE Standard 802.5. This defines a token-passing ring network. The medium is coaxial cable and the interconnection is a physical ring topology with a provision for passive bypass that uses relays.
- IEEE Standard 802.6. This is a project, now under study, to put together a metropolitan area network.

ANSI activities

The ANSI X3T9 Committee has the charter to define I/O interfaces. Several subcommittees are working on standards.

- ANSI X3T9.2 Small Computer Systems Interface (SCSI). Popularly called "scuzzy," this interface defines a scheme to interconnect low-end disk drives and other peripherals to computers.
- ANSI X3T9.3 Intelligent Peripheral Interface (IPI). IPI defines a scheme to interconnect somewhat higher-end peripherals to host adapters over a parallel bus. At the link layer, IPI sends data in the form of packets, much like a local network.
- ANSI X3T9.5 Local Area Networks: Two subcommittees within X3T9.5 are defining different local network standards: Local Distributed Data Interface (LDDI) is in the process of modifying and adopting a 70-Mbit/s coaxial cable network proposed by Digital Equipment Corp. (DEC) based on their CI-network. It uses a star topology. And Fiber Distributed Data Interface (FDDI) defines a 100-Mbit/s fiber-optic ring, which uses a token-passing access scheme.

Standards activity in networking

	ISO	TC97	ANSI	CCITT	IEEE	ECMA	NBS	EIA
APPLICATION	SC16	WG5	X3T5.5	—	—	—	ISO COMPATIBLE	—
PRESENTATION	SC16	WG5	X3T5.5	—	—	—	ISO COMPATIBLE	—
SESSION	SC16	WG6	X3T5.6	—	—	ECMA-75	ISO COMPATIBLE	—
TRANSPORT	SC16	WG6	X3T5.6	—	802	ECMA-72	ISO COMPATIBLE	—
NETWORK	SC6	WG2	X3S3.3	X.25	802	—	—	—
DATA LINK	SC6	WG1	X3S3.2 X3T9	X.21	802	ECMA-82	—	TR30.2 TR40.2
PHYSICAL	SC6	WG3	X3S3.1 X3T9	X.21	802	ECMA-81	—	TR30.1 TR40.1

TC = TECHNICAL COMMITTEE
SC = SUBCOMMITTEE
WG = WORKING GROUP
ISO = INTERNATIONAL ORGANIZATION FOR STANDARDIZATION
ANSI = AMERICAN NATIONAL STANDARDS INSTITUTE
ECMA = EUROPEAN COMPUTER MANUFACTURING ASSOCIATION
CCITT = CONSULTATIVE COMMITTEE FOR TELEPHONE & TELEGRAPH
IEEE = INSTITUTE OF ELECTRICAL & ELECTRONICS ENGINEERS
NBS = NATIONAL BUREAU OF STANDARDS
EIA = ELECTRONIC INDUSTRIES ASSOCIATION
TR = EIA SUBCOMMITTEE

1. Inner ring. *Primary and secondary fiber rings transmit lightwave data in opposite directions. Class A stations—either mainframes or wiring concentrators—connect to both the primary and secondary rings. Class B stations connect only to the primary ring. Fiber cable is terminated with bulkhead connectors.*

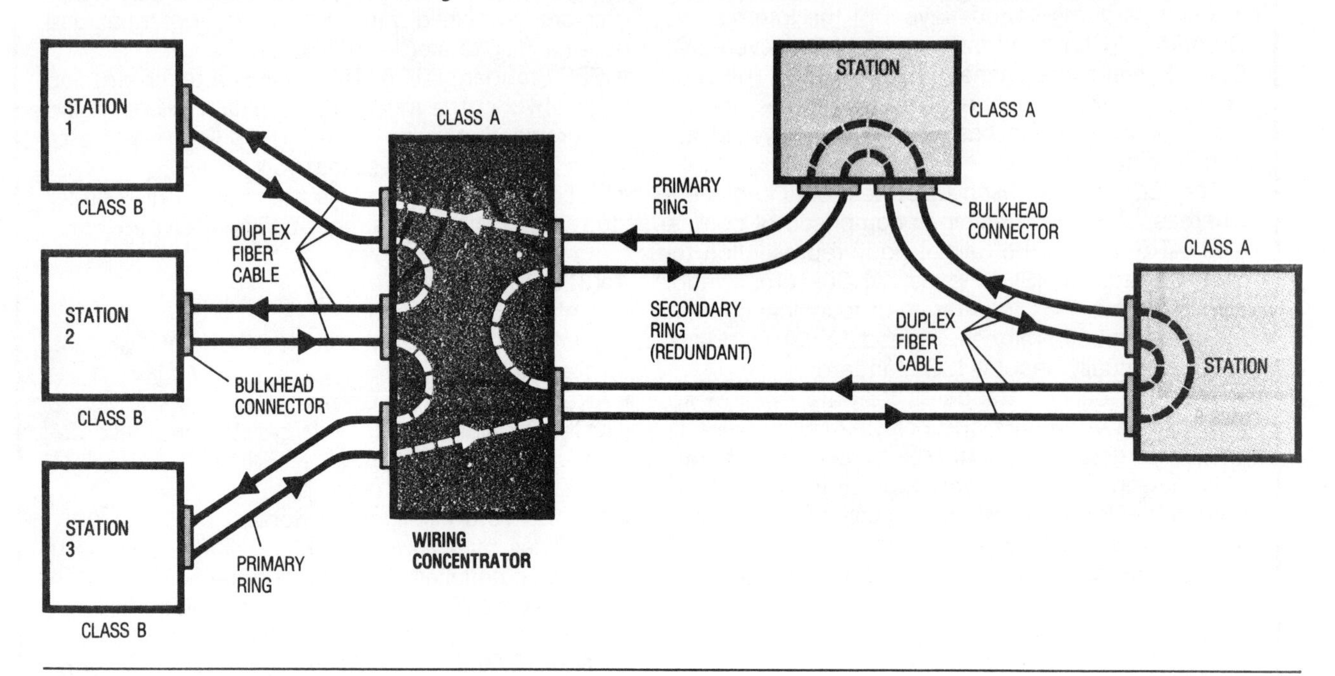

less video traffic. But as the need for these features increases with developments such as teleconferencing, higher data rates seem much more attractive. On a more practical note, low-speed networks are usually adequate for terminals and printers, but for engineering workstations, which require many huge file transfers daily, a high-speed front-end network is almost essential.

Designers have imagined many and varied fiber optic applications for years, but expense has kept many of those plans the stuff of dreams. Now, however, fiber costs are often comparable to those of coaxial cable and are expected to keep dropping. The breakthroughs have come from improvements in technology and the potential for mass production. Until recently, for example, it would have required a laser diode costing several hundred dollars to drive a fiber at over 100 MHz. This speed can be achieved now by using LEDs, priced at less than $10. In fact, one of the objectives of the ANSI FDDI specification group is to define the standard so that it can be implemented with fair-priced components within the reach of today's technology.

When cost is no longer a concern, fiber optics is a clear winner for a number of reasons. Four are:

- *Bandwidth.* Fiber-optic cables allow high data rates—in the range of several hundred megabits per second.
- *Attenuation.* Lightwaves experience relatively low signal loss, resulting in efficient communication over tens of kilometers, without repeaters.
- *Noise susceptibility.* Fiber cables transmit information as light and neither generate nor are affected by electromagnetic interference (EMI). This makes it ideal for use in high EMI environments such as factory floors.
- *Security.* Because it is difficult to tap a fiber cable without interrupting communication, fiber is more secure from interception.

The light-ring standard

As mentioned, the FDDI is a 100-Mbit/s token-passing physical ring using fiber-optic cable. The ANSI X3T9.5 committee specifies this as a local network standard. And various corporate architects of FDDI plan to use it for their own products because the standard includes features that support the many applications required for high marketability.

For example, some would use FDDI for back-end computer room applications where the network need only span several meters. Others intend to use FDDI-based products for connections with circumferences of over 100 kilometers. The FDDI specification places no lower bounds on the number of nodes and the distance between them; at the same time, the upper limits are reasonably large, permitting a wide range of implementations. Some of the main limits are:

- Up to 1,000 nodes on the ring
- Up to 2 kilometers between two nodes
- Up to 200 kilometers ring circumference.

With the maximum 1,000-node configuration, the average node separation will be 200 meters in order to limit the ring circumference to 200 kilometers. Yet several nodes may be separated by up to 2 kilometers as long as the average separation is 200 meters.

These limits are imposed to minimize latency, or the time it takes a signal to travel around the ring. The maximum ring latency is an important parameter for some real-time network applications. And with the proposed FDDI standard, it is held to only a few milliseconds.

2. Fault tolerance. *As shown in A, an FDDI network can sustain a single fault and still maintain the integrity of the entire network. All stations simply reconfigure on the primary ring. If a network similar to that shown in B sustains two faults, it can split into two smaller rings which remain operative internally.*

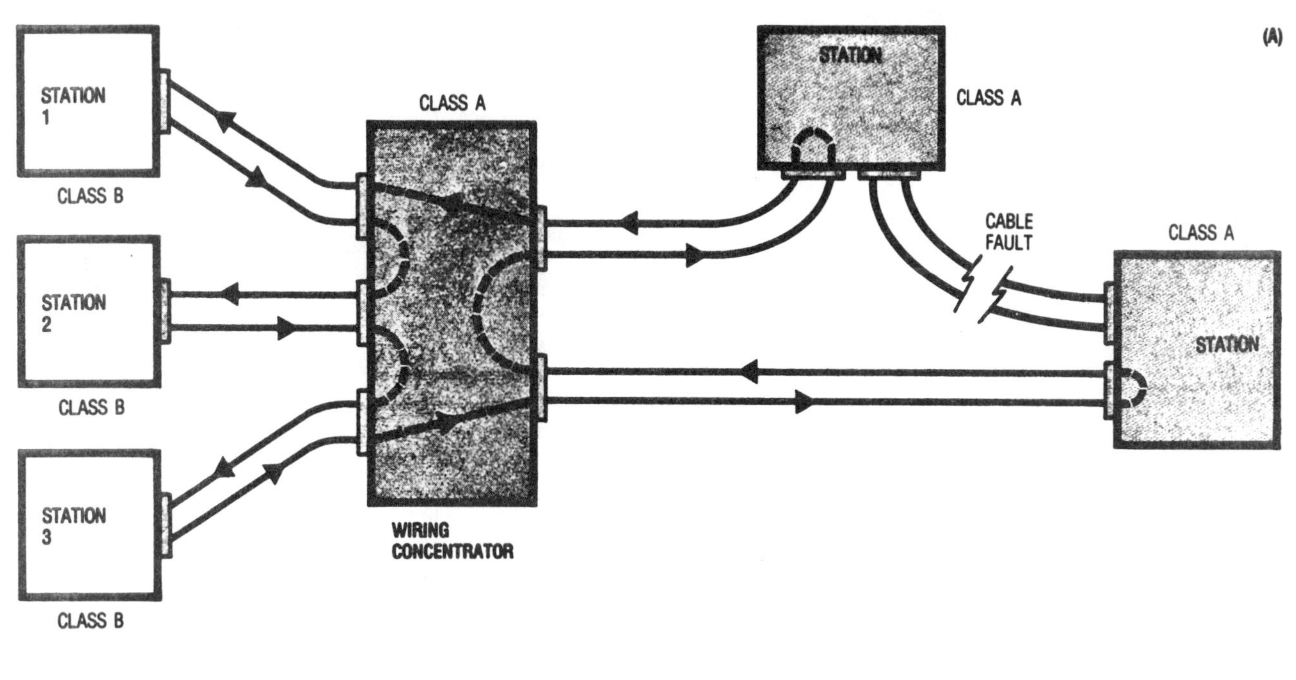

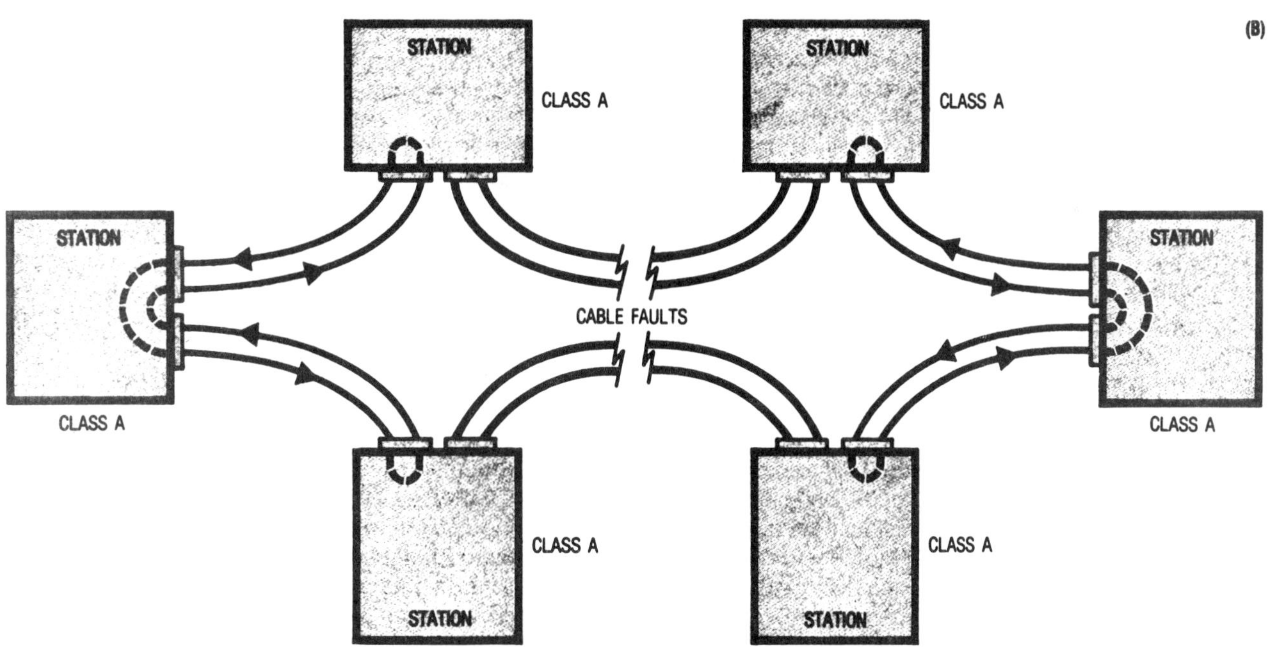

The FDDI ring is a combination of two independent counter-rotating rings, each running at 100 Mbit/s. If both rings operate simultaneously, the effective throughput is 200 Mbit/s. An FDDI scheme can actually use a special case of this where one ring connects all the nodes, and the second counter-rotating ring only a selected few.

Figure 1 illustrates a possible FDDI network configuration with fiber-optic cables forming the inner and outer rings. The paths through which the data travels around the ring are also shown. The ring that reaches all of the nodes is called the secondary ring and carries data in the opposite direction of the primary ring. The primary ring connects only the class A stations (an explanation of station classes can be found below). Such a concentric scheme is useful during ring reconfiguration. If the outer ring fails, for instance, the network can continue operating on the inner ring and still keep the intact portions of the outer ring (Fig. 2a).

In an FDDI network, nodes or stations can be of two

categories, either A or B (Fig. 1). Class A nodes connect to both the inner and outer rings; Class B nodes connect to only the outer one.

The two node classes allow users to tailor network complexity to meet cost objectives. For example, Class B stations need to connect to only one ring so they can be implemented for a lower cost. They are, however, isolated if that ring fails. On the other hand, while Class A stations may require additional hardware to connect to two rings, they offer a level of fail-safeness by being able to swap and continue operations on the good ring should the other fail. Typically stations that need more fault tolerance will be configured as Class A. Less critical stations can be Class B.

Another Class A station is the Wiring Concentrator (WC) illustrated in Figure 1. As its name implies, this device acts as a hub node through which several other stations can be connected. A WC allows a physical ring to be easily maintained, since, like a star network, failing nodes may easily disconnect. The WC can be a service point, with short connections taken out to individual stations, with several WCs so configured in a network. The WC is always a Class A station, with other Class A and B stations connecting to it.

An appealing package

The packaging of the fiber cable also makes the concept of WCs very attractive. As implied in Figure 1, the fiber cable in FDDI would contain two physical fibers packaged in one jacket with a bulkhead connector on either end. For example, for the dual ring connecting the Class A stations, each jacketed cable would contain one fiber for the primary ring and one for the secondary ring. For the Class B stations on the primary ring, the same cable would carry the incoming and outgoing data. Hence, when a Class B station is connected to a WC, only one physical cable need be routed between the two devices. Since the cable carries two fibers, a ring path is physically established.

Although implementing combined media, such as fiber and coaxial cable, is not specified in the FDDI proposal, it is easily accomplished. For example, a dual ring scheme connecting Class A stations can be built using fiber, but the shorter connections between a WC and the Class B stations can be coaxial cable. As long as the data rate is maintained and the token-ring protocol is adhered to, the existence of multiple media in a ring is transparent to the network.

The most typical faults in a network are caused either by failed components or broken cables. Even if a connection is not fully broken, there may be a substantial degradation that shows up as increased bit error rate. Figure 2A shows how an FDDI ring would reconfigure its data paths if a link—or a pair of links—in a dual ring cable became inoperative. The stations would sense the breakage and use the appropriate paths on the secondary ring to keep the network running. In FDDI this reconfiguration would happen automatically within a few milliseconds; the proposed standard defines a station management interface to facilitate this. Also, when a broken link is restored, the station management handshake will allow the ring to automatically return to its original state.

4B/5B coding

5-BAUD SYMBOL	CODE GROUP	LINE STATE ASSIGNMENT
Q	00000	QUIET
I	11111	IDLE
H	00100	HALT (FORCED BREAK)
J	11000	1ST OF SEQUENTIAL SD PAIR
K	10001	2ND OF SEQUENTIAL SD PAIR

5-BAUD SYMBOL	CODE GROUP	DATA QUARTETS (NIBBLES) HEX	BINARY
0	11110	0	0000
1	01001	1	0001
2	10100	2	0010
3	10101	3	0011
4	01010	4	0100
5	01011	5	0101
6	01110	6	0110
7	01111	7	0111
8	10010	8	1000
9	10011	9	1001
A	10110	A	1010
B	10111	B	1011
C	11010	C	1100
D	11011	D	1101
E	11100	E	1110
F	11101	F	1111
T	01101	ENDING DELIMITER (USED TO TERMINATE DATA STEAM)	
R	00111	DENOTING LOGICAL ZERO (RESET)	
S	11001	DENOTING LOGICAL ONE (SET)	

INVALID CODE ASSIGNMENTS		
V	00001	NOTE: THESE CODE PATTERNS ARE INVALID BECAUSE THEY ALLOW MORE THAN THREE CONSECUTIVE ZEROS IN A ROW.
V	00010	
V	00011	
V	00101	
V	00110	
V	01000	
V	01100	
V	10000	

Figure 2B shows the effect of a second failure. In this case, the networks split into two smaller independent networks, both of which remain operative internally.

Nuts and bolts

If a fault occurs in the cable going to a Class B station, that station is cut off from the network and the WC bypasses the node. Situations in which stations connected to the ring lose electrical power or are turned off can be handled by optical bypasses. Electrically operated relays provide pathways that allow the fiber transmissions to bypass a node—so that when power is lost, a mirror directs the lightwaves through an alternative path. A bypass can be provided in either Class A or Class B stations. Most Class A stations that include WCs will probably implement bypasses to get the additional level of fault tolerance. A Class A node without an optical bypass will appear as if all its links are broken when powered off. Optical bypasses (or even electrical bypasses) may be used in WCs at their Class B interfaces to mediate situations where the Class B stations fail.

The specification for FDDI physical layer includes the optical and mechanical characteristics of the fiber and the connectors, the power budgets, the dynamic range required in the receivers, and the encoding/-decoding scheme used.

FDDI specifies three different options for fiber: 100/400 micron diameter fiber (for example, 100 is the diameter of the fiber and 140 is the outer diameter of the cladding or jacket); 62.5/125 micron diameter fiber; and 85/125 micron diameter fiber. For all three, an 850-nanometer wavelength is specified. Bulkhead connectors specify the mechanical interface (Fig. 1).

Several of the low-speed standards, including the IEEE's, use Manchester encoding for baseband transmission. With this method, data and clock information are encoded together so each bit cell or bit period is divided in half—with line transitions occurring mid-way in each bit period. Each time a positive-going transition occurs, a "1" is sent; each time a negative-going transition occurs, a "0" is sent.

Unfortunately, Manchester encoding is only 50 percent efficient. Had it been used with FDDI at 100 Mbit/s, the encoding scheme would have required 200-Mbit/s bandwidth. Accordingly, the LEDs and PIN receivers would have had to operate at 200 MHz.

As a result, FDDI proposes a more efficient encoding scheme, called 4B/5B, to keep the baud rate down. In 4B/5B, the encoding is done on four bits at a time to create a five-cell "symbol" on the medium. The efficiency is 80 percent: to transmit 100 Mbit/s requires a bandwidth of only 125 MHz. The advantage is that inexpensive LEDs and PIN diode receivers, which operate at only 125 MHz, can be used.

The table shows the symbol encoding used in 4B/5B. It is an encoding scheme between 4-bit data "nibbles" and 5-baud symbols. The symbols are transmitted in a Non-Return to Zero Inverted (NRZI) line transmission format. The assignments between the four-bit nibbles and the five-cell symbols are chosen so that a transition is present at least once in three cells on the medium. Given an NRZI format, no more than three zeros could occur in a row, since, with NRZI, the absence of a line transition indicates a "0."

There are eight symbol combinations that violate this requirement, which should never occur in a properly operating ring. There are 32 possible code groups (or symbols) and 8 are invalid, so 24 are left for other interpretations. Sixteen of these correspond to the 16 data-values for a nibble. The remaining symbols are assigned special meaning as control characters at the physical layer. Some of the control symbols are used to derive line states such as "quiet," "idle," or "halt." Others are used as special delimiters for packets or fields within a packet. These include symbols denoted as J, K, T, R, and S. In FDDI these have been assigned specific meanings. For instance, J and K always occur in pairs and act as start delimiters for a packet (Fig. 4). The symbol T is used in conjunction with R and S as an ending delimiter.

Aside from delineating packets, these special symbols play a major role in station management handshake during ring reconfigurations. FDDI uses a token-passing ring consisting of stations serially connected by a transmission medium to form a closed loop. The packets are transmitted sequentially from one station to the next, where they are retimed and regenerated before being passed on to the "downstream" station. (Idle stations can either be bypassed or configured to function as active repeaters.) The addressed station copies the packet as it passes. Finally, the station that transmitted the packet strips it off the ring.

A station gains the right to transmit when it has the "token," which is a special packet that circulates on the ring behind the last transmitted packet. A station wanting to transmit captures the token, places its packet(s) on the ring, and then issues a new token, which the next station can capture for its transmission.

Taking turns

The access scheme in a network determines when a node has permission to transmit. The FDDI access scheme is based on a token packet which represents a permission to transmit. However, to support real-time needs of certain applications it is desirable to ensure that a node obtains a transmission opportunity (that is, assurance of getting the token) within a certain time.

The FDDI access scheme is called timed-token because it has a provision for specifying the time it takes the token to make a cycle of the ring. In essence each node on the ring measures the time it takes for the token to come back to it and compares that time with a prenegotiated target time. If the token comes back sooner than the target time, there is probably a light transmission load on the network. The node can then initiate packet transmissions on the ring as long as it does not exceed the target time. When the token comes back later than the target time, a heavy load on the ring is implied. In such cases the node is only allowed to transmit a high-priority class of packets called "synchronous packets." The node has to wait until the token rotation time (TRT) gets shorter than the target time before it transmits any of its more mundane packets that are not synchronous.

In addition, the FDDI uses the timed-token scheme to allocate the ring's bandwidth. This scheme assumes that the TRT, or the time between two successive token sightings at a station, has a linear relationship to the load on the ring (Fig. 3). The operative TRT T_{opr} is the same at all nodes on the ring. It is guaranteed in a normally functioning ring that TRT will never exceed 2 T_{opr}. The TRT would normally be less than or equal to T_{opr} transient conditions it may exceed it. Hence, nodes that have synchronous traffic (voice, for example) are assured at least one transmission opportunity in every $2.T_{opr}$ period. This is an upper bound on TRT; the TRT itself may vary from one revolution to the next. Thus, synchronous stations need some minimal buffering to support their traffic. The node that needs the lowest TRT determines the T_{opr} for the entire ring through a bandwidth allocation algorithm to be specified. The access scheme is independent of data rate and pro-

3. Upper limits. *TRT is a direct function of loading. T_{opr} is a prenegotiated length of time in which each node normally expects the token to return.*

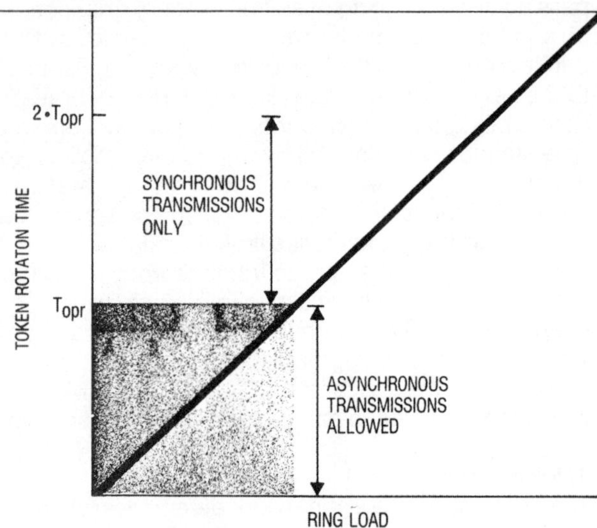

vides an easy transition to higher performance rings. The total synchronous load is the sum of synchronous traffic at the synchronous nodes. Thus, the maximum synchronous load that can be supported, as shown in Figure 3, sets up the configuration limits on the ring.

A TRT less than T_{opr} implies that the load on the ring is light. Asynchronous traffic (file transfers, keyboard commands) can be supported and prioritized at such times. Low-priority packets can be transmitted only when the ring load is light—that is, when TRT is less than a certain threshold for that priority level. In this fashion, the timed-token scheme provides a simple but powerful way to support synchronous and asynchronous traffic on the same ring, with an additional capability of dynamically prioritizing asynchronous traffic as a function of ring load.

Error recovery

Ring malfunctions such as noise, babbling nodes, or configuration violations are reflected in the TRT. And, if the TRT exceeds $2T_{opr}$, then ring malfunction is implied. (FDDI also specifies an early warning timer which times out before $2T_{opr}$ and initiates recovery.) All the nodes then act in concert to recover the ring. Each starts transmitting "Claim Token" packets that contain the TRT value needed by that particular node to support its synchronous traffic. The node with the lowest TRT wins. However, in the case of a broken ring, this process does not go to completion as indicated by a TRT exceeding a threshold value. The nodes start sending out beacon packets, indicating serious ring failure, and any node that receives a beacon repeats it. This enables the fault to be localized and triggers the reconfiguration procedure, thus enabling the ring to function again—albeit at reduced performance. The FDDI standard also specifies the handshake procedures for such things as a station that is either getting onto a running ring or going to a preconfigured setup.

Figure 4 shows the format for an FDDI packet; the token is a special packet and is also shown.

The packet preamble (PA) consists of at least idle symbols. The start delimiter (SD) consists of the symbols J,K (table). The frame control (FC) is 1 byte, and indicates frame type. The destination/source address (DA/SA) can be either 16 or 48 bits long. The address length is specified in the FC field. The information field (INFO) can have from 0 to approximately 9,000 data symbols. An autodin cyclic redundancy check (CRC) comprises the frame check sequence (FCS). End-of-frame (EDF) is followed by frame status (FS), which is provided to the transmitting node by the nodes through which the packets pass.

Comparing

The IEEE 802.5 standard specifies a 4-Mbit/s token-passing ring. When the FDDI subcommittee began work it tried to maintain the services and facilities of 802.5 but modified other sections to obtain data rates up to 100 Mbit/s. A comparison between the two standards will illustrate the factors to be considered when going to higher data rate protocols. Specifically, the physical layer specification is crucial at high speeds. For a data rate of 100 Mbit/s, the group encoding limits the bandwidth to 125 MHz on the medium; as mentioned, a Manchester encoding scheme would have required an increased bandwidth of up to 200 MHz for the same 100-Mbit/s data rate.

FDDI's decentralized clocking scheme requires designing for clock variations between two stations instead of designing for the sum of clock variations on the whole ring. At high speeds, where the bit time is very small, the latter scheme would put tough (and therefore expensive) requirements on the clocking circuitry. Both schemes require latency buffers. However, the buffer in FDDI is divided among the nodes. In IEEE 802.5 each node has a buffer large enough to compensate for all clock variations on the ring. At high speeds the number of bits of buffer goes up and so the 802.5 scheme becomes impractical. The 802.5 centralized clock scheme supports packets of any length. FDDI packets are limited to around 4,500 bytes.

In the 802.5 standard a transmitting node flips a bit in the token—making the bit a start delimiter—and then appends its own packet behind the token. This means that a packet has to be ready and set up for transmission when the token appears. This also means increased hardware and costs. In FDDI the token is a special packet that is stripped off the ring by the node that wants to transmit. When a node takes the token, it puts idles on the ring while the packet is getting set up for transmission. Symbol level manipulation is sufficient in FDDI, unlike in 802.5 where bit-level manipulation is necessary.

From the above it appears that the IEEE scheme is more efficient. However, at high speeds it is the ease of processing, not the efficiency of data transmission, that causes the bottleneck. To ease the speed, size, and complexity requirements on the electronics, the price of a few bytes is an easy tradeoff. In FDDI the token is

4. Data bars. *Information is passed around the ring in frames. The PA field synchronizes the frame with the node's clock. Other fields indicate a frame's beginning, length, destination, source, contents, data integrity, and end. The token is similar to an information packet, but with no information field.*

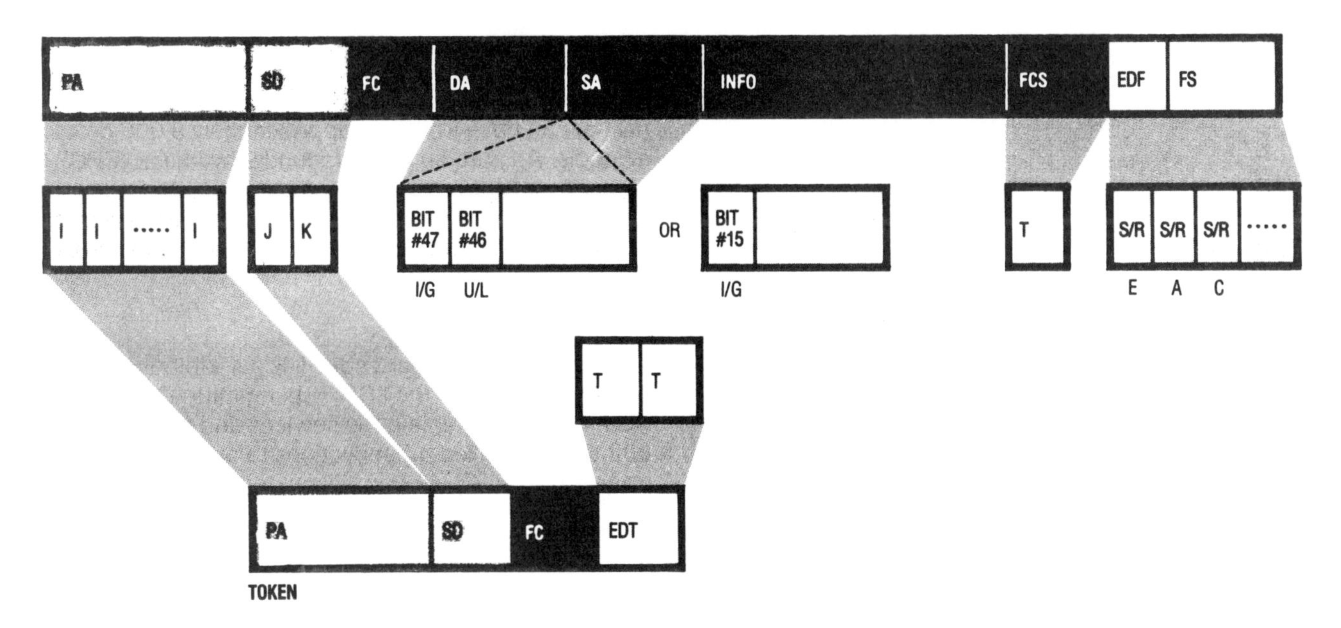

PA = PREAMBLE
SD = START DELIMITER
FC = FRAME CONTROL
DA = DESTINATION ADDRESS
SA = SOURCE ADDRESS
INFO = INFORMATION
FCS = FRAME CHECK SEQUENCE
EDF = ENDING DELIMITER (INFORMATION)
EDT = ENDING DELIMITER (TOKEN)

FS = FRAME STATUS
I/G = INDIVIDUAL/GROUP ADDRESS
U/L = UNIVERSAL/LOCAL ADMINISTRATION OF ADDRESS
E = ERROR DETECTED
A = ADDRESS RECOGNIZED
C = COPIED
= DATA SYMBOLS
= SPECIAL SYMBOLS (I, J, K, T, R, S; SEE TABLE 1)

transmitted immediately after the packet. The 802.5 configured ring waits for the transmitted packet to come back before giving out the token, putting out fill (null data) in the meanwhile. The FDDI scheme is thus more efficient, especially in large rings with a lot of latency.

The FDDI timed-token scheme sets up a traffic framework through a bandwidth allocation scheme. This framework is maintained until some node wants it changed. Synchronous traffic is easy to support on the FDDI ring, and the TRT is the single parameter that controls the ring. In 802.5 each frame has three priority bits (to indicate one of eight levels of priority) and three reservation bits to indicate the priority desired. By suitable manipulation of these fields, synchronous traffic can be supported. Note, however, that traffic is regulated on a per-packet basis.

The dual-ring option specified in FDDI provides the additional reliability and fail-safeness essential for high-performance applications. Because the 802.5 standard is aimed at the low-end market, the dual ring is not specified, though it could be supported.

The success of FDDI will depend on the amount of support it receives from component manufacturers, and the cost reductions achieved as users and manufacturers progress along the curve involved with learning how to implement the standard.

Toward that end, Advanced Micro Devices (AMD) plans to introduce the first chip in its Supernet family of high-speed networking products in mid-1985. The first chip in the family, the Link Protocol Processor (LPP), does most of the buffer management functions, and the FDDI ring-access scheme can be implemented as a module to work with it. ■

Sunil Joshi, section manager for AMD's packet networks division, is involved in product planning for high speed local networks. Venkatraman Iyer is a product planning engineer for that division.

Section 4: Digital Switches And Digital Private Branch Exchanges

4.1 Overview

The digital switch and the digital private branch exchange (PBX) are major alternatives to the LAN for handling a wide variety of local networking requirements. Some of the typical characteristics of these systems are as follows:

- Stations are connected by twisted pair to a central switching unit (star topology).
- Circuit switching is used. The switch establishes a dedicated communications path between two devices wishing to communicate. Bandwidth (data rate) is fixed and guaranteed.
- The switch is actively involved during the call setup phase. During the data transfer phase, data passes transparently through the switch, with only propagation delay.
- Data rates for individual devices are typically limited to about 64 kbps.
- The total capacity, however, may be quite high. A digital PBX may have a total throughput potential in the neighborhood of 500 Mbps.

The digital PBX differs from the digital switch in that it is intended to handle voice traffic as well as data traffic. Additional typical characteristics are as follows:

- Voice is digitized; that is, it is encoded as a digital bit stream. The encoding is done by a device called a codec (coder-decoder), and this function is either dispersed (at the phone) or concentrated (at the switch).
- A hierarchical star topology is often used. In this case, one or more satellite switches are attached to a central switch. This architecture increases system capacity and availability.

Modern digital switches and digital PBXs are based on the use of synchronous time-division multiplexing (TDM). This technique involves preassigning time slots to communicating devices on a shared transmission medium. Since the slots are preassigned, no overhead control or address bits are needed. The slots recur frequently enough to provide the desired data rate.

4.2 Digital Data Switching Devices

The digital switching techniques discussed above have been used to build a variety of digital switching products designed for data-only applications. These devices do not provide telephone service and are generally cheaper than a digital PBX of comparable capacity.

The variety of devices is wide and the distinction between types are blurred. For convenience, we categorize them as follows: (1) Terminal/port-oriented switch, and (2) Data switch.

Before defining these categories, let us look at the functions associated with data switching. The most basic, of course, is the making of a connection between two attached lines. These connections can be preconfigured by a system operator, but more dynamic operation is often desired. This leads to two additional functions: port contention and port selection.

Port contention is a function that allows a certain number of designated ports to contend for access to a smaller number of ports. Typically, this is used for terminal-to-host connection thereby allowing a smaller number of host ports to service a larger number of terminal ports. When a terminal user attempts to connect, the system will scan through all host ports in the contention group. If any port is available, a connection is made.

Port selection is an interactive capability. It allows a user (or an application program in a host) to select a port for connection. This is analogous to dialing a number in a telephone system. Port selection and port contention can be combined by allowing the selection, by name or number, of a contention group. Port selection devices are becoming increasingly common. A switch without this capability only allows connections that are preconfigured by a system operator. If one knows in advance what interconnections are required, fine. Otherwise, the flexibility of port selection is usually worth the additional cost.

An interactive capability carries with it an additional responsibility: The control unit of the switch must be able to talk to the requesting port. This can be done in two ways. In some cases, the manufacturer supplies a simple keypad device that attaches to and shares the terminal's line. The user first dials a connection by using the keypad. Once the connection is made, communication is by the terminal. As an alternative, the connection sequence can be effected through the terminal itself. A simple command language dialogue is used. However, this technique requires that the system understand the code and protocol being used by the terminal. Consequently, this feature is generally limited to asynchronous ASCII devices.

We can now describe the distinction between terminal/port-oriented switches and data switches. In the former, switch attachment points are designated as either terminal or host. Connections are only allowed between a terminal and a host port. For a data switch, there is no such distinction; any attached device can connect to any other attached device.

4.3 The Digital Private Branch Exchange

Evolution of the Digital PBX

The digital PBX is a marriage of two technologies: digital switching and telephone exchange systems. A PBX is an on-premise facility, owned or leased by an organization, that interconnects the telephones within the facility and provides access to the public telephone system. Typically, a telephone user on the premises dials a three- or four-digit number to call another telephone on the premises and dials one digit (usually an 8 or a 9) to get a dial tone for an "outside line," which allows the caller to dial a number in the same fashion as a residential user would dial.

The original private exchanges were manual, with one or more operators required to make all connections from a switchboard. Back in the 1920's, these began to be replaced by automatic systems, called private automatic branch exchanges (PABX), that did not require attendant intervention to place a call. These first-generation systems used electromechanical technology and analog signaling. Data connections could be made through modems. That is, a user with a terminal, a telephone, and a modem or acoustic coupler in the office could dial an on-site or remote number that reached another modem, and data could be exchanged.

The second-generation PBXs were introduced in the mid 1970's. These systems use electronic rather than electromagnetic technology and the internal switching is digital. Such a system is referred to as digital PBX, or computerized branch exchange (CBX). These systems were primarily designed to handle analog voice traffic, with the codec function built into the switch so that digital switching could be used internally. (The codec is the opposite of a modem; it converts analog voice signals into digital data and vice versa.) The systems were also capable of handling digital data connections without the need for a modem.

The third-generation systems are touted as "integrated voice-data" systems, although the differences between third and upgraded second-generation systems are rather blurred. Perhaps a better term is "improved digital PBX." Some of the characteristics of these systems that differ from those of earlier systems include:

- *Use of digital phones*: This permits integrated voice/data workstations.
- *Distributed architecture*: Multiple switches in a hierarchical or meshed configuration with distributed intelligence provide enhanced reliability.
- *Nonblocking configuration*: Typically, dedicated port assignments are used for all attached phones and devices.

It is worthwhile to summarize the main reasons why the evolution described above has occurred. To the untrained eye, analog and digital PBXs would seem to offer about the same level of convenience. The analog PBX can handle telephone sets directly and uses modems to accommodate digital data devices; the digital PBX can handle digital data devices directly and uses codecs to accommodate telephone sets. Some of the advantages of the digital approach are:

- *Digital technology*: By handling all internal signals digitally, the digital PBX can take advantage of low cost LSI and VLSI components. Digital technology also lends itself more readily to software and firmware control.
- *Time-division multiplexing (TDM)*: Digital signals lend themselves readily to TDM techniques, which provide efficient use of internal data paths, access to public TDM carriers, and TDM switching techniques, which are more cost effective than older, cross-bar techniques.
- *Digital control signals*: Control signals are inherently digital and can be integrated easily into a digital transmission path by use of TDM. The signaling equipment is independent of the transmission medium.
- *Encryption*: This is more easily accommodated with digital signals.

Digital PBX Architecture

A variety of architectures has been developed by PBX manufacturers. Since these are proprietary, the details are not generally known in most cases. Here, we attempt to present the general architectural features common to all digital PBX systems.

Figure 4.1 presents a generic digital PBX architecture. Except for features specifically supportive of voice communication, this also depicts a digital data switch architecture. The heart of the system is some kind of digital switching network. The switch is responsible for the manipulation and switching of TDM digital signal streams, using the techniques described in the articles in this section.

Attached to the switch is a series of interface units that provide access to/from the outside world. Typically, an interface unit will perform a synchronous TDM function to accommodate multiple incoming lines. On the other side, the unit requires two lines into the switch for full duplex operation. For input to the switch, the unit performs a multiplex operation. Each incoming line is sampled at a specified rate. For n incoming lines each of data rate x, the unit must achieve an input rate of nx. The incoming data is buffered and organized into chunks of time-slot size. Then, according to the timing dictated by the control unit, individ-

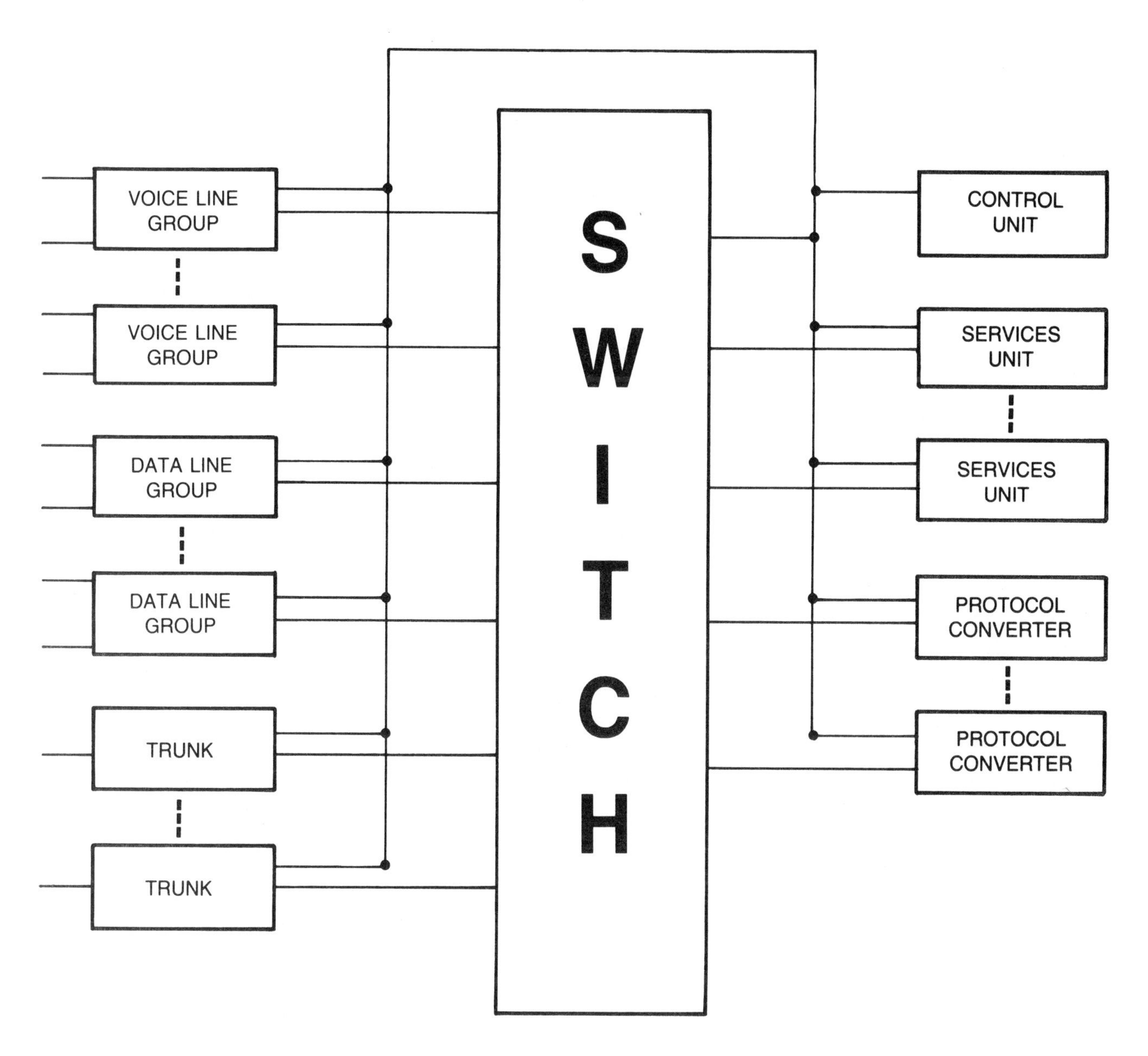

Figure 4.1 Generic CBX Architecture

ual chunks are sent out into the switch at the internal digital PBX data rate, which may be in the range of 50-500 Mbps. In a nonblocking switch, *n* time slots are dedicated to the interface unit for transmission, whether or not they are used. In a blocking switch, time slots are assigned for the duration of a connection. In either case, the time-slot assignment is fixed for the duration of the connection, and synchronous TDM techniques may be used. For output from the switch, the interface unit accepts data from the switch during designated time slots.

Several types of interface units are used. A data-line group unit handles data devices. An analog voice-line group handles a number of twisted pair phone lines. The interface unit must include codecs for digital-to-analog (input) and analog-to-digital (output) conversion. A separate type of unit may be used for an integrated digital voice/data work station, which presents digitized voice at 64 kbps and data at the same or a lower rate. The range of lines accommodated by interface units is typically 8 to 24. In addition to multiplexing interface units that accommodate multiple lines, trunk interface units are used to connect to offsite locations. These may be analog voice trunks or digital trunks, which may carry either data or digitized voice.

The other boxes in Figure 4.1 can be briefly explained. The control unit operates the digital switch and exchanges control signals with attached devices. For this purpose, a separate bus or other data path is used; control signals generally do not propagate through the switch itself. As part of this or a separate unit, network administration and control functions are implemented. Service units would include such things as tone and busy-signal generators and dialed-digit registers. Some digital PBX systems provide protocol converters for connecting dissimilar lines. A connection is made from each line to the protocol converter.

It should be noted that this generic architecture lends itself to a high degree of reliability. The failure of any interface unit means the loss of only a small number of lines. Key elements such as the control unit can be made redundant.

Fourth-Generation PBX

We spoke earlier of the evolution of the digital PBX up through a third generation. As new features and technologies are employed, incremental improvements make difficult the continuing classification of PBXs into generations. Nevertheless, it is worth noting recent advances that will soon begin to show up in PBX products and that, together, might be considered to constitute a fourth generation:

- *Integrated LAN link*: This capability provides a direct high-speed link to a LAN. This allows an optimum distribution of lower-speed devices (terminals) on the PBX and higher-speed devices (computers) on the LAN in a fashion that is fully transparent to the user.
- *Dynamic bandwidth allocation*: Typically, a PBX offers one or only a small number of different data rate services. The increased sophistication of capacity allocation within the PBX allows it to offer virtually any data rate to an attached device. This allows the system to grow as user requirements grow. For example, full-motion color video at 448 kbps or advanced codecs at 32 kbps could be accommodated.
- *Integrated packet channel*: This allows the PBX to provide access to an X.25 packet-switched network.

4.4 Article Summary

The articles in this section are intended to provide the reader with an understanding of how digital switches and digital PBXs work, plus an overview of the various types of devices.

The first article explains the technology and architecture underlying all these types of systems, and explores the key concepts of synchronous time-division multiplexing, space-division switching, and time-division switching.

The next two articles discuss various types of data-only digital switches. The article by Kane is a brief survey of the various devices. "Controlling the Mushrooming Communications Net" focuses on the most general of such devices, the port selector.

The remainder of the articles discuss the digital PBX. "The ABCs of the PBX" is an interesting discussion of the evolution of the digital PBX and its likely future direction. "Office Communications and the Digital PBX" details the requirements for intraoffice communications and discusses the satisfaction of those requirements by a digital PBX. The final article, by Pfister and O'Brien, compares digital PBXs and LANs.

Time Division Switching

J. Bellamy

1.3 THE INTRODUCTION OF DIGITS

Voice digitization and transmission first became feasible in the late 1950s when the economic, operational, and reliability features of solid state electronics became available. In 1962 Bell System personnel established the first commercial use of digital transmission when they began operating a T1 carrier system for use as a trunk group in a Chicago area exchange [23]. Since that time a whole family of T-carrier systems (T1, T1C, T1D, T2, T4) has been developed—all of which involve time division multiplexing of digitized voice signals. Following the development of T-carrier systems for interoffice transmission, Western Electric and numerous independent manufacturers developed digital pair-gain systems for long customer loop applications. However, the pair-gain systems have not been used nearly as extensively as T-carrier systems. Projections for T-carrier usage indicate that 50% of the exchange area trunks will be digital by 1985 [24].

The world's first commercially designed digital microwave radio system was established in Japan by Nippon Electric Company (NEC) in 1968 [25]. In the early 1970s digital microwave systems began to appear in the United States for specialized data transmission services. Foremost among these systems was a digital network developed by Data Transmission Company (Datran).* The first digital microwave link in the U.S. public telephone network was supplied by NEC of Japan for a New York Telephone link between Brooklyn and North Staten Island in 1972 [25]. Digital microwave systems have since been developed and installed by several U.S. manufacturers for use in intermediate length toll and exchange area circuits.

In addition to transmission systems, digital technology has proven to be equally useful for implementing switching functions. The first country to use digital switching in the public telephone network was France in 1970 [26]. The first application of digital switching in the public network of the United States occurred in early 1976 when the Bell System began operating its No. 4ESS [27] in a class 3 toll office in Chicago. Two months after that Continental Telephone Company began operation in Ridgecrest, California of an IMA2 digital toll switch supplied by TRW-Vidar [28]. The first digital end office switch in the United States became operational in July of 1977 in the small town of Richmond Hill, Georgia [29]. This switch was supplied by Stromberg-Carlson for Coastal Utilities, Inc., a small independent telephone company.

1.3.1 Voice Digitization

The basic voice coding algorithm used in T-carrier systems, and most other digital voice equipment in telephone networks around the world, is shown in Figure 1.25. The first step in the digitization process is to periodically sample the waveform. As discussed at length in Chapter 3, all of the information needed to reconstruct the original waveform is contained in the samples—if the samples occur at an 8 kHz rate. The second step in the digitization process involves quantization: identifying which amplitude interval of a group of adjacent intervals a sample value falls into. In essence the quantization process replaces each con-

*The Datran facilities were taken over in 1976 by another specialized common carrier: Southern Pacific Communications.

tinuously variable amplitude sample with a discrete value located at the middle of the appropriate quantization interval. Since the quantized samples have discrete levels, they represent a multiple level digital signal.

For transmission purposes the discrete amplitude samples are converted to a binary code word. (For illustrative purposes only, Figure 1.26 shows 4 bit code words.) The binary codes are then transmitted as binary pulses. At the receiving end of a digital transmission line the binary data stream is recovered, and the discrete sample values are reconstructed. Then a low-pass filter is used to "interpolate" between sample values and recreate the original waveform. If no transmission errors have occurred, the output waveform is identical to the input waveform except for a small amount of quantization distortion: the difference between a sample value and its discrete representation. By having a large number of quantization intervals (and hence enough bits in a code word to encode them), the quantization intervals can be small enough to effectively eliminate quantization effects.

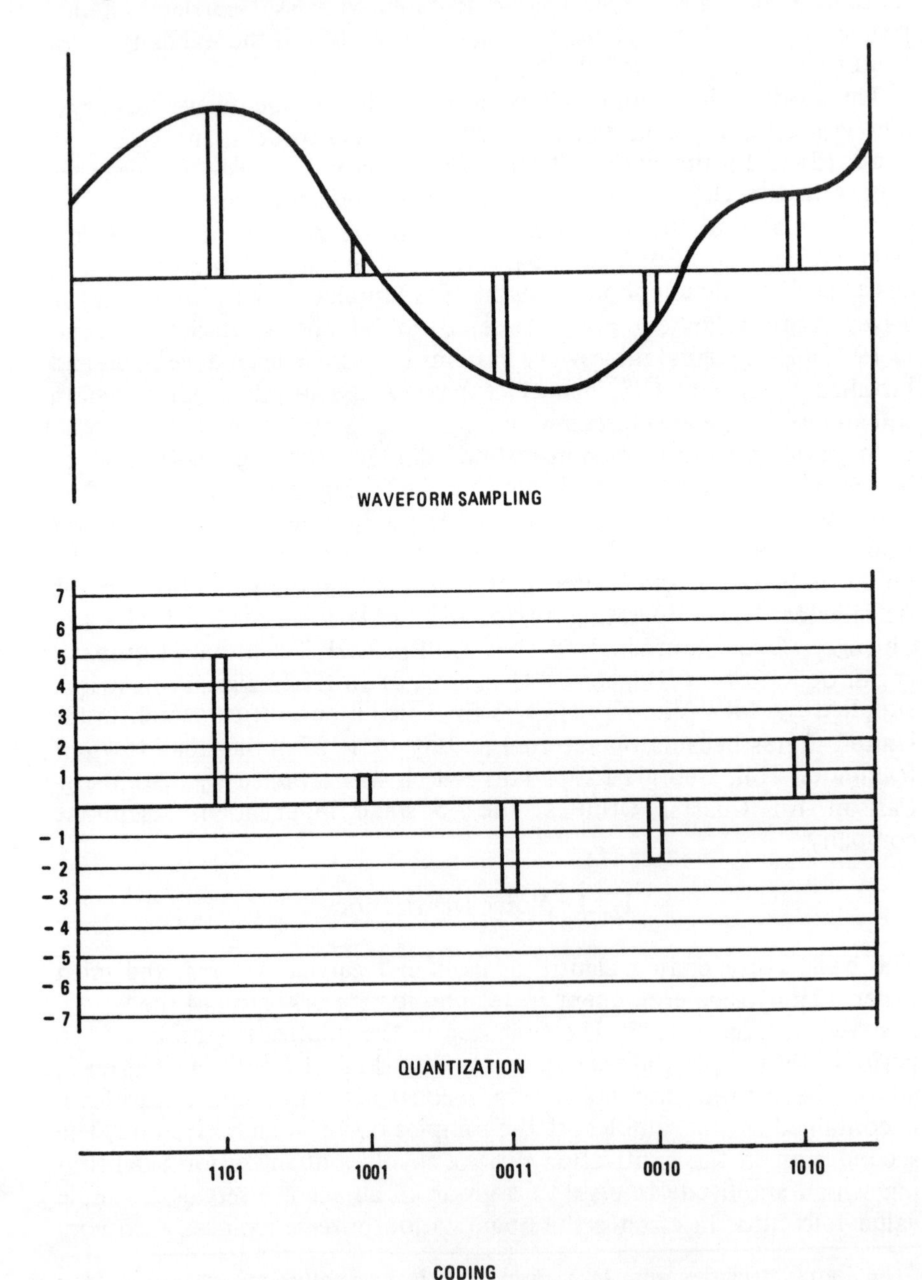

Figure 1.25 Voice digitization process.

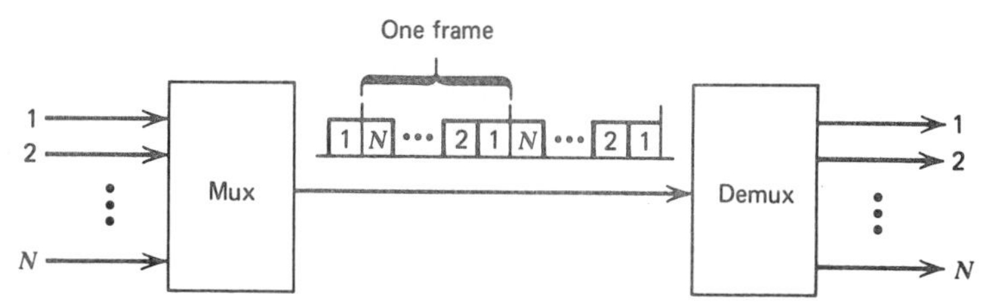

Figure 1.26 Time division multiplexing.

It is worth noting that the bandwidth requirements of the digital signal increase as a result of the binary encoding process. If the discrete, multiple-amplitude samples are transmitted directly, the bandwidth requirements are theoretically identical to the bandwidth of the original signal. When each discrete sample is represented by a number of individual binary pulses, the signal bandwidth increases accordingly. The two-level pulses, however, are much less vulnerable to transmission impairments than are the multiple-amplitude pulses (or the underlying analog signal).

1.3.2 Time Division Multiplexing

Basically, time division multiplexing (TDM) involves nothing more than sharing a transmission medium by establishing a sequence of time slots during which individual sources can transmit signals. Thus the entire bandwidth of the facility is periodically available to each user for a restricted time interval. In contrast, FDM systems assign a restricted bandwidth to each user for all time. Normally, all time slots of a TDM system are of equal length. Also, each subchannel is usually assigned a time slot with a common repetition period called a frame interval. This form of time division multiplexing (as shown in Figure 1.26) is sometimes referred to as synchronous time division multiplexing to specifically imply that each subchannel is assigned a certain amount of transmission capacity determined by the time slot duration and the repetition rate. In contrast, another form of TDM (referred to as "statistical or asynchronous time division multiplexing") is described in Chapter 8. With this second form of multiplexing, subchannel rates are allowed to vary according to the individual needs of the sources. All of the backbone digital links of the public telephone network (T-carrier and digital microwave) use a synchronous variety of TDM.

Time division multiplexing is normally associated only with digital transmission links. Although TDM can be used conceivably for analog signals by interleaving samples from each signal, the individual samples are usually too sensitive to all varieties of transmission impairments. In contrast, time division switching of analog signals is more feasible than analog TDM transmission because noise and distortion of the switching equipment is more controllable. As discussed in Chapter 5, analog TDM techniques are used in some PBXs.

5.3 TIME DIVISION SWITCHING

As evidenced by multiple stage switching, sharing of individual crosspoints for more than one potential connection provides significant savings in implementation costs of space division switches. In the cases demonstrated, the crosspoints of multistage space switches are shared from one connection to the next, but a crosspoint assigned to a particular connection is dedicated to that connection for its duration. Time division switching involves the sharing of crosspoints for shorter periods of time so that individual crosspoints and their associated interstage links are continually reassigned to existing connections. When the crosspoints are shared in this manner, much greater savings in crosspoints can be achieved. In essence, the savings are accomplished by time division multiplexing the crosspoints and interstage links in the same manner that transmission links are time division multiplexed to share interoffice wire pairs.

Time division switching is equally applicable to either analog or digital signals. Analog time division switching is attractive when interfacing to analog transmission facilities, since the signals are only sampled and not digitally encoded. However, large analog time division switches experience the same limitations as do analog time division transmission links: the PAM samples are particularly vulnerable to noise, distortion, and crosstalk. In digital switches, the voice signals are regenerated every time they pass through a logic gate. Thus at some point in switching sizes, the cost of digitizing PAM samples is mandated by the need to maintain end-to-end signal quality. As the cost of digitization continues to decline, digital switching of analog signals is more and more competitive for small switch sizes. If a sufficient number of the signals to be switched are already digital or will be converted to digital at a future date, digital switching becomes more attractive than analog switching, even for the smallest PBXs.

5.3.1 Analog Time Division Switching

A vast majority of PBXs presently available in the United States use time division technology for the switching matrix. Of these, approximately one-half use analog time division switching while the other half use digital time division switching. Figure 5.14 depicts a particularly simple analog time division switching structure. A single switching bus supports a multiple number of connections by interleaving PAM

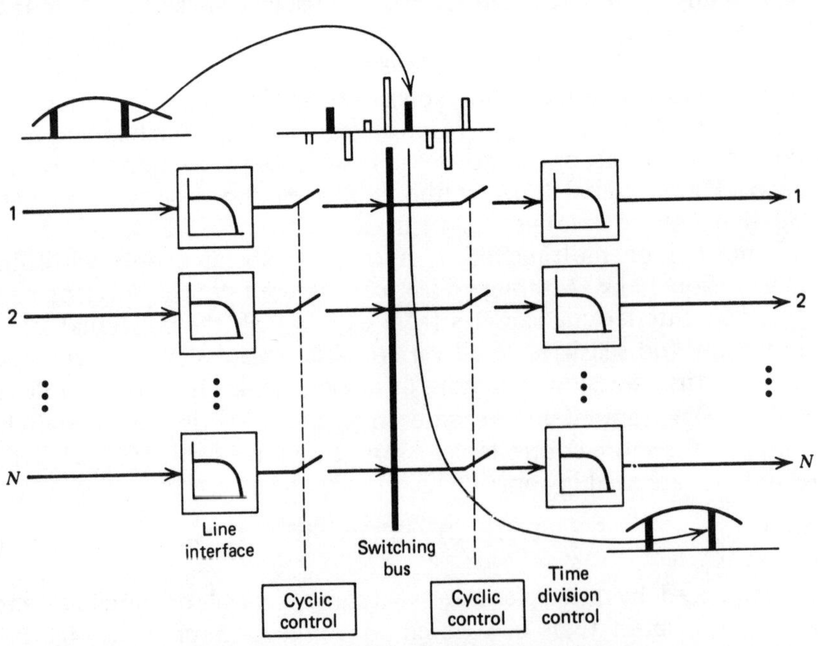

Figure 5.14 Analog time division switching.

samples from receive line interfaces to transmit line interfaces. The operation is depicted as though the receive interfaces are separate from the respective transmit interfaces. When connecting two-wire analog lines, the two interfaces are necessarily implemented in a common module. Furthermore, in some PAM-PBX systems, analog samples are simultaneously transferred in both directions between the interfaces [9].

Included in Figure 5.14 are two cyclic control stores. The first control store controls gating of inputs onto the bus one sample at a time. The second control store operates in synchronism with the first and selects the appropriate output line for each input sample. A complete set of pulses, one from each active input line, is referred to as a frame. The frame rate is equal to the sample rate of each line. For voice systems the sampling rate ranges from 8 to 12 kHz. The higher sampling rates are used to simplify the band-limiting filter and reconstructive filters in the line interfaces.

5.3.2 Digital Time Division Switching

The analog switching matrix described in the preceding section is essentially a space division switching matrix. By continually changing the connections for short periods of time in a cyclic manner, the configuration of the space division switch is replicated once for each time slot. This mode of operation is referred to as time multiplexed switching. While this mode of operation can be quite useful for both analog and

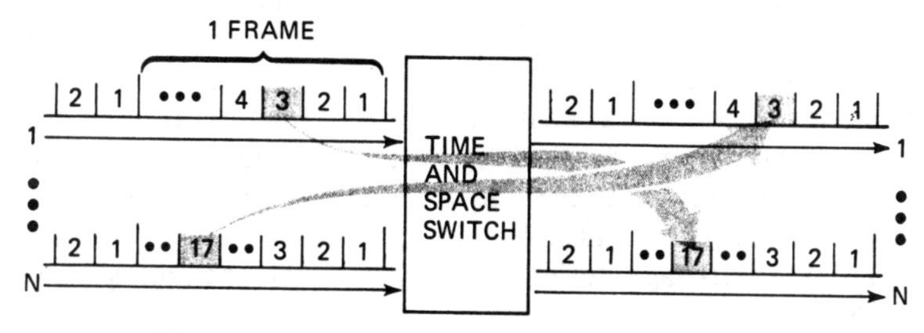

Figure 5.15 Time and space division switching.

digital signals, digital time division multiplexed signals usually require switching between time slots, as well as between physical lines. This second mode of switching represents a second dimension of switching and is referred to as time switching.

In the following discussion of digital time division switching it is assumed, unless otherwise stated, that the switching network is interfaced directly to digital time division multiplex links. This assumption is generally justified since, even when operating in an analog environment, the most cost-effective switch designs multiplex groups of digital signals into TDM formats before any switching operations take place. Thus most of the following discussion is concerned with the internal structures of time division switching networks, and possibly not with the structure of an entire switching complex.

The basic requirement of a time division switching network is shown in Figure 5.15. As an example connection, channel 3 of the first TDM link is connected to channel 17 of last TDM link. The indicated connection implies that information arriving in time slot 3 of the first link is transferred to time slot 17 of the last link. Since the voice digitization process inherently implies a four-wire operation, the return connection is required and realized by transferring information from time slot 17 of the last input link to time slot 3 of the first link. Thus each connection requires two transfers of information: each involving translations in both time and space.

A variety of switching structures are possible to accomplish the transfers indicated in Figure 5.15. All of these structures inherently require at least two stages: a space division switching stage and a time division switching stage. As discussed later, larger switches use multiple stages of both types. Before discussing switching in both dimensions, however, we discuss the characteristics and capabilities of time switching alone.

A Digital Memory Switch

Primarily owing to the low cost of digital memory, time switching implementations provide digital switching functions more economically than space division implementations. Basically, a time switch operates

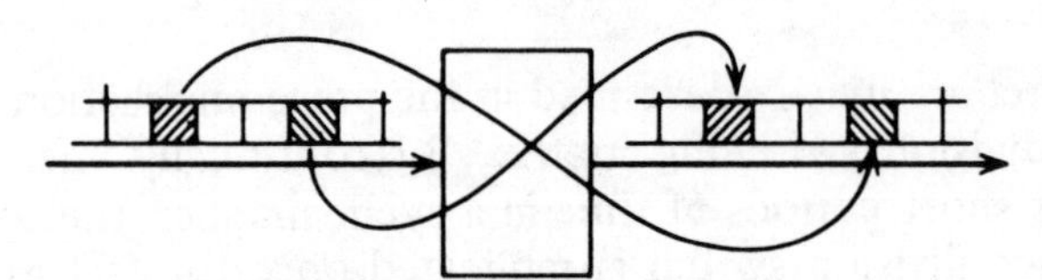

Figure 5.16 Time slot interchange operation.

by writing data into and reading data out of a single memory. In the process the information in selected time slots is interchanged as shown in Figure 5.16. When digital signals can be multiplexed into a single TDM format, very economical switches can be implemented with time switching alone. However, practical limitations of memory speed limit the size of a time switch so that some amount of space division switching is necessary in large switches. As demonstrated in later sections, the most economical multistage designs usually perform as much switching as possible in the time stages.

The basic functional operation of a memory switch is shown in Figure 5.17. Individual digital message circuits are multiplexed and demultiplexed in a fixed manner to establish a single TDM link for each direction of travel. The multiplexing and demultiplexing functions can be considered as part of the switch itself, or they may be implemented in remote transmission terminals. If the multiplexing functions are implemented locally, the multiplexer and demultiplexer may be connected in parallel, directly to the memory. Otherwise, a serial-to-parallel converter is used to accumulate the information in a time slot before it is written into the memory. In either case, a memory write access is required for each incoming time slot, and a memory read access is required for each outgoing time slot.

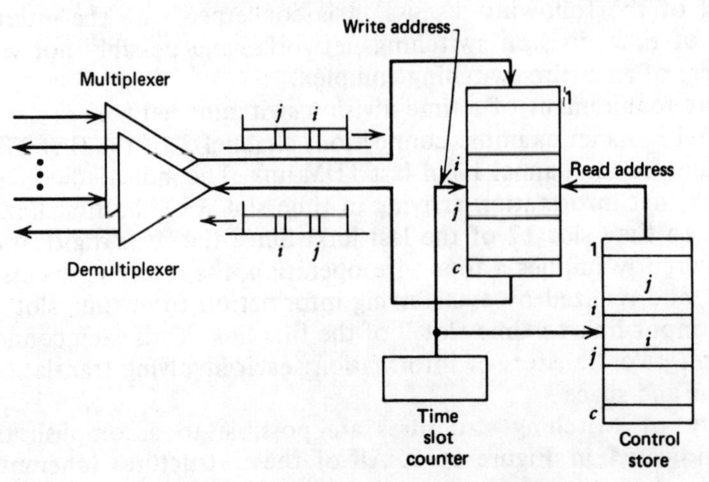

Figure 5.17 Time slot interchange circuit.

The exchange of information between two different time slots is accomplished by a time slot interchange (TSI) memory. In the TSI of Figure 5.17 data words in incoming time slots are written into sequential locations of the memory. Data words for outgoing time slots, however, are read from TSI addresses obtained from a control store. As indicated in the associated control store, a full-duplex connection between TDM channel i and TDM channel j implies that TSI address i is read during outgoing time slot j and vice versa. The TSI memory is accessed twice during each link time slot. First, some control circuitry (not shown) selects the time slot number as a write address. Second, the content of the control store for that particular time slot is selected as a read address.

Since a write and a read is required for each channel entering (and leaving) the TSI memory, the maximum number of channels c that can be supported by the simple memory switch is

$$c = \frac{125}{2t_c} \tag{5.12}$$

where 125 is the frame time in microseconds for 8 kHz sampled voice, and t_c is the memory cycle time in microseconds.

As a specific example, consider the use of a 500 ns memory. Equation 5.12 indicates that the memory switch can support 125 full-duplex channels (62 connections) in a strictly nonblocking mode of operation. The complexity of the switch (assuming digitization occurs elsewhere) is quite modest: the TSI memory stores one frame of data organized as c words by 8 bits each. The control store also requires c words, but each word has a length equal to $\log_2(c)$ (which is 7 in the example). Thus both memory functions can be supplied by 128 $\times$ 8 bit random access memories (RAMs). The addition of a time slot counter and some gating logic to select addresses and enable new information to be written into the control store can be accomplished with a handful of conventional integrated circuits (ICs).

This switch should be contrasted to a space division design that requires 7,680 crosspoints for a nonblocking three-stage switch. Although modern integrated circuit technology might be capable of placing that many digital crosspoints in a few integrated circuits, they could never be reached because of pin limitations. As mentioned in Chapter 2, one of the main advantages of digital signals is the ease with which they can be time division multiplexed. This advantage arises for communication between integrated circuits as well as for communication between switching offices.

If the multiplexer and demultiplexer combination in Figure 5.17 is enhanced to provide concentration and expansion, the system can service much greater numbers of input lines, depending on the average circuit utilization. For example, if the average line is busy 10% of the time, a concentrator/memory switch/expandor operation could support 1000 circuits with a blocking probability of less than .002. The concentration and expansion operations, however, imply a significant increase in the complexity of the system. In fact, these equipments essentially represent time multiplexed space division switches that must be controlled accordingly. The concentrator/memory switch/expandor structure essentially becomes a simple form of a space-time-space (STS) switch discussed later.

Time Stages in General

Time switching stages inherently require some form of delay element to provide the desired time slot interchanges. Delays are most easily implemented using random access memories that are written into as data arrives and read from when data is to be transferred out. If one memory location is allocated for each time slot in the TDM frame format, the information from each TDM channel can be stored for up to one full frame time without being overwritten.

There are two basic ways in which the time stage memories can be controlled: written sequentially and read randomly, or written randomly and read sequentially. Figure 5.18 depicts both modes of operation and indicates how the memories are accessed to translate information from time slot 3 to time slot 17. Notice that both modes of operation use a cyclic control store that is accessed in synchronism with the time slot counter.

The first mode of operation in Figure 5.18 implies that specific memory locations are dedicated to respective channels of the incoming TDM link. Data for each incoming time slot is stored in sequential locations within the memory by incrementing a modulo-c counter with

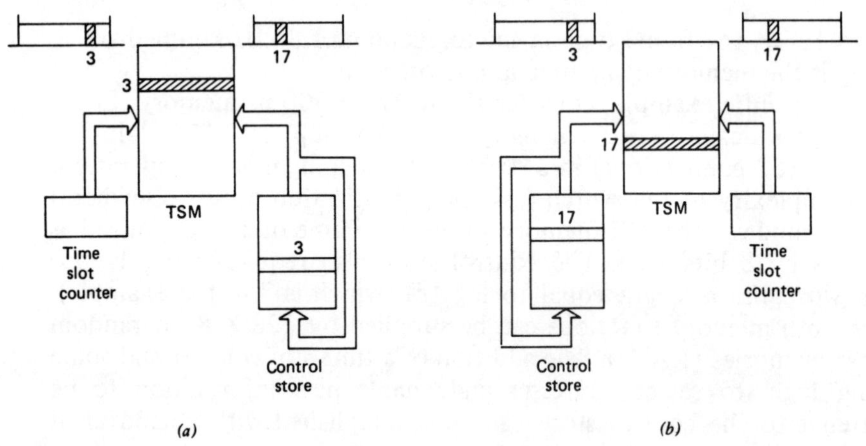

Figure 5.18 Time stage modes of operation. (*a*) Sequential writes/random reads. (*b*) Random writes/sequential reads.

every time slot. As indicated, the data received during time slot 3 is automatically stored in the third location within the memory. On output, information retrieved from the control store specifies which address is to be accessed for that particular time slot. As indicated, the seventeenth word of the control store contains the number 3, implying that the contents of time stage memory (TSM) address 3 is transferred to the output link during outgoing time slot 17.

The second mode of operation depicted in Figure 5.18 is exactly the opposite of the first one. Incoming data is written into the memory locations as specified by the control store, but outgoing data is retrieved sequentially under control of an outgoing time slot counter. As indicated in the example, information received during time slot 3 is written directly into TSM address 17 where it is automatically retrieved during outgoing TDM channel number 17. Notice that the two modes of time stage operation depicted in Figure 5.18 are forms of output-associated control and input-associated control, respectively. In a multiple stage design example presented later, it is convenient to use one mode of operation in one time stage and the other mode of operation in another time stage.

5.4 TWO-DIMENSIONAL SWITCHING

Larger digital switches require switching operations in both a space dimension and a time dimension. There are a large variety of network configurations that can be used to accomplish these requirements. To begin with, consider a simple switching structure as shown in Figure 5.19. This switch consists of only two stages: a time stage T followed by a space stage S. Thus this structure is referred to a time-space TS switch.

The basic function of the time stage is to delay information in arriving time slots until the desired output time slot occurs. At that time the delayed information is transferred through the space stage to the appropriate output link. In the example shown the information in incoming time slot 3 of link 1 is delayed until outgoing time slot 17 occurs. The return path requires that information arriving in time slot 17 of link N be delayed for time slot 3 of the next outgoing frame. Notice that a time stage may have to provide delays ranging from one time slot to a full frame.

Associated with the space stage is a control store that contains the information needed to specify the space stage configuration for each individual time slot of a frame. This control information is accessed cyclically in the same manner as the control information in the analog time division switch. For example, during each outgoing time slot 3, control information is accessed that specifies interstage link number 1

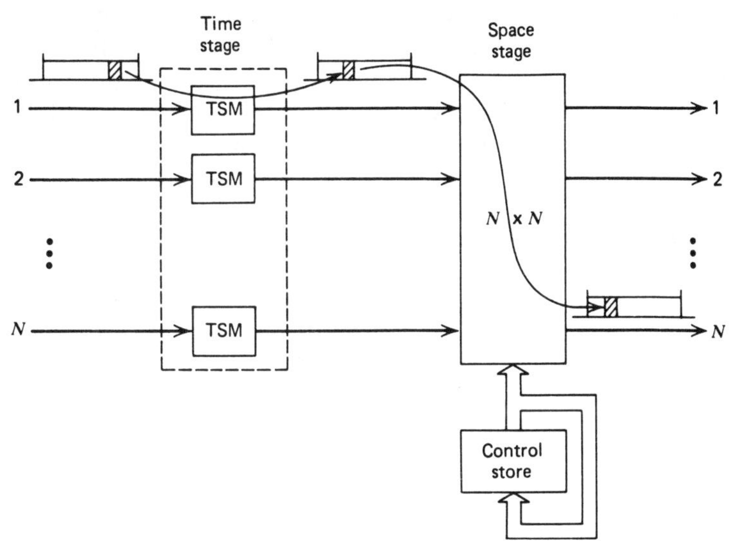

Figure 5.19 Time-space (TS) switching matrix.

is connected to output link N. During other time slots, the space switch is completely reconfigured to support other connections.

As indicated, a convenient means of representing a control store is a parallel end-around-shift register. The width of the shift register is equal to the number of bits required to specify the entire space switch configuration during a single time slot. The length of the shift register conforms to the number of time slots in a frame. Naturally, some means of changing the information in the control store is needed so that new connections can be established. In actual practice, the control stores may be implemented as random access memories with counters used to generate addresses in a cyclic fashion.

Implementation Complexity of Time Division Switches

In previous sections, alternative space division switching structures were compared in terms of the total number of crosspoints required to provide a given grade of service. Other factors that should be considered in a comprehensive analysis are: modularity, pathfinding requirements, effects of failures, serviceability, wiring or interconnection requirements, electrical loadings, and others. Despite the need to assess these other considerations, a crosspoint count is a useful, single measure of a space division switch cost, particularly with electromechanical crosspoints.

In the case of solid state electronic switching matrices, in general, and time division switching, in particular, the number of crosspoints alone is a less meaningful measure of implementation cost. Switching structures that utilize integrated circuits with relatively large numbers of internal crosspoints are generally more cost effective than other structures that may have fewer crosspoints but more packages. Hence a more relevant design parameter for solid state switches would be the total number of integrated circuit packages. If alternate designs are implemented from a common set of integrated circuits, the number of packages may closely reflect the number of crosspoints.

Another useful cost parameter is the total number of IC pin-outs required in a particular implementation. Although this parameter is obviously related closely to the total number of packages, it is generally more useful since it more accurately reflects package cost and circuit board area requirements. Pin-out measurements also provide a direct indication of implementation reliability, since external interconnections are generally less reliable than internal connections of an IC.

Medium scale integrated (MSI) circuits typically provide the equivalent of one crosspoint (AND gate) for $1\frac{1}{2}$ external pins to access the crosspoint. Thus when MSI technology is used, the total number of crosspoints is a useful indication of the total number of pins. We therefore continue to use crosspoints as an implementation cost measurement with the understanding that medium scale integration would be used in all comparative designs. To do so we must be sure that all systems operate at about the same speed, since higher speeds require lower levels of integration.

In addition to the number of crosspoints in space division stages, a digital time division switch uses significant amounts of memory that must be included in an estimate of the overall cost.* The memory count includes the time stage memory arrays and the control stores for both the time stages and the space stages. In the following analyses we assume that 100 bits of memory corresponds to $1\frac{1}{2}$ IC interconnections. (A 1024 bit random access memory typically requires 14 pins.) With this assumption, we can relate memory costs to crosspoint costs by a 100 bits per crosspoint factor. Hence the following analyses of implementation complexity for digital time division switching matrices include the total number of crosspoints and the total number of bits of memory divided by 100.

The implementation complexity is expressed as follows:

$$\text{complexity} = N_X + \frac{N_B}{100} \tag{5.13}$$

where N_X = number of space stage crosspoints
N_B = number of bits of memory

EXAMPLE 5.2

Determine the implementation complexity of the TS switch shown in Figure 5.19 where the number of TDM input lines $N = 80$. Assume each input line contains a single DS-1 signal (24 channels). Furthermore,

---

*It is worth noting that digital memories are inherently implemented with at least two crosspoints per bit. In this case the crosspoints are gates used to provide write and read access to the bits. These crosspoints, however, are much less expensive than message crosspoints that are accessed from external circuits.

assume a one-stage matrix is used for the space stage.

Solution. The number of crosspoints in the space stage is determined as

$$N_X = 80^2 = 6400$$

(The crosspoints on the main diagonal are included since two channels within a single TDM input may have to be connected to each other.) The total number of memory bits for the space stage control store is determined as

$$\begin{aligned} N_{BX} &= \text{(number of links) (number of control words)} \\ &\quad \text{(number of bits/control word)} \\ &= (80)(24)(7) \\ &= 13440 \end{aligned}$$

The number of memory bits in the time stage is determined as the sum of the time slot interchange and the control store bits:

$$\begin{aligned} N_{BT} &= \text{(number of links) (number of channels)} \\ &\quad \text{(number of bits/channel) + (number of links)} \\ &\quad \text{(number of control words) (number of bits/control word)} \\ &= (80)(24)(8) + (80)(24)(5) \\ &= 24{,}960 \end{aligned}$$

Thus the implementation complexity is determined as

$$\text{complexity} = N_X + (N_{BX} + N_{BT})/100 = 6784 \text{ equivalent crosspoints}$$

The implementation complexity determined in Example 5.2 is obviously dominated by the number of crosspoints in the space stage. A significantly lower complexity (and generally lower cost) can be achieved if groups of input links are combined into higher-level multiplex signals before being switched. The cost of the front end multiplexers is relatively small if the individual DS-1 signals have already been synchronized for switching. In this manner, the complexity of the space stage is decreased appreciably while the overall complexity of the time stage increases only slightly. (See the problem set at the end of this chapter.) The implementation costs are reduced proportionately—up to the point that higher speeds dictate the use of a more expensive technology.

Multiple Stage Time and Space Switching

As discussed in the preceding section, an effective means of reducing the cost of a time division switch is to multiplex as many channels together as practical and perform as much switching in the time stages as possible. Time stage switching is generally less expensive than space stage switching—primarily because digital memory is much cheaper than digital crosspoints (AND gates). To repeat, the crosspoints themselves are not so expensive, it is the cost of accessing and selecting them from external pins that makes their use relatively costly.

Naturally, there are practical limits as to how many channels can be multiplexed into a common TDM link for time stage switching. When these practical limits are reached, further reductions in the implementation complexity can be achieved only by using multiple stages. Obviously, some cost savings result when a single space matrix of a TS or ST switch can be replaced by multiple stages.

A generally more effective approach involves separating the space stages by a time stage, or, conversely, separating two time stages by a space stage. The next two sections describe these two basic structures. The first structure, consisting of a time stage between two space stages, is referred to as a space-time-space (STS) switch. The second structure is referred to as a time-space-time (TST) switch.

5.4.1 STS Switching

A functional block diagram of an STS switch is shown in Figure 5.20. Each of the space switches is assumed to be a single stage (nonblocking) switch. For large switches, it may be desirable to implement the space switches with multiple stages. Establishing a path through an STS switch requires finding a time switch array with an available write access during the incoming time slot and an available read access during the desired outgoing time slot. When each individual stage (S, T, S) is nonblocking, the operation is functionally equivalent to the operation of a three-stage space switch. Hence a probability graph in Figure 5.21 of an STS switch is identical to the probability graph of Figure 5.8 for three-stage space switches. Correspondingly, the blocking probability of an STS switch is

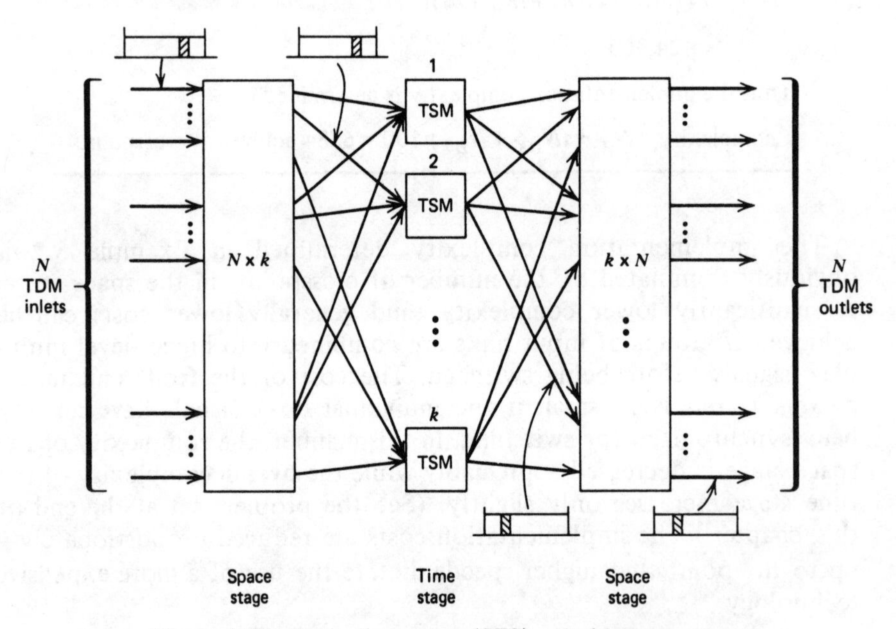

Figure 5.20 Space-time-space (STS) switching structure.

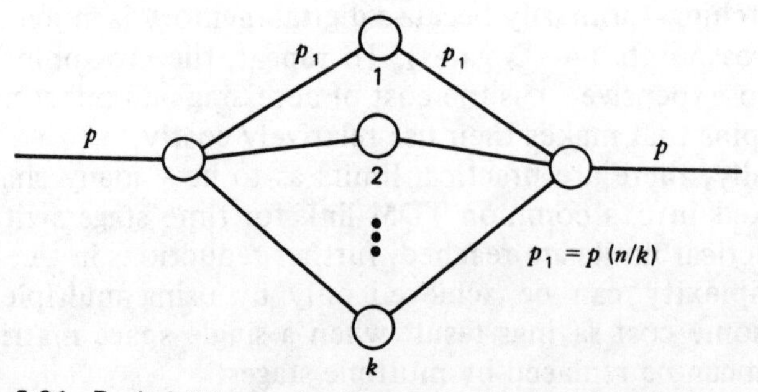

Figure 5.21 Probability graph of STS switch with nonblocking stages.

$$B = (1 - q'^2)^k \tag{5.14}$$

where $q' = 1 - p' = 1 - p/\beta \quad (\beta = k/N)$
k = number of center stage time switch arrays

Assuming the space switches are single stage arrays and that each TDM link has c message channels, we may determine the implementation complexity of an STS switch as*

$$\begin{aligned} \text{complexity} &= (\text{number of space stage crosspoints}) \\ &\quad + [(\text{number of space stage control bits}) \\ &\quad + (\text{number of time stage memory bits}) \\ &\quad + (\text{number of time stage control bits})]/100 \\ &= 2kN + \frac{[2 \cdot k \cdot c \cdot \log_2 N + k \cdot c \cdot 8 + k \cdot c \cdot \log_2 c]}{100} \end{aligned} \tag{5.15}$$

EXAMPLE 5.3

Determine the implementation complexity of a 2048 channel STS switch implemented for 16 TDM links with 128 channels on each link. The desired maximum blocking probability is .002 for channel occupancies of 0.1.

Solution. The minimum number of center stage time switches to provide the desired grade of service can be determined from Equation 5.14 as $k = 7$. Using this value of k, the number of crosspoints is determined as (2)(7)(16) = 224. The number of bits of memory can be determined as (2)(7)(128)(4) + (7)(128)(8) + (7)(128)(7) = 20,608. Hence the composite implementation complexity is 430 equivalent crosspoints.

The value of implementation complexity obtained in Example 5.3 should be compared to the number of crosspoints obtained for an equivalent sized three-stage switch listed in Table 5.2. The space switch design requires 41,000 crosspoints while the STS design requires only 430 equivalent crosspoints. The dramatic savings comes about as a result of the voice signals having already been digitized and multiplexed (presumably for transmission purposes). When the STS switch is inserted into an analog environment, the dominant cost of the switch occurs in the line interface. Modern digital switches are not unlike modern digital computers. The cost of a central processing unit has become relatively small compared to the costs of peripheral devices.

5.4.2 TST Switching

A second form of multiple stage time and space switching is shown in Figure 5.22. This switch is usually referred to as a time-space-time (TST) switch. Information arriving in a TDM channel of an incoming link is delayed in the inlet time stage until an appropriate path through the space stage is available. At that time the information is transferred through the space stage to the appropriate outlet time stage where it is held until the desired outgoing time slot occurs. Assuming the time stages provide full availability (i.e. all incoming channels can be con-

---

*This derivation assumes output-associated control is used in the first stage and input-associated control is used in the third stage. A slightly different result occurs if the space stages are controlled in different manners.

nected to all outgoing channels), any space stage time slot can be used to establish a connection. In a functional sense the space stage is replicated once for every internal time slot. This concept is reinforced by the TST probability graph of Figure 5.23.

An important feature to notice about a TST switch is that the space stage operates in a time divided fashion, independently of the external TDM links. In fact, the number of space stage time slots l does not have to coincide with the number of external TDM time slots c.

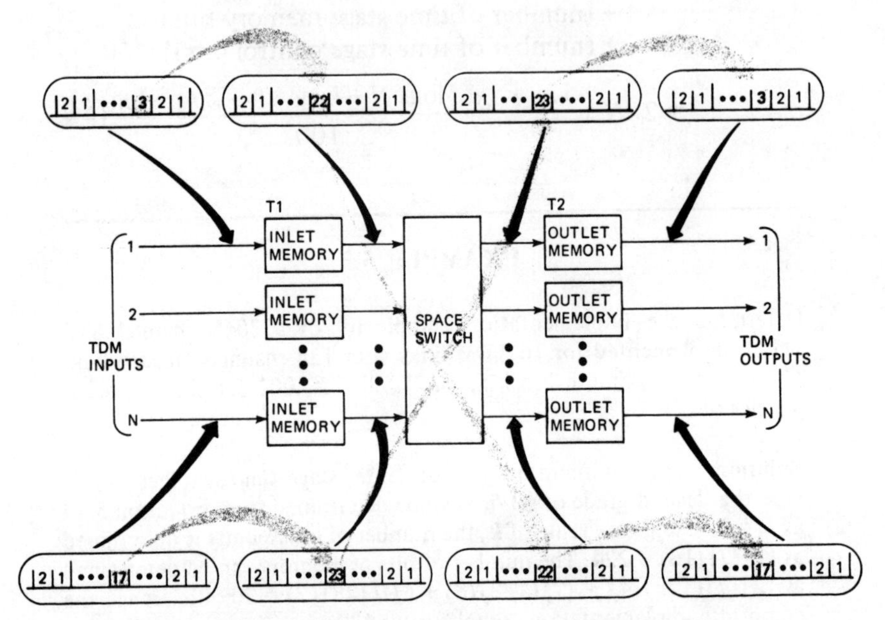

Figure 5.22 Time-space-time (TST) switching structure.

If the space stage is nonblocking, blocking in a TST switch occurs only if there is no internal space stage time slot during which the link from the inlet time stage and the link to the outlet time stage are both idle. Obviously, the blocking probability is minimized if the number of space stage time slots l is made to be large. In fact, as a direct analogy of three-stage space switches, the TST switch is strictly nonblocking if $l = 2c - 1$. The general expression of blocking probability for a TST switch with nonblocking individual stages (T, S, T) is:

$$B = [1 - q_1^2]^l \qquad (5.16)$$

where $q_1 = 1 - p_1 = 1 - p/\alpha$
α = time expansion (l/c)
l = number of space stage time slots

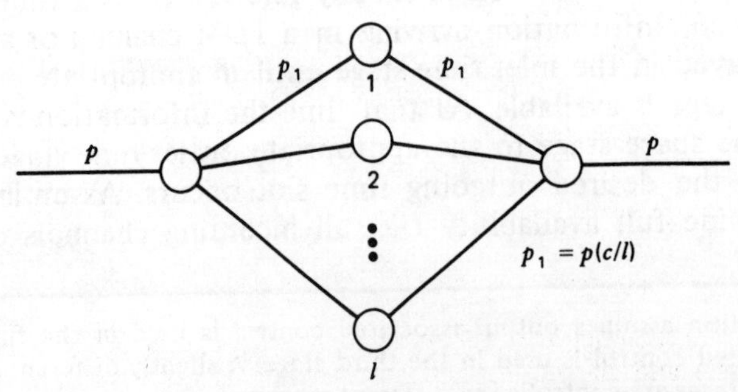

Figure 5.23 Probability graph of TST switch with nonblocking stages.

The implementation complexity of a TST switch can be derived as follows:*

$$\text{complexity} = N^2 + \frac{[N \cdot l \cdot \log_2 N + 2 \cdot N \cdot c \cdot 8 + 2 \cdot N \cdot l \log_2 c]}{100} \qquad (5.17)$$

EXAMPLE 5.4

Determine the implementation complexity of a 2048 channel TST switch with 16 TDM links and 128 channels per link. Assume the desired maximum blocking probability is .002 for incoming channel occupancies of 0.1.

Solution. Using Equation 5.16, we can determine the number of internal time slots required for the desired grade of service as 25. Hence time concentration of $1/\alpha = 5.12$ is possible because of the light loading on the input channels. The implementation complexity can now be determined from Equation 5.17 as 656.

The results obtained in Examples 5.3 and 5.4 indicate that the TST architecture is more complex than the STS architecture. Notice, however, that the TST switch operates with time concentration whereas the STS switch operates with space concentration. As the utilization of the input links increase, less and less concentration is acceptable. If the input channel loading is high enough, time expansion in the TST switch and space expansion in the STS switch are required to maintain low blocking probabilities. Since time expansion can be achieved at less cost than space expansion, a TST switch becomes more cost effective than an STS switch for high channel utilizations. The implementation complexities of these two systems are compared in Figure 5.24 as a function of the input utilization.

As can be seen in Figure 5.24, TST switches have a distinct implementation advantage over STS switches when large amounts of traffic are present. For small switches, the implementation complexities favor STS architectures. The choice of a particular architecture may be more dependent on such other factors as modularity, testability, expandability. One consideration that generally favors an STS structure is its relatively simpler control requirements [10]. For very large switches with heavy traffic loads, the implementation advantage of a TST switch is dominant. Evidence of this fact is provided by the No. 4ESS, a TST structure that is the largest capacity switch built to date.

---

*This derivation assumes that the inlet time stage uses output-associated control (random reads) and the outlet time stage uses input-associated control (random writes). A slightly different result occurs if the time stages operate differently.

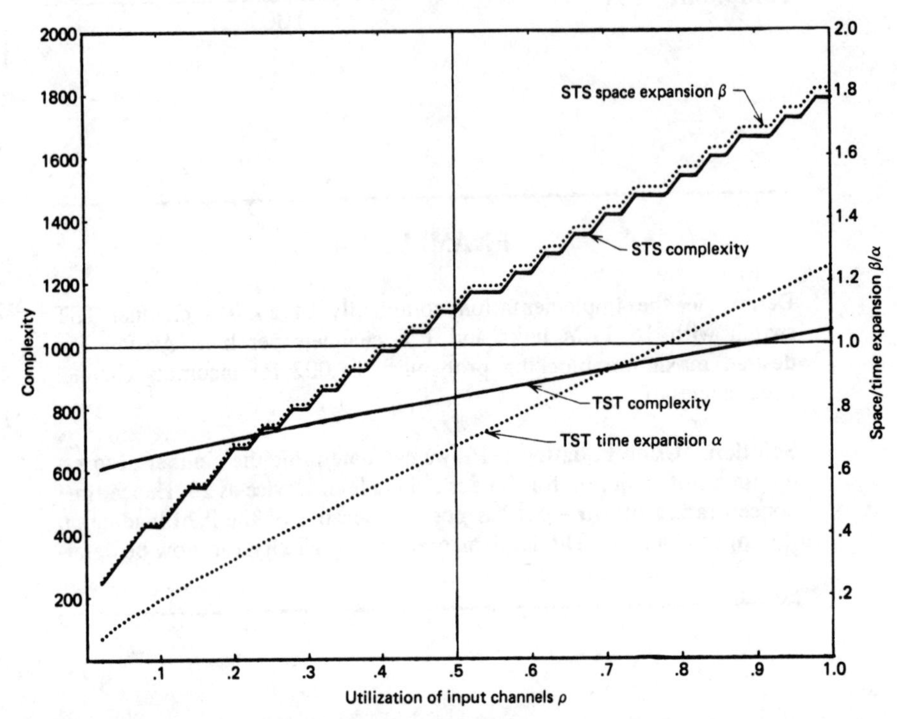

Figure 5.24 Complexity comparison of STS and TST switching structures for a blocking probability of .002.

TSSST Switches

When the space stage of a TST switch is large enough to justify additional control complexity, multiple space stages can be used to reduce the total crosspoint count. Figure 5.25 depicts a TST architecture with a three-stage space switch. Because the three middle stages are all space stages, this structure is sometimes referred to as a TSSST switch. The

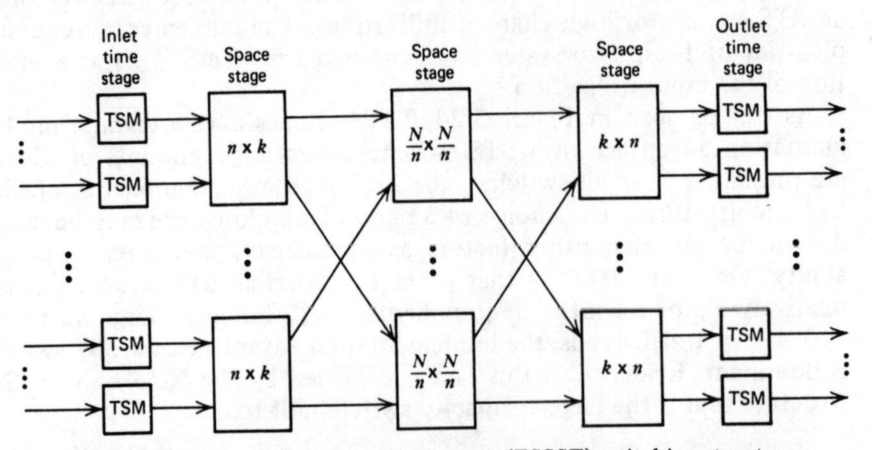

Figure 5.25 Time-space-space-space-time (TSSST) switching structure.

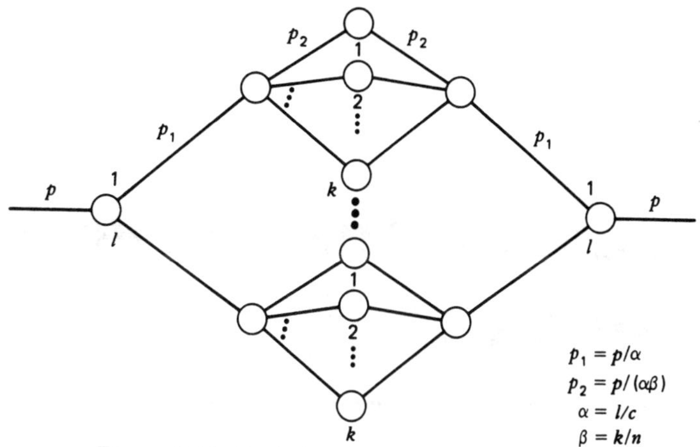

Figure 5.26 Probability graph of TSSST switch.

implementation complexity of a TSSST switch can be determined as follows:*

$$\text{complexity} = \frac{N_X + (N_{BX} + N_{BT} + N_{BTC})}{100} \tag{5.18}$$

where N_X = number of crosspoints = $2 \cdot N \cdot k + k \cdot (N/n)^2$
N_{BX} = number of space stage control store bits = $2 \cdot k \cdot (N/n) \cdot l \cdot \log_2 (n) + k \cdot (N/n) \cdot l \cdot \log_2 (N/n)$
N_{BT} = number of bits in time stages = $2 \cdot N \cdot c \cdot 8$
N_{BTC} = number of time stage control store bits = $2 \cdot N \cdot l \cdot \log_2 (c)$

The probability graph of a TSSST switch is shown in Figure 5.26. Notice that this diagram is functionally identical to the probability graph of a five-stage space switch shown in Figure 5.10. Using the probability graph of Figure 5.26, we can determine the blocking probability of a TSSST switch as

$$B = \{1 - (q_1)^2 \; [1 - (1 - q_2^2)^k]\}^l \tag{5.19}$$

where $q_1 = 1 - p_1 = 1 - p/\alpha$
$q_2 = 1 - p_2 = 1 - p/\alpha\beta$

EXAMPLE 5.5

Determine the implementation complexity of a 131,072 channel TSSST switch designed to provide a maximum blocking probability of .002 under channel occupancies of 0.7. Assume the switch services 1024

*The assumed control orientations by stages are: output, output, output, input, input.

TECH NOTE

Data Communications Network Switching Methods

Features of multichannel intelligent data switching system permit cost-effective data switching of data communications networks

David A. Kane Develcon Electronics Incorporated, Doylestown, Pennsylvania

Today's data communications networks are considerably more complex and larger than the systems in use just a few years ago. Too often, however, these networks have been limited in their rate of growth and usefulness due to the lack of adequate data switching facilities to interconnect system elements. More direct, selective, interterminal communications links are needed to meet the requirements of increasingly intelligent data communications systems. The technology required to effectively interconnect data in these systems has grown in proportion with the advances in data processing's state of the art.

Previously, there were two popular methods of connecting the various hardware in the network: the dial-up lines of common carrier facilities, and dedicated channels and contention hardware. Recently a multichannel, intelligent data switch system has been developed. Connection methods are chosen depending on criteria such as the distances involved and the amount of time a device in the network must remain online with another device.

Common Carrier Facilities

The common carrier or dial-up facilities connect each device in the data processing network to separate multiline rotary exchanges (see Fig 1). This connection enables an unlimited group of users to contend for service port groups through the common carrier switched network—all on a first come, first serve basis.

In a typical timesharing application, the telephone rotary contention allows support of up to four terminals per computer. This permits realization of significant savings in computer port hardware. In addition, there is improved utilization of the computer ports installed. When the computer is busy or connected, the user receives these indications via the telephone rotary. Moreover, terminal users may gain access to different computer systems or support different applications programs on the same computer system, so dial-up access may be used to provide a port selection facility.

Reprinted with permission from *Computer Design* April 1980 issue.

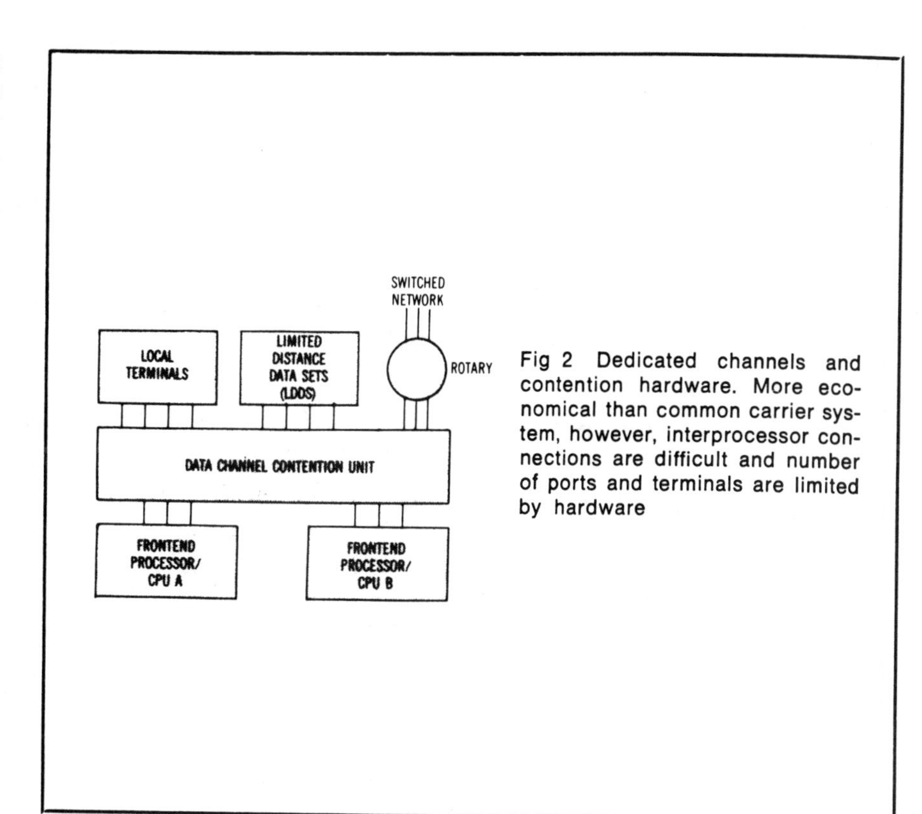

Fig 2 Dedicated channels and contention hardware. More economical than common carrier system, however, interprocessor connections are difficult and number of ports and terminals are limited by hardware

Since dial-up access is dependent upon the telephone, many of this system's advantages are negated by the ever increasing telephone and equipment costs and by limiting performance factors. Because this approach operates on a 2-wire circuit, there are data transmission speed restrictions. Even with the new modems available, the maximum speed is only 1200 baud. Controlled carrier operations with synchronous speeds up to 9600 baud are possible, however, many terminals don't have the required interface control signals for these operations.

With common carrier facilities, no statistical information as to system usage is available. There is no way to exactly determine how many users dialed but were unable to connect with the computers. There are also no statistics for the number of successful calls. If this type of information were available, computer center managers could determine more accurately the efficiency of their operations.

Another problem facing common carrier facility users is the increasingly higher tariffs charged by the telephone company for use of its facilities. Originally the tariffs were based on voice usage. The typical phone call lasted three to five minutes and billings were charged for the number of these short calls. Now, since so many computer users connect to the data terminal by the switched telephone network, phone calls are much longer. Many terminal users are connected for eight or ten hours through the common carrier facility every business day.

The phone company wants to be compensated for this type of usage and now penalizes terminal users with a new tariff in which business usage is measured in increments of five minutes or less. Single message units are charged for each 5-min increment. These tariffs may adversely affect users with PABX and Centrex services. Heavier reliance on these services may result in larger systems—even though voice traffic may not warrant it.

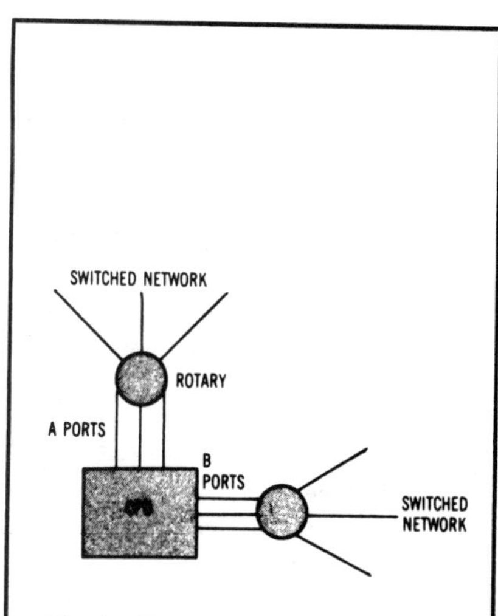

Fig 1 Common carrier system configuration. Multi-line rotary exchanges allow large numbers of users to contend for computer ports through its switched network

Dedicated Channels and Contention Hardware

This method, commonly known as port contention, eliminates some of the problems associated with the dial-up access approach. Service requests are hardware generated. It is more economical—channels are normally leased or owned. The response to service requests is fast. Also, statistical information on system usage may be available.

The dedicated channels and contention hardware approach (Fig 2) does have limiting factors. It presumes that associated equipment are either ports or terminals, and the hardware limits the number of ports and terminals that can be utilized. Inter-processor (port to port) connections are difficult. This method may not provide connect and busy indications.

Multichannel Intelligent Data Switch

There is yet another means of connecting terminals to computers, one that eliminates all of the shortcomings of the other two methods, as well as offers many additional advantages. The technique, called multichannel intelligent data switching, is comparable to the typical central office in a modern switched telephone network. With this approach (see Fig 3), any device in the network can access any other device in the network. Computers

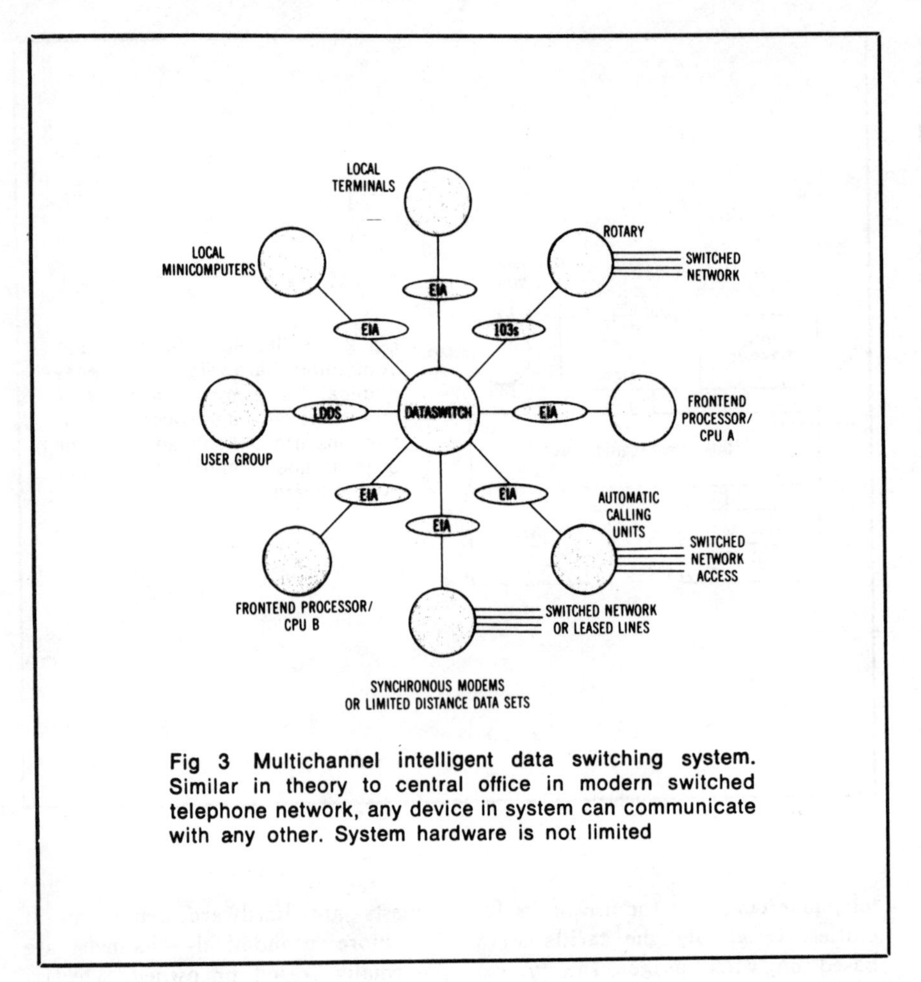

Fig 3 Multichannel intelligent data switching system. Similar in theory to central office in modern switched telephone network, any device in system can communicate with any other. System hardware is not limited

can communicate with terminals, terminals can talk with printers, printers with computers, and peripheral devices can talk with each other.

Through a unique combination of hardware and software the data switch system controls and coordinates all ports, integrating both the dial-up and dedicated access approaches. The system permits non-biased use by operating on a first come, first serve basis. All subscribers (devices in the system) have an equal opportunity to originate requests to any other subscriber. The subscribers contend for a number of incoming channels, or lines, and for computer communications interfaces (ports).

The data switch intercepts a subscriber's request for service, reviews whether the service is available, and then either completes the connection or advises the calling subscriber that the connection cannot be made. Up to 2048 subscribers may be connected, and the system will allow up to 1023 simultaneous full-duplex connections. Communications links in a data communications network incorporating a data switching system may be by dial-up, leased line with limited distance modems, by local terminals, or through any device with an EIA standard RS-232 interface.

Devices with different bit rates or character sets in the network are responded to automatically with a data switching system. A 1200-baud terminal contending for the same deck with a 2400-baud device, will automatically be connected to the first 1200-baud port available in that deck; the 2400-baud device will automatically be connected to the first 2400-baud port available. Essentially, all mixing of transmission speeds is handled by the system. Once port to port connections are made, full-duplex conversations proceed without further intervention. When one party desires to end a connection, the system disconnects both devices simultaneously.

Data switching methods improve computer utilization by expanding data communications line capacities of a realtime computer system. They can be used to optimize computer port utilization for such applications as university campuses, military bases, and hospital complexes where private wires and terminal connections are often required to minimize transmission costs when dedicated channels are uneconomical due to low usage. The data switching method also circumvents the single message unit tariff imposed by the telephone company, without the use of leased or private lines.

Several considerations will insure continued cost-effectiveness, usefulness, and even growth of the system. Maximizing the number of possible terminals, ports, and subscribers will expand the data communications network. The ability to accommodate different codes and transmission speeds ranging from 1200 to 19.2k baud will also assure future growth. The highest possible synchronous and asynchronous transmission speeds will help maximize the cost-effectiveness of the system.

For a truly effective data communications network, the central switching device must be capable of permitting universal access to all devices in the network. In addition, the number of simultaneous connections at any one time should be sufficiently high to allow maximum operating efficiency. Other desirable features include prioritized queuing, account recognition, partyline connections. a password system for data security, English language commands, a broadcast message capability, displaying status messages to operators, memory retention of data in the event of a power failure, and system response to a successful connection.

Summary

A multichannel intelligent data switching system eliminates the short comings of both the common carrier dial-up facilities and the dedicated channels and contention hardware approaches to data switching. The advantages of this type of data switch help lower overall costs of data communications, improve efficiency, and enhance network performance. □

Controlling the mushrooming communications net

Mark Vonarx, Micom Systems Inc., Chatsworth, Calif.

The microcomputer-based intelligent patch panel lets a few computer ports serve more and more users and applications.

Among the many problems facing today's computer-site manager is the explosive growth both in the number and variety of his company's processors and in their effective uses. Typically, most computer systems begin with a single mainframe and local terminals for limited applications. However, before long, a growing demand necessitates adding multiple computers and data communications features, while users clamor for even more data processing services.

The usual results of this growth are:

- Each terminal user is permanently assigned a computer port, even when not active.
- This user cannot connect to a different computer without making cable changes.
- Multiple dial-up telephone rotaries are required for each computer and for each transmission speed. (A dial-up rotary allows a remote-terminal user to call a single number and gain access to one of several auto-answer modems. This modem scans each telephone line for one that is not busy. If all lines are in use, it generates a busy signal.)

An early approach to solving these dilemmas was the use of patch-panel equipment that both enabled a user to manually connect to multiple resources and, with additional cables and switches, provided a level of system monitoring and diagnostics. Since microcomputers can now function in add-on intelligence roles, a new approach is possible: using a micro-based intelligent patch panel (IPP), also called a port selector.

Figure 1 shows a typical IPP configuration, where all users contend equally for computer resources. The necessary transparency of the device allows all users, regardless of connection technique (hard-wired, dial-up, multiplexed), to connect to any of three computers and to different applications within each computer class, all from their terminal keyboards. (Class is defined here as a partitioned physical or programmed resource.) To the user, this connection sequence typically occurs as outlined in the table. (Note that some manufacturers' products do not have all listed capabilities or features.)

The high level of feedback to the user from the IPP typically eliminates the need for intervention by computer-site personnel—especially in the case of the status message during excessive computer downtime, which usually floods the computer site with phone calls.

Additionally, such tutorial response messages as WRONG SPEED, BUSY, WAIT? (contention), and UNASSIGNED delivered in plain English minimize the extent of operator training. Where security is an important consideration, the UNAUTHORIZED response message not only tells the user that he is excluded from a particular resource but also flags the attempted intrusion for the site manager at the system console.

So, from the user's point of view, the intelligent patch panel offers a simple interface for providing feedback on the entire network and, at the same time, conserves computer resources and affords maximum flexibility. Yet the greatest benefit is derived primarily from using the IPP as a control tool. This provides the computer-site manager with a dynamic instrument to monitor and modify his entire network, while allowing for as

1. Contending equally. *In this typical IPP configuration, all users—regardless of connection technique (hard-wired, dial-up, multiplexed)—may connect to any of three computers and to different applications within each computer class from their terminal keyboards. An example of the user's connection sequence is outlined in the table.*

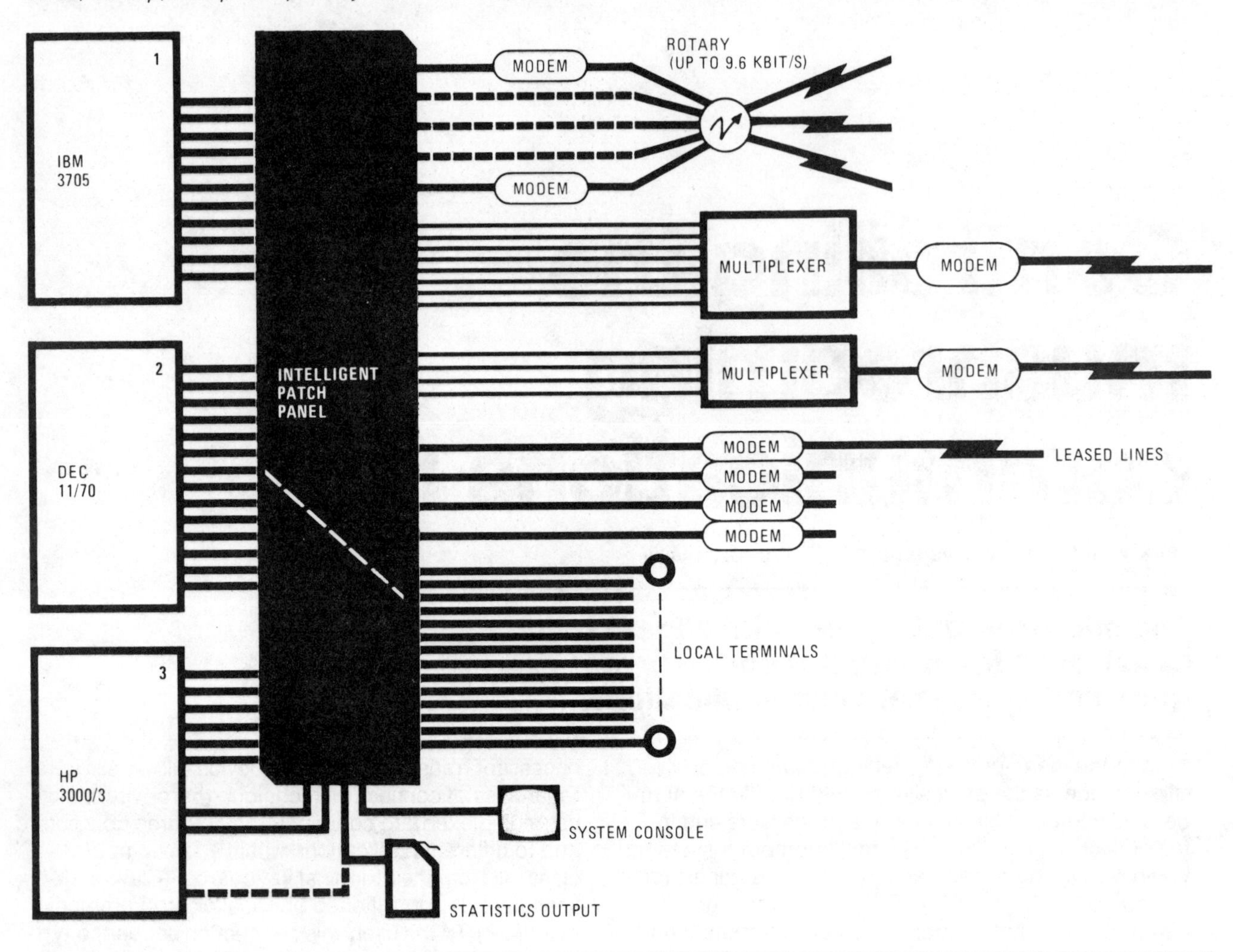

Operator-IPP interactive sequence

OPERATOR ENTRY	SYSTEM STATUS	IPP RESPONSE	EXPLANATION
"CR" (CARRIAGE RETURN)	READY	"CLASS = "	REQUESTS RESOURCE SELECTION
SELECTS 1 TO 127	AVAILABLE	"GO"	CONNECTED TO REQUESTED CLASS
SELECTS 1 TO 127	BUSY	"BUSY, N, WAIT?"	N = NUMBER ALREADY IN QUEUE
"YES" (WISHES TO WAIT)	BUSY	"GO"	CONNECT TO FIRST AVAILABLE PORT
"NO" (DOES NOT WISH TO WAIT)	BUSY	"DISCONNECTED"	CAN SELECT ANOTHER CLASS
SELECTS WRONG SPEED	READY	"WRONG SPEED"	CAN TRY AGAIN
SELECTS UNASSIGNED CLASS NUMBER	READY	"UNASSIGNED"	CAN TRY AGAIN
SELECTS UNAUTHORIZED CLASS	READY	"UNAUTHORIZED"	CAN TRY AGAIN
SELECTS UNAVAILABLE CLASS	CLASS DISABLED	"UNAVAILABLE"	CLASS DISABLED FROM CONSOLE
SELECTS UNAVAILABLE CLASS	CLASS DISABLED	"SYSTEM DOWN TIL 2 PM"	STATUS MESSAGE ENTERED
NO ACTIVITY	TIMEOUT DISCONNECT ENABLED	"DISCONNECTED"	VARIABLE TIMEOUT ENABLED
USER DISCONNECTS	READY	"DISCONNECTED"	USER-INITIATED DISCONNECT

much as twenty-fold growth. As a control tool, the IPP provides four methods of effectively managing computer and communications resources: universal access, contention and user feedback, statistics, and dynamic console control.

Effective resource sharing

Universal access allows all users to focus on a single interface device for all connection techniques and speeds. The hard-wired local terminal—which uses just three of the RS-232-C connections (TRANSMIT DATA, RECEIVE DATA, and SIGNAL GROUND)—can connect to the same resources as the dial-up and multiplexed user, as shown in Figure 1. From the computer-site manager's viewpoint, universal access means that he can select the most cost-effective connection technique regardless of terminal type and interface differences.

Contention and user feedback, as indicated earlier, frees the computer site from the continuous user complaints that typically lead to "pilot errors" by overburdening an undertrained computer-system staff.

Monitoring statistics on the entire network is key in effectively using both computer and communications resources by pinpointing over- and underutilization of each network component—especially in multiple-computer environments. Also, listing such events as connection failures, busy-queue size, and unauthorized entry spotlights trouble areas.

Controlling the network

Dynamic console control is another important attribute of the intelligent patch panel. When problems occur in allocating and controlling resources, dynamic network reconfiguration allows an immediate remedy and, in some cases, experimentation to determine the best possible resource mix.

Today, many users of IPP equipment actually connect the console port of the IPP to a computer port. They then use application programs resident in the computer to monitor and evaluate the statistics output, diagnose problems, and dynamically reallocate resources, even on an hourly basis.

Essentially, then, the IPP informs the computer-site manager of trouble areas that need his attention and allows comparatively easy redress of faults. Thus, a system of limited computer ports or resources can realistically support a user base several times the size of available facilities. And this support is usually even more effective than that attained by unrestrainedly adding resources, which eventually leads to system degradation. [For an in-depth discussion of computer port loading and costs savings, see "Port selectors: trading off the queues for lower network costs" (DATA COMMUNICATIONS, June 1977, p. 59).]

Adjusting the load

In practice, the IPP is even more versatile. For example, as already indicated, with the console control the user can adjust to heavy load periods by reassigning resources and enlarging busy queues, much as power companies do in load shedding. The timeout feature can help identify idle users, who, when spotted, are disconnected by the IPP from access to the computers. In sensitive or secure environments, the UNAUTHORIZED message flags a user who tries to improperly access a restricted resource, and the resulting access data may assist in identifying reckless or harmful users.

Figure 2 demonstrates how a network manager in Los Angeles with a large remote-user base in New York can save on costs if the remote operators contend for both computer ports and communications channels on a multiplexer. Also, the manager in Los Angeles can exercise control over the IPP in New York by using a single multiplexer channel to interface his system console to its port in New York.

Figure 3 is a block diagram of a typical early version

2. Remote control. *A network manager in Los Angeles with a large New York user base can save on communications costs if operators contend for both computer ports and communications channels on a multiplexer. Also, the manager can control the New York IPP by a mux channel connecting his console to its New York port.*

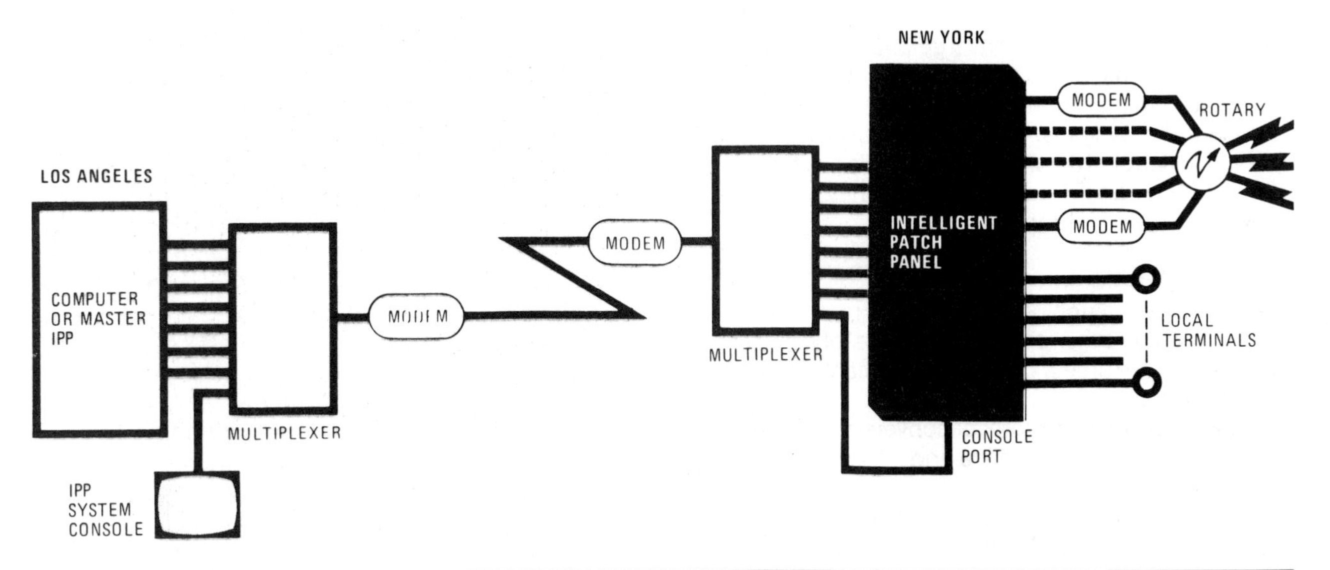

3. Inside an IPP. *Because of its modular architecture and full redundancy, the IPP typically becomes the keystone of a network. This modularity allows the simple "building-block" growth of a relatively small unit into quite a large one. The unit costs from about $10,000 to $100,000 and is available from a number of manufacturers.*

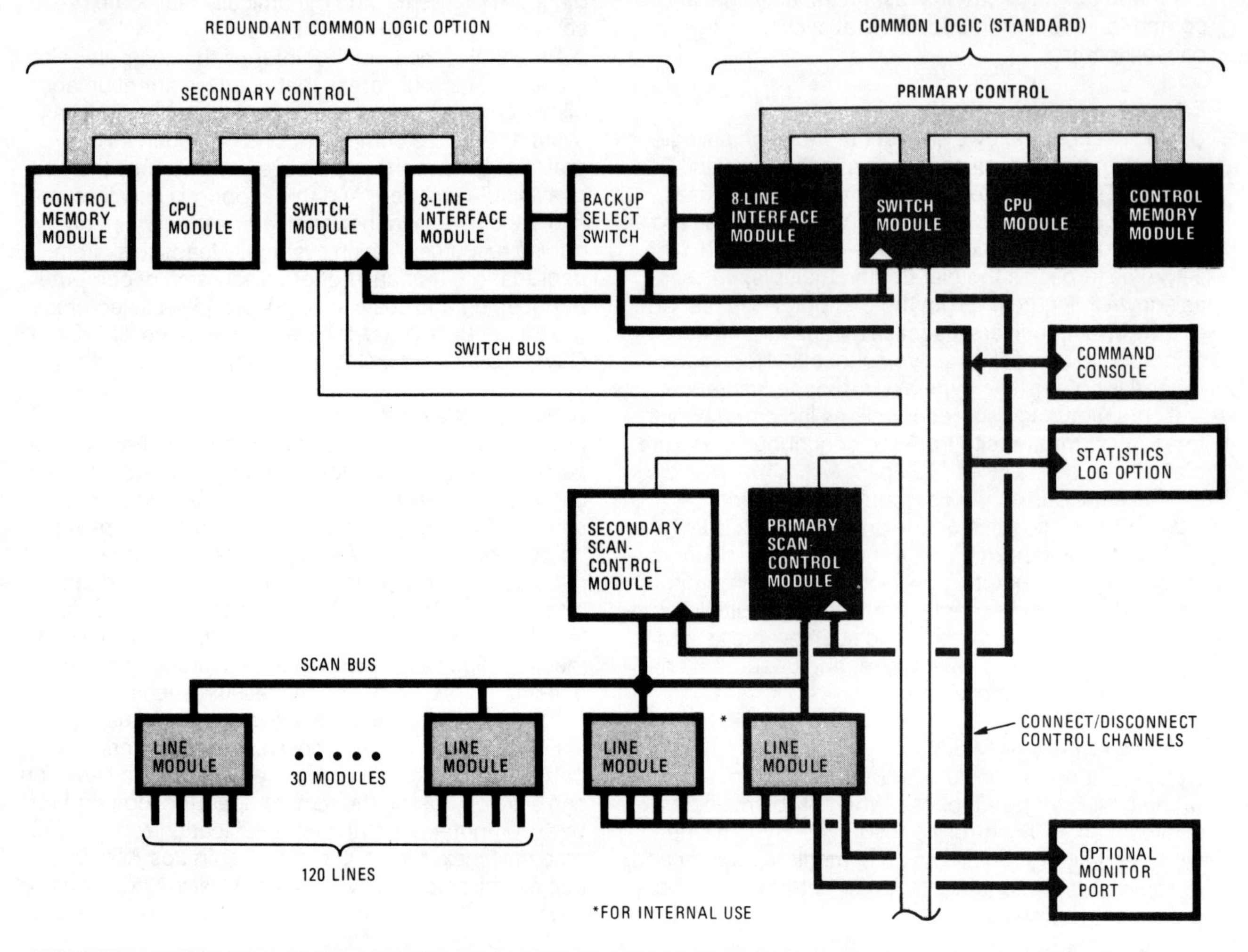

of the microcomputer-based intelligent patch panel. Because of its modular architecture and full redundancy, the IPP often becomes the operational keystone of a data communications network. This modularity allows the simple "building-block" growth of a relatively small unit into quite a large one.

IPPs are available today from a number of manufacturers, including Micom Systems, Gandalf Data, Codex, and Infotron Systems. Prices range from under $10,000 for a small table-top unit with 50 interfaces to over $100,000 for an IPP with full-redundancy, options, and several hundred interfaces.

'Blue-sky' outlook

The intelligent patch panel evokes more wishful thinking than many other products because of its inherent flexibility. The three most frequently mentioned "wish-list" items are:

1. Speed, code, and protocol conversion to make the IPP a truly universal interface and allow its use with large mainframes

2. Preprocessing capability so that certain CPU functions could be off-loaded to the IPP

3. Demultiplexing of remote multiplexers to further enhance network cost savings (such as a remote eight-channel multiplexer connected to a single local IPP interface, with the IPP acting as the local multiplexer)

However, these desirable features also increase the price and complexity of such equipment and push its function into the realm of the large, expensive front-end, or communications, processor.

The intelligent patch panel benefits both the user and the site manager. For the user, the IPP is a simple interface that affords keyboard selection of authorized computer resources and the feedback and control to minimize intervention by computer-site personnel. To the computer-site manager, the IPP gives the information and control necessary to dynamically change the entire network. This results in the most cost-effective configuration, savings in computer ports and operator time, and increased user efficiency.

Finally, because of the nature of any microprocessor-based device, the IPP is inherently programmable, thus allowing for future enhancements and avoiding the rapid obsolescence that seems to have characterized interface and access equipment for so long. ■

The ABCs of the PBX

Leo F. Goeller, Jr. and Jerry A. Goldstone

Private branch exchanges aren't just for communications types anymore. Here's part two of our four-part series on these important devices.

THE ABCS OF THE PBX

by Leo F. Goeller Jr. and Jerry A. Goldstone

A PBX or private branch exchange is a switchboard for business telephones. It differs from the phone company's central office (CO) switch in two very important ways. First, it must in general have someone to say, "XYZ Company, good morning" and then complete the call. Then, if the call reaches the wrong party, some means must be provided to transfer that call to another extension.

At the smaller end of the spectrum, key telephone systems compete with PBXs. A key system may have 50 or more telephones associated with it and many advanced features. There is a philosophical difference, however, between a PBX and a key system: a PBX has a relatively high proportion of calling among telephones it serves, while a key system has most of its traffic with the outside world and is used very little for internal calling. In much larger sizes, Centrex competes, usually by using specially modified central office equipment.

A PBX system (Fig. 1) is composed of four basic parts: switching matrix, control, user terminals, and trunks. The PBX proper includes the matrix and control, along with interface units, usually called line and trunk circuits, that terminate the transmission facilities that extend to user telephones or other switches. In addition, one usually finds "service circuits" in a PBX to apply ringing and call progress tones (busy, reorder, etc.), and to assimilate caller signaling information from telephone dials and tone pads, converting this information to something the control can use.

No matter how complex a modern PBX may become internally, it still works

Excerpted with permission from the *Business Communications Review Manual of PBXs*, published by Business Communications Review, Hinsdale, Ill.

PHOTOGRAPH BY STEVE COOPER

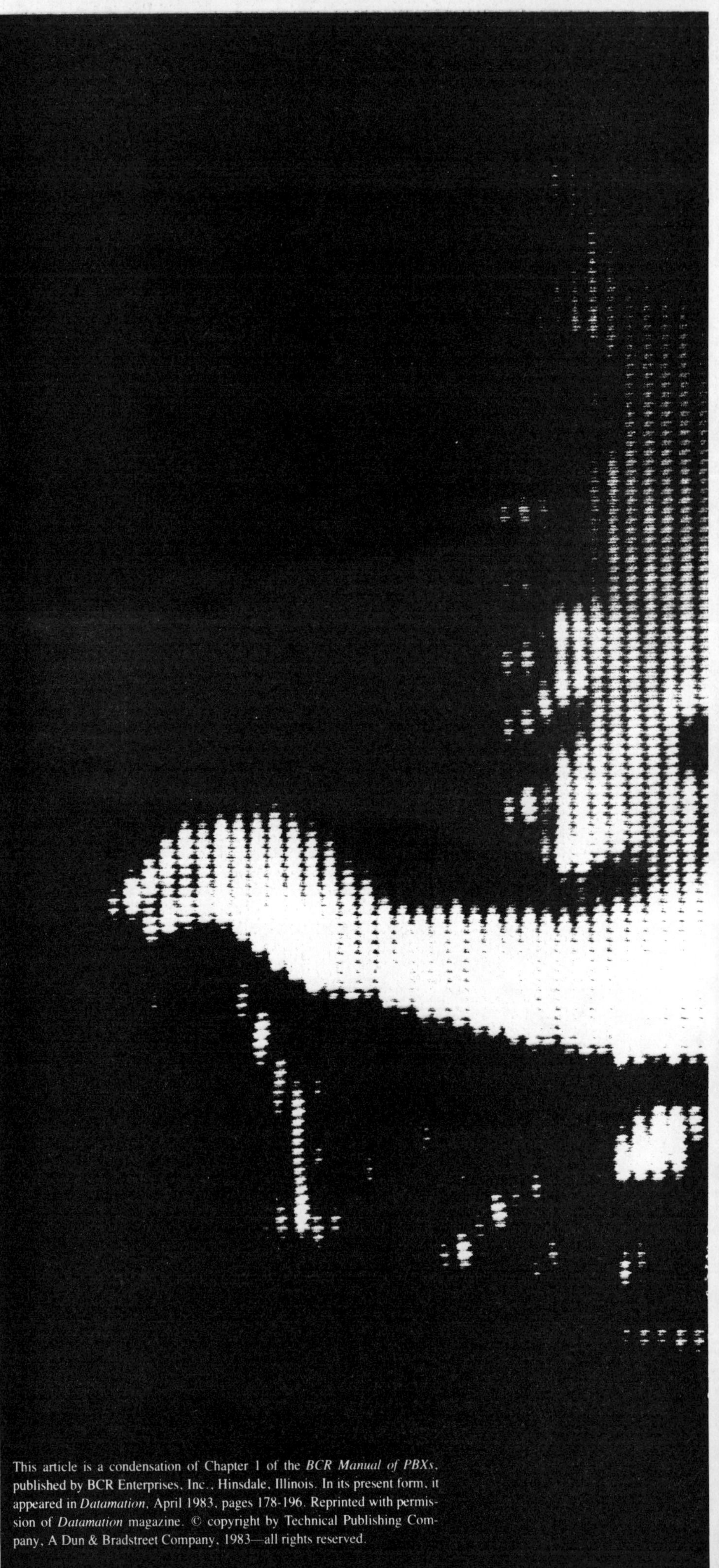

This article is a condensation of Chapter 1 of the *BCR Manual of PBXs*, published by BCR Enterprises, Inc., Hinsdale, Illinois. In its present form, it appeared in *Datamation*, April 1983, pages 178-196. Reprinted with permission of *Datamation* magazine.

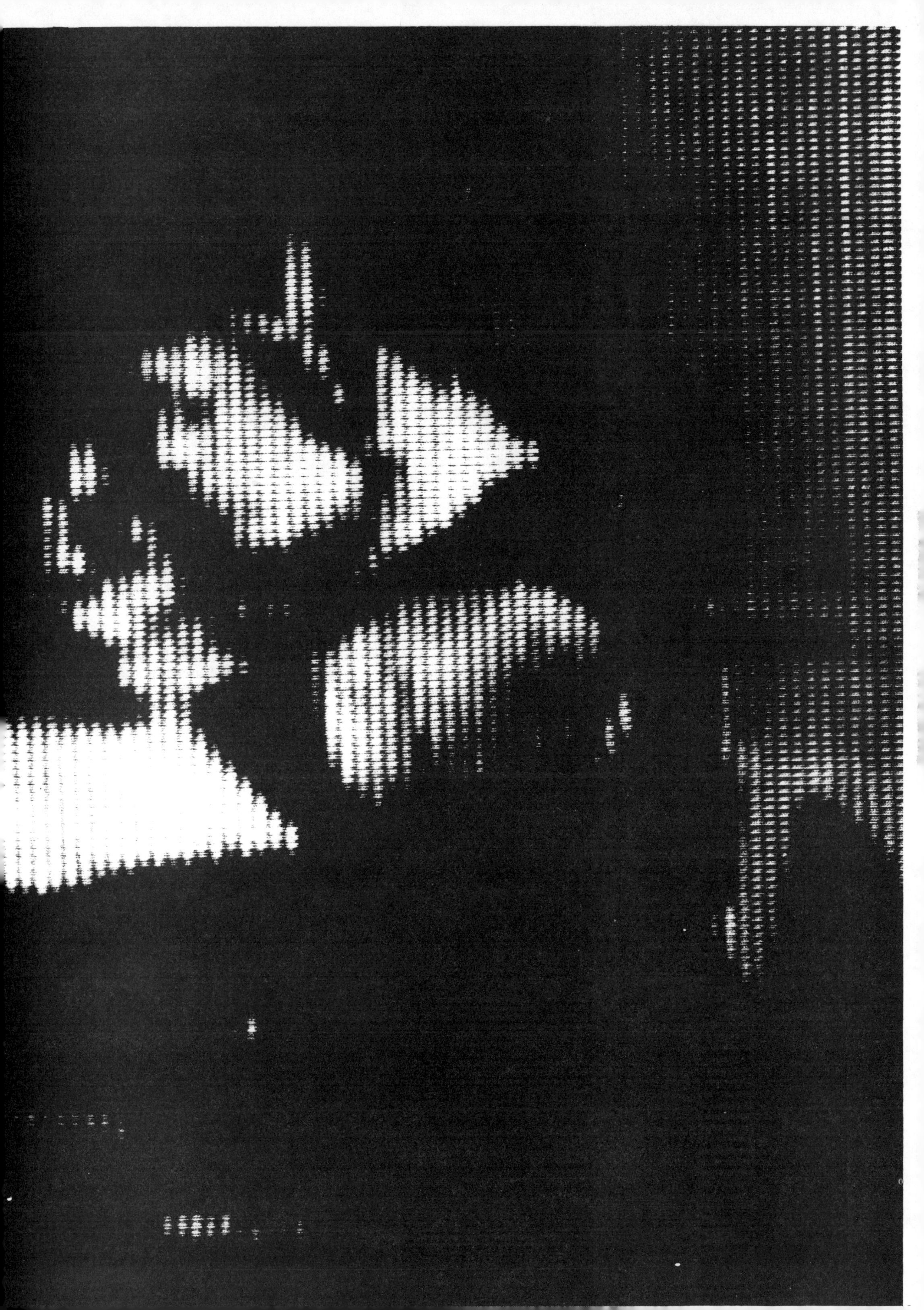

No matter how complex a modern PBX may become internally, it still works very much the way the old manual switchboards did.

very much the way the old manual switchboards did. In the so-called cord board, each line and trunk terminates in a suitable interface circuit that controls one or more signal lamps to alert the attendant and passes the voice path on to a jack that permits easy interconnection.

When a user picks up his phone, the PBX supplies power to the instrument and, by monitoring this flow of power (usually with a line relay), knows to light a lamp to tell the attendant that assistance is needed. The attendant has in front of him a number of pairs of cords that can be used to make connections to lines and/or trunks. These cords perform the precise functions that a modern PBX performs with its switching matrix. The attendant plugs one cord of a particular pair into the jack associated with the calling line and operates a switch that connects his headset to the cord circuit. He then says something like "Number, please" so that the caller knows the attendant is ready to respond to his communication needs. A modern system, of course, uses a dial tone to perform the same function, even though many such systems have replaced rotary dials with tone pads.

The caller then gives the attendant the number he wishes to reach. If it is another extension on the PBX, the attendant takes the other cord of the pair and makes a "busy test" on the called line to make sure it is not busy on another call. If the called line is idle, the attendant then completes the connection to the appropriate jack.

Either the attendant or automatic circuitry detects an answer, terminates ringing, and leaves the calling and called-station users to converse. If either of them needs further assistance, he flashes his switch-hook. That is, he depresses and releases his switch-hook. Each of the two cords in the pair making the connection has a lamp associated with it. Momentary depression of the switch-hook causes the lamp to come on momentarily. This flash signals the attendant to reconnect his headset to the cord circuit to see what assistance is required. When the call is completed and the parties hang up, the cord lamps light, letting the attendant know that the call is over and the cords can be pulled down and made available for another call.

There are still a few manual PBXs in use. They serve their customers well and, because they consist primarily of a very small switching matrix (the cords) and simple line and trunk circuits, they occupy little space and are relatively inexpensive. But perhaps their main advantage, in addition to low cost, is their control. They have the most advanced system control available today, one that is quite flexible and very smart: a human being. A human attendant at a manual switchboard can provide almost all the modern features associated with the new, computer-controlled PBXs. Attendants, available in common to all lines and trunks, meet all the requirements of what is called "common control" in modern switching systems. (Common control can be contrasted with "distributed control" in step-by-step electromechanical systems where each switch has its own control equipment and control is distributed over the entire switching matrix. Common control equipment, shared by all parts of the system, eliminates a great deal of duplication and, when done properly, reduces costs and improves operations.)

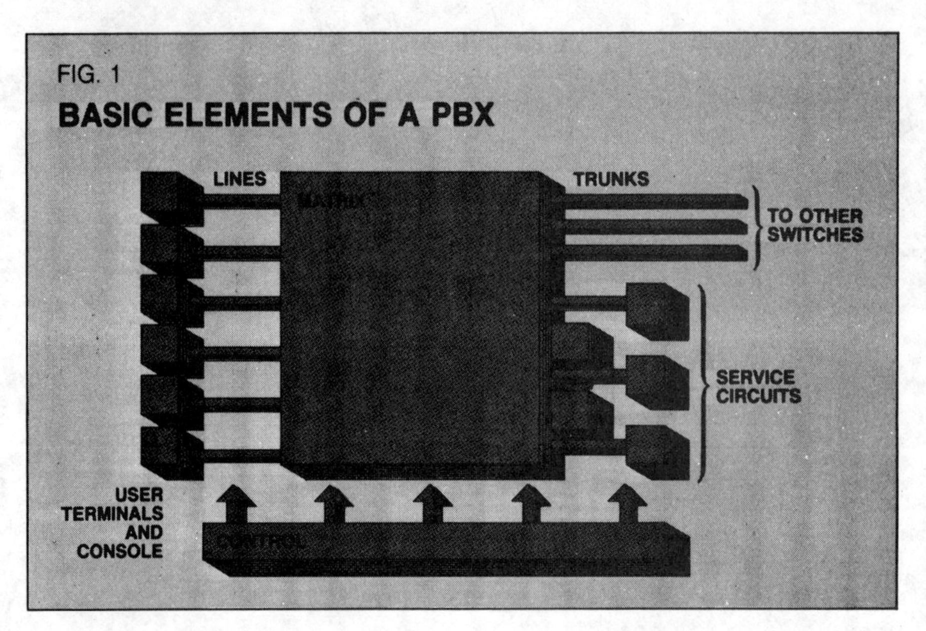

However, people are getting more and more expensive: they like to go to lunch in the middle of the day, they want to go home at night, and they require training. Humans being human, the trend today is to effect as many of the functions of the attendant as possible with automatic equipment, often in the form of a computer acting as a common control.

MODERN PBX FEATURES

A modern PBX still detects the flow of power when the telephone user picks up his instrument. It then makes a connection automatically through the switching matrix to a digit receiver that returns dial tone. The caller dials or keys the called number into the digit receiver (sometimes called a register, a decoder, or something similar). The system responds by making sure the call is permitted and then rings the called line. Upon detection of answer, the calling and called parties are interconnected via the switching matrix for conversation; the system monitors for switch-hook flashes that indicate the need for some additional service, or hang up to free the portions of the switching matrix used on this call for future calls.

A major point of complexity, far more important in PBXs than in most central office switches, lies in terminating the call to some line other than the one requested. Hunting is usually available and widely used in PBXs so that if the boss's line is busy, the call will be routed to his secretary. Modern PBXs have added a variety of call-forwarding features that can be invoked and canceled by the station user. Sometimes privacy features require the return of a special tone to indicate that the called party does not wish to be disturbed. Pickup is a relatively new feature that allows any station in a previously defined pickup group to come off hook and snatch away a call that is ringing unanswered at another station in the group. Camp-on and call waiting may have calls stacked up waiting for an existing conversation to end; automatic callback may have one or more callers waiting for an existing call to be completed so that the system can call them back and then complete to the called party. Obviously, a call encountering camp-on, call waiting, or callback at the terminating line will be dealing with a situation that has several levels of "busy" to contend with. A simple test to see if the line is busy is no longer sufficient. From all this, it is easy to see that the terminating half of the call setup procedure can be quite complex.

Trunk calls are a little more intricate. An outgoing call starts off exactly the same way as an extension-to-extension call, but now the control can complete its part of the job by connecting to any one of several trunks to the local central office. Further, it can, if it wants to, do this long before the caller has finished dialing. Traditionally, callers on a PBX dial 9, get dial tone from the CO, and then dial the telephone number of the called party. This approach was very important in the early automatic PBXs that were constructed from

CHART BY CYNTHIA STODDARD

With the present PBX and central office designs, it is imperative that the CO use ground start circuits.

relays and other electromechanical components. It let the PBX complete its part of the job quickly and easily and turn all the hard work over to the CO. The CO would then store the called number, set up the connection, handle the billing, etc.

The problem with this was the propensity of PBX station users to make personal calls that kept showing up in the bill from the phone company as message units, short-haul tolls, or even long-haul tolls. This led to a central office feature called toll diversion, which automatically terminated all toll calls or diverted them to the switchboard attendant. But because many COs did not have this feature, the restrictor was developed. A restrictor was a box full of switching components that attached to each trunk of the CO and could be programmed with a list of approved calling regions. As time went on, however, it became evident that the restrictor function should be incorporated in the PBX design.

A PBX that incorporates restriction knows which extension is originating the call. Thus the PBX can automatically perform restricting and routing functions based on the "class of service" assigned to the specific extension without the caller having to take any action. External restrictors must treat all calls alike since they have no way of identifying the caller, and external call routers, quite popular during the last 10 years, require the user to identify himself by dialing in an additional group of digits.

Two ways of handling outward calls became possible: cut through and register sender. With memory and control capability being relatively inexpensive in modern PBXs, the register-sender approach has much to recommend it. Many manufacturers, however, still cling to the cut-through approach. Note carefully the difference: with cut through, the system connects as soon as possible to the CO and, in certain circumstances, monitors digits as they go past, while with register-sender operation, the system takes in the entire number and performs restriction, routing, and whatever else may be appropriate and then continues with setting up the call.

In setting up an outgoing call, the PBX sometimes doesn't know when the CO is ready to receive digits, and it almost never knows when the called party answers. Further, it may not know when the call is ended by the called party hanging up. In cut-through operation, the user hears CO dial tone and, ultimately, the called-party answer (or busy tone or whatever); this relieves the PBX of the need to do anything. But the PBX must monitor the internal extension very carefully since this, in many instances, is the only source of information about adding features or ending the call. If the internal extension has been put on hold, the outside party can sometimes hang up without being detected.

When call detail recording equipment is added to or built into the PBX, the inability of the system to determine when a call is answered is a severe problem in making accurate toll bills. On the other hand, machine detection of hang-up is fairly simple if "ground start" trunks are obtained from the CO; ground start trunks also work well to provide an automatic start dialing signal in register-sender operation, although, for a variety of reasons, detection of dial tone directly has much to recommend it.

INCOMING CO CALLS DIFFER

Traditional incoming calls from the CO are quite different from the intra-PBX and outgoing calls we have examined so far. It must be recalled that a PBX trunk is, as far as the CO is concerned, a station line just like the one that goes to a telephone. Thus when the CO wants to complete a call to somebody served by a PBX, it will send ringing down the line (viewed from its end) or trunk (when viewed from the PBX end). Ringing (which is a large, high-power signal at 20Hz and 86 volts) operates a ring-up relay or similar device in the PBX's trunk circuit to make some kind of indication to the system that a CO call is coming in. This indication is forwarded to the console position where the attendant can see and respond to it.

When the attendant signals the system control that the call is to be accepted, ringing is tripped and the call is connected to the console. Tripping ringing causes the CO to put its equipment in the talking state and to start charging. Thus, the calling party pays for the call if it reaches the PBX attendant.

The attendant obtains the called extension number or, more often, the name of the called party, and instructs the control to manipulate the switching matrix to complete the call. The control applies ringing toward the called extension, generally returns audible ringing (ringback) to the calling party, and watches for answer. It is highly desirable that a PBX monitor this ringing situation and return the call to the console after a timed interval if no answer is obtained. It is also desirable that the PBX be able to monitor the trunk circuit for abandon in case the calling party hangs up. Ground start trunks are required for this to be possible. As on any call, the system must monitor the internal party for switch-hook flashes and hang-up.

In many systems, the same CO trunks used for incoming calls are used for outgoing dial 9 calls. This poses a problem that must be understood if serious trouble is to be avoided. The trouble concerns seizure of the same trunk simultaneously by both the CO and the PBX. This situation puts the PBX caller, who has just dialed 9, in direct contact with an incoming call that is almost certainly intended for someone else.

Simultaneous seizure can be minimized at the PBX if the trunk circuit involved is made busy to dial 9 calls as soon as the CO has seized the trunk from the far end. This cannot, in general, be done if all the CO does is apply ringing. Ringing, in most central offices, is on for two seconds and off for four. Thus, if the CO seized the trunk at the start of the silent interval in the ringing cycle, up to four seconds could elapse before the PBX trunk circuit would know. In a busy hour, four seconds is eternity and many dial 9 calls would have a crack at the "idle" trunk. Thus, once again ground start trunks are necessary. They tell the PBX immediately when the trunk is seized from the CO and thus allow the PBX to direct outgoing calls to other circuits. Trunks used in the outgoing direction for dial 9 and incoming for completion to the attendant are usually called combination trunks. With the present PBX and CO designs, it is imperative that the CO use ground start circuits.

Direct inward dialing (DID) is rapidly making Centrex unnecessary, and most modern PBXs offer it. As mentioned above, DID is not particularly difficult at the PBX. Any PBX that can handle dial repeating tie trunks is ready to go immediately. All that is needed is for a CO to be able to send dial pulses; this is harder to come by. In some metropolitan regions, New York City in particular, tandem offices in the public network bypass the local central offices and connect directly to DID PBXs. This lets each PBX be treated as a small central office, and everything works fine.

There are, of course, some practical details. All the old-fashioned step-by-step (SXS) PBXs were quite fast in that they could accept dial pulsing on a tie trunk as soon as the trunk was seized at the distant end. Unfortunately, most modern COs and PBXs are much slower. After detecting seizure, they must find a digit detector to attach to the trunk, or arrange their internal operation to examine the trunk circuit fast and often enough to catch all the dial pulses as they come in. This may take a while. Thus, the distant end must be held off until the PBX is ready. The technique used is called "wink start." The CO (or tandem office) is psyched up to watch for a momentary off-hook signal to be returned. At the end of this one fifth of a second interval of off-hook, the telco end knows it can start sending dial pulses.

Some modern PBXs are always watching their DID trunks (and tie trunks) for incoming dial pulses, and thus are as fast as SXS systems. However, they sometimes have to return a wink start signal anyway to make the CO happy. Thus, we have two problems here: we must know if a PBX is able to send wink start to satisfy the CO, and if it must send wink start to fend off the CO until the PBX is ready to receive digits.

The current trend in PBX design is away from the relatively inexpensive 500/2500-type sets.

When digits are sent to a PBX in a DID situation, the telco sends them at the slowest possible rate: 10 pulses per second, with something more than half a second between trains of pulses that constitute a digit. Thus, to send a four-digit extension number to a PBX, the CO will require at least four seconds. If Touch-Tone had been used, about a half a second would have been needed. There is even a standardized form of dial pulsing, long used between common control switches in the public network and between PBX attendants and common control COs, in which the time could be cut to two seconds. But, for reasons that are unknown, the slowest form of dialing is used. This is particularly amusing in that the Bell System is installing, as rapidly as possible, a new digital method of signaling called CCIS (Common Channel Interoffice Signaling) that may, among other things, cut down signaling time in the public network. The time saved will, of course, be balanced by the slow pulsing into DID PBXs.

A DID call seizes the trunk, gets wink start (if required), and sends the PBX the extension-identifying digits it needs. The PBX then completes the call. That is, the PBX rings the called extension, sends audible ringing (or, if appropriate, busy tone) to the calling party, and monitors for answer. When the call is answered, the answer signal is returned to the CO and the talking connection is established. Note that charging does not start on a DID call until the called party (or somebody else) answers. The telephone company, to be sure it gets paid for the call, will not make the trunk work in both directions until the answer signal is received. The trunk must work in one direction so that the caller can hear audible ringing or busy tone—but it won't work in both directions until after answer has taken place and charging begins.

CARTOON BY SIDNEY HARRIS

THE USER INTERFACE

Telephone sets are the interface between the telephone system and the users. Consoles, in modern equipment seldom more than glorified telephone sets, fall into the same category. Additional interfaces, provided for maintenance and information exchange, are often standard teletypewriters or data terminals although sets or consoles with special displays are sometimes provided. Needless to say, the instrument and the switching system must be able to work with one another if the system is to support communications.

Telephone sets must, in general, convert acoustical energy to electrical energy and vice versa to permit voice communications. For nonvoice services, analogous requirements exist. In addition, the station user must be able to signal toward the system to "place his order," and the system must be able to signal toward the caller to let him know what the system is doing to carry out his instructions. The system must also signal toward the called party to encourage him to answer his phone and, in some instances, to tell him which line he is supposed to answer.

The basic mechanism of the 500-type telephone set, the one in present use throughout the country, was perfected just about the time transistors were announced. Thus, station apparatus has not, as yet, taken any particular advantage of developments in solid-state physics. The 2500-type telephone set, identical to the 500 except for the use of a DTMF (the generic name for AT&T's Touch-Tone trademark) pad for signaling rather than a rotary dial, does, it is true, use transistors for generating the tones. But that is sort of an add-on application.

The 500/2500-type telephone does use some rather early solid-state components to compensate for the distance between the central office and the telephone. The curious result is that the closer to the switch a telephone is, the more it upsets transmission when connecting to trunks. Or, to put it another way, the majority of PBX telephone sets are located where they will harm overall network transmission.

It happens that something less than 20% of all telephones are served by Centrex

Improving transmission at PBX telephones would be one of the easiest ways to improve transmission nationwide.

or PBX systems, while the rest are served directly by central offices on (mostly) a single line basis. It appears, however, that the great majority of toll calls are placed from PBX and Centrex telephones, and these calls are, of necessity, made during the business day when rates are high. Thus, improving transmission at PBX telephones would seem to be one of the easiest ways to improve overall transmission on a nationwide basis. And the easiest way to improve transmission would be to make PBX systems four-wire end-to-end, including the telephone sets.

The current trend in PBX design is away from the relatively inexpensive 500/2500-type sets. The SL-1 PBX from Northern Telecom was the first to go in this direction, and Bell followed quickly with sets for Dimension. Danray also had electronic sets from the beginning. These sets require three or four pairs between the telephone set and the switch, but unfortunately all except Danray use only one pair for voice transmission. One can understand the Dimension using two-wire telephone sets, since Dimension is a two-wire switch. And one can even understand the SL-1 using two-wire telephone sets even though the switch is four-wire internally; after all, Northern Telecom is a telephone-oriented company and tradition is of considerable importance. What is really hard to understand, however, is the new Rolm electronic telephone set. The Rolm switch is four-wire, and the people who designed it were determined to innovate. But their new microprocessor controlled telephone set, the ETS 100, uses two-wire transmission.

Only Tele/Resources and Danray have, to date, seen the logic of four-wire telephone sets. The T/R System 32 is four-wire from station to station, as is the Danray. The only time they are vulnerable to transmission echo is when they connect to two-wire facilities, as when they go to off-premises stations or, more important, to CO trunks.

Conventional 500- or 2500-type telephone sets have a microphone or transmitter for converting acoustical energy to electrical energy to be transmitted via wires. Similarly, they have a receiver for making the opposite conversion. The two are connected via a network, which permits a single pair of wires to be used for transmission in each direction when two separate devices are obviously required at the telephone set to interface a caller's ear and mouth.

The "network" serves an additional purpose. It provides "sidetone." That is, it allows a certain amount of the spoken energy to be fed back to the ear of the speaker (without delay). That is necessary because we are used to hearing ourselves speak (cover both ears and speak aloud to detect the impact of not hearing yourself); if we don't, we change our speaking patterns. As it happens, the sidetone circuit feeds back slightly less sound than we hear through the air; this tends to make us talk a little louder, and provides better volume for the person on the far end of the connection.

The switch-hook, the next device we encounter, makes a path for current from the PBX or CO switch through the telephone set when the caller picks up the handset. The handset, of course, contains the transmitter and receiver, and, when not in use, sits in a cradle on the telephone base. While placed in the cradle, it operates a switch that turns off power; when lifted, the switch closes and completes the path needed for current to flow.

Note that the PBX or CO must always monitor a line for its on-hook or off-hook status. This is called supervision. The switch must know if the user is originating a call, answering a call to his phone, or terminating a call that is already in progress. In recent years, the switch-hook "flash" has regained the importance it had in manual systems. A flash is a momentary on-hook. The system detects it and knows that it is not a hang-up followed by the origination of a new call.

The purpose of the flash is to tell the system that the user wants to send an additional command, a "feature code." Particularly if the system uses DTMF, but often when dial pulsing is used as well, a digit receiver must be connected to unscramble the user's new command. Use of the switch-hook flash and as many as 20 feature codes is common in modern PBXs.

TELEPHONE SET FEATURES

Special telephone sets designed to work directly with the PBX combine PBX capabilities with user convenience. These sets, available from Northern Telecom, the Bell System, and others, usually have a group of buttons that can be either line pickup keys (as in conventional key telephone sets) or feature keys. What usually happens is depression of a selected key tells the system which key is depressed. The system looks up in a table in memory to find out what is going on, and carries out the appropriate action. If a line select key is pushed, the system connects an incoming call for the line to the tel set via the switching matrix; on an outgoing call, charging and restriction are based on the class marks of the line selected. If a feature key has been pushed (the hold button, for instance, although we now have many other possibilities), the system does whatever is required. If visual cues are required by the user, the PBX control causes an appropriate signal to be returned to light or blink the appropriate lamp, to cause the tone ringer to sound, or to provide some other suitable signal.

These modern electronic sets have a number of advantages. First, they are much easier for the user when contrasted with flashing the switch-hook, dialing a number of feature codes, and identifying a variety of call progress tones. Second, they usually need only three pairs, and three pairs will work on any kind of phone from a simple single line set to a 30-button call director. Finally, they permit complete program control of changes in lines picked up, features selected, etc. This kind of control can often be handled from remote locations via a dataset in a dial-up connection or by the customer's communication manager. The saving in OCC (other charges and credits) for moves and changes can be considerable in an active location, and the saving in aggravation and time when the communication manager can effect the change directly rather than trying to honcho an order through a reluctant vendor can hardly be appreciated until it is experienced.

One problem must be noted, however. Single line sets usually require different line cards in the PBX than do these modern sets. This shows that more than a program change is required when one goes from a single line to a multiline set. Further, it is evident that when one changes from a five-button set to a 30-button set, the sets themselves will have to be interchanged even though programming can do most of the rest. In any event, the identification required on each button must be made at the set and not with the program. Even so, the modern sets can be cost effective when properly used.

It should be possible to switch data over public and private voice networks like any other signal. Just how readily this can be done was demonstrated by Danray and taken up by Northern Telecom upon its purchase of Danray. One simply puts an RS232C interface on the electronic telephone set (there are, apparently, better or less expensive interfaces, but 232 exists in vast quantities) and plugs in a terminal or a computer. Danray uses the power pair (one of the three pairs required by their electronic set) to carry off 9,600 bps full-duplex data to a separate auxiliary data switch. The voice telephone is used to set up the connection, but once the data path is set up, the voice equipment is free for make or receive voice calls. This kind of simultaneous voice/data operation seems to be highly favored by those who normally use terminals, particularly over some version of alternate voice/data where the voice phone is tied up with the data connection.

Northern Telecom uses the same approach with the SL-1 PBX, but without a separate data matrix. The SL-1 has a digital time-division switching matrix, and can switch data directly by simply omitting the analog to digital conversion in the data line circuit. Each telephone has two appearances on the

No amount of processor duplication will save the system in the event of a power failure.

switching matrix: one for voice and one for data. Again, the voice phone is free to make and receive calls once it has the data connection established. With the long holding times of data calls (normally found with timesharing in industry), some traffic problems may develop here—but the idea seems to be quite good.

Rolm has done something different. A single voice path through the matrix is submultiplexed into as many as 40 data paths (depending on the speed of the switched data). In addition to adding switching capability with negligible degradation of the system's voice handling capability, this approach appears to be quite inexpensive compared with even relatively low-speed modems.

Many people feel that a telephone set in a business area should have a full alphanumeric keyboard and display and a handset, along with an array of feature and line pickup buttons. This relatively dumb terminal could then interface with the switch, which could include software to permit the set to do whatever is required: be a timesharing terminal, a word processing station, an electronic mail system, or whatever. The cost of modern electronic components would seem to point in this direction.

Consoles are provided with PBXs to permit human assistance when required to complete calls. Early consoles interfaced trunks directly and, working through the trunk appearance on the switching matrix, effected call completion. Today the trend is to use something very much like an electronic telephone set as a console; the switch connects calls needing assistance to the console as to any other telephone, but provides a bit more information by driving suitable displays. Consoles, like electronic telephone sets, can be arranged to have digital signaling paths to the system control to interchange information directly without using the voice path.

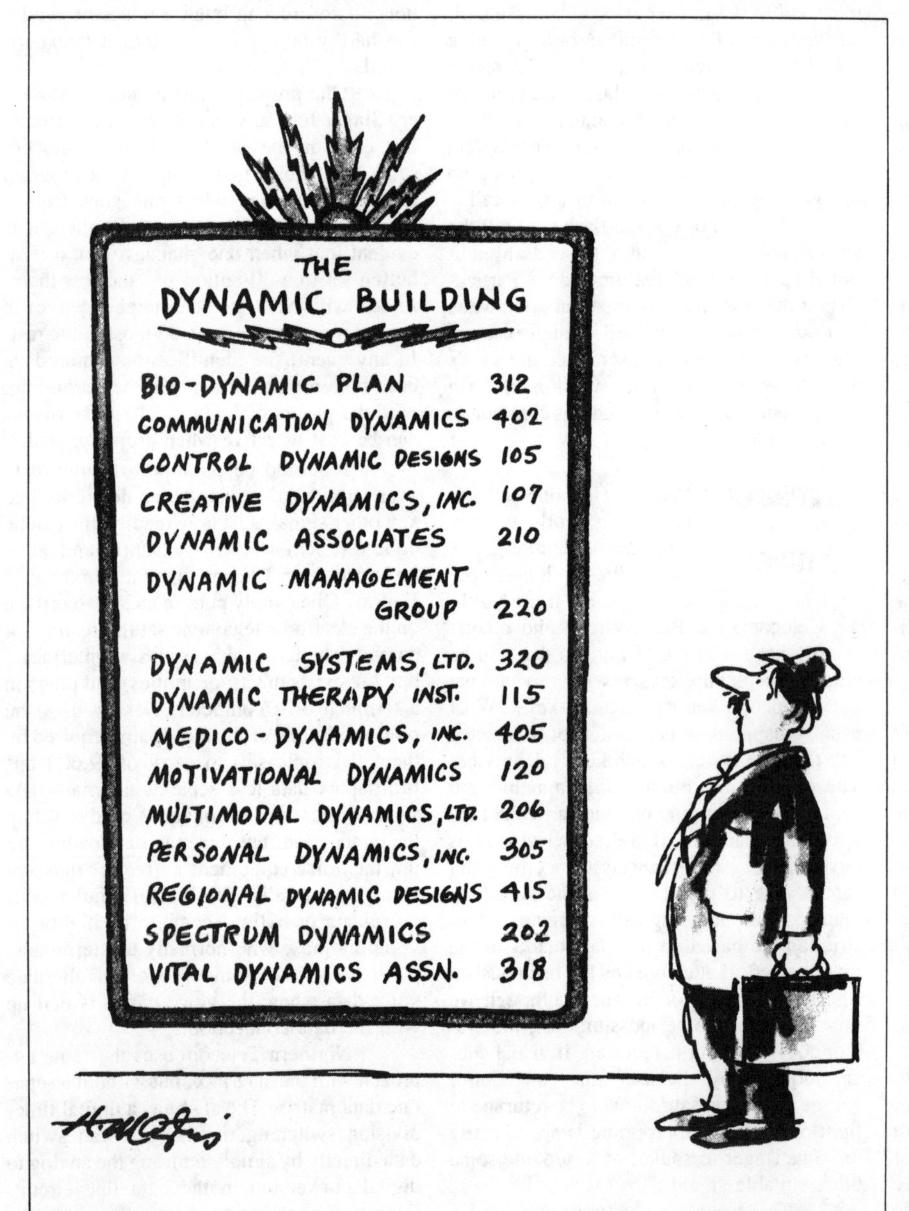

CARTOON BY HENRY MARTIN

SYSTEM CONTROL METHODS

Most modern PBX switches today use a processor of some sort for control. Stored program approaches are now standard, but this hardly tells the whole story. We are confronted with minicomputers and microprocessors, RAM and ROM, backup tapes and disks, and separate standalone mechanisms for call data recording and processing. Like any small computer-controlled industrial system, a PBX is operated by its processor. The processor, backed with program instructions, inspects all lines, trunks, service circuits, and other portions of the system, first for supervisory information (on-hook and off-hook) and then for any additional information that may be needed to make things work (dialed addresses, feature codes, signals from feature/line buttons on electronic telephones, alarm and trouble warning information, etc.). Further, maintenance or other control information may also be coming in.

The control responds to externally generated signals and to internal signals that result from processing information in accordance with data stored in memory. That is, it checks class marks and other instructions and sets up paths through the switching matrix between lines and/or trunks, records information in memory for billing and traffic purposes, and, in general, carries out the functions of an operator at a manual switchboard.

Processors are usually not duplicated for redundancy in small systems; they almost always are in large systems. The breakpoint appears to be at about 400 lines. Duplication for reliability requires additional complexity in that both sets of memories have to be kept up to date, and the computers have to be able to decide which one is in charge. In some systems with duplicated processors, standard business programs (payroll, inventory, etc.) can be run on the standby machine; other systems use the standby machine to handle other functions (such as Rolm's electronic mail) until it is needed. With or without duplication, the system may very well have extra time and memory that could be devoted to store and forward data, etc.

No amount of processor duplication will save the system in the event of power failure. In such an instance, a backup battery is required to keep the system running (or, at least, to save the memory) until the power is restored. If batteries are not provided, some

One of the main advantages of computer control of switching systems is the ease with which new features can be installed.

means may be required to reprogram memory when the power comes back up. Systems using a volatile random access memory (RAM) lose their program when power is cut off, so the system must be able to reload from some reasonably permanent memory when the power is restored. Often a magnetic tape or disk contains the backup program. The backup memory does not always keep track of the calls in progress or the station-programmed features such as call forwarding. Thus, reload sometimes does not get back to the starting point.

One of the main advantages of computer control of switching systems (or other industrial equipment) is the ease with which new features can be installed, services can be upgraded, and changes can be made in the course of regular activity. Note, however, that not all stored-program processor controlled systems permit easy changes. Read only memories (ROMs) are not always changeable in the field—sometimes they have to be unplugged and replaced, while in other instances, they must be altered in a special programming device. ROM memory is quite reliable—it can't be changed by unauthorized personnel very easily, and it is nonvolatile so that it is ready to go as soon as power comes back after a failure. But in most instances, the greater flexibility of making changes from a maintenance terminal, the console, or a special telephone set is of much greater importance. Usually some sort of compromise is used: program instructions that do not change are stored in ROM, while parameters that define special features and translations are keyed in, stored in memory that is easily changed but wiped out with power failure, and duplicated on the backup tape for reload with power restoral. There are almost as many variations as there are PBX systems on the market, and we haven't seen the end of it yet.

Switching matrices can be cataloged under three general headings: space division, frequency division, and time division. In space division, which includes all the older electromechanical systems and some electronic systems, the control finds a path through one or more sets of switches between the line and trunk, sets up that path, and the path, a physical connection that can be traced from point to point, is used by the caller for the duration of the call. When the call is over, the various switches are released for use by other callers.

Frequency division is seldom used, while time division is taking over the field. Unfortunately, time division can be carried out in many different ways, some analog and some digital. And even the digital techniques permit a wide variety. For example, pulse code modulation (PCM) and delta modulation are incompatible with each other, and no two forms of a delta modulation system are compatible.

ANALOG VERSUS DIGITAL

There is a great deal of discussion about the merits of digital versus analog switching. Some people feel that a switch controlled by a digital computer is a digital switch, and they point out quite correctly that most of the features of interest to users are a direct result of stored program control. But this is not what is generally meant when one speaks of digital switching. Digital vs. analog in this context refers to the way the switching matrix operates, and has little to do with the control equipment. Further, it is true that many of the features of interest to users today can be carried out quite well with a switch that has a matrix that works on analog principles.

Analog transmission means that the signal transmitted is a direct analog of the actual signal. In telephony, the actual signal is compressions and rarefactions of air—changes of air pressure that are interpreted as speech. These changes of pressure fall on the microphone or transmitter in the telephone handset, and the microphone converts pressure variations to current variations. Note that the current variations are a direct analog of the pressure variations, increasing and decreasing in exactly the same way. Note also that the power in the current variations is appreciably larger than the power in the sound pressure; there is gain or amplification available in the telephone set. This is the only way long distance telephony could have been practical 25 years before the invention of the vacuum tube.

The electric current can be transmitted over wires, and it can operate more modern equipment to make another analog of the original signal which permits transmission via radio beam. In all these instances, a view of the signal on an oscilloscope would look just the same as if the scope could read sound pressure directly.

Amplification is very important in analog transmission. A small incoming signal must control something that makes a large but directly analogous outgoing signal. The signal will be attenuated by a long cable, but can be amplified again to get back to its proper size. Unfortunately, amplification can't tell the difference between the original signal and that signal plus any noise that may have been picked up along the way. Each time amplification is used, more noise is added to the signal. Ultimately, the signal is submerged in noise. Even a very small variation in the original signal will change it, and all such changes will add up.

A digital signal cannot be continuously variable as can a pressure wave or the analogous current variations produced by the microphone. A digital signal can only take on one of a finite number of values at any instant. It does not have to be amplified, however. The digital signal is measured, its value is determined, and a new signal is made just like the old one. All the noise is stripped off and lost.

This technique is called regeneration and is very old. It was used in telegraph systems before the telephone was invented. Telegraph pulses would be distorted by long wires, and the dots and dashes couldn't be distinguished; then somebody figured that, instead of using one long wire with a key at one end and a sounder and a huge battery at the far end, a number of short wires could be used, end to end, each powered with a smaller battery. The first wire would have a key on one end for sending, and a relay and battery at the far end for receiving. The relay would follow the key properly, and its contacts could act as a key in the next circuit to regenerate a new signal. This regeneration could go from circuit to circuit, outwitting noise and distortion. In a digital telephone system, we convert a voice signal to something that looks like a telegraph signal. Then we can use regeneration rather than amplification and be free of noise and distortion.

The characteristic of digital modulation techniques is that all of the pulses are the same in both amplitude and width. All the system has to do, then, is determine whether a pulse is present or not. A series of standard pulses (or absence of pulses) in successive time intervals can define the amplitude of a voice signal at any instant. This requires more pulses than analog modulation techniques, but simplifies pulse detection and retransmission.

Can a customer tell the difference between an analog and a digital switch? Not on a voice call. Make a connection through relays, reed switches, crossbar, or SXS switches, or with a variety of electronic techniques including the various digital modulation schemes discussed above, and a caller cannot tell which system has been used. On a per-call basis, there is no difference. Why, then, go to all this trouble? Why not stick with SXS, or even stop with 8,000 samples per second where each is of variable height or width?

There are reasons for a PBX to be digital. The public telephone network is about half digital today in an 8-bit PCM format. If these 8-bit words or bytes of PCM are kept intact when they go through switches and trunks, new frontiers open up. It just happens that ASCII uses seven bits, often plus a parity or check bit. Voice channels normally handle 8,000 eight-bit bytes per second; if they can be switched together in built-up connections ultimately extending from one telephone to another, there are possibilities for data transmission that make all present data systems,

The purchase of a digital PBX to obtain all the advantages of the digital future is a bit premature at the present.

including packet networks, seem roughly comparable to the postal service.

THE ULTIMATE PAYOFF

This is the ultimate payoff. With an all-digital network served by digital switches handling digital user stations, voice and nonvoice communications can be mixed as needed on a per-call basis. Note that nonvoice communications are particularly easy to handle: on that day in the future when there is an all-digital network, modems will not be needed. A data signal will just bypass the A/D converters required for the speech part of the telephone and get directly on the bit stream with information precoded to fit. When any dial-up connection can handle 8,000 ASCII characters/sec, new opportunities for business communications not yet even considered will be possible.

Unfortunately, there is a long way to go before such a future will be possible. Most intertoll trunks will remain analog until fiber optics becomes generally available for long-haul PCM circuits. Microwave, satellite, and coaxial cable can handle many more analog circuits than digital at the same cost or bandwidth so they will not vanish easily. Further, protocols required by various data machines to permit them to talk to one another vary from data system to system; indeed, in data communications, one of the principal functions of a node or switch is to convert from one system to another to permit connections between otherwise incompatible equipment. Finally, digital telephone systems need a variety of other signals for synchronization, supervision and control; these tend to make a universal voice/nonvoice system hard to achieve. Thus, the purchase of a digital PBX to obtain all the advantages of the digital future is a bit premature at the present time.

What can a digital switch do for a user today? A few things, some of which may be quite important in special applications. First, distributed switching is now possible with several modern switches. One can take parts of the switch, analogous to line groups in a SXS system, and put them near the telephones. Using T-Carrier techniques, these remote units can connect something like 100 extensions to the main part of the switch with two pairs; this minimizes the three-pair wiring from the remote units to the electronic telephone sets, and the overall economies are considerable in a large building or in a campus-type environment.

The second thing a digital switch can do is switch digital signals internally in digital form, without modems. A digital switch is needed, although Danray, using an analog switch, pioneered the effort as described above. A small interface box is required to take the computer or terminal's digital signal and convert it slightly to conform to the needs of the power pair, which is the channel to the switch, but this little box is relatively inexpensive compared to a high-speed modem. In the newest PBXs, A/D conversion takes place in the telephone set and not at the line card in the switch. Then the data signal can enter the digital world immediately, without the need to utilize power pairs for access.

A modern PBX, from the equipment point of view, is much simpler than the older electromechanical systems. Most of the sophistication is built into the program that instructs the control, and modern digital circuitry has simplified most of what is left. The switching matrix tends to be quite small, and new opportunities are available for convenient design of user terminals. Trunks circuits, going mostly to obsolete (two-wire analog) central offices and to analog long-haul tie trunks, have to meet the outside world on its own terms, but even they tend to take advantage of PBX control and component sophistication.

A modern PBX can do many things the older PBXs could not do, and can open the way to doing things that are done today by completely separate systems. We are right on the edge of a whole range of developments that will change the way business is conducted. But we are not there yet. Thus, one should not rush to buy the current state of the art just because it is more modern. One should understand just what is involved, and make sound decisions on the basis of rational information. And above all, be ready for change. ✻

CARTOON BY JACK CORBETT

Leo F. Goeller Jr. is an independent consultant with Communication Resources in Haddonfield, N.J. He is also on the Board of Members of the Business Communication Review.

Jerry A. Goldstone has been the editor and publisher of *Business Communications Review* for the past 12 years. Copies of the BCR manual can be obtained from the company by writing to 950 York Rd., Suite 203, Hinsdale, IL 60521.

Office Communications and the Digital PBX

I. Richer and M. Steiner
Bolt Beranek and Newman Inc., 50 Moulton Street, Cambridge, Massachusetts 02238, U.S.A.

and

M. Sengoku
Nippon Electric Company, Tokyo, Japan

As part of a study on office automation, we have investigated two related topics: voice and data communications on local office networks, and the use of a computerized PBX as a switch in an office network. Since a computerized PBX might be an effective method for implementing a voice/data office network, we have addressed the important issues of (a) whether voice and data should be handled by the same techniques, and (b) whether these traffic types should be combined on a single network or should use distinct, but interconnected, networks. In studying these topics, we have considered end-user requirements in order to determine the economics and the possible evolution of such networks. We have also evaluated a number of technical problems, including appropriate switching techniques and network topology. Our principal conclusions are that in the near future there are valid technical and non-technical reasons for adding data traffic to the office voice networks, and that the combined network should be based on a star topology.

Keywords: Voice communications, local office networks, computerized PBX.

Ira Richer received the B.E.E. degree from Rensselaer Polytechnic Institute, Troy, New York, and the M.S. and Ph.D. degrees in electrical engineering from the California Institute of Technology, Pasadena, California. After holding postdoctoral positions at the Technical University of Denmark, Lyngby and at Caltech, Pasadena, he joined MIT Lincoln Laboratory, Lexington, Massachusetts, where he was involved in a number of advanced communications projects that spanned orders of magnitude in both the frequency and altitude domains (ELF to UHF, and submachine to satellite). In 1977 he joined Bolt Beranek and Newman (BBN) Inc., Cambridge, Massachusetts. As a senior scientist at BBN, he consults to both commercial and government organizations on a wide variety of network and communications topics.

North-Holland Publishing Company
Computer Networks 5 (1981) 411–422

1. Introduction

"The Technical Office: Analysis and Research"

"Plan Today for Tomorrow's Data/Voice Nets"

"Packet Switching and Office Applications"

"PBXs will Unify Office of the Future"

"Integrated Office Information Systems"

These are the titles of some recent articles and conference papers. Almost daily, we are enticed with such titles (including the one on this paper), each over an article or paper which purports to describe the office of the future. Contained in many of these is a figure showing a box with the words "*Office Network*", and with every possible type of terminal connected to the network – telephones, facsimile devices, "*work stations*", OCR devices, automated typesetters, etc. Rarely, however, does an author dissect the magical box and explain or justify what the communications subnetwork looks like or how it handles its tasks. This dearth of *substantive* information prompted the small study on which this paper is based. The goal of the study was to attempt to deter-

Marianne Steiner is a member of BBN Information Management Corporation (IMC), where she is involved in the planning, marketing and support of office automation systems. She is presently concerned with IMC's newest product, an electronic mail software package. Prior to the formation of IMC Ms. Steiner directed consulting studies at BBN on a variety of network and communication topics including network architecture and office technology. Previously Ms. Steiner worked with the Network Product Management group at Digital Equipment Corporation and the Systems and Programming Division of the Bank of America in San Francisco, CA. Ms. Steiner has an M.E. in Information Science and an M.S. in Applied Mathematics from Harvard University. Her B.S. is from the University of Miami.

Masama Sengoku was born on February 15, 1950. He graduated from Tokyo Electric Engineering College in 1972. He joined Nippon Electric Company, Ltd. in 1972 and is now engineer of the Data Switching Systems Department, Switching Engineering Division. He was engaged in the development of the Digital Data Switching Systems. Mr. Sengoku is a member of the Institute of Electronics and Communication Engineers of Japan.

mine whether it is desirable and feasible to develop a voice/data system, and if so, what the characteristics of such a system might be. The focus was on offices in the United States in the near future (three to five years). Because our interest was in realistic, practicaable possibilities, important aspects of the study were economics, evolution, and market forces as well as technical performance.

This paper presents our principal results on the gross voice and data characteristics of the future office, and on the most promising design alternatives for an office network. However, we shall first present some observations about the interaction of voice and data traffic. In the long term, merging voice and data would be of primary advantage at the management/professional level: it is at this level that voice communications are most important and that the greatest economic incentive lies. To date, there has not been much technological assistance directed at the manager/professional's job and the information flow related to it. The information flow related to the job of a professional or a manager is oriented primarily around interpersonal communications, mostly in meetings and by telephone, but also through written material. The key technology here is communications. We believe that the efficiency and convenience of communications can be enhanced through the availability of voice and data facilities within close reach of the manager's or professional's work space. In the short term, however, we have been able to identify only two specific applications which might require the integration of voice and data communications:

- *voice mail* – a system whereby a caller can leave a spoken message which can be retrieved at the recipient's convenience;
- *dictation* – verbal dictation would be stored and subsequently retrieved for transcription, perhaps by a central pool of secretaries.

We assume that these applications should integrate voice and data techniques because while voice input is more convenient, digital storage is most flexible, enabling messages or dictated text to be manipulated, filed, and retrieved. * Another possibility, of course, is to use the ubiquitous telephone as a more general-purpose input device, for example to enter transactions or to initiate commands to a computer.

A key feature of the above applications is the inherent capability for remote access. Thus, from any telephone, a user could enter or retrieve mail or could input dictation. Of course, in the more distant future, when computers are able to generate text from voice (voice recognition) and to produce high-quality voice from text in *cost-effective* ways, many additional applications will become practical and economical (and the above applications can be augmented appropriately). For the above reasons, we expect the gradual emergence of system configurations that will support the interaction of voice and data in a single application.

The technology for the effective handling of voice communications already exists. In the remainder of this paper, we explore the details of voice and data traffic in the office, and the techniques to best handle this traffic.

2. Office Traffic

In this section we present some statistics on the voice and data traffic in an office. The primary purpose of generating these statistics is to obtain an understanding of the relative magnitudes of the various traffic types and hence of the network requirements. We first consider a hypothetical future office and then give data for Bolt Beranek and Newman Inc. (BBN), which *currently* has significant office data traffic.

2.1. Future Offices

In producing the voice traffic values for a future office, we were able to utilize some general statistics and standard industry guidelines that are available for telephone traffic. On the other hand, since data communications does not presently exist to any great extent in offices, we based our data traffic estimates upon market research reports and user surveys [2] together with some of our own assumptions regarding the data communications environment. However, *the particular assumptions we make are not at all critical to our conclusions.* In fact, in order to be conservative, we intentionally attempted to overestimate the amount of data traffic; the rationale for overestimating will become clearer in the discussion below.

* Dictation utilizing a conventional analog recorder together with control signals from a push-button telephone is currently planned or in use [1].

The principal terminals that we believe will participate in communications on a local office network are:

- telephones for voice communications;
- data terminals for data entry and distributed processing;
- word processors for text editing and electronic mail handling;
- facsimile devices for graphic and hand-written document delivery (primarily inter-office);
- printers for high-speed text output;
- copiers for multiple copies of on-line text documents and also possibly for internal document distribution.

These terminals would communicate with each other; with terminals and computers outside the office; with local minicomputers for data processing and special applications such as electronic mail and text processing; and possibly with local mainframes for database access, file storage, and large scale computing tasks. Note that we have excluded wide-band video devices because we do not believe that their use on office networks will be very widespread in the near future.

Table 1 shows the assumed terminals' characteristics and the number of terminals that might be used in offices of three different sizes. For the purposes of this report, we characterize the size of the office by the number of telephones, since there is usually one telephone per employee, and we denote a small, medium, or large office as having 100, 500, or 2000 telephones, respectively. The average utilization and throughput values in Table 1 are based on the following assumptions:

(1) At each telephone there are 20 calls per eight-hour business day with each call lasting 3 minutes. In a typical two-way conversation, each talker uses the circuit only about half the time, and during that time has short silent intervals between talk spurts. If a mechanism is provided to detect these silences, the throughput requirements for a technique such as packet switching could be reduced by as much as 60%. However, in order to ensure reasonable speech quality and to allow for possible overhead that might be required, we have assumed that the half duplex connection is utilized 100 percent of the time. For voice communications we assumed a digitization rate of 64 kbps, consistent with standard PCM (Pulse Code Modulation) techniques. (The peak data rate is 198 kbps because data might flow in each direction.)

(2) Each word processor is connected for 200 minutes per day (for example, ten sessions of 20 minutes each), and five percent of this time is devoted to actual data communications, with the rest of the time occupied with typing, thinking, reading, and other secretarial activities.

(3) Each data terminal is on-line all day (for example, for data entry or other clerical functions); again, the traffic flows only five percent of the time. Note that word processors and data entry terminals could have a wide range of "intelligence". With much intelligence at the terminal, communications over the network would tend to be in much longer blocks than with dumb terminals; however, to a first order of approximation, the overall throughput would be similar.

(4) Each facsimile device handles 100 pages per day at one minute per page, and 100 percent of the

Table 1
Assumed Terminal and Office Characteristics

	Peak Data Rate (kbps)	Average Utilization (erlangs)	Average Throughput (kbps)	Number of Terminals		
				Small Office	Medium office	Large office
Telephone	128.0	0.13	8.0	100	500	2000
Word Processor	2.4	0.4	0.048	5	50	200
Data Entry	2.4	1.0	0.12	5	50	200
Facsimile	9.6	0.21	2.0	2	10	40
Copier	48.0	0.036	1.7	2	10	40
Printer	9.6	0.36	3.5	2	10	40

connect time is devoted to actual communications. Since facsimile will be used primarily for inter-office communications, we assume that the data rate through the office network is 9.6 kbps for communications over external voice grade telephone lines. Operation at one minute per page therefore assumes that some compression coding is used.

(5) Each copier produces copies from 1000 original documents per day (only the original need be transmitted over the network). We assume that copies would be used mostly for intra-office work and therefore that the original would be transmitted in, say, ASCII form, with 50 kbits per page.

(6) Each printer produces 100 20-page reports each day. (We have assumed here that the transfer rate to the printer is equal to the printer's data rate; an alternate configuration would have a large buffer memory and controller located with the printer at a much higher transfer rate.)

Using the data in Table 1, and assuming that the busy-hour traffic volume is twice the average, we arrive at the busy hour utilization and throughput figures shown in Table 2. The entry for interactive data includes both word processing and data entry. The utilization figures are in erlangs, which is the average number of simultaneous connections. Of course, each connection operates at the data rate appropriate to the communicating devices, and thus each interactive connection requires much less capacity than a voice connection. We see from the table that for each office size, the number of simultaneous data connections might be comparable to the number of voice conversations, but the throughput requirements for voice are substantially greater than those for data.

The data from Table 2 can now be used to estimate the overall traffic handling requirements of the office network. Potentially, there are three relevant switching techniques: circuit switching, packet switching, or a hybrid scheme with circuit switching for voice and packet switching for data. However, because the voice traffic is so much greater than data traffic, we need not perform calculations for the hybrid approach: the results for circuit switching are essentially the same as for hybrid switching.

For circuit switching we obtained the peak number of connections required by using standard telephony (Erlang B) tables for a blocking probability of 0.01 – that is, one percent of the attempted connections would not be completed. We performed a similar calculation for the number of channels required for data traffic and then converted these channels into equivalent full duplex 64 kbps voice channels, assuming that with the overhead necessary for submultiplexing a voice channel, only 48 kbps of throughput could be obtained. (For example, 20 2.4 kbps channels over one voice channel.) The figures we generated assume that full duplex channels are required for data traffic; if the protocols used for data communications require only a half duplex channel, then the data requirements would be somewhat lower.

The sizing for packet switching was obtained from the throughput requirements of Table 2. Clearly, the total capacity must be greater than the average busy hour throughput in order to allow for peak traffic

Table 2
Traffic Volumes for Three Office Sizes

	Busy-Hour Utilization (erlangs)			Busy-Hour Throughput (kbps)		
	Small Office	Medium Office	Large Office	Small Office	Medium Office	Large Office
Voice	25.0	125.0	500.0	1600.0	8000	32000
Interactive Data	9.0	90.0	360.0	1.7	17	67
Facsimile	0.84	4.2	17.0	8.0	40	160
Copier	0.14	0.72	2.9	6.8	34	140
Printer	1.4	7.2	29.0	14.0	70	280

levels, for packet overhead, and for control information, and to ensure a utilization level of less than 100 percent. Thus, we multiplied the total throughput by a factor greater than one to arrive at the required capacity. We assumed, however, that we could take advantage of more statistical averaging as office size increased. Thus, the multiplicative factors used were 1.4, 1.3, and 1.2 for small, medium and large offices, respectively. Note that because there are no real-time high bandwidth devices, response time is not a factor in the sizing calculation.

The overall switching requirements are shown in Table 3. The figures show the number of full duplex, 64 kbps voice channels that would be required for the various alternatives. We now briefly draw some conclusions from the data presented above; we will elaborate on these conclusions in the discussion in subsequent sections. The most striking conclusion we draw from the data above is that voice traffic is substantially greater than data traffic, even though we intentionally attempted to overestimate the data requirements. (It is interesting to note that a similar conclusion about the relative magnitudes of voice and data traffic in long distance information transfer was reached by Cerf and Curran [3].) A related observation is that the peak data throughput in an office is actually quite small, and even for a large office is less than 1 Mbps. The major implication of this conclusion for the design of an office network is that *if a single communications network handles both voice and data, then the network should be optimized for voice.* In addition, in terms of raw throughput, a voice switch for a small office can handle the data traffic for a much larger office. Table 3 also shows that a packet-switching communications network needs only half the capacity of a circuit-switching network. Essentially all of the saving is obtained because we have assumed that a packet switch will take advantage of the half duplex nature of voice traffic, whereas a circuit switch must allocate a full duplex channel to each voice conversation.

As a final point, we remark that the bit rate of high quality, ILI-generated digital voice will be lower than 64 kbps (perhaps 16 kbps) in the not-too-distant future. When these techniques become standardized, they can be used to reduce the required network capacity in almost direct proportion to the decrease in voice digitization rate. Nevertheless, the ratio of voice to data traffic will still be high, and the conclusions stated above will therefore still be valid.

Table 3
Number of full duplex 64 kbps channels required for different size offices for packet and for circuit switching.

	Small Office	Medium Office	Large Office
Circuit Switching			
Voice Only	36	144	527
Voice & Data	39	156	562
Packet Switching			
Voice Only	18	82	300
Voice & Data	1	83	306

2.2. Bolt Beranek and Newman Inc.

In this section we present statistics for current voice and data traffic at BBN's Cambridge facilities. * There are two major reasons for presenting these statistics. First, there is a lot of data traffic at BBN: most reports and documents are generated on-line (*all* secretaries have terminals that link to BBN's computers for editing, storage, and retrieval of text); in addition, *most* staff members and secretaries use an electronic mail system in their everyday business activities. Thus, although BBN may not be a typical office, it represents one possible model for a future office, and the volumes of voice and data traffic provide us with a useful benchmark. Second, we can obtain actual statistics, rather than mere conjectures, of traffic flow: BBN's computerized PBX produces detailed statistics on numbers and types of calls and on call durations, and we can obtain reasonable estimates of data traffic from our knowledge of the BBN working environment. Note that we shall ignore BBN traffic that would not normally flow in a business office – for example, communications involved in preparing computer programs used in BBN's research and development activities.

The configuration at BBN is basically two distinct star networks, one for voice and one for data. For the purposes of this study, the pertinent components of the data network are a central switch, terminals for secretaries and professional staff, mainframes and minicomputers, and printers. There are approximately 800 telephone extensions in Cambridge; however, in order to provide a direct comparison with a medium-size office of the previous section, *all the*

* The data we present is based on measurements and observations made in mid-1979.

figures below are linearly scaled so as to represent an office with 500 extensions.

2.2.1. Voice Traffic

There are two methods of determining the switch requirements necessary to handle voice traffic. As was done in the previous section, the conventional method is to obtain information on the numbers and durations of busy hour internal and external calls, and then to size the switch accordingly. The second method is to observe the number of switch connections at various times and to use the peak value to size the switch. We actually used both methods and arrived at the same results for BBN's traffic: the switch should be capable of providing 70 simultaneous voice channels.

2.2.2. Text Processing

At BBN, there are 40 secretaries, each of whom has a terminal that is on-line approximately three hours per day. However, to allow for peak hour usage, we shall assume that with circuit switching, a dedicated circuit for each terminal must be provided. We shall also assume that all terminals operate at 2.4 kbps (although most terminals at BBN operate at lower speeds), so that two 64 kbps voice circuits can handle all word processing traffic. We estimate the actual data flow by assuming that the average typing speed is 60 words per minute; that approximately 50 percent of the three-hour connect time is used for text input; that because of editing functions, the total traffic is three times the input traffic; and that peak traffic is about twice the average. The total peak data rate is then 2.2 kbps.

2.2.3. Electronic Mail

This medium is heavily used at BBN. We assumed the following average statistics: * half of the employees at BBN use the electronic mail system; each user spends 20 minutes per day reading mail and an additional 20 minutes composing two ten-line messages per day; each message is sent to three recipients; the input/output and peak to average traffic ratios are the same as for word processing. The resulting requirements are three voice channels for circuit-switched connections and a peak data rate of about 1.0 kbps.

* Recent measurements at BBN have shown that these estimates are quite accurate.

2.2.4. Printers

There are seven printers (including high quality output terminals) of various data rates, but with a total maximum data rate of approximately 30 kbps. Because these devices are on-line essentially all day, we shall use this value as an estimate of the peak traffic.

Table 4 summarizes the results for BBN traffic and shows the number of full duplex voice channels required to handle voice and data traffic on a circuit-switching and on a packet-switching basis. We see that BBN's traffic requirements are roughly half those of the medium size office of the previous section although, of course, the ratio of packet- to circuit-switching requirements is the same because of the dominance of voice traffic. Furthermore, for all types of devices, the data traffic at BBN is substantially smaller than that projected in Section 2.1. In summary, the BBN data reinforce the conclusions that were drawn in that section.

2.2.5. Facsimile and Copiers

Although these devices are not part of BBN's data network, we include the statistics for completeness and also to show that the resulting traffic is negligible in comparison with the data traffic given above.

At BBN there are two facsimile machines that together handle about 35 input and 35 output pages per day. During the busiest minute, both machines would be operating, and therefore, the peak data rate is just twice the bit rate of the machines, or 4.8 kbps; hence only 0.1 voice channel is needed for this traffic. (Of course, BBN's facsimile traffic will probably grow as the use of this technique becomes more widespread.)

The copiers at BBN produce about 60,000 copies per month (this excludes BBN's Copy Center, which is used primarily for reproducing long documents and for making many copies; we presume that such a copy center would exist even if copiers were on the network). If the copiers were linked to a data network, then the original copy need be transmitted only once, and if we assume an average of ten copies of each original, with the peak usage twice the average, then the peak traffic is only 1.0 kbps.

2.2.6. Voice Mail

As a final calculation that might be of interest since we are considering voice/data applications in a future office, we shall make some projections on the resource requirements needed to handle a voice mail system. We envision that such a system would use a

Table 4
BBN Traffic (Scaled to 500 Telephones)

	Number of terminals	Required Number of full duplex 64 kbps circuits	Peak throughput (kbps)
telephone	500	70	4500
text processing	40	2	2.2
electronic mail	50 *	3	1.0
printer	7	1	30.0
Requirements for a Voice/Data Network			
circuit-switching		76	
packet-switching		46	

mailbox approach and might have a few of the basic features of a text oriented mail system, but that the voice system would be used only for short messages to individuals who did not answer their telephones or whose telephones were busy. In addition, the voice system would be used for some of the text messages currently transmitted via the electronic mail system. On the basis of statistics gathered by BBN's computerized PBX, we estimate that approximately 1500 call attempts (including internal and external calls) either receive no answer, or receive a busy signal, or are picked up by BBN's Message Center. If we assume that about two thirds of these are either repeated calls or would not be forwarded, then 500 messages per day would be stored by the voice mail system, or about one message per person per day, a reasonable quantity. In addition, perhaps five percent of the present text messages might be sent using the voice system; these messages would be those that are neither sensitive, nor multi-destination, nor very long. Since this amounts to only 25 messages per day, the total is negligible in comparison with that above, and we shall neglect these messages in our calculations.

If we assume that each message lasts about 30 seconds of real time, that each message flows once into storage and once to the recipient, and that the peak traffic is twice the average, then the peak utilization and throughput are 2.1 erlangs and 130 kbps, respectively, for this application. If this traffic were consolidated with the other traffic, three additional voice channels would be required for circuit switching, or two additional channels for packet switching.

However, now consider the storage requirements for these messages. According to the above data, approximately 250 minutes worth of messages are stored *each day* if the digitization rate is 64 kbps, so that approximately 100 megabytes of storage are needed! Clearly, standard pulse code modulation (PCM), which produces this high bit rate, is an inappropriate technology for a voice mail system in a moderate size office. We might note that some possible alternatives are:

– Use of vocoder techniques to remove silent periods and to compress the data by at least an order of magnitude; the vocoder could be dedicated to this application and thus a single device could be shared by all users;

– Use of conventional analog, audio recording techniques (however, unless convenient and nonsequential retrieval methods are provided, analog techniques would be undesirable);

– Use of video disk technology to provide high capacity storage and convenient message access.

3. Design Alternatives

In this section we analyze alternatives related to three high-level design issues. First, we evaluate whether a single network should handle both voice and data, or whether there should be two separate networks, one for voice and one for data, with a communications path between the two. Based upon this evaluation, we then discuss which network topology is preferable – star, ring, bus, or distributed. Finally, we address the switching technique for the preferred topology.

We shall consider these alternatives in light of the following observations:

– Intra-office voice networks are pervasive;

– Intra-office data networks are becoming more necessary and useful; they will be essential to tie together the currently developing variety of office systems to achieve full automation of office processes;

– In a typical business office, voice communications predominate; the ratio of data traffic to voice traffic is extremely low even in highly automated offices;

– At present, there are few applications which combine the use of voice and data in a cost-effective way; in the future, however, combined voice/data applications will become cost-effective and hence more prevalent.

3.1. Separate Networks Versus a Combined Network

On the basis of the observations given above, we can conclude that in the near future, there will be strong interest in intra-office data networks and some interest, but perhaps less utility, in unified voice/data networks. We can find no one strong argument for a single integrated voice/data office network. However, there certainly are reasons for constructing a network that will provide some connection between voice and data devices. Since voice traffic volume is so much greater than data traffic volume and since we assume that an intra-office voice network will always exist, the potential for carrying the data on the already-existent voice network is, at least superficially, extremely appealing, but some concrete justifications are clearly required.

Before outlining the relative merits of separate and combined networks, we present a few thoughts about the traffic patterns in a future office. The data flows in the office will be both for internal and external communications: almost all devices will be involved in some intra-office communications, and many will also utilize some outside communications. Initially the traffic flows within a newly automated office may be somewhat static, but this will change as the variety of devices and applications grows; then the interconnections will become quite dynamic, partially because we anticipate that most communications among terminals will be mediated by a computer or some type of controller (for example, a buffering unit that manages facsimile input/output). In summary, the future terminal will connect to a variety of hosts or terminals, depending upon which provides the particular specialized service required. Also, for data communications external to an office, we believe that with the increased use of distributed processing, an increased fraction of connect time will be devoted to actual communications. In these ways, future data connections will become increasingly similar to current voice connections.

The relative advantages of separate and of combined networks are summarized in Table 5. In evaluating the potential advantages of separate networks in greater depth, we can invoke the following counter-arguments to the three points given in the table:

1. When designing a network (or a product), one should plan for *future* needs (for which a combined network is a better match).
2. Since the volume of data traffic is much less than that of voice, for a given level of performance the data-handling capabilities of a combined network

Table 5.
Relative advantages of separate and combined voice and data networks

Separate Networks	Combined Network
1. At present, there is not much voice-data cross traffic, and the flow patterns of the two are different.	1. In the future, there will be more voice-data cross traffic, and the flow patterns of data will become more similar to those of voice.
2. Separate networks can each be optimized for its own traffic.	2. Data access to external resources is more direct with a combined network (since voice terminals implicitly have such access already).
3. Data and voice have different requirements for delay, throughput, error control, and reliability.	3. With a combined network, a customer might want to purchase a single product with modularity; the customer can then begin with a voice network and later add data capabilities at lower incremental cost.
	4. It may be possible to use existing in-building telephone wiring to carry data traffic.
	5. Since the volume of data traffic is much less than voice, it is incrementally less expensive to provide the capacity for initial as well as for expanded data requirements on a combined voice/data network.

can be sub-optimum without much increase in total cost.

3. There should be no problem in meeting the delay, throughput, and error requirements of both voice and data because (a) if properly designed, the delay through a local network will be very small for all traffic; (b) the volume of data is negligible compared with voice; and (c) existing protocols can be used to handle error control.

The one remaining issue is the different reliability requirements of voice and data. The reliability of the voice network is usually critical to an organization, and telephone systems are designed with this principle in mind. On the other hand, because data handling needs are generally less predictable and more complex, data networks tend to be less reliable. If the addition of data handling capability to a voice network increases the likelihood that the voice traffic will be disrupted, then a combined network will not be accepted in the marketplace. We believe that this is an important issue. However, we also believe that it should be possible to incorporate mechanisms into a combined network that ensure a high degree of reliability. For example, voice and data connections and traffic could be handled differently in order to ensure that if a failure occurs in the data portion, the voice portion is not affected. Also, significant spare capacity could be provided for data traffic in order to avoid problems that might occur when operating near saturation. In other words, it is our opinion that the reliability issue should be manageable with proper design. Thus, in the office environment, the potential advantages of separate networks, as listed in Table 5, either are not significant or can be overcome, and the itemized technical and economic advantages of a combined network outweigh those of separate networks. Our overall conclusion, therefore, is that future office networks should be based upon combining voice and data.

3.2. Network Topology

We now consider the possible topological structure of a combined voice/data network. Four basic alternatives are a star, over which all communications flow through a central controller; a ring, in which data flows sequentially around a loop; a bus, in which data can be broadcast to all devices; and a general distributed topology in which several paths exist between communicating nodes, but not all nodes are connected directly to each other. In evaluating these alternative topologies for local office networks, we rely on the projected office traffic statistics presented in the previous sections, and in particular on the high ratio of voice traffic to data traffic.

We must emphasize strongly that here we are considering the "physical" topology – the arrangement for connecting devices to the "network". In particular, a ring topology, for example, necessarily implies that data flows from one device controller to the next, whereas a star configuration implies that all data flows through a single controller. However, a star controller can take advantage of any of the above alternatives inside its central controller, so that, in principle, a physical star topology could use a central controller that internally uses a ring transmission technique. In fact, within the constraints of distance between a device and its network interface, the contoller for a star network might be able to utilize hardware identical to that developed for other physical topologies.

Within the time frame we are considering, we assume that intra-office voice-only networks will be star networks. Today's voice network in a typical office is centered around a central PBX; a large facility may be organized around multiple PBXs which are interconnected. The market, customer, and technical inertia for the continuing use of star networks for voice is very strong: techniques for central switching are well-proven, and the installation base is enormous. Voice communications have vastly improved over decades of use and continued development; extremely high performance and reliability standards have been achieved, and PBXs are a proven technology for delivering the required quality of service.

None of the other three topologies have been commercially used for intra-office voice networks; however, various data networks have been designed around these topologies. Ring and bus networks are specifically applicable for local area networks, while a distributed topology is applicable for both local and long distance networking. We shall not further consider the general distributed network as a *primary* design alternative for a local office network. In general, a main advantage of this design is that it can parallel the physical topology of the organization. In a large organization, multiple controllers (in the case of a star network), or multiple bus/ring structures will be required to support the volume of traffic or the physical separation of facilities; as such, these networks may evolve to distributed topologies. Other general advantages of distributed topologies are (1) statistical averaging of traffic through network nodes and lines, and (2) high reliability because multiple paths are available. Within a local office environment, however, communications bandwidth is not the costly resource, so this averaging advantage is not relevant. High reliability can be achieved through other means with other designs, so this not a strong advantage. As a primary design, therefore, a distributed topology requires switching complexity with no strong countervailing advantages; however, as an evolutionary capability from single star, bus, or ring networks it might be important.

The characteristics of star and bus/ring networks are compared in Table 6. At the present level of analysis, we believe that the flexibility and the evolutionary considerations listed in Table 6 are perhaps the strongest reasons to develop star network technology (i.e. PBX technology) to support both data and voice. The technology exists now for voice, it is widely used and understood, and the gain for both vendors and users appears to be great, relative to the (probably) low investment. The vendor who can offer a switch for both voice and data can gain an additional market segment, and the user organization can acquire full communications support, probably for a lot less expense than with separate facilities. Product compatibility would be the goal, so that voice "controllers" could be expanded to support data; expansion should be modular so the user can isolate voice and data functionality, or combine it.

A related advantage of a star configuration is that it might be possible to use in-building PBX wiring, thereby reducing not only the cost, but also the time and inconvenience of installing a voice/data network. If an organization owns its own PBX and hence the associated wiring, then these existing wires could also carry data traffic (by a multiplexing technique, for example). Also, if an organization plans to replace a Bell System PBX with a non-Bell unit, then new wiring would generally be installed; in this case, a pair of cables (rather than a single cable) could be routed to each office at little additional cost, the second cable being available for a (possible) data terminal.

3.3. Switching Techniques for a Voice/Data Computerized PBX

In the previous section we presented arguments showing that a combined voice/data network using a star topology is a preferable approach for designing an office communications network. Since most of the traffic on such a network will be voice, we shall call the network's central switch a "computerized PBX" (CPBX), even though this future switch may bear little resemblance to present-day, digital telephone switches. In this section we present some design considerations for the choice of switching technique internal to an office CPBX.

Because of its use in existing PBXs, circuit switching is clearly a prime candidate for use in a CPBX. We use the term "circuit switching" in its broadest sense, namely to signify any switching technique which *pre-allocates* (and hence guarantees) certain resources to a voice or data connection. Thus, circuit switching includes, for example, both space and time division multiplexing. The alternative to circuit switching is "packet switching", where again we shall use the term in a broad sense to denote a method which does not pre-allocate specific resources to users. There are many possibilities here, such as simple ALOHA or carrier sense multiple access (which can be used if the *internal* CPBX topology is a bus). Clearly, the switching technique and the internal CPBX configuration are not independent decisions.

Before comparing these two switching alternatives, wer first note that there are some considerations which do not significantly influence the choice of switching technique, the most basic being performance. For some networks, the performance requirements dictate certain aspects of the switching technique. For example, if many interactive users are to share a single satellite channel, circuit switching (i.e., pre-allocation of bandwidth) is clearly inappropriate, and therefore a variety of "demand assignment" techniques have been proposed. However, for an office network with a single CPBX (or even with several CPBXs), some performance issues disappear. For example, the delay and the error rates should be small regardless of the switching technique that is used. In addition, many of the complexities associated with multi-node packet networks (such as routing and message reassembly) do not occur in a CPBX-based local network. Finally, with circuit switching approaches in which the internal data rate of the switch is much greater than the user data rate (as in time division multiplexing), the hardware must provide some buffering and must construct small blocks of data for transmission through the switch; thus, these approaches must perform some of the same functions performed in a packet switch. In summary, the arguments noted above cannot be

Table 6
Comparison of star and bus/ring topologies for a combined voice/data network

	Star	Bus/Ring
Reliability Controller	limiting resource – impact of failure is great; can be overcome by redundancy	impact of failure should be only a single station outage
Transmission Medium	impact of failure is a single station outage	limiting resource – risk of failure is small, but may be difficult to repair; redundancy is not practical
Growth Capability	limited by controller; large infrequent additions may require overall reconfiguration	limited by bus/ring capacity; each new connection requires new controller
Flexibility	controller can utilize techniques and hardware developed for any physical technology	can have local, specialized functionality
Economics	economy of scale within controller; additional devices may be required for physically long lines	cost of controllers is major factor in assessing viability
Evolutionary Considerations	voice networks are star today (strong market inertia); data traffic is very much less than voice, so it may be minimal cost to add data	none exist – would require massive conversions
Maintainability	more convenient because centrally located; but single complex switch may be more difficult to troubleshoot	distributed maintenance is burdensome (e.g., synchronization of nodes, remote troubleshooting)

invoked *a priori* in order to choose one switching technique over the other.

We now outline the relative advantages and disadvantages of circuit and packet switching. However, because we have not performed a detailed comparison, we must be careful to distinguish between *potential* and clear-cut (or inherent) benefits. In other words, there are certain limitations that existing circuit or packet switching techniques possess for the application under consideration; but if we were to design a new switching technique especially for a voice/data CPBX, we might be able to overcome those limitations. With this point in mind, we can list several benefits associated with curcuit switching:

- it is a proven technology (it already exists for voice)
- because of its widespread use, circuit switching hardware components are more common and should be relatively low priced
- the processing software is less complex than with packet switching (e.g., with packet switching, the switch will need congestion control mechanisms, more sophisticated buffer management capabilities, and silence recognition for voice traffic).

Some of the potential advantages of circuit switching are that it uses less buffer memory (with packet switching there is always some chance that a transmission will be delayed, and hence some additional buffers are needed); that it is easier to isolate voice and data traffic, thereby providing the potential for achieving the required reliability of voice connections in a combined voice/data network (as discussed in Section 3.1); and that support for existing protocols is more readily achieved (since, in effect, a "wire" is dedicated to the connection, the switch appears transparent to the communicating devices). The principal disadvantage of circuit switching is its much greater throughput requirements. This greater bandwidth means that more processor hardware may be needed.

Clearly, the above points are not conclusive for selecting a switching method. On the contrary, we believe that the decisive factor is *cost,* and more detailed analysis is required to evaluate this factor. In a typical CPBX installation, the switch constitutes a significant fraction of the overall system cost, and hence the switching technique should be chosen primarily on the basis of how much the resulting CPBX would cost. In order to properly perform a cost analysis it is necessary to conduct a more detailed study of the traffic characteristics (e.g., flow patterns, message sizes) and of digital voice technology, to develop candidate switching techniques well-matched to the requirements, and to carefully evaluate the hardware and software requirements of these techniques.

4. Summary of Conclusions

In the study reported on here, our goal was to determine the feasibility of integrating voice and data on a single office network. We considered briefly the functional requirements for combining voice and data, and then we analyzed the traffic characteristics of the office in order to determine the magnitude of voice traffic and of data traffic. Subsequently, we considered design alternatives for an office network and its main switching components.

We believe that the requirement for using systems based on both voice and data technologies is most prominent among management and professional level personnel. We have concluded that voice is the preferred input medium for this group of personnel, and digital information is the most convenient and flexible form for processing, storing, and retrieving information. The two most apparent applications for combining voice and data in the immediate future are voice mail and voice dictation, both using digital storage and retrieval techniques. In the more distant future, the widespread availability of computer voice recognition and generation systems capabilities will spur innovation of many more applications which combine voice and data.

To understand the relative magnitudes of the various traffic types that might flow within an office in the future, we generated projections of traffic volumes for voice traffic, text processing communications, electronic mail messages, and communications to/from printers, intelligent copiers and facsimile machines. These traffic projections were based upon market research reports and user surveys, together with some of our own assumptions regarding the data communications environment. We intentionally attempted to overestimate the data traffic in order to be conservative. Nevertheless, voice traffic is shown to be substantially greater than data traffic. The major conclusion we draw from this data is that if a single communication network handles both voice and data, then the network should be optimized for voice. In other words, data traffic should be added to voice networks.

In considering design alternatives for local office networks, we reached several conclusions:

- Future office network designs should be based upon combining voice and data. We find few advantages to separating voice from data, while we believe there are strong technical and economic benefits in a combined network.
- The star topology is deemed the most immediately suitable structure for a combined voice/data intra-office network; such a network would be based around a switch similar to that of the computerized PBX which is currently oriented to voice. Internally, the CPBX could utilize any physical topology.
- Traffic characteristics of both data and digital voice must be studied in more detail; the results of such further study would then provide the basis for identifying candidate switching techniques well matched to the requirements, and for evaluating the resource requirements of these alternative switching techniques. It would then be possible to choose a CPBX design on the basis of delivered performance as well as cost of the switch.
- The circuit-switching schemes currently used within the voice CPBXs may or may not be optimal when switching both voice and data. In order to determine the optimal switching technique, the merits of each must be understood on the basis of resources required in the switch and on the basis of delivered performance; this would then provide the basis for a cost analysis of the switching facilities. Cost is a major decision factor since the switch constitutes a major portion of the cost for a star network.

References

[1] "Country Government Cuts Costs with PBX System," Telecommunications, April 1980, pp. 43–44.
[2] See, e.g., "Managing Global Communications," Creative Strategies International, 1979.
[3] V.G. Cerf and A. Curran, "The Future of Computer Communications," Datamation, May 1977, pp. 105–114.

George M. Pfister and Bradley V. O'Brien,
Perspective Telecommunications Group, Paramus, N.J.

Comparing the CBX to the local network—and the winner is?

The authors rate the two technologies in seven categories. The local net leads in just one —transmission speed.

For the past year or so, a great deal of controversy has arisen over shared-cable—or local—networks. Not only has a conflict been simmering between private branch exchange (PBX) and shared-cable vendors, but a series of "armed camps" have formed within both technology groups.

In the shared-cable group, the confrontations typically involve questions of broadband versus baseband, ring versus bus architecture, or carrier sense multiple access with collision detection (CSMA/CD) versus token passing approaches. In the PBX camp, second or third generation, blocking as opposed to non-blocking, and alternative data integration techniques have overshadowed the previously dominant analog- versus digital-design controversy.

Both users and vendors have been hurled into a state of confusion produced over these controversies. They frequently lose sight of the fact that practical concerns, such as the applications to be supported, the devices to be interconnected, and the site considerations, will dictate the ultimate implementation.

We will examine these practical considerations, and compare the third-generation PBX and the shared-cable approaches. The areas covered will include installation costs and requirements, available bandwidth and throughput, applications to be supported, as well as network topology considerations.

As a first step, definitions and reviews of the third-generation PBX and shared-cable technologies should prove beneficial. The basic concept behind all shared-cable networks is that transmission cables—whether coaxial, twisted pair, or hybrids such as twinax—are inherently capable of carrying very-high-bandwidth data over the relatively short distances involved in intra-site communications networks. Typical distances are less than 1,000 feet for single buildings and less than 5,000 feet for multibuilding campus sites. Over these distances, a twisted-pair cable can carry data at 1 Mbit/s; a baseband-operated coax at 20 Mbit/s; and a radio-frequency-carrier (broadband)-operated coax at 500 Mbit/s.

The key distinction between the different types of shared-cable networks is less the type of cable and more the method of sharing the wide bandwidth provided by the cable. The two basic sharing alternatives are frequency division and time division.

Frequency division multiplexing (FDM) of the transmissions is the simplest method, but not necessarily the least expensive or the most flexible. FDM techniques are usually applied to broadband coax: A pair of stations is assigned a fixed set of frequencies, but newer techniques with frequency-agile modems allow switching to different frequencies, thereby enabling multiple interconnections.

Time division multiplexing (TDM) of the cable capacity is a more complex process but, with the declining cost of digital logic, is becoming more readily available. The allocation of time to individual stations can be centrally assigned as in polled networks, or it can be contended for as in Xerox Corporation's Ethernet baseband-network approach.

Time division can be applied to twisted-pair cables or to baseband or broadband coax. Frequency division and time division are used in combination in several commercial products, such as those from Wang Laboratories, Sytek, and Amdax.

Third-generation PBXs

A third-generation PBX—or CBX (computerized branch exchange)—(Fig. 1) has three basic characteristics: distributed architecture, integrated voice and data, and non-blocking configuration. A distributed

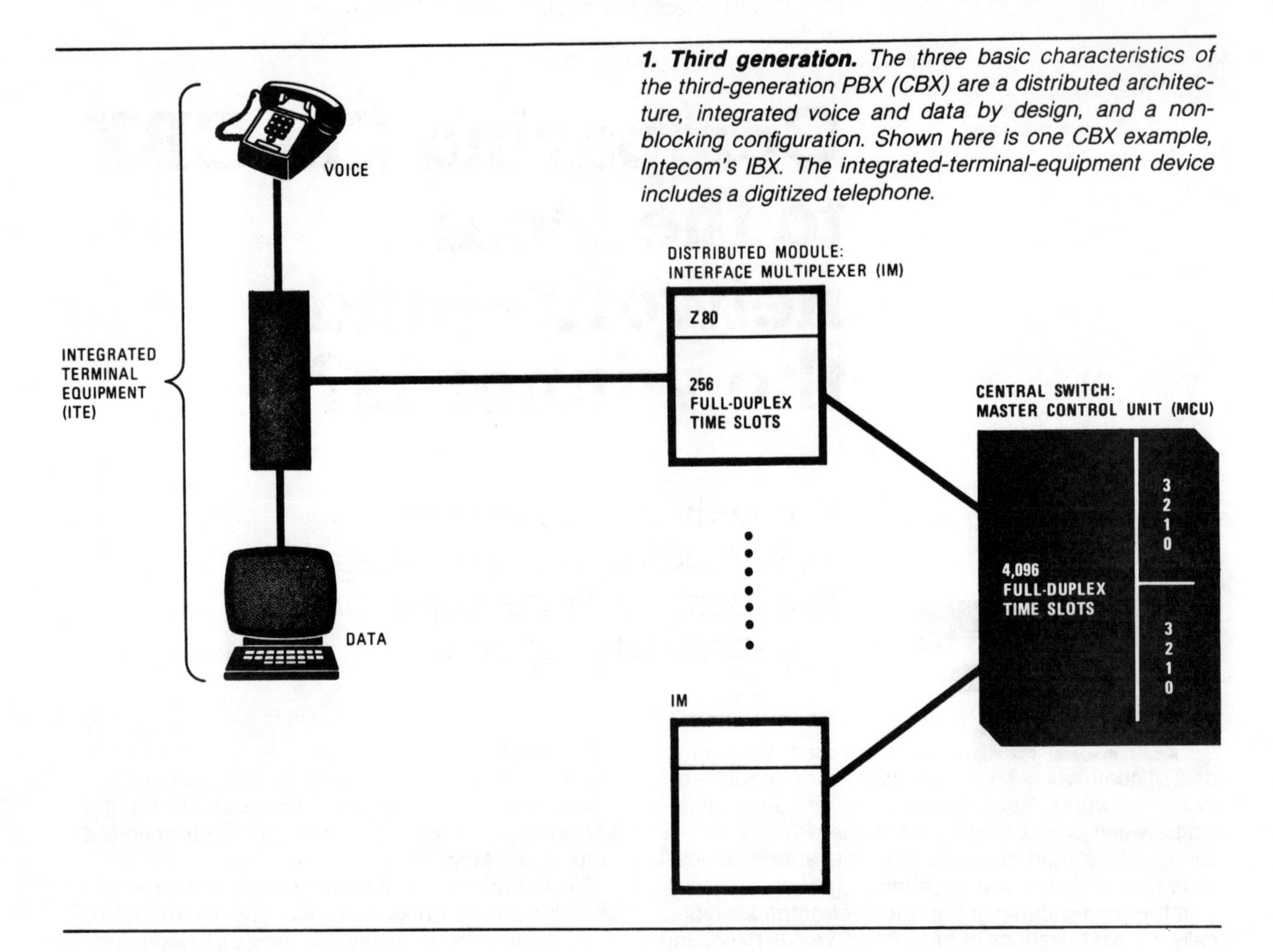

1. Third generation. *The three basic characteristics of the third-generation PBX (CBX) are a distributed architecture, integrated voice and data by design, and a non-blocking configuration. Shown here is one CBX example, Intecom's IBX. The integrated-terminal-equipment device includes a digitized telephone.*

architecture substitutes coaxial or fiber-optic cable for twisted-pair wiring between the central switch and the distributed modules. From a control viewpoint, the distributed module offloads some of the central-switch processor's real-time workload (such as handling "off-hook detect" and other routine functions).

The degree to which control intelligence is offloaded to the module to perform call control and switching is unclear. Autonomous switching in the module, as is the case with Datapoint Corporation's Integrated Switching Exchange (ISX), appears to provide higher reliability, since a module could continue to operate in the event of some other component's failure. However, most CBX designers feel that fully distributed configurations will encounter software and control problems as a result of complex intermodule communications. CBXs such as Intecom's Integrated Business Exchange (IBX), and late-second-generation devices such as the Stromberg-Carlson Digital Business Exchange (DBX) and Rockwell International's Wescom 580 Digital Switching System (DSS), use distributed control. But in these cases the control is hierarchical rather than fully distributed.

Integrated voice and data is an architectural characteristic of the third-generation PBX (or CBX). It differs from the dedicated, alternate-use, port-doubled (double the number of ports needed with both voice and data operation), or submultiplexed approaches typical of late-second-generation devices in that data integration is designed into the CBX. It serves to guarantee processor performance and transmission path availability. The third-generation devices support simultaneous data and voice transmission, with a data rate of up to 56 kbit/s.

Non-blocking architectures will dominate new CBX announcements from now on, because the digital switching technologies necessary to support this mode of operation are now as cost-effective as previous blocked approaches. A non-blocked approach using fixed-time-slot/port assignment also optimizes control processor performance by eliminating complex time-slot-assignment hardware and software. A non-blocking configuration also reduces control overheads in specialized adjunct processors (such as for voice store-and-forward and electronic mail) that could occur for ring-back and queueing situations.

As illustrated in Figure 2, the CBX functions primarily as a circuit-switched transport network connecting the user with specialized processors for voice store-and-forward, voice recognition, and electronic mail, as well as with data processors. Some functions—such as speed, code, and protocol conversions—may be provided in more powerful devices as in Intecom's IBX, which uses 32-bit Perkin Elmer 3210 processors with at least a 1.5-microsecond instruction cycle.

At this point, let us explore the trade-offs between

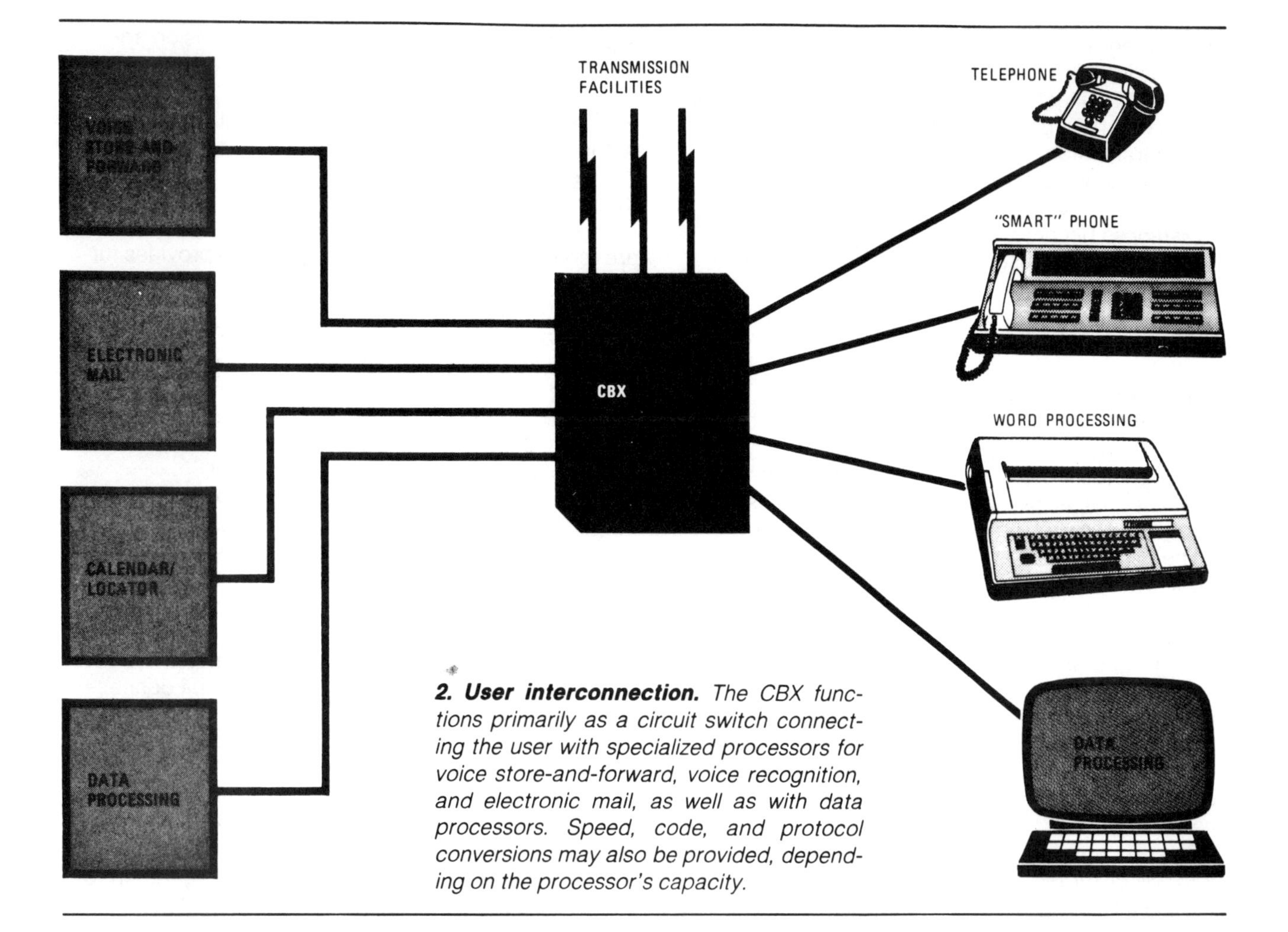

2. User interconnection. *The CBX functions primarily as a circuit switch connecting the user with specialized processors for voice store-and-forward, voice recognition, and electronic mail, as well as with data processors. Speed, code, and protocol conversions may also be provided, depending on the processor's capacity.*

third-generation PBXs and shared-cable networks in the following areas:

- Installation/implementation
- Voice/data integration
- Distance
- Reliability
- Transmission speed
- Available digital bandwidth
- Relative costs

Just about all existing office sites are wired with twisted-pair for distribution of traditional telephone services. An interesting and apparently little-known fact is that all PBXs are installed with at least two pairs of wiring, only one of which is used for voice transmission. The second—and in some cases third—pair is installed for backup should the prime pair be damaged or to allow distribution of another device. As such, most existing PBX installations have available spare twisted pairs for use with port-doubled approaches or all-data PBXs.

The third-generation PBX uses two-pair for voice, data, and control transmissions. Provisions for twisted-pair distribution are usually found in existing buildings, making any PBX installation more readily feasible than if coaxial cable were required. The shared-cable approach usually requires installation of new cable. In some buildings, baseboard or plenum distribution proves most cost-effective. In other buildings where in-floor ducts are used, particularly in "open-office" environments, coax distribution may be prohibitive, if not downright impossible.

Over the last 100 years, PBXs have evolved to effectively handle voice transmission and control. Given the installed base and existing user familiarity, as well as the fact that vendors such as AT&T and GTE will probably enter the office automation market via the PBX, it can safely be assumed that the PBX will remain the dominant technology for voice distribution.

Broadband-cable networks can handle voice, but at a cost. Additional tap and interface devices are required costing about $1,200 per drop, as opposed to a cost of $800-$1,000 per line for voice PBX. Again the CBX gets the nod. It also handles slow to medium (300 to 2.4K bit/s) and medium to fast (4.8 to 56 kbit/s) data transmission. The advantages of cable for data distribution will be discussed later.

Distance considerations

Recent studies indicate that the majority of office-type networks will operate over a wiring distance of less than 1,000 feet, with over 90 percent of the stations within 5,000 feet of each other. These distances are actual cable lengths that average almost double the physical separation of stations.

A third-generation PBX such as Intecom's IBX (Fig. 1) allows digital transmission of voice and data between integrated-terminal-equipment (ITE) devices (such as Intecom's digitized telephones) over distances of up to 2,500 feet. The IBX module, called an interface multiplexer (IM), can be located up to 6,000 feet from the central switch. As a result, the total distance for digital voice or data transmission is approximately 17,000 feet, or almost three miles.

Distances become an important consideration in multibuilding campuses. The distributed architecture of the third-generation PBX allows switch modules to be located in each building, and the modules are interconnected using broadband or fiber-optic cable.

Campus conditions

For intrabuilding situations, shared-cable approaches and CBXs are about equal in the distances they can support. The third-generation PBX proves superior on campuses, especially if fully distributed devices with autonomous switching modules are applicable.

The third-generation PBX is inherently a tree/star topology. As such, it provides a good degree of reliability in that stations, station/module links, modules, and module/central-link components can fail without affecting higher-level or parallel components. Redundancy for critical architectural components, such as modules or module-to-central links, can also be installed for these devices; because of their inherent shared nature, this redundancy is cost-effective. Alternate routing of module/central links is another recommended option.

Shared-cable loops, rings, or buses may be partially or totally disrupted in the event of cable failure. True, multiple cables can be installed to minimize this disruption, but costs are then greater. And the ratio of out-of-service terminals per failure will be higher than with distributed third-generation PBXs.

At the lowest distribution level of a CBX—the station—absolute failure of the wiring disables only a single instrument. In most cases, this is also true of shared cables. But with ring networks and some types of bus devices, failures can be disastrous. The topology of the CBX again proves to be the superior choice.

Speed limitations

The third-generation PBX supports digital voice and data up to about 64 kbit/s. To many users, 64-kbit/s data may seem inexhaustible. However, emerging workstations with high-resolution displays, such as the Xerox Star, and process-sharing devices such as Apollo Computer Inc.'s Domain and Pittsburgh-based Three Rivers Computer Corporation's PERQ, require higher transfer rates.

It should be noted that some CBX vendors will use their product to control intelligent workstations. As a result, proprietary compression protocols are available from vendors such as AT&T, GTE, and Northern Telecom to reduce bandwidth to the 56-kbit/s range. As an alternative, specialized channels may be offered by the same vendors to switch the 1-Mbit/s-and-higher data rates that twisted pair is able to support.

The shared-cable networks are designed to support transmission rates in the Mbit/s ranges. The cable-sharing techniques, especially the time-division approaches, allow this high bandwidth to be shared by devices with "bursty" requirements.

If transmission rates in the over-1-Mbit/s range are required for point-to-point or limited-community-of-interest devices, the shared-cable approach is clearly the winner over the CBX. When specialized services—such as video for training or information distribution—are required, the shared-cable approach provides further advantages.

At first, shared cable appears to have substantially higher bandwidth than third-generation PBXs, since it operates in some implementations with a total basic capacity of 500 Mbit/s. Because of the nature of the various contention or transmission-control techniques, such as CSMA/CD and token passing, channel utilization is, of course, something short of total.

If the digital capacity of an Intecom IBX is multiplied out, 4,000 voice stations at 64 kbit/s and 4,000 data devices at 57.6 kbit/s produce an aggregate transmission capacity of 486.4 Mbit/s [(4,000 x 64) + (4,000 x 57.6)]. Because of the CBX's tree structure, these devices operate as a virtual point-to-point network. Actual throughput more closely approximates maximum than for a shared facility, once a circuit connection is established.

What it costs

The third-generation PBX terminates both digital voice and data for a total cost of about $1,600 per workstation. Data can be added on an optional—or as-needed—basis, allowing a voice-only configuration to be installed at costs comparable to today's late-second-generation PBXs. As mentioned, a termination of a high-speed shared-cable network costs in the vicinity of $1,200 for each data device. If both voice and data were installed on the same cable, the costs would run as high as $2,400 per workstation.

Note that CBXs are less expensive to install if existing wiring is used. Also, twisted pair—which is simpler to handle—should cost less to install due to the lower technology skills required for technicians. Therefore, the CBX again comes out on top.

The Table summarizes the comparison of third-gen-

The scoresheet

CATEGORY	CBX	LOCAL NETWORK
INSTALLATION	✓	
VOICE/DATA INTEGRATION	✓	
DISTANCE	EQUAL	EQUAL
RELIABILITY	✓	
TRANSMISSION SPEED		✓
AVAILABLE DIGITAL BANDWIDTH	EQUAL	EQUAL
COSTS	✓	

Sizing up Dimension

Bell's recent announcement of substantial enhancements for its Dimension PBX product line is significant in a number of respects. The distributed architecture further enforces the distribution of control, function, and networking that will typify most future switches. The distributed communications system (DCS) permits the installation of up to 10 Dimension Custom, 600, or 2000 devices that are then interconnected for voice transmission. Distribution of these nodes is controlled by parallel data links.

This Dimension announcement is also a direct endorsement of the approach taken by Rolm Corporation's VLCBX (VL for very large). The VLCBX utilizes fully distributed and autonomous switching nodes interconnected in a similar fashion.

The accompanying announcement of Message Service confirms the approach of adding applications processing via "outboard" specialized processors. This approach leaves the PBX to do what it does best—provide communications.

The most significant implication of the announcement is the fact that Bell is committing heavy resources to the Dimension product line. Despite a great deal of criticism, the Dimension product is a good one and the authors agree with Bell's strong stand in positioning this product as transitional (four to six years) for office automation applications.

The most frequently stated criticism of Dimension is that it uses an analog transmission technique. Let us see how this "deficiency" could actually be viewed as an advantage.

The analog pulse-amplitude-modulation (PAM) technique used in Dimension allows a single time slot to accommodate both send and receive transmissions. Digital switches require separate time slots for send and receive. One hundred twenty-eight analog time slots implement 128 talking paths, or provide support for 256 ports. One hundred twenty-eight digital time slots implement 64 talking paths, supporting 128 ports.

A fully configured Dimension Custom with 15 modules, each with a 128-time-slot switching matrix, supports 3,840 ports (15 x 128 x 2) in a virtually nonblocking mode (if carefully engineered). The new DCS announcement theoretically extends this to 38,400 ports (3,840 x 10)—well above the 25,000-line limit stated by Bell for DCS.

It should be noted that the Bell announcement also provides strong endorsement for the viability of other late-second-generation devices such as Northern Telecom's SL-1, Rolm's VLCBX, and Rockwell/Wescom's 580 DSS.

The data integration scheme Bell announced on May 18 is a simple port-doubled approach. It provides benefits principally to users of switched dial-up communications in the 4.8-9.6-kbit/s range because of the lower cost of the new data interface device ($45-$55/mo), compared to a Bell modem's $125-$200/mo. The underlying purpose of this data switching announcement is to convince users that Dimension will adequately support medium to high synchronous or asynchronous data rates.

The distributed Dimension announcement should also be regarded as the "death knell" for Centrex, since it provides more advanced functions and sufficient capacity to replace even the largest Centrex systems. Centrex service will ultimately prove undesirable for AT&T as it will belong to the divested Bell operating companies. Its shared nature will preclude intense customer programming, which will lead to processor, peripheral, and terminal add-ons.

eration PBXs and shared-cable approaches. Out of the seven categories, the PBX approach is superior in four areas: installation, voice/data integration, reliability, and costs. In the areas of distance and available digital bandwidth, the two approaches are about equal. For high-speed transmission, the shared-cable approaches are the obvious winners.

This overall CBX superiority should not cause concern for the future of shared-cable networks. Just be aware that the latter takes an unqualified second place in terms of total workstations connected.

The suitability for high-speed graphics, process sharing, and video distribution ensures the success of shared cable. Of much greater consequence, proprietary-exchange procedures among one manufacturer's terminal devices are adequately served by this type of network. Proprietary networks, such as Ethernet, Wangnet, and the IBM 3270 family, will continue to be popular due to user requirements for the manufacturers' devices that are thus supported. A multivendor network, however, is a more complex matter.

It should also be noted that based on the user's requirements, late-second-generation PBXs—which lack the third generation's distributed architecture and integrated voice and data—such as Bell's Dimension, Northern Telecom's SL-1, and Rolm's "CBX," can all satisfy the voice requirements. When coupled with a data PBX, they meet the needs of a large number of users (see "Sizing up Dimension").

One further point becomes clear: If shared-cable networks handle only a limited number of devices, then the baseband approaches such as Xerox's Ethernet are quite restricted in their applications.

While the CBX will dominate the office in implementations, shared-cable networks will have a place for the specialized-terminal types they are intended to support. Acknowledgment of this fact has been becoming more and more clear with announcements of products such as Datapoint's ISX. It was introduced with specified interfaces to the attached resource computer (ARC) shared-cable network. Other major CBX manufacturers have also announced commencement of development efforts to support shared-cable interfaces. Coexistence is proving symbiotic. ■

Section 5: The Network Interface

5.1 Overview

The purpose of a local network is to provide a means of communication for the various attached devices. To realize this purpose, the interface between the network and devices must be such as to permit cooperative interaction. For circuit-switched local networks (digital switches and digital PBXs), the problem is straightforward. The switch provides a transparent connection service that looks like a point-to-point link.

For packet-switched local networks (LANs and HSLNs), a number of issues are raised that relate to the allocation of protocols to the attached devices and to the network. Packet switching implies that the data to be sent over the network by a device are organized into packets that are sent through the network one at a time. Protocols must be used to specify the construction and exchange of these packets. At a minimum for a local network, protocols at layers 1 and 2 are needed to control the multiaccess network communication (For example, these layers would comprise the logical link control (LLC), medium access control (MAC), and physical control functions specified IEEE 802 and introduced in Section 2)

Thus, all attached devices must share these common local network protocols. From a customer's point of view, this fact structures into three alternatives the ways in which devices attach to a LAN or an HSLN: (1) homogeneous/single-vendor approach, (2) "standards" approach, and (3) standard network interface approach.

A homogeneous network is one in which all equipment (network plus attached devices) is provided by a single vendor. All equipment shares a common set of networking and communications software. The vendor has integrated a local network capability into its product line. Customers need not concern themselves with details of protocols and interfaces.

Undoubtedly, many customers will adopt this approach. The single-vendor system simplifies maintenance responsibility and provides an easy path for system evolution. On the other hand, the flexibility to obtain the best piece of equipment for a given task may be limited. Relying on a vendor, without consideration of the vendor's network architecture, for easy accommodation of foreign equipment is risky.

Another approach that a customer may take is to procure a local network that conforms to a standard and to dictate that all equipment be compatible with that standard. The local network would consist of a transmission medium plus an expandable set of "attachment points." This approach, although attractive, has some problems. The IEEE standard for LANs, although final, has not yet been widely implemented. Worse, from the point of view of the present discussion, is that the standard is loaded with options, so two devices claiming to be "IEEE compatible" may not be able to coexist on the same network. The ANSI standard for HSLNs is still in draft form. Thus, there is little hope that incompatible systems will fade away anytime soon.

The promise of local network standards does not lie in the solution of the interconnect problem. Rather, standards offer the hope that the prospect of a mass market will lead to cheap silicon implementations of local network protocols. However, the interconnect problem is an architectural issue, not a protocol issue.

Now, consider that a LAN or an HSLN consists of not only a transmission medium but also a set of intelligent devices that implement the local network protocols and provide an interface capability for device attachment. We will refer to this device as a network access unit (NAU). The NAUs, collectively, control access to and communications across the local network. Subscriber devices attach to the NAU through some standard communications or I/O interface. The details of the local network operation are hidden from the device.

The NAU architecture is commonly used by independent local network vendors (those who sell only networks, not the data processing equipment that uses the network). It holds out the promise that interface options provided by virtually all vendors for communications and I/O operation can be used to attach to a local network.

5.2 Network Access Unit

Typically, the NAU is a microprocessor-based device that acts as a communications controller to provide data transmission service to the attached device. The NAU transforms the data rate and protocol of the subscriber device to that of the local network transmission medium and vice versa. Data on the medium are available to all attached devices, whose NAUs screen data for reception based on address. In general terms, NAUs perform the following functions: (1) accept data from attached device, (2) buffer the data until medium access is achieved, (3) transmit data in addressed packets, (4) scan each packet on medium for the device's own address, (5) read packet into buffer, and (6) transmit data to attached device at the proper data rate.

The hardware interface between the NAU and the attached device is typically a standard serial communications interface, such as RS-232-C. Almost all computers and terminals support this interface. For higher speed, a parallel interface, such as an I/O channel or direct memory access

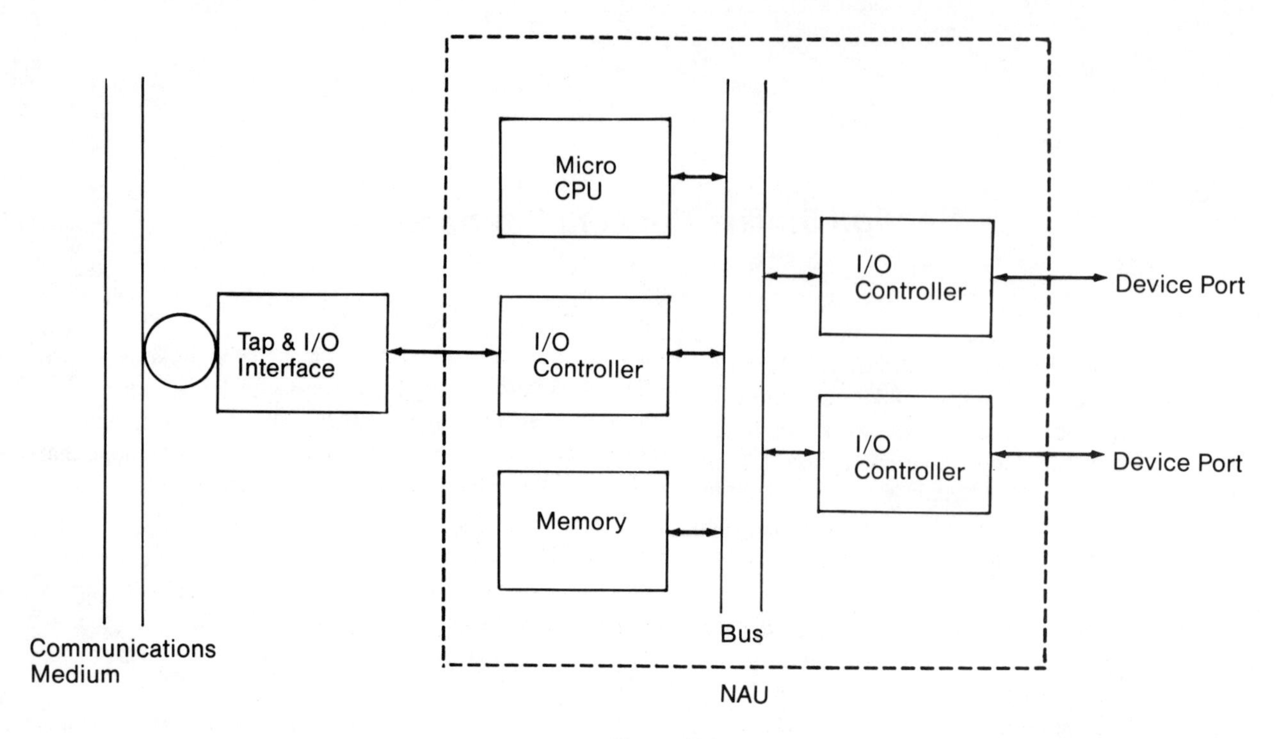

Figure 5.1

(DMA) interface, can be provided.

The NAU can be either an outboard or an inboard device. As an outboard device, the NAU is a stand alone unit, which may have one or more serial communications ports for device attachment. High-speed parallel ports are also used. As an inboard device, the NAU is integrated into the chassis of the data processing device, such as a minicomputer or terminal. An inboard NAU generally consists of one or more printed-circuit boards attached to the device's bus.

Figure 5.1 presents a generic architecture for an outboard NAU. The NAU consists of a number of modules connected by an internal system bus. One I/O controller module controls the interface to the local network medium. Typically, this module will contain the medium access control logic and the physical I/O logic to drive the medium transceiver or modem. Other I/O controllers contain the physical and link layer logic for controlling attached devices. A given controller might handle one or multiple device ports.

The operation of the NAU is controlled by a microprocessor, which makes use of an internal memory to store programs and data. The microprocessor generally executes a simplified operating system and a set of application programs specific to the local network function. For example, the system needs to be able to engage in a dialogue with attached devices to set up and tear down connections to other LAN addresses. Higher-layer protocols, such as a transport protocol, may also be implemented in the NAU.

The architecture for an in-board NAU is similar to that of Figure 5.1. In this case, the device I/O controllers are replaced by an I/O controller that attaches directly to a host computer system bus. Such a controller often employs DMA to exchange data with the host computer's main memory.

From a customer's point of view, an NAU with standard interface options solves, at least at the electrical level, the interconnect problem. From a designer's point of view, the NAU is a useful architectural concept. Whether a network is homogeneous or not, and whether the interface provided to the local network is standard or not, there must be some distributed logic for controlling local network access. Conceptualizing this logic as an NAU clarifies some of the communications architectural issues associated with networking applications on a local network.

The NAU must, at minimum, implement the LAN or HSLN protocols. The articles in this section explore the issue of what, if any, additional communications service the NAU might provide.

5.3 Article Summary

The first article describes the use of an NAU for terminal handling. This seemingly simple case is shown to require considerable functionality.

"Protocols for Local Area Networks" is concerned with protocol residency alternatives: how many layers in the NAU and how many in attached hosts or front-end processors. A number of alternatives are defined and their relative merits are discussed.

The article by Wood looks at a specific broadband LAN implementation. In this system, layers 1 through 4 (physical, data link, network, and transport) are resident in the NAU. The operation of the network and a justification for the approach are provided. This paper provides a perspective on local area network experimentation in 1979. A conclusion from that work was that standard protocols, such as TCP/IP, implemented on powerful microprocessors, should be used and not the flexible transport protocol described in the paper.

Robert Olsen, William Seifert, and Jonathan Taylor,
Interlan Inc., Westford, Mass.

Tutorial: RS-232-C data switching on local networks

Small, specialized controllers--known as terminal servers—establish virtual circuits to link devices to the likes of Ethernet.

During the last two years, vendors, engineers, and designers have used controllers to connect standalone minicomputers and microcomputers to local networks. As a result of their efforts, users are now witnessing the increasing availability of networking software that provides information exchange between compatible and, in some cases, incompatible computers. Computer-to-computer applications include interprocess communications, file transfer, remote file access, and electronic mail.

With recent advances in semiconductor and software technology, smaller, more specialized nodes can be economically connected to local networks, especially to Ethernet because of its potential as a standard. Nodes that offer a specific service to network users and applications are called "terminal servers."

A terminal server connects RS-232-C-compatible devices to a local network. Though it is called a terminal server, the unit is not limited to terminals. As depicted in Figure 1, a terminal server can also handle computer ports, modems, serial printers, microcomputers, and any other data processing device that is RS-232-C-compatible.

Using packet-switching technology, a terminal server provides a means by which users at a data processing installation can access computer and peripheral resources by virtual-circuit links. Virtual circuits appear as direct physical connections between devices. However, they are electronically created, maintained, and terminated by protocol procedures working within the terminal server. Compared to physical circuits, virtual circuits offer users the important advantages of being electronically switchable, enabling communications over extended geographic distances, and resolving communications incompatibilities between sender and receiver (see "Charting channel capacity"). Other benefits include:

- *Overcoming device incompatibilities:* RS-232-C devices with different data rates, frame format, flow-control mechanisms, connectors, and signal pin assignments can be readily interconnected. This means, for example, that a hard-copy terminal that operates at 1.2 kbit/s can be logically connected to a computer port set for 9.6-kbit/s operation. Once the terminal server has been configured to the operating characteristics of the directly attached device, it will resolve device incompatibilities in a manner that is completely transparent to either device.
- *Multiplexed device communications over extended geographic distances:* With an Ethernet terminal server, RS-232-C device communications is multiplexed onto a coaxial-cable transmission line. This permits a substantial reduction in the amount of RS-232-C twisted-pair point-to-point wiring that would otherwise be needed. Devices attached to the terminal server can communicate over distances up to 2,500 meters (1.5 miles) over a single Ethernet, a distance considerably further than that specified by EIA RS-232-C or RS-423. With the aid of a gateway server, geographically distant devices can be interconnected.
- *User commands for electronically connecting and disconnecting devices:* The speed and ease by which connections are made with a network terminal server lets RS-232-C devices become shared resources. A terminal user can, for example, issue a command to the terminal server to establish a connection to a computer port on the network. When the user is finished using the computer, the computer port then becomes available to other users on the network. This circuit-switching facility can yield a considerable cost saving by encouraging more productive use of existing computer ports, serial printers, modems, and terminals.

Reprinted with permission from *Data Communications*, September 1983, pages 231-238.

1. Possibilities. *The name "terminal server" is somewhat of a misnomer. The device also supports microcomputers, printers, and modems, permitting access via RS-232-C ports. It uses packet switching and permits users to access computer and peripheral resources through virtual circuits, which appear as direct physical connections.*

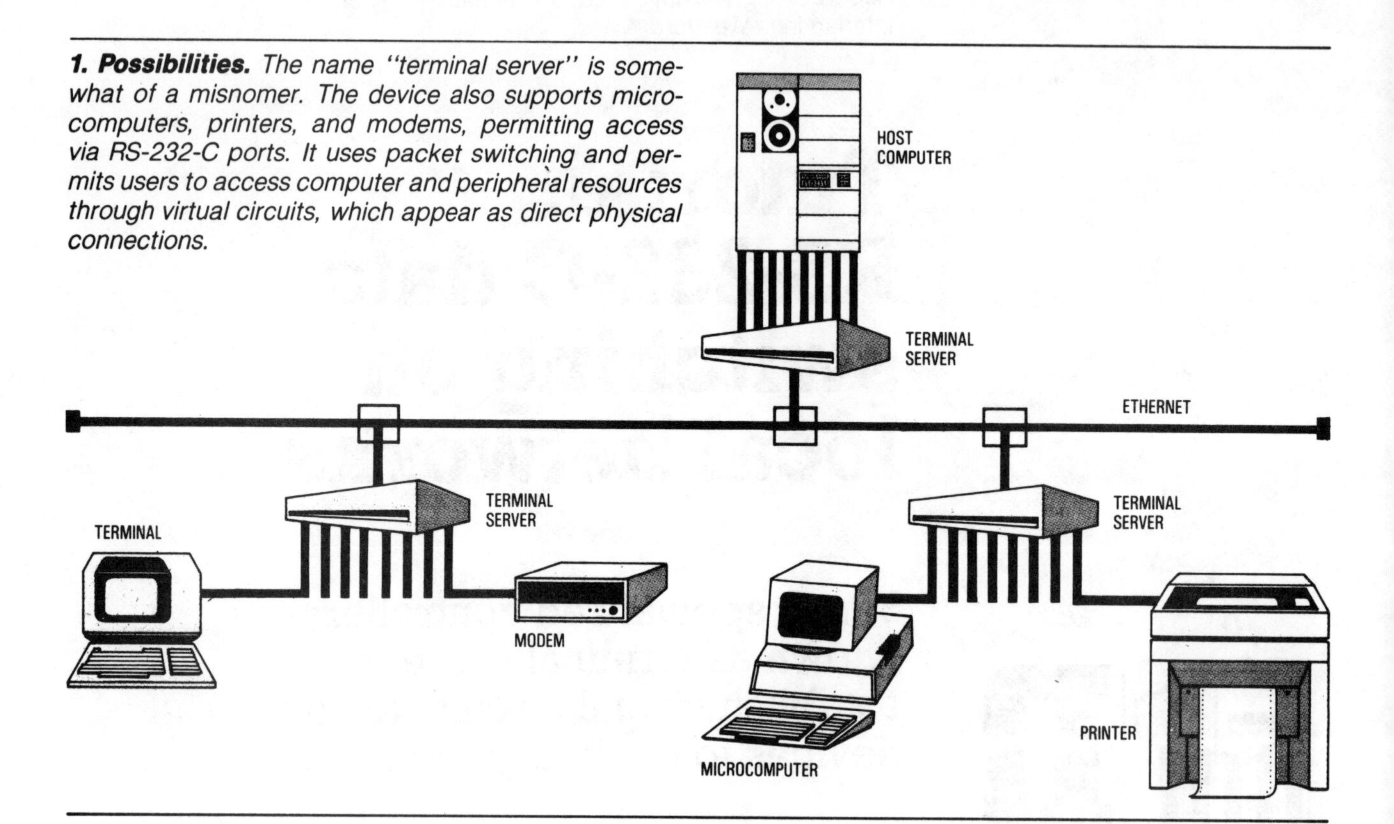

Applications

A network terminal server can solve many of the data communications problems found within a typical data processing installation. Widely used applications of a terminal server are:

■ *Port Switching*—For data processing installations with terminal users requiring access to multiple host computers, a terminal server provides switched virtual-circuit connections. The user issues a "call" command and references the target host by a symbolic name, say, "VAX750." Although access security is generally provided in most computer operating systems, a terminal server provides a password security mechanism to protect against unauthorized user connections to devices on the network that do not contain such security provisions.

■ *Port contention*—For data processing installations that have more terminal users than host computer ports, a terminal server provides users with a way of contending for the limited processor resources. When a terminal user requests a connection to the host computer and its ports are busy, the terminal server will "rotor" to find an open port. If all ports are in use, the user may "camp on" the computer and wait for the first available port. As users log off the computer, ports are freed for use by other terminal users.

The terminal server can handle situations where the user logs off but forgets to disconnect from the host, where the user disconnects but forgets to log off the host, or where the user forgets to both log off and disconnect.

■ *Resource sharing*—For data processing installations where efficient use of expensive RS-232-C devices is desired, the terminal server eliminates the need for physically unplugging and plugging RS-232-C devices together and matching the communications attributes of each device. A terminal server provides user commands for electronically interconnecting devices.

■ *Microcomputer networking*—At many data processing installations, managers prefer that corporate databases be centrally located and controlled by a large host computer. For distributed microcomputing to be effective, users need to store and retrieve files at the host computer and to transfer files between microcomputers. The terminal server provides users with the universal connectivity they require: microcomputers to the host, microcomputer to microcomputer, and microcomputers to printers or other peripheral devices.

■ *Simplified RS-232-C wiring*—A terminal server can resolve RS-232-C wiring problems. Instead of running a large number of point-to-point wires between terminals and computer ports, an Ethernet terminal server multiplexes RS-232-C communications onto a high-bandwidth coaxial cable that can handle thousands of concurrent virtual circuits, and which can span thousands of feet as well.

How it works

A terminal server can contain, for example, four or eight RS-232-C ports. Up to four units (32 ports) might be connected together at their transceiver cable interface so that they share a common transceiver unit connection on Ethernet. This would simplify transceiver-cable wiring problems that occur at such network locations as computer rooms, where a large number of transceiver units are required, although each must be spaced no more than 2.5 meters apart to comply with Ethernet specifications.

To ensure integrity of network operation, a terminal server can place users into two classes; users and network managers. A network manager (a privileged user) may, from any location on the network, configure the operating characteristics of any individual terminal server port (by knowing the password previously assigned to that port), issue the "configure" command, and respond to a series of configuration prompts. Port attributes selected include data rate, frame format, use of modem control lines, use of flow control, device logical names, device operation, and device passwords. The "configure like" command eases the network manager's job of configuring a large number of similar devices attached to the network.

As part of the configuration process, the network manager must specify the connection requirements of the attached device. A terminal server can classify attached RS-232-C devices into one of four types: command device, target device, command/target device, and auto-call device. A command device can issue commands to the terminal server. Typical command devices would include terminals, microcomputers, and auto-answer modems. A target device serves as the target of a virtual-circuit connection request. Typical target devices are host computer ports, auto-dial modems, and serial printers. A command/target device issues terminal server commands and also is the target of an incoming virtual-circuit connection request. This type of operation is suited for such devices as computer ports, auto-dial/auto-answer modems, and statistical multiplexers. An auto-call device requests, at initialization time, a permanent virtual-circuit connection to a prespecified target device.

A switched virtual-circuit connection is established by a user issuing the "call" command and referencing the target port either by its physical address or by one of it logical names. The terminal server uses Ethernet's broadcast delivery technique to provide an entirely decentralized port name/location service. When a user wants a connection to his VAX-11/750, he simply issues the command "call VAX750." The terminal server then broadcasts onto the Ethernet a packet with a "where's VAX750?" message, which is received by all other terminal servers on the network.

Terminal servers with ports having that name respond with their network address information. When multiple ports on the network share a common logical name, the server searches for the first free port in that logical name group. By distributing this name service, the server does not depend on the existence and proper operation of any master station or service.

Once a connection has been established, the terminal server ensures delivery of a byte stream between sending and receiving devices. Communications services provided by the terminal server include:

- *Flow control performed on the incoming byte stream:* This is an essential function in a virtual circuit connection. A device operating at 9.6 kbit/s must be able to respond to the terminal server's flow control for it to successfully communicate with lower-speed devices.
- *Byte stream assembled into packets for transmission:* A 20-millisecond packet-assembly timer assembles bytes into a packet. For the interactive terminal user, typically one byte (or character) is transmitted in a packet. However, for a 9.6-kbit/s block-mode output from a computer, about 20 characters will be assembled into an Ethernet packet.
- *Reliable packet transmission:* To deliver packets reliably, a set of protocols such as the Xerox Network Systems Internet Transport Protocols is used. These transmission protocols allow the terminal server to sequence packet transmissions, check for transmission errors, detect missing packets, identify duplicate packets, and institute any recovery procedures required. In addition, the protocols invoke packet flow control between network stations, as well as providing complete support for internetwork communications.
- *Received packets disassembled into an outgoing*

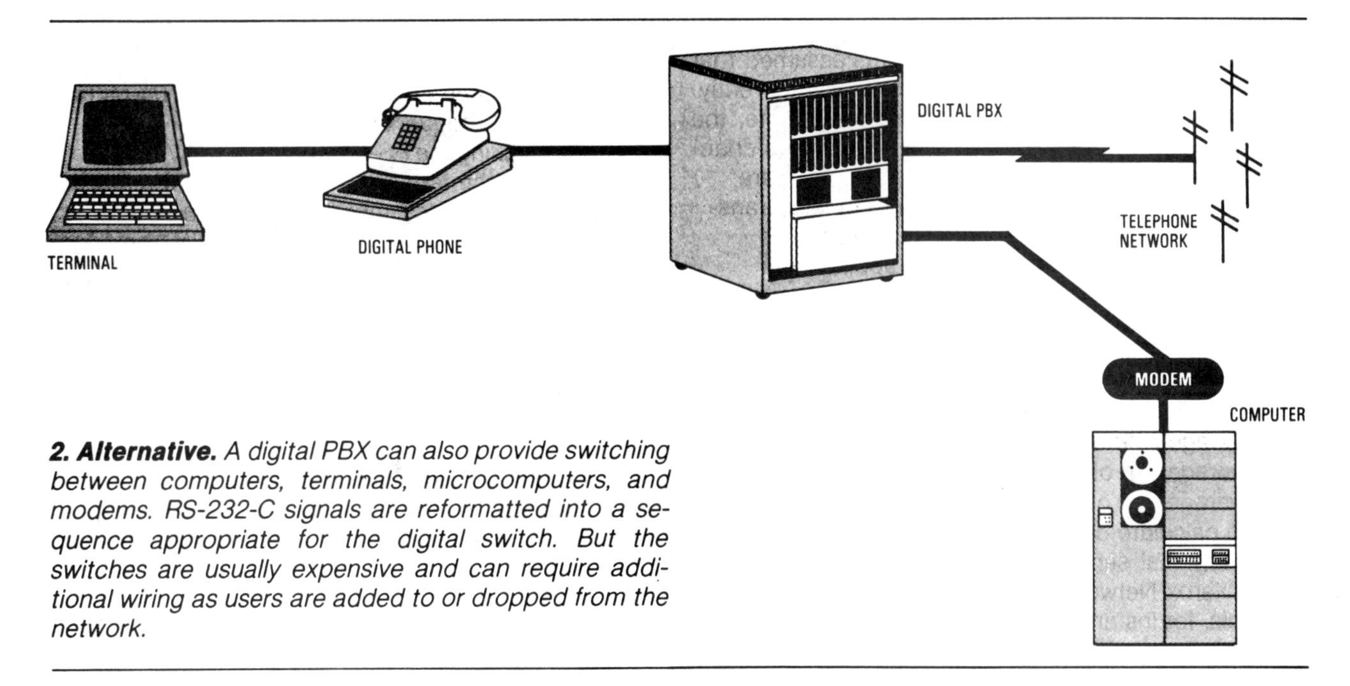

2. Alternative. *A digital PBX can also provide switching between computers, terminals, microcomputers, and modems. RS-232-C signals are reformatted into a sequence appropriate for the digital switch. But the switches are usually expensive and can require additional wiring as users are added to or dropped from the network.*

Charting channel capacity

A terminal server may use Ethernet as the transmission channel for connecting RS-232-C devices by virtual circuits. Although this approach to data switching is becoming increasingly popular, it is still a relatively new concept to most users, and many wonder how many RS-232-C devices Ethernet can support. This number is impossible to calculate because even if all network traffic statistics were known (and remained stationary), today's quantitative analysis tools are not sophisticated enough to handle the complexity of most problems users face. Because of this, analysts often resort to simulation techniques to get the answers they are looking for.

Users without enough programming resources or time to perform a network simulation can use the following technique for determining the number of virtual circuits that can share the channel capacity of the Ethernet (the terminal server used here is the Interlan NTS10). This technique is applied to four timesharing applications in which it is assumed that all the users run the same application concurrently. While the likelihood of this occurring is remote, the analysis provides useful insight into Ethernet's channel capacity. The four applications examined are:

- Half-duplex block-mode device-to-device transfers at 9.6 kbit/s and a 100 percent duty cycle
- Inquiry/update terminal-to-host applications
- Interactive terminal-to-host applications
- Data-entry terminal-to-host applications

Each analysis makes a different assumption about four RS-232-C device transmission statistics:

- Average *size* of an input character stream (A to B)
- Average *rate* of an input character stream (A to B)
- Average *size* of an output character stream (B to A)
- Average *rate* of an output character stream (B to A)

To calculate channel loading, an understanding of the terminal server transmission protocol is useful. The Xerox Network Systems Internet Transport Protocols, for instance, which provide end-to-end delivery of packets between terminal servers, include:

- RIP—routing information protocol for internetwork routing of packets
- SPP—sequenced packet protocol for end-to-end delivery of packets
- PEP—packet exchange protocol for transmission of short message and responses
- ECHO—protocol for verifying the existence and proper operation of terminal server nodes on the network
- ERROR—protocol for delivering transmission error messages

The byte stream from an RS-232-C device is transmitted over the network using SPP. This protocol carries with it 12 bytes of sequencing information (for flow control and reliability checking) preceded by 30 bytes of addressing information by the network-level datagram protocol; the SPP is then encapsulated into an Ethernet frame with 4 bytes of trailer (32-bit cyclic redundancy check). As the frame goes onto the wire, a 9.6-microsecond minimum interframe spacing is required (12 bytes), along with a 64-bit (8-byte) preamble sequence.

For assembling the RS-232-C device's byte stream into packets, the terminal server uses a 20-millisecond (ms) packet assembly timer. When a byte is transmitted to the server from a device, it is held for 20 ms so that additional bytes can be assembled into a single packet for transmission onto Ethernet. After the 20-ms time period expires, a packet containing at least one byte of user information is transmitted. For interactive terminals attached to the server, each packet transmitted onto the network will generally contain only one byte of keyboard data. For sustained transmissions, such as output from a computer port, the number of bytes (or ASCII characters) assembled into a packet is a function of the device's data rate. If that rate is 9.6 kbit/s, a character will be received every 1.04 ms by the terminal server port, and an average of 19.2 bytes of user data will be sent in each packet.

byte stream: The outgoing bytes must be transmitted at the appropriate data rate for the attached device.

- *Device flow control recognized on the outgoing byte stream:* This prevents the attached device from being overrun by the transmitted byte stream.

Alternatives

A terminal server installation is in many respects an application of distributed RS-232-C data switching. Three alternative approaches to data switching are port selectors, PBXs, and host-to-host networks with remote terminal access (for a comparison, see table).

Port selectors have been in use for more than a decade. Terminal lines and computer ports are wired to the central location, where the port selector resides. Circuit switching is performed by time-division multiplexing of the input RS-232-C signals from all active lines and ports. The input digital signals are successively sampled, transmitted over an internal bus, and received at the appropriate output port, where they are reproduced exactly, sample by sample.

Compared with a terminal server's distributed switching approach, the port selector has two major drawbacks:

- The port selector's star topology mandates the use of more linear feet of wiring than is required by an equivalent installation based on distributed terminal servers. This means that wiring an installation is costly, including adding and relocating operators and equipment.
- The port selector contains no intelligence for doing speed, frame-format, and flow-control conversions. This means that a calling terminal must be properly preconfigured with the communications requirements of the computer port being called. For such equipment as interactive terminals and computer ports, this is

Scorecard for Ethernet virtual circuits

	BLOCK MODE, 9.6 KBIT/S, 100%	INQUIRY, UPDATE	INTERACTIVE	DATA ENTRY
AVERAGE SIZE OF INPUT CHARACTER STREAM	19.2 BYTES (19.2 BYTES PER PACKET)	10 BYTES (1 BYTE PER PACKET)	10 BYTES (1 BYTE PER PACKET)	5 BYTES (1 BYTE PER PACKET)
AVERAGE RATE OF INPUT CHARACTER STREAM	50 BYTES PER SECOND	2 BYTES PER MINUTE	5 BYTES PER MINUTE	1 BYTE PER SECOND
AVERAGE SIZE OF OUTPUT CHARACTER STREAM	0	1,920 BYTES (19.2 BYTES PER PACKET) PLUS ECHO OF INPUT	192 BYTES (19.2 BYTES PER PACKET) PLUS ECHO OF INPUT	ECHO OF INPUT
AVERAGE RATE OF OUTPUT CHARACTER STREAM	0	2 BYTES PER MINUTE	5 BYTES PER MINUTE	0
TOTAL CHANNEL BANDWIDTH CONSUMED PER VIRTUAL CIRCUIT	50.880 KBIT/S	3.531 KBIT/S	1.856 KBIT/S	1.344 KBIT/S
NUMBER OF VIRTUAL CIRCUITS PER ETHERNET	138	1,982	3,771	5,208

For the analysis, an assumption is made that is generally accepted in the Ethernet technical community: that Ethernet can be loaded to about 70 percent channel capacity before the channel access time (carrier deference, collision resolution) introduces packet transmission delays that become perceptible to an interactive terminal.

In the use of this 30 percent channel derating factor, the other four Internet Transport Protocols are absorbed, as they tend to be infrequently used in comparison with SPP.

Within SPP, system packets are transmitted whenever flow control and acknowledgment information cannot be piggybacked within traffic going in the opposite direction on the virtual circuit. Operational experience with the terminal server shows that about 25 percent of the packets transmitted are system packets. One is sent as an acknowledgment for every three RS-232-C data packets received.

Results of the analysis are shown in the table. The block-mode application is a sustained 9.6 kbit/s device-to-device half-duplex transfer at 100 percent duty cycle (no flow control). It is important to note that for such an application, greater channel-access delay can be tolerated.

The inquiry/update application assumes infrequent user keyboard transmissions that occur in full-duplex and that also result in a full CRT screen update (1,920 characters) from a host computer that outputs at 9.6 kbit/s.

The interactive application assumes an environment in which a user is editing a file.

The data-entry application assumes an environment consisting of keyboarders working at 50 words per minute.

Each analysis assumes that no other activity is occurring on the network. If such activity is present, then additional channel derating is required.

generally not an insurmountable problem, as the terminal user can experimentally change his data rate to match that of the computer. But for equipment (and users) that are less readily adaptable, severe connection problems will arise. For example, how does the off-site terminal user dialing in via an auto-answer 1.2-kbit/s modem use the port selector to access the same computer resources as his on-site counterparts have use of? Clearly he cannot, unless all on-site resources are also configured to operate at only 1.2 kbit/s.

Retrofitting

PBXs have historically been oriented toward the switching of analog voice circuits by using a time-division multiplexing technique called pulse amplitude modulation. More recent PBX offerings have an all-digital internal design (Fig. 2). Incoming analog voice signals are digitized by a codec chip located inside either the switch or the handset. The codec samples the voice signal at 8 kHz into 8-bit values that are then transmitted onto an internal bus and received at an output voice circuit. For the PBX to be capable of performing RS-232-C data switching, the digital PBX must be retrofitted:

- A box is required at each user device. This box reformats the RS-232-C data into a digital format appropriate for the switch and also functions as a short-haul modem to the switch.
- A line card must be installed at the switch for handling incoming data streams from a number (generally 16) of the remote boxes.
- New software must be loaded into the PBX. At the present time, PBX data switching costs range from $750 to $1,200 per line.

Compared to the terminal server, the digital PBX has

Charting the alternatives

CRITERIA	PORT SELECTOR	DIGITAL PBX	HOST TO HOST REMOTE TERMINAL ACCESS	NETWORK TERMINAL SERVER
SWITCHING LOCATION	CENTRALIZED	CENTRALIZED	DISTRIBUTED	DISTRIBUTED
EASE OF WIRING DEVICES TO SWITCHING EQUIPMENT	DIFFICULT FOR DISPERSED TERMINALS AND HOSTS	EASY FOR TERMINALS LOCATED NEAR TELEPHONE WIRES; DIFFICULT FOR HOST	EASY; CONNECT TERMINALS TO LOCAL HOST AND ATTACH HOST TO NETWORK	EASY; ATTACH SERVER UNIT ON NETWORK AND CONNECT LOCAL RS-232-C DEVICES TO SERVER
CONNECTIVITY OF SWITCHING EQUIPMENT	GENERALLY FULL CONNECTIVITY, THOUGH SOME EQUIPMENT DOES NOT PROVIDE TERMINAL-TO-TERMINAL AND HOST-TO-HOST CONNECTIONS	FULL CONNECTIVITY	TERMINAL ACCESS LIMITED TO DEVICES SUPPORTED BY THE NETWORK SOFTWARE PACKAGE. NO DEVICE-TO-DEVICE COMMUNICATIONS	FULL CONNECTIVITY
SWITCHING TECHNIQUE	GENERALLY TDM CIRCUIT SWITCHING. DEVICE PARAMETERS MUST BE IDENTICAL ON EACH END OF THE CIRCUIT CONNECTION	TDM CIRCUIT SWITCHING. DEVICE PARAMETERS MUST BE IDENTICAL ON EACH END OF THE CIRCUIT CONNECTION	PACKET SWITCHING	PACKET SWITCHING
SWITCH PERFORMANCE	NO DELAY. USE OF HIGH DATA RATES CAN ADVERSELY AFFECT SWITCHING CAPACITY	NO DELAY. USE OF HIGH DATA RATES CAN ADVERSELY AFFECT SWITCH CAPACITY	GENERALLY, THE DELAY IS IMPERCEPTIBLE UNLESS EITHER HOST BECOMES HEAVILY LOADED. FLOW CONTROL IS PERFORMED FOR ATTACHED DEVICES MAKING BLOCK-MODE TRANSFERS	END-TO-END DELAY IS IMPERCEPTIBLE TO THE INTERACTIVE TERMINAL USER. FLOW CONTROL IS PERFORMED FOR A HIGH-SPEED DEVICE COMMUNICATING WITH A LOWER-SPEED DEVICE
USER MAINTAINABILITY	YES, WITH TRAINING. RANGES FROM DIAGNOSTICS TO BOARD-LEVEL REPLACEMENT. A SET OF SPARE BOARDS IS REQUIRED	NO. MAINTAINED ONLY BY VENDOR	YES, WITH TRAINING. RANGES FROM DIAGNOSTICS TO BOARD-LEVEL REPLACEMENT. A SET OF SPARE BOARDS IS REQUIRED	YES, SOME TRAINING IS REQUIRED. RANGES FROM DIAGNOSTICS TO LOW-COST UNIT REPLACEMENT. ONE SPARE UNIT IS REQUIRED
COST PER CONNECTION	$200 to $300 PER LINE ON EQUIPMENT WITH RELIABILITY OPTIONS AND OPERATION TO 9.6 KBIT/S	$750 to $1,000 PER LINE	$2,000 to $5,000 PER HOST	$300 TO $400 PER LINE

three major disadvantages:

- Digital PBXs are not as economical for data switching. If users already have an adequate PBX telephone service, purchasing a digital PBX for the additional task of data switching is difficult to justify financially. Even if a new voice PBX installation is in order, the data options of the voice/data digital PBX currently cost two to three times that of a terminal server installation.
- Like the port selector, few digital PBXs contain (at this time) any intelligence for handling incompatibilities between sending and receiving data devices. The digital PBX simply performs a circuit-switching function and leaves device compatibility concerns to the user.
- Contrary to popular belief, digital PBXs do not necessarily eliminate local network wiring problems just because the phone lines are already in place. In many instances, an additional wire pair is needed to implement the digital PBX. Although some wiring can be eliminated by handling voice and data simultaneously, considerable obstacles remain to connecting data-only devices in a distributed network architecture. As people and equipment are added to or moved around in an organization, the cost of rewiring the PBX must be considered.

Host-to-host

There is considerable activity underway in the area of networking standalone host computers. In addition to remote-file-access and electonic-mail software packages, host-to-host remote terminal access (RTA) capabilities are now becoming available. RTA provides the terminal user with the ability to interact with any computer on the network that runs the same network software package. Because RTA is usually a component of a more complete networking software package that also has host-to-host file transfer and electronic mail, it can be an economical way to obtain distributed RS-232-C terminal-to-host data switching.

Nevertheless, compared with the terminal server, RTA has considerable limitations:

- RTA is generally restricted to local-terminal-to-remote-application connectivity. No device-to-device connection is supported. More important, RTA only works between computers running the same network software package, often written for one specific computer. Support for other hosts and terminals is generally not possible.
- RTA, like the terminal server, uses packet switching to establish virtual-circuit connections. Because RTA is generally implemented on a multitasking, multiuser host, periods of heavy loading can introduce annoying delays in the reception of character echoes from the remote application. For the same reason, block-mode transmissions from an attached intelligent device, such as a microcomputer, may be heavily flow-controlled by the local and remote hosts, resulting in substantial loss in device-to-remote-application communications bandwidth. ■

PROTOCOLS FOR LOCAL AREA NETWORKS

Thomas R. Stack and Kathleen A. Dillencourt

Network Analysis Corporation
Vienna, Virginia 22180

ABSTRACT

Protocol issues in three areas should be considered by application subsystem developers when formalizing requirements and evaluating local area network (LAN) proposals. The first issue area concerns the functional capabilities of elementary protocols provided for local area network application developers. Typically, LAN application subsystems would make use of several of these elementary protocols to accomplish their intended functions. The second issue area concerns the logical separation of control and data transfer functions provided to cooperating application processes through layered protocol interfaces. An implementation interpretation of the ISO reference model of Open System Interconnection for vertically layered protocols is discussed. Protocol software residency is the third issue area addressed. Potential residencies for each protocol software layer are discussed for several network node architectures. An example of protocol layer residency allocation for an architecture consisting of a host processor and a network adapter is presented in greater detail, and its interlayer performance characteristics are discussed.

1. INTRODUCTION

The development of local area networks (LAN) rests on the assumption that applications can be distributed among multiple processors with effective interprocessor communications. Currently, the development of LAN applications in a heterogeneous environment is inhibited by the lack of a good set of commonly available protocols facilitating interprocess communications. This paper discusses protocol issues in three areas which application subsystem developers should consider when formalizing requirements and evaluating LAN proposals.

2. BACKGROUND

A set of protocols specifies how nodes can communicate over networks. Protocols are the procedures and conventions used to regiment the event progression required for orderly, mutually understood interaction between processes. Protocols are developed to satisfy qualitative and quantitative requirements for process interconnection. A primary qualitative requirement is the "useful" work (i.e., functionality) to be provided by the protocol. Some desirable functions are discussed in the next section. Other qualitative requirements include:

- flexibility (to accommodate new uses and features)
- completeness (to properly respond to all relevant network conditions)
- deadlock avoidance/backout mechanisms
- synchronization mechanisms (for interprocess control)
- error detection and recovery
- buffer overflow avoidance
- message sequencing assurance
- duplicate message detection and recovery
- permeance (to implement the protocol uniformly throughout the LAN)
- priority mechanisms
- accounting mechanisms
- security mechanisms
- message delivery guarantees
- data code/format transformations
- computer equipment feature compatibility
- operating system feature compatibility
- communications network feature compatibility

Not all of these requirements are of equal importance for each protocol implementation. For example, a protocol might inhabit a LAN node environment configured into any of the following topologies or hybrids of these topologies:

- star topology - a centralized topology in which lines converge to a central point or points (see Figure 2-1); this topology is also called hierarchical or tree.
- mesh topology - nodes are connected in an arbitrary pattern; each node can have multiple paths to other nodes.
- ring topology - the communications path is a loop with each node connected to exactly two other nodes in a given loop.
- bus topology - the nodes are connected along line segments; this topology is commonly found in LAN's with a shared transmission channel such as a cable-bus.

Typically, routing protocols for mesh topologies are much more complex than routing protocols for the other topologies. Broadcast protocols are relatively simple in most bus and ring topologies. Thus, other protocol requirements, such as message delivery guarantees and message sequencing assurance, may be influenced by the topology chosen.

Reprinted from *Proceedings of the Trends and Applications Conference*, May 1980, pages 83-93.

Quantitative requirements for protocols include:

- throughput - the volume of information that must be transferred during the peak period. This volume is usually characterized by mean message length in octets, the distribution of message lengths, and by the arrival rate of messages.

- delay - the mean and maximum delay that the protocol will add to process responsiveness during the peak period.

- cost - maximum acceptable recurring and non-recurring costs associated with the installation of a protocol in a LAN network.

Quantitative requirements for software reliability and availability are unfortunately not yet generally accepted by vendors.

A protocol may perform functions at the communication link level (such as an HDLC protocol) or at application process level (such as a virtual terminal protocol). Of primary concern to LAN application developers are the application level protocols. Some of the protocols which might be considered elementary to LAN developments are discussed below.

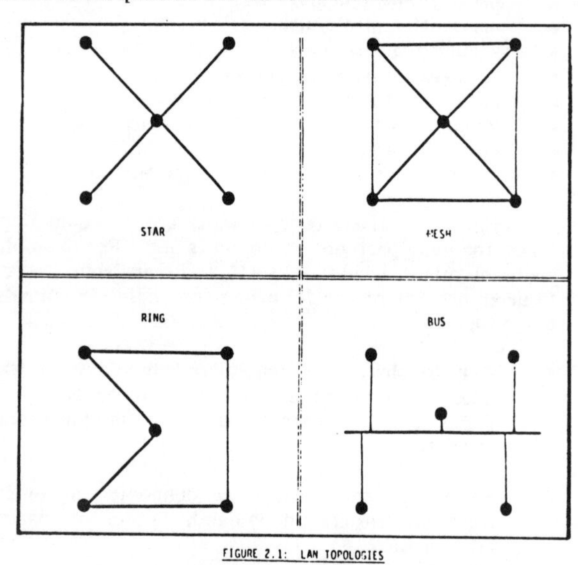

FIGURE 2.1: LAN TOPOLOGIES

3. APPLICATION SUBSYSTEM PERSPECTIVE OF ELEMENTARY PROTOCOLS

The need for a number of elementary high-level protocols providing various types of services is apparent. Three main groupings of such protocols may be defined: application-oriented, executive-oriented, and network-induced. The motivation for this classification is the perspective of distributed systems as extensions of the single-system environment. The goal of elementary protocols is to extend the array of system utilities, programs and operating system services that are available on a single system to the total LAN. Hence, development of elementary LAN protocols is a basic step in evolving high-level operating systems for LANs.

Application-Oriented Protocols

Application-oriented protocols are defined to be interprocess communication rules and data formats which extend the commonly used system programs (languages, editors, library, etc.) of one node to an application process in another node. Such protocols may include:

- File Transfer - allowing a process in one node to access files on another node as though the process were executing in that node. Similar to general system utilities that support media conversion with and without blocking changes, format changes, naming changes, etcetera.

- Editor - allowing a process in one node to store, modify and retrieve text information in a file at another node. Preferably implemented to a specification consistently applied at each node on the network.

- Compile - allowing a process in one node to produce executable programs at another node. Implements a network wide source and object code library and linkage editor.

- Execute - allowing a process in one node to invoke a program at another node by module name, to supply parameters to the program and to receive program output and system notice messages at the sending LAN node process.

- Debug - allowing a process in one node to dynamically debug a program at another node. Preferably allows an application process distributed among two or more LAN nodes to be debugged interactively.

Executive-Oriented Protocols

Executive level protocols are defined to be interprocess communication rules and data formats which extend the operating system services (resource allocation, device or program service, monitor services, etc.) of one node to an application process in another node.

- Command Protocol - allowing commonly used operating system services (ASSIGN, PRINT, TIME, STATUS, etc.) in each node of a network to be invoked uniformly by a process in another node.

- Virtual Scrolling Terminal Protocol - allowing a process in one node to communicate with a process in another node as though the receiving process were a scrolling output device such as a printer or teletype.

- Virtual Screen Terminal Protocol - allowing a process in one node to communicate with a process in another node where the receiving process operates on a randomly addressable collection of two dimensional pages of text using predefined functions and transmitted variables.

- Virtual Graphics Terminal Protocol - allowing a process in one node to communicate with a process in another node where the receiving process operates on a randomly addressable collection of two or three dimensional figures and two dimensional text using predefined functions and transmitted variables.

In this paper, virtual terminals are conceived as being supported by two elementary protocols: a virtual terminal display data transformation protocol and a control protocol. The data transformation protocol maps display commands from the sending process into the prescribed input data formats for the receiver process. The control protocol exchanges non-display information for coordinating the interactions between the sending and receiving processes. The non-display information can include specification of state change or state status request, specification of conditions or events that a process will acknowledge and react to if triggered by the other process(es), and specifications of related information accompanying the control commands to further specify the interaction.

One process might be a real terminal handler process, A, in an intelligent terminal. A process B, in another LAN node associated with A, interacts with A to perform application functions beyond the capabilities of A. B would specify the control conditions and messages that A must send to B whenever it requires B to cooperate in the performance of a task. When A wants to get help from B, it encodes its request into a condition/event code and message format supported by the control protocol.

Both the display data transformation and the control protocols might be designed to support the multiple "models" of virtual terminal discussed above.

Network-Induced Protocols

Network induced protocols are defined to be interprocess communication rules and data formats which facilitate the operation of executive level and application level protocols in a local area network.

- Network Endpoint Declaration Protocol - provides the mechanism for a LAN node to establish or disestablish addressable network ports in a directory thereby allowing qualified processes in other nodes to become associated with processes assigned to this port. The protocol might serve normal and privileged processes in the application space as well as network control functions within the operating system. This protocol provides a mechanism to identify "well known" processes in a network directory.

- Network Access Authorization Protocol - allowing a process to gain access to another process in the network. Includes log-on/log-off support to end users as well as general process interconnection authorization. Interfaced with network security and privacy management information systems.

- Network Directory Service Protocol - allowing a process to request information about a node, another process or an end user. May also support custom menu services for each network user to promote the impression of a single integrated system.

- Transport Control Protocol - allowing a process in one node to establish an association with a process in another node and to exchange messages in a virtual circuit or datagram mode. Usually implemented as an augmentation to the operating system of a network node.

- Interprocess Synchronization - providing a mechanism for two or more processes in two or more nodes to coordinate asynchronously executing functions. This protocol could underlie the virtual terminal control protocol.

- Network System Control Protocol - providing the mechanism for establishing "built-in" maintenance and security subsystems in a LAN environment. It is envisioned that performance, maintenance and security checks should permeate the LAN software as well as hardware subsystem. This protocol facilitates unified specification of performance, maintenance and security related functions.

Summary

The collection of elementary protocols can be combined to deliver an application service. For example, to provide an RJE service, one could employ the execute and file transfer protocols. The execute protocol could implement the control structure for the RJE function including the job control language to initiate execution and the normal or abort message upon termination. The file transfer protocol would ensure that the input and output data files are staged and exchanged efficiently. Other examples could be described to support electronic mail, user menus of authorized processes and other office automation services.

4. RELATIONSHIP TO THE ISO OPEN SYSTEM INTERCONNECTION MODEL

The application perspective of elementary protocols is viewed as a way to present a useful set of tools to realize the development of distributed applications. In this section we relate these protocols to the International Organization for Standardization reference model of Open System Interconnection which we refer to as the OSI model for brevity.

Background

According to the August 1979 documentation release on the OSI model, "Reference Model of Open Systems Interconnection" (ISO/TC97/SC16 N227), the purpose of the model is to provide a basis for coordinating and describing existing and developing standards for system interconnection. The concept of an Open Systen Interconnection refers to "standardized procedures for the exchange of information among terminal devices, computers, people, networks, processes, etc., that are 'open' to one another" by virtue of their mutual use of the procedure described in the reference model. No particular system implementation, technology or interconnection mechanisms are presupposed. In short, the OSI model is concerned with the capability of systems to interconnect and to perform distributed tasks. To promote interconnection standards progress, the OSI model provides an architecture for discussing the layering of protocol dialogue exchanged between interconnected systems.

The basic architecture defines seven layers of protocol in each system to be interconnected to one or more other systems. The seven layers are represented "for convenience" in a vertical sequence. More than one protocol may be defined at a given layer. Protocols interface directly with protocols in adjacent layers and, through lower level protocols, interface indirectly with peer protocols (protocols operating on the same layer). The seven layers and their basic interrelationships are illustrated in Figure 4-1. The seven layers, from the highest layer to the lowest layer, are:

7. Application Layer - This is the highest layer in the reference model of open systems interconnection architecture. Protocols of this layer directly serve the end user by providing the distributed information service appropriate to an application, to its management and to system management. Management of open systems interconnection comprises those functions required to initiate, maintain, terminate and record data concerning the establishment of connections for data transfer among application processes. The other layers exist only to support this layer. Some of the application process is implemented through the use of the application layer protocol. The rest of the application process is user dependent and outside the scope of the OSI model. Three categories of application layer protocols are defined:

   - System Management Protocols - responsible for controlling and supervising open systems (e.g. initiating dialog).
   - Application Management Protocols - responsible for controlling and supervising application processes (e.g. access control).
   - System Protocols - responsible for executing information processing functions on behalf of an application process or user (e.g. RJE, electronic mail).

6. Presentation Layer - The purpose of the presentation layer is to provide the set of services which may be selected by the application layer to enable it to interpret the meaning of the data exchanged. These services are for the management of the entry, exchange, display and control of structured data. The presentation-service is location independent and is considered to be on top of the session layer which provides the service of linking a pair of presentation-entities. It is through the use of services provided by the presentation layer that applications in an open systems interconnection environment can communicate without unacceptable costs in interface variability, transformations or application modification. There are four phases of presentation layer protocol operation:

   - Session establishment phase in which connection is set up
   - Presentation image control phase in which presentation options can be selected by value, by name, by prior agreement or by negotiation
   - Data transfer phase which controls data structure accesses and perhaps executes special purpose transformations such as voice compression or data encryption
   - Termination phase

5. Session Layer - The purpose of the session layer is to assist in the support of the interactions between cooperating presentation-entities. To do this the session layer provides services which are classified into the following two categories:

   - Session Administration Services - binding two presentation-entities into a relationship and unbinding them.
   - Session Dialogue Service - Control of data exchange, delimiting and synchronizing data operations between two presentation-entities. Three types of dialogue are supported:

     - two way simultaneous interaction (full duplex)
     - two way alternate interaction (half duplex)
     - one way interaction (simplex)

To implement the transfer of data between presentation-entities, the session layer may employ the services provided by the transport layer.

4. Transport Layer - The transport layer exists to provide a universal transport service in association with the underlying services provided by lower layers. The transport-service provides transparent transfer of data between session-entities. The transport-service relieves these session-entities from any concern with the detailed way in which reliable and cost-effective transfer of data is achieved. Three types of transport services are identified:

   - A connection-oriented service
   - A transaction-oriented service
   - A broadcast-oriented service

   The transport service is required to optimize the use of the available communications services to provide the performance required for each connection between session-entities at a minimum cost. To achieve optimization, the global demands of all concurrent transport users and the transport layer resource limitations are considered. Multiplexed information streams from lower layer traffic is one of the options available.

3. Network Layer - The network layer provides functional and procedural means to exchange network-service-data-units between two transport-entities over a network-connection. It provides transport-entities with independence from routing and switching considerations, including the case where a tandem subnetwork-connection is used. (Note that CCITT recommendation X.25 defines only a network/user interface at this layer.) The network layer protocol uses underlying data link connections to make network connections invisible to the transport layer protocol.

2. Data Link Layer - The purpose of the data link layer is to provide the functional and procedural means to establish, maintain, and release one or more data links among network-entities. This layer masks the characteristics of the physical layer (such as switched, multipoint, broadcast, polling, contention, etc.) from the network layer.

1. Physical Layer - The physical layer provides mechanical, electrical, functional and procedural characteristics to establish, maintain, and release physical connections (e.g., data-circuits) between link-entities. The physical layer provides for the transmission of transparent bit streams between data link layer protocols across physical connections which are permanently or dynamically established.

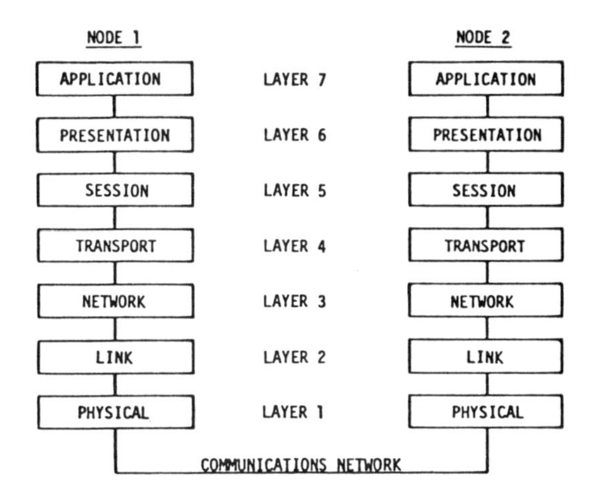

FIGURE 4.1: ISO OPEN SYSTEM ARCHITECTURE

Each of the elementary protocols is classified as a High Level Protocol (HLP), but not every HLP is an elementary protocol. Loosely translated, this means that each elementary protocol maps to one or more of the following ISO OSI model protocol layers: transport, session, presentation or application. One would like to map each elementary protocol onto a single layer of the OSI architecture to promote building block appeal. With some liberal interpretations of the session and presentation layer responsibilities, it can be done.

Fundamental to every protocol is the notion of separation of control and data information. Presentation layer protocols are primarily data handling services for application processes while session layer protocols are primarily control handling services for application processes. If these layers are implemented as, say, subroutine utilities in the application space, then application processes could use the services of each directly whenever required and the session layer could be used to gate data through the presentation layer with simple proven software constructs such as shared variables. An implication of this concept is the modification of the ISO vertical structure illustrated in Figure 4-2. The notions of peer to peer protocol are retained, but the "convenience" of the vertical structure is perturbed. The complexity of the session and the presentation layers is reduced with this change in architecture because the presentation layer is not burdened with control information irrelevant to presentation transformations and the session layer need not concern itself with managing large data transfer "bucket brigades." For example, management of two of the presentation phases, session establishment and session termination can be off-loaded to the session layer.

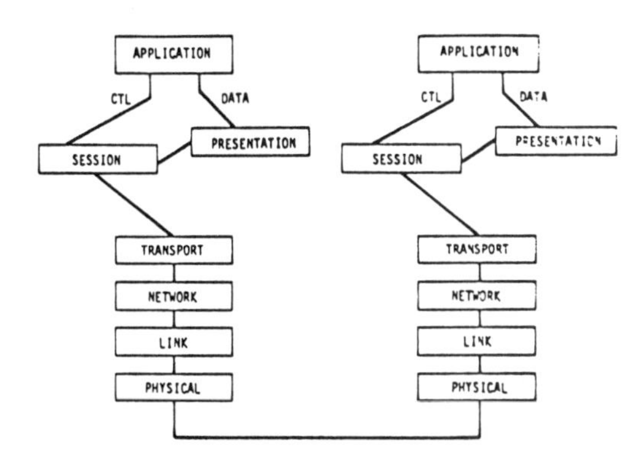

FIGURE 4-2: MODIFIED STRUCTURE ISO OSI MODEL

Note that the control functions performed in the session layer are associated with a single application process. By tightly coupling the session layer to the application layer, we make it possible to implement more simple, application centralized, constructs for reliable, end-process-to-end-process communications. Constructs which perform buffering, duplicate detection, error control, sequence control, flow control and, most importantly, whole process synchronization for distributed applications can be localized at the session layer. That is, a standard session control layer protocol could perform the role of a microcosm operating system for each specific application process in a distributed processing subsystem. With the presentation layer in between, application control would be decentralized between the presentation layer and the session layer complicating development and maintenance. Also, software reliability should improve with this interpretation of the OSI architecture because it should be less complex to implement than the pass through vertical structure implies.

The transport layer would continue to exchange interface control information with the session level, but the presentation layer would share the message pool controlled by the session layer. Thus, the presentation layer would not directly interface with the transport layer.

With this modification to the OSI model, we can map each elementary protocol onto one OSI layer as illustrated in Figure 4-3. Note that the elementary protocols at the application layer have been mapped into system management, application management and system protocol classes defined by the ISO. Also, sublayer protocols for both the session layer and the presentation layer are identified.

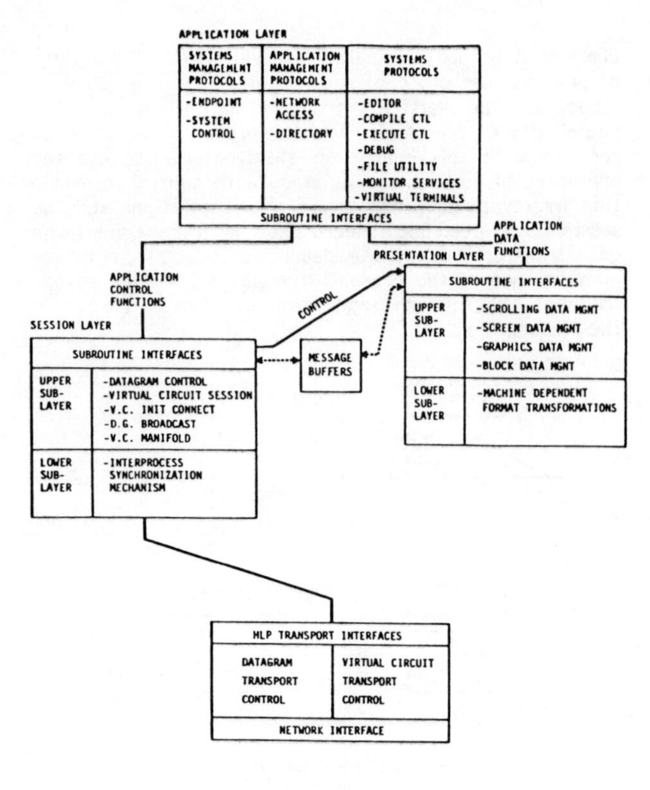

FIGURE 4-3: RELATIONSHIP BETWEEN ELEMENTARY PROTOCOLS AND ISO OSI MODEL HLP LAYERS

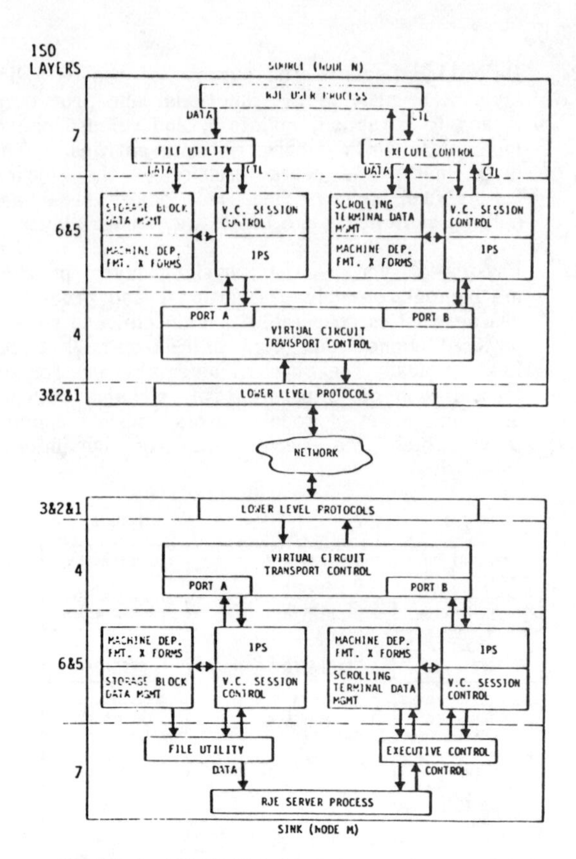

FIGURE 4-4: RJE PROTOCOL BUILT FROM ELEMENTARY PROTOCOLS

An illustration of a conceptual RJE protocol built using some of the elementary protocols is provided in Figure 4-4.

5. PROTOCOL SOFTWARE RESIDENCY

In this section we consider alternative LAN node and protocol software residency architectures. A number of allocations of the ISO protocol layers to typical LAN node configurations are briefly discussed. One allocation where layers one to three reside in a network adapter and where layers four to seven reside in the host is examined in more detail. The adjacent interfaces in this example are discussed in terms of their impact on delay and reliability performance. Where adjacent protocol layers cross hardware interfaces, the types of overhead introduced are discussed.

Potential Protocol Residencies

Four LAN node configurations that can support the seven layers defined in the ISO Open System Interconnection architecture model are illustrated in Figure 5-1. In configuration "A," the host processor supports the network interface, all protocol layers and all protocol using processes. This configuration is the archetype of the late 1960 server nodes like the ubiquitous Tenex host on the ARPANET and of today's small server host. To interface a type "A" configuration to a network is a relatively complex undertaking requiring moderate to severe operating system surgery depending upon the functional and performance requirements of the network interface and/or options chosen. Typically, the host vendor does not offer the interface and in-house or third party software engineers must be retained to develop and maintain the custom software.

A node configuration consisting of a host and a front-end processor is illustrated as "B" in Figure 5-1. This configuration is the archetype of 1970 large scale server hosts. The type "B" configuration retains the vendor's host operating system, but requires modification of the front end software to support the network interface. Also, the front end may be modified to execute one or more protocol layers.

Configuration "C" is externally similar to configuration "B," but represents a significant philosophical difference. Whereas the front-end processor looks unchanged to the host interface hardware and software in configuration "B," the network adapter interface in configuration "C" implies some change in host operating system code to support the hardware interface and software architecture introduced in the adapter. The adapter in configuration "C" is essentially a network standard front-end which accommodates heterogeneity in the hosts it supports whereas the front-end in configuration "B" is an extension of the host which is modified to accommodate the network.

Configuration "D" represents the composite case where the host and its front-end may be integrated as provided by the vendor, and the network adapter is used to accommodate the heterogeneity introduced by the host/front-end configuration. The protocols residing in the front-end for configurations of type "D" are most likely those provided by the vendor although that need not be the case. If the vendor supplied front-end software was not changed, then multiple network

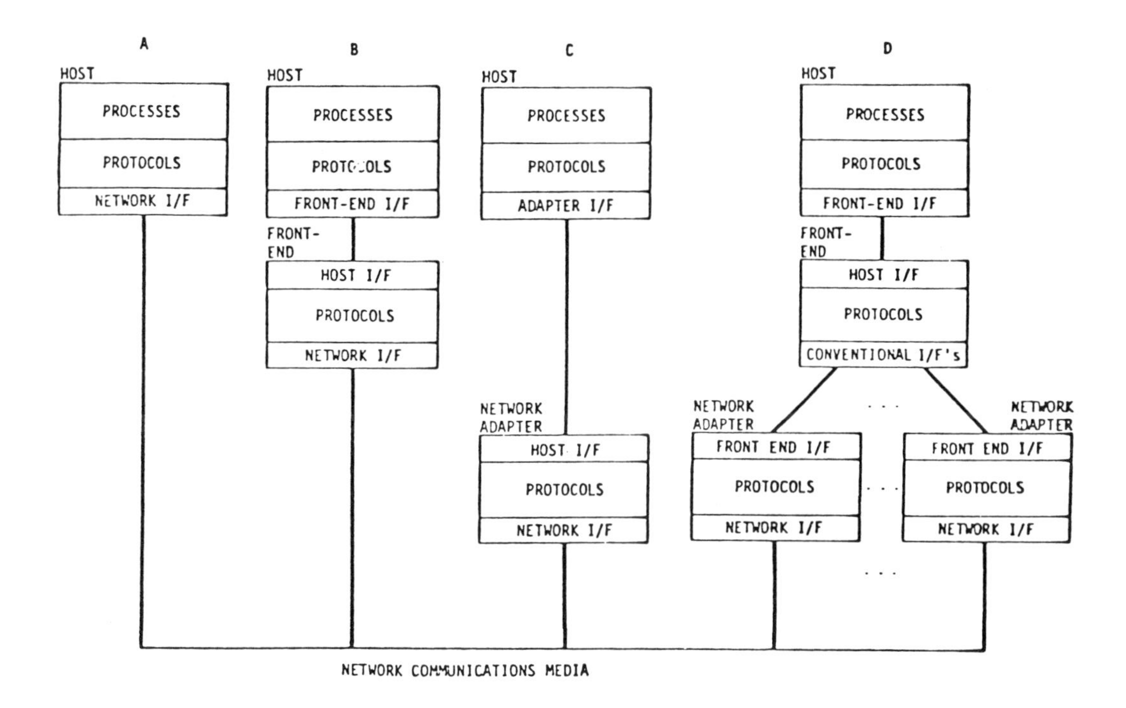

FIGURE 5-1: PHYSICAL RESIDENCY ALTERNATIVES FOR ISO PROTOCOL LAYERS

adapters might be needed to implement multiple logical network connections used by a collection of DDP application processes in the host. If the front-end software was modified, then a single network adapter might satisfy the LAN requirements.

Note that with configurations of type "B," "C," or "D" adjacent protocols may cross a hardware interface. Whenever this occurs, additional software as well as hardware complexity is introduced into the system. This complexity may negatively affect reliability and responsiveness.

A typical host/network-adapter interface is illustrated in Figure 5-2. From a LAN system perspective, the purpose of this interface is to effect information transfer between the highest level protocol operating in the network adapter and the lowest level protocol operating in the host. Each side of the interface introduces four discernable tiers of logic between the two otherwise adjacent protocol layers: two hardware logic tiers and two software logic tiers. The first tier (H1 or A1) consists of the media control and data transfer logic for the interface. For example, if an asynchronous host/network adapter interface were provided, it might be required to conform to RS449, RS442 and X20BIS standards. Tier 2 (H2 or A2) for this same interface would be manufacturer dependent octet I/O transfer logic in either DMA or programmed I/O mode depending upon interface availability and upon cost/performance tradeoffs. Tier 3 (H3 or A3) represents basic driver software logic for the interface including control message exchange, data block send/receive, status checking, interrupt processing and output/input data buffer management. This driver software might be very simple or very complex depending upon functional and performance requirements. Fast interleaved block exchanges across a single hardware interface require complex logic—mostly for the exception handling code needed. Tier 4 (H4 or A4) is an interface handler which interfaces the adjacent protocol software with the basic interface driver. The interface handler conforms to operating system interface conventions and ensures the integrity of protocol control and data information passed between the host and the network-adapter.

Systems that support multiple logical information streams can impose substantial thread management loads upon the interface handlers (or the protocol layer interfacing software). In short, the introduction of a hardware interface between two protocol layers adds additional protocol layers to manage the interface. The complexity and delay attributable to these additional layers depend upon the functional and performance requirements of the divided protocol layers and upon the intensity of the multileaving imposed by the processes operating in the host.

Alternative Residency Allocations

Based upon the four configuration alternatives defined in Figure 5-1 and the seven ISO protocol layers, we can define a large number of alternative protocol residency allocations. However, the number of candidates can be reduced considerably by two reasonable assumptions. First, application layer protocols reside in the host. Second, the physical and link layers always co-reside in the LAN node equipment adjacent to the communications network equipment. Thus, we identify the candidates for protocol residency identified in Figure 5-3.

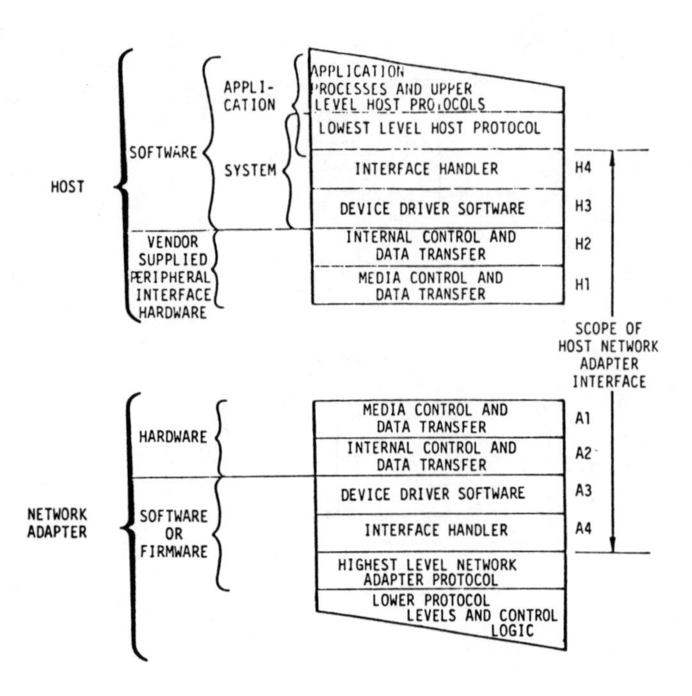

FIGURE 5.2: PHYSICAL SEPARATION OF PROTOCOL LAYERS

There is only one architectural alternative for configuration "A." For some LAN requirements this architecture and allocation is perfectly acceptable. The only remaining issue is which layers reside in the operating system space and which layers reside in the application space. Clearly, the physical and link layers belong in the operating system. Whether the network layer or the network and transport layers belong in the operating system is an interesting research issue not well documented in the literature. The session and presentation layers seem to be natural LAN utilities, probably reentrant utilities, which should reside in the application space with the application layer protocols.

For configuration "B," several alternative architectures are possible. Four architectures are especially intriguing, namely:

B1 : layers 1-2 in FE and layers 3-7 in host
B2 : layers 1-3 in FE and layers 4-7 in host
B3 : layers 1-4 in FE and layers 5-7 in host
B4 : layers 1-6 in FE and layer 7 in host

However, if the motivation for accommodating the network interface function within the existing vendor-supplied host-front end configuration is to maintain maximum vendor support, one might choose option B1 or B2. Then, presumably layers 3 and 4 could reside in the host's application space and interface with the front-end if suitable access methods were offered by the vendor.

The architectural alternatives for configuration "C" are similar to those for configuration "B" except that there are three interesting alternatives, namely:

PROTOCOL LAYER	'A'	'B'	'C'	'D'
1. PHYSICAL	NODE	FRONT END	ADAPTER	ADAPTER
2. LINK	NODE	FRONT END	ADAPTER	ADAPTER
3. NETWORK	NODE	FRONT END OR NODE	ADAPTER OR NODE	ADAPTER, FRONT END OR NODE
4. TRANSPORT	NODE	FRONT END OR NODE	ADAPTER OR NODE	ADAPTER, FRONT END OR NODE
5. SESSION	NODE	FRONT END OR NODE	ADAPTER OR NODE	ADAPTER, FRONT END OR NODE
6. PRESENTATION	NODE	FRONT END OR NODE	ADAPTER OR NODE	ADAPTER, FRONT END OR NODE
7. APPLICATION	NODE	NODE	NODE	NODE

FIGURE 5.3: ALTERNATIVE PROTOCOL RESIDENCY ALLOCATIONS

C1 : layers 1-3 in Network Adapter; 4-7 in host
C2 : layers 1-4 in Network Adapter; 5-7 in host
C3 : layers 1-6 in Network Adapter; 7 in host

Placing just layers 1 and 2 in a special purpose network adapter directly connected to the host does not significantly off-load the host, and while this approach can be taken, the payoff does not seem commensurate with the effort.

The architectural alternatives for configuration "D" would appear to be a combination of those available for configurations "B" and "C." However, it is unlikely that a user would choose configuration "D" only to modify the front-end software to support one or more of the protocol layers. Rather, configuration "D" reduces to a distribution of the protocol layers between the host and the network adapter where the network adapter must be a low cost device - e.g. a microprocessor. Also, each network adapter probably maps to a single logical port for easy interface to the vendor supplied communication access method. For configuration "D," layers 1 and 2 or layers 1, 2 and 3 would seem appropriate for the network adapter. Further work is needed to determine which allocation alternatives are most appropriate for a given LAN node configuration.

Residency Performance Issues

In this section performance issues associated with a particular protocol residency allocation alternative are discussed. The architecture chosen is based upon a configuration of type "C" — a host and a network adapter. To complete the conceptual architecture, layers 1 to 3 are assigned to the network adapter and layer 4 to 7 to the host as shown in Figure 5-4. The transport layer, layer 4, is defined to reside in the operating system space while the session, presentation and application layers, layers 5 to 7, are defined to reside in the application space.

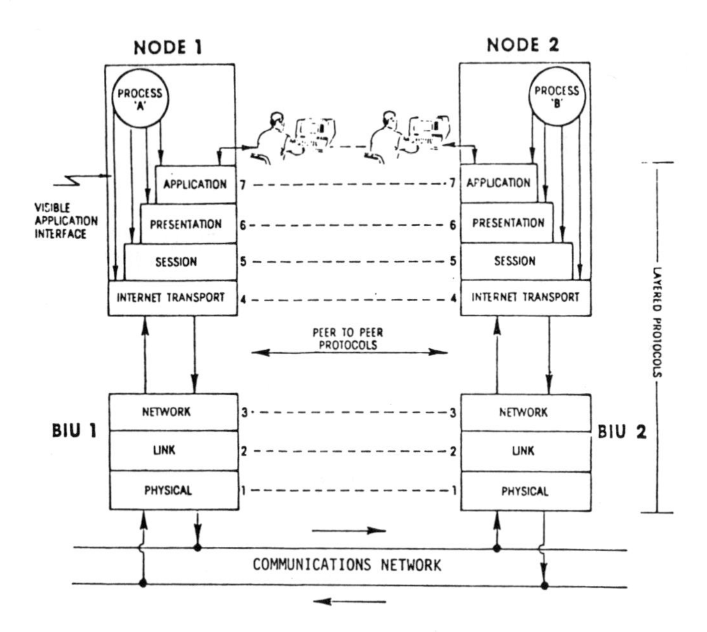

FIGURE 5.4: PHYSICAL SEPARATION BETWEEN LAYERS 3 AND 4

Consider two aspects of performance: response time and reliability. The delays and reliability associated with protocol layers implemented in different architectures are traceable to the functions performed within each layer and across interfaces between adjacent layers. A detailed analysis of the delay and reliability characteristics of a given implementation of an architecture depends upon workload, capacity and complexity issues beyond the scope of this paper. However, it is interesting to consider contributors to delay and reliability at the interfaces between adjacent protocol layers within the context of a single interprocess communication thread.

Consider the contributors to delay for the sample architecture described above as shown in the single thread in Figure 5.5.

When application X has a message for application Y, it queues its data to the presentation layer protocol. If this message is one of many in a dialog with application Y, it may be that all application buffers are full and delays will be incurred either waiting for a buffer to be freed or waiting while the dynamic memory allocation service of the operating system assigns additional buffer space for application X. If this message is the first message of a session between applications X and Y, then delays will be incurred while an association is initiated. Similarly, if application Y or the path(s) to application Y are broken (e.g. software crash along path), then additional delays will be introduced.

While passing control and data between the application space and the operating system space, requests for operating system attention from multiple application processes and system devices can impose contention delays.

Assembly of packets for the outgoing messages might be performed using a buffer pool dedicated to traffic unique to this application's session or using a buffer pool shared by all traffic passing through the host or both. Delays due to buffer unavailability are possible. Note that buffer overflow can be controlled by well chosen flow control procedures throughout the network, but delays due to buffer unavailability may be a direct consequence of flow starts and stops.

Transfer of packets across the transport/network protocol layers in the example can introduce three contributors to delay: buffer unavailability for the device handler/driver in either the host or the network adapter or delays in moving data reliably across the hardware/software interface. The transport protocol layer is expected to reliably deliver information from the higher level protocols used by application X to application Y. Thus, in addition to delays inherent in the host/network-adapter control and data exchange, delays may be introduced due to retransmissions across the interface.

Within the adapter, delays due to internal bus contention may be experienced if peak traffic estimates are exceeded. The consequences could be underrun or overrun errors on block transfers. Recovery from these may require the network to request retransmission of a packet(s) from the host. Processor contention from higher priority traffic activity can result in delays at the network and link protocol layers. Internal network-adapter buffer unavailability delays are also possible.

Delays due to transmission, communications processing and buffer unavailability within the network are extensively discussed in the literature for various architectures.

Delays within the receiving network-adapter are traceable to conditions similar to those discussed above. For example, buffer overruns from the network are possible if peak traffic estimates for the network-adapters are lower than those realized in operation. Delays for retransmission recovery will vary with the communications network design. In some cases, an eventual negative acknowledge will result in a retransmission of the packet whereas in other designs a timeout at the sending device will result in a retransmission.

The type of delays experienced by the receiving host are similar to those discussed for the sending host. However, the delays due to interprocess synchronization at the receiving process, application Y, are particularly interesting. It may very well be the case that minimal delays are experienced along the single thread described from application X to application Y and that the message has been reliably received at application Y's host. However, because application Y is not operating in a state which will input and process the message immediately, the incoming message from application X may remain on a queue for a considerable period of time. Thus, the operation of a distributed application subsystem can be subjected to substantial delays due to application design as well as to computer and communication operating system design.

The reliability contributors for this single thread are also illustrated in Figure 5-5. We note that a subroutine interface is indicated between the application layer and the adjoining presentation (and session) layers. It is interesting to note that generally the integrity of subroutine interfaces across modules in the application space is not questioned. This ubiquitous mechanism lulls us into a false sense of security. Certainly, the operating system questions analogous information transfers with an application across the so-called monitor service

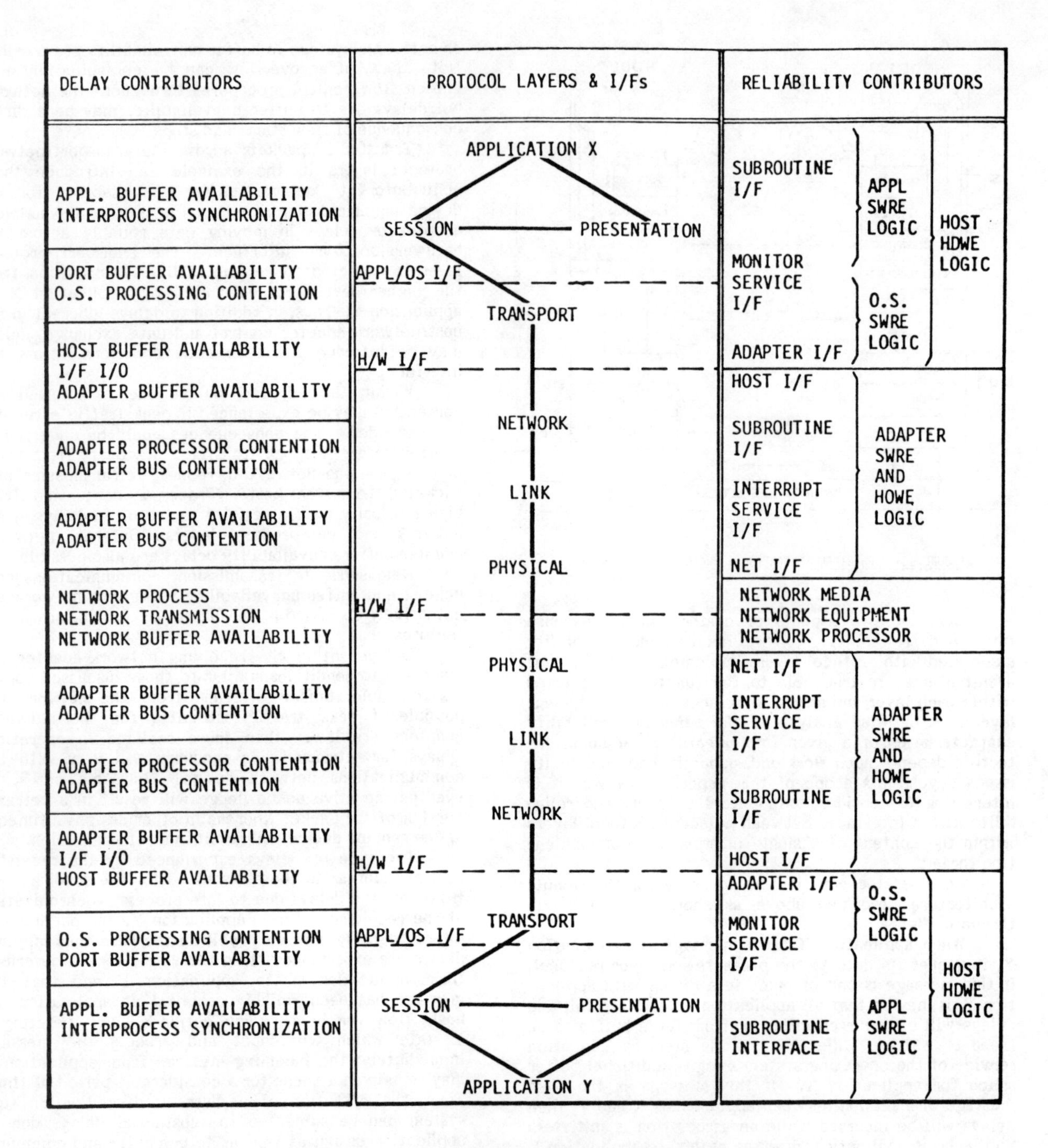

FIGURE 5-5: PERFORMANCE IMPACT AREAS FOR SAMPLE PROTOCOL RESIDENCE ALLOCATION

interface. Computer vendors have long recognized the need for hardware as well as software checks across the operating system space/application system space interface. The need for such checks across the subroutine interface between the application layer and adjoining protocol layers is apparent. At the very least, there should be stringent checking of parameters passed across the interface; the presentation and session layer code might also be implemented as shareable code in write-protected memory.

The interface between the host and network-adapter and between the network-adapter and the network should be instrumented at the hardware and software tiers to facilitate fault detection and isolation. Good engineering practice suggests that software instrumentation should extend throughout the protocol layers.

Further research into modeling protocol residency performance in specific computer communication architectures for given protocol layer specifications would seem to be warranted.

6. SUMMARY

An application subsystem perspective of elementary (building block) protocols was presented. These protocols were divided into three categories: application oriented, executive oriented and network induced. The protocols in the first two categories represent extensions of familiar system functions from the traditional data processing systems environment to the distributed data processing systems environment. Additional system functions to aid application subsystem developers in a LAN environment were introduced in the network induced protocol category. An example of how an application subsystem could employ several of these elementary protocols was presented.

Standards work is progressing on several of these protocols. Few vendors provide any of the protocols discussed and none of the vendors provide all of them as a supported product offering. Several systems engineering houses have staff qualified to provide a customized set of these protocols for a given LAN environment.

The need for control and data transfer function visibility at the application process level was discussed. With a layered protocol architecture, the interfaces between adjacent protocols must be designed to pass selected control as well as data information in either direction. The session and presentation layers of the ISO Open System Interconnection architecture appear to provide an attractive separation of control and data paths between the application layer and its port into the transport layer. This view results in a modification to the vertically structured representation of the ISO protocol layers. The impact of this modified view of the ISO model is largely unexplored.

Protocol software residency decisions can result in a LAN that is functionally sufficient but performance deficient in satisfying requirements. Little progress has been made in quantitatively modeling the residency tradeoff issues for a given LAN node architecture. Some of the possible residency allocations for the ISO protocol layers were illustrated. An allocation in which the three lower layers of ISO protocols reside in a network adapter outside the host processor of the LAN node and the upper four layers reside in the host processor was discussed in some detail. The interfaces between adjacent protocol layers of this architecture were examined and characterized in terms of their contributions to delay or unreliability experienced by an application subsystem. Further work is necessary to define and evaluate the workload performed at each ISO layer to accurately assess the delay and reliability performance characteristics for various protocol residency allocation alternatives.

Practical LAN technology is still primitive in comparison to conceptual goals. Technological developments of a limited nature are steadily progressing, however, and several organizations are planning and acquiring a local area network as their backbone communications plant for integrated office automation services.

REFERENCES

Clark, D., K. Pogran and D. Reed, "An Introduction to Local Area Networks," Proceedings of the IEEE, Vol. 66, No. 11, November 1978, pp. 1497-1517.

Crocker, S. D., J. Heafner, R. Metcalfe, J. Postel, "Function-Oriented Protocols for the ARPA Computer Network," AFIPS Conference, 1972 Spring Joint Computer Conference, Vol. 40, AFIPS Press, Montvale, New Jersey, 1972, pp. 271-279.

Day, J., "Resource Sharing Protocols," Computer, Vol. 12, No. 9, September 1979, pp. 47-56.

Folts, H. C., "Status Report on New Standards for DTE/DCE Interface Protocols," Computer, Vol. 12, No. 9, September 1979, pp. 12-19.

Green, P. E., "An Introduction to Network Architecture and Principles," IBM System Journal, Vol. 18, No. 2, 1979.

ISO/TC97/SC16, Reference Model of Open Systems Interconnection (Version 4), N227, June 1979.

Pouzin, L. and H. Zimmerman, "A Tutorial on Protocols," Proceedings of the IEEE, Vol. 66, No. 11, November 1978, pp. 1346-1370.

Sproull, R. F. and D. Cohen, "High-Level Protocols," Proceedings of the IEEE, Vol. 66, No. 11, November 1978, pp. 1371-1386.

Sunshine, C., "Formal Techniques for Protocol Specification and Verification," Computer, Vol. 12, No. 9, September 1979, pp. 20-27.

Wecker, S., "Computer Network Architectures," Computer, Vol. 12, No. 9, September 1979, pp. 58-72.

A CABLE-BUS PROTOCOL ARCHITECTURE

David C. Wood   Steven F. Holmgren   Anita P. Skelton

The MITRE Corporation, McLean, VA 22102

The benefits of general-purpose local networks are discussed and the requirements that such networks need to satisfy are defined. A generic network architectural model is described and the major design parameters identified. The role of the local network is to provide network transparency for a multiplicity of computer devices. How well this role is performed is a function of the protocol design and implementation.

MITRE's Cablenet is one of several experimental cable-bus networks employing coaxial cable as a shared wideband transmission medium, and using microprocessor based interface units. This paper presents a protocol architecture design based on local network characteristics and the extensive computational capabilities expected from the next generation of microprocessors. We have designed a Flexible Transport Protocol which allows our cable-bus access node to assume a wide range of characteristics; these characteristics can be chosen judiciously to fulfil the needs of a wide spectrum of subscribers.

Introduction

In the early 1970s, packet switching dominated research in computer networks; in the late 1970s, local networks seem to be the focus of research activities. Packet switching networks such as ARPANET evolved from the need to provide nationwide access to large timesharing systems. Local area networks are evolving from a need to interconnect local mainframes, and a proliferation of minicomputers, microcomputers, terminals, and other peripheral devices.

The role of the local network is to provide a "friendly" interface to each of these devices so that they may be unified into a more useful set of tools without unduly affecting device performance. Existing experimental networks vary in tranmission media, and in mechanisms both for accessing the media, and for interconnecting user devices to the network. As the communications technology continues to evolve, new transmission media and transmission mechanisms will be utilized, but the functionality of the local network, will to a great extent be determined by the network interface design. The network interface protocol capabilities and the method of implementing those network interface protocols has a great impact on the 'nature' of the network — it affects ease of use, transition capability, vendor independence, cost, and flexibility of the network.

This paper provides a perspective on local area network experimentation in 1979. A conclusion from that work was that standard protocols, such as TCP/IP, implemented on powerful microprocessors, should be used and not the flexible transport protocol described in the paper.

The next generation of microprocessors appears to hold the key to the success of the local network. If the network interconnection mechanisms are isolated as much as possible from the user devices, and implemented in a distinct, powerful microprocessor-based interface unit, the network will have the required versatility and capability to ensure user transparency for a wide spectrum of user devices and applications.

The MITRE cable-bus local network architecture with its microprocessor-based interface presents an ideal environment for the development and testing of these concepts. The potential of this promising architecture cannot be realized without an appropriate set of communication protocols. A set of cable-bus protocols, with broad applicability to other local architectures, is being designed and implemented at MITRE's Cablenet testbed. This protocol architecture should provide the rich support needed to enable the interface unit to offload network specific protocol implementation. Ideally, this offloading should provide a simplified, and easily implemented, network interface, so that the resultant network interface unit is capable of being 'directed' by devices and processes with diverse requirements.

Reasons for Local Networks

What are the advantages of a planned local network over the unplanned growth of equipment in an ad hoc manner? The benefits are most obvious in a multiple computer environment. The same terminal can be used to access all the computers, instead of having two terminals, side by side, each hard-wired to a different computer, as is sometimes the case today. As well as economizing on terminals, the local network can simplify the user interface by providing a standard log on. The local network provides the same resource sharing potential as long-haul networks, such as transfer of files containing programs, data, etc. Word processing systems can also be connected, so that the same terminals used to access general purpose computers can also be used for document preparation.

Even when there is only a single computer to be connected initially, there are numerous less obvious reasons for planning a local network. An important motivation can be a transition strategy to a future system. Imagine a large computer system with many terminals used for numerous applications. The computer system is obsolete and the organization is faced with the ordeal of converting

Reprinted from *Proceedings of the Sixth Data Communications Symposium*, 1979, pages 137-146.

EHO234-5/85/0000/0268$01.00 © 1979 IEEE

operational applications to a replacement system. By installing a general-purpose local network with the old system, the new system can then be added to the same network. Terminals can access both systems during the transition period while applications are moved over.

Another reason for a local network is an expansion strategy: even though there is only one computer system now, there may be more in the future. A related reason is to provide vendor independence. Numerous computer vendor's have their own local network architectures, often under the guise of distributed processing systems; for example, DEC, Datapoint, Prime. Although these vendor unique systems offer convenient features and simplicity for the user, they also lock the user in to that vendor's equipment.

When a local network is designed for a building, cable or other transmission media will be laid systematically throughout the building. This provides flexibility for adding terminals or computers anywhere in the building, with data communications access being provided in a similar manner to electrical power and telephone outlets. Such a planned installation avoids running a cable through the building each time a new terminal is added; and eliminates the resulting 'spaghetti' near the computer.

The local network can also result in an increase in the number of terminals accessing a computer. Instead of hard wiring each terminal to an asynchronous multiplexer or similar terminal interface, the same number of ports can be shared on a contention basis by only the active terminals. More flexibility still can be obtained with a software demultiplexed packet-mode interface to the computer which avoids the rigid limitation of physical ports. A high-speed interface of this type can enable CRT terminals to be operated at higher speeds, such as 19.2 Kbps, than supported by the conventional terminal interface. Moreover, the character-at-a-time load on the computer caused by terminal handling can also be reduced.

Local Network Requirements

Having discussed the motivation for a local network, let us specify typical quantitative requirements. A local computer network should provide the following:

- interconnection between hundreds of terminals of various types and tens of computers ranging from microcomputers to large systems scattered throughout a building or a collection of buildings;
- the ability to support local terminal to host communications with terminals operating up to 19.2 bps, including terminal virtualization by mapping characteristics for various terminals and computers;
- the ability to interface terminals to the network inexpensively, e.g. not more than several hundred dollars per terminal;
- the ability to support local computer-to-computer communication with data rates of tens of thousands of bps;
- the ability to interface computers via high-speed multiplexed interfaces capable of supporting many virtual connections;
- the ability to offload network specific interface software from mainframe computers via such protocols as X.25 and HFP (Host-to-Frontend Protocol).
- access to remote resources via gateways to other networks.

Recently, a number of experimental networks have been built which address some of the above requirements. The report of the workshop on local area networking held at the National Bureau of Standards in August 1977 includes descriptions of about a dozen local network projects.[1] Further networks are reported in the proceedings of the Local Area Communications Networks Symposium held in May 1979,[2] and elsewhere.[3,4,5] Although many of these networks are designed to support hundreds of terminals, few operational examples of this magnitude exist. One such large installation is the Ethernet at Xerox Palo Alto Research Center.[5]

Virtualization of terminal characteristics involves the same principles which have been used successfully for start-stop terminals on long-haul networks, such as in the ARPANET Telnet[6] and in CCITT Recommendation X.3.[7] Since local networks usually operate at hundreds of kilobits per second, or higher, attaining high-speed computer-to-computer communication should be straightforward given appropriate higher level protocol implementations, but little experimental data has been reported.

The cost of interface devices for attaching terminals to experimental networks is typically $1000; this is high in comparison to current terminal prices. However, this cost is expected to drop to several hundred dollars per terminal when interfaces are commercially available, especially if several terminals are clustered to share an interface.

Computer interfaces tend to be ad hoc at present. Direct memory access (DMA) interfaces, although more sophisticated and tailored to the particular computer, have the advantage of high speed and minimal impact. The increased availability of software for standard network protocols such as X.25[8] and the Transmission Control Protocol (TCP)[9] will simplify host interfacing, although the overhead of such software is not well understood

Interconnection of local networks to long-haul packet networks is being addressed in a number of experiments involving ARPANET. They include Xerox's Ethernet,[10] the Laboratory for Computer

Science network at MIT,[11] and MITRE's Cablenet, described in this paper.

The Local Network Model

The Generic Architecture

A computer network is an interconnected set of independent computing elements. These computing elements interact with one another by exchanging 'bits' of information over a transmission medium. A local network environment generally encompasses a 'limited' area and has a relatively high data rate. With current technology, the distances between computing elements are on the order of several kilometers, and the transmission speeds are on the order of several megabits per second. The major design parameters are:

- o the selection of the physical transmission medium (twisted-wire pair, coaxial-cable, radio microwave, and, recently, fiber optics);
- o the method of accessing the transmission medium (selection, contention or reservation) and the method of controlling that access (centralized or decentralized);
- o the mode of transmission (digital or analog);
- o the juxtaposition of the various access points (nodes) and the degree of connectivity of these nodes (the network topology);
- o and, the method of interfacing the various user devices to the network.

The selection of these parameters will govern the character of the network.

Access and Control of Media. Various combinations of access mechanisms, transport media, and control have been implemented, and in general found to be functionally similar.[12] The access method and medium are obviously communications technology specfic, and this portion of the network, whether implemented in hardware or firmware, should be modular to allow for advancing technology. For a definitive summary of current channel access techniques see Tropper.[13]

Topology. In a long-haul network the computing elements are for the most part widely dispersed, and the fact that the transported information must traverse great distances (10s, 100s, or 1000s of miles) has an impact on the transmission costs, the integrity of the data transmitted, and the transmission delay. Some of the constraints that these considerations place on the network design are alleviated when data transmission distances are less than a few miles. For example, high bandwidth transmission is relatively inexpensive over short distances, therefore, a high degree of connectivity is not necessary to reduce communication costs. Consequently, the ensuing switching complexity that an intricate topology imposes can be eliminated.

Local networks are generally confined to the following topologies: star, ring or loop, and bus. The star has a central node and any number of appendages. One example of a star network would be a network front-end (NFE) interfacing one or more hosts and many terminals to a long-haul network. Failure of the NFE or the central node of a star network impacts on the entire network. The most obvious disadvantage of this configuration is the dependency on the central controlling node. In terms of reliability, i.e., decreased dependence on a single entity, the other architectures are more promising.

A ring or loop architecture is simply a set of computing elements arranged in a circle. The control can be centralized with the loop channel having a primary control node, or distributed, with all nodes having equal status. For a long time, the Distributed Computer System (DCS) at the University of California, Irvine was a unique example of a local ring network.[14] Other examples of a ring architecture are the LCS net at MIT[12] and the Cambridge Ring.[15] For a definitive account of various loop-type networks see Liu[16] and Tropper.[13]

A bus architecture is a set of computing elements arranged in a linear or dendritic (i.e., branched like a tree) configuration with a shared transmission channel; when the transmission medium is a cable (e.g., ribbon, coaxial, or optic fibers) this architecture is commonly called a cable-bus. The bus architecture appears to afford the same functionality as the loop, but the dendritic bus would seem to have an advantage over the loop in a very large building, for example, where, depending upon the geometry of the enclosure, a set of interconnected rings might be necessary.

Network Interface. Although the basic generic model (Figure 1) is always adhered to, the method of implementation, i.e., hardware/software/firmware, differs greatly from network to network. Xerox's Ethernet, for example, implements as much as possible in its Alto host minicomputer to keep hardware costs to a minimum. MIT, on the other hand, is working on a generic local network interface unit, which is microprocessor based, and which will function equally well in both ring and bus architectures with only slight control changes. The MIT model assumes a host specific part in their network interface unit, and network specific software in the host machine.

The method of implementation of the mechanisms which enable communication between devices and the network determines to a great extent the functionality of the network. If these mechanisms are isolated as much as possible from the host computer, or user device, and implemented in a distinct interface unit, one can optimize the functionality of the network.

The speed, capability, and reliability of a local network utilizing this type of hardware architecture is largely determined by the performance of these interface units. Most interface units are microprocessor based.[17,18] The next generation of microprocessors (e.g. Zilog Z8000,[19] Motorola MC68000,[20] and Intel 8086[21]) forecast an interface unit with processing ability comparable to medium sized mini-computers. It should be emphasized that a local network hardware architecture utilizing device independent, microprocessor-based interfaced units, must be paired with a layered set of communication protocols which is capable of supporting such an architecture.

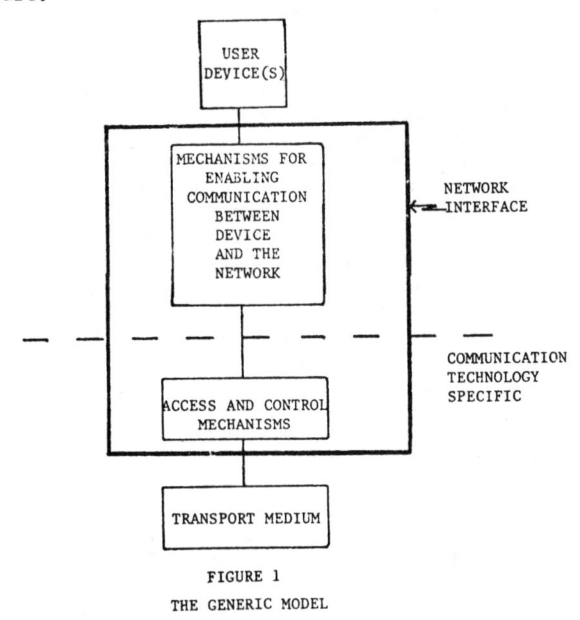

FIGURE 1

THE GENERIC MODEL

Cable-Bus Hardware Architecture

A bus architecture using coaxial-cable for the transmission medium is a popular local network pairing, as in Ethernet, where a single cable is used, and in the various MITRE cable-busses,[17,22,23,24,25] where an inbound cable and an outbound cable are connected at one end, the head-end, and electrically terminated at the distant extremities. The dual cable architecture allots transmitting and receiving to separate cables, the advantage being the doubling of the available channel bandwidth.

Coaxial cable as a transmission medium is very attractive for a number of reasons: it is relatively inexpensive, approximately $500/mile; it can support multimegabit transmissions; and, it is relatively immune to noise. It is well suited for the transmission of digital, as well as analog signals. With a digital baseband signaling transmission scheme, one simply transmits the signal as received without modification. Xerox's Ethernet uses this technique, thus eliminating the cost of modems; very high data rates (3 Mbps) are realized with simple and inexpensive transceivers. With analog transmission the signals are superimposed on a higher frequency waveform which "carries" them. The advantage of using an analog radio frequency transmission scheme is that many parallel channels can be carried on the same cable using various frequencies.

The access mechanisms used in the cable-bus environment have been variations of random-access broadcast schemes. The ALOHA System at the University of Hawaii was the first random-access broadcast network.[26] Using a strategy which has come to be known as "pure aloha", messages were transmitted as desired, and unacknowledged messages were retransmitted. In attempts to increase the bandwidth utilization, various refinements have been introduced, such as a "slotted aloha" scheme, where time slots are allocated to nodes, and a particular node only transmits during discrete dedicated time intervals.[27] While this method decreases the number of retransmissions, it has the disadvantage of 'tying-up' available bandwidth for nodes which may have nothing to transmit. Early implementations of MITRE's cable-bus network (MITRIX) utilized this type of time division multiple access (TDMA) scheme.[22]

A more efficient contention based scheme is employed by Xerox's Ethernet which involves detecting the presence of an unused channel before transmitting, and listening to one's own transmission to enable an early detection of a collision. Sensing the channel availability beforehand decreases the probability of having to retransmit due to collisions, and early collision detection allows one to abort a damaged transmission as soon as possible, thus freeing up the channel. Various schemes have been used to determine the best time for a node that has detected a collision to retransmit. These schemes have been analyzed in the literature and are summarized by Tropper.[13]

A dual-mode slotted digital bus has been designed and built by MITRE/Bedford, and is reported by Meisner.[28] Under this scheme low-duty cycle asynchronous (bursty) users share a common set of contention slots, while high-duty cycle and/or synchronous users are assigned dedicated slots.

The Cablenet Model

MITRE is experimenting with a cable-bus hardware architecture paired with microprocessor-based interface units in an attempt to design and implement a protocol architecture that takes advantage of the predicted microprocessor computational power, and provides the rich support needed to fulfil the local network requirements that were delineated above. Our cable-bus model consists of a set of intelligent hardware interfaces which use a contention-based scheme to aquire temporary ownership of a coaxial-cable in order to transmit messages to other interface units. Although our experience and development is limited to our cable-bus test-bed, it is our feeling that the protocol architecture described in this paper is equally applicable to the broad range of local network ring or bus architectures which align themselves with our local generic model.

It is of prime importance to point out that our cable-bus network is not operating in a vacuum. Our model of many widely dispersed sets of interconnected cable-busses capable of accessing hosts on any one of a set of concatenated local and long-haul networks, each with varying transmission media, characteristics, and capabilities is not unlike Cerf's Catenet.[29]

Cablenet

Cablenet at MITRE/Washington is the test bed for the implementation of these protocols. The network is based on technology developed at MITRE/Bedford.[17]

The system uses standard Community Antenna Television (CATV) coaxial cable and a MOS Technology 6502A microprocessor/LSI-11 pair as cable-bus interface devices. (We envision the next generation interface as being a single entity). The cable-bus uses the dual cable architecture described above, consisting of two parallel coaxial cables, one inbound cable and outbound cable connected at the headend. This architecture takes advantage of the well developed unidirectional CATV components. The topology is dendritic. The MITRE/Washington installation is shown in Figure 2. The interface unit is designed to transmit on the inbound cable and receive on the outbound cable. Certain interface units interface terminals directly to the cable-bus. Other interface units interface computers to the cable-bus.

The broadcast contention scheme, described in the previous section, is used on the cable, with all subscribers concurrently competing for the transmission media. The mechanism used by the interface unit to detect a busy cable is called Carrier Sense Multiple Access (CSMA). Due to signal propagation delay, it is possible for an interface unit to start transmitting without detecting the presence of an instantaneously concurrent transmission by another interface unit. The scheme used to detect simultaneous transmissions (collisions) is called Listen-While-Talk (LWT). To implement the LWT technique, each interface unit reads the initial portion of its own transmission (listens while talking) from the outbound channel, and compares it with the information sent on the inbound channel: if the comparison indicates that the transmission has not been interfered with, the interface unit assumes that the cable-bus has been acquired, disables its receivers, and continues transmission; if the comparison indicates that a collision has occurred, the interface unit backs off for a pseudo-random amount of time, and then attempts to retransmit.

Cable-bus access mechanisms can be finely-tuned to maximize throughput. The performance of various retransmission schemes have been found to be a function of the ratio of the propagation delay (the time that is takes to put the packet on the cable and take it off again) to the packet transmission time.[30] Throughput increases as this ratio decreases, and seems to approach theoretical limits for a packet size of about 1000 bits.[31] It is not clear how a much larger packet size would affect performance, although it is obvious that the packet length can increase with higher data rates. Currently out test bed packet size is 128 bytes; subsequent designs may remove this limitation.

The coaxial cable consists of a copper clad aluminum center conductor, polystyrene dialectric, and an aluminum sheath shield. It has a loss figure of 1.6db per one hundred feet. Analog signals can be effectively transmitted in a frequency range from 5MHZ to 300MHZ. The interface units contain Radio Frequency (RF) modems which modulate a carrier signal to transmit digital information using 1MHZ of the available bandwidth in the 24MHZ frequency range. The remainder of the 294MHZ bandwidth can be used to carry other information channels such as off-the-air TV, FM, closed circuit TV or a voice telephone system. The data rate of our test-bed system is 307.2 KBPS. One mega-bit systems are being made available commercially.

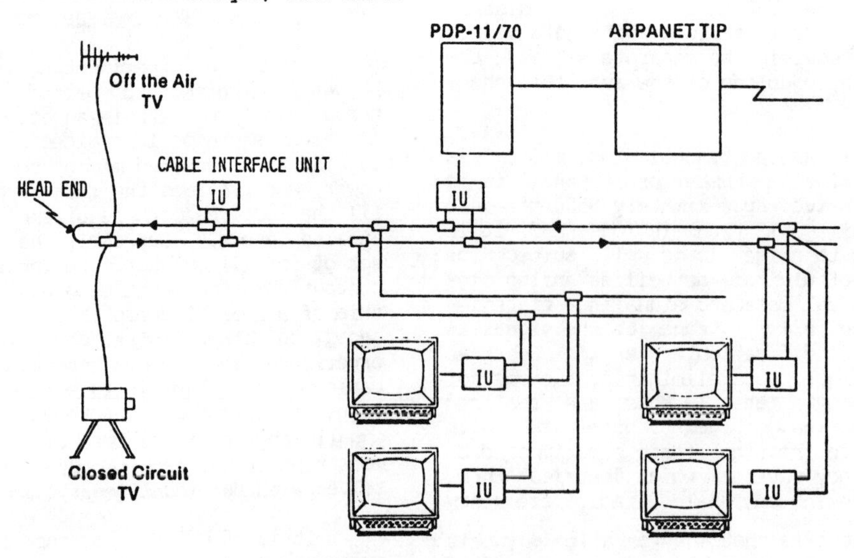

FIGURE 2. CABLENET TESTBED INSTALLATION

Protocol Background

Our local cable-bus protocol architecture relies heavily on protocol design principles which have emerged from the DARPA internet experiments,[29] but due to environmental constraints, such as packet length limitations, and other issues which will become clear in subsequent sections, our protocol architecture model diverges from the DARPA model.

The current thinking in the DARPA Internet community is to utilize an unreliable datagram as the internetwork transport mechanism. The datagram transport mechanism, the Internet Protocol, (IP)[32] is designed to function nicely over a wide range of transmission media, each with individual specific low-level mechanisms. In the basic DARPA model, networks with varying characteristics use the IP as the local transport mechanism as well as the internet transport mechanism. In an interconnected set of networks, an independent datagram mechanism, without flow control or acknowledgments, permits alternate routing and requires a minimum of state information to be retained by the gateways. The datagram transport mechanism is layered under their highly reliable Transmission Control Protocol (TCP),[9] a DoD standard, which provides the flow control and the end-to-end reliability. This structure places the end-to-end checking as close to the user process as possible.

The Ethernet internetwork architecture has in fact adopted this basic layering scheme with significant modifications, but still using an unreliable datagram layered over the Ethernet contention protocol, or alternately, over a variety of other local protocol mechanisms. In the Ethernet PUP protocol architecture an abundance of higher level mechanisms, used either independently, or in concert, access the Ethernet datagram transport layer.[33]

The merging of the cable-bus technology with the microprocessor technological explosion has led to a re-evaluation of these design concepts. An early implementation on our cable test bed of TCP and the IP layered over the cable low-level transport mechanisms resulted in the packet overhead approaching fifty percent. [Packet length restrictions are discussed in the previous section.] This initial experience, coupled with our awareness of the rapidly evolving microprocessor technology, and our desire to fully exploit our multi-mode cable medium, motivated our cable-bus protocol architecture.

Cable-Bus Protocol Design Issues

Protocols designed for a local network environment can be simpler than those designed for a long-haul network, or an internet environment. A discussion of protocol considerations for the local environment can be found in Clark, et. al.[12] An optimal local network protocol design should to an extent take advantage of the network characteristics which are unique to the local environment.

The local network differs from the long-haul network in the following areas:

Bandwidth. The local environment deals with homogeneous nodes, in relatively close proximity, connected by a high bandwidth transmission medium. The local network can support an aggregate network data rate of from several hundred kilobits to several megabits. In this environment the delay for a packet from sender to receiver is on the order of a few milliseconds. In such high performance environments economy of bits is usually not an important factor, however the contention nature of the cable-bus environment dictates that the packet length cannot be unduly long, therefore header length economy is desirable.

Special Capabilities. The local protocols should not preclude taking advantage of any innate hardware specific characteristics, such as a broadcast capability. At the same time specific, and generally media dependent, mechanisms which exist at the very lowest protocol architectural level should be distinct enough so that their evolution with advancing technology will not impinge on higher layers. In our cable-bus environment the mechanisms for detecting the availability of the transmission channel and acquiring it (the CSMA/LWT techniques) are implemented in hardware and firmware at the very lowest level; the transition , e.g., to fiber optics should only effect this level.

Addressing. The addressing scheme should be rich enough to enable intranet message routing as well as the ability to access hosts and processes in distant interconnected networks, but it may be an unnecessary burden for local only traffic to be enveloped in a packet with a global-sized addressing field. It is an additional burden for a processing node to deal with a net address for intranet traffic.

Routing. Routing within the local network environment is far simpler than message routing in the internet, even for the case of similar local networks connected via a bridge. In fact, within the broadcast environment, no special routing is required for internetting. Since a gateway "sees" all cable messages, those with remote network addresses to which it has access are captured and passed on to the remote network. Local cable hosts then simply attach a remote network address to a message, and put it out on the cable. No knowledge of intermediary gateway addresses is required.

Reliability. For maximum efficiency, reliability mechanisms, if possible, should be a function of the transmission medium or the application. Within the cable-bus environment valid arguments exist for placing the reliable communication and flow control functions in a transport layer within the network node. Flow control at this layer is simplified because interface units are communicating with other interface units of like processing speeds, buffering capacities, and round trip delay. Flow control at a higher virtual circuit layer for example must utilize flow control strategies for more widely varying allocation sizes, fluctuations, and require complex retransmission policies which resort to historical tracking of round trip delay. Reliable transmission functions at the transport level are better able to use hardware assists such as the Western Digital HDLC chip to implement CRC creation and validation, as opposed to slower software generated CRC checking.

Internetting. It is essential that the protocols in the local network interwork efficiently with the protocols in the long-haul environment, and that the mechanisms be available to enhance global communication via bridges and gateways. It is expected, however, that traffic between the local network and other networks will be relatively light. Therefore, the burden to translate between local network protocols and remote network protocols should be placed on the gateway. This organization improves performance in the local environment. It enables one to eliminate from the local network needed internetting capbilities, such as fragmenting (the breaking up to packets which may be to big to traverse some networks). It should be emphasized, however, that the set of local protocol functions must be broad enough to support simple translation between remote and local functions.

Cable-Bus Protocol Philosophy

Our design choices have been dictated by our view of the next generation cable-bus interface unit as an extremely powerful processing node. A microprocessor-based interface unit with extensive computational capability would be able to handle a large number of the tasks necessary for internetwork communication. An essential and very basic task of the cable-bus interface unit is accessing the cable (via various contention or time based schemes). Interface units of today also handle reliable transmission of data packets between network nodes. Temporarily expanded addressing would enable the interface transport mechanism to extend communication to include interconnected sets of network nodes. Futher extensions to the interface firmware could include data stream management (the opening and closing of connections), and the mapping of specific terminal characteristics into a standard virtual terminal representation.

In essence, the interface unit on which this protocol architecture is predicated will be a network front-end access node, large enough and powerful enough to contain all the protocol layers necessary for network interconnection, and designed to work in conjunction with a simple host to front-end protocol to enable user access through one, or more, special purpose devices. Thus one can envision an expanded interface unit which is now very close to the user access layer. It is this proximity to the user which allows one to reevaluate the relative placement of protocol functions within such an entity.

Cable-Bus Protocol Architecture

The construction of a protocol architecture to meet these requirements and still remain open-ended enough to evolve nicely to the large number of perceived cable-bus applications is at best difficult. We maintain that it is impossible over the long term. Our approach is to provide a good set of established protocol mechanisms within an extensible structure such that protocols may evolve on a stepwise basis as new protocol mechanisms and cable-bus applications arise.

The protocol architecture is also based on the idea that there are really very few new protocols. Most new protocols are recombinations or reformating of a bounded set of protocol mechanisms which perform such functions as opening a virtual connection or flow controlling data as it passes over a virtual connection.

The protocol architecture that results from this point of view is shown in Figure 3.

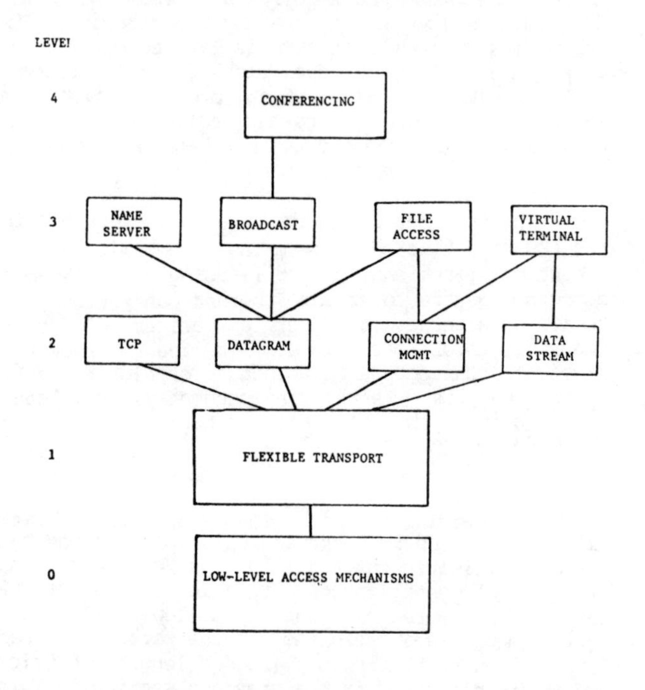

FIGURE 3

CABLE-BUS PROTOCOL ARCHITECTURE

Level 0 provides the cable-bus contention mechanism. This level decides when a packet should be transmitted to the cable and handles packet collisions.

Level 1 provides a flexibly structured set of protocol mechanisms which in combination provide protocol capabilities ranging from raw, unsequenced, unreliable datagrams to a fully sequenced, reliable data stream. This layer (the flexible transport) is described in detail below.

Level 2 represents a series of protocol implementations which are constructed by combining level 1 mechanisms. Note that a Transmission Control Protocol (TCP) implementation rests comfortably at this layer by using only a very few of the level 1 mechanisms. The datagram implementation provides a user interface to the level 1 address mechanisms and adds the capability to perform fragmentation and reassembly of larger sized datagrams. The connection management implementation provides management of virtual circuit connections using a timer based protocol described in Fletcher.[34] The datastream implementation provides a user interface to the reliable, sequencing and out-of-band signaling mechanisms of level 1 to form a reliable, sequenced datastream capability.

Thus level 2 software may exist as a simple combination of level 1 mechanisms providing an interface to the next higher level or it may implement a full set of its own mechanisms using few of the level 1 mechanisms.

Level 3 represents examples of higher level protocols which make use of the functions provided by layers 1 and 2.

The name server implementation provides a mapping between string names of objects and internetwork addresses described in Postel.[35]

The broadcast implementation provides a capability to group a set of users into a conversation such that a message generated by one user is received by all users.

File access provides access to remote file data. File accesses, based on a protocol suggested by Day,[36] allow data transfers to be described as a series of file byte pointer and length requests followed by data responses.

The virtual terminal implementation maps terminal characteristics into standard virtual terminal representations. It includes graphics functions such as line, curve, and shaded polygon drawing as well as the more mundane record mode, stream mode, and terminal option negotiation.

Flexible Transport

The Flexible Transport Protocol[37] defines a set of rules to govern the transport of blocks of data over interconnected cable-bus networks with binary degrees of reliablity, flow control, addressing, and other common end-to-end and transport level mechanisms. These mechanisms are grouped at this level to allow the optional specification of each of the mechanisms in terms of its affect on the format of the resulting protocol header. Each header contains a "bit-map" specifying the "shape" or attributes of the remaining portion of the packet. These attributes are groups of data fields which, if specified, cause the protocol mechanisms referred to above to be invoked. If an attribute is not specified, default processing mechanisms, such as always accepting a packet as in sequence if the sequence attribute is not specified, are invoked. The obvious advantage of this scheme is that if a mechanism is required to support a particular type of data transfer a price is paid in terms of header overhead and processing cycles. No penalty is paid if there is no need for a particular mechanism.

If in the future a general environment exists where the overall packet length is not restricted, the flexible header scheme may easily evolve into a fixed scheme. We should also note that in practice, we don't envision the header length changing from packet to packet, but rather for the attribute specification to be a function of the application process.

The Flexible Transport Protocol supports the following mechanisms:

Packet Assembly/Disassembly. This mechanism provides packet formatting for out-going packets from a global set of variables and a specification of attributes to be applied to any packet data. It also provides for the disassembly of received packets and the passing of any packet attributes and data to a pre-defined sequence of mechanisms within the flexible transport layer.

Packet Addressing. This mechanism provides for the detection of packets addressed to the local host. It detects packets addressed to a remote network if the local host is a gateway to that network. It detects packets addressed to the local host. It locates local port data structures. It also handles broadcast messages should any of the destination host or port attributes of the packet be absent.

Packet Typing. The packet typing mechanism provides for the manipulation of a registered set of packet types which include host reset requests, protocol error messages, and host status messages.

Packet Sequencing. The packet sequencing mechanism provides a means for identifying whether a packet is in sequence, out of sequence, or a duplicate.

Flow Control. The flow control mechanism provides a sliding window describing a range of acceptable sequence numbered packets. It also provides for the acknowledgement of previously received packets.

Out of Band Signal. The out of band signal mechanism provides a means of specifying a location in the data stream where "interesting" information resides.

Figure 4 illustrates the hierarchical structure of the flexible transport attributes. Flow control, for example, makes use of the packet sequencing, and out of band signaling needs to be free of flow control constraints. Packet assembly/disassembly is of course always needed, and one can select any combination of the other mechanisms.

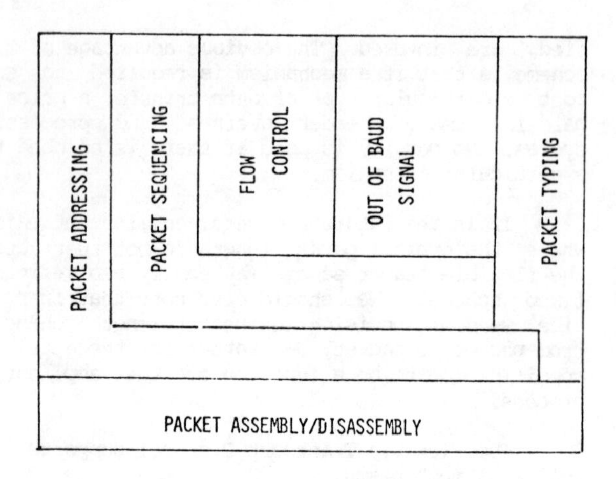

FIGURE 4. FLEXIBLE TRANSPORT LAYER

THE FUTURE DIRECTION

The versatility of the cable-bus and its ability to interconnect a multiplicity of computer devices is very much a function of the protocol design and implementation. A rich protocol structure affords a stable, architecturally sound basis upon which to build.

Once the basic underlying protocol mechanisms described herein have been implemented in Cablenet, we shall incorporate the high-level protocols, such as a resource sharing server which is necessary to yield a high degree of transparency to the user and enable distributed processing. Additionally, the video and voice capabilities inherent in Cablenet need to be explored and integrated with the digital data.

The result of our efforts will be a cable-bus system which: embodies the layered protocol concepts we have described; provides the required nodal processing capabilities; contains the necessary extensibility to enable stepwise replacement of functions with advancing technology; supports a wide variety of devices and communication line disciplines; and, effectively communicates with other networks via network gateways. Our view of the next generation cable-bus interface unit (a Z8000 or Motorola MC68000 board) holds the potential for a fully-automated, distributed, multi-mode network of the future.

References

1. Cotton, Ira W., "Local Area Networking," National Bureau of Standards Special Publication 500-31, April 1978.

2. Meisner, Norman B., (Editor), Proceedings of the MITRE/NBS Local Area Communications Network Symposium, May 1979.

3. McRay, Richard, "Communications Systems at 3M Company," presentation at ACM 78, Washington, D. C., 1978.

4. Ray, Peter, "Office of the Future Approaches at Citibank," presentation at ACM, Washington, D.C., December 1978.

5. Metcalfe,Robert M. and Boggs, David R., "Ethernet: Distributed Packet Switching for Local Computer Networks," Comm. ACM, July 1976, pp. 395-404.

6. Davidson, J., et al, The ARPANET Telenet Protocol: Its Purpose, Principles, Implementation, and Impact on Host Operating System Design, Proc. Fifth Data Communications Symposium, September 1977.

7. CCITT, Recommendation X.3: International User Facilities in Public Data Networks, Public Data Networks, Orange Book, Vol. viii.2, Sixth Plenary Assembly, Int. Telecommunications Union, Geneva, Switzerland, pp. 21-23, 1977.

8. CCITT, Recommendation X.25: Interface Between Data Terminal Equipment (DTE) and Data Circuit-terminating Equipment (DCE) for Terminals Operating in the Packet Mode on Public Data Networks, Public Data Networks, Orange Book, Vol. 2, Sixth Plenary Assembly, Int. Telecommunications Union, Geneva, Switzerland, pp. 70-108, 1977.

9. Postel, J., Transmission Control Protocol, Internet Experiment Note 112, August 1979.

10. Shoch, John, and Stewart, Larry, Internetwork Experiments with the Bay Area Packet Radio Network, Xerox Palo Alto Research Center Technical Report.

11. Cerf, Vinton G. and Kirstein, Peter T., Issues in Packet-Network Interconnection, Proc. IEEE, November 1978, pp. 1386-1408.

12. Clark, David D., Pogran, Kenneth T., and Reed, David P., An Introduction to Local Area Networks, Proc. IEEE, November 1978, pp. 1497-1517.

13. Tropper, Carl, Models of Local Computer Networks, MTR-3783, MITRE-Bedford, May 1979

14. Farber, D.J., et al, The Distributed Computing System, Proc. IEEE COMPCON, February 1973, pp. 31-34.

15. Wilkes, Maurice V., The Cambridge Digital Communication Ring, Proc. MITRE/NBS Local Area Communications Network Symposium, May 1979.

16. Liu, Ming T., Distributed Loop Computer Networks, Advanced in Computers, Vol. 17, Academic Press 1978, pp. 163-221.

17. Hopkins, Gregory T., Multimode Communications on the MITRENET, Proc. MITRE/NBS Local Area Communications Network Symposium, May 1979.

18. Carpenter,R.J., Sokol,J., and Rosenthal, R., "A Microprocessor-based Local Network Node," Proc. IEEE Compcon, September 1978, pp. 104-109.

19. Zilog, Inc., "Zilog Z8000 An Architectural Overview," 03-2028-01, Zilog, Inc., Cupertino, CA 95014., March 1978.

20. Motorola Semiconductor Products, Inc., "MC 68000 Motorola's Advanced Computer System on Silicon," Motorola Product Literature Sheet, Phoenix, AZ 1979.

21. Intel Corp., "MCS-86 Product Description," 9800723B, Intel Corp., Santa Clara CA, 1979.

22. Willard, David., "A Time Division Multiple Access system for Digital Communication," Computer Design, June 1974.

23. DeMarines, Victor A. and Hill, Lawrence W., "The Cable Bus in Data Communications," Datamation, August 1976, pp. 89-92.

24. Dolberg, C.E., "Multimode, Multiservice Local Network", Proc. Intelcom 77, Horizon House International, Atlanta, October 1977.

25. Naylor, J.C., "Data Bus Design Concepts, Issues and Prospects," Proc. IEEE Eastcon, September 1978, pp. 34-39.

26. Abramson, N., The Aloha System--Another Alternative for Computer Communications, AFIPS, Fall Joint Computer Conference 1970, pp. 695-702.

27. Roberts, L.G., Extensions of Packet Communication Technology to a Hand Held Personal Terminal, AFIPS Spring Joint Computer Conference 1972, pp. 295-298.

28. Meisner, Norman B., Segal Joshua H., Dual-Mode Slotted TDMA Digital Bus, Fifth Data Communications Symposium, September 1977, pp. 5-15 - 5-18.

29. Cerf, V.G., The Catenet Model for Internetworking, Internet Experiment Note 48, July 1978.

30. Lam, S.S., A Study of CSMA Protocols in Local Networks, Proceedings of the Fourth Berkeley Conference on Distributed Data Management and Computer Networks, August 1979, p. 141.

31. Kleinrock, Leonard, Packet Switching in Radio Channels: Part 1, Carrier Sense Multiple-Access Modes and Their Throughput Characteristics, IEEE Trans. on Comm., Vol. Com-23, No. 12, December 1975.

32. Postel, J., Internet Protocol, Internet Experiment Note 111, August 1979.

33. Boggs, David R., Shoch, John F., Taft, Edward A., and Metcalfe, Robert M., PUP: An Internetwork Architecture, IEEE Transactions on Communications, Vol. Com-28, No. 1, January 1980, to appear.

34. Fletcher, John G., Watson, Richard W., "Mechanism for a Reliable Timer-Based Protocol," Computer Networks 2 (1978), pp. 271-290.

35. Postel, J., Internet Name Server, Internet Experiment Note 61, October 1978.

36. Day, J., A Proposal for a File Access Protocol, ARPANET RFC 520, 1973.

37. Holmgren, S.F., "Flexible Transprot Protocol," in preparation.

SECTION 6: PERFORMANCE

6.1 Overview

This section looks at the performance of packet-switched local networks. The performance of a LAN or an HSLN depends on a number of key factors, the most important of which are as follows: (1) Network characteristics, which include propagation delay between devices and data rate of the transmission medium, (2) medium access control protocol, and (3) load (traffic) on the network.

The objectives of this section are to report some results from comparative analysis, to provide guidance in assessing overall network performance, and to give the reader a feel for the complexity of the problem.

6.2 Article Summary

The first article, "Local Network Performance," demonstrates that two basic characteristics of a local network, propagation delay and data rate, set an upper bound on performance independent of the medium access control protocol. The article then develops simple performance models for CSMA/CD, token bus, and token ring.

The next article, by Bux, is a description (rather than analytic) report on the delay characteristics of token bus, token ring, and CSMA/CD. The article also examines the end-to-end performance of a file server and timing problems in local network access units. Next, Sastry also examines the performance of token bus, token ring, and CSMA/CD, with the emphasis on throughput rather than delay.

The final article, by Mitchell, looks at the important (tc the user) issue of end-to-end performance. The article presents a general technique and then applies it to a specific case.

Local Network Performance

William Stallings

Significant factors in determining local network performance based on recent studies

February 1984—Vol. 22, No. 2
IEEE Communications Magazine

In recent years, there has been a proliferation of local network products and an intensification of local network R&D activity. Nevertheless, the vast majority of systems conforms to one of two topologies and one of a handful of medium-access control protocols:[1]

- Bus Topology
  ..CSMA/CD
  ..Token Bus
- Ring Topology
  ..Token Ring
  ..Slotted Ring
  ..Register Insertion

Because the number of truly different local network configurations is manageably small, a comparative analysis of local network performance is possible.

The question of performance is of concern in the design or selection of a local network for a specific application. Given a certain collection of devices, with certain traffic characteristics, a fundamental requirement is that the local network has adequate capacity for the expected load. Table I, based on studies by the IEEE 802 Local Network Standards Committee, indicates the type of load that may be offered to a local network by various devices. We would like the local network to be able to sustain a throughput that keeps up with the load, and does so without undue delays.

This paper aims to show which factors are significant in determining local network performance and to summarize recent comparative studies. The first section below shows that two basic characteristics of a local network, propagation delay and data rate, set an upper bound on performance independent of the medium-access control protocol. Next, some simple models are developed for comparing three protocols: CSMA/CD, token bus, and token ring. These are protocols for which standards have been developed [2], and it is likely that most local network products will use a variant of one of them. Finally, some comparative studies are summarized. The results cover CSMA/CD, token bus, and token ring, as well as two other ring protocols — slotted ring and register insertion.

The Effect of Propagation Delay and Transmission Rate

In analyzing local network performance, the two most useful parameters are the data rate (R) of the medium, and the average signal propagation delay (D) between stations on the network. The propagation delay reflects the length of the medium and, in the case of the ring, the number of repeaters and their delay characteristics. In fact, it is the product of these two terms, $R \times D$, that is the single most important parameter for determining the

[1] For the unacquainted reader, these topologies and protocols are defined briefly in an appendix; further details can be found in Stallings [1].

Reprinted from *IEEE Communications Magazine*, February 1984, pages 27-36.

EHO234-5/85/0000/0280$01.00 © 1984 IEEE

TABLE I*
WORKLOAD GENERATED FROM EACH SOURCE TYPE

Type of Source	Peak Data Rate (kb/s)	Duty Factor (%)
Heat/Vent/Air Conditioning/Alarm/Security	0.1	100
Line Printer	19.2	50-90
File Server/Block Transfer	20 000	0.1
File Server/File Transfer	100	10-30
Mail Server	100	30-50
Information Server/Calendar	9.6	1.5
Information Server/Decision Support	56	20-40
Word Processor	9.6	1-5
Data Entry Terminal	9.6	0.1-1.0
Data Enquiry Terminal	64	10-30
Program Development	9.6	5-20
Laser Printer	256	20-50
Facsimile	9.6	5-20
Voice/Immediate	64	20-40
Voice/Store and Forward	32	30-50
Video/Noncompressed	30 000	50-90
Video/Freeze Frame	64	50-90
Video/Compressed	400	20-40
Graphics/Noncompressed	256	1-10
Graphics/Compressed	64	10-30
Optical Character Reader	2.4	50-90
Gateway	1000	0.1-1.0
Host/0.5 MIPS	128	20-40
Host/5 MIPS	1000	20-30

*In Stallings [1].

performance of a local network. Other things being equal, a network's performance will be the same, for example, for both a 50-Mb/s, 1-km bus and a 10-Mb/s, 5-km bus. It will be seen that many widely-used metrics of LAN protocol performance, such as channel utilization and normalized service times, will remain constant if the $R \times D$ product is held constant.

Note that the data rate times the delay product is equal to the length of the transmission medium in bits, that is, the number of bits that may be in transit between two nodes at any snapshot in time. Several examples: assuming a velocity of propagation of 2×10^8 m/s, a 500-m Ethernet system (10 Mb/s) has a bit length of 25; both a 1-km HYPERchannel (50 Mb/s) and a typical 5-km broadband local network (5 Mb/s) run about 250 bits.

A useful way of viewing this is to consider the length of the medium as compared to the typical packet transmitted. This allows one to distinguish protocols geared for a local network from those designed for a multiprocessor backplane bus, which needs to accommodate a maximum of a few bits in transit; and from those for a satellite link, which should accommodate several entire packets in transit. Intuitively, it can be seen that this will make a difference. Compare local networks to multiprocessor computers. Relatively speaking, things happen almost simultaneously in a multiprocessor system; when one component begins to transmit, the others know it almost immediately. For local networks, the relative time gap leads to the need for a complex medium-access control protocol. Compare local networks to satellite links. To have any hope of efficiency, the satellite link must allow multiple packets to be in transit simultaneously. This places specific requirements on the link layer protocol, which must deal with a sequence of outstanding packets waiting to be acknowledged. Local network protocols generally allow only one packet at a time to be in transit, or, at the most, a few for some ring protocols. Again, this affects the access protocol.

The length of the medium, expressed in bits, compared to the length of the typical packet is usually denoted by a:

$$a = \frac{\text{Length of Data Path in Bits}}{\text{Length of Packet}}$$

$$a = \frac{RD}{L}$$

where L is the length of the packet. But D is the propagation time on the medium (worst case), and L/R is the time it takes a transmitter to get an entire packet out onto the medium. So,

$$a = \frac{\text{Propagation Time}}{\text{Transmission Time}}$$

Typical values of a range from about 0.01 to 0.1. Table II gives some sample values for a bus topology. In computing a for ring networks, repeater delays must be included in propagation time.

The parameter a determines an upper bound on the utilization of a local network. Consider a perfectly efficient access mechanism that allows only one transmission at a time. As soon as one transmission is over, another node begins transmitting. Furthermore, the transmission is pure data — no overhead bits. What is the maximum possible utilization of the network? It can be expressed as the ratio of total throughput of the system to the capacity or bandwidth:

TABLE II
VALUES OF a

Data Rate	Packet Size	Cable Length	a
1 Mb/s	100 bits	1 km	0.05
1 Mb/s	1000 bits	10 km	0.05
1 Mb/s	100 bits	10 km	0.5
10 Mb/s	100 bits	1 km	0.5
10 Mb/s	1000 bits	1 km	0.05
10 Mb/s	1000 bits	10 km	0.5
10 Mb/s	10 000 bits	10 km	0.05
50 Mb/s	10 000 bits	1 km	0.025
50 Mb/s	100 bits	1 km	2.5

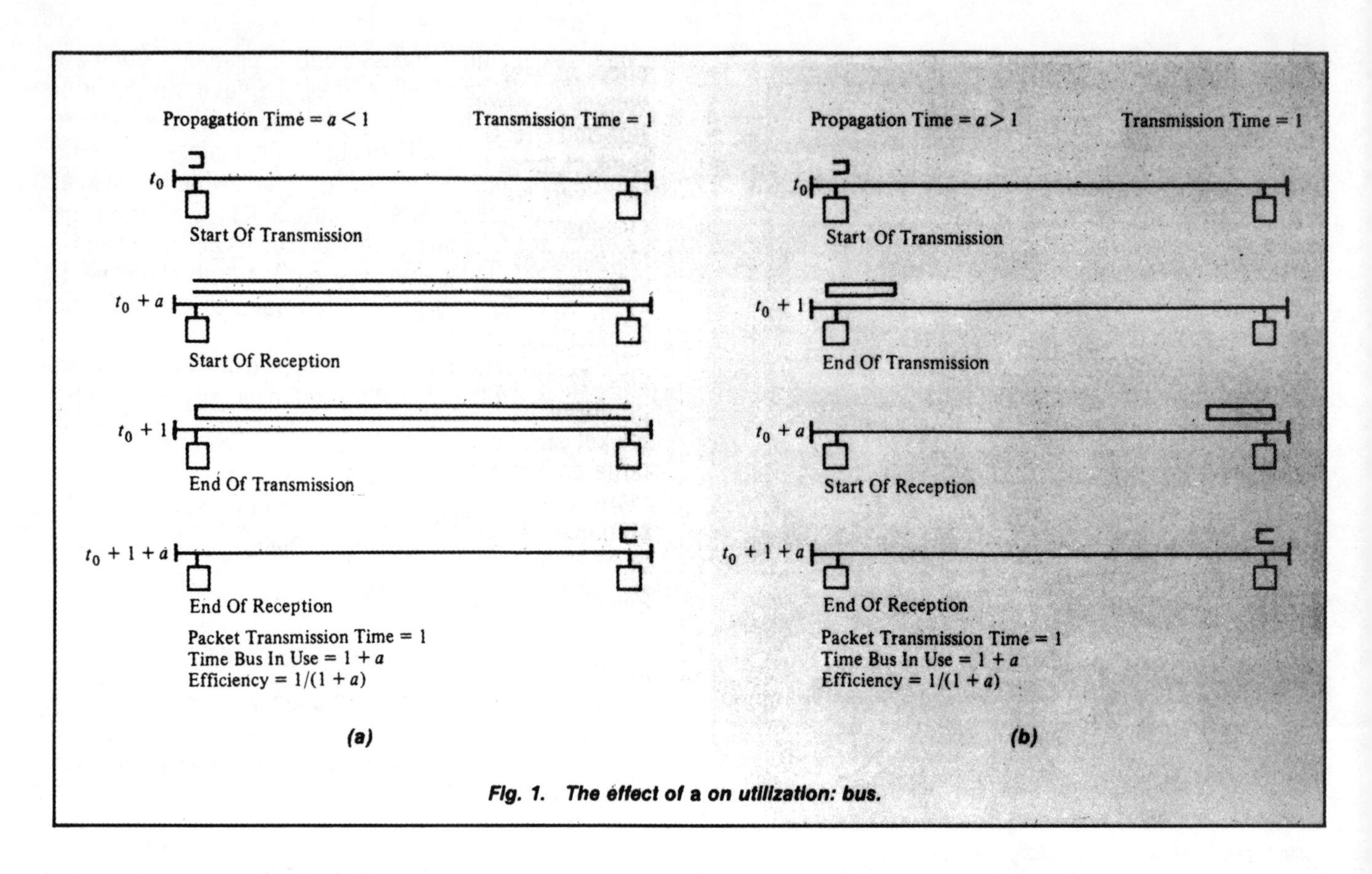

Fig. 1. The effect of a on utilization: bus.

$$
\begin{aligned}
U &= \text{Throughput}/R \\
&= \frac{L/(\text{Propagation} + \text{Transmission Time})}{R} \\
&= \frac{L/(D + L/R)}{R} \\
&= \frac{1}{1 + a} \qquad (1)
\end{aligned}
$$

So, utilization varies inversely with *a*. This can be grasped intuitively by studying Fig. 1; this shows a baseband bus with two stations as far apart as possible (worst case) that take turns sending packets. If we normalize the packet transmission time to equal one, then the sequence of events can be expressed as follows.

1) A station begins transmission at t_0
2) Reception begins at $t_0 + a$
3) Transmission is completed at $t_0 + 1$
4) Reception ends at $t_0 + 1 + a$
5) The other station begins transmitting

Event 2 occurs *after* event 3 if $a > 1.0$. In any case, the total time for one "turn" is $1 + a$, but the transmission time is only 1, for a utilization of $1/(1 + a)$.

The same effect can be seen to apply to a ring network in Fig. 2. Here we assume that one station transmits and then waits to receive its own transmission before any other station transmits. The identical sequence of events outlined above applies.

The implication of (1) for performance is shown in Fig. 3. The axes of the plot are:

- *S*, the throughput or total rate of data being transmitted on the medium, normalized to the bandwidth of the medium.
- *G*, the offered load to the local network; the total rate of data presented for transmission, also normalized.

The ideal case is $a = 0$, which allows 100% utilization. It can be seen that, as offered load increases, throughput remains equal to offered load up to the full capacity of the system ($S = G = 1$) and then remains at $S = 1$. At any positive value of *a*, the system saturates at $S = 1/(1 + a)$.

So we can say that an upper bound on utilization or efficiency is $1/(1 + a)$, regardless of the medium-access protocol used. Two caveats: First, this assumes that the maximum propagation time is incurred on each transmission. Second, it assumes that only one transmission may occur at a time. These assumptions are not always true; nevertheless, the formula $1/(1 + a)$ is almost always a valid upper bound, because the overhead of the medium access protocol more than makes up for the lack of validity of these assumptions.

The overhead is unavoidable. Packets must include address and synchronization bits. There is administrative overhead for controlling the protocol. In addition, there are forms of overhead peculiar to one or more of the protocols. We highlight these briefly:

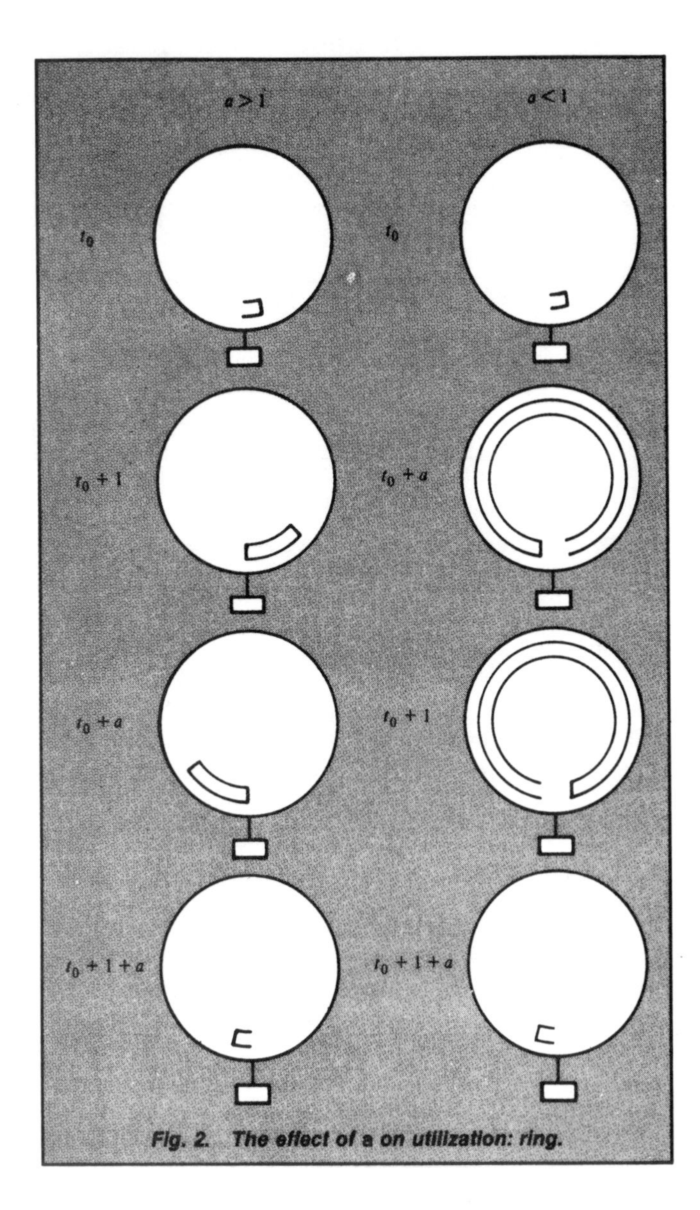

Fig. 2. The effect of a on utilization: ring.

- CSMA/CD — Time wasted due to collisions; need for acknowledgment packets.[2]
- Token bus — Token transmission; acknowledgment packets.
- Token ring — Time waiting for token if intervening stations have no data to send.
- Slotted ring — Time waiting for empty slot if intervening stations have no data to send.
- Register insertion — Delay at each node of time equal to address length; from the point of view of a single station, the propagation time, and hence *a*, may increase due to insertion of registers on the ring.

There are two distinct effects here. One is that the efficiency or utilization of a channel decreases as *a* increases. This, of course, affects throughput. The other effect is that the overhead attributable to a protocol wastes bandwidth and hence reduces effective utilization and effective throughput. For the most part, we can think of these two effects as independent and additive. However, we shall see that, for CSMA/CD, there is a strong interaction such that the overhead of the protocol increases as a function of *a*.

In any case, it would seem desirable to keep *a* as low as possible. Referring back to the defining formula, for a fixed network, *a* can be reduced by increasing packet size. This will only be useful if the length of messages produced by a station is an integral multiple of the packet size (excluding overhead bits). Otherwise, the large packet size is itself a source of waste. Furthermore, a large packet size increases the delay for other stations. Of course, variable-length packets may be used; in that case, performance tends to reflect average packet length [3].

[2]Strictly speaking, acknowledgments are not part of the access protocol but of a higher-level link protocol. However, the ring protocols under discussion allow for acknowledgment by having the sender remove its own packet from the ring. Thus this overhead is avoided.

Simple Performance Models of Token-Passing and CSMA/CD

In this section, we will give some insight into the relative performance of the most important LAN protocols — CSMA/CD, token bus, and token ring — by developing two simple performance models. It is hoped this will aid in understanding the results of more rigorous analyses to be presented later.

For these models, we assume a local network with N active stations, and a maximum normalized propagation delay of a. To simplify the analysis, we assume that each station is always prepared to transmit a packet. This allows us to develop an expression for maximum achievable throughput (S). While this should not be construed as the sole figure of merit for a local network, it is the single most analyzed one, and does permit useful performance comparisons.

First, let us consider token ring. Time on the ring will alternate between data packet transmission and token passing. Refer to a single instance of a data packet followed by a token as a cycle and define:

C = average time for one cycle
T_1 = average time to transmit a data packet
T_2 = average time to pass a token.

It should be clear that the average cycle rate is just $1/C = 1/(T_1 + T_2)$. Intuitively,

$$S = \frac{T_1}{T_1 + T_2} \tag{2}$$

That is, the throughput, normalized to system capacity, is just the fraction of time that is spent transmitting data.

Refer now to Fig. 2; time is normalized such that packet transmission time equals 1 and propagation time equals a. For the case of $a < 1$, a station transmits a packet at time t_0, receives the leading edge of its own packet at $t_0 + a$, and completes transmission at $t_0 + 1$. The station then emits a token, which takes an average time

a/N to reach the next station. Thus, one cycle takes $1 + a/N$ and the transmission time is 1. So, $S = 1/(1 + a/N)$.

For $a > 1$, the reasoning is slightly different. A station transmits at t_0, completes transmission at $t_0 + 1$, and receives the leading edge of its frame at $t_0 + a$. At that point, it is free to emit a token, which takes an average time a/N to reach the next station.[3] The cycle time is therefore $a + a/N$ and $S = 1/(a(1 + 1/N))$. Summarizing,

$$\text{Token } S = \begin{cases} \dfrac{1}{1 + a/N} & a < 1 \\[2ex] \dfrac{1}{a(1 + 1/N)} & a > 1 \end{cases} \qquad (3)$$

The above reasoning applies equally well to token bus where we assume that the logical ordering is the same as the physical ordering and that token-passing time is therefore a/N.

For CSMA/CD, we base our approach on a derivation in Metcalfe [4]. Consider time on the medium to be organized into slots whose length is twice the end-to-end propagation delay. This is a convenient way to view the activity on the medium; the slot time is the maximum time, from the start of transmission, required to detect a collision. Again, assume that there are N active stations. Clearly, if each station always has a packet to transmit, and does so, there will be nothing but collisions on the line. Therefore we assume that each station restrains itself to transmitting during an available slot with probability P.

Time on the medium consists of two types of intervals. First is a transmission interval, which lasts $1/2a$ slots. Second is a contention interval, which is a sequence of slots with either a collision or no transmission in each slot. The throughput is just the proportion of time spent in transmission intervals (similar to the reasoning for (2)).

To determine the average length of a contention interval, we begin by computing A, the probability that exactly one station attempts a transmission in a slot and therefore acquires the medium. This is just the binomial probability that any one station attempts to transmit and the others do not:

$$A = \binom{N}{1} P^1(1 - P)^{N-1}$$

$$A = NP(1 - P)^{N-1}$$

This function takes on a maximum over P when $P = 1/N$:

$$A = (1 - 1/N)^{N-1}$$

Why are we interested in the maximum? Because we want to calculate the maximum throughput of the medium. It should be clear that this will be achieved if we maximize the probability of successful seizure of the medium. This says that the following rule should be enforced: During periods of heavy usage, a station should restrain its offered load to $1/N$. (This assumes that each station knows the value of N. In order to derive an expression for maximum possible throughput, we live with this assumption.) On the other hand, during periods of light usage, maximum utilization cannot be achieved because G is too low; this region is not of interest here.

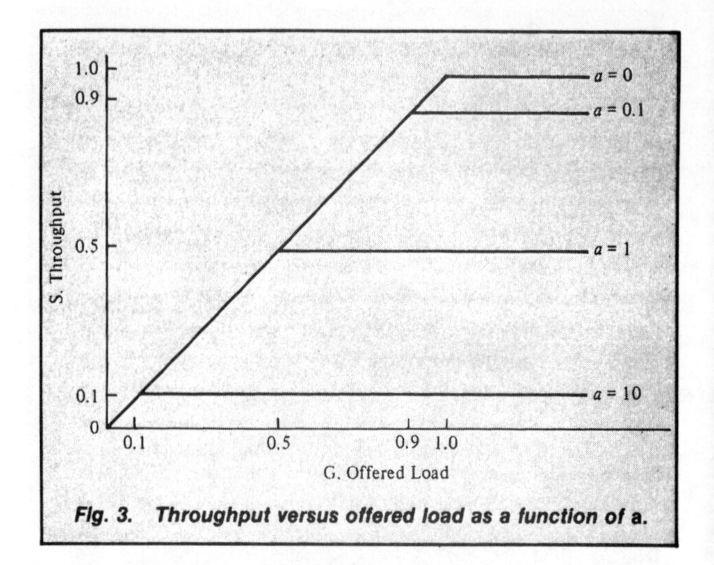

Fig. 3. Throughput versus offered load as a function of a.

Now we can estimate the mean length of a contention interval, w, in slots:

$$E[w] = \sum_{i=1}^{\infty} iPr[i \text{ slots in a row with a collision or no transmission followed by a slot with one transmission}]$$

$$= \sum_{i=1}^{\infty} i(1 - A)^i A$$

The summation converges to

$$E[w] = \frac{1 - A}{A}$$

We can now determine the maximum utilization, which is just the length of a transmission interval as a proportion of a cycle consisting of a transmission and a contention interval:

$$\text{CSMA/CD } S = \frac{\frac{1}{2}a}{\frac{1}{2}a + \dfrac{1 - A}{A}} = \frac{1}{1 + 2a\dfrac{1 - A}{A}} \qquad (4)$$

Figure 4 shows normalized throughput as a function of a for various values of N and for both token-passing and CSMA/CD. For both protocols, throughput declines as a increases. This is to be expected; but the dramatic difference between the two protocols is seen in Fig. 5, which shows throughput as a function of N. Token-passing performance actually improves as a function of N, because less time is spent in token-passing. Conversely, the performance of CSMA/CD decreases be-

[3]The station could transmit at $t_0 + 1$ (tailgating). This is not allowed in the IEEE 802 Standard to simplify control.

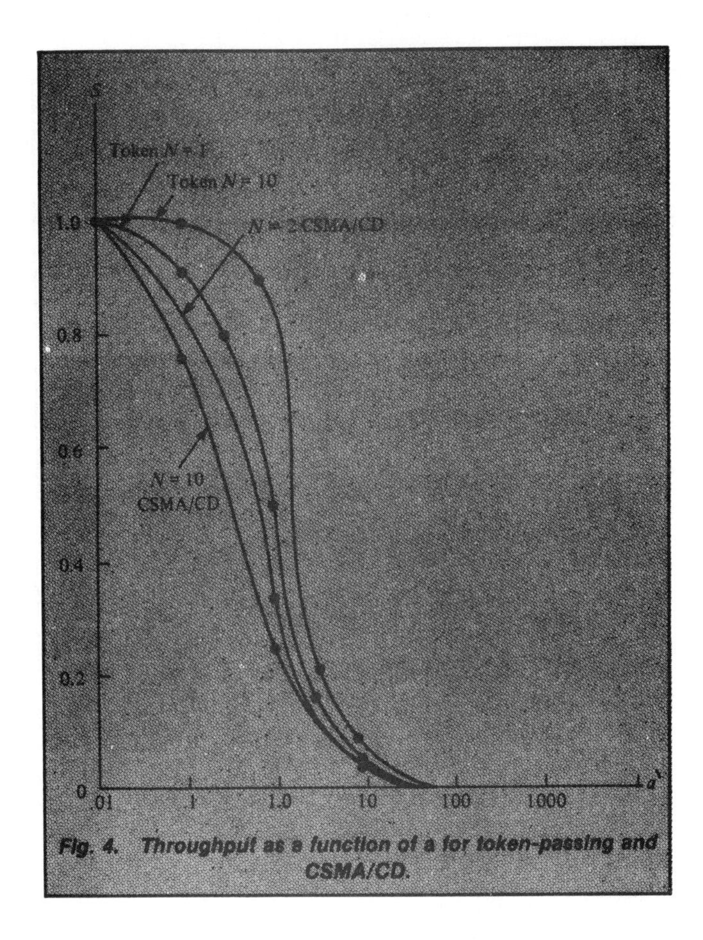

Fig. 4. Throughput as a function of a for token-passing and CSMA/CD.

cause of the increased likelihood of collision or no transmission.

It is interesting to note the asymptotic value of S as N increases. For token:

$$\text{Token} \quad \lim_{N\to\infty} S = \begin{cases} 1 & a < 1 \\ 1/a & a > 1 \end{cases} \tag{5}$$

For CSMA/CD, we need to know that $\lim_{N\to\infty}(1 - 1/N)^{N-1} = 1/e$. Then

$$\text{CSMA/CD} \quad \lim_{N\to\infty} S = \frac{1}{1 + 3.44a} \tag{6}$$

Comparative Results from Analytic and Simulation Models

Although there have been a number of performance studies focusing on a single protocol, there have been few systematic attempts to analyze the relative performance of the various local network protocols. In what follows, we look at the results of several carefully-done studies that have produced comparative results.

CSMA/CD, Token Bus, and Token Ring

The first study was done by a group at Bell Labs, under the sponsorship of the IEEE 802 Local Network Standards Committee [5]. Naturally enough, the study analyzed the three protocols being standardized by IEEE 802: CSMA/CD, token bus, and token ring. The analysis is based on considering not only mean values but second moments of delay and message length. Two cases of message arrival statistics are employed. In the first, only one station out of one hundred has messages to transmit, and is always ready to transmit. In such a case, one would hope that the network would not be the bottleneck, but could easily keep up with one station. In the second case, 100 stations out of 100 always have messages to transmit. This represents an extreme of congestion and one would expect that the network may be a bottleneck. In the two cases, the one station or one hundred stations provide enough input to fully utilize the network. Hence, the results are a measure of maximum potential utilization.

The results are shown in Fig. 6. It shows the actual data transmission rate versus the transmission speed of the medium for the two cases and two packet sizes. Note that the abscissa is not offered load but the actual capacity of the medium. Three systems are examined: token ring with a one-bit latency per station, token bus, and CSMA/CD. The analysis yields the following conclusions:

- For the given parameters, the smaller the mean packet length, the greater the difference in maximum mean throughput rate between token-passing and CSMA/CD. This reflects the strong dependence of CSMA/CD on *a*.
- Token ring is the least sensitive to workload.
- CSMA/CD offers the shortest delay under light load, while it is most sensitive under heavy load to the workload.

Note also that in the case of a single station transmitting, token bus is significantly less efficient

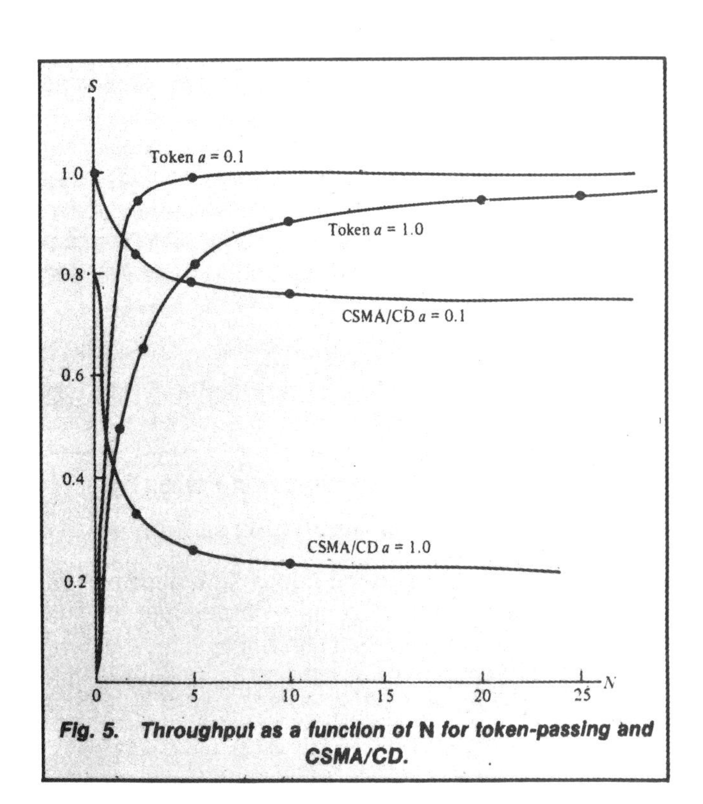

Fig. 5. Throughput as a function of N for token-passing and CSMA/CD.

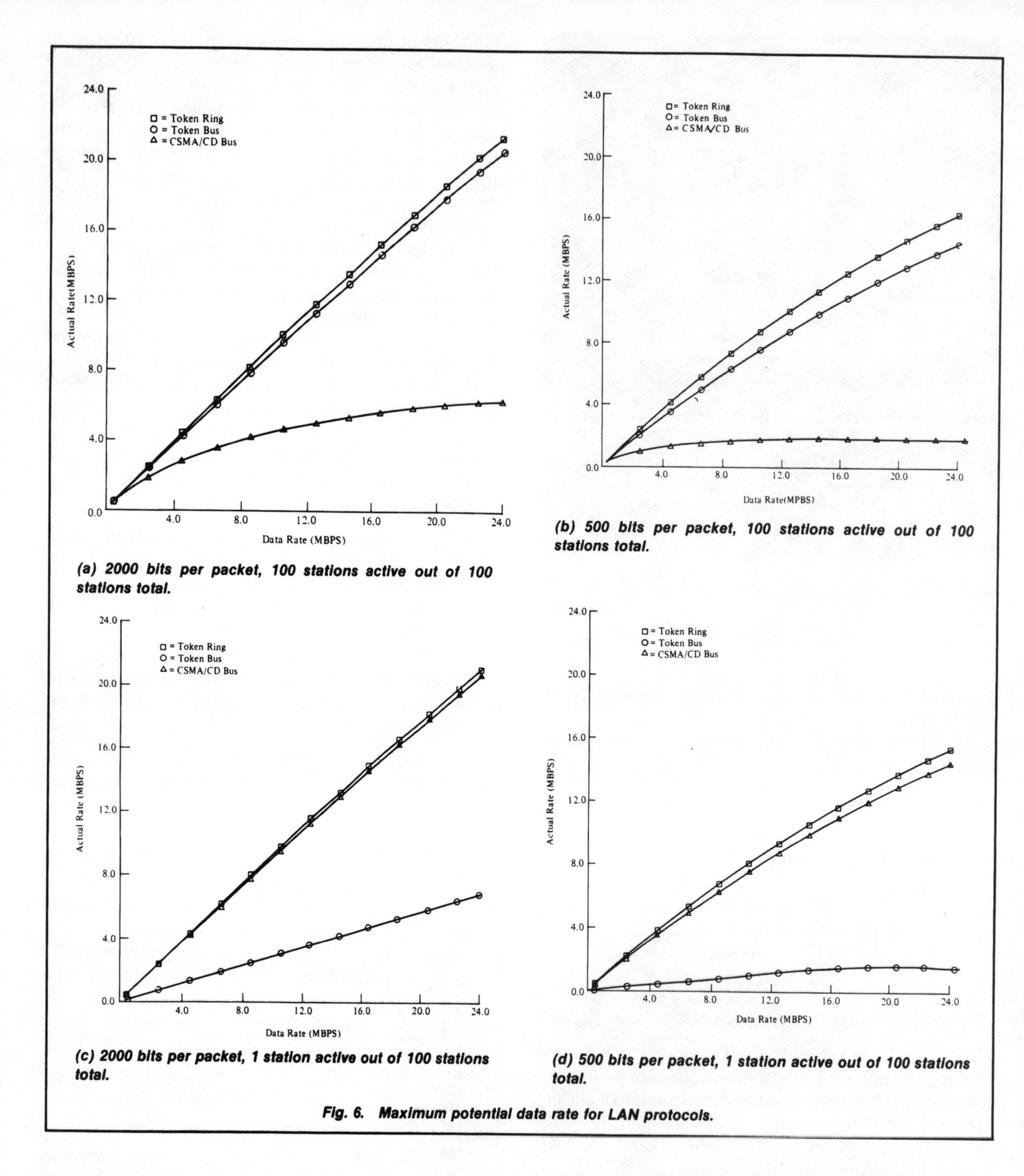

(a) 2000 bits per packet, 100 stations active out of 100 stations total.

(b) 500 bits per packet, 100 stations active out of 100 stations total.

(c) 2000 bits per packet, 1 station active out of 100 stations total.

(d) 500 bits per packet, 1 station active out of 100 stations total.

Fig. 6. Maximum potential data rate for LAN protocols.

than the other two protocols. This is so because the assumption is made that token-passing time equals the propagation delay, and that the delay in token processing is greater than for token ring.

Another phenomenon of interest is seen most clearly in Fig. 6(b). For a CSMA/CD system under these conditions, the maximum effective throughput at 5 Mb/s is only about 1.25 Mb/s. If expected load is, say, 0.75 Mb/s, this configuration may be perfectly adequate. If, however, the load is expected to grow to 2 Mb/s, raising the network data rate to 10 Mb/s or even 20 Mb/s will not accommodate the increase. The same conclusion, less precisely, can be drawn from the simple model presented earlier.

The reason for this disparity between CSMA/CD and token-passing (bus or ring) under heavy load has to do with the instability of CSMA/CD. As offered load increases, so does throughput until, beyond its maxi-

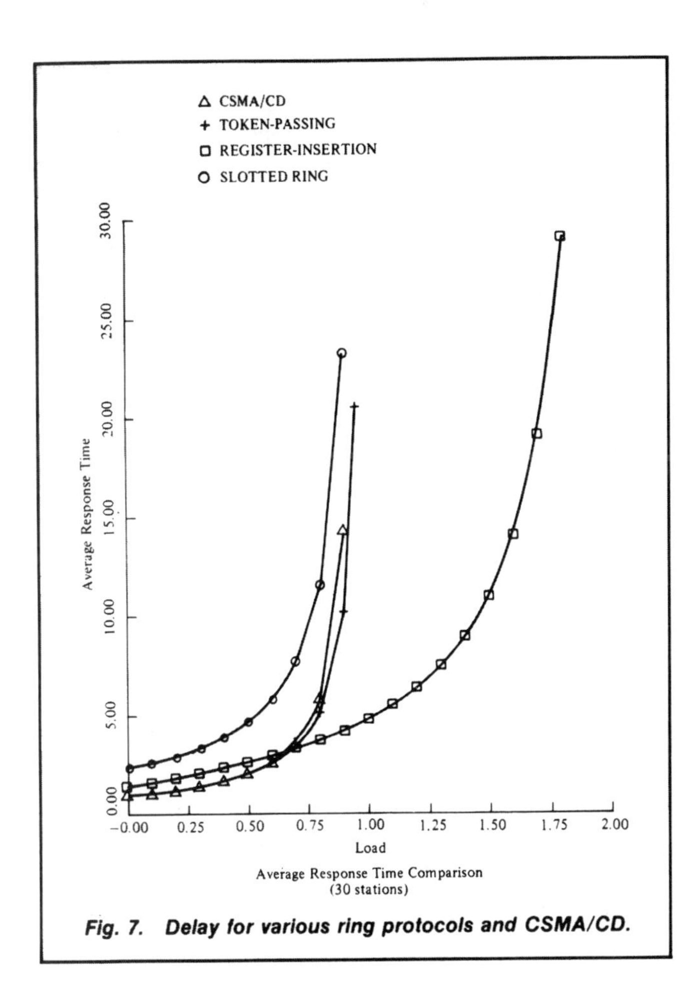

Fig. 7. Delay for various ring protocols and CSMA/CD.

mum value, throughput actually declines as G increases. This is because there is an increased frequency of collisions: more packets are offered, but fewer successfully escape collision. Worse, this situation may persist even if the input to the system drops to zero. Consider: for high G, virtually all offered packets are retransmissions and virtually none get through. So, even if no new packets are generated, the system will remain occupied in an unsuccessful attempt to clear the backlog; the effective capacity of the system is virtually zero. Thus, even in a moderately loaded system, a temporary burst of work could move the network permanently into the high-collision region. This type of instability is not possible with the other protocols.

CSMA/CD and Ring Protocols

It is far more difficult to do a comparative performance of the three major ring protocols than to do a comparison of bus and token-ring protocols. The results depend critically on a number of parameters unique to each protocol. For example:

- Token Ring — size of token, token processing time
- Slotted Ring — slot size, overhead bits per slot
- Register Insertion — register size

Thus it is difficult to do a comparison, and although there have been a number of studies on each one of the techniques, few have attempted pairwise comparisons, much less a three-way analysis. The most systematic work in this area has been done by Liu and his associates [6]. Liu made comparisons based on analytic models developed by others for token ring, slotted ring, and CSMA/CD, plus his own formulations for register insertion. He then obtained very good corroboration from simulation studies.

Figure 7 summarizes the results. They are based on the assumption that $a = 0.005$ and that register insertion ring packets are removed by the destination station, whereas slotted-ring and token-ring packets are removed by the source station. This is clearly an unfair comparison since register insertion, under this scheme, does not include acknowledgments, but token ring and slotted ring do. The figure does show that slotted ring is the poorest performer, and that register insertion can carry a load greater than 1.0. This is because the protocol permits multiple packets to circulate.

Bux [7] performed an analysis comparing token ring, slotted ring, and CSMA/CD. This careful analysis produced several important conclusions (see Fig. 8). First, the delay-throughput performance of token ring vs. CSMA/CD confirms our earlier discussion. That is, token ring suffers greater delay than CSMA/CD at light load but less delay and stable throughput at heavy loads. Further, token ring has superior delay characteristics to slotted ring. The poorer performance of slotted ring seems to have two causes: 1) the relative overhead in the small slots of a local-area ring is very high, and 2) the time needed to pass empty slots around the ring to guarantee fair bandwidth is significant. Bux also reports several positive features of slotted ring: 1) the expected delay for a message is proportional to length (that is, shorter packets get better service than long ones), and 2) overall mean delay is independent of packet length distribution type. Bux has recently extended his analysis to include register insertion [8], achieving results comparable to Liu's.

It is difficult to draw conclusions from the efforts made so far. The slotted ring seems to be the least desirable over a broad range of parameter values, owing to the considerable overhead associated with each small packet. For example, the Cambridge ring, which is the most widely commercially-available ring in Europe, uses a 37-bit slot with only 16 data bits!

As between token ring and register insertion, the evidence suggests that, at least for some sets of parameter values, register insertion gives superior delay performance. Interestingly, there seems to be no commercially-available register insertion product, with the exception of the IBM Series 1 loop, where performance is not an issue. On the other hand, token ring in the United States, with a boost from the IEEE 802 Standard and IBM, and slotted ring in Europe, where many firms have licensed the Cambridge slotted ring, seem destined to dominate the ring marketplace.

The primary advantage of register insertion is the

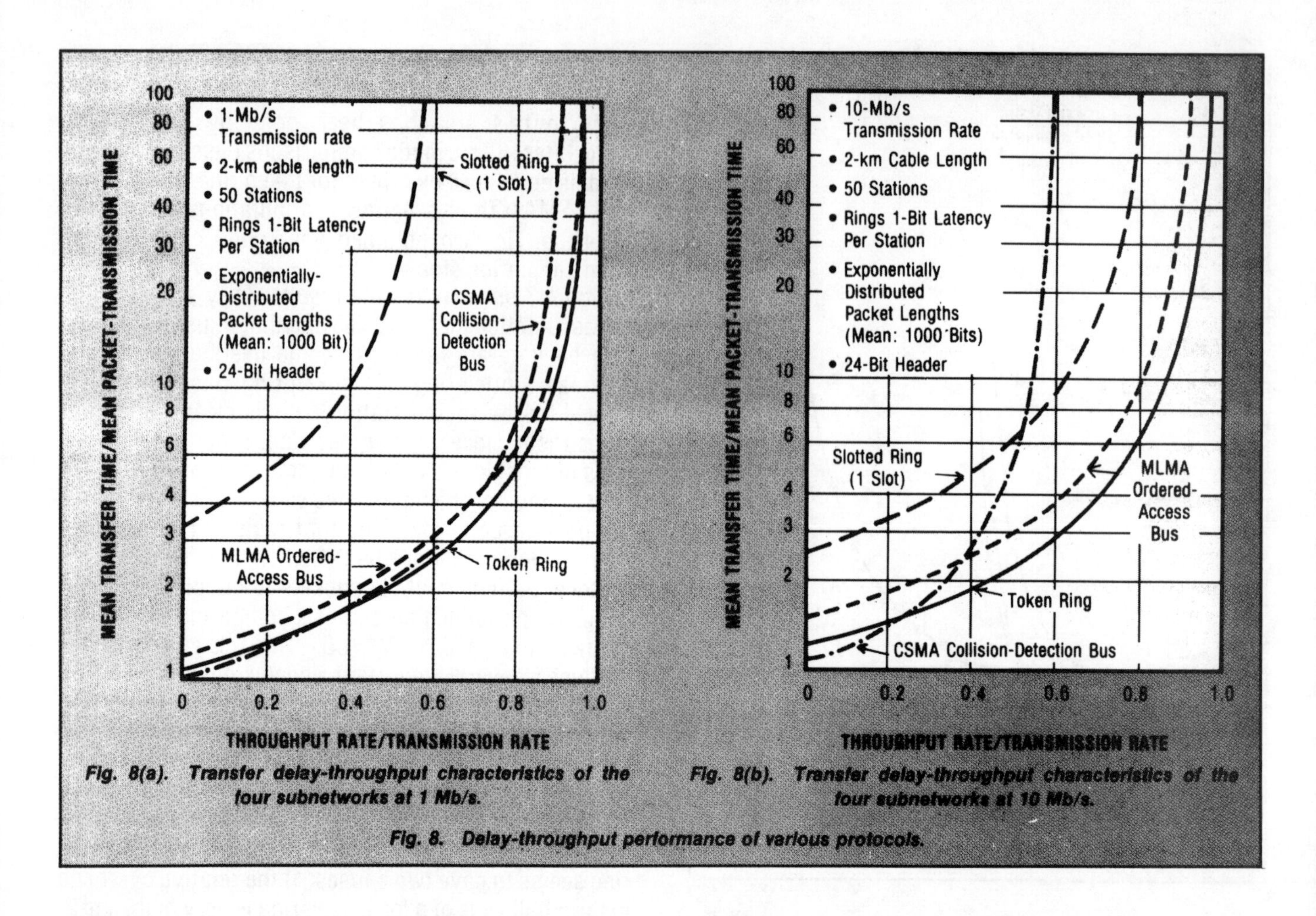

Fig. 8(a). Transfer delay-throughput characteristics of the four subnetworks at 1 Mb/s.

Fig. 8(b). Transfer delay-throughput characteristics of the four subnetworks at 10 Mb/s.

Fig. 8. Delay-throughput performance of various protocols.

potentially high utilization it can achieve. In contrast with token ring, multiple stations can transmit at one time. Further, a station can transmit as soon as a gap opens up on the ring; it need not wait for a token. On the other hand, the propagation time around the ring is not constant, but depends on the amount of traffic.

A final point in comparing token ring and register insertion: Under light loads, register insertion operates more efficiently, resulting in slightly less delay. However, both systems perform adequately. Our real interest is under heavy load. A typical local network will have $a<1$, usually $a<<1$, so that a transmitting station on a token ring will append a token to the end of its packet. Under heavy load, a nearby station will be able to use the token. Thus almost 100% utilization is achieved, and there is no particular advantage to register insertion.

References

[1] W. Stallings, *Local Networks: An Introduction*, New York: MacMillan, 1984.

[2] W. Myers, "Toward a local network standard," *IEEE Micro*, pp. 28–45, Aug. 1982.

[3] F. Tobagi, "Performance analysis of carrier sense multiple access with collision detection," *Computer Networks*, pp. 245–259, Oct./Nov. 1980.

[4] R. M. Metcalfe and D. R. Boggs, "Ethernet: distributed packet switching for local computer networks," *Commun. Ass. Comput. Mach.*, pp. 395–404, July 1976.

[5] B. Stuck, "Calculating the maximum mean data rate in local area networks," *Computer*, pp. 72–76, May 1983.

[6] M. T. Liu, W. Hilal, and B. H. Groomes, "Performance evaluation of channel access protocols for local computer networks," *Proc. COMPCON Fall '82*, pp. 417–426, 1982.

[7] W. Bux, "Local-area subnetworks: a performance comparison," *IEEE Trans. Commun.*, pp. 1465–1473, Oct. 1981.

[8] W. Bux and M. Schlatter, "An approximate method for the performance analysis of buffer insertion rings," *IEEE Trans. Commun.*, pp. 50–55, Jan. 1983.

Appendix — Local Network Terms

Bus — The common name for a local network with a linear or tree topology, in which stations are attached to a shared transmission medium. Transmissions propagate the length of the linear medium or throughout all the branches of the tree, and may be received by all stations.

Ring — A local network in which stations are attached to repeaters connected in a closed loop. Data are transmitted in one direction around the ring, and can be read by all attached stations.

Medium Access Control Technique — A distributed control technique, shared by stations attached to a local network, that determines which device may transmit on the medium at any time.

CSMA/CD — Carrier Sense Multiple Access with Collision Detection. A medium access control technique for bus local networks. A station wishing to transmit first senses the medium and transmits only if the medium is idle. The station continues to sense the medium during transmission and ceases transmission if it detects a collision.

Token Bus — A medium-access control technique for bus local networks. Stations form a logical ring, around which a token is passed. A station receiving the token may transmit data, and then must pass the token to the next station in logical order.

Token Ring — A medium-access control technique for ring local networks. A token circulates around the ring. A station may transmit by removing the token, inserting a packet onto the ring, and then retransmitting the token.

Register Insertion — A medium access control technique for ring local networks. Each station contains a register that can temporarily hold a circulating packet. A station may transmit whenever there is a gap on the ring and, if necessary, hold an oncoming packet until it has completed transmission.

Slotted Ring — A medium access control technique for ring local networks. The ring is divided into circulating slots, which may be designated empty or full. A station may transmit whenever an empty slot goes by, by marking it full and inserting a packet into the slot.

Dr. William Stallings is a frequent lecturer on data communications topics. He is the author of *Local Networks: An Introduction* (MacMillan, 1984); *Local Network Technology* (IEEE Computer Society Press, 1983); *A Manager's Guide to Local Networks* (Prentice-Hall, 1983); and *Data and Computer Communications* (MacMillan, forthcoming).

Dr. Stallings received a Ph.D. from M.I.T. in computer science in 1971. Currently, he is senior communications consultant with Honeywell Information Systems, Inc. He is involved in the planning and design of communications network products and in the evaluation of communications requirements for Honeywell customers. He has been vice-president of CSM Corp., a firm specializing in data processing and data communications technology for the health-care industry. He has also been director of Systems Analysis and Design for CTEC, Inc., a firm specializing in command, control, and communications systems. ■

MAXIMUM MEAN DATA RATE IN A LOCAL AREA NETWORK WITH A SPECIFIED MAXIMUM SOURCE MESSAGE LOAD

A. R. K. Sastry

Rockwell International Science Center
1049 Camino Dos Rios
Thousand Oaks, California 91360

ABSTRACT

This paper considers the collective impact of various parameters of a local area network (LAN) such as propagation delay, interface delay, transmission rate, message length, etc., on the maximum mean data rate (throughput). Due to the interaction of these parameters, the realizable maximum throughput rate depends on the degree of synchronization between instants of time at which the network access and the data to be transmitted become available. If a source is blocked (not allowed to generate data when transmission of a previous message unit is pending), the realizable maximum throughput rate is less than or equal to the nominal maximum throughput rate chosen in the design, while both would be equal for the non-blocked case. The reduction in the throughput for the blocked case can be avoided by introducing a buffer of suitable size at the input of the network interface.

INTRODUCTION

A sub-committeee of the IEEE Project 802 (Local Area Network Standards) recently considered [1]-[3] estimation of the maximum mean data rate as an additional means of characterizing the traffic handling capabilities for the three local area network (LAN) schemes: token-passing ring, token-passing bus, and Carrier Sense Multiple Access with Collision Detection (CSMA/CD). This involves computation of the maximum mean data rates under two extreme traffic conditions, i.e., when (1) only one station is active and (2) all stations are active (which represents the worst-case congestion). The analyses of maximum mean data rates in [1] and [2] assume that each active station is always ready with another message (a data packet or frame) as soon as a previous message is transmitted, irrespective of the LAN transmission rate. It would be more meaningful from a user point of view to examine the implications for a given maximum total message rate. As shown in this note, such an analysis not only identifies the minimum transmission rate required for a particular LAN configuration but also brings out more clearly the impact of the interaction of various network parameters, which might partially explain the observed discrepancies between the theoretical and measured performance [4].

ANALYSIS

Figure 1 shows a user-oriented representation of the throughput (actual useful data delivered) characteristics of a LAN as a function of its transmission (clock) rate.

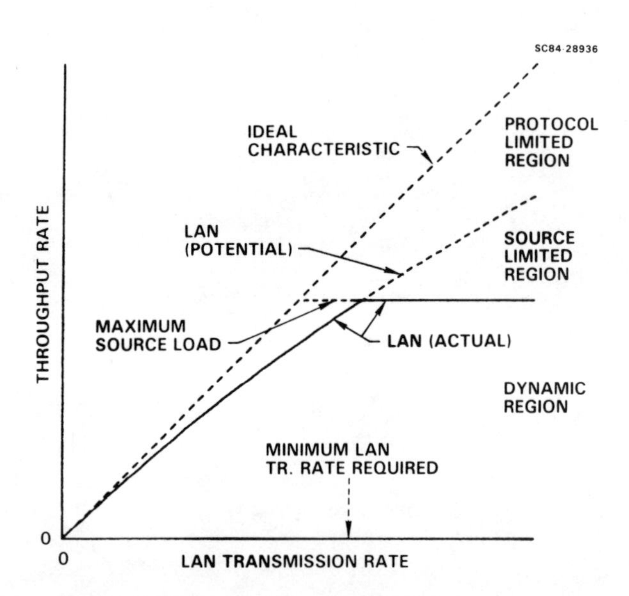

Fig. 1. User–view of qualitative performance of a local area network (LAN) for a given maximum total source data input load.

For a given transmission rate, R bits/s, a given LAN will have a maximum potential throughput rate, M^* bits/s. In most practical situations, for a designed value of M^*, the actual maximum throughput rate, M, $(M \leq M^*)$, is limited by the maximum source data rate, i.e., it would be operating in a "source-limited" region. In this region, the actual total throughput rate depends on the availability of a new packet at each station's interface as soon as it finishes transmitting the previous packet. This availability for a specified source work load results from an intricate relationship among the individual source data rate, the

EHO234-5/85/0000/0290$01.00 © 1985 IEEE

interface delay, the one-way propagation delay, size of the message unit, and the access scheme.

Consider N identical stations (sources) in a LAN, all of them being active, each continuously generating and delivering data (worst congestion case) at a rate of r bits/s to its interface unit connected to the medium. The interface unit handles packet assembly/disassembly functions and any other signal processing, participates in the execution of the medium access protocol, and transmits/receives packets to/from the LAN medium at a transmission rate of R bits/s. Let T_i be the time taken by the interface unit for performing these functions (interface delay) for the transmission of each packet. Also, let T_m be the transmission time for the packet consisting of D data bits and T_p be the largest one-way propagation delay. Then, for a token bus scheme, the maximum mean throughput rate [2], M_b, in bits/s is given by

$$M_b = \frac{D}{(T_m + T_p + T_i)}. \quad (1)$$

We will assume that each station is allowed to transmit only one packet when it holds the token and that the token transmission time and processing times are absorbed in T_i. If a station is synchronously ready with an additional D data bits to be transmitted by the time the token comes back to it, we have

$$\frac{D}{r} = N[T_m + T_p + T_i]. \quad (2)$$

From (1) and (2), we get $M_b = Nr$. However, in a source-limited condition,

$$\frac{D}{r} \geq N[T_m + T_p + T_i], \quad (3)$$

which would mean that the interface unit is not ready with D bits by the time it gets back the token and thus has to pass on the unused token to the next station. Under identical conditions, the same situation would prevail at each station involving a delay of $(T_p + T_i)$. Let $[x]$, denoting the largest integer that is less than x, represent the number of times a station has to pass on an unused token following transmission of a packet and before getting ready with another D bits at its interface. x can be obtained from,

$$\frac{D}{r} = N[T_m + x(T_p + T_i)], \quad (4)$$

noting that (3) and (4) imply that $x \geq 1$.

(i) Blocked case:

Even when the next D data bits are ready and are formed into a packet, the interface unit cannot transmit the packet immediately. It will have to wait until it gets the token again before initiating transmission. Letting $X = [x] + 1$, the waiting time is given by $(X - x)N(T_p + T_i)$. If during this waiting time the source is prevented from sending further data bits (by locking a keyboard of an interactive terminal, for example) there would not be any need for buffering at the interface. Let us call this a "blocked" operation. As shown in Fig. 2a, X would then be a constant for each packet transmission cycle at a given station. We thus have,

$$\frac{D}{r} \leq N[T_m + X(T_p + T_i)], \quad (5)$$

and

$$M_b = \frac{D}{T_m + X(T_i + T_p)}. \quad (6)$$

Notice that X has a minimum value of 1, for which Eq. (6) becomes identical to Eq. (1). Also, using (5),

$$M_b \leq Nr, \quad (7)$$

which means that while Nr could be used for selecting R or vice versa, the actual allowed source load should be bounded by M_b to avoid excessive and accumulating delays. Proceeding similarly and using the basic relationships for token ring and CSMA/CD [2], the corresponding maximum mean throughput rates in bits/s, M_r and M_c respectively, can be shown to be

$$M_r = \frac{D}{T_m + X(T_i + T_p/N)} \quad (8)$$

and

$$M_c = \frac{D}{T_m + (2e - 1)(T_s + T_j) + XT_i}, \quad (9)$$

where, in Eq. (9), T_j is the transmission time for 48 bit collision detection reinforcing jamming pattern, T_s is the slot time equal to max[51.2 μs, $2T_p$], and T_i is the interface delay or interframe gap, whichever is higher. $2e$ collisions per successful transmission of each packet are assumed [2]. In Eq. (8) for token ring, notice that the propagation delay is T_p/N unlike in the token bus in which the entire value of T_p appears for each token transfer. When T_p is small, the difference in performance of the two schemes narrows substantially. Both M_r and M_c are also upper bounded by Nr as in (7).

(ii) Non-blocking case:

If each station is allowed to continue generation of source data bits instead of being blocked during the time

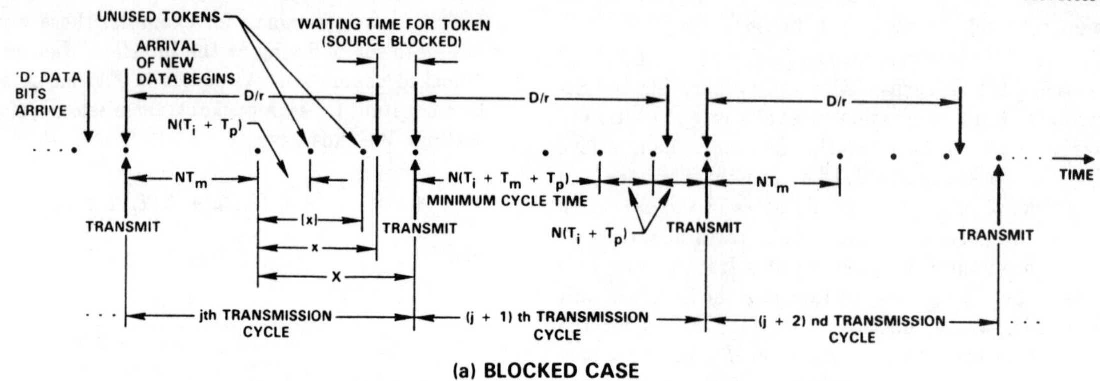

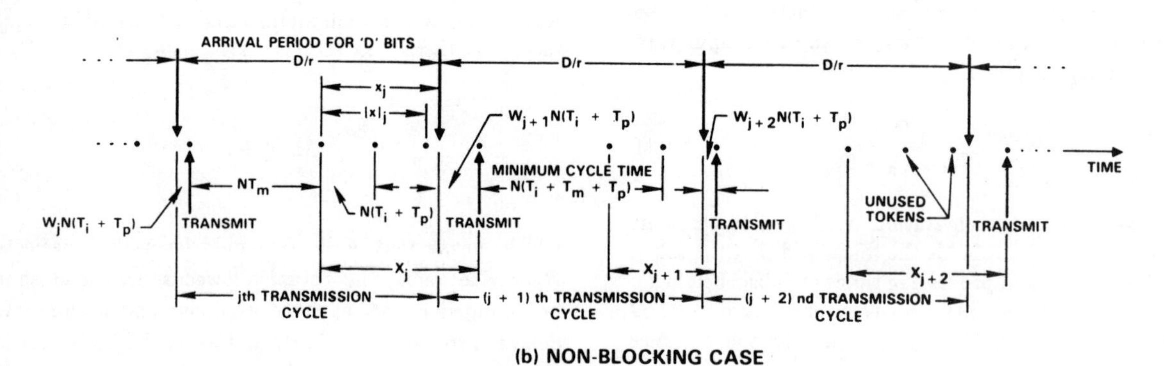

(b) NON-BLOCKING CASE

Fig. 2. Timing relationships between data arrival and transmission processes at the interface unit of a continuously active station (source). (a) source blocked (b) not blocked.

the previous packet is waiting for the token, we would need a buffer of at least D bits long at the interface. From Fig. 2b, it can be seen that if $w_j N(T_i + T_p)$ is the waiting time in the jth transmission cycle ($w_j < 1$ for all j), we can write

$$[x]_j N(T_i + T_p) = \frac{D}{r} - NT_m - [w_j + (1 - w_{j+1})]N(T_i + T_p) \tag{10}$$

where x is as defined in (4). If $(x - [x]) \geq (1/k)$ with $w_j = 0$, $k = 2,3,4\ldots$, $[x]$ would change by ± 1 once in every k successive transmission cycles. Considering that $[x]$ can only assume integral values and that $w_j < 1$ for all j, we can deduce from (10) that

$$-1 \leq \{[x]_{j+1} - [x]_j\} \leq 1, \tag{11}$$

$$w_j = w_{j+k}, \tag{12}$$

and

$$\left(\textstyle\sum_{l=j}^{j+k-1}[x]_l\right)N(T_i + T_p) = \frac{kD}{r} - (kNT_m) - kN(T_i + T_p), \tag{13}$$

for all j. Thus, for example, if $k = 2$, it follows from (11)-(13) that X assumes only two values X_1 and X_2 such that

$$(X_1 + X_2)N(T_i + T_p) = \frac{2D}{r} - 2NT_m, \tag{14}$$

with

$$X_1 = \frac{(D/r) - NT_m}{N(T_i + T_p)} - \frac{1}{2}, \tag{15}$$

and

$$X_2 = \frac{(D/r) - NT_m}{N(T_i + T_p)} + \frac{1}{2}, \tag{16}$$

or vice versa. X_1 and X_2 occur alternately in successive packet transmission cycles and differ by 1, except when $[x] = 0$, i.e., when the the system is not in the source-limited condition, for which case $X_1 = X_2 = 1$. It is clear from (11)-(14) that $\sum_{l=j}^{j+k-1} X_l$ is a constant for any k consecutive transmission cycles and (kD/r) data bits would be transferred during that time. Thus, using (13), and substituting kD, kT_m, and $\sum_{l=j}^{j+k-1} X_l$ in place of D, T_m, and X, respectively, in Eqs. (6), (8), and (9), we get the maximum mean throughput rate, M, for all k as

$$M = Nr \leq M^*, \tag{17}$$

with M and M^* having subscripts b, r, and c for token bus, token ring and CSMA/CD respectively. Notice that Eq. (17) is independent of k. The corresponding bounds M^* for the three schemes can be obtained from Eqs. (6), (8), and (9) using $X = 1$.

When only a single station is active, the token bus scheme will have lower potential throughput rate than the other two schemes since the rest of the $N-1$ stations have to pass on the unused token, causing a minimum delay of $N(T_i + T_p)$ for each packet. Expressions (1)-(9) can be modified using the formulae for the active single station case [2], considering the total maximum message rate as r. When a LAN is designed to carry the total message load when all stations are active, it would certainly be able to carry the message load when only one station is active. In the next section, we will consider only the worst congestion case, which is more important from the point of view of understanding the capability limits of a LAN.

NUMERICAL RESULTS

To illustrate the impact of the interaction of various network parameters on the maximum mean throughput rate, M, some numerical results are presented in Figs. 3-5. The number of overhead bits per data packet is assumed to be 96 bits. Values of various other parameters are indicated in the figures. Figure 3 gives M as a function of the LAN transmission rate R. The dotted curves correspond to the case $X = 1$, which indicates the throughput potential of the respective LANs. When the total maximum message load is held at 10 Mbits/s, token ring and token bus enter the source-limited region after crossing the minimum required R, which are about 11 and 12.5 Mbits/s, respectively. In this region, $M = Nr$ for the non-blocked case. However, for the blocked case, the throughput $M \leq Nr$ exhibits a series of ramps that have progressively decreasing slopes, with the steps occurring whenever x just exceeds integral values. For CSMA/CD, the throughput curve is far below the net offered load, indicating its inability to carry the load even when R is 20 Mbits/s. In a token passing ring, though the token transfer time is expected to be only one bit, data manipulation within the interface could involve significant delays [4]. For this reason, an interface delay of 10 μs is used in this example for the token ring.

Figures 4 and 5 show the effect of propagation delay and interface delay, respectively, on the maximum mean throughput for a fixed LAN transmission rate of 10 Mbits/s. The results are shown at two different total maximum source loads, such that the nature of variation

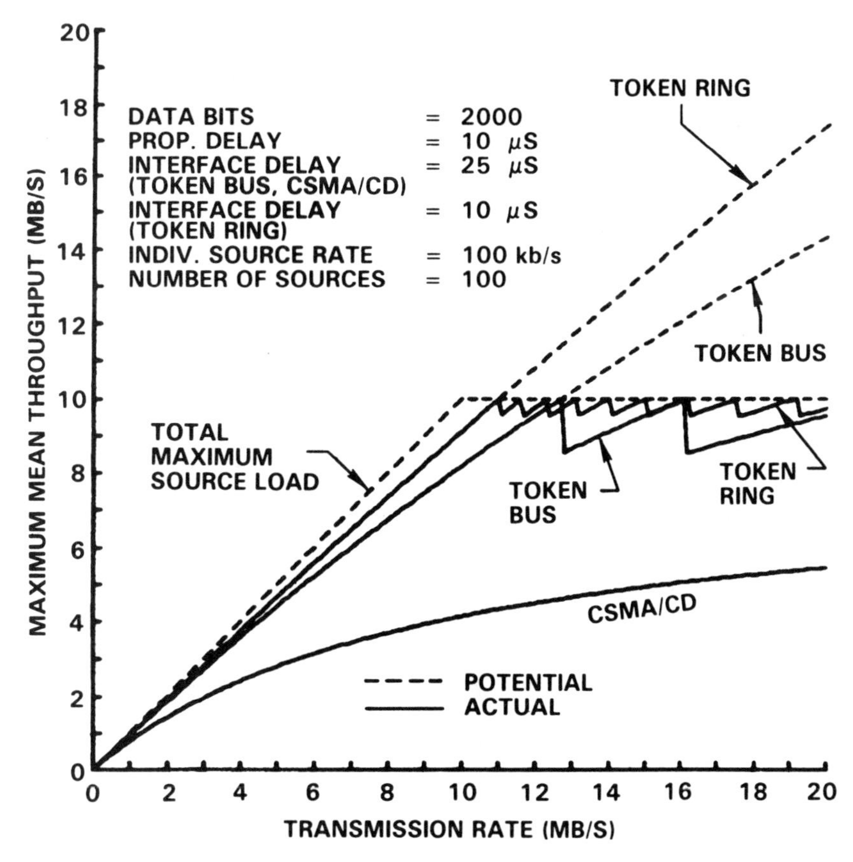

Fig. 3. Maximum mean throughput rate, M, as a function of the LAN transmission rate, R.

in the source-limited region can be seen for CSMA/CD also. For all the three schemes, the step sizes of ramps increase with increase in propagation delay and interface delay and decrease for lower total message rates. Token ring exhibits the smallest step size at low interface and propagation delays, but at higher interface delays all the three schemes have comparable step sizes. However, at high propagation delays, as is to be expected, token ring is the least affected. In Figs. 4 and 5, unlike in Fig. 3 (variation with R), the ramps have negative slopes and the steps occur when the decreasing values of x just take on integral values. Thus, in the source-limited region, Nr is only a design tool for the blocked case, with the actual allowable maximum source load being $M \leq Nr$ (from the ramps), unlike for the non-blocking case for which $M = Nr$. In the protocol-limited region, $M = M^*$ for both blocked and non-blocked cases. By providing an additional buffer (other than that required for processing the earlier D data bits) of length $N(T_i + T_p)$ at the interface, blocking and hence the throughput reduction as depicted by the ramps, can be avoided. Though attention in this analysis is only on deriving the maximum mean throughput rates, a similar phenomenon is also to be expected under actual dynamic message conditions, since most networks are likely to operate under source-limited regions. This could possibly explain part of the observed discrepancy between the predicted and measured performance of a token passing ring [4]. Analytical treatment of the interactions of various parameters under dynamic loading conditions (unlike the extreme conditions considered in this paper) would be quite complex. Simulation and experimental measurements seem to be more desirable approaches.

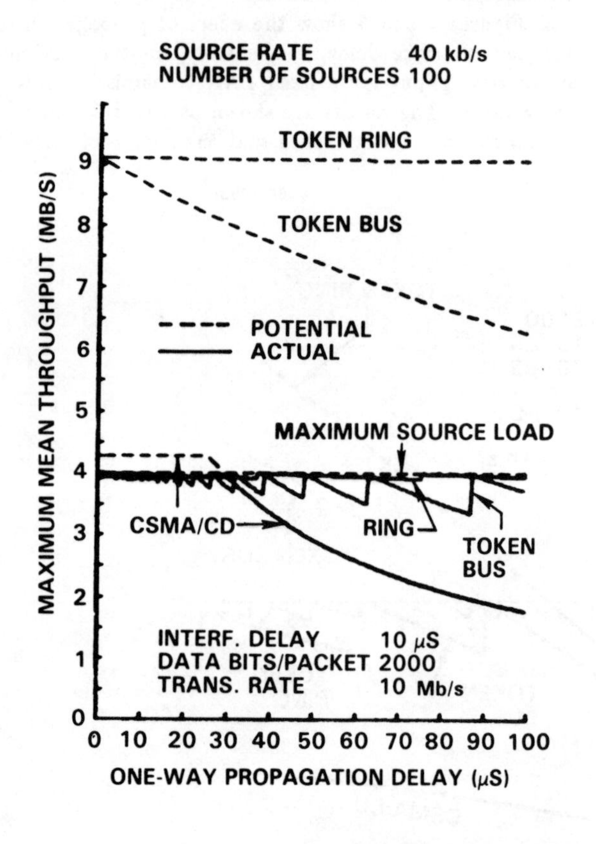

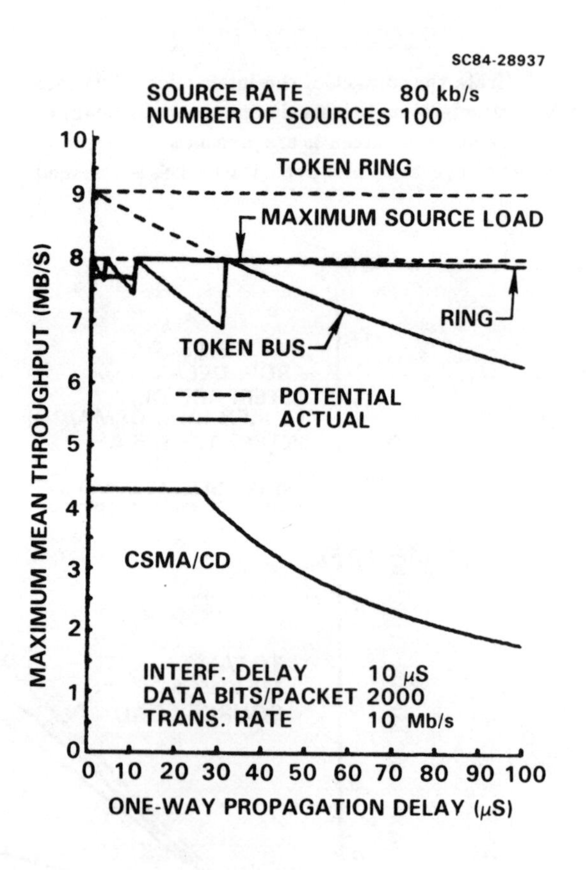

Fig. 4. Effect of propagation delay on the maximum mean throughput rate, M, for a fixed LAN transmission rate, R, of 10 Mb/s, under protocol-limited (dashed curves) and source-limited (solid curves) conditions.

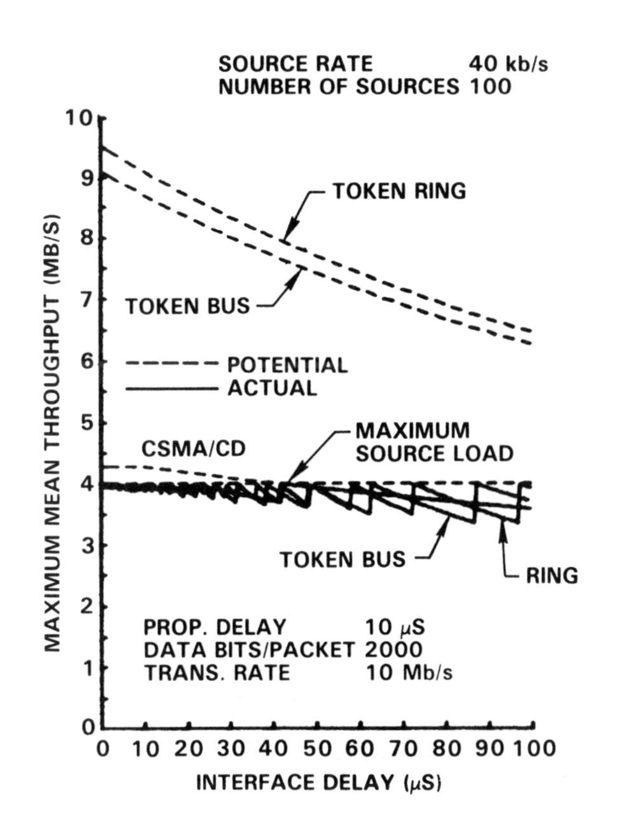

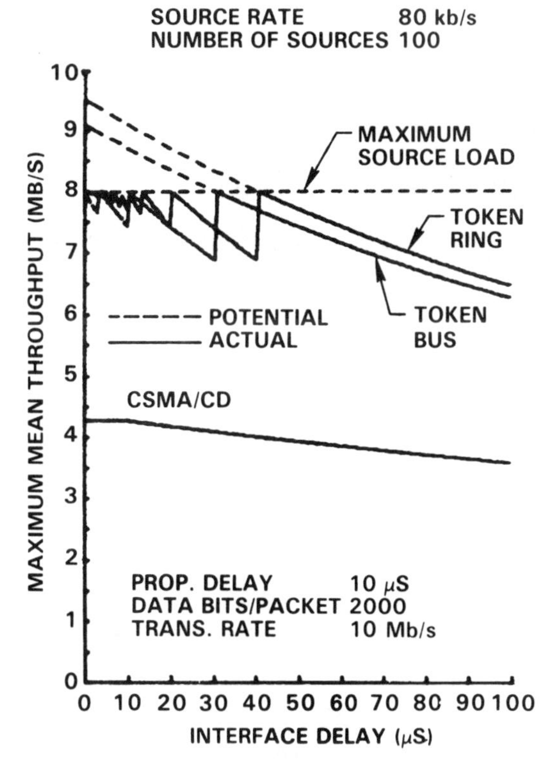

Fig. 5. Effect of interface delay on the maximum mean throughput rate, M, for a fixed LAN transmission rate, R, of 10 Mb/s, under protocol-limited (dashed curves) and source-limited (solid curves) conditions.

CONCLUSIONS

Lack of synchronism between allowed transmission times and availability of messages can reduce the maximum mean throughput in a source-limited regime with a specified maximum total source message load. The extent of reduction depends on the actual values of such parameters as individual source rate, propagation delay, interface delay, LAN transmission rate, and the protocol. Thus, actual allowable total maximum message rates will have to be lower than the design values used in generating the throughput curves. This reduction in throughput could be avoided by adding a buffer at the protocol interface.

REFERENCES

[1]. E. Arthurs *et al*, IEEE Project 802 Local Area Network Standards: Traffic-Handling Characteristics Committee Report, Working Draft, IEEE Computer Society, Silver Spring, Md., June 1982.

[2]. B. W. Stuck, "Calculating The Maximum Mean Data Rate in Local Area Networks," IEEE Computer, pp. 72-76, May 1983.

[3]. W. Stallings, "Local Network Performance," IEEE Communications Magazine, vol. 22, No. 2, pp. 27-36, February 1984.

[4]. J. Sventek, W. Greiman, M. O'Dell and A. Jansen, "Token Ring Local Area Networks: A Comparison of Experimental and Theoretical Performance," Symposium Record, IEEE/NBS Computer Networking Symposium, pp. 51-56, December 1983.

Performance issues in local-area networks

by W. Bux

This paper discusses several important performance problems in the design of local-area networks. The questions discussed relate to various aspects of architecture, design, and implementation: (1) the delay-throughput characteristics of the medium access protocols, (2) the performance of local-area networks on which a file server provides file storage and retrieval services to intelligent workstations, and (3) timing problems in local-area network adapters. Since the paper does not primarily address the performance analyst, it is descriptive in nature; analytic details are omitted in favor of a more intuitive explanation of the relevant effects.

The performance evaluation of local-area networks (LANs) is a multifaceted problem because of the complex interaction among a potentially large number of system components. Therefore, modeling of LANs needs to be performed at various levels, similar to the hierarchical approaches in the analysis of equally complex systems, such as wide-area data networks, telephone networks, or computer systems. This paper summarizes some of the performance analysis work done at the IBM Zurich Research Laboratory in the context of a LAN research project. It discusses various aspects of LAN architecture, design, and implementation. The paper does not primarily address the performance-evaluation specialist; its intention is, instead, to provide a sound intuitive understanding of performance problems that are peculiar to LANs. Theoretical details are omitted, but an extensive list of references to the appropriate literature is given in which the interested reader can find additional detailed information. For an introduction to LANs in general, the reader is referred to Clark,[1] Dixon,[2] or Kuemmerle.[3]

Reprinted with permission from *IBM Systems Journal*, Volume 23, Number 4, 1984, pages 351-374. Copyright © 1984 by International Business Machinery, Inc.

A basic category of LAN performance questions is related to the properties of the medium access protocol, i.e., its throughput-delay characteristics. Investigations of the access protocol can provide valuable insight into the overall efficiency of the mechanism, its sensitivity to essential parameters (transmission rate, cable length, number of stations, etc.), and other important properties, e.g., fairness of access. The second section of this paper is devoted to an overview of the performance characteristics of important LAN medium access protocols.

Models of the above type are suitable to assess the performance characteristics of different access mechanisms (which usually imply a certain network topology) and thus are helpful in finding a good network design. Such models, however, are not appropriate for determining application-oriented performance measures. If one is interested, for example, in the quality of a file service, higher-level protocols, i.e., Logical Link Control, Network, Transport, and Session protocols have to be modeled. Moreover, implementation choices, such as the user-system-to-network interface or buffer management, may have an important effect on the quality of service seen by a user. In the third section, we describe a model of this category, i.e., a file server providing file storage and retrieval services over a LAN to a set of intelligent workstations.

Figure 1 LAN architecture reference model

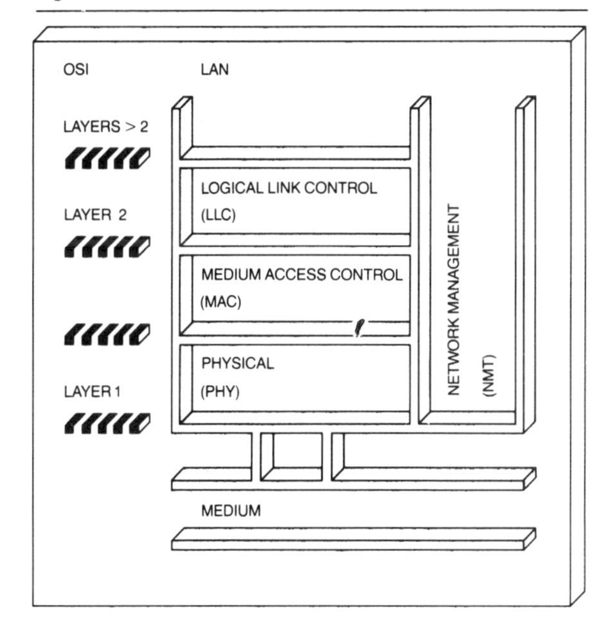

In order to answer detailed questions about the performance of specific components of a system, modeling at a rather deep level of detail may be necessary. A typical example is discussed in the fourth section, where a model of an adapter to a LAN is described. This model was used to study the timing problems associated with the reception of a continuous stream of information.

With these three categories of models, we cover a rather broad spectrum of performance issues related to LANS; nevertheless, there are various important topics we do not address in the present paper. Examples are problems related to the interconnection of local subnetworks, an area where flow and congestion-control problems arise. Furthermore, specific applications, for example, transmission of voice and images, raise challenging performance problems. Additional important areas are traffic measurement methodologies and the traffic-related aspects of network management and configuration.

Delay-throughput characteristics of medium access protocols

The groups concerned with LAN standardization, the Institute of Electrical and Electronics Engineers (IEEE) Project 802 and the European Computer Manufacturers Association (ECMA) TC24, have adopted a LAN architecture model that describes the relationship of LAN architecture and the Open Systems Interconnection (OSI) Reference Model.[3-14] As shown in Figure 1, the OSI data-link layer is split into two sublayers, the medium-dependent "Medium Access Control" (MAC) sublayer and the medium-independent "Logical Link Control" (LLC) sublayer. Peculiarities of the various local-network techniques are thus restricted to the medium, the physical layer, and the MAC sublayer. Consequently, the quality of service at the MAC-to-LLC interface differs between different local-area networks. An important aspect of this service is the delay-throughput characteristic, which will be treated in this section.

We focus on the discussion of the three methods that have been standardized: Carrier-Sense Multiple-Access with Collision Detection (CSMA/CD), token ring, and token bus.[5-9,11-13]

CSMA/CD. Carrier-sense multiple-access with collision detection can be viewed as the offspring of CSMA methods developed for broadcast systems, mainly ground-radio packet-switching systems. Immediate detection of collisions is difficult in radio systems, whereas a rather simple collision-detection technique can be employed on bus systems, at least, if baseband transmission is used. Collision detection helps to improve performance in a short-delay environment. CSMA/CD was first described in Reference 15 as the access protocol of Ethernet.[16] In the meantime, ECMA and IEEE Project 802 have produced standards specifying a CSMA/CD-based local-area network.

The following brief description of the CSMA/CD protocol follows the specification in the existing standards.[5-7,11]

Medium access protocol. The protocol can conceptually be divided into a transmission and a reception part.

In the transmission part, when a station has a frame ready for transmission, it monitors the cable to determine whether any transmissions take place. When the medium is found utilized, transmission is deferred. When the medium is clear, frame transmission is initiated (after a short interframe delay, e.g., 9.6 microseconds).

If multiple stations attempt to transmit at the same time, interference can occur (see Figure 2). Overlap of different transmissions is called a collision. In this case, each transmitting station enforces the collision

Figure 2 CSMA/CD: example of operation (from Ref. 21) ©1981 IEEE

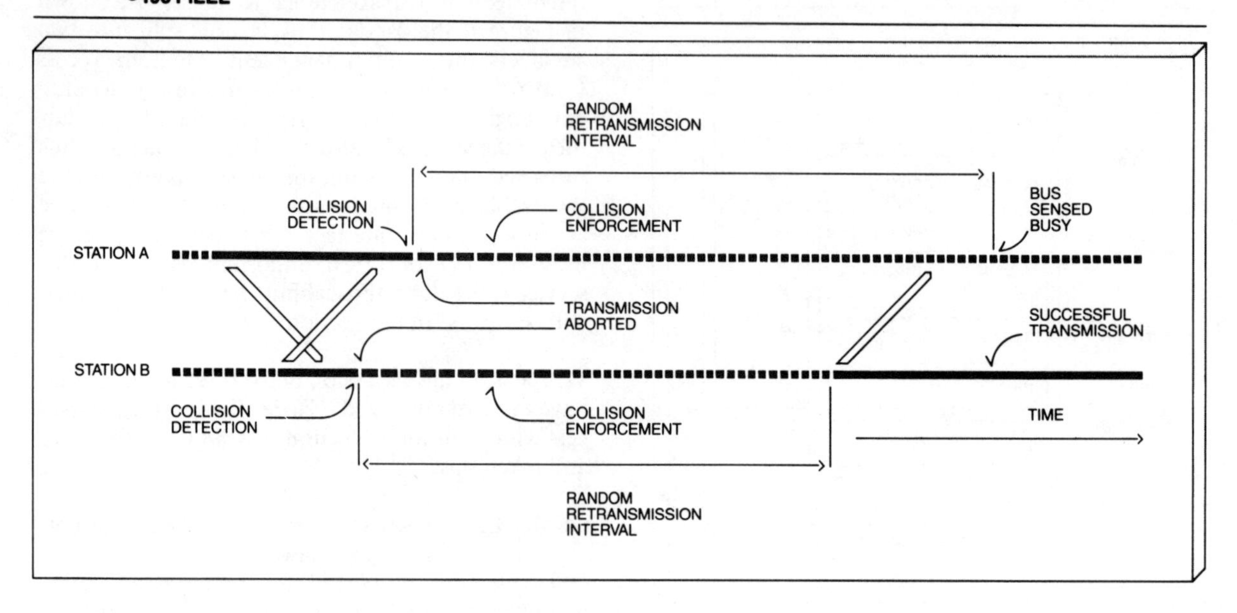

by transmitting a bit sequence called the jam signal. This ensures that the duration of the collision is sufficient to be noticed by all other stations involved in the collision. Then stations schedule a retransmission attempt for a randomly selected time in the future. Retransmission is attempted repeatedly in case of subsequent collisions. Repeated collisions indicate a heavily utilized medium; therefore stations adjust their retransmission activity to the traffic load perceived. This is accomplished by expanding the mean of the random retransmission time on each retransmission attempt.

The scheduling of the retransmissions is determined by a process called "truncated binary exponential backoff." Retransmission times are an integral multiple of the so-called slot time. The slot time must be equal to or greater than the maximum round-trip signal propagation time of the system. For the 10-million-bit-per-second baseband CSMA/CD system, a slot time of 51.2 microseconds has been standardized. The number of slot times to be delayed before the nth retransmission attempt is taken from a discrete distribution that assumes all integer values between 0 and 2^n with equal probability. If ten retransmissions of the same frame fail, the attempt is abandoned, and an error is reported.

The CSMA/CD access mechanism requires transmission of frames of a minimum length. If the frame size is less than the minimum required, a transmitting station must append extra, so-called "pad" bits after the end of the LLC-supplied data. Standardized minimum frame length for a CSMA/CD system with a baseband of 10 million bits per second is 512 bits.

In the reception part, all active stations synchronize with the preamble of an incoming frame and then decode the received signal. The destination-address field of the frame is checked to decide whether the frame should be received by this station. If so, the relevant parts of the frame are copied. The station also checks the validity of the received frame by inspecting the frame check sequence and proper octet-boundary alignment.

Performance characteristics. The performance of CSMA and CSMA/CD systems has formed the subject of numerous studies. The groundwork for the understanding of the performance properties of CSMA was laid in References 17 and 18. CSMA/CD performance has been studied in References 15 and 19 through 23 for different variants of the access principle. To provide a basic understanding of the delay-throughput characteristic of the standard CSMA/CD protocol, an analysis based on the work by Lam[22] appears attractive because the approach is rather straightforward, the underlying assumptions are close to the standardized CSMA/CD protocol, and the results are simple to evaluate numerically.

Figure 3 CSMA/CD delay-throughput characteristic (exponentially distributed information-field lengths)

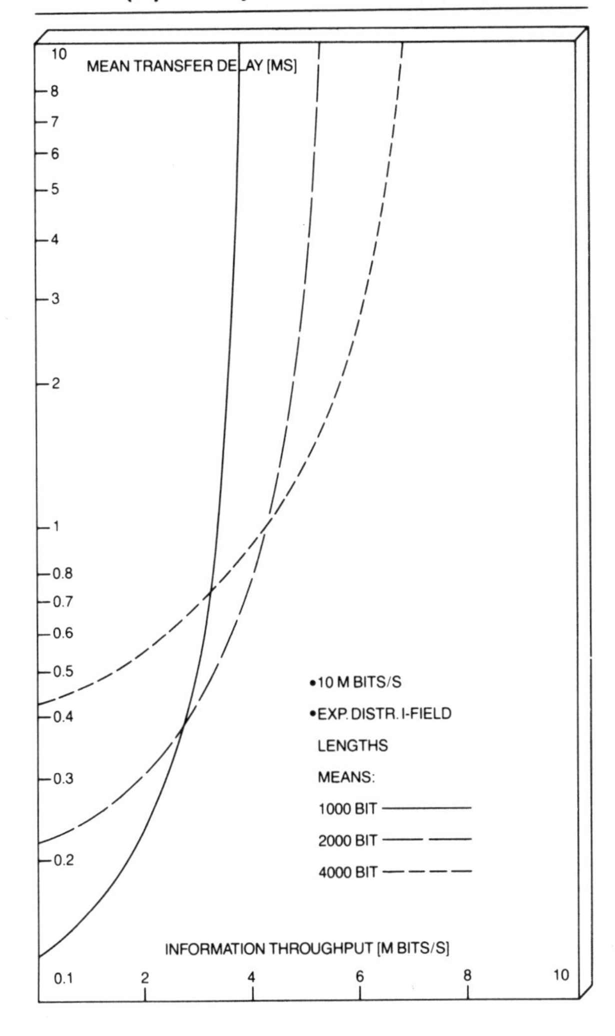

The assumptions underlying the analysis in Lam[22] are as follows. The traffic offered to the network is a Poisson process with a constant and state-independent arrival rate. Each station is allowed to store at most one frame at a time. The generation of a new frame is equivalent to increasing by one the number of stations ready to transmit a frame. Frame transmission times are generally distributed.

The following assumptions are made regarding the medium access protocol: (1) Following a successful transmission, all ready stations transmit within the next slot. (2) Following a collision, stations use an adaptive retransmission algorithm in such a way that the probability of a successful transmission within any of the slots subsequent to a collision is constant and equal to $1/e$ (= 0.368). For a large number of stations, this assumption is well justified.[15-22] (3) Operation is assumed to be slotted in time, i.e., transmission attempts are made only at the beginning of a slot.

Under the above assumptions, the mean queuing delay of the frames was determined in Lam.[22] The examples shown below have been computed with the aid of this solution; however, we modified the analysis in the following three points:

1. It has been assumed in Lam[22] that after every successful transmission, a time interval equal to the end-to-end signal propagation time expires before stations sense end-of-carrier and start to transmit. This represents a slightly pessimistic view of the operation as described in the previous subsubsection. For our results, we assumed that end of transmission is detected with zero delay by all stations.
2. A consequence of assuming a slotted channel is that, even if the channel utilization approaches zero, frames have to wait for half a slot length on the average. Such a delay, of course, does not occur on a nonslotted system, such as the one described in the last subsubsection. We therefore reduce the mean delay according to Lam[22] by half the slot length.
3. As pointed out above, the CSMA/CD access protocol requires a minimum frame length of at least the slot length measured in bits. This fact has not been taken into account in Lam.[22] However, it can be easily incorporated through an appropriate modification of the distribution function of the frame transmission times.

In Figures 3 to 5, we show basic results for delay and throughput of CSMA/CD systems. As parameters for these examples, the values standardized for the 10-million-bit-per-second baseband CSMA/CD system have been used.[5-7,11]

Figure 3 shows the mean transfer delay of the transmitted frames as a function of the information throughput. The frame transfer delay is the time from the generation of a frame until its successful reception at the receiver. The information throughput is defined as the number of bits contained in the LLC-Information field of the frames transmitted per unit time. An exponential distribution for the information-field lengths is assumed. As described above, padding bits are added when the frame length is shorter than the minimum required. We observe from the figure that the delay-throughput characteristic depends strongly on the mean length of the information field. The shorter the frame length, the smaller the delay at small throughput values, but also the smaller the maximum throughput and hence the steeper the increase of the delay curves. The reason for this behavior is that with a decreasing ratio of frame transmission time to slot length, the protocol overhead increases significantly in terms of the fraction of time lost for collisions and their resolution.

In Figure 4, the behavior of the same system, however, for constant information-field lengths of 1000, 2000, and 4000 bits is shown. It can be seen that the delays are smaller than for the exponential distribution. However, the general tendency is the same, in particular, the location of the vertical asymptotes; i.e., the maximum throughput is very insensitive to the information-field length distribution. Generally, the type of this distribution can have an impact on the maximum throughput because of the minimum frame-length requirement. As comparison of Figures 3 and 4 shows, this impact is relatively small for the information-field lengths considered.

How the maximum throughput depends on the transmission speed, given a slot length equal to the standardized value of 51.2 microseconds, is shown in Figure 5. For the different values of the mean information-field length, an area for the maximum throughput is indicated in this figure. The upper and lower boundaries of these areas are determined by two different considerations regarding the situation in the first slot following a successful transmission. In the above-described approach to determine the mean delays, a constant, state-independent frame arrival rate has been assumed. If, under this assumption, the traffic load reaches the system capacity, the probability of a collision after a successful transmission will approach one. As described above, the probability of a successful transmission in one of the subsequent slots is equal to $1/e$. Under this assumption, the lower bound of the maximum throughput regions in Figure 5 has been determined.

A more optimistic assumption is that in an overload case, the probability of a successful transmission in the first slot after a successful transmission is equal to $1/e$. Under this assumption, the average time between subsequent successful transmissions is one slot length shorter than for the more pessimistic assumption first described. The optimistic assump-

Figure 4 CSMA/CD delay-throughput characteristic (constant information-field length)

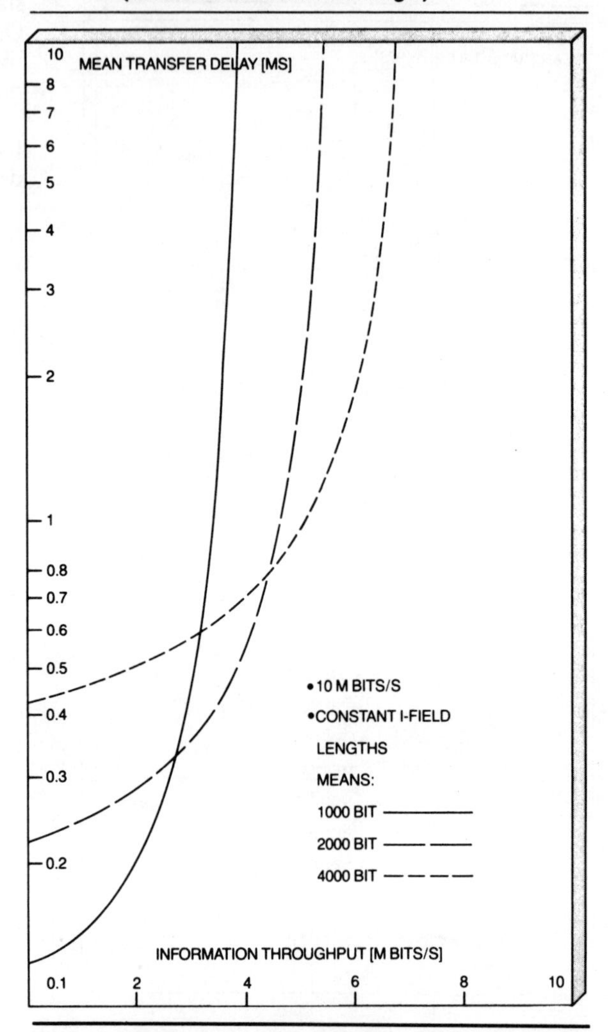

Figure 5 CSMA/CD maximum information throughput versus transmission rate for 51.2-microsecond slot length

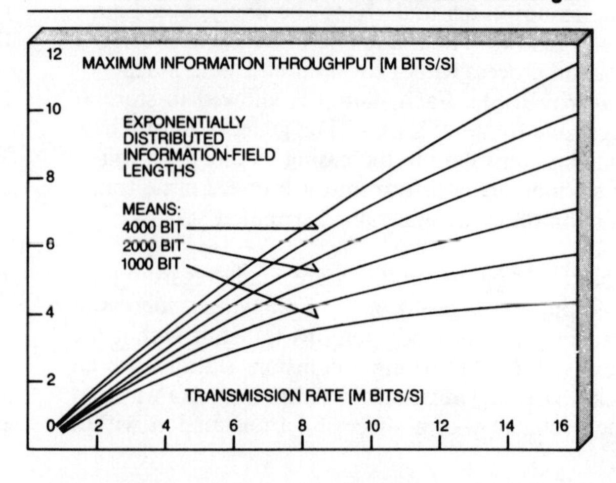

Figure 6 Token-ring queuing model (from Ref. 32, reprinted with permission of North-Holland Publishing Company)

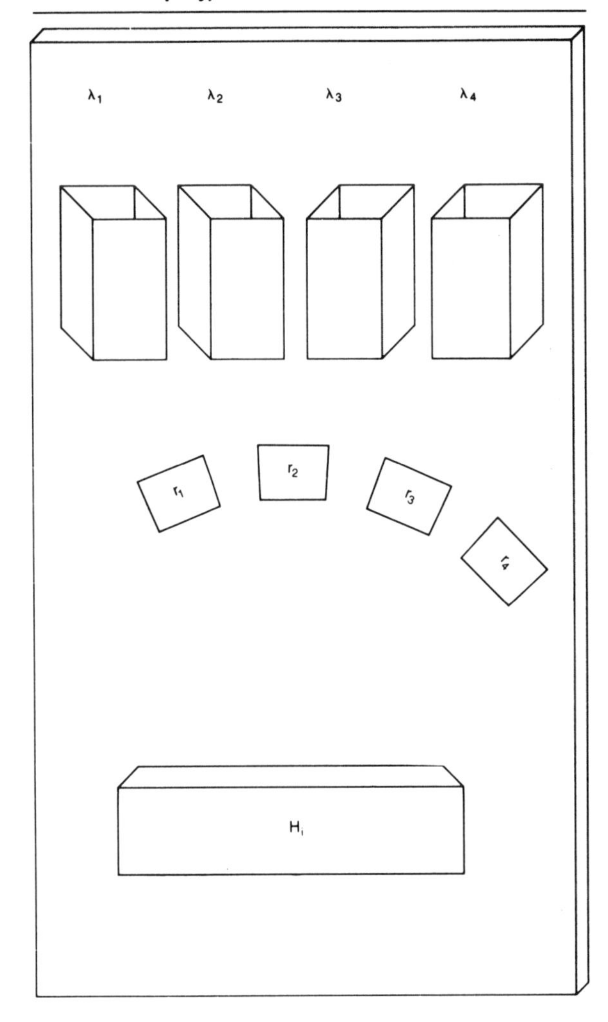

tion underlies the analysis given by Metcalfe and Boggs.[15] This solution has been used to determine the upper bound of the shaded areas in Figure 5. It can be seen that, even under the optimistic assumption, the efficiency of the CSMA/CD protocol decreases significantly with increasing speed, especially in the case of a 1000-bit mean information-field length. Measurements performed on an Ethernet showed a mean frame length of 976 bits.[24]

Token ring. Compared to the other LAN techniques, token rings have a relatively long technical history. Experimental systems showed the feasibility of the ring technique long before alternative methods, e.g., CSMA/CD or token-passing bus systems, were considered.[25-27] However, because of a lack of applications, token rings were not implemented on a broad basis. With the advent of local-area networks, the token-ring principle was reconsidered and found to provide an attractive solution because of its favorable attributes regarding wiring, transmission technology, performance, and the potential for low-cost implementation.[1-3,27-30] Moreover, recent work showed that what had been considered a potential problem of token rings, namely, lack of reliability, can be overcome by a suitable access protocol and an appropriate wiring strategy.[28,29] The above arguments led the standards groups concerned with LAN standardization to consider token rings as one of the candidates for a LAN standard.

The following description is based on the specification of the token-ring operation given in the existing IEEE-802 and ECMA standards.[8,13]

Medium access protocol. A token ring consists of a set of stations serially connected by a transmission medium, e.g., twisted-pair cable. Information is transferred sequentially from one active station to the next. A given station (the one having access to the medium) transfers information onto the ring. All other stations repeat each bit received. The addressed destination station copies the information as it passes. Finally, the station which transmitted the information removes it from the ring.

A station gains the right to transmit when it detects a token passing on the medium. The token is a control signal comprised of a unique signaling sequence that circulates on the medium following each information transfer. Any station, upon detection of a token, may capture the token by modifying it to a start-of-frame sequence, and then appends appropriate control and address fields, the LLC-supplied data, the frame check sequence, and the frame-ending delimiter. On completion of its information transfer and after appropriate checking for proper operation, the station generates a new token which provides other stations the opportunity to gain access to the ring.

A token-holding timer controls the length of time a station may occupy the medium before passing the token.

Multiple levels of priority can be provided on a token ring through an efficient priority mechanism. This mechanism is based on the principle described in Bux et al.[28] whereby higher-priority stations can interrupt the progression of lower-priority tokens and frames by making "reservations" in passing frames. This scheme requires that stations do not issue a new token before having received back the header of their transmitted frame. This so-called "single-token" rule[21,28] also leads to improved reliability of the access protocol because each transmitting station can check the proper functioning of the ring at the beginning of its transmission.

Performance characteristics. The basic operation of a token ring can be described by a performance model as shown in Figure 6. The active stations are represented by their transmit queues. These queues are serviced in a cyclic manner symbolized by the rotating switch that stands for the token.

The time needed to pass the token from station i to station $(i + 1)$ is modeled by a constant delay r_i. On an actual ring, the delay r_i corresponds to the propagation delay of the signals between stations i and $(i + 1)$ (approximately five microseconds per km cable) plus the latency caused within station i by the repeater and by actions such as alteration of the token bit. The station latency is usually in the order of one bit time.

In token rings, the sender is responsible for removing the frames it transmitted from the ring. Therefore, the location of frame destinations on the ring relative to the location of the sender does not affect the ring performance.

Queuing models applicable to token rings have been extensively studied, primarily in the context of polling systems.[20,21,27,31–42] However, analytic results, and especially those that lend themselves to numerical evaluation, are scarce. This is particularly true for models in which the transmission time of a station per access opportunity is limited through a bound on either the token-holding time or the number of frames to be transmitted per token.

Subsequently, we discuss some fundamental results for the token-ring delay-throughput characteristic obtained through simulation and analysis (where applicable).

As pointed out above, a fundamental performance characteristic of any LAN medium access protocol is its sensitivity to transmission speed and distance. Figures 7 and 8 show how token rings perform for various speeds and distances. Figure 7 shows the

Figure 7 Token-ring delay-throughput characteristic (four-million-bit-per-second transmission rate; symmetrical traffic pattern)

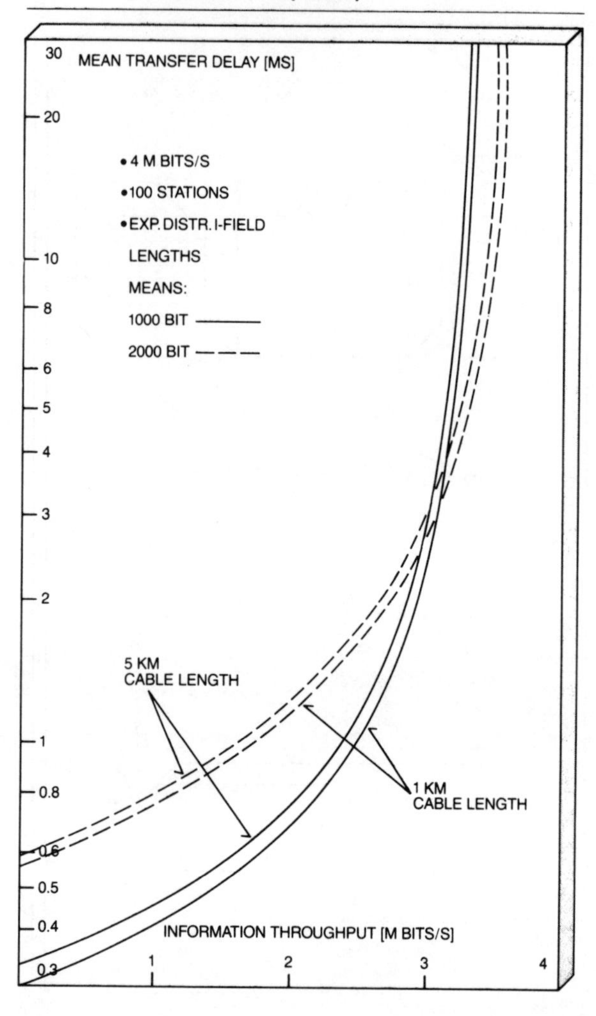

mean frame transfer delay as a function of the information throughput for four-million-bit-per-second rings with one- and five-kilometer (km) cable lengths. It is assumed that all 100 stations generate the same amount of traffic; other traffic patterns lead to very similar results for the delay averaged over all stations. A further assumption is that frames are generated according to Poisson processes. Stations follow the single-token rule described in the last subsubsection; i.e., they wait until the header of their frame has returned before generating a new token. Only one frame per access opportunity can be transmitted. It can be seen that increasing the ring length from one to five km has virtually no impact on the delay-throughput characteristic.

Figure 8 Token-ring delay-throughput characteristic (16-million-bit-per-second transmission rate; symmetrical traffic pattern)

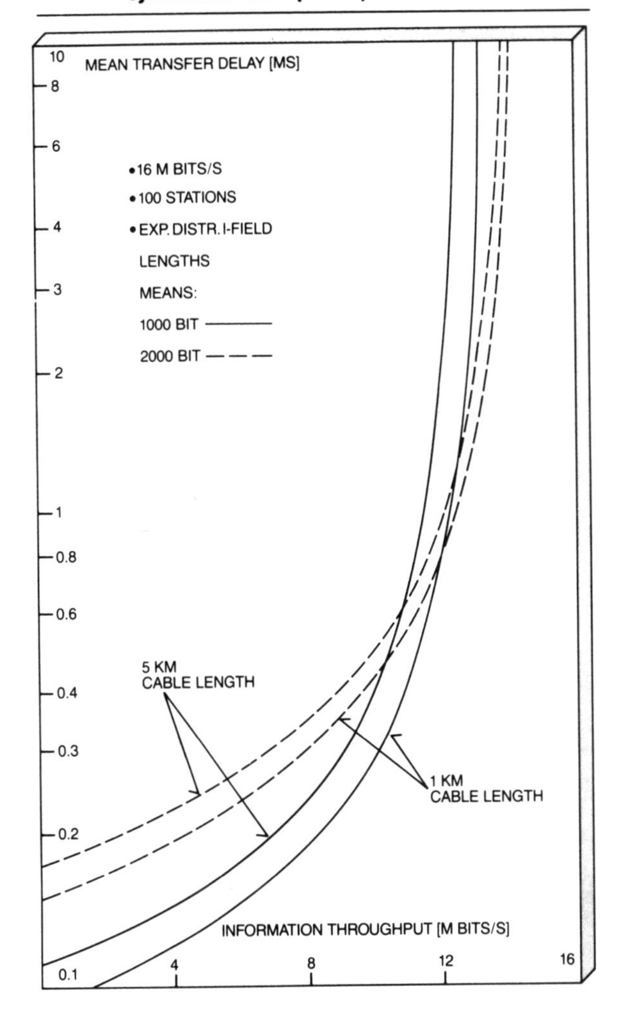

Under the same assumptions, except for a transmission rate of 16 million bits per second, Figure 8 shows the same performance measures as the previous one. Increasing the cable length from one to five km leads to more noticeable differences here, primarily because of the single-token rule; however, the overall effect is still minor.

Overall efficiency of an access protocol is the most basic performance property; a further important criterion is the quality of service given to individual stations, especially in case of unbalanced traffic situations. This service can differ significantly, depending on the rule defining the time a station is allowed to transmit per access opportunity. As mentioned in the last subsubsection, the standards specify the use of a token-holding timer that limits the time a station is allowed to transmit continuously. To demonstrate the impact of this timer, we subsequently consider two extreme cases, a very short timer, such that stations can only transmit one frame per token (Figure 9), and a very long timer, such that stations can always empty their transmit queues completely on each transmission opportunity (Figure 10).

For both examples, Poisson arrival processes have been assumed. However, the arriving data units are not single frames but entire messages, the lengths of which are distributed according to a hyperexponential distribution with a coefficient of variation equal to two. In cases where a message is longer than the maximum information-field length of a frame (256

Figure 9 Token-ring delay-throughput characteristic (one-million-bit-per-second transmission rate, asymmetrical traffic pattern, short token-holding time-out) (from W. Bux, F. Closs, K. Kuemmerle, H. Keller, and H. R. Mueller, "Architecture and Design of a Reliable Token-Ring Network," *IEEE Selected Areas in Communications* SAC-1, No. 5, 756–765 (November 1983). ©1983 IEEE

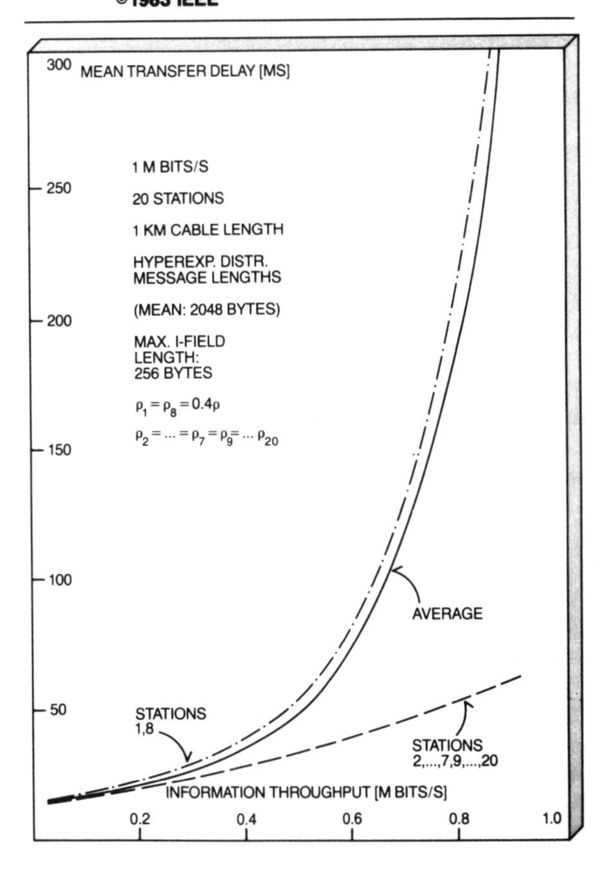

bytes), the message is segmented. In both examples, the assumed traffic pattern is very unbalanced: two of the 20 stations (Nos. 1 and 8) each generate 40 percent of the total traffic; each of the other 18 stations generates only 1.1 percent of the total traffic.

For the single-frame-per-token operation, Figure 9 shows the mean transfer delay of the messages (not frames!) as a function of the total information throughput. Of course, the delay averaged over all stations increases with increasing ring throughput. The same is true for the delay of the messages transmitted by the heavy-traffic stations 1 and 8. However, the delay experienced by the light-traffic stations remains rather small even for very high utilizations. In this sense, the token-passing protocol combined with a single-frame-per-token operation provides fair access to all users.

From Figure 10, it can be seen that the relationship of the delay experienced by light and heavy users is reversed when the token-holding time is long. Here, the mean message transfer delay of light-traffic stations is even higher than the one of heavy-traffic stations. This is due to the fact that messages generated at a heavy-traffic station have a relatively good chance that their station is holding the token and, in this case, are transmitted before frames waiting in other stations. These two examples demonstrate that the token-holding timer can be used to control the station-specific quality of service.

Figure 10 Token-ring delay-throughput characteristic (one-million-bit-per-second transmission rate, asymmetrical traffic pattern, long token-holding time-out)

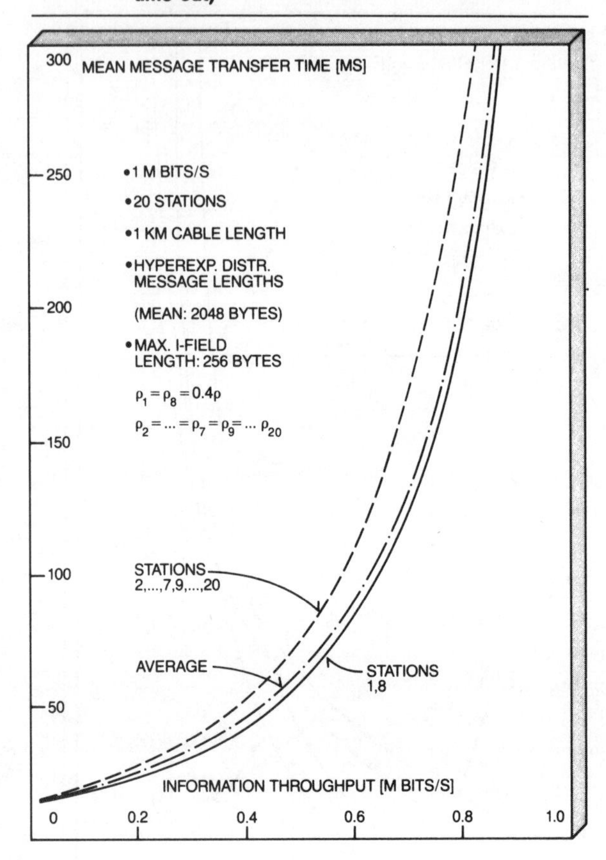

Token bus. The token-bus technique is the third method being considered by the LAN standards bodies. The intention behind developing this technique has been to combine attractive features of a bus topology (e.g., use of broadband transmission) with those of a controlled medium access protocol (e.g., good efficiency under high traffic load, speed-distance insensitivity, and fairness of access).

The subsequent description follows the specification of the token bus given in References 9 and 12.

Medium access protocol. The essence of the token-bus access method can be characterized as follows. A token controls the right to access the medium; the station that holds the token has momentary control over the medium. The token is passed among the active stations attached to the bus. As the token is passed, a logical ring is formed (see Figure 11). Since the bus topology does not impose any sequential ordering of the stations, the logical ring is defined by a sequence of station addresses.

Steady-state operation simply requires the sending of the token to a specific successor station when a station has finished transmitting. A more difficult task is establishing and maintaining the ring (initialization, station insertion in, or removal from, the logical ring). Each participating station knows the addresses of its predecessor and its successor. After a station has completed transmitting data frames, it passes the token to its successor by sending a special MAC control frame, called an "explicit token." The maximum transmission time of any station is controlled by a token-holding timer.

After having sent the token, the station monitors the bus to make sure that its successor has received the token and is active. If the sender detects a valid frame following the token, it will assume that its successor has the token and is transmitting. If the sender does not sense a valid frame from its successor, it must assess the state of the network and, if necessary, take appropriate recovery actions to re-establish the logical ring. Details about establishment and re-establishment of the logical ring are specified in References 9 and 12.

Conceptually, token passing on buses and rings is very similar.

The token-bus access method also allows defining of a priority mechanism, which is not further discussed here.

Performance characteristics. Conceptually, token passing on buses and rings is very similar; hence, the same type of performance model can be used to describe the two techniques. It is obvious, however, that the model parameters are rather different; this is particularly the case for the token-passing overhead. In a token ring, the time to pass the token from one station to the next consists of the signal propagation time between the two stations (approximately five microseconds per km cable) plus the delay caused within a station. As pointed out in the previous subsubsection, the latter delay can be kept as small as one bit time. In contrast to this, on a token bus, passing the token from a station to its successor requires the transmission of an explicit-token frame, which in the standard for the token bus is 152 bits long. To this the signal propagation delay between the two stations has to be added. The third component of the token-passing overhead is the reaction time of the station, i.e., the time a station needs from reception of a token until it has prepared either a token or a data frame for transmission.

In Figure 12, we show the delay-throughput characteristic of one-million-bit-per-second token-bus systems with 100 and 200 stations attached. Further assumptions are: two km cable length, exponentially distributed information-field lengths with means of 1000 and 2000 bits, and zero reaction (processing) delay in the stations. For this example, the traffic is assumed to be completely symmetrical; i.e., all stations generate the same amount of traffic. Furthermore, for this and the following example, a token-holding time is assumed that is sufficiently long for stations always to be able to completely empty their

Figure 11 **Token bus: logical ring on physical bus**

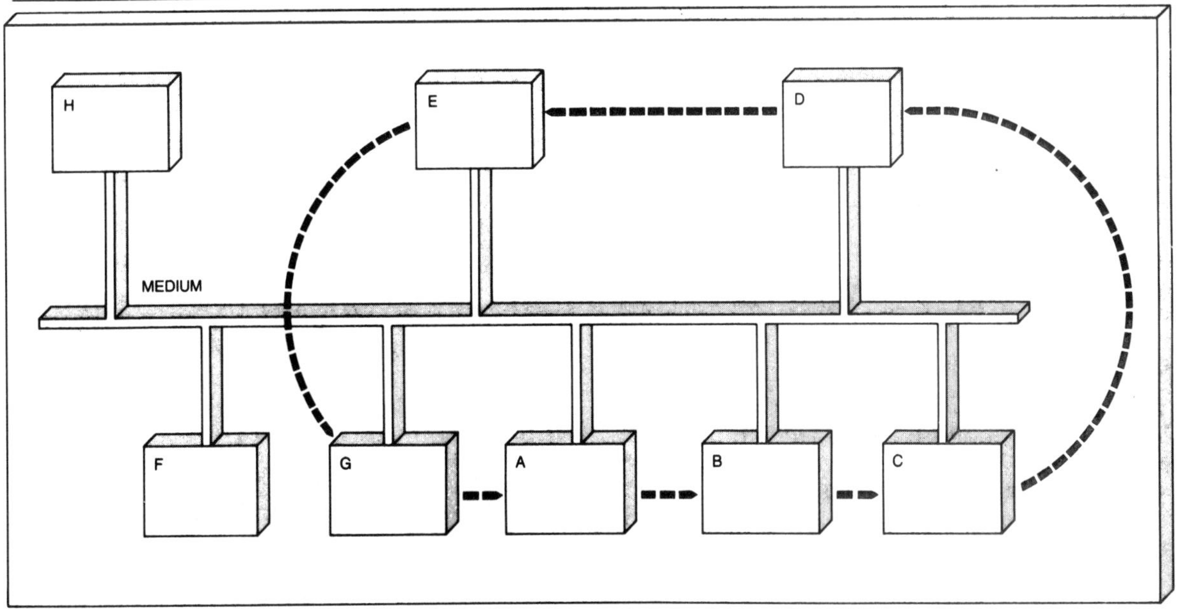

transmit queues at each transmission opportunity. The figure shows that the mean transfer delays are remarkably high compared with one and two milliseconds, respectively, the time it takes to transmit an information field of average length. This is due to the relatively large token-passing overhead of the token-bus technique.

As the next figure demonstrates, the token-passing overhead is reduced in case of asymmetric traffic. The parameters assumed for Figure 13 are a rate of five million bits per second (which is another one of the standardized speeds), a two-km cable length, 100 stations, and exponentially distributed information-field lengths with a mean of 1000 bits. Three different traffic patterns are assumed: (1) a totally symmetrical situation, (2) a situation where two stations each generate 40 percent of the total traffic, the rest being generated by the other stations in equal amounts, and (3) a situation with one station generating 80 percent of the traffic while again the rest is generated by the other stations. For each of these traffic patterns, the figure shows the mean frame transfer delay averaged over all stations as a function of the total ring information throughput. We observe that with increasing asymmetry of the traffic, the average delay decreases slightly, because—per frame transmission—the overhead to forward the token is smaller. It should be noted, however, that this is only true

Figure 12 **Token-bus delay-throughput characteristic (one-million-bit-per-second transmission rate, symmetrical traffic pattern)**

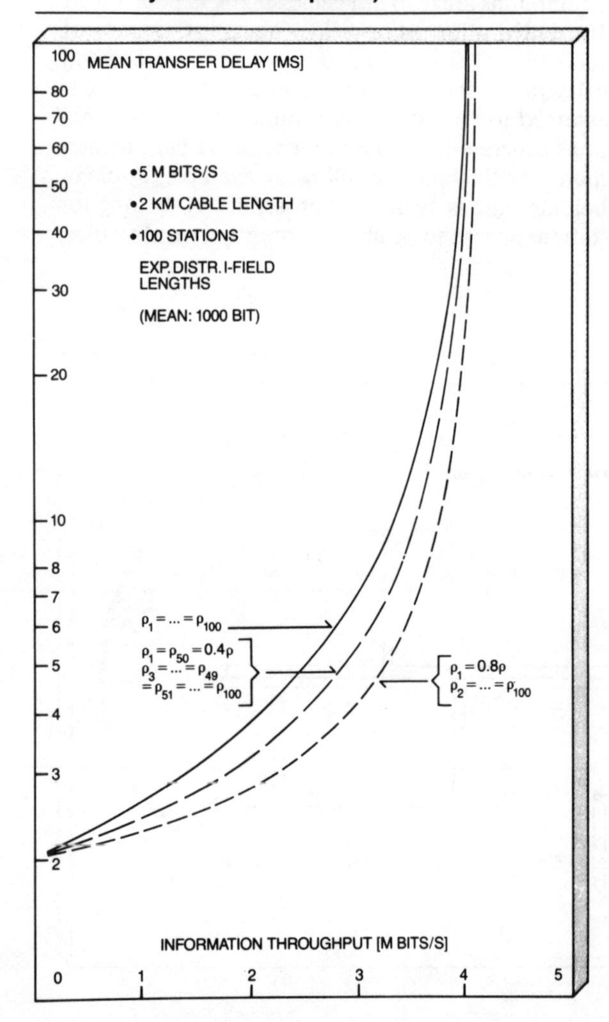

Figure 13 **Token-bus delay-throughput characteristic (mean transfer delay averaged over all stations for different symmetrical and asymmetrical traffic patterns)**

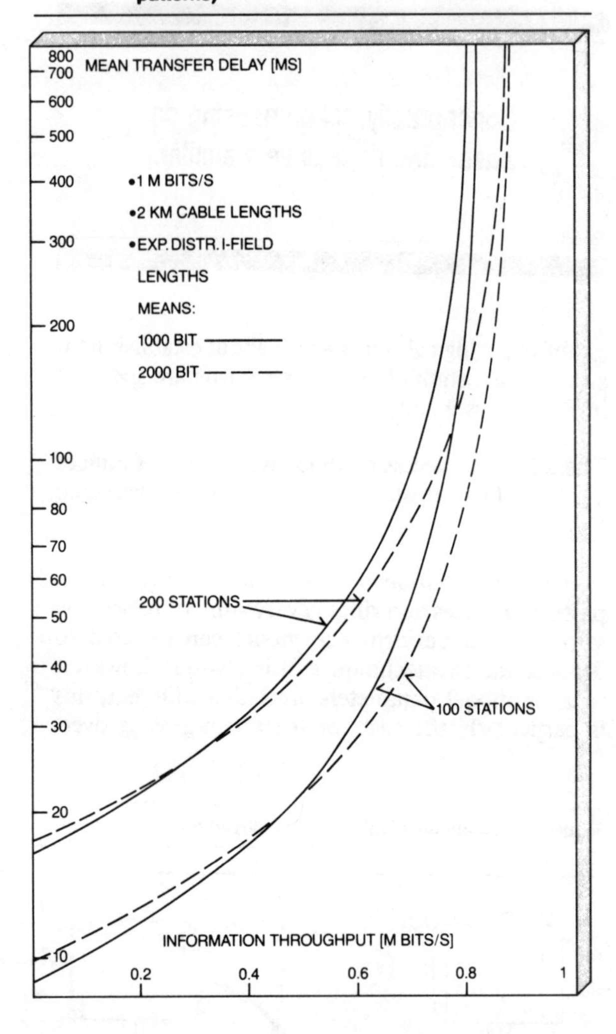

when the token-holding time-out is sufficiently long; for a short token-holding time-out, the effect is reversed.

Other local network techniques. In addition to the three "standard" approaches discussed previously, various alternative LAN techniques have been developed and used. Among the most attractive techniques are slotted rings,[27,43] buffer-insertion rings,[27,44,45] buses with controlled-type access,[37,46–49] or buses employing a combination of random and controlled access.[37,49–53] Because of a lack of space, we cannot discuss these methods in detail; for the interested reader, we subsequently list references in which performance questions related to the above systems are discussed.

The performance of slotted rings is discussed in References 21, 31, 54 and 55. Analyses of buffer-insertion rings can be found in References 56 through 58. Controlled and hybrid-access schemes for buses have been analyzed in References 21, 49, and 59 through 64.

End-to-end flow and error control

Introduction. Models of the type discussed in the previous section are useful in understanding the quality of service provided by the local network at the MAC-to-LLC interface. Apparently, the performance characteristics seen at this interface are not the ones experienced by a user at the application level. To determine application-oriented performance measures, additional levels of architecture need to be modeled, such as an end-system-to-end-system protocol providing means for flow and error control.

The need for flow control arises in cases of a speed mismatch between the communicating partners, limited buffer sizes in the end systems and/or network adapters, and applications where, e.g., one station provides a certain service simultaneously to multiple workstations.

Means to detect and recover from errors are needed for various reasons: (1) Data units can be corrupted by transmission errors; (2) Frames may be lost because of buffer overflow in the receiving end system and/or its adapter; (3) Timing problems in the receivers may cause loss of frames (see the following major section on LAN adapter design).

Protocols providing the functionality needed for flow and error control in LANs are, for example, Class 4 of the ISO/ECMA Transport Protocol,[65,66] or the Type 2 Logical Link Control protocol defined by the IEEE Project 802.[10] Depending on this choice, end-to-end flow and error control is performed in layers corresponding to either layers 4 or 2 of the OSI reference model.

In the next subsection, a scenario consisting of a file server and workstations attached to a local-area ring network is described. The subsection after that describes a model developed to study performance issues of such systems.[67] Results of this study are summarized in the subsequent subsection.

Flow control is implemented by a window mechanism.

Network operation. The configuration of the local-area network under consideration is shown in Figure 14. It consists of user systems (file server and workstations) attached to a token-ring network through ring adapters. Each adapter has a number of transmit/receive buffers. It also contains a processor whose major tasks are to control the data transfer between the ring and the transmit/receive buffers, to manage these buffers, and to control the interface to the user system.

File transfer is performed over a logical connection between the file server and the workstation. The file server can manage multiple connections simultaneously. The protocol under consideration is a subset of the IEEE 802.2 Type 2 Logical Link Control protocol.[10] It provides procedures for connection establishment, connection termination, flow control, and error recovery.

A file is transmitted as a series of Information (I-) frames. For the file transfer environment, information flow on a given connection is unidirectional; i.e., on one connection, I-frames are either sent from the file server to a workstation, or vice versa.

Flow control. Flow control is implemented by a window mechanism; i.e., a sender is permitted to

Figure 14 File-service scenario

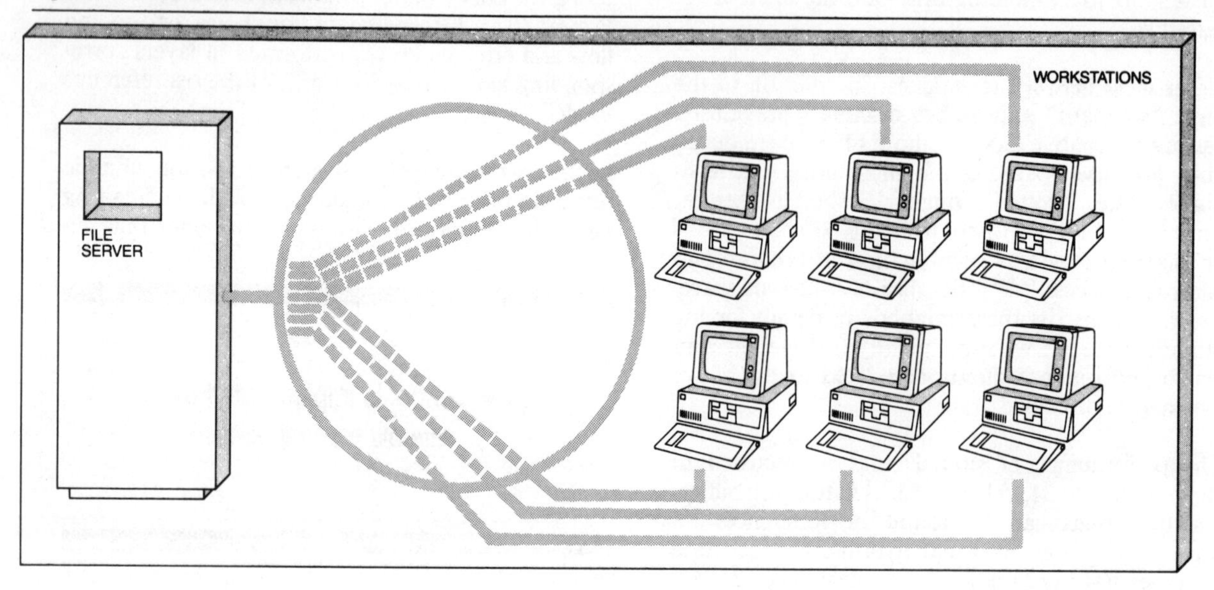

transmit up to W (the window size) I-frames without having to wait for an acknowledgment. The receiver uses Receive Ready (RR-) frames to acknowledge correctly received I-frames and to indicate to the sender that more I-frames can be transmitted.

Error recovery. Any I-frame received with an incorrect Frame Check Sequence (FCS) is discarded. If a received I-frame has a correct FCS, but its send sequence number is not equal to the one expected by the receiver, the receiver will return a Reject (REJ-) frame. The receiver then discards all I-frames until the expected I-frame has been correctly received. The sender, upon receiving a REJ-frame, retransmits I-frames starting with the sequence number received within the REJ-frame.

In addition to REJECT recovery, a time-out mechanism is used. At the instant of transmission of an I-frame, a timer will be started if it is not running already. When the sender receives an RR-frame, it restarts the timer if there are still unacknowledged I-frames outstanding.

When the timer expires, the station performs a "checkpointing" function by transmitting an RR-frame with a dedicated bit (the "P-bit") set to one. The receiver, upon receiving this frame, must return an RR-frame with the "F-bit" set to one. When this RR-frame has been received by the sender, it either proceeds with transmitting new I-frames or retransmits previous I-frames depending on the sequence number contained in the RR-frame received.

Simulation model. A simulation model employed to study the above scenario is illustrated in Figure 15 and subsequently described.[67]

Medium access protocol. The token-ring protocol for medium access is modeled by a multiqueue, single-server submodel with cyclic service (cf. the earlier section on performance characteristics of the token ring). A queue in this submodel represents the frames waiting in the transmit buffers of an adapter.

Ring adapter and system interface. The adapter transmit buffers contain frames to be transmitted onto the ring. The adapter receive buffers temporarily hold frames received from the ring until they can be transferred to the user system. When upon arrival of a frame no receive buffer in the adapter is available, the frame is lost and has to be recovered through the LLC protocol. Transmission errors are assumed to have negligible effect and are not included in the model. Furthermore, it is assumed that timing problems associated with the receive operation, such as the ones described in the next major section, do not exist here.

The adapter processor, together with the system interface, is modeled by a single server with two queues: the receive buffer queue in the adapter and

Figure 15 File-service performance model

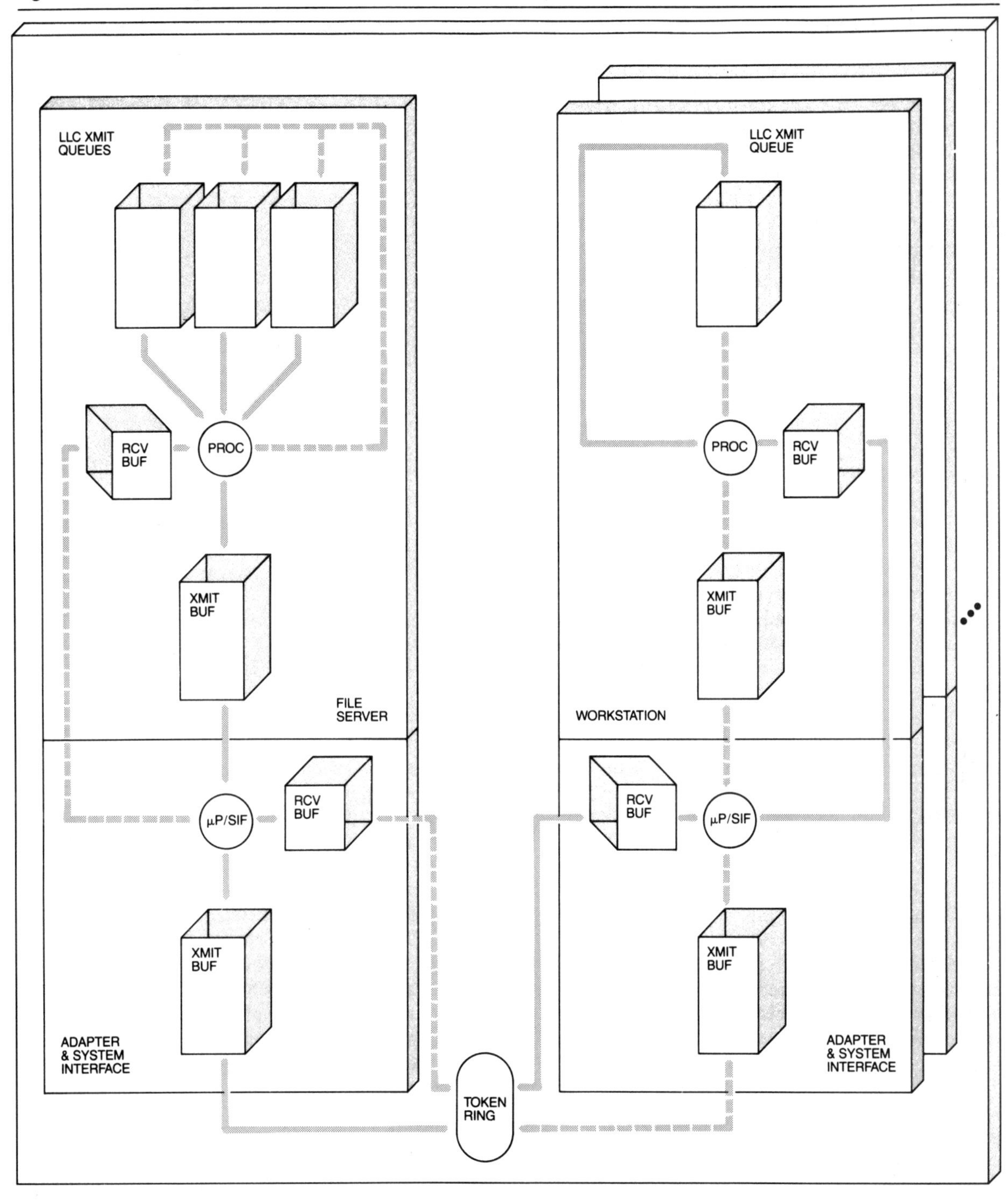

the transmit buffer queue in the user system (see Figure 15). The service time corresponds to the sum of the time to set up a transfer by the adapter processor and the data-transfer time across the system interface. The adapter processor handles frames in its receive buffer with nonpreemptive priority over those in the transmit buffer.

File server. The processor in the file server is modeled by a multiqueue, single-server model. One of the queues is the receive-buffer queue in the file server; the others are for the various connections, containing frames to be prepared for transmission to the workstations. The receive-buffer queue is given nonpreemptive priority over the transmit queues. Among the transmit queues, service is cyclic. Received I-frames are copied to the mass storage of the file server.

Workstations. From the modeling viewpoint, a workstation appears as a special case of a file server with only one file transfer.

It is assumed that both file server and workstations are always able to accept I-frames (i.e., remove them from the LLC receive buffers) and that all traffic sources always have a backlog of I-frames to be transmitted.

Frame lengths and buffer management. The length of I-frames is assumed to be constant and equal to the maximum frame length. This is motivated by our assumption of a permanent backlog of frames at the sources. Each frame is assumed to occupy a complete buffer in the user system or adapter. In the file server, separate sets of buffers are dedicated to the transmit and receive directions; both buffer sets are shared by all logical connections. Similarly, each adapter has two separate sets of transmit and receive buffers.

Results. The results subsequently presented are based on the following selection of parameter values: one million bits per second ring speed, two million bits per second effective system interface speed, 500 bytes constant I-frame length, and 20 microseconds set-up time at adapter processor. We shall refer to a logical connection for file transfer from file server to workstation as a "get-file transfer," and that from workstation to file server as a "put-file transfer." The scenario considered consists of a file server handling an equal number of get-file and put-file transfers. The mean time to process an I-frame (RR- or REJ-frame) at the file server is assumed to be 10 milliseconds (2 milliseconds). The corresponding values for a workstation are 50 and 10 milliseconds. Each adapter/user system has the same number of transmit and receive buffers.

Figure 16 Total throughput and throughput per file transfer versus number of workstations

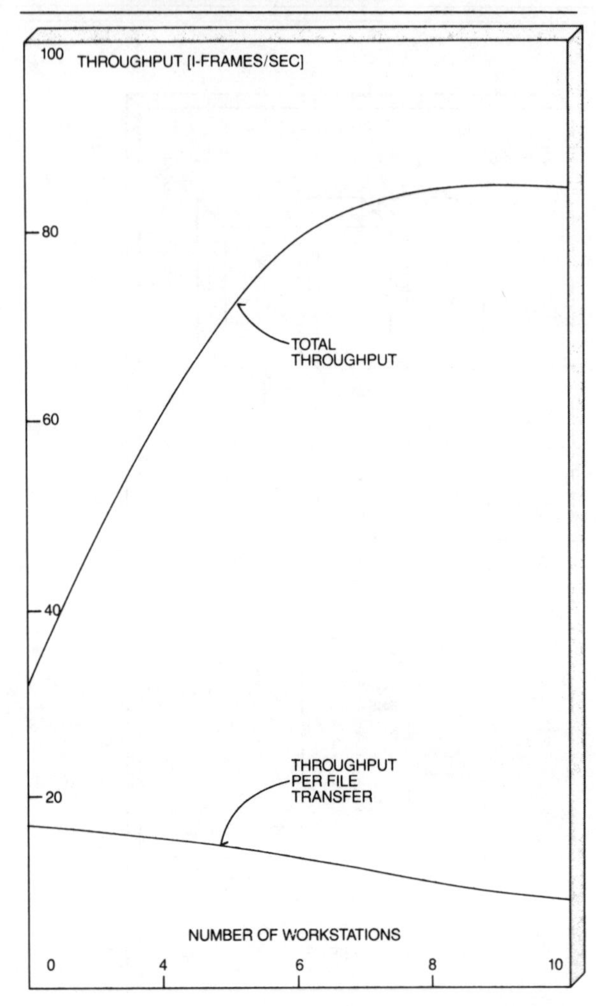

In Figure 16, we show the throughput per file transfer and the total throughput versus N, the number of workstations. The assumed window size is four. Each adapter has four send and four receive buffers. The number of send and receive buffers in the file server is equal to the product of window size and number of workstations; those in the workstations are equal to the window size.

The figure shows that for a small number of workstations, the total throughput increases roughly linearly with N. The reason is that, as long as N is small, the workstations are the bottleneck, and the addition of a workstation does not cause much interference at the file server. When N is large, the bottleneck is shifted from the workstations to the file server. The

Figure 17 Total throughput versus window size

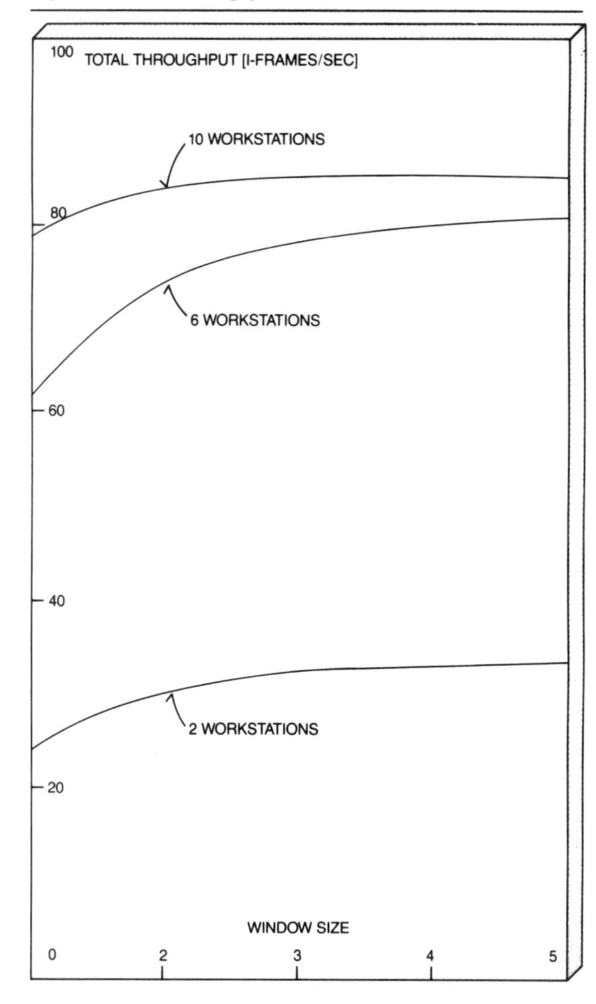

processor of the file server is working at close to full capacity; increasing N does not result in an improvement in total throughput. Since the file-server processor is shared by the various file transfers, the throughput per file transfer is a decreasing function of N.

The ring is not heavily utilized; its utilization increases from 14 percent when $N = 2$ to 34 percent when $N = 10$. Also, the loss probability due to buffer shortage at the file-server adapter is less than 0.2 percent for all cases.

We next study the effect of window size W on the total throughput. In Figure 17, we show the total throughput for different values of W. Three cases are considered: $N = 2$, 6, and 10 workstations. The assumptions regarding the buffer sizes are identical to the ones underlying Figure 16.

For the case of small W, both the workstation and the file-server processors are not busy all the time. An increase in W (e.g., from one to two) therefore results in a noticeable improvement in total throughput. However, when W is larger, either the file server or the workstation processor is busy almost all the time; hence, increasing the window size does not cause an increase in total throughput.

Consider now the effect of file-server buffer size on performance. In Figure 18, we plot the loss probabilities at the file-server adapter versus the number of file-server receive buffers for a configuration with $N = 10$ workstations. The window size is four. Results are shown separately for put-file transfers (loss

Figure 18 Loss probability at file-server adapter versus number of file-server receive buffers

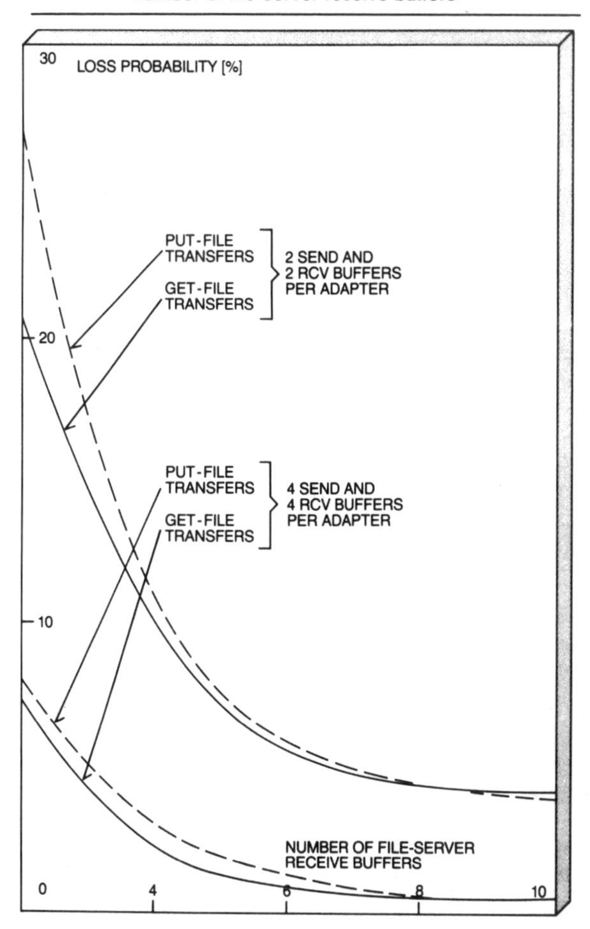

of I-frames) and get-file transfers (loss of RR- and REJ-frames). The results show that a significant fraction of frames is lost when the number of file-server receive buffers is small, but the loss probability decreases quickly with this number. The loss probability also decreases with an increasing number of buffers in the adapter, because in an overload situation, the adapter receive buffers function as an "extension" of the file-server receive buffers.

In view of the fact that the five workstations involved in put-file transfers may have a total number of 20 I-frames simultaneously outstanding, it is surprising that the loss probabilities are rather small already for six file-server receive buffers. This result can be explained as follows. In the implementation of the LLC protocol, each I-frame is separately acknowledged by an RR-frame. Since the file-server processor gives priority to frames received from its adapter, the preparation of frames for transmission is delayed. When the processor is ready to prepare an RR-frame for a put-file transfer, a number of I-frames for this connection may have been received, but only one of them is acknowledged. This RR-frame authorizes the workstation to transmit one I-frame only. It follows that the windows of the workstations and hence the arrival rate of I-frames to the file server are self-regulated.

Generally, high loss probabilities are an indication of insufficient receive buffers at the file server and its adapter. In other words, these receive buffers may have been over-sold to the various logical connections. Under this condition, it is of interest to study the effect of frame losses on throughput. Figure 19 shows the throughput per file transfer as a function of the number of file-server receive buffers for the same scenario as for the previous figure. The put-file transfers suffer significant degradation in throughput when the number of file-server receive buffers is small and hence the loss probability is high (cf. Figure 18). This is due to the fact that both REJECT and time-out recovery result in a delay period before an I-frame with the correct sequence number is retransmitted by the workstation. For lost I-frames and I-frames received out of sequence, no acknowledgments have to be generated (except for a REJ-frame generated when the first out-of-sequence I-frame has been received). Furthermore, out-of-sequence I-frames are not copied, and hence less time is required for processing. This results in more processing resources available to the get-file transfers, which therefore experience an improvement in throughput. Consequently, the total throughput is very insensitive to frame losses because the throughput degradation of the put-file transfers is compensated by the throughput increase of get-file transfers.

Figure 19 Throughput per file transfer versus number of file-server receive buffers

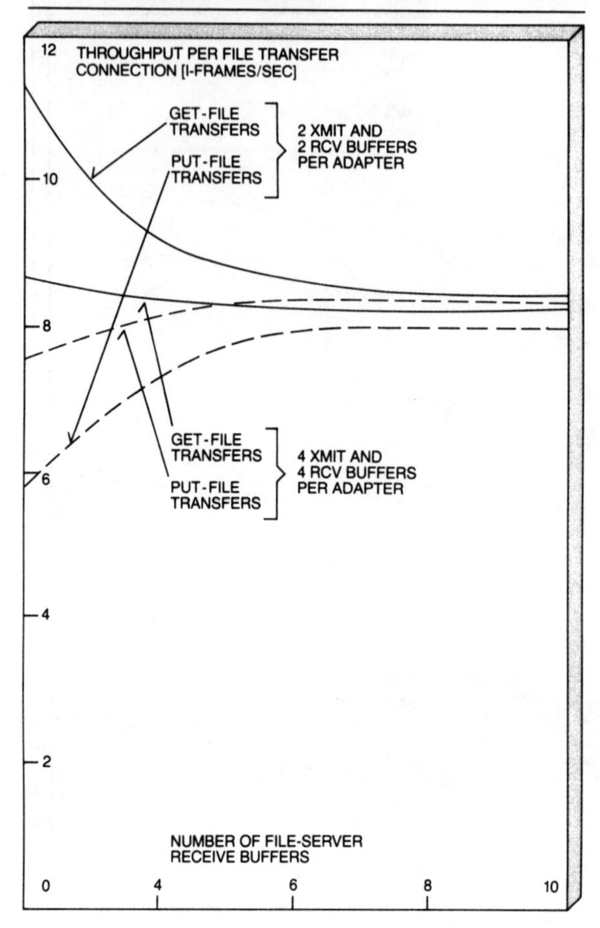

Local-area network adapter design

In a local-area network, user systems are attached to the transmission medium through network adapters, also called network controllers. An essential feature of an adapter is that it is able to receive frames arriving with no or very small gaps between them. If adapters were frequently unable to receive such frames, the performance of the local network—as seen by the user—would be unacceptable. Subsequently, we describe a study, the goal of which was to understand the timing problem associated with the reception of back-to-back frames.[68,69]

Figure 20 Structure of local-area network adapter (from Ref. 68)
©1982 IEEE

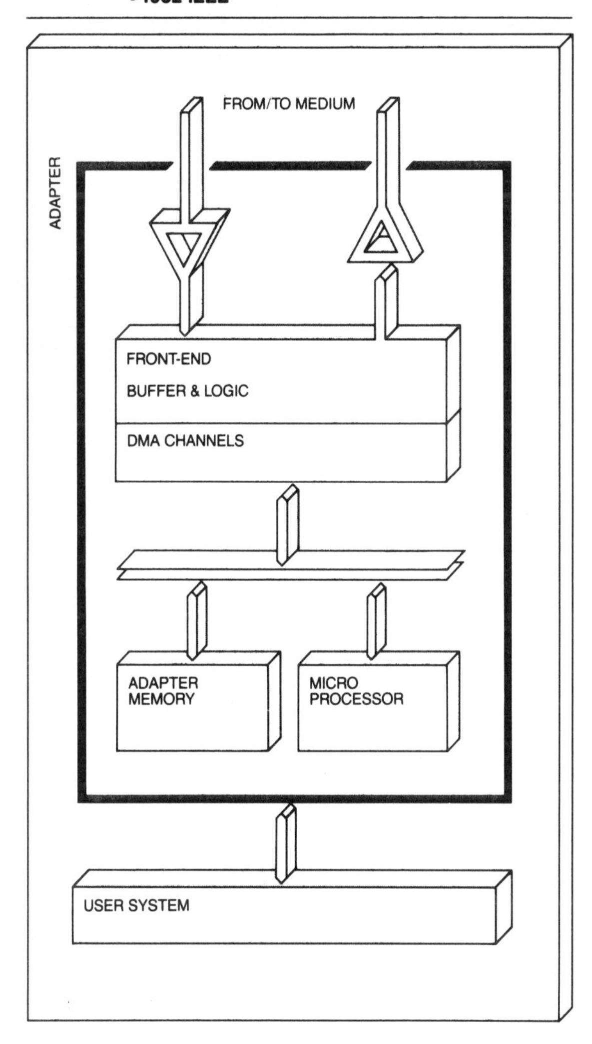

Adapter operation. The structure of the network adapter under consideration is shown in Figure 20. It contains the circuitry necessary to transmit data onto and receive data from the transmission medium and memory for buffering both outgoing and incoming frames. It also has one or more direct memory access (DMA) channels for data transfer between the transmission medium and the adapter memory. Furthermore, the adapter contains a processor that manages the frame buffers and DMA channel(s), and controls the interface to the user system.

When a frame is received, its destination address is compared with the address of the adapter to determine whether the frame is to be copied. If so, the frame is transferred into the adapter memory, provided a DMA channel has previously been set up by the processor. Arriving frames can get lost if no receive buffer is available or if a buffer is available but the processor was unable to set up a DMA early enough. At the end of each DMA transfer, an interrupt to the processor is generated. When servicing this interrupt, the processor searches for a free receive buffer and then sets up the DMA channel to receive into the acquired buffer.

The design goal is that a DMA channel is enabled when the first bit of a frame is received. Obviously, the chance of achieving this goal is higher, the smaller the DMA set-up time and the more DMA channels provided. In addition, one may employ a FIFO buffer at the adapter front-end to temporarily store incoming data in case no DMA channel is enabled. A further possibility to achieve zero (or very small) frame-loss probability is to define the medium access protocol in such a way that a minimum gap is guaranteed between subsequent frames. In this paper, we do not consider the latter possibility, although the analysis can be modified to cover this case.[69]

Data flow on transmit operations is essentially the reverse of the receive operation described above. Since our study concentrates on the most critical part of the adapter operation, namely, frame reception, we do not elaborate on details of the transmit operation.

An alternative to the adapter structure under consideration is a design where received frames are transferred (by DMA) directly into the user system memory without being buffered in the adapter. This, of course, places more constraints on the architecture and performance of the attaching station; an advantage is, however, that intermediate buffering is not needed in the adapter. It should be noted that in such a system, basically the same problem has to be solved regarding the reception of back-to-back frames. Again, a DMA channel must be enabled when the first bit of a frame needs to be buffered.

The model subsequently developed is oriented towards the adapter structure shown in Figure 20. However, the basic mechanism modeled is general enough for the analysis of this model also to be applicable to other adapter structures, e.g., one without buffers.

Performance model. The major assumptions underlying this study are as follows. Frame losses due to shortage of receive buffers are negligible, either because sufficient receive buffers are provided or because the frames received can be moved very rapidly to the user system. A fixed number of DMA channels is always dedicated to the receive direction. We shall restrict our discussion to the situation where a series of frames arrives back-to-back at an adapter. Upon arrival of the first frame, all DMA channels are assumed to be enabled.

The structure of our model is shown in Figure 21; its operation can be described as follows. When the first bit of a frame is to be copied, the state of the front-end buffer is checked; if the front-end buffer is not empty, the frame will be lost. Otherwise, two different situations may occur:

- At least one DMA channel is enabled: In this case, the frame is transferred via one of the enabled

Figure 21 Adapter performance model (from Ref. 68) ©1982 IEEE

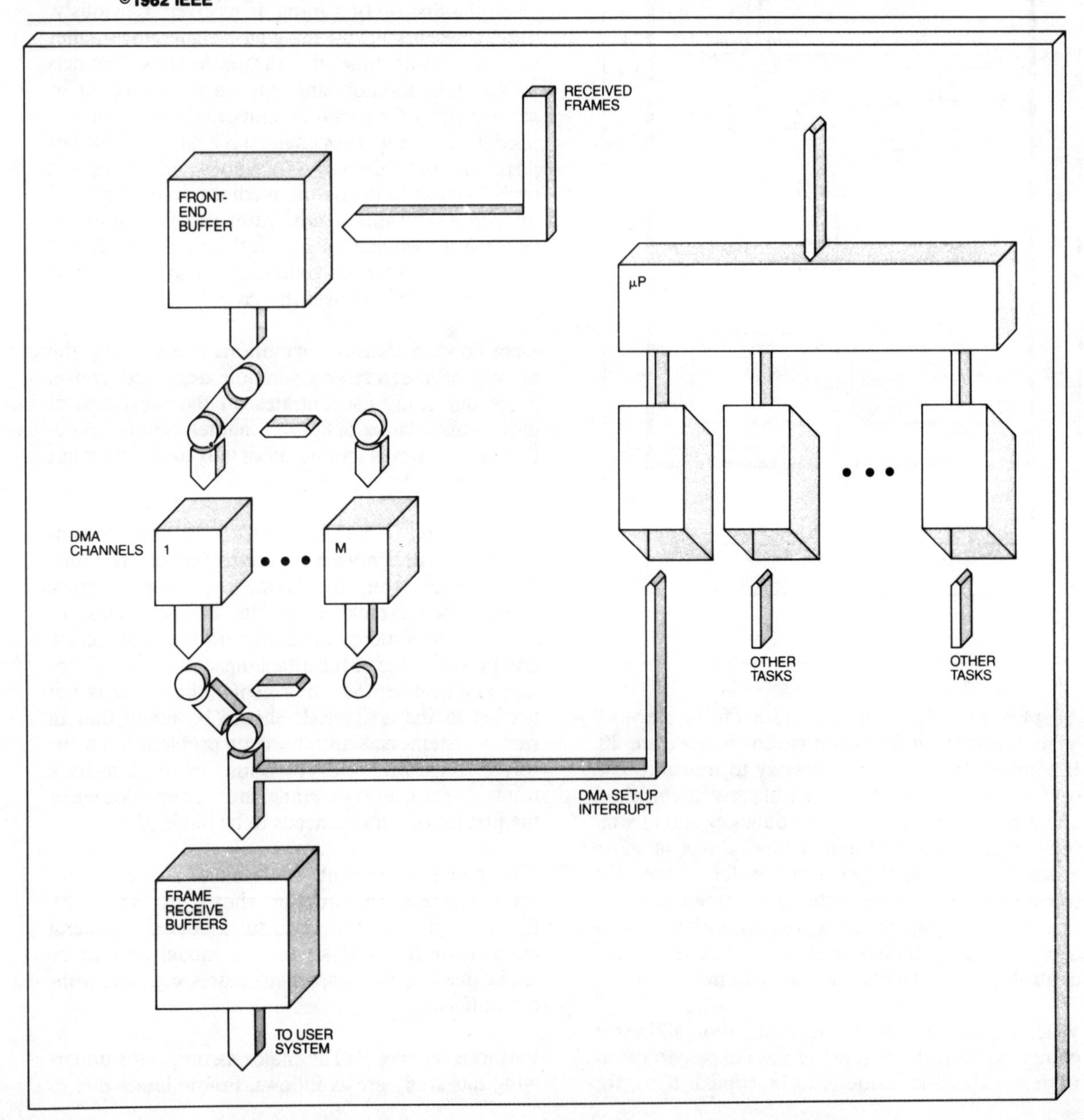

Table 1 Probabilities PB(n) (in percent) that nth back-to-back frame has been lost (one DMA channel; B is in bytes)

	Speed (million bits per second)					
	4		8		16	
	$B = 0$	$B = 10$	$B = 0$	$B = 20$	$B = 0$	$B = 40$
PB (1)	0	0	0	0	0	0
PB (2)	100	0	100	0	100	0
PB (3)	0	0	0	15.0	32.6	65.4
PB (4)	100	0	100	12.7	67.4	27.2
PB (5)	0	0	0	10.8	54.6	17.4
PB (6)	100	0	100	11.4	56.1	41.0
PB (7)	0	0	0	11.6	58.8	32.2
PB (8)	100	0	100	11.5	55.7	26.1

DMA channels into a receive buffer at medium transmission speed.

- No DMA channel is enabled: At medium transmission speed, the frame is written into the front-end buffer. If the front-end buffer is filled before a DMA channel is enabled, the frame will be lost. Otherwise, the newly enabled DMA channel will transfer the contents of the front-end buffer into a receive buffer at DMA channel speed, which is higher than the medium transmission speed. Once the front-end buffer has been emptied, the remainder of the frame is, of course, transferred at medium transmission speed.

An interrupt to the processor is generated at the end of the DMA operation. When servicing this interrupt, the processor acquires a free receive buffer and sets up the DMA channel with the starting address of this buffer. It is assumed that processing of the interrupt takes a constant time and that this interrupt has preemptive priority over the other processing tasks. Our model takes into account that, at interrupt generation time, the processor may still be busy processing an earlier interrupt of the same type, or—in an even worse situation—that previously generated interrupt requests from other DMA channels may still be waiting to be processed.

Analysis. It is relatively straightforward to determine conditions under which back-to-back frames are always successfully received (see Wong and Bux[68,69]). In practice, these conditions may not be met for reasons of hardware/software constraints or cost. If this is the case, knowledge of the probabilities of (a) losing the nth back-to-back frame and (b) being able to receive n back-to-back frames successfully will be very useful in designing an adapter. We subsequently outline how analytic results for these probabilities can be obtained.

The basic approach is to study the time-dependent behavior of a two-dimensional stochastic process $(i(t), j(t))$ defined as follows: $i(t)$ measures the occupancy of the front-end buffer at time t, expressed in terms of the time it takes to transfer the buffered data to the adapter memory at DMA speed; $j(t)$ is the total amount of unfinished work of the adapter processor (relevant to the DMA set-up task). Since the DMA set-up time is constant, the number of enabled/disabled DMA channels can be simply deduced from $j(t)$ at any point in time. Figure 22 shows a sample path of this process and the corresponding states of the DMA channels.

Define an "observation instant" to be a point in time immediately after the last bit of a frame has been copied, under the condition that a DMA channel is available. It is not difficult to see that the process $(i(t), j(t))$ possesses the Markov property[70] at these observation instants. Furthermore, one can determine whether or not a frame has been lost from the state of the process at the previous observation instant. We can therefore obtain answers to our basic performance questions if the state probabilities at the observation instants are known.

Details of the analysis are given in Reference 68; Reference 69 also describes efficient numerical algorithms to compute the relevant performance measures.

Results. For the subsequent results, the transmission speeds considered are 4, 8, and 16 million bits per second. The DMA channel speed D is assumed to be 32 million bits per second. Frame lengths are distributed according to the discrete analog of a truncated hyperexponential distribution;[69] the mean and coefficient of variation of this distribution are 100 bytes and 1.2, respectively. The choice of these values is motivated by the measurement data reported in Shoch and Hupp.[24]

Adapter model with one DMA channel. Consider first the case of one DMA channel. In Table 1, we show the probabilities PB(n) that the nth frame in a sequence of back-to-back frames is lost for a DMA set-up time of 20 microseconds and different medium transmission speeds. The front-end buffer size B is either zero or equal to the product of DMA set-up time T and ring transmission speed R.

Figure 22 Sample path of front-end buffer occupancy, adapter processor and DMA channel activities (from Ref. 68) ©1982 IEEE

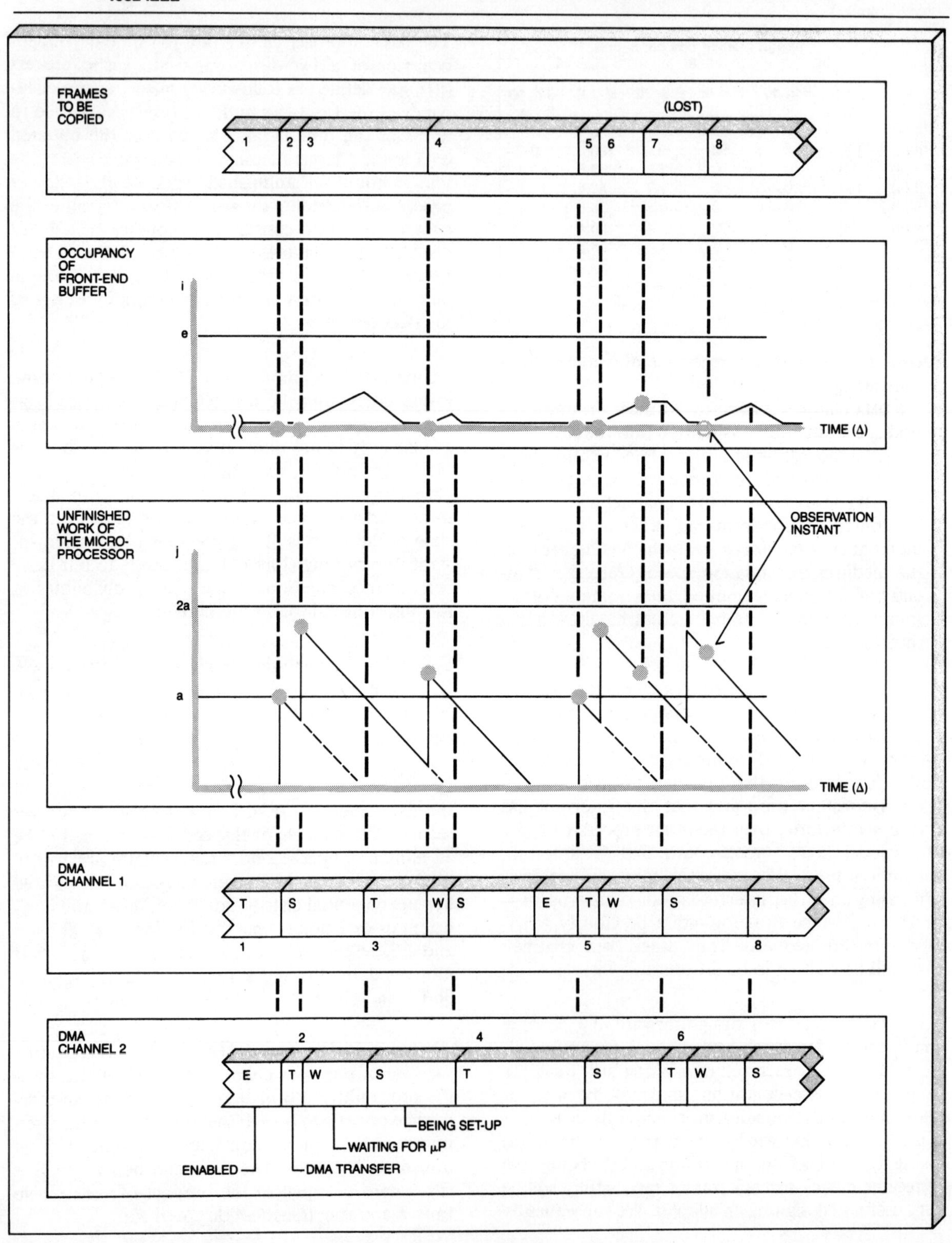

Table 2 Probability NB(n) (in percent) that first n back-to-back frames have been successfully received (one DMA channel; 16-million-bit-per-second transmission rate)

	DMA Setup Time (microseconds)				
	4	8	12	16	20
NB (1)	100.0	100.0	100.0	100.0	100.0
NB (2)	100.0	100.0	100.0	100.0	100.0
NB (3)	100.0	78.6	58.2	44.2	34.6
NB (4)	100.0	61.6	33.8	19.2	12.0
NB (5)	100.0	48.5	19.7	8.7	4.2
NB (6)	100.0	38.1	11.5	3.8	1.4
NB (7)	100.0	20.0	6.7	1.7	0.5
NB (8)	100.0	23.5	3.9	0.8	0.2

Table 3 Probability NB(n) (in percent) that first n back-to-back frames have been succcessfully received (16-million-bit-per-second transmission rate)

	DMA Channels		
	2	2	3
	No F/E buffer	40-byte F/E buffer	No F/E buffer
NB (1)	100	100	100
NB (2)	100	100	100
NB (3)	67.4	100	100
NB (4)	45.4	95.4	100
NB (5)	30.6	90.1	98.7
NB (6)	20.6	85.1	97.1
NB (7)	13.9	80.4	95.5
NB (8)	9.4	75.9	94.0

Apparently, the adapter performs poorly when front-end buffering is not employed. Every other frame is lost for medium speeds of 4 and 8 million bits per second. The results for the case of 16 million bits per second are different because more than one frame may arrive during DMA set-up.

If front-end buffering is employed, all frames are successfully received at the four-million-bit-per-second transmission speed. However, frame loss is observed when the speed is doubled. For the case of 16 million bits per second, the use of front-end buffering results in only a slight improvement in the loss probability. This is an indication that the DMA set-up process is too slow and the processor is the system bottleneck. This observation leads us to subsequently study the adapter performance as a function of the DMA set-up time.

In Table 2, we show the results for NB(n), the probability that the first n frames in a sequence of back-to-back frames have been successfully received for different values of the DMA set-up time T. The medium transmission speed is 16 million bits per second. The front-end buffer size is equal to $T * R$. All frames have been successfully received when $T = 4$ microseconds. For other values of T, frames may be lost, and the results in Table 2 show the performance degradation when T is increased.

Adapter model with two or more DMA channels. Finally, we consider the effectiveness of using more than one DMA channel to prevent loss of frames. For the case of a transmission speed of 16 million bits per second, Table 3 shows results for three different designs: (1) two DMA channels, no front-end buffer; (2) two DMA channels, 40-byte front-end buffer; (3) three DMA channels, no front-end buffer. The DMA set-up time is 20 microseconds.

We observe substantial improvements offered by the use of front-end buffering or the use of an additional DMA channel. The addition of an extra DMA channel is slightly more effective than front-end buffering in alleviating the timing problem associated with DMA setup. Any further increase in the number of DMA channels is not expected to improve performance significantly.

Acknowledgment

The last two major sections of this paper are based on joint work by J. W. Wong and the author. The token-ring simulation results in the second major section were produced by H. L. Truong. Both contributions are gratefully acknowledged. The author would also like to thank K. Kuemmerle for many helpful discussions and for reviewing the manuscript. Much of this paper also appears in *Lecture Notes in Computer Science* (Editors: D. Hutchinson, D. Shepherd, and J. Mariani), published by Springer-Verlag, Heidelberg, Germany, and is reprinted with their permission.

Cited references

1. D. D. Clark, K. T. Pogran, and D. P. Reed, "An introduction to local area networks," *Proceedings of the IEEE* **66**, 1497–1517 (1978).
2. R. C. Dixon, N. C. Strole, and J. D. Markov, "A token-ring network for local data communications," *IBM Systems Journal* **22**, Nos. 1 & 2, 47–62 (1983).
3. K. Kuemmerle and M. Reiser, "Local-area communication networks—An overview," *Journal of Telecommunication Networks* **1**, 349–370 (1982).
4. *ECMA TR/14: Local Area Networks Layers 1 to 4 Architecture and Protocols* (September 1982).

5. *Standard ECMA-80: Local Area Networks (CSMA/CD Baseband) Coaxial Cable System* (September 1982).
6. *Standard ECMA-81: Local Area Networks (CSMA/CD Baseband) Physical Layer* (September 1982).
7. *Standard ECMA-82: Local Area Networks (CSMA/CD Baseband) Link Layer* (September 1982).
8. *Standard ECMA-89: Local Area Networks Token Ring* (September 1983).
9. *Standard ECMA-90: Local Area Networks Token Bus (Broadband)* (September 1983).
10. *IEEE Standard 802.2, Logical Link Control.*
11. *IEEE Standard 802.3, CSMA/CD Access Method and Physical Layer Specifications.*
12. *IEEE Standard 802.4, Token-Passing Bus Access Method and Physical Layer Specifications.*
13. IEEE Project 802 Local Area Network Standards, *Draft IEEE Standard 802.5, Token Ring Access Method and Physical Layer Specifications,* Working Draft (February 1984).
14. International Organization for Standardization, *Data Processing—Open Systems Interconnection—Basic Reference Model,* Draft Proposal ISO/DP 7498 (February 1982).
15. R. M. Metcalfe and D. R. Boggs, "Ethernet: Distributed packet switching for local computer networks," *Communications of the ACM* **19**, 395–404 (1976).
16. *The Ethernet—A Local Area Network Data Link Layer and Physical Layer Specifications,* Version 1.0, Digital Equipment, Intel, and Xerox Corporations (September 30, 1980); available from Digital Equipment Corporation, Maynard, MA, from Intel Corporation, Santa Clara, CA, and from Xerox Corporation, Stamford, CT.
17. L. Kleinrock and F. A. Tobagi, "Packet switching in radio channels: Part I—Carrier sense multiple access modes and their throughput-delay characteristics," *IEEE Transactions on Communications* **COM-23**, 1400–1416 (1975).
18. F. A. Tobagi and L. Kleinrock, "Packet switching in radio channels: Part IV—Stability considerations and dynamic control in carrier sense multiple access modes," *IEEE Transactions on Communications* **COM-25**, 1103–1120 (1977).
19. G. T. Almes and E. D. Lazowska, "The behavior of Ethernet-like computer communications networks," *Proceedings of the 7th Symposium on Operating Systems Principles,* Asilomar Grounds, CA (1979), pp. 66–81.
20. E. Arthurs and B. W. Stuck, "A theoretical performance analysis of polling and carrier sense collision detection systems," *Proceedings of the IFIP Conference on Local Computer Networks,* North-Holland Publishing Company, Amsterdam (1982), pp. 415–438.
21. W. Bux, "Local-area subnetworks: A performance comparison," *IEEE Transactions on Communications* **COM-29**, No. 10, 1465–1473 (1981).
22. S. S. Lam, "A carrier sense multiple access protocol for local networks," *Computer Networks* **4**, 21–32 (1980).
23. F. A. Tobagi and V. B. Hunt, "Performance analysis of carrier sense multiple access with collision detection," *Computer Networks* **4**, 245–259 (1980).
24. J. F. Shoch and J. A. Hupp, "Measured performance of an Ethernet local network," *Communications of the ACM* **23**, 711–721 (1980).
25. D. J. Farber, J. Feldman, F. R. Heinrich, M. D. Hopwood, D. C. Loomis, and A. Rowe, "The Distributed Computer System," *Proceedings of the 7th IEEE Computer Society International Conference,* IEEE, Piscataway, NJ (1973), pp. 31–34.
26. W. D. Farmer and E. E. Newhall, "An experimental distributed switching system to handle bursty computer traffic," *Proceedings of the ACM Symposium on Problems in the Optimization of Data Communications,* Pine Mountain, GA (1963), pp. 31–34.
27. B. K. Penney and A. A. Baghdadi, "Survey of computer communications loop networks: Parts 1 and 2," *Computer Communications* **2**, 165–180 and 224–241 (1979).
28. W. Bux, F. Closs, P. A. Janson, K. Kuemmerle, and H. R. Mueller, "A reliable token-ring system for local-area communication," *Conference Record of NTC '81,* IEEE, Piscataway, NJ (1981), pp. A2.2.1–A2.2.6.
29. W. Bux, F. Closs, P. A. Janson, K. Kuemmerle, H. R. Mueller, and E. H. Rothauser, "A local-area communication network based on a reliable token-ring system," *Proceedings of the International Symposium on Local Computer Networks,* North-Holland Publishing Co., Amsterdam (1982), pp. 69–82.
30. J. H. Saltzer and K. T. Pogran, "A star-shaped ring network with high maintainability," *Computer Networks* **4**, 239–244 (1980).
31. A. K. Agrawala, J. R. Agre, and K. D. Gordon, "The slotted vs. the token-controlled ring: A comparative evaluation," *Proceedings of COMPSAC 1978,* Chicago (1978), pp. 674–679.
32. W. Bux and H. L. Truong, "Token-ring performance: Mean-delay approximation," *Proceedings of the 10th International Teletraffic Congress* (Montreal, Canada), North-Holland Publishing Company, Amsterdam (1983), pp. 3.1-3/1–3.1-3/6.
33. W. Bux and H. L. Truong, "Mean-delay approximation for cyclic-service queueing systems," *Performance Evaluation* **3**, 187–196 (August 1983).
34. R. B. Cooper, "Queues served in cyclic order: Waiting times," *Bell System Technical Journal* **49**, 399–413 (1970).
35. M. Eisenberg, "Queues with periodic service and changeover times," *Operations Research* **20**, 440–451 (1972).
36. O. Hashida, "Analysis of multiqueue," *Review of Electrical Communications Laboratories* **20**, 189–199 (1972).
37. J. F. Hayes, "Local distribution in computer communications," *IEEE Communications Magazine,* pp. 6–14 (March 1981).
38. A. R. Kaye, "Analysis of a distributed control loop for data transmission," *Proceedings of the Computer Communications, Networks, and Teletraffic Symposium,* Brooklyn Polytechnic, New York (1982), pp. 47–58.
39. A. G. Konheim and B. Meister, "Waiting lines and times in a system with polling," *Journal of the ACM* **21**, 470–490 (1974).
40. P. J. Kuehn, "Multiqueue systems with nonexhaustive cyclic service," *Bell System Technical Journal* **58**, 671–698 (1979).
41. I. Rubin and L. F. DeMoraes, "Polling schemes for local communication networks," *Conference Record ICC '81,* IEEE, Piscataway, NJ (1981), pp. 33.5.1–33.5.7.
42. G. B. Swartz, "Polling in a loop system," *Journal of the ACM* **27**, 42–59 (1980).
43. M. V. Wilkes and D. J. Wheeler, "The Cambridge Digital Communication Ring," *Proceedings of the Symposium on Local Area Communication Networks,* Boston (1979), pp. 47–61.
44. E. R. Hafner, Z. Nenadal, and M. Tschanz, "A digital loop communications system," *IEEE Transactions on Communications* **COM-22**, 877–881 (1974).
45. C. C. Reames and M. T. Liu, "A loop network for simultaneous transmission of variable length messages," *Proceedings of the 2nd Annual Symposium on Computer Architecture,* Houston, TX (1975), pp. 7–12.
46. L. Fratta, F. Borgonovo, and F. A. Tobagi, "The Express-net: A local area communication network integrating voice and data," *Proceedings of the International Conference on the Performance of Data Communication Systems and their Applications,* North-Holland Publishing Co., Amsterdam (1981), pp. 77–88.

47. J. O. Limb and C. Flores, "Description of Fasnet, a unidirectional local area communications network," *Bell System Technical Journal* **61**, 1413–1440 (September 1982).
48. E. H. Rothauser and D. Wild, "MLMA: A collision-free multiaccess method," *Proceedings of IFIP Congress 77*, North-Holland Publishing Co., Amsterdam (1977), pp. 431-436.
49. F. A. Tobagi, "Multiaccess protocols in packet communication systems," *IEEE Transactions on Communications* **COM-28**, 468–488 (1980).
50. J. Capetanakis, "Tree algorithms for packet broadcast channels," *IEEE Transactions on Information Theory* **IT-25**, 505–515 (1979).
51. J. Capetanakis, "Generalized TDMA: The multi-accessing tree protocol," *IEEE Transactions on Communications* **COM-275**, 1476–1484 (1979).
52. J. F. Hayes, "An adaptive technique for local distribution," *IEEE Transactions on Communications* **COM-26**, 1178–1186 (1978).
53. W. M. Kiesel and P. J. Kuehn, "CSMA-CD-DR: A new multiaccess protocol for distributed systems," *Conference Record NTC '81*, IEEE, Piscataway, NJ (1981).
54. G. S. Blair, "A performance study of the Cambridge Ring," *Computer Networks* **6**, 13–20 (1982).
55. G. S. Blair and D. Shepherd, "A performance comparison of Ethernet and the Cambridge Digital Communication Ring," *Computer Networks* **6**, 105–113 (1982).
56. W. Bux and M. Schlatter, "An approximate method for the performance analysis of buffer insertion rings," *IEEE Transactions on Communications* **COM-31**, 50–55 (1983).
57. M. T. Liu, G. Babic, and R. Pardo, "Traffic analysis of the distributed loop computer network (DLCN)," *Proceedings of the National Telecommunications Conference*, IEEE, Piscataway, NJ (1977), pp. 31:5-1–31:5-7.
58. A. Thomasian and H. Kanakia, "Performance study of loop networks using buffer insertion," *Computer Networks* **3**, 419–425 (1979).
59. W. Bux, "Analysis of a local-area bus system with controlled access," *IEEE Transactions on Computers* **C-32**, 760–763 (1983).
60. M. Fine and F. A. Tobagi, "Performance of round-robin schemes in unidirectional broadcast local networks," *Proceedings of the ICC '82*, IEEE, Piscataway, NJ (1982), pp. 1C.5.1–1C.5.6.
61. V. C. Hamacher and G. S. Shedler, "Access response on a collision-free local bus network," *Computer Networks* **6**, 93–103 (1982).
62. O. Spaniol, "Modelling of local computer networks," *Computer Networks* **3**, 315–326 (1979).
63. O. Spaniol, "Analysis and performance evaluation of HYPERCHANNEL access protocols," *Proceedings of the 2nd International Conference on Distributed Computing Systems*, IEEE, Piscataway, NJ (1981), pp. 247–255.
64. F. A. Tobagi and R. Rom, "Efficient round-robin and priority schemes for unidirectional broadcast systems," *Proceedings of IFIP WG 6.4 International Workshop on Local Area Networks*, Boston (1979), pp. 47–61.
65. *Standard ECMA-72: Transport Protocol*, 2nd Revision (September 1982).
66. International Organization for Standardization, *Data Processing—Open Systems Interconnection—Connection Oriented Transport Protocol Specification*, Draft Proposal ISO/DP 8073 (June 1982).
67. J. W. Wong and W. Bux, *Performance Evaluation of Logical Link Control in a Local-Area Ring Network*, to appear as an IBM Research Report (1984).
68. J. W. Wong and W. Bux, "Analytic modeling of an adapter to local-area networks," *Proceedings of GLOBECOM 82*, Miami, IEEE, Piscataway, NJ (1982), pp. C.2.3.1–C.2.3.6.
69. J. W. Wong and W. Bux, *Analytic Modeling of an Adapter to Local-Area Networks*, Research Report RZ-1175, IBM Corporation, Research Division, P.O. Box 218, Yorktown Heights, NY 10598.
70. L. Kleinrock, *Queueing Systems*, Vols. I and II, John Wiley & Sons, Inc., New York (1976).

Reprint Order No. G321-5230.

Werner Bux *IBM Research Division, Thomas J. Watson Research Center, P.O. Box 218, Yorktown Heights, New York 10598.* Dr. Bux joined the IBM Zurich Research Laboratory as a Research Staff Member in 1979. He is currently on assignment to the Research Center in Yorktown Heights. His work for the past several years has been in the area of architecture and performance evaluation of local-area networks. He has also been involved in local network standardization through his work in TC24 of the European Computer Manufacturers Association (ECMA). Dr. Bux received the M.S. and Ph.D. degrees in electrical engineering from the University of Stuttgart, Stuttgart, West Germany, in 1974 and 1980, respectively.

A METHODOLOGY FOR PREDICTING END-TO-END RESPONSIVENESS IN A LOCAL AREA NETWORK

by Lionel C. Mitchell

NETWORK ANALYSIS CORPORATION
301 Tower Building
Vienna, VA 22180

ABSTRACT

End-to-end responsiveness in a Local Area Network (LAN) should be examined during the design stage. A methodology for predicting LAN end-to-end responsiveness can be used to evaluate a LAN design prior to its implementation. The methodology presented here provides a structured approach for examining the design parameters of the LAN. The methodology is applied to a particular LAN design, and the evaluation results are presented graphically. Multiple "response versus throughput" curves display the sensitivity of various design parameters.

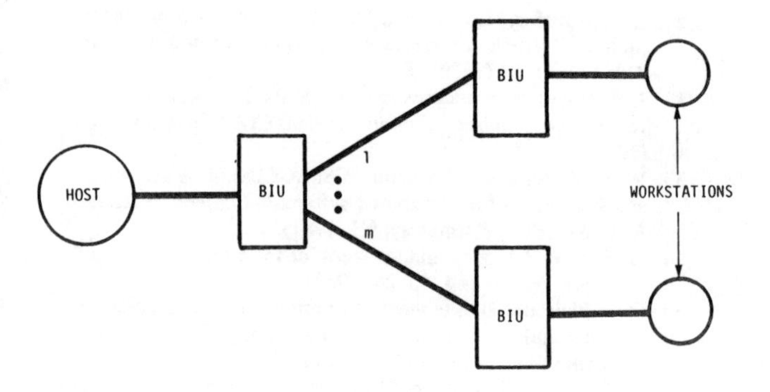

FIGURE 1: LAN ARCHITECTURE EVALUATED

INTRODUCTION

Modeling a Local Area Network (LAN) to predict end-to-end responsiveness provides the designer with valuable insight into the adequacy of the components of the design relative to specific delay requirements. Currently, most of the analytical work dealing with LAN performance have paid particular attention to analyzing the performance of single components of LANs ([1], [2], [3], and [4]) but have not examined end-to-end responsiveness.

This paper discusses a methodology for predicting the end-to-end responsiveness in a LAN and gives an evaluation of a particular LAN design using the methodology. The methodology consists of analytic techniques that quantify end-to-end delay. A basis for estimating delay is established which is consistent with the delay requirement. The components of delay are identified and modeled analytically using network of queues theory and decomposition techniques. Delay sensitivities are examined for variations in LAN design parameters. The particular design that is evaluated is a one mile long, Bus-Tree Topology LAN with a Carrier Sense, Multiple Access method with collision detection (CSMA/CD). Network nodes access a CATV medium via a microprocessor-based Bus Interface Unit (BIU). The generic LAN architecture evaluated is illustrated in Figure 1. The network architecture adheres to the seven protocol layer ISO reference model for Open Systems Interconnection [13].

METHODOLOGY

The methodology for predicting the end-to-end responsiveness of a LAN consists of five steps which provides a structured approach for quantifying delay and evaluating the sensitivity of the network components:

1. Define a single-thread communications path through the LAN to be evaluated against a delay requirement;
2. Identify the delay components of the single-thread path;
3. Characterize the capacity and requirements of the component resources;
4. Represent the single-thread path by a mathematical model;
5. Evaluate the sensitivity of delay to variations in the design parameters.

Single-Thread Definition

The basis for evaluating end-to-end responsiveness against a delay requirement is a single-thread, or logical path, that a block of data traces between nodes. A typical application in a LAN environment with a delay requirement is a Query-Response Activity in which a user at a workstation node inputs a query to a data base that resides on a remote host node. The application process of the host node processes the user's request and sends the response to the user via the LAN facilities. The end-to-end response is defined as the interval of time between the arrival at the host node of the last character of a request from a workstation node and the receipt of the first character of the response at the workstation node.

Note that a workstation could be another computer and a user could be another process.

Delay Components

For the particular design to be evaluated the components of the single-thread that contribute to delaying the response to the user are:

1. Applications Processing,
2. Nodal Communications Software,
3. Node-to-BIU Interface,
4. BIU Communications Software/Hardware/ Firmware,
5. Transmission Plant.

These components are illustrated in Figure 2.

The application processes reside in the host node as well as the workstation node. The application process in the host services the user's request while the application process in the workstation serves to drive the display screen and interaction devices.

The nodal communications software is assumed to reside in both the host and workstation nodes (the methodology pertains to peer-to-peer communications where each node in this case has the minimum capability of an intelligent terminal). This software implements the application, presentation and session layers of protocol [13].

The node-to-BIU interface is assume to be a serial, half-duplex server.

The BIU is assumed to be a microcomputer-based component that implements the transport, network and link layers of protocol in software and hardware. The transport and network layers are the DoD standards TCP and IP, respectively. The link layer is assumed to be HDLC.

The transmission plant consists of a CATV channel capable of operating at T1 speeds (1.544 mbps). The access method is a non-persistent CSMA/CD.

Resource Characterization

The resources of the single-thread path are characterized by their capacity to service requests. The request is characterized by the resource capacity it consumes.

The execution of applications software residing in the host nodes is initiated by requests from users at work stations (or processes in other host nodes). The resources consumed in the execution of the applications software are characterized by the number of instructions executed (path length), the host processing capacity, and the workload mix for the processor. The workload mix represents the concurrent tasks being executed in addition to the single-thread component being evaluated.

The delay attributable to the high-level protocols residing in the node can be characterized using the same methodology as the applications software (i.e., the characteristics are protocol path length, processor capacity and workload mix).

The node/BIU interface between the nodes and the BIU's has waiting, transmission and propagation times as delay components. Since the distance between the nodes and BIUs is typically short, the propagation delay is negligible (in the nano-second range). The waiting plus transmission time is a function of the total traffic for each interface and the transfer rate of the interface.

The lower level protocols that reside in the BIU's can be implemented in software or hardware. For software implementation, the determination of the associated delay is estimated by the methodology used for applications software and node protocols. For the hardware implementations, the associated delay is determined by the service function request arrival rate and the hardware/firmware service rate. It should be noted that the hardware implementations referred to here are not CPU implementations but rather additional logic in the BIU.

The delay associated with the transmission plant is characterized by the capacity of the transmission media, the overhead imposed by the access protocols and the distance between nodes.

Mathematical Model

The delay components of the LAN are modeled analytically as an open network of tandem queues. The delay components are represented by processing activities of the network servers (i.e., the node processor, the BIU processor, the node-to-BIU interface and the transmission plant) and are assigned service priorities (preemptive-resume type). The simplified decomposition approximation method is used for the derivation of the results.

The workstation nodes provide the external source and sink for network traffic under the single-thread assumptions. The transactions generated by a workstation require service from network resources as the request

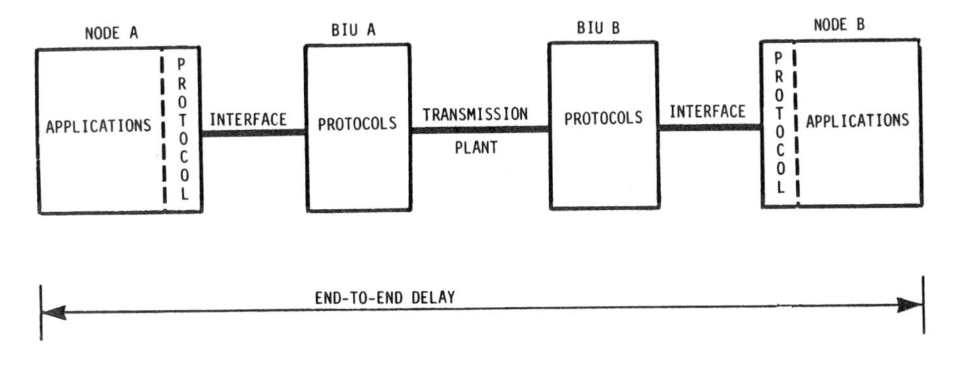

FIGURE 2: SINGLE-THREAD COMPONENTS

travels from the workstation to the host and as the response travels from the host to the workstation. The assumptions for the traffic load parameter for the LAN model are:

- The arrival rate from each set of workstations (connected to one BIU) is uniform over all sets of workstations;
- There is only one transaction type;
- For each query there is exactly one response.

The model described is for data transferred on a block basis as opposed to a character at a time.

The decomposition approximation method of modeling the network of queues was chosen over exact solution methods. A short discussion is given explaining the rationale for choosing this approach.

Exact solution for the joint probability distribution for the number of messages in all queues in a network can be computed using a product form (i.e., the joint probability of the number of packets in all queues is given by the product of the individual queue state probabilities) under certain assumptions [5]* However, the limitations on the service disciplines preclude the use of a preemptive-resume priority scheme which is considered to be a more realistic representation of the node and BIU servers than the service disciplines allowable with a product form solution.

The use of the decomposition approximation method to model computer and data communications network systems is well documented (e.g., see [3], [4], [8], [9] and [11]). This technique consists of solving portions of the queueing network separately and combining the results to produce a solution to the whole model. The decomposition technique exhibits merits which clearly indicate its appropriateness for the LAN evaluation. These include the simplicity of implementaion, the priority handling, and the extensive experience and insight gained in the use of this method in modeling queueing networks. It has been reported that networks which violate the product form solution conditions are surprisingly well approximated by the decomposition approach [11]. In addition, the exponential service assumption, hidden in the decomposition technique, usually results in upper bounds to queue lengths and delays. Thus, the decomposition technique generally leads to conservative estimates of system performance.

The LAN queueing network is decomposed into modules which correspond to the network servers. A description for the model of each module is given below.

The node processor (host and workstatation) is modeled as a single resource, multi-class queueing system. Secondary storage devices are not represented in the model since they are separate, parallel servers which do not add to the end-to-end delay except that the node Central Processor (CP) must handle interrupts for Disk Input/Output (I/O). This latter phenomenon is represented as overhead (NOH) to the node CP. This overhead, which also includes other system administrative functions, is assumed to reduce the nominal capacity of the node CP. The effective processing capacity (NEPC) for a node CP is given by

$$\text{NEPC} = (1-\text{NOH})\ \text{NIPS}, \tag{1}$$

where NIPs = the average number of machine instructions per second that the node CP can execute. (Note that this description does not include non-communications I/O delays but provides an estimate of the delay budget for all other delay sources.

There are five classes of activities modeled for the node processors which are serviced on a preemptive-resume scheme. The activities are described below:

- Link-In: Link level functions for messages inbound from the local BIU;
- Link-Out: Link level functions for messages outbound from the node to the local BIU;
- Protocols-In: High-level protocol functions for messages inbound from the local BIU;
- Protocols-Out: High-level protocol functions for messages outbound to the local BIU;
- Application: Application program processing.

The service time for each activity is characterized by the activity path length (in machine instructions) and the effective processor capacity of the node CP.

The priority structure for servicing the five classes of activities for the host node is assumed to be (from highest to lowest):

1. Link-In,
2. Link-Out,
3. Protocols-In,
4. Protocols-Out,
5. Application.

Note that processing of an application program in a host does not influence the delay associated with executing the high-level protocols resident on the host (because of its priority); however, application processing does add to the end-to-end delay for a transaction.

The priority classes for the workstation node are assumed to be (from lowest to highest):

1. Link-In,
2. Protocols-In,
3. Application,
4. Link-Out,
5. Protocols-Out.

The application processing in the workstation is responsible for moving the response data to the screen. The measure of interest is the number of instructions executed (path length) to place the first character of the response on the screen.

Assumptions for the node component include the following:

- The queueing system has a single waiting line and a single server,

* Assumptions are: 1) All external sources are Poisson; 2)All servers belong to one of the following types: (i) FCFS with exponential service. (ii) Ample service with any rational Laplace transform service distribution. (iii) Single server with LCFS or RR discipline and service distributions have rational Laplace transform.

- Each class of activity constitutes an independent Poisson source with mean arrival rate λ_i;
- The link level protocol is responsible for reliable delivery of messages to the BIU;
- The service times for each class of activity is exponentially distributed with mean service time S_i;
- Each node has an adequate amount of storage such that no data is lost.

The equations for node delay, T_{qj}, for the various classes of node activities, found in [7] and [10], are given by:

$$T_{qj} = \sum_{i=1}^{j} \lambda_i S_i/(1-\sum_{i=1}^{j} \rho_i) + S_j \times 1/(1-\sum_{i=1}^{j-1} \rho_i), \quad (2)$$

where $\rho_i = \lambda_i S_i$. The λi's are determined by solving the balance equations for the network of queues associated with the node component. The number of transactions per second arriving to and departing from the host node is $m\lambda$ where m is the average number of threads (or remote BIU's) that the host is serving concurrently. Thus, m is the multiprogramming level for the host node. Each workstation BIU serves a total of 2 transactions per second (in and out). The node queueing network models are illustrated in Figure 3.

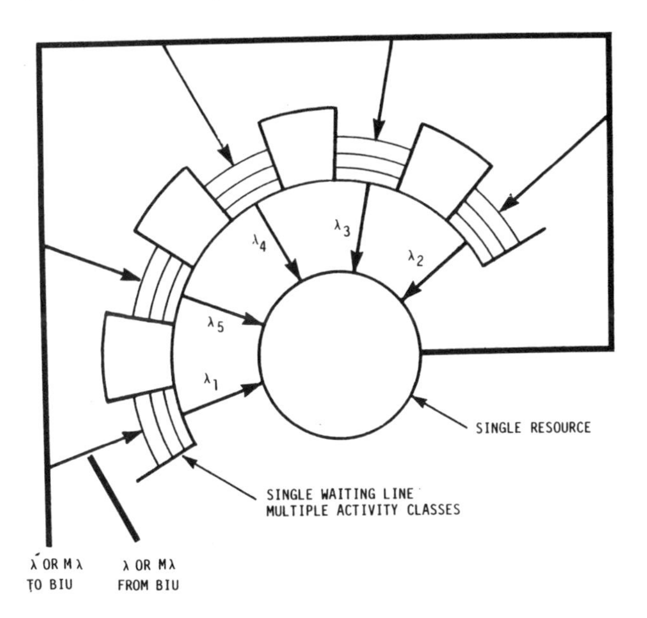

FIGURE 3: NODE QUEUEING DIAGRAM

The Node/BIU interface is modeled as a single-server queue which operates in half-duplex mode. An overhead function (IOH) is assessed on the nominal transfer rate for non-data bits to give the Effective Transfer Rate (ETR) for the interface server:

$$ETR = (1-IDH)\ ITR, \quad (3)$$

where ITR = the nominal Interface Transfer Rate in bits per second (bps).

Assumptions for the interface queueing model are:

- The queueing system has a single waiting line and single server;
- There are two classes of arrivals (messages from the node and messages from the BIU);
- There is no priority structure (i.e., the service discipline is First-Come, First-Served (FCFS);
- Each arrival class constitutes an independent Poisson source with parameter λ_i;
- Each service time distribution is exponential with mean S_i;
- There is adequate storage to prevent loss of data.

The equations for interface delay, T_{qj}, for the interface are given by:

$$T_{qj} = \rho \bar{s}/(1-\rho)+S_j, \quad (4)$$

where

$$\rho = \lambda' \bar{s},$$

$$\lambda' = \lambda_1+\lambda_2,$$

$$\bar{s} = (\lambda_1 s_1+\lambda_2 s_2)/\lambda',$$

For the Host/BIU interface $\lambda_1=\lambda_2=m\lambda$, and for the Workstation/BIU interface $\lambda_1=\lambda_2=\lambda$.

The BIU processors are modeled using the same methodology used to model the node processors (i.e., a single resource, multi-class queueing system with a preemptive-resume priority service discipline). Again, secondary storage servers are not modeled but the overhead for disk interrupts is represented by an overhead factor, BOH, which also includes other systems administration overhead functions. Thus, the effective processing capacity (BEPC) for a BIU CP is given by:

$$BEPC = (1-BOH)\ BIPS, \quad (5)$$

where BIPS = the average number of machine instructions per second that the BIU CP can execute.

The five classes of activities modeled for the BIU processors are serviced according to a preemptive-resume priority discipline. The following is a list of these activities given in the order of their service priority (highest to lowest):

1. Network Link-In: Link level functions for messages inbound to the BIU from the network cable side;
2. Node Link-In: Link level functions for messages inbound to the BIU from the node side;
3. Network Link-Out: Link level functions for messages outbound from the BIU to the network;
4. Node Link-Out: Link level functions for messages outbound from the BIU to the node;

5. TCP/IP: The transport and network functions for messages from the network side and the node side (there is a FCFS discipline within this class of activity).

The queueing delay equations for the BIU are the same as those given for the node and are not repeated here. The probability of a packet error is taken into account in determining the λj's for the link and TCP/IP layer activities. The mathematical assumptions for the BIU model are the same as for those for the node model.

The combination of the physical protocol layer of and the CATV medium is modeled as a separate server. This additional logic implemented in hardware in the BIU is referred to as the Media Access Unit (MAU). The analytic results for the Carrier Sense Multiple Access with Collision Detect (CSMA/CD) model given in [2] and [4] are used to estimate the delay associated with this access scheme. The CSMA/CD access scheme has been modeled extensively ([1], [2], [4], [11] and [12]) and actual measurements of an implementation, [6], show stable behavior for very high sustained throughput.

The assumptions for the queueing analysis of the CSMA/CD access scheme are:

- Poisson arrivals over an infinite population;
- Negligible collision detection time (compared to the bus propagation time);
- Retransmission are treated as independent Poisson arrivals;
- Channel sensing is instantaneous;
- Propagation time between any two nodes is uniform and equal to the maximum value;
- Retransmission of packets is according to the Binary Exponential Backoff probability rule;
- The random interval parameters for the Backoff algorithm is uniformly distributed and the same for all MAU's.

When a packet is ready for transmission, it will be transmitted only if the MAU hardware senses the bus to be idle. This implies that the RF bus is available and the MAU will immediately initiate transmission. It is, possible however, due to the signal propagation delay on the cable, that another MAU will initiate transmission within a time interval small enough to mask the two workstation transmissions. For such a collision to occur, this time interval must be less than the propagation delay between two workstations. The two workstations will detect the collision of their packets shortly after and will abort transmission. The propagation time between any two workstations corresponds to the maximum possible distance (round trip propagation from the source to head end and back to destination) between two workstations on the RF bus.

Whenever a MAU senses a busy bus or aborts transmission due to a collision, it saves the packet in its memory and attempts to retransmit it after a random period. The randomized retransmission interval guarantees that further collisions between the same MAU's will occur at random instead of occuring according to a deterministic pattern which might result in infinite cycles of collisions. The flow chart for the CSMA/CD algorithm is given in Figure 4.

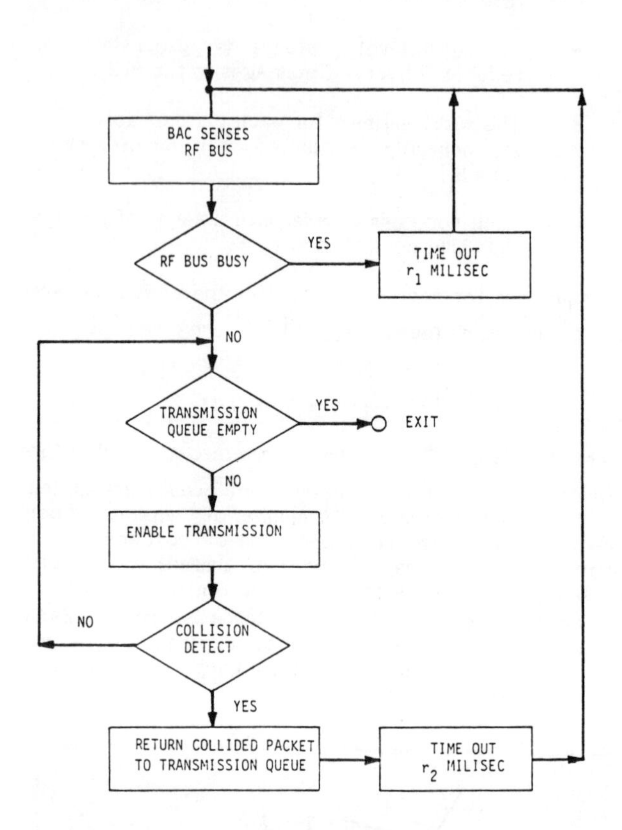

FIGURE 4: CSMA/CD ALGORITHM

For the CSMA/CD access scheme the normalized throughput ($S=\lambda T$) is related to the normalized offered packet traffic, G, (including retransmissions) by the equation:

$$S^* = \frac{G e^{-aG}}{(1+a)G e^{aG}+(1+aG)(1-e^{-aG})^2+1} \quad (6)$$

The average packet transmission delay, D, is given in [4] by:

$$D = (A_1+A_2+A_3)T, \quad (7)$$

where A_1 is the normalized waste time due to collisions, A_2 is the dead time due to retransmissions and rescheduling and A_3 is the propagation and transmission time. Given that N_1 is the average number of times a packet encounters a collision or busy state, N_2 is the average number of times a packet encounters a collision,

* Note that this transcendental equation has to be solved for G by trial and error. A range of values for G which can be used in conjunction with fixed values of S and a is given in [4].

and R_1 and R_2 are the normalized mean retrial intervals after detecting a busy condition and a collision, respectively, it follows that:

$$A_1 = N_2(W+a) \quad (8)$$

$$A_2 = R_2(2^{n_2+1}-1)+(N_1-N_2)R_1 \quad (9)$$

$$A_3 = a+1 \quad (10)$$

where

$$W = \frac{1-e^{-aG}}{G} - ae^{-aG} \quad (11)$$

$$N_1 = G/S-1 \quad (12)$$

$$N_2 = (1+aG)e^{aG}-1 \quad (13)$$

EVALUATION

The analytic model described was coded as a computer program with the various design parameters as user input values (e.g., traffic load, cable propagation, processor overhead and capacity, application program path length, protocol path length and interface transfer rate). The computer program provides a valuable analysis/design tool that can be used by designers in examining the sensitivity of end-to-end delay subject to variation in the design parameters and in predicting weak links and other system limitations.

Bottleneck Identification

The computer program of the LAN model was executed for a preliminary set of parametric values, to identify potential bottlenecks. The computer program generated output is shown in Table 1. The throughput is given as a fraction of the arrival rate generated by one workstation. The response is the single-thread delay previously described. The remaining columns in the table give the relative contribution to delay for the host, the host/BIU interface, the workstation/BIU interface, the host BIU, the workstation BIU, the workstation and the cable (including CSMA/CD), respectively. A potential bottleneck was identified as the workstation/BIU interface which accounts for a large majority of the end-to-end delay in this particular design.

Sensitivity Analysis

The sensitivity of certain parameters was examined by varying their values and examining the effect on end-to-end response for the LAN. The sensitivity analysis which proved to be most interesting were:

- Propagation,
- Protocol Path Length,
- Application Program Path Length.

These sensitivites are shown in Figures 5a, 5b, and 5c relative to an average delay requirement.

The curves for different propagation values show that there is little affect to response for low utilization. However, for higher utilizations propagation has a significant affect on response.

The curves for protocol path length show that the mean delay requirement can be met for seven times the average traffic rate if the path length is less than or equal to 40,000 instructions.

The sensitivity on application program path length shows a very stable system for path lengths less than 200,000 instructions.

Summary

A methodology for predicting end-to-end responsiveness in a local area network and an evaluation of a particular LAN design were presented. The methodology made use of the network of queues theory and decomposition techniques for quantifying response. The methodology can be used to evaluate proposed LAN designs to identify potential bottlenecks and other design weaknesses. In the evaluation presented a bottleneck was identified as the interface between the workstation and the associated BIU. The sensitivity results showed the conditions of propagation, protocol path length and application path length for which the delay requirement was satisfied. Future enhancements to the model will probably include examination of the sensitivity of other parameters (e.g., packet size) and modeling more than one transaction type.

REFERENCES

[1] Tobagi, F.A. and V.B. Hunt, "Performance Analysis of Carrier Sense Multiple Access with Collision Detection", Proc. of the LACN Symposium, May 1979, pp 217-245.

[2] Sherman, R.H., M.G. Gable and G. McClure, "Concepts, Strategies for Local Data Network Architectures", Data Communications, July 1978, pp 29-49.

[3] Lissack, Tsvi, Basil Maglaris and Hubert Chin, "Impact of Microprocessor Architectures on Performance of Local Network Interface Adaptors", Local Networks & Distributed Office Systems Symposium, May 1981.

[4] Maglaris B. and T. Lissack, "An Integrated Broadband Local Network Architecture", Proceedings of the 5th Conference on Local Computer Networks, Minneapolis, October, 1980.

[5] Basket, F., F. M. Chandy, R.R. Muntz and F. Palacios-Gomez, "Open, Closed and Mixed Networks of Queues with Different Classes of Customers", J. ACM 22.2, (April 1975), pp 248-360.

[6] Shoch, J.F. and J.A. Hupp, "Measured Performance of an Ethernet Local Network", Comm. ACM 23.12 (December 1980) pp 711-721.

[7] Kleinrock, L., Queueing Systems, Vol.2, J. Wiley, New York, 1976.

[8] Beizer, Boris, Micro-Analysis of Computer System Performance, Van Nostrand Reinhold, New York, 1978.

[9] Ferrari, Domenico, Computer Systems Performance Evaluation, Prentice-Hall, Englewood Cliffs, New Jersey, 1978.

Traffic Parameters

arrival rate - 0.017 MPS

aggregate load - 100000 BPS

CSMA/CD Parameters

propagation - 30 micro-sec

retrans interval - 5

MSG Lengths

input - 800 Characters
output - 12000 Characters

I/F Xfer rates

host - 800000 BPS
w/s - 9600 BPS

Protocol path length parameters

node protocols

send-12000 Instructions
receive-12000 Instructions

node access link layer
send- 75 Instructions
receive- 75 Instructions

network access link layer
send - 75 Instructions
receive - 75 Instructions

TCP/IP - 12000

multi-prog level - 32

processor capacities

host- 1.100 MIPS
BIU - 0.615 MIPS
w/s - 0.115 MIPS

Host application program path length - 50000 Instructions
Cable utilization - 0.0565
Total normalized traffic including retransmissions - 0.06

		DELAY CATEGORIES						
THROUGHPUT	RESPONSE	HOST	HI/F	WI/F	HBIU	WBIU	W/S	CABLE
0.50	2.0066	0.04	0.01	0.84	0.01	0.02	0.02	0.05
1.00	2.0252	0.04	0.01	0.84	0.01	0.02	0.02	0.05
1.50	2.0444	0.04	0.01	0.84	0.01	0.02	0.02	0.05
2.00	2.0645	0.04	0.01	0.84	0.01	0.02	0.02	0.05
2.50	2.0853	0.04	0.01	0.83	0.02	0.02	0.02	0.05
3.00	2.1071	0.04	0.01	0.83	0.02	0.02	0.02	0.05
3.50	2.1298	0.04	0.01	0.83	0.02	0.02	0.02	0.05
4.00	2.1536	0.04	0.01	0.83	0.02	0.02	0.02	0.05
4.50	2.1785	0.05	0.01	0.83	0.02	0.02	0.02	0.05
5.00	2.2047	0.05	0.01	0.83	0.02	0.02	0.02	0.05
5.50	2.2324	0.05	0.01	0.83	0.02	0.02	0.02	0.05
6.00	2.2616	0.05	0.01	0.82	0.03	0.02	0.02	0.05
6.50	2.2927	0.05	0.01	0.82	0.03	0.02	0.02	0.05
7.00	2.3259	0.05	0.01	0.82	0.03	0.02	0.02	0.05
7.50	2.3615	0.06	0.01	0.82	0.03	0.01	0.02	0.05
8.00	2.4001	0.06	0.01	0.81	0.03	0.01	0.03	0.05
8.50	2.4424	0.06	0.01	0.81	0.03	0.01	0.03	0.05
9.00	2.4892	0.06	0.01	0.80	0.04	0.01	0.03	0.05
9.50	2.5423	0.07	0.01	0.79	0.04	0.01	0.03	0.05
10.00	2.6041	0.07	0.01	0.78	0.05	0.01	0.03	0.05

TABLE 1: EXAMPLE COMPUTER PROGRAM OUTPUT

[10] Martin, James, Design of Real Time Systems, Prentice-Hall, Englewood Cliffs, New Jersey, 1967.

[11] Maglaris, B. and T. Lissack, "Queueing Model for Local Network Interface Adaptors", Technical Report, Network Analysis Corporation, New York, 1981.

[12] Metcalfe, R. and Boggs, D., "Ethernet: Distributed Packet Switching for Local Computer Networks", Comm. of the ACM, 19, No. 7, July 1976, pp 395-404.

[13] ISO/FC97/SC16, Reference Model of Open Systems Interconnections (Version 4), N227, June 1979.

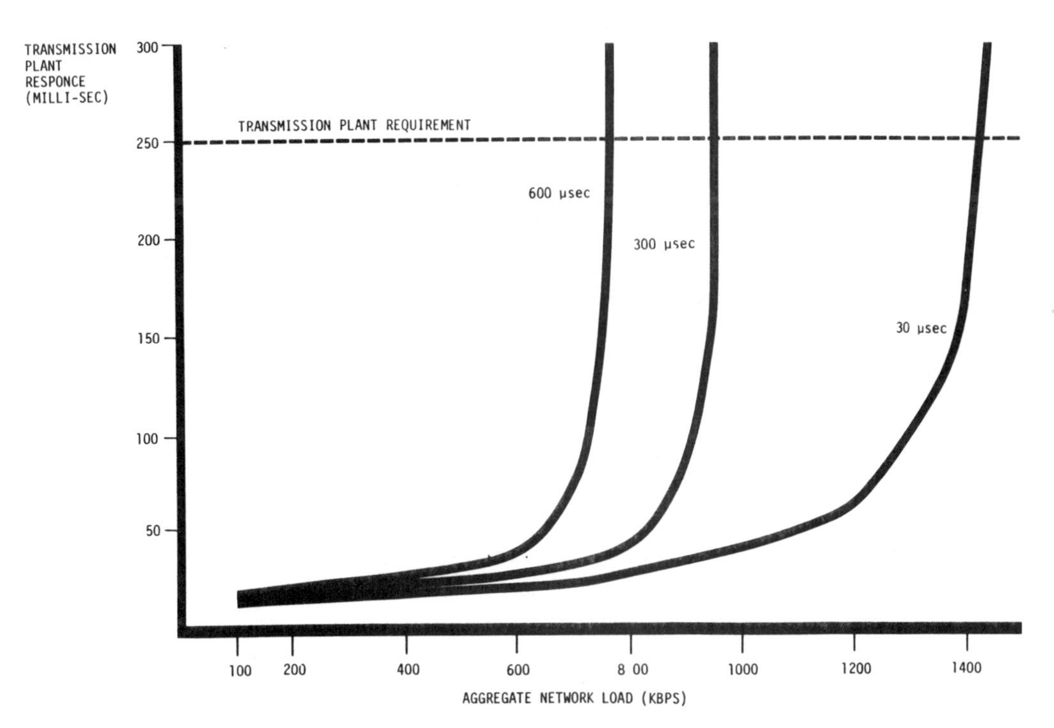

FIGURE 5(A): PEOPAGATION SENSITIVITY

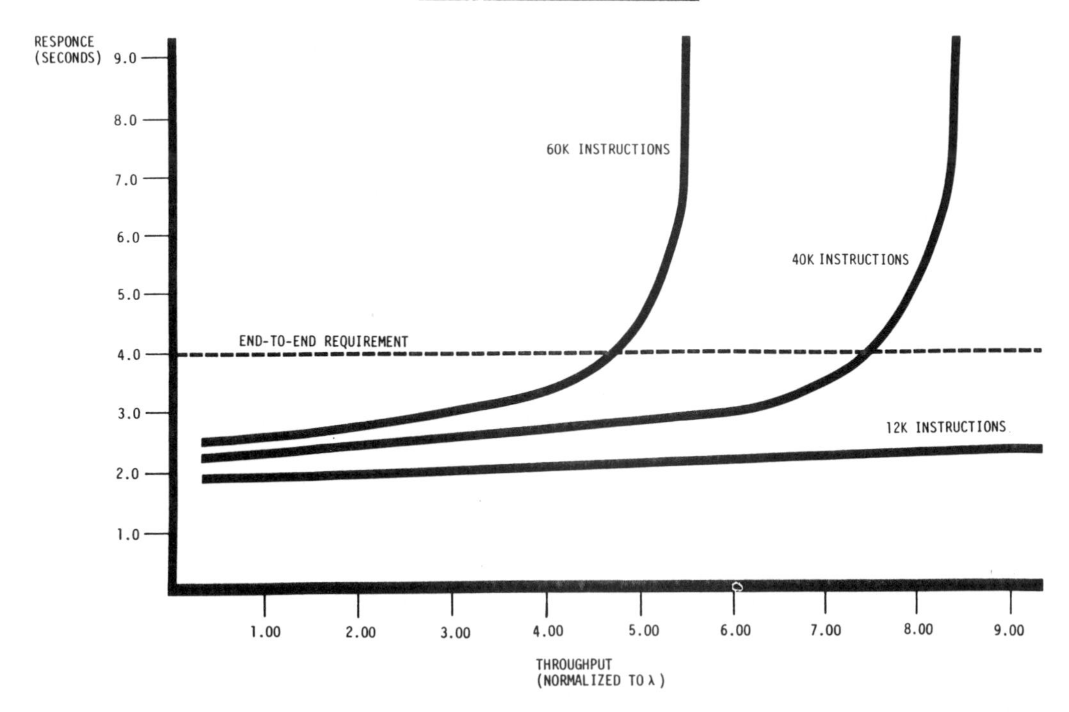

FIGURE 5:(B) HIGH-LEVEL PROTOCOL PATH LENGTH SENSITIVITY

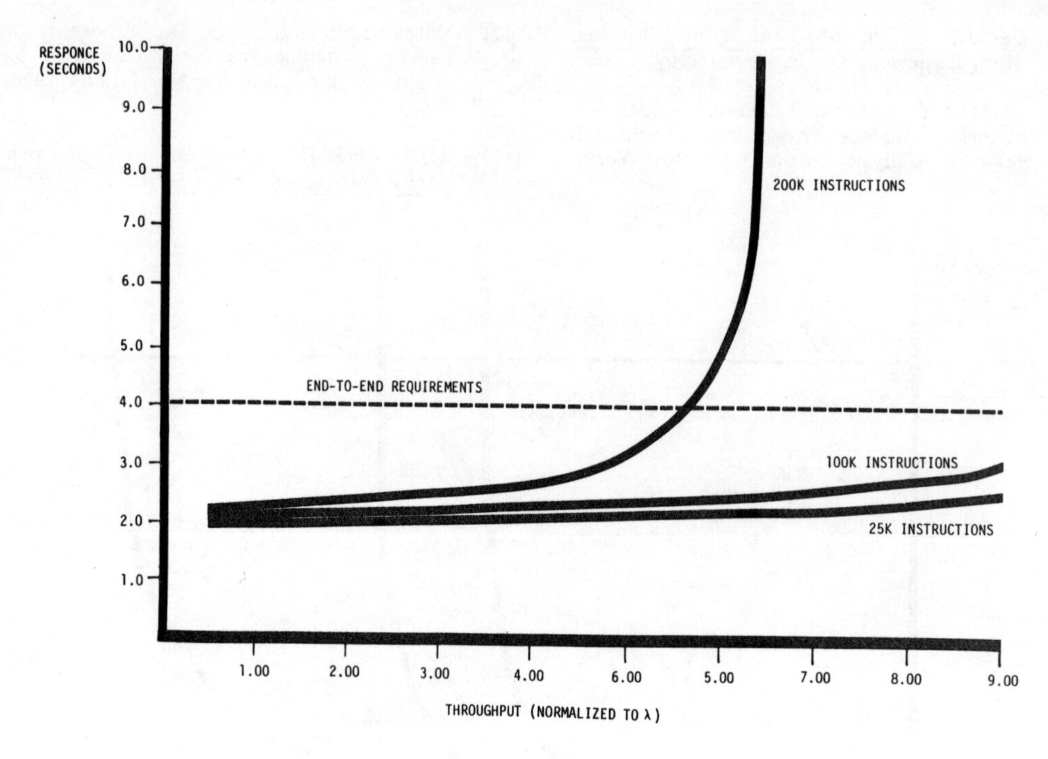

FIGURE 5(C): HOST APPLICATION PATH LENGTH SENSITIVITY

SECTION 7: INTERNETWORKING

7.1 Overview

In many cases, a local network will not be an isolated entity. An organization may have more than one type of local network at a given site to satisfy a spectrum of needs. An organization may have local networks at various sites and may need them to be interconnected for central control or distributed information exchange. Plus, an organization may need to provide a connection for one or more terminals and hosts of a local network to other computer resources.

7.2 Article Summary

"Beyond Local Networks" provides an overview of the key issues involved in extending communication for an attached device beyond the scope of its local network.

"Internetworking and Addressing for Local Networks" appeared as an appendix to draft C of the IEEE 802 standard. It presents a systematic analysis of the various internetwork situations that might arise involving local networks.

The next two articles, by Warner and by Schneidewind, explore some specific problems that arise in attempting to connect a local network to a long-haul network. A number of protocol-related issues are raised and explored.

The final article, by Hawe et al., examines the bridge, a device that is frequently used to interconnect similar LANs.

How bridges and gateways make it possible to switch data among dissimilar networks.

BEYOND LOCAL NETWORKS

by William Stallings

The story of local networks is by now a familiar one to data processing managers. The proliferation of small computers throughout large organizations has created the need for some means of connecting them and enabling them to share data and access to costly peripherals. The local network alone, however, hardly solves all of a manager's interconnection problems.

Like it or not, more than one local network will probably be required to service the wide-ranging mix of computers found in typical corporations. Word procesors in one department, personal computers in another, and mainframes in the back room all need their own kinds of local networks, whether they are sold under that name or not. From simple twisted-pair cabling to hyperfast coax, local networks of many sorts are finding their way into offices and labs, necessitating a new level of communications expertise: internetworking protocols.

This networking of networks takes place within single buildings and across continents as corporations strive to provide company-wide access to electronic files, services, and resources. Electronic mail systems, for instance, gain value geometrically as new users are brought on-line, a procedure that often requires differing local networks to be linked efficiently and transparently.

These various interactions are depicted in Fig. 1. There are a number of local networks, some of which may be in the same building, some not. Local networks may be linked point-to-point (e.g., with a private or leased line) or through a packet-switched network. Devices on the local networks, plus those on the long-haul net, may communicate. The figure shows two types of devices for linking networks, the bridge and the gateway. A bridge is a relatively simple device for linking two local networks that use the same protocols. The gateway is more complex and intended for heterogeneous cases.

To understand the action of the bridge, first consider how communication takes place among stations attached to a single local network. Fig. 2 is an example using a bus-topology local network; the principle is similar for the ring and tree topologies.

Data on a local network are transmitted in packets. So, for example, if station X wishes to transmit a message to station Y, X breaks its message up into small pieces that are sent, one at a time, in packets. Each packet contains a portion of X's message plus control information, including Y's network address. Based on some medium-access protocol (e.g., CSMA/CD or token passing), X inserts each packet onto the bus. The packet propagates the length of the bus in both directions, reaching all other stations. When Y recognizes its address on a packet, it copies the packet and processes it.

Now, suppose two local networks using the same protocols are to be linked. This is accomplished in Fig. 3 using a bridge that is attached to both local networks (frequently, the bridge function is performed by two "half-bridges," one on each network). The functions of the bridge are few and simple: it reads all packets transmitted on network A, and accepts only those addressed to stations on B; it buffers each accepted packet for retransmission on B, using the medium access protocol; and it does the same for B-to-A traffic.

The bridge makes no modifications to the content or format of the packets it handles, nor does it encapsulate them with an additional header. If any modifications or additions were made, we would be dealing with a more complex device—a gateway. This is discussed later. Essentially, the bridge provides a transparent extension to the local network. It appears to all stations on the two local networks that there is a single network, a composite of the two separate nets. All stations may be addressed in the same fashion.

For similar but geographically separate local networks, the desirability of a bridge is clear. It provides a simple and efficient means of interconnecting devices in a number of locations. But the bridge is useful even when all devices are local to each other, for the following reasons:

Reliability. The danger in connecting all data processing devices in an organization to one network is that a fault on the network may disable communications for all devices. By using bridges, the network can be partitioned into self-contained units.

Performance. In general, perfor-

PHOTOGRAPH BY STEVE COOPER

For similar but geographically separate local networks, the desirability of a bridge is clear.

mance on a local network declines with an increase in the number of stations or the length of the wire. A number of smaller networks will often give improved performance if devices can be clustered so that intranetwork traffic significantly exceeds internetwork traffic.

Security. A bridge architecture can enhance network security. For example, sensitive data (accounting, personnel, strategic planning) could be isolated on a single local network. The bridge can prevent those data being sent out to other networks.

Convenience. It may simply be more convenient to have multiple networks. For example, if a local network is to be installed in two buildings separated by a highway, it may be far easier to use a microwave bridge link than to attempt to string coaxial cable between the two buildings.

GATEWAYS MORE COMPLEX When connecting different types of local networks, a gateway is required. As with bridges, paired half-gateways are commonly used, each being attached to its respective local network. A gateway is generally a more complex device than a bridge, for it must accommodate differences between local and long-haul networks. These differences include the following:

- Addressing schemes. The networks may use different end-point names, addresses, and directory maintenance schemes.
- Maximum packet sizes. Packets from one network may have to be broken into smaller pieces to move on another network. This process is referred to as fragmentation.
- Interfaces. The interface to a local network is usually defined through various protocols, including one governing access to the network wire itself. Long-haul networks generally use different protocols (X.25, etc.) than local nets.
- Time-outs. Generally a connection-oriented transport service (e.g., a file transfer, as opposed to electronic mail) will await in acknowledgement until a time-out expires, at which time it will retransmit its segment of data. Generally, longer times are required for successful delivery across multiple networks. Internetwork timing procedures must facilitate successful transmission that avoids unnecessary retransmissions.
- Error recovery. Internetwork services should not depend on or be interfered with by the nature of the individual network's error recovery capability.
- Status reporting. Networks can report status and performance differently, yet it must be possible for the gateway to provide such information on internetworking activity.
- Routing techniques. Intranetwork routing may depend on fault detection and congestion

FIG. 1

INTERCONNECTED NETWORKS

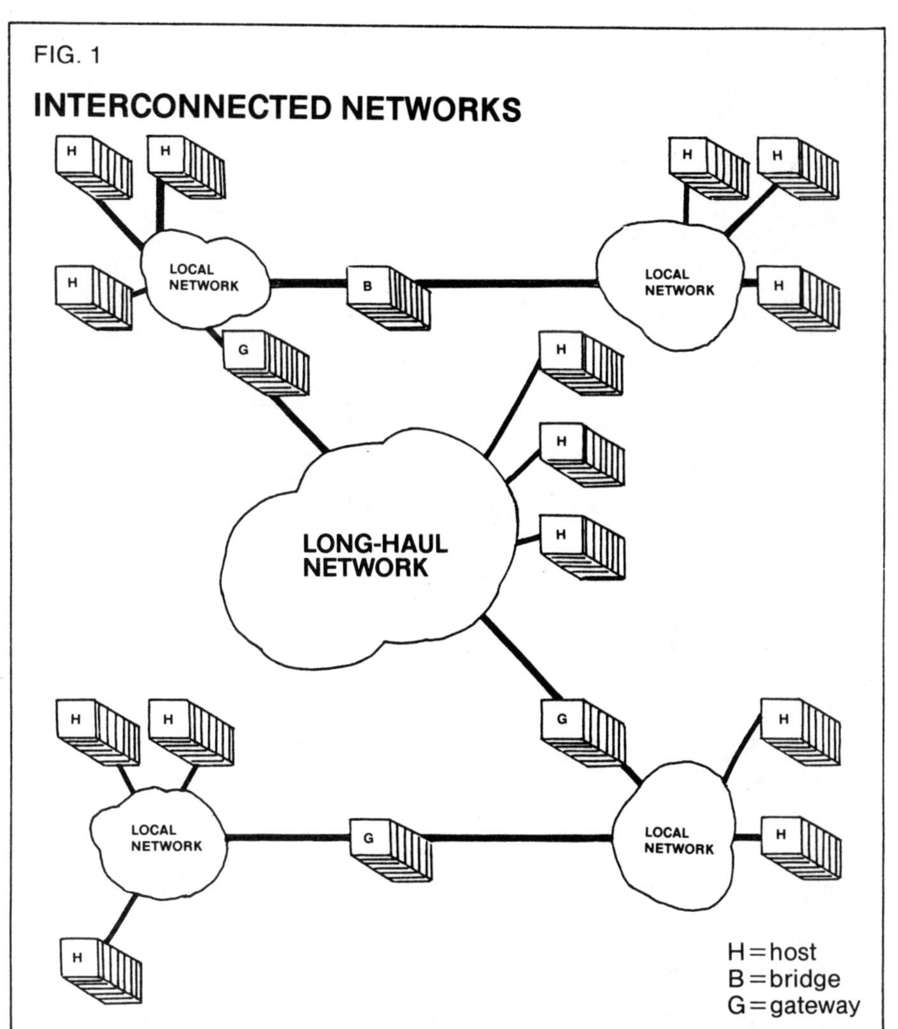

FIG. 2

INTRANETWORK COMMUNICATIONS

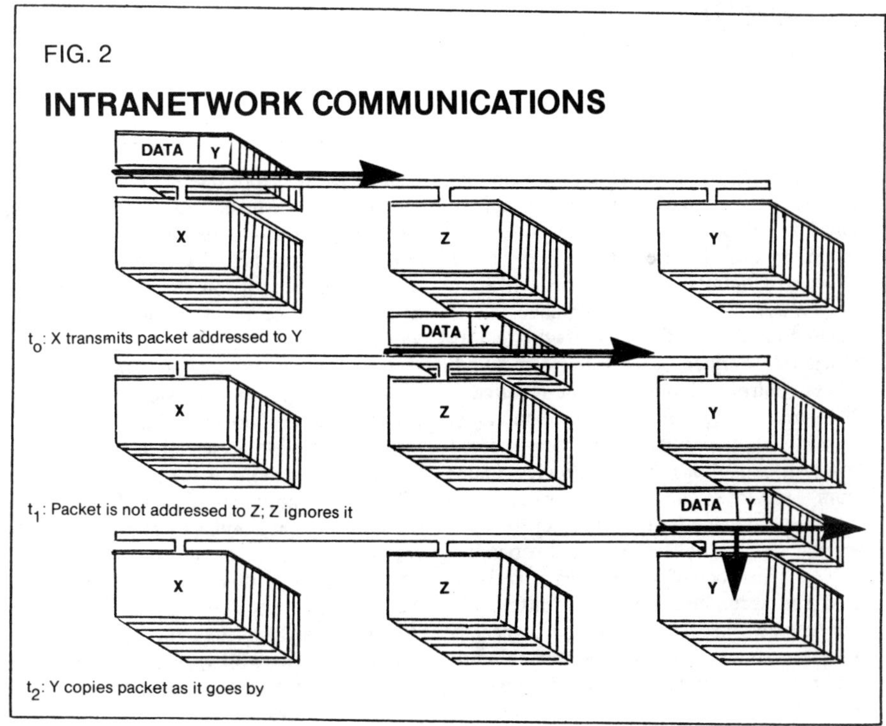

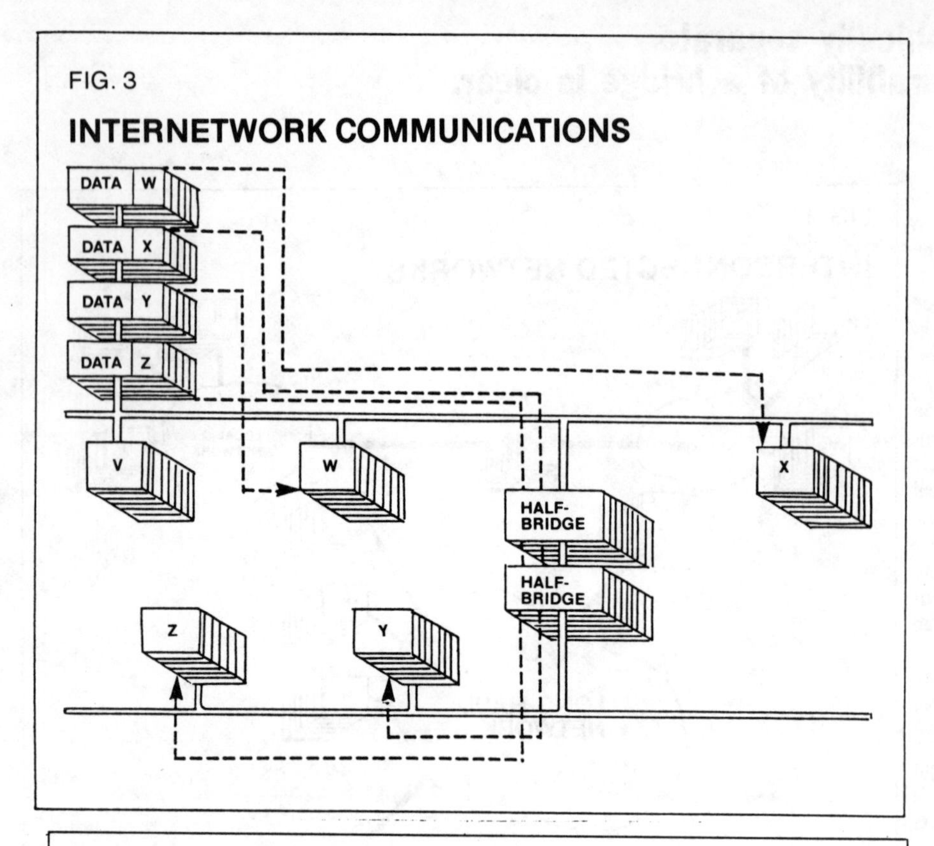

FIG. 3
INTERNETWORK COMMUNICATIONS

FIG. 4

THE ROLE OF IP IN A COMMUNICATIONS ARCHITECTURE

7 APPLICATION	Application services
6 PRESENTATION	Formatting and data presentation
5 SESSION	Connection control
4 TRANSPORT	End-to-end transmission service
IP	Internetwork routing and delivery
3 NETWORK	Internetwork routing and delivery
2 DATALINK	Reliable point-to-point transmission
1 PHYSICAL	Physical and electrical connection

control techniques peculiar to each network. The internetworking facility must be able to coordinate these to route data adaptively between stations on different networks.

- Access Controls. Each network will have its own user access control technique. These must be invoked by the internetwork facility as needed. Further, a separate internetwork access control technique may be required.
- Connection, connectionless. Individual networks may provide connection-oriented (e.g., virtual circuit) or connectionless (datagram) service. The internetwork service should not depend on the nature of the connection service for the individual networks.

A number of approaches have been tried for accommodating these differences among networks. At one extreme, a special-purpose gateway, known as a protocol converter, can be built for each particular pair of networks. Typically, a protocol converter accepts a packet from one network, strips off the control information to recover the data, and then retransmits the data using the protocols of the other network. The disadvantage of this approach, of course, is that a different gateway must be built for each pair of networks.

At the other extreme is the X.75 protocol, which is an extension of the X.25 packet-switch network interface standard that makes it possible to set up a virtual circuit between two stations on the same network. In effect, X.75 provides a logical connection between disjoint stations by stringing together virtual circuits across several networks. The drawback of this approach is that all of the networks must use X.25, a standard not used by most local networks. Furthermore, public-access networks, such as Telenet and Tymnet, do not accommodate X.75 links to private networks.

A more promising approach is the internet protocol (IP), initially developed for Arpanet. Versions of IP have been standardized by both the Department of Defense and National Bureau of Standards. The philosophy of IP is that the gateways and stations share a common protocol for internet traffic, but that the stations and networks are otherwise undisturbed. In terms of the usual open system interconnection (OSI) model for communications architecture, IP fits between the network (routing) and transport (end-to-end delivery) layers (Fig. 4).

IP provides what is known as a datagram service; that is, it will handle each packet of data independently. Multiple packets may arrive out of sequence. If a connection-oriented service is required, communicating hosts must share a common higher-layer protocol. Fig. 5 depicts the operation of IP for data exchange between host A on a local network and host B on a local network through an X.25 long-haul packet-switched network, and shows the format of the data packet at each stage. Each host must have the IP layer, plus some higher layers, in order to communicate. Intermediate gateways need only protocol software up to the IP level.

The data to be sent by A are encapsulated in a datagram with an IP header specifying a global network address (host B). This datagram is then encapsulated with the local network protocol and sent to a gateway that strips off the local network header. The datagram is then encapsulated with the X.25 protocol and transmitted across the network to a gateway. The gateway strips off the X.25 fields and recovers the datagram, which is then wrapped in a local network header and sent to B.

IP makes no assumptions about the underlying network protocol. Each host or gateway that uses IP interfaces with its network in the same fashion as for intranetwork communication.

OPERATION OF AN IP CATANET

A collection of interconnected networks using IP is often referred to as a catanet. Consider two hosts, A and B, on different networks in the catanet. Host A is sending a datagram to host B. The process starts in host A. The IP module in host A constructs a datagram with a global network address and recognizes that the destination is on another network. So the first step is to send the datagram to a gateway (example: host A to gateway 1 in Fig. 5). To do this, the IP module appends to the IP datagram a header appropriate to the network that contains the address of the gateway. For example, for an X.25 network, a layer 3 packet is formed by the IP module to be sent to the gateway.

Next, the packet travels through the

network to the gateway. The gateway unwraps the packet to recover the original datagram. The gateway analyzes the IP header to determine whether this datagram contains control information intended for the gateway, or data intended for a host farther on. In the latter instance, the gateway must make a routing decision. There are four possibilities:

1. The destination host is directly connected to one of the networks to which the gateway is attached.

2. The destination host is on a network that has a gateway that directly connects to this gateway. This is known as a "neighbor gateway."

3. To reach the destination host, more than one additional gateway must be traversed. This is known as a "multiple-hop" situation.

4. The gateway does not know the destination address.

In case 4, the gateway returns an error message to the source of the datagram. In the first three cases, the gateway must select the appropriate route for the data, which it then inserts into the appropriate network with the appropriate address. For case 1, the address is the destination host address. For cases 2 and 3, the address is a gateway address.

Before actually sending data, however, the gateway may need to fragment the datagram to accommodate a smaller packet size. Each fragment becomes an independent IP datagram. Each new datagram is wrapped in a lower-layer packet and queued for transmission. The gateway may also limit the length of its queue for each network it attaches to so as to avoid having a slow network penalize a faster one. Once the queue limit is reached, additional datagrams are simply dropped.

The process described above continues through as many gateways as it takes for the datagram to reach its destination. As with a gateway, the destination host recovers the IP datagram from its network wrapping. If fragmentation has occurred, the IP module in the destination host buffers the incoming data until the entire original data field can be reassembled. This block of data is then passed to a higher layer which is responsible for the proper sequencing of a stream of datagrams and for end-to-end error and flow control.

The internet protocol is most easily understood by looking at its header format (Fig. 6). Data to be transmitted are inserted into a datagram with the IP header. The header is largely self-explanatory. Some clarifying remarks:

Lifetime: in the NBS version, this field indicates the maximum number of gateways a datagram may visit so as to prevent endlessly circulating datagrams. DoD specifies this field in units of seconds, for the same purpose, and also to permit reassembly to be aborted at time-out.

Checksum: this is computed at each gateway for error detection.

Address: specifies a hierarchical address consisting of network identifier plus host identifier.

Options: the only option NBS has defined so far is a security field to indicate the security level of the datagram. In addition, DoD defines source routing, which allows the source host to dictate the routing; record route, used to trace the route a datagram takes; and internet time stamp.

FIG. 5

DATA ENCAPSULATION WITH IP

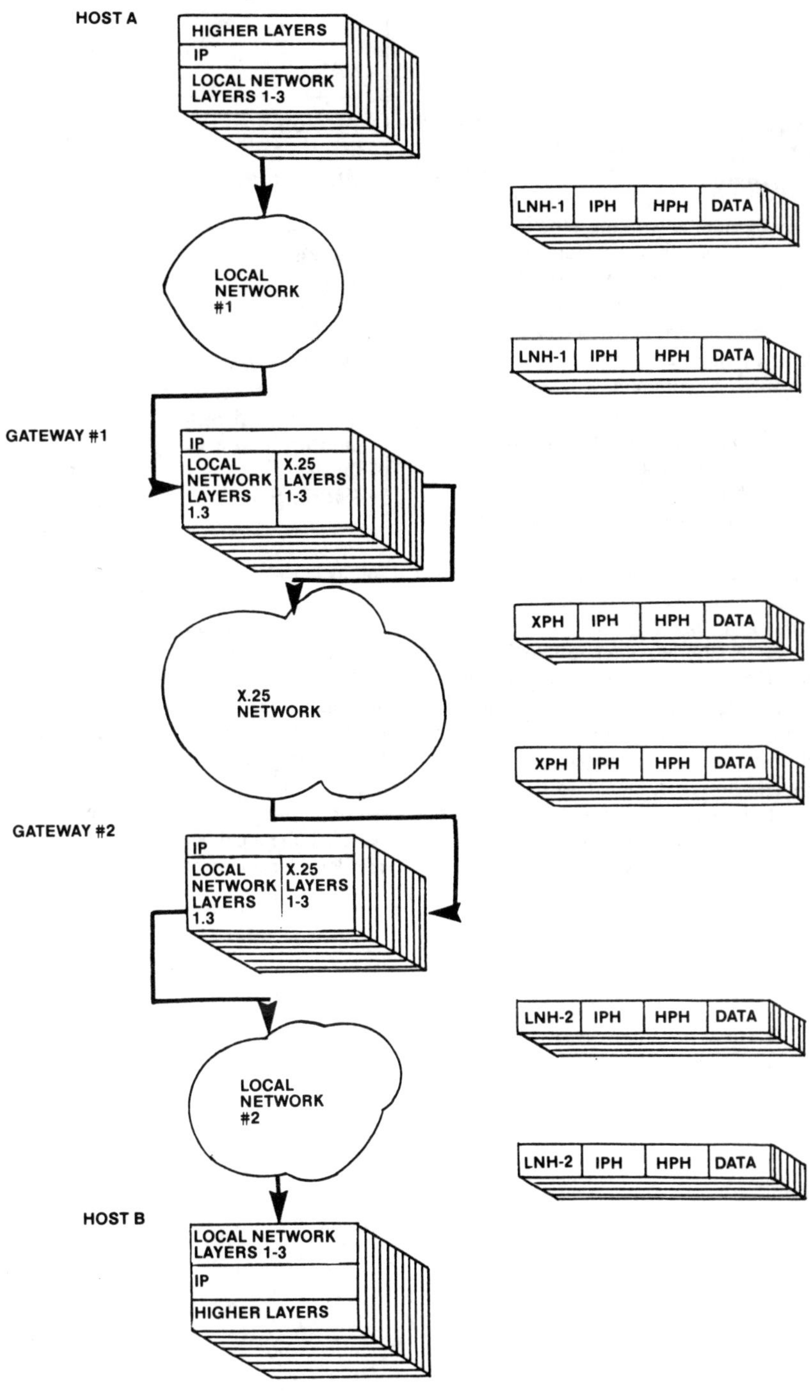

HPH = Higher Layer Protocol Header
IPH = Internet Protocol Header
LNH = Local Network Protocol Header
XPH = X.25 Protocol Header

FIG. 6

IP HEADER FORMAT

NAME	SIZE (in bits)	PURPOSE
Version	4	Version of Protocol
IHL	4	Header length in 32-bit words
Grade of service	8	Specify priority, reliability, and delay parameters
Data unit length	16	Length of datagram in octets
Identifier	16	Unique for protocol, source, destination
Flags	3	Includes more flag
Fragment offset	13	Offset of fragment in 64-bit units
Lifetime	8	Number of allowed hops
User protocol	8	Protocol layer that invoked IP
Header checksum	16	Applies to header only
Source address	64	16-bit net, 48-bit host
Destination address	64	16-bit net, 48-bit host
Options	Variable	Specifies additional services
Padding	Variable	Ensures that header ends on 32-bit boundary

LOCAL NETS AND CATANETS

Most research and experimentation with catanets to date has not involved local networks. While the principles of internetworking remain the same, there are some unique features of local networks that complicate the problem.

Consider the most general case of connecting a local network to a catanet consisting of long-haul networks and other local networks. A common internet protocol is needed to bind these networks together. The difficulty of doing so in a cost-effective way stems from two distinct differences between local and long-haul networks—their speed and how they handle outstanding packets.

Local network links typically operate in the range of 1 megabit to 50 megabits per second. Long-haul networks, on the other hand, generally operate at much lower speeds, usually less than 56 kilobits per second. The local network, moreover, usually uses no intermediate switches to route packets and is fast enough to deliver one packet before another is transmitted. On a long-haul network, however, there may be a number of packets outstanding, or undelivered, while still more are being transmitted.

This type of speed mismatch can result in a local network flooding a slower long-haul network with packets. Without an effective flow control procedure, the long-haul network may simply discard excess packets. A positive feedback mechanism can arise in which the local net sends new packets to the gateway and retransmits unacknowledged old packets.

If packets do not arrive at their destination in the order that they are sent, it may be left to the local network host to buffer and reorder them. This of course is a processing burden on local network hosts.

In conclusion, the manager of local networks needs to be careful when connecting dissimilar networks, for although the technology has made major advances, there are still several pitfalls to avoid.

Dr. William Stallings is a senior communications consultant with Honeywell Information Systems in McLean, Va. He is author of *Local Networks: An Introduction* (Macmillan, 1983).

Appendix D

INTERNETWORKING AND ADDRESSING *FOR* LOCAL NETWORKS

CONTENTS

PART I: LOCAL NETWORK INTERNETWORKING

This appendix was prepared by the Higher-Level Interfaces (HILI) Subcommittee of the IEEE Project 802 Local Network Standards Committee. This material, although not part of the Project 802 specification, is included as an appendix in this specification document to provide insight into how the Project 802 standards can be used and what difficulties are yet to be resolved.

Comments on this appendix can be forwarded to the Project 802 committee, or can be sent directly to the author:

Paul F. Wainwright
1B-317
Bell Laboratories
Holmdel, New Jersey, 07733
201-949-7855

EHO234-5/85/0000/0335$01.00 © 1982 IEEE

PART I: LOCAL NETWORK INTERNETWORKING

1. Introduction

In investigating the internetworking problem, we are taking a top-down view of local network protocols. Our motivation is to provide information to users of the IEEE local network standards that will help them to use local networks in a multi-network environment. This guidance is important since a widely accepted future view of data communications is one where most user equipment is connected to local networks rather than wide-area networks. In this view, local networks may be directly interconnected by one or more local or wide-area networks, as shown in Figure 1. For these reasons, internetworking is an important issue that deserves our attention. Moreover, since internetworking is not generic to local networks but also involves wide-area networks, we need to insure that other appropriate standards bodies (e.g., CCITT, ISO, and ANSI X3S33, X3S37, X3T51, X3T56 and X3T95) include local networks as an integral part of their internetworking efforts.

Overview of Part I:

Section 2 states the objectives of internetworking, while Section 3 analyzes the functions that must be performed for internetworking. Section 4 considers the ISO Reference Model and the appropriate placement of the internetworking functions. Section 5 presents a detailed description of the protocol issues involved in four different types of multiple-network configurations. Section 6 of this paper lists the open issues that the HILI Subcommittee has been discussing, and Section 7 lists our conclusions.

2. Internetworking Objectives

As shown in Figure 1, our main objective in considering internetworking is to enable multiple local networks to be directly interconnectable, and to enable local networks to be connected through wide-area networks. These wide-area networks may include packet-switched, message-switched, and circuit-switched networks. The local networks we are considering are assumed to be consistent with the IEEE 802 standards, although a general internetworking study would need to include other types of local networks as well. The internetworking capabilities should allow flexible topologies, and should minimize the overall protocol development costs and system overhead expenses.

One might ask why we need to be concerned with internetworking in the first place. After all, won't the ISO Reference Model eventually lead to global standards such that all networks use common protocols? The answer is that total homogeneity is neither obtainable nor desirable. This diversity of network protocols is *not* a failure to standardize, but is caused by local economic decisions. It is perfectly logical that in an ideal world, characterized by perfectly designed networks standardized to the utmost, there would still be a considerable diversity. Networks would exist in which 99 percent of the traffic would be local to a single network or cluster of networks. Such individual networks or clusters would be designed in a manner consistent with their primary purpose (to do local switching of data), which may not be consistent with global interconnection or any single global standard. It would still be desirable, therefore, to have a global internetworking scheme that would allow the remaining one percent of the traffic from such networks or clusters to make its way efficiently to other networks.

3. Internetworking Functions

The functions associated with internetworking can be broken into two categories: *basic* and *extended*. Basic functions are those things that must always be done, even if the interconnected networks are of identical type. Basic internetworking functions include such things as addressing across network boundaries, and routing at gateways. (The Global Network Sublayer, as defined below, is usually considered to be responsible for basic internetworking functions.) On the other hand, extended internetworking functions are those things that must be done when the various interconnected networks do not provide the same grade of service. Examples of extended internetworking functions include protocol conversion, packet re-sequencing, segmenting and blocking, and improved error detection (e.g., retransmission). Basic and extended functions exist for both connectionless and connection-oriented protocols, although the exact sets of functions may be different. More work is needed to define the functions that exist in each of these categories.

In considering a protocol architecture, the basic internetworking functions must always be performed at each intermediate point on a data path, as well as at the end points. However, two different philosophies exist for the placement of extended functions. On the one hand, extended functions could be performed only at the end points of a data path, while on the other hand they could be performed only at the gateways to the networks that offer lower grades of service than what is requested (some compromise between these two alternatives might also be possible). These two possible protocol architectures are illustrated in Figure 2.

A: Extended Functions at the End-Points

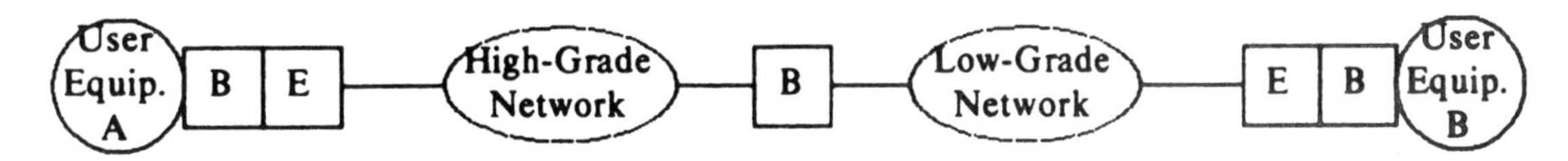

B: Extended Functions Around Low-Grade Network

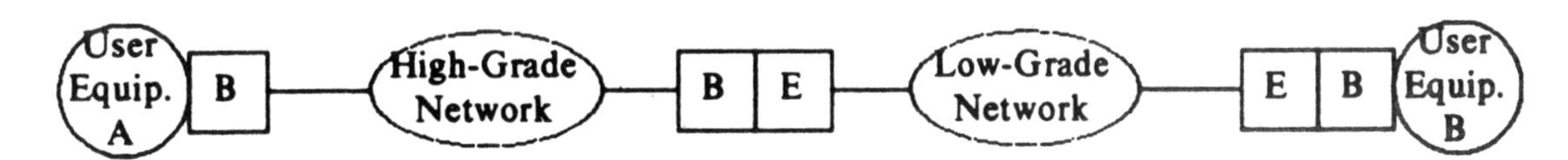

B = Basic Internetworking Functions
E = Extended Internetworking Functions

Figure 2

An advantage to performing extended functions at the end points is that existing (lower-grade) networks would not need to be enhanced in any way. An advantage to performing extended functions in the gateways to lower-grade networks is that the functionality of the higher-grade networks would not be duplicated, and thus the cost of enhancing the lower-grade networks would be assumed only by the users of those networks. Referring to Figure 2, the first case would require User A to implement extended functions despite the fact that it is connected to a high-grade (and therefore high-cost) network. The second case would allow User A to take advantage of the higher grade of service provided by the first network by not duplicating the functionality of the high-grade network. Moreover, performing extended functions at the gateways to lower-grade networks would minimize the need for end-to-end retransmissions due to network failures.

When considering more global system design questions, however, there are several advantages for placing extended internetworking functions in the end points. First, from a system sizing perspective, placement of extended internetworking functions in the gateways would require that gateways contain buffer space and state variables (e.g., for sequencing and error detection) sufficient to serve every correspondent pair that might communicate through it. This is a difficult quantity to judge in a multiple-network environment. Allocating too much buffer space would be economically unjustifyable, while allocating too little would mean possibly denying service to users. Since most end-nodes will be single users, the buffer space needed for internetworking in these nodes can be more precisely estimated than can be done for intermediate nodes, thus leading to a distinct advantage to placing extended functions at the end points.

On the other hand, this same situation can be viewed from an economy of scale perspective in which it could be more economical to concentrate extended functions at gateways.

A second system design consideration in internetworking is the possibility of failure within a gateway. Even with an extremely reliable Link and Network Layer protocol, because packets could be lost by a defective gateway there is no guarantee that a data path is reliable unless there is some sort of end-to-end internetworking protocol with extended functions. (A lot of this would usually be contained in the Transport Layer.)

A third reason for implementing end-to-end internetworking protocols is for flexibility in routing. If successive packets can take different routes, it is possible for them to get out of order despite reliable lower-layer protocols. An end-to-end protocol containing sequencing and error detection would enable dynamic routing to be used freely.

4. Protocol Architecture Considerations

When identifying local network internetworking functions, some consideration must be given to their placement in the ISO Reference Model. Referring to the seven-layer ISO Reference Model (Figure 3), the lowest two layers of protocol are generally tailored to suit the particular network technology being used. On the other hand, the highest three layers are generally independent of the underlying networks, and concern themselves only with end-to-end data transport and control. This leaves two layers -- the Network and Transport Layers -- in which to perform internetworking functions. To date, our discussion of internetworking functions is presented in a general sense, and no attempt has yet been made to assign these functions to either the Network or Transport Layer. Therefore, the goal of internetworking studies should be to determine the proper placement of the basic and extended functions described above within the ISO Reference Model's Network and Transport Layers, and to present guidelines on where these functions should be implemented (i.e., in user equipment or gateways).

Seven Layer ISO Reference Model

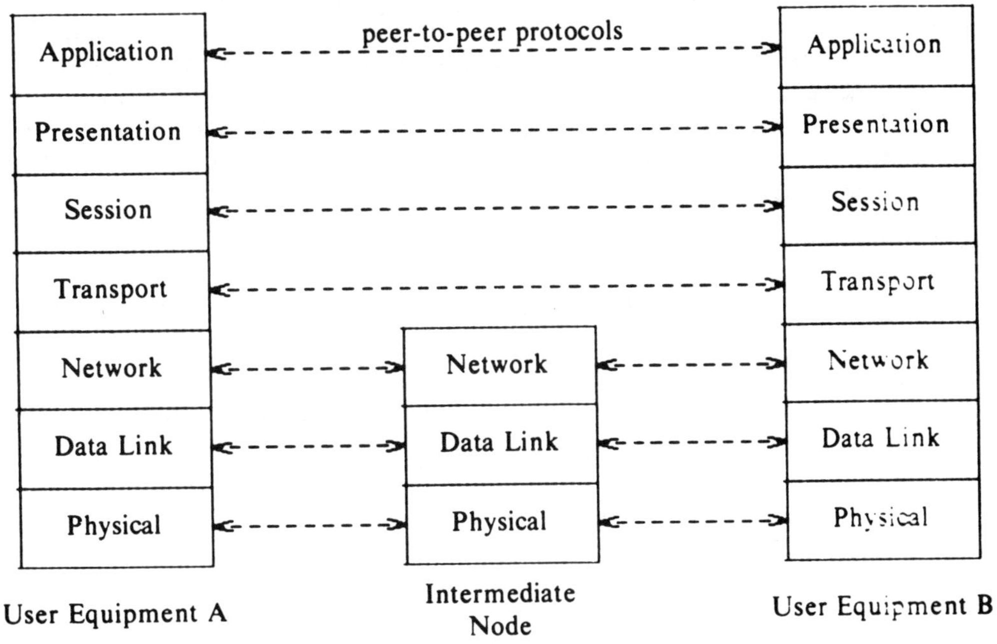

Figure 3

5. Internetworking Scenarios

5.1 Scenario Overview

This section describes the internetworking scenarios that have been formulated by the HILI Subcommittee. The diagrams presented here depict four general categories of local network internetworking:

- A single local network (the degenerate case),
- Two local networks connected together,
- A local network connected to a wide-area network, and
- Two local networks connected through a wide-area network.

These scenarios form a framework for constructing a detailed internetworking study. Such diagrams have been found to be useful in describing the placement of protocol functions both logically within the ISO Reference Model and physically in the user equipment and gateways. These scenarios are not intended to be all-inclusive, but rather serve as a starting point for further internetworking studies.

The scenarios presented here concentrate on the basic functions like addressing and routing, and do not directly deal with the placement of extended functions. However, future work in this area could build on these basic diagrams by including extended functions in the diagrams.

The four scenarios in this section were chosen because all of the basic internetworking functions (so far identified) are exemplified within this group. Thus, careful consideration of these scenarios could be expected to identify the majority of significant issues associated with internetwork communications requiring basic communications functions. The issues that have been identified to date through consideration of these scenarios are listed in Section 6.

Consideration of the possible internetworking scenarios has prompted the separation of the Network Layer into two sublayers, called the *Global Network Sublayer* and the *Communications Services Sublayer*, as shown in Figure 4.[1] The functions performed by the Global Network Sublayer include network and host addressing to enable gateways to perform routing. Specific examples of the functioning of this sublayer will be given below. Functions performed by the Communications Services Sublayer include the traditional layer 3 functions within each individual network.

Modified ISO Reference Model

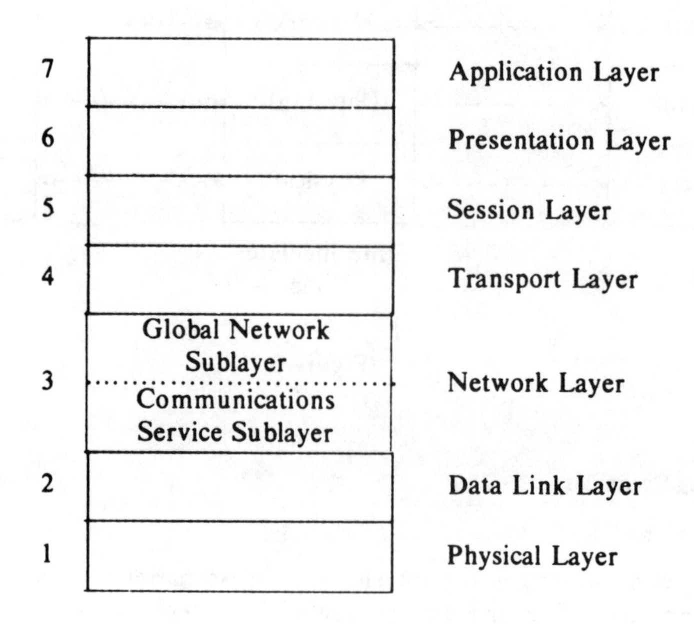

Figure 4

ECMA has recently introduced a 3-sublayer approach to the Network Layer, called Sublayers 3a, 3b, and 3c. Sublayer 3a contains functions normally provided by a given network (e.g., LLC). Sublayer 3b enhances these basic functions to provide a common set of services expected by sublayer 3c. Sublayer 3b may not be needed if 3a's functionality is adequate. Sublayer 3c provides for internetworking.

1. The term *Global Network Sublayer* is used in a generic sense, and is not intended to imply either a connection-oriented or a connectionless internetworking service. Furthermore, the term *Global Network Sublayer* should not be interpreted to imply a particular geographic placement of internetworking functions (e.g., around low-grade networks).

5.2 Description of Scenario Format

This section describes the format of Figures 5 to 8. The "boxes" labeled *User Equipment* or *Gateway* represent devices attached to the networks. These devices could include the following:

- Mainframe, mini, or microcomputers (with attached peripherals),
- Communication processors (e.g., gateways, front-ends),
- Standard peripherals (e.g., printers, disc/tape drives), and
- Terminals.

A given device may be dedicated to performing a single task which supports internetwork communication (e.g., gateway functions or directory services). On the other hand, a given device may be dedicated to serving users, and thus does not *support* but does *require* internetwork communication. A third possibility also exists in which a given device might both perform gateway functions and support users, although none of these dual-purpose devices are pictured in this paper.

Each "box" in Figures 5 to 8 is divided into layers corresponding to the modified ISO Reference Model shown in Figure 4.[2] Only those layers that are necessary to support internetwork communication are shown. Thus, there may be additional (higher) layers in the devices that are not shown since they do not affect internetwork communication. Furthermore, there may be multiple entities within each of the lower layers, but only those entities that are directly involved in internetwork communication are shown. A layer that is cross-hatched indicates that most of the functions ordinarily performed by that layer are not needed by the user equipment or gateway. The narrative description of each diagram indicates the functions performed in each layer.

Service Access Points (SAPs) are indicated by the parentheses between layers. (A SAP is the means by which one layer passes data or control information to one of its neighboring layers.) Not all SAPs are shown.

A high-level view of the frames on each link of the networks is also shown in Figures 5 to 8.

---

2. In these figures, layers 1 and 2 are intended to represent the Physical and Link Layers of a given protocol. For the IEEE 802 protocol, these two ISO layers include the IEEE Physical, Media Access, and Link Layer Control sublayers. These IEEE 802 sublayers are not explicitly shown in this appendix.

5.3 Single Local Network

Figure 5 depicts a protocol diagram for two users on a single local network. In this case, minimum functionality is needed within the Communications Services and Global Network Sublayers because no gateways or packet switches exist along the data path.

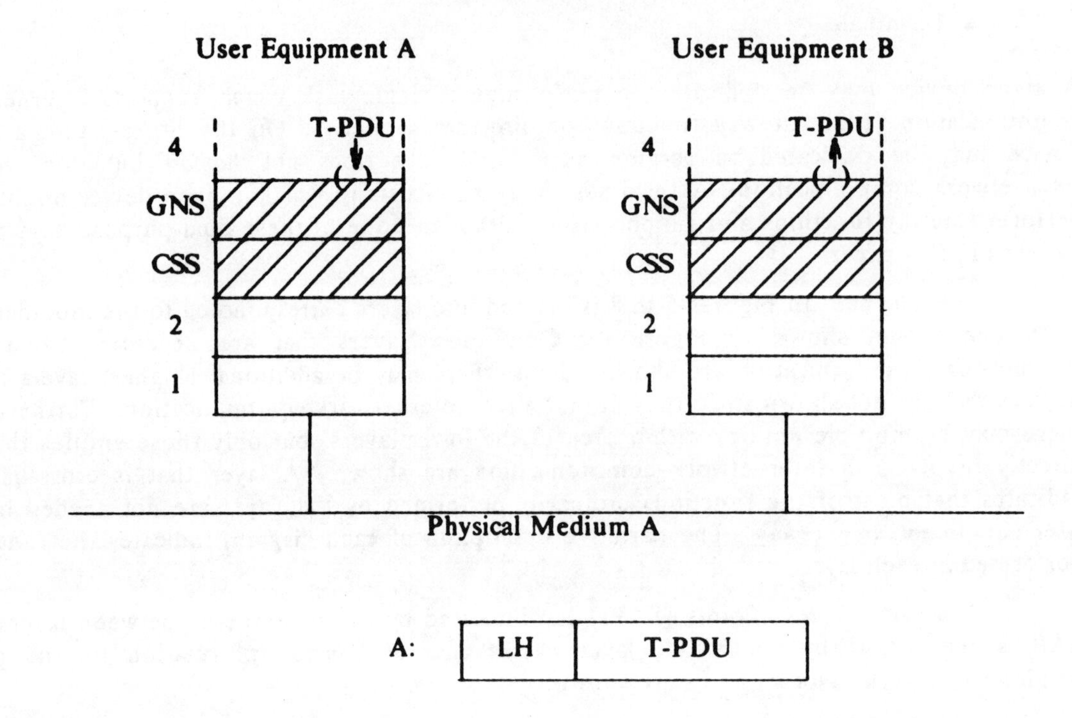

Figure 5

The lower portion of Figure 5 shows the format of packets as seen on the network. For example, if a Transport Layer Protocol Data Unit (T-PDU) is sent from User A to User B, a Link Header is the only major protocol control information that is needed since the Link Layer of User A can directly address the Link Layer of User B.[3] User B's Link Layer removes the Link Header and passes the T-PDU up to its Transport Layer Entity.

---

3. This view may be expanded as we better understand the affect that two-layer hierarchical addressing (as voted in the Seattle meeting) has on the Reference Model.

Only the most basic case is illustrated here. Since many local networks are likely eventually to be interconnected by gateways to other networks, good design suggests that a Global Network Header (as defined in Figure 6) be included even for this single-network case so as to avoid major enhancements upon connecting this single network to a gateway.

5.4 Two Local Networks

Figure 6 shows a protocol diagram for two hosts that are connected to *different* local networks which have a common gateway (the case of multiple gateways with intervening networks is a logical extension of this case).[4] In this case, minimum functionality is needed in the Communications Services Sublayer because the local network Link Layers provide the needed node-to-node communications services. The Global Network Sublayer is needed to perform the end-to-end network routing functions.

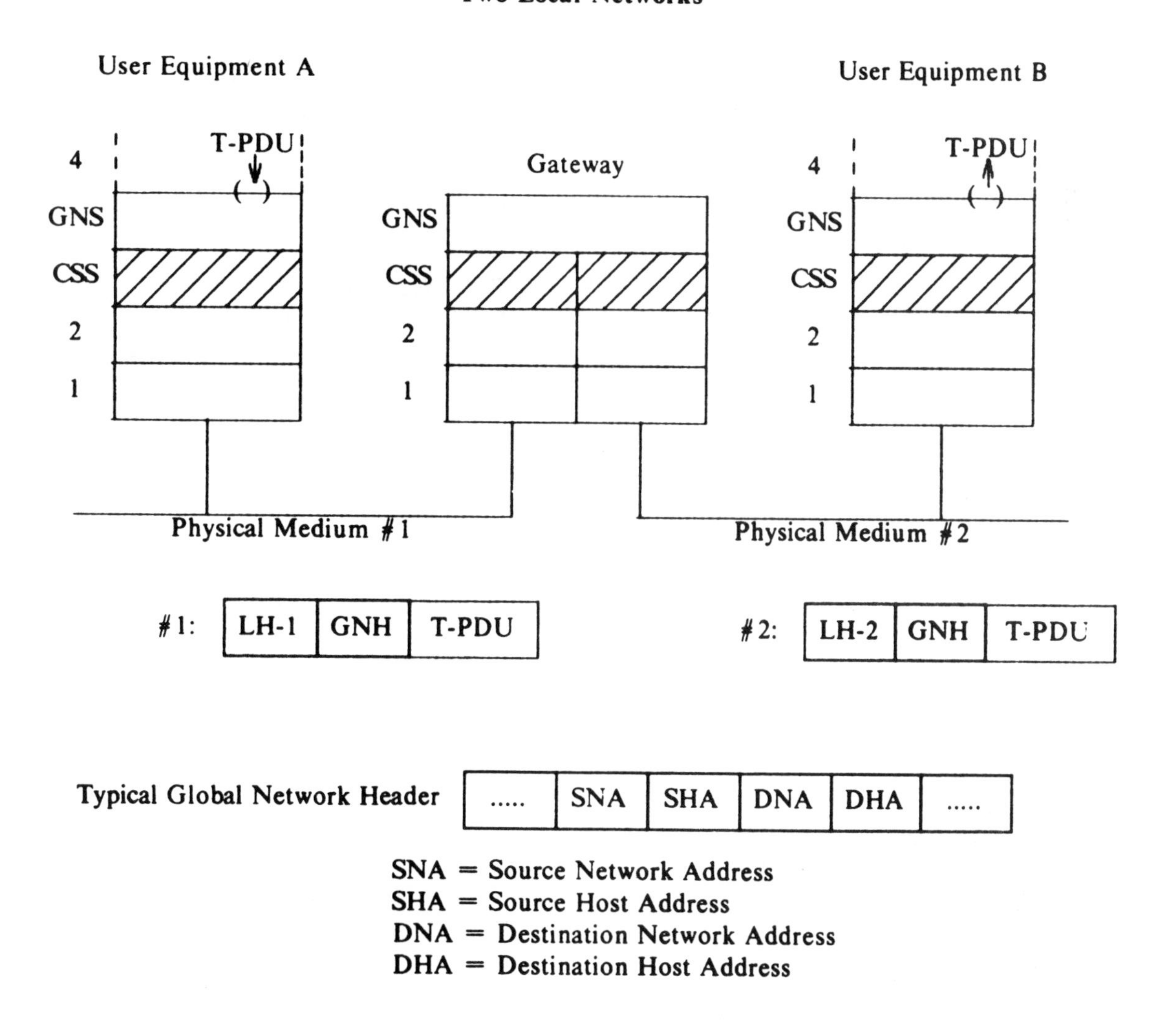

Figure 6

4. The gateway, as shown, is a unique node whose only function is to perform gatewaying. However, gateways could also be implemented as part of a general-purpose node that has access to two or more networks, and performs both gateway functions and supports applications. in general, gateways can be expected to contain internet management protocols that use the services of the lower-layer protocols to perform such functions as maintaining routing tables.

The lower portion of Figure 6 shows the formats of packets as seen on the local networks. A Transport Layer Protocol Data Unit (T-PDU) transmitted from **User A** to **User B** would first be encapsulated by a Global Network Header (GNH) and then by a Link Header (LH-1), as shown on the left of Figure 6. The GNH contains the destination *network* and *host* addresses of **User B** as well as the source *network* and *host* addresses of **User A**, as shown at the very bottom of Figure 6. (It is assumed that **User A** has knowledge of **User B**'s network and host address, or can get them by consulting a Directory Server via a separate interaction.) The Link Header appended by **User A** addresses the gateway.

Within the gateway, the link header is examined and stripped off, and the remaining GNH and T-PDU are passed to the Global Network Sublayer. There, the GNH is examined for the destination *network* address. Since in this case the destination network is directly connected to the gateway, the gateway examines the *host* address and passes the GNH and T-PDU to the appropriate Link Layer entity that provides service to the destination network.[5] (If the destination network were not directly connected, a routing table would be consulted to determine the appropriate routing.) The link entity of the gateway appends a second Link Header (LH-2) that addresses **User B**, using the destination host address from the GNH (this need not be a 1:1 substitution). At **User B**, the Link Header is examined and removed, as is the Global Network Header, and the T-PDU is passed up to the Transport Layer.

This situation may be overly idealistic, since it presumes that no two networks in the entire catenet have the same network address. It may happen that some random collection of networks might be interconnected at some point in the future. If this situation had not been foreseen when the network addresses were assigned, then there could be a serious problem at the gateway because of conflicting network addresses (SNAs and DNAs). Addressing issues are examined in greater detail in Part II of this appendix.

5. The GNH would be unchanged except possibly for a time stamp field, routing field, or lifetime field update. These would be extended functions, and thus have not yet been addressed. The question of segmenting is not yet addressed either since that is also an extended function. Also, network address translation by the gateway (another extended function, not yet addressed) could result in a mapping of network addresses in one catenet to those in a different catenet.

5.5 Local Network to Wide-Area Network

Figure 7 shows a protocol diagram for two users, one connected to a local network, and the other connected to a wide-area network.[6] Although minimum functionality is needed within the Communication Services Sublayer on the local network, a full complement of protocol functions are needed on the wide-area network because of the need to do packet or circuit switching.

Internetworking Scenarios
Case III
Local Network to Wide-Area Network

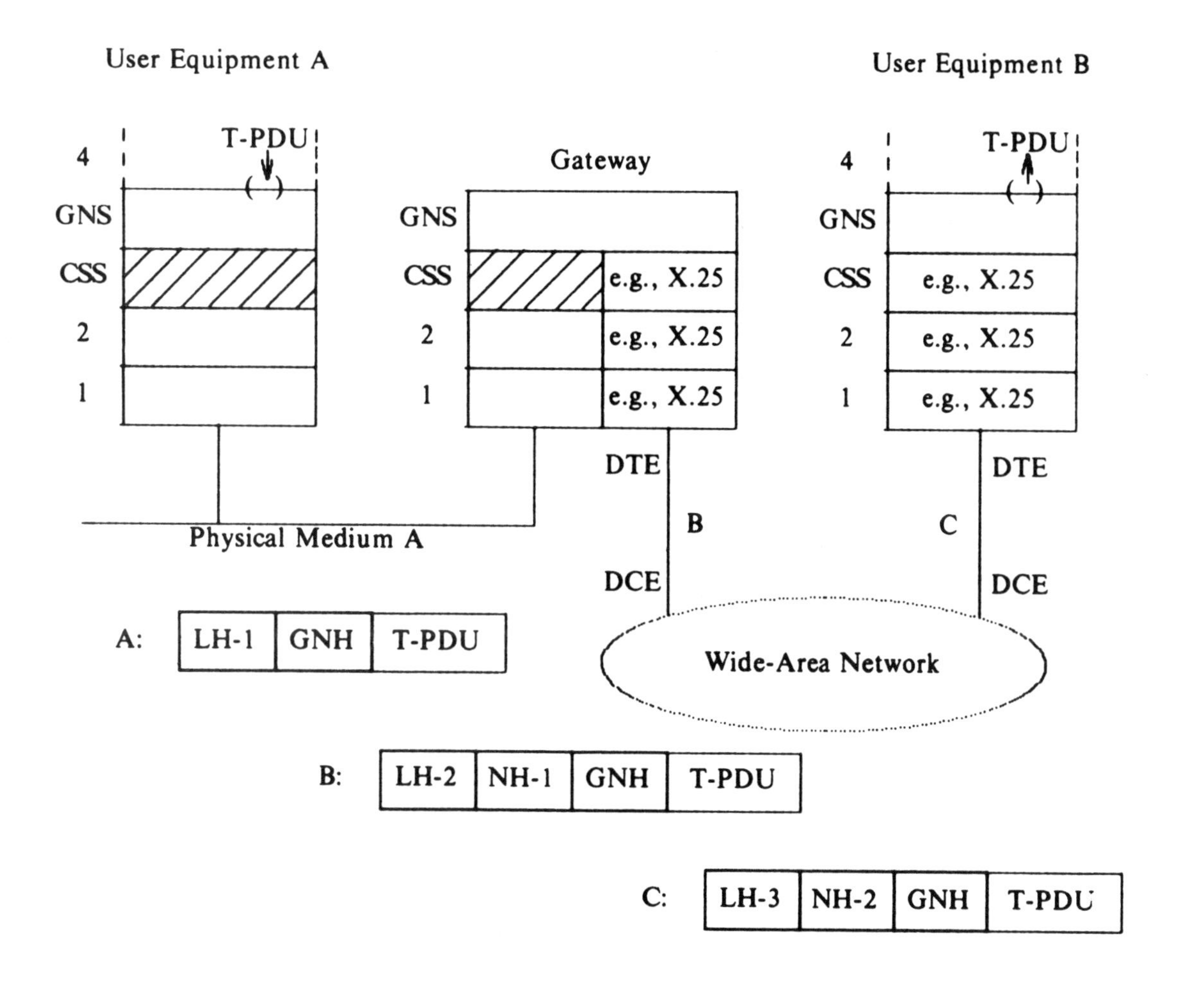

Figure 7

The lower portion of Figure 7 shows the formats of packets as seen on the local network and on the access lines to the wide-area network. As in the case of two local networks, User A encapsulates a T-PDU within a Global Network Header (GNH) and Link

6. By *Wide Area Network*, we mean any non-local data network, including public data networks, private long-haul networks, etc.

Header (LH-1), which is addressed to the gateway. Within the gateway, LH-1 is examined and removed by the Link Layer, and the GNH and T-PDU are passed to the Global Network Sublayer. The GNH is examined for destination *network* addresses, which in this case is a wide-area network, for example, an X.25 packet-switched or an X.21 circuit-switched network.[7] The gateway then performs the full Network, Link, and Physical Layer protocols needed for the wide-area network, including establishing a virtual or real circuit as needed. (The exact mechanism for doing this is for further study.) The GNH and T-PDU are transported by the wide-area network as a Network Layer I-field, and is presented to the Global Network Sublayer of **User B**. Here, the GNH is examined and removed, and the T-PDU is delivered to the Transport Layer of **User B**.

7. X.25 and X.21 are used here as examples only, and do not imply any endorsement of these protocols for use with local networks. This subject is for further study.

5.6 Local Network to Local Network via a Wide-Area Network

Figure 8 shows a protocol diagram for two users, each connected to different local networks which, in turn, are connected by a wide-area network.[8] Although minimum functionality is needed within the Communication Services Sublayer on the local networks, as with the previous case the full complement of protocol functions are needed on the wide-area network.

Internetworking Scenarios
Case IV
Local Network to Local Network via a Wide-Area Network

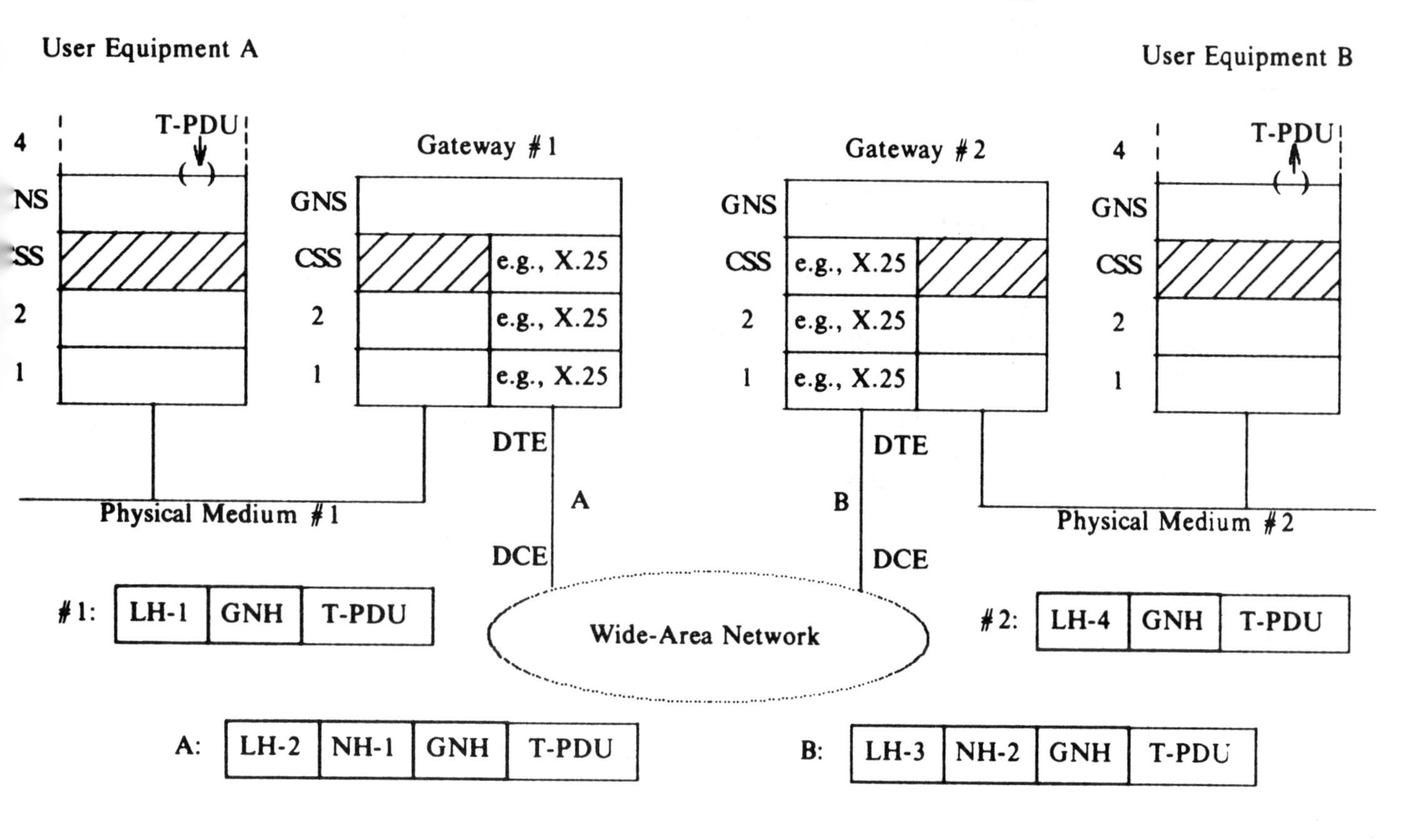

Figure 8

The lower portion of Figure 8 shows the formats of packets on the local networks and on the access lines to the wide-area network. As with the previous case, a Transport Layer Protocol Data Unit (T-PDU) sent from User A is encapsulated within a Global Network Header (GNH) and a Link Header (LH-1), which is addressed to the first gateway. As before, the Global Network Sublayer of the first gateway examines the GNH for destination *network* address. Since the destination network is not directly connected to this gateway, a routing table is consulted and the GNH and T-PDU are routed (in this case) via the wide-area network to

8. The inverse case, two wide-area networks connected by a local network (one possible implementation of a packet switch), is similar to this case. The protocol issues are the same as this case, and can be derived from what is presented here. Thus, the inverse case is not presented as a separate case.

the second gateway. The wide-area network delivers the GNH and T-PDU to the second gateway using the full complement of Network, Link, and Physical Layer protocols.

At the second gateway, the Global Network Sublayer again examines the destination *network* and *host* addresses. The GNH and T-PDU are transmitted to **User B** on the second local network, using the *destination host address* of the GNH as the LH-4 destination address (this need not be a 1:1 substitution). **User B** removes the LH-4 and GNH before passing the T-PDU to its Transport Layer.

6. Internetworking Issues

In the process of studying the scenarios presented above, the HILI Subcommittee has identified certain issues. This section lists the open questions that the HILI Subcommittee has identified for further study.

1. What is the best partitioning of basic and extended internetworking functions within the ISO seven-layer Reference Model? Is the upper (GNS) sublayer of Layer 3 the most appropriate place for basic internetwork functions? Is it the only place? What functions might need to be performed by Layers 6 and 7?

2. How do the services required by the higher layers to support internetworking affect the lower layer protocols? Alternatively, how do the various lower layer services impact the higher-level internetworking protocols? (See the "Protocol Configuration Exercise" in Attachment A.)

3. Since X.25 is an existing international standard, is X.25 Layer 3 a candidate for providing the minimal Network Layer functions needed for local networks? What enhancements would be needed? What about X.21? What about the NBS Internet Protocol?

4. *Within* a local network, given that we have both connection-oriented and connectionless services at Layer 2, exactly what functionality if any is needed at Layers 3 and 4? Which OSI protocols at Layers 3 and 4 would be appropriate with each Link Layer service?

5. How could connectionless service *with* acknowledgement (guaranteed delivery at the Link Layer) contribute to the internetworking solution?

6. What role could a connection-oriented but unrelyable protocol play in providing certain network services such as packetized voice?

7. Conclusions

From the information presented in this paper we conclude that the IEEE 802 work is not necessarily finished at the time the Physical and Data Link Layer standards are accepted and published. We must consider issues that are part of an overall local network standard, although many of these issues are also common to wide-area networks as well. Therefore, the HILI Subcommittee should continue to pursue the following action items:

- Our work with internetworking should be communicated to the other appropriate standards bodies (e.g., CCITT, ISO, and ANSI X3S33, X3S37, X3T51, X3T56 and X3T95), and we should insure that they include local networks in their internetworking work.
- We should better define basic and extended functions for both connectionless and connection-oriented internetworking. (Three categories might be defined: reliable sequenced connection-oriented, unreliable sequenced connection-oriented, and unreliable, unsequenced connectionless.)
- The scenarios that were used to identify the issues associated with the basic internetworking functions should be expanded in order to identify extended internetworking functions and the issues associated with them.
- The geographic placement of extended functions (see Figure 2) should be evaluated. Economy of scale and queueing statistics considerations should be thoroughly documented.
- The relative merits of connectionless and connection-oriented internetwork protocols should be evaluated and documented.
- Internetworking issues should be examined further to determine what affect internetworking has on lower-layer protocols.
- We should specify a few (3 to 5) examples of ways in which existing higher-layer protocols can (or can not) be used on top of the IEEE 802 standards to provide internetworking capabilities. This is sometimes referred to as a "dinner" in the "Chinese menu" of protocols.
- We should examine the appropriateness of X.25 layer 3 for the four internetworking scenarios presented in this paper and current level 3 and 4 protocol work underway in ANSI and ISO.

CONNECTING LOCAL NETWORKS TO LONG HAUL NETWORKS: ISSUES IN PROTOCOL DESIGN

Clifford Warner

Naval Ocean Systems Center
San Diego, California

Abstract

Local networks and long haul networks possess many different physical and technological characteristics. As a result, their performance requirements are best satisfied using very different communication protocols. This paper deals with the protocol design issues which arise when a local computer communication network is interconnected with a long haul network. In particular, the problems involved in connecting a specific local network, the Command Center Network which is now under development by the Navy, to the ARPANET, are discussed.

Introduction

What are the salient characteristics which distinguish a local computer network from a long haul network? Any computer network can generally be viewed as a collection of nodes, at which reside computing resources, and a set of communication channels which the nodes use to communicate with each other.[1, 2, 3] Sharing of resources is accomplished by the transmission and reception of messages which take the form of commands, inquiries, responses, file transfers, etc. These messages are generated and consumed by processes which reside at each node (a common definition of a process is a program in execution).

The nodes consist of host computer and terminal resources. These form the "user-resource" subnetwork. More than one host computer may reside at each node. Terminals may be either local to a host computer, or they may be remote, or a terminal need not be permanently associated with any host computer at all. The computing resources which reside at each node are commonly connected into the network through special purpose communication processors.[2, 3] The communication processors along with the communication links form the "communication" subnetwork. The communication subnetwork may also contain some nodes whose only function is message handling and gateway nodes whose function is to process messages which are sent to and received from an adjoining network. The user-resource subnetwork together with the communication subnetwork comprise the entire computer communication network.

Any computer communication network can generally be defined by the following features: its host computers and terminals, communication processors, topological layout, communication equipment and transmission media, switching technique, and protocol design.[1, 4] These features are chosen to accomplish the function of the network subject to specified performance requirements. The performance measures most commonly quoted include message delay, message throughput, reliability, and cost.[3, 4, 5]

Message delay can be defined as the elapsed time between the creation of a message at its source process and the successful reception of the entire message at its destination process. This definition of delay thus not only includes the delay experienced by the message in travelling through the communication subnetwork, but it also includes the time the message spent being processed by the hosts or communication processors as they implement the network protocols.

Message throughput can be defined as the average number of information bits successfully delivered to the destination process per unit time. With this definition, then, the throughput is affected by the throughput of the various network processors in addition to the throughput of the communication subnetwork.

A computer communication network can be considered reliable if it possesses certain qualities, such as the ability to adapt to changes in network structure, and the ability to recover from lost messages caused by noisy communication channels, incorrect routing, or congestion control mechanisms. This involves the use of acknowledgment and retransmission schemes. Also, providing a multiplicity of paths between nodes is often used to ensure the network's viability in the event of node or link failures.

The cost of a network is determined by the requirements for network resources such as processing speed, memory, and communication channel bandwidth, and by the manner in which these requirements are satisfied (technologies used, etc.).

Long Haul Networks

Long haul networks are predominantly characterized by their topology's large geographic scope. For example, the ARPANET spans the entire continental United States, and extends via satellite links to Hawaii and Europe.[3] The transmission media utilized by long haul networks commonly includes leased telephone lines (typically 9-50 kbits/sec), satellite links, and microwave links.[2] These resources are expensive, particularly if wide bandwidth is required.

The designers of long haul networks have typically implemented complex communication protocols and employed moderately expensive (eg., $50,000) front end communication processors in order to efficiently utilize the communication channel bandwidth.[6] This approach is justifiable from two standpoints. First, the major component of message delay and the major limitation to message throughput in long haul networks is the time required to traverse the communication

Reprinted from *Proceedings of the Fifth Conference on Local Compauter Networks*, 1980, pages 71-76.

channels on the path to a message's destination process.[7] With current technology, the speeds of the hosts and front end processors used by the long haul networks are fast enough that the time required to process a message with a complex protocol is generally not large in comparison to the time required to traverse the communication subnetwork links, and thus does not represent a significant component of message delay or a significant limitation to message throughput. Second, the cost of communication channel capacity for long haul networks is high enough that the use of a moderately expensive minicomputer for communication protocol processing is economically justifiable.

Local Area Networks

Local area computer communication networks possess a topology which is characterized by a relatively small geographical scope. This allows the local network to economically utilize communication links with much different technological characteristics from those used in a long haul network.[6] Typical communication medium technologies available for use in a local network include coaxial cable and optical fibers. With these technologies, and given the small size of a local network, bandwidths on the order of 10 to 100 Mbits/sec are feasible and economical. Even with twisted pairs, bandwidths of 10 Mbits/sec are achievable in a local area network.

Delay, throughput, and cost considerations for a local area network do not call for complex communication protocols. Cost considerations indicate, given the inexpensive wide bandwidth transmission medias available, that moderately expensive minicomputers are no longer economically justifiable. It would not be cost effective to utilize even moderately expensive minicomputers which implement complex protocols designed to efficiently utilize communication channel bandwidth, an inexpensive commodity in a local area network. Rather, less expensive microcomputers would generally be more cost efficient. Thus, given the slower speeds of microcomputers, and given the wide bandwidths of the communication medium, the processing time required to implement a complex protocol will likely no longer be an insignificant component of message delay nor an insignificant limitation to throughput. For example, measurements of the ARPANET Transmission Control Protocol at the University College London (UCM) indicate that their version of TCP has a throughput of approximately 26 kbits/sec.[17] Clearly this would be a severe limitation to throughput across a 10 Mbits/sec bus. Simpler protocols which would require less processing time are thus called for. Simpler protocols may inefficiently utilize communication channel bandwidth, but this is a plentiful resource. The designer of a local area network should be justified in expending a portion of the communication channel capacity in order to reduce message processing time.

It is clear from the above discussion that performance considerations indicate that long haul and local area networks should implement very different communication protocols. Long haul networks call for complex protocols which sacrifice processing time in order to efficiently utilize communication channel capacity, while local area networks call for simple communication protocols which waste channel capacity in order to reduce processing time. This creates a potential conflict of interests if a long haul network is interconnected with a local area network, particularly if each network intends to use the communication protocols it employs for internetwork communication also for communication between hosts both residing completely within it (i.e., for intranetwork communications). The conflict arises as a result of the constraints imposed upon these protocols by the requirement for reliable and coherent internetwork communication, as opposed to the requirement for each network to achieve low delay, high throughput, and low cost in its own intranetwork communications. As an example of this conflict, this paper will discuss the performance issues which arise when a particular local area network, the Command Center Network, which is now under development by the Navy, is connected to the ARPANET.

The Command Center Network

The expected form of the Command Center Network (CCN) has been the subject of previous research.[8, 9, 10] This paper will draw from these works in order to provide a brief description of the CCN.

The CCN interconnects a diverse group of heterogeneous shipboard computers and other Command and Control (C2) information systems in order to facilitate the integration of their resources for presentation to a user, such as a Naval commander of multiple platforms (i.e., ships), or a member of his staff. The resources of most interest which these Command and Control information systems will provide to the network are primarily data bases and other processes containing information on ship positions and identification, and other information of interest concerning the current tactical environment within which the multi-platform unit resides. By providing for automated access to these information resources, the CCN will provide responses to the commander's queries which are not only timely, but which are far more accurate and comprehensive than would otherwise be possible. This capability will greatly enhance the commander's ability to make effective command decisions in a rapidly changing tactical environment.

As currently envisioned these Navy information systems will contribute to the CCN user-resource subnetwork various standard Navy computers, with their associated peripherals, and terminals. These will connect to the communication subnetwork through front end processors which have been termed Network Interface Units (NIU's). The NIU's implement all the protocols which are necessary for communication with the other hosts. The need for front end processors to implement all the communication protocols is necessary in the CCN since most standard Navy computers are already running at full memory capacity, and thus cannot themselves be used to implement the protocols. (This may not be true of future Command and Control information systems which will eventually be included in the CCN.) The topological layout of the CCN is expected to be either a bus or a ring structure. Currently, the bus structure appears to be the probable choice. A depiction of the CCN is given in Figure 1.

The candidates for transmission media to be used in the CCN include coaxial cable, optical fibers, and others. Whatever transmission media is finally selected, it is expected to have a wide bandwidth, on the order of 10 to 100 Mbits/sec.

The ARPANET Transmission Control Protocol

The ARPA internetworking group has developed a reliable host-to-host protocol to be used by computers which

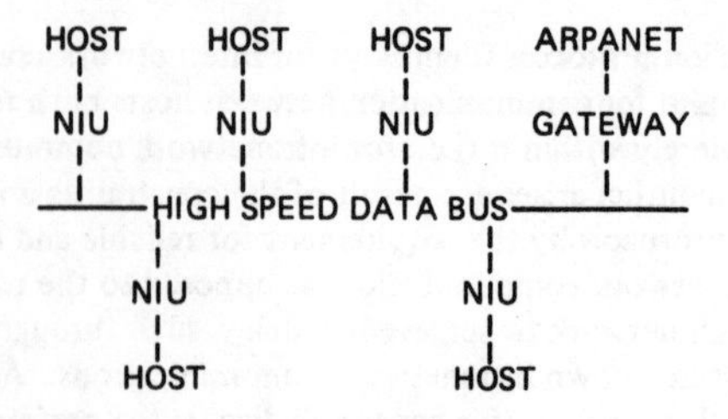

Figure 1. Possible CCN configuration.

reside in the "catenet", an interconnected collection of distinct computer networks. A depiction of the catenet is given in Figure 2. This host-to-host protocol has been called the Transmission Control Protocol (TCP).

The TCP is currently in the process of being implemented as the primary host-to-host communication protocol throughout the ARPANET. In many respects, TCP is well suited to the performance needs of a long haul network such as the ARPANET and not to the performance needs of a local area network. As an example of this, the suitability of the TCP for use as a host-to-host protocol in the CCN is discussed below.

The transmission Control Protocol facilitates the transmission and reception of messages between host computers which reside in an internetwork environment. The internetwork environment is assumed to consist of host computers connected to packet switched networks which are in turn connected via gateways.[11]

The TCP is a member of a layered protocol structure which supports an interprocess communication system for the internetwork environment and provides a virtual circuit between process ports. It interfaces on one side to user or application processes and on the other side to a lower level protocol such as the Internet Protocol. (The Internet Protocol basically attaches internetwork addresses to the packets and fragments packets at gateways when the adjoining network will support only a smaller packet. Thus the Internet Protocol has little or no affect on intranetwork communication performance). The Internet Protocol will typically reside just above the line control protocols for the network.

In addition to its purpose of providing a reliable connection service between pairs of processes, the TCP also has features designed to efficiently utilize the communication

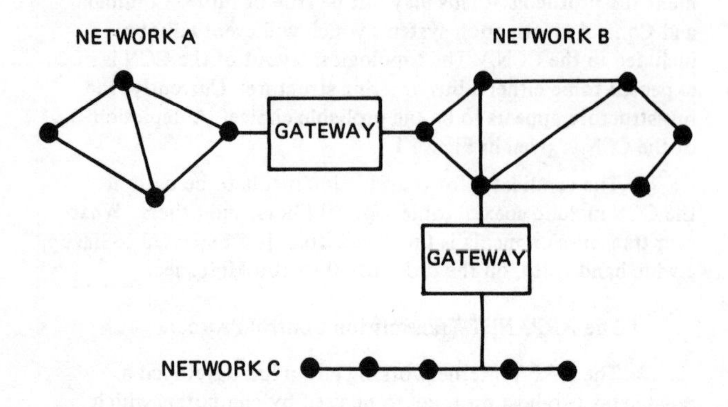

Figure 2. The Catenet.

facilities in a long haul computer communication network in which messages are routed to their destinations over a multihop path. For such a network, the TCP has been designed to give low message delay, high throughput, and provide for cost effective use of the network resources, such as communication channel capacity. The CCN, however, is a local network with features very different from those mentioned above. Delay, throughput, and cost considerations may be better satisfied by using different techniques than are contained in the TCP as it is presently specified. Following is a discussion of TCP, with suggested modifications to the protocol which would make it more suitable as a CCN host-to-host protocol.

TCP Functions

The TCP accepts messages from host processes and performs the following basic functions:

1. Breaking down of messages into packets.
2. Sequencing and reassembly of received packets.
3. Retransmission of lost or incorrectly received packets.
4. Flow control.
5. Detection of duplicate packets.

Packet Switching

TCP accepts a message from a host process and, depending upon the message length, divides it into one or more packets. These packets are relayed in a store and forward fashion until the destination node is reached. Packetizing of messages provides for improved message delay and lower network cost in a network such as the ARPANET. Packet switching decreases message delay by providing for pipelining of message packets,[3] and it utilizes network resources in a cost effective fashion primarily by efficiently utilizing telephone line capacity. Using packet switching, each communication channel is shared between many connections, rather than dedicating a communication channel to only a single connection (whether or not it is in use) as is done with circuit switching. Message switching also shares the communication channels between many connections, but it does not offer the improved message delay achieved by pipelining of packets over a multihop communication path.

While providing for low message delay and the efficient use of communication bandwidth in a network such as the ARPANET, packet switching also allows packets to arrive out of sequence at their destination, thus requiring resequencing to be performed by the destination TCP.

From the standpoint of message delay and throughput, packet switching is not well suited to CCN intranetwork communication. The CCN will consist of a collection of host computers connected by a high speed bus or ring. Whenever a host in the CCN communicates with another host also residing in the CCN, a single-hop connection is established between them (a ring may use repeaters at each node, but messages are not stored at each node and later forwarded on). No opportunity for pipelining exists, thus packet switching offers no improvement in message delay as compared to message switching. Analysis of the Ethernet, a local area network using a contention bus, indicates that their network efficiency (defined as the fraction of time the bus is carrying good packets) increases as packet length increases.[18] The use of a very large packet would imply the use of message switching since most messages would fit into a single packet. Thus, low message delay, efficient communication channel utilization, and protocol simplicity (and thus cost) are all achieved if message switching is used in place of packet switching, or if very large packets are used such that most, if not all, of the messages can be fit into a single packet. This would usually involve merely sending the messages to their destinations intact, eliminating the complexity and degradation in performance which would result from unnecessarily breaking messages into smaller packets and reassembling them at their destination. Breaking up a message into several small packets would also increase overhead in the CCN by requiring a header for each packet instead of only a single header for the entire message.

Sequencing and Reassembly

Since packet switching allows packets in a distributed network such as the ARPANET to arrive out of sequence (this is especially probable when the network becomes heavily congested), each octet of data in a packet is assigned a sequence number at the source TCP. These sequence numbers are used to resequence the packets at their destination TCP prior to being reassembled into a message. If the CCN uses message switching the requirement for resequencing and reassembly is obviously eliminated. If the CCN does employ packet switching, with very large packets, the need for resequencing is still eliminated since alternate routing of messages is not possible over a bus or ring (assuming packets travel in only one direction around the ring). The only way a packet could arrive out of sequence would be either if it were lost due to communication channel noise and later retransmitted, or if the packet ahead of it were lost. However, recovery from lost messages can be handled in the CCN with simple techniques which do not allow messages to arrive out of sequence, eliminating the need for resequencing. One error recovery technique which would accomplish this, and which is simple and well suited to the needs of the CCN, is stop-and-wait ARQ.[12] With this technique, after sending a packet, the sending TCP waits for a positive or negative acknowledgment from the receiving TCP before sending another packet or retransmitting the same packet. With this technique, a delay is incurred between packet transmissions as a result of the time required for acknowledgments to traverse the communication subnetwork. However, the delay required for the acknowledgments to traverse the CCN high speed bus should not be significant.

Even without the need for resequencing, however, messages in the CCN will still need to be provided with a unique identifier for acknowledgment purposes and to enable the recognition of duplicate messages.

Retransmission

Retransmission of messages lost because of incorrect routing or because of errors induced by noisy communication channels is a basic ingredient of any packet switched computer communication network. The TCP protocol uses a scheme whereby retransmission of messages by the source node results from the lack of a positive acknowledgment reception within a time out period. Some computer communication networks also utilize negative acknowledgments to signal to the source node that a retransmission is needed before the time out period has elapsed. The use of negative acknowledgments can thus improve message delay, but it can also decrease throughput as a result of the extra network congestion induced by the negative acknowledgments. Also, negative acknowledgments will not inform the sender of a loss of a message due to incorrect routing, and they can themselves be lost. The use of positive acknowledgments should thus always be used to ensure the delivery of messages to their destinations.

The retransmission of flawed messages should be a part of the CCN protocols. Even though the CCN is a local network, messages will almost certainly, if only rarely, be lost due to communication channel noise, and some messages may be lost due to collisions if a contention bus or ring is used. Some sort of acknowledgment schemes is thus called for. The use of positive acknowledgments with a time out at the sender will be perfectly adequate, and can be included in the simple stop-and-wait ARQ technique discussed above.

Flow Control

The ARPANET TCP protocol uses a window technique for flow control. The receiving TCP sends to the source TCP a window of sequence numbers which it will accept. As messages are received, they are checked to see if they fall within the acceptable range of sequence numbers. If they do not, they are discarded. As messages are received and acknowledged, the window is shifted at both the receiving and sending TCP's so that previously received sequence numbers are shoved outside the acceptable range and new sequence numbers yet to be used are brought in to the acceptable range.

The use of the window technique enables a destination TCP to regulate incoming packet flow, thus preventing the reception of more packets than it can accommodate. During periods when the network is uncongested, the use of an appropriately large window allows packets to be sent from the source TCP well before the destination TCP is ready for them, resulting in an uninterrupted flow of packets and thus higher throughput than would result from the use of a very small window.[7] Since round trip delay over a long haul communication subnetwork is typically an order of magnitude greater than the delay caused by communication protocol processing, a simple protocol that waits for acknowledgment of each packet before transmitting the next packet will cause the communication channels to be idle a large fraction of the time, resulting in poor throughput. However, in a local area network such as the CCN, communication link capacity is not a significant limitation to adequate throughput. Adequate throughput can be achieved if flow control is implemented such that a message is not transmitted from a source host-to-host protocol until the destination host-to-host protocol acknowledges the previous packet. Thus, using this latter technique, protocol simplicity and a resulting increase in throughput (as a result of decreased protocol processing delay) is achieved by eliminating all of the various computations required to check incoming packets to see if they fall in the window, to shift the window as packets are received and acknowledged, and to recompute the window size as network conditions change. Simplicity is also achieved since the need is eliminated for mechanisms which ensure that both the sending and receiving TCP's windows are synchronized.

Detection of Duplicate Packets

The TCP also uses the window technique for detection of duplicate packets. When a duplicate packet arrives, it will lie outside of the window of acceptable packets and be discarded.

However, with the simpler flow control technique suggested above for intranetwork CCN communications, a receiving TCP will only be expecting a single packet sequence number, the number immediately following the number of the preceding packet. Thus, a receiving TCP can detect duplicate packets merely by comparing its sequence number to the one it expects.

CCN and ARPANET Interconnection

The above discussion indicates that the TCP protocol, as it is currently specified, is more complex than is necessary for use in a local area network such as the CCN. Furthermore, measurements of the TCP[17] indicate that it has very poor throughput in comparison to a high speed (10 Mbits/sec) bus such as will be used in the CCN, and thus will not provide optimal CCN intranetwork communication performance. However, since the CCN is to be interconnected with the ARPANET, it must be able to communicate with TCP. This leaves the designers of the CCN with various options.

First, the CCN network could implement TCP for both internetwork and intranetwork communication. This approach would provide for relatively simple communication with hosts residing in the ARPANET, and eliminate the need to develop a host-to-host protocol specifically designed to provide for good performance within the CCN. The simplicity of this strategy is achieved, however, at the expense of definitely suboptimal CCN intranetwork communication performance. The designers of an experimental CCN are currently following this approach.[19] Whether or not it will become permanent is still an open question.

A second solution would be to implement two completely separate host-to-host protocols at each CCN node. TCP would be used to handle communications between a host residing in the CCN and a host residing in the ARPANET, and another host-to-host protocol would be used to handle communication between two hosts both residing completely within the CCN. A primary advantage of this technique is the resultant good performance which should be achieved in both internetwork and intranetwork communications. The obvious disadvantage of this approach is that it would result in the high cost of developing a new host-to-host protocol specifically designed for the CCN, as well as the cost required to implement and maintain two distinct host-to-host protocols at each node.

A third approach, similar to the second approach mentioned above, would be to implement at each node only a CCN host-to-host protocol, placing TCP at the gateway between the CCN and the ARPANET. When a message is to be sent to a host residing in the ARPANET, the gateway would receive the message, process it with the CCN host-to-host protocol, and hand the message to the TCP. The gateway TCP would then deliver the message to its destination ARPANET host. This approach eliminates the cost required to implement and maintain two host-to-host protocols at each CCN host. However, the gateway protocols would generally require a large amount of processing time for each message, and could thus become a bottleneck if a large amount of traffic flows through them.

A last approach would be to implement a CCN host-to-host protocol which retains all of the TCP features not significantly affecting message delay or throughput in the CCN, but which substitutes for the unnecessarily complex TCP procedures. For example, TCP contains fairly elaborate procedures for initial connection establishment and for recovery from host crashes. These techniques may require substantial amounts of processing time. However, they should be used only rarely and thus should not significantly affect delay or throughput. The TCP recovery and connection establishment procedures could thus be implemented intact in a CCN host-to-host protocol with no adverse affect on performance. On the other hand, the flow control, resequencing, and duplicate detection techniques in TCP are too complex for efficient CCN intranetwork communication, and should not be included in a CCN host-to-host protocol. Rather, substitute procedures, such as those previously discussed in the section on TCP, should be used. The resultant modified version of TCP, termed a Local Network Transmission Control Protocol (LNTCP),[20] would be well suited for use in a local area network such as the CCN, yet retain a high level of commonality with the ARPANET TCP.

Each CCN node should be able to implement both the LNTCP and TCP with a limited amount of effort and cost. Being identical in many respects, the two protocols could share substantial protions of software. Those sections of software unique to either LNTCP or TCP could be either executed or bypassed, depending upon the situation. An alternate approach would be to implement only the LNTCP at each CCN host, placing a LNTCP to TCP translator at the gateway to the ARPANET. Since the LNTCP and TCP would be very similar, the gateway translator would be required to perform relatively simple tasks, thus consuming only a limited amount of processing time. The use of a LNTCP should thus allow efficient CCN intranetwork communication, which also maintaining efficient and somewhat simple internetwork communication.

Conclusions

Because of their very different topology, transmission media, and other features; delay, throughput, and cost considerations indicate that long haul networks and local area network should use very different host-to-host communication protocols. Long haul networks require complex protocols which efficiently utilize communication channel bandwidth at the expense of processing time. Local area networks require simple protocols which expend communication channel bandwidth in order to reduce processing time.

The ARPA internetworking group has developed a reliable host-to-host protocol, called the Transmission Control Protocol (TCP), to be used by computers which reside in the "Catenet", an interconnected collection of distinct computer networks. TCP is a complex protocol with features designed to efficiently utilize the communication facilities is a long haul network such as the ARPANET. Any local network interconnected with the ARPANET which uses TCP as its only host-to-host protocol will achieve relatively simple internetwork communications at the expense of definitely suboptimal intranetwork communication performance. An alternate approach would be to implement a Local Network Transmission Control Protocol (LNTCP) which retains many of the features of TCP, but substitutes for the TCP flow control, resequencing, and duplicate detection features, and which uses a much larger packet size than the ARPANET. Such a protocol should provide for efficient local network intranetwork communication performance while allowing for good internetwork communication performance as well.

References

1. Wushow Chow, "Computer Communications Networks—The Parts Make Up the Whole," National Computer Conference, pp. 119-128, May 1978.

2. David J. Farber, "Networks: An Introduction," Datamation, pp. 36-39, April 1972.

3. Leonard Kleinrock, Queueing Systems Volume II: Computer Applications, John Wiley & Sons, Inc., New York, 1976.

4. John M. McQuillan and Vinton G. Cerf, Tutorial: A Practical View of Computer Communications Protocols, IEEE Computer Society, IEEE Catalog No. EHO 137-0, 1978.

5. W.R. Crowther, et al., "Issues in Packet Switching Network Design, " National Computer Conference, pp. 161-175, May 1975.

6. David D. Clark, Kenneth T. Pogran, and David P. Reed, "An Introduction to Local Area Networks," Proceedings of the IEEE, Vol. 66, No. 11, November 1978.

7. Carl A. Sunshine, "Factors in Interprocess Communication Protocol Efficiency for Computer Networks," National Computer Conference, pp. 571-572, 1976.

8. Naval Electronic Systems Command," Statement of Work for Local Command Center Network Development," Naval Ocean Systems Center, Code 8242, San Diego, California, 7 February 1979.

9. Computer Sciences Corporation, "Local Command Control Network Interface Specification," Naval Ocean Systems Center, Code 8242, San Diego, California, September 1978.

10. Glen R. Allgaier, "Command Center Network . . . Backbone of Future Command & Control," Naval Ocean Systems Center, Code 8242, San Diego, California, 1979.

11. Information Sciences Institute, University of Southern California, "Transmission Control Protocol," Defense Advanced Research Projects Agency, Information Processing Techniques Office, 1400 Wilson Boulevard, Arlington, Virginia, 22209, August 1979.

12. H.O. Burton and D.D. Sullivan, "Errors and Error Control," Proceedings of the IEEE, Vol. 60, pp. 1293-1301, November 1972.

13. Ira W. Cotton, "Computer Network Interconnection," Proceedings of the Second Berkeley Workshop on Distributed Data Management and Computer Networks, Lawrence Berkeley Laboratory, University of California, Berkeley, pp. 3-18, May 25-27, 1977.

14. Vinton G. Cerf and Peter T. Kirstein, "Issues in Packet-Network Interconnection," Proceedings of the IEEE, Vol. 66, No. 11, pp. 1386-1408, November 1978.

15. Vinton G. Cerf and Robert E. Kahn, "A Protocol for Packet Network Intercommunication," IEEE Transactions on Communications, Vol. COM-22, No. 5, pp. 637-648, May 1974.

16. Leonard Kleinrock and Holger Operbeck, "Throughput in the ARPANET – Protocols and Measurement," IEEE Transactions on Communications, Vol. COM-25, No. 1, January 1977.

17. Christopher J. Bennett and Andrew J. Hinchley, "Measurements of the Transmission Control Protocol," Computer Network Protocols Symposium, Leige, Belgium, February 1978.

18. Robert M. Metcalfe and David R. Boggs, "Ethernet: Distributed Packet Switching for Local Computer Networks," Communications of the ACM, Vol, 19, No. 7, July 1976.

19. R. Nelson and J. Goodhue, "Architecture for the Experimental Command Center Network, Bolt Beranek and Newman Inc., Report No. 4232, October 1979.

20. C.J. Warner, "Local Network Transmission Control Protocol (LNTCP)," Technical Note 793, Naval Ocean Systems Center, San Diego, California, 15 Dec. 1979.

The approaches to interconnection—network access, network services, and protocol functions—are related and overlap. User requirements and existing specifications determine which one the designer emphasizes.

Interconnecting Local Networks to Long-Distance Networks

Norman F. Schneidewind, Naval Postgraduate School

The demand for broad yet specific network services is an urgent one, and as both local and long-distance networks proliferate, the need for better connections between these disparate systems is becoming critical.

A local network is a data communications system that allows communication between a number of independent devices. These devices can be computers, terminals, mass storage devices, printers, plotters, or copying machines.[1] The network may support a wide variety of applications, such as file editing and transfer, graphics, word processing, electronic mail, database management, and digital voice. Local networks are usually owned by a single organization and operated within a restricted geographical area, most often within a mile radius, at a moderate to high data rate such as 10 million bits per second. A long-distance network, on the other hand, is usually owned by a communications carrier and operated as a public utility for its subscribers, providing services such as voice, data, and video.

An emerging service of long-distance networks is providing the interconnection for local networks and other long-distance networks. Interconnection can provide

- local network to local network communication,
- local network to long-distance network communication, and
- long-distance network to long-distance network communication.

These interconnection possibilities, though exciting, inevitably present designers with the problem of resolving network incompatibilities. There are inherent differences in network characteristics as the result of the diversity of networks that exist to serve the various user communities. These differences have been accentuated by the failure of some networks to adopt standard protocols, by the variety of existing protocols and protocol standards, and by the wide range of incompatible options within existing protocol standards. In addition, designers are faced with a confusing mix of unregulated vendor products (e.g., IBM's System Network Architecture), local networks (e.g., Ethernet), regulated common carrier networks (e.g., Telenet), and newly deregulated communication services (e.g., American Bell).

The changing network scene

To set the stage for discussing the interconnection problem, let's review the evolution of computer networks to their current level of complexity.

Early connections. Before the advent of local networks, network services—supported by a single long-distance network—were viewed as shown in Figure 1. This view had the following major characteristics:

- terminal to computer communication,
- computer to computer communication, and
- terminal to terminal communication.

The orientation was one of data communication rather than networking. The long-distance network provided the terminal or remote-job-entry user with access to

EHO234-5/85/0000/0356$01.00 © 1983 IEEE

remote computers or terminals. This mode of operation was typical of, for example, earlier versions of Arpanet, Decnet, and SNA and of the services provided by data communications carriers such as AT&T and MCI. The network provided access to hardware and software resources that were not available locally.

Emergence of networking. Rapid advances in technology, coupled with the development of local network architectures and protocols, led to the implementation of multiple mini/microcomputer-based workstations. The workstations are tied together by a physical communications medium and supported by protocols for network access and for message transmission and reception. Initially, the terminal was the focal point of activity, accessing hosts in a resource-sharing network such as Arpanet or using a long-distance communications network such as AT&T for connection to a remote computer. Now, the emphasis has shifted to complete, self-contained local networks that access long-distance networks to communicate with other networks and, at the same time, provide communication among the local-network workstations. Thus, contemporary network services feature both inter-local and intra-local network communications (see Figure 2). As far as the long-distance network is concerned, the entire local network looks and functions like a single terminal. Indeed, this is an interconnection design goal.

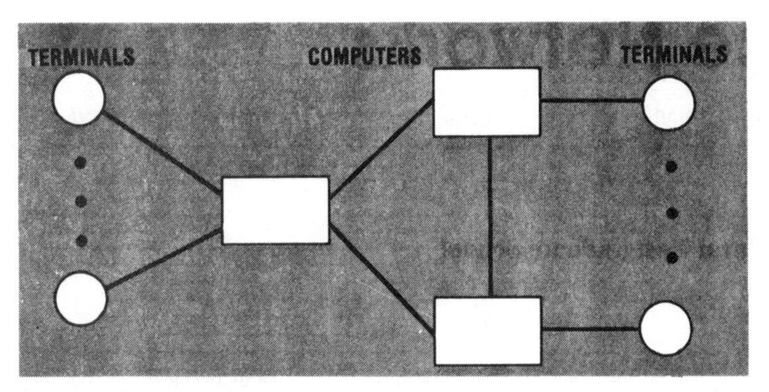

Figure 1. Previous view of computer networks.

Interconnection issues

Local and long-distance networks have significant differences that must be addressed when planning and designing networks consisting of one or more local networks interconnected by one or more long-distance networks.

The differences between local and long-distance networks, summarized in Table 1, lead to major interconnection issues:

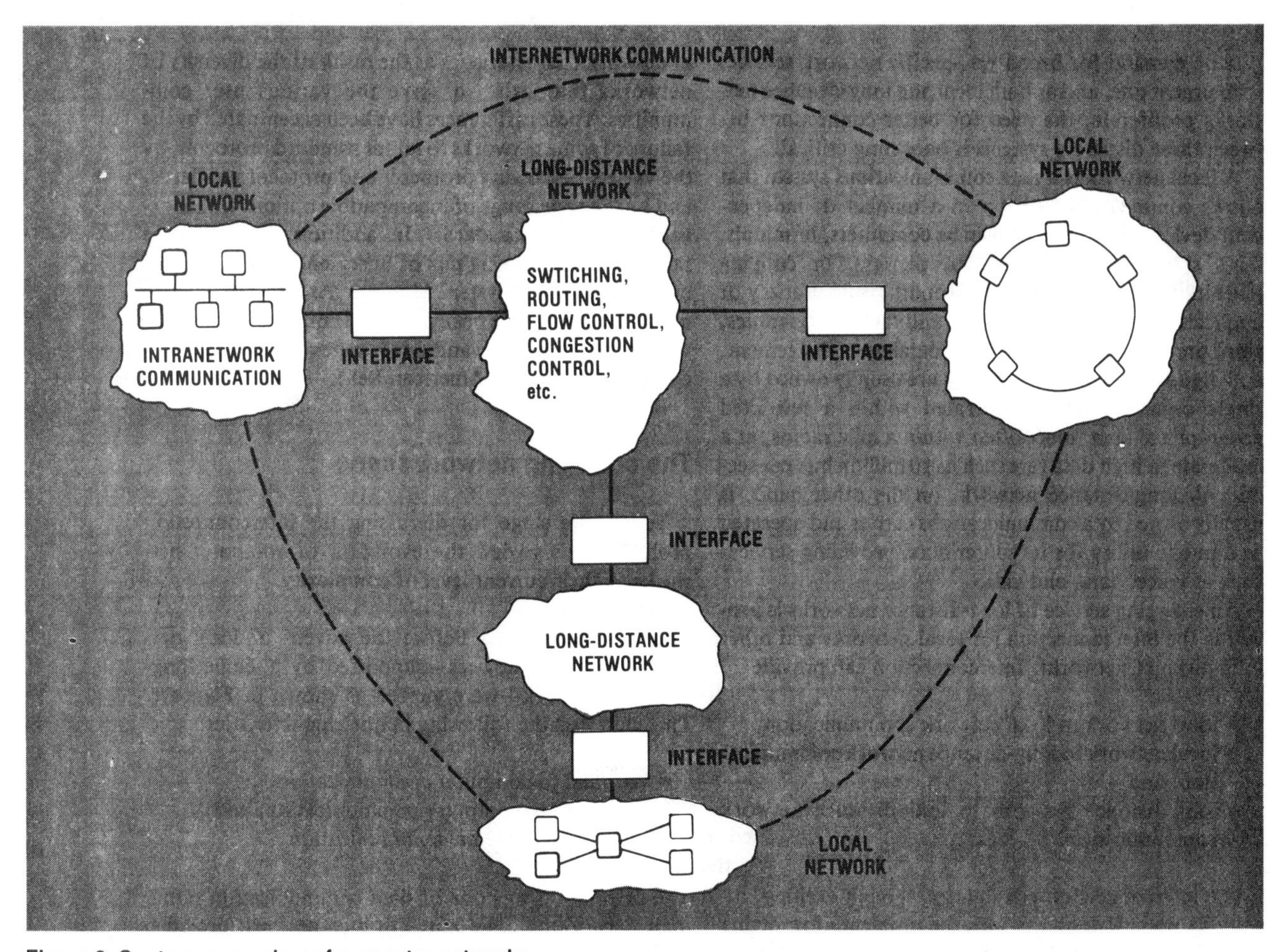

Figure 2. Contemporary view of computer networks.

- How should a local network be physically attached to a long-distance network?
- How should one local network access and communicate with another local network?
- To what extent should protocol and network architecture standards used in one network be used in another network?
- How is the difference in bandwidth, as it affects acknowledgment handling and flow control, to be resolved?
- How is the difference in delay time, as it affects user response time, to be reconciled?
- How should network addressing capability be provided? (A single local network can, of course, have a simpler address structure than a long-distance network, but communication among multiple local networks is the most difficult addressing problem of all.)

Decisions regarding these interconnection issues must be made before, not after, the networks are implemented.

A variety of situations and factors can affect the type of interconnection provided. Sometimes the networks already exist and their specifications are known—for example, when an existing local network is connected to an existing long-distance network to communicate with other local networks. In other situations, however, one or more of the networks must still be specified. A common design problem involves developing specifications for nonexistent local networks that are to communicate via one or more existing long-distance networks.

Thus, the properties of the long-distance network(s) are usually given and part of the local network design problem involves the specification of the interface for connecting the two types of networks. For the designer, this situation presents both a challenge and an opportunity: a challenge because few user organizations—other than communications carriers or the Department of Defense—can control the characteristics designed into long-distance networks; an opportunity because the designer can influence the effectiveness of both intra-local and inter-local communication by the approach he uses to specify the network interface.

In designing the interface, the following important principle applies:

> The more a local network is designed to increase the effectiveness of intra-local network communication, the more the cost of the interface to a long-distance network increases and the more the effectiveness of inter-local network communication decreases.

This principle is an outgrowth of the significant differences in the characteristics that distinguish local and long-distance networks (Table 1). These differences lead to a high-cost, complex interface if each type of network is tailored to the particular needs of its user communities. On the other hand, if the local network is designed to achieve compatibility with a long-distance network, the cost of the interface falls, but local-network throughput and response time suffer. The usual way of resolving this trade-off is to lean heavily in the direction of maximizing local network effectiveness, at the expense of interface cost, because the interface represents a one-time cost while the local network must provide effective service for its users over the lifetime of the network.

The ISO architecture

A significant development in the standards area that exerts considerable influence on network design and intercommunication methods is the International Standards Organization model of architecture for open systems interconnection.[2] (See Figure 3.) The extent to

Table 1.
Comparison of local and long-distance network characteristics.

CHARACTERISTIC	LOCAL NETWORK	LONG-DISTANCE NETWORK
Typical Bandwidth	10 million bits per second.	56,000 bits per second.
Acknowledgment	One message acknowledged at a time.	*N* messages acknowledged at a time.
Message Size and Format	Small (simple header). No need to divide message into packets.	Large (complex header). Need to divide message into packets.
Network Control	Minimum requirement due to small number of links and nodes and simple topology.	Extensive due to large number of nodes and links and complex topology.
Flow/Congestion Control	Minimum due to high bandwidth and simple topology.	Extensive due to low bandwidth and complex topology.
Error Rate	Relatively low. Operated in benign environment.	Relatively high. Operated in noisy environment of telephone network.
Message Sequence and Delivery	Minimum problem due to simple topology (e.g., bus or ring).	Major problem due to complex topology (e.g., mesh).
Standard Architecture	Usually only two or three bottom layers provided.	Frequent use of all or many ISO layers.
Routing	None required due to simple topology	Major problem due to complex topology
Delay Time	Small due to short distance and medium (e.g., coaxial cable).	Large due to distance and medium (e.g., satellite).
Addressing	Simple intra-network communication due to simple topology. Complex inter-network communication due to the use of long-distance network(s).	Complex because of many nodes and links.

which local and long-distance networks adhere to the ISO model has an important bearing on the nature and complexity of the interconnection. The use of many, or all, ISO layers is particularly important for long-distance networks because of their

- complex topology,
- wide geographical coverage,
- large number of nodes and links,
- extensive switching and routing,
- numerous points requiring flow control and congestion control,
- relatively long delays in end-to-end transmission, and
- long distance process-to-process communication requiring complex acknowledgment schemes.

Local networks, on the other hand, have much simpler characteristics and thus less need for the various ISO protocol services. Warner[3] has suggested that forcing a local network design *in total* into the ISO mold could result in significant overhead in terms of (1) a large message size to accommodate multiple headers for the many ISO layers, (2) complicated and unnecessary message acknowledgment procedures, and (3) extraneous hardware and software to support the ISO transport and network layers. However, not using ISO in the local network risks loss of compatibility with ISO-based networks, one of which could be a long-distance network that must interface with the local network.

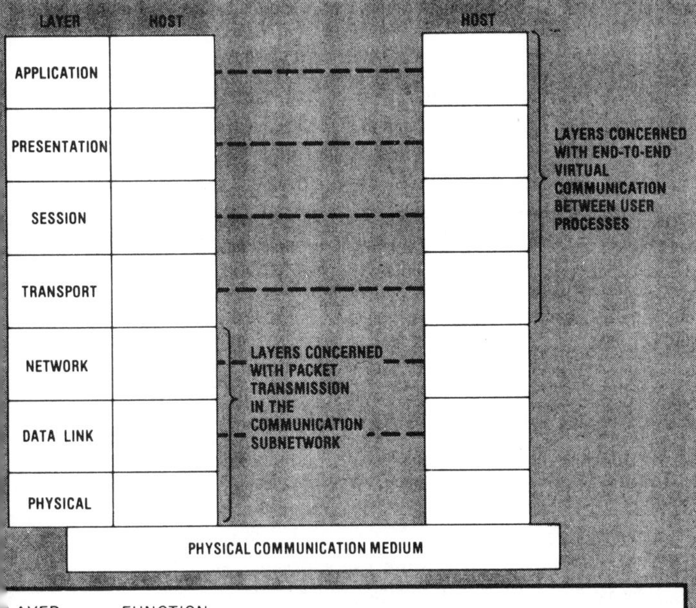

LAYER	FUNCTION
Application	Communication between cooperating user processes
Presentation	Formatting and display of user data
Session	Coordination and administration of user process data exchange
Transport	Reliable end-to-end transfer of data over virtual circuits
Network	Routing and switching of packets in the communication subnetwork
Data Link	Reliable packet transfer between nodes in the communication subnetwork
Physical	Transmission of bits between nodes in the communication subnetwork

Figure 3. ISO model seven-layer architecture.

Approaches for solving the interconnection problem

The three basic approaches to interconnection—network access, network services, and protocol functions—are related and frequently overlap. Bear in mind that a combination of the approaches, described and compared below, may be necessary to interconnect diverse networks effectively.

Network access. The network access approach involves making electrical and physical connections of local networks and user communities via the long-distance network. The predominate considerations in this approach are ones of physical access and interfacing—for example, signal levels, pin connectors, cable length, and transmission medium. But it also emphasizes local-network compatibility with the long-distance network at the bottom three layers of the ISO model. All three layers are needed. *Any* network communication requires the data link layer for reliable internode communication, and a long-distance network requires the switching and routing functions of the network layer.

The main concern in this approach is the user's ability to *access* additional users and resources at a reasonable cost by the most convenient, feasible method. Whether or not the network services obtained as a result of the connection are ideal for the application is of secondary concern.

A number of situations could motivate user interest in the network access approach. Frequently, the motivation is convenience; the service needed—say, for example, an X.25-compatible network—might simply be readily available. Another possibility is that the user's objective is limited. He might not be interested in obtaining computer-based services such as database management, financial forecasting, or engineering computation; perhaps he only wants the services of a *transmission medium* for providing connectivity to other users. Then, the need is for a communications facility whose primary function is the *transport* of data. A data communications carrier is frequently the long-distance network that provides this level of service. A third possibility is that the user's terminal equipment is only compatible with certain networks, so the ability to provide interconnection at the lowest physical level outweighs other considerations.

Ordinarily, the network access approach is used when both the local networks and the long-distance network already exist. Since network characteristics cannot be created or modified, the user's options are limited, and he must be content with a low-cost network that is hardware-compatible with his local networks.

Network services. High-level user services can be obtained with the network services approach to interconnection. Some services, such as database management, could be related to the application and presentation layers of the ISO model; others, such as a high-level communication service like electronic mail, could be related to the transport and network layers.

Obviously, any interconnection approach involves connections between local networks and a long-distance network and thereby provides inter-local network access. However, in contrast to the first approach, the network services approach stresses obtaining specific network services for the user organization, and the details of physical and electrical interfacing, while important, become secondary issues. Necessarily, this approach emphasizes compatibility between local networks and a long-distance network at the higher level layers of the ISO model.

What conditions motivate a user to consider this approach? One situation is when the long-distance network provides a data management or processing service that is not available in the local networks. Often only a large-scale network (e.g., Arpanet) has the host hardware and software capable of providing a desired service. A second situation arises when a high-level, inter-local network communication service is desired. For example, the user organization may want to tie its local networks together, or connect to other organizations' local networks to provide remote interactive processing involving session control and sequenced, error-free message delivery. Typically, this type of service would be obtained from a long-distance network that provides a virtual circuit service. Since the objective is to obtain a specific type of network service, naturally the long-distance network is an existing one. However, the local networks may or may not exist. If they do, protocol conversion will probably be required at the interface between the local networks and the long-distance network. If they don't exist and if ease of interfacing is a primary objective, the desired service may prompt the local network designer to attempt maximum compatibility with the layers and protocols of the long-distance network.

In general, a data communication network is appropriate for the network access approach, but a resource-sharing or value-added network is germane to the network services approach.

Protocol functions. The third method of achieving interconnection provides one set of protocol functions for the local network and another set for the long-distance network, where some functions, or corresponding network layers, are common to both networks. When crossing network boundaries, a transition or "conversion" is made between protocols. The boundary points are typically implemented in hardware with gateways (an interface between two networks) and front-end processors.

This method is used when the user's *primary* objective is to optimize local network communication, by using only those layers and protocols necessary for local network operation, while also providing communication between local networks via the long-distance network. Although the user will not be indifferent to physical access and network services, the dominant objective is to marry two diverse types of networks, which are inherently incompatible, and still retain the effectiveness of each. Protocol conversion is necessary to achieve this objective. The degree of conversion is a function of the differences between the layers and protocols in the two types of networks.

When would a user organization be able to capitalize on this approach? The most likely situation is when the local networks have not been implemented and the user has the opportunity to influence both intra-local network and inter-local network effectiveness by virtue of the protocol functions provided in the local networks; the long-distance network may or may not have been implemented (i.e., it may also be in the planning or development stage). Regardless of the status of the long-distance network, the user organization would, in most instances, have negligible influence over the design of the long-distance network due to the size and dominant position of the long-distance network organization.

In some cases, one protocol can be translated into another. In others, protocols can be held in common among the communicating parties.

This approach is seldom viable when the local networks exist; the likely degree of protocol conversion required, in terms of message format, message size, acknowledgment method, naming, addressing, error control, etc., would make it infeasible.

Comparison of approaches

As stated by Cerf and Kirstein,[4] the common objective of all interconnection methods is to allow all subscribers a means of accessing a host on any of the interconnected networks. They go on to declare that achieving this objective requires that data produced at a source in one network be delivered and correctly interpreted at the destination(s) in another network. This reduces to providing interprocess communication across network boundaries. In some cases, it is enough to translate one protocol into another. In others, protocols can be held in common among the communicating parties.

The efficiency of achieving this objective depends on which approach is utilized. It is not necessary to implement all ISO layers in the local network to achieve effective intra-local network communication, nor is implementation necessary to connect to a long-distance network. However, the number, types, and characteristics of the layers utilized determine the efficiency of inter-local network communication (i.e., communication over the long-distance network).

The network access approach certainly achieves *physical* access to hosts, but the interconnection does not provide access to all the services available in the long-distance network. This approach does not *fully* achieve the requirement of delivering data from the source and having it correctly interpreted at the destination, because complete compatibility between local network protocols and long-distance network protocols may not be possible. For example, it might achieve a datagram service, which requires only the first three ISO layers, but might not be able to realize virtual circuit service, which requires use of the transport layer.

The network services approach does, on the other hand, *completely* satisfy the requirement regarding data delivery and interpretation, but not necessarily efficiently. In this approach, it may be necessary to adopt inefficient local network protocols to achieve compatiblity with the long-distance network. This is the case if the protocols are held in common among the communicating parties, where the "communicating parties" are the local network and the long-distance network.

Table 2.
Comparison of network interconnection approaches.

APPROACH	CHARACTERISTIC	ADVANTAGES	DISADVANTAGES
Network Access	Achieves physical access and protocol compatibility in lower layers of ISO model (e.g., physical, data link, and network layers of X.25).	Relatively inexpensive. May obtain compatibility with international standards.	Only provides compatibility with lower layers of network architecture. Restricted to services of network access method.
Network Services	Obtains use of specific types of services (e.g., virtual circuit service) to satisfy user needs.	The network service is matched to the user need as opposed to simply obtaining physical access to a network. Reduces software development expense.	Restricted to using the same (perhaps inefficient) protocols in all interconnected networks. May be restricted to using a single type of service.
Protocol Functions	Matches number and types of protocols to each type of network.	Uses only those protocols that are necessary in each type of network. High performance. Low overhead.	Expensive software development. Complex network interface.

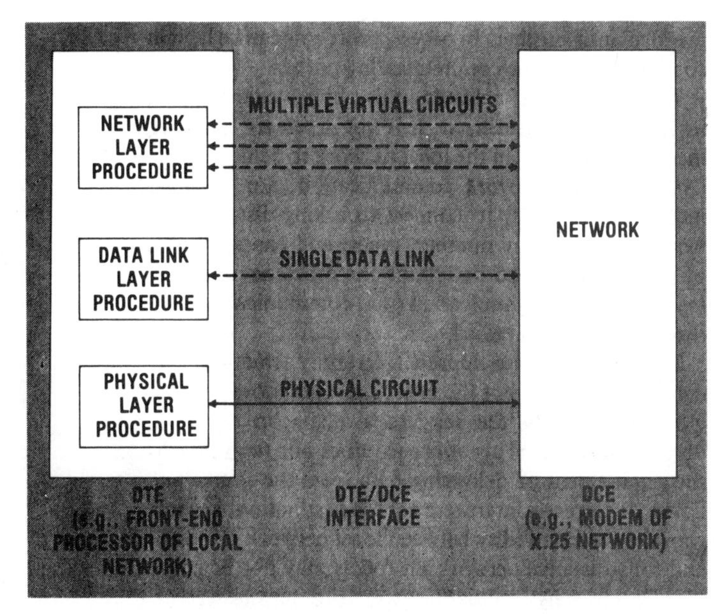

Figure 4. Structure of the X.25 interface (adapted from Reference 5).

The protocol functions approach solves the problem of local-network communications efficiency, but at high hardware and software costs. Its use of the protocol translation technique necessitates a complex network interface.

In general, no matter which approach is utilized, the owner of the local network is responsible for designing the interface and arranging the connection with the owner of the long-distance network, using the specifications of that network as a guide. This work will take place over an extended period of time, and involves development, design, implementation, and maintenance. The three approaches are summarized and compared in Table 2.

Examples of interconnection approaches

Network access. Rybczynski[5] provides an example of the network access approach to interconnection vis-a-vis the X.25 interface standard. X.25 is a standard device-independent interface between X.25-compatible packet networks and user devices operating in the packet mode. The interface point occurs between the user's data terminal equipment, or DTE, and the data communications equipment, or DCE, of an X.25 packet switching network (e.g., GTE-Telenet). Although the DTE is often thought of as an individual terminal or host, it could just as well be a front-end processor of a local network. The DCE could be a modem associated with the communication channel of an X.25 packet-switching node. Multiple local networks connected in this fashion would provide inter-local network communication and the services offered by the X.25 long-distance network. The interface between the DTE and DCE occurs at the first three layers of the ISO model, as shown in Figure 4.

The characteristics of these layers* are as follows:

Physical layer
- full duplex,
- point-to-point, and
- synchronous.

Data link layer
- data link control procedures compatible with the high-level data, link control (HDLC) protocol,
- single data links,
- data transfer,
- link synchronization,
- detection of and recovery from errors, and
- reporting of errors to a higher layer.

Network layer
- packetizing of user and control data,
- network addressing, and
- multiple virtual circuits.

From a practical standpoint the user organization must provide the appropriate hardware and software in

*The X.25 designations for the ISO network and data link layers are "packet" and "frame," respectively; X.25 also uses "level" rather than the ISO term "layer." The ISO terminology is used here to maintain consistency.

its network access unit (e.g., a front-end processor) in the physical, data link, and network layers to be compatible with X.25. This means, for example, providing software to implement HDLC in the data link layer and an RS-232-C hardware interface in the physical layer.

This approach to interconnection emphasizes physical access and the use of the long-distance network as a communications medium for the exchange of messages between local networks. The interconnected local networks must adopt the standards of the long-distance network and install the lower level protocols (e.g., physical, data link, and network layers of X.25) of the long-distance network. This will be beneficial or detrimental for the operation of the local networks, depending on whether the protocol characteristics (acknowledgement, addressing, etc.) enhance or degrade the performance of the local networks. Since this approach only addresses the lower level protocols, the user must provide the upper layer protocols. Also, since network performance is primarily a function of upper-layer characteristics, achievable performance will be uncertain. The major advantage of this approach is its low cost, since the required protocol software exists for many computers.

DDN, the defense data network, illustrates the limitations of the network access approach, specifically with regard to X.25. Although using X.25 is not currently a DDN requirement, it may be added to permit communication with network nodes in the NATO community.[6] The switching nodes used in the DDN (BBN Model C/30s) are designed to be compatible with X.25 in all three layers. However, layer 3 of X.25, the network layer, is not compatible with the layer-3 host-IMP protocol used to support communication between a local network and the DDN. Without the installation of a gateway (i.e., the protocol functions approach), it will not be possible for hosts in the DDN to communicate with hosts in NATO. Thus, although X.25 protocol software exists in DDN, offering the *potential* for a low-cost interconnection, no local network can presently connect to DDN using X.25 protocols; it would not be compatible with all the DDN protocols. Achieving this compatibility would require a protocol converter for translation between the host-IMP and X.25 network layer protocols.

Network services. Another example using X.25 illustrates the relationship between network access and network services. In this example, the real significance of achieving X.25 network access compatibility is to obtain X.25 network services such as switched virtual circuits, permanent virtual circuits, and datagrams.

SVCs and PVCs. Switched virtual circuits, or SVCs, provide a temporary logical circuit between two host processes. A call request action by the process that wants to open a connection is required. An SVC will compete for the use of available network resources, and possibly experience delay in establishing the circuit, but has the advantage of using these resources efficiently. On the other hand, a permanent virtual circuit, or PVC, guarantees network access to the user, obviating the call request procedure, and provides a data path between a fixed pair of network endpoints. The SVC and PVC services are analogous to the switched network and leased lines services offered by data communications carriers.

Datagrams. A datagram service provides transmission of packets in a network where each packet is independent of other packets. There is no guarantee of sequenced delivery of packets constituting a message, nor guarantee of any type of delivery, for that matter. A datagram service is fast and uses network resources efficiently—for example, the destination node can pass a message to a host without waiting to reassemble all of its packets or tieing up valuable buffer space for this purpose. If the user desires guaranteed sequenced delivery, it must be provided by the transport layer residing above the network layer, which is charged with datagram delivery.

It is one thing for users to tolerate an occasional lost packet but quite different to forego sequential delivery.

A datagram service is useful in certain applications where no higher layers are necessary to complete the job of message delivery and where all the data to carry out a function can be contained in a single packet—for example, transaction processing such as a file update, where each update represents an independent action, and narrative message transmission, where each message can be considered an independent entity. In some applications—digitized voice, for example—a datagram service is used primarily because of its speed.

Most practical applications of datagram services require the transport layer to sequence datagrams for delivery to a host process. It is one thing for all the data in a packet to be self-contained (e.g., a Fortran compile command) or to tolerate an occasional lost packet (e.g., digitized voice) but quite different, from the standpoint of the user's operation, to forego sequential delivery; the user wants a Fortran compile done next or the parts of a voice conversation to reach the listener in sequence. (Subsequent sections show how the Department of Defense uses the datagram concept in combination with upper layer functions to provide the desired network services.)

DoD DDN. An application where X.25 takes on great importance is the Department of Defense's Defense Data Network.[6] As related by Corrigan,[7] planners of DDN were confronted with the following situation:

(1) For the most part, vendor protocols are incompatible across different manufacturers' equipment.
(2) However, the DDN must allow for various vendor protocols because many DoD user communities, using a great variety of vendor hardware and software, must be accommodated in the DDN.
(3) Although the Arpanet architecture and protocols, on which the DDN is based, provide many of the capabilities desired for the DDN, they are not completely compatible with the various vendor protocols.

(4) X.25 has been adopted by manufacturers but has not been implemented in the DDN.

Cerf and Lyons[8] point out that, although X.25 is a network access standard for connecting to packet-switched networks, it has the following deficiencies relative to its use in the DDN:

(1) Although datagram service is part of the standard, it has not been implemented in any network. The datagram mode is essential to real-time military applications, such as tactical operations and packet voice.
(2) The availability of only virtual circuit service in X.25, with its required sequencing, introduces intolerable delays in certain real-time applications. In many applications, total data integrity is not essential, but minimum delay is mandatory. Certain military applications require a broadcast mode, which is not compatible with sequenced delivery in a virtual circuit.

Given the diversity of network characteristics, the network services strategy may be good for inter-local network operations but not for intra-local network performance.

Thus, the DoD is faced with a dilemma: compatibility with X.25 is important because many vendors and communications carriers have adopted it, but X.25 does not fully meet DoD's requirements. The DoD's response to this problem is fourfold[8]:

(1) The Internet protocol[9] has been developed for the DDN and is now operational on Arpanet. IP provides a datagram service for those applications which require fast, nonsequenced delivery and addressing and routing capabilities for transmission of datagrams across multiple networks.
(2) The Transmission Control Protocol[9] has been developed for the DDN and is now operational on the Arpanet. Using the services of IP, and the additional capabilities of sequenced delivery, flow control, and end-to-end acknowledgment, TCP provides a virtual circuit service for applications that require interactive terminal to remote host processing.
(3) As a long-range goal, DDN compatibility with X.25 is planned.
(4) The Defense Communications Agency is working with the international standards bodies (e.g., ISO and CCITT) to promote acceptance of TCP/IP in the civilian community and to urge these bodies to give more weight to military requirements, such as real-time response, security, precedence message handling, and survivability, in their standards efforts.

From the above, it can be seen that achieving interconnection among diverse networks can very likely involve a combination of approaches: network access (e.g., X.25), network services (e.g., datagram and virtual circuit), and political and standards activity (e.g., ISO).

The important factor in the network services approach to interconnection is obtaining services available in the long-distance network for the user organization's local networks. Given the diversity of network characteristics, this strategy may be good for inter-local network operations but not for intra-local network performance. Such penalties as high software overhead, due to unneeded flow control, routing, and addressing capabilities, are especially prevalent if all layers of the long-distance network are incorporated into local network communication operations. Even inter-local network efficiency can be poor if service is limited to one type (e.g., fixed-routing virtual circuit service). However, this approach has the significant advantage of providing clean interfaces at the network boundaries, due to the use of the same protocols in all networks. The implication of this is reduced software development costs compared to methods that tailor the protocols to the characteristics of each interconnected network.

Protocol functions. An example illustrating the protocol functions approach is the Navy's Stock Point Logistics Integrated Communications Environment system. The SPLICE concept is being developed as a result of growing demands for automated data processing at Navy stock points and inventory control points. SPLICE is designed to augment the existing Navy stock point and inventory control point ADP facilities, which support the Uniform Automated Data Processing System-Stock Points. The hardware for the UADPS-SP consists of Burroughs medium-size systems. At present there are 20 new application systems being developed that require considerable interactive and computer communication support. These new application systems will utilize minicomputers capable of supporting foreground interactive and computer communication requirements.

Two major objectives led to the development of SPLICE: first, the increased need for the use of interactive database processing to replace the current batch-oriented system; second, the need to standardize the current multitude of interfaces. To reduce total system cost, SPLICE will be developed using a standard set of minicomputer hardware and software. Standardization is particularly important because SPLICE will be implemented at some 60 geographical locations, each having a different mix of application and terminal requirements. The SPLICE processors will be co-located with the host Burroughs system at each Navy stock point and with Burroughs and Univac systems at the inventory control points. A "foreground-background" concept will be implemented with SPLICE minicomputers, which will serve as front-end processors for the Burroughs systems via a local area network interface. The Burroughs computers will provide background processing functions for large file processing and report generation.

The SPLICE project[10] has the following characteristics:

- intra-local area network communication,

- inter-LAN communication over the long-distance DDN,
- conflicting requirements—LAN vs. long-distance network—for communication,
- mandated communications protocols, required for compatibility purposes, that have little relevance to LAN communication,
- local and remote interactive and batch processing, and
- off-loading of certain processing (e.g., database management) from mainframes to minicomputers.

The network configuration (Figure 5) shows the integration of the three interconnection methods—network access, network services, and protocol functions. Network access is achieved via the hardware of the front-end processor in conjunction with the access line and the host-IMP protocol, a network access protocol used in the Arpanet and adapted to the DDN. Basic network services consist of a virtual circuit service for interactive processing and other operations that require reliable, sequenced end-to-end message delivery, plus a datagram service for operations which involve the transmission of independent messages (e.g., the sending of a message in the electronic mail system). The datagram service, implemented in the internet protocol (IP) and operating in the network layer,* supports the transmission control protocol (TCP), operating in the transport layer, to provide a virtual circuit service. The datagram service is used to obtain efficient bandwidth utilization and flexibile message routing. This flexibility is achieved because the messages can be transmitted as independent packets without being constrained to follow a single path and to follow one another in sequence. The TCP sequences the messages and provides reliable end-to-end delivery. The protocol functions approach provides only those protocols in the local area network that are needed to support this type of communications environment. Due to the great differences between local and long-distance network characteristics, protocol requirements differ significantly. This point is illustrated in Table 3, which delineates differences in the utilization of ISO layers and protocols in LAN and DDN communication.

*Some authors classify this as an eighth layer—the internet layer—situated between the transport and network layers.

Sending and receiving messages on the DDN will use all seven layers of the ISO model, as shown in Table 3. The LAN has no need for the services normally provided by the transport and network layers, because routing, switching, and traditional flow control and congestion control services are unnecessary. The presentation layer, implemented in the terminal management module, will accept data from the application process and convert it to LAN format. Conversely, it will accept messages in LAN format and convert them to the appropriate application process format.

Table 3.
Use of ISO layers in LAN design.

LAYER	LAN COMMUNICATION PROTOCOL/MODULE	DDN COMMUNICATION
Application	Application Process Modules	Same as for LAN
Presentation	Terminal Management	Terminal Management
Session	Session Services	Session Services
Transport	— —	TCP
Network	— —	IP
Data Link	Local Communications	Specified by the DDN (Various Protocols)
Physical	Local Communications	

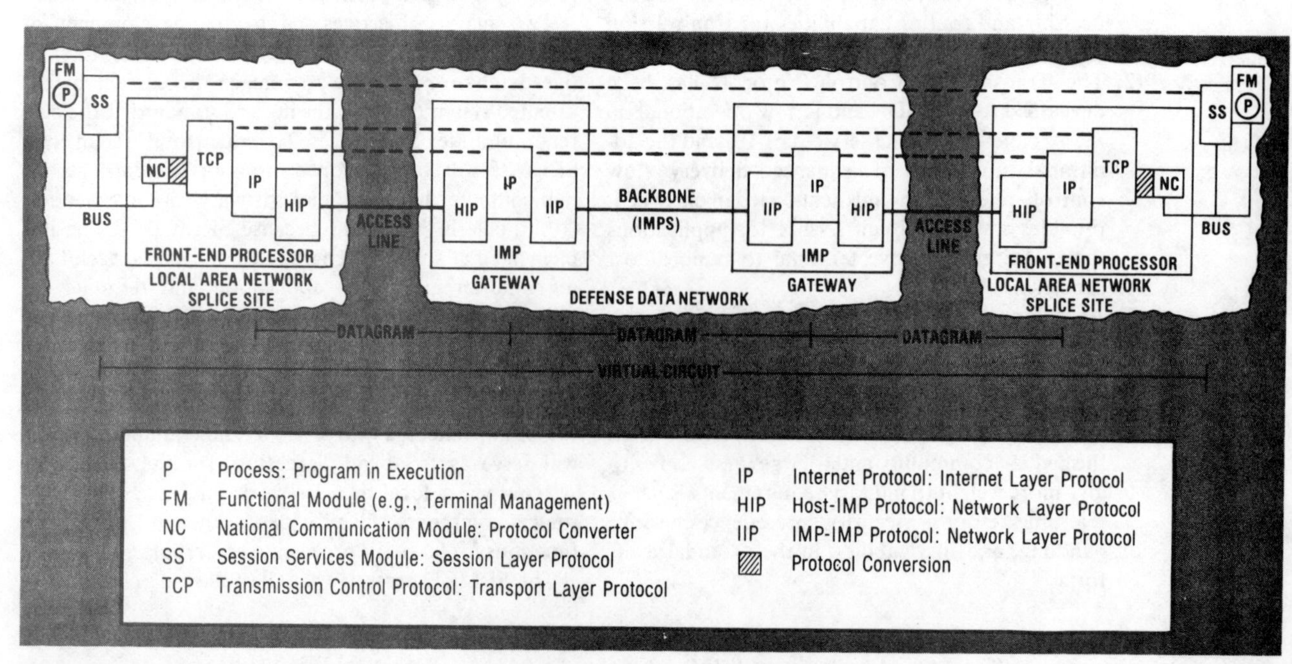

Figure 5. Relationship between local area networks and the Defense Data Network.

To simplify the LAN design, the following message formats are used:

(1) TCP format will be provided to the DDN by the NC module (see Figure 5) whenever communication on the DDN is necessary. A much simpler format will be used for intra-LAN communication.
(2) End-to-end virtual circuit connections and breaking of complete messages into fragments, services normally provided by the transport layer, will be implemented in each of the LAN modules. "End-to-end" in this context refers to the logical communication linkage between two modules separated by a relatively short distance; in some cases the two modules could be in the same hardware unit.

To maximize compatibility and minimize software development, the protocols in the two networks are selected to match as closely as possible, consistent with satisfying the requirements of vastly different communications environments (e.g., routing in the DDN and no routing in the LAN).

The protocol functions approach is used where the inter-local network services and performance provided by the long-distance network (e.g., combination of virtual circuit and datagram services) are satisfactory. It is also used where optimization of intra-local network performance is desired. This is accomplished by using only those layers and protocols that are compatible with and can take advantage of the characteristics of local networks (e.g., single message acknowledgment made possible by high bandwidth). Of course, the user organization must be willing to pay the relatively high software cost of this tailored approach.

It is apparent from the discussion and examples that users may have diverse networking requirements and that local and long-distance networks have opposing characteristics. For most applications, this means that it will be necessary to use a combination of the three approaches to achieve an effective interconnection. ■

Acknowledgment

This work was sponsored by the Fleet Material Support Office and the Naval Supply Systems Command.

References

1. A Status Report, IEEE 802 Local Network Standard, Draft B, Local Network Standards Committee, IEEE Computer Society, Oct. 19, 1981.
2. H. Zimmermann, "OSI Reference Model—The ISO Model of Architecture for Open Systems Interconnection," *IEEE Trans. Communications,* Vol. COM-28, No. 4, Apr. 1980, pp. 425-432.
3. Clifford Warner, "Connecting Local Networks to Long Haul Networks; Issues in Protocol Design," *Proc. Fifth Conf. Local Computer Networks,* IEEE Computer Society, Oct. 1980, pp. 71-76.
4. V. G. Cerf and P. T. Kirstein, "Issues in Packet-Network Interconnection," *Proc. IEEE,* Vol. 66, No. 11, Nov. 1978, pp. 1386-1408.
5. A. Rybczynski, "X.25 Interface and End-End Virtual Circuit Service Characteristics," *IEEE Trans. Communications,* Vol. COM-28, No. 4, Apr. 1980, pp. 500-510.
6. Defense Data Network Program Plan, Defense Communications Agency, Jan. 1982, revised May 1982.
7. Michael L. Corrigan, "Defense Data Network Protocols," *Conf. Record, EASCON 82, 15th Annual Electronics and Aerospace Systems Conf.,* Washington, DC, Sept. 1982, pp. 131-135.
8. V. G. Cerf and R. E. Lyons, "Military Requirements for Packet-Switched Networks and Their Implications for Protocol Standardization," op cit., pp. 119-129.
9. Jonathan B. Postel, "Internetwork Protocol Approaches," *IEEE Trans. Communications,* Vol. COM-28, No. 4, Apr. 1980, pp. 604-611.
10. N. Schneidewind, "Functional Approach to the Design of a Local Network: A Naval Logistics System Example," *Compcon Spring 83 Digest of Papers,* IEEE Computer Society, Mar. 1983, pp. 197-202.

Norman F. Schneidewind is a professor of computer science at the Naval Postgraduate School, where he teaches in information systems and computer science and does research in computer networks and software engineering. Schneidewind is the principal investigator on the Navy's SPLICE computer network project. He has held various technical and management positions in computer system development at SDC, PRC, CUC, Sperry Univac, and Hughes Aircraft.

Schneidewind is a senior member of the IEEE; a member of the Executive Board of the IEEE-CS Technical Committee on Software Engineering, the IEEE Committee on Communications and Information Policy, and the Software Engineering Standards Subcommittee; chairman of the Software Maintenance Workshop; and IEEE-CS representative to the Annual Simulation Symposium.

He received the BSEE from the University of California, Berkeley; MSCS from San Jose State University; and MSOR (Engr), MBA, and DBA from the University of Southern California; and holds the Certificate in Data Processing.

Transparent Interconnection of Local Area Networks with Bridges

Bill Hawe
Alan Kirby
Bob Stewart
Digital Equipment Corporation

ABSTRACT A class of devices known as bridges can be used to provide a protocol-transparent interconnection of similar or dissimilar Local Area Networks (LANs). The motivation for building such devices is briefly described followed by a discussion of their desirable characteristics. We describe the architecture, operating principles, and services provided by a bridge which utilizes a flat address space and is self-configuring. This is followed by a simple resource model of the bridge. The performance of individual LANs is contrasted with the performance of a hybrid network composed of dissimilar LANs connected with bridges.

1. Introduction

As a LAN installation grows, it may exceed the design parameters of an individual LAN. Restrictions such as physical extent, number of stations, performance, and media may be alleviated by the interconnection of multiple LANs. Further, as new LAN architectures are introduced, a simple method of connecting these to existing LANs would be valuable. The traditional method of providing this interconnection borrows techniques from Wide Area Network technology, requiring the use of a common internetwork protocol or protocol translation gateways. We will discuss a class of devices which address these problems in an alternative manner suited to the LAN environment.

1.1 Bridges. A *bridge* (also referred to as a *Data Link relay* [3] is a device which interconnects LANs and allows stations connected to different LANs to communicate as if both stations were on the same LAN (figure 1). For example, node A could send frames to nodes Q, X, or P in the same manner in which it sends frames to node B. The collection of LANs and bridges will be referred to as an *extended LAN*. Any local network (or collection of local networks) that carries traffic between two other local networks operates as a *backbone* with respect to those networks. In its simplest form, a backbone is an interconnecting local network where all of its stations are bridges.

The extended LANs proposed here require no routing or internet information to be supplied by the sending stations. Bridges differ from devices such as amplifiers and repeaters in that they are intelligent filtering devices which store-and-forward frames. Bridges therefore are used to interconnect LANs. Repeaters, on the other hand, are used to interconnect cable segments within a LAN. Bridges also differ from internet routers, which are explicitly addressed by source nodes and which make their forwarding decisions based upon a Network Layer address supplied by the sending node. In terms of the ISO model, a bridge functions within the Data Link Layer (figure 2). Conceptually, a bridge is an n-port device (where $n \geq 2$). However, for simplicity, the rest of this paper will refer to two port bridges.

Bridges make use of Data Link Layer addresses to make forwarding decisions. They have no knowledge of any other address space,

Reprinted from the *Journal of Telecommunication Networks*, Volume 3, Number 2, Summer 1984, with the permission of the publisher Computer Science Press, Inc., 803 Research Boulevard, Rockville,MD 20850, USA.

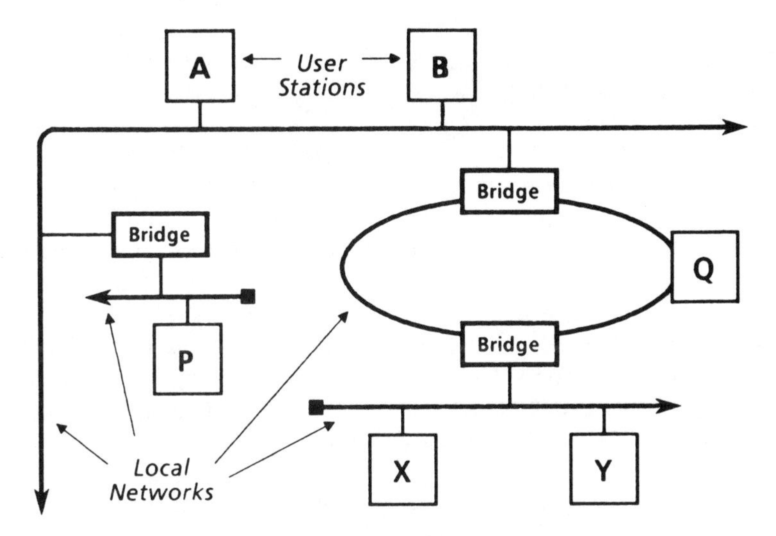

Figure 1. Bridged network configuration.

such as a network or internet address space. Because of this characteristic, bridges are relatively insensitive to the higher layer protocols used by the communicating stations. As will be seen later, the bridge is a useful component in the construction of networks which contain more traditional devices such as routers and gateways which operate above the Data Link Layer.

1.2 Useful Properties. Bridges connecting LANs have several useful properties:

- *Traffic Filtering*—Bridges isolate LANs from traffic which does not need to traverse that LAN. For example, in figure 1, traffic between nodes A and B is not sent on the LANs to which P and Q are connected. Because of this filtering the load on a given

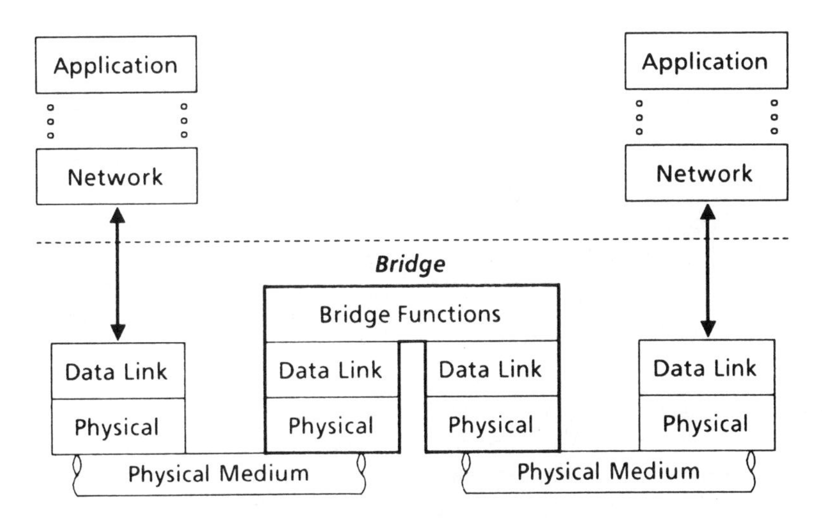

Figure 2. Bridges & data links.

LAN can be reduced, thus improving the delays experienced by all users on the extended LAN.

- *Increased Physical Extent*—LANs are limited in physical extent (at least in a practical sense) by either propagation delay or signal attenuation and distortion. Since the bridge is a store-and-forward device, it forwards frames after having gained access to the appropriate LAN via the normal access method. In this way, the extended LAN can cover a larger extent than an individual LAN. The penalty for this is a small store-and-forward delay.
- *Increased Maximum Number of Stations*—Because of physical layer limitations or stability and delay considerations most LAN architectures have a practical limit on the number of stations on a single LAN. Since the bridge contends for access to the LAN as a single station, one bridge may "represent" many nodes on another LAN or extended LAN.
- *Use of Different Physical Layers*—Some LAN architectures support a variety of physical media (baseband coax, broadband coax, or optical fiber) which cannot be directly connected at the physical layer. Bridges allow these media to co-exist in the same extended LAN.
- *Interconnection of Dissimilar LANs*—LANs of different architecture are typically interconnected with routers or gateways. Often, these devices are complex with only moderate throughput. This may be inappropriate for a LAN environment. It is possible to build a bridge in which its LANs are dissimilar (within constraints to be discussed later). For example, such a bridge would allow stations on an IEEE 802.3 (CSMA/CD) LAN to send frames to stations on 802.4 (token bus) or 802.5 (token ring) [6], [7], [8].

1.3 Desirable Characteristics There are a number of characteristics which an ideal extended LAN should possess. These are goals, all of which, unfortunately, cannot be simultaneously satisfied. These are:

- *Minimize Traffic*—Only traffic generated by user stations should exist on the individual LANs (i.e., no traffic resulting from complex routing algorithms). Further, this traffic should traverse only those LANs necessary to best reach its destination.
- *No Duplicates*—The bridges should not cause duplicate frames to be delivered to the destination(s).
- *Sequentiality*—The combination of LANs and bridges should not permute the frame ordering as transmitted by the source station.
- *High Performance*—In the LAN environment, users expect high throughput and low delay. The extended LAN should preserve these characteristics. In practice, this means that the bridges should be able to process frames at the maximum rate at which they can be received. Since many LANs operate in the multi-megabit per second range, this requires a fast switching operation.
- *Frame Lifetime Limit*—Frames should not be allowed to exist in the extended LAN for an unbounded time. Some higher layer protocols may operate poorly if frames are unduly delayed. This is especially true for protocols designed to depend on the low delay characteristics of a LAN.
- *Low Error Rate*—LANs typically have a low effective bit error rate. Higher layer protocols are often designed with this in mind. This allows the protocols to operate more efficiently since they can assume that errors are infrequent. Extended LANs should not increase this error rate substantially.
- *Low Congestion Loss*—Individual LANs minimize congestion by employing access control schemes which prevent excessive traffic from entering the LAN. Extended LANs are more vulnerable to congestion loss since the bridges may be forced to drop frames when the frames queued to be transmitted match the available buffers. This phenomenon should be minimized by proper design (placement/sizing) of the extended LAN.
- *Generalized Topology*—For purposes of traffic splitting and reliability, it would be useful to allow arbitrary interconnection of LANs via bridges.

1.4 Bridge Types. There are two categories of bridges which are transparent at the Data Link Layer. These are distinguished by the method used to make the forwarding decision.

The best known technique for forwarding is based upon the use of hierarchically organized address space in which the Data Link address of a station is dependent upon its physical location in the extended LAN [16]. This address space is partitioned into fields [8] describing on which LAN in the hierarchy of LANs the station resides. Such a scheme permits the use of a very simple forwarding process in the bridge.

However, there are several problems associated with such a scheme. First, the topology is restricted to a rooted tree (where the LANs are edges and the bridges are nodes). Second, the end nodes must be told their own addresses. This might be accomplished manually or perhaps with a dynamic binding. However, a dynamic binding scheme would require the existence of a protocol to accomplish the binding. In any case, when a station physically moves, its address must change. The difficulty of joining previously disjointed LANs may be significant if manual address administration is used. Third, the depth of the physical hierarchy is pre-defined by the number of fields in the address space.

For the remainder of this paper, we will concentrate on a different type of bridge which uses a flat address space and an adaptive learning algorithm to locate stations. Such a bridge requires no relationship between the address of a node and its location in the extended network. Further, nonrooted tree topologies may be supported. This type of bridge can also operate on a mixed hierarchical/flat address space, giving it significant flexibility in both operation and configuration. Also, such bridges are particularly well-suited to use with IEEE 802 LANs which exhibit consistent global address space administration.

2. Routing Algorithms

The bridge uses *backward learning* [1] with flooding as its backup strategy. Backward learning depends only on local information, inherently available by observing the traffic. Loops are prevented by restricting the topology to a branching tree. The bridge routing algorithm is thus isolated and adaptive. This results in bridges that are simple to install and use.

The bridge routing algorithms depend on a unique address for every station within the extended network. These source and destination addresses are part of the Data Link header. The bridge must receive *all* frames on each local network to which it is connected, *regardless* of a frame's destination address. Also, the bridge must be able to forward a frame with the frame's original source address, not the bridge's source address. These assumptions are the basis for the following descriptions.

Each bridge independently constructs and maintains its own routing data base. The routing data base contains one entry for each station address the bridge knows. Each entry provides an association between a station address and the bridge's local identification of the channel leading to that station. Each entry also contains an age field, used to delete obsolete entries.

Forwarding a frame requires looking up the destination in the routing data base. If the bridge finds the destination, it forwards the frame on the indicated channel, unless that channel was the source for the frame, in which case it discards the frame. If the bridge does not find the destination, it floods the frame on all channels except the one on which it was received. To avoid excessive flooding at startup, a restarted bridge does not forward frames for several seconds, allowing the update process to establish an initial routing data base. Finally, whenever the forwarding process uses an entry, it resets the entry's age.

The bridge updates the routing data base by recording the source address of each received frame, along with the source channel identification and an initialized age. The bridge does not know or care if a channel represents a single LAN or an extended LAN. In order to avoid obsolete entries in the routing data base, and to ensure correctness when stations move, the bridge removes entries that have not been used for several minutes. The timing of this process is not critical. The event occurs infrequently and is therefore low overhead.

In order to avoid frame congestion (and thus frame loss) waiting for a forwarding decision, the forwarding process must be very fast and of high priority. In particular, if there is a requirement to handle worst case traffic loads, the forwarding process must make a forwarding decision within the minimum frame interarrival time from all channels. This avoids instability in the queue for the forwarding process. The update process may be of lower priority, but must make progress so that a bridge does not continue to flood indefinitely. Although the forwarding and update functions are presented here as separate processes, in practice they are somewhat interwoven, being closely allied in the processing of an incoming Data Link protocol header.

To avoid looping, the interconnect topology is restricted to a branching tree. The bridge takes a simplistic approach to avoiding incorrect topologies by sending frames to itself during its listen-only period. If a frame sent on one channel returns on another, the bridge has detected a loop and refuses to begin forwarding. Although this will not detect loops when incorrectly placed bridges start up together, it is a simple way of detecting the most likely case of a new bridge being installed in the wrong place.

3. Services Across Bridges

Bridge routing algorithms should allow accurate and efficient forwarding of data. A bridge only relays data frames. It does not forward Data Link specific control information such as a token. The transparent forwarding of data can take two forms: *pass through* and *translation*.

Pass through is the simplest form of forwarding. It is possible only when the incoming and outgoing LANs have identical frame formats. In this case, the bridge forwards frames unchanged.

Translation is necessary when the LANs have different frame formats. Translation is only possible, however, if the formats are sufficiently similar. In this case the bridge forwards a frame that appears to have originated within the outgoing LAN, but is actually a transformation of the frame from the incoming LAN.

At best, translation involves simple transformations such as different framing, transposing fields, or directly mapping control values. At worst, it requires invention or loss of fields representing unmatched services. For example, in forwarding from a LAN that supports priority to one that does not, the translation process loses the priority information. When forwarding in the opposite direction, the bridge must insert some default priority.

Another potential incompatibility is in frame sizes. One LAN may require a minimum size where another does not, or one LAN may support larger frame sizes than another. In the minimum size case, translation requires adding or removing padding. This works best where padding mechanisms are part of the Data Link protocol; otherwise, some bridge dependent convention must be chosen or translation becomes impossible. Frames that are too large, on the other hand, must be either segmented and reassembled, or simply discarded. Although the former is possible, it is best to accept a maximum extended network frame size and discard oversized frames. This keeps bridge operation simple and fast.

Translation implies the need for address space size compatibility. It also may introduce issues when mapping one space into another. All stations must, therefore, have a unique representation in the address space of any LAN within the extended LAN. A globally administered address space in the extended LAN alleviates this problem.

Certain Data Link specific operations can affect bridge operation in an undesirable manner. For example, if the operation of accepting a frame removed it from the medium (as it could in a ring), a bridge may have difficulty operating in a receive-all manner. Any bridge will change the semantics of a Data Link Layer acknowledgment. From the sender's point of view, a Data Link Layer acknowledgment will have a different meaning depending on whether the destination was reached on the same LAN or through a bridge. In the former case, the acknowledgment means the frame arrived at the destination. In the latter case, it merely means it arrived at the bridge.

3.1 Higher Level Protocols. Higher level protocols have no direct cognizance of the existence of bridges. The protocols may make assumptions about delay, error rate, etc. However, bridges could affect the validity of these assumptions thus removing some transparency. This may adversely affect the operation of the protocols.

By their nature as store-and-forward devices, bridges necessarily introduce delay. It is important that this delay be kept to a minimum. This topic, along with the related topic of congestion control, is treated more fully later in the performance discussion.

Bridges must also avoid introducing frame corruption. A bridge must not subvert the protection of the Data Link's frame check sequence. The most straightforward way for a bridge to preserve the protection is to pass along the frame check as received. This is possible with pass-through forwarding, as long as hardware controller implementations allow it. Passing the frame check through is not possible for translating bridges. In this case, the bridge should take measures such as error detection on the memory and buses to avoid introducing undetectable corruption.

3.2 Incompatible LANs. Bridges can interconnect incompatible LANs, but not as effectively as similar LANs. When LAN addressing, services, or formats are so different that translation is impossible or impractical, the bridge has another option. Bridges can use a simple interbridge protocol to encapsulate incompatible frames. These frames can then be carried through a LAN (or extended LAN) to another bridge for decapsulation and forwarding back into their native environment. This service remains transparent to the source and destination LANs, making them a closed group that "tunnels" through another network. The stations in one closed group cannot communicate with stations in a different closed group, but at least physical coverage can be extended.

Encapsulation has the interesting benefit of preserving all original information, including frame check. On the other hand, it increases bridge complexity and does not attain the degree of compatibility in pass-through or translation forwarding.

4. Resource Models

In order to characterize performance in extended LANs, one must have a model for the resources that can be consumed. Additionally, one must understand the processes which generate work for those resources. In an extended LAN, the resources that affect performance are the Data Links, the buffering capacity, and processing capabilities in the bridges. Figure 3 depicts these resources.

There are also resources in the end stations which affect performance. These are buffer pool sizes, internal bus bandwidths, CPU, and disk speeds, etc. However, for the purposes of this analysis, we ignore those resources since we will focus on the LAN channels themselves. We assume that those other resources

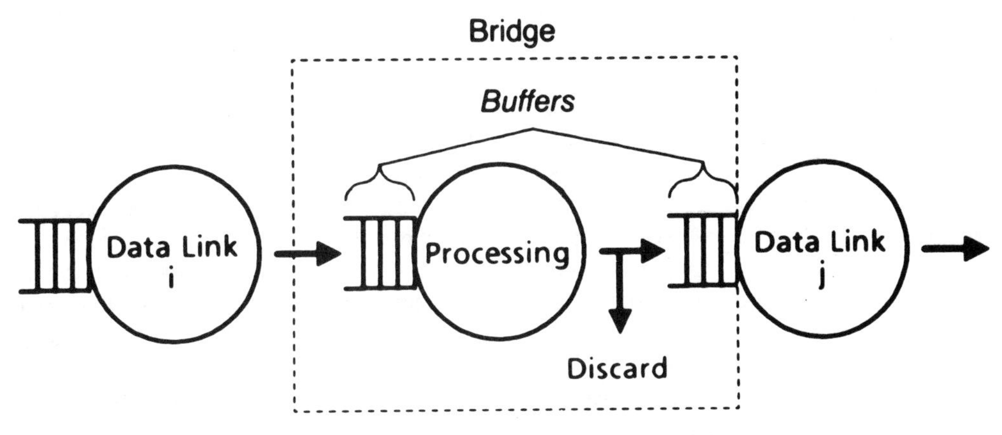

Figure 3. Bridge (2 port) resource model.

are not bottlenecks. In doing so, we imply they do not affect the performance of the LAN channels. This allows the channels to be modeled as "open" queueing systems. Therefore, the traffic sources operate independently of the state of the channel.

In reality, a LAN (or any other network) operates as a "closed" queueing system. This means that the load carried by the LAN at any instant cannot be separated from the performance of the other resources. For example, limited buffering capacity in a low cost end station may result in a large amount of frame loss when receiving traffic from a high performance server. The resultant retransmissions increase the effective load on the LAN channels and any bridges that might be present (not to mention the CPUs). To account for these effects, all resources must be modeled. To avoid this complexity though, we assume the LANs will be the bottlenecks. In the analysis, the system is configured with enough end stations to support the modelled throughput.

4.1 Special Considerations At Bridges. Bridges contend for the resources of a given LAN along with other stations. In some cases, a backbone may contain only bridges. A *subnet* contains end stations and one or more bridges to connect it to a backbone or other subnets. The policies used for the allocation of resources on a subnet or backbone will affect the fairness as perceived by the stations.

In an extended LAN, a bridge acts essentially as a concentrator for N stations. That is, the traffic that actually flows through the bridge is due to N stations. However, it may only be allocated bandwidth on a given LAN as if it were a single station. It may require allocation of resources as if it were N stations since it likely generates more traffic than any one station. One may therefore wish to operate bridges at a higher priority than user stations. This can be done in several ways. On token access LANs, the token holding times, token priorities, etc. can be adjusted to give bridges more of the LAN resources. On CSMA/CD LANs, the collision resolution or backoff algorithms could similarly be adjusted to favor bridges when necessary. On the other hand, under a static allocation of priorities, a bridge with only one station's traffic flowing through it will essentially give that station more than its fair share of resources. The ideal scheme then would be for the allocation to adjust to the demand based on the nature of the stations generating it.

5. Performance Considerations

The performance of an extended LAN is determined by a number of design parameters, including the expected capacity of the backbone and subnets, the overall system capacity, the applied load, frame loss rates, etc. The designer must not only be concerned with providing adequate performance for current usage but must also allow for growth.

Ideally the system is designed to be sufficiently robust to respond to changes in the user population as well as their characteristics. As an example, [9] contains workload information from measurements of users in a program development environment. This can be used directly to estimate the applied load due to N of those users. To do so, however, requires that one also model *all* layers of protocol involved in transferring this information across the extended LAN.

In order to achieve the highest level of performance while at the same time maintaining the desired flexibility in the configuration, low cost to interface, etc., the network designer must understand the tradeoffs in using different LAN technologies in different parts of the extended LAN. Here we consider the differences in the performance of a few popular LAN technologies. In doing so, we consider the parameters which are most important in affecting performance.

Backbone services may require that a large physical extent be covered. Additionally, the backbone may carry several classes of traffic (voice, data, video, etc.), perhaps on separate logical networks. These are reasons that often lead designers to use broadband media as a backbone. Here we are concerned primarily with services supporting high speed frame distribution.

Subnet services usually require high performance as well as ease of configuration, wiring, etc. Subnet operation should not be compromised by stations (such as personal computers) coming up or going down frequently. The entire extended network or subnet should not need to be manually reconfigured to respond to these frequent events.

Another consideration is congestion loss. This can occur in an extended LAN when buffering resources are exhausted in a bridge. This typically is due to transient traffic overloads. There are two reasons. One is when the forwarding process fails to keep up with incoming traffic. The other is when the effective capacity of an outbound LAN is less than the rate of traffic being forwarded on that LAN. In general, it is desirable that frame loss be due to congestion on the outbound LANs, not because of inability to process frames. This simply defines which server will be the bottleneck. It also implies that the forwarding process should operate at a rate at least as great as the total arrival rate on the inbound LANs.

5.1 CSMA/CD Channels. The performance of CSMA/CD channels is determined by several factors. (See [4], [6] and [13] for examples of CSMA/CD systems.) These factors include the number of stations, their locations, the applied load, the propagation delay between stations, and the signaling rate of the channel. As with any channel, the capacity will be diminished by the bandwidth consumed in overhead functions. Overhead includes interframe spacing, addressing and control information in frames, frame checks, and wasted bandwidth due to collisions.

Insight into the bandwidth wasted per collision can be obtained from examining the parameter a [17]. a is the ratio of the average 1-way propagation delay (between *communicating* stations) to the mean frame transmission time. It represents the fraction of a frame that is exposed to a collision. Note that the 1-way propagation delay is a function of the proximity of stations to one another. (Only in the worst case is this half the maximum round trip delay.) For a given frame size and signaling rate, the closer the stations, the lower it will be. When smaller fractions of a frame are exposed to collisions, there is less bandwidth lost per collision. This results in increased efficiency (or capacity) of the channel [15]. Figure 4 shows the general relationship of a to delay.

In general, reducing a can be accomplished by moving stations closer together, sending larger frames, or reducing the signaling rate. The signaling rate is typically fixed (for example, 10 Mbps in the Ethernet). The frame size is a function of the workload, and the station separation a function of the configuration. The presence of bridges may affect a by reducing the effective propagation delay between stations on the same channel since it may be shorter. This will improve the performance of that channel.

The Physical Layer technology will also affect the performance. It has the obvious impact on propagation delay with the implications mentioned above. The geometry of the cable plant will also affect the propagation delay. Star geometries such as those used in fiber optic CSMA/CD systems typically result in increased propagation delay between stations. CSMA/CD on a broadband system is likewise affected. For example, in a broadband CSMA/CD system with collision detection implemented in the stations, the signal must flow up to the headend and back down to the stations before carrier is detected. This means that the slot time will be approximately two times the round trip propagation delay from the furthest station up to the headend.

The implications of the effect that the cable plant geometry has on performance are seen in figure 5. This compares the performance of 10 Mbps CSMA/CD channels on baseband or broadband media. This information is the result of a detailed simulation of the channel [5]. The nodes are spread uniformly across the extent of the network. The maximum extent is 2.8 kilometers. Collision detection is performed at the stations. The mean delay versus offered load is shown for both media for two frame sizes, and includes deferring, collisions, backoffs, transmission, and propagation delays. Each of the curves shown has a different value of a since the frame size and "effective" propagation delay is different for each. Note that as the frame size increases, the lost bandwidth in going from baseband to broadband

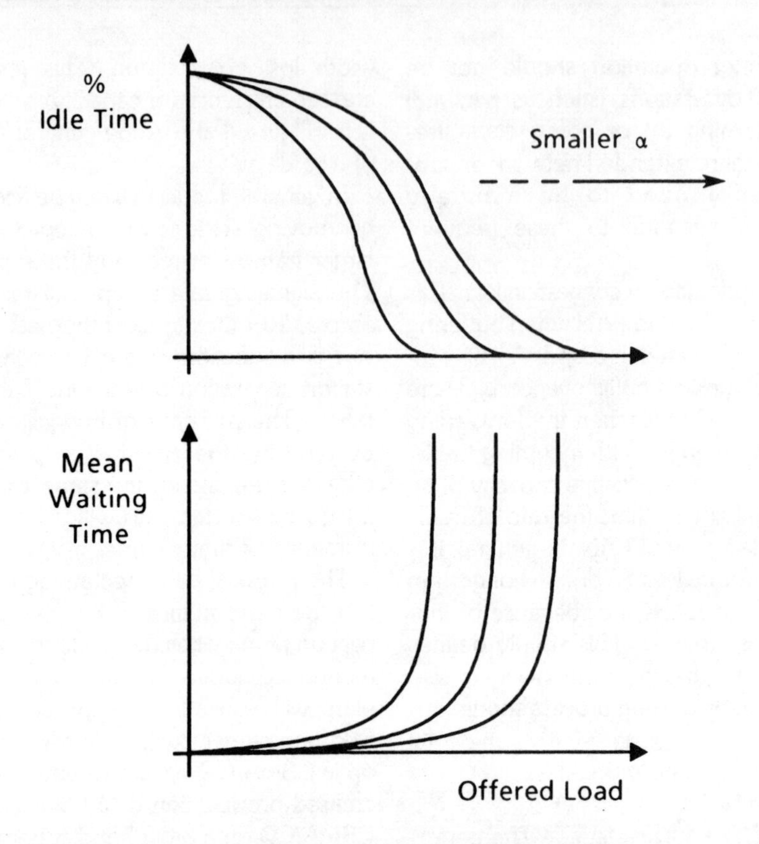

Figure 4. Effect of *a* on CSMA/CD performance.

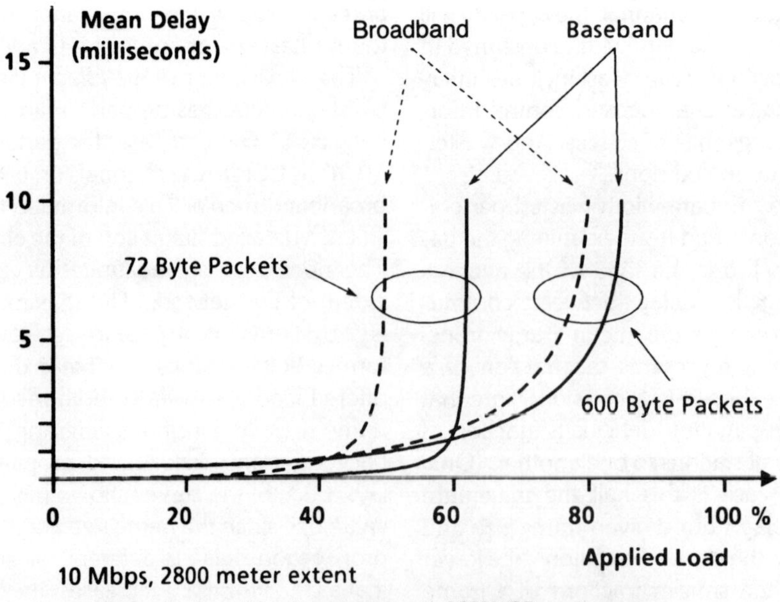

Figure 5. Broadband vs. baseband CSMA/CD performance.

is reduced, because the increased frame size has begun to negate the detrimental effects this particular broadband architecture has on *a*.

5.2 Effect of Bridges on CSMA/CD Channels. Bridges have several effects on the performance of CSMA/CD channels. One is due to the filtering function that prevents traffic from entering a subnet it need not traverse. This reduces the applied load on the channel thus improving performance for the local users of that channel.

Another effect is more subtle. Consider a CSMA/CD system of a given extent (D meters) with N stations distributed uniformly over the extent. Without the use of bridges, all N stations share the resources of that one channel extended over D meters. The delay and capacity are determined then by the applied load as described above. Consider adding a bridge in the center of the system, thus partitioning the system into two channels each with N/2 stations. The collision windows on each of the partitions have been cut in half. This reduces *a* as described above. The net effect then is not only to reduce the load applied to a given channel (through filtering), but also to improve the overall efficiency or capacity of that channel since the extent it must cover is smaller. In other words, the channel gets more efficient while at the same time the load applied to it is reduced. Given these factors along with performance information characterizing the behavior of the channels under load, one can investigate the performance of bridged networks using these channels. (See [5], [12], [15] and [17] for examples of single channel performance).

5.3 Token Access Channels. Token rings and buses use a token to control which station has the right to access the channel. The token is circulated among the stations with each generally allowed to hold it for some maximum predetermined time. Token rings use point-to-point technology between stations and require a physical ring topology. The ring may actually be wired in a star configuration (geometry) to allow for centralized maintenance and the use of existing wiring plans [14].

Just as with CSMA/CD, the performance of these systems is subject to the effects of signaling rate, number of nodes, applied load, propagation delay, etc. However, the token access methods require the active participation of stations that may not have traffic to send. Since each station actively handles the token, the delay at the station affects performance. Additionally, the number active in the ring or bus will determine how long it takes the token to circulate.

Two key parameters of these systems then are the token passing delay and the number of nodes. The token passing delay is a function of the effective size of the token, the signaling rate, the propagation delay between stations and the delay per station. The topology (bus or ring) along with the geometry (star, ring, bus, etc.) must both be considered when calculating the effective propagation delay. The ratio of propagation delay on the channel in a star geometry to that of a bus or ring can vary quite widely. It is possible, depending on the environment, for this effect to be large.

The number of nodes has other effects on system performance. One is that the reliability of the system will decrease as more nodes are added is because it is more likely that a given interface, link, etc. may fail. The wiring strategies mentioned above attempt to address this, and other, configuration problems [14].

Token access protocols typically perform well at heavy load and are often used for real-time systems where a worst case delay (in the absence of bit errors) is to be calculated. Unfortunately, they are not suited for large numbers of nodes for the reasons mentioned above.

As one of the many possible examples of how a system could be configured, consider the use of token access protocols for backbone services. The number of stations need not be large since most would be bridges connecting subnets to the backbone. Large populations of user stations could then be partitioned across subnets using CSMA/CD since it is more flexible to the changing environment at the user stations. Presumably, the backbone would offer good performance at heavy load as long as the number of bridges is not too large [2]. Figure 6 depicts the performance of a 10 Mbps

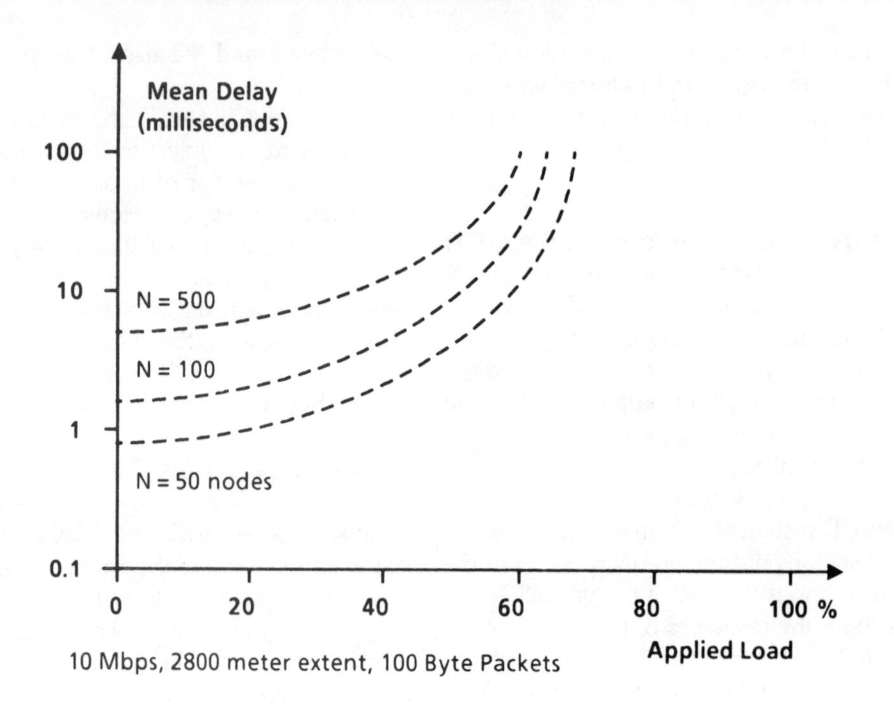

Figure 6. Broadband token bus performance.

broadband token bus using an exhaustive service policy. L is the network extent in kilometers and N is the number of nodes. This uses the model found in [2] which is based on the work in [11].

Performance degradation because of network reconfiguration could be a problem with these protocols. When used as a backbone this may not be serious since the bridges are not expected to go on/off line very often.

6. Performance of Extended LANs

It is important to size the capacity of an extended LAN. Given the characterization of user demands, this is expressed in the number of users that it can "support." The difficulty with using the number of users as the independent variable is that one must account for the resource consumption from all layers of protocol. This is difficult to do in general.

Another problem is that the performance requirements may vary for different higher level protocols. Some may be delay sensitive. For example, terminal access protocols which return echoes end-to-end are quite sensitive to the delay. Other terminal access protocols which allow local editing and echoing are not as delay sensitive. File transfer protocols are not sensitive to the delay but require high throughput. Therefore, to determine the capacity of an extended LAN one must investigate both delay and throughput as applied to the requirements of a particular protocol and application which uses it.

Certain LANs place constraints on the configuration that are due to either Physical Layer limitations (such as the distance over which the line drivers can operate) or the interaction between the Data Link Layer access method and the propagation delay. For example, the Ethernet places a limit on the maximum number of repeaters between any two communicating stations [4]. This constraint assures that the propagation delay budget (which is assumed by the access method protocol) will not be exceeded in any configuration. In an extended LAN, one may also wish to place constraints on the configuration based on the performance expectations of higher layer protocols. For example, a constraint may be that there be no more than N bridges between two stations that use a delay sensitive protocol. In general though, the rules may need to be more complex when an extended LAN is configured with dissimilar LANs. This is because the individual LANs may provide different delay/throughput characteristics.

Another problem when attempting to determine capacity is estimating the amount of traffic that remains local to a given subnet and the amount that leaves a subnet. The worst case occurs when all of the traffic must be forwarded off a subnet through one or more levels of backbones. This creates the largest demand on the resources of the backbone(s). One way to handle this is to assume that all of the locally generated traffic must also be carried by the backbone. Increasing the load will then define the system saturation point. At that point, the resources of the subnets will likely be under utilized. The additional capacity of the subnet can be used for local-only traffic. This defines the limits for the system with respect to the ratio of local to transit traffic that is possible.

6.1 An Example. To illustrate one of the many ways extended LAN concepts can be applied, consider a hypothetical configuration. The purpose of the example is to demonstrate the concepts of the architecture, not to represent a real application. A 10 Mbps broadband token bus extending 16 kilometers is used as a backbone for N 10 Mbps baseband CSMA/CD subnets, each extending 2.8 kilometers. This forms a two-level extended LAN. Figure 7 depicts this configuration.

The processing delay (for the forwarding process only) in the bridges can be neglected if it is a small part of the store-and-forward delay. This assumption is made here. We assume that there are two main classes of traffic to be carried by this extended LAN. One class is terminal/host traffic. (For examples, see [5] and [9].) The other traffic class is comprised of remote file access and transfer.

File traffic on a LAN may have greatly varying characteristics depending on the system architecture. For example, in a client/server system where there is sufficient memory in the file server, there can be a good deal of caching done at the server. This means that accesses done to the file server may return data for a brief period at a rate limited only by the I/O speeds of the server. Less memory at the server, more file transfers than file accesses, or more users sharing the server, will result in arrival rates limited by head contention on the disks at the server.

Terminal traffic can also have greatly varying characteristics. This depends on the nature of the user behavior as well as the terminal communications model. For example, the terminal access protocols may perform echoing over the channel, or it may be done locally at the point the terminal interfaces to the extended LAN. In the case of echoes carried over the channel, the responsiveness of the channel is very important since it may be visible on almost every user keystroke.

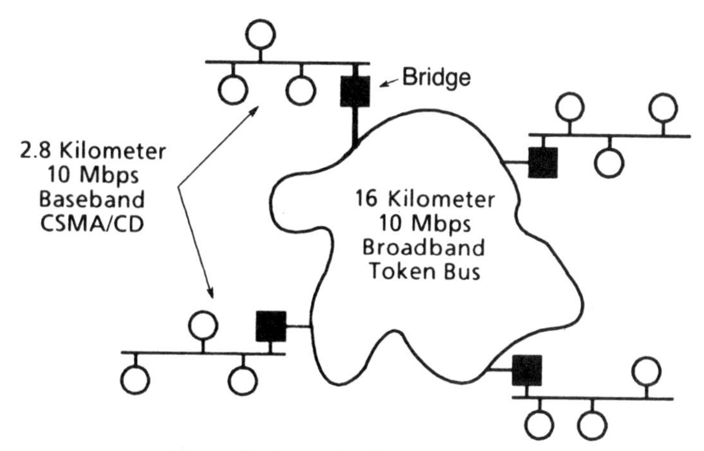

Figure 7. Example of extended LAN.

We select two of the several possibilities for file and terminal traffic outlined above. We assume that disk traffic is characterized as a Poisson process with a mean arrival rate λ_d frames/sec. We assume that frames associated with these sources have a mean size of x_d bytes. The arrival rates and frame sizes include all protocol overheads. We also assume that traffic from terminal access is a Poisson process with a mean of λ_t frames/sec and a mean size of x_t bytes. This also includes all protocol overheads. We use a hybrid model that uses simulation and analytical methods to estimate performance. The CSMA/CD portions of the system are simulated in detail [5] and the token bus performance is computed analytically [2]. Since we also apply the independence assumption [10] and are interested in merely illustrating the example, this hybrid is adequate. However, a more detailed overall model is ultimately required to understand performance fully. This is because we are unable to investigate effects such as congestion loss at bridges with this approach. The amount of loss will depend on traffic patterns, bridge processing speeds, bridge and end station buffering capabilities, higher layer protocol parameters (window sizes, timers, etc.) and higher layer congestion avoidance algorithms (such as dynamic window sizing).

As mentioned previously, it is important to consider both delay and throughput when sizing the capacity of a LAN or an extended LAN. In doing so here, we increase the number of users while observing the delay and utilization of the components of the extended LAN. When the utilization of any resource in the extended LAN reaches 0.9, the user population is no longer increased. (Note that this is utilization not offered load. The offered load is less than 0.9 when this occurs because of the overheads described earlier.) Similarly, if the *mean* delay across the extended LAN exceeds a threshold (T seconds) the user population is no longer increased. We assumed that there are sufficient resources (computers, etc.) added to the extended LAN to support the user population while maintaining the I/O rates for each user class (λ_d and λ_t). This allows the system to be viewed as an open queueing network.

Figure 8 shows several aspects of extended LAN performance. For this figure, $\lambda_d = 25$ frames/sec and $\lambda_t = 5$ frames/sec. $x_d = 600$ bytes, $x_t = 100$ bytes, and $T = 10$ milliseconds. We show three different partitionings of the user population. This includes 10, 20 and 30% of the user stations generating file traffic as defined. The remainder generate terminal traffic also as defined. Plotted in figure 8 are the utilizations of a given CSMA/CD subnet and the token bus backbone. (Note that the utilization will include overhead such as collisions or token passing.) We make the

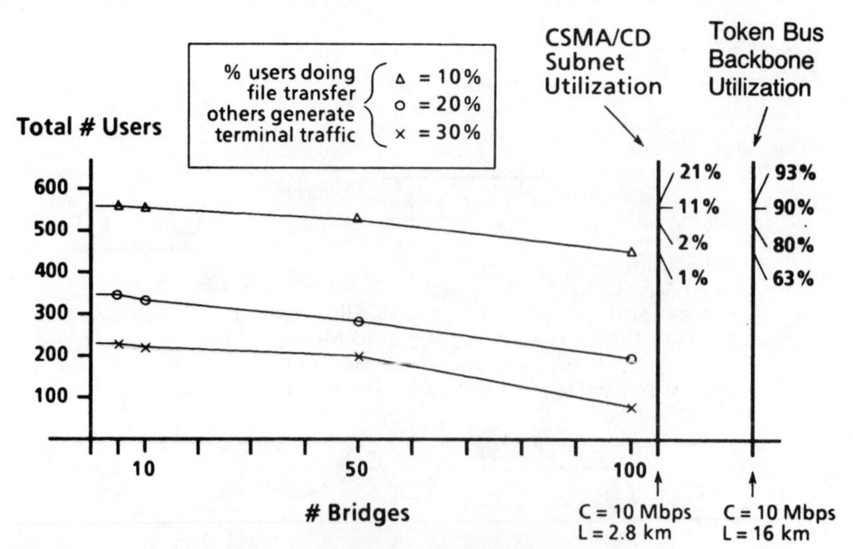

Figure 8. Extended LAN performance.

worst-case assumption here that the user population is divided evenly across the subnets and (as another worse case assumption) that all the subnet traffic must also enter the backbone. This places a lower bound on the supported user population.

Figure 8 demonstrates that there are two regions of performance. One region is where the bandwidth of the backbone is not sufficient to allow for more users. This occurs for small numbers of bridges. The other region is where the token passing delay on the backbone is too large to allow the extended LAN to meet the mean delay goal (*T* seconds). This occurs when the number of bridges is large.

7. Conclusion

We have shown the usefulness of flat address-space, learning bridges in extending LANs. These extended LANs can make use of desirable characteristics which an individual LAN cannot provide. For this architectural approach, we have stated the requirements placed on the bridges including their LAN interface operation, the routing algorithms, etc. We have also described topological constraints and mentioned issues regarding the number of bridges in the extended LAN. Finally, we have discussed the performance aspects of several LANs as well as those issues relating specifically to extended LANs. We have also provided an example of a hypothetical extended LAN and discussed its performance.

Acknowledgment

The authors wish to acknowledge the major technical contributions of Mark Kempf and George Koshy to the concepts in this paper.

References

1. P. Baran, "On Distributed Communication Networks," *IEEE Transactions on Communications Systems*, Vol. CS-12, pp. 1–9, March, 1964
2. Werner Bux, "Local-Area Subnetworks: A Performance Comparison," *IEEE Transactions on Communications*, Oct., 1981
3. R. Callon, "Internetwork Protocol," *Proceedings of the IEEE: Special Issue on Open Systems Interconnection*, Dec., 1983
4. Digital, Intel and Xerox, *The Ethernet: A Local Area Network, Data Link Layer and Physical Layer Specifications*, Version 2.0, Nov., 1982
5. Bill Hawe and Madhav Marathe, "Predicting Ethernet Capacity—A Case Study," *Proc. of Computer Performance Evaluation Users Group Conference*, Washington, D.C., Oct., 1982
6. IEEE Project 802 Local Area Network Standards, "IEEE Standard 802.3 CSMA/CD Access Method and Physical Layer Specifications," Approved Standard, July, 1983
7. IEEE Project 802 Local Area Network Standards, "Draft IEEE Standard 802.4 Token Passing Bus Access Method and Physical Layer Specifications," Draft E, July, 1983
8. IEEE Project 802 Local Area Network Standards, "Draft IEEE Standard 802.5 Token Ring Access Method and Physical Layer Specifications," Working Draft, Sept. 23, 1983
9. Raj Jain and Rollins Turner, "Workload Characterization Using Image Accounting," *Proc. of Computer Performance Evaluation Users Group Conference*, Washington, D.C., Oct., 1982
10. L. Kleinrock, *Queueing Systems, Volume II*, John Wiley & Sons, 1976
11. A.G. Konheim and B. Meister, "Waiting Lines and Times in a System with Polling," *Journal of the ACM*, Vol. 21, pgs. 470–490, 1974
12. Madhav Marathe, "Design Analysis of a Local Area Network," *Computer Networking Symposium*, Washington, D.C., Oct., 1980
13. R.M. Metcalf and D.R. Boggs, "Ethernet: Distributed Packet Switching for Local Computer Networks," *Comm. of the ACM*, July 1976
14. Jerry Saltzer, "Why a Ring?", *Proc of 7th Data Comm. Symp.*, Mexico City, Mexico, Nov., 1981
15. John F. Shoch and Jon A. Hupp, "Measured Performance of an Ethernet Local Area Network," *Comm. of the ACM*, Vol. 23, No. 12, Dec. 1980
16. Norman C. Strole, "A Local Communications Network Based on Interconnected Token-Access Rings: A tutorial," *IBM J. Res. Develop*, Vol 27, No 5, Sept., 1983
17. Fouad A. Tobagi and V. Bruce Hunt, "Performance Analysis of Carrier Sense Multiple Access with Collision Detection," *Computer Networks*, Vol. 4, No. 5, Oct/Nov, 1980

About the Authors

Bill Hawe is a Consulting Engineer in Corporate Research and Architecture at Digital Equipment Corp. He is involved in the modeling and performance analysis of computer networks. He has focused on the evaluation of Local Area Networks (LANs), including simulation modeling of Ethernet and VLSI LAN controllers, analytical models and measurements of gateways, and state descriptive models of Local Area Networking software. Recently, he has been involved in architectural definition and performance analysis of high-performance interconnects for LANs. He participates in the IEEE Project 802 LAN Standards Committee and is also a member of the IEEE 802 performance modeling working group. Prior to joining Digital, he taught courses in computer science, distributed process control, computer networks, and logic design at Southeastern Massachusetts University. While there, he also implemented an X.25 packet switching architecture for personal computers.

Alan Kirby is manager of the Advanced Development group for Networks and Communications at Digital Equipment Corporation. This group is responsible for the development and acquisition of computer communications related hardware and software technologies. His present work relates to high-performance LAN technology, LAN interconnect architecture, and network security. Before joining Digital, Mr. Kirby was Manager of Network Development at National CSS, Inc. There, he was involved in the design and development of a proprietary packet switching network. He received his B.S. degree at Worcester Polytechnic Institute and M.S. degree at the Polytechnic Institute of New York.

Bob Stewart has been with the Networks and Communications group at Digital Equipment Corporation for nearly eight years. For much of that time, he was responsible for the Network Management architecture, as well as two implementations of network management in RSX DECnet. During his time in the Architecture Group, he was the network management contributer for Digital, working with Xerox and Intel on the Version 2 Ethernet Specification. In 1982, he transferred to the Advanced Development Group. Following a study of the Xerox Network System protocols, he became leader of the project which resulted in the extended network bridge architecture. Before coming to Digital, he spent about a year as a software developer with Sycor, a manufacturer of intelligent terminals. Prior to that, he was with Comshare, a time-sharing company, for six years as an operator software developer. He received an A.S. degree from Michigan Christian College, followed by two years in Computers and Communication Science at the University of Michigan. He has also taught commercial courses in network architecture and has a personal interest in home computer software development.

SECTION 8: DESIGN ISSUES

8.1 Overview

The previous sections have not, by any means, exhausted the concepts and issues of interest for local networks. There is a whole host of design issues that have been only briefly mentioned or not touched on at all. This section introduces four of the most important design issues and provides a representative article on each one. The four issues are: (1) network control, (2) reliability and availability, (3) security, and (4) network services.

The need for network control is based on the fact that a computer network is a complex system that cannot create or run itself. The manager of the network must be able to configure the network, monitor its status, react to failures and overloads, and plan intelligently for future growth.

In many LANs and HSLNs, a network control center (NCC) is provided. Typically, this device attaches to the network through a network access unit (NAU) and consists of a keyboard/screen interface and a microcomputer. Except for the smallest networks (less than 10-20 NAUs), an NCC is vital. It supports key operations, administration, and maintenance functions. All of the functions of an NCC involve observation, active control, or a combination of the two. They fall into three categories: (1) configuration, (2) monitoring, and (3) fault isolation.

Configuration functions deal with system initialization and related functions. Examples include down-line loading of software and parameters to an NAU; providing a name/address directory service; and starting up and shutting down of network components. Monitoring functions relate to the collection, analysis, and reporting of network performance and status. Fault isolation functions are automated aids for operator alert and fault identification and location.

As local networks grow in size and capability, the loss of the network becomes more and more costly. Thus, network design must have as a goal high component reliability and high system availability. The key to enhanced availability is to design the network so that individual component failures have little or no effect on the overall network. One of the articles in this section explores ways of achieving this for broadband LANs.

Network security can be defined as the protection of network resources against unauthorized disclosure, modification, use, restriction, or destruction. Security has long been an object of concern and study for both data processing systems and communications facilities. With local networks, these concerns are combined.

Consider a full-capacity local network, with direct terminal access to the network and data files and with applications distributed among a variety of processors. The local network may also provide access to and from long-haul communications and may be part of a catenet. The complexity of the task of providing security in such an environment is clear.

The subject is broad and encompasses physical and administrative controls as well as automated ones. In this section, we include a paper that looks at one important aspect of security: The ability of a network to support users who have various levels of access rights to data.

Finally, we consider the subject of network services. At minimum, a local network must provide a data transfer service for attached devices. There are a variety of other "value-added" services, some of which are discussed in the accompanying article.

8.2 Article Summary

"A Measurement Center for the NBS Local Area Computer Network" looks at one aspect of a network control center, performance monitoring and reporting. The article lists and explains the use of a rather complete set of performance measures. The issue of passive versus active monitoring is also explored.

Of all the types of local networks discussed in this tutorial, broadband LANs have perhaps the most complex reliability/availability requirements. The article by Willard examines an array of techniques for enhancing the availability of such networks, which gives an indication of the scope of the problem. Incidentally, the article by Vonarx in Section 4 exhibits the standard approach (redundancy) taken to enhance the availability of digital switches and PBXs.

The next article, "A Multilevel Secure Local Area Network," looks at a promising new approach to local network security, the trusted NAU. The article explains the requirement, examines alternative approaches, and explores the trusted NAU concept in detail.

Finally, the article by Janson et al. examines in some detail a type of value-added LAN service that is becoming increasingly available.

A Measurement Center for the NBS Local Area Computer Network

PAUL D. AMER

Reprinted from *IEEE Transactions on Computers*, Volume C-31, Number 8, August 1982, pages 723-729.

***Abstract*—This paper describes a measurement center for the NBSNET, a distributed, broadcast local area computer network (LAN) at the National Bureau of Standards. A LAN measurement center allows careful testing and evaluation of a network under normal and varying user-defined conditions. The measurement center consists of three components: an artificial traffic generator, a monitoring system, and data analysis software. The traffic generator emulates varied loads on the network, allowing for controlled experimentation and functional testing. The monitoring system captures measurement information about both artificial and normal network traffic. Analysis software summarizes this information into ten measurement reports following each monitoring period. Implementation issues and problems are discussed.**

***Index Terms*—Broadcast network, CSMA/CD, local network, measurement, multiple access channel, performance evaluation.**

I. INTRODUCTION

A LOCAL area computer network (LAN) is broadly defined in [7] as a set of "computers" whose communication takes place over limited distances between 10 and 10 000 m. Besides micros, minis, and large-scale systems, the set of computers includes terminals, line printers, and other devices requiring and/or providing transmission of data. The communication is accomplished via a variety of media including twisted pairs, coaxial cable, radio broadcast, and fiber optics. Many business applications are ideally suited for LAN technology. For instance, LAN's are recognized as a cost-effective approach to office automation, handling applications such as electronic mail, word processing, and information retrieval.

A recent study performed for the National Bureau of Standards (NBS) predicts LAN's to show the largest growth of all forms of computer-communications over the next decade. Estimations are that by 1985 over 1400 LAN's will be installed by the U.S. Government alone to support intrasite networking communications. The total present-value dollars to be spent on this communications support during the 1981-1985 time period, plus the budgeted dollars in 1985 for future support, will be between $75 million and $117 million [11].

In implementing a LAN, questions arise regarding network functionality and performance. For operational networks, performance can be investigated by designing a local area network measurement center (LAN-MC). A LAN-MC facilitates careful testing and evaluation of a network under both normal and controlled conditions. Such testing is essential for effective use of networks and for their improved future design.

This paper describes a LAN-MC implemented by NBS for the NBSNET. NBSNET consists of two distributed, broadcast LAN's at the Gaithersburg, MD and Boulder, CO facilities connected with a 9600 Bd link. A major component of this MC is a set of ten measurement reports which summarize NBSNET traffic during a monitored period. Although most applicable to broadcast networks such as NBSNET, many of these reports are independent of the underlying network topology and would be useful in designing measurement centers for other LAN architectures. Before proceeding with a description of NBSNET and the reports, we describe the general components of a MC.

II. A LAN MEASUREMENT CENTER

A LAN measurement center has three components: a monitoring system, data analysis software, and an artificial traffic generator. The monitoring system gathers measurement information, such as the size of a message being transmitted, and prepares the information for statistical analysis. Much is known about the characteristics, advantages, and disadvantages of computer system monitors [13]. Based on this knowledge, the best monitor for a LAN is a hybrid monitor employing software to relate network state transitions with their stimuli, and hardware to minimize any overhead network traffic which results from the monitoring activity. Microscopic analysis measures activities in milliseconds and microseconds, thereby characterizing channel activities where communication is on the order of 1 Mbit/s.

The software analysis component of a measurement center summarizes the information captured by the monitoring system either at the conclusion of a measurement period for off-line analysis or during measurement for on-line dynamic analysis. These summaries are statistical overviews of the LAN traffic in the form of performance reports. They provide information such as network delays, traffic distributions, and types of traffic transmitted. This information both supports functional testing of the network and its components and documents LAN performance under varying protocols and other tunable system parameters.

Finally, an artificial traffic generator places varied traffic

Manuscript received March 4, 1981; revised July 27, 1981 and March 4, 1982. This work was supported in part by a grant from the University of Delaware Research Foundation.

The author is with the Institute for Computer Sciences and Technology, National Bureau of Standards, Washington, DC 20234 and the Department of Computer and Information Sciences, University of Delaware, Newark, DE 19711.

loads on a network, thereby allowing for controlled experimentation. For example, a generator can emulate increasing amounts of traffic to observe a network's performance limits under increasing stress. Stress problems therefore can be confronted early in a network's implementation before production activities make modifications costly.

III. NATIONAL BUREAU OF STANDARDS NBSNET

A. Overview

NBSNET is a local area broadcast network which has been operational since October 1979. Users in 20 buildings are connected with the most distant pair separated by approximately 1.5 km. NBSNET employs a carrier sense multiple access with collision detection (CSMA-CD) protocol similar, but not identical to the Ethernet [10].

Logically, NBSNET consists of a single 1 Mbit/s coaxial cable (channel) with multiple ports. Each port consists of a microprocessor-based interface node called Terminal Interface Equipment (TIE). The TIE, described in detail in [1], is programmed to adapt each user device to the network. The TIE has three main components: the user board, the network board, and the TAP.

User boards handle communication between user devices and the network board. In turn, the network board controls the communication to and from the coaxial cable. Output from the network board is coupled to the coaxial distribution cable by the TAP. Each network board supports one to eight user boards. It continuously polls the user boards until one requesting transmission is found. Discussion of the information control flow between users by way of the TIE's is available in [2].

B. Communication Protocol

The following is a discussion of the CSMA-CD protocol as implemented on NBSNET. Key words are italicized. Their definitions are required for understanding the 10 performance reports described in Section IV.

NBSNET employs a *1-persistent protocol* [9]. When a user board has a *packet* to transmit, the board *contends* for the channel. Two cases are possible: 1) if no carrier is sensed, the user *accesses* the channel and begins transmitting, or 2) if the channel is busy with another user's transmission, the user *defers* or waits until the channel becomes idle, at which time it automatically transmits.

In both cases a potential exists for two or more users to overlap their transmissions thereby resulting in a *collision.* A collision can occur in case 1) because the signal propagation delay between users allows for multiple users to sense the channel idle at approximately the same time. A collision can occur in case 2) if two or more users simultaneously defer to another user's transmission. With a 1-persistent protocol, these deferring users are assured of colliding. (Other persistent protocols avoid this problem [9].)

With the TAP hardware, a user listens to its own transmission and detects if it is colliding. Whenever a collision is detected, the user aborts transmission, jams the channel with a special signal to ensure that all other users also detect the collision, and reschedules its transmission according to a randomized backoff distribution. Backoff is randomized to prevent repeated collisions.

If a user's transmission propagates beyond all other users without colliding, the user *acquires* the channel. Case 2) guarantees that no collision can occur for the duration of that transmission. When a user acquires the channel and successfully sends an entire packet, that packet is referred to as a *transmission.*

NBSNET employs a simple positive acknowledgment scheme with a window size of one. A destination, upon receiving a packet, generates an acknowledgment packet, or *piggybacks* an acknowledgment onto another outgoing packet. At that time the received packet has been communicated and is also considered to be a *communication.* (Note that transmission and communication have special meaning in this paper.) For various reasons, such as electrical noise, faulty hardware, or full buffers at the destination, a transmission may not be received and therefore not be a communication. Both transmission and communication imply successful placement of a packet onto the channel, but only the latter implies successful receipt at the destination.

When an acknowledgment is not received from the destination within a predetermined time-out period, the source will retransmit the packet. Hence, each transmission (packet) is either an *original* or a *duplicate* transmission (packet). For most packet types, NBSNET allows up to 7 duplicate transmissions before assuming a malfunction or failure at the destination and breaking the connection. The maximum number of duplicates permitted and the time-outs between duplicate transmissions are tunable protocol parameters.

If a packet is communicated and its acknowledgment is lost, the source will transmit the packet again. All additional transmissions which take place after a packet has been communicated are *redundant* transmissions.

C. Design Issues of Measurement

Local area network behavior is described in terms of discrete events. Measurement tools therefore should be capable of detecting these events and the times when they occur. Svoboda [16] and Ferrari [6] describe the structure, strengths, and weaknesses of various measurement tools. In general, there are four design issues of importance: artifact, location of measurement, traffic generation, and on-line versus off-line analysis. Each is discussed in turn.

1) Artifact: Artifact is the interference on a target system caused by the introduction of a monitoring device [13]. Typically, a portion of a system's resources is allocated to measuring how itself and other resources are performing. For example, if CPU utilization is monitored at 60 percent, perhaps 55 percent is for processing the workload and 5 percent is for controlling the monitor.

Besides minimizing artifact, it is important to know the magnitude of the artifact introduced. When known, this interference can be removed from the final measurements, thus providing an unbiased indication of performance. It may be better to increase artifact to gain additional knowledge of its magnitude.

2) *Location of Measurement:* There are three approaches to measuring the activities of a local area network: centralized, decentralized, and hybrid measurement. These approaches are described below.

a) *Centralized Measurement:* A broadcast network lends itself naturally to a centralized measurement approach [Fig. 1(a)]. Acting in a "promiscuous" mode [10], a modified interface tapping onto the channel can monitor all packets on the network. Therefore, all packet header information as well as additional timing and count information (e.g., interarrival time since last packet, packet size) is available to a central monitor. This approach was employed by Shoch and Hupp in their performance study of an ETHERNET local network [14].

Centralized measurement introduces no artifact and tends to be less costly than other approaches. However, some desirable information cannot be monitored centrally. The timing of when a packet arrives at an interface (from a user device) and the amount of time a user board defers in transmitting a packet are only available at that user board. Similarly, although a centralized monitor can detect a collision, it cannot determine which and how many user boards were involved.

With central measurement, some timings, such as the arrival of a packet onto the network, are biased. An arrival recorded by a central monitor represents the moment when the packet reaches the monitor's TAP, not when the packet enters the channel. To eliminate bias, a central monitor could account for its physical distance from each interface and the propagation delay for signals to cover this distance.

b) *Decentralized Measurement:* In a decentralized measurement approach [Fig. 1(b)], additional memory and real time clocks are incorporated at each network interface. Packets arriving at or departing from an interface can be appropriately time stamped. Information such as collision induced delays and collision counts, which are not available centrally, can be recorded at each interface.

Periodically, each node must transmit its information to a central location for consolidation. In a pure decentralized measurement approach, the central collector does no monitoring; only data collection and reduction. The periodic transmission of measurement information from each node may be as frequent as with every packet (by including measurement information in the transmitted packet), after every r time units (time driven), after every n events (event driven), or upon request from the central collector.

With a decentralized approach all information about the network traffic is available. This includes precise times for transmission and receipt of packets and the source/destination addresses of all colliding packets. Each interface captures the demands placed on the network as they occur and not after a variable delay as with a central measurement device.

Although more accurate, decentralized measurement requires overhead communication for the periodic transmission of data to the central collector. If the transmissions are sent over dedicated lines, extra costs are involved. If sent over the main channel, these transmissions introduce artifact. Artifact can be reduced by less frequent transmission of measurements and by local data reduction (e.g., histograms). However, these alternatives require additional storage and intelligence, respectively, either of which may be prohibitive.

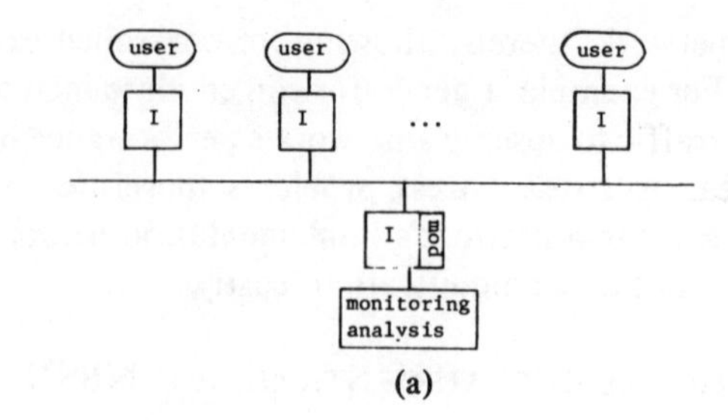

(a)

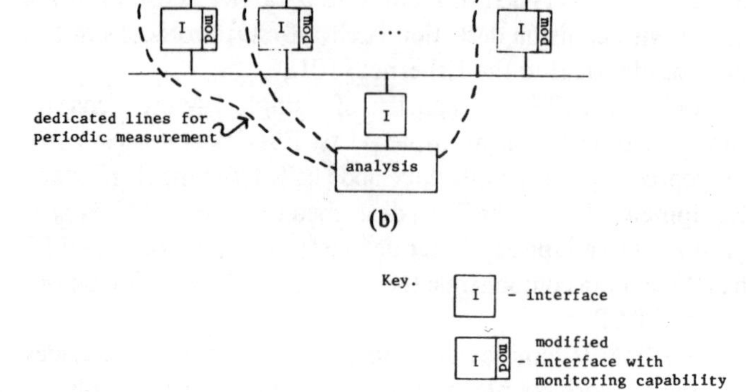

(b)

Key. I - interface

I mod - modified interface with monitoring capability

Fig. 1. Location of measurement in a broadcast network. (a) Centralized. (b) Decentralized.

Depending on experimental objectives, decentralized measurement may require synchronization of interface timers. This problem is a classical one and is discussed in [5]. Finally, because decentralized measurement requires modifications at every interface, implementation and maintenance tend to be more costly than with centralized measurement.

c) *Hybrid Measurement:* Because of the advantages and disadvantages of centralized and decentralized measurement, a hybrid approach was chosen for monitoring the NBSNET (Fig. 2). As much information as possible is collected centrally. Minimal modifications were made to all user interfaces to allow local measurement collection and reduction. These measurements are transferred over the channel to a central site at the termination of each logical connection. Additional modifications were made to those user boards which act as artificial traffic generators. These boards collect timing and collision information (only about artificial traffic) and periodically transmit them to a central site over special inexpensive lines so as not to interfere with the main channel.

A hybrid approach allows accurate and comprehensive measurement. One disadvantage is the complexity of coordinating the analysis of decentralized and centralized measurement. Careful planning minimizes this problem. Independent of the location of measurement, a LAN-MC can be designed for complete or partial measurement. For complete measurement packets must not arrive faster than the measurement system can process them. If packets arrive too frequently, only a sample of the traffic can be collected. This

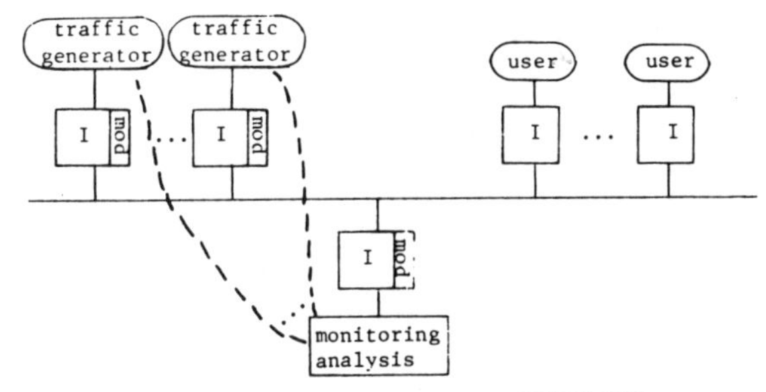

Fig. 2. Hybrid measurement of NBSNET.

significantly affects the algorithms which analyze the data. Timing considerations for the NBSNET measurement system indicate complete measurement is possible [15].

3) *Artificial Traffic Generation:* Analysis of LAN performance requires the ability to generate known artificial traffic loads on a system. Traffic generators are beneficial for two reasons. Normal traffic on a new LAN is typically quite low and rarely stresses its capacity. With traffic generators, however, it is possible to emulate high load conditions. Therefore, network testing and debugging can be accomplished before the network is burdened with production activities when corrections are expensive. Second, traffic generators can produce repeatable traffic patterns. Repeatability facilitates comparison investigations, such as the effect of different communication protocols on network performance.

Traffic generation for NBSNET is accomplished by connecting eight modified user boards to the channel. These generators are programmed to: 1) generate packets with a constant, uniform, or Poisson size distribution, 2) generate packets with constant, uniform, or exponential interarrival times, 3) direct packets to any specified destination, 4) communicate with the monitoring system to synchronize traffic generation and data collection, and 5) permit on-line experimenter control.

4) *On-Line Versus Off-Line Analysis:* Measurement records generated by a monitoring system can be placed in mass storage for off-line future analysis or summarized on the run for on-line monitor display. Current analysis of NBSNET is off-line. When packets are transmitted at a rapid rate, there is limited time to assimilate the data and to simultaneously maintain meaningful statistics on network activity. Except for simple counts, on-line analysis (i.e., performance summaries every 1-2 s) for LAN's is very difficult. This reduces, but does not eliminate, the potential for a complex network feedback system which dynamically adjusts tunable network parameters in response to changing performance and/or workload conditions. NBSNET provides off-line analysis with a delay on the order of 5-10 min following a measurement period.

IV. Measurement Reports

A major problem in designing a local area network measurement center (LAN-MC) is deciding what measurements to collect within a monitored period and what statistics to report. One approach is to measure everything. This implies deriving a database from which the original traffic can be reconstructed completely. Total measurement avoids redesign costs which occur if useful information is omitted from the initial implementation. For most LAN's, however, a total measurement approach requires a prohibitive amount of storage.

A more realistic approach initially determines what managerial and research questions are to be answered by measurement, and what performance reports need be generated. Then one determines the specific network information necessary to satisfy these questions and reports. Finally, the user decides upon an implementation for capturing the information. This is dependent on the network being monitored and the design issue of location of measurement.

Ten performance reports have been implemented for describing NBSNET traffic. The reports were derived in part from the above approach and in part from past experience in measuring long haul networks [3], [8]. They consist of statistics summarizing network activity during any given monitoring period. Each report is classified as either traffic characterization or performance analysis type. Traffic characterization reports indicate the workload placed on the network. This information is a primary source for functional testing of the network. Performance characterization reports indicate the time delays, utilizations, etc., which result from a given load and network configuration. They describe the dependent variables which are observed rather than controlled, and are used for tuning and performance comparisons. A comment section follows each report description where implementation issues are discussed.

A. Host Communication Matrix

The Host Communication Matrix indicates the traffic flow between connected user boards. Tabulated for each source-destination (s-d) pair are the (number, proportion) of (packets, data packets, data bytes) transmitted from s to d. Tabulated for each source (destination) are the (number, proportion) of (packets, data packets, data bytes) transmitted from s (to d). Reported as a summary of the total traffic are the number of (packets, data packets, data bytes) transmitted, the mean number of data bytes per data packet, and the proportion of packets which are data packets.

Comment: Source, destination, and packet type information is part of each packet's header. The number of bytes in a packet is counted by the MC hardware as the packet is tapped off the channel (type: traffic characterization).

B. Building (Group) Communication Matrix

The Building Communication Matrix indicates the traffic flow between buildings or any other user defined groupings of user boards. For example, a group may consist of all user boards connected to the same host. This table condenses the Host Communication Matrix by summing together several groups of rows (columns) into single rows (columns). All tabulated information is identical to that provided in the Host Communication Matrix.

Comment: The NBSNET MC has access to an address-building table which maps user addresses to buildings (type: traffic characterization).

C. Packet Type Histogram

The Packet Type Histogram indicates the distribution of each type of packet transmitted. In measuring NBSNET, packet types are limited only to those defined by the lowest level protocols. Tabulated for each type are (number, proportion) of packets. As summary information (and as a check against other reports), the total number of packets is reported.

Comment: There are currently 12 packet types on the NBSNET. The measurement center counts each packet type by observing the control field of every transmission (type: traffic characterization).

D. Data Packet Size Histogram

The Data Packet Size Histogram records the number and proportion of data packets of particular length classes. Tabulated for each length class *i-j* (say 8–15 bytes) are the (number, proportion) of data packets with (between *i* and *j*, up to *j*) data bytes, inclusive. Values between *i* and *j* estimate the packet size probability distribution, while values up to *j* estimate the cumulative distribution. Reported as summary information are the total number of data packets and data bytes and mean number of data bytes per data packet.

Comment: Data packets are distinguished from other packet types in the packet header control field (type: traffic characterization).

E. Throughput–Utilization Distribution

The Throughput–Utilization Distribution indicates the flow of bytes on the network. Both total bytes transmitted and information bytes communicated are measured. Information bytes are defined to be only those data bytes contained in communications. Overhead such as header bytes and bytes in unacknowledged data packets are not counted since they communicate no information at the packet level. Reported for each user address *i* are: 1) the user channel throughput (bytes per second in all transmissions from address *i*. This count includes synchronization and checksum bytes, but not bytes that are involved in collisions). 2) The user channel utilization (user channel throughput divided by channel capacity). 3) The user information throughput (information bytes communicated per second from address *i*). 4) The user information utilization (user information throughput divided by channel capacity).

Reported as summary information are the total (channel throughput, channel utilization, information throughput, information utilization), and the number of seconds in the measurement period.

Comment: Information statistics describe the beneficial usage of the channel. Information throughput is analogous to the transfer rate of information bits (TRIB), or the number of bits accepted by the receiver divided by time [4]. Total channel utilization excludes the periods when the channel has a signal which is interfered with by noise, faulty hardware, collisions, etc. In computing information throughput, the MC identifies unacknowledged packets by checking packet sequence numbers (type: performance analysis).

F. Packet Interarrival Time Histogram

The Packet Interarrival Time Histogram indicates the number of packet interarrival times which fall into particular time classes. An interarrival time is the time between consecutive carrier (network busy) signals. Reported for each time class *i-j* (say 11–15 ms) are the (number, proportion) of interarrival times (between *i* and *j*, up to *j*) time units, inclusive.

Comment: The MC has a separate timer with 10 μs resolution. This timer is recorded and reset to 0 whenever a carrier signal is monitored. For NBSNET many interarrivals will be less than 1 ms since acknowledgment packets tend to immediately follow receipt of data packets. Other spikes in this histogram are likely to represent service turnaround times for certain processes [14]. For NBSNET, special watchdog packets are transmitted approximately every 2 min to verify inactive connections. Therefore, the longest interarrival time is bounded as long as a connection on the network exists.

Since interarrival times are monitored centrally, they are biased by the propagation delays between interfaces and the MC. These delays are estimated as less than 10 μs. Also, the number of interarrival times will be underestimated since only one interarrival time is collected when multiple arrivals result in a collision. As a result, some times that are tabulated are overstated (type: performance analysis).

G. Channel Acquisition Delay Histogram

The Channel Acquisition Delay Histogram records the times spent by user boards contending for and acquiring the channel. A channel acquisition delay begins when a user board becomes ready to transmit a packet and ends when its first bit is transmitted onto the channel. Included is all of the time spent deferring due to a busy channel and the time recovering and backing off from one or more collisions. Indicated for various time classes *i-j* (say 50–100 μs) are the (number, proportion) of packets whose acquisition delay was (between *i* and *j*, up to *j*) time units, inclusive. Also reported are the total number of packets transmitted, and the (mean, standard deviation) channel acquisition delay time.

Comment: This table reflects the efficiency of a CSMA-CD protocol and the process in which the network board polls each of the user boards. The NBSNET MC collects channel acquisition delays only for packets originating at traffic generators. Modification of all user interfaces for collecting these times was prohibitive. When a packet's transmit flag is set ready for transmission, a timer is reset to 0. When the packet is transmitted (successfully), the timer value is stored locally and then appended to the next packet transmitted (type: performance analysis).

H. Communication Delay Histogram

The Communication Delay Histogram indicates the delays that user boards incur in communicating packets to their destinations. A communication delay begins when an original packet becomes ready for transmission and ends when that packet is received (i.e., communicated) by the destination (which may be several transmissions later). One communication delay exists for each packet communicated. This delay may include several channel acquisition delays.

For completeness, a packet which is never acknowledged and therefore transmitted the maximum number of allowable times, causes an entry in this histogram. This permits analysis of the maximum number of transmissions parameter in terms of time delay. Reported for each time class *i-j* (say 0.5–1 s) are the (number, proportion) of packets which are communicated or which surpass the maximum number of allowable transmissions (herein referred as table entries) whose communication delay time is (between *i* and *j*, up to *j*) time units, inclusive. Also reported are the (total number, mean communication delay, standard deviation communication delay) of {table entries, packets which are communicated, and packets which surpass the maximum number of allowable transmissions).

Comment: By definition, a communication delay excludes the time to generate and communicate an acknowledgment packet back to the original sender. Since the destination begins processing a received packet before (or while) it handles acknowledgment, this time does not reflect the delay in communicating a packet.

As with channel acquisition delays, the NBSNET implementation only captures communication delays for those packets originating at traffic generators. When a buffer's transmit flag is set ready for an original packet, a timer is reset to 0. Each time the last bit of a buffer is transmitted onto the channel, the timer value is saved. When a transmission is acknowledged, the saved value is used to update a local histogram. The histogram is transmitted to a central location after the monitoring period ends. Since No-op packets are not acknowledged, their communication delays are not recorded.

With this decentralized approach, the communication timer value will not include the time to propagate a signal to the destination, nor will it include the destination's software latency to recognize it.

Some factors which influence the communication delay are: the acknowledgement time-out periods before packet retransmission, the maximum number of allowable duplicate transmissions before a connection is broken automatically, and the hardware reliability.

A communication delay differs from the "one hop" delay time defined for measurement of a Packet Radio network (PRnet) [17]. One hop delay is the time interval between when a packet is ready for transmission and its corresponding acknowledgment packet is received. Hence, a one hop delay time includes the time for the destination to communicate its acknowledgment back to the source, while a communication delay time does not (type: performance analysis).

I. Collision Count Histogram

The Collision Count Histogram tabulates the number of collisions a packet of any type encounters before being transmitted. Reported for each collision count value *i* are the (number, proportion) of packets which incurred (*i*, *i* or fewer) collisions before being transmitted. Reported as a summary are the total number of (packets transmitted, collisions) and the (mean, standard deviation) number of collisions per transmission.

Comment: Like the Packet Interarrival Time Histogram, this histogram indicates the efficiency of a CSMA-CD protocol in allowing interfaces to acquire the channel. With NBSNET's 1-persistent protocol, the number of channel contentions for a packet should be one more than the number of collisions incurred in getting the packet transmitted.

Collision count information is available only for artificially generated packets. A collision count is maintained in the header of each packet to be transmitted. Each time a collision is detected, the traffic generator increments the collision count field. When a transmission occurs, the count is sent out as part of the packet and is then monitored by the MC (type: performance analysis).

J. Transmission Count Histogram

The Transmission Count Histogram indicates the number of times a packet is transmitted (original transmission plus duplicate transmissions) before it is communicated to its destination. Redundant transmissions as defined in Section III-B are not included in the histogram since they occur after communication has taken place. Reported for each transmission count *i* are the (number, proportion) of packets whose communication required (*i*, *i* or fewer) transmissions. Reported as a summary are the total number of (packets communicated, packets transmitted, redundant transmissions, piggybacked acknowledgments, No-op packets) and the (mean, standard deviation) number of transmissions required for a communication.

Comment: By observing packet sequence numbers, the MC recognizes the first through last times a particular packet is transmitted and which transmission is the communication. When consecutive transmissions from a particular source–destination pair have identical sequence numbers, then all but the first are duplicate transmissions. The transmission just prior to an acknowledgment is considered the communication. Under ideal conditions, the number of transmissions required per communication is 1 and the number of redundant transmissions is 0.

By counting the number of redundant transmissions, this report indicates what Tobagi *et al.* [17] call the "echo acknowledgment efficiency." With any positive acknowledgment protocol, an interesting metric is how often packets are retransmitted because the acknowledgment was lost even though the packet was communicated (type: performance analysis).

V. Conclusions

Two areas of investigation are planned following verification of the NBSNET-MC. The first area will investigate existing NBSNET low traffic loads for the purpose of uncovering possible errors or inefficiencies. Questions to be answered include the following.

- Is traffic evenly distributed among the network users or are there source–destination pairs with unusually heavy traffic?
- What is the percentage of each type of packet? Are some packet types of unusually high frequency indicating an error or an inefficient protocol?

• What is the distribution of data packet sizes? Are variable size data packets worth the additional overhead or would fixed size packets suffice?

• What are the channel acquisition and communication delay distributions? Are these times excessive?

• Are collisions a factor in getting packets transmitted, indicating possible faulty hardware or protocols?

• What is the information utilization and throughput? How do the information statistics compare with the channel statistics?

The second area will investigate the effects of increasing traffic load and varying packet sizes on network performance. Questions to be answered include the following.

• What is the effect of traffic load on utilization, throughput, and time delays? When, if ever, does traffic load start to degrade system performance?

• Defining a stable network as one whose utilization is a nondecreasing function of traffic load, what is the tradeoff between stability, throughput, and delay?

• What is the maximum capacity of the channel under normal operating conditions? How many active users are necessary to reach this maximum?

• Do larger packets increase or decrease throughput and delay?

• How does constant packet size affect utilization and delay?

Answering these and other questions will help support or dispute the many analytic and simulation results on LAN performance. With an existing network and existing measurement system, it is feasible to determine the validity of the assumptions and simplifications of these past studies.

ACKNOWLEDGMENT

The author gratefully appreciates the active roles that R. Rosenthal, D. Stokesberry, R. Toense, M. L. Fahey, and D. Rorrer played in the design and implementation of the NBSNET Measurement Center.

REFERENCES

[1] R. J. Carpenter, J. Sokol, Jr., and R. Rosenthal, "A microprocessor-based local network node," in *Proc. IEEE COMPCON*, Fall 1978, pp. 104–109.

[2] R. J. Carpenter and J. Sokol, Jr., "Serving users with a local area network," *Comput. Networks*, Oct. 1980.

[3] G. Cole, "Performance measurements on the ARPA computer network," *IEEE Trans. Commun.*, vol. COM-20, pp. 630–636, June 1972.

[4] I. W. Cotton, "Criteria for the performance evaluation of data communications services for computer networks," Nat. Bureau of Standards, Washington, DC, NBS Tech. Note 882, Sept. 1975.

[5] C. Ellingson and R. Kulpinski, "Dissemination of system time," *IEEE Trans. Commun.*, vol. COM-21, May 1973.

[6] D. Ferrari, *Computer Systems Performance Evaluation.* Englewood Cliffs, NJ: Prentice-Hall, 1978.

[7] IFIP Working Group 6.4 on Local Computer Networks, *Statement of Aims and Scope*, June 1979.

[8] L. Kleinrock and W. Naylor, "On measured behavior of the ARPA network," in *Proc. Nat. Comput. Conf.*, AFIPS, vol. 43, 1974, pp. 767–780.

[9] L. Kleinrock and F. A. Tobagi, "Packet switching in radio channels: Part 1—Carrier sense multiple-access modes and their throughput-delay characteristics," *IEEE Trans. Commun.*, vol. COM-23, pp. 1400–1416, Dec. 1975.

[10] R. M. Metcalfe and D. R. Boggs, "Ethernet: Distributed packet switching for local computer networks," *Commun. Ass. Comput. Mach.*, vol. 19, pp. 395–404, July 1976.

[11] Network Analysis Corp. "Impact assessment of standards for LAN: A final report prepared for U.S. Dept. of Commerce," FR.293.01R2, Sept. 1980.

[12] NBSNET User's Information, Nat. Bureau of Standards, Int. Document, Feb. 1980.

[13] G. Nutt, "Tutorial: Computer systems monitors," *Computer*, vol. 8, pp. 51–61, Nov. 1975.

[14] J. F. Shoch and J. A. Hupp, "Measured performance of an Ethernet local network," *Commun. Ass. Comput. Mach.*, vol. 23, pp. 711–720, Dec. 1980.

[15] D. Stokesberry and R. Rosenthal, "The design and engineering of a performance measurement center for a local area network," in *Proc. Comput. Networking Symp.*, Washington, DC, Dec. 1980, pp. 110–115.

[16] L. Svobodova, "Computer system measurability," *Computer*, pp. 9–17, June 1976.

[17] F. Tobagi, S. E. Lieberson, and L. Kleinrock, "On measurement facilities in packet radio systems," in *Proc. Nat. Comput. Conf.*, AFIPS, vol. 45, 1976, pp. 589–596.

Paul D. Amer received the B.S. degree in mathematics from the State University of New York, Albany in 1974, and the M.S. and Ph.D. degrees in computer and information science from The Ohio State University, Columbus, in 1976 and 1979, respectively.

Currently, he is an Assistant Professor on the Department of Computer and Information Sciences at the University of Delaware, Newark. He is also a Faculty Research Assistant at the National Bureau of Standards. At the State University of New York, Albany, he was employed for three years in the Computing Center, with primary responsibility for interacting with faculty and graduate students who used the Center's statistical packages, such as BMD and SPSS. At Ohio State University, his primary research was in the area of computer system performance evaluation. He investigated problems in workload characterization and computer system/service selection employing empirical techniques, simulation, and statistical theory. He was also a Teaching Associate for which he received the 1979 $1000 Graduate Teaching Award. As a Research Assistant at the National Bureau of Standards, he placed his computer selection research within the context of government procurement of interactive computer services. He is also the author of two NBS Special Publications, one of which received the U.S. Department of Commerce Certificate of Recognition. Over the last two years his research has changed emphasis within the area of computer system performance evaluation from system selection to modeling, measurement, and analysis of local area computer networks. This change in direction was motivated by increased importance placed in local network technology by NBS and the predicted boom in the usage of local networks for office automation. His current research activities involve investigation of design issues for measuring any local area network architecture, specifying topology-independent local network performance metrics, and specifying a measurement and control center for a local broadcast network which employs a CSMA/CD communication protocol.

Dr. Amer is a member of the Association for Computing Machinery, SCS, SIGCOMM, SIGMETRICS, and SIGSIM.

Reliability/Availability of Wideband Local Communication Networks

D. G. Willard

The MITRE Corporation
Bedford, MA 01730

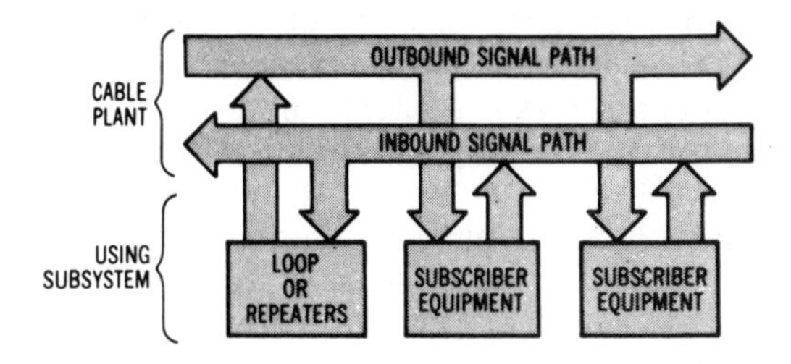

Fig 1 Network segments. Wideband distributed communication network consists of cable plant segment (either single- or dual-cable) and using subsystems (distributed subscriber equipment and centrally located signal processing devices)

The adolescent multimode broadband bus network technology provides operational benefits in local networks that are not possible with conventional communication methods. The very architecture of these systems, however, increases the risk of major consequences when single components fail. Happily, the architecture also provides an opportunity to implement comprehensive monitoring and control procedures at moderate cost. Recognizing potential failure modes, redesigning components to increase reliability, and incorporating certain monitor and control functions will result in a network that provides improved services with higher reliability than can be achieved with conventional communications alternatives.

Local area multimode bus networks can be thought of as consisting of two major system segments: the wideband medium ("cable plant") on which subscriber signals are exchanged, and the devices ("using subsystems") that interface subscriber equipment to the medium (Fig 1). Reliability of the bus network depends on the reliability of the individual components of these segments. Network availability, in turn, depends on the identification and repair procedures used to rectify failures.

Cable Plant Equipment: Failure Analysis

The community antenna television (CATV) cable plant that supports communication signals is usually implemented as tree, star, or a combination of these two basic architectures. Subscribers are effectively connected in parallel for the purpose of retrieving signals from and introducing signals to the network. Consequently, if a portion of the cable plant degrades, a large number of subscribers can be cut off from the network.

Among the major failure modes is a conductive short between center conductor and shield of the coaxial system. This is usually caused by direct shorts on the cable itself, but can be caused by failures in cable components such as taps, amplifiers, and splitters. Not only are the radio frequency (rf) signals prohibited from passing such a short circuit, but because 60-Hz ac is multiplexed onto the cable to power amplifiers, an increased load is drawn from the power supplies. Because commercial practice provides each power supply with overload protection, the ac is either reduced or totally removed.

Fault isolation is difficult under these conditions, since signal tracing techniques are ineffective on coaxial systems; reflectometer processes cannot be employed because the amplifiers are one-way devices for a single frequency. Amplifiers are also made inoperative by the lack of power. The isolation process is made more difficult; large segments of the cable plant are inoperative because many amplifiers are serviced by one power supply. Cable open circuits are similarly difficult to identify and to locate. They do not tend to pull down other segments of the otherwise properly operating cable plant, however, since power supplies are not overloaded.

Cable amplifiers are generally the only active components in the cable signal path and, as such, are primary contributors to the failure rate of local area CATV networks. Measured mean time between failure (MTBF) figures of 50 years have permitted one manufacturer recently to guarantee 20-year MTBFs. Experience has indicated, however, that amplifier failures are not evenly distributed. Failures tend to be bunched into the early (infant mortality) and late (old age) portions of the useful (guaranteed) lifetime. Although architectural design can minimize the effect of single-amplifier failures, many applications would suffer serious consequences if even a portion of the network became inoperative.

Reprinted with permission from *Computer Design* August 1981 issue.

Partial cable failure occurs when a component degrades or some function becomes less than fully operational. An example is the interference caused by extraneous rf signals and/or noise injected into the medium. These signals can ingress through flaws or failures in the coaxial shielding integrity from strong external fields, or they can be produced within the network. The cable plant is a linearly amplified analog medium in which out-of-specification stresses can produce undesired signals. These extraneous signals can interfere directly with acceptable signal detection and themselves contribute to additional system stress. Loose connections, poor solder joints and other intermittents, as well as unstable amplifiers—all can generate noise that will be propagated throughout the network.

Cable Plant Reliability Improvements

Fuses of appropriate value should be inserted throughout the cable plant so that those nearest a short will open. This action removes overload from the power supply and severs the segment of plant that includes the failure. Cable splitters that include provisions for power fusing and satisfy the fusing needs of most cable plant designs are available. This process permits the rest of the plant to continue in service but provides no direct indication of the occurrence or location of the shorting fault. Cable components can also fail "open," but in that case only the affected cable segment becomes inoperative.

Both short and open component failure cases can be automatically identified and isolated with a pilot monitoring subsystem. The basic function of the pilot monitoring process is to loop signals sequentially through selected portions of the cable plant while measuring each returned signal level. If a returned signal is not within tolerance, the integrity of the associated branch is suspect.

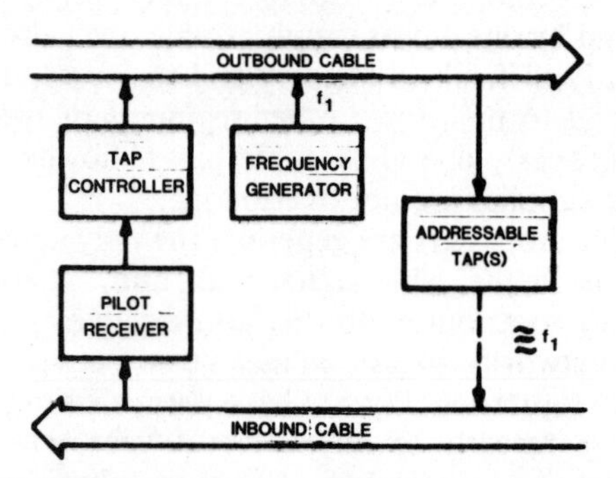

Fig 2 Basic pilot monitoring subsystem. Tap controller located at cable head end causes each remote addressable tap to close, looping only pilot frequency back to head end. Pilot receiver provides measurement of looped signal amplitude to controller for determination of abnormal operation in each branch of cable plant

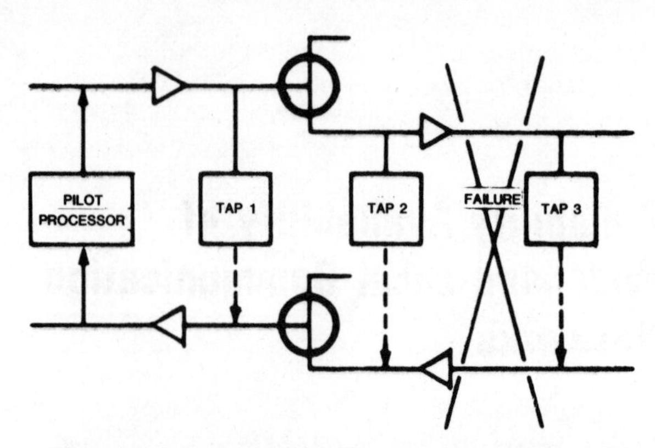

Fig 3 Cable fault isolation. Pilot processor can determine that cable fault has occurred and that it is located between tap 2 and tap 3 locations, since taps 1 and 2 produce normal looped-back pilot amplitudes

In its simplest form, pilot monitoring uses a set of commercially available addressable taps with pilot passing filters. The tap controller and pilot receiver are located at the head end of a 2-cable network, as shown in Fig 2. The controller issues a "close" command to a specific tap and then accepts an amplitude reading from the receiver; this reading is compared with a stored value of expected amplitude. An alert is generated if that value is not within tolerance. The controller then issues an "open" command to that tap, and a new measurement is made to ensure successful opening. The cycle then repeats for each of the other taps in the system.

Different forms of pilot monitoring are possible for other cable configurations. If the pilot monitoring process is applied to a single-cable network, for instance, frequency conversion is required at each tap location. Conversion can be accomplished by frequency translation, a receiver/transmitter combination, or more exotic circuitry.

Automatic processing of data from strategically placed taps can isolate a cable fault to any resolution desired. As an example, Fig 3 illustrates a failure on a 2-cable network between taps 2 and 3 that would be indicated by a successful loop through taps 1 and 2, but an unsuccessful loop through tap 3.

Redundancy is a technique that can be used to minimize the effect of amplifier failures. Inline amplifiers can be effectively paralleled in such a way that the failure of one will reduce the net gain by only 6 dB. Properly implemented, the pilot monitoring subsystem just described can identify which amplifier location has suffered the failure. Replacement of the failed unit can then be effected without disrupting the network. Since the pilot subsystem also identifies and isolates other forms of degradation, it is recommended that the pilot monitoring function be implemented in parallel amplifier installations. However, there is a commercial line of amplifiers that responds to an interrogation signal with a status message transmission. This technique has merit for installations that do not plan to include the pilot monitoring function, but do require rapid identification of amplifier degradation.

An alternate routing technique can be used to circumvent a single-component failure. If a parallel path is provided with appropriate switching, the alternative path can be selected to pass signals around the primary path when it becomes inoperative.

Shielding integrity of the cable plant and spectrum utilization can both be determined by a low resolution, automatic frequency stepped rf amplitude monitor. Each quantum of the spectrum can be compared with stored values of expected signal levels and appropriate alarms generated for unexpected measurements. Such measurements indicate either unauthorized use of bandwidth or the ingression of external signals. Ingression suggests a break in cable integrity, which also permits signal egression.

Subscriber Interface Equipment: Failure Analysis

A properly designed and maintained CATV based cable plant provides a highly reliable and benign environment for the distribution of signals in a local area network. The high signal to noise ratio (S/N) permits high quality analog and low error rate digital signal propagation. Consequently, classic noise associated errors are not a problem in cable based networks. Other problems exist, however.

One digital subsystem that may use the cable network forms a common-channel time division bus on which all intersubscriber communications are exchanged. Several of these buses may exist simultaneously in the larger facilities; each bus has a different rf channel frequency assignment. The following discussion is limited to this class of service.

Common-channel buses are subject to channel jamming. Extraneous inband signals can seriously disrupt traffic flow. The interfering signal can be introduced by either of two mechanisms: improper operation of one of the subsystem subscriber units, or unrelated signals from other network participants or external sources. If the signal is strong enough, it will mask transmissions desired at the subscriber receivers. Interfering signals at normal levels will confuse the receivers and may be misinterpreted as legitimate transmissions.

Little if any effect is felt by the other bus participants if a subscriber is unable to insert a transmit signal onto the channel. Such a condition can occur if the transmit cable connection, the rf modulator, or

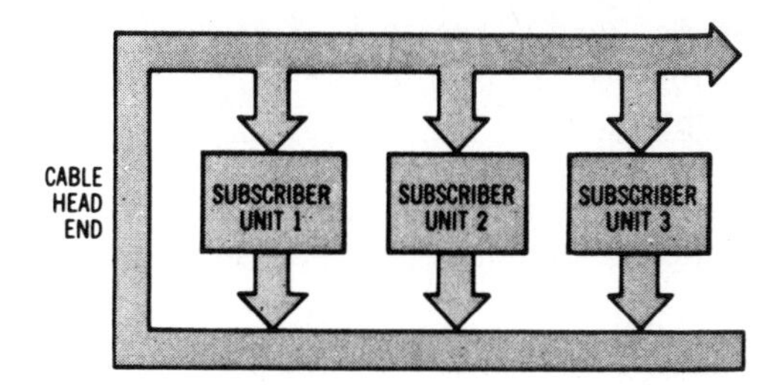

Fig 4 Listen-before/listen-while-talk digital communication bus network. Units intercommunicate by transmitting onto inbound (lower) channel and listening on outbound (upper) channel. These channels are connected (looped) at cable head end. Channel is timeshared among units by unslotted contention protocol in which each unit determines as best it can that channel is unoccupied before starting its transmission (listen-before-talk) and monitors its own transmission for errors and/or contention collisions (listen-while-talk). When collision is detected, each unit involved will invoke retransmission and schedule it after pseudorandom time. In adaptive systems arithmetic mean of this time is chosen as function of collision rate, either by individual unit or by central authority

the control logic fails. However, serious malfunctions can occur if the receive process fails at a subscriber. System timing and the general information necessary for the channel sharing protocol will become unavailable. A subscribing device operating without full receiving capability can issue signals "in the blind," which will cause severe interference to other traffic on the timeshared channel.

In adaptive bus subsystems, signals received in error can produce effects that last longer than the signals themselves. An example of an adaptive subsystem is the listen-before/listen-while-talk bus, in which the mean random backoff parameter is determined as a function of signal collision rate. (See Fig 4.) An error producing interference signal burst can create a large queue of users attempting random delay retransmissions through the collision avoidance process. If it is not carefully implemented, the adaptive backoff parameter protocol can prolong the effects of such a burst.

Bus subscriber units can also develop problems in which distorted operation occurs without full failure. Distorted transmissions can affect all receivers. Such transmissions sometimes result in messages that are not accepted and require retransmission; or they may result in messages that are accepted but are misinterpreted, depending on the strength of the error detection process. Degraded receptions, on the other hand, will also cause missed or misinterpreted messages, but generally at the malfunctioning unit only. These degraded subscriber units have the potential to indirectly cause an unnecessary increase in channel loading because of retransmission attempts that can, in turn, seriously impair subsystem throughput and end to end delay.

Another condition that can completely block communications is a failure at the cable head end location. Since all inbound signals are looped by one or more devices to the outbound path at the head end, most head end failures impede traffic from all subscriber locations equally. Some head end configurations provide a simple wideband loop, others use band limited filters, while others employ repeaters of various complexities. In most installations, either the wideband loop or several active repeaters are employed. Seldom is a single repeater used, since the wideband nature of the medium is usually exploited to propagate various signals simultaneously. Although a wideband loop failure interrupts all services, it is unlikely to occur; thus, in the long run, the wideband loop is less likely to cause problems. On the other hand, a failure of one in a complex of repeaters will affect only its associated channel or subset of channels, but is more likely to fail unless special design precautions are implemented.

Subscriber Interface Reliability Improvements

Buses that contain an inherent monitoring and control capability, such as polling and dynamically assigned slots, can obtain information about the connectivity and technical welfare of each subscribing unit as part of the network control function. (See Fig 5.) Additional technical information can be obtained by interrogating and measuring individual elements.

In contrast, a central network control that can serve as technical control is not available in a distributed control bus system. (See Fig 6.) Some information on the status of the subscriber units can be obtained by passive traffic monitoring. However, full technical monitoring and control requires additional communications and measurement to ascertain whether minimal functions are being performed. In this class of distributed control bus, it is recommended that a periodic status message be issued by each subscriber unit—either automatically or in response to a poll—independent of but containing information about other types of transmission. This report should provide information pertinent to the unit's operation since the last such report. A special facility must then monitor these messages and perform the technical control function.

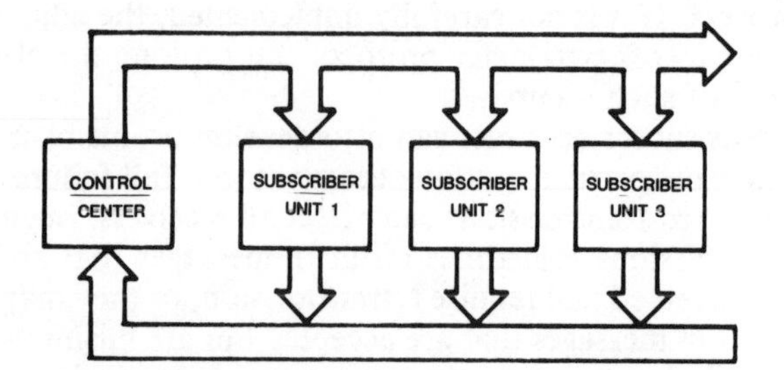

Fig 5 Centralized control network. Here subscriber units exchange information with or through control center. Polling or slotted buses are two such protocols. As byproduct, control center is aware of much of health and welfare of each subscriber unit and hence of that of network

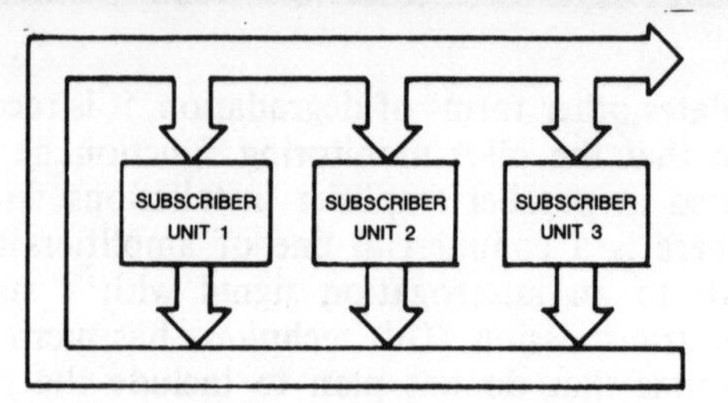

Fig 6 Distributed control network. Subscriber units coordinate exchange of information among themselves without central control authority. Each unit has only parochial view of network health and welfare

Analysis of status messages from individual subscriber units permits the technical monitoring and control facility to judge an appropriate random backoff parameter that is based on the current operation of the complete bus. Continuous modification of the parameter can be broadcast to each subscriber unit as required. This global view is preferred, since an individual unit can modify its parameter based only on a limited view of the bus; consequently, the unit must modify its parameter conservatively.

In both centralized and distributed network control buses, measurements should be made on the quality of the rf signal. It is important to anticipate the degradation in both a subscribing unit's modulator and demodulator. Specialized rf measurement devices provide this data to the technical control facility. Measurement of the transmitted signal from each subscriber unit can be made at any location in the network. Such measurements are nearly useless, of course, unless they can be associated with specific transmitters. One method is to have the measurement device perform this association (ie, digital address decoding). Alternatively, the rf measurement information can be provided to status message interception circuits, where the association will be based on arrival time.

Indirect measurement of each receiver's performance at the subscriber units can also be implemented in the above configuration. The technical control processor can issue cyclic interrogations of each subscriber unit to which a specific response will be issued. If a known rf signal from technical control is progressively perturbated, an operation range can be determined over which the subject receiver performs properly.

To prevent a subscriber unit from transmitting inadvertently because its receiving circuitry is not functioning, the design could include a transmit inhibit function. One method would be to make each unit ascertain that it can hear its status message clearly; otherwise, all other types of transmission will be prohibited. To prevent abnormally long transmissions when the subscriber control logic fails in that mode, each modulator can include a "dead-man" switch to provide an inhibiting function.

Technical Control Considerations

The dichotomy of too little or too much information applies to technical control systems as well as to other forms of monitoring. When the system is performing properly, simple indication of that fact is required. An alert condition calls for a straightforward indicator. However, how the specific cause for alert is presented is critical to successful maintenance. A system that presents only the fact of alert can be designed, but a better system would present the process or logic by which the alert decision was made. The best system design would process all alerts for correlation and present a probable cause.

As an example of these three levels, assume that a cable pilot monitoring function identifies a major cable severance. The simplest system would indicate only that there was a problem on the cable plant. A more complicated design would list all addressable tap locations that report the amplitude of the looped pilot to be low. The best design would determine that, since all out-of-tolerance levels were at the noise level and the locations were all in one building, probable cause for the failure was a break in the cable plant at the building interface.

In a similar manner, the well-designed technical control process would analyze the fact that the amplitude of all status messages on the digital bus had been reduced by 4 dB, and indicate the probable cause as a degradation either of a head end cable amplifier or of the amplitude measurement device itself. Analysis algorithms must be formulated to provide detailed backup information for maintenance personnel.

The technical control facility should not be designed as an integral part of normal systems operations. That is, the complete system of cable plant and using subsystems must continue to function even if technical control is not active. As an example, in a digital bus design that incorporates a centralized adaptive retransmission backoff parameter, each subscriber interface unit must incorporate a fail-safe fallback parameter to be invoked if no such value is received from the central technical control facility. Such design permits the introduction of technical control during any phase of the system's lifetime, and permits modifications to tailor the functions to specific needs.

A single computer based technical control facility is more economical to implement than separate computers for each subsystem. A single-processor configuration is possible if the technical control functions are not built into the subsystem or designed to be time critical. Design should allocate the processing power among the subsystems as necessary. The single-processor configuration can also coordinate and exchange information among individual technical control processes for different subsystems, readily permitting probable cause analysis. For example, probable cause analysis can associate loss of pilot looping with absence of subscriber unit status messages to report the status of a specific section of the network.

A MULTILEVEL SECURE LOCAL AREA NETWORK

Deepinder P. Sidhu
Research & Development
Burroughs Corporation
Paoli, Pennsylvania 19301

Morrie Gasser
The MITRE Corporation
Bedford, Massachusetts 01730

This paper presents a high-level design for a local area network (LAN) that will support subscribers (terminals or hosts) operating at various security levels. Subscribers may be "single-level", which means they are untrusted and can operate at only one security level, or they may be "multilevel" and trusted to operate at a range of security levels [Nibaldi79].

For single-level subscribers, communication is restricted to those at the same security level. This restriction is enforced by trusted interface units (TIUs) used by each subscriber to interface to the LAN, and is based on a security level field in the header of each packet. The TIUs are trusted to enforce and check the security markings in the packets--the hosts or terminals themselves are not.

For multilevel subscribers (a multilevel secure terminal or host), communication is restricted according to the usual security constraints. That is, a multilevel host can transmit at a range of levels between the minimum and maximum. The minimum and maximum are enforced by the TIU for the multilevel host, with the host trusted to choose the specific level of each packet it transmits. Likewise, the multilevel host is trusted to receive packets at the range of its levels and to properly protect the data according to the classification in the packet header. Figure 1 shows a simple multilevel LAN with single-level and multilevel subscribers.

Because the data on the network medium (e.g., coaxial cable) is not encrypted, appropriate physical protection is required. In a broadcast LAN, this would imply that the entire cable and the TIUs would have to be protected to system-high, since all packets on the network are visible at all locations. For subscribers operating at lower security levels (and in less-protected environments) it might not be feasible to protect the medium to system-high at all points, especially since both the TIU-subscriber and TIU-LAN interfaces usually consist of relatively short cables. For example, the physical and procedural controls necessary to provide a DoD Top Secret environment are extremely costly. It would be unreasonable to expect such protection to be required for all the TIUs and the entire LAN medium in a network whose majority of users are unclassified.

To allow for realistic combination of environmental controls we extend the secure LAN architecture to incorporate the concept of separate physical subnetworks whose mediums are each protected to some maximum level that may be less than the maximum level of the entire local network. The subnetworks are connected by "bridges" in such a way that the entire set of subnetworks appear as a single local network to each TIU and subscriber [Clark78]. An example of a LAN composed of several subnetworks is shown in figure 2. Where portions of the medium, TIU-subscriber link, or bridge link must pass through unprotected areas, data is

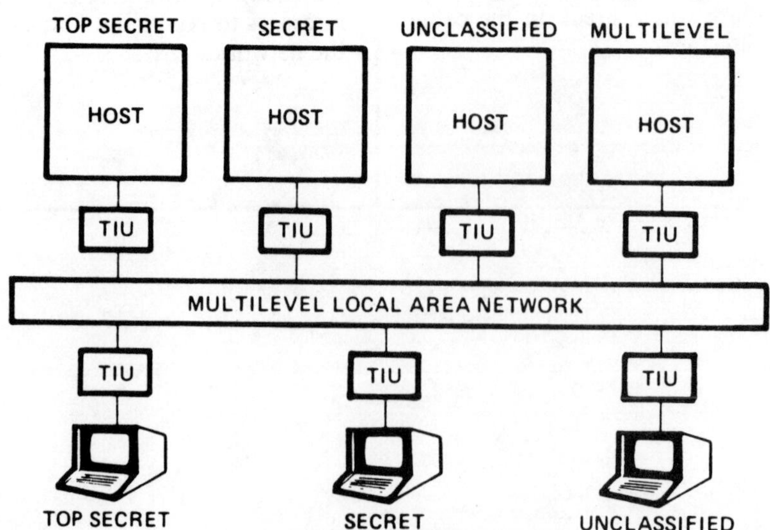

Figure 1. Simple Multilevel LAN

Reprinted from *Proceedings of the 1982 Symposium on Security and Privacy*, 1982, ages 137-143.

EHO234-5/85/0000/0394$01.00 © 1982 IEEE

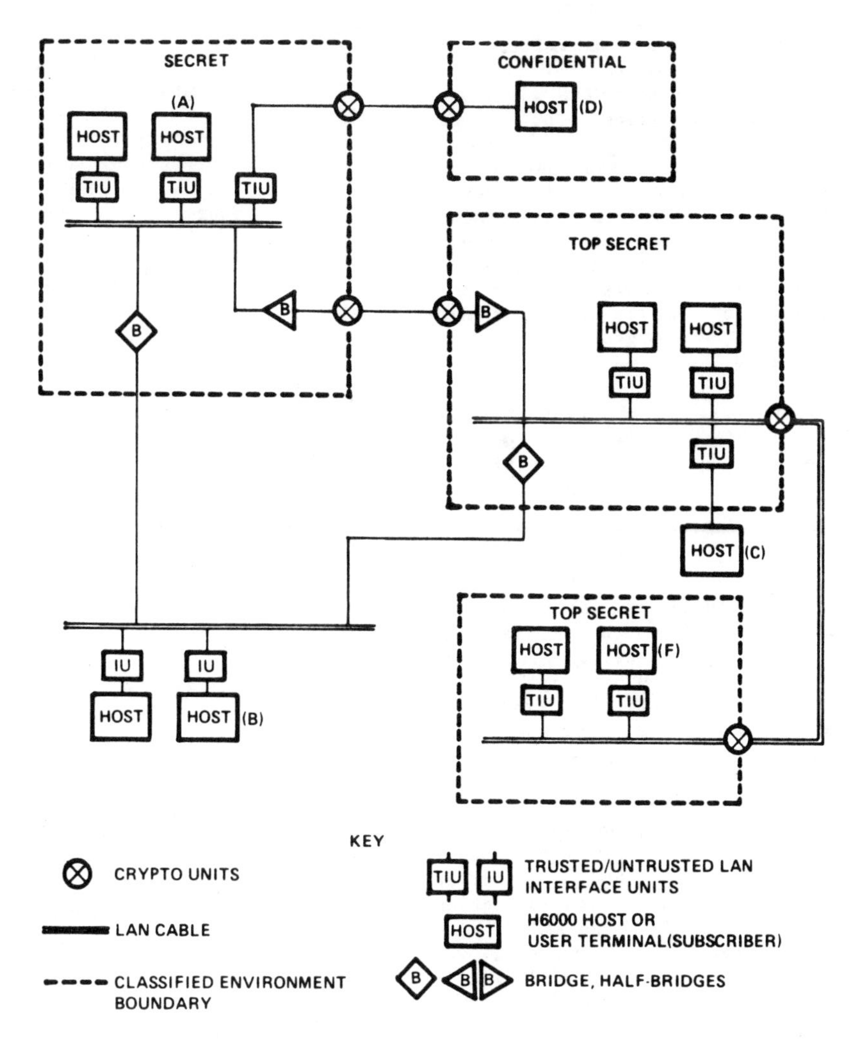

Figure 2. Subnetwork Structure

encrypted using mostly standard link encryption techniques. While this paper does not address encryption as a solution to multilevel data protection, some encryption issues peculiar to this architecture will be discussed below.

The bridges implement a function similar to gateways in wide-area networks but are much simpler. Their job is to route packets between LAN subnetworks with identical protocols. They operate at a level of protocol that makes them transparent to TIUs and hosts or terminals, so that they have no effect on the hardware and software in the TIUs. The bridges perform their routing function based on fixed tables within the bridges and destination addresses in the headers of the packets. They also perform a security check to insure that information from a high level TIU on one subnetwork does not flow to a lower level subnetwork. In this way subnetworks need only be "trusted" (and physically protected) to maintain separation of data within the range of levels of subscribers on that subnetwork. Even unclassified subnetworks can be supported as shown at the bottom of figure 2.

The overall design is intended to be easily implementable with minimal changes to existing off-the-shelf technology and protocols. As such it is felt that it is a practical solution for many installations that have near-term requirements to incorporate a local area network into existing or planned data processing facilities and cannot afford to spend the time or money for more sophisticated long-term options. It is far more flexible than a "system-high" approach where all subscribers must be protected to the highest level [DoD72]. It provides a foundation for multilevel communications at sites that may initially only require communication between single-level entities, but may later upgrade to multilevel hosts and terminals. A proposed implementation would take place in three phases, allowing an initial capability for single-level communication with incremental upgrade to multilevel communication. This phasing matches the anticipated availability of multilevel computers and terminals, where only single-level components are available today, followed by controlled-mode (two-level) hosts, "variable-level" terminals (to be discussed below), and finally multilevel terminals and hosts.

The concept deals with practical matters such as physical protection of the medium, terminals and hosts. It also takes into account the difficulty of certifying large pieces of hardware or software for multilevel operation by reducing to an absolute minimum the components of the system that must be trusted. No "security kernel" or sophisticated trusted mechanisms are required. The design deals with a phased implementation that will satisfy many initial needs in the near future and can later be upgraded, with no disruption of service, for more sophisticated applications as the need for multilevel service increases and a greater volume of traffic must be supported.

The next sections discuss the protocols and the architecture of the TIU and bridge. Some encryption issues are addressed at the end of this paper.

PROTOCOLS

In order to design multilevel security into any network specific protocols must be examined. To insure feasibility of implementation and operation, we are basing our design on an existing protocol that is known to be operational and thus presumably has its bugs worked out. Our goal is to minimize the modifications to the protocol so as not to affect any existing performance studies or implementation techniques. While many of the basic concepts of the approach in this paper are applicable to a number of existing LAN protocols, we have chosen to center our design around the carrier sense multiple access with collision detection (CSMA/CD) protocol that has been proposed for the IEEE standard 802 [IEEE81]. This protocol was chosen because similar protocols are fairly widely (though by no means universally) accepted in industry (Ethernet being the prime example [Ethernet80]). We are not specifying that CSMA/CD is the only protocol that can be used for a multilevel network. However, as design details are presented here it will be apparent where CSMA/CD is specific to this particular design. Certain aspects of the design would have to be modified to use another protocol. When we refer to CSMA/CD in this paper we are specifically referring to the IEEE version, although other versions (e.g., Ethernet) would probably be suitable will little change.

We are not concerned with the issue of whether the LAN medium is a broadband or baseband cable. That is, the physical layer (layer 1 of the ISO reference model [ISO81]) is not an issue for our design, although many aspects of the physical interface (e.g., TEMPEST) must be addressed in an implementation for secure applications. Many of the other aspects of the CSMA/CD protocol not mentioned here remain unchanged from that in the proposed IEEE 802 standard.

Figure 3 shows a simplified format of the IEEE 802 CSMA/CD packet, along with the modified version for our secure LAN. We have subdivided the source and destination address fields into two components, to provide a two-level hierarchical address based on subnetwork number and TIU number. The other

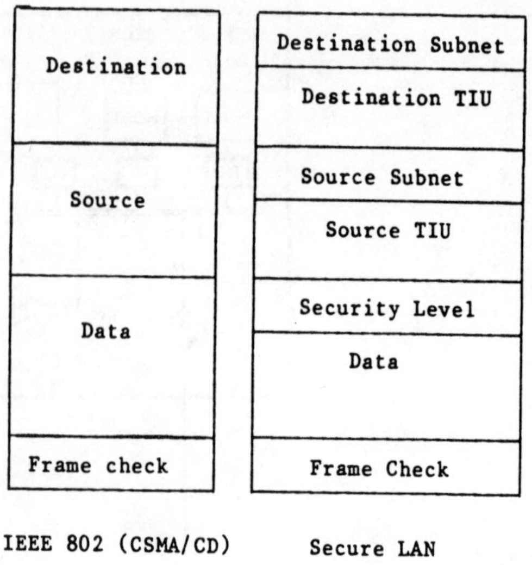

IEEE 802 (CSMA/CD)	Secure LAN
Destination	Destination Subnet
	Destination TIU
Source	Source Subnet
	Source TIU
Data	Security Level
	Data
Frame check	Frame Check

Figure 3. Packet Formats

change is the addition of a security level field at the beginning of the data field. The packet and header length is unchanged, and all the CSMA/CD protocol processing logic is unchanged from that in the standard.

Of course, CSMA/CD is only a low-level link protocol (layer 2 of the ISO reference model), and there are higher layer protocols to be considered in any full implementation. However, our solution is oriented around implementing multilevel security at the link level, with no requirement for any particular protocols at a higher layer. This further minimizes the effect of our approach on any existing software making use of and implementing those higher layers.

Focussing on the link layer alone does have its drawbacks, however. These are seen as minor in an initial scenario where a multilevel LAN would be installed to provide a basic communications capability and also to handle existing security requirements. As the traffic load increases and the type of multilevel processing becomes more sophisticated, the TIUs and bridges on the LAN would be upgraded (in fully compatible manner) so as to provide additional services. These services require the consideration of higher-level protocols, such as the DoD standard Transmission Control Protocol (TCP) with Internet (IP) [Postel81a, Postel81b]. Further discussion of this upgrade capability will be presented in the relevant sections.

TRUSTED INTERFACE UNIT

The TIU is responsible for enforcing the security policy based on the level(s) of its subscriber and the level of packets. TIUs come in three versions, in increasing order of complexity. Initially there would only be the need for single-level TIUs that provide the single-level type of protection for untrusted subscribers discussed earlier. Another version would provide variable-level operation. This means that the TIU is not permanently fixed to communicate at just one level, but can vary its level based on some human operator action. This type of TIU would allow, for example, a terminal to sometimes operate at one security level (to communicate with a certain set of hosts) and sometimes operate at another security level. Hosts whose levels change due to periods processing would also use a variable-level TIU. Finally, there is a multilevel TIU that properly coordinates with its terminal or host to support full multilevel operation.

Single-level TIU

The trusted interface unit shown in figure 4 allows a single-level subscriber (untrusted host or terminal) to communicate with another subscriber at the same security level, via a local network to which subscribers of several levels are connected. The TIU must be physically protected to the level of network-high, and is designed to reliably isolate the traffic at one particular security level from the traffic at all other levels.

We are using the IEEE 802 standard (CSMA/CD) physical and link layer interface on the network, and envision that off-the-shelf hardware will eventually be available, in the form of a chip or circuit board, that facilitates construction of a microcomputer-based TIU for the CSMA/CD protocol. In our security architecture we have anticipated the functions of such hardware and have made an attempt to use it to simplify the TIU implementation, though our design is by no means dependent on its availability.

The header of the CSMA/CD packet begins with a destination address, followed by the source address. The packet ends with a frame check sequence. The function of the CSMA/CD interface is to recognize valid packets received from the network and to transfer the entire packet into the TIU's memory. (We are describing the interface's function as if it were loading data into a microcomputer memory as a DMA device, although there may be variations on this approach.) When the packet has been successfully received and loaded into memory, the TIU CPU is signalled that a successful DMA transfer has occurred.

The CSMA/CD hardware is assumed to be programmed (or "burned in") with the ability to recognize one particular destination address as its own. As data arrives from the network the first few bytes of header are examined and, if the destination is correct, the remaining data is passed through to TIU memory. If the destination is incorrect, or if a collision is detected, the rest of the packet is ignored (not passed into memory). The CSMA/CD protocol is designed so as to detect all collisions while reading the header of the packet (though this attribute is not currently specified in the standard), so that receipt of a correct destination, coupled with no collision, nearly guarantees that the remainder of the packet in memory is valid (i.e., no collision will occur) and is addressed for the current recipient. Once the packet has been read into memory, it is still possible that a frame-check error will be detected by the hardware as the last byte is read. In this case the TIU CPU is not signalled, so the data, even though now resident in memory, will be ignored.

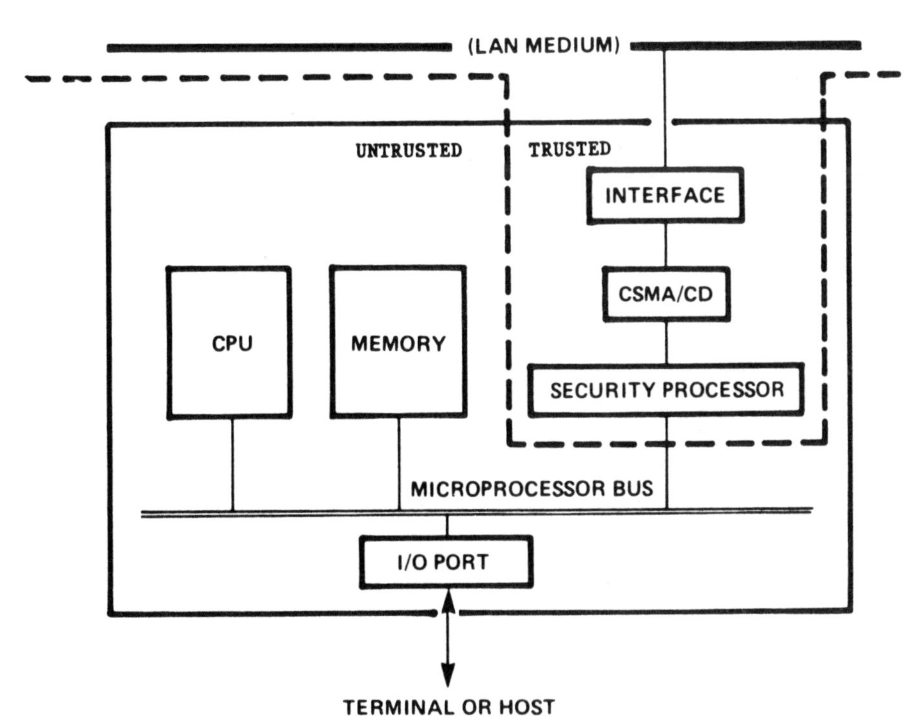

Figure 4. Single-level TIU

On output to the network, a DMA transfer is initiated by the CPU and the interface handles the contention part of the protocol required to get the packet out on the network. It may also, perhaps, handle source address insertion and frame-check computation.

What is important to note is that, between the second field of the header (the source address) and the frame-check sequence, the CSMA/CD interface attaches no particular meaning to the data. For our secure local network we have added an additional field, immediately after the source address, that is the security level of the data. The secure TIU has been designed so as to totally isolate the security-relevant processing (CSMA/CD protocol handling and security field checking) from the remainder of the protocol processing, thus maximizing the flexibility of TIU functions without having to worry about verifying that remainder of the software within the TIU. This concept is particularly important if more complex protocols, such as TCP and IP, are implemented in TIUs. Of course, the security field checking mechanism and many properties of the CSMA/CD protocol handler must be verified.

In the figure we have added a security processor between the CSMA/CD interface and the rest of the TIU, so that there is a distinct trusted/untrusted separation of functions*. On data input from the network, the function of the security processor is to look at the third field of the header, the security level, and only accept the remainder of the packet data if the security level is equal to that of the subscriber. Thus, data will only arrive in the TIU's memory if both the destination and security level are correct. On output to the network, the security processor inserts the subscriber's security level in the packet as the packet is transferred to the network from memory.

We envision the security processor to consist of hardwired logic or perhaps a single-chip computer with an on-board program. This processor has a very simple function since it only processes "good" packets, due to the outboard handling of the contention protocol by the CSMA/CD interface. Also, it need only have the throughput of the subscriber device, not that of the network, since only the subscriber's input and output need be processed. However, depending on the interface characteristics of the CSMA/CD hardware, instantaneous speed might have to be much higher.

Note that, on input from the network, security rules require that no data arrive in the memory of the TIU unless that data is of the proper level. Thus we may be forced to buffer the destination and source fields of an incoming packet within the security processor until we can be sure of the security level, instead of simply passing the fields into TIU memory "on the fly". Also, if a collision has occurred, which will always be detected during reading of the destination or source fields, we may not want to have the partially-read data in memory. Finally, there is the possibility that a packet with a frame-check error will be fully read into memory before the error is detected. There would then be a slight chance that the security level field was corrupted and that the packet should not have been accepted. The probability of this happening is extremely low, since untrusted TIU software cannot force a frame-check error to occur at will, and even if one should occur, there is little likelihood that the error will be such that both the destination and security level have precisely the required values. Furthermore, since the error is a random event, there is no way for malicious software in the TIU to modulate this type of error for covert communication. In any case, full-frame buffering in the security processor could be implemented.

*This separation is similar to the "red/black" separation employed with crypto hardware. In fact, when the "untrusted" side is unclassified, many of the conventional physical red/black separation requirements would have to be adhered to.

The reason only single-level subscribers can be supported with the architecture outlined here is that nothing outside of the TIU CSMA/CD interface and security processor (e.g., terminals, hosts, TIU software) is trusted to maintain separation of data of different levels. This is the most common situation in today's environments.

Variable-level TIUs

A variable-level TIU is the same as a single-level TIU, except that an operator can change the level of the TIU from time to time. This is accomplished via some manual interface to the security processor (e.g., rotary switch). Procedural controls should insure that the host or terminal is appropriately sanitized when the level of the TIU is lowered. This sanitization can be accomplished automatically using a number of techniques. The variable-level TIU might also interface to special-purpose keys on a user's terminal keyboard—keys that are electrically linked to the security processor.

A more complex variable-level TIU for a terminal might allow the operator to communicate the change of security level via the normal keyboard and screen of his terminal. This would entail, however, significantly more complex mechanisms that must be trusted. In figure 4, for example, all of the software in the TIU would have to be trusted, since that code processes keyboard input before it is seen by the security processor. Sophisticated, but well-understood, techniques to implement a logical "trusted communications path" from operator to security processor would have to be employed. Of course for a host that undergoes periods processing to handle classified data of different levels at different times, only a manual interface to the TIU security processor would be appropriate.

Multilevel TIUs

The multilevel TIU for a host or terminal is likely to contain fully trusted software. The security processor in such a TIU would only be able to limit communications to the range of levels at which the host or terminal is authorized to operate. The rest of the TIU would have to be trusted to properly identify the security level of the data to the host within that range, so that the host (which is trusted) can make the correct decisions to provide the necessary protection of the multilevel data. In terms of total functionality and complexity, a multilevel TIU is the same as a single-level TIU. The only difference is in the degree of trust given to the software and hardware in the TIU that is not in the security processor. Thus, the difficulty of building a multilevel TIU over that of a single-level TIU is dependent on software engineering techniques (e.g., verification) rather than on inherent complexity.

BRIDGES

Bridges operate strictly at the CSMA/CD protocol level. A bridge always connects exactly two subnetworks (a simplifying requirement). Its job is to pick packets from one subnetwork, check their destinations and security levels, and send them to the other subnetwork. To prevent congestion, bridges must operate at a speed fast enough to handle a reasonable load of traffic from one subnetwork to another, although multiple bridges could be used to help.

Figure 5 shows the logical operation of the bridge. Note that the destination check is made as the packet is read in from the network before it is buffered, exactly the same as is done by the CSMA/CD interface in the TIU. In the case of bridge, however, more than a single destination must be checked. The set of destinations accepted are stored in a fixed routing table that can be quickly scanned at network speeds. A two-level hierarchical addressing structure is employed to simplify this lookup and reduce the size of the table (see figure 3). Each bridge knows exactly which subnetworks it is responsible for. Thus, packets are buffered in the bridge only if they are definitely addressed to another subnetwork to which the bridge is logically linked.

The security processor in the bridge makes the appropriate security checks on the buffered packets, based only on the levels of the two subnetworks immediately adjacent to the bridge. The bridge does not check final TIU or subnetwork destinations, nor does it verify that the level of the packet is correct with respect to the source. It only checks that the received packet is labelled within the range of levels of the subnetwork from which the packet is arriving, and that that level is within the range of levels of the next subnetwork.

Outgoing packets are handled by the CSMA/CD interface from output buffers in a manner identical to outgoing packets in a TIU.

Because the bridge contains no protocol software outside of the CSMA/CD interface, and the only function it implements is a simple security level check, we see the bridge as simple enough to be fully trusted to perform its job correctly and fast enough to handle a considerable load. The

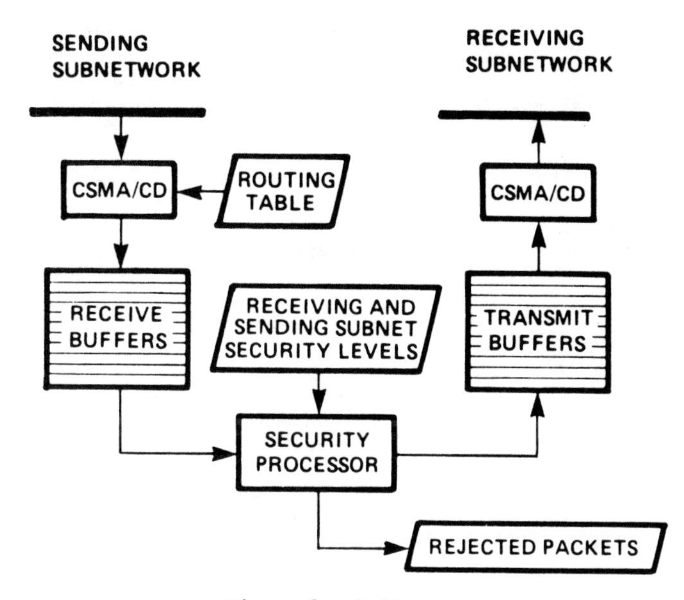

Figure 5. Bridge

buffers in the bridges smooth out temporary overloads. It is not expected that the bridges would be a bottleneck in the overall system except in times of heavy continuous traffic. For this reason the approach is recommended in environments where high traffic density is not expected in the near term. To better deal with greater traffic loads, and to provide more flexibility in addressing and routing, the bridges should provide some form of congestion control as might be implemented in a higher protocol layer such as the DoD Internet Protocol (IP). Such a change should be implemented as a future enhancement (along with corresponding changes to the TIUs to use IP) as it would significantly complicate the amount of trusted software in the bridges and TIUs.

Adding certain key aspects of IP to the bridges, in place of some portions of the CSMA/CD protocol, would allow for internet routing among the local subnetworks and through gateways to wide area networks. This means that the subnetworks would be more like separate networks and the bridges would be more like gateways. IP in the bridges and TIUs would also allow incorporation of the security level field into the header where it is specified as an option in IP, rather than usurping part of the data field of CSMA/CD. Finally, IP would allow a primitive form of congestion control--a bridge could return a control packet to a sender to turn off further transmissions due to overload in the bridge or adjoining subnetwork.

While there are many advantages to putting IP in the bridge, we do not feel at this point that the extra complexity in the TIUs and bridges is desirable in an initial configuration considering the need to trust the software. It may be very likely that an initial installation of a secure LAN would indeed require IP in the TIUs for internetworking [Skelton80], but that IP implementation would reside in the untrusted portion of the TIU and would not be interpreted by the bridges. A smooth transition to installation of IP in the bridges may involve, in part, verifying the existing IP software in the TIUs for multilevel operation.

The two half-bridges shown in figure 2 comprise a special form of bridge required when encryption is necessary between two classified subnetworks. This will be discussed further in the following section.

ENCRYPTION

In Figure 2 several locations are shown where encryption is required. At the top an encrypted line is shown between the confidential host and its TIU that resides in the secret environment. This line would probably employ conventional bit-serial link encryption at the appropriate speed (ignore, at this point the dubious need for encryption on a confidential line).

Another encrypted line is shown on the right side between the Top Secret subnetworks. Encryption here is employed directly between the media of the two subnetworks, without the use of a bridge. This is intended to illustrate encryption of the LAN medium where a cable may pass, for example, between two Top Secret protected buildings. We have not studied the problem of encrypting the LAN medium directly, and what affect it might have on the physical and CSMA/CD protocols. However, our design is not dependent on the ability to encrypt such media, as the subnetworks could be separate and bridges could be used instead.

Near the center of the figure are shown two "split-bridges"—one in the Top Secret environment and the other on the Secret subnetwork. Each half of the bridge communicates with its subnetwork directly using the straightforward CSMA/CD protocol. The two halves of the bridge communicate via a serial line that can be encrypted using conventional means. The functionality of the bridge is allocated between the two halves according to the security requirements. For example, the security processor, which checks that incoming packets from the high side only go to the low side if they have the appropriate security level, must be located on the high side. Buffering for transmission to the low side, and part of the IP protocol handling, if implemented, could be on the low side. Note that the split bridge concept, while introduced here to deal with the encryption problem, is a general solution where two subnetworks cannot be brought into close physical proximity.

The split-bridge is considerably more complex than a single bridge, and it would not be needed in cases where encryption is not required and the media of the two subnetworks could be brought close together. A bridge between a classified subnetwork to an unclassified subnetwork would not have to be split.

CONCLUSION

This secure local area network architecture presented here is one of several means by which multilevel data on a local network can be protected. This design stresses very near-term availability, and as such makes maximum use of well-understood concepts, existing protocols, and off-the-shelf hardware. In order to assist certification for multilevel operation, a minimal amount of trusted software or firmware is required. The TIU design provides a basic trusted multilevel service that allows for implementing in additional TIU software a wide range of applications. This additional software need not be certified or verified. Finally, the architecture is designed to be implemented in phases, providing an initial capability that integrates well into existing operations, and is then upgradable to full service as the need arises.

REFERENCES

Clark78 — Clark, D. D., Pogran, K. T., and Reed, D. P., "An Introduction to Local Area Networks," **Proc. IEEE**, Vol. 66, No. 11, pp. 1497-1517, November 1978.

DoD72 — Department of Defense Directive, DoD 5200.28 "Security Requirements for Automatic Data Processing (ADP) Systems," December 18, 1972.

Ethernet80 — The Ethernet: A Local Area Network Specification, Version 1.0, DEC, INTEL, XEROX, September 30, 1980.

IEEE81 — **Local Network Standards Committee, A Status Report**, Draft B, IEEE Computer Society, October 19, 1981.

ISO81 — ISO/TC97/SC16, "Data Processing—Open Systems Interconnection—Basic Reference Model," **Computer Networks**, Vol. 5, 1981, pp. 81-118.

Nibaldi79 — Nibaldi, G. H., "Specification of a Trusted Computing Base (TCB)," M79-228, The MITRE Corporation, Bedford, MA, November 30, 1979.

Postel81a — Postel, J. (ed.), "DoD Standard Internet Protocol," Defense Advanced Research Projects Agency, 1981.

Postel81b — Postel, J. (ed.), "DoD Standard Transmission Control Protocol," Defense Advanced Research Projects Agency, 1981.

Skelton80 — Skelton, A. P., Nabielsky, J., and Holmgren, S. F., "FY80 Final Report: Cable Bus Application in Command Centers," MTR-80W00319, The MITRE Corporation, McLean, VA, December 1980.

FILING AND PRINTING SERVICES ON A LOCAL-AREA NETWORK

P. Janson, L. Svobodova and E. Maehle*

IBM Zurich Research Laboratory, 8803 Rüschlikon, Switzerland

Abstract

This paper describes the design and implementation of filing and printing services in a distributed system based on a token-ring local-area network. The main emphasis is put on the communication aspects of the client/server scenario: roles of a client and a server in a communication protocol, and the integration of communication protocols with applications.

1. Introduction

Local-area networks provide the basis for systems where human users obtain computing and data-processing services through highly autonomous personal workstations. Intelligent workstations can substantially improve the human interface, both from the point of view of function and of performance. However, intelligent workstations cannot cost-effectively provide all services available today in a large shared system. In particular, expensive hardware devices, such as high-quality printers, must remain shareable. Also, it must be possible to share software resources (information) efficiently and to communicate among users.

Shared resources must be protected and administered in an adequate way. In a centralized system, it is the responsibility of the operating system to control the use of such resources. In a distributed system, shared resources are managed by specialized machines called servers.

The general frame of our work is a distributed processing scenario based on a local-area network, where a workstation is the principal means by which a human user obtains computer services. Specifically, we concentrate on the problem of resource control and communication in the client/server model.**

Servers discussed in the literature include name servers[3,4], authentication servers[5], boot servers[4], and more specialized application-oriented servers[6]. However, the basic servers are a file server and a printer server. A file server is used both to provide information sharing, and for economical reasons. A printer server is principally a controller of a shared hardware resource.

We have designed and implemented a file server, a printer server, and a workstation-based client as the first steps towards building a distributed-system testbed for studying the client/server model. The objective of this paper is to report on the design and implementation considerations of our system.

The structure of the prototype system is described in Section 2. Section 3 focuses on the communication aspects. Section 4 discusses some implementation issues and experience. The present status of the project and the extensions planned are presented in Section 5.

2. The Prototype System

The current configuration of our prototype system is shown in Figure 1. It consists of a file server based on an IBM Series/1 minicomputer, a printer server which controls an IBM 6670 laser printer, and IBM Personal Computers as workstations. These components are connected by a token-ring local-area network.

2.1 Key Features of the Token Ring

Our local-area network is a reliable token ring developed at the IBM Zurich Laboratory[7-9]. This section summarizes the key technical properties of this network.

Physical reliability is achieved through distribution panels, from which local lobes are strung in a radial fashion to the offices (see Figure 2).

* Present address: University of Erlangen, Erlangen, W. Germany.

** The terms "server" and "client" are already well established in the field of distributed computer systems. For definitions, see, for example, References 1 and 2.

"Filing and Printing Services on a Local-Area Network" by P. Janson, L. Svobodova, and E. Maehle from *Proceedings of the Eighth Data Communications Symposium*, 1983, pages 211-220. Copyright 1981, Association for Computin Machinery, Inc., reprinted by permission.

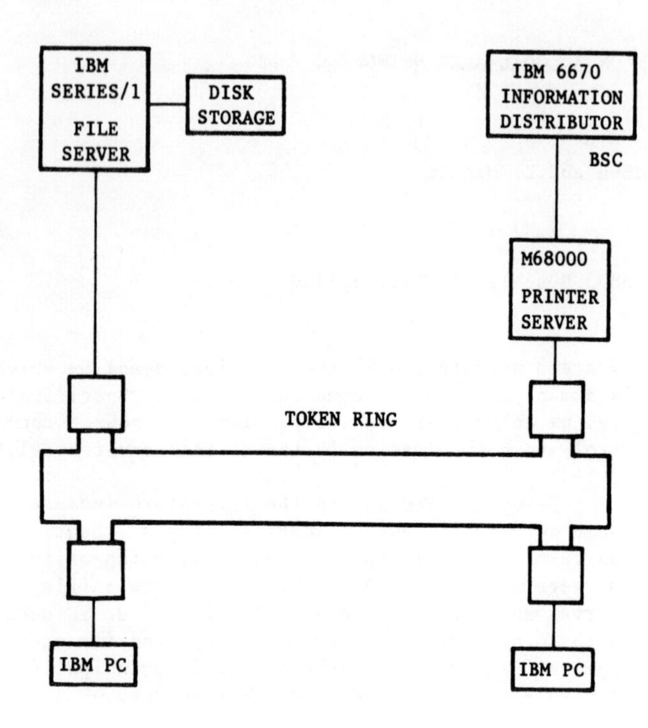

Figure 1

Prototype system.

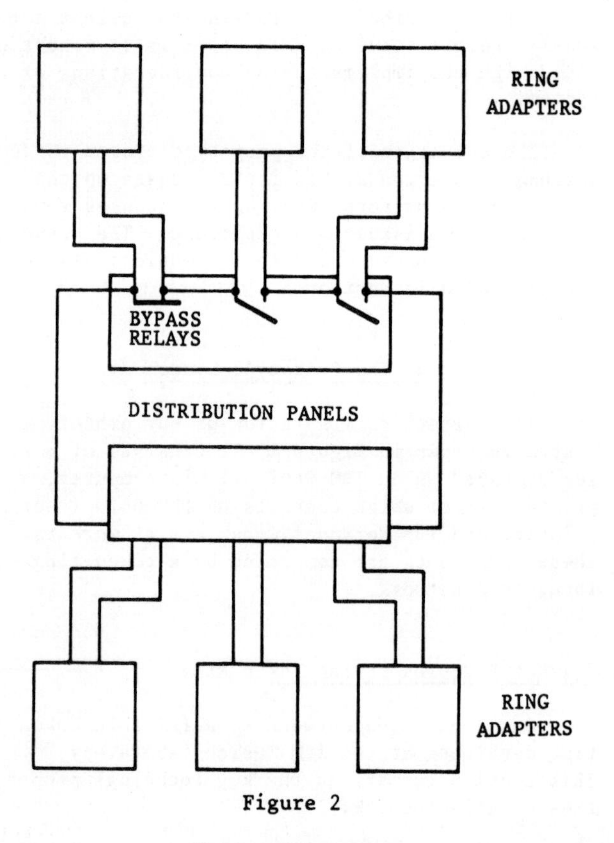

Figure 2

Ring configuration.

Bypass relays in the panels, powered from the attached stations via phantom circuits, allow inactive stations or faulty lobes and adapters to be disconnected from the ring. Distribution panels are installed at strategic points in a building to facilitate maintenance and network reconfiguration. The panels are interconnected by the main ring cable. Devices are attached to the ring via ring adapters that contain the transmission circuitry and execute the token protocol.

Robustness of the token protocol is obtained through a monitor function. The monitor function guarantees that the ring recovers from errors such as lost token (e.g., at system initialization), circulating busy token, and duplicate free tokens. The monitor function is simple enough to be provided in each ring adapter, but for reasons of efficient recovery, it is active in only one ring adapter at any one time. The passive-monitor functions activate themselves in case of an active-monitor failure. A contention-resolution mechanism enforces that only one of them wins the race and becomes the active monitor. It is important to note that the entire monitor function, including the monitor switch-over, is implemented in the adapter, and is transparent to the station attached to it.

Frames transmitted over the ring are protected by a frame check sequence. If transmission errors or station insertion/removal cause a bad frame check sequence, the frame has to be retransmitted. Frame retransmissions, however, are not managed by the ring protocol, but by logical link control or higher-level protocols.

Compared with other access methods used on local-area networks, a token ring has superior delay-throughput characteristics. It does not have the distance and speed limitations of the CSMA/CD protocol, and allows fair sharing of the transmission capacity at high load levels.

The ring provides a building block for supporting reliable distributed systems. However, no ring-specific features of the network, beyond its natural reliability, are exploited in our system design; unlike the Cambridge Distributed System[4,10], our system is independent of the actual network technology, topology, and access protocol.

2.2 File Server

Among the servers proposed and described in the literature, file servers are predominant. A file server is the most fundamental type of server in an information-processing system; it is not only needed to support application programs, but also other types of services.

The charter of a file server can be summarized as:

- provide long-term reliable storage of information, and
- support information sharing.

A survey of existing file servers[2] shows that although most of them support only a low-level model of stored data, their client interfaces are very different. Also, many of the file-server designs aim at a "universal" file server, capable of supporting the following three types of services:
- filing
- paged virtual memory
- database applications.

The designs usually emphasize very high reliability, those aimed at database applications also high concurrency. Consequently, the internal designs are very complex, but most of that complexity has nothing to do with the fact that the system is distributed. We have decided to follow a different path: develop only a simple server, and concentrate on the effects of distribution, namely, communication between clients and servers, which is the essence of the client/server paradigm. In particular, we have been studying:
- design of robust protocols
- low-cost implementations
- the role of file service in other services.

Figure 3 presents three categories of file servers in terms of three design parameters that have the most significant impact on the complexity of a file-server design. Our file server qualifies as a *simple* file server. Clients must send in and retrieve entire files. Consequently, the unit of locking is a file. Operations on individual files are atomic.

	SIMPLE FILE SERVER	UNIVERSAL FILE SERVER	DATABASE MANAGEMENT SUPPORT
UNIT OF DATA ACCESS	FILE	SEQUENTIAL SUBSET OF BYTES	RECORD
UNIT OF LOCKING	FILE	FILE	RECORD OR VARIABLE
SCOPE OF ATOMIC UPDATE	FILE	MULTIPLE FILES	MULTIPLE FILES
		(MULTIPLE SERVERS)	

Figure 3

Classification of file servers.

Since we did not want to study the problems of internal file storage and management, we took an existing filing system, namely, the Tripos hierarchical file system[11] as a base. The file structure will be described in more detail in Section 4.

Figure 4 describes the client interface of the file server. The operations that pertain to files represent the minimum a file server must support. Creation of a file is implicit in the put_file operation.

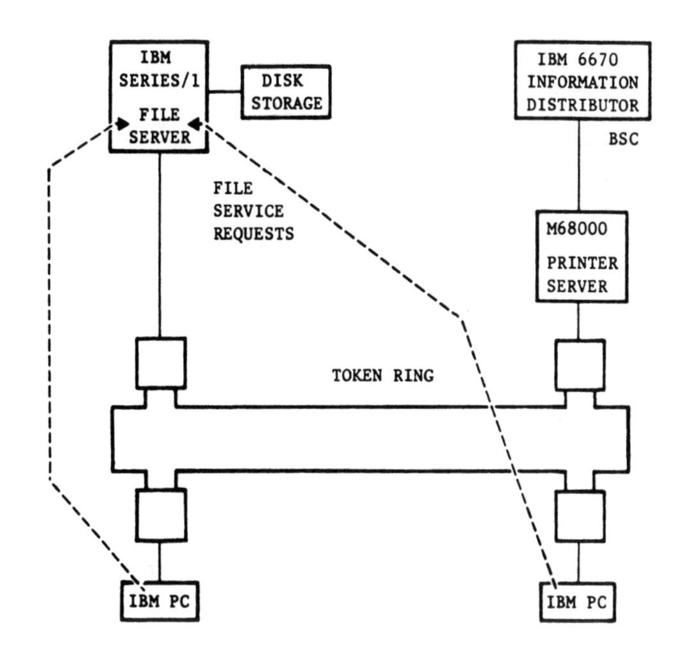

DATA STORAGE/RETRIEVAL	FILE MANAGEMENT
put_file(fn)	make_dir(dn)
get_file(fn)	list_dir(dn)
delete_file(fn)	delete_dir(dn)
	copy_file(fn1,fn2)
	move_file(fn1,fn2)

fn: path name of a file
dn: path name of a directory

Figure 4

File-server interface.

2.3 Printer Server

The printing service has two parts: the control of the actual printing device, and the spooling of files to be printed. Lampson and Sproull gave a brief description of how these two subsystems can coexist on a single machine without full multiprogramming support[12]. In our system, these two parts run on separate machines, which considerably simplifies the implementation.

What we call the printer server is the component that controls the physical printer and feeds it with data obtained from a remote spooler. A similar distribution of function was chosen in the Cambridge Distributed System. In the Cambridge system, the spooling function can be assigned to any processor in the common processor pool.[10] This increases the reliability of the printing service but monopolizes a processor in the pool. In our system, the remote spooler is a simple extension to the file server, and could run on any one or more machines running the file service.

As shown in Figure 5, a print command from a client results in the named file being copied (or sent) to a directory of the file service known as the spooler mailbox. This queueing function of the spooler does not demand any particular action on the part of the file server, which treats the mailbox as any directory in the file system. Although the dequeueing function of the spooler resides in the file service, it is completely passive: it does not make any attempt to spontaneously cause the printing of queued files. Instead, the printer server must prompt the file server to obtain the next file, if any, from the spooler mailbox; once a file has been successfully transmitted to the printer, the file service deletes it from the spooler mailbox.

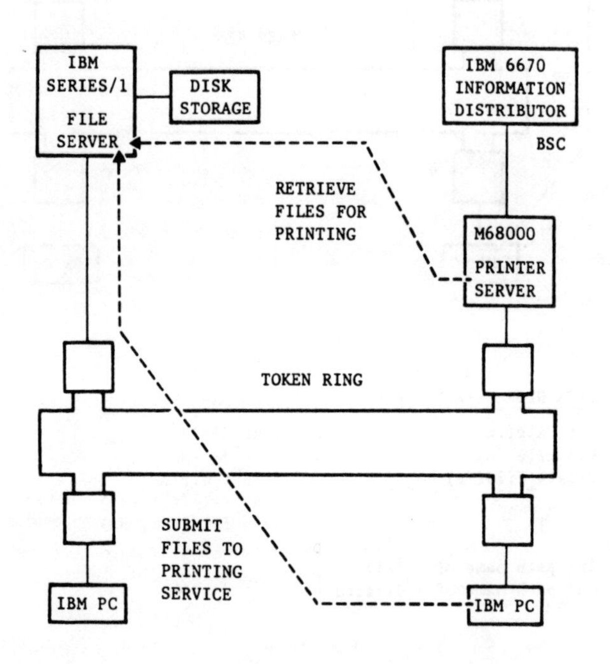

CLIENT:

print(fn) → copy(fn,spooler.mlbx.fn)

PRINTER SERVER:

next_file → get_file(spooler.mlbx.q1)
delete_file(spooler.mlbx.q1)

q1: first file in the spooler queue

Figure 5

Printing service.

In a sense, our printer server is a protocol translator. The data and control information is transmitted to the IBM 6670 laser printer one character at a time, by means of the BSC protocol. On the network side, the printer server uses a block-oriented file-transfer protocol. The printer server does not have its own secondary storage device; it controls the speed of the file transfer and performs only as much buffering as needed to keep the printer busy.

2.4 Workstations

The workstations used in our system are the IBM Personal Computers (PC) running the IBM DOS operating system. Access to the local network services from the PC is provided by the PC client, which is invoked by a special DOS command. At the invocation of this command, the PC, if currently in the stand-alone mode, inserts itself automatically into the ring, by sending appropriate control signals to its ring adapter. The PC client supports a menu-driven interface for direct use by human users.

All of the file-server commands listed in Figure 4 are supported. The put_file commands send a copy of a local file stored on a PC diskette to the file server. A file retrieved from the file server via the get_file command can either be written to a local diskette or displayed on the screen.

The PC client offers two different print commands: one for printing files stored on a local diskette, the other for printing files stored in the file server. As a result of the first command, a copy of the specified local file is shipped directly to the spooler mailbox. The second type of print command causes the file to be copied internally in the file server.

Finally, the PC client offers a simple mail service to facilitate communication with other workstations. This mail service is built on the top of the filing service. The send_mail command sends a copy of a local file to the mailbox ("mail" subdirectory) of the specified user in the file server. PC users can "inspect" (list) the contents of their mailboxes, "view" (display on the screen) individual messages without storing them locally, and "receive" individual messages by moving them to a local diskette.

3. Communication Aspects

In a ring network, frames may be lost due to:

- ring reconfiguration (station insertion or removal)
- transmission errors (bad CRC)
- no free receive buffer in the adapter of the recipient.

The first two events should be relatively rare in a local network. Research performed at our Laboratory has shown that the probability of the last event can be brought down below any target level if the network adapter is properly designed[13].

3.1 Communication Architecture

The communication architecture used in the prototype comprises six layers below the application layer. The lower two layers are based on guidelines that have been emerging lately from the local network standardization committees[14,15], while the higher layers are based on IBM's Systems Network Architecture (SNA)[16,17].

Layer 1, the bottom of the architecture, is the Physical layer. This layer implements the physical media and transmission techniques in the token ring[8].

Layer 2, Link Control (LC), according to emerging local network standards, is divided into two sub-layers: the Media Access Control (MAC) sub-layer, and the Logical Link Control (LLC). The MAC sub-layer specifies frame formatting and media-access protocols. In our prototype, the MAC sub-layer implements the token and monitor protocols outlined in Subsection 2.1.

The LLC sub-layer includes what is known as the elements of procedure according to the HDLC terminology[18]. The proposals of the local network standardization committees recommend that the LLC sub-layer support a so-called connectionless procedure, allowing the unprotected transfer of unnumbered information frames, and optionally a connected procedure, such as ABM (Asynchronous Balanced Mode), for instance[14]. We have implemented only the mandatory connectionless procedure. Thus, in our prototype, LLC supports only one information frame code point: the unnumbered one.

Layer 3, Network Control (NC), in our prototype implements simply a fan-in/fan-out function in every station. The NC layer routes frames (regarded as datagrams at this layer) from access ports to the LLC, and vice-versa.

Our protocols for the next three layers are modeled after SNA. Originally designed for master-slave environments in teleprocessing networks, SNA has evolved and undergone many enhancements, a recent and important one being support for LU 6.2 peer-to-peer communication[17]. Our experimental protocols are based on the peer-to-peer protocols for SNA's Transmission Control (TC), Data Flow Control (DFC), and Function Management (FM) layers.

The SNA TC protocols allow a client and a server to negotiate the parameters of a logical connection called a session through one (or more) two-way handshake(s). The parameters determine such factors as the maximum message size to be used throughout the session and the maximum pacing counts, i.e., the maximum number of messages that can be sent in each direction before an acknowledgement is sent back. As will be explained in the next section, our Transport Control layer also allows a client and a server to exchange information in the form of datagrams, without having to bind a session first.

The DFC layer organizes the traffic between a client and a server as a half-duplex flow of Request/Response Units (RU). Requests carry actual user data while responses carry only acknowledgement or internal network information, such as, for instance, signals controlling the flow on a session.

SNA FM, which implements presentation services as well as powerful resource and network management functions support a collection of transaction-oriented features that can be used to implement atomic and recoverable operations. Some of these features are exploited in our file server.

3.2 Client/Server Communication

Our client/server-communication model supports both datagram (single-shot) and session-based requests. A datagram request is sent in a single ring frame. A reply to a datagram request is also a datagram. A server treats each such datagram as a new request. Thus, in order to be able to use this model, not only must both the information carried by the request and the response fit into a single frame, but the operation requested must be idempotent.

Figure 6 indicates the communication model underlying the client interface of the file server. Of the datagram-based operations, only copy_file is truly idempotent. The other operation are idempotent only from the point of view of their effects on the filing system, but a duplicate request will cause an error reply from the server, since these operations cannot be repeated on a file of the same name. Thus, to be able to use this model, the client must be prepared to handle such error replies correctly. This requirement is not difficult to satisfy: since only the client can create such a duplicate by explicitly resending a request, it is also in the position to interpret correctly a potential error reply.

DATA STORAGE/RETRIEVAL	FILE MANAGEMENT
<-> put_file(fn)	• make_dir(dn)
<-> get_file(fn)	<-> list_dir(dn)
• delete_file(fn)	• delete_dir(dn)
	• copy_file(fn1,fn2)
	• move_file(fn1,fn2)

<-> session-based requests

• datagrams

Figure 6

Implementation of file-service requests.

The session-based requests all involve bulk data transfer. These requests are executed atomically with respect to communication and server failures, but it is not guaranteed that the client will be informed about the final state of a transaction; using Spector's classification of remote reference protocols, the session-based requests qualify as "only-once-type-1" remote reference[19]. A server remembers the state of a client's request only for a limited amount of time; essentially, only until the next request made on the same session, or the end of the session. To protect itself from crashed clients, the server will eventually break an inactive session, thus destroying any information that could be used to determine whether a previous request was committed. However, all of the session-based requests supported by the file server are idempotent, thus once a request has been executed atomically in the server, repeating it has no harmful effects.

3.3 File-Transfer Protocol

The file-transfer protocol consists of two parts: a session control protocol and a block-stream protocol.

The client side and the server side play different roles in each of these parts. In particular, they handle the time-out and retransmission functions very differently. The client always has the initiative; it is the driving force not only as an initiator of a request for service, but also during a file transfer. The server is passive; it responds to requests, data blocks, and prompts from a client, rejects them if they violate the protocol, but does not take any steps to get through to the client. It is the client who must be persistent, and must implement time-out and retransmission to see its requests satisfied.

Interestingly, this situation is in contrast to what is found typically in teleprocessing networks. There, an asymmetry between the user terminal and the host also exists. However, it is the host, usually called the "primary" or the "master", which carries responsibilities such as time-out and retransmission, since the terminal lacks the power to do so; in our scenario, the responsibility lies on the client side, i.e., on the side of the user's workstation in general.

In the server, time-outs are used only to prevent session resources from being tied up by non-responding clients, or clients who do not follow correctly the protocol. The time-out for a session is reset every time the server receives a frame on that session; if the time-out expires, the session is broken, the server releases the local resources allocated to that session, and any on-going file-transfer operation is aborted without side-effects for the file system. This measure protects the server from crashes of the client. However, the client could also tie up server resources uselessly by getting into a loop. Thus, the server must keep track of the number of erroneous interactions with the client, and unbind the session if the count exceeds a predefined limit.

As stated earlier, the major concern on the client's side is to ensure that the task gets done. If no server message is received prior to time-out, all client messages sent since the latest server message was received are retransmitted. These messages may be portions of a file if the client is waiting for an acknowledgement (pacing response), or it may be a pacing response to prompt the server for more data. Upon recognizing a duplicate message, the server *resends* all messages it had sent since the original of the duplicate had been received. The client *ignores* duplicates.

Thus, both the client and the server start a timer every time they start waiting for an action on the part of the other. However, the server's time-out is longer than the client's and they handle time-outs differently. Upon time-out, a client retries its latest transmission while a server aborts the session on the assumption that the client is dead.

3.4 Printing Protocol

The printing protocol has two separate parts. The first involves a transfer of the file to be printed to the spooler mailbox. As explained in Section 2, this step does not necessarily require data transfer over the network. If the file specified is stored in the file server, the file server simply copies that file to the mailbox of the spooler. When the file to be printed is in the local storage of the client, the normal file-transfer protocol described in the preceding section is used to transfer it to the spooler mailbox.

The second part of the printing protocol, controlled by the printer server, is concerned with the file transfer from the spooler to the printing device. This part is further divided into two subparts:

- transfer from the spooler to the printer server, and
- transfer from the printer server to the printing device.

Although called a "server", the printer server is in fact a *client* of the file server, or, more precisely, of the spooling service supported by the file server. The printer server polls the spooler over the network for files to be printed; in reality, it sends a special request to the file server, which is passed to the spooler function. If there is a file in the spooler mailbox at the time such a request is received, it is transferred to the printer server a block at a time; the printer server performs flow control to match the speed of the file transfer to the speed of the actual physical printer. A frame from the spooler to the printer server is passed to the printer one character at a time. A failure to communicate properly with the printing device is signalled immediately to the spooler, and aborts the file transfer. When the printer server has successfully transferred the entire file to the printer, it sends a "commit" response to the spooler; as a consequence, the file is deleted from the spooler queue. Thus, this protocol is truly an end-to-end protocol.

The printer server is persistent in trying to keep the printing service going. It tries to maintain a session with the spooler as long as the printer operates correctly. If the spooler crashes, the printer server rebinds a session at the first possible moment after the spooler has been reinitialized.

4. Implementation

The file server and the printer server were implemented in BCPL[20] under the Tripos operating system[11]. Tripos, designed at the Cambridge University (U.K.), is a portable, real-time, modular operating system for mini and microcomputers. Although very small and offering only limited memory management and user interface support, Tripos provides powerful and efficient multitasking facilities. To a great extent, Tripos is an "open" operating system in the sense of Lampson[12]. The exact configuration can be tailored to the application at hand and the hardware resources available. Tripos has proved very adequate to support non-user-programmable server machines.

The PC client was implemented in the PC Pascal under the IBM DOS operating system. DOS is a single-user single-thread operating system based on diskettes. In addition to the ISO Standard Pascal, PC Pascal provides some further support for system programming (e.g., direct access to physical memory locations) and modular design. The means for modularization is the so-called "unit", which consists of separate interface and implementation divisions. These additional features proved to be very important; they were exploited particularly in the protocol implementation.

4.1 Filing System

The Tripos file system appears as a tree of disk block lists, where each block is self-identifying and refers to its parent or brother. The disk map is never stored on the disk. Instead, every time the system is restarted, it rebuilds the disk map by inspecting the disk from the root block downward. Disk blocks not reachable from the root are considered free. If there exists only a single reference to a block, the block is considered valid. Blocks reachable from more than one place in the file-system structure are considered suspicious, and flagged.

In moving a file from one place in the hierarchical file system to another, Tripos first places a reference to that file in the target directory, then destroys the old reference, and finally updates the disk map. Thus, if the system crashes after the file has been recorded in the new place but before the old reference is destroyed, the map rebuilding procedure will flag the file header. Normally, the operator must decide which reference to drop.

The mechanism just described is used in the file server to support atomic file updates in the following way. A file-update operation is implemented by writing the new version to a time-stamped temporary file in a special directory, and then moving it in one disk write operation to the position of the old version in the tree. This disk write operation realizes the "commit" step of the update. If the system crashed immediately after the commit, it will wake up in a state where the file appears in two directories. The reference in the special directory can safely be dropped to complete the update operation. Atomicity is thus guaranteed. However, Tripos does not offer atomic stable storage as in Reference 21, so a disk failure *in the middle* of a critical disk write operation would leave the file system in an inconsistent state.

4.2 Filing and Printing Services

The Tripos/BCPL environment supports two types of concurrency mechanisms: tasks and coroutines. All tasks and coroutines execute in the same address space. Tasks communicate by sending messages; task scheduling is controlled by Tripos. A task can contain internally any number of coroutines. Coroutines are invoked in a similar fashion to procedures; their scheduling is left to the programmer. Coroutines are much less expensive than tasks in terms of the context-switching overhead.

The network protocols in the file server and the printer server were implemented with efficiency as a key objective, at the cost of sacrificing some of the architectural modularity of the protocols; some of the layers that are clearly distinct in our architectural model, are implemented in the same software module. The principal ways towards low cost communication are minimizing the overhead of context switching, and eliminating data copying between protocol layers. Thus, we concentrated on eliminating task switching along the path of each individual request. Also, whenever possible, we use coroutines rather than tasks to represent concurrent activities. Finally, data sent or received by a client or server are never copied within the communication subsystem; we use buffer windowing similar to Reference 22.

Figures 7 and 8 show the internal structure of the file server and the printer server, respectively.

Since the printer server is dedicated to a single function and contains only a single session at a time, all of the protocol levels have been compressed to a single task that manages all the necessary resources. The data received from the ring are never copied within the printer server: they are passed in the same buffer all the way to the BSC handler and from there directly to the printer.

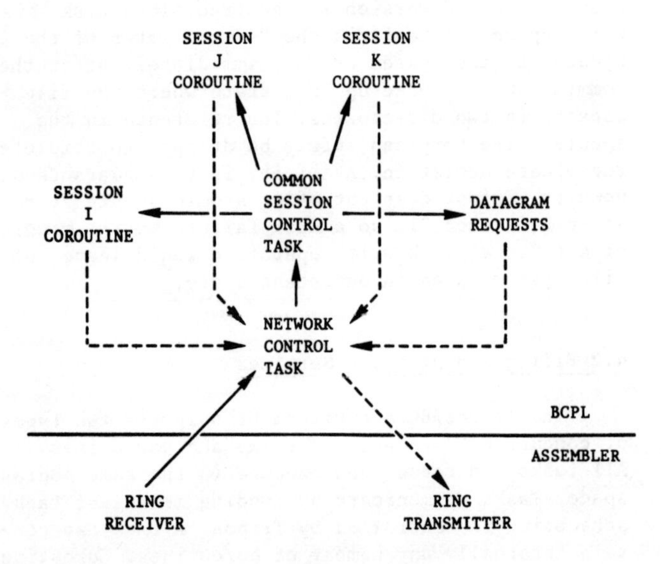

Figure 7

File-server structure.

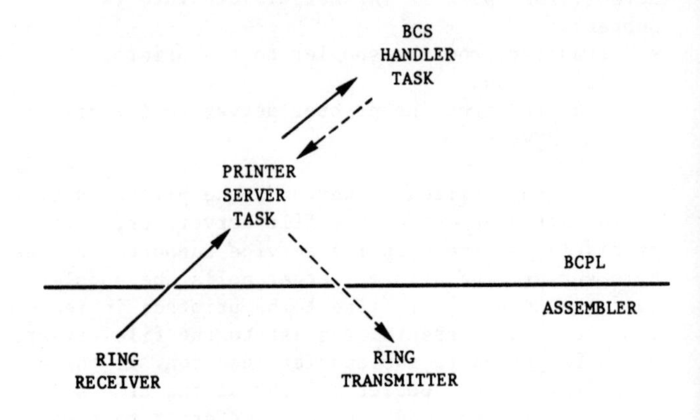

Figure 8

Printer-server structure.

In the file server, the only copy operation is to or from the file-server application itself out of or into disk cache buffers. This operation cannot be avoided unless the ring frame size is coupled direct to the size of disk records, a constraint that clearly cannot hold for all disks, and is therefore unacceptable.

Since we envisioned putting other servers, for example, a name server, on the same hardware as the file server, the communication control was split into two tasks. One task executes the NC protocol, routing frames to and from other tasks representing clients and servers. All of the requests for file services are directed to the file-server task. Within this task, individual session transactions are represented by coroutines. Any session ready to receive data must pass a sufficient number of empty buffers to NC. In addition, the file-server task allocates and passes to NC several empty buffers for datagram requests. All these buffers are interchangeable. NC manages them as a pool, since at the time it receives a frame from the network, it cannot know for which entity it is intended. When it receives a frame for an entity that has no more buffers in the pool, it does not pass the frame to it, but frees the buffer immediately.

4.3 PC Client

One important precondition in the implementation of the PC client was the fact that the current DOS and PC Pascal do not support concurrent processes. Consequently, the entire client is implemented as a sequential Pascal program. This solution is adequate for accessing of network services, due to the passive role of the server in our client/server protocol. Since all actions are always initiated by the client, the client does not have to be prepared to deal with messages asynchronous to its current activities.

Since a workstation is a more "general-purpose" machine than the servers, it is important to facilitate easy modifications and support of different types of communication. Thus, in the implementation of the PC client, we put more emphasis on well-structured, modular code than on performance. Each network layer is implemented as a separate PC Pascal unit; an additional unit is used to control the ring insertion and removal of the PC ring adapter.

4.4 Experience

The servers as implemented today are very small. The file- server code takes 17 kwords of primary memory (16-bit words), out of which 8 kwords are used up by the communication protocols and ring drivers. The communication portion of the printer server represents 4 k of 32-bit words.

Tripos tasks and coroutines proved to be well suited to support the parallelism inherent in real-time communication software, but we should have liked better facilities for managing static storage accessible to multiple concurrent activities (tasks or coroutines). The main shortcomings of BCPL are the lack of typing and the very primitive data structures.

Although the file server and printer server do not share any code, having the same programming environment and tools on both of the machines proved to be very helpful. Specifically, the common model of concurrent activities and the corresponding discipline of synchronization and communication provided a good base for discussing the implementations of the protocols, and simplified the debugging.

The PC client uses 25 kwords (16-bit words) of primary memory, including about 10 kwords of the Pascal runtime support. Among the high-level languages available on the PC, Pascal seemed best suited for our purpose. However, while it is good for producing well-structured and modular code, the lack of concurrency mechanisms made the implementation of the network protocols on the PC more difficult than in the servers.

5. Conclusions

The file server, printer server and PC clients described in this paper are operational.

As stated in the Introduction, our goal is to study the client/server model of distributed computing. From this point of view, the major aspects are the distribution of function, and the communication protocols. We chose to have the printer spooler function implemented as an extension of the file service; the printer server is essentially a protocol translator, which extends the network error and flow control up to the application, that is, to the IBM 6670 controller. The file server provides standard filing services, but at the communication level, the server is driven by the clients.

Our current implementation of the communication protocols is tailored to the function of a particular machine. In both the file server and the printer server, the local resource management is tied closely with the communication control. The passive role of a server in the client/server protocol allowed us to implement the PC client as a sequential Pascal program.

Acknowledgements

Several people contributed to making the system operational. We wish to express our gratitude especially to P. Zafiropulo, who designed and implemented the BSC handler for the printer server, and K. Moritzen, who implemented the user interface of the PC client. Special thanks are due to K. Kuemmerle for his careful reviews and valuable criticism of the paper.

References

[1] Mitchell, J.G., "File servers for local area networks," Lecture Notes, Course on Local Area Networks, University of Kent, Canterbury, England, March 1982, pp. 83-114.

[2] Svobodova, L., "File servers for network-based distributed systems," Technical Report RZ1187 IBM Zurich Research Laboratory, Rüschlikon, Switzerland, November, 1982.

[3] Abraham, S.M., and Dalal, Y.K., "Techniques for decentralized management of distributed systems", *Proc. IEEE COMPCON,* Spring 1980, pp. 430-437.

[4] Needham, R.M., and Herbert, A.J., *The Cambridge distributed computing system,* Addison-Wesley, 1982.

[5] Needham, R.M., and Schroeder, M.D., "Using encryption for authentication in large networks of computers," *Commun. ACM,* Vol. 21, No. 12, December 1978, pp. 993-999.

[6] Birrell, A., Levin, R., Needham, R., Schroeder, M., "Grapevine: An exercise in distributed computing", *Commun. ACM 25,* Vol. 4 (April 1982), pp. 260-273.

[7] Bux, W., Closs, F., Janson, P., Kümmerle, K., and Müller, H.R., "A reliable token-ring system for local-area networks," *Proc. NTC '81,* New Orleans, Louisiana, November 1981, pp. A2.2.1-A2.2.6.

[8] Bux, W., Closs, F., Janson, P., Kümmerle, K., Müller, H.R., and Rothauser, E.H., "A local-area communication network based on a reliable token-ring system," *Proc. Int. Symp. Local Computer Networks,* Florence, Italy, April 1982, pp. 69-82.

[9] Müller, H.R., Keller, H., Meyr, H., "Transmission in a synchronous token ring," *Int. Symp. Local Computer Networks,* Florence, Italy, April 1982, pp. 125-147.

[10] Needham, R.M., "System aspects of the Cambridge ring," *Proc. 7th ACM Symp. on Operating Systems Principles,* Asilomar, California, December 1979, pp. 82-85.

[11] Richards, M., Aylward, A.R., Bond, P., Evans, R.D., and Knight, B.J., "TRIPOS: A portable operating system for minicomputers", *Software Practice and Experience,* Vol. 9, No. 7, July 1979, pp. 513-526.

[12] Lampson, B.W., and Sproull, R.F., "An open operating system for a single-user machine," *Proc. 7th ACM Symp. on Operating Systems Principles,* Asilomar, California, December 1979, pp. 98-105.

[13] Wong, J.W., and Bux, W., "Analytic modeling of an adapter to local area networks", *Proc. GLOBECOM82 Conf.,* IEEE, Piscataway, NJ, pp. 527-532, 1982.

[14] "IEEE 802 local network standard: Draft C", IEEE, May 1982.

[15] "Final draft, ECMA standard on local area networks (token ring)", ECMA Working Paper, December 1982.

[16] Sundstrom, R.J. and Schulz, G.D., "SNA's first six years: 1974-1980," *Proc. Fifth Int. Conf. Computer Communication,* Atlanta, Georgia, October 1980, pp. 578-585.

[17] Gray, J.P., "SNA operating system services to support distributed processing", *Proc. '82 IEEE Int. Large Scale Systems Symp.,* Virginia Beach, VA, October 1982, pp. 161-165.

[18] "HDLC frame structure", "HDLC elements of procedure", and "HDLC balanced classes of procedure", Standards ISO-3309, ISO-4335, and ISO-6256.

[19] Spector, A.Z., "Performing remote operations efficiently on a local computer network," *Commun. ACM,* Vol. 25, April 1982, pp. 246-260.

[20] Richards, M., Strevens-Whitby, C., *BCPL -- the language and its compiler,* Cambridge University Press, 1980.

[21] Lampson, B.W., and Sturgis, H.E., "Crash recovery in a distributed data storage system," XEROX Palo Alto Research Center, Calif., April 1979 (to be published in *Commun. ACM).*

[22] Dion, J., "Reliable storage in a local network," Tech. Rep. No. 16, University of Cambridge, Computer Laboratory, Cambridge, England, February 1981 (Ph.D. thesis).

SECTION 9: GLOSSARY*

Many of the key terms used in this tutorial and the collected articles are defined here. Also included are some important terms from the more general field of computer networking.

ALOHA. A medium access control technique for multiple access transmission media. A station transmits whenever it has data to send. Unacknowledged transmissions are repeated.

AMPLIFIER. An analog device designed to compensate for the loss in a section of transmission medium. It increases the signal strength of an analog signal over a range of frequencies.

ANS X3T9.5. A committee sponsored by the American National Standards Institute (ANSI) that is responsible for a variety of system interconnection standards. The committee has produced draft standards for high-speed coaxial cable bus and fiber optic ring local networks.

BANDWIDTH. Refers to a relative range of frequencies, that is, the difference between the highest and lowest frequencies transmitted. For example, the bandwidth of a TV channel is 6 MHz.

BASEBAND. Transmission of signals without modulaton. In a baseband local network, digital signals (1's and 0's) are inserted directly onto the cable as voltage pulses. The entire spectrum of the cable is consumed by the signal. This scheme does not allow frequency division multiplexing.

BRIDGE. A device that links two homogeneous packet-switched local networks. It accepts all packets from each network addressed to devices on the other, buffers them, and retransmits them to the other network.

BROADBAND. The use of coaxial cable for providing data transfer by means of analog or radio-frequency signals. Digital signals are passed through a modem and are transmitted over one of the frequency bands of the cable.

BUS. A topology in which stations are attached to a shared transmission medium. The transmission medium is a linear cable; transmissions propagate the length of the medium and are received by all stations.

CATENET. A collection of packet-switched networks connected together via gateways.

CATV. Community antenna television. CATV cable is used for broadband local networks.

*Based on Glossary in *Local Networks: An Introduction,* by William Stallings, Macmillan, 1984.

CBX. Computerized branch exchange. A term sometimes used to refer to a digital PBX that is designed specifically to handle both voice and data. See Digital PBX.

CENTRALIZED BUS ARCHITECTURE. A bus topology in which the bus is very short and the links to attached devices are relatively much longer.

CHEAPERNET. A baseband local area network (LAN) that uses a thinner cable and less expensive components than Ethernet or the IEEE 802.3 standard. Although the data rate is the same (10 Mbps), the network span and number of stations is less.

CIRCUIT SWITCHING. A method of communicating in which a dedicated communications path is established between two devices through one or more intermediate switching nodes. Unlike packet switching, digital data are sent as a continuous stream of bits. Bandwidth is guaranteed, and delay is essentially limited to propagation time. The telephone system uses circuit switching.

COAXIAL CABLE. An electromagnetic transmission medium consisting of a center conductor and an outer, concentric conductor.

CODEC. Coder-decoder. Transforms analog voice into a digital bit stream (coder), and digital signals into analog voice (decoder) using pulse code modulation (PCM).

COLLISION. A condition in which two packets are being transmitted over a medium at the same time. Their interference makes both unintelligible.

CONTENTION. The condition when two or more stations attempt to use the same channel at the same time.

CRC. Cyclic redundancy check. A numeric value derived from the bits in a message. The transmitting station calculates a number that is attached to the message. The receiving station performs the same calculation. If the answer differs, then one or more bits are in error.

CSMA. Carrier sense multiple access. A medium access control technique for multiple-access transmission media. A station wishing to transmit first senses the medium and transmits only if the medium is idle.

CSMA/CD. Carrier sense multiple access with collision detection. A refinement of CSMA in which a station ceases transmission if it detects a collision.

DATAGRAM. A packet switching service in which packets (datagrams) are independently routed and may arrive out of order. The datagram is self-contained, and carries a complete address. Delivery confirmation is provided by higher level protocols.

DCE. Data circuit-terminating equipment. A generic name for network-owned devices that provided a network attachment point for user devices.

DIGITAL PRIVATE BRANCH EXCHANGE (PBX). A local network based on the private branch exchange (PBX) architecture. Provides an integrated voice/data switching service. See Private Branch Exchange.

DIGITAL SWITCH. A star topology local network. Usually refers to a system that handles only data but not voice.

DTE. Data terminal equipment. A generic name for user-owned devices or stations that attach to a network.

DUAL CABLE. A type of broadband cable system in which two separate cables are used: one for transmission and one for reception.

ETHERNET. A 10-Mbps baseband local area network (LAN) specification developed jointly by Xerox, Intel, and Digital Equipment. It is the forerunner of the IEEE 802.3 CSMA/CD standard.

FRAME. A group of bits that includes data plus one or more addresses. Generally refers to a link layer (layer 2) protocol.

FREQUENCY-AGILE MODEM. A modem used on some broadband systems that can shift frequencies to communicate with stations in different dedicated bands.

FREQUENCY CONVERTER. In midsplit broadband cable systems, the device at the headend that translates between the transmitting and receiving frequencies. Also known as a frequency translator or a central retransmission facility. See Headend.

FREQUENCY-DIVISION MULTIPLEXING (FDM). A technique for combining multiple signals on one circuit by separating them in frequency.

FSK. Frequency-shift keying. A digital-to-analog modulation technique in which two different frequencies are used to represent 1's and 0's.

GATEWAY. A device that connects two systems, especially if the systems use different protocols. For example, a gateway is needed to connect two independent local networks or to connect a local network to a long-haul network.

GRADE OF SERVICE. For a circuit-switched system, the probability that during a specified period of peak traffic an offered call will fail to find an available circuit.

HEADEND. The end point of a broadband bus or tree network. Transmission from a station is toward the headend; reception by a station is from the headend.

HIGH-SPEED LOCAL NETWORK (HSLN). A local network designed to provide high throughput between expensive, high-speed devices, such as mainframes and mass storage devices.

HOST. The collection of hardware and software that attaches to a network and uses that network to provide interprocess communication and user services.

HYBRID LOCAL NETWORK. An integrated local network consisting of more than one type of local network (LAN, HSLN, digital PBX).

IEEE 802. A committee of IEEE organized to produce a local area network (LAN) standard.

INBOUND PATH. On a broadband local area network (LAN), the transmission path used by stations to transmit packets toward the headend.

INFRARED. Electromagnetic waves whose frequency range is above that of microwave and below the visible spectrum: 3×10^{11} to 4×10^{14} Hz.

INJECTION LASER DIODE (ILD). A solid state device that works on the laser principle to produce a light source for a fiber-optic wave guide.

INTERNETWORKING. Communication among devices across multiple networks.

LASER. Electromagnetic source capable of producing infrared and visible light.

LIGHT-EMITTING DIODE (LED). A solid-state device that emits light when a current is applied. Used as a light source for a fiber-optic wave guide.

LISTEN BEFORE TALK (LBT). Same as Carrier sense multiple access (CSMA).

LISTEN WHILE TALK (LWT). Same as Carrier sense multiple access with collision detection (CSMA/CD).

LOCAL AREA NETWORK (LAN). A general-purpose local network that can serve a variety of devices. Typically used for terminals, microcomputers, and minicomputers.

LOCAL NETWORK. A communications network that provides interconnection of a variety of data communicating devices within a small area.

MANCHESTER ENCODING. A digital signaling technique in which there is a transition in the middle of each bit time. A 1 is encoded with a high level during the first half of the bit time; a 0 is encoded with a low level during the first half of the bit time.

MEDIUM ACCESS CONTROL (MAC). For bus, tree, and ring topologies, the method of determining which device has access to the transmission medium at any time. CSMA/CD and token are common access methods.

MESSAGE SWITCHING. A switching technique using a message store and forward system. No dedicated path is established. Rather, each message contains a destination address and is passed from source to destination through intermediate nodes. At each node, the entire message is received, stored briefly, and then passed on to the next node.

MICROWAVE. Electromagnetic waves in the frequency range 1-30GHz.

MIDSPLIT. A type of broadband cable system in which the available frequencies are split into two groups: one for transmission (5-116 MHz) and one for reception (168-300 MHz). Requires a frequency converter.

MODEM. Modulator/Demodulator. Transforms a digital bit stream into an analog signal (modulator) and vice versa (demodulator). The analog signal may be sent over telephone lines or could be radio frequencies or lightwaves.

NETWORK ACCESS UNIT (NAU). A communications controller that attaches to a local network. It implements the local network protocols and provides an interface for device attachment.

NETWORK CONTROL CENTER. The operator interface to software that observes and controls the activities in a network.

NETWORK MANAGEMENT. A set of human and automated tasks that support the creation, operation, and evolution of a network.

NONBLOCKING NETWORK. A circuit-switched network in which there is always at least one available path between any pair of idle end points regardless of the number of end points already connected.

OPTICAL FIBER. A lightwave transmission medium. Supports very high bandwidth.

OUTBOUND PATH. On a broadband LAN, the transmission path used by stations to receive packets coming from the headend.

PACKET. A group of bits that includes data plus source and destination addresses. Generally refers to a network layer (layer 3) protocol.

PACKET SWITCHING. A method of transmitting messages through a communications network, in which long messages are subdivided into short packets. The packets are then transmitted as in message switching. Usually, packet switching is more efficient and rapid than message switching.

PASSIVE HEADEND. A device that connects the two broadband cables of a dual cable system. It does not provide frequency translation.

PASSIVE STAR. A topology in which each station attaches to a central node by two lines, one input and one output. A signal entering the central node on one input line is split among all output lines. The central node is passive, providing merely an electromagnetic linkage.

PBX. Private branch exchange. A telephone exchange on the user's premises. Provides a switching facility for telephones on extension lines within the building and access to the public telephone network. May be manual (PMBX) or automatic (PABX). A digital PBX that also handles data devices without modems is sometimes called a computerized branch exchange (CBX).

PCM. Pulse code modulation. A common method for digitizing voice. The bandwidth required for a single digitized voice channel is 64 kbps.

PROPAGATION DELAY. The delay between the time a signal enters a channel and the time it is received.

PROTOCOL. A set of rules governing the exchange of data between two entities.

REGISTER INSERTION RING. A medium access control technique for rings. Each station contains a register that can temporarily hold a circulating packet. A station may transmit whenever there is a gap on the ring and, if necessary, hold an oncoming packet until it has completed transmission.

REPEATER. A device that receives data on one communication link and transmits it, bit by bit, on another link as fast as it is received, without buffering. An integral part of the ring topology. Used to connect linear segments in a baseband bus local network.

RING. A topology in which stations are attached to repeaters connected in a closed loop. Data are transmitted in one direction around the ring and can be read by all attached stations.

RING WIRING CONCENTRATOR. A site through which pass the links between repeaters, for all or a portion of a ring.

SLOTTED ALOHA. A medium access control technique for multiple-access transmission media. The technique is the same as ALOHA, except that packets must be transmitted in well-defined time slots.

SLOTTED RING. A medium access control technique for rings. The ring is divided into slots, which may be designated empty or full. A station may transmit whenever an empty slot goes by, by marking the slot full and then inserting a packet into the slot.

SPACE-DIVISION SWITCHING. A circuit-switching technique in which each connection through the switch takes a physically separate and dedicated path.

SPECTRUM. Refers to an absolute range of frequencies. For example, the spectrum of CATV cable is now about 5-400 MHz.

SPLITTER. Analog device for dividing one input into two outputs and combining two outputs into one input. Used to achieve tree topology on broadband CATV networks.

STAR. A topology in which all stations are connected to a central switch. Two stations communicate via circuit switching.

STATISTICAL TIME-DIVISION MULTIPLEXING. A method of time-division multiplexing (TDM) in which time slots on a shared transmission line are allocated to

I/O channels on demand.

SYNCHRONOUS TIME-DIVISION MULTIPLEXING. A method of time-division multiplexing (TDM) in which time slots on a shared transmission line are assigned to I/O channels on a fixed, predetermined basis.

TAP. An analog device that permits signals to be inserted or removed from a twisted pair or coaxial cable.

TDM BUS SWITCHING. A form of time-division switching in that time slots are used to transfer data over a shared bus between transmitter and receiver.

TERMINAL. A collection of hardware and possibly software that provides a direct user interface to a network.

TERMINATOR. An electrical resistance at the end of a cable that serves to absorb the signal on the line.

TIME-DIVISION MULTIPLEXING (TDM). A technique for combining multiple signals on one circuit by separating them in time.

TIME-DIVISION SWITCHING. A circuit-switching technique in which time slots in a time-multiplexed stream of data are manipulated to pass data from an input to an output.

TIME-MULTIPLEXED SWITCHING (TMS). A form of space-division switching in which each input line is a time-division multiplexed stream. The switching configuration may change for each time slot.

TIME-SLOT INTERCHANGE (TSI). The interchange of time slots within a time-division multiplexed frame.

TOKEN BUS. A medium access control technique for bus/tree. Stations form a logical ring, around which a token is passed. A station receiving the token may transmit data and then must pass the token on to the next station in the ring.

TOKEN RING. A medium access control technique for rings. A token circulates around the ring. A station may transmit by seizing the token, inserting a packet onto the ring, and then retransmitting the token.

TOPOLOGY. The structure, consisting of paths and switches, that provides the communications interconnection among nodes of a network.

TRANSCEIVER. A device that both transmits and receives.

TRANSCEIVER CABLE. A four-pair cable that connects the transceiver in a baseband coaxial local area network (LAN) to the controller.

TRANSMISSION MEDIUM. The physical path between transmitters and receivers in a communications network.

TREE. A topology in which stations are attached to a shared transmission medium. The transmission medium is a branching cable emanating from a headend, with no closed circuits. Transmissions propagate throughout all branches of the tree and are received by all stations.

TWISTED PAIR. An electromagnetic transmission medium consisting of two insulated wires arranged in a regular spiral pattern.

VIRTUAL CIRCUIT. A packet-switching service in which a connection (virtual circuit) is established between two stations at the start of transmission. All packets follow the same route, need not carry a complete address, and arrive in sequence.

SECTION 10: ANNOTATED BIBLIOGRAPHY*

As the reader should have gathered by now, the field of local networks is both broad and explosive. No bibliography can hope to be either thorough or timely. The entries in this section were chosen using the following criteria:

- *Relevance*: This tutorial is concerned with the principles and technology underlying local networks. Therefore, few of the references describe specific networks, either experimental or commercially available products.
- *Currency*: Most of the references are of rather recent origin. A good bibliography of material up to 1980 can be found in [SHOC80a].
- *Representativeness*: The interested reader can pursue the topics introduced in this tutorial by consulting the references listed here. They are, however, only representative of the available literature. The articles themselves contain further references for the truly dedicated reader.

10.1 Books

Stallings, W. *Local Networks: An Introduction*, New York: Macmillian, 1984.

This is, in a sense, a companion to this tutorial text, and it follows the same topical organization. It is intended as a textbook as well as a reference for professionals.

Flint, D. *The Data Ring Main*. New York: John Wiley, 1983.

The first half of this book contains an overview of local area network (LAN) technology plus an exposition of internetworking issues. The latter, less technical, half discusses user issues and selection criteria.

Chorafas, D. *Designing and Implementing Local Area Networks*. New York: McGraw-Hill, 1984.

The majority of this book is devoted to a description of some specific vendor offerings. There is also a survey of LAN technology.

Derfler, F. and Stallings, W. *A Manager's Guide to Local Networks*. Englewood Cliffs, NJ: Prentice-Hall/Spectrum, 1983.

A technical overview of local networks for managers, plus guidance on requirements definition, selection, and use.

Rosenthal, R. *The Selection of Local Area Computer Networks,* National Bureau of Standards Special Publication 500-96, November, 1982.

An excellent guidebook for those intending to purchase a local network. Includes detailed guidance for developing a specification for vendors.

Cooper, E. *Broadband Network Technology*. Mountain View, CA: Sytek Press, 1984.

A comprehensive introduction to the technology and practical implementation issues for broadband LANs.

IBM Corp. *A Building Planning Guide for Communication Wiring*. G320-8059, September, 1982.

This booklet describes IBM's cabling system for ring LANs. It provides detailed descriptions and instructions for cable layout and installation.

IBM Corp. *An Introduction to Local Area Networks*. SC20-8203, November, 1983.

An overview of LAN and digital PBX technology, with an emphasis on IBM's token ring research.

Digital Equipment Corp. *Introduction to Local Area Networks*. EB-22714-18, 1982.

An overview of LAN technology with an emphasis on Ethernet.

Freeman, H. and Thurber, K. *Local Network Equipment*. Silver Spring, MD: IEEE Computer Society Press, 1985.

This tutorial text contains reprints of articles describing a broad range of commercially available local networks.

Thurber, K. T. and Freeman, H. A. *Tutorial: Local Computer Networks (Second Edition)*, IEEE Computer Society Press, 1981.

This tutorial text contains reprints of articles describing specific LANs and HSLNs. Most of the networks described are experimental or tailor made rather than being commercially available products.

Franta, W. R. and Chlamtac, I. *Local Networks: Motivation, Technology, and Performance*, Lexington, MA: Lexington Books, 1981.

This is primarily about baseband bus LANs and high-speed local networks (HSLNs).

Tropper, C. *Local Computer Network Technologies*, Academic Press, 1981.

This book is devoted exclusively to a study of the performance of LAN and HSLN medium access control protocols. It summarizes most of the results up to 1981. Consequently, token bus is not included.

Local/Netter Designer's Handbook, Minneapolis, MN: Ar-

*References marked with an asterisk are included in this tutorial text.

chitecture Technology Corp.

This annual publication is an extensive listing of vendors of local network equipment.

Proceedings, Local Computer Network Conference.

A conference held annually in the fall in Minneapolis. Good source of current research results.

IEEE Computer Society. *Logical Link Control: IEEE Std 802.2-1985 (ISO/DIS 8802/2)*. IEEE, 1985.

IEEE Computer Society. *Carrier Sense Multiple Access with Collision Detection (CSMA/CD) Access Method and Physical Layer Specifications: IEEE Std 802.3-1985 (ISO/DIS 8802/3)*. IEEE, 1985.

IEEE Computer Society. *Token-Passing Bus Access Method and Physical Layer Specifications: IEEE Std 802.4-1985 (ISO/DIS 8802/4)*. IEEE, 1985.

IEEE Computer Society. *Token Ring Access Method and Physical Layer Specifications: IEEE Std 802.5-1985 (ISO/DIS 8802/5)*. IEEE, 1985.

The above four are the published specifications of the approved IEEE 802 standards.

10.2 Articles

The articles are listed alphabetically with annotation. Table 10.1 provides a topical key.

ACAM84* Acampora, A. and Hluchyz, M. "A New Local Area Network Using a Centralized Bus." *IEEE Communications Magazine*, August, 1984.

A good technical description of AT&T's Datakit LAN.

AHUJ83 Ahuja, S. "S/NET: A High-Speed Interconnect for Multiple Computers." *IEEE Journal on Selected Areas in Communications*, November, 1983.

Describes a 10-Mbps fiber LAN using an active star switch.

AIME79 Aimes, G. T. and Lazowska, E. D. "The Behavior of Ethernet-like Computer Communications Networks." *Proceedings, Seventh Symposium on Operating Systems Principles*, 1979.

A look at CSMA-type networks.

AKAS84 Akashi, F. and Ohteru, Y. "Efficient Local Area Network Interconnect Using a Bridge." *Proceedings, COMPCON 84 FALL*, September, 1984.

Discusses implementation and performance results for an Ethernet bridge.

ALLA82 Allan, R. "Local-area Networks Spur Moves to Standardize Data Communications Among Computers and Peripherals." *Electronic Design*, December 23, 1982.

An accurate summary of the IEEE 802 standard.

ALLA83 Allan, R. "Local Networks: Fiber Optics Gains Momentum." *Electronic Design*, June 23, 1983.

A view of the state-of-the-art in multiple-access fiber LANs.

AMER82* Amer, P. "A Measurement Center for the NBS Local Area Computer Network." *IEEE Transactions on Computers*. August, 1982.

Describes a rather complete set of performance measures that could be used in monitoring a LAN. Active and passive monitoring techniques are explored.

AMER83 Amer, P. D.; Rosenthal, R.; and Toense, R. "Measuring a Local Network's Performance." *Data Communications*, April, 1983.

Discusses the performance measurement facility described in this tutorial. The focus is more on objectives and operational considerations rather than on means.

ANDR82 Andrews, D. and Schultz, G. "A Token Ring Architecture for Local-Area Networks: An Update." *Proceedings, COMPCON Fall 82*, 1982.

An overview of IBM's approach.

ANSI82 American National Standards Institute. *Draft, Proposed American National Standard Local Distributed Data Interface*, May, 1982.

Text of the draft high-speed local network (HSLN) standard.

ARCH81 Architecture Technology Corp. "Special Report: Network Systems Corporation, HYPERchannel." *LocalNetter*, November, 1981.

Summarizes the HYPERchannel HSLN product.

ARCH82 Architecture Technology Corp. "Special Report: AMTEL Messenger II. A Power Line Local Network Based Product." *LocalNetter*, February, 1982.

Describes a very low cost, low capacity LAN that uses a building's power lines as the transmission medium. No installation costs!

ARTH81 Arthurs, E. and Stuck, B. W. "A Theoretical Performance Analysis of Polling and Carrier Sense Collision Detection Communication Systems." *Proceedings, Seventh Data Communications Symposium*, 1981.

Reports on IEEE 802 performance study.

ARTH82 Arthurs, E.; Stuck, B. W.; Bux, W.; Marathe, M.; Hawe, W.; Phinney, T.; Rosenthal, R; and Tarasou, V. *IEEE Project 802 Local Area Network Standards, Traffic Handling Characteristics Committee Report*, IEEE, June, 1982.

The complete report of the IEEE 802 performance study.

BART84 Bartik, J. "IBM's Token Ring: Have the Pieces Finally Come Together." *Data Communication*, August, 1984.

A good description of the 802.4 specification plus a commentary on IBM's strategy.

BASS80 Bass, C.; Kennedy, J. S.; and Davidson, J. M. "Local Network Gives New Flexibility to Distributed Processing." *Electronics*, September 25, 1980.

Describes the Ungermann-Bass baseband LAN.

BLAI82 Blair, G. S. and Shepherd D. "A Performance Comparison of Ethernet and the Cambridge Digital Communication Ring." *Computer Networks*, pp 105-113, 1982.

The authors conclude that, under some circumstances, slotted ring is superior to CSMA/CD bus.

BOGG80 Boggs, D. R.; Shoch, J. F.; Taft, E. A.; and Metcalfe, R. M. "Pup: An Internetwork Architecture." *IEEE Transactions on Communications*, April, 1980.

An early Xerox internet protocol attempt. Also contains a good discussion of the internet problem for local networks.

BOSE81 Bosen, R. "A Low-Speed Local Net for Under $100 per Station." *Data Communications*, December, 1981.

Describes a low-cost LAN.

BURR83* Burr, W. "An Overview of the Proposed American National Standard for Local Distributed Data Interfaces." *Communications of the ACM*, August, 1983.

Describes ANS X3T9.5, a proposed 50-Mbps local network standard.

BURR84a Burr, W. and Ross, F. "The Fiber Distributed Data Interface: A Proposal for a Standard 100 Mbit/s Fiber Optic Token Ring Network." *Proceedings, FOCI-LAN 84*, 1984.

A description of the proposed standard.

BURR84b Burr, W. and Carpenter, J. "Wideband Local Nets Enter the Computer Arena." *Electronics*, May 3, 1984.

Discusses the ANS X3T9.5 high-speed local network (HSLN) standard and compares it with three commercial products: HYPERchannel, Loosely Coupled Network (LCN), and VAXCLUSTER.

BUX81 Bux, W. "Local-Area Subnetworks: A Performance Comparison." *IEEE Transactions on Communications*, October, 1981.

Compares CSMA/CD, token, and slotted ring. CSMA/CD loses.

BUX82 Bux, W.; Closs, F.; Janson, P. A.; Kummerle, K. Miller, H. R.; and Rothauser, H. "A Local-Area Communication Network Based on a Reliable Token Ring System." *Proceedings, International Symposium on Local Computer Networks*, 1982.

Describes an experimental system that is the basis of IBM's expected product.

BUX83a Bux, W. and Schlatter, M. "An Approximate Method for the Performance Analysis of Buffer Insertion Rings." *IEEE Transactions on Communications*, January 1983.

Extends the work in [BUX81].

BUX83b Bux, W.; Closs, F.; Kuemmerle, K.; Keller, H.; and Mueller, H. "Architecture and Design of a Reliable Token-Ring Network." *IEEE Journal on Selected Areas in Communications*, November, 1983.

Describes the architecture, performance, transmission system, and wiring strategy of IBM's token ring LAN. A good technical exposition.

BUX84* Bux, W. "Performance Issues in Local-Area Networks." *IBM Systems Journal*, No. 4, 1984.

This descriptive (rather than analytic) article discusses delay-throughput characteristics of medium access control protocols, end-to-end performance of a file server, and timing problems in local network adapters.

CELA82 Celano, J. "Crossing Public Property: Infrared Link and Alternative Approaches for Connecting a High Speed Local Area Network." *Proceedings, Computer Networking Symposium*, 1982.

How to connect LANs in buildings separated by public property.

CHEN82 Cheng, W. *Performance Evaluation of Token Control Networks*. PhD thesis, University of Illinois at Urbana-Champaign, 1982.

A very thorough study of token ring performance.

CHER83 Cheriton, D. "Local Networking and Internetworking in the V-System." *Proceedings, Eight Data Communications Symposium*, October, 1983.

Describes the use of gateways to provide LAN internetworking using streamlined protocols for intra-LAN traffic. Contains a good discussion of LAN internetworking performance issues.

CHLA80a Chlamtac, I. and Franta, W. R. "Message-Based Priority Access to Local Networks." *Computer Communications*, April, 1980.

Analyzes an HSLN protocol.

CHLA80b Chlamtac, I.; Franta, W. R.; Patton, P. C.; and Wells, B. "Performance Issues in Back-End Storage Networks." *Computer*, February, 1980.

Looks at HSLN performance.

CHRI78 Christensen, G. S. "Network Monitor Unit." *Proceedings, Third Conference on Local Computer Networking*, 1978.

Describes an NCC for an HSLN that provides a fault-isolation capability.

CHRI79 Christensen, G. S. "Links Between Computer-Room Networks." *Telecommunications*, February, 1979.

Brief description of HYPERchannel.

CHRI81 Christensen, G. S. and Franta, W. K. "Design and Analysis of the Access Protocol for HYPERchannel Networks." *Proceedings, Third USA-Japan Computer Conference*, 1981.

CLAN82 Clancy, G. J., et al. "The IEEE 802 Committee States Its Case Concerning Its Local Network Standards Efforts." *Data Communications*, April, 1982.

A response to the criticism that the standard has too many options and alternatives. It states the case for the need for LAN standards and offers a justification for the committee's approach.

CLAR78 Clark, D. D.; Pogran, K. T.; and Reed, D. P. "An Introduction to Local Area Networks." *Proceedings of the IEEE*, November, 1978.

Despite its date, a good, wide-ranging introduction to LANs.

COOP82 Cooper, E. "13 Often-Asked Questions About Broadband." *Data Communications*, April, 1982.

Short and informative.

COOP83a Cooper, E. and Edholm, P. K. "Design Issues in Broadband Local Networks." *Data Communications*, February, 1983.

Primarily a comparison of mid-split and dual configurations. The article takes into consideration cost, capacity, installation, and reliability.

COOP83b Cooper, E. "Broadband Network Design: Issues and Answers." *Computer Design*, March, 1983.

Looks at implementation and maintenance issues.

COTT80 Cotton, I. W. "Technologies for Local Area Computer Networks." *Computer Networks*, November, 1980.

Another good survey paper for LANs.

COYL85 Coyle, E. and Liu, B. "A Matrix Representation of CSMA/CD Networks." *IEEE Transactions on Communications*. January, 1985.

A new analytical model for CSMA/CD is presented. Because of its power and simplicity, it can be used to investigate the sensitivity of CSMA/CD performance to a variety of parameters.

DAHO83 Dahod, A. M. "Local Network Standards: No Utopia." *Data Communications*, March, 1983.

The author presents a case against local network standards, based on the danger of being frozen into technical obsolescence.

DALA81 Dalal, Y. K. and Printis, R. S. "48-Bit Absolute Internet and Ethernet Host Numbers." *Proceedings, Seventh Data Communications Symposium*, 1981.

Discusses the issue of internet addressing and describes the approach advocated by the Ethernet developers.

DALA82 Dalal, Y. "Use of Multiple Networks in the Xerox Network System." *Computer*, September, 1983.

Looks at the application of the XNS architecture to internetworking with an emphasis on local networks.

DAVI83 Davidson, J. "OSI Model Layering of a Military Local Network." *Proceedings of the IEEE*, December, 1983.

Describes implementation experience with the layering of protocol functions between attached devices and interface units.

DHAW84 Dhawan, A. "One Way to End the Brouhaha Over Choosing an Optimal LAN." *Data Communications*, March, 1984.

Extolls the virtues of the digital PBX.

DIEN83 Diener, A.; Bragger, R.; Dudler, A.; and Zehnder, C. "Database Services for Personal Computers Linked by a Local Area Network." *Proceedings, ACM Conference on Personal and Small Computers*, 1983.

Establishes a set of criteria for evaluating LAN database servers, and discusses hardware and software issues.

DIGA80 Digital Equipment Corp.; Intel. Corp.; and Xerox Corp. *The Ethernet: A Local Area Network Data Link Layer and Physical Layer Specifications*, September 30, 1980.

The formal Ethernet specification.

DINE80* Dineson, M. and Picazo, J. "Broadband Technology Magnifies Local Networking Capability." *Data Communications*, February, 1980.

Describes Sytek's broadband network.

DINE81 Dineson, M. A. "Broadband Local Networks Enhance Communication Design." *EDN*, March 4, 1981.

Covers the same topics as the paper included herein, but provides more technical detail about the RF engineering of the system.

DIXO82 Dixon, R. C. "Ring Network Topology for Local Data Communications." *Proceedings, COMPCON Fall 82*, IEEE, 1982.

Compares token ring to several alternative ring protocols.

DIXO83 Dixon, R.; Strole, N.; and Markov, J. "A Token-Ring Network For Local Data Communications." *IBM Systems Journal*, No. 1, 1983.

A readable overview of token ring, based on IEEE 802.5 and IBM's planned product. Discusses both medium access control and the physical wiring layout.

DONN79 Donnelly, J. E. and Yeh, J. W. "Interaction Between Protocol Levels in a Prioritized CSMA Broadcast Network." *Computer Networks*, March, 1979.

An analysis of the HYPERchannel protocol.

EDN82 EDN Magazine. "Credibility Problems Could Block LAN Growth." *EDN Magazine*, September 1, 1982.

A brief but sobering look at problems users have encountered with LANs.

ENNI83 Ennis G. and Filice, P. "Overview of a Broad-Band Local Area Network Protocol Architecture." *IEEE Journal on Selected Areas in Communications*, November, 1983.

A detailed description of the rather powerful protocol architecture implemented in the Sytek product.

ESTR82 Estrin, J. and Carrico, B. "Gateways Promise to Link Local Networks into Hybrid Systems." *Electronics*, September 22, 1982.

Describes various approaches to designing bridges.

FARM69 Farmer, W. D. and Newhall, E. E. "An Experimental Distributed Switching System to Handle Bursty Computer Traffic." *Proceedings, ACM Symposium on Problems in the Optimization of Data Communications*, 1969.
A paper describing an early token ring system.

FINL84* Finley, M. "Optical Fibers in Local Area Networks." *IEEE Communications Magazine*, August, 1984.
Surveys the various approaches to the use of optical fiber in local network architectures. A good state-of-the-art survey of U.S. and Japanese efforts.

FLAT84* Flatman, A. "Low-Cost Local Network for Small Systems Grows From IEEE-802.3 Standard." *Electronic Design*, July 26, 1984.
Describes Cheapernet, a proposed low-cost version of the IEEE CSMA/CD standard.

FLEM79 Fleming, P. *Principles of Switching*. Geneva, IL: Lee's abc of the Telephone, 1979.
Good, fairly nontechnical description of circuit switching.

FORB81 Forbes, J. "RF Prescribed for Many Local Links." *Data Communications*, September, 1981.
Broadband description.

FORC85 Forcina, A.; Listanti, M.; Pattavina, A.; and Roveri, A. "A Generalized Performance Evaluation of Slotted CSMA Networks." *Proceedings, INFOCOM 85*, 1985.
A new analysis of CSMA and CSMA/CD performance. A discrete time Markov chain is used and results encompass variable as well as fixed packet lengths.

FRAN80 Franta, W. R. and Bilodeau, M. B. "Analysis of a Prioritized CSMA Protocol Based on Staggered Delays." *Acta Informatica*, June, 1980.
Analysis of a high-speed local network (HSLN) protocol.

FRAN82 Franta, W. R. and Heath, J. R. *Performance of HYPERchannel Networks: Parameters, Measurements, Models, and Analysis*. University of Minnesota, Computer Science Department, Technical Report 82-3, January, 1982.
Summarizes results from a long-term project to analyze HSLN protocol performance.

FRAS83 Fraser, A. "Towards a Universal Data Transport System." *IEEE Journal on Selected Areas in Communications*, November, 1983.
A detailed technical description of AT&T's Datakit.

FREE83 Freedman, D. "Fiber Optics Shine in Local-Area Networks." *Mini-Micro Systems*, September, 1983.
An overview article, with emphasis on passive-star technology.

GOEL83* Goeller, L. and Goldstone, J. "The ABCs of the PBX." *Datamation*, April, 1983.
A lengthy discussion of the evolution of the PBX and its likely future direction.

GORD79 Gordon, R. L.; Farr, W. W.; and Levine, P. "Ringnet: A Packet Switched Local Network with Decentralized Control." *Proceedings, Fourth Conference on Local Computer Networks*, 1979.
Describes an early commercial token ring product.

GRAN83 Grant, A; Hutchison, D.; and Shepherd, W. "A Gateway for Linking Local Area Networks and X.25 Networks." *Proceedings, SIGCOMM 83 Symposium*, 1983.
In this approach, the local network appears as a single end point to the X.25 network.

GRAU82 Graube, M. "Local Area Nets: A Pair of Standards." *IEEE Spectrum*, June, 1982.
Summary of the IEEE 802 standard.

GRAU84 Graube, M. and Molder, M. "Local Area Networks." *IEEE Computer*, October, 1984.
A brief overview of the current status of LAN products.

GRNA80 Grnarov, A.; Kleinrock, L.; and Gerla, M. "A Highly Reliable Distributed Loop Network Architecture." *Proceedings, International Symposium on Fault-Tolerant Computing*, 1980.
Describes a technique for enhancing the reliability of a ring by using backward links.

HABE84 Haber, L. "Fiber-Optic Technology Sheds Light on Local Area Networks." *Mini-Micro Systems*, November, 1984.
A survey of current products plans and standards efforts.

HAFN74 Hafner, E. R; Nenadal, Z. and Tschanz, M. "A Digital Loop Communications System." *IEEE Transactions on Communications*, June, 1974.
An early register insertion ring.

HANS81 Hanson, K.; Chou, W.; and Nilsson, A. "Integration of Voice, Data, and Image Traffic in a Wideband Local Network." *Proceedings, Computer Networking Symposium*, 1981.
Addresses the use of a very-high speed (100 Mbps or more) local network and proposes techniques for efficient utilization.

HAUG84 Haugdahl, J. "Key Issues in Selecting Personal Computer Local Networks." *Proceedings, Ninth Conference on Local Computer Networks*, 1984.
Examines some of the key issues involved when considering local networking personal computers.

HAWE84* Hawe, B. Kirby, A.; and Stewart, B. "Transparent Interconnection of Local Area Networks with Bridges." *Journal of Telecommunication Networks, Summer*, 1984.
A consideration of various aspects of bridges, including

desirable characteristics, routing algorithms, protocol issues, and performance.

HERR79 Herr, D. E. and Nute, C. T. "Modeling the Effects of Packet Truncation on the Throughput of CSMA Networks." *Proceedings, Computer Networking Symposium*, 1979.

A very clear and systematic analysis of various CSMA/CD protocols, including nonpersistent, 1-persistent, and p-persistent.

HEYM82 Heyman, D. P. "An Analysis of the Carrier-Sense Multiple-Access Protocol." *Bell System Technical Journal*, October, 1982.

One of the best and most rigorous pieces of analysis that has been published on the subject.

HEYW81 Heywood, P. "The Cambridge Ring Is Still Making the Rounds." *Data Communications*, July, 1981.

Discusses commercial success of a slotted ring system.

HOHN80 Hohn, W. C. "The Control Data Loosely Coupled Network Lower Level Protocols." *Proceedings, National Computer Conference*, 1980.

A commercial HSLN product.

HOLM81 Holmgren, S. F. *Evaluation of TCP/IP in a Local Network*. MITRE Working Paper 81WOO568, September 30, 1981.

Results of an experiment to place network and transport layers in an NAU.

HOPK77 Hopkins, G. T. *A Bus Communications System*. MITRE Technical Report MTR-3515, 1977.

Describes one of the earliest broadband systems.

HOPK79 Hopkins, G. T. "Multimode Communications on the MITRE-NET." *Proceedings, Local Area Communications Network Symposium*, 1979.

Shorter version of [HOPK77].

HOPK80 Hopkins, G. T. and Wagner, P. E. *Multiple Access Digital Communications System*. U.S. Patent 4,210,780, July 1, 1980.

Contains a quite readable system description.

HOPK82 Hopkins, G. T. and Meisner, N. B. "Choosing Between Broadband and Baseband Local Networks." *Mini-Micro Systems*, June, 1982.

Good discussion of pros and cons.

HOPP77 Hopper, A. "Data Ring at Computer Laboratory, University of Cambridge." In *Local Area Networking*, National Bureau of Standards Publication 500-31, 1977.

Describes a slotted ring system.

HOPP83 Hopper, A. and Williamson, R. "Design and Use of an Integrated Cambridge Ring." *IEEE Journal on Selected Areas in Communications*, November, 1983.

Discusses the development process used to implement an integrated-circuit version of the Cambridge ring.

IBM82 IBM Corp. *IBM Series/1 Local Communications Controller Feature Description*. GA34-0142-2, 1982.

A very simple commercial register insertion product, one of the very few.

JAJS83 Jajszczyk, A. "On Nonblocking Switching Networks Composed of Digital Symmetrical Matrices." *IEEE Transactions on Communications*, January, 1983.

A discussion of the design of multistage time and space switching networks for integrated circuit implementation.

JANS83* Janson, P.; Svobodova, L.; and Maehle, E. "Filing and Printing Services on a Local-Area Network." *Proceedings, Eighth Data Communications Symposium*, October, 1983.

Examines in some detail a type of value-added LAN service that is becoming increasingly available.

JEWE85 Jewett, R. "The Fourth-Generation PBX: Beyond the Integration of Voice and Data." *Telecommunications*, February, 1985.

The author proposes that a fourth-generation PBX is characterized by an integrated LAN link, an integrated packet link, and dynamic allocation of bandwidth.

JOEL77 Joel, A. E. "What Is Telecommunications Circuit Switching?" *Proceedings of the IEEE*, September, 1977.

Describes the evolution of this technology.

JOEL79a Joel, A. E. "Circuit Switching: Unique Architecture and Applications." *Computer*, June, 1979.

A broad-brush treatment. Useful as an introduction.

JOEL79b Joel, A. E. "Digital Switching—How it Has Developed." *IEEE Transactions on Communications*, July, 1979.

A more technical version of [JOEL77].

JONE83 Jones, J. R. "Consider Fiber Optics for Local Network Designs." *EDN*, March 3, 1983.

Describes the uses of a fiber optic, passive star configuration that achieves the same functional effect as a baseband bus network.

JOSH84* Joshi, S. and Iyer, V. "New Standards for Local Networks Push Upper Limits for Lightwave Data." *Data Communications*, July, 1984.

A detailed description of a proposed ANSI X3T9.5 standard for a 100-Mbps fiber ring local network.

KANE80* Kane, D. "Data Communications Network Switching Methods." *Computer Design*, April, 1980.

A brief survey of digital data switch systems.

KARP82 Karp, P. M. and Socher, I. D. "Designing Local-Area Networks." *Mini-Micro Systems*, April, 1982.

Looks at network services issues for broadband systems.

KASS79a Kasson, J. M. "The Rolm Computerized Branch Exchange: An Advanced Digital PBX." *Computer*, June, 1979.

Describes a commercial PBX product.

KASS79b Kasson, J. M. "Survey of Digital PBX Design." *IEEE Transactions on Communications*, July, 1979.

Provides a good description of various contemporary PBX/CBX architectures.

KATK81a Katkin, R. D. and Sprung, J. G. "Simulating a Cable Bus Network in a Multicomputer and Large-Scale Application Environment." *Proceedings, Sixth Conference on Local Computer Networks*, 1981.
Provides a rationale for and describes the plan for a study of HSLN performance.

KATK81b Katkin, R. D. and Sprung, J. G. *Application of Local Bus Network Technology to the Evolution of Large Multi-computer Systems*. MITRE Technical Report MTR-81W290, November, 1981.
Reports on the results of study described in [KATK81a].

KELL83 Keller, H.; Meyer, H.; and Mueller, H. "Transmission Design Criteria for Synchronous Token Ring." *IEEE Journal on Selected Areas in Communications*, November, 1983.
Discusses token ring implementation issues, including cable type and layout, transmission, and synchronization with phase-locked loops.

KELL84 Kelley, R.; Jones, J.; Bhatt, V.; and Pate, P. "Transceiver Design and Implementation Experience in an Ethernet-Compatible Fiber Optic Local Area Network." *Proceedings, INFOCOM 84*, 1984.
Describes the system design of one of the few commercially-available fiber LANs.

KILL82 Killen, M. "The Microcomputer Connection to Local Networks." *Data Communications*, December, 1982.
Good discussion of the technology and application of low-cost, low-speed LANs.

KLEE82 Klee, K.; Verity, J. W.; and Johnson, J. "Battle of the Networkers." *Datamation*, March, 1982.
A lighthearted look at baseband versus broadband.

KRUT81* Krutsch, T. "A User Speaks Out: Broadband or Baseband for Local Nets?" *Data Communications*, December, 1981.
A thoughtful comparison.

KUMM82 Kummerle, K. and Reiser, M. "Local-Area Communication Networks—An Overview." *Journal of Telecommunication Networks*, Winter, 1982.
A survey article.

KURO84 Kurose, J.; Schwartz, M.; and Yemini, Y. "Multiple–Access Protocols and Time-Constrained Communication." *ACM Computing Surveys*, March, 1984.
Surveys multiaccess protocols, including CSMA/CD. Examines the performance of such protocols, especially for real-time traffic, such as voice.

LABA78 LaBarre, C. E. *Analytic and Simulation Results for CSMA Contention Protocols*. MITRE Technical Report MTR-3672, 1978.
An important contribution to the CSMA/CD performance analysis literature.

LABA80 LaBarre, C. E. *Communications Protocols and Local Broadcast Networks*. MITRE Technical Report MTR-3899, February, 1980.
A well thought-out discussion of what protocols should reside in the local network access unit.

LEE83 Lee, E. and Boulton, P. "The Principles and Performance of Hubnet: A 50 Mbit/s Glass Fiber Local Area Network." *IEEE Journal on Selected Areas in Communications*, November, 1983.
Explains the principles and provides some implementation details for a fiber LAN that exists in prototype form.

LEVY82 Levy, W. A. and Mehl, H. F. "Local Area Networks." Series in *Mini-Micro Systems*, February, March, July, 1982.
A comprehensive series of articles on LANs, HSLNs, digital switches, and PBXs. High-level discussion of architecture; list of vendors.

LEWI84 Lewis, J. and Baker K. "Alternative to Microwave, Infrared Wins Short-Haul Run." *Data Communications*, November, 1984.
Describes the use of laser for building-to-building links.

LIMB84 Limb, J. "Performance of Local Area Networks at High Speed." *IEEE Communications Magazine*, August, 1984.
An interesting look at the major LAN protocols from the point of view of traffic-handling capacity.

LIND82 Lindsay, D. "Local Area Networks: Bus and Ring vs. Coincident Star." *Computer Communications Review*, July/ October, 1982.
Proposes a configuration similar to AT&T's Datakit and comments on the advantages and disadvantages of this approach relative to bus and ring approaches.

LISS81 Lissack, T; Maglaris, B.; and Chin, H. "Impact of Microprocessor Architecture on Local Network Interface Adapters." *Proceedings, Conference on Local Networks and Office Automation Systems*, 1981.
Study of local network access unit performance.

LIU78 Liu, M. T. "Distributed Loop Computer Networks." In *Advances in Computers, Vol. 17*. New York: Academic Press, 1978.
Good survey of various ring protocols.

LIU82 Liu, M.; Hilal, W.; and Groomes, B. "Performance Evaluation of Channel Access Protocols for Local Computer Networks." *Proceedings, COMPCON Fall 82*, 1982.
Presents results of a comparative performance analysis of token ring, slotted ring, register insertion, and CSMA/CD.

LUCZ78 Luczak, E. C. "Global Bus Computer Communication Techniques." *Proceedings, Computer Network Symposium*, 1978.

Describes various bus protocols.

MAGL80 Maglaris, B. and Lissack, T. "An Integrated Broadband Local Network Architecture." *Proceedings, Fifth Conference on Local Computer Networks*, 1980.

MAGL81 Maglaris, B.; Lissack, T.; and Austin, M. "End-to-End Delay Analysis on Local Area Networks: An Office Building Scenario." *Proceedings, National Telecommunications Conference*, 1981.

MAGL82 Maglaris, B. and Lissack, T. "Performance Evaluation of Interface Units for Broadcast Local Area Networks." *Proceedings, COMPCON Fall 82*, 1982.

The above three papers provide an excellent analysis of end-to-end performance in a CSMA/CD broadband LAN.

MALO81 Malone, J. "The Microcomputer Connection to Local Networks." *Data Communications*, December, 1981.

Looks at the reasons for and approaches to low cost LANs.

MAND82 Mandelkern, D. "Rugged Local Network Follows Military Aircraft Standard." *Electronics*, April 7, 1982.

Discusses MIL-STD-1553, a military LAN standard.

MARA82 Marathe, M. and Hawe, B. "Predicted Capacity of Ethernet in a University Environment." *Proceedings, SOUTHCON 82*, 1982.

Compares analysis with measured results.

MARK82 Markov, J. D. and Strole, N. C. "Token-Ring Local Area Networks: A Perspective." *Proceedings, COMPCON FALL 82*, IEEE, 1982.

Provides good justification for IBM's approach.

MARS83 Marshall, G. "Bridges Link LANs." *Systems and Software*, May, 1983.

Describes bridge operation.

MATS82 Matsukane, Ed. "Network Administration and Control System for a Broadband Local Area Communications Network." *Proceedings, COMPCON FALL 82*, 1982.

A good discussion of desirable features in a network control center.

MCGA85 McGarry, S. "Networking Has a Job to Do in the Factory." *Data Communications*, February, 1985.

Discusses the unique requirements for LANs that support factory automation.

METC76 Metcalfe, R. M. and Boggs, D. R. "Ethernet: Distributed Packet Switching for Local Computer Networks." *Communications of the ACM*, July, 1976.

A classic paper.

METC77 Metcalfe, R. M.; Boggs, D. R.; Thacker, C. P.; and Lampson, B. W. "Multipoint Data Communication System with Collision Detection." *U.S. Patent* 4,063,220, 1977.

The Ethernet patent.

MILL82 Miller, C. K. and Thompson, D. M. "Making a Case for Token Passing in Local Networks." *Data Communications*, March, 1982.

The author argues that token bus is superior to CSMA/CD both in terms of capability and cost.

MITC81* Mitchell, L. "A Methodology for Predicting End-to-End Responsiveness in a Local Computer Network." *Proceedings of the Computer Networking Symposium*, December, 1981.

Examines the issue of end-to-end local network performance. The article presents a general technique and then applies it to a specific case.

MOKH83 Mokhoff, N. "Fiber Optic LANs May Eliminate Future Bottlenecks in Office Communications." *Computer Design*, Fall, 1983.

A survey of fiber-optic components and LAN configurations.

MOKH84 Mokhoff, N. "Networks Expand as PBXs Get Smarter." *Computer Design*, February, 1984.

A survey of local network types, with an emphasis on the digital PBX. Issues of integrating LANs and PBXs are explored.

MYER82* Myers, W. "Toward a Local Network Standard." *IEEE Micro*, August, 1982.

A good technical description.

NABI84 Nabielsky, J. "Interfacing to the 10 Mbps Ethernet: Observations and Conclusions." *Proceedings, SIGCOMM 84*, June, 1984.

Reports on practical experience in connecting devices to Ethernet using a variety of configurations. The performance results indicate that the 10-Mbps data rate is unnecessarily high.

NBS81 National Bureau of Standards. *A Look at Network Management*. Report ICST/LANP-82-1, October, 1981.

A survey of LAN network control issues.

NESS81 Nessett, D. M. *HYPERchannel Architecture: A Case Study of Some Inadequacies in the ISO OSI Reference Model*. Lawrence Livermore Laboratory Report UCRL-53139, April, 1981.

A critical look at the HYPERchannel protocol architecture. Provides some important insights.

OKAD84 Okad, H.; Yamamoto, T.; Nomura, Y.; and Nakanishi, Y. "Comparative Evaluation of Token-Ring and CSMA/CD Medium–Access Control Protocols in LAN Configurations." *Proceedings, Computer Networking Symposium*, 1984.

Using a Markov approach, the authors produce a set of results for the two protocols under varying assumptions.

OLSE83* Olsen, R.; Seifert, W.; and Taylor, J. "RS-232-C

Data Switching on Local Networks." *Data Communications*, September, 1983.
Describes in detail the use of a local network access unit for terminal handling.

PARK83a Parker, R. and Shapiro, S. "Untangling Local Area Networks." *Computer Design*, March, 1983.
Survey article. Discusses pros and cons of various media, topologies, and access control schemes.

PARK83b Parker, R. "Committees Push to Standardize Disk I/O." *Computer Design*, March, 1983.
Describes the functions of the ANS X3T9.5 committee and places its HSLN standardization effort in context with its other activities.

PENN79 Penny, B. K. and Baghdadi, A. A. "Survey of Computer Communications Loop Networks." *Computer Communications*, August and October, 1979.
Probably the best survey of ring protocols.

PFIS82* Pfister, G. and O'Brien, B. "Comparing the CBX to the Local Network—And the Winner Is?" *Data Communications*, July, 1982.
A point-by-point comparison of the LAN to the digital PBX. The authors favor the latter.

PHIN83 Phinney, T. and Jelatis, G. "Error Handling in the IEEE 802 Token-Passing Bus LAN." *IEEE Journal on Selected Areas in Communications*, November, 1983.
A description of the IEEE 802 token bus protocol, with a detailed look at error handling.

PIER72 Pierce, J. R. "Network for Block Switches of Data." *Bell System Technical Journal*, July/August, 1972.
A pioneering slotted ring article.

POTT83 Potter, D. and Amand, J. "Connecting Minis to Local Nets With Discrete Modules." *Data Communications*, June, 1983.
A description of an NAU implementation.

RADI84 Radicati, S. "Managing Transient Internetwork Links in the Xerox Internet." *Proceedings, Second ACM-SIGOA Conference on Office Information Systems*, 1984.
Describes an approach for temporarily establishing and tearing down dial-up circuit and X.25 virtual circuit links in a LAN internet environment.

RAGH81 Raghavendra, C. S. and Gerla, M. "Optimal Loop Topologies for Distributed Systems." *Proceedings, Seventh Data Communications Symposium*, 1981.
The authors propose a reliability-enhancing technique for rings that is optimal in terms of both availability and throughput.

RATN83 Ratner, D. "How Broadband Modems Operate on Token–Passing Nets." *Data Communications*, June, 1983.
Good technical discussion of the RF modem.

RAUC82 Rauch-Hindin, W. "IBM's Local Network Scheme." *Data Communications*, May, 1982.
Concise summary of IBM's ring proposal.

RAWS79 Rawson, E. G. "Application of Fiber Optics to Local Networks." *Proceedings, Local Area Communications Network Symposium*, 1979.
Looks at ways in which fiber optics is practical today. Is still valid.

REAM75 Reames, C. C. and Liu, M. T. "A Loop Network for Simultaneous Transmission of Variable-Length Messages." *Proceedings, Second Annual Symposium on Computer Architecture*, 1975.
Good slotted-ring description.

RICH80* Richer, J.; Steiner, M.; and Sengoku, M. "Office Communications and the Digital PBX." *Computer Networks*, December, 1980.
Details the requirements for intraoffice communications and discusses the satisfaction of those requirements by a digital PBX.

ROMA77 Roman, G. S. *The Design of Broadband Coaxial Cable Networks for Multimode Communications*. MITRE Technical Report MTR-3527, 1977.
Describes in some detail the electronic components of a broadband system and related installation issues. A good, practical account.

ROUN83 Rounds, F. "Use Modeling Techniques to Estimate Localnet Success." *EDN*, April 14, 1983.
A discussion of techniques for modeling CSMA/CD networks. A source listing of a simulation program is included.

SALT79 Saltzer, J. H. and Pogran, K. T. "A Star-Shaped Ring Network with High Maintainability." *Proceedings, Local Area Communications Network Symposium*, 1979.
Describes availability enhancements for a ring. Is similar to IBM's approach.

SALT83* Saltzer, J.; Clark, D.; and Pogran, K. "Why a Ring?" *Computer Networks*, August, 1983.
Examines the benefits of a ring LAN as compared to a bus LAN.

SALW83 Salwen, H. "In Praise of Ring Architecture for Local Area Networks." *Computer Design*, March, 1983.
Discusses the advantages of a token-passing ring with wiring concentrations for reliability. This is the same philosophy as that propounded by IBM.

SAND82 Sanders, L. "Interfacing with a Military Data-Comm Bus." *Electronic Design*, August 5, 1982.
Another article on MIL-STD-1553.

SAST85* Sastry, A. "Maximum Mean Data Rate in a Local Area Network with a Specified Maximum Source Message Load." *Proceedings, INFOCOM 85*, 1985.
Considers the collective impact of various parameters such as propagation delay, interface delay, transmission rate, and message length in the maximum mean through-

put of a LAN. Token ring, token bus, and CSMA/CD are compared.

SCHM83 Schmidt, R.; Rawson, E.; Norton, R.; Jackson, S.; and Bailey, M. "Fibernet II: A Fiber Optic Ethernet." *IEEE Journal on Selected Areas in Communications*, November, 1983.

Describes an Ethernet-compatible fiber-optic star configuration with an active central star repeater.

SCHN83* Schneidewind, N. "Interconnecting Local Networks to Long-Distance Networks." *Computer*, September, 1983.

Explores protocol-related issues in LAN-long haul internetworking. A variety of design approaches are analyzed.

SCHO81 Scholl, T. H. "The New Breed—Switching Muxes." *Data Communications*, June, 1981.

Describes a modified statistical multiplexor that can be used for networking.

SCHW82 Schwartz, J. and Melling, W.P. "Sharing Logic and Work." *Datamation*, November, 1982.

Describes use of a low-cost LAN in an office environment.

SHIR82 Shirey, R. W. "Security in Local Area Networks." *Proceedings, Computer Networking Symposium*, 1982.

An excellent tutorial.

SHOC78 Shoch, J. F. "Internetwork Naming, Addressing, and Routing." *Proceedings, COMPCON 78*, 1978.

Discusses internet issues, with reference to local networks.

SHOC80a Shoch, J. F. *An Annotated Bibliography on Local Computer Networks*. Xerox Palo Alto Research Center, April, 1980.

A good bibliography of material up to the date of publication.

SHOC80b Shoch, J. F. and Hupp, J. A. "Measured Performance of an Ethernet Local Network." *Communications of the ACM*, December, 1980.

Excellent description of a performance measurement experiment.

SHOC82* Shoch, J.; Dalal, Y.; Redel, D.; and Crane, R. "Evolution of the Ethernet Local Computer Network." *Computer*, August, 1982.

A thorough and informative description of Ethernet.

SIDH82a* Sidhu, D. and Gasser, M. "A Multilevel Secure Local Area Network." *Proceedings of the Symposium on Security and Privacy*, April, 1982.

Describes the use of a trusted network access unit to enforce a security policy on a LAN.

SIDH82b Sidhu, D. P. and Gasser, M. *Design for a Multilevel Secure Local Area Network*. MITRE Technical Report MTR-8702, March, 1982.

Describes the trusted interface unit in greater detail.

SIDH82c Sidhu, D. P. "A Local Area Network Design for Military Applications." *Proceedings, Seventh Conference on Local Computer Networks*, 1982.

Another article on the trusted interface unit.

SKAP79 Skaperda, N. J. "Some Architectural Alternatives in the Design of a Digital Switch." *IEEE Transactions on Communications*, July, 1979.

Discusses ways in which the fundamental building blocks of time- and space-division switching are used to configure digital switches.

STAC80* Stack, R. and Dillencourt, K. "Protocols for Local-Area Networks." *Proceedings of the Trends and Applications Conference*, May, 1980.

Concerned with protocol residency alternatives; which protocol layers should be in a local network access unit and which in the attached host. The related merits of various alternatives are discussed.

STAC81a Stack, T. and Dillencourt, K. "Functional Description of a Value-Added Local Area Network." *Proceedings, Computer Networking Symposium*, December, 1981.

Discusses various operating system and application services that can be supported across a LAN.

STAC81b Stack, T. "LAN Protocol Residency Alternatives for IBM Mainframe Open System Interconnection. *Technical Report*, Network Analysis Corporation, 1981.

A further and specific discussion of issues covered in the article in this tutorial.

STAL83* Stallings, W. "Beyond Local Networks." *Datamation*, August, 1983.

An overview of the key issues involved in extending communication for an attached device beyond the scope of its local network.

STAL84a* Stallings, W. "Local Network Performance." *IEEE Communications Magazine*, February, 1984.

Develops a simple set of performance models for CSMA/CD and token-passing, and then surveys the results of a number of comparative LAN performance studies.

STAL84b* Stallings, W. "Local Networks." *Computing Surveys*, March, 1984.

A comprehensive survey.

STAL84c Stallings, W. "Digital Signaling Techniques." *IEEE Communications Magazine*, December, 1984.

A discussion of various signaling techniques that can be used on baseband local networks, including Manchester and differential Manchester.

STAL85 Stallings, W. "A Tutorial on the IEEE 802 Local Network Standard." *Journal of Telecommunication Networks*, Fall, 1985.

A detailed technical description of the standard.

STEW84 Stewart, B.; Hawe, B.; and Kirby, A. "Local Area

Network Connection." *Telecommunications*, April, 1984.
A good discussion of the function and performance of a bridge.

STIE81 Steiglitz, M. "Local Network Access Tradeoffs." *Computer Design*, October, 1981.
The author makes a case for token bus over CSMA/CD.

STIE85 Stieglitz, M. "X.25 Standard Simplifies Linking of Different LANs." *Computer Design*, February, 1985.
Describes an approach to the use of an X.25 gateway to link a LAN to other LANs and to hosts and terminals via an X.25 wide-area network.

STRO83* Strole, N. "A Local Communications Network Based on Interconnected Token-Access Rings: A Tutorial." *IBM Journal of Research and Development*, September, 1983.
Describes IBM's planned ring local network products, the basis for the IEEE 802.5 standard.

STUC83a Stuck, B. "Which Local Net Bus Access Is Most Sensitive to Traffic Congestion?" *Data Communications*, January, 1983.
Reports on an IEEE 802 performance study, with an emphasis on the approach. CSMA/CD, token bus, and token ring were examined.

STUC83b Stuck, B. "Calculating the Maximum Mean Data Rate in Local Area Networks." *Computer*, May, 1983.
Same topic as [STUC83a], with an emphasis on results.

STUC84 Stuck, B. "An Introduction to Traffic Handling Characteristics of Bus Local Area Network Distributed Access Methods." *IEEE Communications Magazine*, August, 1984.
A detailed examination of CSMA/CD and token bus under a variety of assumptions.

SUNS79 Sunshine, C. "Network Interconnection." *Proceedings of Local Area Communications Network Symposium*, 1979.
A thought-provoking checklist of design issues for local network internetworking.

SUNS83 Sunshine, C.; Kaufman, D.; Ennis, G.; and Biba, K. "Interconnection of Broadband Local Area Networks." *Proceedings, Eight Data Communications Symposium*, October, 1983.
Discusses a design for interconnecting large numbers of devices across multiple LANs. The key issue is routing.

TANG85 Tang, Y. and Zaky, S. "A Survey of Ring Networks: Topology and Protocols." *Proceedings, INFOCOM 85*, 1985.
A brief survey of a variety of ring-based topologies and access protocols for local networks. The authors classify and compare 24 existing ring networks.

THOR80* Thornton, J. "Back-End Network Approaches." *Computer*, February, 1980.
Looks at the application of high-speed local networks to back-end data base applications, and describes HYPERchannel.

THUR79 Thurber, K. J. and Freeman, H. A. "Architecture Considerations for Local Computer Networks." *Proceedings, First International Conference on Distributed Computer Systems*, 1979. (Reprinted in [THUR81])
Develops a taxonomy for local networks and classifies a number of systems.

TOBA80a Tobagi, F. A. and Hunt, V. B. "Performance Analysis of Carrier Sense Multiple Access with Collision Detection." *Computer Networks*, October/November, 1980.
A detailed mathematical derivation.

TOBA80b Togabi, F. A. "Multiaccess Protocols in Packet Communication Systems." *IEEE Transactions on Communications*, April, 1980.
A widely-referenced article that surveys the performance results for CSMA/CD and related protocols.

TOBA82 Tobagi, F. A. "Distributions of Packet Delay and Interdeparture Time in Slotted ALOHA and Carrier Sense Multiple Access." *Journal of the ACM*, October, 1982.
A rigorous, highly mathematical derivation.

TOBA83 Tobagi, F.; Borgonovo, F.; and Fratta, L. "Expressnet: A High-Performance Integrated-Services Local Area Network." *IEEE Journal on Selected Areas in Communications*, November, 1983.
A unidirectional bus architecture and a proposed access protocol that provide good performance at high data rates. A promising approach for high-speed local networks.

TSAO84 Tsao, D. "A Local Area Network Architecture Overview." *IEEE Communications Magazine*, August, 1984.
A brief overview of existing LAN architectures.

VONA80* Vonarx, M. "Controlling the Mushrooming Communications Net." *Data Communications*, June, 1980.
Describes an intelligent port selector type of digital data switch. Design for redundancy is emphasized.

WAIN82* Wainwright, D. "Internetworking and Addressing for Local Networks." *IEEE Project 802 Local Network Standards, Draft C*, May, 1982.
A systematic analysis of protocol issues relating to the various internetwork situations involving local networks.

WARN80* Warner, C. "Connecting Local Networks to Long-Haul Networks: Issues in Protocol Design." *Proceedings of the Fifth Conference on Local Computer Networks*, December, 1980.
Explores protocol-related issues in attempting to internetwork LANs and long-haul networks. The article highlights the relevant differences between the two types of networks.

WATS80 Watson, W. B. "Simulation Study of the Configuration Dependent Performance of a Prioritized, CSMA Broadcast Network." *Proceedings, Fifth Conference on Local Computer Networks,* 1980.

Another look at HSLN protocol performance.

WAY81 Way, D. "Build a Local Network on Proven Software." *Data Communications,* December, 1982.

Discusses the NAU-device interface.

WILK79 Wilkes, M. V. and Wheeler, D. J. "The Cambridge Digital Communication Ring." *Proceedings, Local Area Communications Network Symposium,* 1979.

A worthwhile description of a widely-used slotted ring system.

WILL81* Willard, D. "Reliability/Availability of Wideband Local Communication Networks." *Computer Design,* August, 1981.

Examines a variety of techniques for enhancing the availability of broadband LANs.

WOLF78 Wolf, J. J. and Liu, M. T. "A Distributed Double-Loop Computer Network." *Proceedings, Seventh Texas Conference of Computing Systems,* 1978.

An approach to enhancing ring availability.

WONG84 Wong, J. and Bux, W. "Analytic Modeling of an Adapter to Local Area Networks." *IEEE Transactions on Communications,* October, 1984.

A study of the performance of LAN interface units with respect to their ability to absorb packets from the LAN. Some generally useful results are reported.

WOOD79* Wood, D. "A Cable-Bus Protocol Architecture." *Proceedings of the Sixth Data Communications Symposium*, November, 1979.

Looks at the protocol architecture of a broadband LAN. In this system, the layers up through transport are resident in a local network access unit.

WURZ84 Worzburg, H. and Kelley, S. "PBX-based LANs: Lower Cost per Terminal Connection." *Computer Design*, February, 1984.

Discusses digital PBX architecture, then compares it to the LAN, and looks at integrated PBX-LAN systems.

TABLE 10.1 REFERENCE KEY

1. Introduction

CLAR78	LEVY82
COTT79	PARK83a
EDN82	STAL84b
GRAU84	THUR79
KUMM82	TSAO84

2. Local Area Networks

ACAM84	COOP83b	GRAU82	KELL84	MILL82	SAND82
AHUJ83	DAHO83	HABE84	KILL82	MOHK83	SCHM83
ALLA82	DIGA80	HAFN74	KLEE82	MYER82	SCHW82
ALLA83	DINE80	HEYW81	KRUT81	PENN79	SHOC82
ANDR82	DINE81	HOPK77	LEWI82	PIER72	STAL84c
ARCH82	DIXO82	HOPK79	LIND82	PHIN83	STAL85
BART84	DIXO83	HOPK80	LIU78	RATN83	STIE81
BASS80	FARM69	HOPK82	LUCZ79	RAUC82	STRO83
BOSE81	FINL84	HOPP77	MALO81	RAWS79	TANG85
BUX82	FLAT84	HOPP83	MAND82	REAM75	WILK79
BUX83b	FORB81	IBM82	MARK82	ROMA77	
CLAN82	FRAS83	IEEE82	MCGA85	SALT79	
COOP82	FREE83	JONE83	METC76	SALT83	
COOP83a	GORD79	KELL83	METC77	SALW83	03. High-

3. High-Speed Local Networks

ANSI82	CHRI79	PARK83b
ARCH81	HANS81	THOR80
BURR83	HOHN80	TOBA83
BURR84a	JOSH84	
BURR84b	LEE83	

4. Digital Switches and Digital PBXs

DHAW84	JOEL77	KASS79b	SKAP79
FLEM79	JOEL79a	MOKH84	VONA80
GOEL83	JOEL79b	PFIS82	WURZ84
JAJS83	KANE80	RICH80	
JEWE85	KASS79a	SCHO81	

5. The Network Interface

DAVI83	NESS81	WAY81
ENNI83	OLSE83	WOOD79
HOLM81	POTT83	
LABA80	STAC80	
NABI84	STAC81	

6. Performance

AIME79	CHRI81	KURO84	OKAD84	TOBA82
ARTH81	COYL85	LABA78	ROUN83	WATS80
ARTH82	DONN79	LIMB84	SAST85	WONG84
BLAI82	FORC85	LIU82	SHOC80b	
BUX81	FRAN80	LISS81	STAL84a	
BUX83a	FRAN82	MAGL80	STUC83a	
BUX84	HERR79	MAGL81	STUC83b	
CHEN82	HEYM82	MAGL82	STUC84	
CHLA80a	KATK8la	MARA82	TOBA80a	
CHLA80b	KATK8lb	MITC81	TOBA80b	

7. Internetworking

AKAS84	DALA82	RADI84	STEW84	WARN80
BOGG80	ESTR82	SCHN83	STIE85	
CELA82	GRAN83	SHOC78	SUNS79	
CHER83	HAWE84	STAL83	SUNS83	
DALA81	MARS83		WAIN82	

8. Design Issues

AMER82	HAUG84	RAGH81	SIDH82c
AMER83	JANS83	SHIR82	STAC81
CHRI78	KARP82	SIDH82a	WILL81
DIEN83	MATS82	SIDH82b	WOLF78
GRNA80	NBS81		

AUTHOR BIOGRAPHY

Dr. William Stallings is a senior communications consultant with Honeywell Information Systems, Inc. He has designed a number of data and computer communications networks for Honeywell customers. Previously, Dr. Stallings was Vice President of CSM Corp., a firm specializing in data processing and data communications technology for the health care industry. He has also been Director of Systems Analysis and Design for CTEC, Inc., a firm specializing in command, control, and communications systems.

Dr. Stallings has a PhD from M.I.T. in computer science and a B.S. from Notre Dame in electrical engineering. He is the author of numerous technical papers and the following books:

- DATA AND COMPUTER COMMUNICATIONS, Macmillan, 1985
- COMPUTER COMMUNICATIONS: ARCHITECTURES, PROTOCOLS, AND STANDARDS, IEEE Computer Society Press, 1985
- INTEGRATED SERVICES DIGITAL NETWORKS, IEEE Computer Society Press, 1985
- LOCAL NETWORKS: AN INTRODUCTION, Macmillan, 1984
- A MANAGER'S GUIDE TO LOCAL NETWORKS, Prentice-Hall, 1983